NO OTHER GUIDE HAS AS MUCH TO OFFER ... THESE BOOKS ARE A PLEASURE TO READ.
Gene Shalit on the *Today Show*

★ ★ ★ ★ ★ (5 star rating) "Crisply written and remarkably personable. Cleverly organized so you can pluck out the minutest fact in a moment. Satisfyingly thorough."
Réalités

"The information they offer is up-to-date, crisply presented but far from exhaustive, the judgments knowledgeable but not opinionated."
New York Times

"The individual volumes are compact, the prose succinct, and the coverage up-to-date and knowledgeable ... The format is portable and the index admirably detailed."
John Barkham Syndicate

"They contain an amount of information that is truly staggering, besides being surprisingly current."
Detroit News

"These guides address themselves to the needs of the modern traveler demanding precise, qualitative information ... Up-beat, slick, and well-put-together."
Dallas Morning News

"... Attractive to look at, refreshingly easy to read, and generously packed with information."
Miami Herald

"These guides are as good as any published, and much better than most."
Louisville (Kentucky) *Times*

Other Books in the Get 'em and Go Series

Canada
Caribbean, Bermuda, and the Bahamas
Disneyland
Europe
Hawaii
Mexico
South America
United States
Walt Disney World

CONTRIBUTING EDITORS

Jeremy Addis
Tom Barrington
Isabel Bass
Cathy Beason
Susan Braybrooke
Karen Cure
James Davie
Michael Dervan
Robin Dewhurst
Bonnie Dudley Edwards
R. D. Eno
Ronald Faux
Michael Finlan
Trevor Fishlock
Bryn Frank
Ida Grehan
Emily Greenspan
Susan Grossman
David Hanly
Ben Harte
David Hoyle
Paul Hughes
Peter Johnston
John B. Keane
Michael Leech
Nancy Lyon
Carole Martin
Robin Mead
Anne Millman
Ann Nugent
Tony O'Riordan
Allan Rokach
David Owen
Alan Reeve-Jones
George Stacpoole
Colm Toibin
Marcia Wallace
Sean White
David Wickers
Diane Wood
Carol Wright

COVER   Paul Posnick

SYMBOLS   Gloria McKeown

MAP   Etta Jacobs

A Get 'em and Go Travel Guide

GREAT BRITAIN and IRELAND 1983

Stephen Birnbaum
EDITOR

Claire Hardiman
EXECUTIVE EDITOR

Kristin Moehlmann
Associate Editor

Denise DeGennaro
Assistant Editor

HOUGHTON MIFFLIN COMPANY BOSTON 1982

For Alex

This book is published by special arrangement
with Eric Lasher and Maureen Lasher.

Copyright © 1982 by Houghton Mifflin Company

All rights reserved. No part of this work may be reproduced
or transmitted in any form by any means, electronic or
mechanical, including photocopying and recording, or by
any information storage or retrieval system, except as
may be expressly permitted by the 1976 Copyright Act or
in writing from the publisher.
Requests for permission should be addressed
in writing to Houghton Mifflin Company,
2 Park Street, Boston, Massachusetts 02108.

ISBN: 0-395-32871-3 (pbk)
ISSN: 0162-5497 (Get 'em and Go Travel Guides)
ISSN: 0278-0860

Printed in the United States of America

W 10 9 8 7 6 5 4 3 2 1

Contents

ix **A Word from the Editor**

1 **How to Use This Guide**

GETTING READY TO GO

A mini-encyclopedia of all the practical travel data you need to plan your vacation down to the final detail.

When and How to Go

9 What's Where
11 When to Go
18 Traveling by Plane
27 Traveling by Ship
31 Touring by Car
34 Touring by Rail
39 Touring by Bus
41 Package Tours
47 Camping and Caravanning, Biking, and Hiking

Preparing

53 Calculating Costs
56 Entry Requirements and Documents
57 Planning a Trip
59 How to Pack
60 How to Use a Travel Agent
62 Insurance
64 Hints for Handicapped Travelers
67 Hints for Traveling with Children
70 Hints for Single Travelers
73 Hints for Older Travelers
75 Medical and Legal Aid and Consular Services

On the Road

79 Traveler's Checks, Credit Cards, and Foreign Exchange
82 Accommodations and Reservations

CONTENTS

- 89 Tipping
- 90 Shopping
- 93 Sports
- 95 Time Zones and Business Hours
- 96 Mail, Telephone, and Electricity
- 97 Drinking and Drugs
- 98 Customs and Returning to the US

Sources and Resources

- 101 Tourist Information Offices
- 104 Theater and Special Events Tickets
- 104 Camera and Equipment
- 106 Genealogy Hunts
- 110 Books and Magazines
- 111 Words to the Wise

PERSPECTIVES

A cultural and historical survey of Britain and Ireland's past and present, their people, politics, and heritage.

Britain

- 115 History
- 131 Literature
- 140 Architecture
- 144 Traditional Music and Dance
- 149 Food and Drink

Ireland

- 156 History
- 164 Literature
- 172 Architecture
- 174 Traditional Music and Dance
- 177 Food and Drink

THE CITIES

Thorough, qualitative guides to each of the 21 cities most often visited by vacationers and businesspeople. Each section, a comprehensive report of the city's most appealing attractions and amenities, is designed to be used on the spot. Directions and recommendations are immediately accessible because each city guide is presented in consistent form.

183	Bath	299	Galway
194	Belfast	307	Glasgow
201	Brighton	320	Kilkenny
212	Bristol	328	Limerick City
223	Cambridge	335	London
236	Canterbury	362	Oxford
244	Cardiff	372	Stratford-upon-Avon
253	Chester	382	Waterford
263	Cork	390	Wexford
272	Dublin	398	York
288	Edinburgh		

DIVERSIONS

A selective guide to more than 15 active and cerebral vacations including the places to pursue them where the quality of experience is likely to be highest.

For the Body

- 413 Great Golf
- 417 Tennis
- 419 Horsing Around
- 429 Wonderful Waterways and Coastal Cruises
- 435 Gone Fishing
- 445 Freewheeling by Two-Wheeler
- 453 Stalking and Shooting
- 455 Great Walks and Mountain Rambles

For the Mind

- 466 Marvelous Museums
- 476 The Performing Arts
- 487 Feis and Fleadh: The Best Festivals
- 498 Antiques and Auctions
- 510 Ancient Monuments and Ruins

For the Experience

522 Pub Crawling
532 Rural Retreats
545 Teashops and Tea Gardens
549 Mead and Meat Pies: Historical Banquets
552 Shopping Spree

DIRECTIONS

The most spectacular routes and roads; most arresting natural wonders; and most magnificent castles, manor houses, and gardens — all organized into 19 specific driving tours.

Great Britain

567 Southeast England
581 Channel Islands
587 Southwest England
604 The Cotswolds
613 The Lake District
624 Scottish Lowlands
637 Scottish Highlands — p 641
648 Scottish Islands
662 Wales

Northern Ireland

679 Antrim Coast

Irish Republic

690 Southeast Ireland: Dublin to New Ross
698 Southcentral Ireland
707 West Cork
711 Ring of Kerry and the Beara Peninsula
724 Dingle Peninsula
731 Clare
738 Connemara
746 Southern Mayo
752 Donegal

761 **Index**

A Word from the Editor

The publication of this new guide to Great Britain and Ireland represents the beginning of a new phase for our travel guide series. Having covered rather broad geographic areas in our first half-dozen guides, with this volume we embark on a program of treating the world's most popular travel destinations in somewhat greater depth.

Such treatment only reflects an increasingly apparent trend among travelers—the frequent return to treasured foreign travel spots. Once upon a time, even the most dedicated travelers would visit distant parts of the world no more than once in a lifetime—usually as part of that fabled old Grand Tour. But greater numbers of would-be sojourners are now availing themselves of the increasingly easy opportunity to visit favored parts of the world over and over again.

So where once it was routine to say that you'd "seen" a particular country after a very superficial, once-over-lightly encounter, the more perceptive travelers of today recognize that it's entirely possible to have only skimmed the surface of a specific travel destination even after having visited that place more than a dozen times. Similarly, repeated visits to a single site permit true exploration of special interests, whether they be sporting, artistic, or intellectual in nature. Multiple visits also allow an ongoing relationship with foreign citizens sharing similar interests, and an opportunity to discover and appreciate different perspectives on a single field of endeavor.

For those of us who spent the last several years working out the special system under which we present information in this series, the luxury of being able to devote nearly as much space as we like to just a quartet of countries is as close to guidebook heaven as any of us expects to come. But clearly, this is not the first guide to what were once called the British Isles—one suspects that guides of one sort or another have existed at least since Caesar's legions crossed the English Channel. Guides to Great Britain and Ireland have existed literally for centuries, so a traveler might logically ask why a new one is necessary at this particular moment.

Our answer is that the nature of travel to Great Britain and Ireland, and even the travelers who now routinely make the trip, have changed dramatically of late. For the past 2,000 years or so, travel to and through Britain and Ireland was an extremely elaborate undertaking, one that required extensive advance planning. Even as recently as the 1950s, a person who had actually been to England, Scotland, Ireland, or Wales could dine out on his or her experiences for years, since such adventures were quite extraordinary and usually the province of the privileged alone.

With the advent of jet air travel in the late 1950s, however, and of increased-capacity, wide-body aircraft during the 1960s, travel to and around once distant lands became extremely common. In fact, in two decades of nearly unending inflation, air fares may be the only commodity in the world that has actually gone down in price. And as a result, international travel is now well within the budgets of mere mortals.

Attitudes, as well as costs, have changed significantly in the last couple of decades. Beginning with the so-called flower children and hippies of the 1960s, international travel lost much of its aura of mystery. Whereas their parents might have chosen a superficial sampling of London or Dublin, these young people, motivated as much by wildly inexpensive "youth fares" as by the inclination to see the world, simply picked up and settled in various parts of Europe for an indefinite stay. While living as cheaply as possible, they usually adopted with great gusto the local lifestyle and generally immersed themselves in things European.

Thus began an explosion of travel to and in Great Britain and Ireland. And over the years, the development of inexpensive charter flights and packages fueled and sharpened the new American interest in and appetite for more extensive exploration.

Now, as we turn the corner into the 1980s, those same flower children who were in the forefront of the modern travel revolution have undeniably aged. While it may be impolite to point out that they are probably well into their untrustworthy 30s (and mostly firmly enmeshed in establishment activities), their original zeal for travel remains unabated. For them it's hardly news that the way to get to Dover is to head toward Canterbury, make a right, and then wait for white cliffs to appear. Such experienced and knowledgeable travelers have decided precisely where they want to go and are more often searching for ideas and insights to expand their already sophisticated travel consciousness. And—reverting to their youthful instincts and habits—they are after a deeper understanding and fuller assimilation of the British and Irish milieus. Typically, they visit single countries (or even cities) several times and may actually do so more than once in a single year.

Obviously, any new guidebook to Great Britain and Ireland must keep pace with and answer the real needs of today's travelers. That's why we've tried to create a guide that's specifically organized, written, and edited for this more demanding modern audience, one for whom qualitative information is infinitely more desirable than mere quantities of unappraised data. We think that this book and the other guides in our series represent a new generation of travel guides, one that is especially responsive to modern needs and interests.

For years, dating back as far as Herr Baedeker, travel guides have tended to be encyclopedic, seemingly much more concerned with demonstrating expertise in geography and history than in any analysis of the sorts of things that genuinely concern a typical tourist. But today, when it is hardly necessary to tell a traveler where London is, it is hard to justify devoting endless pages to historical perspectives. As suggested earlier, it's not impossible that the guidebook reader may have been to Great Britain and Ireland nearly as often as the guidebook editor, so it becomes the responsibility of that editor to provide new perceptions and to suggest new directions to make the guide genuinely valuable.

That's exactly what we've tried to do in our series. I think you'll notice a different, more contemporary tone to the text, as well as an organization and focus that are distinctive and more functional. And even a random examination of what follows will demonstrate a substantial departure from the standard guidebook orientation, for we've not only attempted to provide information of a different sort but we've also tried to present it in a context that makes it particularly accessible.

Needless to say, it's difficult to decide precisely what to include in a guidebook of this size—and what to omit. Early on, we realized that giving up the encyclopedic approach precluded the inclusion of every single route and restaurant, which helped define our overall editorial focus. Similarly, when we discussed the possibility of presenting certain information in other than strict geographical order, we found that the new format enabled us to arrange data in a way that we feel best answers the questions travelers typically ask.

Large numbers of specific questions have provided the real editorial skeleton for this book. The volume of mail I regularly receive seems to emphasize that modern travelers want very precise information, so we've tried to address these needs and have organized our material in the most responsive way possible. Readers who want to know the best restaurants in Cardiff or the best golf courses in Scotland will have no trouble whatever finding that data in this guide.

Travel guides are, of course, reflections of personal taste, and putting one's name on a title page obviously puts one's preferences on the line. But I think I ought to amplify just what "personal" means. I do not believe in the sort of personal guidebook that's a palpable misrepresentation on its face. It is, for example, hardly possible for any single travel writer to visit thousands of restaurants (and nearly as many hotels) in any given year and provide accurate appraisals of each one. And even if it were possible for one human being to survive such an itinerary, it would of necessity have to be done at a dead sprint and the perceptions derived therefrom would probably be less valid than those of any other intelligent individual visiting the same establishments. It is, therefore, impossible (especially in an annually revised and updated guidebook *series* such as we offer) to have only one person provide all the data on the entire world.

I also happen to think that such individual orientation is of substantially less value to readers. Visiting a single hotel for just one night or eating one hasty meal in a given restaurant hardly equips anyone to provide appraisals that are of more than passing interest. No amount of doggedly alliterative or oppressively onomatopoeic text can camouflage a technique that is specious on its face. We have, therefore, chosen what I like to describe as the "thee and me" approach to restaurant and hotel evaluation and, to a somewhat more limited degree, to the sites and sights we have included in the other sections of our text. What this really reflects is personal sampling tempered by intelligent counsel from informed local sources, and these additional friends-of-the-editor are almost always residents of the city and/or area about which they have been consulted.

Despite the presence of several editors, a considerable number of writers and researchers, and numerous insightful local correspondents, very precise editing and tailoring keep our text fiercely subjective. So what follows is purposely designed to be the gospel according to Birnbaum, and it represents as much of my own taste and insight as is humanly possible. It is probable, therefore, that if you like your cities genteel and your mountainsides uncrowded, prefer small hotels with personality to huge high-rise anonymities, and can't tolerate fresh fish that's been relentlessly overcooked, we're likely to have a long and meaningful relationship. Readers with dissimilar tastes may be less enraptured.

I also should point out something about the person to whom this guidebook is directed. Above all, he or she is a "visitor." This means that such elements as restaurants have been specifically picked to provide the visitor with a representative, enlightening, stimulating, and above all, pleasant experience. Since so many extraneous considerations can affect the reception and service accorded a regular restaurant patron, our choices can in no way be construed as a definitive guide to resident dining. We think we've listed all the best places, in various price ranges, but they were chosen with a visitor's viewpoint in mind.

Other evidence of how we've tried to tailor our text to reflect changing travel habits is most apparent in the section we call DIVERSIONS. Where once it was common for travelers to spend a foreign visit nailed to a single spot, the emphasis today is more likely to be directed toward pursuing some active enterprise or special interest while seeing the surrounding countryside. So we've selected every activity we could reasonably evaluate and organized the material in a way that is especially accessible to activists of either an athletic or cerebral bent. It is no longer necessary, therefore, to wade through a pound or two of extraneous prose just to find the very best crafts shop or the quaintest country inn within a reasonable radius of your destination.

If there is a single thing that best characterizes the revolution in and evolution of current holiday habits, it is that most travelers now consider travel a right rather than a privilege. Travel today translates as the enthusiastic desire to sample all of the world's opportunities, to find that elusive quality of experience that is not only enriching but comfortable. For that reason, we've tried to make what follows not only helpful and enlightening but the sort of welcome companion of which every traveler dreams.

Finally, I should point out that every good travel guide is a living enterprise; that is, no part of this text is cast in bronze. In our annual revisions, we refine, expand, and further hone all our material to serve your travel needs even better. To this end, no contribution is of greater value to us than your personal reaction to what we have written, as well as information reflecting your own experiences while using the book. We earnestly and enthusiastically solicit your comments on this book *and* your opinions and perceptions about places you have recently visited. In this way, we will be able to provide the most current information—including the actual experiences of the travel public—and to make those experiences more readily available to others. So please write to us at 60 E 42nd St., New York, NY 10165.

We sincerely hope to hear from you.

STEPHEN BIRNBAUM

How to Use This Guide

A great deal of care has gone into the organization of this guidebook, and we believe it represents a real breakthrough in the presentation of travel material. Our aim has been to create a new, more modern generation of travel books and to make this guide the most useful and practical travel tool available today.

Our text is divided into five basic sections, in order to best present information on every possible aspect of a vacation in Britain or Ireland. This organization itself should alert you to the vast and varied opportunities available as well as indicating all the specific, detailed data necessary to plan a trip. You won't find much of the conventional "quaint villages and beautiful scenery" text in this guide; we've chosen instead to use the available space for more useful and purposeful information. Prospective itineraries tend to speak for themselves, and with so many diverse travel opportunities, we feel our main job is to explain them and to provide the basic information—how, when, where, how much, and what's best—to allow you to make the most intelligent choices possible.

What follows is a brief summary of the five sections of this book and what you can expect to find in each. We believe that you will find both your travel planning and en route enjoyment enhanced by having this book at your side.

GETTING READY TO GO

This mini-encyclopedia of practical travel facts is a sort of know-it-all companion that provides all the precise information you need to go about creating a trip. There are entries on more than 30 separate topics, including how to travel, what preparations to make before you leave, what to expect in the different countries, what your trip is likely to cost, and how to avoid problems. The individual entries are specific, realistic, and cost-oriented.

We expect that you will use this section most in the course of planning your trip, for its ideas and suggestions are intended to facilitate the often confusing planning period. Entries are intentionally concise in an effort to get directly to the meat of the matter. This information is further augmented by extensive lists of sources for more specialized information and some suggestions for obtaining travel information on your own.

PERSPECTIVES

Any visit to an unfamiliar destination is enhanced and enriched by understanding the cultural and historical heritage of that area. We have, therefore, provided just such an introduction to Great Britain and Ireland, their past and present, people, architecture, literature, music and dance, and food and drink.

2 HOW TO USE THIS GUIDE

THE CITIES

Individual reports on the 21 cities most visited by tourists and businesspeople have been researched and written by professional journalists on their own turf. Useful at the planning stage, THE CITIES is really designed to be taken with you and used on the spot. Each report offers a short-stay guide to its city within a consistent format: an essay, introducing the city as a historic entity and a contemporary place to live; *At-a-Glance,* a site-by-site survey of the most important (and sometimes most eclectic) sights to see and things to do; *Sources and Resources,* a concise listing of pertinent tourist information, meant to answer a myriad of potentially pressing questions as they arise—from the address of the tourist office to where to find the best night spot, to see a show, to play golf, or to get a taxi; and *Best in Town,* our cost-and-quality choices of the best places to eat and sleep on a variety of budgets.

DIVERSIONS

This very selective guide is designed to help travelers find the very best places in which to pursue a wide range of physical and cerebral activities without having to wade through endless pages of unrelated text. With a list of more than 15 theme vacations—for the body, the mind, and the experience—DIVERSIONS provides a guide to the special places where the quality of experience is highest. Whether you seek golf or fishing, luxurious hotels or atmospheric pubs, each entry is the equivalent of a comprehensive checklist of the absolute best in Britain and Ireland.

DIRECTIONS

Here are 19 itineraries that range all across the countryside, along the most beautiful routes and roads, past the most spectacular natural wonders, through the most historic cities and countryside. DIRECTIONS is the only section of the book to be organized geographically, and its itineraries cover the touring highlights of England, Scotland, Wales, Northern Ireland, and the Irish Republic in short, independent journeys of 3 to 5 days' duration. Itineraries within each country can be connected for longer trips or used individually for short, intensive explorations.

Each entry includes a guide to sightseeing highlights; a cost-and-quality guide to accommodations and food along the road (small inns, castle hotels, hospitable farms, country and off-the-main-road discoveries); and suggestions for activities.

Although each of the sections of the book has a distinct format and a special function, they have all been designed to be used together to provide a complete package of travel information. To use this book to full advantage, take a few minutes to read the table of contents and random entries in each section to give you an idea of how it all fits together.

Pick and choose information that you need from different sections. Assume, for example, that you have always wanted to take that typically English vacation, a walking tour through rural England, but you never really knew how to organize it or where to go. Turn first to the hiking section of GETTING READY TO GO as well as the chapters on planning a trip, accommodations, and climate and clothes. These short, informative entries provide plenty of practical information. But where to go? Turn next to DIRECTIONS. Perhaps you choose to walk the 100-odd-mile Cotswold Way. Your trip will certainly begin and end in London, and for a complete rundown on that fabulous city, you should read the London chapter of THE CITIES. Finally, turn to DIVERSIONS to peruse the chapters on sports, hotels, antiques, and other activities in which you are interested to make sure you don't miss anything in the neighborhood.

In other words, the sections of this book are building blocks to help you put together the best possible trip. Use them selectively as a tool, a source of ideas, a reference work for accurate facts, and a guide to the best buys, the most exciting sights, the most pleasant accommodations, the tastiest food—*the best travel experiences* that you can have.

GETTING READY TO GO

When and How to Go

What's Where

The islands that make up Great Britain and Ireland — which together used to be known as the British Isles — lie in the North Atlantic immediately off the northwest coast of France, separated from the Continent by the English Channel, the Strait of Dover, and the North Sea. Dover, on the southeast tip of England, and Calais, in the northwestern corner of France, are only 25 miles from each other. Included in the scattering of tiny islands nearby that are part of Great Britain are the Channel Islands; the Isle of Man; the Orkneys, Hebrides, and Shetlands off the coast of Scotland; and others.

England, Scotland, and Wales (Great Britain) together with Northern Ireland are the major entities that compose the United Kingdom. Northern Ireland, a province of the UK, consists of six counties — Antrim, Armagh, Down, Fermanagh, Londonderry, and Tyrone — and covers an area of some 5,000 square miles in the northeastern part of the island of Ireland. There are 26 counties in the Irish Republic. In total, the United Kingdom covers some 94,000 square miles and has a population of 56 million, 1.5 million of whom live in Northern Ireland. Physically, England dominates its island, covering well over half the area that extends from the southern coast along the English Channel to Newcastle, at the edge of the Scottish Lowlands. Wales abuts England on the west, projecting into St. George's Channel, which separates it from Ireland. Scotland forms the northern third of the island. The Irish Republic covers some 27,000 square miles, the lion's share of the island it shares with Northern Ireland; it has a population of 3 million.

ENGLAND

Broadly speaking, England is rather flat in the south and east and mountainous in the north and west. Like all generalizations, however, this one has a striking exception — the southwestern peninsula, which is dominated by two large wild moorlands, Dartmoor and Exmoor. The more southerly, Dartmoor, is a granite-based, desolately beautiful region of rugged hills and bogs; the gentler Exmoor is a heather-clad plateau creased by deep valleys cradling tiny, whitewashed villages.

The south and east of England are low-lying lands crossed by ranges of rolling hills and gently sculpted by slow-moving rivers. The highlands here are paradoxically called "the Downs." Much of the area is now "Londonized," but you'll still find delightfully rural and provincial towns.

To the north, the lowlands merge imperceptibly with the Midlands, a mining and manufacturing region centered on Birmingham. The landscape, although often marred by industry, is subtly attractive, especially around the Derbyshire hills and the Peak National Park. The Midlands slope away to East Anglia, a large tract of flat and beautifully still countryside, whose citizens retain a strong regional identity. At the coast the land slips quietly into the North Sea; here, there are many deserted beaches; peaceful wildlife reserves; and the famous Broads, haunt of sailors and fishermen.

The great backbone of England is the Pennine Hills, which run north from South Yorkshire to Scotland. Although surrounded on three sides by heavily populated cities, the Pennines remain remarkably wild. To the west is the Lake District, where volcanic rocks and glaciation have combined to produce a stunning landscape of mountains, woods, and lakes. England's highest mountain, Scafell Pike (3,210 feet), dominates this region, loved by hikers and campers. In the east, the North York Moors, cut by fast-flowing rivers into a patchwork of dales, reach northward to a very secluded corner of England, Northumberland. No industry has ever penetrated here, or large town ever grown up. Even the roads hesitate; only river valleys like Coquetdale penetrate the heart of this wild region.

SCOTLAND

Emerging without fuss from northern England, the Lowlands of Scotland are a region of broad valleys and rounded green hills, quite unlike the stereotypical image of wild Scotland, but no less beautiful. Farther north, however, above the Highland Boundary Fault, that wilder Scotland begins; here are the towering mountains, cascading waterfalls, and deep forests. The Fault runs right through Loch Lomond, Britain's largest stretch of inland water, which is dotted with tiny islands. In the east are the Trossachs ("the Bristly Country"), an uncivilized thicket of birch, oak, and heather crowding Lochs Katrine, Archay, and Venachar. This is the heart of the romantic Sir Walter Scott region, immortalized in his long poem, *The Lady of the Lake*.

North again are the Highlands proper, running from Fort William in the southwest, up the coast to Cape Wrath at the northern tip of the country to the Highland capital, Inverness. The mountains here are often snow-capped in summer, and the rivers have sliced through the harsh slopes to feed dense pine forests. In the far west the Atlantic has taken charge and carved long rugged fingers from the land, leaving sea-filled valleys between them. Off that remote coast are the Hebrides — a group of rocky islands flung into the ocean. Largest and perhaps best of all is Skye, "the Faery Isle," a volcanic wonderland softened by rivers and mists that is still serenely remote from the present century and breathtakingly beautiful.

WALES

Wales is ringed with huge castles, reminders of those days when its people were kept under strict control by their nervous English neighbors. The need for caution has gone, but the sense of difference between the two countries still persists and is reflected by the striking change of scenery as you cross from the green and gentle hills and valleys of English "Border Country" to the rugged mountains of Wales.

The Brecon Beacons of the south and center are the heart of wild Wales. Their highest point, Pen-y-Fan, is 2,906 feet above sea level and the roads give up long before reaching its heights. But pony trails abound, and it's very easy to forget civilization as you trot along past slate outcroppings and thundering waterfalls. The Pembrokeshire coast in southwestern Wales is considered the most spectacular in all Britain. Here, the mountains rush headlong into the sea, only sometimes softened by sandy bays and quiet creeks. The industrial towns of Port Talbot, Swansea, and Cardiff are located along the southern coast. The people there make their living refining and shipping the coal and iron ore carved from mines in the steep and isolated valleys of South Wales.

Wales is at its most dramatic, however, in the far northwest. Here, its highest mountains, the Snowdon Massif (3,560 feet at the highest peak) look down over range upon range of slate-brown mountains and valleys, rushing rivers, and huge lakes. The drive from Barmouth on the coast inland to Dolgellau follows the Maddach Estuary, with the Cadair Idris mountains towering above you. This experience will banish forever any misconceptions you may have of Britain's countryside being flat and tame.

But to experience the full beauty of Snowdonia, you must leave the car and walk or climb in the mountains themselves.

NORTHERN IRELAND

Most people who have never visited Northern Ireland — or Ulster, as it is often called — think of it as a drab, gray, and beleaguered country. Although it's true that "the troubles" persist, the scenery is far from drab and the welcome as warm as any you will receive. In the southeast, the majestic Mountains of Mourne really do sweep down to the sea around Kilkeel — you'll see at once why they are sung about. Along the Antrim coast, fierce and perpendicular headlands leap into the ocean on all sides, but inland are green and lush pastures watered by serene loughs (a lake in Ireland is a *lough*, the same as a *loch* in Scotland) and hugged by gently heaving hills. Lough Neagh, the largest lake in the United Kingdom, covers 153 square miles in the middle of the country and is bordered by five of the six counties. A major feature of the landscape in the southwest corner of Ulster is the watery, forested county of Fermanagh, which has more than 150 islands in its largest lake, Lough Erne.

IRISH REPUBLIC

Prim whitewashed cottages surrounded by verdant pastures and flowering hedgerows — this is the conventional image of Eire. But, in fact, Irish terrain is remarkably more varied for so small a country and can change abruptly in a matter of miles. In the northwest — counties Donegal, Mayo, and Galway — the landscape is stark and the vegetation brushy. Innumerable stone walls march without hesitation up steep mountainsides, where shaggy cattle graze stubbornly on the rocky land. To the south, the forbidding hills of northern County Clare, which appear to be almost paved with stone, give way to rolling, velvety meadows and powdery strands. The highest mountains in Ireland are in the southwest — on the Dingle, Kerry, and Beara peninsulas. Here sandstone ridges such as the Macgillycuddy's Reeks and the Caha and Slieve Mish mountains were shaped by Ice Age glaciers, which also left behind scores of lakes and valleys. More gentle are the southern coast of Ireland — a seascape of quiet coves, saltwater marshes, and little fishing villages — and the southeastern coast, a resort area popular for its sunny weather and sandy beaches. Just south of Dublin is the scenic Glendalough Valley, ringed by mountains, watered by two lakes, and scattered with ancient Christian ruins. The midlands, an area stretching roughly from Dublin west to Limerick, is a low-lying plain with many lakes and bogs. The green fields here are rived with black trenches from which turf has been cut, and the air is sweet with the smell of turf fires.

When to Go

For North Americans as well as Europeans, the period from mid-May to mid-September has long been — and remains — the peak period of travel, the traditional vacation time. As far as the weather is concerned, Great Britain and Ireland are at their best then: cooler and more comfortable than many other, less temperate, destinations on the Continent where an eventual heat wave is a foregone conclusion. It should be superfluous to point out, however, that neither country is a single-season vacation area, and more and more vacationers who have a choice are considering the advantages of off-season travel. Though many of the lesser tourist attractions may close for the winter — especially from December through Easter in rural areas — the major ones are open and they are less crowded, as are the cities. Off-season, British and Irish life is seen at its most natural, a lively social and cultural season is underway, and, of course, it's cheaper.

For some, the most convincing argument in favor of off-season travel is the economic one. In fall, air fares drop and hotel rates go down. Relatively inexpensive package tours become available and the independent traveler can get farther on less, too. Europe is not like the Caribbean where high season and low season are precisely defined and rates drop off automatically on a particular date. But many British hotels lower rates or offer cut-rate "mini-break" packages (for stays of more than one day, especially over weekends) from October through April, and hotel rates in Ireland tend to be at their lowest from January through March. Savings can be as much as 20%, unless high-season rates prevail because of an important local event — such as the Spring Show in Dublin. Of course, many smaller guesthouses and bed-and-breakfast houses (B&Bs) close off season in response to reduced demand, but there are still plenty of places to stay.

CLIMATE: Most people want to travel when the weather is best. To the extent that it is mild, with no beastly hot summers or bone-chilling winters eliminating chunks of the calendar from the options, the weather in both Great Britain and Ireland cooperates to make them multiseasonal destinations. Warm currents from the Gulf Stream soften extremes of temperature and even provide the surprising touch of palm trees in downtown Dublin and in western Scottish gardens.

The climate is hardly perfect, however. For one thing, you probably won't come home with a suntan, even in summer. There is a reason for those renowned peaches-and-cream complexions and the reason is moisture, meaning frequently overcast skies, or even rain. To avoid disappointment, expect the worst, and you might be pleasantly surprised at how infrequently it actually happens. Remember, also, that though winters are not the marrow-freezing scourges of the northern US and Canada, they are damp, and central heating is usually inadequate by North American standards. Mid-October through mid-March is admittedly not an ideal time for touring the Scottish or Irish countryside, though it may be suitable for those with special outdoor interests such as fishing and hunting.

London is very much a city of the temperate zone. With occasional exceptions, summers tend to be moderately warm, with few days above 75°F (24°C), and winters moderately cold, with few days dropping below 30°F (-1°C). Spring and autumn tend to be comfortable, with little more than a sweater or light overcoat required. Umbrellas or raincoats are necessary, but legends about London's incessant rain are exaggerations. The truth is that the weather in London is often unreliable and unpredictable, with beautiful mornings turning into dreary afternoons and vice versa. Yet London has less rainfall than Rome, which is known as a sunny city. It simply thins its rain out and spreads it over more days: not hard, driving rains, but showers.

Though changeability is typical of British weather, it is safe to say that the farther north and west you go from the heart of England, the wetter it gets. This is because winds moving from west to east drop their rain over Britain's mountainous backbone and proceed over the rest of the country a good deal drier. In Edinburgh, a day with no rain is a rarity, even in summer. Mists are not unknown either, and when the wind blows, put millstones in your shoes. On the other hand, temperatures usually don't go below freezing in winter or over 70°F (21°C) in summer. A mackintosh with a zip-in lining that fits over everything you own is a recommended survival kit. In the Scottish Highlands and islands, chances for good weather are best May through September. Cloudy days are a matter of course, but this doesn't mean the sun never shines. Days get very long in the summer and there is daylight well into the June night in northernmost areas.

Ireland's climate tends to be even more consistently showery than Britain's. Because of westerly winds coming from the Atlantic, it, too, has heavier rainfall in the west than in the east, but because of the country's small size, it has relatively uniform temperatures throughout. Summers are cool and winters are mild. In Dublin, average winter temperatures range from 39° to 45°F (4° to 7°C), with January and February the coldest months; average summer temperatures range from 61° to 70°F (16° to 21°C), with July and August the warmest months. Lightweight wools are worn even in summer. April is the driest month in Ireland and May and June are the sunniest months.

The chart below lists seasonal temperature ranges for specific British and Irish cities and should give a better idea of what weather conditions to expect and, therefore, what to pack.

AVERAGE TEMPERATURES (in °F)

	January	*April*	*July*	*October*
Aberdeen, Scot.	36°–43°	40°–49°	52°–63°	43°–54°
Bath, Eng.	38°–49°	40°–54°	54°–67°	41°–52°
Belfast, N. Ire.	36°–43°	40°–54°	52°–65°	45°–56°
Brighton, Eng.	43°–49°	43°–56°	58°–65°	47°–52°
Bristol, Eng.	40°–47°	38°–56°	54°–67°	45°–58°
Cambridge, Eng.	34°–43°	40°–58°	54°–72°	43°–59°
Cardiff, Wales	36°–45°	41°–56°	54°–68°	47°–58°
Chester, Eng.	38°–45°	40°–54°	54°–68°	45°–58°
Cork, Ire.	36°–49°	41°–56°	54°–68°	45°–58°
Dover, Eng.	36°–45°	43°–54°	58°–68°	49°–59°
Dublin, Ire.	34°–47°	40°–56°	52°–68°	43°–58°
Edinburgh, Scot.	34°–43°	40°–52°	52°–65°	45°–54°
Galway, Ire.	40°–49°	43°–54°	56°–68°	49°–58°
Glasgow, Scot.	34°–41°	40°–54°	52°–67°	43°–56°
Inverness, Scot.	34°–43°	38°–50°	52°–63°	43°–54°
Killarney, Ire.	41°–50°	45°–56°	54°–70°	49°–59°
Limerick, Ire.	36°–47°	41°–56°	54°–67°	45°–58°
Liverpool, Eng.	36°–45°	41°–52°	56°–67°	47°–56°
London, Eng.	36°–45°	40°–56°	56°–72°	45°–58°
Manchester, Eng.	36°–43°	41°–56°	56°–70°	45°–58°
Oxford, Eng.	34°–45°	41°–58°	54°–72°	45°–58°
Stratford-upon-Avon, Eng.	36°–47°	41°–56°	52°–76°	43°–59°
York, Eng.	36°–47°	41°–54°	58°–72°	43°–56°

SPECIAL EVENTS: Many travelers may want to time a trip to coincide with a special event. The highlight of a sports lover's trip may be attendance at the British or Irish championships of his or her game. For a music lover, a concert in a great cathedral may be a thrilling experience and much more memorable than seeing the same church on a sight-seeing itinerary. A folklore festival can bring nearly forgotten traditions alive or underscore their continuing significance in modern life.

In both Great Britain and Ireland, the calendar of such events is a busy one from spring through fall, but there is still much that is happening in winter. In London, the cultural season proceeds at a pace that few other cities can match. Museums and galleries mount special exhibitions; ballet and opera take place at Covent Garden and the Coliseum; concerts are held at the Royal Festival Hall, Royal Albert Hall, and Queen Elizabeth Hall; and the theater is everywhere. Other cities and towns, whatever their size, promote their own smaller cultural programs. Winter is also the height of the soccer and rugby season throughout the island, and curling and other winter sports are underway in Scotland. The grouse-hunting season in the Highlands opens in mid-August and runs to mid-December. In Ireland, a land of horse lovers, there's racing going on practically all year round, fishing for one species or another is also possible

14 GETTING READY / When to Go

all year, and winter is the hunting season. Somewhere a bloodstock sale, a rugby match, or a festival of drama, music, or dancing is taking place.

The events below are the major ones, listed according to the months in which they usually occur. Since there can be some variation from year to year, check with the British Tourist Authority, the Northern Ireland Tourist Board, or the Irish Tourist Board for the exact dates of anything you wouldn't want to miss.

GREAT BRITAIN

February

Crufts Dog Show—Over 8,000 canine entries compete for the "best of show" title. London.

March

Oxford vs. Cambridge Boat Race—Since 1829 and Cambridge is ahead. The big event in intercollegiate rowing takes place on the Thames between Putney and Mortlake and can be viewed from the towpath. London.

April

Grand National Steeplechase—World's most famous jumping race, with all Britain betting on the outcome. Aintree Racecourse, Liverpool.

Shakespeare Theatre Season—Shakespeare's plays performed in the town of his birth by the outstanding cast of the Royal Shakespeare Company. Season runs until January. Stratford-upon-Avon.

Badminton Horse Trials—Major event on the equestrian calendar: dressage, cross-country, and show jumping. Badminton.

May

Chichester Festival Theatre Season—Drama festival with four plays running for 5 months in modern Festival Theatre. After London, a good place to catch top-flight British productions. Chichester.

Pitlochry Festival Theatre Season—Five months of summer theater in a Scottish Highlands resort. Pitlochry.

Brighton Festival—Music and theater plus fringe events and fireworks in this seaside resort. Some performances in the Royal Pavilion. Brighton.

Chelsea Flower Show—Acres of flowers, shrubs, trees, and flower arrangements set up on the grounds of the Royal Hospital. London.

Bath Festival—Two weeks of choral and chamber music, art and film shows, lectures, garden and walking tours throughout the lovely Georgian town. Bath.

Glyndebourne Festival Opera—Over 2 months of first-rate opera. At intermission festival-goers in formal dress dine in the restaurant or picnic on the lawn. Near Lewes.

June

The Derby—The world's most famous horse race, run since 1780 when Lord Derby didn't make the winner's circle but did win the toss of a coin that gave his name to the event. Epsom Downs, Epsom.

Aldeburgh Festival—A 2-week music festival founded by composer Benjamin Britten. Concerts — emphasis is on new works — take place in churches, houses, and in the Snape Maltings Concert Hall. Aldeburgh.

York Mystery Plays and Festival of the Arts—Recreation of fourteenth-century mystery plays by 200 citizens of York. Held every 4 years (the next one is in 1984), it takes over 3 weeks and includes an arts festival with symphony and chamber concerts, choral music, and ballet. York.

Trooping the Colour—The Queen's official birthday parade and the pageantry of royal Britain at its best; from Buckingham Palace to Horse Guards Parade and back. London.

Royal Ascot–Part of the London season, the June meeting at Ascot Racecourse is attended by the Queen, members of the royal family, and high society in hats. Ascot.

Wimbledon Lawn Tennis Championships–The world's most prestigious tennis tournament and another part of the London season — there's a royal box at center court. London.

July

Henley Royal Regatta–The international rowing regatta is watched from grandstands or from boats moored to the riverbank; another fashionable gathering on the London social calendar. Henley-on-Thames.

City of London Festival–Orchestral, choral, and chamber concerts in St. Paul's Cathedral, the Mansion House, the Guildhall, the Tower of London, and other spots within the square-mile City of London. London.

Llangollen International Musical Eisteddfod–An extremely popular festival of choral music, folk music, and dancing that draws more than 10,000 competitors from over 30 countries yearly to a small town in Wales. *Eisteddfod* is the Welsh word for "session," and this one is 5 days of song in foreign tongues and colorful national costumes. Llangollen.

British Grand Prix–Top British motor race. Held in even-numbered years at Brands Hatch, near Dartford, and in odd-numbered years at Silverstone, near Towcester.

Royal International Horse Show–International show jumping and other events. Wembley Stadium, London.

British Open Golf Championship–One of golfing's great moments. First played in 1860, it now moves annually from course to prestigious course in England and the sport's ancestral home in Scotland.

August

Royal National Eisteddfod of Wales–A celebration of the Welsh language and culture and the chance to hear some of those famous Welsh choirs; arts and crafts contests and the "chairing of the bard" ceremony. Site alternates yearly between North and South Wales.

Cowes Week–International sailing festival at the headquarters of British yachting. Cowes, Isle of Wight. (Begins on July 31.)

Three Choirs Festival–Founded in the early eighteenth century and considered Europe's oldest continuing music festival — in this case, choral music. Held annually in rotation in the three cathedral cities of Gloucester, Worcester, and Hereford.

Edinburgh International Festival–Four festivals crammed into one 3-week extravaganza: the main music and drama festival with performing artists of world renown; the Festival Fringe, shoestring to big-time productions by amateurs and professionals who come at their own expense; the Edinburgh Military Tattoo, a nightly concert spectacle of pipe bands and kilted regiments on the esplanade of Edinburgh Castle; and the Edinburgh Film Festival. Edinburgh.

September

Farnborough Air Show–Aerospace exhibition and display of flying. Farnborough.

Braemar Royal Highland Gathering–Best known of the Scottish Highland gatherings takes place near Balmoral Castle under the patronage of the Queen; piping, dancing, and Highland games such as "putting the stone" and "tossing the caber." Braemar.

October
Horse of the Year Show–A major show-jumping event. Wembley, London.

National Mod–The Mod is to Scotland what the Eisteddfod is to Wales — a week of song, dance, and storytelling, this time in Gaelic. Site varies from year to year.

State Opening of Parliament–The Queen rides in the Irish State Coach from Buckingham Palace to the Houses of Parliament; ceremony inside is closed to the public but the procession can be seen en route. London. (It is sometimes held at the beginning of November.)

November
London to Brighton Veteran Car Run–Antique cars leave Hyde Park Corner, London, and drive to Brighton in celebration of the turn-of-the-century day on which a law requiring cars to be preceded by a man waving a red flag was dropped from the books.

Lord Mayor's Procession–Colorful parade of the newly elected Lord Mayor who rides from the Guildhall to the Royal Courts of Justice in an antique, horse-drawn carriage attended by costumed bodyguards. London.

IRISH REPUBLIC AND NORTHERN IRELAND

March
St. Patrick's Week–Celebrations throughout the Republic give the patron saint his due. Parades and other festivities in Cork, Dublin, Dundalk, Kilkenny, Killarney, Sligo, Waterford, and Wexford. In Northern Ireland, there's an important pilgrimage to Slemish Mountain, County Antrim, where the saint tended sheep as a boy, as well as musical and other events in and around Downpatrick, where he is said to have established Ireland's first monastery.

April
World Championships in Irish Dancing–Dancers from around the world compete with Ireland's best, chosen in national championships in February. Dublin.

May
Spring Show and Industries Exhibition–A week-long trade and livestock show with daily horse jumping competitions — like a huge country fair in the heart of Dublin and one of the city's two biggest annual events. Dublin.

Cork International Choral and Folk Dance Festival–An international choir competition with folk dancing exhibitions. Cork.

Pan Celtic Week–Representatives of Scotland, Wales, Cornwall, the Isle of Man, Brittany, and Ireland compete in song, dance, and sports. Killarney.

Fleadh Nua–Pronounced "flah," this is a festival of traditional music, the second most important one in Ireland. Ennis.

Maytime Festival and *Carrolls Theatre International*–Music, sports, social events, and an international drama festival. Dundalk.

June
Festival of Music in Great Irish Houses–Two weeks of classical concerts in beautiful eighteenth-century mansions. Dublin.

Annual Mourne Wall Walk–A sort of hiking marathon in which entrants pit themselves against the high peaks of the Mountains of Mourne, following a 22-mile-long course with a total ascent of 10,000 feet. Dunnywater, Annalong.

July

Writers' Week–Lectures, workshops, competitions, and camaraderie for writers. Listowel.

Killarney Bach Festival–A weekend of his organ music, chamber and orchestral pieces, choral works, as well as lectures. Killarney.

Orangemen's Day and the Sham Fight–Colorful parades in Belfast and other cities and a sham fight at Scarva in County Down commemorate the Battle of the Boyne.

August

Dublin Horse Show–An outstanding sporting and social event attracting horse fans and the smart set from around the Emerald Isle, across the Irish Sea, and from Europe and America. International jumping competitions daily, auctions, band concerts, arts and crafts exhibits, folk dances, dinner dances — it's the gathering of the year. Dublin.

Puck Fair–Actually, a 3-day livestock sale, and an excuse to keep the Guinness flowing. Men of the village capture a wild billy goat who, beribboned, watches over the festivities from a pedestal above the square. Killorglin.

Ancient Order of Hibernians' Processions–Parades, religious services, and sports events commemorate Lady Day. Various cities in Northern Ireland.

Yeats International Summer School–Two weeks of lectures, seminars, and discussions of his work and its background, an entire course with a certificate on completion. Tourists can participate with single admission tickets. Sligo.

Fleadh Cheoil na hÉireann–An All-Ireland Fleadh and the year's most important gathering of traditional Irish musicians. Some compete and some just play, and for 3 days there is music everywhere. Site changes from year to year.

Ould Lammas Fair–A very popular and traditional Irish fair held annually since its sixteenth-century inception. Ballycastle.

September

Rose of Tralee International Festival–One of the country's biggest bashes. A folk festival, dancing and singing, and endless opportunities for merriment occur around the central event: the selection of the Rose of Tralee from a bouquet of fair, young lasses of Irish descent who congregate at County Kerry from around the globe. Tralee.

All-Ireland Hurling Final and All-Ireland Football Final–Two rousing finales to a season of Gaelic sports. The hurling final is traditionally held in Croke Park on the first Sunday in September and the Gaelic football final follows two Sundays later. Dublin.

Waterford International Festival of Light Opera–Amateur groups from Britain and Ireland vie to give the best performance of a musical or operetta, and for 2 weeks the pubs stay open late. Waterford.

October

Dublin Theatre Festival–A fortnight of new plays by Irish playwrights plus imported productions and plenty of opportunity to discuss them. Dublin.

Cork Film Festival–An important week on the calendar of international film festivals; European premieres of feature films and competition for the St. Finbarr trophy for the best short film. Cork.

Castlebar International Song Contest–Devoted to popular music, it's one of the most important song contests in Europe. Castlebar.

GETTING READY / Traveling by Plane

Galway Oyster Festival–The Lord Mayor opens the first oyster of the season, inaugurating two days of feasting on oysters, brown bread, and Guinness stout. Galway.

Wexford Opera Festival–Rarely performed eighteenth- and nineteenth-century operas are staged in the small, restored Georgian Theatre Royal, and recitals, concerts, exhibitions, and balls go on elsewhere. The 12-day gala has an international reputation. Wexford.

November

Belfast Festival at Queen's–Three weeks of classical music, folk music, jazz, opera, ballet, drama, and film at Queen's University. Belfast.

Traveling by Plane

The air space between North America and Europe is the most heavily trafficked in the world. It is served by dozens of airlines, almost all of which sell seats at a variety of prices under widely different terms. It is not uncommon for half a dozen passengers sitting side by side on the same wide-body jet to have paid fares varying by hundreds of dollars for their respective seats, and all too often the traveler paying more would have been equally content with the terms of a cheaper ticket.

You probably will spend more for your air fare than for any other single item in your travel budget. To find the least expensive seat, there are certain facts you should know about the kinds of flights available, bargain arrangements, and the latest wrinkles in the scheduled and charter airline scene.

SCHEDULED FLIGHTS: Airlines offering regularly scheduled flights from the United States to Great Britain, many on a daily basis, are:

Aer Lingus
Air Florida
Air India
Braniff International
British Airways
British Caledonian
Delta

El Al
Icelandair
Northwest Orient
Pan Am
TWA
Western
World

Gateways – The number of US cities serving as gateways for direct flights to Great Britain has been growing and will continue to expand in the future. At present, direct flights (no change of plane between the starting and terminating cities, though the flight may not necessarily be nonstop) depart from Anchorage, Atlanta, Baltimore, Boston, Chicago, Dallas/Fort Worth, Denver, Detroit, Houston, Los Angeles, Miami, Minneapolis/St. Paul, New York, Philadelphia, San Francisco, St. Louis, Seattle, and Washington, DC. British cities served by direct flights from the US are London, Glasgow, and Manchester, with flights to London landing at either Heathrow or Gatwick airports, flights to Glasgow landing at Glasgow's Prestwick Airport, and those to Manchester at Manchester International Airport.

Aer Lingus operates daily scheduled flights to Ireland from New York (no Tuesday service in winter), and less frequent direct flights from Boston. All Aer Lingus flights land first at Shannon International Airport in the west of Ireland, then terminate at Dublin Airport in the east. Other airlines that currently have direct scheduled flights one or more days a week are Northwest Orient, from Boston and New York to Shannon, Transamerica, from Los Angeles and New York to Shannon, and Air Florida from Miami to Shannon.

GETTING READY / Traveling by Plane 19

Fares – Perhaps the most common misconception about fares on scheduled airlines is that the cost of the ticket determines how much service you'll receive on the flight. This is true to a very limited extent. A far more realistic rule of thumb is that the less you pay for your ticket, the more restrictions and qualifications you'll be subject to before you get on the plane (as well as after you get off).

These qualifying aspects usually relate to which months you travel, how much in advance you purchase your ticket, the minimum and maximum time you must remain abroad, whether you're traveling as a member of a group, and whether you're willing to travel on an airline-specified date within a predetermined week or to stand by — literally — on the chance that a seat will become available. Your ticket will fall into one of seven fare categories being offered by scheduled carriers flying between the US and Great Britain and Ireland. From most to least expensive, these are:

1. First class
2. Economy
3. Excursion
4. Advance purchase excursion (APEX or Super APEX)
5. Group inclusive travel (GIT)
6. Standby
7. Budget

In a class by itself is the Concorde, the supersonic jet developed by France and Britain that cruises at speeds of 1,350 miles per hour and makes transatlantic crossings in half the time of subsonic jets. British Airways offers Concorde service to London from New York and Washington, DC; Air France flies from those cities to Paris. Service is one class (lavish care, with champagne and caviar all the way) and the fare is expensive, about 20% above first-class fare on a subsonic carrier. Some discounts have been offered, but time is the real gift of the Concorde: It makes a New York to London run in 3½ hours.

1. *First Class:* More than twice the price of an economy ticket, and quite a lot to pay for free earphones and a glass of subpar champagne in your own special section of the plane. But the atmosphere is certainly classier — especially on the wide-body jets — and there are the added comforts of spacious seats and more leg room. Boeing 747s offer an upstairs lounge, and the service is far more attentive than in the economy section of the plane. No advance booking or minimum stay is required and there is no cancellation penalty. Unlimited free stopovers are allowed, an incredible bonus on a long trip. If you're planning to visit countries besides Great Britain or Ireland, you could stop over in any number of cities en route to your most distant destination, provided that certain set, but generous, maximum mileage limits are respected.
2. *Economy:* You travel on any scheduled flight you wish and your ticket is valid for a year. Unlike first class, which costs the same year-round, economy fares vary seasonally from a basic period in effect most of the year to a peak period that can be from 5% to 20% more expensive. The peak season is usually from mid-May to mid-September for eastbound travel and from mid-June to mid-October westbound. There are no minimum stay requirements, advance booking is not necessary, and there is no cancellation penalty. In general, normal economy fares allow unlimited stopovers, but normal economy is fast becoming an obsolete category as airlines switch to a system of two different price levels. Since passengers paying full economy fare are in the same compartment as passengers paying considerably less on discount fares, airlines have been introducing special frills to compensate those paying the full price. Seating is in the forward part of the economy class compartment and the section may or may not be separated from the rest of the economy seats by an actual partition. Liquor and headsets are free and there may

be more selections on the menu, as well as a separate counter for speedier check-ins. As in the old full-fare economy, stopovers are free and unlimited. This new class is known as premium economy or business class, though many airlines have different names for it. Pan Am calls it Clipper Class; British Airways refers to it as Club Class; at World Airways, it's Executive One; at TWA, it's Ambassador Class; and at Aer Lingus, Executive Class.

The remaining economy fare in this dual system is likely to be called "special" economy or, simply, economy. On a recent New York to London round trip, it cost about 15% less than business class, the saving effected by limiting the frills and the stopover privileges. Restrictions vary from airline to airline, but it is common to limit stopovers to one in each direction and to add a surcharge (usually $25) for each one. Not all airlines have adopted the new system. Many have retained a single economy fare that may resemble either of the two new classes in price and flexibility.

3. *Excursion:* The two basic excursion-fare types — the 14- to 21-day excursion and the 22- to 45-day excursion — have coalesced into one 14- to 60-day excursion and even this is fast disappearing on the US to Great Britain or Ireland route. If you find it, it may not be the bargain it once was, which is why the law of supply and demand is causing its extinction. Numerous other, cheaper, discount tickets have been introduced since excursions came into being and, with the introduction of the new "special" economy fares discussed above, excursions now exist that cost more than the very fares they were meant to discount. On a 14- to 60-day excursion you must stay away at least 14 days and no more than 60. There is no advance booking requirement and no cancellation penalty. A stopover, but not a free one, is usually permitted in each direction. There are usually two price seasons, though there may be three. Excursion fares apply to round trips only and have "open jaws," which means you can fly to one city and depart from another, arranging and paying for your own transportation between the two.

4. *Advance Purchase Excursion:* When an excursion ticket must be bought in advance, it becomes an APEX or a Super APEX. Almost all airlines flying to Great Britain and Ireland have one or the other or both, usually good for a minimum of 7 days abroad and a maximum of from 60 days to 6 months. Whether APEX or Super APEX, the ticket must be paid for in its entirety 21 days in advance of departure, and its price will vary seasonally from the basic period through an intermediate shoulder period to the peak summer period (a future fourth season is possible). The difference between APEX and Super APEX is in the stopovers allowed: One, free or costing $25, may be available on the APEX. The Super APEX allows none at all and for this reason is the cheaper of the two. The drawback to advance purchase excursions is that they penalize travelers who change their minds. The return flight must be reserved at the time you buy the ticket, and if for some reason you must change it while abroad (no medical excuses are accepted), you pay the difference between the round-trip APEX fare and the round-trip economy fare. In other words, by changing your return reservation after travel has begun, you change your entire round-trip fare from the APEX to the economy category. There is also a $50 penalty for changing or canceling a reservation before travel begins. These fares can masquerade under a variety of names: British Airways' Dollarstretcher and Aer Lingus's Green Saver fares are all advance purchase excursions.

5. *Group Inclusive Travel:* This is for passengers traveling as a group, taking the same flight and prepurchasing a minimum number of ground arrangements at their destination(s). The number of participants may be as few as 5 or as many as 40. The required time abroad varies according to the type of group, but frequently is limited to 3 weeks. The actual fares will also vary, again depending on the mini-

GETTING READY / Traveling by Plane

mum number in the group, but the air cost will be spelled out in brochures distributed by wholesalers and tour operators who are handling the group tour arrangements.

6. *Standby:* Travel to Europe became especially popular in the fall of 1977 when Britain's Laker Airways (now defunct) was given authority to operate exceptionally low cost, regularly scheduled daily flights between London and New York. Passengers on those early flights could purchase tickets only on the day of departure, on a first-come, first-served basis, and there was no guarantee that they would get on that day's flight, on the next one, or even the next one.

Since then, other carriers have added standby service, which in procedure operates much like the original Laker one. You must stand by anew for each departing flight, though the likelihood of success is increased by the number of airlines offering unsold seats on a standby basis. If you can't get on one airline's first flight of the morning, you can go from terminal to terminal to stand by for flights operated by other carriers later in the day. Obviously, it is much better to attempt flying standby during the off-season when space is not as tight as it is during peak travel periods — and this is especially true since airlines have been cutting back flights in order to fly as full as possible. Standby procedures vary from airline to airline, and an airline may even vary its procedure from airport to airport. Once aboard, however, you'll have the same meal service and frills (or lack of them) enjoyed by others in the economy compartment. As with economy fares, standby fares apply to one-way or round-trip travel, the tickets are bought at basic or peak season rates, and they are valid for a year. Most airlines have a special telephone number to call for a regularly updated report on seat availability.

7. *Budget:* These fares usually are available for a limited number of seats on selected flights. The ticket must be purchased no later than 3 weeks before the beginning of the week in which you intend to travel. When you buy it, you tell the airline the week you want to fly, but you cannot designate the exact day. Seven to ten days before departure time, you are told the date and time of your flight. The main drawback for anyone on a 2-week vacation is that conceivably you could fly to your destination on the last day of week one and be scheduled to return on the first day of the next week with no time to see the country — unlikely, but it could happen. Budget prices are often the same as standby prices, and because the fare requires a lot of handling by the airline, it is becoming a thing of the past.

Not all scheduled carriers offer tickets in all of the seven fare categories. And it should be noted that there is little, if any, difference in the prices charged by the main carriers for a ticket in the same fare category between the same two cities — despite a government policy of airline deregulation now in progress. At present, the similarities are more an effect of the economics of the marketplace than anything else, with airlines hastily matching any new package of fares and conditions proposed by competitors or being priced out of business. But while bargain offers proliferate, the cost of jet fuel soars, often diminishing the value of discounts to consumers. Some airlines, however, consistently manage to offer bargain rates. These tend to be smaller carriers that can provide a lot for less because of lower overhead, uncomplicated route networks, and other limitations in their service.

Transamerica (formerly Trans International Airlines), once a charter airline only, has added scheduled flights that are usually cheaper than those of the strictly scheduled carriers on the same routes. The airline currently has only two gateway cities (New York and Los Angeles) and two destinations (Shannon, Ireland, and Amsterdam, the Netherlands) for international scheduled flights, and departures are limited to once, twice, or three times weekly depending on route. (There are no flights from Los Angeles

22 GETTING READY / Traveling by Plane

in the winter.) World Airways flies six or seven times weekly from Baltimore/Washington, DC, to London and Frankfurt, and it offers a good selection of fare categories. Icelandair (formerly Icelandic), though it has always been a scheduled airline, also has limited gateways and limited destinations. It long had the cheapest airfare to Continental Europe on its New York to Luxembourg route, but its fares to London — the airline sells tickets in the economy, APEX, and Super APEX categories — are comparable to those offered by any of the other, larger carriers.

Discount fares can appear and disappear quickly. Special promotional fares, for instance, may be offered when an airline inaugurates a new route. A foreign carrier will often match or undercut the fare other airlines are offering into its own country. Watch for these, but also remember that not all discounts are advertised. It is essential to shop around, to check with several airlines, and to call each one several times — you will most likely receive quotes that vary from day to day and from reservations clerk to reservations clerk. When you think you've obtained a good deal, make your booking, but be sure to read the fine print for specifications about duration of stay, cancellations, and so on.

Keep in mind that the cheapest fare may not always be the best one if you plan to venture far afield in Europe. Until recently, flights between European cities booked in Europe were quite expensive and were best avoided by careful use of stopover rights on transatlantic round-trip tickets. Buying an expensive business class ticket to your farthest destination, for example, and taking advantage of its unlimited stopovers, often turns out to be cheaper than buying a bargain ticket (with no stopovers allowed) and booking yourself to the extra cities desired on European flights. This may no longer be true, however. At press time, more and more European-based carriers were slashing their intra-Europe rates, offering "creative" fares that could be purchased only in Europe. (Frequently, it was hard for a traveler to get an exact quote on this side of the Atlantic, but it was not unusual for the reductions to represent a 50% discount over the fares the same airlines had charged the year before.) An example of such a "creative" fare is Aer Lingus's European Connection — one flat round-trip rate from Shannon or Dublin to almost all European cities served by the airline. Unlike the other new intra-Europe fares, this had to be booked prior to departure from the US, and it was available only to holders of a transatlantic Super APEX ticket on Aer Lingus.

Finally, if you don't have the time and patience to investigate personally all possible air departures and connections for a proposed trip, remember that a travel agent can be of inestimable help. A good agent has at hand the information on what flights go where, when, and what optional categories of tickets are available on each. An increasing number also have automated reservation tie-ins with a major carrier, in which case information on seat availability on all flights for the day you want to leave can result in reservation and confirmation in a matter of minutes.

Reservations – When making plane reservations through a travel agency, ask the agent to give the airline your home phone number as well as a daytime business number. All too often the airline has only an agency number as the official contact for changes in flight plans. Especially during the winter, weather conditions sometimes hundreds or even thousands of miles away can wreak havoc with flight schedules. The airlines are fairly reliable about getting this sort of information to passengers if they can reach them, but often they can't if the agency is closed for the night or the weekend. Specify to your travel agent that you want a home phone contact provided to the airline, and if you have any doubts, call the airline and do it yourself.

Most return reservations from international destinations are automatically canceled after the required reconfirmation period (usually 72 hours before the flight) has passed. If you look at the back of your airline ticket, you'll see the need to reconfirm specifically spelled out. Every travel agent or airline ticket office should hand each traveler a

GETTING READY / Traveling by Plane 23

reminder to reconfirm return flights, but this seldom happens and travelers are often disappointed. Don't let yourself be lulled into a false sense of security by the "OK" on your plane ticket next to the number and time of a returning flight. That only means that a reservation has been entered: *A reconfirmation is still necessary.*

Seating – Where you sit can make a real difference in your comfort on the flight. Airline seats are usually assigned on a first-come, first-served basis at check-in time. Seat reservations arranged through a travel agent are often ignored, so get to the airport early. Before making your choice, ask to see a seating plan. You won't ordinarily have much choice about the kind of plane you fly, but remember that for long flights 747s and 1011s are more comfortable than DC10s. For shorter hops, a DC10 is perfectly comfortable. Some other hints: Generally speaking, seats in the middle of the economy section, over the forward part of the wing, give you the smoothest ride on a 747, and seats toward the front of the aircraft are the quietest. Seats immediately behind the exits and in front rows of each section offer the most leg room, and be careful of seats in the last row, since they seldom recline all the way. Sleeperette seats — found in first class on Pan Am, for instance — allow passengers to stretch out for the flight.

Smoking – The Civil Aeronautics Board has adopted minimum standards to ensure that nonsmokers will not be "unreasonably burdened" by passengers who smoke. For a wallet-size guide, which notes in detail the rights of nonsmokers according to CAB regulations, send a stamped, self-addressed envelope to ASH, CAB Cards, 2013 H St. NW, Washington, DC 20006. The guiding principle is that nonsmoking sections must be enlarged to accommodate all passengers who wish to sit in them. CAB regulations, however, apply only to US carriers.

Flying with Children – Portable bassinets are usually available for travelers with infants, and they work best when used at the very front of the aircraft. On long flights, the bulkhead seats are usually reserved for families traveling with small children. For the person who wishes to avoid children, it is wise to remember that families generally do not sit in the smoking areas.

Seat Size – If you have a weight problem, you may face the prospect of a long plane ride with special trepidation. You should be aware, therefore, that center seats in the three-seat alignments of wide-body 747s and DC10s are about 1½ inches wider than those on either side, so heavyweights can be as comfortable in the middle as in window or aisle seats. The seats just behind the first-class cabin partition usually have extra leg room, though the most leg room of all is afforded by seats just behind the emergency exit doors. Overweight travelers should also be aware that if the standard seat belt doesn't span their girth, all airlines have belt extensions. And if your size problem is really severe — that is, if you need more than one seat — the CAB has a regulation that requires an airline to sell you two seats for the price of one and a half.

Meals – It is possible to order many kinds of special meals for your flight if you give the airline 24 hours' notice. The range of available cuisines and dietetic foods includes high protein, vegetarian, kosher, baby or child's plate, low calorie, low cholesterol, and low sodium.

Getting Bumped – A special air travel problem with scheduled flights is the possibility that an airline will accept more reservations than there actually are seats on a given flight. This is entirely legal and is done to compensate the airlines for prospective passengers who don't show up for a flight for which they have reservations. If the airline has oversold the flight and everyone does show up — either on a domestic flight or on your way overseas from the United States — the airline is subject to stringent rules laid down by the CAB to protect travelers. The same rules apply to a return flight to the United States if you're flying with a US-owned carrier and your reservation was made in the US. Compliance is optional for foreign carriers operating into the US.

The CAB rules require that the airline first seek ticketholders willing to be bumped voluntarily from their seats for a negotiable sum paid by the airline. If, however, there are not enough volunteers, the airlines may bump passengers involuntarily according

24 GETTING READY / Traveling by Plane

to a priority seating plan approved by the CAB and available to passengers at all ticket counters. These passengers must be paid denied-boarding compensation equivalent to the one-way fare to their destination (but not less than $37.50 or more than $200) if the airline can get them there within 2 hours of the original arrival time on a domestic flight or 4 hours on an international flight. If the airline cannot get them there until later than that, the compensation must be doubled. The CAB also allows airlines to offer bumped travelers a voucher for a free flight instead of the denied-boarding compensation. The passenger can choose either the money or the voucher, the dollar value of which may be no less than the monetary compensation to which the passenger would be entitled. The voucher is not a substitute for the ticket the bumped passenger may have been unable to use — the airline continues to honor that as well.

Baggage – Travelers flying from the US to Europe may face two different kinds of regulations. On a US flag airline or on a major international carrier, CAB baggage regulations doubtless will be in effect. Each passenger is allowed only one carry-on bag, which must fit easily under a seat on the plane. Its combined dimensions (length, width, and depth) must be less than 45 inches. In addition, each first-class passenger is allowed to check two bags, neither of which may exceed a total of 62 inches (combined length, width, and depth). Economy passengers are also allowed two bags in the cargo hold, neither one to exceed 62 inches and the total combined dimensions of *both* together not to exceed 106 inches. Charges for additional bags are assessed at a flat rate.

On European local or trunk carriers, however, you may find your luggage subject to the old weight determination under which economy-fare passengers are allowed only 44 pounds total of luggage without additional charge. First-class passengers are allowed 66 pounds total.

Luggage should be labeled inside and out and all tags from previous trips should be removed in order to avoid confusion. If your bags are not in the baggage claim area after your flight, or if they're damaged, report the problem to airline personnel immediately. Some airlines disclaim liability for missing or damaged luggage that is not reported in writing within 4 hours of the arrival of the flight, but CAB regulations allow up to 45 days on domestic flights and 21 days on international flights. (Though it seems likely that most people would report loss or damage without delay, the regulation protects those who, because of illness or some other complication, cannot do it immediately.) Fill out a report form on your lost or damaged luggage and hold on to a copy of it and your claim check. If you must surrender the check to claim a damaged bag, get a receipt for it to prove that you did, indeed, check baggage on the flight. Most airlines have emergency funds to dispense to passengers stranded away from home without luggage, but if it turns out your bags are truly lost and not simply delayed, do not there and then sign any paper indicating you'll accept a settlement offer. Since the airline is responsible for the value of your bags within certain statutory limits, you should take time to assess the extent of your loss (see *Insurance*, GETTING READY TO GO). It's a good idea to keep records indicating the price you paid for the bags and their contents because these help to eliminate arguments in establishing the amount of either loss or damage.

It's important to keep in mind that CAB regulations are subject to change because of deregulation and changes in the airline industry in general. Before you fly, double-check with your airline on all rules that affect you.

CHARTER FLIGHTS: By actually renting a plane or at least booking a block of seats on a specially arranged flight, charter operators can offer travelers air transportation — often coupled with a hotel room, meals, and other arrangements — at costs lower than most economy or excursion fares on scheduled flights. Charters were once the only air fare bargains available, but this is no longer the case. Various discount, standby, and budget fares on scheduled airlines are often just as low, especially on the most competitive routes. Flights to Britain are becoming harder to spot among the charter listings because travelers to Britain can take advantage of discount fares on almost every

GETTING READY / Traveling by Plane 25

airline flying there and can depart conveniently from any number of gateway cities across the US. (Charters have always been attractive to people living in out-of-the-way places because they frequently take off from nearby airports, saving travelers the inconvenience and expense of getting to a major city to begin the trip.) And even the APEX fares to Britain, while not as low as the occasional charter that can be found, have extremely flexible conditions, allowing a stay abroad as short as 7 days or as long as 6 months. Charter flights to Ireland, however, still exist because until quite recently there were few alternatives for the cost-conscious. Standby and budget fares on scheduled flights to Ireland were few and far between, and even now the nearest gateway city may still be halfway across the continent from a prospective traveler's home. Where demand persists, charter operators will fill it, renting the planes or the seats from scheduled airlines or from specialized charter airlines, and offering the flights to the public directly through advertisements or travel agents. You buy the ticket from the operator or the agent, not from the airline owning the plane.

Charter travel once required that an individual be a member, of fairly long standing, of an organization, club, or other "affinity" group whose main purpose was not travel. Now "public charters" have been approved by the CAB, making charters more competitive by giving their operators some of the flexibility of the scheduled airlines. Public charters are open to anyone, whether a member of a group or not, they have no advance booking requirements, and they have no minimum-stay requirements. They allow the passenger to book one flight to cross the Atlantic and to book another one-way passage coming back. (Note: These are CAB regulations, that is, American regulations, and they do not control charter laws in other countries. For example, if you want to book a one-way foreign charter back to the US, you may find advance booking rules are in force.) Operators can offer air-only charters, selling the flight alone, or they can offer charter packages, including the flight plus a combination of land arrangements such as accommodations, meals, tours, or car rental. Some things to keep in mind about the charter game:

1. If you are forced to cancel your trip, you can lose most and possibly all of your money unless you have cancellation insurance, which is a *must* (see *Insurance*, GETTING READY TO GO).
2. If too few passengers book, charter flights can be canceled by the operator up to 10 days before departure. Your money is returned in this event, but you may have too little time to make new arrangements.
3. Most charters have little of the flexibility of regularly scheduled flights regarding refunds and the changing of flight dates; if you book a return flight, you must be on it or lose your money.
4. Charter operators are permitted to assess a fuel surcharge of up to 10% of the air fare, if rising fuel costs warrant it, after you have paid for your flight.
5. By virtue of the economics of charter flights, your plane will almost always be full, so you will be crowded, though not necessarily uncomfortable.

Bookings – If you do take a charter, read the contract carefully and note:

1. Instructions concerning the payment of the deposit and the balance, and to whom the check is to be made payable. Ordinarily checks are made out to an escrow account, which means the charter company can't spend your money until your flight has been completed. The charter company should be bonded (usually by an insurance company), and you should know the name of the bonding agent. If you want to file a claim against the charter company, the claim should be sent to the bonding agent.
2. Stipulations regarding cancellation by the consumer. You may forfeit much or all of your payment if you cancel closer to the departure date than allowed.

3. Conditions under which the operator has the right to cancel the charter. (Other than CAB-set periods of notice of cancellations, the only justification for cancellations is a natural disaster or a political upheaval.) Remember that if an operator can't fly at the specified time or via the designated route, no last-minute substitutions may be made. The charter must be canceled and your money must be refunded immediately.

Consumer Information – Current charter operations are in some disarray because of government deregulation, the serious competition of discount fares on scheduled airlines, and also because a number of operators have been successfully sued by consumers for not coming across with the promised goods — usually when a charter flight was purchased in conjunction with on-the-ground accommodations as part of a package. From a consumer standpoint, the need to select a reliable charter company has never been greater. When you consider a charter flight or package, ask your travel agent who runs it and then check out the company. The Better Business Bureau in the home city of the company you are considering can tell you the number of complaints, if any, lodged against the company in the past, as can the CAB.

The CAB will also do what it can to assist air travelers who have complaints. You must write a formal letter requesting assistance and your letter must be specifically addressed to the CAB. It is not enough to simply send a copy of a letter of grievance that was addressed to an airline, travel agent, or tour operator, though you may send such a copy if it is accompanied by a cover letter to the CAB. Write to the Bureau of Compliance and Consumer Protection, Civil Aeronautics Board, 1825 Connecticut Ave. NW, Washington, DC 20428 (phone: 202-673-6047). The CAB also has local offices in Chicago, Miami, Dallas, Los Angeles, and Seattle. A good source of information on the regulations governing the airlines is *Air Travelers' Fly-Rights,* available free of charge from the Public Affairs Office of the CAB at the above address (or call 202-673-5990). Two excellent sources of specific information on upcoming charter flights, as well as general hints on air travel, are *How to Fly for Less* by Jens Jurgen (Travel Information Bureau, PO Box 105, Kings Park, NY 11754; $5), and *Travel Smart,* a monthly newsletter (Communications House, 40 Beechdale Rd., Dobbs Ferry, NY 10522; $23 a year).

ON ARRIVAL: Heathrow, Britain's main international airport, is 15 miles from central London and the trip into town can be easily made on the London underground (subway) from Heathrow Central Station at the airport itself. Piccadilly Line trains leave every 4 to 7½ minutes, depending on the time of day, and operate 20 hours a day (18 hours on Sunday). Stops are convenient to most of London's main hotel areas, and the line feeds into the rest of the London underground network. The fare varies according to destination: Heathrow to Piccadilly Circus, about a 45-minute trip, costs £1.80. By comparison, taxi fare from Heathrow to downtown London is about £12. Buses also connect Heathrow with London and suburbs. Gatwick Airport, 27 miles from central London, is not linked to the underground but it does have its own rail station. Trains leave for London's Victoria Station every 15 minutes from 6 AM to midnight and once per hour thereafter. The trip takes under 40 minutes and costs £2.90, compared to a taxi ride of about £24. Flights from the US also serve Manchester and Glasgow. Manchester International Airport is 10 miles from central Manchester; express buses leave the International Arrivals Terminal every half-hour for the Chorlton Street Bus Station and the Victoria Rail Station. Fare for the approximately 30-minute trip is £1. Glasgow's Prestwick Airport is 35 miles from the center of the city, reached by bus to the Anderston Cross Bus Station in about 1¼ hours; fare £2.10.

If you arrive at Ireland's Shannon International Airport in the west, CIE (Córas Iompair Éireann, the National Transportation Company) buses will take you to the Limerick Railway Station in downtown Limerick, 15 miles away. Departures are every half-hour during morning and evening hours of peak traffic, otherwise once an hour (to midnight). The bus ride is about 45 minutes long and the fare is IR£1.45. If you prefer to take a taxi, you'll pay about IR£6. From Limerick there are an average of six trains a day to Dublin, a 2½ hour trip to the east coast. CIE buses connect Dublin Airport, 6 miles north of the city, with Busaras (Dublin's Central Bus Station) on Store Street every 20 minutes up to midnight; the fare is IR£1.20. The taxi fare to a similar city-center location will be about IR£5.

Daily air service between London and Dublin is provided by both British Airways and Aer Lingus, and internal services are abundant in both countries. In Great Britain, at least eight domestic airlines have scheduled flights to major cities and islands. British Airways runs many shuttle flights daily between London and Glasgow, Edinburgh, and Belfast. (An express bus service connects with most flights arriving at Belfast Airport. The journey time to Great Victoria Street in the center of the city is 40 minutes and the fare is £1.45.) In Ireland, Aer Lingus provides domestic service between Shannon and Dublin, and between Dublin and Cork. A private commuter carrier called Avair operates between Shannon or Dublin and Belfast. Aer Arann schedules flights between Galway and the Aran Islands in Galway Bay.

Traveling by Ship

Alas, the days when steamships reigned as the primary means of transatlantic transportation are gone, days when Italy, France, Sweden, Germany, Norway, the Netherlands, and England — and the US — had fleets of liners that offered luxurious week-plus trips across the North Atlantic.

But one ship remains for this type of service: Cunard's *Queen Elizabeth 2*. For seagoing enthusiasts, the *QE2* is the most luxurious vessel afloat — as well as one of the largest — and remains pretty posh even after more than a decade of cruising the waters of the world. Transatlantic crossings between New York and Southampton, England (sometimes via Cherbourg, France), are scheduled frequently from April through December and they do not come cheap. Last year the one-way, per-person cost of the 5½-day trip was from $1,120 (for the cheapest, two-in-a-cabin, transatlantic-class accommodations) to $5,855 (for one of the most luxurious travel experiences imaginable). Cunard has brought an ocean voyage aboard a luxury liner within reach of the ordinary traveler, however, by introducing an air/sea package in conjunction with British Airways. The one-way ticket to Europe by sea includes an allowance toward return air fare that — depending on when you travel, how long you stay, and where you live — can amount to a free flight home. If you want to splurge, you can even fly home on the supersonic Concorde, provided you make up the considerable difference between your air allowance and the Concorde fare. For information, contact Cunard, 555 Fifth Ave., New York, NY 10017 (phone: 212-880-7500).

Another interesting transatlantic crossing possibility for those who have the time is what is referred to in the industry as a "positioning" cruise. This is the sailing of a US- or Caribbean-based vessel from its winter season berth to the city in Europe from which it will be offering summer cruise programs. Eastbound positioning cruises take place at particular times in the spring; westbound return in the fall. Since ships do not make the return trip until ready to position themselves for the next cruise season, most lines offering positioning cruises have some sea/air arrangement that allows passengers to fly home economically.

Norwegian America line's *Vistafjord* has been making positioning crossings for a number of years. Its 1980 crossing was a 15-day cruise from Port Everglades, Florida, via New York to Le Havre, London, and Hamburg for a respectable $1,360 to $2,740 per person in a double cabin. With return by air to New York, the price ranged from $1,654 to $3,034. The *Vistafjord* then proceeded to Scandinavian ports and Leningrad on a Baltic Sea cruise that could be tacked onto the transatlantic passage. The ship's 1981 crossing went from Florida to Barcelona. Information: Norwegian American Cruises, 29 Broadway, New York, NY 10006 (phone: 212-422-3905).

Among the other cruise ships that have called at British ports en route from winter to summer berths is the Royal Viking Line's *Royal Viking Sea*. In 1980, it took 10 to 11 days from Fort Lauderdale to Southampton ($1,330 to $3,120) and Amsterdam ($1,475 to $3,458), with prices again per person in shared accommodations. A cruise through the Norwegian fjords, through the Shetland and Orkney islands of Scotland, then into the Irish Sea to Dublin and back to Southampton and Amsterdam could be bought with or without the Atlantic crossing and the Atlantic portion alone was also available with accommodations for a few day's stay in London before a flight back to the US. The ship made no transatlantic crossing in 1981, but will sail from New York to Southampton in 1982, when the *Royal Viking Sky* will also sail to Southampton from Fort Lauderdale. Information: Royal Viking Line, One Embarcadero Center, San Francisco, CA 94111 (phone: 800-227-4246).

The coastal waters of Great Britain and Ireland are busy with ships in transit between the two and on their way elsewhere, but, except for mini-cruises in specific areas, they are rarely explored on extended pleasure trips. A ship that sailed these waters in 1980 and 1981 was the *Orpheus,* on a 2-week special-interest cruise from Southampton offered by Swan's Hellenic Cruises, a British company. Ports of call were Dover and Hull in England; Leith and the Orkney and Shetland islands in Scotland; Galway, Glengarriff, and Cobh in Ireland; Holyhead, Wales; and the Isles of Scilly and the Channel Islands. Lecturers were aboard to discuss the history and archaeology of the places visited. Cost of the cruise in 1981 ranged from $2,089 to $3,516 per person, double occupancy, and there was no air/sea arrangement for those joining from the US. For information on future cruises, contact Swan's US representative: Esplanade Tours, 38 Newbury St., Boston, MA 02116 (phone: 800-343-7184).

Freighters – An alternative to cruise ships is travel by freighter. These are cargo-carrying ships that also take a limited number of passengers (usually about 12) in reasonably comfortable accommodations. The idea has romantic appeal, but there are a number of drawbacks to keep in mind. Though freighters are usually cheaper than cruise ships, they are not the cheapest means of crossing the Atlantic (excursion or even economy air fare is cheaper). Accommodations and recreational facilities vary, but freighters are not cruise ships and aren't designed to amuse passengers, so it is important to enjoy the idea of the freighter itself. Schedules are erratic, and the traveler must fit his or her schedule to that of the ship. Passengers have been known to wait as much as a month for a promised sailing, so if time is short, this is obviously a serious disadvantage. Freighters from the US to British or Irish ports are at present nonexistent and service to northern European ports such as Le Havre, Rotterdam, Amsterdam, and Bremerhaven is intermittent. At this time, service to the Mediterranean is easier to obtain. Two organizations provide tips, schedules, and other information for the prospective passenger:

1. *Pearl's Freighter Tips:* Run by Pearl Hoffman, a well-experienced hand in freighter travel. Mrs. Hoffman actually finds sailings for her customers, handles bookings, and provides all kinds of background advice. 175 Great Neck Rd., Great Neck, NY 11021 (phone: 516-487-8351; 212-895-7646).
2. *TravLtips Freighter Associations:* Provides a log of freighter schedules around the country. PO Box 188, Flushing, NY 11358 (phone: 212-939-2400).

Inland Waterways – Cruising the canals and rivers of Europe is becoming more and more popular, probably in reaction to the speed of jet travel and the rush to do as much

GETTING READY / Traveling by Ship

as possible in a minimum period of time. A river cruiser, barge, or traditional canal narrowboat averages only about 5 miles an hour, covering in a week of slow floating the same distance a car would travel in a few hours of determined driving. Passengers see only a small section of foreign countryside, but they see it with a detail and intimacy simply impossible through any other means of conveyance.

Both Great Britain and Ireland have waterways ideal for cruising. The River Thames is a favorite itinerary, navigable for 125 miles; another follows the quiet flow of the River Avon from Stratford-upon-Avon to Tewkesbury, where it joins England's longest river, the Severn. Also popular are the rivers, lakes, and interconnecting waterways of the Norfolk Broads in East Anglia; the quiet, less trafficked Fens, just west of the Broads; and several hundred miles of old narrow canals in the Midlands that were crucial to the development of the Industrial Revolution. Here, only traditional narrowboats — from 30 to 70 feet long but never more than 6 feet 10 inches in the beam — can navigate, because the canals, some as narrow as 20 feet, have locks a uniform 7 feet across. In Ireland, the River Shannon and its lakes, Lough Ree and Lough Derg, cut north to south through a good part of the country, and the Grand Canal traverses its heart from Shannon Harbour to Dublin. A branch of the canal runs south to meet the River Barrow, navigable on to Waterford. Above the Shannon's source, the scenic lakeland of 50-mile-long Lough Erne is also popular with cruisers.

There are two ways to cruise the inland waterways: by self-skippered boat or by booking aboard a hotel boat. If you choose to be your own skipper, you will be shown how to handle the craft, and told whom to call if you break down, but once you cast off, you and your party — the boats hold from 2 to 12 people — will be on your own. You do your own cooking or eat at pubs along the way, help lock keepers operate the gates, and even operate untended locks yourself.

The alternative is to cruise on a hotel boat — a converted barge or narrowboat. These carry up to 12 guests in Great Britain, in addition to the crew. (Hotel narrowboats often travel in pairs, with crew aboard the first and guests following behind.) You can charter the boat and have it all to yourself or join other guests aboard. Cruises are usually from 3 days to a week long and accommodations can be simple or quite luxurious. When reading the brochure, note the boat's facilities (most have private cabins but shared bathrooms) as well as the itinerary and any special attractions. Some cruises feature gourmet food; some make a point of visiting historic spots; and some seek out good locations for antique shopping.

Cruising the Inland Waterways of Europe, a very attractive book by Jarrett and Stanley Kroll (Harper & Row; $19.95), describes many European itineraries and tells how to plan and carry out your cruise. The BTA publishes *Inland Waterway Holidays,* a free booklet listing companies that offer boats for hire or hotel boat cruises, and the Irish Tourist Board publishes an information sheet, "Cruising on Inland Waterways," with particulars on Irish companies — the majority of which rent self-skippered boats. The firms listed below will provide information or arrange your whole holiday afloat in Great Britain and Ireland or in other countries of Europe:

1. *Bargain Boating, Morgantown Travel Service:* Books self-skippered boats in Great Britain and Ireland. 127 High St., Morgantown, WV 26505 (phone: 304-292-8471).
2. *Floating Through Europe:* Books hotel boat cruises in Great Britain; operates its own hotel barge on the Thames and a pair of hotel widebeats on the Avon. 271 Madison Ave., Suite 10007, New York, NY 10016 (phone: 212-685-5600).
3. *Skipper Travel Services:* Books self-skippered boats and hotel boat cruises in Great Britain and Ireland. 210 California Ave., Palo Alto, CA 94306 (phone: 415-321-5658).

Ferries – Numerous ferries link Great Britain and Ireland with each other and with the rest of Europe. Nearly all of them carry both passengers and cars — you simply

30 GETTING READY / Traveling by Ship

drive on and drive off in most cases — and nearly all of the routes are in service year-round. Space for cars should be booked as early as possible, especially for July and August crossings, even though most lines schedule more frequent departures during the summer months.

Among the ferries to Great Britain is the fleet of Sealink ships operated by British Rail in conjunction with the Dutch Zeeland Steamship Company, the Belgian Maritime Transport Authority, and the French National Railroads. Sealink connects Hoek van Holland (Netherlands) with Harwich; Oostende (Belgium) with Dover and Folkestone; and the French ports of Calais and Boulogne with Dover and Folkestone, Dunkerque with Dover, and Dieppe with Newhaven.

Other ferry services between Europe and Great Britain operate from Bergen, Stavanger, and Kristiansand (Norway) to Newcastle, and from Kristiansand to Harwich; from Gothenburg (Sweden) to Newcastle and Felixstowe; from Esbjerg (Denmark) to Newcastle and Harwich; from Hamburg and Bremerhaven (West Germany) to Harwich; from Scheveningen (Netherlands) to Great Yarmouth, from Rotterdam to Hull and Felixstowe, and from Vlissingen to Sheerness; from Zeebrugge (Belgium) to Hull, Felixstowe, and Dover. Ferries from French ports operate from Calais and Boulogne to Dover; from Le Havre to Portsmouth and Southampton; from Cherbourg to Portsmouth, Southampton, and Weymouth; from St. Malo to Portsmouth and Plymouth; and from Roscoff to Plymouth. In addition, there are ferry links from the Faeroe Islands, from Helsinki and Leningrad, from the Polish ports of Swinoujscie and Gdynia, and from Santander, Spain.

Seaspeed hovercraft, operated by British Rail and the French National Railroads, carry both cars and passengers on a cushion of air across the Channel between Calais or Boulogne and Dover (Hoverlloyd hovercraft serve the Calais to Ramsgate route). Since hovercraft travel a few feet above the surface of the water, they can be obstructed by waves and are grounded when the Channel is rough. When weather is good, however, they make the Calais to Dover trip in 32 to 35 minutes (compared to the 1½ to 1¾ hours the trip takes by ferry) and the Boulogne to Dover crossing in 37 to 45 minutes (1¾ hours by ferry).

Ferries to Ireland from the Continent leave Le Havre several times weekly year-round for Rosslare Harbour; Cherbourg twice weekly March through October for Rosslare Harbour; and Roscoff once weekly year-round for Cork. Between Great Britain and Ireland there are daily, year-round Sealink services from Fishguard, Wales, to Rosslare Harbour and from Holyhead, Wales, to Dun Laoghaire. Both trips take about 3½ hours. Other ferry lines link Pembroke to Cork or Rosslare Harbour, and Liverpool to Dublin. A daily jetfoil service between Liverpool and Dublin (B & I Line) takes passengers only and cuts the traveling time along this route from an average 7 hours to 3¼ hours. Ferry services to Northern Ireland connect Liverpool to Belfast in 10 hours, and the Scottish port of Cairnryan to Larne in 2 to 2½ hours' time. The Sealink ferry travels between Stranraer, Scotland, and Larne in 2¼ hours.

Regularly scheduled car and passenger ferries travel from various mainland ports to the Orkney and Shetland islands, the Inner and Outer Hebrides, the Isle of Man, and the Isles of Scilly. Sealink ferries connect the mainland to the Channel Islands and the Isle of Wight, and for holders of the BritRail Pass, travel to the latter is free.

Most ferry arrivals and departures are well-served by connecting passenger trains or buses, and in the case of Sealink ships and Seaspeed hovercraft, passengers can buy through train tickets from London to Dublin, Brussels, or Paris that include the ferry portion of the trip. The London to Paris route on through services by train/hovercraft/train takes about 6¼ hours; London to Brussels by train/hovercraft/bus, about 7¼ hours; London to Dublin by train/ferry/train, from 9½ to 10¼ hours. Many ferry operators offer round-trip excursion packages at reduced rates, and there are reduced rates for midweek travel during high season or for off-season travel.

Touring by Car

Once you've mastered the trick of keeping to the left side of the road, you'll find both Great Britain and Ireland ideally suited for driving tours. Distances between major cities are reasonable and the historical and cultural density is such that a visitor can use the flexibility of a car to maximum advantage, covering large amounts of territory visiting major sites or spending the same amount of time equally absorbed motoring from village to village. (See DIRECTIONS for our choices of the most interesting driving itineraries.)

But driving isn't a cheap way to travel. Gas prices are higher in Europe than in North America, and car rentals are not necessarily cheaper. Most people will make arrangements for their rental from the US, and it is important to explore every alternative before making your choice.

RENTING A CAR: There are several options for getting wheels abroad, including leasing, but most people simply rent a car, and do so in one of three ways — as part of a fly/drive package; through a US-based travel agent or international rental firm; or, once they are overseas, from a local car hire company. Essentially, the first two involve the same sort of thing: The car comes as part of a larger package, arranged and paid for before you leave.

Fly/Drive – Airlines, charter companies, travel packagers, and sometimes even independent travel agents offer fly/drive — often called self-drive or go-as-you-please — packages to Great Britain and Ireland. Besides return air fare and a car waiting at the airport, a typical fly/drive package used to include one night's free lodging in the gateway city. Increasingly, in place of the night's lodging, a block of prepaid accommodations vouchers is included, one for each night of the stay, and you are supplied with a list of hotels that accept them. Tour prices vary according to the category of hotels used and there are budget plans using accommodations such as bed-and-breakfast homes or farmhouses. The greater the number of establishments participating in the scheme, the more freedom you have to range at will during the day's driving and still be near a place to stay for the night. Generally, except for the first night's stay, which will be reserved before you leave the US, it is up to you to make day-to-day advance reservations en route.

Most packages are for 1 or 2 weeks, which means 5 to 12 days of actual driving, with unlimited mileage included. Car rentals are usually based on a six-tier price system, with six sizes of cars — variations of budget, economy, regular, and luxury — listed as A through F, the latter being the largest and most expensive. Most often the tour price quoted is for a small car of group A, though larger cars are usually available at additional cost. Larger cars also consume more gas, but they may be more comfortable, especially for two or more people on a longer trip. Be warned: Very few European-make cars have automatic transmissions, and those that do will most likely be F cars. Automatic transmissions must be specifically requested at the time of booking your package and, again, you will pay more and use more gas.

Some additional fly/drive hints: Use a good map to work out your itinerary well in advance, and plan on driving no more than 125 to 150 miles a day. If London is part of your tour, schedule it at the end, not the beginning, of the trip. This allows you to get into the countryside on your first day, presumably your objective, but gives you a place to stay near the airport on your last night, highly convenient. The car will probably be more of a nuisance than a help in London, so drop it off before you check into your hotel and take public transportation to the airport.

Rentals from the US – Travel agents can arrange foreign rentals for clients, either with local firms or with large US-based international operations. Several of the larger

GETTING READY / Touring by Car

British and Irish firms are represented in the US and it isn't necessary to go through a travel agent to deal with some of them. Godfrey Davis Car Hire, Britain's largest company, is represented by Dial Travel, 1735 Eye St. NW, Washington, DC 20006 (phone: 800-424-2862). Kenning is represented by American International Rent-a-Car, 4241 Sigma Rd., Dallas, TX 75234 (phone: 800-527-0202). Swan National is at 1133 Broadway, New York, NY 10010 (phone: 212-929-0920). Dan Ryan Rent-a-Car, one of the larger Irish companies, is at 10401 N Pennsylvania Ave., Oklahoma City, OK 73120 (phone: 800-654-3090), and Murray's Rent-a-Car, another large Irish firm, is represented in the US by National Car Rental, 7700 France Ave. S, Minneapolis, MN 55435 (phone: 800-328-4300). Procedures for renting a car through these representatives vary. In some cases you prepay nothing and are given only a written confirmation stating that a car is reserved. In other cases, you may pay either a deposit or even the full rental fee, in this way guaranteeing that the dollar rate quoted is what the rental actually costs you no matter what currency fluctuations may occur before you turn in the car.

Familiar US-based companies have pick-up and drop-off points throughout Britain and Ireland, and anyone can reserve a rental car by calling the international division of Hertz (phone: 800-654-3131), Avis (phone: 800-331-2112), Budget (phone: 800-228-9650), or others. Most companies quote weekly flat rates based on unlimited mileage, with renter paying for gas. (If you can't get an unlimited mileage deal, don't rent from that firm.) The rate is guaranteed against currency fluctuation and is prepaid in the US. Taxes and drop-off charges (if the car is left in a city other than the one in which it was picked up) are paid later. (Note: The tax rate in Britain is 15%; in Ireland, 10%.) There are legitimate bargains in car rentals when you know how to shop for them, and a good place to start your hunt is with Part 2 of the *Official Airline Guide* issued Jan. 1, March 1, May 1, July 1, Sept. 1, and Nov. 1. You'll find one in almost every travel agency. Compare the prices of all the major car rental firms. When you've narrowed your choices to two or three companies, you (or your travel agent) can confirm current rates and make reservations by calling the firm's toll-free number (also listed in the guide).

Local Rentals – The least expensive option is to rent a car once you arrive in Britain or Ireland, checking out local rates as carefully as you would if you were renting in the US. Every major city has dozens of small, local rental firms with rates that will be less than the international operations; in some cases you will have to put money up front for every day you intend to use the car, but most firms accept — and prefer — credit cards. Obviously, local rentals are a more attractive proposition in cities such as London or Dublin only if you are willing to invest the time to do some shopping once you get there. The car hire section of the local yellow pages is a good place to start. The BTA booklet *Vehicle Hire,* which you can pick up before you go, lists addresses and prices of US firms in Britain and Northern Ireland as well as those of large and small British firms and it, too, can serve as a useful basis for comparison.

If you intend to rent a car only occasionally, relying mainly on other means of transportation, bear in mind that Godfrey Davis operates Rail Drive booths in 73 British railroad stations. A car can be reserved before you board the train and it will be waiting for you at your destination. There is a 10% discount on rentals to BritRail Pass holders. (A special BritRail Pass/Godfrey Davis package that includes unlimited train travel and up to one car rental a day for the duration of the pass is sold by BritRail Travel International offices in North America. See *Touring by Rail,* GETTING READY TO GO.) Swan National has outlets at major bus stations where cars can be booked to be picked up upon arrival in other cities and British Airways (in conjunction with Godfrey Davis) and British Caledonian Airways have similar linked-hire schemes.

DRIVING: A US citizen driving in Great Britain or Ireland must have a valid driver's license from his or her state of residence; proof of liability insurance is also required shorter ones. It saves about one-third the normal fare on a day's outing if you depart after the morning rush hour and return after the evening rush has subsided. Weekend returns also save about one-third the normal fare if you leave on a Friday, Saturday, or Sunday, and return on the Saturday, Sunday, or Monday of the same weekend. Monthly returns and other discounts are available, so inquire before buying any ticket. To save even more money, consider buying one of the variety of rail passes allowing unlimited travel within a set time period. Some are meant for foreign tourists only and must be bought before you go (see below).

Most of the Inter City trains have either a restaurant car, where a full lunch or dinner costs about £5 to £7 excluding wine and tip, or a buffet car offering simpler, less expensive snacks and drinks, including alcoholic ones. If you're sure you will want to eat en route, however, it's a good idea to inquire beforehand exactly what meal service is offered on the train you'll be traveling. Seats in the dining car should be reserved either before boarding or through the steward very early in the trip.

Sleeping cars are found on night trains to Scotland, the north and west of England, and Wales. Since the sleeper supplement is a standard £9 addition to the price of a first-class ticket (£7 in second class), they provide a relatively inexpensive night's rest — especially when the saving of a hotel bill is considered. You will have a single compartment to yourself in first class (couples share connecting single compartments); in second class you'll share double accommodations, one in the top bunk, the other below. Lone travelers are paired with a stranger of the same sex though they may occasionally have a compartment all to themselves. In either first or second class, there is a wash basin in the compartment, and a morning wake-up is provided by the attendant who leaves hot coffee or tea and biscuits at the door, free of charge. As a matter of course, you'll be awakened one-half hour before your stop, but if that is not enough time for you, tell the attendant the night before at what time you want to get up. Passengers traveling to the end of the line may stay in their bunks until 7 AM or 7:30 AM, even if the train is scheduled to arrive earlier than that.

Naturally, it is best to travel light enough to keep your suitcase with you on the overhead rack, but if you have quite a bit of luggage, it can be loaded on to the baggage car found on nearly every train. No claim ticket is issued, so label your things inside and out. If you are getting off at an intermediate station, make your way to the baggage car as you approach your stop and supervise the unloading yourself. It is not the attendant's responsibility to do it for you even if you have printed your destination conspicuously on the bag. Most stations have porters or self-service carts, though you may find either or both in short supply when you need one. Baggage can be checked overnight at the Left Luggage facilities in most stations or in 24-hour lockers in some.

Both first- and second-class seats on most Inter City trains can be reserved in advance, either before you leave home or after your arrival in Great Britain. Reservations reduce flexibility, of course, but they are advisable during the summer on certain popular routes such as London-Edinburgh, London-Glasgow, London-Manchester, and London to points southwest. Sleeper reservations are necessary and should be made as far in advance as possible. Reservations can be made through travel agents or BritRail Travel International offices in North America (addresses below) or, in Great Britain, at British Rail Travel Centers set up to help passengers with bookings and information on all services offered by British Rail. The Travel Center at 4/12 Regent St. in London (open 9–5, Monday through Friday) offers the broadest services; others are at most of London's main railway stations, at Heathrow and Gatwick airports, and at railway stations in many other cities.

The multiplicity of London's train stations requires an explanation. There are 11 principal ones, each the starting point for trains to a particular region, with occasional overlapping of routes. The ones the tourist is most likely to encounter include King's Cross, departure point for Northeast England and Eastern Scotland including Edinburgh; St. Pancras, for trains going due north from London as far as Sheffield; Euston,

36 GETTING READY / Touring by Rail

serving the Midlands, North Wales including Holyhead and ferries for Dun Laoghaire, Ireland, Northwest England, and Western Scotland including Glasgow; Paddington, for the West Country and South Wales including Fishguard and ferries to Rosslare, Ireland; Victoria, for Gatwick Airport and, along with Charing Cross Station, for departures to Southeast England; and Liverpool St. Station, for departures to East Anglia and to Harwich for ferries to the Continent and to Scandinavia. Though stations are interconnected via London's underground (subway) system, allowing passengers to avoid busy surface streets while transferring from one to the other, you should still leave plenty of time to make the change. Note also, for your travels in other parts of Britain, that London is not the only city with more than one station.

Drivers should be aware of British Rail's car carrying trains, called Motorail, operating principally between London and Scotland, between London and the West Country, and between London and South Wales for connections to Ireland. Motorail allows car owners to take to the rails for long distances while their car travels with them on a flatcar. Book well in advance for this, especially in the summer. Another service for motorists are the Rail Drive booths, located in 70 rail stations throughout Great Britain, and operated by Godfrey Davis-Europcar. Passengers can reserve a car before boarding the train and find it waiting for them at the station of their destination. Special rates apply for holders of the BritRail Pass and Rail Drive packages can be arranged through BritRail Travel International offices in North America before you leave home.

Britainshrinkers are another British Rail enterprise. These are all-inclusive escorted tours out of London, either day trips or overnighters, combining fast rail travel with more leisurely sight-seeing by bus. The Britainshrinker to Brighton, for example, departs London's Victoria Station at 9:10 AM on Fridays, includes a morning visit to the Royal Pavilion — with time for browsing and lunch by the sea — and an afternoon visit to Arundel Castle, and arrives back at Victoria Station at 6:15 PM the same day. There are ten other 1-day itineraries and five overnight tours of 2 or 3 days duration. Britainshrinkers, available March through October only, can be booked through BritRail Travel International offices in North America or at the British Rail Travel Centers in London stations.

Sealink ships, operated by British Rail in conjunction with the rail or shipping lines of its neighbors, cross the Channel and the North Sea to Belgium, the Netherlands, and France, and the Irish Sea to Ireland. They also link the Isle of Wight and the Channel Islands to the mainland. While many other private shipping companies provide the same car and passenger ferry services, Sealink connections allow a traveler to buy a through train ticket from London to Paris, Brussels, Amsterdam, or Dublin, with no need to make separate arrangements for the sea portion of the journey. Travel is by rail to the water, where the ship waits, equipped or not with sleeping cabins depending on the length of the trip. Passengers walk to the ship and, on the other shore, they board a waiting train to complete the journey — referred to as the "boat train." Seaspeed hovercraft, run jointly by British Rail and the French National Railroads, skim across the surface of the water with their cargo of passengers and autos, crossing the Channel in 37 minutes on the Dover-Boulogne route and in 32 minutes on the Dover-Calais route.

Sealink connections to Dublin leave London's Euston Station for Holyhead, Wales, proceed from there by ferry to Dun Laoghaire, Ireland, and terminate at Dublin's Connolly Station. Sealink connections to southern Ireland leave Paddington Station in London and cross the Irish Sea from Fishguard, Wales, to Rosslare Harbour. Another Sealink service leaves Stranraer, Scotland, for Larne, Northern Ireland.

Ireland – In the Irish Republic, the government-owned Córas Iompair Éireann (CIE, or the National Transportation Company) operates the railroads as well as the country's intercity buses. Main rail routes radiate from Dublin to Belfast, Northern Ireland, and to Sligo, Westport, Galway, Cork, Limerick, Killarney and Tralee, Water-

GETTING READY / Touring by Rail 37

ford, and Wexford. There are also services between Dublin and the ferry ports of Dun Laoghaire and Rosslare, and between Rosslare and Limerick. Shannon Airport is connected by bus with Limerick from where there are several trains daily to Dublin and Cork.

Dublin has three principal train stations — Connolly, Heuston, and Pearse — and, as in London, it is important to be sure from which station your train will leave. Distances are not great: From Dublin to Belfast, Northern Ireland, on the *Enterprise* city-to-city express is a 2½-hour trip, and trips from Dublin clear across the heart of the country to Galway or south to Cork take 3 hours. Because of these distances, there is no need for sleeping cars on Irish trains, but you will find either a restaurant or a buffet car or, at the least, light refreshments available on most main routes.

The two classes of travel are called standard and super-standard in Ireland, and most main routes have both classes. If not, the one you'll find will be standard class. Fares are based on standard-class service; for super-standard service a supplement of IR£4.50 is paid, the same for any one-way trip whatever its length. Where seat reservations are possible, as on certain main routes, they can be made as far as 3 months in advance, though not from North America.

Baggage can be checked through to your destination between any two stations in the Republic, but not between the Republic and Northern Ireland. Nor can you check baggage into Ireland from Great Britain or vice versa. Since you keep it with you, keep it light, because porters are not easy to find as you get on and off the Irish Sea ferries. Most stations have Left Luggage areas where baggage can be checked overnight.

Trains between Dublin and Belfast are operated in cooperation with Northern Ireland Railways whose own routes in the northern "six counties" (Ulster) are few: Belfast to Londonderry via Coleraine, Belfast to Bangor, and Belfast to Larne. Travel on these is either standard class or first class.

Passes – The Eurailpass, the first and best known of all rail passes, is not valid for travel in Great Britain or Northern Ireland, though in 1980 the Republic of Ireland became the newest member of the Eurail network. There is no dearth of alternative rail passes in Great Britain or Northern Ireland, however, and they not only save you a considerable amount of money, they can also save you time. Since they are validated by an information clerk on the day of your first trip, they spare you the trouble of standing in ticket lines — which can be very long in the peak travel season.

The BritRail Pass is the most extensive, offering unlimited travel throughout England, Wales, and Scotland (including passage on BritRail's Sealink ships to the Isle of Wight and on the steamers plying Lake Windermere, the largest of the English lakes). BritRail Passes are issued for either first-class or economy travel for periods of 7, 14, or 21 days, or for 1 month, with children from 5 to 13 years traveling at half fare in each of the eight categories. The BritRail Youth Pass, for those 14 through 25, allows unlimited travel in economy accommodations, and the BritRail Senior Citizen Pass allows anyone 65 or over to travel in first class at economy rates. The BritRail Pass can also be bought as the BritRail Seapass to Ireland or to the Continent. This costs more, the extra charges covering either one-way or round-trip travel between Great Britain and Ireland by train and Sealink ship, or between Great Britain and the Continent via train and Sealink ship or Seaspeed hovercraft. The Youth Pass and the Senior Citizen Pass are also available in any of these combinations, all of which must be bought before going abroad, either from a travel agent or through BritRail Travel International offices in North America.

There is no doubt that the BritRail Pass is a bargain. At 1982 rates, the price of the 7-day adult economy pass was less than one round-trip fare between London and Edinburgh. Unfortunately, the usefulness of the pass stops at the Irish shore, nor is there any other pass that is valid for travel in both countries. The Eurailpass, entitling holders to 15 or 21 days, or 1, 2, or 3 months of unlimited first-class travel throughout

GETTING READY / Touring by Rail

16 European countries, is accepted on Irish trains, but unless you are combining a visit to Ireland with sight-seeing on the Continent, it is not as economical as Ireland's Rambler Ticket. Rambler Tickets are good for unlimited travel in standard class (you pay a supplement for super-standard if and when you want it), and come in four versions: 8 or 15 days by rail alone or 8 or 15 days by rail and bus. The latter combination should be considered, since trains in Ireland do not take you everywhere, and rail and bus routes are well integrated. The tickets can be bought either before you leave from CIE Tours International (address below) or after you arrive at the Dublin, Limerick, Cork, Waterford, and Galway railway stations or the CIE Booking Office, 59 Upper O'Connell St., Dublin. (The Youth/Student Rambler Ticket, for those between the ages of 16 and 26, must be purchased before going overseas; it is good for 8, 15, or 30 days.) The Rambler Ticket can be used only in the Irish Republic, not in Northern Ireland, and though it allows unlimited bus travel, use of city bus lines is excluded.

Some other passes are worth investigating if you plan to thoroughly explore a limited region. The Scottish Highlands and Islands Travelpass, for instance, provides unlimited train and bus travel in the Scottish Highlands plus ferry service to the larger Scottish islands, and includes round-trip transportation between either Glasgow or Edinburgh and the Highlands area. A 10-day Travelpass can be obtained through BritRail Travel International offices in North America; 8- or 12-day versions can be obtained in Great Britain. All are valid from March through October only. Other rail passes — among them the Freedom of Scotland ticket, the Freedom of Wales ticket, the Rail Runabout Ticket (for Northern Ireland), and regional Railrovers — are designed primarily for use by British citizens who cannot take advantage of the BritRail Pass. They are sold locally and limited to the selected region, usually on a seasonal basis. For rail buffs, there is even the Joint Tourist Ticket, good for as many scenic trips as desired on seven of the eight very quaint narrow-gauge steam railways of Wales. Tickets are issued for 7 days and can be bought at any of the railways at the time of your first trip, though you can write ahead for details, timetables, or the ticket to Joint Tourist Ticket, Wharf Station, Tywyn, Gwynedd LL36 9EY.

Further Information – The *Eurail Guide* by Marvin Saltzman (the Saltzman Companies; $8.95) discusses routes, rates, and all the ins and outs of Eurailpasses and other special rail deals around the world in complete detail. It contains information on Great Britain, too, though the Eurailpass is not valid there, and is an excellent buy for the serious rail traveler. The most revered and most accurate worldwide railway book is the *Thomas Cook International Timetable* ($14.95), a weighty compendium of over 500 pages, issued every 2 months. It includes schedules for Great Britain and Northern Ireland and for the Irish Republic , as does the equally hefty *Thomas Cook Continental Timetable* ($14.95). Thomas Cook also publishes an excellent *Rail Map of Europe* ($5.45, plus 75¢ postage) and all three are sold by the Forsyth Travel Library, PO Box 2975, Shawnee Mission, KS 66201.

BritRail Travel International offices in the US provide information on all British Rail services, make reservations, and sell tickets and rail passes. Addresses are: 630 Third Ave., New York, NY 10017 (phone: 212-599-5400); 510 West Sixth St., Los Angeles, CA 90014 (phone: 213-626-5104); and 333 North Michigan Ave., Chicago, IL 60601 (phone: 312-263-1910). BritRail's *Travel Times,* a booklet-sized summary of the main Inter City train services between major tourist centers in England, Wales, and Scotland, is available free from these offices. To buy a Rambler Ticket, or for information on train travel in Ireland, contact CIE Tours International, 590 Fifth Ave., New York, NY 10036 (phone: 212-977-9300 or toll-free, 800-223-8944). This office also makes available a free timetable of train services in the Irish Republic.

Touring by Bus

Going from place to place by bus may not be the fastest way to get there, but that may possibly be the only drawback to bus travel. A persuasive argument in its favor is its cost: Short of hitchhiking, traveling by bus is the cheapest way to cover a long distance. On the average, a bus ticket between two cities in the United Kingdom costs about half the price of the corresponding train ticket; in the Irish Republic, about two thirds of the train fare. For this amount, you will travel comfortably, if not always speedily, to your destination, enjoying an equally scenic view. The bus trip from London to Edinburgh takes 10 hours, for instance, and you could cover the same territory in 4½ to 4¾ hours aboard a high-speed train, but since high-speed trains are not in operation everywhere, the time differential on most routes is not as extreme. Buses can also take you to outposts remote from the railroad tracks, if you're so inclined, especially in Ireland where train service is more limited than it is in Great Britain. A map of the bus routes of either country is not much different from a road map: If the way is paved, you can be sure a bus — some bus — is assigned to travel it. The network of express buses — those traveling long distances with few stops en route — is only slightly less extensive. Because of this, both Great Britain and Ireland are particularly well-suited to bus travel.

It should be noted that to the British, only the bus that takes you from stop to stop in town is known as a bus; the vehicle that takes you from city to city or on a tour is called a coach. With the exception of Scotland and Northern Ireland, express coaches throughout the United Kingdom are operated by National Travel (NBC) Ltd., headquartered in London's Victoria Coach Station. In Scotland, the major bus companies come under the heading of the Scottish Bus Group, and in Northern Ireland, Ulsterbus operates the buses.

National Travel and the Scottish Bus Group offer a number of discounts on their already quite economical bus fares. A round-trip ticket (called a return ticket) usually costs twice the one-way fare, but if you're coming back the same day you can buy a day return that costs only 10% more than the one-way (called single) ticket. Ask also about midweek and weekend returns for savings that are less extraordinary, though still worthwhile. And if you're planning to use the bus regularly, consider buying one of the bus passes discussed below.

London's main bus depot is the Victoria Coach Station on Buckingham Palace Road. The National Travel information office in the station (phone: 730-0202) supplies information and timetables and handles bookings. If you are leaving from London during peak travel periods it is advisable to book well in advance.

In the Irish Republic, the state-owned Córas Iompair Éireann (CIE, or the National Transportation Company) operates the trains, the long-distance or provincial buses, and the city buses of Dublin, Cork, Limerick, Waterford, and Galway. As in Great Britain, there are reduced rates for midweek and weekend return trips and a number of bus passes are available. CIE's main booking office in Dublin, at 59 Upper O'Connell St. (phone: 300-777), provides timetables, maps, and information on how to get anywhere in Ireland by bus or train, as well as tickets. The buses leave from the Central Bus Station (Busarus) on Store St.

CIE also operates a series of half- or full-day tours by sight-seeing bus from major cities. From Dublin, for instance, there are 25 different tours, including three city sight-seeing itineraries. Tours leave also from Killarney, Limerick, and Galway. They begin as early as April in some areas and are run through September or October, though

40 GETTING READY / Touring by Bus

many are run at the height of the summer only. Departures are daily or several times weekly and prices range from IR£2.50 to IR£13.50. Brochures detailing the tours are available from CIE Tours International, 590 Fifth Ave., New York, NY 10036 (phone: 800-223-8944).

Bus passes – Several bus passes that allow unlimited travel within a specific time period make the bus even more of a bargain in Britain and Ireland. Unlike some rail passes, none of the bus passes have to be bought before you go, though most of them can be bought here and it's a good idea to investigate them as you plan your trip.

For Great Britain, there's the Britexpress Travelcard, offered by National Travel (NBC) Ltd. and good for travel between 60 cities and towns in England, Wales, and Scotland on the National Express coach network and some Scottish Bus Group services. The card, available in 5- or 10-day versions, is a slight variation on the pass theme in that it is good for 5 or 10 separate days of unlimited travel spaced any way you please over a period of a month. There are student (14 to 26 years) rates, and cards for children cost half the adult rate. The Britexpress Travelcard can be bought through a travel agent before you leave or in Britain, upon production of a passport, at National Travel booking offices in bus stations throughout the country or at the National Travel office in Victoria Coach Station. The same company offers a slightly different Wanderbus ticket, good for a day of unlimited travel from the first bus of the morning to the last bus at night. It is valid anywhere in England and Wales south of the Mersey and Humber rivers (that is, south of an approximate line drawn from Liverpool to Hull) and is bought at local bus stations. It is also valid on the Green Line bus network in London. Children under 14 travel at an additional discount.

Not strictly a bus pass, the Scottish Highlands and Islands Travelpass allows unlimited travel by bus and rail in the Highlands area and on ferry services to the Scottish islands. It is good, too, for travel on the post buses that in some rural areas of Scotland carry mail and the occasional passenger. The Travelpass, valid from March through October, is issued for a period of either 8 or 12 days if bought in Great Britain (from British Rail offices, Scottish Bus Group offices, Caledonian MacBrayne Ltd. offices, or by writing to Travelpass, c/o Pickford Travel, 25 Queensgate, Inverness, Scotland) and for a 10-day period if obtained through BritRail Travel International offices in North America. Prices for the pass are almost a third lower off season (March, April, May, and October).

Since the same company (CIE) runs both buses and trains in the Irish Republic, it is only natural that Irish passes are valid for both bus and train travel. The Rambler Ticket is sold in 8- or 15-day versions, and either version is available for rail travel alone or in a bus and rail combination. The tickets can be bought from CIE Tours International in the US (address above), at railway stations in Ireland, and at the CIE Booking Office in Dublin. They are valid only in the Irish Republic.

The Freedom of Northern Ireland ticket is a bus-only pass, valid for 7 days' travel on all Ulsterbus services in Northern Ireland from April through September. Buy it at bus stations in Northern Ireland or at Ulsterbus Ltd., 10 Glengall St., Belfast BT12 5AB.

Though bus timetables can be picked up overseas, it may be useful to have them on hand to help you plan before you go. For a comprehensive timetable of services in England, Wales, and Scotland, write to the Editor, National Express Services Guide, National Travel (NBC) Ltd., Victoria Coach Station, Buckingham Palace Rd., London SW1W 9TP. This is a large volume of over 600 pages, weighing more than 4 pounds. You can also write to the same address for information about schedules and fares for some 500 destinations throughout Britain, but always with London as the point of departure and point of return. The *Provincial Bus Timetable* of CIE routes in the Irish Republic is available free from CIE Tours International. For services in Northern Ireland, write to Ulsterbus Ltd., Great Victoria St., Belfast, BT2 7AB. Specify the region you are interested in or ask for the complete package of timetables (no charge).

Many city bus lines have their own tourist discount schemes that are a help to anyone who expects to do a lot of moving around in town. Not only do they save money, they also spare the bearer the bother of digging in pockets and handbags for small change. London Transport, the authority that runs the city's buses and underground (subway) trains, offers a multitude of such passes, but the main ones are the Go-as-You-Please ticket for 3, 4, or 7 days of unlimited travel on the bus or the underground; the Red Bus Rover, a one-day ticket for the bus system only (there's also a one-day Central Tube Rover for the underground only); and the Red Bus Pass, for one month of unlimited travel on the city's buses. Other cities — among them, Edinburgh, Glasgow, and Cardiff — have other bus bargains, so if you're interested, always ask before you buy — there's bound to be something available. If you don't use one of the unlimited travel tickets, remember that in London and Dublin there is no flat bus fare. The rate varies with the distance traveled and there is usually a conductor to tell you how much you owe. Remember, also, to always "queue up" at the bus stop not only in Great Britain, but in Ireland, too.

For an extensive listing (with prices) of available bus and rail passes, request the booklet *Tourist Tickets and Discount Cards* from the British Tourist Authority.

Package Tours

If the thought of buying a package for travel to and through Europe conjures up visions of a race through ten countries in as many days with a busload of frazzled fellow passengers as companions, you should be aware that packages are not what they used to be. For one thing, not all packages are package tours, and the one you buy does not necessarily have to include any organized touring at all, nor will it necessarily provide you with traveling companions either. If it does, however, you'll find that people of all sorts — and just like yourself — are taking advantage of packages today because they are economical and convenient, save the purchaser an immense amount of planning time, and offer so many variations in destinations and arrangements that it's virtually impossible for the Europe-bound traveler not to find one that fits at least the majority of his or her preferences. With continuing inflation, packages have emerged as one of the best of travel buys.

In essence, a package is a combination of travel services that can be purchased as a single booking. It may include any or all of the following: transatlantic transportation, local transportation (and/or car rentals), accommodations, some or all meals, sightseeing, entertainment, transfers to and from the hotel at each destination, taxes, tips, escort service, and a variety of incidental features that might be offered as options at additional cost.

In other words, a package may be any combination from a fully escorted tour offered at an all-inclusive price to a simple fly/drive booking allowing you to remain on your own. Its principal advantage is that it saves you money: Invariably the cost of the combined arrangements is well below the price that would be paid if all the elements included were bought individually. An important additional feature is that because you can purchase all these elements at the same time, you are left free to devote your full attention to traveling — the burdensome details of your trip already taken care of.

Packages are put together by wholesale tour operators, some retail travel agencies, airlines, hotels, and charter organizers, and the combinations are almost limitless. Perhaps the most common minimum arrangement is transatlantic air transportation and some ground travel feature, usually hotel accommodations. The most complete is likely to be a fully escorted tour in which the price includes everything except personal expenses (laundry, bar bills, shopping) from the time you leave home until you

42 GETTING READY / Package Tours

return. An important thing to keep in mind is that some kind of prebooked land arrangement at your destination may reduce the cost of your airline ticket by qualifying it for a group rate (see *Traveling by Plane*, GETTING READY TO GO). The resulting price of the airline ticket is certain to be well below its cost if it were purchased separately.

The lower prices that are possible through package travel come about as a result of high-volume participation. The tour packager negotiates for services in wholesale quantities — blocks of airline seats or hotel rooms, group meals, busloads of ground transportation, and so on — and they are made available at a lower per capita price because of the large number of each being purchased for a given time period. Here again, the net prices for the individual tour elements are considerably below what an individual would pay if purchasing them on an independent basis, and, even with markups and commissions, the tour price to retail customers is still reasonably below what they would pay if planning such a trip on their own. The prepackaging, however, is subject to various restrictions governing the duration of the trip and usually requires full payment before departure.

What goes into a package depends on who is organizing it. The tours put together by wholesale and retail agents can run the gamut from deluxe everything to simple tourist-class amenities or even bare-bones necessities. Fly/drive and fly/cruise packages are usually the joint planning efforts of airlines and, respectively, car rental organizations and cruise line operators. There are also hotel packages organized by hotel chains or associations of independent hotels; resort packages; custom-designed individual tours (frequently expensive, depending on the class of facilities), and of course charter flight programs, which may range from little more than air fare and a minimum of ground arrangements to a full-scale tour or vacation organized under the aegis of a membership group. Special-interest tours, increasingly popular for second-time visitors, can be once-only programs organized by particular groups through a retail agency or regular offerings packaged by a tour operator. They can feature food, music or theater festivals, a particular sporting activity or event, a special commemorative occasion, even scientific exploration. Reliable travel agents will be aware of specialized tours and will be able to book them for you or at least provide information.

To determine whether or not a package — or more specifically, which package — fits your travel plans, start by evaluating your interests and your needs, deciding how much and what you want to see and do. Gather whatever package tour information is available for dates that fit your time schedule and read the brochures carefully. Remember that because of rapidly rising air fares, brochures seldom include the price of the airline ticket in the price of the package. Applicable air fares from various gateway cities are usually listed separately, as extras, and have to be added to the total price of the ground arrangements. Before doing this, get the latest quote from the airline, because the air fares in the brochure may well be out of date by the time you read them. Check the brochures for the following:

1. What's included in the price — and what isn't.
2. Are the prices guaranteed; that is, if costs increase between the time you book and the time you depart, can surcharges be added?
3. Departure dates.
4. Variations in the itinerary — and price — for tours at different times of the year.
5. Supplements for people traveling alone. Package prices given are almost always for one person sharing a double room, and the supplement for single accommodations can raise the price considerably.
6. Specifications on whether all or "some" meals are included, since in the latter case you'll have to allow more for personal expenditures.
7. Class of hotels included.
8. Amount of refund in case of cancellation before departure.
9. Whether the operator may cancel the tour if too few people sign up.

Read the responsibility clause (usually at the end of the descriptive literature) very carefully. Here the tour operator frequently expresses the right to change services or schedules as long as you are offered equivalent arrangements; this clause also absolves the operator of responsibility if circumstances beyond human control affect the operation of the tour.

One of the consumer's biggest problems is finding enough information to judge the reliability of a tour packager, since individuals seldom have direct contact with the firm putting the package together. Usually, a retail travel agent intervenes between customer and tour operator, and much depends on the candor and cooperation of the agent. You should ask a number of questions about the tour you are considering. For example: Has the agent ever used the package provided by this tour operator before? How long has the tour operator been in business? Which and how many companies are involved in the package? If air travel is by charter flight, is there an escrow account in which deposits will be held, and, if so, what is the name of the bank?

This last question is very important. The law requires that tour operators deposit every charter passenger's deposit and subsequent payment in a proper escrow account. Money paid into such an account cannot legally be used except to pay for the costs of a particular package or as a refund if the trip is canceled. To ensure the safe handling of your money, make out your check to the escrow account — by law the account number must appear in the brochure and it's usually found in that mass of minuscule type on the back. Write the details of the charter, including the destination and dates, on the face of the check; on the back, print the words "For Deposit Only." Your travel agent may prefer that you make your check out to him, saying that he will then pay the tour operator the fee minus his commission. But it is perfectly legal to write your check this way and the agent should have sufficient faith in the tour operator to trust him to send the proper commission. If your agent objects too vociferously to this procedure, consider taking your business elsewhere, because if you don't make your check out to the escrow account you lose your escrow protection should the trip be canceled or the tour operator or travel agent fail.

Sample Packages to Great Britain and Ireland – There are dozens and dozens of packages available to Great Britain and Ireland today, visiting one or both of the countries, exploring a selected region, or stopping in London or Dublin only. Especially broad is the choice of escorted sight-seeing tours by motorcoach — anywhere from 7 days to 3 weeks or more in length — with an array of itinerary possibilities available. Typically, breakfast plus one dinner daily are included, and the hotel accommodations used are first class or better, with private baths or showers in all rooms, though some tour wholesalers offer cheaper alternatives to their standard tours by downgrading the quality of the lodgings.

There are even escorted bus tours with accommodations in tents, admittedly for the young and often with an upper age limit. One example is the 28-day Britannia tour of Britain, open to anyone 18 to 30 years old, offered by a British packager, Continental Coach Tours (London) Ltd., and marketed in the US by Intercollegiate Holidays, Inc., 501 Madison Ave., New York, NY 10022 (phone: 212-355-4705). Other companies offering similar tours are listed in *Camping and Caravanning, Biking, and Hiking,* GETTING READY TO GO.

An equally common type of package available to Great Britain and Ireland is the fly/drive arrangement, often described in brochures as a self-drive or go-as-you-please tour. What's usually included is the use of a rented car and a block of as many prepaid hotel vouchers as needed for the length of your stay, along with a list of participating hotels at which the vouchers are accepted. Most often, only your first night's accommodation will be reserved; from then on you book a room one stop ahead as you drive from place to place. In other cases, all the hotels are booked before you leave (or you can opt to book them, for a fee), requiring that you stick closely to a suggested route. Sometimes if the hotels used are first class or are members of a chain, the staff may make advance reservations for you day by day. Most operators offering these packages offer budget versions as well. There are plans using only simple bed-and-breakfast houses or farmhouses, plans mixing standard hotels with farmhouses, plans allowing an extended stay at one hotel or farmhouse (with some meals included in this case) or even in your own thatched Irish cottage. There are also fly/rail combinations: Arthur Frommer Holidays, in conjunction with British Airways, has "Britain Without Cash" packages that include rail tickets for specific 1- or 2-week itineraries in Great Britain and prepaid vouchers for hotel rooms, reserved before you set out, and for three meals a day. These packages are also available as fly/drive arrangements.

As one of the world's greatest cities, London is by itself of interest to visitors and many tour operators have packaged it that way. Basically, the package includes transfers between airport and hotel, a choice of hotel accommodations (with breakfast) in several price ranges, plus any number of other features that you may not need or want but would lose valuable time arranging if you did. Among these are one or two half-day conducted sight-seeing tours of the city; passes for unlimited travel by subway or bus; discount cards for shops, museums, and restaurants; membership in and admission to clubs, casinos, and discotheques; and car rental for some or all of your stay — usually a week, though 3-, 5-, and even 14-day packages are available. City combinations are possible: The 9-night package to London and Edinburgh offered by BTH Holidays is an example.

With the addition of theater tickets, the basic London package turns into a show tour, one of the most popular city programs. Arthur Frommer Holidays and British Airways have a 7-night show tour, for instance, that includes transfers, hotel accommodations, 4 days of unlimited subway or bus travel, tickets to 3 plays or musicals, one banquet dinner in a theme nightclub, an escorted evening pub tour, membership and admission to two casinos and three discotheques, plus discount cards for shops and restaurants. TWA and Air India also offer show tours (TWA's includes a half-day city sight-seeing and a full-day excursion to Stratford-upon-Avon).

Among the many special-interest tours that have been put together for visitors to Britain are the 10-day Wimbledon tennis packages operated by Fourways Travel Ltd., with tickets for 6 days of matches included. Another type of special-interest package, almost a staple among packages to Great Britain and Ireland, is the golf tour. The main ingredient is a chance to play at some of the oldest and best courses in the world: St. Andrews, Turnberry, Gleneagles, Troon, and Carnoustie in Scotland; the Killarney, Ballybunion, Portmarnock, and Royal Dublin courses in the Irish Republic; the Royal Portrush and the Royal County Down courses in Northern Ireland. A fly/drive arrangement is usually involved, with rental car, hotel accommodations for a week or two, often one dinner per day, and some greens fees included. There are packages allowing you to spend an entire week at one course, to play only Irish or only Scottish courses or to combine them, and special packages permitting you to both play golf and attend the British Open when it's held. BTH Holidays, together with British Airways and Aer Lingus, offers several golf packages that provide rental cars to get you from course to course; Golf Intercontinental also offers packages. Caledonian Tours has both self-drive packages and tours by escorted motorcoach, and the latter include escorted sight-seeing itineraries for the nongolfers in the group. Other golf packages are available from Tom Maloney Tours (Irish courses only), Bestway Golf Tours (for 3 days of golfing and 3 days viewing the British Open), and Dial Travel (for a short 3-day holiday at a Scottish course).

Inland waterway trips on canal boats or river barges are another type of special interest package that can be enjoyed in either Great Britain or Ireland. They're becoming increasingly popular and are discussed at length in *Travel by Ship*, GETTING READY TO GO. For enthusiasts of other outdoor activities, there are week-long horseback riding holidays at a choice of four equestrian centers in Ireland (Lismore Travel, 106 E 31st

GETTING READY / Package Tours 45

St., New York, NY 10016; phone: 212-685-0100); week-long horse treks of Ireland's Connemara Trail or the Dingle Peninsula, as well as week-long stays at a riding school in County Wexford, or at Castle Leslie, Glaslough, in Co. Monaghan, with 3 hours of riding daily, but no instruction (Hamilton Travel and Incentive Corporation, 422 Madison Ave., New York, NY 10017; phone: 212-751-9360), or a week of salmon and trout fishing in the Highlands of Scotland (Dial Travel, address above). A hiking trip through the moors and bogs of Ireland, rural England, or remote areas of Scotland is another possibility. Mountain Travel has developed 2- to 3-week itineraries that range in difficulty from easy, with much moving from point to point by Landrover, to strenuous, with an average 5 to 10 miles of walking a day. Contact Mountain Travel, 1398 Solano Ave., Albany, CA 94706 (phone: 415-527-8100).

Among special-interest packages of the nonsporting variety is an 11-day escorted motorcoach tour, Great Houses and Gardens of England and Wales, part of a series of Art Treasures Tours led by experts in their field and offered by W. F. & R. K. Swan, a well-known British tour operator. Swan is represented in the US by Esplanade Tours, 38 Newbury St., Boston, MA 02116 (phone: 617-266-7465). Dailey-Thorp Travel, Inc. (654 Madison Ave., New York, NY 10021; phone: 212-486-9555), specializes in music and opera tours, and its offerings include events in England, Scotland, Wales, and Ireland, as well as on the Continent. Admirers of Barbara Cartland may be interested in one of the Romantic Tours offered by The World of Oz (The Cortell Group, 3 E 54th St., New York, NY 10022; phone: 212-751-3250) in conjunction with British Airways. The week-long tour of England features a tea with the prolific author herself at her Camfield Place estate and a lunch with her daughter, Countess Spencer, at her Althorp Park home.

European Packages Booked in Britain – For years, experienced travelers have known that some of the cheapest tours of Europe could be booked abroad and that British tour operators offered the best of all possible deals. Often, for less than half the price of an air ticket from London to Athens and back, the smart shopper could pick up the flight plus a week's worth of adequate, if spartan, accommodations. Then the expenses of British packagers began to rise with inflation and the bargains became less enticing. But many British operators continue to cater to the budget end of the market and they still frequently manage to put together the better deal (which becomes even more attractive to Americans when the exchange rate is favorable). With their local clientele in mind they tend to specialize in tours from London to the Continent, with savings realized by scheduling a certain percentage or all of the nights in lodging without private bath. The assortment of budget tours of their own country and Ireland is less broad. Their basic tours, though competitively priced, frequently do not fall into the budget category, but more and more companies are adding a selection of 3- or 4-day mini-tours that save money because they cover only a limited area. Some of these are so economically priced that two or more of them together can still cost less than a single, longer, standard tour covering approximately the same territory.

The following are some of Britain's major high-volume or economy-minded tour operators. Several have representatives in the US to handle American bookings, but most of these representatives prefer to deal with travel agents rather than individuals. Note that because of the extra costs involved in making arrangements from this end, packages booked here can run 10% to 15% more than if booked while in Britain; and if you attempt to book through the British office by mail, your request will most likely be referred back to the US representative.

1. *Cosmos Tours:* In 1982 this firm offered 36 tour series with 1,000 departures, specializing in low-cost but fully reliable motorcoach tours to Europe and priding itself on offering most meals. On its tours of Britain and Ireland, the policy is

usually breakfast and dinner only, and the number of nights spent with private bath varies with each tour. Cosmos will match singles wishing to share a room, sparing both travelers the single supplement. The company's US office is at 69-15 Austin St., Forest Hills, NY 11375 (phone: 212-268-8088) and it accepts bookings from travel agents only. The London sales office is at 180 Vauxhall Bridge Rd., London SW1V 1ED (phone: 834-7412).

2. *Frames Tours:* Reasonably priced coach tours of both Europe and Great Britain and Ireland are available, and though the company is not primarily budget-oriented, it does a series of mini-tours in England, Scotland, and Wales, and to Paris. It also offers hotel packages in London. Frames's New York office, which accepts bookings only through travel agents, is at 1633 Broadway, New York, NY 10019 (phone: 212-977-5140). Its London address is Frames House, 33 Elizabeth St., London SW1 (phone: 730-3330).

3. *Glenton Tours:* This long-established company is a specialist in low-cost motor-coach tours of Great Britain (45 itineraries) — though one of its tours is a 10-day exploration of Ireland. Most tour prices are based on accommodations with private bath. In 1982, Glenton offered two tours to Europe. The US representative is Bestway Holidays, 84-01 Jamaica Ave., Woodhaven, NY 11421 (phone: 800-221-0099); bookings are preferred through a travel agent rather than from the general public. Head offices in London are at 114 Peckham Rye, London SE15 4JE (phone: 639-9777).

4. *National Travel (NBC) Ltd.:* This company specializes in motorcoach tours of Great Britain and Ireland. It has standard tours, budget tours (without private facilities), and a series of mini-tours comparable to those offered by Frames. National Travel's US representative is The Kemwel Group, Inc., 106 Calvert St., Harrison, NY 10528 (phone: toll-free, 800-221-3276; or 914-835-5454). They accept bookings from individuals and travel agents. London headquarters are at Victoria Coach Station, Buckingham Palace Rd., London SW1W 9TP (phone: 736-3466).

5. *Thomson Travel Ltd.:* Great Britain's largest tour operator is big enough to own its own airline, Britannia Airways. Its coach tours travel from home turf to Europe, including the USSR, and as far afield as the foothills of the Himalayas. On some tours all overnights are in rooms with private bath; on others, fewer than half are in accommodations with private facilities. Thomson's only US office, in Chicago, offers nonstop US-originating (from Chicago only) 8-day packages to European cities, London among them, as well as an escorted 16-day tour of Britain. Thomson is also known for a broad selection of Mediterranean holiday packages that include round-trip air fare (from Britain) and a week or two or more of villa or apartment rental. For information on Thomson's Chicago-originating packages, see your travel agent or contact Thomson Vacations, 401 N Michigan Ave., Chicago, IL 60611 (phone: 312-467-0300 or toll-free, 800-621-9543). For everything else (note that Thomson does not yet have tours of its own territory or of Ireland in its Britain-based catalog), write to Thomson Travel, Greater London House, Hampstead Rd., London NW1 7SD (phone: 387-9321).

6. *Townsend Thoresen:* Best known as the major ferry service for crossings from Great Britain to Northern Ireland and the Continent, this firm in recent years has branched out with motorcoach tours of Europe (none of Britain or Ireland) ranging in duration from 2 to 14 days. Its tours provide basic comforts if not always a private bath. Bookings in the US are handled by the company's agent, Express International, PO Box A, Main St., Saltillo, PA 17253 (phone: 814-448-3945, or, for reservations only, 800-458-3606), which will deal with either travel agents or the public. Its office in London is at 127 Regent St., London W1R 8LB (phones: 437-7800; 734-4431).

7. *Trafalgar Tours:* Like Frames, this is not strictly a budget company. In addition to an extensive selection of tours to traditional destinations on the Continent, travel programs are available for Scandinavia, Eastern Europe, and Israel. Tours range from Superior Europe and Great Britain and Ireland, to Globe Trotters ($50 a day for travelers under 35—includes Club Med), to Money Stretchers, to budget Cost Savers. Trafalgar's US offices are in New York (30 Rockefeller Plaza, New York, NY 10020; phone: 212-586-1785) and California (PO Box 19189, 18872 MacArthur Blvd., Suite 450, Irvine, CA 92715; phone: toll-free, 800-854-0103). Bookings will be accepted only through travel agents and only at the 800 number. In London, the office is at 9–11 Bressenden Pl., London SW1E 5DF (phone: 828-4388).

Some other British tour operators to investigate for budget packages include Swinards and Wallace Arnold, and not to be discounted is Thomas Cook, the best known of all tour operators headquartered in London. Its name is practically synonymous with the Grand Tour of Europe, but Cook's tours span the world, with itineraries ranging from deluxe to moderate, including some of the budget variety as well. Cook has a number of offices in major cities of North America; its US headquarters are at 5 World Trade Center, New York, NY 10048 (phone: 212-938-0950). Its main headquarters are in London at 45 Berkeley St., Piccadilly, London W1A 1EB (phone: 499-4000).

Camping and Caravanning, Biking, and Hiking

CAMPING AND CARAVANNING: In Great Britain and Ireland, sites for camping and caravans (as recreational vehicles are called) are plentiful. Most are open from Easter through October and they fill quickly at the height of the summer season, so it's a good idea to arrive early in the day if you haven't been able to reserve a pitch in advance. Caravanning is extremely popular with European vacationers and many parks cater more to the caravanner than to the tent dweller, but in neither country are campers or caravanners restricted to the official sites. Using private property, however, requires the permission of the landowner or tenant first — as well as the responsibility to leave the land exactly as you found it in return for the hospitality. When in difficulty, remember that tourist information offices throughout Britain and Ireland can direct you to sites in the areas they serve.

Many comprehensive guides to sites are available. The British Tourist Authority publishes *Britain: Camping & Caravan Sites,* a guide to over 1,800 sites in England, Scotland, Wales, and Northern Ireland, listing the charges for and facilities of each. The book also lists companies renting caravans, tents, and other camping equipment and is available from the British Travel Bookshop, 680 Fifth Ave., New York, NY 10019 ($8.95, plus $1.50 handling). The AA guide *Camping and Caravanning in Britain,* published by the Automobile Association of Great Britain, Fanum House, Basing View, Basingstoke, Hampshire RG21 2EA, England, is also available from the British Travel Bookshop ($6.95, plus $1.50 handling) and from other bookstores. It lists about 1,000 campsites inspected and rated by the AA and provides other information of interest to campers including an unrated list of rental companies. A leaflet describing camping and caravan sites in Britain's Forest Parks is available free from the Forestry Commission, 231 Corstorphine Rd., Edinburgh EH12 7AT, Scotland. The Northern Ireland Tourist Board publishes the free booklet *Caravan & Campsites,* listing over 100 sites; it is

GETTING READY / Camping and Caravanning

available from Tourist Information Centres in Northern Ireland and from all BTA offices. The Irish Tourist Board also publishes the yearly guide *Caravan & Camping Parks,* listing all sites meeting the board's minimum standards. Listings include a grading of the facilities, descriptions of the sites, and fees. The booklet is distributed free of charge in North America.

The International Camping Carnet, issued by the French camping organization Fédération Internationale de Camping et Caravanning, is a pass that is useful in Europe, entitling the bearer to discounts at some sites and often accepted in place of a passport when the campground owner wants to hold a document as security until you've paid your bill. It is not necessary for camping in Great Britain and Ireland, but it does open the gates to the sites operated exclusively for their members by two major groups, the Camping Club of Great Britain and Ireland and the Caravan Club. The Camping Club (11 Lower Grosvenor Pl., London SW1W OEY) publishes a guide to its own and other British and Irish sites, and provides information and assistance to members, foreign visitors with the carnet, and foreign visitors without the carnet who become temporary members. The Caravan Club (East Grinstead House, London Rd., East Grinstead, West Sussex RH19 1UA) publishes a guide to its sites plus over 3,500 farm sites. The International Camping Carnet is available in the US from the National Campers and Hikers Association, 7172 Transit Rd., Buffalo, NY 14221, for a fee of $20, which includes camping information and membership in the association.

Camping equipment is available for sale or rent throughout Great Britain and Ireland, and rentals can be booked in advance through any number of outfitters. The above mentioned guides to camping and caravanning contain lists of outfitters and the national tourist offices in the US can supply information on reliable dealers. Rentals of recreational vehicles can also be arranged from the US through several companies, including:

1. *Auto-Europe,* 21 E 40th St., New York, NY 10016 (phone: 800-223-5555, toll-free; or 212-578-4400).
2. *Dial Travel,* 1735 Eye St. NW, Washington, DC 20006 (phone: 800-424-9822, toll-free; or 202-223-6492).
3. *Europe by Car,* 630 Fifth Ave., New York, NY 10020 (phone: 800-223-1516, toll-free; or 212-581-3040).

Reservations should be made well in advance as the supply is limited and the demand great. Generally, two types of vehicles are offered: minibuses customized in various ways for camping, often including elevated roofs; and larger coach-type vans. Towed vehicles can be hired overseas, but are not usually offered by companies in the US.

If you plan to rent a caravan in Britain or Ireland and use it on the Continent as well, make sure that whatever you drive is equipped to deal with the electrical and gas standards of all countries on your itinerary. There are differences, for instance, between the bottled gas supplied in Britain and on the Continent. You should either have a sufficient supply of the type your camper requires or equipment that can use either type. If you're towing a camper, note that nothing towed is automatically covered by the liability insurance of the primary vehicle. As towing is an additional strain on car and driver, both should be in top physical condition. Whether driving a camper or towing, it is essential to have some idea of the terrain you'll be encountering en route, since grades can sometimes be too steep for certain vehicles to negotiate and some roads are off limits to towed caravans.

A packaged camping tour abroad is a good way to have your cake and eat it too. The problems of advance planning and day-to-day organizing are left to someone else, yet you still reap the savings benefits that shoestring travel affords. These packages are usually geared to the young, with ages 18 to 35 as common limits. Transfer from place to place is by bus as on other sight-seeing tours, but overnights are in tents and meal arrangements vary. Often there is a food fund that covers meals in restaurants or in the camp; sometimes there is a chef and sometimes the cooking is done by the participants themselves. An organization called Camping Tours of Europe, 1615 Northern Blvd., Suite 400, Manhasset, NY 11030 (phone: 516-365-9400), markets the European camping tours of six British tour operators. Other companies offering camping tours are Intercollegiate Holidays, Inc. (tour of Ireland only), 501 Madison Ave., New York, NY 10022 (phone: 212-355-4705), and the International Travel Guild, 330 Sutter St., San Francisco, CA 94108 (phone: 415-397-7160).

Horse-drawn Caravans – A caravan vacation in an entirely different spirit is possible in Ireland, one country where it is common to tour in a horse-drawn wagon. The vehicle is barrel-shaped in Gypsy style and has bunks for up to four people and a gas stove for cooking. No experience in handling the horse is required: The company that rents the caravan teaches harnessing and unharnessing plus the basics of horse care before you set out. Not much ground can be covered this way (rentals are usually by the week) but the caravan bases are generally located in very scenic areas that are pleasant to explore in depth. Most companies provide a route to follow, pointing out where to find bathroom facilities and the best spots to stop for the night. Cost of renting the caravan varies from about IR£95 to IR£140 in low season to about IR£135 to IR £230 in summer — which includes oats for the horse but not supplementary charges for any grazing the animal might do as you park for the night. The Irish Tourist Board has a list of operators to contact to reserve a horse-drawn caravan, something you should do well in advance if you want to have one at the height of the summer.

BIKING: For young or energetic travelers, the bicycle offers a marvelous way to see a country, especially where the terrain is conducive to easy cycling as it is in Great Britain, one of the most popular of European destinations for foreign tourists on two wheels. Much of the country is rolling hills and, except for the environs of industrialized cities, nearly traffic-free secondary roads can be found almost everywhere, threaded neatly through picturesque stretches of countryside. There is even less traffic in Ireland, a country that tends to be flat to rolling in its middle, hilly on the coast, and scenic throughout. Biking has its drawbacks, of course: You can carry little baggage, travel is slow, and you are exposed to the elements, which in both Great Britain and Ireland means a mild climate with cool evenings — and the ever-present possibility of showers.

Whether you travel independently or join an organized cycling tour, a valuable book to help you prepare for all contingencies is *Bicycle Touring in Europe* by Karen and Gary Hawkins (Pantheon Books; $4.95). The BTA's booklet *Britain on Two Wheels* provides information on taking your own bicycle (including motorcycles or mopeds and scooters) to Britain and lists companies that rent bikes in all areas. (Note: Because of insurance regulations, few companies in Great Britain rent powered cycles to North Americans. Those that do are listed in the booklet.) In Ireland, there are over 100 Raleigh Rent-a-Bike dealers and some of them permit bikes to be rented at one outlet and returned to another. The tourist boards of both the Republic and Northern Ireland distribute a leaflet listing the dealers, or you can write for it directly to Irish Raleigh Industries, 8 Hanover Quay, Dublin 2, Ireland. Mopeds, motorcycles, and scooters cannot be rented in Ireland.

Detailed maps are a necessity on a biking tour, allowing you to find scenic byways as well as the route that goes around the mountain, not up it. Maps are available from a number of sources, but those of the Bartholomew National series (on a scale of 1:100,000 — 1 centimeter of map equals 100,000 centimeters or 1 kilometer of road) or GT series (1:253,440 — 1 centimeter of map equals approximately 2.5 kilometers of road) are particularly useful for Great Britain and Ireland. These can be ordered from John Bartholomew & Son Ltd., 12 Duncan St., Edinburgh EH9 1TA, Scotland, or, if you are a member, through either the Cyclists Touring Club or the British Cycling

Federation. Both are British groups that accept Americans as members. The Cyclists Touring Club, Britain's largest cycling association, not only runs organized tours for cyclists, but also has a number of planned tours available in pamphlet form for bikers traveling on their own. It will also help members plan custom-made tours for themselves. For information on joining, write to the CTC at Cotterell House, 69 Meadrow, Godalming, Surrey GU7 3HS, England. The British Cycling Federation exists primarily to promote bicycle racing but it, too, provides a touring service for members and has planned numerous touring routes throughout Great Britain and the Continent. Contact the British Cycling Federation at 70 Brompton Rd., London SW3 1EN. When the going gets rough, remember that arduous parts of the journey can be avoided by loading your bicycle on the luggage van of a train. Bicycles are generally transported free on British trains, except on Inter City 125 routes, Motorail car-carrying services, or boat trains to the Continent. It's a good idea to check with the station the day before your departure. On Irish trains, they travel at one-quarter the standard (second-class) fare.

More than one organization offers bike tours of Great Britain and Ireland. An advantage of such a tour is that shipment of equipment — your bike — is handled by organizers and the shipping fee is included in the total tour package. Otherwise, it is necessary to ship through an airline and there are no standard procedures for this. Some international carriers provide shipping cartons for bikes (you will have to disassemble it, but if you are contemplating a tour you should be familiar enough with your bike to do this with ease) and charge a nominal shipping fee. Other airlines don't provide cartons and charge as much as $50. Another attraction of *some* organized tours is the existence of a "sag wagon" to carry extra luggage or you and your bike, too, when you can't pedal another mile. Accommodations on tours can vary from campgrounds and hostels to hotels, and as a result, tour prices also vary.

Among the groups sponsoring yearly bike tours to Europe are the American Youth Hostels and its local chapters or councils. The 1982 summer program of the national organization (1332 I St. NW, Washington, DC 20005; phone: 800-424-9426) included a 44-day adult tour of Ireland and Britain for those 18 and over, and a youth version of it for those under 18, as well as a 16-day adult tour of the English countryside. Other tours began in London and included parts of England before moving on to continental Europe. The Metropolitan New York Council of American Youth Hostels (132 Spring St., New York, NY 10012; phone: 212-431-7100), a local AYH affiliate with a particularly broad tour program, offered four itineraries to Great Britain and/or Ireland in 1982. Three of these were for teenagers only and one, a 17-day tour of Ireland, was for adults only. Accommodations on both the adult and youth programs are in camps, hostels, or student hotels. Cyclists not traveling on tours should nevertheless familiarize themselves with the activities of the AYH organization since membership in it is a prerequisite for staying at most youth hostels abroad. *The International Youth Hostel Handbook, Volume One: Europe and the Mediterranean* describes some 2,500 hostels overseas, with a location map, and is available through the AYH national office ($6, plus $1.50 handling) or through some of the local councils. There is no age limit to membership in AYH, and hostels abroad (except in Switzerland and Bavaria) do not impose age restrictions for use of their facilities.

The International Bicycle Touring Society is another nonprofit membership organization that regularly sponsors bicycle tours around the US and Canada and overseas. Tours to England and Scotland were among the foreign itineraries on the 1982 program. Participants must be over 21 and are usually between 30 and 60 years old. A sag wagon goes along and accommodations are in inns and hotels. The IBTS is at 2115 Paseo Dorado, La Jolla, CA 92037. You may also want to investigate the tours of Britain and the Continent offered to members of Britain's Cyclists Touring Club (address above). Join early if you decide to participate.

GETTING READY / Camping and Caravanning 51

Some other organizers of bicycle tours to Europe, including British or Irish destinations, are:

1. *The Great Outdoor Adventure Company,* PO Box 311, Kansas City, MO 64141 (phone: 816-531-4066). Offered 2-week tours of England and Ireland in 1982, in addition to other European itineraries. Sag wagon accompanies tours, and accommodations are in hotels.
2. *Gerhard's Bicycle Odysseys,* 1137 Southwest Yamhill, Portland, OR 97205 (phone: 503-223-2402). Will offer one, and possibly two, 2-week tours of Ireland in 1983. Sag wagon; accommodations in hotels and most meals.
3. *Adventure Center,* 5540 College Ave., Oakland, CA 94618 (phone: 415-652-8747). Offers bicycle tours of Ireland, with overnights in farmhouses, and of the Cotswolds area of England. Other European destinations and other types of accommodations available.

HIKING: The British Tourist Authority, the Irish Tourist Board, and the Northern Ireland Tourist Board distribute information sheets on walking and mountaineering and there are several other sources of information for those intent on getting about on their own steam. The Ramblers Association, 1/5 Wandsworth Rd., London SW8 2LJ, publishes *Guides to Local Walking,* listing guidebooks and maps for walkers, and *Long Distance Footpaths,* with details of a number of long-distance routes. The British Mountaineering Council, Crawford House, Precinct Centre, Booth St. E, Manchester, England, furnishes advice on mountaineering and rock climbing and a list of qualified guides. The Federation of Mountaineering Clubs of Ireland, 3 Gortnamona Dr., Foxrock, Dublin 18, can be contacted for information and advice, and will provide a list of general and regional walking and climbing guidebooks that can be ordered through its office or bought at bookstores in Ireland. *Irish Walk* guides, a series of six regional guidebooks published by Gill and Macmillan, are sold in bookstores throughout Ireland, north and south. Each contains full details of the best hill walks in the area, maps, and notes on climate, flora and fauna, and mountain safety.

If you are hiking on your own, without benefit of a guide or a group, a map of the trail you plan to use is a necessity. Ordnance Survey Maps on the scale of 1 inch to 1 mile cover the whole of Britain, and Ordnance Survey Tourist Maps of particularly popular areas show the contours of the land by variations in color. The British Travel Bookshop carries a selection of the maps or, for a catalog of all maps available, write to Ordnance Survey, 22-24 Caxton St., London W1, England. For similar maps of Ireland, write to the Ordnance Survey Office, Phoenix Park, Dublin; and for Northern Ireland, contact Ordnance Survey of Northern Ireland, 83 Ladas Dr., Belfast BT6 9FJ. Having studied the map, choose a route in keeping with your physical condition, and stick to the defined path unless you are an experienced hiker and know the area well. Let someone know where you are going and when you expect to be back — if the hike is impromptu, leave a note on your car. Always know your own limits.

All you need to set out on a simple hike are a pair of sturdy shoes and heavy socks; jeans or long pants to keep branches, nettles, and bugs off your legs; a canteen of water; a hat to protect you from the sun; and, if you like, a picnic lunch. It is a good idea to dress in layers, so that you can peel off a sweater or two to keep pace with the rising sun and put them back on as the sun goes down. Make sure, too, to wear clothes with pockets or bring a pack to keep your hands free. Some useful and important pocket or pack stuffers include a jackknife, waterproof matches, and a compass.

If you prefer to travel as part of an organized group, see the July/August issue of *Sierra* magazine for the Sierra Club's annual list of foreign outings, or contact the Sierra Club Outing Department, 530 Bush St., San Francisco, CA 94108 (phone: 415-981-8634). Each year the club sponsors one or two walking trips of 2 to 3 weeks in length in Great Britain or Ireland (such as "The Green Hills of England and Scotland" on the 1982 calendar). Distances are traveled in minibuses and overnights are in inns, bed and breakfast farmhouses, or, occasionally, campgrounds. Mountain Travel, a company specializing in adventure trips around the world, offered seven 11- to 18-day walking tours to Great Britain and Ireland in 1982 (as well as two 11-day sailing trips out of Inverness). Itineraries are graded according to difficulty, travel between areas of interest is by minibus, and accommodations are in guesthouses, castles, or inns. Contact Mountain Travel, 1398 Solano Ave., Albany, CA 94706 (phone: 415-527-8100).

Preparing

Calculating Costs

Once upon a time, after prospective transatlantic travelers had set aside the shekels for air fare, they could look forward to the rest of their money going a long, long way, comparatively speaking, in Europe. The irony is that now that budget, standby, cut-rate, and no-frills fares have made getting there affordable as never before, staying there has become the problem. Inflation rates and, until very recently, exchange rates have conspired to drive the traveler's day-to-day costs to heights that only a few years ago would not have been believed. But before you put away your passport in despair and start looking for cheaper destinations, consider the fact that even as the dollar was taking the beating of its life against currencies around the world, more Americans were traveling abroad than ever before, and much of the traffic was transatlantic. Very few of them were in a tax bracket that would allow them to say "Hang the expense." Rather, they managed by prudent marshaling of their funds and by careful and exhaustive planning.

Britain's reputation as one of the more expensive European countries to visit is due more than anything else to prices in its capital, London, which the *London Financial Times* rated as one of the most expensive cities in the world — at least for the business traveler. It remains to be seen how long this label will stick, but in the meantime, British tourism authorities have mounted a campaign to call the attention of potential visitors to the many low-cost options available for almost every entry in the traveler's budget. Some BTA publications stress this theme, among them a *Bed & Breakfast in Britain* brochure, an introduction to a most reasonable and pleasant way to bring down the high cost of housing for the tourist, and *Great Value Britain,* a booklet discussing bargains in everything from accommodations and meals to sight-seeing and shopping. In the same spirit, the Irish Tourist Board — and Ireland enjoys a reputation as one of the more economical European destinations, though no longer truly cheap — distributes a leaflet describing 80 of the country's free attractions.

There are many variables that affect the cost of a vacation, but the major expenses are transportation, accommodations, and food, the latter two of which are especially affected by fluctuations in the exchange rate — that is, how much of a given foreign currency the dollar will buy. A number of other expenses must be allowed for: local transportation, sight-seeing, shopping, and miscellaneous items such as admission tickets, drinks, local taxes, and tips.

The easiest way to put a ceiling on the price of all these things is to consider buying a package tour. If it is a totally planned and escorted one, with almost all transportation, rooms, meals, sight-seeing, local travel, tips, and the like, included and prepaid, you will know beforehand almost exactly what the trip will cost and the only surprise will be the one you spring on yourself by succumbing to some irresistible but expensive souvenir rather than the trifles you intended. The various types of packages available are discussed in *Package Tours,* GETTING READY TO GO, but a few points bear repeating here. Not all packages are package *tours.* There are loosely organized arrangements in which some features (transatlantic transportation, rooms, transfers) are included but

54 GETTING READY / Calculating Costs

others such as sight-seeing and dining are left to your own discretion. More and more, even experienced travelers are being won over to the idea of packaged travel, not only for the convenience and the planning time saved, but above all for the money saved. Whatever elements you choose to have in your package the organizer has gotten for you wholesale — and they are prepaid.

The possibility of prepaying for elements of your trip is an important point to consider even if you intend to be strictly independent, with arrangements entirely of your own making and all bought separately. You may not be able to match the price of the wholesale tour package, but at least you will have introduced an element of predictability into your accounting, thus reducing the risk that some budget-busting expense along the way might put a damper on the rest of your travel plans. With the independent traveler in mind, we suggest below some of the ways to pin down the cost of a trip beforehand, but there are two further variables that will influence the cost of your holiday whether you buy a package or do it all yourself. One is timing. If you are willing to visit during the less-trafficked off-season months when transatlantic air fares are lower, you'll find the rates at many hotels lower also. Keep in mind those periods that are generally referred to as the shoulder months, between the traditional low and high seasons (approximately late March to mid-May and late September through November). Costs are only a little less than in high season but the weather should be agreeable and you won't be bucking the crowds that can force a traveler without a hotel reservation into the most expensive hostelry in town in peak months. Another factor that will influence the cost of your trip is whether you will be traveling alone or as one of a pair. The prices quoted for package tours are almost always based on double occupancy of hotel rooms and the surcharge — or single supplement — for a room by yourself can be quite hefty. If you are shopping for a hotel room on your own you'll find that there are many more double rooms than single rooms and that the price of a single is roughly two-thirds that of a double.

Transportation – Air fare is really the easiest cost to pin down, though the range and variety of flights available may be confusing initially. A detailed explanation of the various categories is given in *Traveling by Plane,* GETTING READY TO GO. Essentially the traveler can choose from one of several categories of scheduled flights — ranging in expense from first class, which presumably no vacation traveler needs, to budget and standby — or charters.

In earlier sections of GETTING READY TO GO we discussed the various means of travel within Europe: rented car, bus, or train. The most important factor in determining which of these to use is the amount of traveling you plan to do and the length of time you will be abroad. If you intend to move about a great deal between cities, a pass allowing unlimited travel by rail or bus or both is likely to be the most economical form of transport. The passes are quite reasonably priced and those that can be bought before you go are especially attractive ($107 for a 1-week adult economy class BritRail Pass in 1982; $80 for an 8-day adult rail and bus Irish Rambler Ticket) provided they are valid in all the areas you plan to visit. If road touring is your object, you should look carefully into fly/drive arrangements versus straight rentals and into renting from a small, strictly local firm versus renting from a larger company. The advantage of dealing with the smaller firm may be lower rates, that of dealing with the larger one the possibility of prepayment in the US (see *Touring by Car,* GETTING READY TO GO). Always look for the flat rate based on unlimited mileage.

Accommodations – Room costs run a very wide gamut. Most expensive — and that can be $100 and up for a double room in London — will be international hotels with a full complement of business services. (There is no sacred edict that states travelers must put up at deluxe hotels, however, and by skipping over the great small hotels, inns, and guesthouses, you might be missing a very special experience.) At the opposite end of the scale are the bed-and-breakfast houses, where you can spend the

GETTING READY / Calculating Costs 55

night in surroundings that may be homey or spartan, but are almost always clean and adequate. B&B's average about £6 or £8 per person per night in Britain or Ireland, but they are not easy to find in London where, as in any metropolis, space is at a premium and few private homes have the spare room to rent to passing strangers. Nevertheless, budget accommodations in central London do exist and, recognizing the need, travel agents, tour packagers, airlines, and tourist boards are doing what they can to make their whereabouts known. Two additional options open to anyone staying for an extended period of time are the "holiday let" or "self-catering holiday" and the home exchange. In the first case, you actually rent an apartment; in the second, you and a foreign family exchange homes for an agreed-upon period of time.

If you don't want to remain fixed in one spot but still want to eliminate the element of surprise from your accommodations budget, you can take advantage of the hotel voucher schemes that frequently come as part of a fly/drive package. You receive a block of prepaid vouchers and a list of hotels that accept them as total payment for a night's stay, but if you want to upgrade your lodgings from time to time, there is often another set of hotels that accept the same vouchers upon payment of a supplement.

In Britain, slightly lower hotel rates can be expected off-season — from October through April. Many hotels offer "mini-break" packages, that is, a discount for a stay of 2 or more nights, usually over a weekend, and though these discounts may be in effect any time of the year, they are most common when demand is low. In Ireland, rates are lowest from January through March. (For a detailed discussion of the range and variety of places to stay in Great Britain and Ireland, see *Accommodations*, GETTING READY TO GO.)

Food – Restaurant dining — particularly in the better eating establishments of major tourist cities — is, comparatively speaking, going to hit your purse, wallet, or credit card hardest. If you're an independent traveler and taking all of your meals out, allow roughly $40 to $50 a day for food. That includes breakfast, because increasingly in large urban hotels, the breakfast that comes with the price of the accommodations is Continental (coffee and rolls), or there is an extra charge for the full English or Irish breakfast. That amount should also cover taxes and a service charge and perhaps a carafe of table wine at dinner — but you won't be splurging. The estimate is based on fixed menu meals, which can at least provide a tasty and occasionally imaginative food selection, but no predinner cocktails. If you want to order a dinner of your choice in one of the major cities, be prepared for the tab to rise much higher. All of this is no reason for you to stop your trip, however — you'll notice we said that *dining* is going to hit your wallet hard. If you're up to a steady diet of fish and chips, you can get by on less. And there is some relief out in the countryside where the breakfast that comes with the bed in the typical B&B can still be a filling one, apt to hold you straight through midday, though travelers on a severe budget would be advised not to skip lunch. Pub lunches in general are becoming more and more imaginative everywhere and they're probably the best food buy you'll encounter.

Our restaurant choices are listed in the *Best in Town* sections of CITIES and in the *Checking In* and *Eating Out* sections of each tour route in DIRECTIONS. The basis for selection has been to give the best value for the money. The restaurants are rated as expensive, moderate, or inexpensive, and approximate price ranges for those labels in the given area are supplied.

Local Taxes – A sales tax or VAT (Value Added Tax) is affixed to both goods and services. In Great Britain, the standard rate is 15%, whether on overnight room accommodations or on goods purchased in local stores. In Ireland, the tax on accommodations is 15%, on goods 15% to 25%. Ask in advance whether the room price quoted includes the tax — it should in Ireland, but in Britain it may or may not, though prices should be displayed in a way that shows clearly what is what. The VAT on purchases can be avoided by having the goods sent directly to your home address. In addition, some stores in Britain operate an Over-the-Counter Export Scheme whereby you pay the tax, have a VAT relief form validated by a customs clerk as you leave the country, mail the form to the store, and receive a rebate in return.

Service Charges – Increasingly, hotels and restaurants include a 10% to 15% charge on the cost of rooms and food to cover gratuities. Again, this may not be specified at the time of making reservations, so ask in advance. At restaurants, visitors should ask if a service charge is included in the bill submitted at the end of a meal. Even when such charges are included, an additional tip is appropriate if the service has been exceptional or if the service charge is minimal.

Other expenses, such as the cost of local sight-seeing tours, will vary from city to city. Official tourist information offices are plentiful in both countries and most of the better hotels will have a concierge or someone else at the front desk able to provide a rundown on the cost of local tours and full-day excursions in and out of the city. Special discount passes for tourists providing unlimited travel by the day or the week on regular city transportation are available in most large cities. An Open to View ticket ($19 from BTA offices in the US) provides a month of free admissions to 560 castles, stately homes, and other historic sites in Britain that are privately owned or the properties of the National Trust or the Ancient Monuments division of the Department of the Environment; both these bodies are charged with the preservation of national treasures. The ticket comes with a booklet listing the properties and the hours they are open. Entrance to major museums is usually free.

Finally, for savings on shopping, dining, and nightlife, consider buying a Countdown Card, entitling the bearer to a 10% discount on payments in cash at many stores, restaurants, nightclubs, and discos in both Great Britain and Ireland. A 3-month card costs $10 and is obtainable from Countdown Card, Inc., 11 E 47th St., New York, NY 10017 (phone: 212-888-1144), or from Countdown Ltd., 88–92 Earls Court Rd., London W8. The card comes with one of two guides to outlets that offer the reduction. You must specify which guide you want: either *Countdown London* or *Countdown Europe*, which includes London plus the rest of England, Scotland, Wales, the Irish Republic, and other countries. The first guide comes with the card free; the second costs an extra $2.

Entry Requirements and Documents

A valid US passport is the one document required for travel to either the United Kingdom or the Irish Republic and, of course, you must have one for reentry into the US. No visas are necessary. As a *general* rule, possession of a US passport entitles the bearer to remain in these countries for up to 3 months as a tourist; study, residency, or work necessitate acquiring completely different documents and considerably more laborious procedures are involved.

Vaccination certificates are required by authorities only if the traveler is entering from an area of contagion as defined by the World Health Organization. Because smallpox is considered eradicated from the world, there are only a few countries that continue to require visitors to have a smallpox vaccination certificate. You will certainly not need one to travel to the United Kingdom or the Irish Republic, or to return to the US.

Passports are valid for 5 years from the date of issue and the document itself cannot be renewed; passport holders must turn in expired passports to receive new and valid ones. This can take as little as 2 weeks or as much as a month, and certainly, anyone applying for a passport for the first time should allow at least 4 weeks for delivery. Normal passports contain 24 pages, usually adequate for 5 years' worth of visas and entrance and exit stamps, but frequent travelers can request a 48-page passport at no extra cost.

Passport renewal can be done by mail, but anyone applying for the first time must do so in person at one of the following places:

1. The State Department Passport Agencies in Boston; Chicago; Detroit; Honolulu; Los Angeles; Miami; New Orleans; New York City; Philadelphia; San Francisco; Seattle; Stamford, CT; and Washington, DC.
2. A federal or state courthouse.
3. Any of the 1,000 post offices across the country with designated acceptance facilities.

Application blanks are available at all these offices and must be presented with:

1. Proof of US citizenship. This can be a previous passport. If you are applying for your first passport and you were born in the United States, your birth certificate is the required proof. If you were born abroad, a Certificate of Naturalization, a Certificate of Citizenship, a Report of Birth Abroad of a Citizen of the United States, or a Certification of Birth is necessary.
2. Two 2 × 2-inch front-view photographs in color or black and white, with a light, plain background, taken within the previous 6 months. These must be taken by a photographer rather than by a machine.
3. Cash, check, or money order for the $5 execution fee and the $10 passport fee.
4. Proof of identity. Again, this can be a previous passport, or a driver's license, a Certificate of Naturalization or of Citizenship, or a government ID card with a physical description or a photograph. Failing any of these, you should be accompanied by a friend of at least 2 years' standing who will testify to your identity. Credit cards or social security cards do not suffice as proof of identity.

Passports can be renewed by mail on forms obtained at designated locations only if the expired passport was issued no more than 8 years before the date of the application for renewal and if it was not issued before the applicant's 18th birthday. Send the completed form with the expired passport, two photos (signed along the left-hand side as well as on the back), and $10 (no execution fee required here) to the nearest passport agency office.

Every individual, regardless of age, must have his or her own passport. Family passports are no longer issued.

■ **SHOULD YOU LOSE YOUR PASSPORT ABROAD:** Immediately report the loss to the nearest US consulate. You can get a full 5-year replacement (until recently, 3-month temporary passports were issued) directly from the consulate, but you must fill out a "loss of passport" form and follow the same application procedure — and pay the same fees — as you did for the original. It's likely to speed things up if you have a record of your passport number and the place and date of its issue.

Planning a Trip

For most travelers, a week-plus trip to Great Britain and/or Ireland can be too expensive for an "I'll take my chances" type of vacation. Hence a little planning is crucial. This is not to suggest that you have to work out your itinerary in minute detail before you go, but by considering where you want to go, what you want to do, and how much you want to spend, you'll find it much easier to avoid delays, unexpected expenses, and the need to alter your plans because of unforeseen developments.

58 GETTING READY / Planning a Trip

In thinking out your trip, start with the following basics:

1. How much time will you have to spend?
2. Do you want to visit one, a few, or many different places?
3. During what time of the year do you plan to travel? (It can make a considerable difference in what's open at your destination(s) as well as in the cost of transportation and accommodations.)
4. How much money do you have to spend on your trip?
5. Do you want an unstructured trip (in which you'll be on your own when you get to your destination), or would you prefer the company and schedule of an escorted tour?

With firm answers to these major questions, start reviewing literature on the areas in which you're most interested. The British and Irish tourist boards in the US are ready sources for brochures or other information on features of their respective cities and countrysides (their addresses are listed in *Tourist Information Offices*). Other good sources of information are airlines, hotel representatives, and travel agents, who should be well supplied with literature from wholesalers and tour operators who organize packages and other travel arrangements to Europe. In other words, up-to-date travel information is plentiful and you should be able to accumulate not only everything you want to know about the places you plan to visit, but also about the tours and packages that are available to each. See *Package Tours*.

You can now make almost all of your own travel arrangements if you have the time to follow through with hotels, airlines, tour operators, and so on. But you'll probably save considerable time and energy if you have a travel agent make reservations and arrangements for you. The agent also should be able to advise you of alternative arrangements of which you may not be aware. Only very rarely will these services cost you any money and they may even save you some (see *How to Use a Travel Agent*). Well before departure (depending on how much in advance you make your reservations), the agent will supply you with a packet that includes all your tickets and hotel confirmations, and often a day-by-day outline of where you'll be when, along with a detailed list of whatever flights or trains you're taking.

Before your departure, find out what the weather is like at your destinations at the time of year you'll be visiting. This will help you decide what to include among the items you'll be packing (for details on weather and packing, see *How to Pack*). And if you're planning an extended stay in a particular city or section of the countryside, you'll find it useful to read a bit about the area's history, its food specialties, people, and places of interest, especially if you are visiting for the first time.

While vacation arrangements are fun and exciting, don't forget the things that must be done at home to prepare for your absence. Before you leave, attend to these household matters:

1. Arrange for your mail to be forwarded, held by the post office until you return, or picked up at your house daily by a friend or neighbor. Someone should check your door occasionally to collect any unexpected deliveries. Piles of leaflets, circulars, packages, or brochures are an announcement to thieves that no one is home.
2. Cancel all deliveries (newspapers, milk, and so on).
3. Arrange for your lawn to be mowed at regular intervals.
4. Arrange for the care of pets.
5. Etch your social security number in a prominent place on all appliances (televisions, radios, cameras, kitchen appliances). This considerably reduces their appeal to thieves and facilitates identification.
6. Leave a house key, your itinerary, and your automobile license number (if you are

GETTING READY / How to Pack 59

---

driving) with a relative or friend. Notify police that you are leaving and tell them who has your key and itinerary.
7. Empty the refrigerator and lower the thermostat.
8. Immediately before leaving, check that all doors, windows, and garage doors are securely locked.

To discourage thieves further, set up several variable timers around the house so that lights (and perhaps even the television or a radio) go on and off several times in different rooms of the house each night.

Make a list of any valuable items you are carrying with you, including credit card numbers and the serial numbers of your traveler's checks. Put copies in your luggage to facilitate identification in case of loss. Put your name and business address — *but never your home address* — on a label on the exterior of your luggage.

Review your travel documents. If you are traveling by air, check to see that your ticket has been filled in correctly. The left side of the ticket should have a list of each stop you will make (even if you are only stopping to change planes), beginning with your departure point. Be sure that the list is correct, and count the number of carbons to see that you have one for each plane you will take. If you have confirmed reservations, be sure that the column marked "status" says "OK" beside each flight. Have in hand vouchers or proof of payment (preferably from the hotels themselves) for any reservations for which you've paid in advance; this includes hotels, transfers to and from the airport, sight-seeing tours, car rentals, special events, and so on.

How to Pack

The goal is to remain perfectly comfortable, neat, clean, and adequately fashionable wherever you go, but to actually pack as little as possible. The main obstacle to achieving this end is habit: Most of us wake each morning with an entire wardrobe hanging in our closets, and we assume that our suitcase should offer the same variety and selection. Not so; only our anxiety about being caught short makes us treat a suitcase like a mobile closet, and you can eliminate even the anxiety (and learn to travel lightly) by following two firm packing principles:

1. Organize your travel wardrobe around a single color — blue or brown, for example — that allows you to mix, match, and layer clothes. Holding firm to one color scheme will make it easy to eliminate items that don't harmonize; and by picking clothes for their adaptability and compatibility with your basic color, you will put together the widest variety of wardrobe with the fewest pieces of clothing.
2. Use laundries to renew your wardrobe. Never overpack to ensure a supply of fresh clothing — shirts, blouses, underwear — for each day of a long trip. Businesspeople routinely use hotel laundries to wash and clean clothes and, if these prove too expensive, there are laundromats in most towns of any size.

Climate and Clothes – Although Britain and Ireland are farther north than most of the US — London, sitting astride latitude 51°30', is about even with Québec's Gaspé Peninsula — the climate is generally much milder. The Gulf Stream, which warms the coasts of both countries, brings moderate temperatures year-round, with few subzero winters or blistering hot summers. Daily temperatures in Britain's coldest months (December, January, February) hover around 35° or 40°F (2° or 5°C) and summers generally average about 70°F (21°C). Similarly, Ireland's winter tempera-

60 GETTING READY / How to Use a Travel Agent

tures rarely dip below 40°F (5°C) and summer temperatures usually rise no higher than 70°F (21°C). The stereotype about English and Irish weather being wet is true — it rains often throughout the year and even on fairly clear days the weather feels damp.

The temperate climate makes packing rather simple, if not altogether lightweight. A versatile item of clothing you'll find indispensable in both Great Britain and Ireland is a raincoat, preferably with a zip-out lining and a hood. The removable lining lets you adapt to temperature changes and the hood is better suited (and less cumbersome) than an umbrella for the fine, misty rain. Other appropriate apparel would be a warm wool sweater or jacket, even in summer (tweeds are worn year-round). And finally — since the best touring of castles, cathedrals, and countryside is on foot — pack a comfortable pair of walking shoes. Generally speaking, your fall wardrobe will probably have everything that's needed for the trip. For more detailed weather information, see *When to Go*, GETTING READY TO GO.

Fashion – In London, you'll see a lot of chic, trendy dressing, and in Dublin, more relaxed, conservative attire. For a special dinner at one of the finest restaurants in either city, men should take along a suit or sports jacket and women a suit or cocktail dress. Otherwise, be guided by your own tastes and wear whatever makes you feel comfortable.

Packing – A recommended packing procedure is the so-called layer method, designed to get everything in and out of a bag with as few wrinkles as possible. Heavy items go on the bottom and sides, and corners are stuffed with such articles as socks, underwear, shoes, handbags, and bathing suits. Then layer on the more easily wrinkled items, such as shirts and slacks, dresses and skirts, even jackets. Pack them with as few folds as possible. On the top layer put immediate needs, such as pajamas, sweater, raincoat, and the like. Make the layers even and the total contents of your bag as full and firm as possible to keep things from shifting around during transit.

Traveling Wrinkle-Free – While packing, interleave each layer of clothes with plastic cleaning bags, which will help preserve pressed clothes while they are in the suitcase. Unpack your bags as soon as you get to a hotel. Nothing so destroys freshly cleaned and pressed clothes as sitting for days in a suitcase. Finally, if something is badly wrinkled and can't be professionally pressed before you must wear it, hang it overnight in a bathroom where the bathtub has been filled with very hot water; keep the bathroom door closed so the room becomes something of a steam room. It really works miracles.

Some Final Packing Hints – Try to select toiletries and cosmetics that come in plastic containers. Glass-bottled liquids should be placed in plastic bags. If traveling overnight, put a few necessary toiletry items in a purse, a shoulder bag, or some other small, easily carried case. Add an emptied airline bag to your suitcase; you'll find it handy for overnight trips, beach outings, or for carrying purchases home. Don't ever put necessities such as medicine, travel documents, cash, or credit cards in your checked luggage; keep them in a piece of hand luggage that you carry.

How to Use a Travel Agent

A reliable travel agent remains your best source of service and information for planning a trip abroad whether you already have a specific itinerary that only requires reservations or need extensive help in sorting through the maze of air fares, tour offerings, hotel packages, and the scores of other arrangements that may be required for a trip overseas.

You should know what you want from a travel agent to be able to evaluate what you are getting. It is perfectly reasonable to expect your travel agent to be a thorough travel specialist, with information about your destination, and, even more crucial, a command of current air fares, package tours, charters, ground arrangements, and other wrinkles in the travel scene.

To make the most intelligent use of a travel agent's time and expertise, you should know something of the economics of the industry. As a client, you traditionally pay nothing for the services performed by the agent; it's all free, from advice on package tours to reserving a river cruise. Any money that the travel agent makes on the time spent arranging your itinerary — booking hotels, resorts, or flights, or suggesting activities — comes from commissions paid by the suppliers who provide these services — the airlines, hotels, and so on. These commissions generally run anywhere from 8% to 11% of the total cost of the service, though certain new no-frills discount fares earn an agent somewhat less. In some cases an agent may ask you to pay a fee for very personalized attention such as planning a custom-made itinerary or making reservations at places that do not pay commissions, such as a small country inn or guesthouse. In most instances, however, you'll find that agents provide their traditional services at no charge to you.

This system implies two things you should be alert to concerning your relationship with any travel agent.

1. You will get better service if you arrive at the agent's desk with your basic itinerary already planned. Know roughly where you want to go, what you want to do, and how much you want to spend. Use the agent to make bookings (which pay commissions) and to advise you on facilities, activities, and alternatives within the parameters of the basic itinerary you have chosen. You get the best service when you are requesting commissionable items. As there are few commissions on camping or driving-camping tours, an agent is unlikely to be very enthusiastic about helping to plan one. The more vague your plans, the less direction you can expect from most agents. If you walk into an agency and say "I have two weeks in June, what shall I do?" you will most likely walk out with nothing more than a handful of brochures. So do your homework.

2. Be watchful. There is always the danger that an incompetent or unethical agent will send you to a place that offers the best commissions rather than the best facilities for your purposes.

You should choose a travel agent with the same care with which you would choose a doctor or lawyer. You will be spending a good deal of money on the basis of the agent's judgment, and you have a right to expect that judgment to be mature, informed, and interested. At the moment, unfortunately, there are no real standards within the travel agent industry to help you gauge an agent's competence or expertise. The quality of individual agents varies enormously. Several states are toying with the idea of licensing agents, which would at least ensure that anyone acting as a travel agent has met some minimum standards, if not guarantee absolute competence. Though there are as yet no laws regulating travel agencies, an industry organization, the American Society of Travel Agents (ASTA), guarantees that any member agency has been in business at least 3 years or done $500,000 worth of business in the year before membership was granted. More useful is the knowledge that any travel agent who completes the 2-year course at the Institute of Certified Travel Agents in Wellesley, Massachusetts, will carry the initials CTC (Certified Travel Counselor) after his or her name. This indicates a relatively high level of expertise, though it's sad to note that only about 20% of travel agents operating in the US have this certificate.

Perhaps the best way to find a travel agent is by word of mouth. If the agent (or agency) has done a good job for your friends over a period of time, it probably indicates a certain level of commitment and concern. But always ask not only for the name of the company but for the name of the specific agent with whom they dealt, for it is that individual who will serve you, and quality can vary widely within a single agency.

Once you've chosen an agent, be entirely candid. Budget considerations rank at the top of the candor list, and there's no sense in wasting the agent's (or your) time poring over itineraries that you know you can't afford. Similarly, if you like a fair degree of comfort, that fact should not be kept secret from your travel agent, who may assume that you wish to travel on a tight budget even when that's not the case.

Insurance

It is unfortunate that most decisions to buy travel insurance are impulsive and are usually made without any real consideration of the traveler's existing insurance policies. Too often the result is the purchase of needlessly expensive short-term policies that duplicate existing coverage and reinforce the tendency to buy coverage on a trip-by-trip basis rather than to work out a total and continuing travel insurance package that might well be more effective and economical.

Therefore, the first person with whom you should discuss travel insurance is your own insurance broker — not a travel agent or the clerk behind the airport insurance counter. You may well discover that the insurance you already carry — homeowner's policies and/or accident, health, and life insurance policies — protect you adequately while you travel, and that your real needs are in the more mundane areas of excess value insurance for baggage or trip cancellation insurance.

To make insurance decisions intelligently, however, you should first understand the basic categories of travel insurance and what they are designed to cover. Then you can decide what you should have in the broader context of your personal insurance needs, and you can choose the most economical way of getting the desired protection — through riders on existing policies; with one-shot short-term policies; through a special program put together for the frequent traveler; through coverage that's a part of various travel club benefits; or with a combination policy sold by insurance companies through brokers, tour operators, and even travel agents.

There are five basic categories of travel insurance:

1. Baggage and personal effects insurance.
2. Personal accident and sickness insurance.
3. Charter flight cancellation insurance.
4. Flight insurance (to cover death or injury).
5. Automobile insurance (for driving your own or a rented car).

Baggage and Personal Effects Insurance – If baggage and personal effects are included in your current homeowner's policy, check with your broker about the necessity for a special floater to cover you for the duration of a trip. The object is to protect your bags and their contents in case of damage or theft anytime during your travels. If this is not part of your present policy, you must decide if you need more protection than is included in the terms of any international airline ticket. International airlines only provide limited coverage for loss of or damage to baggage, though in recent court cases these preestablished limits have been successfully challenged. Limits of liability vary from airline to airline; the most common terms for international flights are $9.07 per pound or $20 per kilo, up to $400. (Read the fine print on your ticket for the exact terms set forth by the airline on which you are flying.) And remember: These figures represent *maximum* payments and are not awarded automatically; payments ultimately will be made on the basis of the actual value of your luggage and its contents.

If you are carrying goods worth more than the maximum protection offered by the airline, you should consider excess value insurance, available from the airlines at 10¢ to 15¢ per $100 of protection. This insurance can be purchased at the airline counter when you check in, though you should arrive early to fill out the necessary forms and to avoid earning the enmity of other passengers checking in who will be kept waiting while you transact your insurance purchase. Excess value insurance is also included in certain of the combination travel insurance policies discussed below.

- **ONE NOTE OF WARNING:** Be sure to read the fine print of any excess value insurance policy; there are often specific exclusions, such as money, tickets, furs, gold and silver objects, art, and antiques. And remember that insurance companies ordinarily will pay only the depreciated value of the goods rather than their replacement value. To best protect the items you're carrying in your luggage, have photos made of valuables, and keep a record of the serial numbers of such items as cameras, typewriters, radios, and so on. This will establish that you do, indeed, own the objects. If your luggage disappears en route or is damaged, deal with the situation immediately, at the airport, train station, or bus station. If an airline loses your luggage, you will be asked to fill out a Property Irregularity Report before you leave the airport. If your property disappears elsewhere, make a report to the police at once.

Personal Accident and Sickness Insurance – This covers you in case of illness on the road (hospital and doctor's expenses, lost income, and so on). In most cases it is a standard part of existing health insurance policies, though you should check with your broker to be sure that your policy will pay for medical expenses incurred abroad.

Charter Flight Cancellation Insurance – Charter passengers are usually required to pay the full price of their tour (whether it includes a flight only or a flight plus accommodations and other land arrangements) a substantial period of time in advance of departure. Although cancellation penalties vary (they are listed in fine print in every tour brochure and before you purchase a package tour you should know exactly what they are), rarely will a passenger get more than 20% of this money back if forced to cancel within a few weeks of leaving. Therefore, if you book a charter, you should have cancellation insurance to guarantee full refund of your money should you, a traveling companion, or a member of your immediate family get sick, forcing you to cancel your trip or *return home early*. The key here is *not* to buy just enough insurance to guarantee full reimbursement in the case of cancellation. The proper amount of coverage should be sufficient to reimburse you for the cost of having to catch up with a tour after its departure or having to travel home at the full economy air fare if you have to forgo the return flight of your charter. There is usually quite a discrepancy between your charter air fare and the amount you would have to pay to travel the same distance on a noncharter carrier.

Cancellation insurance is available from travel agents and tour operators in two forms: as part of a short-term, all-purpose travel insurance package (sold by the travel agent); or as specific cancellation insurance designed by the tour operator for a specific charter tour. Generally, the tour operator's policies are cheaper but less inclusive. Read any policy carefully before you buy it, and again be sure the policy you choose provides enough money to get you home from the farthest point on your itinerary should you have to fly on a scheduled flight. Also, be sure to check the specific definition of "family members" and "preexisting medical condition." Some policies will not pay if you become ill from a condition for which you have received treatment in the past.

Flight Insurance – Airlines have carefully established limits of liability for the death or injury of passengers. For international flights these are printed right on the ticket:

a maximum of $75,000 in case of death or injury. But remember, these limits of liability are not the same thing as insurance policies; they merely state the *maximum* an airline will pay in the case of death or injury, and every penny of that is usually subject to a legal battle.

This may make you feel that you are not adequately protected. But before you buy last-minute flight insurance from an airport vending machine, as many passengers do, consider the purchase in light of your total existing insurance coverage. A careful review of your current policies may reveal that you are already amply covered for accidental death, sometimes up to three times the amount provided for by the flight insurance you're buying in the airport.

Be aware that airport insurance, the kind you typically buy at a counter or from a vending machine, is among the most expensive forms of life insurance coverage available anywhere, and that even within a single airport, rates for approximately the same coverage can vary. Often the vending machines are more expensive than coverage sold over the counter, even when policies are with the same national company.

If you buy your ticket with an American Express, Diners Club, or Carte Blanche credit card, you are issued automatic life and accident insurance at no extra cost. American Express automatically provides $75,000 in free life insurance; Diners Club, $75,000; and Carte Blanche, $60,000. Each of these cards offers additional coverage at extremely reasonable prices. For $3, American Express cardholders can buy $250,000 worth of flight insurance; Diners Club members, $250,000 (an advance application must be submitted prior to purchase of the ticket); and Carte Blanche cardholders, $150,000.

Automobile Insurance – Public liability and property damage (third-party) insurance are compulsory in the United Kingdom and the Irish Republic whether you drive your own car or a rental. Every car rental contract includes this coverage, but has a deductible of about $500. The optional collision insurance provision, however, covers the deductible in case of an accident. Both the British and Irish tourist authorities strongly recommend taking out the collision insurance, which only tacks on about $5 per day to your rental and can save you unnecessary worry during your trip. Your contract (with appropriate insurance box ticked off) will suffice as proof of insurance. A US driver's license that has been in effect for a year is acceptable identification on the road. An International Insurance Certificate (called a Green Card), available from insurance brokers in the US, used to be required throughout Great Britain, Ireland, and all of Europe; it is now necessary only for driving in Italy and in Communist countries.

Combination Policies – Short-term insurance policies, which include personal accident and medical coverage, trip cancellation insurance, and baggage and personal effects insurance, are available through retail insurance agencies, automobile clubs, and many travel agents. These combination policies are designed to cover you for the duration of a single trip.

Hints for Handicapped Travelers

Roughly 35 million people in the US alone suffer from some sort of disability. At least half this number are physically handicapped. Like everyone else today, they — and the uncounted disabled millions around the world — are on the move. More than ever before the disabled are demanding facilities they can use comfortably, and they are being heard. Accessibility, both here and abroad, is being brought up to more acceptable standards every day.

Planning – It is essential to make travel arrangements well in advance and to specify

GETTING READY / Hints for Handicapped Travelers 65

to all services involved the degree of your disability or restricted mobility. Fortunately, there are some excellent organizations to help you begin. Rehabilitation International/ USA (RIUSA) is a national organization that provides information and services to the disabled and is affiliated with similar organizations in over 60 foreign countries. RIUSA publishes the *International Directory of Access Guides,* a regularly revised, free listing of almost 350 access guides both domestic and international with information on where to write for them. For the latest edition of the guide, contact RIUSA, Access Guide, Rehabilitation/World, 20 W 40th St., New York, NY 10018 (phone: 212-869-9907).

The Travel Information Center at Moss Rehabilitation Hospital is a free service designed to help handicapped people plan trips. It cannot make travel arrangements but will supply information about particular cities or countries or any special interests you have. Write to the Travel Information Center, Moss Rehabilitation Hospital, 12th St. and Tabor Rd., Philadelphia, PA 19141 (phone: 215-329-5715).

To keep abreast of developments in travel for the handicapped as they occur, you may want to join the Society for the Advancement of Travel for the Handicapped (SATH), a nonprofit organization whose members include travel agents, tour operators, and other travel suppliers, as well as consumers. SATH publishes a monthly newsletter and can provide information on travel agents or tour operators in the US and overseas who have experience or an interest in travel for the handicapped. Contact SATH, 26 Court St., Brooklyn, NY 11242 (phone: 212-858-5483).

An excellent book to consult is Louise Weiss's *Access to the World: A Travel Guide for the Handicapped* (available from the author, 154 E 29th St., New York, NY 10016, for $7.95, plus $1 handling). Ms. Weiss provides extensive information on transportation and hotels and offers sound tips for the disabled traveler abroad. Another book of note is *TravelAbility* by Lois Reamy (Macmillan; $11.95). It is geared mainly to travel in the US but gives lots of information useful to handicapped travelers whatever their destination.

The British Tourist Authority's *Britain for the Disabled* (free) contains helpful information on a variety of topics concerning the handicapped; and the section on Great Britain and Northern Ireland in RIUSA's International Directory of Access Guides mentioned above is especially comprehensive. Many of the publications listed were prepared by and are available directly from the Royal Association for Disability and Rehabilitation (RADAR), 25 Mortimer St., London W1N 8AB, to whom you may want to write for an up-to-date price list. Another source for information and publications is the Central Council for the Disabled, 25 Mortimer St., London W1N 8AB. A central source of information on facilities in the Republic of Ireland is the National Rehabilitation Board, 25 Clyde Rd., Dublin 4, Ireland, publishers of *Dublin for the Disabled.*

For details on the accessibility of hotels, consult the annual official accommodations guides of the British Tourist Authority and the Irish Tourist Board, both of which use the "symbol of access" to point out accommodations suitable for wheelchair-bound guests. The British guide *Britain: Hotels and Restaurants* (the symbol of access is also used in the restaurant lists) is sold for $12.95 at the British Travel Bookshop; and the *Guide to Approved Accommodations in Ireland* (including hotels, guesthouses, country houses, farmhouses, and hostels) is available free from the Tourist Board. Another guidebook that uses the symbol of access to designate hotels with bedrooms accessible by wheelchair is the 1981 *Michelin Red Guide to Great Britain and Ireland,* sold in general bookstores or available from the Michelin Tire Co., Guides and Maps Dept., Box 5022, New Hyde Park, NY 11042; $12.95).

A good guide for visitors to London is *London—A Guide for Disabled Visitors,* published by the London Tourist Board ($2.75), available at the British Travel Bookshop.

66 GETTING READY / Hints for Handicapped Travelers

It should be noted that almost all of the material published with disabled travelers in mind deals with the wheelchair-bound traveler for whom architectural barriers are of prime concern. A problem that will restrict the movement of another category of handicapped, blind people, is the very strict enforcement of anti-rabies laws in both the United Kingdom and the Irish Republic. Any dogs brought into either country must spend 6 months in quarantine — and seeing-eye dogs are not exempt. Guide dogs can be trained in one month, however, and blind travelers planning extended stays in Great Britain should write to the Guide Dogs for the Blind Association, 113 Uxbridge Rd., London W5, England.

Air Travel – Disabled passengers should always make reservations well in advance and should provide the airline with all relevant details of their condition when doing so. These details include information on mobility, toileting, whether or not you use oxygen, and whether airline-supplied equipment such as a wheelchair or portable oxygen will be necessary. Be sure that the person you speak with understands fully the degree of your disability — the more details provided, the more effective the help that can be given. Then, the day before the flight, call back to make sure that all arrangements have been taken care of, and on the day of the flight, arrive early so that you can be boarded before the rest of the passengers. Carry a medical certificate with you, stating your specific disability or the need to carry particular medicine. (Some airlines require the certificate and you should find out the regulations of the airline you'll be flying well beforehand.) In most cases, you can be wheeled as far as the plane, and sometimes right onto it, in your own wheelchair; if not, a boarding chair may be used. Your own wheelchair will be folded and put in the baggage compartment and should be tagged as escort luggage to assure that it's available at planeside immediately upon landing rather than in the baggage claim area.

For an access guide to 282 airports here and abroad, write for *Access Travel: Airports,* from the Airport Operators Council International, 1700 K St. NW, Washington, DC 20006. It includes detailed information on Heathrow, Gatwick, and Stansted airports in England; Aberdeen, Edinburgh, Glasgow, and Prestwick in Scotland; and Dublin and Shannon airports in Ireland. With the exception of Dublin and Shannon, the same airports are discussed in a series of airport access guides prepared by the British Airports Authority and called *Who Looks After You at Heathrow Airport?* (or Gatwick Airport, Stansted Airport, and so on). To receive a copy, write to the British Airports Authority, 2 Buckingham Gate, London SW1E 6JL, filling in the name of the airport that interests you.

Travel by Ship – Cunard's *Queen Elizabeth 2* is considered to be the best-equipped ship for the handicapped — all but the top deck is accessible. The *QE2* crosses the Atlantic regularly from April through December, from New York to Cherbourg, France, and its home port of Southampton, England.

Travel by Car, Bus, or Train – The best solution to getting around is to travel with an able-bodied companion who can drive. Another option is to hire a chauffeur-driven auto. As for doing the driving yourself, it is extremely difficult in Europe to find rental cars adapted with hand controls for the disabled. One company that does supply them is Kenning Car Hire Ltd., at 477–479 Green Lane, Palmers Green, London N13. Kenning is represented in the US by American International Rent-a-Car, 4241 Sigma Rd., Dallas, TX 75240 (phone: 800-527-0202). The cars cannot be taken to Ireland, however.

Bus travel is not recommended for travelers who are totally wheelchair bound unless they have someone along who can lift them on and off or they are members of a group tour designed for the handicapped and using a specially outfitted bus. Local personnel may be willing, but there are often regulations prohibiting them from actually picking up a passenger. If you have some mobility, however, you'll find employees usually quite happy to help you board and exit.

Travel by train is becoming more feasible especially in Britain where many newer trains have removable seats that can accommodate a wheelchair up to 24½ inches wide. The number of destinations (London to Liverpool, Manchester, Glasgow, Edinburgh, Bristol, and South Wales among them) is still limited and lavatories on even these trains are still not accessible, though most trips are not long; most stations, however, have restroom facilities for the handicapped. On other trains, passengers can arrange to travel in the guard's van, that is, the baggage car. The ride will not be scenic but it will get you there. Wheelchair passengers travel at one-half the normal second-class, one-way fare (unless they occupy a normal seat) and arrangements, either to ride in the guard's van or to have seats removed, or for an escort at stations, must be made through the area manager in advance. *British Rail: A Guide for Disabled People,* an access guide to railway stations, is available through RADAR or the Central Council for the Disabled (addresses above). For more information on British trains, contact BritRail Travel International offices in New York, Chicago, or Los Angeles; for information on Irish trains, contact CIE Tours International, 590 Fifth Ave., New York, NY 10036 (phone: 800-223-8944, toll-free; or 212-977-9300).

Tours – The following travel agencies or tour operators specialize in making group or individual arrangements for the Europe-bound handicapped traveler and all have experience in travel to Great Britain or Ireland. Those arranging tours have all offered trips to these destinations in the past, though because of the special requirements of handicapped travel, the same packages may not be offered regularly. Programs designed for the physically impaired are run by specialists who have traveled in advance or have thoroughly researched hotels, restaurants, and places of interest to be sure they present no insurmountable obstacles.

1. *Evergreen Travel Service,* 19505 L, 44 Ave. W, Lynnwood, WA 98036 (phone: 206-776-1184). Handles both tours and individual arrangements.
2. *Flying Wheels Travel,* Box 382, Owatonna, MN 55060 (phone: 507-451-5005). Handles both tours and individual arrangements.
3. *Handi-Tours,* Calladine & Baldry Travel, Yorkdale Shopping Centre, Suite 153, Dufferin St. & Hwy. 401, Toronto, Ontario M6A 2T9, Canada (phone: 416-789-7656). Tours and individual arrangements.
4. *Handy-Cap Horizons,* 3250 E Loretta Dr., Indianapolis, IN 46227 (phone: 317-784-5777). A travel club for the handicapped or elderly, their families and friends (membership is $10 per person per year) that escorts its members on group tours.
5. *Rambling Tours Inc.,* PO Box 1304, Hallandale, FL 33009 (phone: 305-456-2161). Group tours only.

Hints for Traveling with Children

What better way to be receptive to the experiences you will encounter than to take along the young, wide-eyed members of your family? And what better place to take them than Great Britain and Ireland where you'll find tales of King Arthur's Court and Robin Hood, not to mention the leprechauns, fairies, and little people lurking around every bend. Your children's company does not have to be a burden or their presence an excessive expense. The current generation of discount air fares makes flights to these countries a good deal cheaper than a decent summer camp. Or why not send them to summer camp in the Irish countryside while you do some touring? Gaeltacht vacations are offered for children during the summer months in Irish-speaking regions; here they can learn a bit about the language, folklore, and traditions of the Irish people. Riding holidays and pony

68 GETTING READY / Hints for Traveling with Children

trekking, as well as traditional camps, are popular in England, Scotland, Wales, and Northern Ireland.

If, however, you'd like to keep the family together, you can rent a cottage or visit a family farm in the countryside. The British and Irish tourist offices have information on how to make arrangements for any of these vacations.

A family trip will be an investment in your children's futures, making geography and history come alive to them, and a sure memory that will be among the fondest you will share with them someday. Their insights will be refreshing to you; their impulses may take you to unexpected places with unexpected dividends. At whatever age, the experience will be invaluable to them. It is necessary, however, to take some extra time to prepare for the trip.

Here are several hints for making a trip with children easy and fun.

1. Children should be part of planning the trip, and preparations should begin about a month before you leave, using maps, atlases, travel magazines, and travel books to make clear exactly where you are going and how far away it is. Part of the excitement of the journey will be associating the tiny dots on the map with the very real places the children visit a few weeks later. You can show them pictures of streets and scenes in which they will stand within a month. Don't shirk history lessons, but don't burden them with dates. Make history light, anecdotal, pertinent, but most of all, fun. Read them Irish folklore, teach them a Highland fling, set them to tracing their ancestral roots.
2. Children should be in on the planning of the itinerary, and where you go and what you do should reflect some of their ideas. If they know enough about architecture and geography before they go, they will have the excitement of recognition when they arrive, and the illumination of seeing how something is or is not the way they expected it to be.
3. Give children specific responsibilities. The job of carrying their own flight bags and looking after their personal things, along with some other light travel responsibility, will give them a stake in the journey.

Packing – Choose your own and your children's clothes wisely. Take only drip-dry, wrinkle-resistant articles, comfortable shoes — sneakers or sandals — and a few things to keep warm and dry. But limit packing to a minimum. No one likes to carry added luggage, and you'll be surprised that, when abroad, clothes are about the last thing on your mind.

It is a good idea to bring along as many handy snacks as you can squeeze into the corners of your suitcases. These should include things like raisins, nuts, sucking candy, and crackers (especially for the tots). Don't worry if your supply is quickly depleted — airports and train stations are well stocked with such items.

Along with these few edibles, pack a special medical kit (see *Medical and Legal Aid Abroad*) and some packaged towelettes for dirty fingers. Have your children choose a few favorite toys to bring along. Pens, crayons, and paper take up the least amount of room and can be put to use during long car trips or train rides. You might also encourage your children to draw what they see around them. Any way you can think of to help them assimilate their new experiences will increase their enjoyment.

Planning – Give children who can read books on Britain and Ireland. The British Travel Bookshop (680 Fifth Ave., New York, NY 10019) has a "discovering series" and some of the titles will especially appeal to children — *Kings and Queens* and *Preserved Railways* ($2.80 each, plus $1.50 handling). It also offers the beautifully illustrated *Four Countries, One Kingdom* ($4.25, plus $1.50 handling), a history book for children 11 and older, and *Stonehenge and Avebury* ($1.95). *Facsimile Book Shop* (16 W 55th St., New York, NY 10019) specializes in Irish books and records and has

GETTING READY / Hints for Traveling with Children 69

paperbacks and cassettes on Irish fairies, genealogy, history, and folklore. Other large series that cover Great Britain and Ireland and are available in general bookstores include: *Talking of Wales* by Trevor Fishlock (Faber and Faber)—available from the *Rivendell Bookshop*, 149 First Ave., New York, NY 10003; Time-Life's colorful and informative picture series called Great Cities, which includes London and Dublin; the delightful *Artstart* series by Ernest Raboff (Doubleday), which includes the life and works of painters from Raphael to Picasso; and Newsweek's *Great Museums of the World* series (Norton).

Getting There and Getting Around – Take time to investigate the many discount and charter flights available as well as the package deals and special rates offered by the major airlines. Sometimes booking is required up to 2 months in advance. Are there special reductions for children? The answer, happily, is almost always yes. Children under 2 usually travel free on airplanes as long as you keep them on your lap. (Don't despair, though. If there are empty seats around you, no one will object to your putting your child down. Armrests on airplanes are generally removable.) Children ages 2 through 12 usually travel at two-thirds the adult fare. If you notify the airline in advance, they will provide a special infant seat. Special meals for children are also available with advance notice. For landings and takeoffs, have a bottle or pacifier on hand for the infants and some gum or sucking candy for older children. This will keep everyone swallowing properly and ensure against earaches caused by rapid changes in air pressure. Newborn babies, whose lungs may not be able to adjust to the altitude, should not be taken aboard an airplane. (Note: Some airlines refuse to carry pregnant women in their eighth or ninth month, for fear of the hazards of an in-flight birth. Check with the airline ahead of time.)

By ship, children (ages 1 through 12) usually travel at half fare. If you plan to travel by train through Britain and Ireland, you might consider purchasing one of the economical train passes that feature reduced children's rates. Great Britain's BritRail Pass allows children 5 through 13 to travel at half fare and the Irish Republic's Rambler Ticket cuts train (and bus) costs in half for children under 12. The Eurailpass, also valid in Ireland, offers free passage for children under 4; children under 12 ride at half price. Buy these passes before you leave the US. Northern Ireland Railways' unlimited travel pass, the Rail Runabout, is half price to children under 16; the Freedom of Northern Ireland bus pass (available April through September) is also discounted substantially for children under 16. Both are bought in Northern Ireland. The Britexpress Travelcard, bought either in Britain or through travel agents in the US, lets children under 14 years ride the bus in England, Scotland, and Wales at half the price of an adult card.

Accommodations and Meals – Often a cot will be placed in a hotel room at little or no extra charge. If you wish to sleep in separate rooms, special rates are sometimes available for families in adjoining rooms. You might want to look into accommodations along the way that will add to the color of your trip; there are, for instance, many country inns, farmhouses, and cottages throughout the British and Irish countrysides that could prove a delightful experience for the whole family. And don't forget castles, many of which double as hotels. Your children will love them. Camping facilities are often situated in beautiful, out-of-the-way spots and are generally good, well equipped, and cheaper than any hotel you will come across.

What to See and Do – For specific suggestions on what to see and do in the various cities, see the individual city reports in CITIES. There are several excellent publications that focus on the interests of the young visitor and provide helpful hints for parents. The BTA puts out two such booklets: *Young Visitors to Britain* lists riding schools, camps, museums, and will even tell your child how to find a British pen pal; the 82-page *Children on Holiday* not only lists activities for children but indicates hotels with special amenities for parents, such as a resident nanny. Also ask the BTA about an organization called Universal Aunts, Ltd. This group has a wide range of services including picking a child up at an airport or train station, babysitting, and conducting children's tours. *Discovering London for Children* by Margaret Pearson ($2.80, plus $1.50 handling, from the British Travel Bookshop) is an entertaining and useful sightseeing guidebook for parents. The entry for each of the popular London landmarks has a short historical sketch in addition to basic information on admission charges, days open, and how to get there. The Irish Tourist Board puts out two brochures that can help in planning a trip to Ireland with your children: the *Land for Youth and Learning Study Planner* and *Trip Planner*. They also publish dozens of fact sheets on every topic of interest, i.e., folklore, summer schools, camps, and regions where Irish is still spoken.

There are some general things to remember when traveling with children. First and foremost, don't forget that their attention span is far shorter than an adult's. They don't have to see every museum to learn something from their trip; watching, playing with, and talking to other children can be equally enlightening experiences. Try to break up the day into short, palatable segments: no more than a morning or afternoon dedicated to any one activity, be it travel or sight-seeing. Also, remember the places that children the world over love to visit: zoos, country fairs, amusement parks, beaches, and nature trails, many of which are listed in the publications previously mentioned.

Hints for Single Travelers

Just about the last trip in human history in which the participants were neatly paired was the voyage of Noah's Ark. Ever since, passenger lists and tour groups have reflected the same kind of asymmetry that occurs in real life, as countless individuals set forth to see the world unaccompanied (or unencumbered, depending on your outlook) by spouse, lover, friend, or relative.

There are some things to be said for traveling alone. It forces you to see more; it requires that you be self-reliant, independent, and responsible. It necessitates that you be more outgoing, and, therefore, you tend to meet more people than you would have had you been traveling in a pair. Unfortunately, it also turns you into a second-class citizen.

For the truth is that the travel industry is not yet prepared to deal fairly with people who vacation by themselves. Most travel bargains, including package tours, hotel accommodations, resort packages, and cruises, are based on *double-occupancy* rates. This means that the per-person price is offered on the basis of two people traveling together and sharing a double room. (Hotels can afford to offer such deals at no loss because, theoretically, two people traveling together will eat and drink more.) For exactly the same package, the single traveler will have to pay a surcharge, called the "single supplement," which can add 50% to 75% to the basic per-person rate.

Don't despair, however. There are scores of inexpensive guesthouses, small hotels, and B&Bs throughout Great Britain and Ireland. These smaller accommodations offer a cozy atmosphere and prices that are still quite reasonable for the single traveler. Given your unencumbered state, you may want to consider an organization catering to people interested not only in seeing the sights abroad but also in meeting the people en route. The United States Servas Committee keeps a worldwide list of hosts willing to take visitors into their homes as guests for a 2-night stay. (See the section on Home Stays, *Accommodations and Reservations*, GETTING READY TO GO.) If you prefer to have your arrangements taken care of for you, a number of options have emerged. Cosmos, the British tour operator specializing in budget motorcoach tours of Europe, offers a guaranteed-share plan whereby singles who wish to share

GETTING READY / Hints for Single Travelers

rooms are matched by the tour escort with like-minded individuals and charged the basic tour price. Those wishing to stay on their own, of course, pay the single supplement. Cosmos tours can be booked in the US through your travel agent. Enterprising travel agencies and other organizations have created travel clubs and packaged singles-only tours for every age group. Some charge minimal membership fees; others offer their services free. But the basic service offered by all is the same — to match the unattached person with a compatible travel mate. Following is a list of some of these agencies:

1. *Widow's Travel Club:* Despite the name, this club serves both women and men, single, divorced, or widowed. Travelers are asked to fill out questionnaires regarding their destinations, likes and dislikes, and so on. Annual membership fee is $25. Beatrice L. Green, Room 3716, Time-Life Bldg., Rockefeller Center, New York, NY 10020 (phone: 212-586-0307).

2. *Gramercy's Singleworld:* About two thirds of this agency's clientele is under 35 and over half this number are women. There are no age limits, however, and Singleworld does organize tours and place singles on existing packages regardless of age. The annual membership fee is $15. 444 Madison Ave., New York, NY 10022 (phone: 212-753-7595).

3. *Womantour:* This organization is run by Estilita Grimaldo, who arranges group and individual travel programs for women. The annual membership fee is $15. 5314 N Figueroa St., Los Angeles, CA 90042 (phone: 213-255-1115).

Two specific groups of single travelers deserve special mention: women and students. There are countless women who travel by themselves in Britain and Ireland. Such a venture need not be feared. Traveling alone in these countries is no different from living alone at home; in fact most British and Irish cities are considerably safer than many American cities. And, in some cases, friendlier: You will generally find people to be very courteous, generous, and welcoming. One lingering inhibition many female travelers still harbor is that of eating alone in a public place. The trick here is to relax and enjoy your meal and surroundings; although you may run across the occasional unenlightened waiter, solo diners are no longer an uncommon sight nor scorned. If you still feel apprehensive, Dena Kaye offers some lively, helpful advice on solo travel in her book *The Traveling Woman* (Doubleday; $11.95).

A large number of single travelers, needless to say, are students. There are many benefits for students abroad, and the way to begin to discover these is to consult the Council on International Educational Exchange, 205 E 42nd St., New York, NY 10017 (phone: 212-661-1414). This organization, which administers a variety of work, study, and international travel programs for students, is the US sponsor of the International Student Identity Card. Reductions on trains, air fare, and free entry to most museums and other exhibits are only some of the advantages of the card. To apply for it, write to the CIEE; application requires a $6 fee, a photograph, and proof that you are a full-time student (this means a letter or bill from your school registrar with the school's official seal).

Special transportation discounts are available to students and youth in both Britain and Ireland. CIE, the Irish Republic's National Transportation Company, has a Youth/Student Rambler Ticket for those between the ages of 16 and 26. It allows the holder 8, 15, or 30 days of unlimited travel by rail or by a combination of rail and bus. The ticket must be purchased before going overseas (from CIE Tours International, 590 Fifth Ave., New York, NY 10036; phone: 212-944-8828 or 800-223-8944). Also, from April through September, Dublin Tourism sells special tickets to those taking summer courses in Ireland. These tickets allow unlimited travel on Dublin city and suburban trains and buses for 2 weeks ($12 fee). Eurail's Youthpass, for those

72 GETTING READY / Hints for Single Travelers

under 26, is accepted in the Irish Republic, but is not really economical unless you are traveling through several other countries on the Eurail network (which does not include Great Britain).

In Great Britain, British Rail offers the BritRail Youth Pass for anyone between the ages of 14 and 25. The Youth Pass permits unlimited train travel in economy class throughout England, Scotland, and Wales for 7-, 14-, or 21-day or 1-month time periods. It is also valid on the Sealink (owned by British Rail) ships to the Isle of Wight and on the Lake Windermere steamers. For an extra charge, there is a Youth Seapass version that provides one-way or round-trip sea travel between Britain and the Continent or Britain and Ireland in addition to all the other benefits of the BritRail Youth Pass. To buy a pass, contact your travel agent or the BritRail Travel International office at 630 Third Ave., New York, NY 10017 (phone: 212-599-5400), or in Los Angeles or Chicago, 21 days before departure. Because the passes must be purchased before you leave the US, you will have to have some certainties in your itinerary in order to choose the most economical version.

For accommodations, keep in mind that youth hostels are plentiful throughout Great Britain and Ireland. These are a sure place to meet people your own age and are generally clean, well located, and always cheap. For short stays of up to 4 nights (sometimes longer, if you call ahead and make arrangements with the house parents), hostels of the Youth Hostels Association, located all around Britain, are open to those who carry a YHA card. To get the card, write to American Youth Hostels, 1332 I St. NW, Washington, DC 20005 (phone: 800-424-9426). The membership fee is $14 for anyone over 18; $7 for anyone under. If you go without a YHA card, you can get an International Youth Hostels Federation guest pass for $12 by contacting the British and Irish associations mentioned below. The British Tourist Authority publishes two helpful booklets: *Britain: Youth Accommodation* and *Young Visitors to Britain*. These list hostels (which allow stays of 1 to 3 nights) and university facilities (where longer stays of 1 or 2 weeks are permitted). For more information, contact either the BTA or the British Universities Accommodation Consortium, PO Box 32, University Park, Nottingham N97 2RD, England. There are four regional YHA groups in Great Britain and Ireland that publish handbooks on hostels in their particular area. For hostels in England and Wales, contact the YHA at Trevelyan House, 8 St. Stephen's Hill, St. Albans, Hertfordshire AL1 2DY (phone: 55215), or at 14 Southampton St., London WC2E 7HY (phone: 836-8561); in Scotland, Scottish Youth Hostel Association, 7 Glebe Crescent, Stirling FK 2JA; in Northern Ireland, Youth Hostel Association of Northern Ireland, 56 Bradbury Pl., Belfast BT7 1RU; in the Irish Republic, Irish Youth Hostel Association (An Oige), 39 Mountjoy Square, Dublin 1 (phone: 745734). Hostels in Ireland and Northern Ireland are a bit more rustic than those in Great Britain; guests must provide their own cutlery, towels, and linens.

The YMCA and the YWCA also run economical sex-segregated accommodations and have separate offices to contact for information. You can get a list of Ys in Great Britain by writing to the National Council of YMCAs, 640 Forest Rd., Walthamstow, London E17; or to the YWCA, 2 Weymouth St., London W1 (636-9722). For a listing of Ys in London, write YMCA, 31 Craven Terrace, Lancaster Gate, London W2 (phone: 723-0071); YWCA, 16 Great Russell St., London WC1 (phone: 580-4827 or 636-7512). These agencies will not make bookings for you; make reservations directly with the Y you choose.

There are many private houses and farms throughout the countryside that make a pleasant home base and provide a chance to meet local people. The Northern Ireland Tourist Board publishes its own useful booklet titled *Farm and Country Holidays*, listing country homes and working farms as well as a brochure called *Northern Ireland Town and Seaside Houses;* for the latter, write to 74 Seacliff Rd.,

Bangor, Co. Down. The Irish Tourist Board also has information on these accommodations. On some farms you'll get a room and a hearty breakfast for about $12 to $15 per day.

And there's always camping. Virtually any area of the countryside in Great Britain or Ireland has a place for you to pitch your tent and enjoy the scenery. There are numerous national parks, and, with permission, you can camp on private acres of farmland. Many of the campsites have showers, laundry rooms, public phones, eating facilities, shops, and tents to rent. In Dublin or Cork the tourist offices have information on where to rent a backpacker's kit for about $5 per person per day. Both the Irish and British tourist authorities have booklets listing sites, their facilities, and available equipment rental; some sites rent tents by the day.

If you're at least 18 years old and a full-time student in a US college or university, you can work in Ireland for up to 4 months and in Britain for up to 6 months at any time of the year. For information on the types of jobs available and where they're located, contact the Council on International Educational Exchange (address above). The pay is low, but it will help cover the cost of your trip.

Summer study programs are popular and courses diverse: literature, language, history, politics, folklore, music, painting, and crafts. For information on specific courses, colleges, their costs, and requirements, send for *Discover Young Ireland* from the Irish Tourist Board, and *Study in Britain* from British Information Services, 845 Third Ave., New York, NY 10022 (212-752-8400).

We also recommend *Let's Go: Britain and Ireland,* published by Harvard Student Agencies, Thayer Hall B, Harvard Yard, Cambridge, MA 02138; $6.25. It's an excellent source for student (or budget) travelers.

Hints for Older Travelers

Reduced air fares, special package deals, and more free time are just some of the factors that have given some 23 million Americans over age 65 a chance to see the world at an affordable price. Senior citizens are an ever-growing segment of the travel population, and the trend among them is to travel more frequently and for longer periods of time. Retired travelers can also take advantage of off-season travel, avoiding crowds and escaping higher prices. For example, summer is peak season in these countries, but by traveling right before or right after — April, May, September, and October — you'll still have good weather and be able to take advantage of lower rates if they're offered.

Planning – When packing, bear in mind that you will not always find central heating in guesthouses, restaurants, and other public places. Bring along a warm sweater (even summer evenings can be cool) and a raincoat (see *How to Pack* and *When to Go,* GETTING READY TO GO) — but remember that one secret to happy traveling is to *pack lightly*. Most common toilet articles, in familiar brands, are available just about anywhere you go. Be sure to take with you any medication you need, enough to carry you through without a prescription for the duration of your trip; pack it separately in a carryall in case your luggage is lost or detoured, along with a note from your doctor for the benefit of airport authorities. It is also wise to bring a few common medications with you — aspirin and something for stomach upset may come in handy. If you are diabetic or have cardiac problems, carry your medical records. Remember that Medicare will not cover you abroad — but Britain's free medical care is extended to foreign guests in (but only in) emergencies. A number of organizations exist to help you avoid or deal with a medical emergency overseas. For further information on these services, see *Medical and Legal Aid Abroad,* GETTING READY TO GO. A word of caution

GETTING READY / Hints for Older Travelers

— don't overdo it. Allow time for some relaxing each day to refresh yourself for the next scheduled sight-seeing event. Traveling across time zones can be exhausting. Plan on spending at least one full day resting before you start touring. If you're part of a group tour, be sure to check the planned itinerary thoroughly. Some package deals sound wonderful because they include all the places you've ever dreamed of visiting. In fact, they can become so hectic and tiring that you'll be reaching for a pillow instead of your camera.

Some of the benefits available to older travelers require advance notification. There is a wide range of special discounts and group travel opportunities available and you should take ample time to familiarize yourself with them. The following associations will help you see the world.

1. *National Council of Senior Citizens:* The emphasis of this organization is on developing low-cost travel opportunities for its members. Their charter trips are well organized and less exhausting than many others since you stay at one hotel for the duration, but can take optional 1-day sight-seeing trips. Other trips include daily sight-seeing excursions. The roster of tours is different each year, as it depends on membership response, so you'll have to inquire about Britain and Ireland. The annual membership fee is $6 per individual or $7.50 per couple. 1511 K St. NW, Washington, DC 20005 (phone: 202-347-8800; for travel information, 202-638-5011).

2. *National Association of Mature People:* Membership is available to anyone 55 years or older throughout the country, at $5 per year for either an individual or a couple. They, too, offer a changing schedule of tours every year. PO Box 26792, Oklahoma City, OK 73126 (phone: 405-848-1832).

Many tour operators specialize in group travel for older persons. Grand Circle Travel, Inc., which caters exclusively to the over-50 traveler, packages a huge variety (no continent is left untrod) of escorted tours, cruises, and extended vacations in one spot. It has numerous itineraries to Great Britain and Ireland. Contact Grand Circle at 555 Madison Ave., New York, NY 10022 (phone: 212-688-5900, or toll-free 800-221-2610), or at 215 Long Beach Blvd., Long Beach, CA 90801 (phone: 213-432-8704, or toll-free 800-421-3733). Gadabout Tours, operated by Lois Anderson, sometimes offers escorted tours to England, Scotland, Wales, and Ireland. For further information, write Gadabout Tours, 700 E Tahquitz-McCallum Way, Palm Springs, CA 92262 (phone: 714-325-5556). Frames, a British tour operator, has special discounts on three different tours of Great Britain if you're 55 or over. Although it's located in England, you can book a Frames tour through your travel agent.

Discounts – BritRail offers a Senior Citizen Pass for those 65 and older. It permits unlimited first-class train travel through England, Scotland, and Wales at the economy fare. It is also valid on Sealink ships to the Isle of Wight and on the Lake Windermere steamers. The Senior Citizen Seapass gives you all the benefits of the rail ticket in addition to one-way or round-trip passage to Ireland. Both tickets are available for 7, 14, or 21 days or 1 month and must be purchased before entering Great Britain. Northern Ireland Railways' Rail Runabout Ticket, bought in Northern Ireland and good for 7 consecutive days of unlimited train travel, is half price to senior citizens.

There are no other reduced transportation rates strictly for senior citizens at this writing, but the regular discount passes on trains and buses in Great Britain and Ireland are very economical. Refer to the *Touring by Rail* and *Touring by Bus* sections of GETTING READY TO GO.

Medical and Legal Aid and Consular Services

MEDICAL AID: The surest way to return home in good health is to be prepared for common medical problems en route. So before we describe the health facilities available in Great Britain and Ireland, here are some tips to consider while still in the US.

Prepare a compact and personal medical kit including Band-Aids, first-aid cream, nose drops, insect repellent, aspirin, an extra pair of prescription glasses or sunglasses if you wear them, Lomotil or an equivalent for diarrhea, Dramamine or an equivalent for motion sickness, a thermometer, and a supply of those medicines you take regularly. In the corner of your kit, keep a list of all the drugs you have brought and their purpose as well as a copy of your doctor's prescriptions (or a note from your doctor). This could come in handy if you are ever questioned by police or airport authorities about why you are carrying drugs. It is also a good idea to ask your doctor to prepare a medical identification card that includes such information as your blood type, your social security number, any allergies or chronic health problems you have, and your medical insurance number. Check with your insurance company on the applicability of your policy while abroad. (Older travelers should note that Medicare does not make payments out of the country.)

The *Medic Alert Foundation* sells identification tags that specify that the wearer has a health problem that may not be readily apparent to a casual observer. A heart condition, diabetes, epilepsy, or severe allergies are the sorts of things that these badges were developed to communicate, conditions that, if unrecognized at a time when emergency treatment is necessary (a time when you may be unable to speak for yourself), can result in tragic treatment errors. In addition to the identification emblems, the foundation maintains a central file (telephone number clearly inscribed on the ID badge) from which your complete medical history is available 24 hours a day via a telephone call. The one-time membership fee of from $15 to $48 depends upon the type of emblem you select — from stainless steel to 10K gold-filled. For information contact: Medic Alert, PO Box 1009, Turlock, CA 95381-9986 (phone: 209-668-3333; or toll-free, 800-344-3226).

Assist-Card International is sold only through travel agents and provides a number to call — 24 hours a day, 365 days a year — where complete emergency medical assistance can be arranged, including ambulance or air transportation to the proper treatment facilities, local lawyers for a case that is the by-product of an accident, and up to $5,000 in bail bonds for a judicial proceeding that is similarly the result of an accident. The organization will also arrange for a flight home if a traveler is unable to complete a trip, and will pay any necessary fare differential. Fees for the Assist-Card vary according to the length of the trip abroad, ranging from $25 for a 5-day card to $150 for a 90-day itinerary. For information about these and other travel services, contact: Assist-Card Corporation of America, 745 Fifth Ave., New York, NY 10022 (phone: 212-752-2788 in New York, or toll-free elsewhere, 800-221-4564).

SOS also offers a program to cover medical emergencies while traveling. Members are provided with telephone access — 24 hours a day, 365 days a year — to a worldwide, monitored, multilingual network of medical centers. A phone call brings assistance ranging from telephone consultation to transportation home by ambulance or aircraft, and in some cases transportation of a family member to the place where you are hospitalized. The service can be purchased for a week ($12.50; additional coverage

GETTING READY / Medical and Legal Aid

is $1.60 per day), a month ($36), or a year ($140), and includes a $1,000 insurance policy with a $25 deductible. Formerly available only on a corporate basis, it is now being offered to individuals. For information contact: International SOS Assistance, Inc., Two Neshaminy Interplex, Suite 208, Trevose, PA 19047 (phone: 215-244-1500; or toll-free, 800-523-8930).

Intermedic, a division of Executive Health Examiners, provides access to a directory of physicians in 170 cities in over 90 countries including Great Britain and Ireland. The annual fee is $6 for an individual and $10 for a family. Each physician listed has provided Intermedic with data on his or her medical education, professional experience, and hospital affiliation; and each has indicated a willingness to respond promptly to calls from traveling Intermedic members. They have also agreed in writing to a ceiling on fees for any initial visit. For information contact: Intermedic, Inc., 777 Third Ave., New York, NY 10017 (phone: 212-486-8974).

The National Health Service, the public health service of Great Britain and Northern Ireland, provides free medical aid for tourists in *emergencies,* but not for subsequent treatment. When a traveler is treated for a preexisting chronic condition, health care is free only if the attending physician determines that urgent treatment is necessary. There is a charge for all other care, though visitors staying long enough (more than 3 months) may register with the National Health Service and be entitled to the same free medical treatment the British receive. Free emergency services for travelers are currently under review and may not be available in the future. Check with the BTA before you travel. In the Irish Republic, where the General Medicine Service provides either free hospital coverage or free total health care for nearly all citizens, tourists (except from Common Market countries) must pay for all treatment, even in emergencies. If you have medical insurance in the US, check with your insurance company before you go — it may be good for short-term coverage in Ireland.

If a bona fide emergency occurs in Great Britain, the fastest way to receive attention may be to take a taxi to the emergency room (called "casualty department" in England) of the nearest public teaching hospital — the type most likely, except in small towns, to provide 24-hour emergency service. An alternative is to dial 999, the free nationwide emergency number used to summon the police and fire trucks and ambulances. Since British ambulance dispatchers are accustomed to taking calls from doctors only, state immediately that you are a foreign tourist and then the nature of your problem and your location.

In Ireland, three cities — Dublin, Galway, and Cork — have teaching hospitals. Night emergency service rotates among hospitals and you should call 999, the nationwide emergency number here, too, to find out which one in a given area is on duty. The same number can be dialed for an ambulance, but as in Britain, a taxi may be a faster way to reach help. Ambulances in both countries are meant primarily for transportation, and beyond the attendant's expertise in cardiopulmonary resuscitation, few are equipped to give treatment en route.

If you need a doctor for something less than an emergency in Great Britain, there are several ways to find one. Ask at your hotel or check the local post office where neighborhood NHS physicians are supposed to be listed (though they often aren't). You can also dial 999 for help in locating a doctor. What you will get is the name of a general practitioner, since in Britain, specialists almost always see patients upon referral only. If you're in London, an additional way to find a doctor is to call the consular division of the US embassy, which keeps a list of local doctors in private practice. (Most British doctors work within the National Health Service system, though they are allowed to see private patients. Some practice privately only, and there are more of these in London than elsewhere in England, and many more in England than in Scotland or Wales.) For many travelers, this is the best solution. For one thing, a private doctor may be willing to see you more quickly than the local NHS general practitioner. For another, if you know it's a specialist you need, one in private practice will usually see you without a general practitioner's referral. When you do get the appointment, you'll be going to the doctor's "surgery" (office), where he or she keeps surgery hours.

In the Irish Republic GMS doctors may also treat visitors as private patients. To find one in a nonemergency situation, consult the regional health board (there are eight of them) for a list of GMS general practitioners approved for the area served. The office of the Eastern Health Board, which serves Dublin, is at 1 James's St. (phone: 757951). Private practice is quite common in Ireland, but even doctors working within the General Medicine Service — not on a prepaid salary as British physicians are — tend to schedule tourists quickly. In addition, though general practitioners deliver primary care here, too, there is no violation of protocol in approaching a specialist directly. Call the appropriate department of a teaching hospital or, in Dublin, the US consulate, which also maintains a list of doctors. Remember that if you are hospitalized in the Republic, you will have to pay even in an emergency. You can choose to be put in a private wing, but a bed on the ward is much cheaper.

Pharmacies in both countries are called "chemists." It is difficult, if not impossible, to find one willing to fill a foreign prescription. Exceptions are made in emergencies — a diabetic needing insulin, for instance — but even in an emergency you will more than likely be supplied only enough of a drug to last until a local doctor can write a prescription. Take what you need with you, including contraceptives. In the Irish Republic, these products are not readily available.

For further information on doctors, hospitals, and health care in Britain, Ireland, and the rest of Europe, read *Traveling Healthy* by Sheilah M. Hillman and Dr. Robert S. Hillman (Penguin Books; $7.95).

LEGAL AID ABROAD: It is often far more alarming to be arrested abroad for an infringement of the law than at home. Not only are you alone among strangers, but the punishment can be worse. Granted, the American consulate can advise you of your rights and provide a list of lawyers, but it cannot interfere with local due process.

The best advice is to be honest and law abiding. If you are issued a traffic ticket, pay it. If you are approached by drug hawkers, ignore them. Penalties for possession of marijuana and other narcotics are generally far more severe than in the US.

CONSULAR SERVICES: There is one crucial place to keep in mind when outside the US — namely, the United States consulate. If you are injured or become seriously ill, the consulate will direct you to medical assistance and notify your relatives. If, while abroad, you become involved in a dispute that could lead to legal action, the consulate, once again, is the place to turn. And in case of natural disasters or local civil unrest, consulates around the world handle the evacuation of US citizens if such a procedure is necessary. Keep in mind, though, that nowhere does the consulate act as an arbitrator or ombudsman on an American citizen's behalf. The consul has no power, authorized or otherwise, to subvert, alter, or contravene the legal processes, however unfair, of the country in which he or she serves. Nor can a consul oil the machinery of a foreign bureaucracy or provide legal advice. The consul's responsibilities do include providing a list of lawyers, information on local sources of legal aid, assignment of an interpreter if the police have none, informing relatives in the US, and the organization and administration of any defense monies sent from home. If a case is tried unfairly or the punishment seems unusually severe, the consul can make a formal complaint to the authorities. In a case of what is called "legitimate and proven poverty" — of an American stranded abroad without funds — the consul will contact sources of money such as family or friends in the US, make application for aid to agencies in foreign countries, and, as a last resort, arrange for repatriation at government expense. Consuls will not lend money.

Do not expect the consulate to help you with trivial difficulties such as canceled reservations or lost baggage. The consulate is primarily concerned with the day-to-day administration of services such as issuing passports and visas; providing notarial services; the distribution of VA, social security, and civil service benefits to resident Americans; depositions; extradition cases; and reports to Washington of births, deaths, and marriages of US citizens. In the Irish Republic the US consulate is at 42 Elgin Rd., Ballsbridge, Dublin (phone: 688777); in Great Britain, at 24 Grosvenor Sq., London W1 (phone: 499-9000); and in Northern Ireland, at Queen's House, 14 Queen St., Belfast BT1 6EQ (phone: 28239).

On the Road

Traveler's Checks, Credit Cards, and Foreign Exchange

It may seem hard to believe, but one of the greatest (and least understood) costs of travel is money itself. If that sounds simplistic, consider the fact that you can lose as much as 30% of the value of your dollars simply by changing money at the wrong place or in the wrong form. So your single objective in relation to the care and retention of your travel funds is to make them stretch as far as possible. And when you do spend money, it should be on things that expand and enhance your travel experience, not on unnecessaries. This requires more than merely ferreting out the best air fare or the most charming budget hotel. It means being canny about the management of money itself. Herewith, a primer on making your money go as far as possible.

TRAVELER'S CHECKS: Most people understand the necessity of protecting travel funds from loss or theft by carrying them in the form of replaceable and/or refundable traveler's checks rather than cash. An equally good reason to carry them is that they invariably get a better rate of exchange than cash does — usually by at least 1%. The reasons for this are rather technical, but it is a fact of travel life that you should not ignore.

That 1% won't do you much good, however, if you have already spent it buying your traveler's checks. Several of the major traveler's check companies charge 1% for the privilege of using their checks; others don't. Checks purchased at branches of Barclays Bank in New York City are free; Thomas Cook checks issued in US currency are also free. If you purchase traveler's checks at a bank in which you maintain significant accounts (especially commercial accounts of some size), you may find that the bank will absorb the 1% fee as a courtesy.

The traveler's checks listed below are readily recognized and convertible in all areas of Great Britain and Ireland. However, there are some important facts to be aware of when using traveler's checks: Don't assume that restaurants, smaller shops, or other establishments in hamlets and villages are going to have change for checks in large denominations; don't expect change in US currency except at banks and international airports; and, most important, while it's possible to get refunds for lost or stolen checks during regular business hours, weekend refunds can be quite difficult.

It's not a bad idea to buy a *small* amount of pence and pounds in advance of your departure. But note the emphasis on small, because exchange rates for these "tip packs" are uniformly vile. Their advantages are threefold: You become familiar with the currencies (really the only way to guard against being cheated during your first few hours in a new country); you are guaranteed some money should you arrive when a bank or exchange counter isn't open or available; and you don't have to depend on hotel desks, porters, or taxi drivers for change. Tip packs are available from most banks, American Express, or by mail, for a minimum of $50, from Deak-Perera, 41 E 42nd St., New York, NY 10017 (phone: 212-883-0400).

GETTING READY / Traveler's Checks, Credit Cards, Foreign Exchange

A tip pack is the only foreign currency you should buy before you leave. Although foreign currency traveler's checks are available from American Express, Thomas Cook, and Deak-Perera, the exchange rates are usually worse than you will get in banks abroad, and the wisest advice is to carry the bulk of your travel funds abroad with you in US dollar traveler's checks.

With adequate proof of identification (a passport), traveler's checks are as good as cash in almost all hotels, restaurants, stores, and banks. For safety, keep your purchaser's receipt and an accurate listing of your checks (by serial number) in a place that's separate from the checks themselves; the availability of the receipt will facilitate refund arrangements if the checks are misplaced, lost, or stolen. Here is a list of the major companies issuing traveler's checks and their fees and replacement policies:

1. *American Express* — 1% purchase fee. Refunds available during business hours from American Express offices or banks that sell American Express traveler's checks. Night, weekend, and holiday emergency refunds of up to $100 available at specified locations. To report lost or stolen checks, call toll-free, 800-221-7282; in New York State, call collect 212-248-4584.
2. *Thomas Cook* — No purchase fee for checks issued in US dollars. Refunds available same day during business hours from Cook, AAA, Hertz Rent-a-Car, and some banks that sell Cook traveler's checks. To report lost or stolen checks, call toll-free 800-223-7373; in New York State, call collect 212-921-3795.
3. *Citicorp* — 1% purchase fee. Refunds available same day during business hours from Citibanks and other banks offering Citicorp traveler's checks. To report lost or stolen checks, call toll-free 800-221-2566; in New York State, call collect 212-546-5700.
4. *Bank of America* — 1% purchase fee. Refunds available immediately during business hours at office where checks are sold; no weekend service. To report lost or stolen checks, call toll-free 800-227-3460; in Alaska and California, call collect 415-622-3800.
5. *Visa* — Fees determined by financial institutions selling the checks. They're free when purchased at Barclays Bank in New York City. Refunds available by calling a 24-hour refund referral number, which will give you the nearest refund location: in the Continental US, outside California, toll-free 800-227-6811; in California, 800-632-0520; and from Alaska or Hawaii, 800-227-6830; from anywhere else in the world, call collect 415-574-7111.
6. *MasterCard* — 1% purchase fee. The newest entry into the traveler's check sweepstakes, and now available from a number of banks around the US and at Thomas Cook offices around the world. To report lost or stolen checks, call toll-free, 800-223-9920, in the US; from anywhere else in the world call collect, 212-974-5696 (24 hours a day).

CREDIT CARDS: In Great Britain and Ireland, MasterCard (formerly Master Charge in the US) is sometimes called Access; Visa is also known as Barclaycard in Great Britain.

One of the thorniest problems of using credit cards abroad has to do with the rate of exchange at which any purchase is charged. The fact is that the exchange rate in effect on the date that you make a foreign purchase has nothing at all to do with rate of exchange at which your purchase is billed to you on the invoice you receive months later in the US. American Express blithely confirms this fact. The amount it charges is ultimately a function of the exchange rate in effect on the day your charge is received at an American Express service center, and no one at American Express cares much about what may have happened to the relationship between the foreign currency and the dollar in the intervening period. There is, incidentally, a 1-year limit on the time that a service establishment can take to forward its charge slips to American Express's clearinghouse.

GETTING READY / Traveler's Checks, Credit Cards, Foreign Exchange 81

Similarly, foreign purchases billed to Diners Club are involved in a kind of lotterylike charge formula, whereby three banks are called on the day foreign exchange transactions arrive. Diners Club then gives its customers the "best" rate, although best for whom is unexplained. Visa waits for charges to get to its San Francisco clearinghouse, where foreign transactions are completed twice each month, and the customer is charged whatever the prevailing exchange rate is on the transaction day. Again, the exchange rate on the day you make your purchase has no meaning whatsoever.

The principle at work in this credit-card-exchange-rate roulette is simple, but very hard to predict. You make a purchase at a particular dollar-versus-local-currency exchange rate. If the dollar gets stronger in the time between purchase and billing, your purchase actually costs you less than you anticipated. If the dollar drops in value during the interim, you pay more than you thought you would. There isn't much you can do about these vagaries except follow one very broad, very clumsy rule of thumb: If the dollar is doing well at the time of purchase, its value increasing against the local currency, use your credit card on the assumption it will still be doing well when billing takes place. If the dollar is doing badly, assume it will continue to do badly and pay with traveler's checks. If you get badly stuck, your only recourse is to complain.

In any case, all types of credit cards are handy additional means to avoid carrying a lot of cash. However, establishments you may encounter abroad may not honor *all* major cards. Therefore, you'll find it helpful to have several different credit cards with you on your trip to cover some of the costs of shopping, restaurant meals, or other expenses. Following is a list of credit cards that have wide international use, with some of their key features of greatest significance to travelers:

1. *American Express* — Emergency personal check cashing at American Express or representatives' offices (up to $200 cash in local currency, $800 in traveler's checks); extended payment plan for plane tickets with 18% interest on unpaid balance; $75,000 free automatic insurance on any flight for which ticket was charged to card; additional $250,000 insurance also available at low cost. Contact: American Express, 125 Broad St., New York, NY 10004 (see yellow or white phone book pages for local customer service number).
2. *Diners Club* — New Doublecard allows separate billing for business, personal expenditures; Cash Advantage line of credit; $75,000 free automatic insurance on flights using tickets charged to the card; up to $400,000 additional low-cost insurance; no-fee currency conversion; personal check cashing up to $250 at participating hotels; emergency cash. Contact: Diners Club, 10 Columbus Circle, New York, NY 10019 (212-559-2900).
3. *Carte Blanche* — Extended payment plan for airline tickets and tours, with yearly interest of 19% on unpaid balance; $60,000 travel accident insurance policy. Contact: Carte Blanche, 3460 Wilshire Blvd., Los Angeles, CA 90010 (toll-free phone: in California, 800-282-5886; outside California, 800-421-0081).
4. *Visa* — Cash advance available at 57,000 banks worldwide based upon credit limit, usually $300 to $5,000; interest charge on unpaid balance; other details now set by issuing bank. Check your local bank for information.
5. *MasterCard* — Cash advance available at affiliated banks worldwide, with credit limits ranging from $300 to $1,500 and up; interest charge on unpaid balance; other details now set by issuing bank. Check your local bank for information.

FOREIGN EXCHANGE: Rule number one is as simple as it is inflexible. Only change your money at banks, where your dollars always buy the greatest amount of foreign currency. Unless someone holds a gun to your head, never, repeat never, exchange dollars for foreign currency at hotels, restaurants, or retail shops, where you are sure to lose a significant amount of your dollar's buying power.

Rule number two: Estimate your money needs carefully; if you overbuy you lose twice — buying and selling back. Every time you exchange money, someone is mak-

82 GETTING READY / Accommodations and Reservations

ing a profit, and rest assured, it isn't you. Use up your foreign currency before leaving. Britain has lifted the exchange control regulations that for a number of years restricted the amount of British currency you could take out of the country, while the Irish Republic allows you to leave with no more than IR£100 in Irish notes (there's no limit if you're traveling to Great Britain, the Channel Islands, or the Isle of Man).

Rule number three: Don't buy money on the black market. The exchange rate will be better, but it is a common practice to pass off counterfeit bills to unsuspecting foreigners who aren't familiar with the local currency.

Rule number four: Learn the local currency quickly and keep aware of daily fluctuations in the exchange rate. These are listed in major newspapers, including the *International Herald Tribune,* for the preceding day. Rates change to some degree daily. For rough calculations it is quick and safe to use round figures, but for purchases and actual currency exchanges, you should carry a small pocket calculator that allows you to use the exact rate.

The basic currency unit in both Britain and Ireland is the pound — either the pound sterling or the Irish pound (or punt). Though the Irish pound once maintained parity with the pound sterling, it is now linked to EEC currencies; British money and Irish money are no longer interchangeable and they have different exchange rates vis-à-vis the American dollar. In both countries, however, the pound is divided into 100 units called pence. These are distributed in 50p, 10p, 5p, 2p, and 1p coin denominations (the British have a ½p coin). Paper money is issued in £20, £10, £5, and £1 notes (the Irish also have £100 and £50 notes). You may find shillings still in circulation in Britain — leftovers from the predecimal currency system — which are equal to 5p. And be aware that in Northern Ireland, shops, hotels, and restaurants no longer accept Irish currency.

Accommodations and Reservations

From elegant, centuries-old resorts to modest and inexpensive guesthouses, you can be comfortable and well cared for on almost any budget in either Great Britain or Ireland. Britain, and London especially, is admittedly full of deluxe establishments providing expensive services to people with money to burn. But recently, British tourism officials and travel agents have begun to focus attention on the many budget alternatives available in an effort to convince prospective American visitors that inflation and the vagaries of the dollar abroad need not keep them at home. And although the price tag has risen considerably on accommodations in Ireland, it remains one of the more affordable countries in Europe and the Irish are fighting to keep it that way.

Our accommodations choices are included in the *Best in Town* sections of the CITIES and in the *Checking In* and *Eating Out* sections of each tour route in DIRECTIONS. They have been selected for a variety of traveling budgets, but the lists are not comprehensive, and with some diligent searching — before you leave and en route — you will turn up an equal number of "special places" that are uniquely yours.

A good first step in finding a place to stay is consulting the brochures and booklets we cite in the discussions below. Most of these are available from the British and Irish tourist offices; where appropriate, we've given prices and noted those which must be purchased from the British Travel Bookshop (680 Fifth Ave., New York, NY 10019).

ACCOMMODATIONS:
Hotels, Guesthouses, and Inns – Although there is no official rating system for British hotels, they tend to fall into rough categories. Hotels can be large or small, chain-operated or independent, new and of the "international standard" type or well-

established and traditional in both appearance and approach. There are resort hotels with recreation facilities and motels with almost no facilities. Breakfast is usually included in the quoted price of any room, and it is usually a full one of juice, coffee or tea, rolls, cereal, and eggs and bacon, though there is a growing tendency in the larger urban hotels to substitute a Continental breakfast (coffee and rolls) or to charge separately for the full one. Most rooms in better hotels come with private baths; the closer to the budget end of the scale and beyond the city centers, the more likely it is that the room will have a wash basin with hot and cold water and access to a public bathroom in the hall. A service charge of 10% to 15% may be added to bills in addition to a compulsory 15% Value Added Tax. Hotels, motels, guesthouses, and inns with four rooms or more are required to display minimum and maximum room prices in a manner that clearly shows what is included. If not clear, be sure to ask in advance what the final tab will be since the extras can add considerably to the bill. (To reduce it, consider traveling off-season, and investigate the hotel "mini-breaks" offered by many British chains. These packages allow a discount for stays of 2 nights or more, usually weekends, and can be in effect at any time of the year.) The BTA's annual *Britain: Hotels and Restaurants* ($12.95) lists over 3,000 hotels throughout the country with room prices inclusive of extras. It includes establishments in Northern Ireland, too, though the Northern Ireland Tourist Board's annual *Northern Ireland: All the Places to Stay* is a more complete listing (60p). Note that unlike hotels in Great Britain, those in Northern Ireland are graded according to an official rating system similar to the one (described below) followed by the Irish Tourist Board in the Irish Republic.

Guesthouses are to Britain what pensions are to the Continent. Also called private hotels or board residences, they are generally small, family-run, and most often in the budget category. A special group of commended guesthouses provides outstanding service and costs more; see *Commended Country Hotels, Guest Houses and Restaurants,* a BTA publication, which sells for $7.50. Also see *Where to Stay in Scotland: Hotels and Guesthouses* ($3.80). Both are available, with a $1.50 each handling charge, through the British Travel Bookshop. Unlike hotels, guesthouses do not provide meals for nonguests and unlike inns, they are not licensed to serve alcohol. The standard practice is for breakfast to be included in the room price and some, though not all, offer an evening meal if desired. Prices are typically from $12 to $25 per person, and for this, there is usually no private bath nor is there always running water in the bedroom. Guesthouses are found everywhere and especially at seaside resorts where the vacationing British keep them heavily booked all summer long.

Inns are also of particular interest to travelers attracted by the prospect of sampling the lodging of another age. There are inns dating back to medieval times and many more not quite so old that have nevertheless been in business for centuries. An inn was, first of all, a wayside watering place for travelers passing on foot, horseback, or by coach, but laws requiring the innkeeper to provide food for the drinkers and accommodations for the diners turned innkeepers into hoteliers. The focal point of an inn is still its public bar, and the number of rooms is usually, therefore, limited; some in city centers do not provide accommodations at all. What remains of bygone days is the charm of thatched roofs, timbered facades, cobblestone courtyards, beamed ceilings, and the occasional four-poster bed. Heating and hot and cold water in the rooms have been added, though private bathrooms are usually lacking. Inns are found in any price range, from $15 per person and up. The BTA's *Stay at an Inn* ($2.45) lists a selection of them found in historic towns all over Britain.

Most of the rooms for rent in the Irish Republic are listed in one of two publications issued yearly by Bord Fáilte, the Irish Tourist Board. The *Guide to Approved Accommodations in Ireland* details regularly inspected accommodations registered with the Tourist Board and maximum prices are quoted. Hotels are graded in five categories

(A*, A, B*, B, and C), but behind those letter grades may be found anything from a luxurious, turreted castle redolent of Irish history to a large, modern, and functional high-rise or a simple, family-run hostelry. Guesthouses are similarly rated (A, B, and C), and though it is sometimes difficult to distinguish between some of the smaller, family-run hotels and the guesthouses, the latter are almost always family enterprises and tend to be more informal and personal in their hospitality. The official dividing line is the meal service: The hotel dining room is open to nonresidents. Guesthouses cater exclusively to their guests, and in some cases will serve breakfast only (generally a full one and included in the room price), though usually a partial or full board plan by the day or the week will be available. Guesthouses, too, can vary in atmosphere from old, reconverted Georgian residences to brand-new, built-for-the-purpose premises. Bathroom facilities vary considerably: in an A* hotel, most rooms have private bathrooms; in an A guesthouse, some rooms with private bath may be available; in either hotel or guesthouse, where a private bath is lacking, the room will have hot and cold running water. In all Irish accommodations, the 10% Value Added Tax must be included in the room price quoted. A service charge of from 10% to 15% is usually added to hotel and guesthouse bills.

Castle Hotels – Among the most interesting of Britain's and Ireland's accommodations are the castle and country house hotels, specializing in the traditional atmosphere and hospitality typical of a great country estate. Formerly country homes, ancestral mansions, and family castles before their conversion to hotels, they are noteworthy for their architectural features and surrounding gardens or parklands, their river- or lakeside settings, or locations in dell, dale, and mountain. The real attraction, however, is the history associated with so many of them and their antique decor, undisturbed by the modern amenities (TV, private baths) that have been added. Prices are not economy class — from $30 to $60 and up per person, including breakfast. Both the British and Irish tourist offices publish booklets describing the castle hotels available; these are titled, respectively, *Castle and Country House Hotels* and *Ireland's Castle Hotels.*

B&Bs – Britain's "bed-and-breakfast" houses provide precisely what the name implies. Though any hotel, inn, or guesthouse does the same, it is unusual for a B&B to offer the extra services found in other establishments, and consequently, the B&B route is the cheapest way to go. With the exception of London, where they are scarce, they are found anywhere there are extra rooms to let in a private house and a landlady or landlord willing to attend to the details of this homespun form of hospitality. Private baths are rare; in recompense, the breakfasts are hearty, home-cooked, and as often as not, served along with some helpful tips on what to see and do and a bit of family history to add to the local lore. Prices average from about $12 to $15 per person per night, breakfast included. Few BTA publications list B&Bs but those of the regional tourist boards often do; for example, the Scottish Tourist Board publishes *Where to Stay in Scotland: Bed and Breakfast* ($3.65, available at the British Travel Bookshop).

The Irish Tourist Board offers a guide that lists accommodations in town and country homes. Though not cited as such, these are the Irish equivalent of British B&Bs, the extra rooms of private homes to which adjustments have been made to meet the Tourist Board's inspection standards. Rarely will you find a private bathroom, but there is hot and cold running water in nearly all rooms in homes approved by the Tourist Board and listed in the guide. Costing from about $10 to $14 per night, breakfast included, B&Bs are perfect places to spend 1 or 2 nights as you tour the countryside, though you can stay longer since many offer weekly rates for partial board and some for full board.

Farmhouses – In both Great Britain and Ireland, farm families put up guests on a similar basis: for a night or two or by the week, with weekly half-board plans available. Listings with the Irish Tourist Board, in the BTA's *Farmhouse Accommodations* and

GETTING READY / Accommodations and Reservations

Wales Farm Holidays, and the Northern Ireland Tourist Board's *Farm and Country Holidays* carry a brief description of each farm, allowing travelers to pick a traditional one or a modern one, a dairy farm over a sheep farm, one with ponies to ride, or one near a river for fishing. If the peace and quiet and the coziness of the welcome are appealing, a farmhouse can be an ideal base from which to explore a region by car or by foot, and an especially good idea for those traveling with children.

Home Exchanges – An alternative for families content to stay in one place while on vacation is a home exchange. It is an exceptionally inexpensive way to ensure comfortable, reasonable living quarters with amenities that no hotel could possibly offer. Often the trade includes a car; almost always it means living in a new community in a manner the average hotel guest never experiences. Several companies publish directories of individuals and families willing to trade homes with others for a specified period of time. In some cases, you must be willing to list your home in the directory; in others, you can subscribe to the directory without listing your own home and negotiate directly with the owners of the home you want. There is no guarantee that you will find a listing in the area in which you are interested, but each of the directories below has hundreds or thousands of listings in North America and in Europe, including Great Britain and Ireland.

1. *Adventures in Living:* Listing in an annual directory and two annual supplements costs $25 a year. Some rentals are also listed. PO Box 278, Winnetka, IL 60093.
2. *Holiday Exchanges:* Monthly listing for $20 for 6 months, plus 6 months' worth of backlistings. PO Box 878, Belen, NM 87002 (phone: 505-864-8680).
3. *Vacation Exchange Club:* Some 6,000 listings, about one third of which are in Great Britain and Ireland. Subscriptions cost $21 a year for two directories: one in late winter, one in the spring. 350 Broadway, New York, NY 10013 (phone: 212-966-2576).

Flats, Homes, and Cottages – Another alternative to hotels for the visitor content to stay in one spot for a week or more is to actually rent a house or apartment (called a "flat" in Britain and Ireland). Known as a "holiday let" or a "self-catering holiday," a furnished rental has both the advantages and disadvantages of living "at home" abroad. It is certainly cheaper than a first-class hotel for the same period of time (though luxury rentals are available, too); it has the comforts of home, including a kitchen, which means savings on food; it gives a sense of the country that a large hotel often cannot. On the other hand, a certain amount of housework is involved because if you don't eat out, you have to cook, and though some holiday lets come with a cleaning person, most don't.

The BTA publishes *Holiday Homes,* a free booklet that gives information on rental agencies and properties in Great Britain. The Irish Tourist Board distributes booklets prepared by regional tourism organizations in Ireland listing houses and apartments for rent along with the names of the owners to contact to make arrangements. Finally, there are companies in the US that arrange rentals in Europe; they handle booking and confirmation paperwork, generally for a fee included in the rental price. Those listed below have many properties in Great Britain, fewer in Ireland:

1. *AAD Associates:* Apartments, private homes, and seasonal accommodations in university residences in Wales and England, including London. PO Box 3927 Amity Station, New Haven, CT 06525 (phone: 203-387-4461).
2. *At Home Abroad:* British farm and country houses, one Irish castle, and a few London townhouses available. Photographs of properties can be requested by mail for a $35 registration fee. 405 E 56th St., Apt. 6H, New York, NY 10022 (phone: 212-421-9165).
3. *Inquiline Inc.:* Directory of available rentals costs $5.95. Large program in Lon-

don and other areas of England; Scotland and Ireland are also represented. Cedar Rd., Katonah, NY 10536 (phone: 914-232-7516).
 4. *Interchange/Villas International Ltd.:* Specializes in London flats, but can arrange rentals elsewhere in Great Britain and Ireland. 213 E 38th St., New York, NY 10016 (phone: 212-685-4340 or 213-271-0575).
 5. *ITP Worldwide Luxury Villa Holidays:* Rents large, fully-staffed luxury country houses in England and villas in Europe. Weekly rates from $1,344 to $4,494. 101 Bradley Pl., Suite 204, Palm Beach, FL 33480 (phone: 305-833-6943 or 800-327-4505).
 6. *Rent Abroad Inc.:* London flats, some other properties in England available. Registration fee of $10 includes receipt of literature and photographs by mail. PO Box 5183, Westport, CT 06881 (phone: 203-277-9376).

Living in a flat or house are "self-catering" options found in both countries, but renting a thatch-roofed cottage is generally possible only in Ireland. Located mostly in small towns on the southwest seaboard, these traditional dwellings have a romantic appeal all their own. On the practical side, however, they are fairly inexpensive, can be rented by the week, month, or summer season, and have modern kitchens and baths. These factors combine to make the cottages a sensible choice for families with small children. For a brochure, write Shannon Development, 590 Fifth Ave., New York, NY 10036 (phone: 212-581-0480), or contact Rent-an-Irish-Cottage Limited, Shannon Airport House, Shannon International Airport, Co. Clare, Ireland.

Home Stays – Travelers are often impressed by the hospitality extended to them in small family-run guesthouses and B&Bs in Britain and Ireland. Often, catering to guests is not the proprietor's sole or even main means of support, and more than once you'll come away feeling you've been one of the family. This being the case, it is sometimes difficult to draw a line between a stay as a paying guest in a commercial establishment, and a "home stay" — where you also pay for your accommodations and any food or extras you consume. There is a distinction, however, basically one of intent on the part of both the hosts and the guests: You must want to get to know each other and be willing to exert the extra effort to do so.

Beyond that, there are other differences. Almost always, you, alone or with your family, will be the only party staying with your hosts. And though the cost of meals (except breakfast) is not included in the cost of the stay — because most travelers want to sample at least a few of the local restaurants — when you do eat at home, you sit down at the table with the rest of the family. It is quite common especially to have the first night's dinner at home and it is not unusual for hosts to arrange a dinner party later in the stay so you can meet some of their friends. There can be further participation in family activities, too, depending on how much of your time you want "organized" and always remembering that your hosts are most likely not on vacation as you are.

The better services that arrange home stays visit prospective hosts and choose only those genuinely interested in meeting foreigners and making their stay a memorable experience. The host, in fact, is probably better screened than you, the guest. The usual procedure is for you to fill out a questionnaire giving personal information such as the names and ages of family members, occupations, special interests, plus character and/ or credit references. The service then selects a few possibilities and lets you make the final decision. Often there is a minimum stay (usually 3 to 5 nights) and sometimes a maximum (2 weeks, for instance, though most travelers don't want to stay that long in one place while touring overseas). The entire cost of the stay is usually paid in advance, whereas any charges for meals or other extras are paid in cash to the host on departure. To avoid embarrassment, the service advises you beforehand what the host will be charging for any meals you do decide to take.

The following organizations arrange home stays with British families, and one of them has a few Irish families who open their homes to guests, too. Last year costs of these programs ranged from $40 to $90 per night per couple, with an average of from $50 to $65 per night. Single rates are also available and there are reductions for children.

1. *At Home in England,* 10 W 86th St., New York, NY 10024 (phone: 212-595-2087). About 90 homes in England, including central London, and Scotland.
2. *AAD Associates,* PO Box 3927, Amity Station, New Haven, CT 06525 (203-387-4461). About 50 homes, primarily in England, principally London, and a few in Wales and Scotland.
3. *In the English Manner,* 643 Carolina St., San Francisco, CA 94107 (phone: 415-821-4555 or 415-346-4400). About 65 houses and castles in Great Britain, 20 cottages in the Cotswolds and Scotland, and 20 deluxe apartments in central London.

If the thought of paying anything for your keep means to you that you are not truly a guest, there is another organization — the United States Servas Committee, Inc. — that maintains a list of hosts throughout the world willing to throw open their doors to foreigners entirely free of charge. The aim of this nonprofit cultural program is to promote international understanding and every effort is made to discourage freeloaders. Servas will send you an application form and the name of the nearest of some hundred interviewers around the US for you to contact. After the interview, if you're approved, you'll receive documentation certifying you as a Servas traveler. There is a membership fee of $30 for an individual and there is also a deposit of $15 to receive the host list, refunded on its return. The list gives the name, address, age, occupation, and other particulars of the hosts, languages spoken, and the dates they are willing to receive guests. From then on it is up to you to write them directly and Servas makes no guarantee that you will be accommodated. If you are, you'll normally stay 2 days and will be offered breakfast and dinner. Servas stresses that you should choose only people you really want to meet and that for this brief period you should be interested mainly in your hosts, not in sight-seeing. It also suggests that one way to show your appreciation once you've returned home is to become a host yourself. The minimum age of a Servas traveler is 18 (however, children under 18 who are with their parents travel free), and though quite a few are young people who've just finished college, there are travelers (and hosts) in all age ranges and occupations. At present there are over 300 listings in Great Britain and Ireland. Contact Servas at 11 John St., Room 406, New York, NY 10038 (phone: 212-267-0252).

RESERVATIONS: Advance hotel reservations are recommended year-round in the major cities. In high season — June through September — the advice to book ahead extends to resorts and popular tourist sites from coast to coast and across the Irish Sea. To the extent that you are able to settle on a precise itinerary beforehand, it is best to reserve accommodations before you go. The simplest way is to leave it all to a travel agent who will provide this service for free if the hotel, inn, or guesthouse in question pays agents a percentage. The British and Irish accommodations guides use a symbol to show which of the establishments listed do pay such a commission. If the one you pick doesn't, the travel agent may charge a fee to cover costs or you may have to make the reservation yourself.

The do-it-yourself method is fairly simple if you intend to stay mainly in hotels that are members of chains or groups, whether British or Irish ones with US representatives or American ones with hotels overseas. Naturally, the more links in the chain, the more likely that an entire stay can be booked with a minimum number of letters or phone calls to one central reservations system. Either a travel agent or the British and Irish tourist offices will be able to tell you who in the US represents a particular hotel.

To reserve a room in a hotel that's not represented in the US, it may be necessary

88 GETTING READY / Accommodations and Reservations

to telephone or write directly. Be sure to give full details of your requirements and several alternate dates, if possible. You will probably be asked to send a deposit in the amount of one night's lodging, payable by foreign draft; in return, be sure to get written confirmation of your reservation. One shortcut, if the request is made a minimum of 4 weeks in advance, is to write to the Central Reservations Service of the Irish Tourist Board, which will reserve, free of charge, any of the accommodations listed in its official accommodations guides. Contact the Central Reservations Service, Irish Tourist Board–Bord Fáilte, PO Box 273, Dublin. A similar service for reserving London hotels only (and stays of at least 2 nights) is provided by the London Tourist Board, 26 Grosvenor Gardens, London SW1W ODU, and requires a minimum of 6 weeks' notice. A £1 fee is charged, which is later deducted from the hotel bill.

If the hotel you want has no rooms available for your chosen dates, take heart. Making reservations early is usually the best advice but sometimes, making them later gives equally good results. What was unavailable 6 months in advance may suddenly become available 6 days — or even 6 hours — before your arrival. Should that not occur, there will almost always be some cancellation in one hotel or another on the date you arrive and there are services geared to help you find them. Tourist Information Centres (TIC's) in most British ports of entry (seaports, airports, railroad terminals) will reserve a room in the locality for a small fee (usually no more than 60p) or a refundable deposit (about £3) or both. The London Tourist Board's Tourist Information Centre in the Heathrow Airport Underground Station books hotels only, whereas the Tourist Information Centre in Victoria Railway Station will book hotels and budget accommodations such as guesthouses and hostels. The desks of numerous hotel booking agencies, charging similar fees or deposits, are also found in rail stations and airports. These can make same-day or advance reservations for London or other parts of Britain, as can the central reservations offices of the various hotel chains and groups. In the Irish Republic, Tourist Information Offices located throughout the country and at Shannon and Dublin airports and the ferry ports of Dun Laoghaire and Rosslare Harbour (the latter open May through September only) will make a reservation for a small fee to cover costs. In Dublin proper, offices are at 14 Upper O'Connell St.

Britain's Tourist Information Centres and Ireland's Tourist Information Offices can also be put to use by those who prefer to give full rein to their wanderlust unhampered by hotel reservations made too far in advance. In Great Britain, any TIC displaying a Tourist Accommodation Service sign (a bed appears on it) can supply information and book a room in its locality once you've arrived there. Some provide a further Book-a-Bed-Ahead (BABA) service. Go early in the day before starting out for your destination and, for a fee of from 50p to £1.25, a staff member will phone ahead to make a reservation — provided you're going to an area that also has a BABA service. The network is thickest in Scotland, Wales (where it's called a Bed Booking Service), and Northern Ireland, less so in England. You must claim your room early: Bookings are provisional and are usually released at 6 PM each evening. Book-a-Bed-Ahead can also handle B&B accommodations, though these are found just as easily by keeping an eye out for the signs on windows and gateposts or, in small villages, by asking any policeman or shopkeeper who in the area rents rooms. In Ireland, all Tourist Information Offices are equipped, for a small fee, to help with advance reservations in other parts of the country.

A word about overbooking: Although not unique to Britain or Ireland, the international travel boom has brought with it some abuses that are pretty much standard operating procedure in any industry facing demand that outstrips supply. Hotels overbook rooms on the assumption that a certain percentage of no-shows is inevitable. When cancellations don't occur and everybody with a reservation arrives as promised, you can find yourself in the position of holding a valid reservation for which no room exists.

There's no sure way to avoid all the pitfalls of hotel overbooking, but there are some ways to minimize the risks. First, always carry evidence of your confirmed reservation with you. This should be a direct communication from the hotel to you or your travel agent and should specify the exact dates and duration of your accommodations and the price. Absolutely the weakest form of confirmation is the voucher slip a travel agent routinely issues, since it carries no official indication that the hotel has verified your reservations.

Even better is the increasing opportunity to guarantee hotel reservations by giving the hotel (or its reservation system) the number of your credit card and agreeing that the hotel is authorized to charge you for that room no matter what. It's still possible to cancel if you do so before 6 PM of the day of your reservation (sometimes 4 PM in resort areas), but when you do cancel under this arrangement, make sure you get a cancellation number to protect you from being billed erroneously.

If all these precautions fail and you are left standing at the reservation desk with a reservation that the clerk won't honor, you have a last resort: Yell as long and as loudly as necessary to get satisfaction. The person who makes the most noise gets the last room in the house.

Tipping

Throughout Britain and Ireland, the practice of including a service charge —generally 10–15%—as part of basic hotel and restaurant bills is virtually constant. It has the advantage of eliminating any question about how much and whom to tip, but it confounds North Americans who are not always used to the custom. The threat is that a traveler unaware of the "service included" policy may leave additional gratuities that are redundant and unnecessary.

A restaurant menu will usually state whether a service charge is added automatically to the bill, but if you don't find this notice indicated, don't hesitate to ask the waiter at the time your bill is presented. If the tip has been added, no further gratuity is expected— though it's a common practice in Britain and Ireland for diners to leave a few extra pence on the table. The emphasis is on "few," and 20–50p is more than enough. If no service charge has been included on your bill, tip approximately 15% of the basic amount. Europeans don't normally tip this much, but Americans seem to feel more comfortable with a figure that roughly approximates the level of gratuity common in the US and Canada. By all means, leave less than this amount if you want to penalize poor service, or leave a bit more to reward excellent and especially efficient attention. In the finest restaurants, where a multiplicity of servers are present, plan to tip 5% to the captain in addition to the standard 15% for your waiter. The sommelier who has opened and served your wine is entitled to a gratuity of approximately £1 per bottle.

It's not necessary to tip the maitre d' of any restaurant unless he has been especially helpful in providing a table or has helped to arrange a special party. In instances where tipping the maitre d' is appropriate, the range of tips normally varies between £2 and £5. In allocating gratuities at a restaurant, pay particular attention to what has become the standard credit-card charge form, which now includes separate places for indicating gratuities for waiters and/or captains. If these separate boxes do not appear on the charge slip presented to you, simply ask the waiter or captain how these separate tips should be indicated.

There is virtually no tipping in pubs—unless you become something of a regular and care to offer the barman an occasional drink. It is not uncommon, however, to leave a few pence for a barmaid; and if you are served at a table in a bar or cocktail lounge, a small gratuity—10–20p—is not unusual.

As in restaurants, you will normally find a service charge of from 10 to 15% included in your final hotel bill at most British and Irish hotels. No additional gratuities are required—or expected—beyond this billed service charge. It is unlikely, however, that you will find a service charge added to bills in small guesthouses or modest bed-and-breakfast establishments. In these cases, let your instincts be your guide; no tipping is expected by members of the family who own the house, but it is a nice gesture to leave something for others—such as a dining room waiter or a maid—who may have helped you. A gratuity of 20–50p per night is adequate in these cases.

If a hotel does not automatically add a service charge, it is perfectly proper to ask to have an extra 10–15% added to your bill, to be distributed among those who served you. This may be an especially convenient solution in a large hotel, where it's difficult to determine just who out of a horde of attendants actually performed particular services. If you prefer to distribute tips yourself, a chambermaid generally is tipped at the rate of 50p per day, or £2 to £3 per week. Tip the concierge or hall porter for specific services only, and the amount of such gratuities should depend on the level of service provided. Doormen and/or porters are generally tipped at the rate of 30p per bag for carrying luggage, and you may want to add a small additional amount if a doorman helps with cab or car. Other miscellaneous tips to hotel staff depend entirely on the service rendered.

Once upon a time, taxi drivers in Britain and Ireland would give one a rather odd look if presented with a tip for a taxi fare, but times have changed and 10–15% of the amount on the meter is now a standard gratuity. The minimum taxi tip should be about 10p in Britain, and perhaps half again as much in Ireland. Porters in airports expect to be compensated at the rate of about 30p per bag in Britain, and 40p in Ireland. Ditto porters who carry your bags in railway or bus stations.

Theater ushers are not tipped in either country, though it is common to purchase a program from the person who shows you to your seat. Sight-seeing tour guides are usually tipped, and members of a tour may discuss a total amount among themselves and contribute equally to this gratuity.

Shopping

Browsing through the department stores, street markets, auction houses, fabulous small shops, and crafts centers of Great Britain and Ireland will undoubtedly be one of the highlights of your trip. You may not be quite as ebullient about prices as you might have been a few years ago, but there is still plenty of value left for the money and enough quality and craftsmanship to make many an item irresistible. To help steer you toward the best, several sections of this book are devoted to shopping. In CITIES, individual city reports include a listing of specific stores, boutiques, and markets, as well as descriptions of special shopping streets where they exist. And in DIVERSIONS, there are sections that tell not only where to find antiques and other collectibles, but also—for those who have yet to experience this stimulating form of acquisition—how to buy them at auctions.

What to Buy – Cashmere sweaters and Shetland wool knits are enduring British classics, as are Harris tweeds, ancestral tartans, and cotton and silk Liberty prints, whether sold by the yard or made up into fashionable clothes. Burberrys and Jaeger are good labels, and there are lesser-priced sports clothes at Marks and Spencer stores around the country. Harrods in London is Europe's largest department store and it should be on your sight-seeing list even if it's not on your shopping list. Its motto, *Omnia, Omnibus, Ubique* (Everyone, Everything, Everywhere), gives a pretty good idea of the range of its activities. Shopping can also be mixed with sight-seeing in the famous food department at Fortnum and Mason, purveyor of groceries to the Royal Family—which may explain the formality of swallow-tailed coats on its salesclerks (pronounced "clarks"). There are still some antiques left in Britain, in spite of the shiploads consigned to US dealers. In London, try the Bermondsey–New Caledonia Market—a dealers' market—very early Friday mornings for a chance at what might turn up in an expensive shop later in the day, unless you spot it first. The showrooms of Sotheby's and Christie's, probably the most famous art and antique auctioneers in the world, are open for viewing. If you attend the daily sales, however, don't move a muscle or blink an eye unless you've brought money—lots of it. New and used china comes from quality suppliers such as Minton, Royal Doulton, Staffordshire, Aynsley, and Wedgwood, and new and used books from any number of shops on London's Charing Cross Road, including one (Foyles) with a stock of over four million volumes.

In Ireland, crafts are thriving. Products in traditional and modern styles and combinations of the two are found in craft centers, workshops, and stores throughout the country. Details are in the *Craft Hunter's Pocket Guide,* available free from Irish Tourist Board offices in the US, and in the *Crafts and Craftsmen* shopping guide for Northern Ireland, published by the Local Enterprise Development Unit and also available free from BTA offices or from Lamont House, Purdy's Lane, Belfast BT8 4TB. Typical of the work currently being done are the traditional, highly prized white wool sweaters and berets knit on the western seacoast and on the Aran Islands, earthenware pottery in modern but natural shapes, and exceedingly well executed silver and gold jewelry in contemporary styles. Donegal tweed has been handloomed for centuries on the Donegal coast of northwest Ireland, and a jacket made of it could be one of the most durable you've ever owned. Pearly Belleek china, luminous Waterford crystal, and Irish lace or linens endow any table with elegance, and Irish smoked salmon goes well with such a setting.

How to Shop Abroad – The goods are still enticing, but gone forever are the incredibly low prices enhanced by a dollar consistently stronger than any European currency. Quality goods are not necessarily cheaper in a fashionable boutique in the capital city of the country from which they came than they are in an equally fashionable US store. To be sure, do some homework before you go and arrive prepared with a list of the goods you want—as specific as possible, with brands or labels—and the cost of each in the US. In some cases, you will find it cheaper to buy abroad, but frequently you will find it is not, and knowing the difference exactly is crucial to a successful shopping trip. Once you've arrived, it is still necessary to comparison shop as much as time permits, bearing in mind that articles can be cheaper closer to their point of origin, and cheapest of all in the factory that makes them, if it sells to the public. You'll get a better price on Donegal tweeds, for instance, at small factories and shops in County Donegal than in Dublin, and Scottish woolens and knitwear are cheaper at mill outlet stores in Scotland than in shops in either Edinburgh or London. On the other hand, Waterford glass cannot be bought at the factory (though you can tour it), and since its wholesale price is standard within Ireland, its retail price will vary from shop to shop depending on markup only. In England, the Royal Doulton, Spode, Minton, and Wedgwood factories at Stoke-on-Trent do have retail shops on the premises, but, in order not to undercut their own retailers, they do not sell at discounted prices. (Two of them—Wedgwood and Spode—have "seconds" shops where you can pick up china with slight imperfections at up to half off the ordinary retail price.)

If your itinerary won't allow combing the countryside in search of sources, and if you can time your visit accordingly, perhaps the best bargains in almost anything British may be had at sale time: two weeks in January and one week in July when the majority of London's department stores and specialty shops offer their wares at substantial reductions. Londoners wait for the sales, not to mention the rest of the British and hordes of shoppers from the Continent, so expect some of the usual local reserve to disappear as all engage in a frantic fight for some of the world's most coveted merchandise.

Duty-Free Shops – If common sense tells you that it is always cheaper to buy goods in an airport duty-free shop than to buy them at home or in the streets of a foreign city, you'd best be aware of some basic facts. Duty-free, first of all, does not mean that the goods you buy will be free of duty when you return to the US. Rather, it means that the shop has paid no import tax acquiring goods of foreign make because the goods are not to be used in the country, which is why duty-free goods are available only in the restricted passengers-only area of international airports or are delivered to departing passengers on the plane. In a duty-free store, you save money only on goods of foreign make because they are the only items on which import tax would be charged in any other store. There is usually no saving on locally made items and, therefore, little reason to hold off from buying local souvenirs until you reach the airport. There may, in fact, be a definite drawback to buying local goods in airport duty-free shops, since the shops usually pay high airport rents, and the goods may well be more expensive than they would be in a downtown store. The real bargains are foreign goods, but—let the buyer beware—not all foreign goods are automatically cheaper in an airport duty-free shop. Spirits, smoking materials, and perfumes are fairly standard bargains, but when buying cameras, watches, clothing, chocolates and other foods, and luxury items, be sure to know what they cost elsewhere. Terrific savings do exist (they are the reason for such shops, after all), but so do overpriced and overrated items that an unwary shopper might find equally tempting.

There are several airport duty-free shops in Great Britain and Ireland, but Shannon International Airport's Duty-Free Shop was the world's first and remains one of the most renowned. Here, there are savings to be had on foreign goods—Lalique crystal, Swiss watches, French perfumes—though not necessarily on Irish-made goods. If you haven't been able to scout out your souvenirs at the source, however, they should cost no more at Shannon than at Irish shops in downtown areas and certainly less than they would back home. And it may be convenient to buy them here rather than carry them with you throughout your trip, provided you're willing to take a chance on finding the desired item in the right size and color and provided you arrive at the airport in enough time to do your shopping. Shannon also operates a mail-order service that can be used long after you've left Ireland. You'll have to pay the import duty on items you order, but since your purchases are free of a retail store's markup, you will still pay less than you would in a stateside specialty shop. You can get the mail-order catalog as you pass through Shannon or you can request it from Shannon Development, 590 Fifth Ave., New York, NY 10036 (phone: 212-581-0480). If you study a copy before you go, you'll be better equipped to compare the quality and prices of the merchandise you'll encounter as you shop overseas.

Value Added Tax – Commonly abbreviated as VAT, this is a tax levied by various European countries and added to the purchase price of most merchandise. The standard VAT rate in Great Britain and Northern Ireland is 15% (children's clothes, books, food, and transportation exempt), while in the Irish Republic it is either 18% or 30% —the higher rate applies to luxury goods such as watches, jewelry, furs, glass, and cameras (food, clothing, and transportation exempt). The tax is intended for residents of the country (and is already included in the price tag), but visitors are required to pay it unless they have purchases shipped directly by the store to an address abroad. In Ireland, this is the only way to avoid paying VAT; in Great Britain, there are two additional "retail export" schemes meant to benefit visitors. The Personal Export Scheme is somewhat limited: It allows purchases (generally of £25 or more) to be made exclusive of VAT if the items are sent directly to the port from which you will depart but does not apply to anyone leaving the country by air. Under the Over-the-Counter Export Scheme, you pay the tax, take the packages with you, and then take steps to have the tax refunded. To do this, show the salesperson your passport (always carry it with you when you shop) and ask for a VAT relief form. As you leave the country —and it must be within 3 months of the date of purchase for this scheme to work— have the form validated at the customs desk that usually adjoins passport control. When you arrive home, mail the form back to the store and the store will send you your VAT rebate. This scheme is limited to small articles that can be carried in your hand luggage, so if you're buying something larger than that, ask the storekeeper what procedure to follow. Not all stores operate the scheme and some will require a set minimum purchase before undertaking the paperwork involved or will deduct a small charge from your refund to cover their expenses.

Sports

Castles and churches, museums and monuments are all part of the European experience, testimony to what fired the mind and stoked the soul of a country in days gone by. Another part of the experience is meeting the people. Day by day, you will see them going calmly about their daily lives. To see them at their most energetic, however, it helps to see them involved in the pastimes they are most passionate about: in other words, sports. In Great Britain and Ireland these include games that are hardly known in the US as well as games that are the ancestors of our own national pastimes. Among them, along with where and when to see both the players and the spectators at their enthusiastic best, are the following:

Soccer – If attendance records are a guide, this is the most popular sport in Britain, where it's called football and was called football long before the Americans began to play anything remotely resembling it. After rugby came on the scene, the London Football Association was formed in 1863 to protect the purity of the original football, which then became known as "association football," and eventually as "soccer," through constant repetition of the abbreviation for the word "association." Whatever it's called, this is the game that fills the papers with predictions and details of players' salaries, and draws huge crowds—lately very unruly ones—to the stadiums. The season runs from August to April, with games played on Saturday afternoons or evenings. To see what it's all about, follow the crowds to the grounds of some of the most popular professional clubs in the London area: Arsenal, Highbury Stadium, Avenell Rd., N5 (phone: 226-0304); Chelsea, Stamford Bridge, Fulham Rd., SW6 (phone: 385-5545); Tottenham Hotspur, 748 High Rd., N17 (phone: 808-1020); West Ham United, Boleyn Ground, Green St., E13 (phone: 472-0704). Top teams outside London are Manchester United, Liverpool, and Ipswich. In May (the first or second Saturday), the Football Association Cup Final, an event the equivalent of the World Series, takes place at Wembley Stadium, London (phone: 902-1234), before a crowd of 100,000. Football tickets are usually bought at the stadium about an hour before the match, but for the Cup Final they're sold in advance to club members and very few are on public sale. Rest assured it will be on the telly.

Rugby – A schoolboy at the great English public school at Rugby invented something new in 1823 by picking up the soccer ball (football) and running forward with it, contrary to the rules. Soccer was basically a kicking game, but carrying the ball and tackling became part of the new sport, formalized in 1871 when the Rugby Football Union came into being. Exported to the US, rugby developed into American football, which it resembles—somewhat. In Britain, rugby is an amateur sport, played from September to April on Saturday afternoons by school and university teams, county teams, hospital teams, and by anyone else who can bring together the requisite 15 players per side. Anyone who's seen the game will remember the "set scrum," one means by which play begins, when forwards of opposing teams, like two compact and only apparently disorderly phalanxes, push and shove against each other for possession of the ball. Rugby has been described as a "ruffian's sport, played by gentlemen," and play proceeds in a rugged fashion without protective equipment. The most important matches—including international ones such as England vs. Wales, Scotland, or Ireland—are played in southwest London at Twickenham, stadium and headquarters of Rugby Union's controlling body (Whitton Rd., Twickenham; phone: 892-8161). Cardiff, Wales, is another stronghold and the place to see a match there is in Cardiff Arms Park. In Edinburgh, go to the Murrayfield Rugby Ground; and in Dublin, Lansdowne Road.

Rugby League, an offshoot of Rugby Union, is both an amateur and a professional sport played according to a different set of rules by teams of 13 players. Its stronghold is in the north of England—Lancashire and Yorkshire, principally—but the Rugby League Cup Final takes place at London's Wembley Stadium in May.

Cricket – Soccer and rugby move at a fast pace, but anyone on a tight schedule may not have time to take in a cricket match, which takes a leisurely 3 to 5 days to finish, though some 1-day competitions have been introduced. British—in fact English—to the core (it's been dated as far back as the twelfth or thirteenth century and rules existed by 1744), the very name of the game has come to signify fair play, and what is "not cricket" is conduct not befitting a gentleman and a sportsman. (Cricket never made it in the American colonies though an early form of baseball was similar to it.) The season runs from mid-April to early September and matches are played by university teams and by professional county teams. International, or test, matches take place annually. The most famous ever was that won by Australia over Britain in 1882, the morning after which London's shocked *Sporting Times* ran an obituary for British cricket, announcing that its remains would be cremated. Since then, any Great Britain–Australia test match is played for the "Ashes," which repose in an urn that never leaves the Cricket Memorial Gallery at Lord's Cricket Ground, London—not even if Australia wins. Lord's Cricket Ground, home of the Marylebone Cricket Club, the sport's governing body, is *the* place to see a game (St. John's Wood Rd., London NW8; phone: 289-1615). Next best place is The Oval (Kennington, London SE11; phone: 735-2424), home of the Surrey County Cricket Club and site of the 1882 humiliation.

Polo – No one is sure where it came from—somewhere in central Asia probably—but it got to Britain via India where enthusiastic British army officers discovered it and brought it home. The first match seems to have been played on the outskirts of London in 1871. From the beginning it has been a rich man's sport, since it takes a lot of money to maintain a string of polo ponies and a string of them is necessary: The game is a fast and punishing one for the horses and the player will change mounts more than once during a game. There are some 500 players in Britain, and the fact that Prince Charles is among them helps to keep the game very much alive. The Hurlingham Polo Association (60 Mark Lane, London EC3R 7TJ) is polo's governing body. To see a match, go to Smith's Lawn, Windsor Great Park, Windsor, or to Cowdray Park, Midhurst, West Sussex, on summer weekends.

Curling – Scotland participates in the football and Rugby Union frenzy, but it has its own pastimes, too. Besides golf, which began here, there is curling, a major winter sport that probably began here, and if not, at least developed here. Curling has been almost as successful an export as golf, and there are now many more curlers in Canada than in Scotland, but the Scots have been curling since the sixteenth century and the Royal Caledonian Curling Club, founded in 1838, is the governing body of the sport. In this game, the player slides a curling stone—up to 44 pounds of round, polished, and flattened granite, with a handle at the top for the grip—across the ice toward a goal or tee, using a broom to sweep the way clear in front of the stone as it swishes home. The sweeping melts the ice a bit, drawing the stone on. There are four players per team and the team that wins is the one with the most stones closest to the tee.

GETTING READY / Time Zones and Business Hours

Curling rinks are found all over Scotland, in cities such as Glasgow, Edinburgh, Aberdeen, Dundee, and Inverness, as well as in smaller cities and at the winter sports complex at Aviemore, where championship games take place.

Highland Games – You'll see plenty of kilts and plenty of sheer brute strength at these traditional annual athletic meets. The history of the games goes back as far as the eleventh century. They take place along with clan gatherings and bagpipe and dance competitions all over the Scottish Highlands during the summer and the calendar is especially busy in August and early September. Even the Queen attends the Braemar Royal Highland Gathering, the best known of the Highland games, held not far from Balmoral Castle on the first Saturday in September. Most of the games are running and throwing events and they're usually entered by professionals. The main event at many a gathering is a sport called "tossing the caber," actually a tree trunk of considerable weight that must be "tossed" from a vertical position—if the athlete can manage it. The caber at the Braemar games, all 19 feet and 120 pounds of it, has been tossed, but rarely. Rules of the Scottish Games Association require that the caber start out bigger and heavier than any of the athletes can handle but that it can be cut down if it can't be tossed. Once someone has been successful, however, the caber stays as it is. Besides Braemar, other important games are the Isle of Skye Highland Games at Portree, the Cowal Highland Games at Dunoon, and the Aboyne Highland Games.

Gaelic Football – The Irish have two national sports, both thrillers. They developed their own form of football and it's the fastest and roughest one of all, though not nearly as rough as it used to be when a game was more an outburst of territorial rivalry than a sport. A particularly vicious encounter prompted the formation of the Gaelic Athletic Association in 1884 and with it a set of rules. Thus purged of its brutality but not of its passion, the game emerged resembling both soccer and rugby, but more the latter than the former. Teams represent Ireland's 32 counties and as the season progresses through the summer, hardly an Irish soul remains unmoved by the spectacle. The All-Ireland Football Final packs them into Dublin's Croke Park (phone: 74-31-11) for the day of reckoning, traditionally the last Sunday in September.

Hurling – The other Irish national game is fast and dangerous and unique to the Emerald Isle. Played on a field by two teams of 15 players each, the instrument of aggression is the hurley, or *camán*—a 3-foot-long wooden blade of a stick with a curved tip to catch, run with, then use to hurl a leather-covered ball, or *sliotar*, toward the goalpost. The ball moves faster than the speed of light, the hurley sticks whirl, and opportunities for insult or injury are rife. Also a summer game, the hurling season unfolds with the Gaelic football season and reaches its own conclusion at Croke Park in the All-Ireland Hurling Final—usually the first Sunday in September. The football final follows at the end of the month and closes out the sports calendar.

Time Zones and Business Hours

TIME ZONES: Both Britain and Ireland fall into the Greenwich Mean Time zone. Measured from Greenwich, England, at longitude 0°0', it is the base from which all other time zones are measured. Areas in zones west of Greenwich have earlier times and are called Greenwich Minus; those to the east have later times and are called Greenwich Plus. For example, New York City is 5 hours earlier than Greenwich, England (Greenwich Minus 5); when it is noon in Greenwich, it is 7 AM in New York.

These two nations move their clocks an hour ahead in late spring and an hour back in the fall, corresponding to Central European Time and to daylight-saving time in the US; therefore the same differential between time zones is maintained year-round.

British and Irish timetables use a 24-hour clock to denote arrival and departure times, which means that hours are expressed sequentially from 1 AM. For example, the departure of a train at 6 AM will be announced as "0600"; whereas one leaving at 6 PM will be noted as "1800." A departure at midnight would be "2400."

BUSINESS HOURS: In Great Britain and Northern Ireland, most businesses are open Mondays through Fridays from 9 AM to 5:30 PM; in the Irish Republic they open a half-hour later, but close at the same hour. Shops follow the same timetable, except that they are also open on Saturdays and in small towns and villages there is at least one weekday when they close at 1 PM. Some stores in Dublin skip the early closing and simply don't open on Mondays; a few in London close early on Saturdays. Larger stores in British and Irish shopping centers usually extend their hours till 8 or 9 PM 2 days a week.

Banking hours in England and Wales are from 9:30 AM to 3 PM. Banks in Scotland and in Northern Ireland operate from 9:30 AM to 3:30 PM, but break for lunch from 12:30 to 1:30. In Ireland, banks are open Mondays through Fridays from 10 AM to 12:30 PM and from 1:30 till 3 PM. On Thursdays, Dublin banks extend their hours until 5 PM and branches throughout the country have later closings at least one day a week. Two exceptions to the general rule are the Dublin Airport bank, which is open daily April through September from 7:30 AM to 11 PM and October through March (closed Christmas Day) from 8:30 AM to 9:30 PM; and the Commercial Bank at Grafton and Dame Streets, which is open Saturdays from 10 AM to 1 PM. Most British and Irish banks are closed Saturdays, Sundays, and public holidays (called bank holidays).

Post offices in Great Britain are open Mondays through Fridays from 9 AM to 5:30 PM and on Saturdays from 9 AM until 12:30 or 1 PM. In Ireland, the main post office in Dublin, on O'Connell St., is open daily from 8 AM to 11 PM, while post offices in the smaller towns are usually open Mondays through Saturdays, from 9 AM to 5:30 PM.

Mail, Telephone, and Electricity

MAIL: "Poste Restante" is the equivalent of our general delivery and is probably the best way to have your mail sent if you do not have a definite address. The central or main post office in each city or town handles Poste Restante, so make sure you call at the correct office when inquiring after your mail.

American Express holds mail free of charge for clients only. You must be able to show an American Express card, traveler's checks, or a voucher proving you are on one of the company's tours to avoid paying for mail privileges. Those who aren't clients must pay the equivalent of about $1 in local currency each time they ask if they have received mail whether they actually have a letter or not. There is also a forwarding charge of $3 for clients and nonclients alike. A list of American Express addresses in Britain and Ireland is contained in the pamphlet *Services and Offices* available from the nearest US branch of American Express.

US embassies and consulates abroad do not accept mail for tourists. They will, however, help out in emergencies, if you need to receive important business documents or personal papers, for example. It is best to inform them either by separate letter or cable, or by phone if you are in the country already, that you will be using their address for this purpose.

TELEPHONE: Direct dialing within the country, between nations, and overseas is possible in both London and Dublin. There are a lot of digits involved once you start dialing outside the national borders, but by avoiding operator-assisted calls, costs are cut considerably and rates are reasonable. Except for calls made through hotel switchboards. One of the most unpleasant surprises foreign travelers encounter is the amount they find tacked on to their hotel bill for telephone calls, because foreign hotels routinely add surcharges that can be the equivalent of a daily room rate. It's not at all uncommon to find 300% or 400% added on to telephone charges.

Until recently, the only recourse against this unconscionable overcharging was to call collect when phoning from abroad, or to use a telephone credit card (available through a simple procedure from any local US phone company). But now American Telephone & Telegraph, which was unjustly blamed for these overcharges, has put together Teleplan, to set limits on surcharges for calls made by hotel guests from their rooms. Teleplan is currently in effect in virtually all the hotels in Ireland, in all the Trusthouse Forte hotels in England, and in Marriott properties in both places. Teleplan agreements stipulate a flat amount for credit card or collect calls (currently between $1 and $6) and a flat percentage (between 20% and 25%) on calls paid for at the hotel. For further information, write for the brochure *Teleplan vs. Hotel Telephone Surcharges,* Overseas Promotion Coordinator, AT&T Long Lines, PO Box 602, Morris Plains, NJ 07950–9990.

Until Teleplan becomes universal, it's wise to ask the surcharge rate *before* calling from your hotel. Similarly, it's still a good idea to use your telephone credit card, if you have one, and if not, to place your call collect. If neither of these choices is possible, make your international calls from the local post office or special telephone center to avoid the surcharges, which seem to be restricted to international hotels. You can always place a call abroad and ask the party to call you right back. AT&T Long Lines also offers the brochures *Britain—Worth Calling Home About* and *Ireland—Worth Calling Home About*.

While the British telephone system is fairly reliable, making connections in Ireland can sometimes be hit or miss—all exchanges are not always in operation on the same day. If you dial a number and can't get through, you'll just have to try later or the next day. So be warned: If you have to make an important call—to make a reservation in another city, for instance—do it a few days ahead of time.

ELECTRICITY: A useful brochure about electricity is *Foreign Electricity Is No Deep Dark Secret,* published by the Franzus Company (352 Park Ave. S, New York, NY 10010). It provides information about converters and adapter plugs for electrical appliances to be used abroad but manufactured for use in the US. The United States runs on 110-volt, 60-cycle alternating current; Great Britain, Northern Ireland, and the Irish Republic all run on 220- or 240-volt, 50-cycle alternating current. The large difference between US and European voltage means that without a converter, the motor of a US appliance used overseas would run at twice the speed it's meant to and would quickly burn out. You can solve the problem by buying a lightweight converter to transform foreign voltage into the domestic kind acceptable to your appliance (there are two types of converters, depending on the wattage of the appliance in question), or by buying dual-voltage appliances that convert from one to the other at the flick of a switch (hair dryers of this sort are common). The difference between the 50-cycle and 60-cycle currents will cause no problem—the appliance will simply run more slowly—but you will still have to deal with differing socket configurations before plugging in. Sets of plugs for use worldwide can be bought at hardware stores.

Drinking and Drugs

DRINKING: It is more than likely that some of the warmest memories of your trip will be moments of conviviality shared over a drink in a neighborhood pub. You'll find that hard liquors, wines, and brandies are distilled to the same proof and often are the same labels as those you'll find at home; however British and Irish beers and ales tend to be about 5% higher in alcoholic content and have quite a different flavor from those brewed in the US.

You'll want to try each country's specialties. Scotch whisky and English ale are the favorites in British pubs. Whisky may be tempered with a little water or ice, and ale comes cellar-chilled or sometimes refrigerated. In the pubs of Ireland, Guinness stout, a dark, syrupy beer with a thick creamy head and a pronounced bitterness, is the favorite. (For a more thorough discussion of British and Irish beverages, see *Food and Drink*, PERSPECTIVES, and *Pub Crawling*, DIVERSIONS.)

Pub hours in Britain and Ireland vary slightly and confuse everyone. In general, pubs in England, Scotland, Wales, and the Irish Republic open for business in the late morning, shut down in late afternoon (3 PM to 5 PM), and then reopen around dinnertime. Occasionally you can find an open pub in the late afternoon.

As in the US, national taxes on alcohol affect the prices of liquor in Britain and Ireland. Prices for mixed drinks are about the same as at home. Local beers and ales are as satisfying as they are well known and reasonably priced, so take this opportunity to savor them at the source.

Two caveats: The legal age for drinking is 18 in both Great Britain and Ireland. Those under 18 are allowed into pubs but, of course, cannot be served alcoholic beverages. When setting off to do some serious pub crawling, leave your car behind and make alternate plans for transportation back to the hotel. There are strict laws against drunk driving in both Britain and Ireland and they are adamantly enforced.

DRUGS: There is a ready supply of marijuana and other drugs in major cities just as there is in the US, but don't be deluded into believing that this easy access denotes a casual attitude on the part of authorities. The moderate legal and social acceptance that marijuana has won in the US has no counterpart in either country. The best advice is, simply, don't mess with drugs; and for heaven's sake never cross a border carrying any illegal or controlled substance. Customs officials make routine, random searches and will throw the book at any offender, which can mean imprisonment for possessing the smallest amount of a drug. (If you carry medicines that contain a controlled drug, make sure you have a current doctor's prescription.) There isn't much that the US government through its consular representative will do for drug offenders beyond providing a list of lawyers. Having broken a local law, your fate is in the hands of the local authorities.

Ironically, you can get in almost as much trouble coming through US customs with over-the-counter drugs picked up abroad that contain substances that are controlled in the US. Cold medicines, pain relievers, and the like, often have codeine or codeine derivatives that are illegal except by prescription in the US. Throw them out before you leave for home.

Customs and Returning to the US

In November 1978 customs allowances for US citizens returning from abroad were revised for the first time since 1965. The most meaningful change for the tourist is the increase in the individual duty-free exemption: You may now bring in articles totaling $300 in value (up from $100) without paying duty on them, provided they accompany you and are for personal use. A flat 10% duty based on the "fair retail value in country of acquisition" is assessed on the next $600 worth of merchandise brought in for personal use or gifts. Any amounts over $900 are dutiable at a variety of rates, with those on more commonly imported products listed in the brochure *Know Before You Go* issued by the US Customs Service. For this useful pamphlet—part of a trip kit, which also includes hints for travelers, several Department of Agriculture pamphlets, and *GSP and the Traveler*, which provides a list of items that are importable duty-free in unrestricted quantities—contact the US Customs Service, Public Information Department, 6 World Trade Center, New York, NY

10048 (phone: 212-466-5550). The travel packet is also available from any US customs office.

Families traveling together may make a joint declaration to customs, a procedure that permits one member to exceed his or her duty-free exemption to the extent that another falls short. Families may now also pool purchases dutiable under the flat rate amount. A family of three, for example, would be eligible for up to a total of $1,800 at the 10% flat duty rate (after each member had used up his or her $300 duty-free exemption) rather than three separate $600 allowances. This grouping of purchases is extremely useful when considering the duty on a high-tariff item, jewelry or a fur coat, for example. Individuals are allowed 1 carton of cigarettes (200) and 1 liter of alcohol if over 21. Alcohol above this allowance is liable for both duty and the tax imposed by the Internal Revenue Service. Antiques that are 100 or more years old, and you have proof from the seller of that fact, are duty-free, as are paintings and drawings if done entirely by hand.

Personal exemptions can be used once every 30 days and in order to be eligible an individual must have been out of the country for more than 48 hours. If the exemption has already been used once within any 30-day period, or if your trip is less than 48 hours long, the duty-free allowance is cut to $25. The allotment for individual gifts mailed from abroad has been raised to $25 per gift from $10. These gifts do not have to be declared and are not included in your duty-free exemption.

Tourists have long been forbidden to bring in foreign-made US-trademarked articles (if the trademark is recorded with customs) without written permission. It's now possible to enter with one such item as long as it's for your personal use.

Clearing customs is a simple procedure. Forms are distributed by airline or ship personnel before arrival. If your purchases total no more than the duty-free $300 limit, you need only fill out the identification part of the form and can make your declaration orally to the customs inspector. If entering with more than $300, a written declaration must be submitted. It is illegal not to declare dutiable items; you are smuggling, and the penalty can be anything from stiff fines and seizure of the goods to prison sentences. It simply isn't worth doing. Just as you wouldn't exchange money for foreign currency in the back alleys of foreign cities, so should you avoid any suggestions from foreign merchants that they help you secure a bargain by deceiving customs officials. Such transactions are frequently a setup using the foreign merchant as an agent of US Customs. Another agent of US Customs is TECS, the Treasury Enforcement Communications System, a computer that is being used to store all kinds of pertinent information on returning citizens. There is a basic rule to buying goods abroad, and you should never contravene it: If you can't afford the duty on something, don't buy it. Your list or verbal declaration should include all items purchased abroad as well as gifts received abroad, purchases made at the behest of others, repairs, and anything brought in for sale. Items that you mail or have shipped home for your own use are dutiable. For a copy of a booklet called *International Mail Imports,* which defines both duty-free and taxable items, write to the Department of the Treasury, US Customs Service, Washington, DC 20229.

Gold, gold medals, bullion, and up to $5,000 in currency or negotiable instruments may be brought into the US without being declared. Sums over $5,000 must be declared. Drugs are totally illegal with the exception of physician-prescribed medication. It's a good idea to travel with no more than you actually need of any medication and to have the prescription on hand in case any question arises either abroad or reentering the US.

Customs implements the rigorous Department of Agriculture regulations concerning the importation of vegetable matters, seeds, bulbs, and the like. Living vegetable matter may not be imported without an import permit and everything must be inspected, permit or not. Processed foods and baked goods are usually okay. Regulations on meat products generally depend on the country of origin and manner of processing.

Customs agents are businesslike, efficient, and not unkind. During the peak season, clearance can take time, but this is generally because of the strain put on capacity by a number of jumbo jets disgorging their passengers at the same time, not unwarranted zealousness on the part of the customs people.

Sources and Resources

Tourist Information Offices

Below is a list of national tourist offices in the United States and in Great Britain and Ireland. These organizations can provide travel and entry information and literature is usually free. When requesting travel brochures and maps, state your particular areas of interest regarding hotels, restaurants, special events, tourist attractions, guided tours, and sports facilities. Offices are generally open Mondays through Fridays.

There are numerous regional tourism organizations as well as more than 700 Tourist Information Centres located in towns throughout England, Scotland, Wales, and Northern Ireland, and more than 70 Tourist Information Offices in the Irish Republic. These furnish information and handle inquiries by mail and, where numbers are given, also by telephone. Some are open in summer only and others year-round. For a complete listing of all local information centers, seasonal and otherwise, contact the national tourist offices.

IN THE US:

British Tourist Authority, 680 Fifth Ave., New York, NY 10019 (phone: 212-581-4700); 612 S Flower St., Los Angeles, CA 90017 (phone: 213-623-8196); John Hancock Center, Suite 3320, 875 N Michigan Ave., Chicago, IL 60611 (phone: 312-787-0490); Plaza of the Americas, North Tower, Suite 750, Dallas, TX 75201 (phone: 214-748-2279).

Irish Tourist Board, 590 Fifth Ave., New York, NY 10036 (phone: 212-246-7400); 230 N Michigan Ave., Chicago, IL 60601 (phone: 312-726-9356); 1880 Century Park E, Suite 314, Los Angeles, CA 90067 (phone: 213-557-0722); 681 Market St., San Francisco, CA 94105 (phone: 415-781-5688).

Northern Ireland Tourist Board, 680 Fifth Ave., New York, NY 10019 (phone: 212-581-4700).

ENGLAND:

British Tourist Authority, "Welcome to Britain" Tourist Information Centre, 64 St. James's St., London SW1A 1NF (phone: 01-499-9325).

London Tourist Board, 26 Grosvenor Gardens, London SW1W ODU (phone: 01-730-3450).

English Tourist Board, 4 Grosvenor Gardens, London SW1W ODU (phone: 01-730-3400).

Cumbria Tourist Board, Ellerthwaite, Windermere, Cumbria LA23 2AQ (phone: 096-62-4444).

East Anglia Tourist Board (includes Cambridgeshire, Essex, Norfolk, and Suffolk), 14 Museum St., Ipswich, Suffolk 1P1 1HU (phone: 0473-214211).

East Midlands Tourist Board (includes Derbyshire, Leicestershire, Lincolnshire,

Northamptonshire, and Nottinghamshire), Exchequergate, Lincoln LN2 1P2 (phone: 0522-31521).

Heart of England Tourist Board (includes Gloucestershire, Hereford and Worcester, Salop, Staffordshire, Warwickshire, and West Midlands), The Old Bank House, Bank St., Worcester WR1 2EW (phone: 0905-29511).

Northumbria Tourist Board (includes Cleveland, Durham, Northumberland, and Tyne and Wear), 9 Osborne Ter., Jesmond, Newcastle upon Tyne NE2 1NT (phone: 0632-817744).

North West Tourist Board (includes Cheshire, High Peak District of Derbyshire, Greater Manchester, Lancashire, and Merseyside), The Last Drop Village, Bromley Cross, Bolton BL7 9PZ (phone: 0204-591511).

South East England Tourist Board (includes East Sussex, Kent, Surrey, and West Sussex), Cheviot House, 4–6 Monson Rd., Tunbridge Wells, Kent TN1 1NH (phone: 0892-40766).

Southern Tourist Board (includes parts of Dorset, Hampshire, and the Isle of Wight), The Old Town Hall, Leigh Rd., Eastleigh, Hampshire SO5 4DE (phone: 0703-616027).

Thames and Chilterns Tourist Board (includes Bedfordshire, Berkshire, Buckinghamshire, Hertfordshire, and Oxfordshire), PO Box 10, Abingdon, Oxfordshire OX14 3HG (phone: 0235-22711).

West Country Tourist Board (includes Avon, Cornwall, Devon, West Dorset, Somerset, and Wiltshire, and the Isles of Scilly), Trinity Ct., 37 Southernhay E, Exeter, Devon EX1 1QS (phone: 0392-76351).

Yorkshire and Humberside Tourist Board (includes Humberside and North, South, and West Yorkshire), 312 Tadcaster Rd., York, YO2 2HF (phone: 0904-707961).

CHANNEL ISLANDS:

Alderney Recreation and Tourism Committee, States Office, Alderney (phone: 0481-82-2994).

Guernsey Information Bureau, PO Box 23, St. Peter Port, Guernsey (phone: 0481-23552).

Herm Island Administrative Office, Herm Island, Via Guernsey (phone: 0481-22377).

States of Jersey Tourist Information Bureau, Weighbridge, St. Helier, Jersey (phone: 0534-78000).

Sark Tourist Information Officer, Sark (phone: 0481-83-2262).

ISLE OF MAN:

Isle of Man Tourist Board, 13 Victoria St., Douglas, Isle of Man (phone: 0624-4323).

ISLE OF WIGHT:

Isle of Wight Tourist Board, 21 High St., Newport, Isle of Wight PO30 1JS (phone: 0983-524343).

SCOTLAND:

Scottish Tourist Board, 23 Ravelston Terr., Edinburgh EH4 3EU (phone: 031-332-2433).

Borders Regional Council, Department of Physical Planning, Newtown, St. Boswells Melrose, Roxburghshire TD6 0SA (phone: 083-52-3301).

Central Regional Council, Tourism Department, Viewforth, Stirling FK8 2ET (phone: 0786-3111).

Dumfries and Galloway Tourist Association, Douglas House, Newton Stewart, Wigtownshire DG8 6DQ (phone: 0671-2549).

Fife Regional Council, Fife Tourist Authority, Fife House, North St., Glenrothes KY7 5LT (phone: 0592-754411).

Grampian Regional Council, Department of Leisure, Recreation, and Tourism, Woodhill House, Ashgrove Rd. W, Aberdeen AB9 2LU (phone: 0224-682222).

Highlands Regional Council, Development Dept., Regional Buildings, Glenurquart Rd., Inverness 1V3 5NX (phone: 0463-34124).

Highlands and Islands Development Board, Bridge House, 27 Bank St., Inverness IV1 1QR.

Lothian Regional Council, Dept. of Leisure Services, 40 Torphichen St., Edinburgh EH3 8JJ (phone: 031-229-9292).

Strathclyde Regional Council, Dept. of Leisure and Recreation, McIver House, Cadogan St., Glasgow G2 7QB (phone: 041-204-2900).

Tayside Regional Council, Dept. of Recreation and Tourism, Tayside House, 28 Crichton St., Dundee DD1 3RD.

WALES:

Wales Tourist Board, Brunel House, 2 Fitzalan Rd., Cardiff CF2 1UY (phone: 0222-499909).

Mid Wales Tourism Council (includes parts of Dyfed, Gwynedd, and Powys), The Owain Glyndwr Centre, Machynlleth, Powys SY20 8EE (phone: 0654-2653).

North Wales Tourism Council (includes Clwyd and most of Gwynedd), Glan y Don, Civic Centre, Colwyn Bay, Clwyd LL29 8AR (phone: 0492-56881).

South Wales Tourism Council (includes parts of Dyfed and Powys, Gwent, Mid, South, and West Glamorgan), Darkgate, Carmarthen, Dyfed SA31 1QL (phone: 0267-7557).

IRISH REPUBLIC:

City of Dublin Region, 14 Upper O'Connell St., Dublin 1 (01-747733).

Eastern Region (includes Dublin, Kildare, Louth, Meath, and Wicklow counties), 1 Clarinda Park N, Dun Laoghaire, Co. Dublin (phone: 01-808571).

Southeastern Region (includes Carlow, Kilkenny, southern Tipperary, Waterford, and Wexford counties), 41 The Quay, Waterford (phone: 051-75823).

Cork/Kerry Region, Tourist House, Grand Parade, Cork (phone: 021-23251).

Midwestern Region (includes Clare, Limerick, and northern Tipperary counties), 62 O'Connell St., Limerick (phone: 061-47522).

Western Region (includes Galway and Mayo counties), Aras Fáilte, Ireland West House, Galway (phone: 091-63081).

Donegal/Leitrim/Sligo Region, Stephen St., Sligo (phone: 071-5336/7/8).

Midland Region (includes Cavan, Laois, Longford, Monaghan, Roscommon, and Westmeath counties), Dublin Rd., Mullingar, Co. Westmeath (phone: 044-8761).

NORTHERN IRELAND:

Northern Ireland Tourist Board, River House, 48 High St., Belfast, BT1 2DS (phone: 0232-31221); in Belfast Airport (Aldergrove), Belfast (phone: Crumlin 52103).

Theater and Special Event Tickets

Both the British Tourist Authority and the Irish Tourist Board can supply information on the many special events and festivals that take place in Britain and Ireland, though they cannot in all cases provide the actual program or detailed information on ticket prices. In more than one section of this book you will come across mention of events to spark your interest — everything from music festivals and special theater seasons to sporting championships — along with addresses to write for descriptive brochures, reservations, or tickets. Since many of these occasions are sometimes booked well in advance, if there is something you would surely not want to miss, you should think about having your booking in hand before you go. If you do write, remember that any request from the US should be accompanied by an international reply coupon to ensure a response (send two of them for an airmail response—you can obtain the coupons from any post office). Actual tickets can usually be paid for by an international postal money order or by foreign draft.

Tickets for London shows, sports events, and opera, ballet, and concert performances that are part of the regular cultural seasons in London and elsewhere can be bought before you go from the following agencies. (They may also be able to supply tickets to some of the more popular special events.)

1. *KPI Tours & Travel,* 1290 Ave. of the Americas, New York, NY 10104 (phone: 212-397-3200). Service charge of $6 per ticket. Does not handle events in Ireland.
2. *London Stages,* 9763 W Pico Blvd., Los Angeles, CA 90035 (phone: 213-879-4997). Service charge of $4 per ticket. Handles events in London and Stratford-upon-Avon only. No Covent Garden tickets.

Camera and Equipment

Vacations are everybody's favorite time for taking pictures. After all, most of us want to remember the places we visit — and show them off to others — through spectacular photographs. Here are a few suggestions to help you get the best results from your travel picture-taking.

BEFORE THE TRIP: If you're just taking your camera out after a long period in mothballs, or have just bought a new one, check it thoroughly before you leave to prevent unexpected breakdowns and disappointing pictures.

1. Shoot at least one test roll, using the kind of film you plan to take along with you. Use all the shutter speeds and f-stops on your camera, and vary the focus to make sure everything is in order. Do this well in advance of your departure so there will be time to have film developed and to make repairs, if they are necessary. If you're in a rush, most large cities have custom labs that can process film in as little as 3 hours.
2. Clean your camera thoroughly, inside and out. Dust and dirt can jam camera mechanisms, spoil pictures, and scratch film. Remove surface dust from lenses and camera body with a soft camel's-hair brush. Next, use at least two layers of crumpled lens tissue and your breath to clean lenses and filters. Don't rub hard and don't use compressed air on lenses or filters because they are so easily damaged. Persistent stains can be removed by using a Q-tip moistened with liquid lens

GETTING READY / Camera and Equipment

cleaner. Anything that doesn't come off easily needs professional attention. Once your lens is clean, protect it from dirt and damage with an inexpensive skylight or ultraviolet filter.

3. Check the batteries in the light meter, and take along extra ones just in case yours wear out during the trip.

EQUIPMENT TO TAKE ALONG: Keep your gear light and compact. Items that are too heavy or bulky to be carried with you will likely stay in your hotel room.

1. Most single lens reflex (SLR) cameras come with a conventional 50mm lens, a general purpose lens good for street scenes taken at a distance of 25 feet or more and full body portraits shot at normal distances. You can expand your photographic options with a wide-angle lens such as a 35mm, 28mm, or 24mm. These are especially handy for panoramas, cityscapes, and large buildings or statuary from which you can't step back. For close-ups, a macro-lens is best, but a screw-on magnifying lens is an inexpensive alternative. Telephoto and zoom lenses are bulky and not really necessary unless you are shooting animals in the wild. If you want one such lens that gives a range of options, try a 35mm to 80mm zoom; it is relatively light, though expensive. Protect all lenses with a 1A or 1B skylight filter, which should be removed for cleaning only. And take along a polarizing filter to eliminate glare and reflection, and to saturate colors in very bright sunlight.

2. Travel photographs work best in color. The preferred and least expensive all-around slide films are Kodachrome 64, Fujichrome, and Agfachrome. For very bright conditions, try slower film like Kodachrome 25. In places that tend to be cloudy, or indoors with natural light (as in museums), use a fast film such as Ektachrome 400, which can be "pushed" to ASA 800 or 1600. Films tend to render color in slightly different ways. Kodachrome brings out reds and oranges. Agfachrome mutes bright tones and produces fine browns, yellows, and whites. Fujichrome is noted for its yellows, greens, and whites. Anticipate what you are likely to see, and take along whichever types of film will enhance your results.

   If you choose film that develops into prints rather than slides, try Kodacolor 100 or 400 for bright, sunny days. For environments where there isn't much contrast — in the shade or on dark, overcast days — use Kodak Vericolor. Remember that multiple prints made from slide transparencies are generally better than those made from print negatives.

   How much film should you take? If you are serious about your photography, pack one roll of film (36 exposures) for each day of your trip. Film is especially expensive abroad, and any leftovers can be bartered away or brought home and safely stored in your refrigerator. Bring exposed film home for processing. It is cheaper and safer than developing it abroad. If you are concerned about airport security x-rays damaging your film, store it in lead-lined bags sold in camera shops. In addition, always carry film on board with you to preclude the possibility of theft, loss, or damage. In case your camera will be inspected, keep it empty of film when passing through security.

3. A small battery-powered electronic flash unit is handy for very dim light or at night, but only if the subject is at a distance of 15 feet or less. Flash units cannot illuminate an entire scene, and many museums do not permit flash photography, so take such a unit only if you know you will need it. If your camera does not have a hot-shoe, you will need a PC cord to synchronize the flash with your shutter.

4. Invest in a broad camera strap if you now have a thin one. It will make carrying the camera much more comfortable.

5. A sturdy canvas or leather camera bag — not an airline bag — will keep equipment organized and easy to find.

6. For cleaning, bring along a camel's-hair brush that retracts into a rubber squeeze

bulb. Also, take plenty of lens tissue and plastic bags to protect cameras against dust.
7. Buy an inexpensive lens cap "leash," or pack some extra lens caps — they're the first things to get lost.

SOME TIPS: For better pictures, remember the following pointers:

1. *Get close* — Move in to get your subject to fill the frame.
2. *Vary your angle* — Get down, shoot from above, look for unusual perspectives.
3. *Pay attention to backgrounds* — Keep it simple or blur it out.
4. *Look for details* — Not just a whole building, but a decorative element; not just an entire street scene, but a single remarkable face.
5. *Don't be lazy* — Always carry your camera gear with you, loaded and ready for those unexpected moments.

Genealogy Hunts

It's possible to trace your ancestors by mail, or to do your research stateside using the thousands of reels of microfilmed records on file at the Church of Latter Day Saints' genealogical library in Salt Lake City. Or you can hire a professional genealogist. But nothing is quite as satisfying as flipping through the records on your own and actually visiting the area where your ancestors lived. Thanks to an abundance of records kept throughout the ages in Britain, the descendants of yeoman and middle-class families can trace their heritage back to the 1400s; but even if your pedigree is not quite so grandiose, there's a good chance that you'll be able to worship in a church where some great-great-great-great-grandfather was married, or walk up to the house where his children were born, or read a will written in his own hand, or photograph his moss-covered gravestone in some peaceful country churchyard. When you're doing the research in person, the process is more efficient than by mail, since you can follow up clues on the spot.

It goes without saying, however, that you can't even begin to search abroad until you've laid the groundwork at home. You need to know not only the name of your emigrant ancestor, but also the dates of his birth and emigration. You must also have a general idea of where he came from. The names of his relatives can also be useful. From there, you'll be able to consult parish registers and the archives of various public record offices and genealogical libraries throughout Britain. Note: Don't forget about the realignment of counties that took place in 1974; many records were relocated at that time.

ENGLAND AND WALES

In the mid-sixteenth century, England united with Wales, so, although the Welsh have their own language, the two countries' records are essentially one and the same.

The search is easiest if your ancestor emigrated after 1837, when civil registration of births, marriages, and deaths was introduced in both countries. St. Catherine's House, London, houses the records, and like most in Britain, they're indexed, but to get particulars you have to request a certificate, the preparation of which takes a day or two.

Birth certificates give date and place where the event occurred; the child's forenames; his father's name and occupation; his mother's name and maiden surname; her usual residence if the birth took place elsewhere; and the name and address of the person providing the information.

Marriage certificates give the names of the contracting parties; their ages (most of

GETTING READY / Genealogy Hunts 107

the time, that is; and you must remember that some people stretched the truth a bit); their fathers' names and occupations; the date and place of the marriage; and the names of the witnesses.

A death certificate records the date, place, and cause of death, plus the deceased's name, age, occupation, and usual residence (if different from the place of death), and the name and address of the person furnishing the data.

The details on a birth certificate usually tell you enough so that you can look for the parents' marriage certificate, and the marriage certificate will usually give you the information you need to find the records of the births of the two parties.

Once you know the addresses, you may get further information from returns of the censuses taken decennially from 1841 on and now housed at the Public Record Office, Chancery Lane, London. Partial information about the returns is available from 1901 on; complete data is available if a century has passed since the census date.

These and other British records should lead you, if your American research did not already, to the period before 1837. In this era, it's the registers of the 14,000 parish churches in England and Wales that are your most valuable source. Gaps in their listings of baptisms, marriages, and burials do exist, but some volumes date from as early as 1538, when the law requiring the clergy to keep such records went into effect. Copies of many of them are at the Society of Genealogists, a private genealogical library open to the public for a fee at 37 Harrington Gardens, London SW7 4JX; the library has catalogues of the copies that can be found here and elsewhere. Where no copies exist, you can find out the originals' whereabouts from the appropriate County Record Office. (Lists of County Record Offices' addresses are available at Her Majesty's Stationery Office, London.) When you do locate the parish, use *Crockford's Clerical Directory* to find the name and address of the clergyman who currently has custody of the records. Make an appointment as far in advance as possible so that you can be sure that the clergyman will have time to show you his records.

The above-mentioned County Record Offices provide other valuable information. Many well-to-do folk were married by license in the good old days, and records of the proceedings can often be found in the County Record Offices. (Others are housed in the Lambeth Palace Library, London SE1 7JU, and the Guildhall Library, Aldermanbury, London EC2P 2EJ, which has an unrivaled collection of the material on London.)

Various centralized indexes of vital records, available in genealogical libraries, can also be useful. *Boyd's Marriage Index,* which covers the period from 1538 to 1837, is only one.

Among the genealogist's best tools are wills, especially in Wales, where, until the mid-nineteenth century, surnames changed with each generation as in Scandinavian countries. The information you find in a will can often clarify relationships of people whose names you've found mentioned elsewhere, and the particulars are almost always reliable. Sometimes you can make up charts for several generations of a family from just one will. If the document you need was proved since 1858, you'll find it at the Principal Registry of the Family Division, Somerset House, Strand, London WC2R 4LB. Before 1858, wills were proved in a variety of courts, depending on the deceased's holdings. If they were varied and widespread, the will was generally proved in the Prerogative Court of Canterbury (PCC), if the deceased lived in the southern half of England; or, if he lived in the north, in the Prerogative Court of York. The PCC records, which begin in 1383 and are indexed, are at the Public Record Office, Chancery La., London; the York court records, which date from 1389, are at the Borthwick Institute, St. Anthony's Hall, York, and are indexed only until 1688.

When, sooner or later, you hit a snag in your research, you can get help at the Society of Genealogists. In addition to the parish register transcripts, it houses a vast general index of names, a 7-million-entry marriage index, and a collection of documents relating to some 13,000 families, plus material for Scottish, Welsh, and Irish families and for English families abroad. When you need professional help, consult the College of Arms, Queen Victoria St., London EC4V 4BT. Also write for *Tracing Your Family Ancestry—Wales* from the Wales Tourist Board, Dept. TAC, PO Box 1, Cardiff CF1 2XN. The British Travel Bookshop carries *Discovering Your Family Tree* (England) and *Discovering Surnames* (Irish, Scottish, and Welsh), $2.80 each, plus $1.50 handling.

SCOTLAND

Many Scots, including whole boatloads of prisoners who were boarded against their will, crossed the Atlantic in the seventeenth and eighteenth centuries during the political turmoil that followed the deposition of the Catholic king James II and the struggle of his son Charles Edward Stuart, or "Bonnie Prince Charlie" (1720–1788), to regain the throne. Flora Macdonald, who helped in the escape of this romantic fellow after his defeat, in 1746, at Culloden Moor, was just one of the Scottish immigrants of this period.

Tracing these families, and others, can be relatively simple here, for in addition to the fact that the records are remarkably thorough to begin with, they're all centrally located. New Register House on Princes St., Edinburgh EH1 3YT, contains not only the records of births, marriages, and deaths made since the beginning of compulsory registration in 1855, but also about 4,000 old parish registers, some dating from the sixteenth century, most one and two hundred years older, both in the original and on film. The fact that married women are often listed under their maiden names makes your work just that much easier. To make matters better yet, New Register House is also the repository for the returns of the decennial census from 1841 onward; census records are available here after 70 years rather than 100 as in England.

Wills, justiciary records, deeds, services of heirs, and other legal documents are also in Edinburgh, at the Scottish Record Office. Registers of sasines, a Scottish document dealing with the descent of land, are also available here.

Although these records may be all you need, there are also many books, articles, and unpublished materials that may help you work out any knotty problems you encounter. Organizations like the Scots Ancestry Research Society, 3 Albany St., Edinburgh 1 (phone: 031-556-4220), and the Scottish Genealogy Society, 21 Howard Pl., Edinburgh EH3 5JY (phone: 031-556-3844), can help you directly or provide you with the names of professional searchers. Margaret Stuart's *Scottish Family History* (1930), Joan Ferguson's *Scottish Family Histories Held in Scottish Libraries* (1960), and G. F. Black's *Surnames of Scotland* (1946) may also prove helpful. You may also be interested in contacting the Scottish Tartans Society, Davidson House, Drummond, Comrie, Perthshire PH6 2DW (phone: 07647-779), a noncommercial cultural organization that maintains an enormous fund of information about tartans.

THE REPUBLIC AND NORTHERN IRELAND

It was the great potato famine of 1846–1848 that drove 4 million Irish across the Atlantic, but several thousand came before that, and hundreds of thousands have come in the years since then. In general, just where you look for the records of your forebears will depend on whether they came from the north or the south.

All Protestant marriages on the island were recorded beginning in 1845, and civil registration of births, deaths, and Roman Catholic marriages began in 1864.

When you're researching ancestors who lived in the south, you'll find those records from the earliest days to the present in the Custom House, Dublin 1. Records of births, marriages, and deaths that occurred before formal record-keeping commenced were kept by the parishes. Half of the registers where you'll find such details are still in the keeping of various parish priests and ministers. Unfortunately, the other half, which had been deposited in the Four Courts Building in Dublin, burned up in the great fire of 1922, along with most probate records and the census records for the years from 1813 to 1851.

This may make your research difficult, but you don't necessarily have to abandon the trail, because various other records still exist. So-called Tithe Applotment Books, containing, among other things, the names of people whose holdings were subject to tithes during the first half of the nineteenth century, can be useful. You'll find them in the collections of the Public Record Office, Four Courts, Dublin 7. This office also has a variety of other genealogical and land tenure records, some dating to the 1600s, along with copies of many Church of Ireland parish records, wills, abstracts of wills, indexes to wills, and so on. Deeds, leases, mortgages, settlements, and other records of transactions relating to property, dating from as early as 1708, are recorded at the Registry of Deeds, Henrietta St., Dublin 1.

When all else fails, visit the National Library, Kildare St., Dublin 2. Here you'll find not only all manner of books, manuscripts, directories, family histories, and genealogical and historical journals, but also national and provincial newspapers, and various deeds, letters, and other papers relating to a number of Irish families. The library's Genealogical Office in Dublin Castle has still more information. If your ancestors were Presbyterian, you can get help from the Presbyterian Historical Society, Church House, Fisherwick Place, Belfast 1 (phone: 23936).

If your ancestors lived in the north of Ireland, you may find the records you need in either Dublin or Belfast. Records of births, marriages, and deaths from the beginning of civil registration until 1922 are still in the Custom House in Dublin, while post-1922 records are in Belfast at the General Register Office, Oxford House, 49–55 Chichester St., Belfast BT1 4HL. Although the 1922 fire destroyed many old wills, some thousands of copies, notes, and extracts, as well as the Tithe Applotment Books and many other documents relating to the people of the six counties are preserved at the Public Record Office of Northern Ireland, 66 Balmoral Ave., Belfast BT9 6NY. On the other hand, the records of the Registry of Deeds in Dublin and of the Genealogical Office in Dublin Castle can be useful. When your trail turns cold, you can get help from the Irish Genealogical Association, 162A Kingsway, Dunmurry, Belfast (phone: 629595), or from the Ulster Historical Foundation, 66 Balmoral Ave., Belfast BT9 6NY (phone: 661621). The Irish Genealogical Association has an agent in the US, Doris A. Ward, 42 Larchmont Rd., Asheville, NC 28804; and Donna Hotaling, 2255 Cedar La., Vienna, VA 22180, organizes heritage tours to Northern Ireland.

Especially useful, no matter where in Ireland your ancestors hailed from, is *The Handbook on Irish Genealogy*, published by Heraldic Artists, Ltd., 9A Trinity St., Dublin 2. It contains lists of parish registers for the Roman Catholic, Church of Ireland, and Presbyterian churches, plus useful maps, and more. Other Irish genealogical materials are available from Historic Families, 8 Fleet St., Dublin 2; *The Irish Ancestor, An Illustrated Journal* may also help. Write Miss Rosemary ffolliott (sic), Pirton House, Sydenham Villas, Dundrum, Dublin 14.

If you'd prefer to leave the legwork to someone else, write to the Shannon Development Company, 590 Fifth Ave., New York, NY 10036, for its questionnaire. Based on the information you supply, a genealogist in Ireland will trace your family roots and an 8-day Irish Heritage Vacation specially geared to your history will be arranged. You can also request the helpful leaflets *How to Trace Your Own Family Roots* and *The Origins of Irish Surnames* from Shannon Development and *Tracing Your Ancestors* from the Irish Tourist Board.

SPECIAL PROBLEMS

If your ancestor did not belong to the established church of the land, you may have difficulties at first, but there are special genealogical societies and/or guides for just about any sect you can name. The records of the Society of Friends, for instance, are a dream — superbly indexed and organized. Archives of the Huguenots, the French Protestants who came in great waves around 1685 following the revocation of the Edict of Nantes, have been collected by the Huguenot Society of London (54 Knatchbull Rd., London SE5) and the universities' libraries at Oxford and Cambridge and the Guildhall and Lambeth Palace libraries in London. Research into Jewish ancestry can be slow going because of frequent name changes. The Jewish Historical Society of England, 33 Seymour Pl., London W1H 5AP, is a great resource.

For help locating societies that concern themselves with other groups, contact the big genealogical libraries in the country of your ancestors' origin.

Books and Magazines

Throughout GETTING READY TO GO, numerous books and brochures have been recommended as good sources of further information on a variety of topics. In many cases these have been publications of the British Tourist Authority or the Irish Tourist Board, and are available free through their offices. Others can be found in the travel section of any good general bookstore. In addition, there are several bookstores and mail-order houses — such as the British Travel Bookshop mentioned frequently in the foregoing text — that specialize in books about Great Britain or Ireland, especially those not published in the US. Their addresses are given here:

1. *The Berkshire Traveller Press,* Stockbridge, MA 01262 (phone: 413-298-3778). Mail order only. Stocks an extensive selection of guides published by the British Automobile Association (AA) and by regional British tourist boards, as well as many of the BTA publications for which there is a charge.
2. *British Travel Bookshop,* 680 Fifth Ave., New York, NY 10019 (phone: 212-765-0898). Carries a complete line of books and maps on all areas of Britain, including AA- and BTA-produced material and other books by major and little-known British publishers.
3. *British Gifts,* PO Box 26558, Los Angeles, CA 90026. Mail order only. Stocks a large selection of maps and books on Britain, including AA and BTA publications.
4. *Facsimile Book Shop,* 16 W 55th St., New York, NY 10019 (phone: 212-581-2672). Carries just about any kind of book pertaining to Ireland — literature, history books, guide books — along with records, cassettes, and maps.
5. *Irish Books & Media,* 683 Osceola Ave., St. Paul, MN 55105. It's not a bookstore, but a mail-order house specializing in all kinds of books from Ireland—history, fiction, biographies, as well as travel.
6. *Keshcarrigan Bookshop,* 90 West Broadway, New York, NY 10007 (phone: 212-962-4237). Sells a variety of Irish books and records and is a good place to look for out-of-print volumes.
7. *The Rivendell Book Shop,* 149 First Ave., New York, NY 10003 (phone: 212-533-2501). Specializes in books on Cornish, Welsh, Irish, and Scottish religion, mythology, and folklore. Records are also available.

The following stores specialize in travel also, but not in travel to any particular country or continent. You'll find books on Great Britain and Ireland on the shelves along with guides to the rest of the world, and you may even come across some old Baedekers.

1. *The Complete Traveller,* 199 Madison Ave., New York, NY 10016 (phone: 212-679-4339). Travel guides and maps, old and new.
2. *Forsyth Travel Library,* 9154 W 57th St., Shawnee Mission, KS 66201 (phone:

913-384-3440). Travel guides and maps, over the counter and by mail order.
3. *Gourmet Guides,* 1767 Stockton St., San Francisco, CA 94133 (phone: 415-391-5903). Travel guides and maps, along with cookbooks.
4. *The Happy Wanderer Travel and Book Center,* 194E Yorba Linda Blvd., Placentia, CA 92670 (phone: 714-528-2502). Books and maps, plus travel paraphernalia from luggage to voltage converters.

Before or after your trip you may want to subscribe to magazines that specialize in information about Britain or Ireland. *In Britain,* a monthly, and *Ireland of the Welcomes,* a bi-monthly, are both published by the respective tourist boards; the magazines usually spotlight various parts of the countryside and contain sketches about contemporary and historical personalities. Subscriptions: *In Britain,* Box 1238, Allwood, Clifton, NJ 07012 ($22.95 for 1 year— or send $3 for one issue to the British Travel Bookshop); *Ireland of the Welcomes,* PO Box 84, Limerick, Ireland ($10 for 1 one year, $18 for 2). *Inside Ireland,* published independently by two women, Brenda Weir and Gill Bowler, is a quarterly newsletter that reports on a wide variety of topics — shopping, real estate, the arts, restaurants and pubs, and the like. A subscription ($30 for 1 year) also entitles you to use their information service and to receive special supplements dealing with genealogy, accommodations, and other subjects. For a sample copy of the newletter ($1), write: *Inside Ireland,* 46 Lower Baggot St., Dublin 2, Ireland.

Words to the Wise

"Two people divided by the same language" is how Oscar Wilde described the transatlantic relationship between Britain and the US. He had a point. Below are some common British and Irish terms followed by their standard American translations.

aubergine: eggplant
bespoke: custom-made
biscuit: cookie or cracker
black spot: blind curve in the road
bonnet (car): hood
boot (car): trunk
candy floss: cotton candy
car park: parking lot
chemist's shop: drugstore
chips: french fries
coach: long-distance bus
cotton: thread
cotton wool: absorbent cotton
crisps: potato chips
cul-de-sac: dead end
dual carriageway: divided highway
dynamo (car): generator
face flannel: washcloth
flat: apartment
flyover: overpass
gear lever: gearshift
hire purchase: installment plan
jar: a glass of whiskey, stout, or other alcoholic beverage

GETTING READY / Words to the Wise

left luggage office: baggage room
lift: elevator
loo, lavatory, WC: bathroom
mackintosh, mac: raincoat
nappy: diaper
off licence/wine merchant: liquor store
overtake: pass
petrol: gasoline
pram: baby carriage
public school: private school
queue: stand in line
rasher: slice of bacon
reception: front desk
return ticket: round-trip ticket
roundabout: traffic circle
silencer (car): muffler
single ticket: one-way ticket
stalls (theater): orchestra seats
stone: measure of weight equal to 14 pounds
surgery: doctor's or dentist's office
trunk call: long-distance call
underground, tube: subway
wellingtons: rubber boots

PERSPECTIVES

Britain

History

Who built Stonehenge? Alas, we do not know. Britain is an island and its early history is a tale of invasions and immigrations. In one of these waves the earliest inhabitants of Britain disappeared, leaving behind great stone circles like those at Stonehenge and Avebury built about 2,000 BC, and primitive flint tools, but no trace of their language.

The Bronze Age reached Britain sometime after 1600 BC, brought by a race of people known as the "Beaker Folk," identified by their tools fashioned from Cornish tin and Irish copper, and pottery of a distinctively idiosyncratic shape.

THE CELTS

In the seventh century BC there arrived on the island the first tribes of whom there is a definite historical record. These were the Celts, a race of warriors, artists, and bards who decorated their shields with intricate abstract designs and forged their weapons from iron. They brought with them a priestly caste called the Druids who led them in worshiping a pantheon of nature spirits in groves of trees and administered the tribes' systems of law and education. Remains of an Iron Age village can be seen at Maiden Castle in Dorset.

About 75 BC the Belgae (present day Belgium is named for them) settled in England. A chief of the Belgae, Cymbeline (ca. AD 5–AD 40), who gave his name and very little else to a play by Shakespeare, is the first identifiable figure in British history. He minted coins that bore his own image and established a tribal capital at Colchester. Cymbeline died just before the second Roman invasion in AD 43.

THE ROMANS

Julius Caesar landed in Britain at Dover with an expeditionary force in 55 BC primarily to cut off communication between tribal chiefs on the island and those in Gaul. But it was not until Claudius's personal expedition nearly a century later that a permanent garrison was established and that conquest began in earnest.

At first the Celtic tribes resisted the Romans fiercely, chiefly under Caractus, son of Cymbeline, who was captured and taken to Rome, and Boadicea, the first of a series of remarkable women in British history, who was the chief of a Norfolk tribe, the Iceni. It was only after Boadicea's defeat and suicide by poison in AD 61 that the Pax Romana finally prevailed in the southern part of England.

In the north, skirmishes continued for decades, prompting Emperor Hadrian, who had visited Britain in 121, to have built (ca. 122–127) the 73½-mile-long wall that stretches from the Tyne River in northeast England to Solway Firth in southwest Scotland and is named for him.

Until 450, Britain south of the wall was the Roman province of Britannia, a source for the empire's Cornish tin, grain, and slaves.

The impact of Roman civilization was indelible, not least in the establishment of a capital where the Thames River becomes narrow enough to ford. They named it Londinium — London. Other towns flourished too, among them Eboracum (York), Lindum (Lincoln), Devana Castrum (Chester), and Aquae Sulis (Bath), where sections of the ancient baths can still be seen. In addition, the conquerors built for military purposes the famous Roman Roads, among them the Fosseway, part of which is today a quiet country road in southern Warwickshire.

The street plans of many English towns betray Roman origins, although the schools where Greek and Roman law were taught and the villas with their remarkably sophisticated central heating systems lie buried beneath rubble and grass.

ANGLES, SAXONS, AND JUTES

In the middle of the fourth century, piratic raids of the Province of Britannia by the Scoti, an Irish race, and the Picts, inhabitants of present-day Scotland, increased, while a series of Saxon tribes of the Teutonic race penetrated the southeast of the country. Cut off from supply routes by the Teutonic conquest of Gaul and faced with the disintegration of the empire in Rome, the Roman legions withdrew from Britain. Lacking a trained army of their own, the native Celts fled to the western fringes of their land, where their descendants flourish today. The territory they left was occupied not only by the Saxons, but also by their kinfolk from northern Germany, the Jutes, and by the tribe that gave its name to the southern half of Britain, the Angles. These loosely knit tribes gradually coalesced into what became known as the Heptarchy — the seven kingdoms of Wessex (the West Country), Essex (Southeastern England north of London), Sussex, Kent, East Anglia, Mercia (the Midlands) and Northumbria (Northern England). Occasionally one king among the seven would achieve primacy and it was during the supremacy of Ethelbert of Kent that Augustine the Monk (St. Augustine of Canterbury) arrived in southeast England in 597.

CHRISTIANITY

There had been Roman Christians in the service of the Empire, among them the father of Patrick, the Apostle of Ireland, and Irish missionaries had established isolated Christian settlements on the Celtic fringe in the northwest of England and the west of Scotland. But the descendants of the Teutonic invaders in most parts of England had not been converted.

Much of English history can be told in a series of anecdotes and the first is probably that concerning the conversion of England. The story goes that Pope Gregory I (St. Gregory the Great) was walking in Rome one day when he spotted some handsome flaxen-haired youths in chains.

"Who are they?" he asked.

"Angles," he was told, "pagans."

"Not Angles," the Pope replied, "angels!" And he decided that their country belonged to Christ.

Thus, Augustine the Benedictine, charged with the task, presented himself to King Ethelbert, who gave the monk and his companions some land at Canterbury, and founded the see that is still first in authority in England.

Contact with the Celtic church led to conflict. The customs of the Roman monks were less austere than those of the Irish and they calculated the date of Easter by different means. When they met at the Synod of Whitby in 664 the differences were settled and the Celtic church submitted to Rome, which was to dominate England spiritually for the next 870 years.

There followed a golden age of monastic learning and religious art, especially manuscript illumination. Missionaries from the British church were known all over Europe. Theodore of Tarsus, Archbishop of Canterbury from 690–699, introduced the Roman system of bishoprics and parishes and initiated national synods that brought the rival kingdoms together for the first time. How well he succeeded is proven by the title of St. Bede's *Ecclesiastical History of the English People,* published ca. 731, which suggests that by this date the inhabitants of the country were accustomed to thinking of "England" as a unit.

Certainly the Mercian king Offa (reigned 757–796) thought so. He was the first king to sign himself on charters as *Rex Anglorum* (King of the English), the existence of other kings notwithstanding. Offa is perhaps best remembered for Offa's Dyke, the entrenchment he built as a barrier against the Welsh on the border of England and Wales. Parts of the dyke are well preserved. Offa's burial place, Offchurch in Warwickshire, is an exquisite village not far from Stratford-upon-Avon.

It was in Offa's reign that the first of the Danish raids on the English coast took place. These were followed by a series of Viking onslaughts, until only the Kingdom of Wessex, under the first English national hero, Alfred the Great (849–899), was offering resistance. Alfred is remembered by all English schoolchildren for a particular legend. The story goes that after a particularly unsuccessful skirmish with the Danes he was forced to flee to the Somerset fens where he took refuge with an old peasant woman who did not recognize him. The woman gave him shelter and food and asked him to watch some oaten cakes that she had placed on the fire. Alfred began to think of his next campaign and the cakes started to burn. When the old woman returned she scolded the shabby king roundly. Whether or not the story is true it is certain that his mind was frequently occupied with defeating — or compromising with — the Danish invaders. At the Peace of Wedmore in 878 defeat and compromise came hand in hand. Having temporarily bested the Danes, Alfred extracted a promise from their chief, Guthrun, that he would become a Christian and leave England in peace, and they divided the country between them. The line of demarcation ran roughly from southeast to northwest, with

Alfred taking the southern part, including London. The northern part was ceded to Danish immigrants and became known thereafter as the Danelaw, the territory where the rules and customs of Denmark flourished.

Alfred was not only a warrior, he was also a scholar; as the first translator from Latin to English of St. Bede's *History,* he is acknowledged to be one of the fathers of English literature. He invited European scholars to his court, instituted schools, and directed the foundation of the *Anglo-Saxon Chronicle,* ca. 891, the sole source of much of our knowledge of early Christian England.

Alfred's son, Edward (reigned 899–924), began the reconquest of the Danelaw, which was completed under Edward's son, Athelstan (reigned 924–939). The Vikings were christianized and absorbed into Anglo-Saxon society. One Dane, Oda, became Archbishop of Canterbury in 924.

In 991 the Viking raids began again, led by Sven Forkbeard, king of Denmark. By 1013 Sven was acknowledged ruler of England and the English king Ethelred the Unready fled to Normandy. Sven's son Canute (reigned 1017–35), although the son of a conqueror, was revered by subsequent generations of Englishmen, largely because of his treatment of some sycophantic courtiers. Legend has it that among Canute's entourage were some who considered him to be — or said that they considered him to be — semi-divine. They claimed that if he wished he could turn back the tide. When the rumor came to Canute's ears he took his court to the shore where he sat in his throne commanding the tide to recede. When it didn't, he reminded the offenders of the difference between the honor that belonged to God and that which belonged to the king.

Canute, through his sons, also ruled Norway and Denmark. When he died, ruling such a large northern empire proved too difficult for his heirs. In 1042 Danish rule ended in England and Ethelred's son, Edward (reigned 1042–66), came from Normandy to claim his crown.

The saintly Edward, known as the Confessor, had little taste or flair for kingship. His main preoccupation was with religion (in 1065 he founded the Church of St. Peter which later became famous as Westminster Abbey), and he was politically and physically dominated by the powerful Earl Godwin of Wessex, whose son Harold succeeded the childless Edward to the throne in 1066.

THE NORMAN CONQUEST

When Harold Godwinsson (1022?–66) arrived at Hastings to meet the Norman invaders, he was already the triumphant victor over his brother Tostig and Harold III of Norway in a decisive battle at Stamford Bridge on September 25, 1066. He was killed at the Battle of Hastings on October 14, by a Norman arrow that penetrated one of his eyes. A 23-foot-long embroidery attributed to William the Conqueror's wife, Matilda, illustrates the incident. Called the Bayeux tapestry, it is housed in the Bayeux Museum in Normandy.

By Christmas Day, the Conqueror, William I (1027?–87), the illegitimate son of Robert I of Normandy and a tanner's daughter, had been crowned king of England. There were to be other invasions of England, but this was the last to succeed. It is from this point on that England stops being constantly on the defensive, and becomes a country determined to expand. The culmination of this desire was reached in the vast empire ruled from London in the reign of Victoria.

Resistance to William was never very effective. The Saxon rebels, ill-equipped and generally disorganized, were no match for the Norman cavalry clad in chain mail and garrisoned in fortified keeps. The most famous outlaw was Hereward the Wake, a Saxon chieftain from Lincolnshire, who made one valiant last stand in the fens of the Isle of Ely. Hereward's exploits made him a folk hero. He is known as the Last of the English.

Perhaps the greatest legacy William left was the *Domesday* (or *Doomsday*) *Book,* a record of a survey made in 1085–86 of every parcel of land in England, who owned it, and who had owned it.

William was succeeded in England by his son, William II (reigned 1087–1100), called William Rufus because of his ruddy complexion. William II made enemies of the church by the sale of church lands, and of the people by ruthless taxation. He was killed while hunting in the New Forest by what history has politely termed a stray arrow, and was followed by his brother, Henry I (reigned 1100–1135), known as Henry Beauclerk (the fine clerk), for his ability to read and write. During Henry's reign an accounting system for administering the income and expenditure of the realm was introduced. This system was the nucleus of the modern exchequer. Henry also appointed justices to travel into the provinces to see that the laws of the realm were administered fairly, causing him to be known as the Lion of Justice. Henry's only son, William, died in 1120 in what has become known as the Wreck of the White Ship in the English Channel. Legend has it that after the death of his heir, the king was never again known to smile. His only remaining child was a daughter, Matilda (1102–67), who at the age of 23 became the widowed empress of Germany and at 26 the countess of Anjou. In 1126, 1131, and again in 1133, Henry had required a group of powerful English barons — and, most notably, his nephew Stephen of Blois (1097–1154) — to acknowledge Matilda as Henry's successor to the throne. On Henry's death in 1135, Stephen repudiated his oath and had himself declared king. The result was an era of civil war and anarchy during which, men said, "the heavens slept." Following the death of Stephen's son, Eustace (1153), Matilda's son Henry was accepted as heir apparent.

Henry II (1135–89), by his marriage to the remarkable Eleanor of Aquitaine and through his succession to possessions in Normandy and Anjou, was the lord of a large part of France, a fact that was to dominate English history for nearly 250 years. Henry is best remembered for his quarrel with Thomas à Becket, his former crony, which brought to a head the conflict between church and state.

THE CHURCH IN THE MIDDLE AGES

The church in Henry's time was an almost autonomous organization existing side by side with the secular authority represented by the king. The right to invest archbishops and bishops with symbols of their office had been won for the church by Thomas's predecessor, St. Anselm, in 1107, making the pope, and not the king, supreme authority in ecclesiastical matters. The visible power of the church in Henry II's day was everywhere. Many of the cathedrals that are one of England's glories today were in their infancy in Henry's reign: Durham Cathedral, the most perfect example of Norman architecture in Britain, was consecrated in 1093, Ely in 1083, Winchester in 1093, and Norwich in 1096. In addition the great Cistercian abbeys of Rievaulx, Jervaulx, and Fountains, and the Benedictine houses at Selby and Whitby and other places served to remind the king of the power of the church. The crisis with Becket reached its climax over who should prosecute those men in Holy Orders who had broken the law — "criminal clerks," as they were called. The crown and its justices, said Henry. The church, said Thomas. It was more than a matter of church and state, however. Thomas à Becket had been Henry's closest friend and as Chancellor of England had lived as a sybarite. On his appointment to the archbishopric of Canterbury his personal habits had become austere and the authority he acknowledged was not Henry's but that of the church. Henry, so the story goes, was heard to mutter, "Will no one rid me of this troublesome priest?" and shortly afterward Thomas was murdered by four knights of Henry's entourage. The murder shocked the whole Christian world. Within 3 years Thomas had been canonized and Henry was forced to do penance at his shrine. Canterbury became a place of pilgrimage surpassed in Europe only by Santiago de Compostela in Spain. Its importance was immortalized in Chaucer's *Canterbury Tales,* while the crisis between the two former friends has inspired numerous biographies and dramas, the most famous of which are Anouilh's *Becket* and T. S. Eliot's *Murder in the Cathedral.*

Henry's son Richard I, called Richard the Lion-Hearted (1157–99), has appealed to movie-makers rather than dramatists — especially as the king who reigned during the exploits of the legendary Robin Hood. Although he was king for 10 years, Richard spent only 2 of them in England. In the popular imagination Richard is a benign and just monarch, the very antithesis of his sinister brother, John Lackland. The truth about Richard is more complicated. He was chivalrous, brave, war loving, and homosexual. His devotion to the Third Crusade seems to have arisen from a taste for military combat as much as a desire to bear witness to the glory of God. The most romantic story concerning Richard tells of his release from captivity in Germany. On his way home from the Crusade in 1190 he was taken prisoner by Leopold II, margrave of Austria. Richard's favorite troubador, Blondel de Nesle, wandered through Europe singing a song known only to the two of them. As he sang outside Dürstein Castle, Blondel heard a voice responding to his song and was able to tell Richard's friends where he was incarcerated.

There are no romantic stories about King John (1166–1216). He is best known as the king who was forced to accept the Magna Carta by his barons at Runnymede in June 1215. The charter set forth the principle that the king was not absolute and that he was required to observe the rights of subjects and communities. There is no written constitution in Britain and to this day the Magna Carta is one of the most important documents in British constitutional history.

John's son, Henry III (1207–72), succeeded to the throne as a 9-year-old boy. The quarrels with powerful barons that had marred his father's reign were even more serious during that of Henry. In 1258, a group of noblemen under the leadership of Henry's brother-in-law, Simon de Montfort, forced Henry to acknowledge the Provisions of Oxford, which effectively handed over power to a council of 15 members. Henry repudiated the provisions in 1261 and thereby started a 6-year struggle with his barons, during which de Montfort was killed at the battle of Evesham in 1265.

In spite of the constant atmosphere of crisis between the king and the barons, cultural life in England flourished during Henry's reign. Three great colleges of Oxford University were founded during this period: University College (1249); Balliol (1263); and Merton (1264). At the same time the Franciscan philosopher and scientist Roger Bacon (ca. 1214–94) made Oxford the greatest center of learning in Europe.

Henry's son, Edward I (1239–1307), found himself more often in conflict with his Welsh and Scottish neighbors than with his barons. He completed the conquest of Wales in 1282, and in 1301 had his son (later Edward II, 1284–1327), who had conveniently been born in the castle at Carnarvon in North Wales, declared prince of that country. The title Prince of Wales has usually been given to the eldest son of the sovereign ever since. Edward's struggle to become overlord of Scotland was ultimately less successful, although history remembers him as the Hammer of the Scots and he removed the ancient coronation stone of the Scottish kings from Scone, the Scottish royal seat. It now sits under St. Edward's chair in Westminster when the sovereign is crowned.

Edward II is best remembered from the play by Elizabethan dramatist Christopher Marlowe that depicts the monarch's infatuation with his favorite, Piers Gaveston, earl of Cornwall, and his murder in particularly brutal circumstances at Berkeley Castle in Gloucestershire. His son, Edward III (1312–77), came to the throne in 1327 when he was 15 years old, though he was effectively controlled by his mother, Isabella, and her lover, Roger de Mortimer, earl of March, until the latter's execution in 1333.

THE HUNDRED YEARS WAR

Much of Edward's reign was focused on the series of wars that became known as the Hundred Years War, caused by disputes over English holdings in France; trouble between the great weaving cities of Flanders, which were allies of the English, and their French overlords; and French aid to the Scots. To exacerbate matters Edward assumed the title king of France, claiming that the salic law, which debars succession to or through females, applied in France. (It did and even if it didn't, there were at least five senior claimants). The title king of France remained incorporated in the English crown until the reign of George III in the nineteenth century. The two most famous battles of the Hundred Years War — Crécy in 1346 and Poitiers in 1356 — did much to establish the reputation of the king's heir, Edward, the Black Prince, as a legendary figure of heroism and chivalry in English history.

The other single dominating feature of Edward III's reign was the Black Death, the epidemic disease that according to some estimates reduced the population of England by one-half. The resulting labor shortage accelerated the change from a society of laborers bound to a single master to one where free-lance services could be offered, and the country never again returned to the system of servile tenure. When during the reign of the Black Prince's son, Richard II (1377-99), landlords tried to resurrect that system, they were repulsed by the Peasants' Revolt of 1381. (It was led by two men of Kent, Wat Tyler and Jack Straw; a pub called *Jack Straw's Castle* now stands on the high point of Hampstead Heath, London, where he is said to have assembled his followers.)

Richard's reign ended in abdication; he was replaced by his first cousin, Henry Bolingbroke (IV), son of John of Gaunt (who was duke of Lancaster and fourth son of Edward III). Taking advantage of Richard's unpopularity, Henry had himself "elected" king by Parliament, thereby bringing the house of Lancaster to the throne.

Between 1400 and 1406 Henry had to contend with four rebellions against his authority. His son Henry V (1387-1422) (Shakespeare's Prince Hal) avoided such occurrences by concentrating his subjects' minds once again on the long drawn-out struggle with France. Following his victory at Agincourt on October 25, 1415, over vastly superior French forces, Henry was assured of the support of his countrymen for the house of Lancaster. He had himself declared regent of France and heir to Charles VI, whose daughter, Isabella, he married.

The son they produced, the ill-fated Henry VI (1421-71), succeeded his father in 1472 when he was barely 9 months old. "Henry VI, in infant bonds crowned king/Of whose state so many had the managing/That they lost France and made his England bleed," wrote Shakespeare accurately in his epilogue to *Henry V*.

Henry VI's appetite for war was minimal. He was more concerned with religion and literature, and in spite of the virtually endless turmoil of his reign, managed to found Eton College near Windsor in 1440 and King's College at Cambridge in 1441. The military successes of his father in France were gradually whittled away, as France rallied under Joan of Arc (burned 1429) and other leaders. By the end of the Hundred Years War in 1453, Gascony, Maine, Normandy, Bordeaux, and Bayonne were controlled by the French, leaving Calais as the only English possession in France.

In England, the great nobles made rich by the wars and by the recently introduced farming of sheep kept increasingly large retinues that amounted to small private armies. These semi-independent chieftains fought with one another and terrorized their neighbors uncontrolled by the king or the council that ruled in his name. In 1450, tired of the virtual anarchy around them, about 30,000 men from Kent and Sussex marched on London under one Jack Cade and demanded that Henry's kinsman and heir, Richard, duke of York, be admitted to the ruling council. During two brief periods during which Henry was judged insane, Richard acted as Lord Protector of the realm. In 1454 when the king recovered, Richard was unwilling to yield his power and there followed what is probably the most famous family feud in history, the Wars of the Roses (1455-85).

THE WARS OF THE ROSES

To understand the rationale behind this struggle it is necessary to resort to some genealogy. Both Henry VI and Richard were descended in the direct male line from Edward III, Henry via Edward's fourth son, John of Gaunt (duke of Lancaster), Richard from the fifth son, Edmund (duke of York). In addition, however, Richard was descended through his mother from Edward's third son, Lionel, duke of Clarence, giving him the superior claim according to the English laws of succession. The white rose on the crest of the house of York and the red rose adopted as the badge of the house of Lancaster gave this dreary 30-year quarrel its name.

Henry's antipathy to war notwithstanding, his wife, Margaret of Anjou, was determined to secure the inheritance for their son, Edward, born in 1453, even after Henry was taken prisoner following the battle of Northampton in 1460 and had acknowledged Richard as his heir. A year later Richard was dead and his son was proclaimed king as Edward IV (lived 1442–83) and the kings of the house of Lancaster were declared by Parliament to have been usurpers. Except for a brief period in 1470–71 when Henry was restored, Edward managed to hold on to his throne for 20 years, although until the death of Henry (probably by murder) in the Tower of London in 1471, the picture was one of battles, victories, reversals, and more victories.

A dozen years later in 1483 another king of the Yorkist dynasty, Edward V, who had succeeded his father when he was 12 years old, was to die in the tower. Whether he and his younger brother (known to history as the "little princes in the tower") were murdered by command of their uncle, Richard III (1452–85), has never been satisfactorily established. We do know that Richard was prepared to go to the extraordinary lengths of marrying his niece, Elizabeth of York, Edward V's sister, to secure his position. (He was refused.) Although Richard's dealings with his people were remarkable for his sense of justice and his accessibility (Shakespeare's monster is largely a brilliant invention), the old dynastic rivalry ruined him. In 1485, at Bosworth Field in Leicestershire, he was killed in battle by the forces of Henry Tudor, earl of Richmond, the surviving heir to the claims of the house of Lancaster. The crown of England was found in a bush, and the Wars of the Roses ended.

THE TUDORS

Henry Tudor (1452–1509) was crowned as Henry VII and married Elizabeth of York, thus uniting the two houses. His reign was remarkable for an expansion in learning and knowledge of the outside world. William Caxton's printing press had been established at Westminster in 1477 and Thomas Malory's *Le Morte d'Arthur* published in 1485. Under a patent from Henry VII dated March 15, 1496, John Cabot sailed from the West Country port of Bristol and reached North America in the vicinity of Cape Breton in Canada. English claims on the American continent were later based on this discovery.

Henry Tudor's son Henry VIII (1491–1547) is probably the best-known king in English history, not least for his six wives. Henry's struggle with the papacy over his divorce from Katherine of Aragon and his marriage to Anne Boleyn has tended to obscure his early religious fervor. In 1421 he wrote the *Assertion of the Seven Sacraments,* a rebuttal of Martin Luther. For his pains he received the title Defender of the Faith from Pope Leo XI, a title which the English sovereign bears to this day.

Twelve years later in 1534 the Defender of the Faith became the founder of the Church of England when Henry caused the Act of Supremacy to be passed. The act declared that the king and his successors were the supreme head of the church and clergy in England. Among those executed for refusal to take the oath confirming the act were the Bishop of Rochester, St. John Fisher, and Henry's erstwhile friend and chancellor, St. Thomas More. Religious orders were dissolved and many great abbeys and monasteries sold to the highest bidder. The hauntingly beautiful ruins of Fountains Abbey in Yorkshire and Tintern Abbey in Wales date from this period. Henry's marital exertions notwithstanding, all his descendants were dead by the end of 1603.

In the meantime there were three more Tudor monarchs. The first was Edward VI (1537-53), Henry's sickly son by Jane Seymour, who gave his name to the King Edward VI Grammar Schools, i.e. free college preparatory schools around England, the most famous of which is the school that William Shakespeare attended in Stratford. Edward was succeeded by Henry's daughter by Katherine of Aragon, Mary I, whose attempt to restore Catholicism and consequent decimation of the Protestant bishops caused her to be known as Bloody Mary. And finally there was Elizabeth I, the Virgin Queen (1533-1603). During Elizabeth's reign the European renaissance came into full bloom in England, most notably in the person of William Shakespeare (1564-1616). The school where he learned his little Latin and less Greek still stands in Stratford and is one of the most perfect spots in the country for soaking up the atmosphere of Elizabethan England.

This period also saw the ascendancy of England's sea power as demonstrated by Sir Francis Drake, who became the first Englishman to circumnavigate the globe (1577-80), and Sir Walter Raleigh, who in 1596 sailed 300 miles up the Orinoco River in Central America. The English superiority at sea culminated in the defeat in 1588 of the Great Armada from Spain — a fleet of 362 ships and 3,165 cannon — which had been sent to conquer England in the name of Catholicism.

Both Elizabeth and her people were victims of inflation. An influx of precious metals from the New World and the expansion of the wool trade had brought enormous changes to the economic structure of England. The value of the revenues that by tradition and hereditary right accrued to the Crown dwindled. To save money Elizabeth was frequently obliged to take to the road, traveling with her court from great house to great house to be entertained at the cost of the leading noblemen of England. One such "progress," or journey, to Lord Leicester's at Kenilworth Castle, has been immortalized in the novel *Kenilworth* by Sir Walter Scott.

The poor took to the road too in Elizabeth's reign, though in rather less luxury than the queen. Land that had traditionally been put under the plough was enclosed for sheep pasturage, which required a smaller labor force. The displaced laborers — "sturdy beggars" as they were known — wandered from place to place seeking employment and, quite incidentally, inspired the children's nursery rhyme, "Hark, hark, the dogs do bark, the beggars are coming to town . . ."

In 1601 Parliament passed the Poor Law charging individual parishes with the welfare of the needy.

Elizabeth's reign was marred only by the execution of her cousin, Mary Queen of Scots (1542-87), at Fotheringhay Castle in Northamptonshire. Mary had been a rallying point for Catholics after Elizabeth had been declared a bastard by Pope Paul IV. Mary's apparent implication in a plot to assassinate Elizabeth forced the Tudor queen to sign her death warrant, a decision which biographers tell us was to haunt her for the rest of her life.

It was to James VI of Scotland, who as Mary's son was the real heir in any case, Elizabeth left the throne in her will, and he hurried to London to be also crowned King James I of England in 1603. His accession united the two kingdoms in his person though they were to have separate parliaments for another 104 years.

THE STUARTS

There had been a Stuart on the throne of Scotland ever since Robert II succeeded in 1371. Robert was the grandson through his mother of the famous Robert the Bruce who, according to legend, regained hope and courage after defeat in battle by observing the patience with which a spider wove its web. He was the descendant also of King Duncan who had been slain by Macbeth in 1040, who in turn was the descendant of the ancient Irish High Kings. For several hundred years the single outstanding feature of Scottish history was one of wars with England, often in alliance with France. Mary Queen of Scots was herself half French, had spent her childhood in France, and was the widow of a French king before marrying James VI's father. In Scotland to this day there are French words in use — *gigot* for a leg of lamb comes to mind — that are not heard in England outside French restaurants.

James I was pedantic — the Wisest Fool in Christendom men called him — superstitious, and susceptible to the flattery of many male favorites. The warm reception the English offered him initially cooled when it became clear that he did not understand the English parliamentary system or the religious changes taking place. He managed to offend both Puritans and Catholics by his intransigence, and the latter prepared to assassinate him when he opened Parliament on November 5, 1605. The gunpowder to be used in the plot was discovered in the cellars of the Houses of Parliament and one of the conspirators, Guy Fawkes, was arrested. On any November 5, Guy Fawkes Day, visitors can see bonfires dotting the countryside and effigies of Fawkes being burned.

James authorized the publication of the Bible that bears his name and is one of the masterpieces of written English.

Charles I (1600-1649), who succeeded James in 1623, had even less success in dealing with Parliament than his father. In 1628 it adopted the Petition of Right, a statement of civil liberties that prohibited the billeting of soldiers with civilians; arrest on unspecified charges; martial law in peacetime; and all forms of taxation not approved by Parliament itself. Charles assented to the petition in return for financial subsidies for which he was desperate, then promptly violated it by exacting by force the ancient taxes known as "tonnage and poundage."

From 1629 to 1640 he ruled without Parliament; in 1641 it issued the Grand Remonstrance, which set out in full its grievances against the king. On January 3, 1642, Charles went to the House of Commons in an attempt to arrest five of its members. He failed and the Commons withdrew to the Guildhall in the heart of the city of London where they were protected by citizens of the metropolis. Charles made his way to York where he was joined by 65 members of the Commons and 32 peers. When he raised the standard at Nottingham in August 1642, the Civil War had begun.

THE CIVIL WAR 1642-46

English schoolboys used to reenact the Civil War between the Cavaliers (the Royalists) and the Roundheads (Puritan Parliamentarians under Oliver Cromwell) the way American schoolboys play cowboys and Indians. The romantic hero in this otherwise bleak period was Prince Rupert of the Rhine, Charles's nephew, who distinguished himself first of all at the bloody battle of Edgehill in northern Oxfordshire. Charles's strength was further diminished by defeats at Marston Moor in 1644 and Naseby in 1645. In 1647 he fell into the hands of parliamentary forces, and was tried and convicted of treason "for laying war against Parliament." On January 30, 1649, he was beheaded in Whitehall, London, an act regarded by Royalists then and now as regicide.

THE COMMONWEALTH 1649-60

The Commonwealth was dominated from the start by Oliver Cromwell, who in 1653 assumed the title of Lord Protector. The title and office of king as well as the House of Lords were abolished. Parliament met regularly but acted merely as the instrument for Cromwell who was virtually a dictator, rigidly enforcing the puritanical laws that had been enacted and using the army to collect taxes. When he died in 1659 his son, Richard, became Protector. Richard managed to hold the office for only a few months since he was unable to control the army. He became known to history as Tumbledown Dick.

THE RESTORATION

Puritan supremacy and military control engendered a strong reaction and by the spring of 1660 public opinion was clearly in favor of inviting Charles II to return to England from the Continent, to which he had fled. His resumption of the crown, however, was subject to certain conditions; these were accepted by Charles in the Declaration of Breda (April 14, 1660), in which he proclaimed among other things an amnesty to all not especially excluded by Parliament. When Charles entered London on May 29, 1660, there were several days of rejoicing. His reign is remembered in the popular imagination as a kind of English bacchanalia. Public dancing was permitted once more and the theaters were reopened.

The licentious mood of the times was superbly chronicled by Samuel Pepys (1633–1703), the Prince of Gossips, in his diaries.

The era was not entirely frivolous however. In 1662 the Royal Society, generally agreed to be the world's most celebrated organization for stimulating scientific research, was founded. In 1665–66, Sir Isaac Newton formulated the theory of gravity, thus changing our understanding of physical laws.

More somber was the Great Plague of April 1665 and the Great Fire of London, which burned 450 acres of the city between September 2 and 9, 1666. It is because so many structures were destroyed by the fire that there exists today the present St. Paul's Cathedral as well as 40 or so other beautiful churches designed by the brilliant architect, Sir Christopher Wren, in an effort to rebuild London.

Charles left no legitimate heirs, although by one of his many mistresses, he is the ancestor of the new Princess of Wales, the former Lady Diana Spencer.

Charles's brother, James II (1633–1701), assumed the throne in 1685. He was a convert to the Roman Catholic faith in a country where Parliament had passed in 1673 the Test Act, which excluded from public office all those who refused, among other things, to take communion according to the rite of the Church of England. He was moreover formed in the same autocratic Stuart mold as his father and grandfather. By his first wife, he fathered two daughters, both brought up as Protestants. A subsequent marriage (after his conversion) to a devout Catholic, and the birth of his son, James, on June 10, 1688 (known in history as the Old Pretender), proved intolerable to both the Tory and Whig parties in England. On June 29 seven Whig and Tory leaders invited William of Orange (who was James's son-in-law and also his nephew) to come to London and take the throne. He arrived there on December 19 and on December 22 James fled to France.

William and his wife, Mary, were crowned in February 1689 and reigned jointly until Mary's death in 1694, after which William reigned alone until 1702. In 1701, when it seemed clear that both William and his successor, Princess Anne (James II's younger daughter, later Queen Anne; reigned 1702–14), would die childless, Parliament passed the Act of Settlement declaring that the sovereigns of Great Britain were to be Protestant. The crown was settled on Sophia of Hanover, a granddaughter of James I, and her Protestant heirs.

Some Scottish Jacobites — supporters of the house of Stuart; *Jacobus* is Latin for James — objected to the act and planned to offer the Scottish throne to James Stuart, the Old Pretender. To avoid this, in Queen Anne's reign an Act of Union was passed (1707), establishing one parliament for the United Kingdom and adopting one flag, the crosses of St. George and St. Andrew known as the Union Jack.

THE HANOVERIANS

In spite of the union, Jacobite risings were launched in 1715 just a few months after the son of Sophia of Hanover came to the throne as George I (reigned 1714–27) and again in 1719. Both failed miserably and Jacobite aspirations lay dormant until 1745 when the Young Pretender, James's son, Charles, popularly called Bonnie Prince Charlie (1720-88), landed in Scotland and penetrated as far south as Derby in England before he and his army were dispersed.

Neither George I nor his son George II (reigned 1727-60) cared much for living in Britain and public affairs fell increasingly into the hands of ministers. Chief among these was Sir Robert Walpole (1676-1745), First Lord of the Treasury to George I and George II and generally recognized as the first British "Prime Minister and First Lord of the Treasury." It is from Walpole's day that the British cabinet has usually been drawn from the party forming the majority in the House of Commons.

Ministers controlled not only affairs in the United Kingdom but an increasingly vast overseas empire based largely on the European demand for sugar and tobacco, and on the slave trade. By the Treaty of Paris (1763), which ended the Seven Years War between Britain and France, the United Kingdom gained Canada and all the French territories east of the Mississippi, Grenada in the West Indies, Florida, Senegal, and confirmation of her possessions in India.

Twenty years later, by another Treaty of Paris (September 23, 1783), Britain was forced to acknowledge the independence of the United States. This act represented the final repudiation of the North American policy of George III (1738-1820). Throughout the struggle with the colonists the king had displayed a stubbornness and shortsightedness that were not always characteristic of the way he tried to rule at home. By 1782, however, much of the popularity he had once enjoyed in England had waned. His acquiescent minister, Lord North, who had mismanaged the war with the colonies, resigned, and in 1783 George, whose mental instability was becoming more obvious, was forced to accept the younger William Pitt (1759-1806) as prime minister. Pitt's rise to power marked the end of any significant influence that the British sovereign could exercise over Parliament.

The loss of the United States was assuaged by the addition to the colonial map of Australia and New Zealand, discovered by Captain James Cook in 1771, and by the territories won as a result of the Napoleonic Wars, 1803-15. These wars had added two names to the long litany of English heroes: Lord Nelson, victor of the sea battle of Trafalgar on October 21, 1805, and the Duke of Wellington, who defeated Napoleon at Waterloo, June 18, 1815. The territories awarded to Britain in the subsequent carve-up of the world included Ceylon, Trinidad, Tobago, Malta, Mauritius, and the Cape Colony of South Africa.

THE INDUSTRIAL REVOLUTION

The final defeat of Napoleon naturally inspired a period of national rejoicing. It also added 400,000 men to the ranks of the unemployed — and the dissatisfied.

Since George III's accession in 1760, England had changed radically. Technology based on the use of wood for fuel and wind and water for power had given way to one in which power was based on steam, particularly for raising coal from mines. The appearance of James Watt's steam engine in 1769 marked the summit of this development.

The all-important cotton textile industry was revolutionized by a series of inventions that resulted in a tremendous increase in output. The landscape in the mining areas of the North and the Midlands changed completely. The Midland coal fields became known as the Black Country.

In Lancashire large cotton mills sprang up across the county. Birmingham, equidistant from England's main ports, became a large manufacturing center.

People poured from the countryside to find jobs in the new urban industrial areas. Legislation controlling conditions of employment was nonexistent. Women and children as well as men could be required to work for as long as they were able to stand up. With a pool of cheap female and child labor available, male breadwinners and their families often starved. By 1843 in Queen Victoria's reign (1837–1901) there were 200,000 inmates in workhouses.

The sort of life led by the poor in the early nineteenth century has been brilliantly exposed in the novels of Charles Dickens (1812–70).

REFORM

The population shifts caused by the Industrial Revolution had done nothing to change the way that Britain was represented geographically in Parliament. "Rotten boroughs" — districts where the population had declined considerably — still returned two members whereas big industrial cities such as Birmingham elected none.

Ninety-nine percent of the 400,000 soldiers demobilized in 1815 had no vote. They were moreover to suffer like their fellow countrymen from two pieces of legislation designed to favor the rich, especially landowners. One was the 1815 Corn Law, which virtually excluded all foreign corn from Britain, thereby raising the price of bread. The other was the abolition of the 10% income tax in 1816. The popular agitation, food riots, and calls for reform that followed culminated in the Peterloo Massacre of 1819 when armed horsemen cut down listeners at a large open air parliamentary reform meeting at Manchester.

The reign of George IV (1820–30) saw two pieces of legislation that signaled that Parliament and the small segment of the population that it represented (about 420,000 out of 23 million people) were resigned to change. One was a more favorable Corn Law (1828) permitting grain to be imported at any time and fixing the duties so that prices remained reasonably low. The other was the Catholic Emancipation Act (1829), which restored to Catholics many of the privileges that had been removed by the Test Act, including the right to sit in Parliament.

It was the Great Reform Bill of 1832 in the reign of William IV (1830–37) that marked the beginning of democracy in Britain. Although it added only 800,000 people to the rolls, it redistributed 143 seats. Among the large cities finally enfranchised were Manchester and Birmingham.

Parliament's social conscience prevailed. The following year, in 1833, slavery was abolished in the colonies and a Factory Act was passed forbidding the employment of children under 9 and regulating work hours.

Under two of Queen Victoria's prime ministers, Benjamin Disraeli (1804–81), a Conservative, and William Gladstone (1809–98), a Liberal, Reform

Bills in 1867 and 1884 added close to 3 million male voters to the electoral rolls, most of them from the working classes.

Women over 30 were given the vote in 1918, but it was not until 1928 that they shared the franchise equally with men and were permitted to vote at 21.

The Victorian era produced a number of remarkable men and women besides those responsible for electoral reform, among them Florence Nightingale (1820–1910), the founder of modern nursing; the poet Lord Tennyson (1809–1902), who is buried in Westminster Abbey; and the social reformer Lord Shaftesbury (1801–85). It was also the era when Karl Marx (1818–83) sat for years in the Reading Room of the British Museum writing *Das Kapital* while the peaceful revolution he declared impossible got under way all around him.

The enfranchisement of urban workers under Disraeli and Gladstone resulted in the formation of the Labour Party in 1900, which has always tended to prefer a mild, pragmatic form of socialism to the more revolutionary kind proposed by Marx. Since 1924 the Labour and Conservative parties have alternated in office with almost predictable regularity except for periods of National Government — government with ministers drawn from all major parties — during times of national emergency. The last of these was from 1940 to 1945, during World War II, under the leadership of Winston Churchill (1874–1965) whose panache as a wartime leader made him a hero along the lines of Nelson and Wellington.

The House of Lords — the upper house of Parliament — lost the last vestiges of its power in 1911 during the administration of Prime Minister David Lloyd George (1863–1942). In that year the Parliament Act was passed denying the lords any power over a bill involving finance and circumscribing the delay they could exercise over other legislation.

The creation of hereditary peers (i.e., lords who can pass on to their heirs their titles and the privileges of sitting in the House of Lords) was discontinued in the 1960s when a system of life peerages was introduced to provide the chamber with able men and women who could contribute to national debates. The House still provides the government with senior ministers however. Lord Carrington, Foreign Secretary in the administration of Britain's first woman Prime Minister Margaret Thatcher (appointed 1979), is a hereditary peer who sits in the House of Lords.

The other hereditary institution, the Crown, appears likely to flourish. Victoria's heirs, Edward VII (1901–10), George V (1910–36), Edward VIII (1936; abdicated and became the duke of Windsor), George VI (1936–52), and Elizabeth II (1952–present) have all succeeded to the throne quite smoothly. Even the sting of the abdication crisis was quickly overwhelmed by the impending catastrophe of World War II.

The monarchy today has little more than the power "to be consulted, to encourage, and to warn," as political theorist Walter Bagehot wrote in 1867. But although the monarch no longer has the right to dissolve Parliament, she has the right to refuse to dissolve it. That is to say that if a prime minister should resign because of lack of support in the House of Commons the monarch has the right to ask someone else to form a government if she believes that that person can command a majority in the House.

Perhaps the most useful function of the monarchy in the twentieth century is its role as the head of the Commonwealth, that loosely knit group of countries that were formerly a part of the British Empire.

As the ranking member of the Commonwealth and a comparatively recent member of the European Economic Community (the Common Market), Britain forms a political bridge between its former possessions and Western Europe.

Of all the territories Britain has controlled it is only with Ireland, the one it could never truly dominate, that there remain seemingly insoluble problems.

Literature

Until the late eighteenth century, it was fashionable for cultivated British travelers to be appalled by much of the local scenery. They dismissed mountain landscapes as "horrid" — a word that, to Latin scholars of the day, meant "uncouth" or "shaggy." They preferred to pull down the carriage blinds, or better still, to remain in London.

Then along came Wordsworth and Scott. William Wordsworth (1770–1850) set forth the Lake District as nourishment for the eye, and found in mountaintops an inspiration for the spirit. Meanwhile, Walter Scott (1771–1832) quite consciously turned the Scottish Highlands and borders to literary ends in his novels and poems. Thus, in the nineteenth century, cliffs suddenly became glamorous, mountains fashionable, and ravines a romantic enthusiasm. Nineteenth-century excursionists filled the Scottish Trossachs, armed with Scott's popular narrative poem, *The Lady of the Lake*.

Even today, our perceptions of British landscapes are shaped by the experience of literature. What would the world think of the Lake District if Wordsworth, Coleridge, and Southey had not lived and worked there? Similarly, the novels of Thomas Hardy (1840–1928) have bestowed a cosmic significance on the heaths and tumuli of Dorset: "To persons standing alone on a hill during a clear midnight such as this, the roll of the world eastward is almost a palpable movement" *(Far from the Madding Crowd)*.

Authors such as Hardy impose an image of their own creation on a countryside. The reader traveling through the region cannot escape it. Is he seeing Dorset or is he experiencing Hardy's Wessex? A more fantasy-minded tourist might even pursue the haunts of the fictional characters. For example, Dorchester, where Hardy was educated and where he lived for the first 40 years of his life, is the Casterbridge of his novels; Woolbridge Manor, near Wool, has been identified as the Wellbridge Manor of *Tess of the D'Urbervilles;* and in Bindon Abbey you can see the empty stone coffin in which Angel Clare laid Tess.

The traveler in a more cheerful mood might follow Mr. Pickwick and the Pickwick Club on their Dickensian travels. Eatanswill, of the Eatanswill Election, where Mrs. Leo Hunter gave her fancy-dress breakfast, is actually Sudbury, in Essex. And so on . . .

A BRIEF CHRONOLOGY: MEDIEVAL TIMES

"Anon." was the first English author, and among the first literary figures were monastic chroniclers who — working chiefly at Canterbury, Peterborough, and Winchester — laboriously compiled *The Anglo Saxon Chronicle,* that mixture of history, rumor, and poetry drawn from earliest times to the twelfth century. England then was a country of marsh and forest.

Chaucer (ca. 1345–1400), the author of *The Canterbury Tales,* is the first great name among English poets. He is known to have gone to France with Edward III's army, to have served in the medieval equivalent of the diplomatic service, and to have been appointed, in 1374, controller of customs in the City of London. There he lived above Aldgate, one of the eastern gateways to that then walled city. Aldgate is now just another commercial street, and the closest one can come to Chaucer is a plaque on an undistinguished building in Whitechapel that marks his former residence.

During the fifteenth century, in Westminster, William Caxton set up his famous printing press, the first in England. English literature in the vernacular was given a tremendous boost, and the reading public greatly increased. *The Canterbury Tales* was one of the works that were set on Caxton's press. Another was Sir Thomas Malory's *Le Morte d'Arthur,* a prose translation of a French story that has permeated English literature. The legend of King Arthur is memorably retold in Tennyson's *Idylls of the King* and in *Camelot,* the modern musical version. Sir Thomas wrote his Arthurian work in Newgate Prison, where the wayward knight was jailed for a variety of crimes that included assault, extortion, jail breaking, poaching, a cattle raid, armed robbery, and attempted murder. Newgate Prison is no more; the Old Bailey, London's Central Criminal Court, now stands in its place.

SHAKESPEARE AND STRATFORD-UPON-AVON

In the sixteenth century, during the reign of Queen Elizabeth, Shakespeare burst upon the stage, and the English language reeled. There are those who would argue that Shakespeare, an actor with no education beyond that provided by Stratford's grammar school, could not have written Shakespeare's plays. They must be the works of Francis Bacon — too well born to admit their authorship. Or else, they must be the works of Christopher Marlowe — too widely believed murdered in a tavern brawl to risk the publicity. But let us accept, along with the vast majority, that the Shakespeare who wrote the plays, and who seems to have coined half the English language, was that same young man who came to London from Warwickshire in the 1580s and found employment as an actor.

The Elizabethan age already was one of popular enthusiasm for the theater — an English enthusiasm that has continued to the present day. But the theaters were regarded with suspicion by city government, and so they were built in what were then the rural suburbs of London. The first, The Theatre, was erected in 1577 at Shoreditch, to the east of the city. The Globe was in Southwark, on the far bank of the Thames. Just north of the City — for sixteenth-century London has now become merely the banking quarter of a much greater whole — a blue plaque is set into a blank wall in an undistinguished street. It reads: GOOD MASTER EDWARD ALLEYN'S FORTUNE THEATRE STOOD ON A SITE NEAR HERE IN 1600.

The stage was then patronized by men of culture and by the populace, the "groundlings" — by the circle and the pit. Thus the Shakespearean plays alternated elevated themes with scenes of low comedy. With a flourish of trumpets the captains and the kings depart, stage left; enter stage right the drunken porters, the punning clowns.

Although his theatrical career was centered in or near London, Shakespeare has put Stratford-upon-Avon on the map. If Shakespeare had not been born there, Stratford would be no more than a Warwickshire market town, much like a hundred other small English towns.

In 1769 the actor David Garrick — mindful, no doubt, of how much he owed his own career to parts like Richard III — superintended the first annual celebration of Shakespeare's birthday. Stupendous rainfalls dimmed the event slightly; several persons were drowned and several events had to be abandoned. Nevertheless, the town caught on as a focus of literary pilgrimage. No building associated with Shakespeare is not a museum. The site of his own demolished house has become a memorial garden, and even Anne Hathaway's cottage has been visited by millions paying tribute to literature.

April 23, the feast day of England's patron saint, George, is also celebrated, by happy chance, as the birthday of its patron poet. On the nearest Saturday to that date, the whole town still turns to ceremony: The diplomatic corps journeys up from London; flags of all the nations are flown; processions are formed; and wreaths are laid. Even before Garrick, Stratford was becoming a place of literary enthusiasm. A subsequent owner of New Place — an imposing residence in the center of Stratford that Shakespeare bought in 1597, retired to in 1610, and died in in 1616 — was much harassed by curious tourists. Strangers would knock at his door and want to see the mulberry tree under which the great man wrote. So, in 1756, the new owner cut the mulberry tree down. (A local opportunist bought the timber and turned it into souvenirs, for which there was already a demand.) In 1759, mainly to spite his fellow townsmen, he demolished the house itself. Its site is now a garden, stocked with the trees, herbs, and flowers mentioned in the plays.

Meanwhile, the curious — having paid their orthodox respects at the tomb in Stratford Church — were already visiting Shakespeare's birthplace in Henley Street. There were no birth certificates in those days; but Stratford must be reckoned Shakespeare's birthplace, since his parents, John and Mary Shakespeare, are known to have been living there in 1564. The house was passed from his granddaughter (and last direct descendant) to his great-nephew's family, to whom it belonged until 1806. In the late eighteenth and early nineteenth century, the tenants of the house were not above exhibiting spurious relics, and at least one made a good income from favoring visitors with fragments cut from "Shakespeare's very own chair."

On Thursday, September 16, 1847, the house was put up for auction as "the truly heart-stirring relic of a most glorious period, AND OF ENGLAND'S IMMORTAL BARD." The sale was not unforeseen. Committees had been set up, and theatrical benefits and charity concerts had been held to raise money. The house was bought for £3,000.

It was a solid sixteenth-century house, half-timbered and mullioned, built of local materials. A surprising amount of the original fabric remains: the flagstones knew Shakespeare's feet; the timbers were familiar to his hand.

The original intention was to entrust the house to the government. Instead, the committees found themselves perpetuated as the Shakespeare Birthplace Committee (recognized by Act of Parliament in 1891 as the Shakespeare Birthplace Trust). Between 1857 and 1864 much was done to restore the house to its original condition. An eighteenth-century brick facing on part of the building was removed. Dormer windows were restored in accord with the evidence of the earliest engraving (published in 1769). The adjoining properties were removed to reduce the risk of fire, for when Shakespeare was born the house was part of a row.

In the ensuing years the same Trust acquired the home of Shakespeare's wife, Anne Hathaway; Hall's Croft, a medieval house in which the poet's daughter Susanna lived after her marriage; and Mary Arden's house, birthplace of the poet's mother at Wilmcote, a few miles northwest of the town. The trust has also established the Shakespeare Centre and a reference collection.

In 1879 the *Shakespeare Memorial Theatre* was built beside the river. Burned down in 1926 (the surviving library wing is a monument to the florid architectural piety of the nineteenth century), it was replaced by the present theater in 1932. This is the home of the *Royal Shakespeare Company,* which presents the plays of Shakespeare and others in both London and Stratford.

In the villages that surround Stratford, idyllic cottages are inhabited by nationally known actors and actresses. With Shakespeare himself as the principal local industry, the town has an abundance of hotels, many with Shakespearean names, and a superabundance of gift shops and craft centers.

THE SEVENTEENTH CENTURY

Meanwhile, a whole school of metaphysical poetry was flourishing — with religious subject matter; neatly turned verse; and sharp, direct, and often elaborate metaphor. John Donne (1573–1631) was the central figure among these poets. In youth he was a dissolute man about town; in age, a saintly City preacher and dean of St. Paul's Cathedral. You will find his effigy in St. Paul's — it is one of the few monuments to have survived the 1666 Fire of London. Characteristically, he sat for it in life, wearing his shroud.

Donne was the first chaplain of Lincoln's Inn, one of the Inns of Court to which English barristers belong. Each of the Inns of Court has many literary associations, for many English authors have studied law. An appetite for the picturesque will take the visitor to London to Lincoln's Inn. There, when a senior member dies, it is the custom for the chapel bell to be tolled, and the visitor might call to mind Donne's most celebrated lines: "Never send to know for whom the bell tolls; it tolls for thee."

The seventeenth century was also the time of John Milton (1608–74), a giant in English literature, a university man (Christ's College, Cambridge), and a poet in Latin and Hebrew as well as English. Born in London, Milton lived there when he wrote *Paradise Lost* and its sequel, *Paradise Regained.* He was buried in St. Giles, Cripplegate, a medieval church that survives in the middle of the extravagantly modern architecture of London's Barbican. He was a first-rate scholar, and one of the last men ever to master just about all that was known. (Today, of course, that is impossible.) When he was a very young man, he decided to become the greatest English poet of all time — and he did.

THE EIGHTEENTH CENTURY

A dominant figure of the second half of the eighteenth century was Dr. Samuel Johnson (a doctor of laws) — essay writer, pamphleteer, novelist, and author of the very influential *Dictionary of the English Language* (1755). Dr. Johnson is, perhaps, most renowned as one of the greatest conversationalists who ever lived. Fortunately, much of his talk was faithfully recorded for us by his biographer, James Boswell. To cite just one example, Dr. Johnson once declared, with typical authority, "When a man is tired of London, he is tired of life, for there is in London all that life can afford."

This man, who rejoiced so vigorously in the sociability of literary London, lived for a time (1749–59) in a house in Gough Square, an alley to the north of Fleet Street. That house still stands and here the visitor may intrude into the past, for it is open to the public. The house contains not only a collection of portraits and letters but also something much less tangible, the flavor of the man's life.

THE NINETEENTH CENTURY

The last century was a time of many literary greats — so many, that we cannot even attempt to mention all of them. They ranged from the Romantic poets — Wordsworth, Coleridge, Byron, Shelley, and Keats — to such novelists as Charles Dickens, the Brontë sisters, and Jane Austen. It can hardly have occurred to Jane Austen that Chawton Cottage, where she lived from 1809 to 1817, would become a place of public show, for her work was secret and her novels were published anonymously. Jane Austen died in obscurity in 1817, at the age of 42.

The cottage still stands in the Hampshire village of Chawton, where Austen lived with her widowed mother and her sister Cassandra. Today it is owned by the Jane Austen Trust. While living there she revised *Sense and Sensibility* and *Pride and Prejudice* and wrote *Emma* and *Persuasion.* She worked in the common sitting room, where she was always ready to slip her paper under a blotter when she heard that famous creak of the door. (The door is there; the creak has gone.) This sitting room, though a small and unassuming room in a small and seemly house, has seen the creation of those perfect portraits of provincial life and universal character.

Long before the Austens moved in and fitted it up, Chawton Cottage may have been a posting inn; the road that idles past was then the main road to Winchester. It is known that the house declined into laborers' dwellings before it was restored by the Trust. Today, however, it is as nearly as possible the house that Jane Austen knew. Some of the original furniture has found its way back. On the table stands part of a dinner service whose purchase is recorded in a surviving letter. Her bedroom upstairs still overlooks the yard, the bakehouse/laundry, and the outhouse containing her mother's donkey cart.

There may be souvenirs on sale in the parlor, letters in frames on the walls, yet one feels that at any moment Jane Austen may return from walking up to the big house. No matter that the village pond opposite has long been filled in. No matter that the motorway whines past a few hundred yards away.

A scant mile from Chawton is the town of Alton, with its main street bedizened with shopfronts. Here it is still possible to imagine the younger Miss Bennets *(Pride and Prejudice)* walking in search of officers, to imagine good Miss Bates *(Emma)* about her marketing.

Finally, there is Bath — the place where nearly all her marvelous characters "take the waters." Before she moved to Chawton and after her father retired from his rectorship, Jane Austen's family actually lived in Bath. One of their homes, 4 Sydney Place, is marked with a plaque. The beauty of Bath today is that so little has changed. Fashionable society abandoned Bath in about 1840 and began to take other waters abroad. So where the honeyed stone terraces of the eighteenth century end, the suburbs of the 1920s begin. Apart from a vast new hotel in the center of town, few thought it worthwhile to tear down, redevelop, or embellish nineteenth-century Bath.

If Jane Austen were to do anything so uncharacteristic as to haunt a place, her sprightly specter in sprigged muslin would find everything in Bath just as she remembered it. And one could do worse than follow her as one's guide — to walk, "with great elasticity," down Milsom Street with Catherine Morland, to wait opposite Union Passage for John Thorpe to pull up in his gig, to loiter outside the Pump Room until Isabella and Catherine appear in hotly indifferent pursuit of young men (all from *Northanger Abbey*) . . . or to enter the Assembly Rooms and see exactly where Anne Elliot encountered Captain Wentworth *(Persuasion)*.

Bath remains to this day a trim, precise city, peopled by characters, whether fictional or historic, who lived at precise addresses. Dickens's Mr. Pickwick and his party settled in lodgings in Royal Crescent; Mr. Pickwick, like Isabella and Catherine, frequented the Pump Room. It was out of a house in Royal Crescent that his friend Mr. Winkle was locked while only half awake and half dressed. It was from No. 11 Royal Crescent that the playwright Sheridan went off with the singer Elizabeth Linley. Does it matter which is fiction and which is fact?

Fiction has inspired many a reader to dream about the Yorkshire moors. The most renowned of these dreamers, the nineteenth-century American poet Emily Dickinson, wrote "I never saw a moor/I never saw the sea" — and indeed, she never did. Airplane and railroad, however, have brought many a twentieth-century visitor to the heather-studded moors.

And with good reason. Even if the domineering Reverend Patrick Brontë had never been incumbent of the Yorkshire village of Haworth in the 1840s, the moors around it would now be accounted scenic. But the Reverend Mr. Brontë had three daughters (not to mention a dissolute son who was Emily's model for the fictional Heathcliff). By writing *Wuthering Heights, Jane Eyre,* and *The Tenant of Wildfell Hall,* Emily, Charlotte, and Ann Brontë imbued mere topography with literary associations and implications; and the Brontë

Society, restoring the parsonage and opening it to the public, has turned a minor entry in the gazetteer into an international shrine.

You can draw your own map of nineteenth-century literary Britain — almost infinitely. For example, Salisbury in Wiltshire is a much visited town. It has a cathedral; it has history; it has Stonehenge nearby. But as good a reason as any for visiting Salisbury is the small fact that "wandering one midsummer evening round the purlieus of Salisbury Cathedral," Anthony Trollope (1815–82) "conceived the story of *The Warden.*" And from *The Warden* grew all of Trollope's Barchester novels.

Thomas Hardy's birthplace is a small thatched cottage on the outskirts of Dorchester. It is approached by a 10-minute walk through woods; the interior is open by appointment only, and then only the parlor.

No doubt the greatest English novelist of all, however, was Charles Dickens, whose work greatly influenced a legion of writers — including one as remote from him in time and place as Dostoyevsky. Dickens began life as a journalist, and wrote his novels at a hectic rate in weekly parts. Like Shakespeare, Dickens was enormously popular. Many thousands of readers on both sides of the Atlantic eagerly awaited those weekly installments.

Dickens (1812–70) lived much of his life in London. The tourist who goes down to the Thames at Blackfriars where the cars now speed along the riverbank, cannot be sure whether he is seeking out the young David Copperfield, sent to wash and label bottles at Murdstone and Grinby's warehouse, or the young Charles Dickens, miserably employed in a blacking factory a little farther upstream. But success came to the young Dickens. And he established his reputation — with the completion of *The Pickwick Papers,* and the writing of *Oliver Twist* and *Nicholas Nickleby* — at about the time he, his wife, and his young son came to live at No. 48 Doughty Street, near the Gray's Inn Road (1837). The house, now owned by the Dickens Fellowship, is open to the public.

Walter Scott (1771–1832), as any traveler in Scotland discovers, made much of this country in his own image, or at least in the image of ancient romance, which he marshaled in his novels. His novels take the characters of history — some of it quite recent in his day — and turn them into a more compelling reality. It would be difficult for many people to say whether the character of, for example, Jeannie Deans, heroine of *The Heart of Midlothian,* was an invention or not. For it is a novel, like so many of Scott's, full of real events (in this case Edinburgh's Porteous Riots of 1736) and historical characters, among them Queen Caroline.

One finds the same imprecision about location. In *The Bride of Lammermoor* the castle, Wolf's Crag, is taken by many to be Fast Castle on the east coast. The author himself wrote evasively that the position of Fast Castle "seems certainly to resemble that of Wolf's Crag as much as any other, while its vicinity to the mountain ridge of Lammermoor renders the assimilation a probable one." (Mountain ridge is a bit steep for the Lammermuir Hills, but that is the effect that Scott has on scenery.) Certainly Ellen's Isle in Loch Katrine owes much of its fame to its park in *The Lady of the Lake.*

There is no imprecision about Scott's own residences. For most of his active life he lived in Edinburgh, at 39 Castle Street, a house identified by a small statuette above the door. Otherwise, it is inaccessible, for it is now a legal office. From there, having made a fortune and lost it, he finally retired to the baronial pile he had designed at Abbotsford, near Galashiels. This is now a monument to Scott the novelist and antiquarian, opened to the public by his descendants.

Relics of Scott, Robert Louis Stevenson, and Robert Burns are in Edinburgh in a museum called Lady Stair's House, romantically situated in an alley off the High Street. Much of Burns's literary output was produced in Edinburgh, although Ayrshire, from whence he came, and to which he returned, is scattered with memorials to him, and places associated with him.

Robert Louis Stevenson (1850–94) was perhaps the writer who described the city of Edinburgh with the greatest sympathy. He was born at 8 Howard Place, then on the northern fringes of the town, but grew up at 17 Heriot Row, just across Queen Street Gardens from 39 Castle Street. From the Heriot Row windows he looked down on Leerie the lamplighter *(A Child's Garden of Verses)*. In consumptive adulthood he lived in Bournemouth (Hardy's Sandbourne), in America, and in Samoa. But he always looked back to Edinburgh.

Even *Treasure Island* is said to have its Edinburgh associations: The map of the island, it is claimed, was based on an island in a small ornamental pond in Queen Street Gardens. *Kidnapped,* that most Scottish of books, follows the Lowlander David Balfour in his flight with Alan Breck, during the aftermath of the Jacobite uprising of 1745. *Kidnapped* is an exhilarating adventure yarn, but its account of the journey from the western coast of Mull, through Appin, over Rannoch Moor and down through Balquhidder to Stirling also constitutes an excellent guidebook for any visitor to the Highlands.

THE TWENTIETH CENTURY

The London of today has grown into an amorphous region. But even its remotest suburb has some literary interest, some chance association with authorship. Among its greatest literary interpreters have been Charles Dickens and Virginia Woolf. The novels of Dickens were written at a journalistic gallop; Virginia Woolf composed hers with agonizing care. Her novels are often accounted "difficult," but in them, and in her shorter writings, she creates a scene, composed of random moments in time, which lives more strongly than the actual streets she is describing. One cannot board a No. 11 bus down the Strand without remembering Elizabeth Dalloway's taking an impetuous, allusive omnibus ride from Westminster to Chancery Lane *(Mrs. Dalloway)*.

Virginia Woolf was a Londoner. She was born, in 1882, at 22 Hyde Park Gate, a tall confident house that still overlooks the south side of the park. After her father's death she moved to Bloomsbury, living first with her brother and sister, later with her husband, Leonard Woolf, in a number of houses: 46 Gordon Square, 29 Fitzroy Square, 52 Tavistock Square (Dickens, too, had once lived in this square; both their houses have been demolished), and finally in Mecklenburgh Square.

Her eye was acute, and her imagination imposed its own enhancing order on the streets and squares of the London of 60 years ago. In *Mrs. Dalloway* she has pinned down Mayfair — every brick, every leaf — on an early summer morning. In *Night and Day* and *Jacob's Room* she has done the same for the Strand, Bloomsbury, and Holborn.

There may be little of the picturesque in the town of Eastwood and the Nottinghamshire coalfields, but D. H. Lawrence was not only born there but set many of his novels in the area and peopled the novels with characters drawn from life. You can walk the streets of Eastwood and pass from *The White Peacock* to *Women in Love* to *Sons and Lovers*. Here, in Devonshire Drive, is the very house in which the Brangwen sisters lived. Here at Gresley, just a few hundred yards off the M1 motorway, is the church where they came to watch the wedding *(Women in Love)* . . .

The nineteenth century was the great age of English theater. Ornate palaces were built in every suburb and provincial town and theatrical companies toured the country by way of the recently developed railways. However, the nineteenth century produced no great playwrights until the last couple of decades, when Oscar Wilde and George Bernard Shaw began to write for the stage.

Yet Shaw, who lived until 1950, rightly belongs to the twentieth century. And it was Shaw himself, with that unflappable sense of his own importance, who left his house at Ayot St. Lawrence, just north of London, to the National Trust. This was his home from 1906 until 1950, and it came to the Trust exactly as he had lived in it, with his books, his papers, and his furniture.

Harold Nicolson's *Diaries and Letters* records the rather macabre story of how he, as Chairman of the Trust, went down to inspect Shaw's bequest in 1950. There he found "all his hats, and coats and nailbrushes etc." and, on the garden paths, spread a few days before, the ashes of Shaw himself, "like the stuff put down for slugs."

A WORD ABOUT BLUE PLAQUES AND THE NATIONAL TRUST

Unleashed on his or her literary trail, a visitor to London will find a number of buildings marked with blue commemorative plaques. Some, on modern structures, merely hint that someone — Coleridge or Dryden — "lived in a house on this site." Others designate a surviving house: These very steps up to this very door represented security to some great writer; this doorknob was familiar to his or her hand; these, perhaps, were the very panes of glass through which he or she viewed the passing world. A few literary figures are remembered by more than a plaque affixed to a wall. The National Trust is the custodian of many a literary shrine; it preserves and opens to the public such important homes as No. 24 Cheyne Row, London, where Thomas Carlyle lived from 1834 until his death in 1881; Wordsworth's birthplace in Cockermouth, Cumbria; and Lamb's House, Rye, East Sussex, where Henry James spent the summers from 1898 until his death in 1916, and where he wrote *The Ambassadors* and *The Golden Bowl*.

Architecture

Britain has castles and cathedrals that can hold their own with those of Europe, but its domestic architecture — stately homes, farms, cottages, and parish churches — best expresses the character of the people and the progress of British life through the ages. Many stately homes are open to the public and can be visited and viewed in detail. Take a half-day's trip out of London — no matter the direction — and you can enjoy the rich heritage of old homes and cottages that everywhere remain part of Britain's daily life. Many a village pub — where you can stop for a beer, lunch at the bar, or partake of a more formal dining room repast — will date from Elizabethan times or earlier. (Some say the Old Chesil Rectory pub at Winchester is the oldest in the country.)

Many of these indigenous buildings have grown or have been altered over the years, so that their style is not pure, nor their history unalloyed. Tales of their derivation may be as varied as the people you talk to about them — but their authenticity and their central role in the life of their localities are beyond dispute.

Walk through the village streets, go into the pubs, spend some moments in the parish churches, and you will begin to experience the flavor of English life, as articulated in its buildings. Get off the main road, take almost any byroad in Kent, Surrey, or Sussex, and you will be surprised at the number of old village centers that survive on the very fringes of the major metropolitan areas in this very crowded land.

Remains of Roman villas can be seen here and there in England; a particularly fine one is found at Bignor in Sussex.

In addition, quite a number of Saxon churches or parts of churches survive in England, predating the Norman Conquest of 1066. The earliest Saxon churches were built of timber with neither aisles nor towers. Later versions, such as Bradford on Avon in Wiltshire or Earl's Barton in Northamptonshire, have blunt, crudely decorated towers and reproduce in stone the earlier types of wooden ornamentation. An interesting part-Saxon church, in the attractive sailing village of Bosham on Chichester Harbour, Sussex, is said to commemorate the spot where the Saxon king Canute "told the sea to go back." And many churches in East Anglia have the round towers that hark back to Saxon times.

Brought in by William the Conqueror in 1066, Norman architecture is equivalent to the style known on the Continent as Romanesque. In Britain, the Norman period extended from the Conquest to the latter part of the twelfth century, when the Gothic style was born. Norman abbey churches and cathedrals are numerous in England, for the period of the conquest was a period of building and rebuilding.

Romanesque structures of this period are typically heavy and solid, with round arches. Architectural historian Nikolaus Pevsner described their Englishness as "an articulation . . . that conveys to us at once a feeling of certainty and stability ... There is no wavering here — as there was none in the ruthless policy of William the Conqueror in subduing and normalizing England. Blunt, massive, and overwhelmingly strong are the individual forms which architects used in these early buildings, sacred as well as secular."

Winchester Cathedral (1080–90) is an example of early Norman architecture; Durham Cathedral (1093–1130) is High Romanesque. The latter anticipates the Gothic style in its vaulting over the choir. This is probably the earliest example of rib vaulting in Europe. Pevsner cites the White Tower at the Tower of London and the keep of Colchester Castle in Essex as examples of the massive, almost brutal English secular architecture of the Norman period.

During the latter part of the twelfth century Gothic architecture flowered in England as it did in Europe. With its pointed arches, flying buttresses, fully developed rib vaulting, and its elaborate stained glass windows, this style introduced a new concept of religious space. The Gothic combined structural clarity with a coherent expression of interior space and an honest use of materials. So much engineering skill was martialed in its soaring surge toward heaven, that even today "Gothic" and "cathedral" are almost synonymous in most people's minds.

The earliest English example of developed Gothic is the east end of Canterbury Cathedral, which was started by William Sens in 1175. Lincoln (begun 1192) and Salisbury (about 1220) are fine, mature examples of the early English Gothic period. Wells (dedicated in 1239), with its carved west front, was one of the few to escape the ravages of Oliver Cromwell. In the fourteenth century its famous inverted arches were added to support the tower, which was then in danger of collapse.

Wells marks the transition to the decorated style of the middle Gothic period. This was the period when the famous octagon at Ely Cathedral was built to replace an earlier tower that had collapsed into the church. (Some of the most dramatic feats of ecclesiastical architecture were corrections of earlier structural deficiencies!) Many of the boldest and most celebrated castles in Wales were also erected at the end of the thirteenth century, among them Harlech, Conway, and Caernarvon.

The Gothic period went out with the perpendicular style, which was almost the antithesis of its immediate predecessor. Here the emphasis was on strong, simple vertical and horizontal elements, large windows with fine, repetitive tracery, and fan vaulting. St. George's Chapel, Windsor (1474), and King's College Chapel, Cambridge (1446–1515), are supreme examples of this architectural period. Do not miss King's College Chapel. The whole of Cambridge, easily accessible by train from London, is well worth a visit — but King's College Chapel, with its powerfully simple exterior and delicately ornate interior, speaks directly to the heart. If you get there in the afternoon, try to catch evensong at about 3 or 3:30, sung in candlelight by one of the finest men-and-boy's choirs in the world.

The return to classical (especially Italian) principles and influences, known as the Renaissance, swept Europe in the fifteenth century, began to appear in England during the reign of Henry VII, and took hold in the reign of Henry VIII.

Throughout the Tudor and Jacobean periods, several influences combined to shape English architecture: the devotion to large, mullioned windows, typical of the perpendicular Gothic style; the French and Italian Renaissance preoccupation with symmetry; and decorative motifs — especially an ornamentation known as strap-work, that originated in the Netherlands. Longleat House in Wiltshire (1568), Hardwick Hall in Derbyshire (1591–97), Hatfield House in Hertfordshire (1608–12), and Audley End in Essex (1603) each in its own way demonstrates a balance between these architectural forces.

Inigo Jones (1573–1652) — painter, stage designer, and architect — introduced the purity of Palladian forms to English architecture, marking this important transition with his Queen's House, Greenwich (1616). But it was Sir Christopher Wren (1632–1723), England's most renowned architect, who created England's own unique expression of classical and baroque architecture. Wren's masterpieces are fortunately very much in evidence today, notably St. Paul's Cathedral and numerous fine city churches. Many of Wren's structures suffered severe damage in the blitz of World War II, and have since been faithfully restored and rebuilt.

The classical purity of Palladianism reappeared in Bath, with John Wood the Elder's (1704–54) planning of Queen Square and with his son John Wood the Younger's (1728–81) design of Royal Crescent. Also in the classical tradition was John Nash (1752–1835), whose Regent Street and Regent's Park frontages in London are world famous. There are Georgian or Regency Squares in many cities, but perhaps the most beautiful are in Dublin. These too are designed in the spirit of classical symmetry.

Architecturally, the late eighteenth century and most of the nineteenth century must be characterized as a period of historical revival and a looking back to the past for inspiration. At first, neoclassicism appeared with a return to "first principles," meaning the nobility and simplicity of Greek art. As the nineteenth century advanced, neoclassicism was abandoned in favor of the revival of specific — and sometimes superficially applied — styles of the past.

Pattern books were produced to enable architects to provide their patrons with buildings designed in the style of their choice, whether this was Gothic, Norman Provincial, Greek Revival, or French Renaissance. Among the eighteenth- and nineteenth-century stylistic revivals, however, there were vigorous and original architects and approaches to architecture, that, to some extent, anticipated the future. Robert Adam (1728–92), generally considered a master of the purest neoclassical expression, in fact interpreted Greek and Roman themes in a highly personal way. His Syon House, Middlesex, is an example of the delicacy of his detail and the transparent quality of his space. Sir John Soane (1753–1837), who clothed his buildings in overtly neoclassical forms, could not quite conceal his romantic and picturesque leanings. His No. 13 Lincoln's Inn Fields, London (now the Sir John Soane Museum), is not to be missed.

At the same time, in the mid-nineteenth century, another influence was sweeping away much of the fabric of the past. Industrialization brought new construction techniques, using iron and glass with apparently limitless possibilities, and causing as much anxiety as optimism. Joseph Paxton exploited this technology in his daring design of the famed and ill-fated Crystal Palace

(1851). Structural tours de force were also displayed in a number of new iron bridges.

Initially, these developments caused architects to retreat in fear into increasingly effete imitations of the past, leaving the real breakthroughs in design to the engineers. But ultimately, modern architecture was born in response to both the perils and the challenges of the machine.

At first this response took the form of an attempt to master or to arrest the power of the machine by a deliberate return to hand craftsmanship in every aspect of life. Author, art critic, and social reformer John Ruskin thought that handicrafts would reawaken the medieval pride in collective work and ameliorate the impersonal effects of industrialization. And in 1861, British designer, socialist, and poet William Morris formed the Arts and Crafts Movement, which aimed to bring the beauty of individual craftsmanship into every home in the land. Morris's home, The Red House at Bexley Heath in Kent, was designed by Philip Webb in 1859, and set a standard for the picturesque style of residential architecture that was to follow.

Richard Norman Shaw (1831–1912) and Charles Annesley Voysey (1857–1941) were the chief exponents of the picturesque architectural style. Sometimes, a certain austerity appeared in their work that can be regarded as foreshadowing the modern movement in England. In Glasgow, Charles Rennie Mackintosh (1868–1928) was also influenced by Morris, and created his own highly original, historically premodern designs. His most notable works include the teashops he did for Miss Cranston and the now-famous Glasgow School of Art (1897–99).

Two parallel developments, the work of the Chicago School in America, and that of the Bauhaus in Germany, finally brought modern architecture to the attention of the whole world. In Chicago in the 1880s and 1890s, the skyscraper evolved — a tall building with steel skeletons that removed any load-bearing function from the walls. A parallel development was the elevator. These two inventions changed the face of corporate architecture.

At about the same time, at the Bauhaus in Germany, architect Walter Gropius (1883–1969) was introducing a new architectural aesthetic based on industrial technology and modern materials. He preached the doctrine that a building's form must be lean and clean, derived from and expressive of its essential function.

Britain was comparatively slow to embrace the international style of the modern movement. However, in the 1950s, such men as Sir Leslie Martin, Eric Lyons, and Lord Llewelyn-Davies were pioneers in prefabricated schools and housing. The postwar housing at Roehampton has achieved world renown. Britain has also been in the vanguard of modern town planning, taking a leadership role in the evolution of the concept of the garden city or the new town. These self-contained communities do not depend, as the typical suburbs do, on London or on other metropolitan centers. Sir Ebenezer Howard (1850–1928) was the father of this movement, and Letchworth, started in 1903, was the earliest garden city and is worth a visit. Welwyn Garden City, Hampstead Garden Suburb, and, more recently, Cumbernauld New Town in Scotland, are interesting examples of the evolution of the idea of the new town.

The bombing of London, especially in the area around St. Paul's, created opportunities for postwar urban development. A number of high-rise towers have been built, against the strenuous opposition of those who viewed them as destructive to London's lovely skyline, and to the scale and environmental quality of the city. The towers have gone up, nonetheless, though few have any architectural distinction. The Barbican Development, the new Stock Exchange, and Chartered Accountants Hall are some of the most interesting high-rises in the City of London area. New Zealand House, Thamesmead, Brunswick Center, The Economist Building, and the Institutes of Education and Law are also new London buildings worth a second look.

Having attempted in a few short pages to trace the history and development of English architecture — with its chief exponents and some pivotal buildings of each period — we must return to the starting point — to England's domestic architecture. The grand and not-so-grand country houses, the town squares, the villages, country towns, inns, and farmhouses — these are the soul of English architecture. One sees them wherever one travels. Many grand and more modest houses are open to the public. Although there are a number of books about them, the best source of basic information is the British National Trust, which owns and operates so many.

As you travel through England, you will be struck by regional differences in building styles and materials. If you study some of these buildings, you will learn something about their local character and about the periods of their origin. Especially striking are the black-and-white timbered houses of Cheshire and Shropshire. Gawsworth Hall near Macclesfield, Little Moreton Hall near Congleton, and the Feathers Inn, Ludlow, are three of the finest. In Kent, the oasthouses for drying the hops to make beer are indigenous architectural forms worth a detour to see.

The Cotswolds (chiefly Gloucestershire) are noted for the yellowish-gray stone used on almost all buildings, old and new. Some Cotswold villages, such as Bibury, Broadway, Castle Combe, and Stow-on-the-Wold represent English vernacular architecture at its most enchanting. Here brick, flint, tile, slate, timber, and thatch make their appearance throughout the country. Their color palettes and patterns weave themselves into their background with an environmental integrity that we strive for in modern forms and materials and cannot find.

Traditional Music and Dance

There's more to dance in Britain than Scotland's Highland Fling: England and Wales both have traditions of their own which mirror distinctive cultures. It all adds up to a rich inheritance — surprising, perhaps, in so small an island.

The origins of British ceremonial dance are said to lie in pagan and primitive rituals — in magic and myths, in seasonal celebrations, and in fertility and luck-bringing rites. Historians argue about dates and derivations, but certainly some of the oldest surviving ceremonial dances are rooted in the

Stone, Neolithic, and Iron ages. Later the dances were variously influenced by the invading Celts, Jutes, Angles, Saxons, and Scandinavians.

Probably the earliest music for dance was provided by the chanting of the dancers, and rhythmic sounds produced on any domestic or hunting implements at hand. Primitive instruments included drums, bagpipes, other pipes such as flute and recorder, and reed instruments.

In pagan times ritual dancing was essential to existence, and later both ritual and social folk dances were enjoyed as a form of merrymaking and as a relief from the daily battle for survival. The early Christian church abhorred pagan revelry, as did the Puritans in later times, but neither group succeeded in putting an end to dancing. It was the Industrial Revolution in the nineteenth century that did the most damage, shifting communities toward a more impersonal lifestyle. All was not lost, however.

Imagine a tranquil village amidst England's verdant Oxfordshire countryside on a warm spring day, the village green lined with spectators intently watching six dancing men who are dressed in white trousers and shirts, with bells tied below their knees, wearing black bowler hats decorated with flowers and ribbons, and carrying white handkerchiefs. In this scene you have one of the most famous of all surviving English ritual ceremonial dances, the Cotswold morris.

The costume described is the one worn by the Bampton morris dancers, who perform annually in Bampton each Spring Bank Holiday Monday. The dancers are accompanied by a single musician, playing either a fiddle or a melodeon (a Viennese accordion), and by two "characters," one of whom bears a cake impaled on a sword and the other, a Fool, who carries a pig's bladder and teases people. The whole performance is wrapped in an atmosphere of jollity, with everyone reacting good-humoredly to the Fool's mocking taunts and acting as if they believe that tasting the cake will bring good luck.

There are other traditional Cotswold morris teams near Bampton, which also perform locally in spring and summer, in Abingdon, Chipping Camden, and Headington. The dancers usually wear white costumes, black shoes, and bells; they carry either handkerchiefs or, for use in rhythmic "combat," wooden sticks — but there are many differences in the colorful accessories peculiar to the individual teams. There are variations too in each team's dances, and although the steps themselves are simple, the skill lies in coping with the changing rhythms and patterns; any irregular ringing of the bells soon draws attention to the offender. Though the dancers are amateurs they take enormous pride in their performances.

No one is certain whence came the word *morris*. There was a widely held belief that it derived from the dark-skinned Moors of Spain, and though this is now dismissed, it did seem to make sense in connection with another tradition, the Processional Morris of the Britannia Coconut Dancers, for which the dancers blacken their faces.

The Britannia Coconut Dancers or, as they are often called, the Britannia Nutters, perform throughout the Saturday before Easter in the Lancashire town of Bacup. The eight men of the team carry mill bobbins and garlands of colorful rags. They dress in a ritual disguise of white hats, red and white decorated shirts, black breeches, long white socks, and clogs, and dance through the streets to the accompaniment of a brass band.

Since the sixteenth century traditional instruments that accompanied morris dancing have been the pipe and tabor (a small drum), which are played simultaneously by a single musician; but fiddles, melodeons, and concertinas are also popular nowadays.

Sword dances are a tradition of the northeast, having developed in all probability from the weapon dances of the ancient Romans, which in turn were once part of a pagan rite possibly even older than the forerunners of the morris dance. Sword dances used to be associated with sword plays, and though the plays as such have now disappeared the dances still contain an element of drama that is exemplified by the retention of characters such as Tommy (a king) and Betsy (a half-man, half-woman creature).

There are two distinct types of sword dance, the long sword (stiff), which is danced in Flamborough (Humberside), Grenoside and Handsworth (South Yorkshire), and Loftus, Skelton, and Guisborough (Cleveland); and the short or rapper sword (flexible), which is the specialty of the Royal Earsdon Sword Dancers at Earsdon near Newcastle-on-Tyne.

The steps consist of complex mixtures of walks, runs, and (in the rapper) fast "jigging with shuffles." Swords are linked to symbolize the unbroken ring of life, and periodically they are plaited together into a many-sided lock, which is then held up by the captain of the team for the approval of the crowd. The rapper sword dance has no counterpart elsewhere. It is a more athletic dance than the long sword dance, which might be said to resemble the style of "soldiers at the double."

Sword dances are performed between Boxing Day (the first weekday after Christmas) and Plough Monday (the first or second Monday in January), to the accompaniment of a single musician with pipe, accordion, or fiddle, by teams of five to eight men. Dancers wear either military-type uniforms or white shirts and stylish versions of miners' "long shorts" with colorful sashes and rosettes for decoration.

The 'Obby 'Oss Procession may be seen in two towns in the West Country: Padstow (Cornwall) and Minehead (Somerset). Both ceremonies are held in early May and involve men dressed as horses parading through the town with their attendants. Of the two, the Padstow 'Obby 'Oss ceremony on May 1 is the more celebrated. It starts at midnight the night before when selected "mayers" go round the town singing, and then early next morning they decorate the streets with festive greenery. The 'Oss emerges midmorning and dances through the streets for the rest of the day accompanied by the mayers, a teaser, and a memorable May Day tune, played on melodeons, accordions, and drums. Superstition plays an integral part in these dances, and the locals enter into the ceremonies with enthusiasm, convinced that the 'osses are lucky.

Each year, on the first Monday after the first Sunday after September 4, you can see the ancient Abbots Bromley (Staffordshire) horn dance. It is believed to have originally been a fertility ritual, but this is played down nowadays — the villagers prefer to associate it more with the traditions of the deer hunt. Six male dancers, dressed in Tudor costume, carry reindeer horns,

PERSPECTIVES / Traditional Music and Dance

and since three are clothed in white and three in black it is supposed that they symbolize good and evil. Four characters escort the dancers, the Fool, the Hobby Horse, the Maid Marian (a man-woman figure), and Robin Hood with his bow and arrow, and they all parade through the village streets entertaining the crowds with plenty of dancing and tomfoolery. The Horse ensures that the two musicians with melodeon and triangle are kept up to snuff by persistently and rhythmically clacking his jaws!

There is another form of dance tradition in England quite separate from these ritual ceremonial dances, the social or country dances. These are done purely for enjoyment, by men and women together, and even by children. They developed in the rural communities and, quite separately, in the ballrooms and drawing rooms of the aristocracy.

Among the most popular country dances were those which celebrated May Day. To this day people still enjoy the traditions that have developed from the old customs, such as dancing round the Maypole and choosing the May Queen. Oldest of all the surviving dances is the world-famous Helston furry dance, which is performed each year on or about May 8 in Helston (Cornwall) to celebrate the passing from darkness (winter) into light (spring). The dance, which is accompanied by the Helston Town Band, is processional and during the day there are three separate processions: for children, for formally dressed adults, and for anyone in the mood to make merry.

In the sixteenth century court dances were formal and dignified, but during the reign of Elizabeth I the courtiers were introduced to rustic dances, first as entertainment and then for participation; and almost inevitably the traditions began to mingle and lived on under the collective title of country dances.

These dances enjoyed their greatest popularity in the eighteenth century, after which they gradually went out of favor. In the early twentieth century they were revived by Cecil Sharp. With tireless enthusiasm he collected and chronicled hundreds of dances, tunes, and songs. He founded the English Folk Dance Society, which later became the English Folk Dance and Song Society and which rekindled interest everywhere. From this countless affiliated clubs have sprung, and nowadays you may be sure that every night somewhere in town or country there are informal dances or *ceilidhs* (evenings of traditional music, song, and dance).

If you come to England looking for folk dance and music you would do well to begin your search at Cecil Sharp House, home of the English Folk Dance and Song Society (2 Regents Park Rd., London NW1 7AY, phone: 485-2206). They welcome visitors and will let you browse in the library among the specialized books (predominantly British and American). There are also magazines, photographs, tapes, pamphlets advertising events and festivals, and a bookshop — and if you peep into the main hall you may even see some dancing! Overseas members currently pay an annual subscription of £5.85.

In Scotland there are no longer either ritual ceremonial dances or dance-dramas: The only traditional dances that survive come from the Highlands and undoubtedly most famous of all is the Highland fling.

The name comes from the flinging action made by the working foot as it moves sharply inward to the lower calf of the supporting leg. Though its origins probably lie in battle traditions it is an elegant dance. But there must be a "fire in the feet," and the dancer, his weight balanced on his toes, must make intricate cutting, beating, kicking, and flinging movements with enough verve and agility to astonish his audience.

Seann triubhs ("shabby trousers") is another favorite Highland dance. It is said that during the '45 Rebellion (the Jacobite uprising of 1745) men had to wear tartan trews (trousers) instead of kilts, and this dance is symbolic of that period and the attempts that were made to "shake off" the trousers. However much truth there is in that story, *seann triubhs* is an extremely graceful traveling dance that mixes cutting, beating, and kicking movements with pirouettes, balances, and attractive circlings of the arms.

There is only one hilt-and-point sword dance in Scotland that resembles the English tradition: the Papa Stour sword dance, still performed in the Shetland Island of Papa Stour. The Highland sword dance is performed between the angles made by two swords placed on the ground in the form of a cross, and though the dancer must show plenty of vigor he also has to be extremely delicate so as to avoid touching the swords with his feet as they beat, step, and jump.

Elaborate costumes are worn for these dances, consisting of kilt, velvet jacket (or shirt and tie), plaids (lengths of tartan placed over the shoulders), a sporran (animal-skin pouch) attached to a chain round the waist, and ghillies (soft flat black shoes). Women wear similar costumes, but without the sporran. Traditionally the most popular accompanying instrument is the bagpipe, though jew's-harp, fiddle, and melodeon are also common. The best place to see Highland dancing is at one of the many Highland Games that take place between mid-July and mid-September. The Games of Braemar and Dunoon are especially popular for dancing.

Just when country dances began to go out of vogue in England in the early nineteenth century they became immensely popular in Scotland, and have remained so to this day, although had it not been for the formation in 1923 of the Scottish Country Dance Society, less authenticity might have prevailed.

These dances are vivacious or graceful, and in the main they fall into three groups, strathspeys, reels, and jigs, with hundreds of variations of each. The men wear kilts and the women white dresses and tartan sashes. Originally the bagpipe was the most popular accompanying instrument, but it has now been superseded by the fiddle.

Scottish country dancing has a worldwide following these days, and many foreign visitors join the (now) Royal Scottish Country Dance Society's annual summer school at St. Andrews. There are performances and casual gatherings all over Scotland throughout the year as well as competitions, festivals, and displays at Highland Games. During the summer months, there is even dancing in the streets of Edinburgh. For more information contact Miss M. M. Gibson, the Royal Scottish Country Dance Society, 12 Coates Crescent, Edinburgh EH3 7AF (phone: 225-3854), and the Scottish Tourist Board, 23 Ravelston Terr., Edinburgh EH4 3EU (phone: 332-2433).

Surprisingly, since the Welsh are renowned for their musical traditions, there is less apparent love of dance, and little is known about the early folk dances. In the Middle Ages there were many popular dances including chains, rounds, reels, and morris dances, but with the establishment of the Chapel in Wales in the late eighteenth century these merrymakings were forced to a halt. The people were obliged to concentrate on religion, and consequently their musical talents became vested in their great choral tradition.

The instrument that dominates is the harp. Wales boasts the triple harp which, with its three rows of strings, is considered by some to be the finest harp in existence. Undoubtedly it lends itself to dancing, though the fiddle and flute are also popular. The only dance that has survived in an unbroken tradition is the clog and broom dance. It is vigorous, and quite tricky to perform: The dancer makes fast tapping steps around the broom as it lies on the ground, or he may pick it up and jump over it. Nowadays some of the best dancers delight in introducing inventive tricks into it.

It was not until 1949, with the formation of the Welsh Folk Dance Society, that attempts were made to salvage what was left of the dances. It also has made great efforts to ensure that authentic costumes survive, and these are usually quaint and charming: breeches, waistcoats, and shirts for men; and pretty blouses, long skirts with lace aprons, and caps, or the well-known, tall, flat-topped black hats for women.

You'll find plenty of dance displays at the International Musical Eisteddfod in July at Llangollen or the Royal National Eisteddfod of Wales (which alternates each August between North and South Wales), and the many smaller ones which crop up all over Wales during the summer. Information can be obtained from Mrs. Jean Huw Jones, Dolawenydd, Betws, Ammanford, Dyfed SA18 2HE (phone: 2837), and the Wales Tourist Board, 3 Castle St., Cardiff CF1 2RE (phone: 27281).

Food and Drink

The image most Americans have of British food is that of a massive roast beef, surrounded by plainly cooked vegetables, baked potatoes, and a little gravy. No elaborate sauces or violent flavors. Unfortunately, cost has driven the roast beef of old England into decline, but you can still sample its splendor in "carvery" rooms in the major London hotels, where huge joints of beef, pork, and lamb are featured. Many "medieval banquet" restaurants also serve meals styled to resemble feasts of the past — from the sixteenth century to Victorian times. These, however, aim more for drama than for authenticity, and the visitor must go elsewhere for genuine "Old English" dishes. In an effort to promote traditional foods and recipes, the British Tourist Board created the "Taste of England, Scotland, and Wales" distinction. You'll see this noted on many menus, and tourist board booklets list the establishments that serve traditional fare.

BREAKFAST: A SUBSTANTIAL MEAL

"Breakfast first, business later," declared British writer William Makepeace Thackeray. Standard breakfast fare includes grapefruit or juice, eggs, and bacon, with tomatoes, mushrooms, or sausages, followed by toast, marmalade, and tea or coffee.

Some country house hotels have preserved the Edwardian tradition of serving kidneys and kedgeree. (The latter, a fish and rice mixture flavored with curry, is particularly good for soaking up any excesses of the night before.) A mixed grill of lamb chops, sausages, liver, kidney, mushrooms, and tomatoes also may be served as a late breakfast dish, and potted and cold meats, brawn (a cold, pressed pig meat), and finnan haddock are also popular.

Regional sausages, such as Cumberland ring sausages, can still be found. And in Lancashire and Scotland, Suffolk, or black, pudding is famous. It's made with pig's blood and served sliced with grilled bacon and eggs. Potato cakes, crisply fried, are served in some places, and in Wales and north Cornwall, a seaweed called "laverbread" is fried with the bacon.

Is it any wonder that novelist Somerset Maugham once commented that to eat well in Britain, one should eat breakfast three times a day?

TEA: A BRITISH TRADITION

"Everything stops for tea" is an English saying, and rare is the worker who can get through his day without tea breaks. The afternoon tea meal was started in about 1780 by the duchess of Bedford as a gossipy way of filling in the time between early lunch and late dinner. A whole industry of teacups, special china, cake stands, embroidered cloths, linen, and tea forks for the cakes grew up, and a ritual evolved around a silver teapot and sugar bowl with little tongs.

This graciousness has disappeared in today's hurried times. Visitors, however, can still test out Rupert Brooke's lines "Stands the church clock at ten to three?/And is there honey still for tea?" Honey or country preserves, particularly strawberry jam, go with scones, which are rather like the American biscuit. Other cakes include Victoria sponge rock and fairy (iced) cakes, Battenburg, and Madeira. In Scotland, teas are substantial, and they include fruitcakes like Dundee and tea breads, which are halfway between cakes and breads in consistency. In Wales, bacon, fish, pancakes, and *bara brith* ("speckled bread") are eaten.

In Devon and Cornwall, tea is served with thick, clotted cream, and regional cakes follow sandwiches and scones. "Tea" also refers to the early evening meal in the north, and in country districts (especially in Shropshire) one may still find signs for "farm teas." These are often quite substantial — including salads, ham, or fish. The "strawberry tea" is a happy summer event during the Wimbledon tennis fortnight and the Henley regatta: A bowl of fresh strawberries and cream is served with tea.

In the smaller villages and towns, there used to be many shops where local ladies served tea and homemade cakes; this was considered a respectable occupation for "spinsters" ever since a Miss Cranston set up the country's first tearoom in Glasgow's Sauchiehall Street in 1904. These days, teashops come and go, and some consider tea to be an endangered meal.

Nevertheless, the afternoon tea ritual is still maintained in its glory by hotels like the *Lygon Arms* in Broadway, which serves crumpets and tea cakes in winter. And tea at the *Ritz* in London is the tops: Here monogrammed Irish linen covers the high little round tables (the stiffly corseted Edwardian ladies sat higher than today's women) and thin cucumber, cress, or smoked salmon sandwiches and delicate pastries are served. A choice of Indian and China teas is traditional. (For a more extensive selection of teashops and tea gardens see DIVERSIONS.)

THE MAIN COURSE

As we have said, Britain is famous for its good roast meats, such as chicken, turkey, and duckling, as well as game in season — pheasant, grouse, quail, partridge, venison, and hare. However, there are many outstanding meat dishes besides the traditional roast, including meat pies, puddings, and stews.

In the little Cotswold village of Broadway, the butcher shop called *Collins* still practices the old art of making raised pies. Typically, the pies have carefully molded, high sides and are filled with game from local shoots. So special are *Collins*'s pies that *Harrods* and *Fortnum and Mason* keep specially monogrammed pie molds there.

Perhaps more familiar to most Americans is the steak and kidney pie, which when served in London sometimes also contains mushrooms or oysters. More economical recipes use cheaper cuts of meat. For example, Lancashire hot pot utilizes the neck end of lamb, and tripe and onions is a northern favorite. On the banks of the Mersey River the word *scouse* may be heard more than seen on a menu. It is a diminutive for *lobscouse,* a lamb, beef, and vegetable stew and is such a favorite with Liverpudlians that they are nicknamed Scouses. And Robert Burns called the Scottish favorite, haggis, the "chieftain o' the puddin race." It is a dish made of the innards of a sheep, minced with suet and oatmeal, and it's traditionally served with "tatties and neeps," or potatoes and turnips. Haggis is now often offered on hotel menus as an appetizer.

In the Midlands, where ham and bacon are especially loved, little pieces of bacon turn up in boiled, hot, gray peas. Pork crackling is rendered down to make "scratchings" and is often sold in pubs in packets and eaten like potato chips. The great hams of the country are in York, where they are cured by dry salting. York hams are said to have derived their original flavor from smoking in the oak sawdust of timbers used in the building of York's cathedral. Bradenham ham, made since 1781, is dry-cured, pickled in molasses for a month, and matured for 3 months thereafter. Suffolk Seager ham is rounded with a dark brown finish. It is cured in brine, black treacle, and molasses and then it is smoked.

The Dunmow flitch is a side of bacon traditionally presented every 3 years to the most harmoniously married couple in this Essex town. You may also come across the bacon "clanger," a pastry roll of bacon, onion, and herbs that originated in Oxfordshire. Sometimes it has a sweet filling at one end and is savory at the other, so that a worker in the fields could take his whole meal in one neat pack.

Practicality mixed with poverty was the origin of the Cornish pasty that was made for the tin miner (many of whom immigrated to Colorado, where pasties are still served at the miners' festival). Triangular in shape, so it can slip into a pocket, the pasty contained potato, vegetables, and whatever scraps of meat were available. It was said that the pasty was hard enough to withstand a fall down the mine shaft.

And now a word about the trimmings: *Tracklement* is the lovely old English word for a condiment to go with meat. Cumberland sauce with ham or pâté is one old delight, red currant jelly goes with lamb, and there are many chutneys. Mustard is the major meat accompaniment, declared by George I to be his favorite. *Colman's* mustard shop in Bridewell Lane, Norwich, is a replica of a nineteenth-century grocer's shop and sells many blends. Other English mustards include *Taylors,* English vineyard mustards, and whole grain mustards by *Evelyn and Crabtree.* Horseradish cream — they say the best horseradish root comes from country graveyards — is a pungent root that is grated, mixed with cream, and served with roast beef.

Because it's an island, Britain has a plentiful supply of fish and seafood. Cod is king and it is usually served up as the ubiquitous fish fingers. Turbot is served with hollandaise sauce, and Dover sole and mackerel traditionally served with gooseberry sauce. Herrings, pilchards (which are popular tinned in oil for teas), bloaters from Yarmouth, and sprats are traditional fish. Salmon is the luxury fish, caught in Scotland and in bigger English rivers like the Wye. In summer it is served poached hot with hollandaise sauce or cold with mayonnaise and cucumber. Smoked salmon is a glory that is principally found in Scotland, and smoked mackerel and trout are served as appetizers with horseradish sauce.

Oysters from East Anglia and Cornwall, shrimp from Lancashire's Morecambe Bay, lobsters, mussels, and Dublin Bay prawns are all popular, if expensive. Londoners like small shellfish such as whelks or cockles; these are skewered on a pin and sold from stalls in the East End. They also enjoy eels, jellied or made into pies with a green parsley sauce. Whitebait may open a meal, and on the Severn River in spring, elvers (baby eels) are eaten in competitions to see who can consume the most.

Fish and chips, the age-old British favorite, can be enjoyed in impressive, chandelier-hung surroundings at *Harry Ramsden's* in Guisley, Yorkshire. Other recommended places for a fish-and-chip pilgrimage are the *Gainsboro* at Hull, *Bryan's* fish restaurant at Headingly, and *Mother Hubbard's* at Girlington near Bradford.

Eleanor Roosevelt once remarked, "The English have ten green vegetables and eight of them are brussels sprouts." Although vegetables are often a weak spot on the British menu, there are some exceptions. Spring is heralded by the arrival of little new potatoes cooked with a sprig of mint and served with melted butter. Cold mashed potatoes and leftover cabbage are often mixed together and fried for breakfast or for light family meals. In England this is known as "bubble and squeak" and in Scotland as "rumbledethumps" — because of the elbow grease that goes into beating it. And "pan haggerty" — thinly sliced potatoes, onions, and grated cheese — is pan fried in Northumbria. Early in the summer there is samphire, a marsh plant that is eaten like asparagus in East Anglia. Asparagus itself is ready in June and is expensive, but like strawberries and salmon, it's a sign of the British summer.

DESSERTS

A "good pud" is a threat to dieters, but traditional puddings live on in Britain, aided by memories of the nostalgic treats of childhood. Before North Sea oil and central heating, Britons kept warm with a whole repertoire of suet puddings: Kentwell pudding, in which a lemon and butter and sugar were encased in suet pastry; spotted dicks, suet with dried fruit; or castle, treacle, mattress, and cabinet puddings. Bread and butter pudding cooked with dried fruit and milk was another favorite, and Christmas pudding served after the turkey is probably the richest of all: It's dark with fruit and alcohol and it is served with custard, rum, or brandy butters.

Not all puddings are heavy. Syllabub was made originally by pouring fresh cow's milk from a height onto lemon and wine mixtures. Junkets are a light, creamy affair made in the West Country: indeed, visits to the dairy to eat this became so popular that the word *junket* is now synonymous with a party outing. Another confection was a puree of rhubarb and gooseberries mixed with thick cream. And trifle is a year-round favorite — it's sponge cake, soaked in sherry, layered with raspberry jam or fruit, and topped with custard and cream.

A most famous pudding — which can also be eaten cold with jam for dessert — is the Yorkshire pudding usually served with roast beef. Yorkshire women claim only they can make it properly, though a local competition to find the champion pudding maker was won by a Chinese chef.

But puddings are by no means the only dessert specialties to be found in Britain. Many baked products can be sampled and bought from the weekly Women's Institute markets (a list is available from the National Federation of Women's Institutes, 39 Eccleston St., London SW1W 9NT). These small, friendly regional markets are a good way to meet local people.

Gingerbread, a specialty of the Lake District, is made daily in *Sarah Nelson's* shop in Grasmere. In this area, gingerbread alphabets were once used to teach children to read. Shortbread is Scotland's favorite, while in Richmond, Surrey, "maids of honour tarts," named for Anne Boleyn's ladies, are still sold. The *Old Bakewell Pudding* shop in Bakewell, Derbyshire, sells tarts with almonds and raspberry jam. Yorkshire's parkin, based on oatmeal, treacle, and ginger, is made traditionally on November 5, Bonfire Night. Also in Yorkshire, apple pie is a favorite dish customarily eaten with a slice of cheese. The locals are fond of the rhyme: "Apple pie without a slice of cheese is like a kiss without a squeeze."

As for fruit, Scottish raspberries from Speyside are excellent in flavor. Outstanding among the late summer fruits in Britain are apples, pears, and plums, particularly damsons and greengages. Britons often mix soft fruits with black and red currants to make a "summer pudding;" the fruit is puréed and put in a crust made of dried bread.

BREADS AND CHEESES

Among British breads are bloomers, baps (soft Scottish breakfast rolls), coburgs, cobs, pistols (round-shaped loaves), and cottage loaves (two rounds on top of each other). Biscuits (cookies and crackers) include Dorset knobs — dried, rusklike tidbits that go with cheese — and Bath Olivers — thin water biscuits invented in the eighteenth century for dieters by Dr. Oliver, Bath's first spa physician.

England has nine national cheeses, of which Stilton is king. A veined blue cheese from Leicestershire, it is traditionally served with port. Cheshire cheese, which comes in patriotic red, white, and blue versions, was much loved by Samuel Johnson; his favorite Fleet Street pub in London is named *The Cheshire*. Lancashire cheese spreads and toasts well. Derby is the rarest, and sage Derby, veined with the herb, was originally made for Christmas. Caerphilly was once made in Wales, and now it's made in Somerset. Easily digestible, Caerphilly was the chosen snack of coal miners cramped at the pit face. Cheddar from the Mendip Hills goes well in a fruit pie pastry.

"New" cheeses are brought out regularly. These include red Windsor, veined with red wine; Cotswolds, a double Gloucester with onions and chives; Walton, a blend of Cheddar and Stilton; Ilchester, a cheddar mixed with beer, spices, and chives; and Labra, the first ewe's milk cheese to be made since the Middle Ages.

In certain areas, you can visit farms to see cheeses being made. In Scotland many national cheeses are made in Orkney, including Dunlop, Caboc (rolled in oats), and Castle Stuart blue cheeses.

A NOTE ON BEVERAGES

The pub or "local" is a Briton's home away from home; it's an informal place to talk and drink. Most British beer is warm and heavy, so often the lagers served chilled are more to the visitors' taste. Local breweries persist and such brews as Adnams of Southwold with their Fishermen's ale, Doddington, Theakstons, Ruddles, Toby Cobbold of Ipswich, and Greene King of Bury St. Edmunds are served mainly in their regions. "Real ale" bars are springing up around the country these days — even at some railway stations. A few unusual pub drinks are black beer from Leeds, which is made from malt and cane sugar mixed with rum, whisky, or lemonade; shrub, which was used as a West Country mix to sweeten sea-tainted rum in the old smuggling days; and lovage, an herbal pick-me-up that is also from the West Country.

Cider is a traditional drink from the West Country and Hereford. It's based on fermented apples and is sold fresh. (The sweetness varies.) Some leading cider producers own pubs that specialize in cider. In the West Country, some pubs sell "scrumpy," the raw farm-brewed cider that has a deceptive ox-felling power; so much so, that the police are not eager that it be sold to tourists. Mead is a honeysweet drink dating from before Christian times. It is still made in Cornwall and on the island of Lindisfarne, where the factory is open to the public.

Although Britain has always been thought of as a beer-drinking country, wine is rapidly becoming popular as well. Today you can find wine lists that offer selections from California to Australia, and from Chile to Charente. In addition, Britain is reviving its native vineyards, which declined during the Middle Ages, when most of France — and French wine — was under the control of the English crown. The English Vineyards Association numbers over 400 growers, who produce 180,000 bottles per year. Among the best-known names are Hambledon and Pilton Manor in Somerset, both of which have days when they are open for visitors. Adgestone from the Isle of Wight is one of the most prized wines, and Beaulieu comes from Lord Montagu's estate in Hampshire. Merrydown in Sussex also produces English country wines made from elderberries, red currants, and apples.

And though pubs advertise Harvey Wallbangers and other cocktails, the more conservative Briton will have a sherry before a formal meal and a glass of port (known as the "Englishman's drink") afterward. On hot summer days, many find a gin and tonic cooling, and a whisky and soda is good any time. But even though gin, vodka, and other spirits are made in Britain, Scotch is the most popular — more than 200 brands are produced and consumed. So much Scotch is sold that they say the duty on its sale pays for the nation's defense budget! (For a more complete discussion of beers, ales, and liquors, as well as the selection of the best watering holes in Britain, see *Pub Crawling,* DIVERSIONS.)

Ireland

History

Imagine that you are standing on a windswept headland, a country of lush green glens behind you, the tumultuous sea at your feet. A beautiful girl approaches you, an orphan, she says, but of noble lineage, who tells you a tale so full of romance and heroism and piety and cruelty and *Sturm und Drang* that you cannot decide whether to laugh or cry but find yourself listening enraptured to her compelling voice.

This is Ireland, and the Irish themselves are inclined to surrender to her charms. For centuries, they have been compounding a political and social mythology out of songs, legends, and history, and the heroes of that mythology — Finn MacCool, Brian Ború, Patrick Sarsfield, Wolfe Tone, Daniel O'Connell, and Charles Parnell — remain the controlling models for modern Ireland's political and social behavior. When Patrick Pearse, a leader of the 1916 Easter Rebellion, invoked the Ulster hero Cu Chulainn while British troops beseiged his little band in the Dublin General Post Office, he rallied his men with an image from the nation's antiquity. The revival of the Irish language, a cornerstone of government policy, affirms the continuity of the Irish Republic with its remotest antecedents. No other nation in Europe requires an understanding of its most distant past to complete an understanding of its present.

THE CELTS

The Celts were a family of Indo-European warrior aristocracies related by language, religion, mastery of horsemanship, and a flammable temperament that kept them always at each other's throats. From their arrival in Ireland between 500 and 50 BC, the Celtic clans warred ceaselessly among themselves for territory, tribute, and cattle. Sensitive and superstitious, they were terrorized by their priests (druids) and master-poets (*filidhe;* pronounced fee-lee), whose curses carried weight with the gods and in whose memories reposed the only record of tribal histories, genealogies, and myth. These learned, almost Brahmanic castes maintained their own training academies and provided the only source of social unity among the various tribes.

The family was the fundamental Celtic social unit from which all rights and authority flowed. Tribal alliances were matters of military convenience rather than treaty, and not until the fifth century AD did the Irish establish the semblance of a central power. Even then, the High King, ruling from the Hill of Tara, drew his authority not from law but from the tacit consensus of the legislative assemblies of tribal chieftains and nobles. The O'Neill High Kings, whose dynasty endured until the eleventh century, invoked a national spirit by convening the first such assembly — though each tribe had previously conducted its own and continued to do so. The O'Neills also raised a standing army (the Fianna), but even after the Ulaid of Ulster — last of the Celtic tribes to resist Gaelic dominance — were subdued in 851, their control of Ireland remained tenuous.

Gaelic civilization flourished unconsumed by the Roman Empire in what W. B. Yeats would call "the Celtic Twilight." Its decentralized social structure evolved without interference, and when, in the fifth century, Christianity was introduced by St. Patrick, the new church adapted itself at once to this design. Abbeys and monasteries patronized by local chieftains and entirely independent of diocesan authority became the seats of church power; out of touch with Rome, the Irish clung to old doctrines long after they had been abandoned or revised elsewhere in Christendom. Yet, the monasteries nourished a lively intellectual life; graduates of the poetic academies, attracted by the ascetic ethos, flocked to the monasteries and abbeys, learned to write, and created the stunningly illuminated manuscripts in which the oral literature of the nation was first written down. By decree of Columcille (St. Columba), a Gaelic prince, poet, and founder of the first native order, lay poets were officially employed in every royal court after 575. The literary arts thus enjoyed the patronage of both church and state.

When the barbarians inundated Europe in the fifth century, Christian learning crawled to high ground in Ireland. As the deluge subsided, Irish missionaries ventured over the European continent, founding monasteries, restoring literacy, and resuscitating the faith amid the ruins of Hellenic civilization. John Scotus Erigena (which means "Irish-born") and his contemporary, Sedulius Scotus, taught in the palace schools founded by Charlemagne and the monasteries of Ireland received students from abroad; but while this lively traffic earned Ireland the epithet "Isle of Saints and Scholars," it turned Rome's efforts to reforming the doctrinally wayward church and bringing it under central control.

In 795, Ostmen, the predatory Vikings, commenced their raids along the Irish coast, leveling monasteries and torching whole libraries. These Norse pirates built a string of garrisons along the eastern coast, proclaiming themselves kings and establishing Ireland's first cities and ports. The fractious Gaels were helpless to dislodge these ferocious and well-organized intruders. Late in the tenth century, an obscure chieftain from Clare, Brian Ború, overthrew the Danish king of Limerick and, by three usurpations, dispossessed the O'Neills and declared himself High King of Ireland. For a few short years, Brian united the tribes of Ireland behind his leadership; he routed the Danes from their chief stronghold, Dublin, at the Battle of Clontarf in 1014. Brian, alas, lost his life in the battle, and the Irish relapsed into squabbling over succession to the Tara monarchy.

THE NORMAN INVASION

Though their dominance had been broken, the Norsemen remained in Ireland as sailors and merchants, intermarrying with the Gaels and assimilating the native culture. In 1166 they joined with the chiefs of Leinster to overthrow their king, Dermot MacMurrough, who fled to England where he formed an alliance with some Norman adventurers whom he hoped would restore him to his realm. In 1169, these mail-clad buccaneers landed on the Baginburn headland in Waterford, and in 2 years had seized Leinster for their leader, Richard Fitz-Gilbert de Clare, known as "Strongbow." MacMurrough died soon after. Before these brilliant, methodical soldiers the Irish had no defense. In 1171 Strongbow and the rest of the Normans resentfully acknowledged themselves subjects of Henry II, and the High King Rory O'Connor recognized Henry as his sovereign in return for control over all unconquered areas. Ireland had become the property of the English crown.

The Normans marked their holdings with a line called the "Pale," a thin strip of land on the eastern coast. But as Norman and Gael intermarried, the former became, as the saying goes, more "Irish than the Irish themselves." (The Irish referred to the Normans as "Old Foreigners," while the English called those who had gone native "degenerate English.") By 1261, the Gaels had adopted Norman military techniques, putting an end to their conquests, while the Normans had taken up the Gaelic language and culture, maintaining poets and commissioning manuscripts like any native chieftain.

The rapprochement displeased the English. In 1297, to consolidate the colony and muster troops from it for his Scottish wars, Edward I convened an Irish Parliament at Kilkenny, which was hostile to the Gaels and assimilated Normans. By 1366, the Parliament had promulgated statutes to separate the "races," but these were largely ignored by a very mixed population. The Normans had built cities, introduced English common law, and mingled names like Bourke, Butler, and Carey with O'Brien, O'Neill, and O'Donnell. Culturally distinct from England and uncomfortable as colonials, the Normans declared parliamentary independence in 1460.

THE PLANTATION

The Reformation and the Tudor monarchy put an end to their adventure. In 1541, Henry VIII compelled the Irish Parliament to recall his sovereignty. He then asserted his authority to govern the Irish church, as he had already done in England, and imposed the "plantation" policy, under which native Irish and some "degenerate English" landholdings were seized and regranted to loyal English fortune seekers. Resistance to the policy centered in Ulster, where the chieftains Red Hugh O'Donnell and Hugh O'Neill, setting aside old rivalries, formed the Tyrone Confederation and, in the first of Ireland's revolutions, rose against Henry's "new earls" (as those who literally bought titles and rights to the land were called). Promises of Spanish assistance were obtained, and from 1594 to 1603 the Tyrone Confederation rebelled with some success against the English. In 1601, a Spanish fleet sailed into Kinsale on the southern coast, and the English Lord Mountjoy turned to attack them, whereupon O'Donnell and O'Neill swept down from the north to besiege the besiegers. The Spanish pressed for a decisive engagement; O'Neill argued for attrition, but O'Donnell forced the issue. The Battle of Kinsale was fought on Christmas Eve, 1601, and the Hispano-Gaelic alliance, insufficiently prepared, went down in defeat. The defeated earls, O'Donnell and O'Neill, were permitted to return to Ulster; but after a few years of suffering English rule, they sailed in self-imposed exile to the Continent in 1607, an event often called the "Flight of the Earls."

The plantation policy went forward apace. In Ulster, barely one tenth of the land was retained by its native inhabitants; the rest was planted with Presbyterian colonists from Scotland, dissenters in their own country. In 1641, Norman soldiers, unemployed and wandering the countryside, enlisted with the Irish chiefs of Ulster in another uprising. The Irish Parliament, now sitting at Dublin, expelled its Catholic members, who gathered at Kilkenny to proclaim a provisional government.

Presiding over this revolution was Owen Roe O'Neill; nephew of Hugh and a statesman of some sophistication, he envisioned for Ireland a centralized and autonomous native government. After Owen Roe's victory over parliamentary forces at Benburb in 1646, Charles I, facing Cromwell's insurgence at home, offered a treaty that would have reversed the plantation policy; but the Catholic clergy, holding out for emancipation from the Protestant crown, persuaded Owen Roe to reject it. After deposing the king in 1649, Cromwell turned to the reconquest of Ireland, and in September stormed the town of Drogheda, slaughtering 3,500 inhabitants in reprisal for earlier revolutionary terrorism. Owen Roe's death in November signaled the collapse of the resistance. Limerick and Galway capitulated in 1652, and 30,000 Irish soldiers followed their chiefs into exile in what the Irish remember as "the Flight of the Wild Geese."

The Cromwellian Act of Settlement in 1652 extended the plantation policy; Irish lands were seized and distributed among demobilized English soldiers and the financiers of the reconquest. The Catholic Church was outlawed and its properties confiscated. Towns were seeded with English burgesses and native merchants were relocated to the perimeters. The common people were reduced to virtual slavery as tenants on lands immemorially theirs. By 1655, what remained of the Gaelic nation languished among the stony acres west of the Shannon. By 1688, Protestants, though they comprised a tiny minority of its population, owned 78% of all the land in Ireland.

STUART vs. ORANGE

With the ascension of James II, a Catholic, in 1685, England's policies in Ireland were somewhat liberalized. But James was deposed in 1688 and fled to France. In 1689 he moved to Ireland, where he hoped to establish, in this Catholic nation, a base from which to recover his throne. Catholic France rallied to the Jacobites (as his followers were called) and sent a fleet to Kinsale in 1689. But Protestant Europe as determinedly supported William of Orange, James's Protestant successor. Things came to a head on July 1, 1690, when a mixed army of Danes, Germans, French Huguenots, and English overwhelmed the Jacobites at the Battle of the Boyne. The Irish army, under Patrick Sarsfield, fell back and retrenched beyond the Shannon. They then sallied forth to meet the Protestants at the Battle of Aughrim, and, when defeated again, Sarsfield gathered the remains of his army behind the walls of Limerick and indomitably withstood two lengthy English sieges before finally obtaining favorable terms of surrender, which London was largely to ignore. Sarsfield and his men, like the earls some 40 years before them, fled in exile to France. (Sarsfield joined the French army and died in battle in 1693, crying: "Oh, that this were for Ireland.")

ROBERT EMMET, WOLFE TONE—IRISH PROTESTANT PATRIOTISM

The hope of Irish freedom dashed, England imposed the Penal Codes in 1695, the apartheid statutes by which Catholics were denied nearly all rights at law and reduced to serfdom. (In the words of one Lord Chancellor: "The law does not take into account the existence of such a person as an Irish Roman Catholic.") Yet while the Penal Codes ensured the privileges of the Ascendancy, they also effectively tied most of the Protestant gentry — but not the Protestant magnates — to the land, while tariffs restricted the economy. Furthermore, although the Dublin Parliament was supposedly autonomous in most areas, in fact it merely rubber-stamped the acts of Westminster. All Catholics and many Protestants chafed under the English yoke. In 1791 the Protestant patriot Wolfe Tone founded the United Irishmen, which — inspired by the French revolution — attempted to bring together Catholics and Protestants in common cause against the English government. The movement gained strength quickly in Ireland, but was suppressed in 1794. Wolfe Tone fled to Paris to raise an army of liberation, and, in 1798, Ireland's third revolution broke out in Wexford. Tone and a French fleet hurried to its aid, but the ragtag rebels, led by two priests, John Murphy and Michael Murphy, were crushed at Vinegar Hill (Waterford) before the fleet could arrive. The French, surrounded at Castlebar (County Mayo), surrendered, and Tone, denied an honorable execution before a firing squad and condemned instead to the gallows, slit his throat. In 1801, the Act of Union abolished the Irish Parliament and absorbed Ireland into a United Kingdom. Revolution erupted for the fourth time in 1803, led this time by Robert Emmet, but it collapsed in confusion on the brink of success, and Emmet, whose stirring speech from the scaffold embedded itself in the Irish memory, was hanged.

CATHOLIC EMANCIPATION

In 1793, a Catholic Relief Bill had ostensibly restored all Catholic rights except that of holding elective office, an omission that rendered the rest meaningless. In 1823, Daniel O'Connell, the brilliant Kerry lawyer and orator, organized the Catholic Association which, by tithing its members a penny a month, became an organ of legal defense and agitation and the underground government of the Gaelic nation. O'Connell was a peerless organizer, and when defiant voters in Clare elected him to Westminster in 1828, the orchestrated mass movement behind him so intimidated England that he was seated, accomplishing full Catholic emancipation in a stroke.

In 1830, leading a substantial Irish voting bloc in Parliament, O'Connell embarked on a campaign to repeal the Union. Committed to reform within the constitution, activism within the law, and loyalty to the crown, O'Connell threw his party's support behind the Whigs, counting on their backing the repeal movement if they displaced the Tories. But Prime Minister Melbourne's Whig government, once elected, reneged, supported by a Protestant Ascendancy determined to protect its property and power under the Union by force if necessary. The Irish masses stood ready to take up arms at the first word from O'Connell; the Young Ireland party, led by journalist Charles Gavin Duffy and poet Thomas Davis, urged O'Connell to abandon his pacifist principles and lead them in revolution. O'Connell had no such intention. Instead, in 1842–43, he organized and addressed a series of "monster meetings" — rallies in support of repeal; at the one held at Tara, nearly a million people assembled peacefully to hear him speak in the open air. The meetings were perfectly legal, but the English government — mindful of O'Connell's tremendous influence — sent troops to surround the meeting held at Clontarf and threatened violence if the crowd did not disperse. Though he was within his rights, and though the assembly could probably have overwhelmed the soldiers, O'Connell canceled the meeting. The next year, he and Duffy were arrested and convicted of sedition. Though the House of Lords later reversed the verdict, O'Connell emerged from 2 months in prison largely stripped of his influence. He split with Young Ireland in 1846; momentum passed to its leaders, and he died in 1847.

THE IRISH FAMINE

In that year, the potato, staple of the common people, succumbed to blight for the second time and the Great Famine descended over Ireland. It was a catastrophe beyond description; starvation, dysentery, and cholera decimated the population, and thousands fled to America. Ireland lost about 2 million people between 1845 and 1855, yet Britain stuck to its free trade philosophy and intervened as little as possible on the theory that private enterprise would eventually sort things out. Relief aid actually decreased as the famine worsened. Yet, throughout this Irish holocaust, food was exported from Ireland to pay rents to absentee landlords in England. Great estates went bankrupt and passed into the hands of profiteers who thought nothing of evicting their destitute and starving tenants.

In 1848, under the leadership of William Smith O'Brien and spurred by the writings of John Mitchel (who had been deported to Australia for publishing the seditious journal *United Irishman*), what remained of Young Ireland staged and bungled an armed insurrection. Its participants followed Mitchel to Australia. For almost a decade, the nationalist movement lay dormant and the Irish language and economy languished through neglect. Industrialization was financed by London only in Ulster, which attached itself commercially to the industrial northwest of England, alienating itself still further from the rest of Ireland, where there were virtually no manufacturers. Circumstances were preparing Ulster for separation.

HOME RULE

After the collapse of the repeal movement, the nationalists regrouped behind the Home Rule proposal, which would have restored at least a measure of autonomy to the Irish nation. After 1875, the leader of the Home Rule party at Westminster was Charles Stewart Parnell, an Irish Protestant and charismatic leader who implemented the policy of "obstruction," or withholding his considerable political support to gain concessions for Ireland. Parnell's tactical brilliance secured the admiration and cooperation of William Gladstone, the Liberal Prime Minister; despite their efforts, however, the Home Rule Bill was twice defeated in Parliament. Shortly thereafter, Parnell suffered a serious blow to his reputation: Two British civil servants were murdered in Dublin's Phoenix Park, and *The Times* published a forged letter allegedly from Parnell condoning the killings. Then, in 1888, a divorce proceeding revealed Parnell's liaison with a colleague's wife; he was condemned by Protestant England and Catholic Ireland, his followers dropped away, and he died in disgrace 3 years later at 45.

Nationalist leadership passed to the Sinn Féin (Ourselves Alone), a party founded in 1902 by Arthur Griffith, who favored an independent Irish Parliament. Despite the resistance of Ulster's Orangemen, a society formed to protect the privileges and liberties of Protestants, and the organization of the paramilitary Ulster Volunteers, a Home Rule Bill was finally enacted in 1914. But the Orange militants had succeeded in amending the bill to give Ulster's six counties, with their Protestant majority, the option of seceding from Ireland and remaining in the Union. The outbreak of World War I fatally delayed implementation of the bill, and Ireland, on the eve of its independence, stood divided against itself.

EASTER RISING

The Easter Rebels of 1916 looked to England's enemy, the Germans, for aid as Hugh O'Neill had looked to the Spanish and Tone to the French. Organized as the Irish Volunteers, their emissary to Berlin, Roger Casement, was captured by the British while returning to warn that German support would not be forthcoming. (Casement was convicted before a military court and hanged.) This was on Good Friday, 1916. The Volunteers canceled what was to have been a national insurgence, but the Dublin contingent, hopeless of success, rose to martyrdom on Easter Monday. The 1,200 Volunteers seized strategic buildings around the city; on the steps of the General Post Office, leader Patrick Pearse read the proclamation of an Irish Republic. British troops, ordered to dislodge the rebels, left central Dublin in ruins. Seventeen rebel leaders — including Pearse, Thomas McDonough, John McBride, Joseph Plunkett, and James Connolly — died before a firing squad. Public outrage at the executions persuaded the British to commute the sentences of William Cosgrave, later president of the Free State, and Eamon de Valera, later president of the provisional government of the republic.

The martyrs, none of them important figures before death, became national heroes afterward. In the elections of 1919, Sinn Féin scored a landslide victory in parliamentary elections, but the deputies refused to take their seats, convening instead the Dáil Éireann (Assembly of Ireland) under de Valera's presidency and proclaiming the Republic once again. England implemented Home Rule, exempting from it the six counties of Ulster, but the Dáil would accept nothing short of total independence. Ireland burst into violence: The IRA under Sinn Féin leader Michael Collins waged a bloody guerrilla war with the Black and Tans, England's paramilitary police force to whom countless atrocities were attributed; British police fired on the crowds at a sporting event in Dublin's Croke Park; army barracks came under regular attack. The ordinary functions of government dissolved in subversion. In 1921, Griffith and Collins negotiated a treaty with Britain by which a new state, Saorstát Éireann (Irish Free State) was created as a Dominion in the Commonwealth and under the crown. The Dáil accepted the treaty, but de Valera rejected it and was repudiated by the Dáil. Griffith became the Free State's first president, and Collins, fearing a civil war, made overtures to de Valera, assuring him privately there would be no oath of allegiance to the crown in a new Irish constitution. But de Valera remained adamant and organized an "underground Republic" with himself as president, Sinn Féin as its party, and the IRA as its militia; it would acknowledge neither the crown nor the partition of Ireland.

IRISH FREE STATE

In 1922, incensed by a Free State constitution that embodied the terms of the treaty, IRA troops occupied the Four Courts, the building in Dublin that houses the superior courts of Ireland. Under enormous pressure from Britain, the Free State moved in troops and gunboats, and a few days later commenced a series of raids on Republican headquarters in Dublin hotels. Republicans and Free Staters were at war. Political unity once again escaped the Irish, and the country quaked with assassinations and skirmishes. Griffith died in August and Collins a few days later in an ambush near Cork. In 1923, de Valera declared a cease-fire. He agreed to enter the Dáil in 1927, whereupon Sinn Féin drew away from him to the leftist frontier of Republican intransigence. De Valera founded a new party, Fianna Fáil, whose members he urged to take the oath of allegiance to the crown as he had done — with "mental reservations." Fianna Fáil acquired a majority in 1932 and a new government, headed by De Valera, was formed. A new constitution was promulgated in 1937, declaring the nation the Republic of Eire and abolishing the oath. In 1949, Eire withdrew from the Commonwealth; at the same time, Britain, to establish a legal basis for partition, referred the question to the heavily Protestant Ulster Parliament at Stormont, which put the issue of Union before a popular referendum whose outcome was never in doubt.

PARTITION

Since then, the industrialized cities of Northern Ireland — Belfast and Derry — and many of the larger towns have divided into sectarian camps. In the

1960s, a Catholic civil rights movement agitated for Catholic representation at Stormont in proportion to the Catholic population, which brought a violent response from the Protestants, to whom the cause seemed synonymous with reunification with the Republic. The IRA, now an extra-legal militia outlawed even in the Republic, came to the defense of the Catholic camp. Confronted by virtual civil war which Stormont was powerless to stop since it represented only one side, Britain suspended the Northern Ireland legislature in 1972. Stepping between the warring factions, the British army became a target of IRA hostility, along with the paramilitary Ulster Defense Force. But now, bound by the legal precedent of the 1949 referendum, Britain has no way of withdrawing from Ulster without a majority mandate, and Ulster has no way of forming a government to which both sides can consent and thereby impose law and order without British intervention.

Ulster-Protestants are proud of their heritage and fearful of losing not only property but some of their rights and liberties as British subjects under the Irish Republican constitution, which embodies the moral doctrines of the Catholic Church. Efforts within the Republic to conciliate Ulster by expunging from the constitution clauses — such as that against divorce — offensive to Protestants have proven futile. Further, Ireland's economy is weak and agricultural, plagued by unemployment and inadequate social services; while Northern Ireland is industrial and shares the benefits of the British welfare system. The Republicans, however, have never acknowledged Britain's authority over any portion of Ireland, and regard partition as an act of gerrymandering by an illegitimate power. The intransigence of both sides makes reconciliation seem unlikely.

Literature

In Ireland, the magic of language has from the earliest times conferred a special and exalted status on those who command it. The poets of ancient Ireland had a reputation for supernatural powers and may have belonged to a caste that practiced sorcery. Even in the modern era, men of letters have been accorded high political honors unheard of in other countries. Douglas Hyde (1860–1949), one of those responsible for the revival of the Irish language and literature through the founding of the Gaelic League in 1893, became president of the Republic in 1938, and the poet and Nobel laureate W. B. Yeats (1865–1939) served as a senator from 1922 to 1928. In addition, the Irish language has imparted to the English speech of the country a haunting music and a distinctive, cantering rhythm.

The *filidhe* (master-poets of the Celts) earned their prestige by subjecting themselves to a rigorous course of training at bardic academies where the curriculum demanded memorization of lengthy sagas and learning composition in complex meters. Many graduates of the academies were attracted by monastic life, and their manuscripts and magnificent calligraphy and illumination made them Europe's preeminent students of literature. Between the eighth and sixteenth centuries these monks transcribed the oral traditions of which they were the living archives and, by keeping them in circulation, preserved them for posterity.

From various manuscript sources scholars can reconstruct the two great saga cycles, that of the Red Branch warriors of Ulster province and that of Finn MacCool and his Fenian band (the Fianna). The Ulster cycle constitutes a portion of the tribal history of the Uliad, who gave their name to the northernmost of Ireland's five provinces, and seems to have become current during the first century BC, though a quantity of older lore had been incorporated in the cycle. The king of the Ulidians in the cycle is Conchobar (pronounced Con-a-choor), whose castle stood at Emain Macha near modern Keady, County Armagh. But the protagonist is Cu Chulainn, the Hound of Ulster, offspring of the sun god and hero of the tribe.

The cycle centers around the Tain Bo Cualinge (The Cattle-Raid of Cooley), an epic narrative in which the semilegendary Queen Maeve of Connaught leads an expeditionary force toward Cooley (near Dundalk) to steal Conchobar's prized Brown Bull. Cu Chulainn single-handedly holds the invading army at bay while the Ulstermen recover from a 9-days' illness.

Cu Chulainn adds to the conventional virtues of courage and honor an impulsive disdain for any check to his appetites. He is the arch-individualist, a larger-than-life figure who postpones his first encounter with the Connaughtmen to keep a date with a woman, and who slays in single combat his best friend and his only son despite the promptings of human tenderness. His daring and determination together with a roguish impetuosity established a comic tradition in Irish literature.

Cu Chulainn was specifically a hero of the men of Ulster. But, between the commencement of the O'Neill dynasty and the height of the Norse incursions, Irish society was challenged to transcend the old clan loyalties for the sake of military unity. This was achieved politically in the person of Brian Ború and in literature through the Fenian cycle, which was the first truly national, rather than tribal, epic.

Finn MacCool, his son Oscar, his grandson Ossian, and his comrades Diarmiat and Cailte commanded the Fianna, the standing army of professional warriors said to have been mustered to the service of Cormac Mac Art, son of the founder of the Tara monarchy, in the third century AD. The Fenians were, from the outset, national rather than tribal heroes. Unlike the Ulster cycle, composed mostly in prose and incorporating myths in a highly learned manner, the Fenian cycle springs directly from popular folklore and employs a ballad meter to which the music of the common people easily adapted itself. It is more immediate and dramatic. Its characteristic form is the monologue or dialogue and its setting is the Christian era into which some Fenian hero has survived to speak, often to St. Patrick, of bygone days of glory. Not originally a product of the bardic academies, the Fenian cycle did not enter the courtly repertoire until the twelfth century, by which time it had already displaced the Ulster sagas in popular favor.

In contrast to Cu Chulainn, champion of a civilized nobility, the Fenians choose to live outside the pale of settlements and courts, preferring the woods and wilds. They are hunters rather than soldiers, akin to the gods of nature and place worshiped in the vernacular religion. It is from the Fenian tradition that Irish poetry receives its extraordinary sensitivity to nature:

166 PERSPECTIVES / Literature

> Arran of the many stags,
> The sea strikes against its shoulder . . .
> Skittish deer are on her peaks,
> Delicious berries on her manes . . .
> (From *The Colloquy of the Old Men,* a Fenian romance from a fifteenth-century manuscript, translated by Myles Dillon)

From the stories themselves flow the lyrical richness of Irish poetry, the sweetness and nostalgia of popular folk song, and the whole romantic spirit, dash, and panache of Irish history. The Fenian cycle inaugurates a dramatic and intensely personal literary style, which became the expressive mode of the Irish nation and provided the archetype of the outlaw brotherhood in which the nineteenth-century revolutionaries cast themselves.

The *filidhe* and its elite tradition were destroyed by the social upheavals caused by the plantation policy which replaced Irish landowners with English and later Scottish colonists prepared to offer allegiance to the crown. It was not until the eighteenth century, however, that it was finally extinguished. As late as 1781, a young schoolteacher from Clondagach, County Clare, who had educated himself in the metrical complexities of bardic composition, published an epic satire in the Irish language called *The Midnight Court,* in which the women of Ireland indict the men for contempt of matrimony and obtain a conviction in the court of the Fairy Queen. The poem is elegant, racy, and dreamlike, but its ribaldry proved too strong for a public taste narrowed by oppressive works that were pious and patriotic. The poem was suppressed, though portions of it can be heard recited from memory in some modern Irish-speaking households. Merriman, last of the *filidhe,* wrote nothing more and died in 1805.

Literature in English has been written in Ireland since the fourteenth century, but many of the Anglo-Irish literati owe little to the national traditions. Irish was the native tongue, and the native populace, denied and excluded from educational institutions by the Penal Codes, produced a glorious but impermanent body of unwritten poetry.

The chief educational institution in Ireland was Trinity College, Dublin, founded in 1591 as a university for the Protestant gentry. Trinity was the intellectual nursery of an extraordinary series of writers whose work places them more properly in a history of English rather than Irish literature. Yet their remarkable singularity of expression was one that could only have been nurtured in an environment where talk, conversation, language, provided the main indoor entertainment.

Chronologically, the first of these writers was Jonathan Swift (1667–1745), author of *Gulliver's Travels,* who is buried in St. Patrick's Cathedral, Dublin, of which he was dean. Next was William Congreve (1670–1729), author of one of the greatest comedies in the English language, *The Way of the World.* Then comes Oliver Goldsmith (1730?–74), the son of a Church of Ireland clergyman who is most famous for his play *She Stoops to Conquer* and his friendship with Dr. Samuel Johnson. Finally there is Oscar Wilde (1854–1900), the flamboyant author of the play *The Importance of Being Earnest* and the novel *The Picture of Dorian Gray.*

Two Dubliners who did not attend Trinity need to be mentioned in this category. One is Richard Brinsley Sheridan (1751–1816), the descendant of a famous Anglo-Irish family, whose masterpieces include *The Rivals* and *The School for Scandal*. The other is George Bernard Shaw (1856–1950), widely considered to be the greatest dramatist in the English language after Shakespeare. Shaw spent his first 20 years living in seedy gentility in Dublin. Even after he left to take up residence (and literary sovereignty) in London he never failed to involve himself in Irish affairs whether it concerned Parnell's divorce or Casement's homosexuality. Indeed he is one of the few writers in history who is as famous for his political curmudgeonry as he is for his great works. *(St. Joan; Pygmalion; Heartbreak House)*. A statue of him by Prince Paul Troubetskoy stands outside the National Gallery of Ireland to which he left a substantial part of his fortune.

Occasionally the Protestant Ascendancy did produce a writer who was truly Irish in sympathy. One of these was Thomas Moore (1779–1852). Moore was a friend and the eulogizer of Robert Emmet (executed 1803), the prototype of the sort of Irishman who is both Protestant and nationalist. Emmet himself deserves a place in Irish literature for his speech from the scaffold which contains the immortal words, "Let no man write my epitaph . . ." Moore was a literary, though not a militant, patriot who wrote in the plaintive style of Irish folk song, often to popular airs. Songs like "The Minstrel Boy" and "The Harp That Once Through Tara's Halls" were ambassadors from romantic Ireland to the English gentry and helped revise their image of the Irish as crude and barbarous.

In 1842, *The Nation* magazine began publishing the poems and translations of James Clarence Mangan and Samuel Fergusson. Their work, infused with the energy and misty grandeur of the Irish language, excited interest in ancient literature, particularly the Fenian cycle. Its vibrant tapestry of hunts and fatal love, journeys to the underworld, battles between mortals and ghosts, sojourns in fairyland, and tone of wistful longing for the lost ardor of youth appealed to the romantic temperament of the times.

But the burgeoning political and literary movement did not achieve the status of a renaissance until the appearance of the work of W. B. Yeats (1865–1939), whose early imitations of folk poetry grafted French symbolism onto Irish folklore. Introduced to the Ulster cycle by his friend and patroness of the Irish Literary Renaissance, Lady (Augusta) Gregory, Yeats became fascinated by the figure of Cu Chulainn and meditated upon this image of the kind of reckless and heroic action he admired but shrank from in many poems.

William Butler Yeats was an unlikely Irishman. Son of an atheist father, the portraitist J. B. Yeats; grandson of the dandyish Church of Ireland rector at Drumcliff, County Sligo; brother of the expressionist painter Jack Yeats — William Butler Yeats was a member of various occult societies, an admirer of the English and a defender of the Ascendancy, a member of London literary society, and in his youth, one of those bohemian aesthetes whose tastes and style were schooled by the lyrical poetry of A. C. Swinburne, the humanist doctrines of Walter Pater, and the heroic fantasies of William Morris. Yet, he was also an ardent supporter of Charles Parnell, briefly a member of the Fenian Brotherhood, and a student of Irish folklore. Debarred from religious belief by the skepticism inherited from his father, Yeats invented a personal cosmology in which the clash and union of opposites, represented by the phases of the moon, become the dynamic force in history. ("By opposition, square and trine . . ." he says in the poem "In Memory of Major Robert Gregory.") The great poems of his middle years take their intellectual structure from this esoteric and enchantingly bizarre mythology, which perfectly expressed the contradictions of his own nature. Passionately attached to the peasantry, in whom he saw the wellspring of Ireland's creative energy, Yeats was equally passionately the champion of the Ascendancy, whom he regarded as Ireland's intellectual elite capable of giving coherent shape to the emotions of the masses. In his last years he abandoned his highly personalized mysticism to return with new freedom to the subject matter of his earliest days. Pathologically shy, Yeats was nevertheless proud and a trifle vain of his striking good looks. He became one of Ireland's leading public men and it was, ironically, this status rather than his years of obsession with mysticism and folklore that inspired his greatest poem, "Among School Children," with its famous last line "How can we know the dancer from the dance?"

Yeats often found himself embroiled in controversy because of the parochialism of the Dublin public, whose tastes were circumscribed by oppression and a conservative church. Yeats's own verse was not the source of his troubles; rather it was his defense of his friends and colleagues — Synge, Joyce, O'Casey. That he was a patriot, albeit an eccentric one, a celebrant of the Easter Rising, and, in his youth, a slightly uncomfortable agitator, did not go unrewarded; in 1922 he was appointed a senator of the Irish Free State. In debate, he spoke magnificently and pugnaciously against censorship, and also against the constitutional prohibition of divorce, which he characterized as an insult to the Protestant minority. He helped to found the Abbey Theatre, now a national institution, but when angry mobs stormed the stage, infuriated at a reference to women's undergarments in Synge's *Playboy of the Western World,* Yeats stepped before the curtains and sternly reproached them. When they did it 20 years later over the appearance of a prostitute in O'Casey's *The Plough and the Stars,* Yeats confronted them a second time, booming at them: "You have disgraced yourselves again!" Ireland loves drama, and Yeats provided drama in abundance. In return, Ireland grudgingly offered him its adoration for the splendor and valor of his quixotic idealism.

Yeats believed that great poetry must be rooted in place and "The Lake Isle of Innisfree," "The Fiddler of Dooney," "The Man Who Dreamed of Faeryland," and others of his early poems are set close to Sligo town. But the most important landmarks in his verse are Knocknarea, atop of which stands the pile of stones known as Queen Maeve's Cairn, and Ben Bulben, the limestone mesa on the other side of Sligo Bay. Between these two mountains, spectral horsemen called Dananns were said to ride each night:

> The host is riding from Knocknarea
> And over the grave of Clooth-na-Bare;
> Caoilte tossing his burning hair,

> And Niamh calling *Away, come away* . . .
> ("The Hosting of the Sidhe," ca. 1899*)

To these horsemen, Yeats, buried in Drumcliffe churchyard at the foot of Ben Bulben, addressed himself in his epitaph:

> *Cast a cold eye*
> *On life, on death.*
> *Horseman, pass by!*
> ("Under Ben Bulben," 1938)

Yeats's work is among the glories of modern literature (he won the Nobel Prize in 1923), yet he was unstintingly generous and supportive of other writers. He encouraged the younger Anglo-Irish writer, John Millington Synge, to rediscover his roots by visiting the Aran Islands in Galway Bay. Synge's sojourn on Inishmaan, as well as in other Irish-speaking regions, inspired him to combine the realism of Ibsen with the wild, fantastical speech of the Irish countryside in plays that treated the life of Ireland's impoverished rural proletariat with Chekovian irony and unsentimental honesty. Synge never romanticized, and his plays have no heroes. Christy Mahon, protagonist of *The Playboy of the Western World*, finds himself suddenly a celebrity in a strange village after confessing to the murder of his own father, and the object, thanks to his prestige, of the affections of Pegeen Mike, the daughter of a publican. When Christy proves innocent of the crime, Pegeen turns on him in a paroxysm of disappointment because, having shown himself to be more tender than wicked, he lacks the notoriety to elevate her life beyond its drudgery; in the last line of the play, having "lost her only playboy of the western world," she realizes, too late, that she loves him. In *Riders to the Sea*, set in the Aran Islands, an old woman accepts the drowning of her last surviving son with a chilly stoicism that is at once tragic and appalling. Synge's is a vision without comfort, as bleak as Dreiser's, and as perversely comic as Chekhov's.

Synge died in 1909 at the age of 38, but not before he had given the Abbey Theatre and the playwrights of Ireland a dramatic style, often vulgarized, alas, into "peasant-quality" plays in which quaintness and condescending coyness displace Synge's unsparing realism. Synge invented a dialect in which the idioms and constructions of Irish are rendered directly into English. So exquisite a tool did this dialect become that Synge used it to splendid effect in his translations of Petrarch and Villon. But no other playwright could manage the trick.

Synge's example, and Yeats's solicitous encouragement, bore fruit in the work of the next great Abbey playwright, Sean O'Casey (1884–1964). Born in the Dublin slums, O'Casey, a Protestant, was the first figure of the Literary Renaissance to spring directly from the proletariat and to make the urban working class the subject of his attention. O'Casey needed no synthetic dialect; the speech of Dublin came naturally to him. His politics, however, came

---

*"The Hosting of the Sidhe," from *The Collected Poems of W. B. Yeats* (New York: Macmillan, 1956). © The Macmillan Company 1956. Reprinted by permission of Macmillan Inc., Macmillan London Ltd., M. B. Yeats, and Anne Yeats.

as a mild shock to his colleagues — most especially Yeats, whom O'Casey remembered with wry affection in his memoirs — for he professed to be Communist. Equally shocking to the public was his insistence on showing Dublin's raw backside. The presence of a prostitute in *The Plough and the Stars* together with the meeting of revolutionary patriots in the unholy precincts of a pub, provoked riots at the play's premiere. Two years later, embittered at *The Plough's* reception and furious because Yeats refused to produce his next play, *The Silver Tassie,* O'Casey moved to England, never to return. Nothing he wrote thereafter quite equaled his early works, which also included *Juno and the Paycock* and *Shadow of a Gunman.*

O'Casey's social passion, his sense of grievance, and his identification with his working-class characters left him more vulnerable than Yeats and Synge to sentimentality; yet, his affection for the outlaw and the outcast recalls the Fenian tradition and rescues his early plays from bathos. O'Casey's spiritual successor among Irish playwrights was Brendan Behan (1923–1964). Housepainter, drunkard, and self-made intellectual, Behan, between 1956 and 1958, disposed of his mammoth talent in three works — *Borstal Boy,* his memoir of life in a British reformatory where he was imprisoned for revolutionary terrorism on English soil; *The Quare Fellow,* a drama of prison life under the pall of an inmate's imminent execution; and his magnum opus, *The Hostage,* after which he subsided into notoriety and drink.

Behan's last words, spoken to the nun at his hospital bedside, were: "God bless you, sister, and may all your sons be bishops." He lived and wrote with Rabelaisian gusto. In 1937, he joined the outlawed Irish Republican Army and gave his youth to the cause, although he grew to distrust the fanaticism he saw in it. *The Hostage* is a kind of tragic farce in which an IRA contingent, commanded by a bizarre Ascendancy enthusiast, seizes a young British soldier and holds him hostage in a Dublin brothel on Nelson Street where the residents include, among the working girls, two outrageous homosexuals, a devout and lascivious spinster, and an innocent housemaid who falls in love with the hostage. The Republicans threaten to kill the prisoner in order to force the reprieve of two of their own facing execution in a Belfast jail. The play is punctuated by songs that lampoon Irish piety, by dances and jokes, and, finally, by the gunfire of a police raid in which the hostage is tragically killed. Characters frequently address the audience, the accompanist remains onstage throughout, and no pretense is made that this is anything but theater; yet it captures the emotions anyway having dispensed with every theatrical convention except the heart's truth.

James Joyce (1882–1941), the titan of Irish prose, exempted himself from the Literary Renaissance — he referred to Yeats's Celtic Twilight as the "Cultic Toilette" — and at age 22 expatriated himself to the Continent. He took with him a handsome but intellectually unprepossessing shopgirl, Nora Barnacle, who became for him the personification of Dublin, in the environs of which Joyce set everything he ever wrote.

Joyce's insistence on fixing his most obscure works to the real, even trivial, details of the city he remembered, amounted to the most creative obsession in modern letters. As a young man, growing up in a middle-class home, educated in Catholic prep schools and at Trinity College, Joyce had been attracted to the realism of Ibsen and learned Norwegian to read his plays in the original.

Ulysses, the huge novel that established Joyce's preeminent reputation, follows Leopold Bloom, a Dublin Jew, his wife, Molly, and young Stephen Daedalus, Joyce's surrogate, in their minute-by-minute progress through a single day — June 16, 1904 — in Dublin. Joyce employed a stream-of-consciousness technique to record the random associations of his characters' thoughts. Readers were shocked by the eroticism of these interior monologues, and the book was until quite recently banned in Ireland. Yet Dubliners who managed to obtain copies were fascinated by the many living personalities parading across the pages and by the accuracy with which Joyce had observed and remembered the city, its features, and its speech. What few realized was how brilliantly Joyce had transformed the details of Dublin life — newspaper articles from June 16, 1904, brand-name household goods, idioms of local patois — into symbols of Europe's mythological and psychic heritage represented by *The Odyssey*, the novel's controlling metaphor. Nor do many readers appreciate Joyce's love for his characters until Molly Bloom's long interior soliloquy on the edge of sleep.

On "Bloomsday," June 16, of every year, dedicated Joyceans gather in Dublin to retrace the routes followed by *Ulysses*'s characters: from the Martello Tower (a Napoleonic era fortress) where Joyce, like Stephen Daedalus, lived in his student days, through the city, past nearly every point of interest or importance, to Eccles Street, where the Blooms resided. Fans of Joyce's next and last book, *Finnegans Wake*, are rather few. It is probably the most frustrating and impenetrable book ever written, for here language itself is the subject. Nearly every one of the book's 237,600 words has several meanings at once. Joyce, master of nearly every European language, enlisted them all to create this huge stream-of-consciousness work — the sleeping, dreaming thought-flow of the Earwicker family of Dublin, whose matriarch, Ann (known also as Anna Livia Plurabelle), is at once the spirit of the Liffey and the form of the book.

Joyce's works belong to the Red Branch line — comic, cosmic, larger-than-life — but Samuel Beckett, briefly his secretary in the 1930s and another Dublin expatriate to the Continent, belongs to no tradition though he shows the influence of Joyce and Synge. A founding member of the avant-garde, and Ireland's third Nobel Prize winner (after Yeats and Shaw), Beckett's enigmatic plays and novels seem less overtly Irish than the works of his compatriot although here and there in *Waiting for Godot* one hears echoes of the Irish music hall, and the astute reader or listener will realize that *Play* is set in Foxrock, a Dublin suburb. Beckett, the quintessential absurdist, displays in works as dauntingly obtuse in starkness as *Finnegans Wake* the characteristic daring and individualism of the Irish.

Ireland has dispensed fine writing to the world — this is no provincial tradition — with astonishing abundance in this century. Among the lesser-known luminaries, some of whom have fallen into the shadows of the gods, are Frank O'Connor, memoirist, essayist, translator, and chronicler nonpareil of literary Ireland; Patrick Kavanagh, Ireland's only beat poet; Louis MacNeice, the Belfast poet; Flann O'Brien *(At Swim Two Birds)*, surrealist virtuoso; Denis O'Donoghue, the literary critic; playwrights Brian Friel and Hugh Leonard, who have enjoyed notable successes on Broadway; poets Thomas Kinsella and Seamus Heany; and, to run on and on, Padraic Colum, Denis Johnstone, Iris Murdoch, Brian Moore, Edna O'Brien, Liam O'Flaherty, Sean O'Faoilain . . . as though all the vital energies of the nation, pent up through 700 years of oppression, were erupting. The spectacle of the Irish literary explosion is without parallel in history.

Architecture

Ireland is full of picturesque ruins and ancient structures, which is part of its charm for Americans unaccustomed to architecture older than a few centuries. Along every Irish road and river lie Stone Age tombs, ruined abbeys, decayed or restored castles, Palladian-style manor houses, and stately Georgian mansions. And the thatched and whitewashed or fieldstone cottages in the remoter regions are most appealing with their timeless, homespun simplicity.

The oldest structures, some of which have been dated to 3,000 BC, are the megalithic monuments — the tumuli and stone circles at Carrowmore in County Donegal and Carrowkeel in County Sligo; the passage grave complex at Brugh na Boinne in County Meath; and the decorated standing stones and dolmens scattered about the countryside. Whether these monuments were built by an indigenous people or by immigrants is not known, but they are similar to those found in Europe and England; Stonehenge is perhaps the best-known example. It is thought that these structures were prehistoric shrines, and that the Celts, who began arriving in Ireland around 500 BC, also endowed the sites with religious or magical significance.

The earliest Celtic structures are the *dúns*, fortresses enclosed by dry-stone walls and often built atop megalithic shrines or ring-forts. The walls served both to keep cattle in and protect the settlement from attack. The most famous and impressive of the fortresses is Dún Aengus on the Aran isle of Inishmore in Galway Bay. Dún Aengus is a semicircle; its open side is a cliff that drops precipitously 266 feet to the roiling Atlantic, giving the impression that the missing half of the circle had collapsed into the ocean in some terrible cataclysm. Other notable ringed fortresses include Tara in County Meath and Grianán of Aileach in County Donegal.

Early Celtic dwellings were built of timber and wattle and have not survived. In treeless areas people lived in stone dwellings; their *clocháns* (beehive huts) were constructed in corbelled fashion, with the stones overlapping each other. The early Christian churches were also built in the beehive style, although some variations were introduced — such as a rectangular shape and a pitched roof. Two examples are Skellig Michael off the Kerry coast, and the Gallerus Oratory in County Kerry; both are thought to date to the eighth century.

The round tower is another relic of early Christian architecture. Ranging in height from 70 to 120 feet, slightly tapered, and topped by a conical roof, these were bell towers as well as places of refuge where monks hid from

Viking invaders. (The doorway was located high above the ground and when under attack the inhabitants withdrew the adjoining ladder for safety.) A fine example of an early Christian round tower is the freestanding, eleventh-century structure at Glendalough in County Wicklow.

Irish monastic and ecclesiastic architecture further developed with the introduction to Ireland of the Romanesque style during the twelfth century. It was embraced with some enthusiasm by native artisans, and ornate stone carvings — human and animal heads, chevrons, interlace, and foliage — decorate the arches, doorways, capitals, and sometimes windows of the churches of this period. The Chapel of Cormac, situated on the Rock of Cashel in County Tipperary, is the earliest Irish Romanesque structure in the country and Clonfert Cathedral in County Galway is perhaps the most ornate; both have heavily embellished portals.

The invasion of the Normans in 1170 changed the face of Irish architecture forever, for they brought with them from England and Wales the designs and styles, proportions, shapes, and decorative devices prevalent there. Eager to colonize, they began a flurry of cathedral- and castle-building that lasted from the twelfth to the seventeenth century. The numerous churches constructed during this period tended to be large and Gothic in style, with tall lancet windows and pointed arches; St. Patrick's Cathedral in Dublin is a fine example. The typical Norman fortress had a square stone keep enclosed by curtain walls linking four circular corner towers. King John's Castle in Limerick City, built in 1210, combines all of these features. The towerhouse, a structure favored by both Norman and native Irish, dates to between the fifteenth and seventeenth century. Most of them were built, however, just after the Statute of 1429 which offered a £10 subsidy to any person building such a tower within the Pale. The so-called £10 houses were fortified dwellings built of stone, four or five stories high, with narrow slitted windows and a steeply pitched roof. A very simple Norman-built towerhouse is Donore Castle in County Meath.

During the late seventeenth century, domestic dwellings began to look less like fortresses and more like the classical mansions popular in England. This meant that houses were often built of brick, with hipped roofs and dormer windows, as exemplified by Beaulieu in County Louth. Very soon, however, the Irish and English imagination was captured by Palladianism, a reinterpretation of the design principles evolved by Italian architect Andrea Palladio in the mid-sixteenth century. The arrangement of columns and arches in the facade of Bellamont Forest in County Cavan is a typical Palladian motif.

The eighteenth century saw the architectural expansion and enhancement of Ireland's urban centers — Belfast, Cork, Dublin, Limerick, and Waterford. During this period Dublin received a heady endowment of new buildings designed in the classical style — incorporating elements from ancient Greek and Roman architecture — such as Trinity College, the Four Courts, the Custom House, and the Parliament buildings (now the Bank of Ireland). Georgian architecture was also popular, and elegant Georgian squares — gracious greens presided over by tall brick town houses with pillared doorways and distinctive fanlights — appeared not only in Dublin (Fitzwilliam and Merrion squares), but also in Limerick City (Newtown Pery) and in Belfast (Donegall Square). Neoclassicism remained in vogue during the nineteenth century, although Irish architects also flirted briefly with various revivals of the Gothic style (St. Finbarr's Cathedral in Cork), Italianate (the Custom House in Belfast), and Edwardian (Belfast City Hall).

The common dwellings of Ireland remained virtually unchanged from earliest Celtic times: They were usually only one room heated by a central fireplace that vented its smoke through a hole in the roof. Stables and byres were built adjacent, although animals sometimes shared the living quarters in the interest of warmth. The central hearth style with hipped roof was most common in the eastern counties, while homes in the northwest had a bed alcove and room extensions. In the southwest, gables appeared, rising above the thatching, which replaced stone as the common roofing material. Two-story dwellings did not appear until the late nineteenth century, when, after the depopulation caused by the famine, efforts were made to eliminate the thatched cottages altogether and replace them with more modern accommodations.

Today, the art of thatching has been practically lost, though many old vernacular houses are still in use. Departing visitors whose route back to Shannon Airport takes them through Adare, County Limerick, can see an especially pretty row of thatched houses on their way through town, and chances are they'll also see a thatcher at work, because the roofs are meticulously kept. The traditional style has also been revived somewhat in villages of thatched cottages — with open fireplaces and flagstone floors, as well as electricity, modern heating, and plumbing — built for the use of vacationers. But more than likely, what the visitor will remember most is the haunting picture of the same simple dwellings scattered forlorn and deserted throughout the Irish countryside, left to decay when their owners left for a better life elsewhere. The history of Ireland is indeed told in its architecture.

Traditional Music and Dance

The harp is the instrument most associated with Ireland from ancient times; it was used for centuries by learned bards who entertained the royal Gaelic courts with recitations of poetry and sagas.

After the dissolution of the Gaelic courts ordered by the Cromwellian Act of Settlement in 1652, the bards scattered to the countryside, where they mingled with folk poets, and a general intermarriage of their styles ensued. The classical airs that evolved from such collaboration — "The Coolun," "Roisin Dubh," and "Eileen Aroon" — present a refinement and gravity uncommon in folk music.

The harpers traveled among the houses of the rural gentry, playing traditional songs and creating new ones on commission. The greatest of these harpers was Turlough O'Carolan (1670–1738), whose compositions wed a certain European sophistication (perhaps acquired in Dublin) with a native Irish sensibility: Though his melodies are quite lengthy and complex, they also flirt now and again with the popular gapped scales, never losing touch with the folk spirit. Some have become staples of modern Irish ensembles.

PERSPECTIVES / Traditional Music and Dance 175

Another instrument always associated with Ireland is the bagpipe. The *uilleann* (pronounced ill-en) pipes differ from those played in Scotland in that the bellows is pumped with the elbow, a softer reed is used, the drones are slung across the leg of the seated player, and there are keys that change the drone notes when depressed with the heel of the right hand, enabling the player to produce chords. The *uilleann* has been called the "Irish organ," for it is capable of extremely rich, resonant sound, though, with its straps and harnesses, it resembles an instrument of torture. The west of Ireland, particularly County Clare, was until recently the home of fine Irish piping; but the recent rise in popularity of Irish music throughout the world has persuaded numbers of young Irish (who might otherwise have belabored guitars) to take up the arduous study of this noble and exacting instrument.

While traditional dance music is played on pipes as well as fiddles, the "big airs" — the slow and majestic classical tunes — are especially moving when played on the expansive pipes. Of the older generation of pipers, only Seamus Ennis is still alive, though many recordings of great pipers like Willy Clancy and Leo Rowesome are available. Three of the best younger pipers are Paddy Maloney, of The Chieftains, Finbar Furey, of the Furey Brothers, and the virtuosic Joe McKenna. The McPeakes of Belfast were three generations of harpers, pipers, and singers led by Frank McPeake, reputed to have been the first piper skilled enough to sing to his own accompaniment.

The piper produces the melody — trills, grace notes, and other flourishes — by moving his fingers to open or close the holes of the chanter, or pipe. Flutes and pennywhistles are played in the same way, without tonguing. The great Sligo fiddler Michael Coleman, who emigrated to America and recorded here in the 1920s, evolved a similar ornamental style for his instrument, one which has since become the standard. The musical embellishments used by fiddlers, pipers, flutists, and pennywhistlers perfectly suits the structure of Irish dance music — the jigs, reels, and hornpipes — in which a sinuous and fluid melody rushes along with scarcely a pause for breath, diving and soaring with dizzying exuberance. The stuttering throb of the *bodhrán* (a hand-held drum beaten with a double-headed stick) gives the music an irresistible rhythmic momentum more like jazz or flamenco than anything in the other Celtic musical traditions.

The music of County Kerry tends to be less hectic and more regularly cadenced than that of the rest of the country. Some scholars believe it represents an older style. Polkas and schottisches, not found elsewhere in Ireland, are performed in Kerry, as are longer, more elegant dances. A fine example of the latter, which will seem more classical and less Irish to the average listener, and more like the harp music of Carolan, is the work of Eugene O'Donnell, the fiddler.

The Connemara region on Ireland's far western coast, a rocky and forbidding region north of Galway City, is famous for its singers and for its stately, mysterious ballads. The vocal technique resembles that of piping and Sligo fiddling; some of the notes are changed or the tempo slowed and the melody is delivered with a multitude of embellishments. The effect can be quite fascinating, as if you were listening to dance music in slow motion. The recordings of Joe Heany of Carna provide excellent examples of the ballad style.

Ensembles of singers or musicians are not traditional in Ireland. Solo playing was the rule until the 1920s when record companies began to demand lively and audible renditions of dance tunes to supply the dance market in America; this prompted musicians to seek accompanists. During the 1950s, Sean O'Riada, a "serious" composer and harpsichordist, hearing the *ceildhe* (dance) bands that had begun to form and sounded, as someone wrote, "like a tree full of blackbirds," conceived the idea of arranging Irish music for an orchestra of traditional instruments. He gathered a group of fiddlers, pipers, accordionists, whistlers, flutists, and drummers in Dublin and taught them their parts by ear (few could read music). The delightful result was Ceolteori Cualain, the first sophisticated folk music ensemble, for whom O'Riada provided many orchestrations, which — though they were enriched with harmonies, counterpoint, even rudimentary fugues — never lost their simplicity and drive.

During the 1960s, the Clancy Brothers and Tommy Makem found an audience among folk music fans in America, and introduced them to a species of Irish music worlds away from "Mother Macree" and the other products of the Hibernian division of Tin Pan Alley. Their repertoire included revolutionary and patriotic songs (as well as that pungent Irish subgenre, the antiwar song), sea chanties, and children's songs, all of them delivered with robust good humor and taste. Since the disappearance of the harpers in the nineteenth century, music had rarely been a professional undertaking among the Irish, but the Clancys stimulated a new interest, and before long, Ireland was in the midst of a ballad boom. Among the more successful groups were The Dubliners, a group of four — later five — men including Ronny Drew, a flamenco guitarist and master of the Dublin street-ballad, and Barney McKenna, a wizard who pioneered the application of the Sligo style to the tenor banjo. The Dubliners have proven a durable institution, though, like most Irish musicians who want to earn a living by their art, they have had to seek audiences in England and on the Continent.

After the death of Sean O'Riada, a party of his alumni formed The Chieftains to carry on his style and bring it to a wider audience. They tightened the O'Riada sound and began running tunes together in patchwork medleys, sometimes juxtaposing contrasting sounds for dramatic effect. The Chieftains fathered a generation of such ensembles in Ireland and Scotland as well as America, where "Celtic" bands have begun to proliferate. Among the best Irish bands are Planxty, Sweeny's Men, The Bothy Band, and De Danann; they preserve the charm and melodic richness of traditional music but deliver it with the instrumental daring and emotional impact of rock.

Music clubs have lately begun to spring up in various Irish cities so that now musicians — who previously gathered only in a few pubs or at government-sponsored summer music festivals — may perform regularly. Concerts are rare, though, and you must search pretty far in the country to find local pubs where musicians play (see *Where to Hear Traditional Irish Music*, DIVERSIONS). For years, music was like conversation to the Irish: They would no sooner pay for a song than for a chat.

Food and Drink

Ireland's location and climate have combined to produce an agricultural abundance: Its lush grasslands support a thriving livestock industry, resulting in good beef, lamb, and pork; its extensive waters yield a fine harvest of fish and seafood: sole, plaice, mackerel, sea trout, salmon, lobster and crab, prawns and scallops, oysters and mussels; its soil and mild climate nurture barley, wheat, sugar beets, and potatoes — as well as other vegetables, when Irish farmers can be persuaded to grow them.

At its best, Irish food is fresh, nourishing, and prepared simply. There are some regional variations and a few local specialties, but the real geographical division is between the coast and the interior. On the coast, which is heavily touristed, food is on the whole good and presentation attractive. The flat heart of the country has barely emerged from the dark English provincial ages that dominated food in Ireland for a century and a half. The "commercial hotel" — the haven of the turn-of-the-century English business traveler — established a horrendous food pattern that is only now breaking up. A typical meal here consisted of Windsor soup (a nondescript liquid full of floury lumps) and overdone roast beef, crowded on the plate by watery, overcooked vegetables and bathed in a thicker version of the soup called "gravy." This repast concluded with a heavy pudding doused in a nasty, viscous, yellow liquid miscalled "custard." You will rarely find this meal now in its pristine horror, but elements of "commercial" cooking still survive in the midlands and the wary traveler must forage around a little for better food.

That dire warning noted, we will now discuss *real* Irish food. The timing of meals in Ireland is important. The Irish food day is divided into three main meals and almost as many side events. The weight-conscious visitor will simply have to pick and choose and be firm.

A typical Irish breakfast starts with porridge (a flavorsome boiled oatmeal topped with cream) and continues through a main course of bacon and eggs accompanied by toast and orange marmalade. The eggs you can have any style and the bacon is good though not cooked crisply. You may also be served a black or white pudding (both are kinds of blood pudding) or even kidney or liver. Tea is recommended over coffee; with rare exceptions the Irish do not make coffee well. They make their tea strong and with milk; inform them if you want it weak and with lemon.

A breakfast alternative offered on the coast is plaice, a delicate-tasting flounder-style fish, or fresh mackerel if they are running. Try both for a new and delightful breakfast experience.

Instead of toast you may be served a coarse, wholemeal "brown bread" — homebaked, nutty, and delicious — or "soda bread" — plain white, usually made *without* raisins (unlike the unauthentic version often served in American restaurants).

The midmorning snack — a cup of tea or coffee with a biscuit (cookie) or sweet bun — is very popular in urban Ireland: Some temples to the practice are *Bewley's Oriental Cafés* in Dublin (sinfully sweet sticky buns and coffee topped with Jersey cream), *Lydon House* in Galway, and *Thompson's* in Cork. Over much matins, much business is conducted, gossip exchanged, and romances started or continued.

To dine or not to dine is a big question for the traveler. For most Irish people, particularly those in the countryside, dinner is the main meal, taken about one o'clock, and usually consists of soup, meat (beef or chicken), vegetables (peas, cabbage, carrots, and usually potatoes), and dessert (the Irish call them sweets). The latter are generally puddings or pastries. Here or there, you may encounter carrageen sweets; these are molded jelly with extract of Irish moss, a species of seaweed, flavored with lemon rind and served with heavy cream or fruit. They are mild and subtle and entirely pleasant. Cheese is often offered as an alternative to dessert. Irish cheese is good and some hotels have a tempting cheeseboard that includes French and other European varieties. If you are staying with an Irish family, follow custom — otherwise do as you like. Most hotels and restaurants feature dinner in the afternoon, and a saving grace is that although fundamentally the same meal as that served in the evening it costs up to 50% less.

The alternatives to a full dinner are luckily multiplying in Ireland. Hotel coffee shops or lounges will serve cold plates of smoked salmon, chicken, salads, or sandwiches. The Irish pub — which hitherto concentrated on one thing, drink — is gradually extending its menu from sandwiches (which are thin and bready by American standards), to include soup, cold plates, salads, and hot meat pies. Watch for signs that say "Pub Grub." Another option in some towns are fish-and-chip shops; the fish (usually whiting) is good, the chips delicious, and the price low.

Or you may prefer to skip lunch and sustain yourself until the main evening meal by having afternoon tea. This fine English institution is, like many other colonial relics, slowly fading from Ireland. Afternoon tea is undeniably a spiritual refreshment; it can rise to ritual, however, when it includes delicate finger sandwiches of ham, chicken, or cucumber; strips of toast with honey; chocolate eclairs; heavy fruitcakes; or wedges of apple tart with cream. You can indulge in such an experience at *Hunters Hotel* in Ashford, County Wicklow; or *Rathmullan House,* in Rathmullan, County Donegal.

The domestic Irish evening meal is usually tea or supper — "high tea" if you want to distinguish it verbally from the afternoon version. In winter it might be quite a substantial meal — a mixed grill (sausage, bacon, kidney, a small piece of steak, and a lamb chop), steak and French fries, or fish in the coastal areas; in summer, it may be something lighter, such as boiled eggs with toast or bread and jam, or a plate of sliced cold chicken or ham. Tea is rounded off with cake, a fruit tart, pudding, or scones.

Among the traditional Irish dishes you should lunge for when they are offered are oxtail soup, Irish stew (simmered layers of onion, potato, and mutton), and fresh salmon — in season — for which the country is famous. Seafood, surprisingly, has only recently become popular in Ireland, though the coastal waters abound with prawns, lobster, mussels, and oysters. Each

October, at the beginning of the oyster harvest, a festival is held in Galway City, during which bushels of bivalves meet their doom in a deluge of porter (a dark beer). Briefly thereafter, oysters become available in the shops. Another delicacy sometimes served in restaurants is the periwinkle, a tiny sea snail that is boiled, picked from the shell with sewing needles, and eaten. Dipped in melted butter laced with garlic, the winkle need not blush before the escargot.

At fairs or horse races, you may notice little bags of dried seaweed being sold as though it were candy; this is dulse, and it makes a tasty, salty "chaw" — a fine accompaniment to a glass of stout.

This brings us to the subject of drink. The favored beverage is stout, or porter, a dark, pungent brew with a head like thick cream and a reputation for being able to support life single-handedly. Guinness is the largest brewer, though other brands are locally obtainable outside Dublin. (Guided tours are no longer conducted at the Guinness brewery on St. James's Gate, but an audiovisual show is offered and visitors are still invited to sample the famous stout.) Good lager and ale, like stout, are drawn at room temperature; the Irish regard the American custom of taking such beverages icy cold with the wry detachment of the anthropologist. They privately think it is a custom suitable only for savages. A dash of sweetened lime juice in a glass of beer makes a refreshing drink called, of course, lager and lime.

Most Irish bartenders do not mix drinks, and wines, except for brandy, are not widely available. The spirits of choice are gin, Scotch, and Irish whiskey. The whiskey distributed for home consumption is far smoother than the youthful export stuff, though of slightly lower proof. It is, like the great malt whiskeys of Scotland, a straight liquor, unblended, and it has a distinctive fruity bouquet and trace of sweetness. Don't miss a chance to sample that famous after-dinner treat — Irish coffee, a tantalizing concoction of hot coffee and whiskey topped with a thick layer of gently whipped cream. (For a more complete discussion of beers, ales, and liquors, as well as a selection of the best watering holes in Ireland, see *Pub Crawling*, DIVERSIONS.)

THE CITIES

BATH

Bath was meant to be a beautiful city, and it is. Anchored in the valley of the River Avon and reverberating up seven surrounding hills in the southwest corner of the Cotswolds, its location alone would have been promising. But for more than 1,600 years, the ancient city — known as Aquae Sulis to its Roman founders — remained undistinguished except as the site of Britain's only hot springs, a place to come and "take the waters." It was a tremendous eighteenth-century urban planning effort that made Bath the splendid Georgian city that it is today. Then the haphazard parts, including the striking abbey, were unified along classical lines in tier upon tier of crescents, terraces, and squares climbing from the banks of the river. As a result, Bath still calls itself the best-planned town in England, and visitors who see its warm, honey-colored stones set against the rich green of lawn, tree, and wooded hillside will probably agree.

The city's past emerges from legend with the Romans who, in approximately AD 54, established an elaborate system of baths here along with a temple to Sulis Minerva, a combination of the Celtic deity, Sul, and the Roman goddess of wisdom, Minerva. The town grew to become a famous health resort and remained one until the Romans left Britain in the early fifth century. After that, Aquae Sulis declined rapidly and the Roman baths sank back into the warm mud.

The Saxons built an abbey in 781, such a fine one that it was chosen as the site of the coronation in 973 of King Edgar as the first king of England in a ceremony that has remained a model for the coronation of all subsequent English kings and queens. The city's fame was short-lived, however, though the sick continued to be drawn to medieval baths raised over the salubrious mineral springs by builders unaware of the ancient prototypes buried underground. As the visitors soaked in the Cross Bath (dating back to the ninth century), the King's Bath (built smack on top of the Romans' reservoir in the twelfth century), and others, Bathonians made a better living in the wool trade — Chaucer's Wife of Bath was one of the successful local makers of cloth.

With the patronage of royalty in the late seventeenth century, Bath began to regain its reputation as a first-class spa. The wife of King James II, Mary of Modena, bore a healthy son after a stop at the Cross Bath. His daughter, Queen Anne, later made several trips. Once kings and queens and their entourages, members of court, country gentry, and notables from all walks of life began to take the cure or just luxuriate, Bath was suddenly fashionable among the well and the sick.

Today's city of elegant squares and crescent streets is the labor of love of three eighteenth-century gentlemen who were now to make their appearance on the scene. Richard "Beau" Nash came in 1705. He was an honest gambler from Wales, a social catalyst who found his calling when he took on the job of master of ceremonies, in charge of public entertainments. Nash was the equivalent of a present-day fund raiser and public relations person on Bath's behalf. He found the money to pave roads, light streets, and endow the Royal Mineral Water Hospital, which survives as the Royal National Hospital for Rheumatic Diseases. He became an arbiter of taste and comportment, laying down rules of etiquette that were not to be broken. Duels were suppressed, smoking in public prohibited, improper dress ridiculed, corruption in the sedan chair business wiped out. Within a generation, the sheer force of his personality had made Bath the second capital of English society.

A Cornish postal clerk named Ralph Allen arrived next. He eventually became postmaster, made a fortune from the mail business, and bought the limestone quarries on the southern hill of the city, Combe Down. Bath's pale stone was as yet untested for building purposes, so Allen engaged a Yorkshire architect, John Wood, as technical adviser. It was a master stroke. Thus supplied with financial backing and the material with which to build, the talented Yorkshireman proceeded to impose architectural order on the gay whirl of the city, designing not simply single buildings but entire rows, circles, and squares of them in accordance with the neoclassical principles of the Palladian style. Queen's Square, North and South Parade, and the Circus are all his.

Wood's grand conceptions were not realized in full, not even by his son, another John Wood, who carried on the father's work and added his own to the Bath landscape. The younger Wood's Assembly Rooms enclosed the Georgians' amusements and dalliance in aesthetically suitable wrappings. While the frivolity endured, they were the essence of Bath. But his ultimate expression was the Royal Crescent, a beautiful scimitar of a street whose grandeur seems almost out of keeping with a city this size, one that was never in itself of great consequence in the affairs of state, though almost anyone who was of consequence — in government, the arts, or society — spent time here.

Visitors to Bath today see much of it as the Georgians left it, despite bombing damage during World War II, the growth of population (now at 84,000), and the development of light industry. Bathonians have carefully safeguarded their heritage, preserving not only individual landmarks but the congeniality of the whole, and they've done this without creating a museum city. The quaint, restored shopfront you pause to admire may not be anything of note, just a pristine, but busy, Laundromat. Twentieth-century traffic moves through certain main streets in continuous streams, while elsewhere there are plenty of pedestrian walkways to give the feeling of a city truly built in a gentler age. This is a feeling that's hard to shake in Bath — as if one would want to. Instead, reinforce it by walking up to the Royal Crescent at dusk. As the honey-colored stones fade to gray, the lights of the city twinkle across the dark shadows of Royal Victoria Park as softly as gas lamps.

BATH AT-A-GLANCE

SEEING THE CITY: The up-and-down setting of this city on seven hills provides more than one spot for an overall view. If you have a car, drive north up Lansdown Road and see Bath unfold beneath you or, even better, go to the opposite side of town: From Widcombe Hill you face directly onto Bath Abbey, the Royal Crescent, and the Pump Room, the sights that make the city famous.

SPECIAL PLACES: Bath's tourism "musts" are conveniently situated right in the heart of town. The hot baths of Aquae Sulis may have given the city its start in the first century, but the most commanding building is undoubtedly the later abbey, the massive square-towered edifice that dwarfs its surroundings from almost every angle. Still later came the Assembly Rooms, the Pump Room, and glorious streets, squares, and crescents that have helped to make Bath the architectural gem that it is.

Roman Baths – The baths are Britain's most complete Roman remains, fed by the country's only hot water springs. The establishment, with its magnificent Great Bath, flourished between the first and fifth centuries AD as one of the most famous health resorts of the Roman Empire, then fell into ruin. The springs themselves — gushing to the surface at a temperature of 110°F and a rate of more than 300,000 gallons a day — remained in use for various later baths, however, including the King's Bath, built by twelfth-century Normans over the Roman reservoir and spring, next to the by-then buried Roman baths. Rediscovery of the latter began in the eighteenth century and they are still being excavated today. The treasures preserved in the accompanying museum include coins, gemstones, pewter tableware, mosaics, and a gilt-bronze head of the goddess Sulis Minerva, to whom a temple on the site was dedicated. Many of the objects were found in the most recent excavations beneath the floor of the King's Bath, where the ancients had thrown them as offerings to the sacred spring. (Among the more unusual finds are the curses inscribed on lead invoking the aid of the goddess in bringing grief to an enemy.) Excavations now proceed in the area of the original temple precinct, underneath the Pump Room. Open daily. Admission charge includes entrance to the Roman Baths and the Pump Room. Abbey Churchyard (phone: 61111 or 65028 evenings and weekends).

Pump Room – Upstairs from the baths, this grand hall was built at the end of the eighteenth century. It was one of the town's social centers and continues as a meeting place for both natives and tourists. The mineral water that used to be pumped to the fountain in the bay window was the same therapeutic drink that Sam Weller of *Pickwick Papers* thought tasted like "warm flat-irons." You can no longer sample it, but in recompense, have some Bath buns and coffee and listen to the Pump Room Trio play its daily (except Sunday) morning concert on the platform under the balcony with the potted palms (or in the nearby Concert Room, depending on the progress of the temple excavations). Open daily. The admission charge to the Roman Baths includes the Pump Room; a combined ticket admits you to the Assembly Rooms and the Museum of Costume on Bennett St. as well. Abbey Churchyard (phone: 61111 or 65023 evenings and weekends).

Bath Abbey – A Saxon abbey and a Norman cathedral occupied this site before the present church was begun in 1499. The cathedral had fallen into ruin when Bishop Oliver King, Bishop of Bath and Wells, was inspired to rebuild the church by a dream, which is represented by the angels ascending ladders into heaven carved on the west front. Though its predecessor was much larger, Bath Abbey is no disappointment. Inside, daylight pours through sparkling panes of glass in the tall clerestory windows (the church is sometimes called the "Lantern of the West" for this reason), illuminating the famous fan vaulting, a pale and delicate example of English perpendicular architecture. The nineteenth-century east window over the altar, unusual for its square-topped shape, was damaged in World War II and restored by the great-grandson of its original designer. Note also the medieval carving of the Prior Birde Chantry next to the sanctuary and, at the northeast corner of the church, the modern Edgar Window showing the coronation of the man thought to have been the first king of England, in 973. Abbey Churchyard.

Assembly Rooms – Designed by John Wood the Younger, these opened in 1771 as a fashionable gathering place where concerts, dancing, card games, and light refreshments could be enjoyed in surroundings of appropriate elegance. Such light-mindedness was scorned in the Victorian age, and from the mid-nineteenth century onward the Bath Assembly Rooms fell into disrepair, then were restored to their former splendor in 1938 only to be gutted, except for the shell, by a World War II bombing raid. What the visitor sees today is a faithful reconstruction of the rooms carried out with the aid of detailed eighteenth-century engravings. The ballroom, lit by five crystal chandeliers that were safely stored elsewhere at the outbreak of the war, looks like a giant blue and white Wedgwood confection and the tearoom is no less delectable a creation in a golden tone. To see what might have been worn for activities in these rooms, go downstairs to the Museum of Costume where there is an array of eighteenth-century finery along with earlier and later exhibits making up one of the largest costume collections in the world. Open daily. Admission charge. Bennett St. (phone: 61111 or 65023 evenings and weekends).

Royal Crescent – The sheer stateliness of Bath's showpiece of residential architecture rarely fails to impress. The Royal Crescent is the supreme achievement of John Wood the Younger and is considered to be the finest crescent in Europe. Begun in 1767, it consists of 30 pale amber Georgian stone houses whose 114 Ionic columns support a continuous cornice the length of the curving whole. Ironwork fences, the sidewalk, and the cobblestone street repeat the curve, wrapping it around a sweeping segment of Royal Victoria Park. The Bath Preservation Trust has restored No. 1 Royal Crescent as a Georgian residence and it is open to the public daily except Mondays, March through October. Admission charge. At the end of Brock St. (phone: 28126).

The Circus – Another example of Georgian town planning, this is possibly the greatest achievement of John Wood the Elder, who began it in 1754. It is a stately ring of regally proportioned and identically faced stone town houses surrounding a circular green of lawn and huge spreading plane trees. Each of its three sections is composed of 11 houses fronted by columns in Doric, Ionic, and Corinthian tiers. Wood designed one of the houses — Nos. 7 and 8 — for William Pitt, MP for Bath and later Prime Minister of England, and many other celebrities have lived here over the years, including the painter Thomas Gainsborough (No. 17) and the explorer David Livingstone (No. 13). At the north end of Gay St.

Bath Carriage Museum – In the eighteenth century, the residents of the Circus kept their horses and carriages in these coach houses and stables in Circus Mews. Today, what is billed as Britain's finest collection of antique horse-drawn carriages (there are over 30 of them) takes up the same space, along with a display of harnesses and liveries. Step outside during the summer season, and a carriage will be waiting to take you around the Circus and the Royal Crescent and back. Open daily. Admission charge (rides extra). Circus Mews (phone: 25175).

Pulteney Bridge – Bath's version, on a smaller scale, of the Ponte Vecchio in Florence. Built in 1770 by Robert Adam, this shop-lined structure on three arches connects Grand Parade and Bridge Street to Argyle Street, and even if you don't window-shop, you'll be across it before you know it. Below the bridge is the boomerang-shaped Pulteney Weir, recently redesigned for the purposes of flood control.

Holburne of Menstrie Museum – The former Sydney Hotel (built in 1796–97) houses a superb collection of silver, glass, porcelain, bronzes, furniture, and paintings by English masters such as Sir Joshua Reynolds and Thomas Gainsborough. A wide range of twentieth-century craftwork, including textiles, pottery, furniture, and calligraphy, is on display in a crafts study center. Open daily throughout the year; afternoon teas are served in the garden in summer. Admission charge. Great Pulteney St. (phone: 66669).

Prior Park – A handsome Georgian mansion overlooking the city, Prior Park was designed for Ralph Allen by John Wood the Elder. Allen had bought the local Combe Down stone quarries and Wood was a proponent of the Palladian style in architecture. When stone and style came together in early buildings such as Prior Park, begun in 1735, it was a forecast of things to come for Bath. Alexander Pope and Henry Fielding visited here — Allen is the Squire Allworthy in Fielding's *Tom Jones* — but today Prior Park is a boys' school. The gardens and chapel are open daily from May to September. About 1 mile southeast of Bath (phone: Combe Down 832752).

American Museum in Britain – If you're in the mood for Americana, this museum has 18 period rooms ranging in source from a seventeenth-century New England saltbox to a mid-nineteenth-century New Orleans mansion, plus such other curiosities as a Massachusetts tavern of colonial vintage (fresh gingerbread is served throughout the day), the captain's cabin of a Yankee whaling boat (complete with creaking sound effects), and an old-fashioned country store. The rooms are in Claverton Manor, a stately neoclassical home of 1820. Open April through October daily except Mondays; rest of the year by appointment. Located 2.5 miles east of town (phone: 60503).

■ **EXTRA SPECIAL:** Just outside Bath, the Kennet and Avon Canal winds lazily along leafy banks. Opened in 1810, the long-neglected canal has now been re-dredged and brought back to life for pleasure craft. On Saturday and Sunday afternoons in spring and summer, a waterbus plies between Bath and Folly Swing Bridge, the prettiest section of the canal. In the spring you stand an excellent chance of passing broods of newborn ducklings and cygnets splashing about under their mothers' watchful gaze. If you're not in Bath over a weekend, you can enjoy a cruise on the River Avon aboard the *Scenic I,* which runs daily on the hour from 11 AM to 7 PM upstream from Pulteney Weir opposite the Parade Gardens. For details on other boat trips, check with the information center.

SOURCES AND RESOURCES

On-the-spot details about Bath can be obtained from the Information Centre (phone: 62831) opposite the Roman Baths and Pump Room in the Abbey Churchyard. An excellent *Bath Official Guide Book* is available for about 50p from the information center and most bookstores. Christopher Ansley's *New Bath Guide,* a satirical look at eighteenth-century Bath society, was an immediate hit when published in 1766 and it is still carried in some local bookstores.

For Local Coverage – The daily (except Sundays) *Bath & West Evening Chronicle* has details of events taking place in the city.

GETTING AROUND: Both the bus station and the train station are at the southern end of Manvers Street. From either, it is a short (provided you are not burdened by luggage) walk up the street to the Orange Grove round-about where a left turn will take you into the Abbey Churchyard, the center of the city. The Roman Baths, the Pump Room, and the Information Centre are here and most of the rest of the places you'll want to see are no more than a few minutes' walk away. Delightfully, many of Bath's streets are traffic-free pedestrian islands. City of Bath honorary guides — known as the Mayor's guides — will take you on a free, approximately 1.5-hour walking tour if you wish; they're carefully trained, unpaid volunteers, and they frown on tips. Tours depart daily except Saturdays in summer, Sunday mornings only in winter. For exact times, consult the notice board outside the Pump Room entrance or ask at the information office. Be aware, too, that there are short, but very helpful, guided tours of the Roman Baths (the time of the next departure is posted by the Great Bath).

Bus and Train – Trains depart from the Bath Spa railway station on Manvers Street. For information, call British Rail (phone: 63075). The *Bristol Omnibus Company* runs the city buses and long-distance coaches, most of which leave from the bus station, also on Manvers Street. The same company operates 2-hour guided bus tours daily (except Saturdays) during the spring and summer. For bus information or to book a tour, call the station (phone: 64446).

MUSEUMS: In addition to those mentioned in *Special Places,* others of note are:

Museum of Bookbinding – A reconstruction of a nineteenth-century bindery. Open Mondays through Saturdays, July to September; at other times by appointment. Manvers St. (phone: 66000).

Burrows Toy Museum – Children's games, dolls, and other toys of the last two centuries. Open daily. York St. (phone: 61819).

Camden Works – The contents of a Victorian brass foundry, aerated mineral water factory, and engineering works preserved lock, stock, and barrel. Closed Fridays. Julian Rd. (phone: 318348).

Geology Museum – Fossils from the rocks of North Somerset. Closed Sundays. 18 Queen Sq. (phone: 28144).

Victoria Art Gallery – Paintings, etchings, prints, porcelain, and a collection of Bohemian glass. Closed Sundays. Bridge St. (phone: 61111 or 65024 evenings and weekends).

SHOPPING: Bath is an excellent shopping center. The usual gift shops that proliferate wherever tourists congregate are especially tasteful here. Antique shops are numerous, and in addition to the individual ones, there are antique markets where the private shopper may spot something exquisite before the dealer from London or overseas does. The *Great Western Antique Centre,* Bartlett St., is one of these, open Mondays through Saturdays from 9:30 AM to 5 PM. Its many stalls sell everything from victrolas and antique tiled stoves to old buttons still on the card. The *Bartlett Street Antique Market,* just across the street, is another, full of stalls doing business Tuesdays through Saturdays from 9 AM to 5 PM. The *Bath Antique Market,* Guinea La., is a Wednesdays-only (7 AM to 3 PM) occurrence attracting dealers from all over the west of England.

A short selection of Bath's many fine shops, including those selling antiques or collectibles, follows. The majority of the city's stores stay open 6 days a week, closing on Sundays, but there are a few that also close on Mondays.

Bath Stamp & Coin Shop – For collectors or beginners. Pulteney Bridge (phone: 63073).

Corridor Stamp Shop – As above, but stamps only. Look for it, if only to make sure you pass through the narrow, glass-covered arcade where it is located. 7a The Corridor (phone: 63368).

The Gay Venture – Two small shops around the corner from each other, both crammed with smallish objects — antique jewelry, dolls, and boxes and bottles to hold small quantities of things. 7a York St. and 5 Church St. (phone: 64092).

The Gift Horse – Glass paperweights, board games, and other British-made gifts. 14 Union Passage (phone: 66093).

Jolly's – A department store selling everything from fashion to food. Milsom St. (phone: 66201).

Linen & Lace – Edwardian blouses, Victorian nightdresses, plus the old lace cushions and bed linens on which to swoon. 15 George St. (phone: 334040).

E. P. Mallory & Son Ltd. – Again, two shops. Old jewelry and silver at 5 Old Bond St. (phone: 65443); modern jewelry, silver, and china at 1/4 Bridge St. (phone: 65885).

Mementos of Bath – Souvenirs of the Roman Baths and the rest of Bath — even a record of the Pump Room Trio. Roman Baths (phone: 61111).

Timothy Solloway – Fine linens, British and imported, for kitchen, bed, and, of course, bath. 3 Church St. (phone: 66463).

SPECIAL EVENTS: The highlight of the year is the *Bath International Festival of Music,* 2 weeks of musical events of exceptional quality in late May and early June. For concerts and operas, the festival makes use of the town's handsome old halls, including the Assembly Rooms, the Guildhall Banqueting Room, and the Theatre Royal, while choral and organ performances take place in Bath Abbey or in nearby Wells Cathedral. Advance booking is required, and bookings can be made by mail from the first week in April. For details, write to the Bath Festival Office, Linley House, 1 Pierrepont Pl., Bath BA1 1JY. The *Royal Bath and West Show,* the biggest agricultural show in the West Country, is held each year at the end of May. It started in Bath but now takes place 20 miles south of the city at Shepton Mallet. Several antique fairs are held in Bath each year. Most notable is the West of England Antiques Fair, which takes place in May at the Assembly Rooms.

SPORTS: The *Sports and Leisure Centre* on the Recreation Ground has facilities for swimming, squash, badminton, table tennis, and other activities, plus a sauna and a solarium. Across the river via North Parade Bridge (phone: 62563).

Cricket – The *Bath Cricket Club* (phone: 25935) plays at the North Parade Cricket Ground across the river and just to the south of the Sports and Leisure Centre. You'll see matches between local teams there on weekends during the cricket season. If you happen to be visiting Bath in June when the *County Cricket Festival* is held, you'll see some even better teams compete on the Recreation Ground. Consult the newspaper or the monthly events list put out by the information center for specifics.

Fishing – For the license, apply at the Wessex Water Authority, Broad Quay; for the fish, either the River Avon or the Kennet and Avon Canal.

Golf – The *Bath Golf Club* (phone: 63834) is about a mile east of town at Sham Castle (the folly, or false ruin, built by Ralph Allen in 1760 to improve the view from his town house). The *Lansdown Golf Club* (phone: 22138) is about 2 miles north of town on Lansdown. Both clubs accept visitors.

Horse Racing – The *Bath Races* take place a few times each month from April through September at the racecourse on Lansdown, 2 miles north of town.

Rugby – The *Bath Rugby Football Club* (phone: 25192) plays its home games on the Recreation Ground. Again, the monthly events list keeps track of the dates and times.

Soccer – *Twerton Park,* about a mile west of Bath via the Lower Bristol Rd., is the scene of the *Bath City Football Club* (phone: 23087) games. Consult the events list.

Swimming – The pool at the *Sports and Leisure Centre* on the Recreation Ground is open year-round.

THEATER: *Bath's Theatre Royal,* in The Sawclose at the end of Barton St. (phone: 62821) dates from 1805 and has reopened after major renovations. Once again it provides an intimate setting for comedy, drama, musicals, opera, ballet, concerts, and a traditional Christmas pantomime. The theater also stages pre-London openings and is a regional base for the National Theatre.

MUSIC: Concerts of classical music presented in unusual surroundings by leading artists are part of the 2-week Bath International Festival of Music beginning in late May (see *Special Events*). Throughout the rest of the year, music by local and visiting groups can be heard at the *Theatre Royal* and elsewhere. During the summer, the Pump Room Trio holds forth with concerts of light orchestral music in the Parade Gardens on weekday afternoons, and there are band concerts in the same place on Sunday afternoons. Pubs with live jazz nightly or several nights weekly include *The Entertainer,* North Parade, next door to the Fernley Hotel (phone: 61603), and *The Bell,* 103 Walcot St. (phone: 25998).

NIGHTCLUBS AND NIGHTLIFE: The quiet dignity of the place means that Bath is unlikely to win an award as Britain's most swinging city. What happens, happens in the pubs, and in night spots such as *The Beau Nash Club,* Kingston Rd. (phone: 65966), which has two dance floors, including one reserved for roller disco.

SINS: When you've partaken of Bath buns in the Pump Room, indulge yourself further with a Sally Lunn (a hot yeast bun — another local specialty) at *Sally Lunn's House* on North Parade (phone: 61634). Sally's house is supposed to be the oldest in Bath, and the buns have been served here since she herself, a pastry cook, first dreamed them up in the seventeenth century. Do not renounce the topping of raspberry jam and whipped cream. For more obvious sins, consult the barman or hotel porter.

BEST IN TOWN

CHECKING IN: As befits one of Britain's principal tourist cities, Bath has a number of memorable hotels and a few truly outstanding ones. Unfortunately, some of them have the NO VACANCY sign up all summer long, and if you want to visit Bath in July or August in particular, you must book in advance. The Tourist Information Centre, Abbey Churchyard (phone: 60521 for accommodations), will do its utmost to help if you have difficulties and will usually come up with something, even if it is a simple (but usually excellent) bed-and-breakfast establishment where you may have to share a bathroom with fellow guests. Because this is such a popular tourist center, room costs tend to be higher than in many other cities. Expect to pay $80 or more for a double room with breakfast at hotels listed in the expensive category; between $50 and $75 at those listed as moderate; and under $50 at any listed as inexpensive.

Beaufort – Bath's most modern hotel has 123 rooms and is built over a municipal parking lot on the banks of the Avon. There is no period charm here; it rates for efficiency, convenience, and comfort. Walcot St. (phone: 63411). Expensive.

BATH / Best in Town

Francis – In an entirely different spirit, the 90-room *Francis* forms the southern side of Queen Square, built by John Wood the Elder between 1729 and 1736. Damaged by World War II, the hotel has been rebuilt in its original style, and furnishings reflect the period. Reserve well in advance and be sure to ask for a room facing the park. Queen Sq. (phone: 24257). Expensive.

Priory – Without a doubt, this is one of Britain's best country hotels. A gothic-style house built in 1835, its 15 rooms are furnished with antiques, and in the quiet gardens is a heated swimming pool in use from spring through fall. It's located about a mile from the center of Bath. Closed Christmas week. Weston Rd. (phone: 331922). Expensive.

Royal Crescent – The centerpiece of the Royal Crescent, this elegant and historic Georgian hotel is part of Bath's architectural heritage. There are 29 super-deluxe rooms, but to really splurge, spend a night in one of the extra-special apartments. The Sir Percy Blakeney Suite, for example, has a seventeenth-century canopied bed, pale blue sofas, an oriental carpet, and a white and gold ceiling of intricate gesso swirls. 15 & 16 Royal Crescent (phone: 319090). Expensive.

Lansdown Grove – A modernized Georgian mansion, this is on Lansdown hill, facing south over the city. The 44 rooms are pleasantly decorated and some have balconies from which to further enjoy the view. Lansdown Rd. (phone: 315891). Moderate.

Fernley – This is a nineteenth-century building opposite the Parade Gardens, next door to *The Entertainer* pub, and very near the Abbey Churchyard. About half of the 49 rooms have private baths. 1 North Parade (phone: 61603). Moderate.

Gainsborough – A mile from the center, here is a small B&B set in a garden. All 15 rooms have private baths. Weston La. (phone: 311380). Moderate.

Pratt's – As historic as any hotel in Bath, *Pratt's* is located in South Parade, a Wood design of the 1740s. It has 50 modern, comfortable rooms, but not all with private baths. South Parade (phone: 60441). Moderate.

Royal York – Queen Victoria slept here in 1830, when she was still a princess and the hotel was still an old coaching inn. More than half of the 56 large rooms have private baths. George St. (phone: 61541). Moderate.

County – Friendly and unpretentious, this 25-room hotel has a restaurant, grill room, and three bars. Only two of the rooms have private baths. 18–19 Pulteney Rd. (phone: 66493). Inexpensive.

EATING OUT: The range of restaurants in Bath is broad: English, French, Italian, Greek, Indian, Chinese, and many more. And since this is one of Britain's principal tourist cities, the price range is broad, too. You can drop a bundle easily if you wish, but there are opportunities to economize. You'll pay $55 to $60 and up for a meal for two with wine at restaurants listed below as expensive; from $35 to $55 at the moderate ones; and less than $35 at the inexpensive ones. In addition, there are numerous wine bars and fast-food establishments where two people can eat simply for less than $10.

Hole in the Wall – It doesn't sound like much, but this beamed and flagstoned restaurant in the basement of a Georgian building has been one of Bath's most prestigious eating spots for a number of years. The cuisine is mostly French and usually superb, and there is great variety. Reservations are advised, especially for Saturday night. Closed Sundays and 2 weeks after Christmas. 16 George St. (phone: 25242). Expensive.

Old Mill – This is a hotel restaurant on the River Avon about 2.5 miles from town. Good English cooking is the specialty — traditional Sunday lunches are served here, too. Tollbridge Rd., Batheaston (phone: 858476). Expensive.

Priory Hotel – Dinner is a grand occasion here and you can choose to have it either in the Georgian *Brown Dining Room* with period furniture and paintings or in the *Terrace Restaurant* overlooking the courtyard. Cuisine is French — even to the nationality of the pigeons roasted in butter with garlic cloves, brandy, cream, and finely chopped foie gras. Weston Rd. (phone: 331922). Expensive.

Flowers – On the ground floor of three beautifully converted eighteenth-century courtesans' houses, this restaurant is brightly decorated in pastel colors and its walls are crammed with art work. Traditional English food is the specialty. Closed Sundays and Mondays. 27 Monmouth St. (phone: 313774). Expensive to moderate.

Bruno's – Not at all Italian, this intimate, candlelit, cork-walled restaurant does English and French dishes and does them very well. The lemon sole with lychees in a sauce of cream and wine is notable among several other fish and game specialties. Closed Sundays. 2 George St. (phone: 63341). Moderate.

Popjoy's – Beau Nash lived with his mistress Juliana Popjoy in this Georgian house, hence the name of the restaurant. It's one of the very best in Bath, with high-quality English dishes made from seasonal produce. Aperitifs are served in Beau Nash's first-floor dining room. Closed Sundays. Beau Nash House, Sawclose (phone: 60494). Moderate.

La Pentola – Down the stairs at the river end of North Parade, the stone-vaulted barrel of a room that is the restaurant's dining area was once a cellar for the patrician home above. The fare is strictly Italian and rated as among the town's better values. Closed Sundays and Mondays. 14 North Parade (phone: 24649). Moderate.

Wood's – The two dining rooms, basically Georgian including the fireplaces, have been attractively updated with modern cane seating and finished off in tones of beige, burnt orange, and dark red. English and French cooking are featured and it's advisable to book. Closed Sundays and Mondays. 9 Alfred St. (phone: 314812). Moderate.

Barcelona – Small, unpretentious, and Spanish. There are hot snacks only at lunch, but for dinner, specialties such as mussels, grilled king prawns, and, of course, paella appear. Closed Mondays. 31 Barton St. (phone: 63924). Moderate to inexpensive.

The Canary – Peer through the multipaned windows fronting the narrow street and you'll see a profusion of small tables set in a bower of flowery wallpaper, plus many happy customers. This is a busy, licensed teashop serving one-dish meals such as quiche, omelettes, and salads. Closed evenings. 3 Queen St. (phone: 24846). Inexpensive.

Clarets Restaurant and Wine Lounge – A downstairs wine cellar and restaurant with contemporary styling and a youngish, sophisticated clientele. Open 7 days a week for drinks, meals, snacks, or just coffee. In summer, tables are set up outside. 6 Kingsmead Sq. (phone: 66688). Inexpensive.

Francis Hotel – Even if you're not staying here, stop by for the buffet lunch in the elegant surroundings of the hotel's *Roman Bar*. Pile your plate with cold cuts and salad, add a pint of ale, and consume it smugly — it's not at all a bad deal. Queen Sq. (phone: 24257). Inexpensive.

The Terrace – The row of half-circle windows overlooking the Great Bath belongs to the long and narrow *Terrace Restaurant*. Lunch only is served year-round, and in summer, afternoon tea. Pump Room, Abbey Churchyard (phone: 61111). Inexpensive.

Walrus and Carpenter – Beefburgers, chili con carne, and steaks are the choices in this attractive restaurant on a corner near the *Theatre Royal*. It's open evenings only, from 6 to 11. 28 Barton St. (phone: 314864). Inexpensive.

The Moon and Sixpence – This is an attractive self-service wine-bar restaurant situated in a restored courtyard. During the summer, outdoor tables surround a lovely fountain. Just off Broad St. (phone: 60962). Inexpensive.

SHARING A PINT: At first glance, *The Saracen's Head,* 42 Broad St., looks like an ersatz antique. In fact, it is said to be the oldest pub in town. The building was completed in its present form in 1713 and Charles Dickens stayed here in 1835 while it was still an inn (the display case in the wall has a few items from his time). While bending your elbow, be sure to appreciate the original plasterwork in the beamed ceiling. Around the corner on Green St., there's the *Old Green Tree,* and if business is brisk, you'll have to squeeze in. Its tiny bar, smoking lounge, and snug are paneled in dark wood and all is very friendly, intimate, and cozy. *The Grove,* newly opened in a renovated Regency building on Grand Parade opposite the Pulteney Weir, looks like a restaurant in someone's living room. Actually, it, too, is a pub, and although bar snacks are served all day, you can sit graciously at those tables with just a drink. *The Grapes,* Westgate St., occupies a lovely old building — white walls, dark beams, etched glass in the doorway — and the mood is lively. *The Huntsman,* North Parade, manages to be almost all things to all people. The main lounge bar of this establishment is filled at lunch with office workers and with tourists who come for the great variety of fast, honest food. Downstairs, the noisy Cellar Bar is frequented by students and other youth. Upstairs, there's a quiet restaurant. The *Huntsman* is sprawling and comfortable, and the entrance toward the river is claimed to be the oldest shopfront in Bath.

BELFAST

As capital city and seat of the Northern Ireland Parliament, Belfast has made international headlines for the last decade. Most Americans are aware that since 1969 the city has been plagued by terrorist activity, and visitors to Belfast are likely to find a low-profile British Army presence. As you leave Aldergrove Airport you'll encounter a checkpoint, and another at the city center, where all packages and bags are searched before entering. The Irish seem to take all this in stride and carry on their lives in a normal manner. And, because most of the violence is directed toward specific political targets, tourists have not been drawn into it. A look at Belfast's history would, however, prove invaluable for travelers trying to appreciate "the troubles."

Belfast, or *Béal Feirste* in Irish, means "the ford at the mouth of the river," in this case, the Lagan. It was the natural harbor and strategic defense position formed by the River Lagan and Belfast Lough that prompted various marauders over the centuries — Anglo Norman, Scottish, and Irish — to establish a castle here. By the sixteenth century, the area was controlled by the O'Neills, earls of nearby Tyrone. After the final defeat at Kinsale in 1601 of the great Irish chieftain Hugh O'Neill, the lands were confiscated by the English Crown; in 1603, they were granted by Elizabeth I to Sir Arthur Chichester, governor of Carrickfergus, who built a new castle and supplanted the native Irish with English and Scottish colonists. (This was the era of "the plantation of Ireland.") In 1613 Belfast was granted a charter of incorporation and allowed two (Protestant) representatives to the British Parliament. In the years that followed the Catholic Irish rose up in revolt several times, but were always crushed; they suffered particularly under the harsh Penal Codes, which usurped their property, outlawed their religion, and denied their civil rights.

Soon after the revocation of the Edict of Nantes in 1685, Belfast was washed by a new wave of settlers — this time, French Huguenots fleeing religious persecution. They brought with them improved weaving methods, which spurred the town's fledgling linen industry into rapid expansion throughout the eighteenth century. During this period Roger Mulholland, a local architect, drew up a plan dividing the town into a grid of streets for construction and development. The grid included Donegall Square and was bordered roughly by Wellington Place and Chichester, Great Victoria, May, and Howard streets. Along these avenues many elegant Georgian buildings were erected by Belfast's prosperous linen merchants.

The city continued to burgeon during the nineteenth century, aided by the

Act of Union (which made Ireland part of Britain) and by the resurgence of its shipbuilding industry. Belfast was fancifully called "the Athens of the North" for its many patrons of the arts, and most of its gracious architecture (designed by the famous Charles Lanyon) dates to this era. Unfortunately, the city's prosperity was not shared by all its citizens; the Irish Catholics were still excluded from representation in London, better housing, and sometimes even employment.

In 1920, after much bloody struggle by the Irish for self-government, Britain enacted the Home Rule Bill, which established two new Parliaments — one each in Dublin and Belfast. In 1921, a treaty was signed, formally creating an Irish Free State consisting of the 26 southern counties and leaving it to the 6 northern counties to choose between union with this state or with Britain. The Protestant-dominated Belfast Parliament chose the latter, and the new province of Northern Ireland was born.

Today, second in size only to Dublin, Belfast is a sturdy, red brick, industrial city ringed by beautiful bluish-purple hills that shelter ancient castles and echo with Irish folklore. A visit to bustling Belfast — a city that might change Ireland's future — should be followed by a journey along the historic Antrim Coast — an area that shaped Ireland's past.

BELFAST-AT-A-GLANCE

SEEING THE CITY: The best views of Belfast are seen from the top of Cave Hill, 2 miles north of the city. To the south is the Old City, dominated by the copper-domed City Hall in Donegall Square; to the west is Lough Neagh, the largest lake in Ireland. Carrickfergus, Holywood, and Bangor also can be seen from the hill, and on a clear day you might be able to see the Isle of Man.

SPECIAL PLACES: Many of the streets in the eighteenth-century Old City have been made pedestrian walkways and shopping arcades, where automobiles are prohibited. This poses no problem, as Belfast is a small city best seen by foot.

CITY CENTER

City Hall – A statue of Queen Victoria stands in front of this ornately pillared and corniced red stone structure capped by a 173-foot-high copper dome. Completed in 1906, its interior is richly decorated in the elaborate Edwardian style with stained glass and marble. Donegall Sq. S.

St. Malachy's Church – This is a fine example of the lavish Gothic-style Roman Catholic churches built in Ireland during the nineteenth century. Note especially its remarkable fan-vaulted ceiling, virtually dripping with intricate and lovely plasterwork, similar to that found in Henry VII's Chapel at Westminster Abbey in London. Alfred St.

Royal Courts of Justice – An imposing building, finished in 1933, the "four courts" is constructed of Portland stone and was a gift from Britain. Chichester St.

Albert Memorial – Looking a little incongruous among parking lots and office buildings, this 35-meter memorial honoring Prince Albert (Queen Victoria's consort) is built in the shape of a clock tower and has settled slightly to one side, which earned it the nickname "Belfast's leaning tower." At the river end of High St.

Custom House – This squarish and solid-looking building was designed by architect Sir Charles Lanyon in the richly corniced, somewhat grand Italianate style, which was popular in Ireland in the mid-nineteenth century. Sculptures of Britannia, Neptune, and Mercury decorate the pediment on the seaward side. High St.

Belfast Cathedral – This church, which has been under construction since 1899 and therefore combines many architectural styles, is distinguished by some fine Irish-Romanesque carving and sculpture. Donegall St.

ENVIRONS

Port of Belfast – Cranes and cables poise against the sky above this busy city port; the largest in Ireland, it handles a variety of cargo ships and tankers. Shipbuilding is the city's primary occupation and numerous ocean liners have been repaired or constructed here, including the famous *Titanic,* which collided with an iceberg and sank in 1912.

Stormont – A mile-long road leads uphill through the estate, with its extensive gardens of bright scarlet Korona roses, to the moribund Parliament House, once the seat of Northern Ireland's legislature. Two statues on the grounds remind you of Ulster's political reality: One, at the juncture of the approach avenues, is of Lord Carson, the Dublin lawyer who kept Belfast British during and after World War I; the other, in the main entrance hall of the Parliament building, is of Lord Craigavon, Northern Ireland's first prime minister, best known for his fiercely anti-Republican slogans, "Not an inch" and "No surrender." Upper Newtownards Rd., just east of the city.

Belfast Castle – Of very recent vintage (1870), this mansion — with its turrets, tower, gables, and ornate carving — is a fine example of the romantic Scottish baronial style imported to this area during the plantation of Ireland. Given to the city in 1934 by a former mayor of Belfast, the earl of Shaftsbury, the estate is now open to the public. Antrim Rd., north of the city.

Cave Hill – About 2 miles north of the city, Cave Hill is a lovely afternoon's diversion. You can take a stroll through the Hazelwood Gardens and Bellevue Zoological Gardens, or climb to the craggy hill's summit (1,188 feet) and MacArt's Fort, an ancient earthwork.

Queen's University – When founded in 1845, the school was associated with colleges in Galway and Cork; in 1909, it broke away to become independent. Its original red brick, Tudor-style buildings designed by Charles Lanyon are now only a small fraction of the many buildings that make up the university complex. In November the Belfast Festival at Queen's is held at the university, with a multitude of events offered — film, music, and drama. The *Queen's Film Theatre* is also open to the public. University Rd.

- ■ **EXTRA SPECIAL:** Right next door to Queen's University, Belfast's Botanic Gardens is a splendid 38-acre estate dominated by the Charles Lanyon–designed Palm House, an unusual wrought-iron and glass-domed building sheltering tropic plants. Also located within the gardens is the Ulster Museum, which has a fine collection of paintings by English and Irish artists; a section devoted to Irish glass and silver; a display of artifacts and treasures salvaged from the *Girona,* the Spanish galleon that sank off the Antrim coast in 1588; an archaeological exhibit of Bronze and Stone Age tools and crafts; and a gallery explaining the development and technology of the linen industry. University Rd.

SOURCES AND RESOURCES

The Northern Ireland Tourist Board (River House, 48 High St., Belfast BT1 2DS; phone: 46609) offers information, maps, and leaflets on the area. At city hall you can pick up the *Belfast Official Tourist Handbook,* and at bookshops you can buy *Discover Northern Ireland* by Ernest Sandford (£3.50) as well as the booklet *Let's Eat Out* (40p), listing all the eating establishments in Northern Ireland. For help in tracing your ancestral roots, contact the Irish Genealogical Association, 162 Kingsway, Dunmurry, Belfast BT17 9AD (phone: 629595).

For Local Coverage – The *Belfast Telegraph* and the *Newsletter* are both published daily.

GETTING AROUND: As we have said, Belfast's inner core has been closed to private cars, so you will be limited to taking a bus or walking in this area. You may wish to travel outside the city, however, and so listed below are facilities for doing just that.

Bus – For points south, go to the Ulster Coach Station on Great Victoria St.; for points north, to the one on Oxford St. For information about schedules and departures, call 20011.

Car Rental – You'll find several car rental agencies represented at Aldergrove Airport, including *Avis,* 173 Airport Rd. (phone: 52333); *Godfrey Davis,* 181 Airport Rd. (phone: 52123); and *Hertz* (phone: 52533). In the city are *Agnew,* 511 Lisburn Rd. (phone: 663231); *Belfast Car Hire,* 27–31 Grosvenor Rd. (phone: 27211); and *McCausland Self-Drive,* 108 Great George St. (phone: 35171).

Taxi – There are taxi ranks at the main bus and rail terminals and at city hall. Or, call *Fast Taxi* (phone: 58011); *Dial-A-Cab* (phone: 797711); *Able Taxi* (phone: 41999); or *Fonacab* (phone: 33333).

SHOPPING: The highlight of Belfast's shopping scene is its antique shops. Especially recommended are: *Fortwilliam London Lodge,* which carries Victoriana, silver, and jewelry (Fortwilliam Pk.); *John and Charlotte Lamb,* known for eighteenth- and nineteenth-century furniture, paintings, and silver (Shore Rd.; by appointment only); *Sinclair's Antique Gallery,* specializing in fine jewelry and silver (Arthur St.); and *The Bell Gallery,* which handles Irish paintings (Bradbury Pl.). Very little linen is made in Belfast now, but *Smyth's Irish Linen,* 20 Wellington Pl., is the best outlet for quality linens made elsewhere. *Simpson Brothers Ltd.,* 6 Callender St., handles needlework, textile crafts, and Irish linens. For those particularly interested in handcrafts, the free booklet *A Guide to Northern Ireland Crafts and Craftsmen* provides the names, addresses, and specialties of Irish artisans in the six counties as well as Belfast. Write to: Local Enterprise Development Unit, 19 Linenhall St., Belfast BT2 8B5.

SPECIAL EVENTS: The *Ulster Harp National,* Northern Ireland's most important steeplechase, is held at Downpatrick Race Course in February. The boisterous *Battle of the Boyne Parade* (also called Orangemen's Day), the largest in Ireland, marches through Belfast every July 12. In late summer the city holds its *International Rose Trials* at Sir Thomas and Lady Dixon Park, an event that draws rose aficionados from all over Britain and Ireland. The *Belfast Festival* at Queen's University in November is an international arts symposium, with presentations of music, drama, and films.

SPORTS: Fishing – Despite all the commercial shipping coming in and out of Belfast, fishing can be very good in Belfast Lough. It is best known for its coalfish, pollack, and whiting, but small skate are sometimes taken at Ballymaconnell Point, near Bangor, and it's worth trying for cod from the rocks around Blackhead Lighthouse. The area is best fished, however, from a small boat with an outboard motor.

Golf – There are ten 18-hole courses: *Balmoral,* 518 Lisburn Rd. (phone: 668514); *Malone,* Ballydrain, Dunmurry (phone: 612758); *Helen's Bay* (phone: Helen's Bay 3253); *Fortwilliam,* Downview Ave. (phone: 71770); *Clandeboye,* Conlig, Newtownards (phone: Bangor 5767); *The Knock,* Dundonald (phone: Dundonald 3251); *Carnalea,* Station Rd., Bangor (phone: Bangor 5004); *Belvoir Park,* 73/75 Church Rd. (phone: 641159); *Royal Belfast,* Craigavad, Holywood (phone: Holywood 2368); and *Bangor,* Bangor (phone: Bangor 3922).

Sailing – The nearest place to hire a sailboat is the *Ulster Sailing School,* Carrickfergus Harbour (phone: Carrickfergus 65022 or 62215).

Swimming – A number of indoor and outdoor pools are available, including *Falls Road Swimming Pool* (phone: 24906); *Grove Swimming Pool* (phone: 748599); *Templemore Swimming Pool* (phone: 57540); and *Ormeau Swimming Pool* (phone: 21904).

Tennis – Belfast city council has tennis courts, primarily tarmacadam hard courts, in the following city parks: Ormeau, Woodvale, Alexandra, Victoria, Musgrave, Waterworks, Wedderburn, Orangefield, and Ballysillan.

MUSEUMS: In addition to the Ulster Museum and Art Gallery, mentioned in *Extra Special,* Belfast has others of note. They are:

Ulster Folk and Transport Museum – This is a 136-acre, indoor/outdoor complex in Cultra, 7 miles northeast of the city, illustrating Ulster life. In the park, there's a reconstructed village with a linen mill, blacksmith's forge, weaver's cottage, and farmhouses of different styles that illustrate Northern Ireland's social history. Don't miss the first-class collection of Victorian photographs or the exhibit of William Conor's urbanscapes in Cultra Manor, former home of Sir Robert Kennedy, an Ulster diplomat. Small admission charge. Off the Bangor Rd., Cultra.

The Arts Council Gallery – Local artists' work is featured. Bedford House, Bedford St.

The Octagon Gallery – This gallery also exhibits the best work done by local artists. 1 Lower Crescent St.

THEATER: The *Grand Opera House,* adjacent to the Hotel Europa on Great Victoria St., which was refurbished and reopened in late 1980, is Belfast's finest theater. Drama, ballet, concerts, and other entertainments are scheduled throughout the year. For recorded information, call 49129; for advance booking, call 41919. The *Lyric Players Theatre,* Ridgeway St. (phone: 660081 or 669660), features Irish drama and the classics. The *Arts Theatre,* Botanic Ave. (phone: 24936 or 42819), offers popular plays and musicals. The *Group Theatre,* Bedford St. (phone: 29685), presents mostly amateur theatricals, some of which are quite good.

MUSIC: *The Ulster Orchestra* and the *Belfast Philharmonic* give concerts at Ulster Hall, 30 Bedford St.; inquire about tickets at the box office. On Monday nights during the school term, the *Queen's Folk Music Society* presents traditional Irish music at 29 University Sq.

NIGHTCLUBS AND NIGHTLIFE: Belfast's nightlife lacks sparkle. Bars shut down at 11:30 PM. The best bets are the *Penthouse* at the *Europa Hotel* for dancing, or *Abercorn,* a nightclub at 23 Malone St. There are Saturday night dinner dances at the *Culloden Hotel,* Craigavad, and the *Stormont Hotel,* 587 Upper Newtownards Rd.

BEST IN TOWN

CHECKING IN: Belfast, like other Irish cities, offers a range of accommodations, from sleek, modern hotels to charming, old hostelries. Expect to pay $60 and up for a double in a hotel listed as expensive; and between $40 and $60 in moderate. Staying at a guesthouse can be considerably less expensive — rates run about $18 per person. A listing of such lodgings is included in the brochure *All the Places to Stay,* available from the Northern Ireland Tourist Board.

Culloden – Situated on 12 acres of secluded gardens and woodland overlooking Belfast Lough, this one-time bishop's palace may be Northern Ireland's most luxurious hotel. Its beautifully appointed rooms are done in silks and velvets, and the elegant dining room and public areas are filled with antiques. The bar is in part of what was once the bishop's chapel. A new wing has recently been added with 46 rooms. Craigavad (phone: Holywood 5223). Expensive.

Belfast Europa Hotel – This is a modern high-rise hotel right in the city center, near the Opera House and other sites of interest. Its restaurants and bars are popular meeting places for Belfasters, and there's dancing in the nightclub on Friday and Saturday nights. Great Victoria St. (phone: 45161). Expensive.

Stormont Hotel – This hotel is about 4 miles out of town and just across the road from the Parliament Houses and Stormont Castle. It has 50 modern bedrooms and ample parking facilities. The dining room features Irish specialties, and dancing on Saturday nights. 587 Upper Newtownards Rd. (phone: 658621). Expensive.

Wellington Park Hotel – In the prettier part of Belfast, this is a refurbished Georgian building with modern bedrooms and a restaurant. A good choice during the International Arts Festival. 21 Malone Rd. (phone: 661232). Expensive.

The Old Inn – The thatched portion of the inn was built about 1614 and smugglers were said to have used the inn down to the close of the eighteenth century. Many pieces of handsome old furniture are used throughout the inn, and what the rooms lack in size they make up for in charm. The Old English suite has twin brass four-poster beds, and the Azalea Suite has cupboard beds with drapes. Some rooms do not have private baths, but each has a washbasin. In the back of the inn is a tea garden overlooking Crawfordsburn Glen. Just off the Bangor Rd., 15 Main St., Crawfordsburn (phone: Helen's Bay 853255). Expensive to moderate.

EATING OUT: Most Belfast hotels have their own dining rooms. For dinner out, try *Restaurant 44,* 44 Bedford St., or *Thompson's Restaurant,* 47 Arthur St. (phone: 23762). Several other fine restaurants are located in Belfast's suburbs and surrounding small towns. These include: *The Barn,* 120 Mon-lough Rd., Saintfield (phone: 510396); *Carriage Restaurant,* Station Sq., Helen's Bay (phone: 852841); *Clanbrassil House,* Sea Front Rd., Cultra (phone: Holywood 3147); *The Hansom Cab,* 35 Railway St., Lisburn (phone: 74652).

In addition, the Northern Ireland Tourist Board publishes a booklet called *Let's Eat Out in Northern Ireland* (about 60p) that includes an extensive list of eating places in Belfast.

SHARING A PINT: Just across Great Victoria Street from the Europa are two atmospheric old pubs, *The Crown,* with a big stone fireplace and stained-glass windows, and *Robinson's,* with a polished wood snug and mahogany bar. *Kelly's Cellars,* Bank St., and the *American Bar,* Dock St., both offer traditional Irish music. Also try the *Washington Bar,* Howard St.; the *Red Hand Bar,* Lower North St.; and *Hannigan's,* 9 Fountain St.

BRIGHTON

Brighton straddles 7 miles of breezy English Channel coast and although it is England's oldest and most famous resort, it is also a colorful, cosmopolitan town in its own right, with great character, style, and vitality. No winter ghost town this; it bustles all year through.

Brighton has never been prim. In less permissive days when a naughty weekend was still naughty, Brighton was the place for it. Only an hour on the train from London left the maximum time for an illicit interlude in one of the numerous private and discreet hotels. Famous men kept their mistresses here in elegant bay-fronted houses bordering quiet seaview squares. The city people brought their manners, fashions, and entertainments with them and nicknamed their coastal capital "London-on-Sea." This attitude lingers. Brighton has more than its fair share of amusements, hotels, restaurants, theaters, pubs, shops, and sports facilities. It also has a great number of eccentrics and oddballs who wander around unremarked, basking in the town's liberalism and adding to its charm.

None of this happened by chance, for Brighton was established by one of the greatest eccentrics of all time — the Prince Regent who eventually became King George IV of England. This spoiled, wayward, and extravagant libertine first visited Brighton in 1783, lured by the new fashion for sea bathing hailed as a cure-for-all by another eccentric, Doctor Richard Russell of nearby Lewes. The prince loved the place and promptly set about building the most amazing and exotic palace in Europe, just across the fields from the narrow, cobbled streets that once made up the original medieval fishing village of Brighthelmstone.

Famous worldwide for its bizarre beauty, the Royal Pavilion he conjured up sits like a blue and white oriental fantasy in the middle of a formal English garden. Outside, it resembles a Mogul palace; inside, the decor carries a fancy for chinoiserie to the ultimate of lavishness. It became the hub of the Prince Regent's glittering and cultured social circle, but not everyone at first thought it beautiful. Wags at the time commented not only on its onion domes, but also referred to turnips and a "considerable number of bulbs of the crown-imperial, the narcissus, the hyacinth, the tulip, the crocus, and others . . ." To one critic it seemed the dome of St. Paul's had gone to Brighton and pupped. When the Prince Regent was king (1820 to 1830), he lost interest in the completed palace but his successor, King William IV, enjoyed summers here and Queen Victoria stayed here, too, but reportedly was not amused.

The Royal Pavilion set the tone for the future: Regency Brighton was extravagant and gay. The narrow streets of the fishing village became the home of hostelries, restaurants, and boutiques. Theaters, music halls, parks, and gardens sprouted around the Pavilion and Brighton became the country's most fashionable resort, graced by a splendid pier at each end of the seafront.

Its popularity has continued from those Regency days. Although most of its 5.5 million visitors a year now come only for the day or weekend instead of the traditional fortnight, a new university and arts college, an impressive new yachting marina, and a growing convention trade have all combined to add a new dimension to the town and make it far more vital and cultured than most resorts. Brighton also has a distinct cosmopolitan flavor, thanks to its proximity to the Continent. French, German, Italian, Spanish, and Scandinavian students were quick to take advantage of the distance, using the town as a first base for their English-language schooling.

Most visitors still head directly for the beaches, but these are for the hardy rather than the sun worshiper. They are of shingle stones rather than sand and the tides can be strong, fueled by bracing breezes. To the west, the beaches are cleaner, quieter, and fringed with the lawns of Brighton's stately and (dare one say it) staid neighbor, Hove.

The central beaches are boisterous, friendly, and the first to become crowded with families. Here are the amusement arcades, bumper cars, fish and chip cafés, cockles and whelks stalls, paddling pools, putting greens . . . in short, all the slightly sleazy glories of the traditional seaside resort that are not to be missed. The crowning glory of this candy-floss mile is the Palace Pier, complete with café, vintage slot machine museum, fishing platforms, and boat rides as well as endless slot machines and fun-fair thrills. Sadly, the West Pier — far prettier but less well placed for attracting day-trippers — has been closed for some time and will eventually be demolished, if it doesn't fall down first.

Heading east past the center of town, England's famous white cliffs begin their gradual climb toward Dover. The beaches become rockier and narrower and virtually disappear at high tide. But at low tide they are a veritable delight for shrimp catchers and seapool ponderers. The quaint and largely unspoiled village of Rottingdean, 4 miles east of the center of Brighton in the gentle, rolling hills of the Sussex Downs, is the perfect focal point for these uncommercialized, untamed beaches that still belong to the true sea lover.

Lining Brighton's main seafront and stretching into spacious garden squares behind it are hundreds of hotels and guesthouses, large and small, good and bad. Most are in Regency style with bay fronts, balconies, and wrought-iron trimmings, but there are some good modern hotels as well, a result of the thriving conference trade. Beyond the seafront, the heart of the town lies focused on the narrow streets of the original village and the shopping streets that grew up around it and the Royal Pavilion. Cosmopolitan Brighton lives in these "Lanes," with art shops, book shops, boutiques, and antique stalls, and, of course, the best restaurants, cafés, pubs, and wine bars. There's something for every taste and pocketbook here and the whole area of the Lanes is perfect for people-watching or browsing. Locals use this part as much as visitors, even in high summer, and if prices are a little inflated, perhaps the atmosphere is worth it!

Real local color is still farther afield, however, and is very easy to miss. It centers on Gloucester Road and Kensington Gardens, in the area between Brighton's railway station and the Dome. This whole section was once nearly a slum until a timely preservation order made it trendy. Now the little flat-fronted laborers' houses are snapped up by aspiring executives who commute to London. It is also the main student quarter and the starting point for many of the newest fashions, and it is certainly the best place for spotting the real eccentrics or one of the many famous actors who live or retire here. It is still possible to find bargains in the junk shops, and the local pubs and cafés might be scruffy but they are also genuine, frequented by some of the resort's most fascinating people.

Between this highly metropolitan scene and the seaside razzmatazz Brighton offers a whole range of entertainments, holiday sports, and sights. Few visitors allow themselves sufficient time to see it all, let alone the beautiful Sussex countryside surrounding the town. But the beauty of this lovely, liberal place is that you can spend as little as a day or as much as a year here and still come away satisfied.

BRIGHTON AT-A-GLANCE

SEEING THE CITY: The best view is from the end of the Palace Pier, which is at the junction of Marine Parade and the Old Steine. On the clearest days you can see the whole sweep of the coast from Worthing to Beachy Head. To the west, the Peace Statue marks the boundary of Brighton and the start of Hove Lawns. To the east is the impressive seawall of the Marina with the white cliffs above. In between is the entire Brighton seafront. Don't neglect the pier itself, a splendid Victorian structure of iron and steel, wood and glass, lined with amusement halls, slot machines, sun decks, fishing platforms, and endless candy-floss and hot donut stalls. The Palace Pier is open every day of the year, hours depending on the season. There is a small admission charge.

For a spectacular, if expensive, night view, hotels such as the *Metropole* or the *Norfolk Continental,* both on King's Rd., have rooftop rooms for dinner or dancing.

SPECIAL PLACES: You'll be doing a lot of walking — browsing through the old quarter, ambling along the seafront promenade, visiting the dazzling Brighton Pavilion — within a fairly centralized area of an otherwise sprawling town. For the sights outside the center, take the local bus, unless something more characteristic, such as the electric railway or the open-topped excursion buses mentioned below, is indicated.

CENTRAL BRIGHTON

Royal Pavilion – A Mogul palace bedecked with minarets, onion domes, terraces, and trellises, this was the creation of Brighton's prime mover and shaker, the Prince Regent who became King George IV of England. It was begun modestly in 1786 and was rebuilt in its present extravagant form by the English architect John Nash (who also laid out Regent's Park and Regent Street in London and redesigned Buckingham Palace) from 1815 to 1821. The state and private apartments are arranged with superb Regency- and Chinese-style furniture and works of art, including many original pieces on loan from Queen Elizabeth. Open daily (phone: 603005).

204 BRIGHTON / At-a-Glance

If at all possible, visit during July, August, or September when the Regency Exhibition makes the Pavilion even more spectacular than usual, with the huge Banqueting Room set with silver, gold, porcelain, and glass from the period. Other marvelous rooms include the Saloon, the North and South Drawing Rooms, the King's Apartments, and the Great Kitchen, which has the original mechanical spits, over 500 pieces of copperware, and tables showing the preparation of a banquet. The magnificent Music Room, tragically destroyed by fire in 1975, is still being restored. The Royal Pavilion Lawns have deck chairs and regular summer performances by the Pavilion Trio band. The Royal Pavilion is also the scene of some of the musical events of the Brighton Festival, held in May. Open daily, from late September to June, 10 AM to 5 PM; from early June until late September, open 10 AM to 7:30 PM; closed Christmas, Boxing Day, and for 2 days prior to the Regency Exhibition. Admission charge. Town center, above the Old Steine (phone: 603005).

The Lanes – The roughly square mile of narrow, paved alleys that made up the original village can only be visited on foot. This area is Brighton's Old Town and it's full of atmosphere and character, with countless shops for buying or browsing, including particularly good ones for books or antiques. Shop around to find the best price, however, especially if you're looking at antique jewelry. Entrances to the Lanes are all clearly marked and the easiest to spot are on East Street, North Street, Ship Street, and Middle Street. Look for Duke's Lane, just off Ship Street, cunningly created out of backyards and filled with boutiques. Brighton Square, another of the more modern additions, is the center of the Lanes, with trees, benches, and a café-bar ideal for watching the world go by, Continental style.

King's Road – This is the main seafront road. Steps and slopes lead down from it to the central beaches and the lower promenade with cafés, amusement halls, and all the traditional seaside entertainment. Fish and chips wrapped in newspaper, jellied eels, peanuts, ice cream, cotton candy, and Brighton rock candy are the things to eat, washed down with a pot of tea that will be served on a tin tray if you want to take it to the beach for a picnic. It's cheap and very cheerful, but rent a deck chair because you might find bits of tar on the pebbles. The Palace Pier end of the King's Road is most rowdy. Opposite the beach at East Street, the Old Fish Market is still used (and smells like it) and the adjoining beaches are used by local sailing clubs. Toward Hove, the scene becomes more sedate, with singsong pubs replaced by boating ponds and putting greens. If you prefer grass to stony beaches, the Lawns at Hove are the place to take the sun and sea.

Volk's Railway and Peter Pan's Playground – Britain's first public electric railway opened in 1883 and still runs along the edge of Brighton's easterly beaches. The track starts 200 yards east of Palace Pier and extends 1 mile to the western perimeter of the Marina. The ride is inexpensive, and passengers travel in little wooden carriages with open sides and yellow roofs. Take it out to the Marina, then stroll back at sea level along Madeira Drive, passing Peter Pan's Playground and Fun Fair. The alternative is to return via the high-level Marine Parade with its ornate Victorian ironwork — the walk is quieter and gives better views. There is a temperamental lift opposite Peter Pan's but don't rely on it working. Volk's Railway runs from Easter until October; Peter Pan's Playground is open from Easter through September.

Brighton Art Gallery and Museum – Close to the gardens of the Royal Pavilion and housed in buildings originally intended as stables for the palace, the gallery contains Brighton's fine collection of old masters and English watercolors, and a good collection of pottery and porcelain. It also has the most important collection of twentieth-century Continental and English decorative art in the country. Worth seeing as well — the history of Brighton's seaside. Open Tuesdays through Saturdays; afternoons only on Sundays; closed Mondays. Free. Church St. (phone: 603005).

Brighton Marina – This ambitious construction, the largest yachting marina in Europe, was built against the odds of gale force winds and tumultuous seas and opened in May 1979, by the Queen. Immense breakwaters protect the inner harbor and have an enviable record for fishing catches. The marina has berths for over 2,000 yachts, a selection of historic boats, a chandlery, and a boatyard. Special events are arranged throughout the year. Open every day from 9 AM until dusk. Reach it by Volk's Railway, a number 7a bus from Old Steine, or by car — there is good parking. Small admission charge. Marine Dr., 2 miles east of the Palace Pier (phone: 693636).

Saint Nicholas's Churchyard – Brighton is full of quiet green corners tucked away out of sight of the main roads and easy to miss. St. Nicholas's Churchyard is one of the prettiest and is perfectly placed for a rest after shopping in nearby Western Road. It's a short walk up the steep hill of Dyke Road (which starts just above the Clock Tower) to the shallow brick steps that lead into the peaceful grounds surrounded by the gray flint walls characteristic of the area. The church itself is not always open but has a twelfth-century Norman font and some excellent stained-glass windows. The top end of the churchyard leads into a small park.

ENVIRONS

Preston Manor – Two miles out from the Old Steine along the main London Road is this charming eighteenth-century country house set in beautiful parkland. It has original furnishings of the seventeenth to nineteenth centuries, including some fine silver and paintings, all arranged as they would have been during the life of the family that owned it. Open Wednesdays through Saturdays 10 AM to 5 PM; Sundays 2 PM to 5 PM; closed Mondays and Tuesdays except bank holidays. Small admission charge. Buses number 5 or 15 from the Old Steine take about 10 minutes (phone: 552101).

Booth Museum of Natural History – Not too far away from Preston Manor, this is an entirely different kind of museum. It houses a large collection of British birds, stuffed and displayed in their natural habitats, plus an exhibit of skeletons illustrating evolution. Open weekdays except Thursdays 10 AM to 5 PM, Sundays 2 PM to 5 PM. 194 Dyke Rd., close to the Seven Dials (phone: 552586).

British Engineerium – Various Victorian steam engines — and the impressive Easton and Anderson steam engine of 1876 — puff efficiently away every weekend in the engine houses of this "living steam" museum. A huge number of Victorian mechanical inventions and other engineering exhibits are displayed in the beautifully restored nineteenth-century water pumping station. Open daily except Christmas 10 AM to 5 PM. Small admission charge. Nevill Rd., Hove, 3 miles from Brighton center (phone: 559583).

Stanmer Park – A natural park in the downland of Sussex is the setting for a village preserved as it was at the turn of the century. There are farmyards, a duck pond, a woodland park, and a manor house to visit. Most parts are open daily. Lewes Rd., 4 miles northeast of Brighton center, just before the University of Sussex campus.

Devil's Dyke – This famous beauty spot is 700 feet above sea level. The devil is supposed to have dug a chalk pit here to let in the sea and drown the pious folk of Sussex. The attempt failed but the view is spectacular. Near Poynings, 8 miles from Brighton center.

■ **EXTRA SPECIAL:** When the weather allows, open-topped excursion buses run along the seafront to Rottingdean, a picturesque Sussex village set on the cliff tops in downland countryside. Steps and slopes lead to the undercliff walk edging narrow rocky beaches and to the open-air saltwater swimming pool — a sun trap that catches reflections off the white cliffs above it. A very pretty High Street has some good pubs and curio shops as well as the general stores typical of a small village. The *Plough Inn* is on the village green. Rudyard Kipling lived in Rottingdean and adjoining his house on the green is *The Grange,* a small art gallery and museum that has displays of his letters and books as well as Sussex folklife collections, toys, and frequent temporary exhibitions. The Grange is open Mondays, Tuesdays, Thursdays, and Fridays 10 AM to 6 PM; Saturdays 10 AM to 5 PM; and Sundays 2 PM to 5 PM in winter, 2 PM to 6 PM in summer (phone: 31004). Rottingdean village is 4 miles east of Brighton, easily reached by several buses, including the open-topped ones.

SOURCES AND RESOURCES

The main Tourist Information Centre is at Marlborough House, 54 Old Steine, near North St. (phone: 23755). There is an information kiosk open in the summer only on King's Rd. at West St. Hove's Tourist Information Centre is at the Town Hall, Church Rd. (phone: 775400). All three carry books, maps, guides, and leaflets. The official town guide (10p) gives a brief outline of attractions and lists accommodations. It has an adequate map but a better one will cost 45p, or there's a street-by-street guide for about £1, both available at local book stores and newsstands. *In and Around Sussex* (25p) is good for attractions up to 30 miles from Brighton. There is also a guide for disabled visitors. The tourist information center has these. The BTA publishes a good general leaflet available free of charge at its US offices.

For Local Coverage – The *Brighton Evening Argus* is on sale everywhere from about 3 PM onward, usually with a good entertainment section. There is also a weekly *Brighton and Hove Gazette* and a weekly *What's On* sold at newsstands.

GETTING AROUND: Central Brighton is ideal for walking — the best parts are all fairly close. Outside the main center, the town gets hilly.

Bus – This is the best way to get around both the town and the county. Local buses run from the Old Steine. Regional Southdown Motor Services buses leave from the Pool Valley Bus Station where the timetable is on display. Some buses require the exact fare so take loose change with you or buy a Travelcard for unlimited weekly travel. Fares start at 10p. For information on local buses, call 606141; for regional services, 606600.

Tourbus – From mid-June to mid-September, guided tours aboard double-decker buses provide a good introduction to the city. Tickets and timetables are available at the Tourist Information Centre.

Taxi – There are reliable taxi stands at the railroad station and at the intersection of East and North streets. You may be able to hail a cab in the street and they are good at responding to telephone calls. To order one, phone *Streamline Cars* at 27282.

Car Rental – All main firms are represented but traffic is congested, and car parking is scarce and by meter in the center. Unless you're planning an excursion, you're better off without a car.

MUSEUMS: In addition to those mentioned in *Special Places,* museums of interest are:

Hove Museum of Art – Coins, medals, watches, dolls, and miniatures as well as a good modern exhibition. 19 New Church Rd., Hove (phone: 229410).

Aquarium and Dolphinarium – Performing dolphins in the 1,000-seat dolphinarium and a varied display of freshwater, marine, and tropical fish, sea lions, and turtles in the mock Gothic underground galleries of Britain's largest aquarium. At presstime, the new "Brighton Experience" audiovisual theater was scheduled to open shortly. Marine Parade (phone: 604234).

SHOPPING: Churchill Square is Brighton's pride — a new, modern precinct with all the major chain stores including *Habitat,* the furniture and housewares store. It's next to the original shopping street of Western Road, near its eastern end. In the vicinity of Churchill Square, Western Road runs into North Street, giving almost 2 miles of prime shopping, with the cheap and cheerful shops and stalls of Gardner Street, Bond Street, and the Lanes leading off North Street. The best guide to the city's odd and unusual shops is an entertaining booklet called "You Can Get It in Brighton," available at the Tourist Information Centre for £1.50. Best buys are antiques, bric-a-brac, secondhand books, and local paintings and crafts, plus the traditional English glass, china, and woolens. Some shops close for half a day on either Wednesdays or Thursdays though this practice is gradually dying out. Shops to look for include the following:

Friends – A fascinating leather shop, either for buying things ready-made or the materials to make them yourself. The store also does first-class repairs to all leathergoods. 29 Bond St. (phone: 27607).

Hanningtons – The smartest store in town, selling furniture, china, and glass, as well as men's and women's clothing. North St. (phone: 29877).

Kokoro – A rare antiquarian bookshop with some precious volumes, historic documents, and manuscripts. 36 Duke St. (phone: 25954).

Lawleys – Good for china and glass. 25 North St. (phone: 26068).

Ralph Lewis Gallery – Excellent exhibitions of local artists' watercolors, ceramics, pottery, woodcarvings, and hand-made scarves, all reasonably priced. The owner, a local artist and author, talks about them with great enthusiasm. 1 Union St., the Lanes (no phone).

SPECIAL EVENTS: The *Brighton Festival* in May provides a full program of music, theater, dance, and other entertainment, all detailed in the festival program available from February on. For information, write to the Brighton Festival Office, Marlborough House, Old Steine, Brighton, East Sussex BN1 1EQ, England.

The *London to Brighton Veteran Car Run* takes place in early November. Antique cars — the "Old Crocks" — make their annual pilgrimage from Hyde Park Corner in London to Madeira Drive in Brighton in celebration of the day in 1896 when a law requiring all motorcars to be preceded by a man waving a red flag was finally dropped. A *Historic Commercial Vehicle Rally,* every year in May, is a runner-up to the Old Crocks. Trucks, fire engines, ambulances, and the like take part.

SPORTS: You can wear yourself out at the *King Alfred Sports Centre* playing badminton or table tennis, bowling, swimming in the two indoor sea-water pools, luxuriating in the private baths or taking a sauna, then finishing off in the restaurant or bar. Open all year. Kingsway, Hove (phone: 734422).

Cricket – For a modest entry fee you can watch a match — called a fixture — at the *Sussex County Cricket Ground,* Eaton Rd., Hove. The local tourist office has a calendar of fixtures.

Fishing – Good catches are sea whiting, mackerel, occasionally plaice, and very occasionally cod. The best place to fish is at the *Brighton Marina* (phone: 693636). Pay 35p a session at the office or hire a boat for £7 from the fishing tackle shop. During the summer, only angling club members can fish from the Palace Pier: Try your luck at the groynes (breakwaters) instead. Those toward Hove, where there are fewer boats and swimmers to disturb you and the fish, are preferable. No charges or permits for this.

208 BRIGHTON / Sources and Resources

Golf – The *East Brighton Golf Club,* Roedean Rd., has one of the best courses in the area, with magnificent views over sea, downs, and Marina. Visitors are welcome. Several buses from the Old Steine pass it (phone: 603989). The municipal *Hollingbury Park Golf Club,* Ditchling Rd., has 18 reasonable holes open to all. Number 26 bus from the Old Steine takes you right there (phone: 552010). If you prefer to take the game very casually, try the two pitch-and-putt courses on either side of the Roedean school on the way to Rottingdean. You can rent clubs, balls, and tees, and hit away happily without embarrassment.

Greyhound Racing – *Coral Stadium,* Nevill Rd., Hove, has races three times a week (twice in winter) from 7:45 PM. Telephone 731028 or 720757 for a table in the excellent restaurant.

Horse Racing – The *Brighton Races* meet 17 times a year between April and October at the *Brighton Racecourse,* Race Hill (phone: 29801, ext. 426).

Soccer – There's a good local support for the *Brighton and Hove Albion* — known locally as the Seagulls. Games are played from late August to mid-April at the Brighton and Hove Albion Ground on Goldstone Rd., Hove (phone: 739535).

Tennis – Twelve parks have public courts. The main ones are in *Preston Park,* 10 hard courts in all, easily seen from the London Road. Another 10 courts are on the other (west) side of the road away from the main park in a section called the Rockery. There's no racquet hire, nor can you book any of the public courts. Just take a chance and turn up, but be prepared to wait during July and August.

Windsurfing – The *Southern Windsurfing School,* on the beach just west of the Palace Pier, has courses for beginners and the more advanced (but be ready for onlookers from the pier). Board hire is also available. Arch 185, King's Rd. (phone: 21968 from Easter to September; all-year number is 606-2013 in London).

THEATER: The *Theatre Royal,* New Rd. (phone: 28488), has pre-London runs and variety with weekly changes in the bill. Some good, some bad. Other productions are at the *Gardner Centre Theatre,* a modern theater-in-the-round at the University of Sussex, Falmer (phone: 685861).

MUSIC: You can hear all kinds. Big pop and rock concerts are at the 5,000-seat *Brighton Centre,* Russell Rd. (phone: 202881). The *Dome,* 29 New Rd., slightly smaller with 2,000 seats, stages classical, light, pop, rock, and variety events, including some with international celebrities (phone: 682127). The rooms of the *Royal Pavilion* are used for recitals and chamber concerts not only during the Brighton Festival but also throughout the year. You'll see them well advertized in the local press and on posters around town. *St. Peter's Church,* London Rd., has occasional organ concerts, and several pubs have folk, jazz, and rock groups and informal singsongs.

NIGHTCLUBS AND NIGHTLIFE: This tends to be bright, breezy, and informal, with the emphasis on the young and noisy. Apart from the pubs, which are crowded in summer, activity centers on *Kingswest,* an entertainment complex on King's Road close to the West Street intersection. It contains three nightspots. *Busbys* (phone: 25899) is for the smartly dressed (no jeans) over-21 crowd. *Jenkinson's Cabaret Bar* (phone: 25897) caters to a younger and more trendy clientele, but still no jeans. The music is live, usually pop and rock. The *Top Rank Suite* (phone: 25895) varies from night to night, sometimes live music, sometimes disco. Check the *Argus* for details. There are two casinos: one in the *Metropole Hotel,* and *Sergeant York's,* 88 Queen's Rd., near the station (phone: 26541). Several hotels and restaurants have dinner dances or cabarets.

SINS: The first public nudist beach in the country opened officially in Brighton in April 1980. If you can defy the winds, the pebbles, and the rubberneckers (or you'd rather be one yourself), the beach is just to the west of the Marina.

BEST IN TOWN

CHECKING IN: The best hotels are those with a sea view and even inexpensive ones can be found overlooking the eastern or western ends of the beaches. At an expensive hotel a twin room with private bathroom and TV will cost about $55 to $60 per person, including breakfast, tax, and service. A moderate hotel will be about $35, and the simplest private hotel (guesthouse) will be from $15 to $25, but this will not include a private bathroom. The better hotels offer reduced weekly rates in June, July, and August, when there is no convention business in town and many also offer winter weekend bargains. Do not turn up without a reservation from August through June, which is traditionally convention season. There are also holiday flat-lets available with prices from $90 to $350 per flat per week, depending on the size.

The Bedford – Tall, modern, spacious, comfortable, and a little impersonal, but one of the best in town. It has 124 rooms. King's Rd. (phone: 29744). Expensive.

The Grand – Right in the center of the seafront, this is an old and very attractive hotel with Victorian architecture at its best in the lobby and landings. The rooms, 178 of them, are modern and comfortable. King's Rd. (phone: 26301). Expensive.

The Metropole – A large, modernized period hotel, it has good facilities, including its own health club and casino, plus garage. It also has an attached exhibition hall and since it's the main conference hotel in Brighton, it's one of the first to fill. King's Rd. (phone: 775432). Expensive.

Norfolk Continental – Toward the Hove end of the seafront and recently reconstructed, it still sports its attractive and bright Regency-style exterior. This is a busy place of 70 rooms, with its own wine-cellar bar, pub, and American bar with live music over the weekend, plus a rooftop nightclub and restaurant. King's Rd. (phone: 738201). Expensive.

Olde Place – If you can't stay here, or prefer to be in the center of town, this traditional, oak-beamed village inn is still worth a visit for a meal. High St., Rottingdean (phone: 31051). Moderate.

Old Ship – On the seafront close to the Lanes, much of its original style and charm is intact, especially in the 200-year-old banqueting room used by the Prince Regent. The 151 rooms vary from simple singles to lavish antique-four-poster-bedded delights. King's Rd. (phone: 29001). Moderate.

Prince Regent – There are many smaller hotels in this elegant, airy square facing the West Pier. This one was recently restored in full Regency style, and the accent is on friendly service. 29 Regency Sq. (phone: 29962). Moderate.

Royal Crescent – One mile out of the center, this 66-room hotel has a strong Regency flavor, a friendly atmosphere, and excellent views. It's close to the Kemp Town area with some interesting little shops nearby. Marine Parade (phone: 606311). Moderate.

Wheeler's Sheridan Hotel – This is a landmark of red Edwardian brick at a noisy corner of the seafront, but its location is outweighed by its plushness — velvet, brass, and crystal — and atmosphere. Its 56 rooms are very popular with regular customers, so book ahead. 64 King's Rd. (phone: 23221). Moderate.

Le Flemings Hotel – It's small but it's enterprising, with music and dancing in the bar, comfortable furnishings, and a pretty courtyard. Regency Sq. (phone: 27539). Inexpensive.

Orient Hotel – Here, in a street full of them, is one of Brighton's better small private hotels. It's a few yards from the seafront and a good value. 8–10 Oriental Pl. (phone: 25082). Inexpensive.

Touring Hotel – Two miles out from the center, close to Preston Manor and Park, this is a good stop for the motorist. It's a modern, attractive 20-room hotel with parking and it's close to the main London-Brighton Road. 216 Preston Rd. (phone: 507853). Inexpensive.

EATING OUT: Brighton is fortunate in having a greater variety of restaurants than most cities its size. You'll find just about every style of cooking you could want, including the usual range of Indian, Chinese, and Italian, and better-than-average Greek. Local fish is delicious, whether it costs 50p and is served in a newspaper or sets you back £10 in an exclusive fish restaurant. There are some good fun spots with cheap fast food and there's a healthy sprinkling of better restaurants with excellent and imaginative fare. At the cheaper restaurants you can still get a simple English 3-course set meal for under $10 per person. In the moderate ones, a meal with a fair amount of skill in its preparation and presentation will cost about $20, including house wine. The most expensive in town will cost about $28 to $35 each, including wine, with service on top.

English's Oyster Bar – If you can treat yourself only once, do it here. The restaurant is 150 years old, converted from 400-year-old fishermen's cottages in the Lanes. Reservations necessary. Closed Christmas and Boxing Day. 29–31 East St. (phone: 27980). Expensive.

French Connection – Once a Georgian fisherman's cottage, this is now an intimate and romantic restaurant known for its unusual French and English dishes. Service is especially friendly. Closed Sundays and Christmas week. 11 Little East St. (phone: 24454). Expensive.

Le Francais – For those who take French cuisine very seriously, here is a smart, formal restaurant that does the same. Specialties are from Normandy, but go easy if you can and save room for the desserts. Dinner only. Closed Christmas. 1 Paston Pl., Kemptown area (phone: 680716). Expensive.

Wheeler's Oyster Rooms and Restaurant – The seafood is unsurpassed and it's served in Edwardian-style elegance. Reservations are necessary, since this is one of the oldest and best-known restaurants in the region. Closed Christmas and Boxing Day. 17 Market St. (phone: 25135). Expensive.

Lawrence – A tiny, tasty place and it's easy to miss. Fish is best but there are also unusual dishes, cooked on request. Dinner only. Closed Sundays, Tuesdays, and Christmas. 40 Waterloo St. (phone: 772922). Moderate.

Le Grandgousier – This is tiny, too, and informal. Everyone shares one huge table and tucks into the simply-cooked food. The choice is limited but it's great fun and good value. Closed Saturday lunch and all day Sunday, but usually open until midnight for dinner. 15 Western St. (phone: 772005). Moderate.

Spartacus – No place is complete without a Greek taverna and here's a good one. Try the *bouzouki* music, belly dancing, singing, dancing, and plate-smashing. Open every night until 2 AM (midnight on Sundays). 38 Preston St. (phone: 24682). Moderate.

Zorba's – This is very much like *Spartacus* and worth knowing about when its neighbor is full. 34 Preston St. (phone: 21453). Moderate.

BRIGHTON / Best in Town

Al Forno – Simple and crowded, this Italian place is great for pizzas and pastas. Eat outside during the summer. Closed Mondays, Sunday lunch, and Christmas. 36 East St. (phone: 24905). Moderate to inexpensive.

Browns – The atmosphere is light, bright, and busy, with sanded floors, white walls, and palms. This is the best of the hamburger-spaghetti palaces, open every day with continuous service. Ship and Duke Sts. (phone: 23501). Inexpensive.

Caprice Carvery – You'll have to leave the center of Brighton, but it's well worth the trip — you may carve as much as you want from the roasts. Open daily. Third Ave., Hove (phone: 778737). Inexpensive.

Golden Girl – This is a good example of the traditional seaside café offering top value in plain cooking and fast service. It has no license to serve drinks, but full meals are available from noon until night. Open daily except Christmas. Manchester St. (phone: 603147). Inexpensive.

Woodforde's – It's in simple, farmhouse style, and it's known for its toasted sandwiches, pancakes, and homemade cakes served for brunch, lunch, and tea. In the evening there's a dinner menu, but bring your own wine. Closed during the day in winter and on Sundays year-round. 6 George St. (phone: 687453). Inexpensive.

SHARING A PINT: It's difficult to choose from the wide selection of pubs in Brighton. Best for atmosphere and interest include the *Abinger,* 142 King's Rd., 200 yards from the West Pier. It has an unusual split-level design with alcoves and balconies overlooking the sea. The *Belvedere,* 159 King's Rd. Arches, close to the Palace Pier, is a boisterous, beachside bar — don't dress up. The *Colonnade Long Bar,* New Rd., is next to the Theatre Royal and used during intermissions; it has Victorian decor and a good selection of playbills. Don't miss *Cricketers* on Black Lion St., the town's oldest pub. The original parts, dating back to 1549, include the stables and coachyard, and there are old mirrors and marble and brass tables. The *Bedford Tavern,* 30 Western St., is simple and unassuming but if you're passing by, pop in to see its collection of heraldry. Go to *Dr. Brighton's,* on King's Rd. by Market St., for the real old gaiety bar atmosphere of red velvet, engraved mirrors, and live old-time piano music. The *Druid's Head,* Market Pl., The Lanes, is an old-world pub with beams and decorative horse brasses. Once a smugglers' haunt, it now belongs to the fashionable young set. The *King and Queen,* Marlborough Pl., an amusing imitation of a Tudor beer garden, overlooks the Old Steine Gardens. It's good for families — there's an aviary for diversion. The *Royal Pavilion Tavern,* Castle Sq., is a popular central pub with old oak panels and beams and extensive hot and cold snacks. In Rottingdean, the *Black Horse,* High St., is a genuine village pub, with a comfortable and friendly large bar and the original snug — the tiny bar for women.

BRISTOL

A century ago, as described in the pages of Robert Louis Stevenson's *Treasure Island*, a wide-eyed visitor could wander the docks of Bristol, sniffing in the smell of tar in the salt air, marveling at the figureheads of ships that had been far over the world and the "many old sailors, with rings in their ears, and whiskers curled in ringlets, and tarry pigtails, and their swaggering, clumsy sea-walk . . ." It was a scene that any movie mogul would have been proud to conjure up on a Hollywood back lot.

Naturally, Bristol looks like that no more. Now it's a large and relatively modern city with isolated patches of antiquity, plenty of new office buildings, lots of traffic, and much that is happening almost everywhere but in the city docks. Walk along the quayside today and you'll see the characteristic old warehouses decrepit and deserted, or restored to new use as museums and arts and exhibition centers. Freight yards are empty, cranes idle, and the great ships of yesteryear are merely suggested by the presence of faded barges, modest pleasure craft, and, sometimes, naval warships. The impression is not one of beauty, in fact, until the visitor comes upon one of Bristol's massive medieval churches, all the more imposing for its twentieth-century surroundings, or stumbles into one of its narrow cobbled streets, or penetrates the spirit of those old and derelict docks.

Bristol had been an important port since the eleventh century. During the Middle Ages, its merchants and seafarers traded in wine, stacking the wharves and cellars with Bordeaux from France, sherry from Spain, and port from Portugal. By the fifteenth century it was known for an enterprising maritime boldness that attracted sailors from Europe bent on discovery. John Cabot came from Italy, found backing by a local merchant, and set sail in 1497 to become the first explorer to reach the American mainland. The customs officer who awarded Cabot a pension was Richard Amerycke, and to this day some Bristolians believe that it was he, and not Amerigo Vespucci, who gave his name to the New World.

Cabot was followed by other explorers, then by thousands of early American settlers who stepped off European soil here and sailed to a new life. Having played its part in the discovery of America, Bristol did its share in developing it, financing colonization efforts, trading in Virginia tobacco and West Indian sugar. A less glorious chapter in its history was its involvement in the black slave trade, on the proceeds of which Bristol merchants grew fat, while the Quakers and John Wesley and his Methodists, who were all influential here, railed against it.

Unlike most seafaring cities, the docks in Bristol are not at the edge of town but right in the heart of it, and for all those centuries, the ships, like cars lined up at parking meters on Main Street, dominated the Bristol scene. That they do no longer is the result of an error of judgment on the part of the earliest Bristolians. The city grew at the confluence of the Avon and Frome rivers, 7 miles inland from where the Avon — which rises and falls with almost the highest tide in the world — flows out into the Severn estuary. Fear of piracy caused the medieval inhabitants to plant themselves far upstream, a less than ideal location that made docking a tricky business of picking the right moment to set out upriver or risk getting stuck in the mud at low tide. Even berthed ships were in danger of breaking up in the tidal sweep.

To remedy this, the city channeled the Avon into a new cut in the early eighteenth century, creating a "floating harbor" with a constant level of water for ships to tie up in. But by then, much transatlantic trade had already been lost to Liverpool. Ironically, the situation was not helped by the presence of Isambard Kingdom Brunel, the pioneering British engineer who built the largest vessels of his day, thereby inspiring even larger ones — which couldn't make it up the Avon to Bristol. By the end of the nineteenth century, new docks had been built downstream at Avonmouth and Portishead, and Bristol's reputation as an international port was safe. But the waterways in the center of town are now all but deserted and the dockside bustle takes place miles away.

The cityscape underwent a further change as a result of World War II. The blitz of 1940–41 damaged some 90,000 buildings, including the medieval core (the original castle that used the Avon and the Frome as its moat had been razed centuries before on the orders of Cromwell). Throughout history the tallest structures in Bristol had been the spires and towers of churches, but with postwar reconstruction came the first tall office blocks. Now it is necessary to walk between walls of concrete and glass for a glimpse of the churches, as fine as those in any medieval city, and the other reminders of Bristol's heritage — remains of early monasteries and Georgian squares and terraces — that survive.

For many devotees, Bristol's most charming part is suburban Clifton, perched on the Clifton and Durdham Downs above the city and the Avon Gorge. Begun as a dormitory in the healthful high air for visitors to the Hot Well spa at the foot of the gorge, Clifton then became a fashionable place to live. The spa had only a brief moment of glory in the early eighteenth century (Bath was more popular), but Clifton was left with Georgian crescents to compete with those of Bath, and large, graceful Victorian villas. When the wealthy moved out early in this century, Clifton lost its cachet, but many of its houses have since been restored and it is now a quiet residential quarter with shops and bistros and a villagelike atmosphere appealing to young sophisticates.

Still, Clifton is far from the reality of a commercial, manufacturing city of nearly half a million people. The more distant suburb of Filton, the hub of Bristol's aircraft industry (the supersonic Concorde came off the production line here), is closer to the old spirit of adventure, perhaps, but the heart of the city is really in the waterways, its most characteristic visual feature. Though they contain plenty of dingy clutter — through which swans have the

BRISTOL-AT-GLANCE

SEEING THE CITY: From the top of the Cabot Tower on Brandon Hill there is a spectacular bird's-eye view of the center of Bristol and much of the surrounding area. It's quite a climb, however, and the view is almost as good from the base of the tower. The panorama is dominated by church spires, venerable stone buildings, and waterways, and it provides a surprise. Bristol has a generous amount of open space for a city whose past has been linked so strongly with commercial and maritime matters, and you'll see a lot of greenery among the old buildings and new office blocks.

SPECIAL PLACES: The best starting point for exploring Bristol is the vast rectangle known to the locals as "the Centre." If it's not marked as such on your map, look for its boundaries: St. Augustine's Parade and Broad Quay to the west and east, Colston Avenue to the north, and the Bridgehead (or Quay Head) to the south at the tip of St. Augustine's Reach. In recent years the Centre has been taken over by cars, but if you can bear the exhaust fumes and the incessant roar of traffic, you are well placed here to reach the older sections of town, the waterfront, the dignified buildings of College Green, and the shops of Park Street. Most buses to other parts of the city also stop here, and there are plenty of waiting taxis. A plaque on the Bridgehead commemorates the spot from where John Cabot set out on his historic voyage of discovery to the New World, and the park benches around the statue of Neptune provide a welcome chance to sit down while deciding in which direction to set out yourself.

CENTRAL BRISTOL

Bristol Cathedral – The Cathedral Church of the Holy and Undivided Trinity was founded in the twelfth century as an Augustinian monastery. The Norman chapter house, which dates from this earliest period, should not be missed. Other older parts are the thirteenth-century Elder Lady chapel and the fourteenth-century choir and Eastern Lady chapel (with the Jesse window), while the nave is the work of a Victorian architect faithful to the original style. Particularly interesting, if you have the time to study them, are the sixteenth-century misericords in the choir on which monks — who were not allowed to sit during services — leaned. They're beautifully carved and all different, some with serious and some with humorous scenes. College Green (phone: 24879).

The Council House – This graceful, curved, twentieth-century red-brick building across the street from the cathedral is the headquarters of Bristol's municipal administration. The golden unicorns on either end of the roof are symbolic of the city, also to be found on its coat of arms. Since this is a working building, tours of the interior are by special arrangement and for groups only. College Green.

The Georgian House – Once the home of a merchant wealthy from West Indian trade, this is now a museum maintained as though the merchant and his family still lived in it. It was built in 1790 and the furnishings, all of local manufacture, are Georgian in period. Open Mondays through Saturdays from 10 AM to 5 PM (closed from 1 to 2 PM). 7 Great George St. (phone: 299771, ext. 237).

City Museum and Art Gallery – The museum has extensive collections in the fine

BRISTOL / At-a-Glance

and applied arts, archaeology and history, geology and natural history, but visitors pressed for time will find exhibits of Bristol blue — and green, amethyst, and white — glass not too far beyond the lobby. The building next door to the museum, looking much older than it is, is the twentieth-century neo-Gothic Wills Memorial Building of the University of Bristol. It houses the 10-ton Great George bell, which sounds hourly in E flat. Open Mondays through Saturdays from 10 AM to 5 PM. Queens Rd. (phone: 299771).

King Street – This cobbled street was laid out in the 1660s and remains one of the most picturesque in Bristol. The pink buildings at its western end are the Merchant Venturers' Almshouses, built in the seventeenth century for retired seamen. Next is the eighteenth-century Old Library, now a restaurant. Farther along, the Palladian-style Coopers' Hall, a guildhall built in 1743, has become the entrance to the Theatre Royal, since 1766 one of the leading stages in the country and the present-day home of the Bristol Old Vic Company. Several other seventeenth-century edifices line the street, which ends with a group of buildings as appealingly half-timbered and gabled as you'll see anywhere. Built in 1664, these houses eventually became *Ye Llandoger Trow,* an inn where Daniel Defoe is supposed to have met the man he transformed into Robinson Crusoe, and which still operates as a pub and restaurant. King Street stops at an original stretch of Bristol quayside known as the Welsh Back.

Corn Street – The four bronze "nails," or trading tables, on which sixteenth- and seventeenth-century merchants counted out their money ("paid on the nail") characterize this section of Bristol. The heart of the medieval city was at the crossing of Corn, Broad, High, and Wine streets and the area later became Bristol's center of banking and commerce. Corn Street, especially, is an amalgam of worthy and workaday eighteenth- and nineteenth-century buildings. Two to compare are the Exchange (1743), behind the nails, designed by John Wood the Elder as a market and meeting place for merchants, and the ornately carved palazzo (1854) across from it, now Lloyd's Bank. Behind the Exchange is the St. Nicholas Market, a warren of stalls covered over in the eighteenth century and still going strong daily except Sunday. Several interesting churches include All Saints (Corn St.), with Norman foundations; St. Nicholas's (St. Nicholas St.), dating from the 1760s and now a museum; and Christ Church (Broad St.), an eighteenth-century replacement of an earlier church. (The mechanical men who strike the quarter hours on its clock were on the older building, too.) Walk to the end of Broad Street and you'll come to St. John's Gate, the only survivor of Bristol's nine medieval gateways.

John Wesley's New Room – In contrast to the other, imposing churches to be visited in Bristol, the world's first Methodist chapel is a spare and simple house of worship. John Wesley built it in 1739 and he and his brother preached here for 40 years. Their living quarters are upstairs. Open 10 AM to 4 PM (closed from 1 to 2 PM); closed Wednesdays and Sundays. 36 The Horsefair.

THE DOCKS

St. Mary Redcliffe – The church Queen Elizabeth I described as "the fairest, goodliest, and most famous parish church in England" was built mostly in the fourteenth and fifteenth centuries near enough to the Avon docks to be a merchant seaman's last and first call at the beginning and end of a voyage. It is an outstanding example of perpendicular architecture and it positively presides over what has since become a rather dull stretch of the Bristol cityscape. Inside, the nave and choir soar to a ceiling ornamented with more than 1,200 carved and gilded bosses. As you enter, note the unusual hexagonal shape and the very pretty stained-glass windows of the outer north porch, which dates to 1290, and the black marble pillars of the late-twelfth-century inner north porch, the oldest part of the church. Redcliffe Way.

SS *Great Britain* – Following the SS *Great Western,* the SS *Great Britain* was the second nautical accomplishment of the great Victorian engineer, Isambard Kingdom Brunel. When it floated out from Bristol in 1843, it was not only the first iron-hulled screw steamship in the world, it was also the largest liner on the seas. The *Great Western,* which had been the first transatlantic steam vessel, is no more; the *Great Britain,* fortunately, is. Shipwrecked and abandoned in the Falkland Islands in 1886, its return to the city in 1970 was a nostalgic and emotional occasion and it is now being restored in the dock where it was built. Open daily from 10 AM to 6 PM in summer and to 5 PM in winter. Admission charge. Great Western Dock, Gas Ferry Rd., off Cumberland Rd. (phone: 20680).

CLIFTON

Clifton Suspension Bridge – Bristol's most famous landmark is another of Isambard Kingdom Brunel's achievements. The bridge has a 702-foot span, 245 feet above the high water level of the Avon Gorge, and though it adds an attractive focal point to the Clifton scene, it is entirely functional. Before it opened in 1864, people crossed the river in a basket on a cable. Since then, pilots have flown underneath it and suicides have been attempted from it. The city's favorite story is that of the young woman who jumped after a lover's quarrel in 1885 — she parachuted gently in her petticoats to a soft landing in the mud and lived to a ripe old age.

Clifton Cathedral – The Cathedral Church of Saints Peter and Paul is the headquarters of the Roman Catholic diocese of Clifton. Completed in 1973, it is considered an important work of contemporary church architecture, designed to reflect the most recent changes in the form of liturgical worship. Visitors are welcome inside to see its modern works of art. Pembroke Rd. (phone: 738411).

Clifton and Durdham Downs – Bristol's largest and most popular open space covers more than 400 acres on the north side of the city. Bristolians play football on the Downs in winter, cricket in summer, and walk on the green expanse year-round.

Zoological Gardens – The Bristol zoo is one of the best in Britain. It has more than 1,000 animals, birds, reptiles, and fish, but it is most famous for its white tigers. There are also extensive gardens. Closed Christmas Day. Admission charge. Clifton Down (phone: 38951).

ENVIRONS

Blaise Castle House Museum – Blaise Castle itself is nothing but a Gothic-style "folly," a sham structure built in 1766 to decorate the grounds of this estate. Blaise Castle House Museum, set up in the estate's real eighteenth-century mansion, is a folk museum of costumes, toys, crafts, and other reminders of West Country life in days gone by. The landscaped grounds contain woodlands, walkways, and a number of attractions for children. Open 2 PM to 5 PM Wednesdays through Saturdays. Henbury, 4 miles northwest of Bristol (phone: 506789).

■ **EXTRA SPECIAL:** You can sample dockside Bristol easily enough on foot by walking from the Bridgehead along Narrow Quay, over the Prince Street Bridge and onto Prince's Wharf, beyond which is Wapping Wharf with the SS *Great Britain* at its far end. During the summer, the Bristol horsebus, an old-fashioned, horse-drawn open carriage, clop-clops from the Bridgehead on a short tour of the city and docks. (At presstime, the continuation of the horsebus tours was uncertain.) Another choice is the ferry. During the season it plies the Floating Harbour from Narrow Quay, making various stops including the *Great Britain.*

SOURCES AND RESOURCES

The City Information Centre (phone: 293891) on Colston St., next to the Colston concert hall, can supply brochures, maps, and general information. It's open Mondays through Fridays from 9 AM to 5 PM and on Saturdays from 9 AM to 12:30 PM. The center distributes free month-by-month events leaflets and also Bristol's *What's On Diary,* a free publication issued nine times a year with details of local events, restaurants, and nightlife. For 40p, you can pick up the *Bristol Official Visitors Guide,* which is a comprehensive introduction to all aspects of the city and includes several walking tours to cover its sights. Other walking tour guides are available, including a "Walkabout" series on individual routes. *The Bristol Heritage Walk* brochure describes a route that is marked on the streets it follows. If you're in town from July through September, try one of the regular walking tours led by Bristol's Corps of Guides. They leave once a day from the "nails" outside the Exchange on Corn St. and from Neptune's Statue, cost 50p per person, and last approximately 1.5 hours. The exact time of departure is posted outside the information center or the Exchange.

For Local Coverage – The morning *Western Daily Press* and the *Bristol Evening Post* are the two local dailies.

GETTING AROUND: You may want to take a bus or taxi to Clifton, but the rest of Bristol is walkable, with one word of warning. Traffic speeds around and out from the Centre in all directions, and little provision seems to have been made for pedestrians to interrupt it. There are a few traffic lights (all pedestrian operated) and a few striped zebra crossings (where the pedestrian has the right of way once he or she steps from the curb), but you'll see many a Bristolian paused on the verge of a dash at the sight of any break in the two-way onslaught. If you do as the Bristolians do, be careful.

Bus and Train – The *Bristol Omnibus Company* operates bus services within the city and throughout the surrounding area and also conducts sight-seeing tours during the summer months. Most city bus routes include a stop in the Centre; long-distance coaches operate out of the bus station on Marlborough Street, north of the Broadmead shopping center. For information on bus schedules, call 553231 from 8 AM to 9 PM, or 558211 for details on tours; to buy a timetable, drop in at the Bristol Omnibus office in Colston Centre (a modern building across from the City Information Centre). For train information, call Temple Meads Railway Station (phone: 294255), located at Temple Gate, from 8 AM to 10 PM.

Taxi – You'll have no trouble getting a taxi in the Centre for the trip out, but for the return, you'll probably have to call one. Numerous cab companies are listed in the Yellow Pages.

Car Rental – The major national and international companies are represented.

MUSEUMS: In addition to those discussed in *Special Places*, Bristol has a number of other interesting museums. Entrance is free to all those maintained by the city.

Bristol Industrial Museum – Machinery, especially that connected with transport — including horse-drawn carriages and a model of the Concorde cockpit — displayed in a transit shed in the city docks. Prince's Wharf (phone: 299771, ext. 290).

Harvey Wine Museum – An illustration of how wine is made, plus collections of old wine bottles, wineglasses and decanters, and silver decanter labels. The well-known wine company has set up the museum, which can be visited by appointment only. 12 Denmark St. (phone: 298011).

The Red Lodge – A sixteenth-century house preserved with its eighteenth-century alterations and furnishings of both periods. Great George St. (phone: 299771, ext. 236).

St. Nicholas's Church Museum – A church converted to an ecclesiastical museum of silver, vestments, and church art including an altarpiece by William Hogarth. Admission is free, but there is a charge to do a rubbing in the Brass Rubbing Centre downstairs. Baldwin St. (phone: 299771, ext. 243).

SHOPPING: Bristol's stores are many, drawing shoppers from all over the west of England and from South Wales. You'll find almost anything, though the emphasis is on the needs of the local shopper rather than tourist preferences. Broadmead is a very large, modern shopping center around a pedestrian mall — department stores, supermarkets, and other stores are legion here. Smaller, more expensive shops are found along Park Street, Queens Road, and Whiteladies Road. For local color, browse through the vegetables, crockery, parakeets, and other things in the St. Nicholas Market any day except Sunday. On Thursdays and Fridays from 9 AM to 3:30 PM, an antiques and crafts market takes place in the nearby Exchange. For more antiques and small boutiques, visit The Mall and its environs in Clifton, also. The Clifton Antiques Markets, 26/28 The Mall, is open from 10 AM to 6 PM Tuesdays through Saturdays.

Alexander Gallery – Fine art dealers and publishers. 122 Whiteladies Rd. (phone: 739582).

Bristol Craft Centre – Jewelers, potters, weavers, leatherworkers, an embroiderer, and others market what they make on the same premises at 6 Leonard La., an exceedingly narrow passage from Corn St. to Small St., entered from the opening beside 31 Corn St. (phone: 23182).

City Museum and Art Gallery Shop – Handmade reproductions of Bristol blue glass ware are on sale here, as well as posters, prints, and other souvenirs. Queens Rd. (phone: 299771).

Clock Shop – Barometers, cutlery, china, glassware, and souvenirs of Bristol as well as clocks. 38 The Horsefair (phone: 23072).

Debenhams – An excellent department store with goods from furs to furnishings. The Horsefair (phone: 291021).

Dingles – Also a department store, more exclusive than the above. Queens Rd. (phone: 215301).

George's – Three very good bookshops, all on Park Street: No. 89 for general books, No. 81 for academic books, and No. 52 for fine arts books (phone: 276602).

House of Lewis – Men's custom tailors. 47 College Green (phone: 23897).

SPECIAL EVENTS: The water and wine that played such a part in Bristol's past come together fittingly one week in May in the *World Wine Fair and Festival*, the city's biggest annual event. Exhibitors come to the Bristol Exhibition Complex, two refurbished warehouses on the Floating Harbour just below the Bridgehead, from all over the world, stands are set up for visitors to sample wines not usually available for general consumption, and fireworks displays light up the city docks. The docks are also the focus of other events, including the *Bristol Boat Show* in April or May, the *Embassy Grand Prix* power boat race in May or June, and the *Bristol Harbour Regatta and Rally of Boats* in July and August. In September, the sky over Ashton Court Estate, 825 acres of park on the other side of the Clifton Suspension Bridge, is full of multicolored hot-air balloons taking part in the *Bristol International Balloon Fiesta*.

SPORTS: Four sports centers provide facilities for squash, badminton, bowls, and various team games. The largest of these is the *Whitchurch Sports Centre,* Bamfield, Whitchurch (phone: 833911), south of the city. Whitchurch is open 7 days a week, has a sauna and bar, and is also the scene of spectator events such as basketball and hockey games and karate matches.

Cricket – The *Gloucestershire County Cricket Club* (phone: 46743) plays at the *County Ground,* Nevil Rd., from the end of April through the beginning of September.

Greyhound Racing – Mondays, Wednesdays, and Fridays (1:30 PM) are racing days at the *Eastville Stadium.*

Rugby – The *Bristol Rugby Club* (phone: 514448) is based at the *Memorial Ground,* Filton Ave.; the *Clifton Rugby Club* (phone: 500445), at Cribb's Causeway.

Soccer – The *Bristol City Football Club* on the grounds at Ashton Gate (phone: 632812); the *Bristol Rovers Football Club* plays at the *Eastville Stadium* (phone: 511050). Most games are on Saturdays at 3 PM.

Swimming – Bristol has 11 indoor pools open 7 days a week (closing at noon on Sundays). The outdoor pool at Oakfield Place, Clifton, is open 7 days a week from mid-May to early September.

THEATER: Bristol has made a name for itself in British theatrical history. The famous *Theatre Royal,* King St. (phone: 24388), opened in 1766, is the oldest continuously active theater in Britain. Since World War II it has been the home of the Bristol Old Vic Company, one of the most respected repertory groups in the land. The Bristol Old Vic does both classic and new plays, but if you have a choice, see a Shakespearean or other old comedy, because they're especially suited to the splendor of the Georgian setting. The company also plays at the *New Vic,* a second, modern auditorium next door (but sharing entrance and box office with the *Theatre Royal*). While almost as large, the *New Vic* is meant for informal and experimental theater and can be used for theater-in-the-round. Finally, you'll see smaller productions at the *Little Theatre* (phone: 291182), situated inside Colston Hall on Colston St., where the Little Theatre Company presents its productions as well. The Bristol Old Vic Theatre School (phone: 733535) gives several performances yearly at all the aforementioned theaters or at the *Vandyck Theatre* on Park Row, home of the University of Bristol Drama Department. As the first such department in a British university, this is another part of Bristol's theatrical tradition. The *Bristol Hippodrome,* St. Augustine's Parade (phone: 299444), seats 2,000 and hosts touring companies such as the Royal Shakespeare Company and the National Theatre Company. It is also the stage for visiting opera and ballet.

MUSIC: *Colston Hall,* Colston St. (phone: 22957), is Bristol's main venue for all types of musical performances, from classical to pop. The Bournemouth Symphony Orchestra and the Bournemouth Sinfonia play a regular season of concerts — the Harveys Bristol Series — from October to April. Touring opera and ballet companies stage their productions at the *Bristol Hippodrome,* St. Augustine's Parade (phone: 299444), and concerts of twentieth-century music are the specialty of the *Arnolfini Arts Centre,* 16 Narrow Quay (phone: 299194), which showcases the contemporary in all the arts. Recitals are held in many of Bristol's churches, including Bristol Cathedral, Clifton Cathedral, St. Mary Redcliffe, the Lord Mayor's Chapel on College Green, and St. George's Church on Charlotte St. University of Bristol students put on concerts, often at lunchtime, in the *Wills Memorial Building,* Queens Rd.

NIGHTCLUBS AND NIGHTLIFE: Bristol's nightlife can stand up to comparison with that offered by any city outside London. There are more than 20 nightclubs, including *Yesterdays*, 15 King St. (phone: 297670), which has five bars, two discotheques, a restaurant, and a fast-food counter; the *Reeves Club and Cabaret Room* at Arno's Court Hotel, 470 Bath Rd. (phone: 711461); and *Platform One*, Clifton Down Station (phone: 739171).

BEST IN TOWN

CHECKING IN: Bristol is not the prime tourist destination that prestigious Bath is, but as an important commercial center and the object of many an expense-account traveler, it's no cheaper than its neighbor. A wide range of accommodations is available, however, and if you book in advance, you should be able to find a room at the right price almost any time of the year. Look in Clifton for the broadest choice of reasonably priced small hotels and guesthouses. Few of Bristol's hotels are right in the center of town and those that are tend to be in the expensive category. As a rough guide, expect to pay more than $75 a night for a double room at an expensive hotel, between $50 and $75 at a moderate one, and $30 to $50 at an inexpensive one. A hearty English breakfast should be included in the rate, but a growing number of the top hotels now offer room only.

Dragonara – Swish, modern, and luxurious, it's close to the city center and to the railroad station. Traffic races by out front and the setting is unglamorous, but the beautiful church of St. Mary Redcliffe does dress up the neighborhood. There are 210 rooms. Redcliffe Way (phone: 20044). Expensive.

Grand – This large, lovely Victorian has had a face lift and now sports a scrubbed stone exterior above the row of brown and gold striped awnings that line the street. Grand and gracious inside, and very well located in the historic center. Broad St. (phone: 291645). Expensive.

Holiday Inn – Just like any other *Holiday Inn* you know. This modern, multistory hotel has 300 spacious rooms, a sauna, indoor swimming pool, gym, restaurants, bars, and a disco. It's convenient to the Broadmead shopping center, with a courtesy car operating to and from the railroad station. Lower Castle St. (phone: 294281). Expensive.

Unicorn – It's smarter than its unappealingly modern front on Prince Street would lead you to believe. Go around back and you're right among the cobblestones, chains, and bollards of Narrow Quay and the harbor. Contemporary styling inside (193 rooms) and a popular waterfront bar. Prince St. (phone: 294811). Expensive.

Avon Gorge – This solid white block of Victoriana perches on the edge of Clifton overlooking the Avon Gorge and the Clifton Suspension Bridge. At present, there are 74 rooms (expansion in progress), but if you don't get one gorge-side, enjoy the view at tea on the terrace. Sion Hill, Clifton (phone: 738955). Moderate.

Hawthorns – In Clifton, only about half a mile from the Park Street shops. It has 163 rooms (though not all with bath) and a wide range of entertainment. Woodland Rd., Clifton (phone: 738432). Moderate.

St. Vincent Rocks – This Regency hotel is a smaller (48 rooms) and slightly more moderate (not all rooms have private bath) alternative to the *Avon Gorge Hotel* down the road. It, too, overlooks the gorge and has an enviable view of the Clifton Suspension Bridge. Sion Hill, Clifton (phone: 739251). Moderate.

Dunraven – Farther out than the others (about a mile from the center — bus or taxi necessary) and facing Durdham Downs, this discreet, cream-colored Georgian building has 34 sparklingly clean and well-maintained rooms. None have private baths but all have hot and cold running water. 42 Upper Belgrave Rd., Clifton (phone: 737475). Inexpensive.

Glenroy – Comfortable and small (28 rooms), and part of one of Clifton's attractive nineteenth-century squares. Very few of the rooms have private bath. 30 Victoria Sq., Clifton (phone: 739058). Inexpensive.

Seeley's Hotel – A serviceable place, this, too, is in Clifton, not far from the Park Street shops. About half of the 60 rooms have private bath and all have TV, radio, and tea-making facilities. 19–27 St. Paul's Rd., Clifton (phone: 738544). Inexpensive.

EATING OUT: As one of the largest cities outside London, you'd expect Bristol to be well endowed with good restaurants, and it is. There are some excellent eating places in the hotels and some equally good ones outside, in central Bristol and Clifton, offering traditional English, Chinese, French, Indian, Italian, or other cuisine. In addition, the city has two floating pub-restaurants. To sample local fare, try Severn salmon, Cheddar-cooked ham, jugged hare, and pigeon pie. A meal for two with wine will cost more than $45 at a restaurant listed as expensive, $35 to $45 at one listed as moderate, and less than $35 at an inexpensive one.

Gorny – Friendly service and imaginatively cooked food are what draw people to this Swiss-French restaurant run, in fact, by a German. Open for dinner only Tuesdays through Saturdays; closed the month of August and a week at Christmas. When it's open, booking is essential. 13 Cotham Rd. (phone: 426444). Expensive.

Restaurant du Gourmet – Three floors of a terraced house make up this French restaurant. The atmosphere is intimate but the menu is extensive. Closed Sundays and Mondays; dinner only on Saturdays, when you should be sure to reserve a table. 43 Whiteladies Rd. (phone: 736230). Expensive.

Harveys – The wine cellar of the famous firm of wine merchants is no ordinary place: frogs' legs among the appetizers, specialties such as beef Wellington or venison cutlets with juniper berries and gin, and four sauces for the duck. The bill of French and English fare is bountiful and the wine list will never cramp your style. Closed Saturday lunch, Sundays, and public holidays. 12 Denmark St. (phone: 277665). Expensive.

Kiln – Part of the *Dragonara Hotel,* this unusual round restaurant is actually a 200-year-old kiln for the making of Bristol glassware. Regional specialties are featured — if you can corral a party of ten, have the whole roast suckling pig. Desserts on Elizabethan nights (Fridays in winter) have such jollifying names as raspberry fool, Eton mess, and tipsy cake. Dancing on Fridays and Saturdays; closed Sunday nights. Redcliffe Way (phone: 20044). Expensive.

Michael's – Here you can feast on such delicacies as cream of Stilton soup, roast quail with grapes, and passion fruit sorbet. The ornate Victorian dining room, converted from an old garage, is filled with flowers, curios, and tables of assorted shapes and sizes; the bar with chaise longues, stuffed birds, and a fireplace. Reservations are advisable. Open for dinner Tuesdays through Saturdays and for lunch on Sundays from mid-September until Easter. 129 Hotwell Rd. (phone: 276190). Expensive.

Colley's Supper Rooms – Arrive punctually at 8 PM for a wonderful six-course supper. There is no menu in the conventional sense, but plenty of variety. Judging by the fact that the place is often booked solid weeks ahead, people are happy with the arrangement. Closed Sundays and Mondays. 153 Whiteladies Rd. (phone: 730646). Moderate.

Lochiel – Formerly a Scottish mail boat, it's now a floating restaurant, moored in the Floating Harbour. The dining room, below aft, has been restored in the style of a luxury liner. Its small four-course menu, based on local, seasonal produce, changes every week. St. Augustine's Reach, Canon's Rd. (phone: 292447). Moderate.

Rajdoot – Authentic Indian cuisine — including the charcoal, clay-oven barbecues of tandoori cooking — are served in an elegant setting. Open for lunch and dinner daily, though not for Sunday lunch. Reservations are essential for the evening meal. 83 Park St. (phone: 28033). Moderate.

Orangery – In the *St. Vincent Rocks* hotel, this restaurant has a wall of windows from which to admire the Clifton Suspension Bridge and, though enclosed, is decorated rather like a light and airy sunporch. One of the specialties is a steak, mushroom, and oyster pie, made with Guinness and named for Brunel, the builder of the bridge. Sion Hill (phone: 739251). Moderate.

Bloomers – The eighteenth-century Old Library premises are now fresh and folksy inside, with lights hanging low over antique pine tables, chairs copied from those in an old farmhouse kitchen, and lots of potted plants. Stick to a hamburger or meat pie or have one of the more imaginative entrées. King St. (phone: 291111). Inexpensive.

Trattoria da Renato – Actors and actresses from the Old Vic across the street congregate here. The walls are covered with their photos and the tables are attractively covered with pink napery topped by white lace. Food is Italian. Closed Saturday lunch and Sundays. 19 King St. (phone: 298291). Inexpensive.

SHARING A PINT: The *Full Moon,* 1 North St., is supposed to be the oldest pub in Bristol — something by that name was already marked as "a very ancient hostellerie" on a map of the city in the thirteenth century. If you go in the summer, sit outside at the tables in the old stableyard. Jazz pubs are a special feature of Bristol nightlife and one of the best is the *Old Duke,* at the Welsh Back end of King St. It is jamming and jammed 6 nights a week from 8:30 PM (Sundays noon to 2 PM). If you can't get in, go across the street to *Ye Llandoger Trow,* where there are three small bars (and two second-floor restaurants) in the seventeenth-century building, one with a beautifully carved fireplace and the coziest of table-nooks under the stairs. Another popular pub left over from the seventeenth century is *Ye Shakespeare,* 78 Victoria St., a note of charm in an otherwise plain neighborhood. In Clifton, *The Royal Oak,* 50 The Mall, is the place to go for traditional brews and atmosphere — stone walls, oak beams, and seating at high-backed oak settees. While you're at it, you might just as well drink a toast of Bristol milk (sherry), so-called according to a seventeenth-century clergyman, author, and wit, because it was the "first moisture" tasted by infants in this wine-importing city.

CAMBRIDGE

Cambridge's bold claim to being the most beautiful city in Britain is based on the majestic architecture of its several colleges. The distinction is not often disputed (except by its rival, Oxford, the country's other bastion of knowledge and medieval design). Each year, millions of visitors flock to this small city to marvel at its masterpieces of cut stone, stained glass, and carved wood, and to breathe its rarefied and scholarly atmosphere. They also come to Cambridge for an experience Oxford cannot match: a quiet punt ride up the "Backs" on the River Cam, which slides lazily past the colleges' back lawns (hence the name), and is edged by lush green banks and drooping willows. One nineteenth-century tourist, Henry James, described the Backs as "the loveliest confusion of gothic windows and ancient trees, of grassy banks and mossy balustrades, of sun-checquered avenues and groves, of lawns and gardens and terraces, [and] of single arched bridges spanning the little stream . . ." Lesser tourists have come to much the same conclusion on postcards written to the folks back home.

This city of great tranquillity and beauty has long historical roots. Cambridge was first established in AD 43 as a Roman camp on a hill overlooking a natural ford in the River Cam at its upper navigable limit. The camp blossomed into a trading town, as the Romans built roads connecting Colchester, the garrison town to the southeast, with Lincoln, a settlement in the north. In the fifth century, the area was overrun and conquered by the Saxons. St. Bene't's (a contraction for St. Benedict's) Church dates to this period; its Saxon tower remains standing today. In the eleventh century, the Normans, too, invaded Cambridge, and under instructions from William the Conqueror built a castle to defend the town against rebels led by Hereward the Wake.

Details about early scholarly stirrings in Cambridge are vague. There was a monastery in the nearby town of Ely, and, in 1209, when students retreating from a hostile townsfolk streamed here from Oxford, these monks may have set up a center of learning. Whatever the case, by the mid-thirteenth century, the university was firmly established and by 1284 the first college founded, then called St. Peter's and later known as Peterhouse. During the fourteenth and fifteenth centuries, eleven more colleges were founded and several hostels were built to house the students.

Today, education is Cambridge's main industry (there are 35 colleges and about 12,500 students), but the university, like the one at Oxford, retains its original medieval organization. Each of the colleges is a self-governing entity within a decentralized university system. Each drafts its own rules and holds title to its own property. While the university provides lectures and awards degrees, it is the individual colleges that control admissions, determine the subjects an undergraduate should "read" (study), and conduct examinations.

Strictly speaking, of course, the term "university" refers not to its imposing granite structures, but rather to the community of people involved — the chancellor, masters, and fellows and scholars, to be exact. The chancellor, aided by various administrative personnel, governs the university as a whole. Each college is presided over by a master, who heads a staff of fellows (commonly referred to as "dons"). The dons conduct weekly tutorials (discussions of an assignment with a student), give lectures, and do their own academic research. The position of don is as much an identity as a job; one tried to explain the mystique in this way: "Being a don at Cambridge is more than a job. It is a way of life. If he will never be rich, he is at least his own master . . . He lives in surroundings compared to which any other city whose university tempts him to move appears so often shabby and ugly. That is why so few move."

Many scholars feel the same attachment to Cambridge — with good reason. Ever since the Middle Ages the colleges have traditionally provided for their members' every need. Each self-sufficient enclave includes a dining room, with an imposing high table where the master and fellows dine apart from (and a bit above) the undergraduates; a chapel; a library; and common rooms as well as private rooms where students live. More important, many colleges have remained unchanged over the centuries. Cambridge has spawned some of the most influential figures in politics, the arts, and science — people like Cromwell, Pepys, Newton, Darwin, Wordsworth, and Byron. What undergraduate would not delight in writing at Samuel Pepys's desk or wielding the same silverware as Oliver Cromwell?

Cambridge, like any institution that reaches so far into the past, is plagued as well as enriched by traditions out of step with the modern world. Perhaps because of its monastic beginnings, the university has always disciplined students rather rigorously. For example, until fairly recently, the college gates were locked at 11 PM. As each college is surrounded in a rather prisonlike way by high walls often crowned with a row of spikes, there was no easy way to get in if you tarried too long. This hardly deterred spirited carousers, however, and the famous night climbs of Cambridge have spawned many a British mountaineer.

As a result of this and other episodes, the emphasis at Cambridge upon dignity and discipline has become somewhat legendary. Consider the oft-told tale of the student who tried to turn the ancient rules to his own advantage. In studying the university statutes he discovered that he had the right, while sitting for an examination, to demand a tankard of ale from the proctor. His request was grudgingly granted and the ale brought in . . . but not without a price. For it seems that the statute, which dates back to the fourteenth century, also made it compulsory to wear a sword after dark. The next evening the student was found and fittingly — if somewhat uncomfortably — attired.

CAMBRIDGE AT-A-GLANCE

SEEING THE CITY: Head straight for Great St. Mary's, the University Church in King's Parade, and climb to the top for a fine view of the city. For an alternative perspective stroll up Castle Mound, once the site of Cambridge's castle, whose stonework was gradually removed over the years and used in the construction of the colleges.

SPECIAL PLACES: Every tour of Cambridge should begin at its heart — the colleges, all of which are open in part to the public. A word of warning, however: The colleges are not museums, but private places where people live and work, and Cambridge's 2.5 million yearly visitors create an enormous problem, especially in spring and summer when students are preparing for exams. To some extent, the situation would be like finding your own backyard on the itinerary of every tour of England. What's more, the colleges receive no income from tourists, so visiting their courts (the counterparts of Oxford's quads) should be considered a great privilege and quiet behavior only common courtesy.

In general, visitors are allowed to walk around the courts (but not on the grass, which remains the privilege only of fellows); visit the chapels and some gardens; and occasionally go into other designated areas, such as libraries or dining halls. Members of the college live off a "staircase," as the names at the bottom will indicate, but unless you are visiting a friend or relative in residence you won't be allowed to wander into these private quarters. The colleges are also sometimes closed to visitors — for example, when examinations are being taken. Notices to this effect are posted at the gate; if in doubt, check with the porter in the college lodge.

The selection of colleges below is by no means exhaustive, but it does include those most interesting architecturally and most centrally located. If you have time to visit only a few of them, King's College and Trinity College should be at the top of the list. Nearby Queens' and St. John's (and perhaps the entire area between them) would be both worthwhile and easy to reach, and you'd still have time to explore the Backs. Some of the colleges not mentioned below are Peterhouse (founded in 1284); Gonville and Caius, pronounced "Keys" (1348); St. Catherine's (1473); Sidney Sussex (1596); and Downing (1800). Then there are the three colleges founded for women, namely Girton (founded in 1869, out of town and far removed from the lusty male population); Newnham (established in 1871 — novelist Margaret Drabble studied here); and New Hall (built in 1954 and probably Cambridge's most controversial building — judge it for yourself). Lastly, the three most recently founded colleges are Churchill (inspired by Sir Winston's wish to encourage scientific and technological studies and founded in 1960, way out of town); Fitzwilliam (founded in 1966 and affectionately referred to as Fitzbilly); and Robinson, opened by the Queen in 1981.

THE COLLEGES

Corpus Christi College (1352) – Because the Old Court has changed little since it was built in the fourteenth century, it provides a glimpse at medieval college organization. Then four students shared a room but each had his own study cubicle — hence the difference in the size of the windows. In the sixteenth century, one of the cubicles would have been used by the great English dramatist, Christopher Marlowe, when he was a student here. The library, containing a priceless collection of Anglo-Saxon manuscripts (nearly 40 of them, saved from the libraries of monasteries dissolved by Henry VIII and including an important copy of the *Anglo-Saxon Chronicle*) is open on some afternoons, and the chapel is open daily. Be forewarned: the college is said to have a resident ghost. Trumpington St.

Pembroke College (1347) – The college was founded by Marie de Valence, countess of Pembroke, and some of the buildings of her time survive. The chapel (built later, in 1663–66) was Sir Christopher Wren's first building, designed while he was a professor at Oxford. Wren's uncle, who had been imprisoned in the Tower of London and intended the chapel as thanksgiving for his release, told his nephew that since he was a mathematician, he ought to be capable of building a chapel. Wren was and did, in a classical style new to Cambridge. The college is also known for its gardens. Trumpington St.

Queens' College (1448) – Founded by Margaret of Anjou and Elizabeth Woodville, the respective queens of Henry VI and Edward IV, Queens' has a lovely red-brick First Court built in the fifteenth century and decorated with a sundial in the seventeenth century. But its pièce de résistance is the New Court. The cloister around it, also fifteenth century, supports a wonderful example of sixteenth-century domestic architecture called the President's Lodge (Queens' does not have a master), an evocative building of timber and plaster that is put to good use in May Week as a backdrop for the college's productions of Shakespeare. Also of interest is the Mathematical Bridge, a copy of an original (1729) that was held together on geometrical principles without nails, nuts, or bolts, but which, once taken apart by some curious Victorians, couldn't be put back together again without the fastenings. Sir Basil Spence's Erasmus Building (1959) was one of the first modern contributions to college architecture (Erasmus, the Renaissance theologian, lived at Queens' in 1511–14). Queens' La.

King's College (1441) – Of the grand design that Henry VI had for the college he founded, only the chapel was ever realized. It was not until 1724, when the Fellows' Building was added, that an actual court began to take shape where Henry intended one; until then, students lived in an older court that is no longer part of the college. But the magnificent Gothic chapel, begun in 1446 and completed 90 years later, largely as the founder planned it, is not only Cambridge's best-known building, it is also often acclaimed the finest building in England — and all this majesty had been meant initially for the private worship of only seventy scholars. The initial stage of construction ended in 1461 when Henry was deposed (the level that had been reached at that point is visible in a change in color of the stone). Edward IV and Richard III financed further work, but it was Henry VII who began the final stage and left money for its completion, which explains the rose of his Tudor father and the portcullis of his Beaufort mother, symbols carved everywhere as decoration. The chapel has the largest fan-vaulted ceiling in existence; original sixteenth-century stained glass, the gift of Henry VIII, in all but one (and part of another) of its windows; and an intricately carved wood organ screen bearing the initials of Henry VIII and Anne Boleyn, another gift. Behind the altar is Rubens's *Adoration of the Magi,* donated in the 1960s after having set a record for the highest price ever brought by a painting at auction. The chapel is open daily, but be prepared for unpredicted closings due to choir practice or recording sessions. The King's College Chapel Choir is very well known, so if you get a chance, go and listen. Notices of forthcoming concerts are usually posted on the doorway. Evensong services are held at 5:30 PM on weekdays (excluding Mondays) and 3:30 PM on Sundays during school terms only. King's Parade.

Clare College (1338) – Though one of the oldest colleges, its original buildings were destroyed by fire and the present ones date only to the seventeenth century. They rank among the university's most handsome, however, and Clare's bridge is the oldest (1640) and one of the prettiest on the Cam. The college is also known for the elegance of its eighteenth-century wrought-iron gates and for the delightful Fellows' Garden on the other side of the river. The college hall is normally open to visitors when not in use and the garden is normally open from 2 to 4:30 PM on weekdays. Trinity La.

Trinity Hall (1350) – Originally, all the colleges were called halls and the people who lived in them were the college. Gradually, the latter word became more inclusive in meaning and by the nineteenth century, most of the halls had changed their names. Because a Trinity College already existed, Trinity Hall is the only Cambridge college known by its old name. Traditionally the college for lawyers, its Front Court dates to the fourteenth century, but it was refaced in the eighteenth century. You'll get a better idea of Trinity's early days by seeing the sixteenth-century Tudor brick library, especially pretty in summer when the flowers bordering it are in bloom. Trinity La.

Trinity College (1546) – Founded by Henry VIII, Trinity is the largest college in Cambridge and home to more than 800 students. The school has a distinguished roster of alumni: Francis Bacon, John Dryden, Isaac Newton, Thomas Macaulay, Alfred Lord Tennyson, Bertrand Russell, six British prime ministers, over 20 Nobel Prize winners, and Prince Charles, not to mention Lord Byron, who was eventually "sent down," or expelled, for rooming with a pet bear and bathing naked in the fountain at the center of the Great Court, which was the source of the college's water supply. The Great Court, the largest court or quad in either Cambridge or Oxford, is the creation of Thomas Nevile, master of the college in the late sixteenth and early seventeenth centuries. He also began Nevile's Court; the long cloister on the north side is where Newton worked out his theory of sound (stand at its west end and stamp your foot to hear the echo he timed to measure the speed of sound). Nevile's Court became complete only at the end of the seventeenth century with the addition of Christopher Wren's library — and the sight of the sun resplendent on the glass of the Wren Library's many windows is still one of the most memorable in Cambridge. The library is open to the public from 2:15 to 4:45 PM Mondays through Fridays and on Saturdays during the school term from 10:30 AM to 12:30 PM (it's lavish with carved wood inside and some of its treasured manuscripts are usually on display). Nevile's dining hall (again, Cambridge's largest) is between the two courts and is normally open to visitors from 10 AM to 2 PM, except on Sundays. Trinity St.

St. John's College (1511) – An enormous, rather austere place, this is the second largest of the Cambridge colleges, with buildings spanning the centuries. The beautiful gate house, ornate with the arms of the founder, Lady Margaret Beaufort (mother of Henry VII), is in its original state, the Second and Third courts date back to the sixteenth century, but across the River Cam are the nineteenth-century neo-Gothic New Court and the ultramodern Cripps Building. The two parts of the college are connected by the covered Bridge of Sighs (1831), picturesque despite the bars on the windows to keep undergraduates inside. William Wordsworth was a St. John's student; he later wrote of its "three gloomy courts," in the first of which (much altered since the founding) he had an "obscure nook." St. John's St.

Magdalene College (1542) – Built in the fifteenth century to house Benedictine monks studying at Cambridge, Magdalene (pronounced Mawdlen) was founded as an actual college in the sixteenth century, and its First Court has buildings of both centuries. It is a favorite of the British aristocracy, but its most famous student was Samuel Pepys, who left his library to his old school, including the manuscript of his famous diary. The library — arranged in presses Pepys himself provided — is open Mondays through Saturdays from 11:30 AM to 12:30 PM, and from 2:30 to 3:30 PM. Across the street from the college are old buildings that Pepys himself would have seen. Magdalene St.

Jesus College (1496) – This is another college with a religious background. Founded on the site of a convent that dated back to the twelfth century, Jesus, too, has parts that are older than it is, including the chapel — though the pre-Raphaelite stained glass (by Edward Burne-Jones and Ford Madox Brown) and ceilings (by William Morris) came about during a nineteenth-century restoration. The college is approached via a long, brick-walled avenue known as the "chimney," but once past the fifteenth-century gate tower, the grounds are spacious, with gardens and a delightful Tudor Cloister Court. Alistaire Cooke, journalist and commentator on the American scene, was a Jesus undergraduate, as were Laurence Sterne and Samuel Taylor Coleridge. Jesus La.

Christ's College (1505) – This was the first of the two colleges Lady Margaret Beaufort founded at Cambridge, and as at St. John's, her coat of arms above the gate makes a highly ornamental entranceway. John Milton was a student at Christ's College (he wrote many early poems here and a later one, "Lycidas," was written in memory of a college fellow) and so was Charles Darwin. The beautiful Fellows' Garden (open 2 to 4 PM on weekdays) contains a mulberry tree traditionally associated with Milton. St. Andrew's St.

Emmanuel College (1584) – Sir Walter Mildmay, Queen Elizabeth's Chancellor of the Exchequer, founded this college on the site of a thirteenth-century Dominican friary that had been dissolved by Henry VIII. Monastic buildings were converted to college use (the friary church became the dining hall), then other buildings followed, including the chapel and its colonnade (1668–73) designed by Sir Christopher Wren. Emmanuel was meant to educate clergymen and it became a center of Protestant theology, but because of their Puritan sympathies, many of its graduates emigrated to America in the early seventeenth century. Among these was John Harvard, who died at the age of 31 leaving $1,600 and 320 books for the foundation of Harvard University. St. Andrew's St.

OTHER CAMBRIDGE SIGHTS

The Fitzwilliam Museum – The private treasure trove that Viscount Fitzwilliam donated to the university along with the funds for a building to house it, is one of the oldest public museums in the country. First opened in 1848, it contains Middle Eastern, Egyptian, Greek, and Roman antiquities, and European ceramics, manuscripts, paintings, drawings, and miniatures of all periods. The paintings and drawings — from Flemish and Italian old masters through French Impressionism to modern English Art — are in the gallery upstairs, open between 2 and 5 PM; the rest is in the downstairs gallery, open from 10 AM until 2 PM. The museum also sponsors temporary exhibitions. Trumpington St. (phone: 69501).

The Senate House – This classical Georgian building of the 1720s was designed by the English architect, James Gibbs (the same who designed the Fellows' Building next to the King's College Chapel), and it, too, belongs to the university. When illuminated at night, its Corinthian details make it look almost like an edible confection, and each June it becomes the suitably stylish setting for the ceremony of General Admission to Degrees — graduation, that is. King's Parade.

The Round Church – Built in the same distinctive shape as the Holy Sepulcher Church in Jerusalem, the Norman Round Church dates back to about 1130. It is one of only five Round Churches still surviving in England. Bridge St.

The Folk Museum – Crafts, tools, kitchen and farm equipment, toys, and furniture are among the many objects on display in a series of rooms meant to illustrate life in Cambridge and the surrounding countryside in the last few hundred years. The building itself was formerly a pub *(The White Horse Inn)* and in the courtyard is an eighteenth-century shopfront, one of several large relics salvaged from Cambridge's past. Open Tuesdays through Saturdays, and on Sunday afternoons. Admission charge. Corner of Castle and Northampton Sts. (phone: 355159).

Brass Rubbing Centre – Don't let the thought of working in a cold, damp, and dimly lit church put you off the idea of brass rubbing; in Cambridge, there's a cozy do-it-yourself workshop with 70 brasses to choose from. The brasses are replicas of monuments to real people (mostly minor gentry — the very wealthy invested in more elaborate stoneworks) dating back to the time of the Crusaders. The price for making your own rubbing ranges from £2 to £6 depending on the size of the brass you choose and includes the use of all materials plus basic instruction for novices. If you can't summon the necessary effort — and brass rubbing is hard work — the center also sells finished rubbings. Open 10 AM to 5 PM, Tuesdays through Saturdays (Mondays also, in July and August). Wesley Church Library, King St. (phone: 61318).

The Scott Polar Research Institute – The small museum here is dedicated to the famous explorer and to polar exploration. Letters, diaries, and photographs of Robert Falcon Scott's expedition to the South Pole are on display along with souvenirs of other expeditions and exhibits describing the geography and geology of the Antarctic and current polar research. Open Mondays through Saturdays from 2:30 to 4 PM. Lensfield Rd. (phone: 66499).

The Botanic Gardens – These are the university's research gardens, open to the public on weekdays and summer Sundays. You'll find the hothouses very inviting on cold days (in winter the Cambridge east winds seem to blow uninterrupted all the way from Siberia). Entrances on Bateman St., Trumpington Rd., and Hills Rd. (phone: 350101).

American Military Cemetery – More than 3,800 American servicemen who fought World War II from British bases are buried in these beautifully landscaped grounds. The names of another 5,125 who lie in unknown graves are inscribed on the Memorial Wall. On the Madingley Rd., 4 miles outside the city (phone: 210350).

- **EXTRA SPECIAL:** One of the most stylish ways to enjoy Cambridge is to hire a punt — a long, flat-bottomed, square-nosed boat that is both steered and propelled by means of a long pole that you push into the mud of the river bottom. It sounds difficult, looks easy, and, in practice, is somewhere between the two. Be prepared for ridicule from the onlookers along the grassy banks, especially if you go around in circles or, heaven help you, get the pole stuck in the mud and forget to let go. Either explore the Backs, a beautiful stretch of river behind the college and past splendid lawns, gardens, and drooping willows, or go on a lengthier excursion up the river to Grantchester for tea. The two routes are separated by a lock. Scudamore's Boat Yards, a famous Cambridge name in punting, offers punts for self-drive hire at two locations, one at Quayside, off Bridge Street, and another at Mill Lane, near Silver Street (but go to the latter if you're aiming for Grantchester). The cost is £1.60 an hour with £5 deposit. Don't forget to stand at the back of the boat, especially if you have recently been to Oxford where they stand at the front. The deposit is deductible *if* you return. There is also chauffeured punt service with champagne, strawberries, and cream.

SOURCES AND RESOURCES

The Tourist Information Center, located on Wheeler Street (phone: 358977), is open Mondays through Fridays from 9 AM to 6 PM (9 AM to 5:30 PM November through February) and on Saturdays from 9 AM to 5 PM. From May through September, it is also open on Sundays (10:30 AM to 3:30 PM). The center offers guided tours of the colleges and through the intricate maze of small streets and alleyways around them. The tours, which last approximately 1.5 hours, depart daily most of the year and on Saturdays only from mid-November through March. You can check the departure schedule by calling the number above. Tickets cost 95p and can be bought at the center no more than 24 hours before the tour begins. Tours of "historic" Cambridge are also given in the summer on Wednesday and Friday evenings at 7; these also cost 95p and leave from the center.

The center sells a comprehensive selection of guides to Cambridge. These include the

230 CAMBRIDGE / Sources and Resources

Cambridge Official Guide, A Brief Guide to Cambridge, Country Walks Around Cambridge, and *Places of Interest Outside Cambridge.* Available free are a city map and pamphlets on the area's events, where to eat, accommodations, campsites, bike rental, car rental, bookshops, and antique shops.

Most of Cambridge's bookstores (see *Shopping*) carry a broad range of guidebooks including many "picturebooks" filled with lush photographs. Try to find *Look at Cambridge* and *Historic Cambridge* by John Brooks; *Cambridge* by Kenneth Holmes; and *Royal Cambridge* by Marion Colthorpe, which describes the many royal visits to the city since Queen Elizabeth I.

For Local Coverage – Check the *Cambridge Evening News*, the city's daily paper, or *The Varsity*, the university's weekly rag.

GETTING AROUND: Cambridge and London are linked by frequent trains from Liverpool Street Station, travel time about 1.5 hours. The Cambridge railway station is a long walk away from the center of town, so take the bus that waits in the front of the station or a taxi (which will cost roughly 75p).

Taxi – Two of the biggest taxi companies are *Camtax*, 26 Victoria Rd. (phone: 313131), and *United*, 123a Hills Rd. (phone: 352222). Apart from the trip into town from the station or visits to places outside the city such as the American Military Cemetery, you're unlikely to need a cab, since most of the places of interest in town are within walking distance of each other.

Bicycles – Most students and some academics travel around by bike. You can rent one from *Geoff's*, 164 Mill Rd. (phone: 249374), or from *University Cycle and Electrical*, 93–95 King's St. (phone: 311560). A day's hire will run about £1.50, and a week's £3–4.

Car Rental – Try *Kennings*, a national chain, at 24/26 Hills Rd. (phone: 61538) or *Godfrey Davis* at 315 Mill Rd. (phone: 248198).

Bus – For slow but inexpensive links to other towns in East Anglia and London, try the bus; the station is on Drummer St. Local buses are few and far between — don't bother with them unless you're planning on a long stay.

MUSEUMS: In addition to those described in *Special Places*, Cambridge has a number of other interesting museums. The best of these are:

The Whipple Science Museum – Early microscopes, telescopes, astronomical and navigational equipment, surveying instruments, slide rules, and electrical apparatus. Open Mondays through Fridays, 2 to 5 PM. Free School La. (phone: 358381).

University Museum of Zoology – Displays on marine life, birds, insects, and mammals, as well as fossil specimens. Open Mondays through Fridays, 2:15 to 4:45 PM. Downing St. (phone: 358717).

Museum of Classical Archaeology – Casts of Greek and Roman sculpture. Open Mondays through Fridays, 9 AM to 1 PM and 2:15 to 5 PM. Little St. Mary's La. (phone: 65621).

The Sedgwick Museum of Geology – Geological specimens by the hundreds. Open Mondays through Fridays, 9 AM to 1 PM and 2 to 5 PM. Downing St. (phone: 51585).

Kettles Yard Art Gallery – Permanent collection of modern art including works by Henri Gaudier-Brzeska, Ben Nicolson, and Christopher Wood, and changing exhibits of contemporary art and crafts. Permanent collection open daily 2 to 4 PM; exhibition gallery open Mondays through Saturdays from 12 to 6 PM, Sundays 2 to 4 PM. Northampton St. (phone: 352124).

SHOPPING: The marketplace in Market Square, on ever-so-flat Market Hill, has been a shopping area since medieval times. The stalls, sheltered by brightly colored canopies, are open for business year-round Mondays through Saturdays. Most sell fruits and vegetables and inexpensive clothing but one or two sell items of interest to visitors, including gifts and secondhand books.

Cambridge abounds in bookstores that stock much more than just academic tomes. *Heffers of Cambridge,* an establishment with many branches, has its main bookstore at 20 Trinity St. (phone: 358351); other branches include a children's bookshop at 30 Trinity St. (phone: 356200); paperback shops at 13 Trinity St. (phone: 61815) and 31 St. Andrew's St. (phone: 54778); and a shop selling Penguin books only at 51 Trumpington St. (phone: 358351). *Bowes and Bowes* has presided over its corner location on Trinity and Market sts. for the last 400 years; *Deighton, Bell & Co.* at 13 Trinity St. (phone: 353939) offers rare and fine books; and *G. David,* a Cambridge institution for secondhand books, is at 16 St. Edward's Passage (phone: 354619).

The city has two main shopping thoroughfares. The first starts at St. John's Street and continues down Trinity Street, along King's Parade (with colleges on one side and old shop buildings on the other, some dating to the sixteenth century), and into Trumpington Street. The second begins at Magdalene Bridge and runs down Bridge Street, Sidney Street, St. Andrew's Street, and Regent Street.

The Friar's House – Crammed with fine crystal and porcelain, and the best selection of collector's paperweights in East Anglia. Open 7 days a week. Bene't St., behind King's Parade (phone: 60275).

Ryder and Amies – Caters to the university's demand for badges, plaques, cufflinks, crested ties, and college rugby shirts (various colors); also carries Shetland tweed ties and tartan berets. 27 King's Parade (phone: 350371).

W & G Taylor – Tweeds and tartan items, as well as a range of deerstalker hats and 6-foot-long, striped scarves (available in different colors, depending upon college allegiance). 5 Trinity St. (phone: 350510).

Barretts – A 200-year-old china and glass emporium with a vast selection of crystal (Waterford, Stuart, Webb, Edinburgh) and china (Wedgwood, Royal Doulton, Minton, Spode, Royal Crown Derby, Royal Worcester). 2 St. Mary's Passage (phone: 66711).

Cambridge Fine Art – Nineteenth- and twentieth-century oil paintings and watercolors; will ship to the US. 68 Trumpington St. (phone: 68488).

Primavera – Pottery, glass, cards, tiles, clothes, toys, corn dollies, clay Suffolk cottages, and many other pretty items. 10 King's Parade (phone: 357708).

SPECIAL EVENTS: Most university events take place during the school terms — there are three a year — and more toward the end of the term than the beginning. The most celebrated is *May Week,* which actually takes place in June and is closer to a fortnight than a week. It is the busiest time on the social calendar, enhanced by a general feeling of relief at the end of the working year, particularly in the wake of final examinations. Many college and university societies put on displays of their activities, the most delightful of which are the plays and concerts held on the college lawns (to which the public may go). Each year several colleges hold elaborate balls — the May Balls — at which members and their guests (though outsiders can sometimes buy tickets — ask at the porters' lodge) dance from dusk till dawn, enjoy champagne buffets, and, if still going strong, punt up to Granchester for breakfast.

Late in June, the *Midsummer Fair* takes place on Midsummer Common — as it has since the Middle Ages. During the last two weeks in July, the city sponsors the *Cambridge Festival,* the most important part of which is a series of concerts and recitals in such historic settings as the King's College and St. John's College chapels and the Senate House. There are also art exhibitions, dramatic presentations, a fireworks display, and an Elizabethan feast. The weekend-long *Folk Festival* closes the month.

SPORTS: Both the university and town hold regular sporting events throughout the year. During the winter months, soccer and rugby are the most popular, and in the summer, cricket. The college playing fields are dotted around the town; you'll find many of these indicated on the tourist office map. Schedules of events are posted on the notice boards in the porters' lodges of the individual colleges.

Fishing – In the Cam, naturally. A rod license can be obtained for about £2 wherever you rent tackle.

Golf – There are public courses at Gog Magog and Bar Hill.

Rowing – A major university sport, rowing reaches a crescendo in March when eights from Oxford and Cambridge clash on the Thames in London. The rest of the year, college boat clubs, as well as local school and town clubs, row upriver from Midsummer Common. You'll often see eights, fours, pairs, and single sculls practicing on the river, but watch out for the almost equally frequent coach bicycling along the towpath. With one hand gripping the handlebars and the other clutching a megaphone, he won't be looking where he's going, so be sure to keep out of his way. Traditional racing can't be done on the Cam, because it isn't wide enough for two boats to row side by side. Instead they race in a line. Sometimes as many as 15 boats participate in a single competition, each starting off a one-and-a-half-length interval behind the other. The object is to catch up with the one in front and overlap the stern — hence the name of the race, "Bumps." University *Bumps* take place in February and during May Week (in June), city *Bumps* in July, on a course between Baitsbite Lock and Stourbridge Common. The best place to watch is from the towpath at Fen Ditton.

Walking – Choose from among the area's several enjoyable walking trails — along the Cam towpaths; across the meadows to Grantchester, so beloved by the poet Rupert Brooke; down the Coe Fen Nature Trail (which starts at the bridge near the rough car park off Barton Road). Other trails are recommended in the Tourist Information Centre's booklet, *Country Walks Around Cambridge*.

THEATER: The *Arts Theatre* at Peas Hill (phone: 352000) puts on modern and classic plays, ballet, opera, light opera, and other musical productions by local and touring companies. It also stages the annual Footlights Review in June, a satirical presentation that gave birth to such eminent wits as David Frost, Dudley Moore, Jonathan Miller, and John Cleese. The university's *Amateur Dramatic Club (ADC) Theatre* on Park St. (phone: 59547) has an excellent reputation and puts on a broad selection of plays during the school term.

MUSIC: Cambridge plays host to many concerts and recitals throughout the year including performances of large choral works by the Cambridge University Music Society and the King's College Chapel choir; organ recitals in Great St. Mary's and the King's College Chapel; and many other solo appearances. Details and times are posted on notice boards in the college porters' lodges, as well as in several restaurants, cafés, bookstores, and the various faculty buildings. You'll find rock and disco music at the Corn Exchange, a large covered area on Wheeler Street, once a market and now used for a variety of functions.

CAMBRIDGE / Best in Town

NIGHTCLUBS AND NIGHTLIFE: Despite the city's youthful population, there isn't much taking place in the small hours, mainly because the undergraduates have to be back in their dorms by then. The best disco in town is *Ronelles* in Heidelberg Gardens, Lion Yard. Drinks here are reasonably priced and you can get a simple meal for about £3.50. Thursday night is for the "oldies" — those over 25; Wednesdays are free for women. (Note that no jeans are allowed and men must wear jackets and ties.)

SINS: Cambridge doesn't have a red-light district. The greatest sin in such an academic environment, surpassing even lust, is sloth, whether it's lounging around in the sunshine on the lawns; loafing in a punt (while someone else struggles with the pole); or else lying propped on one elbow, a glass of beer at hand, watching a game of cricket at Fenner's, the university's cricket grounds. If you prefer to indulge in gluttony, try a sticky and scrumptious Chelsea bun from the famed *Fitzbillies Cake Shop* on Trumpington St., just across the road from the Fitzwilliam Museum.

BEST IN TOWN

CHECKING IN: Cambridge offers few moderate or expensive hotels, but numerous inexpensive bed-and-breakfasts. During the summer and particularly toward the close of the school year (the end of May/beginning of June) when the influx of tourists is further bolstered by parents and other relatives visiting students, you'll find it difficult to get a room. For May Week you'll need to reserve at least 2 months in advance. Although the tourist office provides a booking service for visitors who arrive without a room reservation, don't expect it to perform miracles on short notice. In Cambridge and environs you'll pay $65 and up for a double room at an expensive hotel; between $45 and $65 at a moderate one; under $45 at an inexpensive one.

Garden House Hotel – The town's most luxurious four-star hotel, it's close to the city center yet situated in 3 acres of gardens that reach down to the river. At dusk, you can sip cocktails on the lawn before tackling the extensive menu, including typical English dishes. All the 55 bedrooms (there are 5 suites, each named after a Cambridge college) have private bathroom and shower, and most have small balconies overlooking the gardens and river. Granta Pl. (phone: 63421). Expensive.

Gonville Hotel – Located next to the green called Parker's Piece, this is a modern hotel lacking in atmosphere but with a good restaurant. Light refreshments are served on the sheltered patio during summer. Gonville Pl. (phone: 66611). Expensive to moderate.

University Arms Hotel – An imposing structure on the edge of Parker's Piece, the *Arms* has belonged to the same family since 1891. The oak-paneled dining room, which overlooks the park and has a grand fireplace, also boasts an impressive wine list that includes several house wines bottled by the proprietor. There are three bars, one with 100 different types of whiskey. 120 rooms, all but 14 with bathroom. Regent St. (phone: 51241). Expensive to moderate.

Arundel House Hotel – This converted Victorian terrace building overlooks the river and Jesus Green and offers a cozy atmosphere, friendly service, and all modern conveniences. 53 Chesterton Rd. (phone: 67701). Moderate.

Blue Boar Hotel – The first recorded mention of this venerable place was in a 1693 document reporting that a party of church wardens spent 2 shillings on beer here to celebrate the Queen's birthday. It has, needless to say, been modernized since then and all 48 rooms (11 with private bathrooms) have telephone, radio, TV, and tea- and coffee-making facilities. Trinity St. (phone: 63121). Moderate.

Cambridgeshire Hotel – It more than compensates for its out-of-town location with a plethora of sports facilities — an 18-hole championship golf course, tennis courts, squash courts, sauna, and a large, heated, indoor swimming pool. All 100 rooms have private bath or shower. 4.5 miles northwest of Cambridge on the A604 (phone: Crafts Hill 80555). Moderate.

Royal Cambridge Hotel – Spanning several Regency houses, this completely modernized hotel is situated on the main London-to-Cambridge road (A10), close to the city center. 85 rooms, many with private bathrooms. Trumpington St. (phone: 51631). Moderate.

May View Guest House – With an excellent location overlooking Jesus Green, this B&B is tastefully decorated and the breakfast is a hearty start to anyone's day. 12 Park Parade (phone: 66018). Moderate to inexpensive.

Five Gables Farm – This Tudor farmhouse has oak beams, working fireplaces, and a relaxing rural setting. Buck's La., Little Eversden, about 7 miles southwest of Cambridge (phone: Comberton 2236). Inexpensive.

Homestead – Mrs. Byerley, the landlady here, used to run a pub and knows how to provide a warm, friendly welcome. Her three bedrooms are large by B&B standards, and all have TVs. 23 Tenison Ave. (phone: 62854). Inexpensive.

EATING OUT: Although Cambridge is generally poorly rated as a "gourmet" town, it is well served by several eating houses in the inexpensive (less than $20 for dinner for two) and moderate (between $20 and $35) categories. Most of these offer extremely good value and large helpings — the latter is an especially important consideration in a town where most of the potential customers are students.

Don Pasquale – One of the city's top restaurants, with a somewhat Italian menu. The pheasant roasted with capers, onions, parsley, and white wine sauce is especially recommended. 12 Market Hill (phone: 67063). Expensive.

Shades – A highly versatile menu, mainly English dishes, served in an upstairs restaurant (snacks are available downstairs in the wine bar). The desserts, which are occasionally dreamed about in lectures, can be consumed while admiring the view of King's College from the window. Closed Sundays and Mondays. 1 King's Parade (phone: 59506). Expensive to moderate.

Fagin's – A French restaurant, richly decorated on the inside with retired cinema seats and marble-topped tables. 33 Bridge St. (phone: 62054). Moderate.

Taj Mahal – The best of Cambridge's dozen-plus Indian restaurants. Iranian and Malaysian food is also served. 37 Regent St. (phone: 353855). Moderate.

Eraina – A cosmopolitan taverna with a menu composed of multiple choices, including Italian, Chinese, Austrian, and Greek dishes, as well as charcoal-broiled steaks, roasts, and a selection of 21 omelets. A favorite among local office workers. Closed on Sundays. 2 Free School La. (phone: 68786). Moderate to inexpensive.

Varsity – Another Greco/Cambridge restaurant, with Franco/Anglo influences, and chips served more or less with everything. The clientele is composed mainly of students enjoying a break from college dinners. There are three dining rooms; the main floor is the best for people-watching. 35 St. Andrew's St. (phone: 356060). Moderate to inexpensive.

Fitzwilliam Museum Coffee Room – Pâté with tasty breads, homemade quiche, cheesecake, French pastries, and good coffee are among the fare. Closed Sundays and Mondays; otherwise open 10:30 AM to 4 PM. Trumpington St. Inexpensive.

Martin's – Its rock cakes and homemade doughnuts are in constant demand; cold dishes and a few hot ones also available at midday. (The steak and kidney pie here is made as it should be.) The place is filled with students during the school term, but looks a little empty and sad at other times. Closed evenings and Sundays. 4 Trumpington St. (phone: 61757). Inexpensive.

Nettles – A minuscule vegetarian-health-food café with a delicious range of foods, including nut pâté and *muesli* with goat's milk. Open only during lunch hours (10 AM to 3 PM); closed Sundays. 6 St. Edward's Passage. Inexpensive.

Sweeney Todd's – A newly established pizza and hamburger joint located in an old water mill — you can watch the water gushing over the wheel as you eat. Newnham Rd. (phone: 67507). Inexpensive.

Wilson's Granary – Bargain rates and attractive, Laura Ashley–type atmosphere; cauliflower au gratin, quiche, curried eggs, and prawns among its regular offerings. There is an à la carte restaurant and carvery upstairs. Closed Sundays. 14 Trinity St. (phone: 356845). Inexpensive. (Restaurant and carvery moderate.)

For cream teas try *The Orchard* at Grantchester (open summers only; closed Wednesdays); *The Barn* at Fen Ditton (open Saturdays and Sundays only during the summer); and *Hobb's Pavillion,* a converted cricket pavilion overlooking Parker's Piece and named after one of England's all time greats (closed Sundays and Mondays). An even creamier affair can be enjoyed at the *Copper Kettle,* 4 King's Parade, where the treats include American-style cheesecake and baba au rhum with pineapple and fresh cream.

SHARING A PINT: Cambridge has many more pubs than colleges, and most of them serve real ale. The *Eagle* on Bene't St. is one of the oldest in the country. A seventeenth-century coaching inn, it has a gallery overlooking a courtyard where outside drinking (and eating) is popular during the summer. A ceiling in one of the bars displays American Air Force squadron numbers from World War II. The *Baron of Beef* on Bridge St. is a woody, beamy, "olde worlde" student haunt. Tucked away at the end of Thompsons La., the *Spade and Beckett* has a peaceful garden looking onto the river. The *Fort St. George in England,* Midsummer Common, is a gathering spot for rowing enthusiasts; you can sip ale and watch the boats at the same time. Try a Scotch egg — a hard-cooked egg wrapped in sausage meat, dipped in breadcrumbs, and deep fried.

CANTERBURY

Despite the vast damage inflicted by World War II bombing raids (and subsequent rebuilding and development), there remains enough sheer history in Canterbury to give the impression of time's having stopped somewhere along the line and only recently started again to admit the automobile, electricity, and indoor plumbing. The cathedral, begun in the eleventh century and finally completed in the sixteenth, towers moodily over the pubs and shops crouching nearby; half-timbered, whitewashed little houses line the narrow streets; and the River Stour, long ago plied by seagoing ships, now drifts slowly past brilliant flowerbeds and under arching stone bridges. Countless ghosts walk the passageways unseen, and after dark you can almost hear the chanting of monks on their journey from cloister to dining hall.

Of course, Canterbury's history reaches far beyond the Middle Ages. The first settlement of any size known to have flourished in the area dates to about 300 BC. In about 75 BC, these poorly organized natives were conquered by the Belgae, a tribe from across the Channel; still later, in 54 BC, Roman troops led by Julius Caesar stormed and took one of the Belgic fortified camps. A full-scale invasion was launched by Emperor Claudius during the next century, and it was after this victory that the Romans settled in permanently. They called the place Durovernum Cantiacorum and built roads connecting the city with other settlements to the north and south. You can still see traces of the Roman period around Canterbury. For example, the medieval city walls were built upon the original Roman foundations and an intricately tiled Roman pavement is found in Butchery Lane.

During the fifth century Britain was invaded and conquered by the Saxons; by 560 the city had forsaken its Roman identity to become Canterbury (actually Cantwarabyrig), the capital of the Saxon kingdom of Kent, ruled by Ethelbert. It was with the arrival in 597 of St. Augustine — sent by the Pope to convert Ethelbert and his subjects to Christianity — that Canterbury assumed its new and final role of cathedral city. For in the years that followed, Augustine became Archbishop (and primate of all England); founded the Abbey of Sts. Peter and Paul (now called St. Augustine's Abbey); and established the first cathedral.

The city was racked by several invasions during the ensuing years — the Vikings, Danes, and Normans all destroyed much that they found and built anew (including the cathedral). The incident that really put the city on the map, however, was the murder of Thomas à Becket in 1170.

Becket, for years a trusted advisor to King Henry II, was named archbishop of Canterbury in 1162. Thus began a long power struggle between the two over who was the final authority on church matters. Regarded by some as a traitor, Becket was slain in his own cathedral by four of the king's knights. He was soon canonized a saint and the place where he fell declared a shrine. People from all over the world began to flock here by the thousands to honor the martyr. So popular was the pilgrimage to Canterbury that Geoffrey Chaucer chose it as the narrative vehicle for his bawdy classic, *Canterbury Tales,* in which each pilgrim tells his story as the group journeys together to the shrine.

Canterbury can claim many literary connections in addition to this most famous one to Chaucer: The dramatist Christopher Marlowe was born here in 1564 and educated at the King's School; you may be able to catch a performance of one of his plays at the Marlowe Theatre on St. Margaret's Street. Some three centuries later, the playwright and novelist W. Somerset Maugham, also a King's alumnus, sent the protagonist in *Of Human Bondage* to school here. R. H. Barham, the nineteenth-century humorist, was born in St. George's Parish and set parts of his series *The Ingoldsby Legends* in Canterbury. Joseph Conrad, although Polish-born, became one of England's great adventure writers and is buried near Westgate. St. Dunstan's is the setting for several episodes of Charles Dickens's novel *David Copperfield;* in fact, the hotel called The House of Agnes on St. Dunstan's Street is supposedly the building Dickens had in mind when he described the home of Agnes Wickfield.

A day's stroll will take you past most of these landmarks, retracing the real or fictitious footsteps of the city's illustrious native sons. If you just let your imagination run a bit as you wander through Canterbury's prim gates and gardens, you'll soon begin to sense its less decorous past — when the pious thronged the city's crowded streets, the taverns roared a welcome, and the scaffold threatened the woebegone wrongdoer.

CANTERBURY AT-A-GLANCE

SEEING THE CITY: As you approach Canterbury — by car on Rt. A2 from London, from Dover in the southeast, or from Whitstable a few miles to the north — you are immediately aware of the towering hulk of the cathedral, floodlit by night and somberly gray in the daytime, and no less impressive than it was at the true dawn of England's history. There are three viewpoints you shouldn't miss. The first, for a panorama, is the high-point plateau called Eliot Causeway on the campus of the University of Kent-at-Canterbury, about 2 miles along the road to Whitstable. Admission is free, but visitors are not particularly encouraged. The second is the summit of the Westgate Tower, a massive piece of fortification abutting the City Wall. Admission, 15p. The third is the roof of elegant *Riceman's Department Store,* close to the central bus station and in an area where most of the ancient buildings were wiped out by bombing. Because of its insularity it affords a splendid view of all that fortunately remains. Admission by courtesy of the management.

SPECIAL PLACES: Although you've seen the splendor of the cathedral from a distance, you haven't experienced the vastness of its frontage. Walk along the busy shop-lined stretch of Mercery Lane, leading from the middle of High Street, and into the broad patio called Buttermarket. Immediately opposite is the Christ Church Gate; through here you enter another world. From west to east ranges the South West Tower, built in 1460, and behind it the added North West Tower of 1840. Then comes the Nave, dating from 1400, and east of that the noble Bell Harry Tower, raised in 1500. Next are the South East Transept, originating in 1126, and the Choir, put up during the restoration of 1184. The dates given relate only to the superstructure; the main work was started more than 400 years earlier. There will be other "special places" of your own choosing, but it is here, in the open, away from the clamor of traffic and trade, that you first experience the sensation of stepping into medieval history.

CANTERBURY CATHEDRAL

The traceable story goes back to the time of Ethelbert, king of Kent, who in 597 granted the site now occupied by the cathedral to St. Augustine, the Christian missionary from Rome. Building began in 602. Little is known of subsequent events until the disastrous fire of 1067, the year following the Conquest, after which the cathedral was completely rebuilt from its foundations. The history of the present fabric therefore starts with the work of reconstruction carried out by the first Norman archbishop, Lanfranc, in 1070. A hundred years later the infamous murder of Archbishop Thomas à Becket led to continuing pilgrimages and the common acceptance of Canterbury Cathedral as the "Mother Church of the realm."

The Nave – Take a good look at this cavernous, majestic, peaceful enclosure. Designed in about 1400 by Henry Yevele, the architect of Westminster Hall and the nave of Westminster Abbey, it is an example of Perpendicular Gothic and has long been regarded as one of the greatest architectural masterpieces in the world. An interesting and unexplained oddity is that if you stand near the center, at the western end, and view the whole length of the building through the choir screen, the presbytery, and Trinity Chapel, you will notice that the cathedral is not set in a straight line. The eastern part inclines toward the south, or, from your point of view, the right. Exactly behind you is the West Window, with its figure of Adam in the act of digging. This dates from 1178, and is probably the earliest action picture in existence, by which is meant that until then all church windows showed only immobile and flat outlines not in sequence. Similar illustrated windows appear in all parts of the vast church, forming a rich gallery of medieval artwork. The brilliant jewel-tone windows high in the clerestory look merely decorative from floor level, but with good binoculars you can see more detail, and the fascinating and often lighthearted tales unfold like a present-day newspaper cartoon. The so-called "Poor Man's Bible" illustrates scenes from the Old and the New Testaments for the illiterate populace, miracles supposedly performed at Becket's shrine, and homely little accounts of thirteenth-century life.

The Tomb of the Black Prince – Edward of Woodstock, son of King Edward III, became Prince of Wales, but was outlived by his father and never succeeded to the throne. He is remembered as a hero of the battles of Crécy and Poitiers and a tireless patron of the cathedral. It was under his sponsorship that Henry Yevele was able to carry out major rebuilding in the crypt and also design the Westgate and a considerable portion of the city walls. In 1363 the Black Prince married Joan, the Fair Maid of Kent; this match and the subsequent marriage of their daughters to almost all claimants to the throne, resulted in the start of the York and Tudor dynasties. His shrine and tomb, with all the royal knightly regalia displayed nearby, may be seen in the south aisle of Trinity Chapel. It is considered among the most splendid memorials in England.

The Crypt – This is the oldest part of the cathedral, with a low roof and rounded arches in pure Norman style, its rather frightening severity relieved by grotesque and deliberately humorous carvings on the capitals (top part) of the pillars. Some of these are undoubtedly caricatures of church dignitaries of the time.

The Martyrdom – The site where Thomas à Becket was slain by four French knights — Fitzurse, de Moreville, de Tracy, and le Breton — on December 29, 1170, is in the northwest transept at the western end of the crypt. The four, with their retainers, were sent on this evil mission because Archbishop Becket refused to place the demands of his king, Henry II, above those of the church. A shrine venerating the saint was erected after his death, although only the original steps remain, worn down by countless thousands of feet over the centuries.

The Choir (or Quire) – This might be called the jewel of the cathedral, because of the sparkling beauty of its glasswork, the oldest examples of which are the Twelve Miracle Windows.

The Cloisters, the Chapter House, the Green Court, the King's School – To see the cathedral's entire interior takes the better part of a day, but be sure to make time for the peripheral buildings that date from when the whole was a Benedictine monastery. The Cloisters, leading from the Chapter House, are virtually "corridors in the vale of time." If as you stroll through the passageway called the Dark Entry you encounter the ghost of a certain Nell Cook, don't be alarmed — you're not the first. The story of her origin is obscure and her occasional appearances are rarely sinister — so far anyway. Beyond the Green Court, and traditionally associated with the cathedral itself, is the King's School, the oldest public school in the land. (The term "public" is really a misnomer for "private"; this is a very expensive and exclusive private boy's school.) The King's School is architecturally notable for its handsome Norman staircase.

WITHIN THE OLD CITY WALLS

About half of the initial wall structure still stands; the walkway atop it makes a fascinating hike in good weather. Look north for the cattle market, which is close to the shopping center and has been used since the reign of Alfred the Great. Close by you can see the 150-year-old *Invicta*, a steam-powered locomotive designed by George Stephenson, and a working remnant of one of the earliest passenger railways in the world.

The Westgate – The next most imposing of Canterbury's historic buildings is at the extreme end of St. Peter's Street, following on from High Street, 5 minutes' walk in a westerly direction from the cathedral. As a relic it is magnificent, but it has a grisly history: Construction of the Westgate Towers was started at the order of Simon of Sudbury in 1380, during the reign of Richard II. In the following year, it became the city gaol, which it remained until 1829. Today it is a museum exhibiting a collection of arms and armor, shackles, manacles, fetters, and instruments of torture; and the old prison cells still retain their original doors and fittings. Even the timbers of the dreaded gallows are here, a macabre reminder that prisoners were hanged for sometimes quite trivial offenses. Open daily, except Sundays, from April to September, 10 AM to 1 PM and 2 PM to 5 PM; October to March, 2 PM to 4 PM.

Dane John – Nothing to do with Danes, but a prominent feature of central Canterbury, with its prehistoric mound giving fine views of the red-tiled Tudor houses in the neighborhood. The name comes from the Norman-French word *donjon*, meaning a castle or keep, or — more chillingly — a dungeon. Dane John lies southwest of the cathedral, about 5 minutes' walk from Christ Church Gate.

The Norman Castle – A vast ruin now, but it still possesses one of the largest Norman keeps in the country. It was built between 1070 and 1094 and has been several times surrounded and captured and was once the royal prison for the County of Kent. Like the Westgate, it has a grim history of cruelty and mayhem. When the fanatical Mary I was on the throne, many Protestants were imprisoned here before being burned at the stake for their religious opinions. The Norman Castle is at the junction of Castle St. and Rheims Way.

OUTSIDE THE PERIMETER

St. Dunstan's – The section of Old Canterbury beyond the Westgate and leading toward the railway crossing on Whitstable Road. A good place of call is *The House of Agnes,* now a hotel in St. Dunstan's Street (see *Best in Town*), reputedly the one Dickens had in mind as the house of Agnes Wickfield in *David Copperfield*. The interesting old *Falstaff Inn* is nearly opposite, and a door or so away is a small, cozy pub called *The Bishop's Finger*. (The name refers to the ring worn by medieval bishops, not to the rude but ancient gesture of contempt.)

St. Augustine's Abbey – Founded by St. Augustine, with the support of King Ethelbert, in AD 602. Largely a ruin, but an important and still beautiful relic of Canterbury's past, particularly the finely restored Fyndon Gate. Reached from the Quenin Gate of the cathedral.

ENVIRONS

Chilham Castle Keep – Fifteen minutes by car, due south of Canterbury. Chilham Castle, the home of Viscount Massereene and Ferrard, is one of the finest houses in Kent. The Jacobean house is not open to the public, but the splendidly preserved Norman keep remains an attraction for visitors throughout the year. Stop here, not just for its quite glorious setting in 300 acres of forest, but also for a taste of Elizabethan dining. Food is served in the hall of the keep, drinks in the dungeon — but be reassured that the uniformed staff are only there for service and decoration! (To reserve a table, call 022776-561.)

Fordwich – Drive to Sturry, 4 miles north of Canterbury on Rt. A28. Turn right at the signpost. The tiny one-time Cinque Port on the River Stour is less than a minute away. It is an exquisite little town of some 300 inhabitants, and is remarkable for having the smallest town hall in England, delightful to look at and scarcely bigger than a farmworker's cottage. Nobody knows how old the structure is, but the records show that extensive repairs were carried out as recently as 1474. Here again, you'll see instruments of torture. The stocks are outside in the courtyard, their oaken clamps worn slim from centuries of use; the small prison is in one corner; and overlooking the river stands the crane that once lowered condemned miscreants into the water for drowning. Beside it is the ducking-chair for the correction of shrewish wives, and in the town hall itself you can inspect the room set aside for drying them off. An excellent place for lunch is the *George and Dragon,* round the corner from the town hall (see *Best in Town*).

- **EXTRA SPECIAL:** Every year, during the third week of July, a series of choir and orchestra concerts are given at The King's School and in the environs of the cathedral. The musical performances are very well done and performed in glorious surroundings, but wear something warm — it can get very chilly in the evenings. Buy tickets at *Riceman's Department Store* (see *Shopping*).

SOURCES AND RESOURCES

The Tourist Information Center is at 22 St. Peter's St. (phone: 66567), close to the Westgate Towers. It stocks the usual helpful guidebooks, brochures, and maps, and is open daily from 10 AM (closed Sundays). Guided tours of the city leave Longmarket daily at 2:15 PM, from May until September; the fee is 60p. To arrange additional or out-of-season tours, consult the tourist office.

For Local Coverage – The *Kentish Gazette* weekly includes a useful "Town Crier" supplement, which lists all local events; consult also the *Kent Herald* and the *Kentish Observer*. You can find all three at Kent County Newspapers Ltd., 9 St. George's Pl. (phone: 68181).

GETTING AROUND: As Canterbury is very small, the best form of transportation is your own two feet. However, you may decide to visit some of the outlying areas, in which case you'll need to know about alternate modes, discussed below.

Bus – From the bus station on St. George's Lane (near *Riceman's Department Store*), you can catch buses to Dover, Folkestone, Deal, and Margate (all about a half-hour's ride). Call for information: 66151.

Taxi – Quick and courteous cab service is available at all times. Try *Austen's Taxis* (phone: 54105); *Bishop's Taxis* (phone: 65566); *Canterbury Radio Taxis* (phone: 60333); or *Taylor's Taxis* (phone: 56363). (Remember you need a 5p coin for the telephone.)

Car Rental – There are many car rental firms in Canterbury; among them are: *Autorentals* (phone: 69366); *Aviary Car Hire* (phone: 60378); *Canterbury Motor Co. Ltd.* (phone: 51791); *Rent-a-Car* (phone: 66131). There is adequate, low-cost car parking in the city.

MUSEUMS: Religious articles are displayed in Canterbury's churches and cathedral. The city's most interesting museums are *The Royal Museum and Art Gallery*, 18 High St. (the Beaney Institute), which incorporates *Buff's Regimental Museum* and chronicles the area's history and archaeology; the *Westgate*, St. Dunstan's St., which has a collection of weapons and armor; and the *Roman Pavement*, Butchery La., which shelters the remains of a Roman mosaic floor and other artifacts. For information on any of these three, call 52747.

SHOPPING: Canterbury's compact size makes it a shopper's dream. For a wide selection of the basic necessities, try *Riceman's Department Store*, opposite the bus station; *Debenham's*, on Guildhall St.; or *Marks and Spencer*, 4 St. George's Pl. If your hobby is antiques, spend a morning in Palace St. — turn right out of Christ Church Gate of the cathedral, and first right again. There are many antique shops along here; a few to look for are: *The Lighthouse*, No. 4; *Cumagain Antiques*, No. 6; *Gerrards of Canterbury*, No. 8; *Caboodles*, No. 12; *Five Centuries Antiques*, No. 18; *The Aristocrat*, No. 19; *Parker-Williams Antiques*, No. 22. Pottery collectors should be sure to stop in at *The Canterbury Pottery* on the far side of Buttermarket, just before Mercery La. For a special experience walk down to *The Old Weavers' House*, at 1–3 King's Bridge, across from the County Hotel in High St. This is one of the most spectacular seventeenth-century houses in the city; and features a weaving room, a tea garden, coffee shop, and ducking stool poised over the Stour. Stone jewelry, crafts, and brass rubbings' are sold here, and river tours can be arranged.

SPORTS: Cricket – Canterbury is cricket territory; to watch this very British game at its best, go to the *Kent Country Cricket Club* at St. Lawrence Ground, off Old Dover Rd. (phone: 63421). Tickets are available at the gate.

Golf – The well-kept, 18-hole *Canterbury Golf Club*, Littlebourne Rd. (phone: 63586), is open to the public. Players with established handicaps are preferred, but novices not discouraged. Clubs may be rented.

Swimming – The Kingsmead indoor swimming pool on Kingsmead (phone: 69817) is open to the public. Admission fee.

Horseback Riding – Horses can be hired at two stables located about 5 miles due north of Canterbury: *High Rews Equestrian Centre,* Canterbury Rd., Herne Common (phone: Herne Bay 62678); *Homecroft Riding Stables,* Canterbury Rd., Herne Common (phone: Herne Bay 2065).

THEATER: Canterbury has only one commercial playhouse, the *Marlowe,* on St. Margaret's St. (phone: 64747). The *Gulbenkian Theatre* of the University of Kent on St. Giles La. (phone: 69075) is generally open to the public; its offerings include plays, recitals, concerts, and lectures. Check the newspapers for schedules.

NIGHTCLUBS AND NIGHTLIFE: There aren't any of the former and there isn't any of the latter. Try Margate on the coast.

SINS: Another dismal failure. Any sins actually committed should either be kept to yourself or reported to the Dean and Chapter.

BEST IN TOWN

CHECKING IN: In Canterbury, you must book well in advance, because the city plays host to about 2 million visitors during the summer months. Most of the hotels listed below are smallish, but make up for this shortcoming with their cheerful and attentive service. None, however, is in the luxury class. For a double room in the hotels we list below, expect to pay $50 to $85 per night in those noted as expensive; $30 to $50, moderate; and $20 to $30, inexpensive.

County – First licensed in 1629, it is considered the best in Canterbury, and is richly decorated and furnished in antiques. The hotel's restaurant specializes in Continental cuisine. 74 rooms; parking available. High St. (phone: 66266). Expensive.

Slatters – Unremarkable in decor but modern and comfortable, this hotel is continuously busy. Because it's located next to the Marlowe Theatre, visiting theatrical personalities can sometimes be spotted in the bar. 30 rooms; parking. St. Margaret's St. (phone: 63271). Expensive.

Abbots Barton – At this large country house surrounded by its own attractive grounds, you'll find a quiet, old-fashioned ambience; good food; and solid, comfortable furniture. In short, it's the perfect home base for families. Facilities include 51 bedrooms (41 with private baths) and parking. New Dover Rd. (phone: 60341). Moderate.

Eastwell Manor – This turreted, rambling hostelry has 20 spacious rooms, extensive gardens, and an accomplished kitchen. Ashford (phone: 0233-35751). Expensive.

The George and Dragon – This charming old sixteenth-century inn near the River Stour has thirteen rooms. Its restaurant, which serves Continental cuisine at dinner, also offers a very fine hot-and-cold buffet lunch. Fordwich, near Sturry (phone: 710661). Moderate.

The Georgian Guest House – If you're a little eccentric, you'll find yourself one of the family at this B&B. 69 Castle St. (phone: 61111). Inexpensive.

CANTERBURY / Best in Town

EATING OUT: Although it's a country town, Canterbury boasts a few very fine restaurants, where you can have an expertly prepared meal for a reasonable price. There are also some cozy little eateries in the surrounding area, which you may decide to include on a day tour out of town. In general, a meal for two, excluding wine, tips, and drinks, will run about $35 to $50 in a place listed as expensive, $20 to $35 in a moderate one, and under $20 in an inexpensive one.

The Duck Inn – This snug little restaurant, warmed by a roaring fire, is noted for its very good French cooking. It's about 5 miles outside Canterbury, near the village of Bridge on the road to Dover. The best approach is to take a taxi. Reservations necessary. Closed Mondays and Tuesdays. Pett Bottom (phone: 830354). Expensive.

The Beehive – In the Middle Ages, the *Beehive* was a pub conveniently located across the way from the cattle market; in the eighteenth century, it was a smugglers' lair. Today it's one of Canterbury's best restaurants — a small and intimate place specializing in Continental food. Reservations necessary. 52 Dover St. (phone: 61126). Expensive.

Ristorante Tuo e Mio – This is just the place for a rich, satisfying Italian lunch or dinner, topped off with a sinful zabaglione. Parking is not too good, so walk instead. Reservations necessary. 16 The Borough (phone: 61471). Expensive.

Canterbury Shellfish – The nearby Channel ports have supplied Kent with fresh fish and seafood for centuries, so while you're here you should definitely sample the day's catch. Note the hours: 12 to 2:30 PM and 6 to 10:30 PM. Reservations necessary. 78 Broad St. (phone: 65442). Moderate.

The House of Agnes – Referred to in Dickens's *David Copperfield*, it's now a hotel as well as a restaurant. The kitchen prepares good hearty English home cooking. Reservations necessary. 71 St. Dunstan's St. (phone: 65077). Moderate.

Flap Jax – This is the place for homesick Americans — the menu features steaks, chicken, waffles, pancakes, and hamburgers. Stop for breakfast or lunch during a day tour of the area. It's in Hythe, 6 miles west of Folkestone. Reservations recommended. 32–34 High St. (phone: 0303-69898). Inexpensive.

SHARING A PINT: For a special experience, stop by the *Millers Arms*, Mill La. (phone: 52675); it's an authentic oak-beamed, flagstone-floored pub that even has its own minuscule brewery. Then there's the *Three Compasses*, 18 St. Peter's St. (phone: 62753), which is somewhat more formal and sometimes inclined to be stuffy, but serves good pub grub. Possibly the friendliest and most atmospheric pub is the *Olive Branch*, 39 Burgate (phone: 62170), opposite the cathedral gates.

CARDIFF

"A proper fine Towne" was how the seventeenth-century cartographer Christopher Saxton described Cardiff. And today it's a proper fine city: handsome, spacious, and genial, with a definite sense of its own importance. It is, after all, the capital city of the principality of Wales. And it has a capital feel about it. You sense right away that it is at the center of things. It is a busy headquarters for commerce, industry, government, the arts, and communications. And it has perhaps the most attractive city center in all of Britain — the "Welsh Washington," as it's called.

From London you can be delivered to Cardiff's front door in under 2 hours by the 125 mph super-train, nicknamed the "Welsh Bullet." And the big station sign says *Caerdydd*/Cardiff in salute to the two languages of Wales, hinting at the history, pride, and fascination of this singular land. Welsh, spoken by one fifth of the principality's 2.8 million people, is Wales's distinction among nations; and its story is a central part of the history of the Welsh people.

In Cardiff you'll see the language (it's older than English and dates from the sixth century) written on all manner of signs. You're sure to see the word *Croeso* — "welcome" — and the Welsh mean it. And you'll hear the language spoken in the streets and shops and on radio and television.

But you won't hear it a lot. For one thing Cardiff is in southeast Wales, and the strongly Welsh-speaking areas are in the north and west. Cardiffians though have their own distinctive twang, one of the many strands from which the city's character is woven. It is a multilayered and cosmopolitan place, an outward-looking, modern European city of warm people, as well as a storehouse of the history of a fascinating area.

Cardiff was awarded capital city status by Queen Elizabeth in 1956, at a time when nationalist feeling in Wales was demanding some recognition of the principality's special identity within the United Kingdom. Other towns applied for the honor, but only Cardiff (population now 277,000) had the scale, background, and facilities to make it a realistic contender.

Diligent Romans built a no-nonsense little Cardiff beside the River Taff as part of their network of conquest. It served as a fort and trading post. The Roman stones, still visible today, were already old when the Normans arrived in the eleventh century and built their own castle.

On a mound they raised a keep, a noble medieval fist, and it remains intact: one of the finest examples of its kind in Britain. Castle, moat, and green are right in the city center and Cardiffians like to saunter or doze on the green on summer days.

King Edward I of England conquered stubborn Wales in the thirteenth century. But a century or so later, in 1404, the Welsh political comet Owain Glyndwr fanned the embers of resistance, started a war of independence, and sacked Cardiff. Eventually he lost his struggle, but five centuries later Cardiff was generous enough to erect a marble statue of the hero in its opulent city hall.

Roundheads took the town from Royalists in Britain's seventeenth-century civil war. But for nearly 200 years after that life was peaceful enough. Cardiff bloomed quietly, a market town, seaport, and occasional bolt-hole for pirates prowling the Bristol Channel.

Then the Industrial Revolution came. Up in the winding green valleys, spoking from Cardiff's hub, men tore out coal to fuel factories, furnaces, mills, ships. The coal was sent to Cardiff, first by mule, then barge, then rail, for onward shipment to British cities and the world.

The new Cardiff soared on the dizzy spiral of the great coal rush, the central event in post-1800 Welsh history. The riches of the valleys poured in. The Taff ran black. Tycoons multiplied. With Welsh coal at the heart of British economic expansion Cardiff became the world's greatest coal port. The Cardiff Coal Exchange is still there in dockland, monument to an age, a stately Victorian edifice in Coalowner Gothic. Look at it, and in your mind's eye you can see the frock-coated financiers making their fortunes.

In its heyday, Cardiff's dockland was called Tiger Bay. It was a teeming, noisy, rumbustious Dodge City of pubs, little houses, and bordellos. Today, old Tiger Bay has gone; for it was a time as well as a place. The slums have been cleared and the area is often cited as an example of an integrated multiracial community of long standing. And its people prefer you to use its proper name: Bute Town.

During Cardiff's Victorian and Edwardian expansion, its top citizens consolidated its position as chief city of Wales. Among lawns, shrubs, and boulevards they built their halls of government and culture: city hall, county hall, museum, law courts, university, and others, all laid out in a grand magisterial sweep. Meanwhile, the burgeoning middle classes built lovely villas in places like Cathedral Road.

One of the most pleasant things about Cardiff is that it is a good place for walking. Its heart remains village-sized. And the castle, the business center, shops, restaurants, pubs, hotels, station, rugby stadium, museum, theaters, galleries, and parks can all be reached comfortably on foot.

You can traverse the city by way of parks, greens, and footpaths; and the stroll across Llandaff Fields to Llandaff, the secluded village-within-the city, with its cathedral, pubs, and cottages, is a great favorite.

One of the famous parks, though, is not a park at all: Cardiff Arms Park is a temple of rugby football, a game to which Welshmen devote blood, sweat, and tears. On big-match Saturdays the city seems to vibrate with emotion, song, and excitement. The Red Dragon flag of Wales is hoisted aloft and almost everyone seems to have a leek or a daffodil, the national emblems, pinned to hat or coat. To be in Cardiff on one of these days is to experience a certain kind of Welshness, humorous and exuberant, in the raw.

CARDIFF AT-A-GLANCE

SEEING THE CITY: Right in the middle of town is the best place to get a feel for Cardiff: the castle. It is open almost every day of the year. Cross the moat bridge, go through the gate house, turn left, and make for the clock tower. From here you get a sentry's-eye view of the castle itself, the River Taff, the Arms Park, Sophia Gardens, and busy shopping streets. You can also see the famous "animal wall" — a row of sculptures of beasts and birds perched on battlements. You can see Bute Park, stretching off in the direction of Llandaff cathedral; and the pristine towers, domes, and greenery of Cathays Park (pronounced *Catt-hays*). Much the same view can be had from a slightly different vantage point, the roof garden of the castle. This is a piece of delicious Victorian extravagance, with its delightful shrubs, murals, mosaics, and fountains. On the northwest edge of Cardiff is The Wenallt, an area of rolling woodland from which you get a superb view of Cardiff, laid out on its coastal plain, and of the Bristol Channel.

SPECIAL PLACES: Although Cardiff owes much of its importance and growth to coal, there has been over the years a conscious effort to keep its center ungrimy. The city fathers of the last century dreamt they dwelt in marble halls — and set about making that dream come true. The Cardiff they made is, at its center, a place of gracefulness and greenery. And its compactness means that, for the most part, you can park the car and walk to the principal sights; and are never far from a little restaurant or a jolly pub; or a shady tree or stretch of grass where you might like to do as the locals do and chat, read, gaze, or snooze.

CITY CENTER

Cardiff Castle – Nineteen hundred years of history are stored here. The Roman walls are 10 feet thick and, as you can see, the stone keep on its *motte*, or mound, was built to last when it was erected in the thirteenth century to show the local people who was boss. The castle has always been lived in, and the third marquess of Bute, one of Wales's great coal moguls, ordered the renovations and extensions that give the place its unique appearance. He commissioned the architect William Burges to design a nobleman's indulgence. The result is the baroque and charming place you enjoy today, full of color, exquisite murals, carvings, and painted ceilings and windows. There is a table with a hole in it, through which a vine emerged, enabling the marquess and guests to pluck fresh grapes. Part of the castle is now used for civic receptions and banquets: It is a wonderfully eccentric place for the drinking of champagne. Other rooms and towers house the museum of the Welch Regiment. A visit to the castle includes a well-worth-it conducted tour, although you can wander on your own if you prefer. Admission charge. (phone: 31279).

National Museum of Wales – A short walk from the castle, or from the main shopping area, is one of Britain's finest museums. Built of Portland stone, huge and airy, it offers a broad-ranging and detailed introduction to Wales in all aspects. It has a remarkable collection of carved Celtic standing stones and crosses; a host of national treasures; and a gallery housing, among much else, the work of artists like Augustus John and his sister Gwen, and an outstanding collection of Impressionist paintings. Apart from its large permanent collection, the National hosts touring art exhibits. Open daily from 10 AM, Sundays from 2:30 PM. Free. (phone: 397951).

City Hall – Next to the museum, it is distinguished by its clock tower and ornate stonework. Inside is the Marble Hall with its statues of the great men of Welsh history.

Cathays Park – Pink-surfaced avenues, blossom, shrubs, walks, statuary, and buildings of an almost Athenian aspect. Welsh people are rightly proud of it.

ENVIRONS

St. John's Church – A landmark in Cardiff since the fifteenth century, with its tall pinnacled tower in the Perpendicular style. It is the heart of the city's commercial and shopping district and is 2 or 3 minutes' walk from the castle.

Llandaff Fields – On these tree-avenued meadows in summer you'll see boys playing cricket, maybe dreaming of playing first-class cricket one day at Sophia Gardens, the handsome ground in the city center. This is a lovely setting for the game that is a British passion and a mystery to foreigners. Why not go for a few hours and enjoy trying to understand the ritual? In winter the boys will be playing rugby and dreaming of playing in the red shirt for Wales at Cardiff Arms Park.

Llandaff – Two miles from the city center. You can reach it by walking across Llandaff Fields, or by bus. Llandaff is a charming enclave: Somehow it has retained a sleepy village air with its neat and solid Victorian houses, inns, whitewashed deanery, and a village green from which a path leads to the cathedral, beautiful and discreet in its hollow. St. Teilo founded a settlement here in the sixth century, which is how Llandaff got its name: *Llan* (church) and *taff*, from the River Taff. The cathedral dates from the twelfth century. It fell into disrepair and was at one time a beer house and cattle shelter. It was restored in the nineteenth century, wrecked in an air raid in 1941, and restored once more. One of its most striking features, and still controversial, is Epstein's aluminum figure of Christ, which dominates the nave. Llandaff is worth making time for.

Old Bishops Palace – In keeping with the rest of Llandaff: peaceful gardens among ancient walls, a place for reflection.

Bute Town – Cardiff's famous and notorious Tiger Bay of days gone by. Time was when seafaring men from many parts of the world settled in this dockland area and created a vibrant, tough, and often seamy and squalid community. Things have changed a lot, and though Bute Town is still a lively, mixed community, it prides itself on its respectability. The coal trade isn't what it was, of course; but the docks are still very important. And it's interesting to see the imposing shipping and banking offices, and the Coal Exchange, built in the great days of the coal rush. There's a new museum here, the Welsh Industrial and Maritime Museum (phone: 371805) exhibiting the machinery that powered early industrial growth, and other pioneering equipment. Admission free. From the High Street or the bus station in the city center you can get a bus to the museum, in the heart of Bute Town.

Roath Park – One hundred acres, with an attractive lake. You can rent a rowboat very cheaply (just keep away from the serious young lads fishing from the banks); admire the geese camped on the island; and pause at the miniature lighthouse, a memorial to the Antarctic hero, Captain Scott, who sailed from Cardiff to make his ill-fated expedition to the South Pole.

Dyffryn Gardens – These are a few miles west of the city center, on Rt. A48 at St. Nicholas. On the way down the winding country road (where you can get a good feel for the lovely Vale of Glamorgan) you can stop at the Tinkinswood long barrow, one of the finest examples of a neolithic burial chamber to be found in Wales: It has a 40 ton capstone. Dyffryn House (phone: 593328) is a spacious mansion with 80 acres of spacious grounds to match. It has masses of flowers, shrubs, and trees. And it has a teahouse. So it's a perfect place in which to wind down and draw breath. It is open from April to October and admission is 60p. You can reach Dyffryn by bus from the station, nos. 251, 252, or 302.

■ **EXTRA SPECIAL:** Out on the edge of the Vale of Glamorgan, 4½ miles from the city center, at St. Fagan's, is one of Cardiff's most pleasant treats, the *Welsh Folk Museum* (phone: 569441). You can spend an absorbing day here and be astonished that time seems to fly by so quickly. In the 100-acre estate around the Tudor mansion (closed for renovation until sometime in 1983) are an original cottage, farmhouses, barns, a smithy, a tollhouse, a chapel, tannery, cockpit, woolen factory, and other buildings. Each one once stood in some part of rural Wales, was carefully taken apart, its stones and slates and beams numbered, then reconstructed in the sheep-grazed meadows of St. Fagan's. The furnishings and equipment are authentic too, and you can wander through the houses, upstairs and downstairs, to see how Welsh people lived through the centuries. You'll note the cozy fireside beds and the love spoons that young men carved for their sweethearts: The more intricate the carving the deeper the passion! St. Fagan's tells the story of the people of Wales. The attendants are jolly, helpful, and all Welsh-speaking. In addition to the authentic buildings, St. Fagan's has a large museum and a restaurant. Open daily from 10 AM, Sundays from 2:30 PM; admission charge. Take the no. 32 bus, which leaves from the station every hour on the hour.

SOURCES AND RESOURCES

In the Welsh language the name of the Wales Tourist Board is *Bwrdd Croeso Cymru* —literally translated as Wales Welcome Board. It gives you an idea of how the Welsh feel about showing visitors their land. The board's office in Cardiff is in the center, across the road from the castle, at 3 Castle St. (phone: 27281), and here you can get maps, guidebooks, leaflets, and personal advice and directions. The paperwork is high quality and the advice is bright and friendly. You can also get information about Cardiff from the Public Relations Officer, City Hall, Cardiff (phone: 31033).

The Wales Tourist Board publishes an excellent, clear, and colorful map of Wales. And there are good cheap maps and guides to Cardiff available at newsagents and bookshops like *W. H. Smith and Menzies*. You'll find a wide selection of books about Wales in *Lears* on St. Mary St., *Siop y Triban* in Wyndham Arcade, and *Oriel* in Charles St.

For Local Coverage – The city's Public Relations Office publishes brochures, books, and a useful guide called *Events in Cardiff* each month. And you can get information about restaurants and entertainments from the Wales Tourist Board. On a day-to-day basis you will find movies, theaters, and concert listings in the *Western Mail,* published every morning except Sunday, and the *South Wales Echo,* Cardiff's afternoon paper.

GETTING AROUND: Buses – At its heart Cardiff is a walker's city. But there's an excellent bus network that operates until late at night. Cardiff Transport (phone: 396521) runs a good variety of tours, using open-topped double-decker buses, starting from Greyfriars Road, where there's an information kiosk.

Trains – Good rail services to the suburbs, outlying towns, valleys, and villages. And of course fast inter-city services. Local trains run from both Central and Queen Street stations. Information from British Rail, Central Station (phone: 28000).

Taxi – Cabs don't cruise as a rule. The Wales Tourist Board has a good taxi list, and there are plenty of firms in the Yellow Pages. *Glamtax* (phone: 21687), *Castle Cabs* (phone: 394929), and *City Centre Cars* (phone: 394394) are among those offering 24-hour service. There are cab ranks at Central station and the Friary in the city center.

CARDIFF / Sources and Resources

Car Rental – Most major national and international firms have offices in Cardiff: *Hertz* (phone: 24548); *Avis* (phone: 42111); *Godfrey Davis* (phone: 45448).

MUSEUMS: In addition to those described in *Special Places,* the following museums are of interest.

Turner House Art Gallery, Plymouth Rd., Penarth (phone: Penarth 708870).

Oriel Art Gallery, exhibitions change about every 3 weeks. 53 Charles St. (phone: 395548).

Chapter Centre for the Arts, touring exhibitions of contemporary works. Market Rd., (phone: 396061).

SHOPPING: There is no need to embellish the facts: The shopping in Cardiff is excellent. There's a wide range of goods, expensive and bargain, in big stores, little stores, and friendly boutiques. Much of the shopping center is a pedestrian precinct. And one of the capital's attractions is its system of shopping arcades; these make browsing a pleasure in any weather. Watch for Welsh woolen products, beautiful bedspreads, flannel, pottery, and woodwork.

Howells of Cardiff – Is one of the major department stores and sells almost everything. A good range of glassware, china, and gifts. Also a smart delicatessen and restaurant. St. Mary St. (phone: 31055).

David Morgan – Another big department store in the city center. The Hayes (phone: 21011).

Things Welsh – Pottery, crafts, woolens, metalwork, all of good quality. Duke St. Arcade (phone: 33445).

Welsh Rural Crafts – A good selection of crafts. Royal Arcade (phone: 26728).

Pethau Cain – Traditional Welsh crafts. Pontcanna Pl., Llandaff Fields (phone: 372263).

Cardiff Indoor Market – All the bustle, noise, and color of Wales, with a wide range of goods and accents. Welsh lamb is a specialty in the butchers' stalls; *bara brith,* a kind of fruit bread, is offered at the bakers' stalls. And try some *laverbread,* a Welsh delicacy. It's a thick black seaweed, something of an acquired taste, delicious with ham or bacon. Another Welsh favorite you'll find here is cockles. Open Mondays to Saturdays, closed on Wednesday afternoons. Entrance in St. Mary St.

Antique Market – Browsing is fun here. Open Thursdays and Saturdays. Mill La.

SPECIAL EVENTS: The *Cardiff Searchlight Tattoo* is a military pageant held every 2 years in the arena of Cardiff Castle. The castle is also the setting for the annual horse jumping championships, every June. The *Llandaff Festival of the Arts* is growing in stature and is held every June. A big rugby match is always a special event: You're unlikely to get tickets for an international, but less important matches are just as passionate and exciting.

SPORTS: Visitors are welcome to use the wide range of sporting facilities at the *Western Leisure Centre* (phone: 593592) and the *Heath Sports Centre* (phone: 755607).

Golf – The *Cardiff Golf Course* is open to the public. Sherbourne Ave.

Riding – You can rent horses at *Equitation and Riding Centre,* Poncanna Fields, a few miles west of Cardiff.

Rugby – This is a national passion and the immensely popular *Cardiff Rugby Club* plays at the *Cardiff Arms Park National Rugby Stadium.*

Skiing – There's an artificial slope at Fairwater Park, where you can also rent ski equipment (phone: 561793).

Sailing – There's boat rental and anchorage at *Penarth,* 5 miles south of Cardiff.

Swimming – Go to the Wales Empire Swimming Pool on Wood St. (phone: 22296), where you can also have a Turkish bath and sauna.

THEATRE: *The New,* in Park Pl. (phone: 32446), stages productions by the internationally renowned Welsh National Opera, ballet, pre-London plays, and pantomime in the winter. *The Sherman,* in Senghennydd Rd. (phone: 25855), is a modern theater that puts on plays by major professional groups and sometimes by local amateur groups. The small "workshop" theater is known for its fringe productions. Show schedules can be found in the local papers.

MUSIC: "Praise the Lord — we are a musical nation," one of Dylan Thomas's characters said. And Cardiff does its best to live up to that with a regular program of concerts. *St. David's Hall,* a newly opened 2,000-seat national concert and conference center on Working St., presents a wide variety of musical entertainment—classical, jazz, rock, and folk—as well as sports, films, lectures, and other "large-scale" events. Midday concerts can be heard in *City Hall* and at the *BBC Wales* concert hall in Llandaff.

NIGHTCLUBS AND NIGHTLIFE: Cardiffians take their evening pleasure with some enthusiasm. They like to go out to dinner and take quite a long time over the meal: They're not fast-food folk. And they like propping up a bar, talking and listening to music. You'll find it easy to join them in any of these activities. Cardiff also has a number of nightclubs; these include *Mont Merence,* 45 Charles St. (phone: 29142); *Bumpers,* Castle Arcade (phone: 32654); *Papagio's,* Hayes Bridge Rd. (phone: 25646); and *Club Incognito,* 41 St. Mary St. (phone: 44004).

SINS: For the wheelers and dealers, there's gambling at *Les Croupiers,* 32 St. Mary St. (phone: 22810), and at *Kings Casino Club,* 7 High St. (phone: 387580). You might find striptease or topless bars here or there in the city, but Cardiff is not renowned for these art forms.

BEST IN TOWN

CHECKING IN: Wales has always been popular with travelers, and some of its hotels are justly famous. Moreover, standards have been improved considerably during the past few years. If you want the tops in comfort and class in Cardiff you'll have to pay top dollar, but in the more modest places you will find great comfort, excellent home-cooked food, a warm welcome, and a bill that doesn't make you pale. Consult the tourist board, which has lists of recommended and inspected hotels. A double with breakfast in a hotel in the expensive category will cost $70 to $90; in the moderate, $50 to $70; and in the inexpensive, as low as $20.

The Angel – Considered the best, with a gracious, spacious air and an attentive staff. 97 rooms. Right in the center of town, at Castle St. (phone: 32633). Expensive.

The Post House – Up-to-date and very comfortable. Located a bit out of town at Pentwyn, so you really need to have a car. Good eating and other facilities. 150 rooms (phone: 731212). Expensive.

CARDIFF / Best in Town

The Park – A good hotel in the middle of town. Large, amiable, popular, and a favorite with business people. 99 rooms. Park Place (phone: 23471). Expensive to moderate.

The Beverley – Comfortable and friendly with a good restaurant. 19 rooms. 75 Cathedral Rd. (phone: 43443). Moderate.

The Centre – Smart, modern, and comfortable rooms with all the facilities. Bilingual signs and notices are a pleasant nod of respect to the old language. 160 rooms. Westgate St. (phone: 388681). Moderate.

The Royal – One of Cardiff's long-established and most dependable hotels. 68 rooms. In the center of town on St. Mary St. (phone: 23321). Moderate.

Cedars Hotel – In a pleasant and quiet suburb, it's comfortable and has a restaurant. 25 rooms. Fidlas Rd., Llanishen (phone: 752163). Inexpensive.

The Ellincliffe – This is representative of a number of good, clean, comfortable, and rather homely hotels, not far from the city center. It has a restaurant and a liquor license. 160 Cathedral Rd. (phone: 30420). Inexpensive.

EATING OUT: Cardiff is a cosmopolitan city and this is reflected in its restaurants, tastes, and menus. While you're here, though, be sure to try the local specialties, such as Welsh lamb. Likewise don't miss fresh Welsh salmon or *sewin,* a kind of trout. Pluck up courage and taste *laverbread* — remember it's not bread but seaweed. For starters, you'll find *cawl* (broth) in its various forms delicious. And to round off, homemade pies and fruit tarts are usually good. Some restaurants, mainly the less expensive ones, serve food throughout the day and evening. Others stick to the usual lunch and dinner hours, and these places accept major credit cards. Eating out in Cardiff is less expensive than in London. Expect to pay $35 and up for dinner for two, including wine and tips in places listed as expensive; $20 to $35 in a moderate restaurant; and under $20 for an inexpensive meal.

The Angel – This hotel restaurant has more than a touch of class and good food. Service is a shade slow, but who's rushing? Castle St. (phone: 32633). Expensive.

Gibson's – One of the capital's most enjoyable restaurants, at which the proprietress almost always scores a bull's-eye with her French-style cooking. There's a good atmosphere, a friendly staff, and wines to match. Reservations required. A little off the beaten track at 6 Romilly Crescent (phone: 41264). Expensive to moderate.

Harvesters – Be sure to bring a robust appetite — the food here is good and filling. Try the pea soup and dare to have jugged hare; it's magnificent. Reservations recommended. 5 Pontcanna St. (phone: 32616). Expensive to moderate.

Positano – This is a good, traditional Italian restaurant. Church St. (phone: 35810). Expensive to moderate.

Savastano's – The reason Jimmy Savastano's place is usually busy, and the customers keep on coming back, is because it provides a happy, delicious, and informal eating experience. Italian specialties; veal dishes are especially good. Reservations recommended. 300 North Rd., Gabalfa (phone: 30270). Expensive to moderate.

The Spot – Another good Italian place where you can also have well-prepared fish. Church St. (phone: 44958). Expensive to moderate.

Yr Ystafell Gymraeg – The name means "The Welsh Room," and not surprisingly, the restaurant is furnished with Welsh antiques. You'll find many enjoyable native dishes here: Choose from cockles, laverbread, lamb, and goose. The steak and kidney pie is lovely and so is the cawl. Reservations recommended. 74 Whitchurch Rd., Gabalfa (phone: 42317). Moderate.

The Frenchman – An informal eatery, it has a wine bar atmosphere. In summer you can have lunch outside. Park Pl. (phone: 28899). Moderate to inexpensive.

Grains Diner – One of the new breed of health food restaurants, it has a farmhouse-kitchen decor and serves nourishing well-prepared food such as vegetable casseroles, fish, and lamb. *Grains* doesn't have a liquor license, but you're welcome to bring your own — and Morgan's Wine Store is conveniently located across the street. 5 Romilly Crescent (phone: 21905). Inexpensive.

Field's – Another health food place, *Field's* serves up savory pancakes and all sorts of tasty things made with nuts and fresh vegetables. Good fun. 99 Wyeverne Rd., Cathays (phone: 23554). Inexpensive.

Lexington – Americans say that this hamburger joint is as good as the best back home. Bright and breezy atmosphere, with All-American desserts like apple pie and cheesecake, too. Queen St. (phone: 42278). Inexpensive.

The Louis – It's open all day and serves excellent meals from a large menu. Just the place for traditional high tea, with friendly waitresses and plenty of room. St. Mary St. (phone: 25722). Inexpensive.

Riverside – A successful Cantonese restaurant, this place is a cut above average and offers a great variety of dishes, all cooked by talented hands. Reservations recommended. 44 Tudor Rd., Riverside (phone: 372163). Inexpensive.

Tandoori Mahal – Typical of the many Indian restaurants in Cardiff, this restaurant offers authentic tandoori (clay-oven) cooking served by a friendly staff. 98 Albany Rd., Roath Park (phone: 491500). Inexpensive.

SHARING A PINT: Cardiff has pubs for all tastes—quiet, noisy, intimate, brash. And it has its own beer, made at Brain's brewery (that's the malty smell in the air in St. Mary Street!). The bar in the *Angel Hotel* is quite posh; the clublike back bar in the *Park Hotel* is busy at lunchtimes and early evenings. The *Old Arcade,* in Church St. (phone: 31740), is a typical large, friendly, Cardiff pub. The *Conway,* in Conway Rd. (phone: 32797), is a favorite, lively haunt of young Welsh-speaking people. Out at *St. Fagan's* is the elegant *Plymouth Arms* (phone: 569130), where you can eat well, too.

CHESTER

The red sandstone walls surrounding the old city of Chester are the only city walls in Britain to have come down to the twentieth century very nearly intact. For the last three centuries they have been a pleasant place to walk to get a better view of one of the most medieval-looking of British cities. Before that, however, these walls did their share of preserving it. Though it's now been more than 300 years since Chester's streets have seen any fighting, the walls are a reminder that it has been a military city for all its nineteen centuries of existence.

The original town — called Deva or Castra Devana, fortress on the Dee — was laid out by the battle-tested veterans of the Roman Twentieth Legion when Britain became the newest province of the Empire only decades after the Crucifixion. Centuries after the Romans had abandoned Britain, Edward I set out from here to crush the rebellious Welsh, binding them into submission in the thirteenth century with a chain of coastal fortresses from Flint to Caernarvon. Later still, Chester's position astride the route to Ireland was of strategic importance to Charles I, who expected reinforcements from his armies there, during the mid-seventeenth-century Civil War between the King and his Parliament. Charles watched the defeat of his army at the battle of Rowton Moor and fled the city, only to go on to eventual execution.

Since Roman times, there have always been soldiers in Chester. Even now it is the home of an active unit, the Royal Irish Rangers, and the permanent depot of its own county regiment, the Cheshire Regiment, first formed three centuries ago. This military presence has stamped itself firmly on the city. The four main streets follow the line of the main roadways laid out inside the Roman fort almost 2,000 years ago, and where they meet at Chester Cross, the Church of St. Peter is built on the foundations of the Roman headquarters building and the residence of the military commander. The lines of many of the smaller back streets echo the layout of the Roman barracks, granaries, and storehouses.

Even the Rows, Chester's above-ground-level network of shopping walkways, may owe their origins to the city's distant past as a military fortress. According to one of the more convincing theories (no one really *knows* why they were built), the ruins of the buildings left by the Romans were so massive that their Saxon successors preferred to build on top of them and in front of them rather than labor to remove the weighty stonework. The surviving rows follow the four main streets — Bridge Street, Watergate Street, Northgate Street, and Eastgate Street — that existed within the Roman fortress, and even the one exception, a now-vanished set of rows down Lower Bridge

Street, lies along the Roman road from the fort to the Dee crossing — a road that would also have been lined with Roman buildings. (Complaints that shops in the rows were dark — Daniel Defoe was among the complainers — led to a theory that they were deliberately built to keep the wares of Chester's merchants from scrutiny in broad daylight, but this theory is not taken seriously.)

Chester's military history has left a practical legacy. Before mechanization, armies marched — whatever Napoleon might have said — on their own two feet, and this is a city designed as much for today's pedestrian, shopper, or tourist, as it was for yesterday's infantryman. The almost-complete circuit of the city walls, built on the north and east over the original Roman ramparts but extended to the south and west by Saxon engineers to take the city's defenses closer to the river, links with the Rows to form a network of walkways completely free from the traffic below. In addition, the four main city streets are now being turned into a pedestrian area, and though it will be some years before cars are finally banished, traffic levels within the walls are already low enough to give a feeling of the city before the coming of the automobile.

One reason Chester still possesses so many links with the past is that it has been in decline, in a sense, ever since the Middle Ages. Originally a major port, the silting-up of the Dee eventually killed the seaborne trade with Ireland and America. Remedies were tried, but in the end, shipping moved to an obscure fishing village called Liverpool on the nearby River Mersey, and with it went the industrialization and urbanization that would have obliterated the old Chester forever.

Instead, the city found a new role as a prosperous market town, a trading center between northwest England and North Wales, and a destination for some half a million tourists a year who are treated to the sight of as picturesque a town as any in old England. Boswell told Johnson it pleased his fancy more than any town he ever saw, and Nathaniel Hawthorne wrote of its "houses of very aged aspect, with steep, peaked gables."

Yet in spite of the abundance of black and white half-timbering, Chester's buildings are today largely the work of Victorian restorers and rebuilders. Fortunately, they were enthralled by the traditional Cheshire "magpie" decoration, and their revival designs give the city a unity of style that bridges the centuries. Among the Georgian brick and Victorian plaster are genuine ancient houses such as the Old Leche House and Bishop Lloyd's House dating from the sixteenth and early seventeenth centuries. Near them is God's Providence House — so called because its inhabitants survived the plague in centuries gone by — built in the same era but rebuilt, more richly decorated, 200 years later. It's entirely typical of Chester that the real and the reproduction are so intermingled and, sometimes, virtually indistinguishable.

CHESTER AT-A-GLANCE

SEEING THE CITY: In a city as tightly packed as Chester, there's no single spot for a panoramic vista. The Grosvenor Bridge across the Dee, the longest single masonry arch in the world when it opened in 1831, gives a good view down onto the racecourse and the river and across to the city skyline behind the western ramparts of the city walls. But for a closer view of the city's bustle, pick a spot on the Rows overlooking Chester Cross, where you can lean on the old balustrades and watch the world go by. Twice each day during the summer, at noon and 3 o'clock, Town Crier Michael Chittenden stands by the Cross in tricorn hat, scarlet cloak, and knee breeches—a replica of the nineteenth-century uniform of the City Bellman—to bring the citizens up to date on the day's events.

SPECIAL PLACES: Chester's compact layout, not to mention its tougher-than-average parking problems, make it an ideal city to explore on foot. Pubs, restaurants, museums, and shops are all within a few minutes' walk of one another. For the more energetic, the 2-mile circuit of the city walls (see *Extra Special*) is a useful connecting link to the cathedral and the river, where tree-lined walks and rows of benches make an ideal spot to end a walking tour.

The Rows – Chester's above-pavement-level pedestrian shopping "streets" or galleries were built in the Middle Ages over the main roads of the original Roman fortress. Bridge Street and Eastgate Street Rows have the most cosmopolitan shops, Northgate Street Rows have survived, with gaps and changes of level, but Watergate Street Row has the strongest flavor of the past, with its antique and curio shops and magnificent old houses such as Old Leche House. This was built in the mid-sixteenth century as the town residence of the Leche family, so called because they were originally "Leeches," or surgeons, to King Edward III in the 1300s. Another magnificent house is Bishop Lloyd's House, built in the early seventeenth century for Dr. George Lloyd who was Bishop of Sodor and Man from 1600 to 1604 and Bishop of Chester from 1604 to 1615. The elaborate carvings (including the three-legged crest of the Isle of Man) and the broad windows on the front were a local fashion, which turns up again in the Falcon Inn and the Bear and Billet Inn on Lower Bridge Street, where the original Rows have all but vanished. Leche House is now an antique shop; you must arrange a visit to Bishop Lloyd's House in advance.

The Cathedral – Not originally a cathedral at all, this was founded in 1093 by Hugh Lupus, the Norman earl of Chester and alleged nephew of William the Conquerer, as the Benedictine Abbey of St. Werburgh. The abbey was broken up in 1540 when Henry VIII dissolved England's monasteries, and the following year the church became the city cathedral. You can still see the monks' dining room, the cells where they studied in the old cloisters, and part of the shrine to St. Werburgh (an Anglo-Saxon abbess who died ca. AD 700), which attracted pilgrims from all over the north of England during the Middle Ages. Outside, the new bell tower (1975) is the first separate one to be added to an English cathedral in 500 years. St. Werburgh St.

The Castle – At the city end of the Grosvenor Bridge, these colonnaded buildings don't look much like a castle today. The original Norman fortress on its superb defensive position overlooking the river and the Old Dee Bridge was completely transformed between 1788 and 1822 to house the Assize Courts. Behind the Georgian court building (now housing Chester's Crown Courts), the 750-year-old Agricola Tower is the only part of the medieval castle that survives. It can be viewed on request — ask at the Cheshire Military Museum — and the court buildings can be seen from the Public Gallery when the courts are in session. Castle St.

Abbey Square – The low arch of the fourteenth-century Abbey Gateway, where the Chester Miracle Plays were performed in the Middle Ages, is on the eastern side of Town Hall Square. Through the gateway is Abbey Square, a peaceful oasis of cobblestones and Georgian houses, scarcely changed in 200 years. From the opposite corner of the square, Abbey Street leads to the Kaleyard Gateway, a gap in the city walls that once gave access to the abbot's private garden.

Old Dee Bridge – Until the opening of the Grosvenor Bridge 150 years ago, all traffic across the river had to use this narrow medieval bridge, built on the site of the Roman crossing more than seven centuries ago. It leads from the city to the old suburb of Handbridge, called Treboeth or "Burned Town" by the Welsh who burned it more than once during cross-border raids before they were subdued in the thirteenth century.

The River Dee and the Groves – The name comes from that given by the Romans to both town and river — Deva. Below the city walls is the Groves, Chester's tree-lined riverside promenade, with seats used by fishermen, by audiences for the Sunday brass-band concerts, and by picnickers watching the boats. Here you can rent motorboats and rowing skiffs (but watch out for the weir just above the Old Dee Bridge) or you can leave the navigation to others and book a trip on one of the large passenger launches going upriver to Heronbridge and the tranquil charm of Eccleston village. You can come back by boat, by city bus from Eccleston, or by foot along the riverbank path through the Meadows on the Handbridge side.

■ **EXTRA SPECIAL:** Chester's walls are nearly complete, which makes them unique in Britain, and a first-class way to explore the city. Start by climbing to the top of the Eastgate arch, crowned by the clock commemorating Queen Victoria's Diamond Jubilee in 1897 and symbolizing Chester to exiles all over the world. Follow the wall southward and near the modern Newgate arch. You'll see the foundations of one of the corner towers of the original Roman fort. Across Vicar's Lane is the excavated half of the amphitheater the Romans used for gladiatorial contests as well as for drills and weapons training, while next to the Newgate, the old Wolfe or Wolfeld Gate gives an idea of just how narrow the Roman and medieval city gates must have been. Beyond the Newgate arch you come eventually to six short flights of steps — the Wishing Steps. According to local tradition, if you make a wish, run from the bottom to the top, then down and back again without drawing breath, your wish will come true!

As the walls swing west, there's a good view of the river and the old bridge. After crossing the Bridgegate arch, rebuilt and widened like the other city gates in the eighteenth century, you come to the only gap in the walls, beside County Hall. Look for the signposts on the other side of the hall and rejoin the ramparts as they turn north beside the Castle. You pass the racecourse on the Roodee — a recreation area first used for racing in 1540 — and the Watergate arch before you reach the old Bonwaldesthorne's Tower in the northwestern corner of the defenses and the Water Tower at the end of a spur wall. When the Water Tower was built in the fourteenth century, the river was so close it flowed through the archway.

The northern face of the walls is the most impressive of all, since the original ditch that ran full circuit was widened and deepened here in the eighteenth century as part of the Chester Canal. You'll pass the Goblin Tower, nicknamed Pemberton's Parlour after a local rope-maker who sat in comfort to watch his workers toiling below, then, close to the Northgate, a bastion called Morgan's Mount, after the commander of a royalist battery placed here in the Civil War siege of 1645. If you look out over the parapet, you'll see the precarious Bridge of Sighs spanning the giddy drop to the canal. It was used to take prisoners from the Northgate Jail across to the Chapel of St. John for a last service before their execution.

Finally, the northeastern corner of the walls is crowned by King Charles's Tower, built on the site of the original Roman tower. Here Charles I is supposed to have stood while his army was crushed on the field of Rowton Moor in September 1645. He fled afterward, begging the city to hold out for 10 more days. When Chester finally surrendered to Parliament 5 months later, its citizens were starving and weak from disease, but its walls still held the enemy at bay.

SOURCES AND RESOURCES

You'll find local guides, handouts, lists of events, maps, and a monthly *What's On* bulletin at the Tourist Information Centre at the Town Hall (phone: 40144). Guided tours of the city leave here every morning at 10:45 AM; official guides have a city badge or letter of authorization from the Town Hall. If you want to spend an evening in an English home, you can arrange it by calling Mr. and Mrs. Ball (phone: 9162117), Mr. and Mrs. Evans (phone: 671392), or Mr. and Mrs. Read (phone: 3396615), who organize this free, friendly service, any day after 5 PM.

For advice on where to eat, the *Chester Good Lunch Guide* (50p) is just about the best value as it covers the city and surrounding area (for dinners as well as lunches) in great detail.

For Local Coverage – There are three newspapers reporting on local events: the *Chester Chronicle*, whose files include issues that give as-it-happened coverage of the American Revolution, and the *Chester Observer*, both of which appear on Fridays, and the *Chester Courant* on Tuesdays. There is also some coverage in the *Liverpool Daily Post* (mornings) and the *Liverpool Echo* (evenings).

GETTING AROUND: Bus – The Chester Corporation operates services inside the city area. See the Tourist Information Centre for details. Crosville Motor Services, with an enquiry office (phone: 24158) at the Delamere Street bus station, operates services outside the city.

Taxi – Chester's complex parking arrangements make cabs a good idea in the city area. Cab stands are in front of the Town Hall and outside the Railway station on City Road. You can flag down the licensed black taxicabs anywhere you see them, or you can book cabs in advance from *Chester Radio Taxis* (phone: 372372).

Car Rental – For travel outside the city, it makes sense to rent a car. There are local offices of *Avis*, 128 Brook St. (phone: 311463), and *Hertz*, Sealand Rd. (phone: 374705).

MUSEUMS: Chester has several museums devoted to preserving and presenting its long history. Among them are:

Grosvenor Museum – The main museum, named, like so much else in the city, after the family of the eleventh-century Norman earl of Chester Hugh Lupus, whose nickname was "Hugh the Fat Hunter" or "Hugh le Gros Veneur." It contains many relics of Chester's Roman past, natural history exhibits, paintings, and silver. Grosvenor St. (phone: 21616).

Cheshire Military Museum – Three centuries of the Cheshire Regiment, including service in America and India, and the campaign under General Sir Charles James Napier who annexed the Indian province of Sind for the British in 1843 and announced his success with the terse Latin *Peccavi*, meaning "I have sinned." Chester Castle.

British Heritage Exhibition – Reconstruction of how the Rows looked (and smelled) in Victorian days, and a center where you can buy brass rubbings or try your hand at making your own. Vicar's La. (phone: 42222).

Chester Heritage Centre – A slide show on the history of Chester, before-and-after photographs of the restoration of its buildings, and a changing exhibition on the city's heritage. St. Michael's Church, Bridge St. Row (phone: 317948).

King Charles's Water Tower – Models and relics of Civil War Chester. City Walls.

SHOPPING: Most of the best shops are along the elevated walkways of the Rows and the arcades leading off them, above the traffic and covered from the weather. Antique shops and silversmiths (see *Sins*) are especially good, as are the clothes shops, from expensive fashion stores to an ever-changing but constantly-replaced selection of ultracheap boutiques.

Laura Ashley – Victorian-style dresses, children's clothes, wallpaper, and fabrics. Watergate Row (phone: 316403).

Blakes – Old family bakehouse, virtually unchanged since Victorian days. Shop early in the day as the delicious home-baked bread and misshapen but tasty cakes and pies tend to sell out by midafternoon. Watergate St. Row (phone: 25933).

Brown's of Chester – The city's premier department store, founded in the reign of the same George III who presided over the loss of the American colonies. It's now owned by Debenham's store chain, but much of the old style still survives. Particularly good for women's clothes and perfumes. Eastgate St. (phone: 20001).

Celtic Crafts – Traditional Welsh crafts, woolens, blankets, tapestry, slate and wooden ornaments, pictures, and toys. Northgate St. (phone: 318423).

Duttons – Three shops in one: an old-established family grocer, a health food shop, and a wine store. Godstall La., off Eastgate St. opposite Brown's (phone: 21488).

Galt Toys – Children's toys, fairly expensive, but excellent in quality, finish, and design. Bridge St. Row (phone: 26559).

William Jones – Specialty foods — coffee, Chinese and Indian teas, chocolates, sausages and pies, cheeses, bacon. In Owen Owen's Bridge St. store (phone: 21555).

Three Kings Studios – Pottery by resident artist Tony Eaton, along with work from more than 70 local artists and craftsmen. Lower Bridge St. (phone: 317717).

SPECIAL EVENTS: There's top-class flat racing at the *Chester Races* three times a year: the 3-day Chester Cup meeting the first week of May, 2 days in mid-July, and in late August or early September. *Beating Retreat,* a military ceremonial with a display of massed bands, takes place on the Castle grounds in late May. The *Chester Festival,* from late June to early July, is a 2-week program of music, theater, exhibitions, and other events all over the city, and the *Chester Summer Music Festival,* later in July, is a week's worth of orchestral concerts, recitals, and choral works.

SPORTS: Chester's multisport leisure center, *Northgate Arena,* opened in 1977. It has squash courts, badminton courts, and a swimming pool with palm trees, rocks, children's paddling area, and training pool. Corner of Victoria Rd. and St. Oswalds Way (phone: 380444).

Cricket – For those who want to experience the mysteries of the national game for themselves, *Chester Boughton Hall Cricket Club* has home matches every Saturday afternoon and some Sundays from May to late September at the Filkins Lane ground.

Golf – There are clubs for hire at the 9-hole municipal golf course at Westminster Park (phone: 673071). Visitors with a temporary membership also have access to the

18-hole courses at the *Chester Golf Club,* Curzon Park (phone: 677760); the suburban *Upton-by-Chester Golf Club* (phone: 381183) and *Vicars Cross Golf Club* (phone: 35174); and the *Eaton Golf Club* at Eccleston (phone: 674385).

THEATER: Local repertory productions and some touring productions take place in the *Gateway Theatre,* Hamilton Pl. (phone: 40393), and in the *Clwyd Theatre* at Mold, 12 miles away (phone: 95-55114). Liverpool's wider choice of theaters is only 45 minutes away by car.

MUSIC: Occasional concerts are to be heard in the Town Hall, the cathedral, the *Gateway Theatre* (see above), or at the *Clwyd Theatre* in Mold (phone: 95-55114). The local *Chester Symphony Orchestra* or visiting artists and ensembles do the honors. Much more happens in summer when the 2-week Chester Festival (late June to early July) features some musical events and the week-long Chester Summer Music Festival (July) is devoted to it.

NIGHTCLUBS AND NIGHTLIFE: The choice is rather limited. *Maxwells Night Spot,* City Rd. (phone: 24710), and *Angels,* Love St. (phone: 43448), are predominantly discos with occasional live music, as are *The Edwardians,* 39–41 Watergate St. (phone: 20619), and *Tiffanys,* 144 Foregate St. (phone: 314981). For a more refined atmosphere, the *Plantation Inn Hotel,* Liverpool Rd. (phone: 374100), has dinner and dancing every evening from 7:30 PM, and the *Rowton Hall Hotel,* Whitchurch Rd. (phone: 35262), has a dinner dance every Saturday from 8 PM. In the city, there are dinner dances on Saturday nights at the *Grosvenor Hotel,* Eastgate St. (phone: 24024). For folk music buffs, there's a folk evening every Monday at 8:30 PM in the *Bear and Billet,* Lower Bridge St. (phone: 21272) and at 8 PM every Friday in the *Bull and Stirrup,* Upper Northgate St. (phone: 24912).

SINS: If avarice means coveting beautiful things from the past or present, then this is the place to indulge the foible. For centuries, Chester's silversmiths were so famous that the city had its own Assay Office off Watergate Street where the Chester hallmark was stamped on their handiwork. Today you can buy fine-quality gold, silver, and jewelry from specialists like *Boodle and Dunthorne,* by the Grosvenor Hotel on Eastgate St. (phone: 26666); from *Lowe's,* 11 Bridge St. Row (phone: 25850); or from *Brown's,* 2 Eastgate Row (phone: 24357). For antiques in the wider sense, try the shops down Watergate Row. Among them, *Erica and Hugo Harper* at No. 27 (phone: 23004), *Wellesley Wilson* at No. 29 (phone: 23836), and *Chester Antiques* at No. 49 (phone: 311768) sell anything from a silver spoon to a full dinner service, from a delicate miniature to something as substantial as a Georgian table or a Welsh dresser.

BEST IN TOWN

CHECKING IN: Hotels in Chester fall into three categories: the old and expensive, the new and moderately expensive, and the small and inexpensive. For the top-of-the-range hotels in the city center, expect to pay up to $100 for a double room with bath. This includes breakfast, which rates as a meal in its own right. Out-of-town hotels and motels charge about $60 for a double, but with breakfast extra. Best values are found at the smaller hotels which charge about $40 per night for a double.

Grosvenor Hotel – Built between 1863 and 1866, the Grosvenor has a reputation as Chester's best hotel, an old and luxurious establishment with superb service. Some reports say it's been slipping lately, though Britain's ex–prime minister Sir Harold Wilson and Monaco's Princess Grace have been recent guests. The 40 single rooms and 60 doubles all have private bath. Eastgate St. (phone: 24024). Expensive.

Blossoms Hotel – Edwardian with later facelifting outside, modernized inside, this remains a hotel in the traditional manner — sweeping staircases, thick carpeting, and comfortable rooms. There are 78 of them, 57 with private bath. St. John St. (phone: 23186). Expensive to moderate.

Queen Hotel – Built to serve the adjacent railway station, this is a classic Victorian hotel. It has been recently refurbished and its 91 rooms all have private baths. City Rd. (phone: 28341). Expensive to moderate.

Abbots Well Moter Inn – This is an elegant hotel-motel on the eastern edge of the city. It has a good restaurant and 104 rooms, all with private bath. Whitchurch Rd. (phone: 32121). Moderate.

City Walls Hotel – An elegant Georgian house next to the walls on the western side of the city, this little place has 20 rooms, all with bath. 14 Stanley Pl. (phone: 313416). Moderate to inexpensive.

Ye Olde King's Head – One of the city's oldest inns (it dates back to the sixteenth century) with a lovely timbered dining room. There are only 11 guestrooms, none with private bath. 48 Lower Bridge St. (phone: 24855). Moderate to inexpensive.

Abbotsford – Business and holiday guests both stay at this small (16-room) family hotel located in an area that seems to specialize in smaller hotels and guesthouses. It's close to the Northgate Arena and although it may lack the facilities of the bigger city-center hotels, it's a good buy. Victoria Rd. (phone: 26118). Inexpensive.

Golden Lion – Three rooms are for rent in this old, friendly pub on the main A483 road in the center of Rossett village, 5 miles south of Chester. Breakfasts and evening meals are served. Rossett (phone: 570316). Inexpensive.

Cavendish Hotel – This is actually a beautifully restored and elegantly furnished Edwardian house set in its own landscaped gardens on the edge of town. 44 Hough Green (phone: 675100). Inexpensive.

Pied Bull – Passengers used to board the stage for London at this old coaching inn. It's a cheerful pub with five guest rooms. Northgate St. (phone: 25829). Inexpensive.

EATING OUT: Chester's choice of restaurants is surprisingly good. You could eat in a different place every night for a month and still not cover the whole list. Generally, prices are lower than in larger cities: $50 for two, including wine, is the absolute top. Most restaurants will set you back less than $30, and by choosing carefully you can get away with a meal for two for $20 or less. Some of the foreign restaurants — Swiss, French, Italian, Greek — offer a lot for the money, and the best value of all must be the hot and substantial Indian curries and the more exotic Chinese specialties.

Craxton Wood – A delicious meal in the French restaurant of this country house hotel might consist of crab in Pernod, *truite en papillote,* fresh vegetables, and a Black Forest cherry tart. Closed Sundays, Christmas, and Boxing Day, the last 2 weeks in August, and the first week in September. Puddington, 5 miles north of the city on the main Parkgate Rd. (A540) (phone: 3394717). Expensive.

Rossett Hall – This is a luxury restaurant in a Georgian country house, with first-class cooking and top-quality local cheeses. Closed Sunday evenings. Follow the A483 road south 5 miles to the village of Rossett, then look for Rossett Hall behind the long wall on the right-hand side of the road in the center of the village. Wrexham Rd., Rossett (phone: 570867). Expensive.

Grosvenor Hotel – The main hotel dining room serves classic French cooking (trout, veal, lamb) and does it impeccably. It's open all year except Christmas and Boxing Day. Down in its *Grosvenor Bar,* there are other hot and cold lunchtime dishes (closed Sundays). Eastgate St. (phone: 24024). Expensive in the main restaurant, moderate in the bar.

Boat Inn – Every inch of the 15-mile drive to this country pub and restaurant is worth it. The setting above the beautiful upstream reaches of the Dee is incomparable. Pheasant and fresh Dee salmon are on the menu in season, along with vintage clarets and Burgundies. Follow A483 to Wrexham (12 miles south), then take A539 and look for the sign for Erbistock. Erbistock, Clwyd (phone: 097873-243). Expensive to moderate.

Courtyard Restaurant – Informality and a high standard of cooking come together nicely here, close to the cathedral behind a small archway and the tiny courtyard from which the restaurant gets its name. For lunch, there's a hot and cold buffet or the à la carte menu to tempt you. Closed Sundays, bank holidays, Christmas, and Boxing Day. 13 St. Werburgh St. (phone: 21447). Moderate.

Jean's Kitchen – The setting is an unpromising one in a neighborhood shopping center, but this bistro-style place is good enough to be recognized by both English and French experts. Closed Sundays. 1 Newton Close, St. Anne St. (phone: 381313). Moderate.

Jade Cantonese Restaurant – Most Chinese restaurants in Britain are Cantonese (via Hong Kong), but this is the only one in Chester to offer a full Cantonese menu. Behind its rather garish facade, there are delicious subtle flavors, crisp vegetables, and a genuine mixture of Chinese diners among the clientele. Closed Sundays. 43 Watergate St. Row (phone: 21455). Moderate to inexpensive.

Shangri-La Restaurant – The exotic fare is Bangladeshi and it's excellent value for the money. The portions are heroic and the bargain is better still if you order a different dish for each person and then share them all, from the mild *dansakhs* to the scorching *vindaloos.* 27 Lower Bridge St. (phone: 46354). Moderate to inexpensive.

Aphrodite's – Here you can dine in the same room as Charles I, though not from the same menu. This Greek restaurant is in the recently-restored Gamul House, which was the home of Sir Francis Gamul, mayor of Chester and host to the king during the mid-seventeenth-century Civil War siege. Greek specialties such as dolmades and moussaka, and Greek and Cypriot wines, are served in the main restaurant, smaller portions at lower prices in the street-level taverna. Closed Sundays. Gamul Terrace, Lower Bridge St. (phone: 319811). Inexpensive.

Great American Disaster – As close as you're likely to get to a genuine hamburger and definitely the only place in Chester for anything approaching American cooking. Other specialties are steak and chicken, french fries (chips), baked potatoes, salads, apple pie, American beer, coffee, Coke. 14 Lower Bridge St. (phone: 318973). Inexpensive.

Sidoli's Restaurant – Upstairs, beyond the ground-floor ice cream parlor and pizzeria, there's a restaurant serving real Italian food, including special 5-course suppers on Fridays and Saturdays. The ice cream is homemade. Restaurant closed Sundays (though the ice cream parlor is open); pizzeria closed Sundays and Mondays. Northgate St. (phone: 44068). Inexpensive.

Needham's Fish and Chip Shop – Real English fish and chips at their best are on the limited menu, which also lists chicken, pies, and curry. Comfort is minimal: Eat at small tables in the adjacent dining room, or take the fish and chips out and eat 'em the proper way, from the paper. Tasty and unbeatable value. 21 Lower Bridge St. (phone: 26472). Very inexpensive.

SHARING A PINT: Pubs are the center of Chester life. In the old days they were simply places to drink and chat, but now most of them serve food, too, and the best of them give even good restaurants a run for their money. The *Boat House,* at the upstream end of the Groves next to the school and club boathouses, used to be a real rowing man's pub, with faded photographs of long-gone oarsmen and autographed oarblades on the wall. Now a noisy, cheerful, busy River Bar has been added, full of young people and music, but with an unmatchable view of the Dee. The *Bear and Billet* on Lower Bridge St. is a beautiful seventeenth-century half-timbered house turned into a popular and friendly pub offering food as well as drinks. It once belonged to the earls of Shrewsbury who enjoyed the profits from the tolls of the adjacent Bridgegate. (Before going in, look up: Payment was often in kind, hence the doors high in the gable where a hoist was used to lift goods to and from the roof storehouse.) *Duke's,* set in modern surroundings in Mercia Sq., is one of the new generation of wine bars. It serves wine by the glass, draught and bottled beers, plus a hot dish-of-the-day. *The Albion Inn,* close to the walls on Park St., is just the opposite, a real, old-fashioned, cozy, back-street Chester pub with draught beer from the wood and the traditional steak and kidney pie, black pudding and mushy peas, bread and cheese, and treacle tart. The *Lock, Stock and Barrel,* on Cow Lane Bridge, off Frodsham St., is a multipurpose pub converted from an old granary warehouse, where you can have a meal, a snack, or a drink in a delightful canal-side setting. *The Town Crier,* opposite the railway station on City Rd., is a newly renovated establishment that serves traditional ales as well as meals.

CORK

The Irish Republic's second city is a bustling, flavorsome, highly individual place, quite different from Dublin in appearance and atmosphere. Though it lacks the capital's Georgian uniformity, it makes up for the defect in visual variety, mixing the romance of mock-Gothic outlines with the moderation and proportion of the classical style. Dublin is flat and Cork is up and down on hills; Dublin is a somber tone, Cork variegated, light and dark, as its local stones. And while Dublin, as capital, was burdened with an alien tradition of subservience, Cork cultivated a spirit of defiance that earned it the nickname Rebel Cork. It is a busy, assertive, self-made place where Jack is as good as his master and frequently tells him so.

The making of Cork was the River Lee, which flows not only through, but in and around, the city as it approaches its great estuary. In its valley it formed a great marsh with islands that became, as in Venice, the foundation of the town and the source of its Gaelic name, *Corcaigh,* meaning "a marshy place." The first actual settlement was, as might be expected, a little Gaelic monastery founded in the sixth century by an obscure but still beloved abbot-bishop named Barra of the Fair Hair, or Finbarre. The monastery, on a hill south of the river where the present St. Finbarre's Cathedral stands, grew in power and it was probably its reputation for wealth that enticed the Vikings in their longboats up the estuary and through the sinuous marsh. They first founded a trading post here in the eighth century and within 50 years they had fortified one of the islands to become the right and tight little city of Cork.

In time, the Vikings became subjects of the Gaelic prince of the area, MacCarthy Mor, but they nevertheless maintained a degree of independence in their island city under their own *jarl,* or ruler, until the Norman invasion forced them to switch allegiance. In the turbulent centuries that followed, the inhabitants of Cork City acquired a reputation for independent-mindedness even to rebellion. King John (as prince) gave them a charter in 1188, they were back under the MacCarthys by 1195, they were given a more prestigious charter by the king in 1199, and another new one in 1241, but in 1495 they nearly seized the crown itself when they received the pretender to the throne, Perkin Warbeck, and escorted him to England to proclaim him king of England and lord of Ireland.

While Dublin's monuments are castle and parliament house and the homes of the great nobles, Cork within its island walls had shops and warehouses and banks. It was essentially a trading town and still is. In the eighteenth century, it became the great supply port for the American colonies, sending out beef and bacon and butter, and during the Napoleonic Wars, it was the larder of the British army and navy. Gradually, rows of houses began to rise along the winding creeks between the islands and at last Cork expanded beyond its walls and up the sides of the river valley.

As the merchants made money, they developed an appreciation of civilized amenities. Cork silver and glass became tasteful and elegant. A Cork school of painters developed; the neoclassical subjects of James Barry and Robert Fagan, the townscapes of Nathaniel Grogan, and the historical panoramas of Samuel Forde and Daniel Maclise can be admired in the Crawford Municipal Art Gallery. Talk has always been a strong art form in Cork; the accent is singsong and musical, but it conceals a sharp verbal wit used to deadly effect on native and visitor. The wordsmiths met in drinking clubs and debating societies and produced a circle of essayists and poets including William Maginn, a Johnsonian schoolmaster and satirist, and Francis Sylvester O'Mahony ("Father Prout"), a mocking ex-priest, both of whom scored in the literary reviews when they emigrated to London, and a gentle lyric poet, J. J. Callanan, who died young in Lisbon.

The nineteenth century also produced some distinguished architecture in Cork. First the brothers Pain, pupils of John Nash, came from London and built bridges, jails, a courthouse, some lovely town houses with gentle Regency bowfronts, and the delightful Gothic fantasy, Blackrock Castle, at the end of the Marina walk. They were succeeded by the Deane family, builders of churches, banks, and Cork's University College. From their firm, in turn, emerged Benjamin Woodward, a genius of the neo-Gothic whose best work is in Dublin and Oxford.

Cork in the twentieth century is chronicled in the short stories of Seán O'Faoláin and Frank O'Connor, both natives. It is still a work-a-day city; shops, warehouses, and factories are part of its fabric. But it is also a good talking town, a great eating-out town, a sports-mad town. During the War of Independence (1919–1921) it was a wellspring of nationalistic fervor, losing two majors and many public buildings to the cause. Since then, it has withstood the worst assaults of modernization, though its cramped island site has given it some real traffic problems, which the city's 120,000 inhabitants manage to live with in their own spirited way. They are a most competent people whose response to good fortune and bad is a mocking laugh and a musical burst of anecdote.

CORK AT-A-GLANCE

SEEING THE CITY: The north slope of the river valley is dominated by the tower of St. Anne's Church, better known simply as Shandon steeple. Cross the river and climb the tower to an outside balcony. The city will be at your feet, the flat marsh area with its busy streets surrounded by what Edmund Spenser called "The spreading Lee, that like an island fayre/Encloseth Corke with his divided floode." The Lee here forms a north channel and a south channel, and between them is the compact central island known as the "flat of the city." Patrick Street, or St. Patrick Street, which is the main artery crossing the island, was itself once an open river channel, as were the Grand Parade and the South Mall. In the eighteenth century you would still have seen ships afloat in these channels, but by 1800 the waterways had been turned into thoroughfares for the traffic on foot, hoof, and wheel that crowded into the city's business district. Quieter, more reflective parts of Cork are the slopes that rise to the south and north of the central island. The Gothic towers of St. Finbarre's Cathedral and the graceful Gothic quadrangles of the university are on the far slope, and churches, convents, and hospitals are to the right and left beneath you on the near slope.

SPECIAL PLACES: The "flat of the city" is the hub of activity in Cork, and a walk along Patrick Street (affectionately called "Pana" by the locals, with a dying fall on the "a") and its subsidiary arteries is as traditional an activity as the European evening promenade. Going east to west, it is properly done on the left path, in order to have a view of the better-preserved right side of the street with its delicately bow-fronted eighteenth-century houses (the left side had to be replaced when British troops burned the street in 1920). Patrick Street leads to the Grand Parade, which runs straight to the south channel of the river and has some traditional weather-slated bowfronts remaining from the eighteenth century. At the south channel, the Grand Parade meets the South Mall, now the financial district. Here, a few characteristic merchants' houses remain from the days when the South Mall was still an open waterway. Doors at street or water level open onto basement storerooms so that boats could be unloaded easily, and high outside steps lead up to the merchants' living quarters above their merchandise. Walking is the best way to see the flat of the city, and when you are ready to cross to the north or south banks, you'll find numerous bridges spanning the still-flowing channels.

FLAT OF THE CITY

Father Matthew Statue – This memorial to Father Theobald Matthew, the "apostle of temperance," is the work of the celebrated nineteenth-century Irish sculptor, John Henry Foley, who also created the monument to Daniel O'Connell in Dublin and was one of several artists responsible for the Albert Memorial in London. Father Matthew, a superior of the Capuchin Order in Cork, was known not only for his crusade in the cause of temperance but also for his work among the poor, especially during the mid-nineteenth-century famines. The statue is a central point of reference in Cork City. Patrick St. at Patrick Bridge.

Crawford Municipal School of Art and Gallery – School and gallery are housed in a red brick building put up in the early eighteenth century as the city's Custom House. The gallery contains a select collection of works by painters of the twentieth-century Irish School: Orpen, Lavery, and Yeats; a good representation by artists of the earlier Cork School: Barry, Grogan, Forde, and Maclise; and some fine examples of Cork silver and glass. Open Mondays through Fridays from 9:30 AM to 5:30 PM, Sundays from 9 AM to 1 PM. Emmet Pl.

Church of Saints Peter and Paul – Opened in 1868, this excellent Gothic revival church by E. W. Pugin is typical of Cork in its casing of red sandstone and its dressing of white limestone. Off Paul St.

Coal Quay Market – This outdoor flea market is open for business daily (except Sundays), not on the quays, but on a street running from the Grand Parade to Coal Quay. No longer colorful and not exactly sweet-smelling, it takes place in front of a market building with good classical frontage, now privately owned. Corn Market St.

English Market – Fruit, vegetables, fish, and meat — including local specialties such as drisheen (blood pudding or blood sausage) and tripe — are displayed and sold in a stylish late-eighteenth-century market arcade under a cast-iron and glass roof. When the market is in full swing, daily except Sundays, the scene is animated and the stallholders are full of Cork esprit and chat. Entrances off Patrick St., Princes St., and Grand Parade.

Court House – The Pain brothers, James and George Richard, designed this stately Corinthian-porticoed building, erected in 1835. Sir Walter Scott, among others, admired it. Washington St.

South and North Main Streets – When Cork was still enclosed by walls, its main gates were located at the South Gate Bridge and the North Gate Bridge. Between the two ran the spine of the medieval city, worth walking today for its atmosphere redolent of food and housewares shops. The much-altered eighteenth-century Protestant Christ Church, South Main St., is on the site of a medieval parish church that dated back to the Normans and was probably the church in which Edmund Spenser married Elizabeth Boyle, his Irish bride, in the sixteenth century. Another of Cork's medieval parish churches (there were two of them) was off North Main Street, in the vicinity of which there are also many lanes — such as Portney's Lane — that once housed merchants and craftsmen.

Mercy Hospital – When it was built in the eighteenth century, this was the Mansion House of the mayor of Cork. The handsome building with its Italianate front is the work of the Sardinian architect Davis Ducart; the good stucco ceiling inside is by Patrick Osborne of Waterford. The building is now a hospital, but it's open to visitors during normal business hours. Henry St.

Holy Trinity Church – The church of the Capuchin friars, also known as the Father Matthew Memorial Church, is from the 1830s. Internally, it is a charming Regency Gothic creation by George R. Pain. The lantern spire by Coakley, which complements it externally, is a graceful later addition enhanced by the riverside setting. Father Matthew Quay.

NORTH BANK

St. Patrick's Bridge – This mid-nineteenth-century bridge is a very satisfactory classical construction in white limestone. The view from it — upriver over the city's churches, convents, and other institutions, and downriver to the ships — is quintessential Cork. Patrick's Hill, a precipitous street housing fashionable doctors, leads up the north bank from the bridge and it's almost worth the climb for another view over the city. End of Patrick St.

St. Anne's Church, Shandon – The quaint pepper-box tower of this Protestant church, built from 1722 to 1726, is the symbol of Cork. Shandon steeple rises in square tiers to its cupola and weather vane crowned by a golden fish and, as in the old jingle — "Red and white is Shandon steeple/Partly coloured like the people" — it has two red sides and two white sides, a combination that is a signature of many Cork buildings. From the top of the steeple you can look out over the river valley and note the source of the color scheme: one slope of red sandstone and an opposite one of silvery white limestone. The Shandon churchyard is the last resting place of Francis S. O'Mahony, a fitting spot, because it was he, under the pen name "Father Prout," who wrote "The Bells of Shandon," a song that made both bells and church famous. Open from 9:30 AM to 6 PM in summer, from 10:30 AM to 4:30 PM the rest of the year. Church St.

St. Mary's Dominican Church – Kearns Deane, a member of the very prominent family of Cork architects responsible for several of the city's classical buildings, designed this church with the solid portico in 1832. Inside, there is a carved ivory madonna of fourteenth-century Flemish origin. Pope's Quay.

St. Patrick's Church – A flurry of construction in the classical style took place in early nineteenth-century Cork. Another good example is this church by George R. Pain (1836) at the foot of the handsome hillside suburbs of Tivoli and Montenotte. The elegant lantern is modeled on the Temple of the Winds in Athens. Lower Glanmire Rd.

SOUTH BANK

Red Abbey – Nothing is left of the abbey of the Canons of St. Augustine except the tower of its church. It is the solitary relic of the early Cork monasteries and, indeed, of medieval Cork. When the duke of Marlborough besieged the city in 1690, he put a cannon on the tower and directed his fire at the city walls across the south channel of the Lee. Before leaving the spot, walk around the corner to Dunbar Street for a look at St. Finbarre's South, known also as the South Chapel, an unusually early (1766) Catholic church (there are very few eighteenth-century Catholic churches in Ireland) with an altarpiece by John Hogan, one of the most important Irish sculptors of the last century. Off Mary St.

Elizabeth Fort – The massive curtain walls are what is left of a seventeenth-century fort that once housed the Cork garrison. Today, a modern police station stands incongruously within the walls. Off Barrack St.

St. Finbarre's Cathedral – Though somewhat foreshortened on its confined site — where the city's patron saint chose to put his monastery in the sixth century — this Protestant cathedral is considered to be a brilliant essay in French Gothic by William Burges, an English architect who also designed Cardiff Castle and the quadrangle of Yale University. It was built between 1867 and 1879 to replace an earlier church, which itself replaced a medieval church damaged in the siege of 1690. (Only a cannonball remains of that one, found 40 feet above the ground in the tower.) Burges's three spires are most successful and his interior detail is rich and inventive. Bishop St.

University College – The main quadrangle is a gem of nineteenth-century collegiate architecture (reminiscent of the colleges at Oxford) by Thomas Deane and his partner, Benjamin Woodward. Later additions do not quite maintain the initial high standard, but the Honan Chapel on the grounds, architect James J. McMullen's 1915 revival of twelfth-century Irish-Romanesque style, has interesting exterior details and is stuffed with treasure inside: stained-glass windows, embroideries, tabernacle enamels, and a joyous mosaic floor. The chapel usually closes during school holidays. Western Rd.

■ **EXTRA SPECIAL:** The *Cork Film Festival* is an accredited event on the international film festival calendar. The emphasis is on short films of all descriptions — general interest and documentary, animated, art, and industrial films — in competition for the bronze St. Finbarre trophy, but you'll also see the Irish premieres of many feature-length films here, plus something special each year such as a retrospective of the work of a major contemporary director or a tribute to the film industry of a particular country. Cork is a serious film festival, with all the visiting actors and actresses, film makers, journalists, and earnest film fans that such events attract, but it is also an excuse for a party, the focus of which is the Film Festival Club, the after-screening center of discussion and conviviality. The festival, once held in June, now runs for 8 days in September or October, and the booking of tickets begins approximately one month in advance. A season ticket covers admission to all the films and lectures, and with the addition of an extra sum, includes membership in the Film Festival Club. Holiday packages including bed and breakfast accommodations in hotels and guesthouses are available, but if you want to attend only a few screenings, that's possible, too. For information, write to the Cork Film Festival, 38 MacCurtain St., Cork (phone: 502221).

SOURCES AND RESOURCES

The Cork/Kerry tourism office, Grand Parade (phone: 23251) offers information, guidebooks, maps, and leaflets. You can purchase two helpful booklets here, *Cork North and East and Cork City* (15p) and the excellent *Tourist Trail* (50p), a walking guide to Cork. For books and pamphlets on the city's history and background, visit Liam Ruiseal's bookshop around the corner on Oliver Plunkett St.

For Local Coverage – The *Cork Examiner* is the one they call "de payper." It's the morning daily, full of local color. The *Evening Echo,* essential for entertainment information, comes out every evening and the *Cork Weekly Examiner,* a potpourri of current local happenings, appears every Tuesday.

GETTING AROUND: In the "flat of the city," walking is easier and faster than going by bus or car because of congested traffic, restricted parking, and one-way circuits. Car drivers should observe the local disc parking system — it works. Books of disc tickets cost £1 in tobacco and newspaper shops.

Bus and Train – A good city bus service radiates from the Father Matthew Statue. County buses, long-distance buses, and day tours leave from the Bus Station in Parnell Pl., a block east of the statue. Trains leave from Kent Station, Lower Glanmire Rd., on the northern bank of the Lee. For bus and train information by phone, call 504422.

Taxi – Cab ranks are located at the stations and in the middle of Patrick St., opposite the Savoy Centre and the Victoria Hotel. Otherwise, you can call one from your hotel (phone: 21568 or 22317).

Car Rental – All major international and national firms are represented. Consult the Yellow Pages.

MUSEUMS: Paintings and sculpture by Irish artists and others are in the *Crawford Municipal Art Gallery* (see *Special Places*). The *Cork Public Museum,* Fitzgerald Park, contains interesting displays of Cork history from the earliest times to the present, and the surrounding park has a pleasant riverside walk and sculptures by the late Seamus Murphy, a well-known Cork stonecarver-turned-sculptor. The museum is closed Saturday afternoons and Sundays; the park is open daily. (Contact the tourist office for the exact hours, which vary with the season.) Off Mardyke Rd., a promenade parallel to Western Rd.

SHOPPING: As to be expected of the Republic's second largest metropolitan area, Cork is an excellent shopping center, offering a variety of goods. Major department stores are on Patrick Street; small shops and boutiques abound on Princes and Oliver Plunkett streets. Some of the more rewarding places to stop off during the course of a spree are the following:

Barry's Tea – A provision shop par excellence. It stocks not only exquisite teas and preserves but the delightful Hadji Bey Turkish Delight, a candy that's made in Cork. Princes St. (phone: 20995).

Cash's Department Store – Cork's equivalent of Dublin's *Switzer's* sells a general range of linens, woolens, tweeds, glassware, and other goods. 18 Patrick St. (phone: 26771).

Cork Antique Market – Antiques to bric-a-brac. Open Fridays and Saturdays from 10:30 AM to 5:30 PM. 7 Tuckey St.

Cork Arts Society Gallery – Frequent exhibitions by local artists. 16 Lavitt's Quay (phone: 505749).

Queen's Old Castle – A traditional department store elegantly converted to a varied shopping mall that includes cafés for the weary. Grand Parade.

Savoy Centre – Also a shopping mall, this one splendidly set in the art deco surroundings of a former cinema. Among the shops and cafés, note especially the *Cork Craftsmans Guild* with an extensive selection of pottery, handknits, metalwork, and anything else a talented group of southern Irish craftspeople may be inspired to create. Patrick St.

Stephen O'Shaughnessy – Jewelry by himself. 22 Patrick St.

SPECIAL EVENTS: Cork is a festival town. In early May it hosts the week-long *Cork Choral Festival* with colorful and tuneful choirs competing from all over the world. Its well-established *Film Festival* of short and feature-length films (see *Extra Special*) takes place in September or October, and in late October the town is hopping and bopping with the *Jazz Festival.* For information, contact the tourist office on Grand Parade.

SPORTS: Golf – Several hospitable golf courses surround the city and welcome visitors daily or every weekday. The 18-hole *Cork Golf Club* is at Little Island (phone: 821451), about 6.5 miles from the center. Others to try are the *Douglas Golf Club* (phone: 291086), about 3 miles away, and the *Muskerry Golf Club* (phone: 85104), about 8 miles away. At Monkstown, a village on the western shore of Cork Harbour, the clubhouse of the *Monkstown Golf Club* (phone: 841225) is a seventeenth-century castle. Greens fees average $5 to $10.

Greyhound Racing – Betting is brisk 3 nights weekly at the *Cork Greyhound Stadium* on Western Rd. (phone: 43013).

Hurling and Gaelic Football – Cork's *Páirc Uí Chaoimh* stadium on the Marina Walk east of town is the headquarters of Gaelic hurling and football in the south. Matches — of one or the other game — take place most Sunday afternoons through the summer season, and Rebel Cork is a power to be reckoned with in hurling especially.

Riding – Three stables are convenient to the city: *Highland Lodge Riding School,* Monkstown (phone: 841037); *Brooklodge House Riding School,* Glanmire (phone: 821169); and the *Rock Farm Equestrian Centre,* Little Island (phone: 821024). Rates are from $6 to $12 per hour.

Rugby and Soccer – Both are played at the *University Grounds,* Mardyke Walk. See the sports pages of the *Cork Examiner* for match times.

Sailing – Cork Harbour is a sailor's paradise and the *Royal Cork Yacht Club* (phone: 831440), now with headquarters downriver in Crosshaven, welcomes visitors from other clubs.

THEATER: The *Cork Opera House,* Emmet Pl. (phone: 20022), is a modern replacement of a romantically decayed theater that burned down in the 1950s. Drama and musical comedies, opera, and ballet are all staged here. The *Irish Ballet Company,* born and headquartered in Cork but usually to be found touring the country, performs at the Opera House in February (phone: 20112 for ballet information). The *Everyman Playhouse,* Father Matthew St. (phone: 26287), offers seasons of new plays, foreign and Irish.

MUSIC: For a small city, Cork is fairly rich in music. There are regular lunch-hour concerts of classical music in summer, evening ones the rest of the year. The *Cork Music Lovers Diary,* available at the tourist office, tells the what and where, or call the Cork School of Music (phone: 20026). Traditional Irish music is provided several nights a week during the summer at the new Cork/Kerry Tourism *Entertainment Centre* behind the tourist office on Grand Parade. See the tourist office for both schedules and tickets.

NIGHTCLUBS AND NIGHTLIFE: The disco scene is lively. Recommended are *Mr. Bojangles* at the Savoy Centre, *Swingers* on Oliver Plunkett St., *Krojaks* in Carey's La. off Patrick St., *Chandras* on Grand Parade. Check the hotels for cabaret and dancing and see the *Evening Echo,* the best paper for entertainment listings, for other events.

SINS: Ask a sailor.

BEST IN TOWN

CHECKING IN: Cork can be jam-packed in high season, so reservations are recommended. Hotels vary from the sleek modern one on the outskirts to the downtown dowagers that have been upgraded with bathrooms and coffee shops. Expect to pay $70 and more for a double in the expensive category (and this may not include breakfast); rooms in the moderate category run from $50 to $65; in inexpensive, $40 or less. If you arrive without a reservation, you will not be left out in the cold. The tourist office in Grand Parade will always help and Cork has a range of good, inexpensive guesthouses at $25 and less for a double.

Arbutus Lodge – If you want to get as close as possible to what some consider the best restaurant in Cork and perhaps in Ireland, head for this elegant mansion amid gardens overlooking the city and the river. There are 20 rooms, good but small, and all have bath. Montenotte (phone: 501237). Expensive.

Jurys – On the banks of the River Lee on the western approaches to the city, this is starkly modern. Baths, phones, and TV in all 140 rooms. A heated pool, sauna, and gym are in a newly added pavilion. Western Rd. (phone: 26651). Expensive.

Imperial – The dowager of them all, stately in the middle of the South Mall and close to everything, took shape on the drawing board of Thomas Deane. The grande dame is not as starchy as she looks and her French restaurant, *La Duchesse,* is very competent. Meals are served to the accompaniment of piano music. South Mall (phone: 23304). Moderate.

Metropole – This dowager, too, manages to keep up appearances. Behind the Victorian facade of brick and limestone are 125 rooms, all with color TV and phones, most with bath. On the north bank close to the railway station and ferryport. MacCurtain St. (phone: 508122). Moderate.

Silver Springs – Another modern hotel on the fringes. Rooms are no-nonsense ones, all 72 with baths. If you are lucky, yours will have a delightful view of the river and passing ships. There is a handy coffee shop as well as a restaurant. Glanmire Rd. (phone: 507533). Moderate.

Moore's – This is a comfortable and homey choice in a downtown location. A fair proportion of the 39 rooms have private bathrooms. Morrison's Island (phone: 227361). Inexpensive.

EATING OUT: Cork, to say it again, is a good eating-out town, largely because the locals eat out quite a bit. Do not ignore the hotel dining rooms; some of them offer very good value and one in particular may be the best in Ireland. In addition to the restaurants below, the natives frequent good restaurants half an hour or so from Cork (see *Kinsale* in the West Cork tour route in DIRECTIONS). Dinner for two without wine or tips will cost $40 and up in places listed as expensive; $20 to $35 in the moderate ones; under $20 in the inexpensive ones.

Arbutus Lodge Restaurant – Having won all the awards, it still keeps up its standard for excellent and innovative cooking. Seafood is superb. Most things are. Try the "tasting" menu if it is on — you'll be treated to a sample of up to a dozen different dishes. A distinguished wine list delights even the toughest customers. Major credit cards are accepted. Reservations recommended. Montenotte (phone: 501237). Expensive.

Lovetts – French cuisine is served in this period house in the suburbs. Seafood is especially recommended. Major credit cards are accepted and reservations are suggested. Churchyard La., off Well Rd., Douglas (phone: 294909). Expensive.

Oyster Tavern – This is a traditional chophouse and an inner-city favorite. The whitebait and sole are memorable. Busy, so you may have to wait in the bar, which is pleasant. Market La., off Patrick St. (phone: 22716). Moderate.

Murphs – A youthful clientele gathers here at this eatery that's strong on hamburgers and salads as well as steaks and seafood. In mezzanine of Savoy Centre, Patrick St. (phone: 504059). Inexpensive.

SHARING A PINT: Cork's pub system is unusual for Ireland in that it is made up, as in Britain, of independent houses and "tied" ones linked to a particular brewery. Some bars serve only Beamish stout, some only Murphy's (the local brews); the independent ones serve both and Guinness as well. Up to the mid-50s you could tell who sold what from the outside. Beamish pubs had a classic black and gold nameplate and were called *The Malt Shovel, The Black Swan, The Winning Post,* and *The Office* — ("I was delayed at the Office, dear.") The Murphy pubs had a cream and brown trim and usually sailed under their owners' names. Then some irreverent design genius came along and put them both in nondescript contemporary lettering. Inside, however, they keep their individuality. At *Rearden's Cellar Bar,* Washington St., the atmosphere is nineteenth century, the conversation tends to the academic, and the emphasis is on wine. The *Long Valley,* Winthrop St., is a traditional pub where you can sample both Beamish and Murphy's stouts. *Le Chateau,* right in the middle of Patrick St., is crowded but pleasant. On Drawbridge St., just beside the Opera House, audience and actors meet for good talk and the occasional song at the *Grand Circle. Beechers Inn,* Faulkners La., is convenient to the office of the *Cork Examiner,* so the usual liquids come with the customary quota of newspaper rumors. Across the river on the hill beside the old Elizabeth Fort, *The Gateway,* Barrack St., is supposed to be the oldest pub in Cork. It dates back to the seventeenth century and it is credible that the Duke of Marlborough drank here; certainly legions of his military followers through the centuries did. And *Henchy's,* 40 St. Luke's, is a fine place to sip a pint and listen to the distinctive Cork accent.

DUBLIN

This friendly city is steeped in a history often troubled, sometimes splendid; a city of wide Georgian streets, elegant squares, magnificent doorways; of memorable sunsets that bathe the eighteenth-century red brick facades until the houses seem to glow with their own fire and the very windows seem made of gold; a city of ancient churches and cathedrals thrusting their hallowed spires and towers against the skyline; a city where the English language acquires a unique dimension, and where the dark, creamy-headed Guinness stout flows abundantly in companionable pubs. This is a city like no other European capital. It is set like a jewel in the great curving sweep of Dublin Bay; behind, to the south, rise the Dublin hills and the Wicklow Mountains. Through the city the River Liffey — James Joyce's Anna Livia Plurabelle — wends its leisurely way to the sea, spanned, as it passes through Dublin, by eleven bridges.

Once, there was only one bridge. Indeed, it was not so much a bridge as a mere ford in the river, and it stood approximately where the Father Matthew Bridge stands today. It was built by the first Celtic inhabitants of what is now Dublin. When they came here, we cannot be sure; what is certain is that, by AD 140, they were well established on this site. The Celts themselves probably referred to the spot by a name that endures to this day in the official Gaelic Baile Atha Cliath, the Town of the Ford of the Hurdles.

It was not, however, until the coming of the Vikings, or Norsemen, that Dublin as we now know it began to take shape. The old Celtic settlement had at no time been a place of national importance; its significance was as a ford of the Liffey en route to the ancient royal capital of Tara. In the year AD 837, 65 Viking longboats sailed into Dublin harbor and up the mouth of the River Liffey. These early Viking settlers established themselves a little downstream from the old Celtic settlement, on a spot where the Poddle, which now flows underground, entered the Liffey, causing it to form a dark pool, or *dubh linn*. The Vikings referred to their settlement by these two Gaelic words, and the angelicized version became the city's modern English name. Dublin rapidly became the focal point of the Viking invasion of Ireland. Then, as the Vikings began to see that trading was ultimately more profitable than plunder and as they began to settle and intermarry in their new homeland, Dublin became a major center for their extensive European trade. Not long after their arrival they were converted to Christianity and in 1034 erected a cathedral, which became the nucleus of present-day Christ Church. The cathedral stood in the center of Viking Dublin and allows us to place the ancient city accurately.

Just over three centuries after the coming of the Vikings, new invaders swept Ireland. In 1169 the first contingent of Normans landed on the beach of Bannow, in County Wexford. Two years later, the powerful baron Richard Gilbert de Clare, otherwise known as Strongbow, arrived at the gates of Dublin with a thousand men. The city was taken by storm; its Viking king and inhabitants were forced to flee. Thereafter Dublin became the center of the English conquest, as it had become the center of the Viking conquest.

Not long afterward, it became necessary to fortify the city. For this purpose Dublin Castle was built not far from the old Viking cathedral. The cathedral itself had been taken over by Strongbow not long before, and a new and larger edifice erected in its place. The city walls were built along with the castle. (Their remains can be seen at St. Audeon's Arch, below Christ Church.) Thus medieval Dublin began to take shape, small in size and surrounded by walls.

In shape and in size Dublin did not alter greatly until the arrival of a new viceroy, or king's representative, in 1662 heralded Dublin's rise to a definitive national importance. Dublin, under James Butler, duke of Ormonde, became and remained the central arena for Ireland's social, political, and cultural life.

Butler, believing that the stability of a government should be reflected in public works, began municipal improvements almost immediately. The solitary, medieval Dublin Bridge was joined by four new bridges across the river; the Phoenix Park (to this day the largest enclosed urban park in the world) was walled and several new streets were built.

Dublin's importance as a city and as a seaport increased enormously in that time. It was, however, in the eighteenth century that Dublin was truly to flourish. During this century it became one of the most brilliant and sparkling capitals in all Europe. The strong movement toward parliamentary independence that took place at this time was reflected in the splendid Parliament House (now the Bank of Ireland in College Green), commenced in 1729, the first in a series of great public buildings. Extensive rebuilding was carried out on Dublin Castle and Trinity College. The Wide Streets Commission was set up. It was as if the city were proudly preparing for the unprecedented position of importance it would occupy when, in 1782, parliamentary independence was conceded to Ireland by the British Parliament.

Great buildings followed one another in dizzying succession — Leinster House, the Royal Exchange, the Mansion House, the Four Courts, the Custom House. Irish classical architecture, in all its gravity, beauty, and balance, reached full maturity. It flowered in public buildings and private houses, spacious squares and elegant streets. This was Georgian Dublin (various king Georges sat on the British throne in the period): the Dublin of Henry Grattan, Oliver Goldsmith, Jonathan Swift, Bishop Berkeley and Edmund Burke, David Garrick and Peg Woffington. Handel himself conducted the world première of his *Messiah* in this glittering city, whose center was concentrated in the area between Dublin Castle and the Parliament House.

Architecturally, Dublin reached its zenith in the eighteenth century. Henceforward, its brilliance was to be sculpted in the written word rather than in stone. The nineteenth century saw an end to the halcyon days of Home Rule; with the dismantling of the Parliament, Dublin's political and social life suffered a blow from which it was not to recover easily. By contrast, its literary life began to flower. In the nineteenth century two great literary movements were born in Dublin — the Gaelic League and the Irish Literary Renaissance. Between them, the two movements revived and romanticized the early legends and history of Ireland. The literary renaissance — spearheaded by William Butler Yeats, Lady Augusta Gregory, Douglas Hyde, and John Millington Synge, to name but a few — placed a splendid and indelible mark on twentieth-century English literature. (Equally renowned are Irish or Ireland-born writers not directly associated with the Gaelic League renaissance, men like Samuel Beckett, who won the Nobel Prize for Literature in 1969 and who was born in Dublin in 1906; George Bernard Shaw, who wrote in England but was born in Dublin; and Brendan Behan.) The movement found its greatest expression in the creation of the Abbey Theatre, associated forever with the brilliant plays of Sean O'Casey; for many years the Abbey was the most famous theater in the world. The Gaelic League, on the other hand, had more popular appeal; with its dream of the restoration of the Gaelic language and the reestablishment of a separate Irish cultural nation, it provided a great deal of the inspiration for the Easter Rebellion of 1916.

This uprising was concentrated in Dublin. It sparked the 5-year War of Independence, which culminated in the Anglo-Irish Treaty of 1921 (whereby Ireland gained the status of Free State). The signing of the treaty was followed by Civil War in 1922–23, during which many buildings that had escaped damage in 1916 suffered badly. Today, happily, all the heirlooms of the eighteenth century have been restored to their original grandeur.

Dublin today, with a population of 680,000, is far larger than it has been at any other stage of its history. Nevertheless, it is still an eminently walkable city. The crossroads of medieval and eighteenth-century Dublin remain the center of interest. Within a half-mile radius of the Bank of Ireland on College Green lie the cathedrals, the museums, Dublin Castle, the great Georgian public buildings, the parks, and the shops. All are neatly enclosed by the Royal Canal to the north and the Grand Canal to the south.

Besides sight-seeing, a visitor should sample Dublin's abundant cultural offerings, especially its theaters. But the true focal point of Dubliners' social life is the pub, and it is there you must go to find them. Dublin can be a comfortable, "down home" place to visit, so slow down and enjoy it. If you do, you will find that there is an endearing earthiness about Dublin, a quality which inspired James Joyce to refer to his native city in off-color, though affectionate, terms as "strumpet city in the sunset" and "dear, dirty Dublin."

DUBLIN AT-A-GLANCE

SEEING THE CITY: A view of this essentially flat city is offered by the rooftop *Carvery Restaurant* in the *Burlington Hotel* (see *Checking In*). Or see Dublin from afar in the neighboring Wicklow Mountains.

SPECIAL PLACES: Central Dublin is very compact. Since traffic can be slow moving, by far the best way to see the city is on foot. A good idea is to take one of the CIE (Córas Iompair Éireann, National Transport Company) city sight-seeing tours. These last for about 3 hours and are an excellent and enjoyable way of getting one's bearings. They leave from the Central Bus Station, Store St. (phone: 74-63-01). Then, armed with Dublin Tourism's splendid, signposted *Tourist Trail,* the determined sight-seer should set off on foot to see and experience as much of Dublin as time allows.

SOUTH DOWNTOWN

Merrion Square – This is the loveliest of all Dublin's Georgian squares, a study in balance and elegance, evoking the graciousness of a vanished age. Note particularly the variety of fan-lighted doorways. Have a look at number 1, where the young Oscar Wilde lived with his celebrated parents, the surgeon Sir William Wills Wilde and poetess "Speranza"; number 42, home of Sir Jonah Barrington, eighteenth-century barrister and raconteur; number 58, where Daniel O'Connell lived, "the Liberator" who won Catholic Emancipation in 1829; number 70, home of tragic Sheridan Le Fanu, author of sinister tales such as *Uncle Silas* and *Through a Glass Darkly* — after his wife's death in 1858 he shut himself up there, appearing only after nightfall to walk, a solitary cloaked figure, in the shadows of Merrion Square; number 82, where William Butler Yeats, poet and Nobel Prize winner, lived. Today, the only house in the square used as a private dwelling is number 71, where well-known couturière Sybil Connolly has her home and studio.

Leinster House – When young Lord Kildare, earl of Leinster, chose to build a mansion here in 1745, all of fashionable Dublin protested, for at that time the north side of the city was the fashionable side. Undaunted, he went ahead with his plan, asserting that "Where I go, fashion will follow." His prophecy came true. The house Lord Kildare built is said to resemble the White House, whose architect, James Hoban of Carlow, studied in Dublin after the completion of Leinster House. The building was purchased in the nineteenth century by the Royal Dublin Society, and in 1921 the Parliament of the new Irish Free State chose the building as its meeting place. Today Leinster House continues to be the meeting place of the Dail (House of Representatives) and Seanad (Senate). When the Dail is in session, you may watch the proceedings from the visitors' gallery. Apply for tickets at the main gate. Kildare St., Merrion Square (phone: 78-99-11).

The National Museum – When Leinster House belonged to the Royal Dublin Society, it became the nucleus of a complex of cultural buildings — the National Gallery, the National Library, the Museum of Natural History, and the National Museum. These are all worth visiting, but the National Museum especially should not be missed. There is a collection of gold objects dating from the Bronze Age to early Christian times almost without parallel in Western Europe. No admission charge. Kildare St. (phone: 76-55-21).

St. Stephen's Green – Not far from Merrion Square lies St. Stephen's Green, one of the loveliest of Dublin's many public parks. It is pleasantly laid out on 22 acres with gardens, a waterfall, and an ornamental lake. It's an excellent place to come in summer, to sit and watch working Dublin take its lunch; bands play on the bandstand in July and August.

The Mansion House – Dublin preceded London in building a Mansion House for its lord mayor in 1715. In the Round Room the Declaration of Irish Independence was adopted in 1919, and the Anglo-Irish Treaty of 1921 was signed there. The Round Room is normally open to visitors; it is a very popular center for exhibitions. Dawson St. (phone: 76-28-52).

Trinity College – Dawson Street descends to meet Trinity College, the oldest university in Ireland, founded by Elizabeth I of England on the site of the twelfth-century Monastery of All Hallows. Alumni of the college include Oliver Goldsmith, Edmund Burke, Jonathan Swift, Bishop Berkeley (pronounced "bark-lee," who also lent his name to incorrectly pronounced Berkeley in California), William Congreve, Thomas Moore, Sheridan Le Fanu, and Oscar Wilde, to name but a few. No trace of the original

Elizabethan structure remains; the oldest surviving part of the college dates from 1700. The Long Room, Trinity's famous library, is the longest single chamber library in existence. It contains a priceless collection of 800,000 volumes and 3,000 ancient manuscripts and papyri. The library's chief treasure is the *Book of Kells,* an eighth-century manuscript transcription of the four Gospels described as the "most beautiful book in the world." No admission charge. Closed Saturday afternoons and all day Sundays. College Green (phone: 77-29-41).

Parliament House – Facing Trinity College is the monumental Parliament House, now the Bank of Ireland. Built in 1729 and regarded as one of the finest examples of the architecture of its period, this was the first of the great series of eighteenth-century public buildings in Dublin. As its name implies, it was erected to house the Irish Parliament in the century that saw the birth of Home Rule. College Green (phone: 77-68-01).

Dublin Castle – As you move away from College Green, Dame Street leads westward toward the older part of the city, where the early Viking and Norman settlers chose to establish themselves.

Castles have gone up and down on the site of the present castle. A Celtic *rath* was almost certainly followed by a wooden Viking fortress and this in turn was supplanted by the great stone castle erected by John of England in the thirteenth century. The castle was for 400 years the center of English rule in Ireland; for much of this time it had as grim a reputation as the Tower of London. Although the present building is essentially eighteenth century, one of the four towers that flanked the original moated castle survives as the Record Tower. Fifteenth-century Bedford Tower was the state prison; today it houses the Heraldic Museum and the unique Genealogical Office, where visitors with Irish ancestry can (for a fee) have their family tree traced. The Georgian State Apartments, formerly the residence of the English viceroys, were beautifully restored between 1950 and 1963 and are now used for state functions. St. Patrick's Hall in the State Apartments was the scene of the inauguration of Ireland's first president, Douglas Hyde; here, too, President John F. Kennedy was made a freeman of Dublin.

The Bedford Tower, the Chapel Royal, and the State Apartments can be visited for a small admission charge. Dublin Castle (phone: 71-17-77).

Christ Church Cathedral – Not far from Dublin Castle, the massive shape of Christ Church Cathedral crowns the hill on which the ancient city stood. Founded in 1038 by Viking King Sitric Silkenbeard of Dublin, Christ Church was demolished in the twelfth century and rebuilt by the Norman Richard Gilbert de Clare (Strongbow), who is buried within its walls. The cruciform building has been much restored through the centuries, but the beautiful pointed nave and the wonderful stonework remain virtually unchanged. These walls have witnessed many dramatic scenes in the course of Irish history. Christ Church today is the Church of Ireland (Protestant) Cathedral for the Diocese of Dublin. The vaulted crypt remains one of the largest in Ireland. In front of this cathedral Dubliners traditionally gather to ring in the New Year. The cathedral and crypt can be visited. Christ Church Pl. (phone: 77-80-99).

St. Audeon's Arch and the City Walls – The thirteenth-century church of St. Audeon is Dublin's oldest parish church. It was founded by early Norman settlers, who gave to the church the name St. Ouen, or Audeon, after the patron saint of their native Rouen. Close to the church is a flight of steps leading down to St. Audeon's Arch, the sole surviving gateway of the medieval city walls.

St. Patrick's Cathedral – Christ Church stood within the old walled city. One of her twelfth-century archbishops, John Comyn, felt that while he remained under municipal jurisdiction he could not achieve the temporal power for which he thirsted. Accordingly, he left the city walls and built a fine palace within a stone's throw of Christ Church. Today St. Patrick's is the national cathedral of the Church of Ireland. By the nineteenth century both cathedrals were in a state of considerable disrepair. Henry Roe, a distiller, came to the aid of Christ Church, restoring it at his own expense; Sir Benjamin Lee Guinness of the famous brewing family came to the assistance of St. Patrick's — hence the saying in Dublin that "Christ Church was restored with glasses, St. Patrick's with pints!"

The early English interior of St. Patrick's is very beautiful; the nave is the longest in Ireland. The cathedral's particular fascination, however, lies in its wealth of monuments, especially the Geraldine Door, the Cork Memorial, and the monument to Dame St. Leger. The greatest interest of all, though, is in the long association with St. Patrick's of Jonathan Swift, author of *Gulliver's Travels* and dean of the cathedral for 32 years. Within these walls he is buried, beside his loving Stella. On a slab near the entrance is carved the epitaph he composed for himself, which Yeats described as the greatest epitaph in literature. Open to visitors. St. Patrick's Cathedral (phone: 75-48-17).

Guinness Brewery – Founded in 1759 by Arthur Guinness with the sum of £100, Guinness's today is the largest exporting stout brewery in the world. Visitors are welcomed although, due to major reconstruction, they are no longer invited on a tour of the brewery. An audiovisual presentation is offered instead, after which visitors can sample the Dark Fantastic to their hearts' content. No admission charge. St. James's Gate (phone: 75-67-01).

NORTH DOWNTOWN

The Four Courts – Almost across the river from Guinness's lies the stately Four Courts of Justice, dating from the apogee of the eighteenth century. The building was begun by Thomas Cooley and completed by James Gandon, the greatest of all the Georgian architects. Court sittings (Supreme and High) are open to the public. No admission charge. Inns Quay (phone: 72-55-55).

St. Michan's Church – Not far from the Four Courts is St. Michan's, a seventeenth-century church built on the site of a tenth-century Viking church. The eighteenth-century organ is said to have been played by Handel when he was in Dublin for the first ever public performance of the *Messiah*.

Of more immediate interest, perhaps, is the extraordinary crypt, with its remarkable preservative atmosphere: Bodies have lain here for centuries without decomposing and you can, if you feel so inclined, shake the hand of an 8-foot-tall Crusader! Open Mondays through Fridays and Saturday mornings. Small admission charge. Church St.

Moore Street – A left turn past the historic General Post Office leads down Henry Street; the second turn to the right off Henry Street is Moore Street. In this street, among the fruit and flower sellers, you can hear the true voice of Dublin — lively, warm, voluble, speaking an English that is straight Sean O'Casey.

The Municipal Gallery of Modern Art – Beyond the Garden of Remembrance (a memorial to those who died for Irish freedom), on the north side of Parnell Square, is Charlemont House, designed by Sir William Chambers in 1764. Lord Charlemont, for whom the house was designed, was a great patron of the arts; it is fitting that his house became, in recent times, the Municipal Gallery of Modern Art. The gallery should not be missed; it has an outstanding collection of Impressionist paintings, and more recent artists such as Picasso, Utrillo, and Bonnard are well represented, to say nothing of such prominent Irish painters as Sir William Orpen, John B. Yeats (the poet's father), and Jack Yeats. Closed Mondays and Sunday afternoons. No admission charge. Parnell Square (phone: 74-19-03).

The Abbey Theatre – Alas, the original Abbey Theatre, founded by Yeats and Lady Gregory on the site of the old city morgue, is no more. In 1951, at the close of a performance of O'Casey's *The Plough and the Stars* — a play that ends with Dublin blazing in the aftermath of rebellion — the theater itself caught on fire and was burned to the ground. The New Abbey, designed by Michael Scott, one of the country's foremost architects, opened in 1966 on the site of the original building. The lobby, which can be seen daily (except Sundays), contains interesting portraits of those connected with the theater's early successes. Performances nightly (except Sundays). Abbey St. (phone: 74-45-05).

The Custom House – This masterpiece of Georgian architecture adorns the north bank of the Liffey, to the east of O'Connell Street. It was the chef d'oeuvre of James Gandon and is one of the finest buildings of its kind in Europe. The Custom House is occupied by government offices and is not open to the public; it should, nonetheless, be seen at close range: the carved riverheads that form the keystones of the arches and entrances are splendid. Custom House Quay (phone: 74-29-61).

THE SUBURBS

The Phoenix Park – Lying northwest of the city center, the Phoenix Park is the largest enclosed urban park in the world. Within its walls are the residences of the president of the republic and the US ambassador. The park covers 1,760 acres, beautifully planted with a great variety of trees. Among the attractions are the lovely People's Gardens, the herd of fallow deer, the horse-race course, and the Zoological Gardens. Dublin Zoo is said to be the most beautiful zoo in Europe; it also has a most impressive collection of animals and holds several records for lion breeding. The park and zoo are open daily.

The Chester Beatty Library – Founded by an American, naturalized British resident in Ireland, this library is considered to be the most valuable and representative private collection of Oriental manuscripts and miniatures in the world. The "copper millionaire with a heart of gold," Chester Beatty willed his marvelous library to the people of Dublin. Open Tuesdays through Fridays. No admission charge. 20 Shrewsbury Rd., Ballsbridge (phone: 69-23-86).

Malahide Castle – In a north city suburb of Dublin, Malahide Castle has only recently been opened to the public. For eight centuries this was the home of the Talbots of Malahide. Magnificently furnished in period style (mostly eighteenth century) with part of the very valuable National Portrait Collection on view, it is well worth a visit. Malahide, County Dublin (phone: 45-23-37).

■ **EXTRA SPECIAL:** The beautiful Boyne Valley is one of Ireland's most storied and evocative sites, and it makes an easy and interesting day trip. Leave Dublin by the Navan road, passing through Dunshaughlin (which takes its name from a church founded by St. Seachnall, a companion of St. Patrick). Six miles south of Navan, signposted to the left, is the Hill of Tara. Although only some grassy mounds and earthworks recall a splendid past, it is impossible to remain unmoved by the site's history: This is "Royal Tara," where High Kings of Ireland were crowned on the Lia Fail (the Stone of Destiny) before time began. And it was here, at the tribes' great triennial Feis of Tara, that laws were enacted and revised. Now, as Moore writes in his immortal song, "No more to chiefs and ladies bright / The harp of Tara swells / The chord alone that breaks at night / Its tale of ruin tells."

Returning to the Navan road, you will pass the striking ruins of sixteenth-century Athlumney Castle on the east bank of the Boyne, about 1.5 miles from Navan. Continue on through Donaghmore, with its remains of a twelfth-century church and a round tower. Nearby, below the Boyne Bridge, lies Log na Ri — the Hollow of the King — where people once used to swim their herds of cattle ceremoniously across the river, to protect them from the "little people" and from natural disasters.

The village of Slane lies on one of the loveliest stretches of the Boyne. There are some delightful Georgian houses, but the history of this small town goes back far beyond the eighteenth century. It was on the hill that overlooks Slane that St. Patrick lit the Paschal Fire on Holy Saturday, AD 433, and drew upon himself the wrath of the High King's druids. Patrick emerged victorious from the ensuing confrontation, and Christianity began its reign in Ireland. On the slopes of the hill are the remains of an ancient earthen fort and the ruins of a sixteenth-century church. Quite apart from archaeological interest, the climb up Slane Hill is well worth the effort — rewarding the energetic with fine views across the tranquil Boyne Valley to Trim and Drogheda. Just outside the town lies the estate of Slane Castle, a nineteenth-century castellated mansion in which the present occupant, Lord Mountcharles, has opened a fine restaurant (phone: 041-24207).

Downstream from Slane is Brugh na Boinne — the Palace of the Boyne — a vast necropolis over 4,000 years old. Here, beneath a chain of tumuli, kings of Ireland were laid to rest in passage graves of remarkable complexity. The tumuli of Dowth, Knowth, and Newgrange in particular are of major interest, both for their extent and the amazing diversity of their sculptured ornamentation. Newgrange is one of the finest passage graves in all of Western Europe, and it has been opened to the public. There is a permanent archaeological exhibition and guided tours are available. Closed Mondays.

Continuing down the Boyne Valley, you reach Drogheda, an ancient town that has witnessed many a dramatic scene in the course of Irish history, the most famous of which was the defeat of James II by William of Orange on July 12, 1690. Other reminders of its past include: the thirteenth-century St. Laurence's Gate, the only surviving of the original ten gates in this once walled city; the ruins of thirteenth-century St. Mary's Abbey; the Norman motte and bailey of Millmount, and the fine Millmount Museum; St. Peter's Church, where the head of St. Oliver Plunkett, martyred archbishop of Armagh, is enshrined.

Five miles north of Drogheda, you reach Monasterboice, an ancient monastic settlement noteworthy for one of the most perfect high crosses in Ireland — the intricately carved tenth-century Cross of Muireadach. Southwest of Monasterboice are the impressive ruins of Mellifont Abbey. Dating from 1142, this was the first Cistercian foundation in Ireland and heralded a whole new style of ecclesiastical architecture. Note especially the remains of the gate house, and the octagonal lavabo.

Return to Dublin via the N1.

SOURCES AND RESOURCES

For on-the-spot information and assistance, call the Dublin Tourism Tourist Information Offices, at Dublin Airport and 14 O'Connell St. (phone: 74-77-33). The Tourist Information Offices will advise you on all aspects of your stay in Ireland and will make theater bookings and hotel reservations anywhere in the country. They also publish *Dining in Ireland* (available at Tourist Information Offices and most bookstores).

The *Tourist Trail*, published by Dublin Tourism and available at their offices, is an excellent walking guide to the city. Another invaluable Dublin Tourism publication is *Dublin—Useful Information.* The best city map is the Ordnance Survey Dublin Map; less-detailed, but generally adequate maps are also available.

For Local Coverage – *In Dublin,* published fortnightly, covers every conceivable activity in Dublin, including theater, cinema, music, exhibitions, sports, and cabarets. *What's On In Dublin* is published monthly by Dublin Tourism and is available at their offices. Main daily newspapers are: the *Irish Times,* the *Irish Independent,* and the *Irish Press;* main evening papers are the *Evening Herald* and the *Evening Press.*

GETTING AROUND: Bus – *CIE (Córas Iompair Éireann, National Transport Company)* operates rail and bus transport not only in Dublin but nationwide. There is no subway in Dublin, but cross-city bus routes are extensive. Fares are not paid on entering; they are collected after the passenger is seated. Exact fares are not required.

Day tours from Dublin are operated by *CIE* from the Central Bus Station, Store St. There is a wide range of tours available (phone: 74-63-01).

All information regarding bus and rail travel throughout the republic can be obtained by telephoning 78-77-77. An official bus and rail timetable is available at newsstands.

Taxi – There are stands at many points throughout the city, especially near main hotels, and cabs can also be hailed in the streets. Your first conversation with a Dublin cabdriver will assure you that you are in fact in Ireland. Among the companies that operate a 24-hour radio service are *Blue Cabs* (phone: 76-11-11), *Irish Taxi Co-op* (phone: 76-66-66), and *National Radio Cabs* (phone: 77-22-22).

Car Rental – Many Dublin firms offer excellent self-drive facilities. Advice and brochures are available from tourist offices.

MUSEUMS: In addition to the museums mentioned in *Special Places*, Dublin is also the home of the *Dublin Civic Museum*, South William St., and the *Museum of Childhood*, The Palms, 20 Palmerstown Park, Rathmines (private collection of antique dolls and toys). The latter has a small admission charge (phone: 97-32-23).

SHOPPING: Neatly balanced on two banks of the Liffey, Dublin has two downtown shopping areas: one around O'Connell Street and Henry Street, and the other centered in Grafton Street and its environs. Stores on the more elegant south side of the river are excellent, with friendly service and a wide range of high-quality products, and the compact area in which they are confined makes shopping very easy. Powerscourt House Centre, just off Grafton Street, has a number of fashion, antique, and craft shops situated in a courtyard built around an elegant Dublin townhouse. Good buys are the chunky Aran sweaters (expensive, but they will last a lifetime), Donegal tweed, Waterford and Galway crystal, and Belleek china. *Brown Thomas* and *Switzer's* are the main department stores on Grafton Street; *Arnott's*, *Roche's*, and *Clery's* are fine stores in the O'Connell and Henry streets area. Henry Street also houses a host of inviting jewelry shops. And the famous *Kilkenny Design Centre* has a marvelous store on Nassau Street, with a wide range of Irish-designed goods — blown-glass, silver, ceramics, rugs, furniture, pipes, toys, candles, woven items, and more, even Irish edibles. There are good buys in old prints along the south bank of the Liffey near O'Connell Street, and the best bargains in woolens are just across the river. Among some recommended shops are:

Laura Ashley – Fashion and fabrics for the home, adults, and children, by the English designer. 7 Dawson St. (phone: 714247).

Bernadette Madden – A good selection of batiks. Open daily by appointment. 12 Herbert Pl.

Bewley's Cafés Ltd. – Coffees and chocolates are the specialties at the several cafés of the Bewley organization. One is at 78–79 Grafton St. (phone: 776761).

Chez Nous – Handmade sweets and other confections. 15 Lad La. (phone: 762503).

Cleo Ltd. – Hand-knitted and handwoven cloaks, caps, and shawls. 18 Kildare St. (phone: 761421).

Sybil Connolly – Ireland's reigning couturière; her romantic ballgowns of finely pleated Irish linen are indeed special. 71 Merrion Sq. (phone: 767281).

Paul Costelloe – Designer of ready-to-wear for women. 42 Drury St. (phone: 711598).

Pat Crowley – Silky and seductive blouses and dresses. 14 Duke St. (phone: 710219).

Eason & Son Ltd. – Jam-packed with tomes and paperbacks, maps, records, and stationery. 40–42 Lower O'Connell St. (phone: 741161).

Pat Flood – Modern silver and gold jewelry in traditional Irish designs. 12 Fade St. (phone: 770829).

Irish Cottage Industries – Sweaters, tweeds, and anything else hand-knit, hand-crocheted, handwoven, or hand-braided. 44 Dawson St. (phone: 713039).

H. Johnston Ltd. – Traditional blackthorn walking sticks. 11 Wicklow St. (phone: 771249).

Kapp and Peterson – Tobaccos and hand-carved pipes for men and women. 55 Grafton St. (phone: 712120).

Kevin & Howlin Ltd. – Clothing for men, ready-made and made-to-measure. 31 Nassau St. (phone: 770257).

Joseph Monaghan – Dublin's gold-medal tailor. 98 St. Stephen's Green (phone: 753598).

Mullins of Dublin – For coats of arms emblazoned on parchments, plaques, even door knockers. 36 Upper O'Connell St. (phone: 741133).

Waltons Musical Instrument Galleries – Bagpipes and Irish harps as well as records. 2–5 N Frederick St. (phone: 707805).

The Weavers Shed – Handwoven fabrics, by the yard or made up. 9 Duke La. (phone: 773716).

SPECIAL EVENTS: Outstanding annual events include *St. Patrick's Day* on March 17, of course, with a parade and many other events; an *Irish Music Festival (Feis Cheoil)* in May; the *Festival of Music in Great Irish Houses* in June, for concerts by international celebrities in Georgian mansions near Dublin; *Bloomsday,* June 16, when fans of James Joyce gather from around the world to follow the circuitous path through Dublin that takes Leopold Bloom from morning until late at night in *Ulysses;* the *Dublin Horse Show,* the principal sporting and social event of the year, in August; and the *Dublin Theatre Festival* in October, featuring new plays by Irish authors in a series of exciting first nights. For details about these and other events, inquire at the Tourist Office (see above).

SPORTS: Bicycling – Irish Raleigh Industries operates *Rent-a-Bike* at a number of city firms (phone: 77-43-95).

Gaelic Games – Football and hurling are two fast and enthralling field sports; important matches are played at *Croke Park.* For details, see the calendar of events in *In Dublin* or call Croke Park (phone: 74-31-11). The hurling and football seasons reach their conclusion at Croke Park with the All-Ireland Hurling Final and the All-Ireland Football Final, two Sundays in September.

Golf – There are over 30 courses within easy reach of Dublin; visitors are welcome at all clubs on weekdays, but gaining admission can be more difficult on weekends. Two of the finest courses in the world, *Portmarnock* and *Royal Dublin,* are just north of the city, and these should not be missed.

Greyhound Racing – An exciting spectator sport, this can be seen regularly at two tracks, each an 8-minute ride from the city center: *Shelbourne Park Stadium* and *Harold's Cross Stadium.* Details in *In Dublin* or at the Tourist Office.

Horse Racing – *Phoenix Park* is the site of races in the city, but the course is straight, not circular, which makes for frustrating viewing. You may see the start, the middle, or the end, but you won't see the whole race. Better is the very famous racecourse, *Curragh,* about a mile outside the town of Kildare in County Kildare. It's less than an hour's drive from Dublin. Leopardstown, six miles south of the city, has a very modern racecourse.

Horseback Riding – A list of riding establishments registered with the Irish Horse Board and located close to Dublin is available at Tourist Offices.

Tennis – There are a number of public courts around Dublin, where visitors can play for a very low hourly fee. The most central is *Herbert Park,* Ballsbridge (phone: 68-43-64).

THEATER: For complete program listings see the publications under *For Local Coverage.* There are eight main theaters in the city center; smaller groups perform in the universities, in suburban theaters, and occasionally in pubs and hotels. The main theaters are the *Abbey* and the *Peacock,* both at Lower Abbey St. (phone: 74-45-05); the *Gate* (the theater of Michael MacLiammoir and Hilton Edwards), Cavendish Row (phone: 74-40-45); the *Gaiety,* South King St. (phone: 77-17-17), mostly for revues, musicals, and opera; the *Olympia,* Dame St. (phone: 77-89-62), for everything from revues to straight plays; the *Eblana,* Store St. (phone: 74-67-07), a small theater offering mostly modern comedy; the *Focus,* Pembroke Pl. (phone: 76-30-71) for Russian and Scandinavian works; the *Project Arts Centre,* 39 E Essex St. (phone: 71-33-27), very avant-garde.

For children, the *Lambert Puppet Theatre* in the suburb of Monkstown will prove irresistible. Clifton La., Monkstown (phone: 80-09-74).

It is always advisable to reserve in advance for theater in Dublin. You can make bookings at the theaters, at tourist offices, and at the information desks of *Switzer's* and *Brown Thomas* department stores, Grafton St. Some of the theaters accept telephone reservations.

MUSIC: The recently opened *National Concert Hall,* Earlsfort Terrace, off St. Stephen's Green (phone: 71-18-88), is the new center of Dublin's active musical life and the new home of the *RTE (Radio Telefis Éireann) Symphony Orchestra. RTE* performances are held regularly, as are a variety of other concerts. For schedule information, phone the concert hall or check local publications. In April and September the *Dublin Grand Opera Society* holds its spring and winter seasons at the Gaiety Theatre. Traditional Irish music is a must. Sessions are held at many places around town by an organization called *Comhaltas Ceoltóirí Éireann* (phone: 80-02-95); ballad sessions are held nightly except Sundays in the *Abbey Tavern,* Howth, 10 miles north of the city on the coast (phone: 32-20-06). Many pubs have music on an informal basis — *O'Donoghue's* in Merrion Row is one of the most famous (and least comfortable). Try also *Toner's* and the *Baggot Inn,* both in Lower Baggot St., *Slattery's* in Capel St., and *The Merchant* in Merchant's Quay. There are many other listings in *In Dublin.*

NIGHTCLUBS AND NIGHTLIFE: There is little in the way of large-scale cabaret-cum-dancing in Dublin; swinging Dublin tends to congregate on the discotheque scene. Premises range from the large, lively places where an escort is not necessarily required to small, intimate clubs. Most discotheques only have wine licenses.

Among the more established discotheques on a rapidly changing scene are the large and lively *Annabel's* in the *Burlington Hotel; Raffles* in the *Sachs Hotel; Barbarella's* and *Zhivago,* both off Merion Row; *Silks* in the Phoenix Park racecourse; *Blinkers* at Leopardstown racecourse. Smaller, more intimate clubs are mainly to be found in the Leeson Street area: try *Club Elizabeth, Bojangles, Samantha's, Styx,* and *Aphrodite's.* The most famous traditional cabaret in Dublin is the long-established *Jury's Cabaret;*

nightly, except Mondays (phone: 76-75-11). Also good are the *Braemor Rooms,* Churchtown (phone: 98-86-64), and the *Irish Cabaret* at the *Burlington Hotel* (phone: 60-52-22).

SINS: Drinking is the pet vice of the Irish; local sources say the Liffey runs dark with Guinness and "even the damned island is shaped like a diseased liver!"

Dublin's "sin strip," Leeson Street, is not outstandingly — but perhaps sufficiently — sinful.

BEST IN TOWN

CHECKING IN: An American journalist once described how he was awakened by the telephone one morning in a long-established, deluxe Dublin hotel: "Good morning sir, this is your 8:30 wake-up call." "I didn't ask for an 8:30 call," snapped the journalist. "I asked to be called at 7:45!" "Oh. Well, it's 9:00 now, anyway, sir. I hope that'll be all right, sir. . . ." The story is probably apocryphal, but it illustrates the peculiarly unhurried atmosphere to be found in some of the city's older hotels — an atmosphere that is simultaneously frustrating and captivating. It must be said that Dublin does not boast a truly deluxe, first-class hotel. In contrast, a plethora of streamlined, modern hotels have sprung up in recent years on the city's perimeter. These sometimes, but by no means always, sacrifice a little of their warmth for efficiency. There is something, then, for everyone, and in every price range.

For really inexpensive accommodations, try some of the Grade-A guesthouses on the edge of the city; about $20 will pay for a room and full Irish breakfast.

Because the value of the pound fluctuates considerably, our price estimates can only be approximate. Expect to pay between $60 and $80 for a double room in hotels classified as expensive; $30 to $60 is moderate; below $30 is inexpensive.

Note: The Tourist Board offers a list of hotels they have inspected and graded; they also have a computerized reservation service all over Ireland (see *Sources and Resources*).

The Berkeley Court – This new baby of the P. V. Doyle Group has proved itself outstanding since it opened in 1978. Situated close to the city in the leafy suburbs of Ballsbridge, the *Berkeley* combines old-world graciousness with modern efficiency. Contemporary and antique are blended in an impeccable decor. Service is exceptionally warm. There are 200 rooms, an excellent dining room, and a good coffee shop. Lansdowne Rd. (phone: 60-17-11). Expensive.

The Shelbourne – This long-established hotel is a nice mixture of the dignified and the lively. Undeniably stately in its appointments, the *Shelbourne* attracts a sizable and varied section of Dublin's "beau monde," from socialites to literati. The *Lounge,* overlooking St. Stephen's Green, is a favorite rendezvous. The dining room is pleasant, if unexciting; the bar is delightful. Standards in the 166 bedrooms tend to be uneven; some are splendid, others small. St. Stephen's Green (phone: 76-64-71). Expensive.

The Burlington – Just outside the city center, this is Ireland's largest hotel with 420 bedrooms. Amenities include an indoor heated swimming pool, sauna, massage parlor, hairdressing salon, and nightclub. There are several restaurants: the *Rooftop Carvery,* commanding fine views over Dublin; the luxurious *Sussex Room,* serving high-quality Irish and international cuisine; the *Georgian Grill,* offering fast-service snack meals. Upper Leeson St. (phone: 60-52-22). Expensive.

Jury's – Another modern hotel, located in Ballsbridge, this was formerly the *Inter-*

Continental; it has improved immeasurably since *Jury's* took it over. The 314 bedrooms are large and well appointed, although bathrooms are rather small. Despite the hotel's size, there are nice personal touches, such as an Alka-Seltzer left beside the bathroom glass for guests who have dined too well in one of the excellent restaurants. The *Embassy Room* offers Irish and international cuisine; the new *Kish* restaurant, within the *Pavilion,* has a very extensive seafood menu. The *Pavilion* also has a cocktail bar, indoor swimming pool, and spacious lounge area. There is also the 23-hour *Coffee Dock.* For entertainment, *Jury's* offers Ireland's longest-running and most famous cabaret. The *Dubliner Bar* is particularly pleasant. Northumberland Rd. (phone: 76-75-11). Expensive.

Bloom's – Centrally located, this new hotel of the Ryan chain was opened in 1979. It is an intimate and elegant hotel with a high commitment to service. There are 86 rooms with color TV, air-conditioning, trouser pressing, free mixers and ice, and direct-dial telephones. Every corridor has an ice cabinet and a shoeshine. There is a tea lounge decorated with plants, the *Anna Livia Gourmet Restaurant,* the *Blazes Boylan Coffee House,* and *Bloom's Bar* (note the names from Joyce). Anglesea St. (phone: 71-56-22). Expensive.

The Tara Tower – Ten minutes' drive from the city center, on a well-serviced bus route, this modern hotel is comfortable and very reasonably priced. The 100 bedrooms are all well equipped, with radio, television, and telephone; many overlook Dublin Bay just across the road. The lobby is small, but there is a good restaurant and a grill that remains open until midnight. Merrion Rd. (phone: 69-46-66). Moderate.

The Montrose – Similar to but larger than the *Tara Tower,* the *Montrose* is near the National Radio and Television Studios and across the road from the new Belfield campus of University College, Dublin. Also about 10 minutes' drive from the city center, on a well-serviced bus route. Its 190 bedrooms are quite comfortable, and there is a good restaurant. Other amenities include a grill, bars, health center, hairdressing salon, and souvenir shop. Stillorgan Rd. (phone: 69-33-11). Moderate.

The Clarence – This centrally located hotel is on the Liffey and near shopping areas. It has 70 comfortable bedrooms, most with baths, and a restaurant. 6-8 Wellington Quay (phone: 77-61-78). Moderate.

The Mount Herbert – Close to the city center, the *Mount Herbert* is a well-run family-owned guesthouse. It has 88 bedrooms (77 with bath); the restaurant is quite good. No bar (wine license only). Very pleasant atmosphere. 7 Herbert Rd. (phone: 68-43-21). Inexpensive.

The Ariel – Most of the 15 rooms of this homey guesthouse have baths. 52 Lansdowne Rd. (phone: 68-55-12). Inexpensive.

Egan's Montrosa – With 19 rooms, all with baths, this is another comfortable guesthouse. 7 Iona Park (phone: 30-36-11). Inexpensive.

Iona House – Another guesthouse with eight rooms, all with baths. 5 Iona Park (phone: 30-62-17). Inexpensive.

EATING OUT: Where food is concerned, Ireland, first and foremost an agricultural country, has outstanding raw materials, but truly distinctive and extensive Irish cuisine really does not exist. There are, of course, traditional dishes such as Irish stew, Dublin coddle, bacon and cabbage, but this kind of dish is a rara avis on the menu of most of the better restaurants, being looked down upon as too common to prepare for discriminating diners.

Where the serving of its enviable agricultural produce is concerned, Ireland has nothing to be ashamed of — top restaurants can compare with the best anywhere.

Dublin offers a wide range of first-class restaurants, a somewhat more restricted range of moderately priced establishments, and a number of fast-service, inexpensive eating places. It should be noted that few hotel restaurants are mentioned in the list that follows; generally speaking, really interesting cuisine in Dublin is to be found in small, privately run restaurants.

Dinner for two with wine will cost between $40 and $55 in expensive restaurants; $20 to $40 is moderate; below $20 is inexpensive.

Berkeley Court – One of the best of the hotel restaurants, this is a truly elegant, lavishly appointed room; its prize-winning chef produces highly satisfactory cuisine. Lansdowne Rd. (phone: 60-17-11). Expensive.

Snaffles – Tucked away in the basement of one of Dublin's most elegant old Georgian houses, with less the air of a restaurant than that of the private dining room of some comfortable country house. The cooking is vintage Irish country house, simple and excellent. Superbly prepared game and fowl, including such rarities as plover, are specialties. Don't miss the spinach. Reservations essential. 47 Lower Leeson St. (phone: 76-22-27). Expensive.

Mirabeau – Located about 8 miles southeast of Dublin, this restaurant is touted as one of the best and the most expensive in Ireland. Owner and chef Sean Kinsella personally welcomes guests at the front door and offers a large selection of freshly made soups, fish, and curry dishes, as well as inviting desserts. A dinner here is well worth the short drive. Closed Sundays. Marine Parade in Sandycove (phone: 80-98-73). Expensive.

The Lord Edward – Strictly for seafood lovers (no meat on the menu), this restaurant is located in a tall, Victorian building opposite historic Christ Church Cathedral, in the older part of the city. The seafood is prepared and served in the classic French style. Closed Sundays and bank holidays. Reservations are essential. 23 Christ Church Pl. (phone: 75-25-57). Expensive.

King Sitric – A superb small restaurant, right on the bay, serves perfectly cooked fish and excellent wines in a tastefully restored old house. The service is excellent. They also specialize in game birds such as grouse and snipe. East Pier, Howth (phone: 32-52-35). Expensive.

Le Coq Hardi – Run by owner/chef John Howard, twice Gold Medal winner in the prestigious Hotelympia/Salon Culinaire contest, this is a small and gracious establishment in the basement of the *Lansdowne Hotel* (with which it has no connection) on Pembroke Road. Its extensive à la carte menu offers many house specialties such as Mr. Howard's renowned *caneton à l'orange*. Closed Sundays and closed for lunch Saturdays. Reservations essential. 29 Pembroke Rd., Ballsbridge (phone: 68-90-70). Expensive.

The Grey Door – Opened in 1978, it has already achieved an enviable reputation for fine Russian and Finnish cuisine. The wine list is good and the more adventurous imbiber can sample such rarities as Russian champagne. The setting behind this elegant doorway in the heart of Georgian Dublin is intimate, rather like dining in a private home. Closed Sundays. 23 Upper Pembroke St. (phone: 76-32-86). Expensive.

The Tandoori Rooms – As the name suggests, Eastern food is the specialty here, but there are plenty of Western dishes and an extensive wine list. The place is very personally run by genial Mike Butt. Closed Sundays. 27 Lower Leeson St. (phone: 762286). Expensive.

Restaurant na Mara – The name means "restaurant of the sea," and this long-established eatery specializes, of course, in seafood. The building itself is an elegantly converted railway station (owned by the National Transport Company). Closed Sundays and Mondays. 1 Harbour Rd. in Dun Laoghaire, just south of Dublin (phone: 806767 or 800509). Expensive.

Oliver's – Also in the harbor town of Dun Laoghaire, this is one of the few restaurants around Dublin that is open on Sundays. Small and friendly, it features fresh seasonal food. Reservations advised. 62 Upper George's St., Dun Laoghaire (phone: 802204). Expensive.

Sandford House – Located about 10 minutes from the city center, in the suburb of Ranelagh, the *Sandford House* serves good, moderately priced food in very comfortable surroundings; occasionally there's live piano music. Another of the few restaurants open on Sundays. Sandford Rd., Ranelagh (phone: 974383). Moderate.

Locks Restaurant – This provincial-style restaurant is on the banks of the Grand Canal near Portobello Bridge. Only the freshest produce is used for the French and Scandinavian dishes served here. 1 Windsor Ter., Portobello (phone: 75-20-25). Moderate.

The Blackboard – Tucked away behind Grafton Street, this place will satisfy the appetite of the hungriest shopper. It specializes in grills and excellent puddings. The decor is unpretentious and you are likely to find yourself sharing one of the long tables downstairs with strangers, but the food is good and the service quite friendly. Closed Sundays. 2 Balfe St., behind Woolworth's of Grafton St. (phone: 77-34-68). Moderate to inexpensive.

Pancake HQ – The emphasis here is on salads, seafood, hamburgers, and steaks, and lavish dessert pancakes are a specialty of the house. The atmosphere is cheerful, and the clientele tends to be fairly young and lively. Closed Sundays. 5 Beresford Pl. (phone: 744657). Inexpensive.

Kilkenny Kitchen – This bright, self-service restaurant in the Kilkenny Design Centre makes a perfect stop for morning coffee, lunch, or afternoon tea (no dinner) during a day of shopping. The menu is limited, but there's a tasty choice of dishes and very good salads. Closed Sundays. Kilkenny Shop, Nassau St. (phone: 777066). Inexpensive.

National Gallery Restaurant – Impressive location in the National Art Gallery. Open daily for lunch and for dinner on Thursdays. Merrion Square (phone: 76-52-68). Inexpensive.

Murph's – Irish-American food served at reasonable prices in this chain of lively restaurants, owned by two Irish-American brothers. A la carte throughout the day until midnight (2 AM in Baggot Street). Interesting decors. Closed Sundays and public holidays. 99 Lower Baggot St. (phone: 68-12-05); 18 Suffolk St. off Grafton St. (phone: 68-13-49); 21 Bachelor's Walk (on the waterfront, near O'Connell St.) (phone: 74-57-69). All inexpensive.

Captain America's Cookhouse – Specializes in "genuine American hamburgers"; not bad at all. Open daily. 1st Fl., Grafton Court, Grafton St. (phone: 71-52-66). Inexpensive.

SHARING A PINT: Until you have been in a pub, you have not experienced Dublin. Here Dubliners come to pursue two serious occupations: drinking and conversation. Many pubs are ugly modern, complete with Muzak and plastic, but plenty of traditional pubs remain — noisy, companionable places where you can pursue friendly ghosts of bygone Dublin in an unhurried atmosphere. Some favorites are the *Horseshoe Bar* in the *Shelbourne Hotel,* St. Stephen's Green (phone: 76-64-71), favored by the uppity, horsey set; the *Bailey,* at 2 Duke St. (phone: 77-30-55), a literary pub that actually displays the door of nearby 7 Eccles St., where Joyce's Molly and Leopold Bloom lived; *O'Donoghue's,* off St. Stephen's Green, for Irish ballads; the *Palace Bar* on Fleet St., a traditional haunt of journalists and literati; *Mulligans* of Poolbeg St., renowned for the quality of its pint, appreciated equally by the dock workers and students (from nearby Trinity College), who form its main clientele; the *Stag's Head,* Dame Ct. (a great haunt of the legal profession), which serves hearty hot lunches at reasonable prices; *Neary's,* Chatham St., which offers delicacies like smoked salmon and oysters in season; the *Brazenhead,* Bridge St., and *Davy Byrne's,* 21 Duke St., for plain drinking and gab; *Doheny and Nesbitts* on Merrion Row, which is always known simply as "Nesbitts" — try the bar, not the modernized upstairs lounge; and last, but very far from least, the utterly delightful *Ryans,* Parkgate St., with its shining mirrors, its courteous barmen, and its snugs where guests can drink quietly.

WINE BARS: A relatively recent development in Dublin, wine bars offer light meals and good wines at moderate prices. Some exceptionally pleasant examples of the genre are:

Kilmartin's – Originally owned by a turf accountant (or bookie), its new owners retained both the name and the racing-style decor. Run by two young women, both Cordon Bleu cooks, Kilmartin's offers a limited but excellent menu. The house wine is particularly good. 19 Upper Baggot St. (phone: 68-66-79).

Shrimp's – Tiny, but charmingly decorated, it is not the place to air your most intimate thoughts. The food, however, is tempting and you can choose from a good range of wines. 1 Anne's La. (phone: 71-31-43).

Mitchell's – Situated in the cellar (where else!) of Mitchell's Wine Merchants, this is where swinging Dubliners lunch. The menu is somewhat limited, but the helpings are large, the cooking quite good, and the desserts mouth-watering. Alas, it's not open in the evenings. Get there before 12:30, or you'll find yourself in for a long wait at lunchtime (which you can while away by sampling some of Mitchell's splendid wines). 21 Kildare St. (phone: 68-03-67).

EDINBURGH

Beautiful and famous metropolises like Rome or San Francisco may be built on hills, but Edinburgh, a stark and in some ways still medieval city whose streets have often flowed with blood, has the distinction of being built on extinct volcanoes.

Astride one of these, high above the houses where Edinburgh's 436,271 inhabitants dwell, looms Edinburgh Castle, a portentous fairy-tale structure that often causes visitors to gasp for breath the first time they see it. It seems almost supernatural, with ancient stonemasonry rising out of volcanic rock as if there were no dividing line between the two.

From the seventh century onward there was a fortress where Edinburgh Castle now stands, and as life in the Middle Ages became more civilized, life within the fortress spilled over onto the long sloping ridge — carved by glaciers ages after the volcanic era — that runs downward from Edinburgh Castle to the foot of Arthur's Seat, another extinct volcano crowning Edinburgh's central park. The ridge, with its clusters of high stone and wood tenements, its one thin, snakelike public street, its cathedral, and its tollbooth was and still is the securing knot at the center of Scotland's legal, commercial, and artistic fiber.

Walking around central Edinburgh today is sheer joy. You don't even need a map; you can't go wrong. Every time you come to a hilltop you see a glorious, sweeping fusion of earth, sky, and sea, and every time you look up an alley you see fantastic steeples, jagged, smoking, chimney-potted skylines, or beauteous rotund domes. The city lights its most imposing public buildings at night, and they are legion, spread out over a series of precipices and valleys. Nature provides incredible sunsets, the product of Scotland's unique slowly fading evening light (the "gloaming") and rapid change in the evening temperature. Legend and romance are at every hand. Somebody famous lived in almost any residence you pass.

At the head of the legend-and-romance brigade are arch-Presbyterian John Knox and Mary, Queen of Scots, who together dominated life in the Edinburgh of the late sixteenth century. (Not that they dominated it together. When Mary arrived in Edinburgh in the autumn of 1561 as Scotland's very young and very Catholic new queen, Knox described the event in his diary as God having fouled the air with black fog and seeping rain.) The political and religious strife attendant upon Mary's reign is notorious, as are her two marriages and the three deaths associated with them, the last of these her own (she was beheaded by her cousin Queen Elizabeth I of England, to whom she had fled for asylum). Mary lived in Holyrood Palace, by the abbey at the base of Arthur's Seat. John Knox lived up the ridge from her near St Giles's

Cathedral within the city gates. Both residences are extant and open to the public today.

Their Edinburgh reached its full flower around the end of the seventeenth century, when the tenements along the ridge had grown 15 (or more) tottering stories high and housed uncounted numbers of people, all of whom threw their garbage into the central street, warning those below with nothing more than the terse cry *"Gardez-loo!"* Buildings frequently collapsed. Water could be had only from one of the city's six wells, called *pennywells* (their sites are still marked today), and inhabitants would line up with buckets from 3 AM on to be sure of some water. If you were rich enough, you paid someone to get your water for you. These cramped and malodorous conditions, plus a plethora of alehouses and a police force made up of decrepit Highlanders back from European wars, no doubt had something to do with the locals' favorite sport, rioting on fete days, parade days, and the king's birthday. Riots occasioned by more serious events were frequent also and occurred regularly in every age up to the Victorian and even beyond. Famous instances are the assassination of a wealthy councillor, John MacMorran, by dissatisfied youths at the Royal High School (sixteenth century); "Cleanse the Causeway," a battle in the streets between two noble families, the Douglases and Hamiltons (seventeenth century); the Jenny Geddes affair, in which a Presbyterian fishwife caused pandemonium by throwing a stool at a dean who was reading the new Episcopal service book in St. Giles's Cathedral (the first event in the British Civil War, seventeenth century); the Porteous Riots, immortalized by Sir Walter Scott in *The Heart of Midlothian* (eighteenth century); and the trial of William Burke, whose sale of his victims' corpses to the University of Edinburgh's medical luminaries did so much to further the international reputation of that great institution (nineteenth century). Religious riots have scarred the city's history repeatedly, although the last one was back in the 1930s.

Obviously this wizened medieval town had to spread out somehow, and luckily, in the second half of the eighteenth century, its by now thoroughly Protestant God sent it an increase in trade and prosperity. City fathers erected a wealth of new buildings on another ridge to the north — known as the New Town, connected to the Old Town by bridges. The classically proportioned beauty of New Town buildings, many of which were designed by the world-renowned British architect Robert Adam, is a testament to what is generally regarded as Edinburgh's golden age, part of the so-called Scottish Enlightenment. It was a great age not only for architects but for writers, publishers, philosophers, and politicians. Throughout the city, taverns became seminars. Among many other well-known people of the time, David Hume, Adam Smith, and James Boswell were Edinburgh men.

Today's Edinburgh has lost some of its traditional vibrancy and color, though it is certainly safer and cleaner. The near stranglehold the Presbyterian Church of Scotland attained on the social institutions during Queen Victoria's reign meant that industriousness, temperance, and respectability — the middle-class virtues — took supreme command of the city. About 60% of the present inhabitants are white-collar workers, an unusual proportion which helps keep the local flavor staid.

Nonetheless, signs are that things are livening up. In the last 3 years an avalanche of trendy pubs, nightspots, discos, and restaurants has shattered the city's sober air. Edinburgh has always been favored by geography, situated as it is on the Firth of Forth, an inlet in the North Sea, and surrounded by woods, rolling hills, and lochs (lakes). It is not only a national capital but a port whose chief exports include whisky, coal, and machinery; a large brewing center; and a center for nuclear and electronics research. And though the idea of a Scottish Assembly at Edinburgh—favored by a majority of Scottish voters—was set aside on a technicality a few years ago, a groundswell of agitation for Scotland's greater control of her own affairs remains. Who can say whether Edinburgh's second golden age is at hand? Perhaps not all its volcanoes are extinct.

EDINBURGH AT-A-GLANCE

SEEING THE CITY: Edinburgh has many wonderful views; on a clear day you can see for miles in all directions from the top of any of its extinct volcanoes. To the north lies the sparkling Firth of Forth and, beyond it, the ancient kingdom of Fife. To the south are the lovely Pentland Hills and surrounding plowed farmlands. Look eastward, where the giant Bass Rock, off the coast of Berwickshire, meets your eye. Look westward, and you can see across the whole nation to Ben Lomond, nearly on the west coast of Scotland! If you have a car, drive up Arthur's Seat (the road begins just by Holyrood Palace), park at Dunsapie Loch, and walk to the uppermost height (a steep and furzy climb — wear flat shoes and watch out for falling sheep). If you have no car, see the city from Edinburgh Castle.

SPECIAL PLACES: The "Royal Mile" is the name given to the oldest part of the city, the road that runs downhill from Edinburgh Castle to Holyrood Palace. It comprises four contiguous streets: Castle Hill, the Lawnmarket, High Street, and the Canongate. Since the entire citizenry of Edinburgh lived and worked for centuries either on or just off these four streets, the Royal Mile is practically groaning with objects and sites of historic fascination: sixteenth- and seventeenth-century houses, well preserved, with their adjacent courtyards and closes; residences of famous writers and distinguished thinkers; St. Giles's Cathedral, the High Kirk of Edinburgh, with its seventeenth-century spire in the shape of the Scottish crown; excellent museums; the classical City Chambers; and the building where Scotland's Parliament met from 1639 until union with England's in 1707.

THE ROYAL MILE

Edinburgh Castle – The oldest building in Edinburgh is part of the castle structure, a tiny ethereal chapel built by Queen Margaret, the wife of the Malcolm who features in *Macbeth*. King James VI of Scotland (later James I of England) was born here. The Scottish Regalia, including Sceptre and Crown, are on display. These disappeared after the union of Scotland with England and were found, over a hundred years later, by Sir Walter Scott (who was leading a government commission appointed to look for them) in an old locked box. Emotion ran so high that his daughter, who was present on the occasion, fainted when he lifted the lid. Also in the castle is the Scottish National War Memorial, honoring Scots who died in the two world wars.

Outlook Tower Visitor Centre – A short distance east of the castle, climb up 98 steps, walk outside, and find yourself face to face with church spires. The camera obscura, actually a periscope, throws a revolving image of nearby streets and buildings onto a circular table, while one of the tower's denizens gives an excellent historical talk. Downstairs is a very good book shop carrying everything from Lady Antonia Fraser's best-selling biography of Mary, Queen of Scots, to gleaming coffee-table volumes about one of the national obsessions, Scotch whisky. Open daily, 9:30 AM to early evening. Admission charge. Castle Hill (phone: 226-3709).

Parliament House – Built between 1632 and 1640, after Charles I suggested it replace the Collegiate buildings of St. Giles's Cathedral, this historic sanctum once housed Scotland's Parliament and is today the country's supreme court. Until 1982 tourists could enter only by written permission. Its showpiece is the Great Hall, with a fine hammer-beam roof and walls laden with portraits by Raeburn and other famous Scottish artists. Closed Saturdays through Mondays. Upper High St. (phone: 225-2595).

St. Giles's Cathedral – A church of some sort has stood here for over 1,000 years. The medieval building here was named for the Athenian saint Egidius (Giles). St. Giles's has often been showered by flying religious fur, especially at the time of the Reformation. In 1559–60 soldiers were put on guard at the church and many of its treasures hidden in private Catholic homes; Protestant nobles nonetheless ravaged the altars. Later, English troops came to their aid and, using ropes and ladders, stripped St. Giles's from top to bottom. It was at this stage that John Knox, a prime mover in this sequence of events, was made minister of St. Giles's. His unmarked grave is believed to be somewhere under the cobbles of Parliament Square, just outside St. Giles's. Open daily. Upper High St. (phone: 225-4363).

The Mercat Cross, or Market Cross – Near the east door of St. Giles's stands a monument erected by W. E. Gladstone, prime minister of Britain off and on from 1868 to 1894. Here was the crossroads at which proclamations were read out and public hangings took place, at least until well into the eighteenth century. It was also the commercial focal point of old Edinburgh, the place being so thick with butchers, bakers, merchants, burgesses, lawyers, tinkers, tailors, farmers, drovers, and fishmongers that the town council issued ordinances requiring each trade to occupy its own separate neighboring street or close (hence the names you see on the entrances to the closes as you go down the Royal Mile: Fleshmarket Close, Advocates' Close, and so on). City tradesmen never obeyed these ordinances, however, and the Mercat Cross remained as colorful as ever until the city began to spread out in the second half of the eighteenth century. High St., by St. Giles's.

Advocates' Close and Anchor Close – These are typical of the many narrow alleys that gave access to the inns and taverns that were so much a part of Edinburgh's eighteenth-century cultural life. Doors to these places (taverns no longer) were topped by stone architraves dating from the sixteenth century and bearing inscriptions like "Blissit Be God of Al His Gifts" or "Spes Altera Vitae" (these two examples are still in Advocates' Close today, neglected by city guidebooks, longing for you to admire them). In Anchor Close was Dawnay Douglas's, where the poet Robert Burns habitually drank. Entrances to both closes are from High St.

John Knox's House – Legend says that Scotland's fieriest preacher of all time lived here, but historians say no. However, legend has won out and this attractive fifteenth-century dwelling was preserved when most of its neighbors were razed during the widening of High Street in 1849. Closed Sundays. Admission charge. 45 High St. (phone: 556-6961).

Acheson House – When King Charles I was crowned at Edinburgh in 1633, Sir Archibald Acheson, baronet, was his secretary of state. Acheson built this house, a small courtyard mansion, the only one of its kind in Edinburgh, in the same year. It was the height of elegance in its day, yet 100 years later it had become a popular brothel and 200 years after that was inhabited by 14 families, though it had been built to house one. Communist Party members met in secret in its drawing room in the early 1930s.

It was bought and restored by the marquess of Bute in 1935, whereupon, despite its history, it was leased to the Canongate Kirk for a manse! Today it houses the Scottish Craft Centre, where you can buy all sorts of attractive, handmade items. Closed Sundays and Mondays. Free. 140 the Canongate (phone: 556-8136).

Canongate Kirkyard – You'll see this opposite Acheson House. Pause long enough to read the long list — which the city has mounted on a plaque — of notables buried there. The Canongate.

Scottish Stone and Brass Rubbing Centre – You can rub any of the brasses or stones on show, no experience necessary. Materials are provided for a fee that probably won't come to over £4. The brass commemorating Robert Bruce, king of Scotland from 1306 to 1329, is magnificent. And your own finished products will make beautiful gifts. Open daily except Sundays. Canongate Tollbooth Annex, 163 Canongate (phone: 225-1131).

Holyrood Palace – A royal retreat since the beginning of the sixteenth century, the palace is where Queen Elizabeth II stays when she is in residence in Edinburgh today. It is made of stone, a huge, imposing round-towered edifice befitting kings and queens. Most of what you see of it now was built by Charles II from 1671, but it is chiefly associated with Mary, Queen of Scots, who lived in it well before that for six contentious, sensational years. The old part, still extant, contains her bedroom and the supper room in which David Riccio, her secretary, was brutally murdered before her very eyes by a gang of armed men that included her jealous husband, her cousin Lord Darnley. By the side of the palace, within its spacious grounds, are the picturesque ruins of Holyrood Abbey and the lodge known as Queen Mary's Bath House, where the eminent lady reputedly bathed in red wine. A guide will take you through it all, sparing no gory details. Closed Sundays November through March. Admission charge. Closed when the queen is in town. At the bottom of the Canongate (phone: 556-7371).

BEYOND THE ROYAL MILE

Princes Street Gardens – Princes Street is modern Edinburgh's Main Street, its Broadway, and its Fifth Avenue. The gardens stretch nearly the street's whole length on the south side, where the old Nor' Loch, which was used in medieval times as the castle moat, once stood. The city spends thousands of pounds every year to keep the gardens opulent with flowers. In summer months (June-September) there are concerts, children's shows, variety acts, and do-it-yourself Scottish country dancing (to professional bands) here. Gates close at dusk. Princes St.

National Gallery of Scotland – Smack in the middle of Princes Street Gardens, on a man-made embankment called the Mound, is this exquisite museum, opened in 1859. It contains paintings by British and European masters from the fourteenth century to Cézanne. Open daily. Free. The Mound (phone: 556-8921).

Scott Monument – Sir Walter Scott is certainly one of Edinburgh's favorite sons — his face even decorates all Bank of Scotland notes, even though he was the most famous bankrupt in Scottish history (he wrote the Waverley novels to retrieve his losses). The elaborate 200-foot Gothic-style monument on the east end of Princes Street Gardens helps make Edinburgh's skyline the ornamental marvel it is. Its 287 steps take you to the summit. (Don't attempt it if you suffer vertigo.) Closed weekends. Admission charge. Princes St. (phone: 225-2424, ext. 6607).

The New Town – To the north of Princes Street lies the largest neoclassical townscape in Europe, built between the 1760s and 1830s. Assiduous conservation means that little has changed externally in these streets, squares, and crescents. Three of the more interesting ones are Charlotte Square (designed by Robert Adam), Moray Place, and Ann Street. The New Town Conservation Centre (13A Dundas St.; phone: 556-7054), arranges guided tours of the area; closed weekends.

The Georgian House – On the most spacious, gracious square in the elegant New Town, the National Trust for Scotland has furnished a house in period style and opened it to the public. The kitchen is especially remarkable, a wonderland of now-defunct utilitarian objects that would have belonged to a typical high-income late-eighteenth-century ménage. Fascinating audiovisual sessions on the history and topography of the New Town come with the admission price. Open daily April through October; weekends only November to mid-December; closed mid-December through March. 7 Charlotte Square (phone: 226-5922).

Edinburgh Zoo – Opposite the Pentland Hills, away from the city center, en route to the western suburb of Corstorphine, you'll find a zoo with a view and the world's most famous penguins, the largest colony in captivity. Every afternoon at 3:30, from April to October, they perform their delightful Penguin Parade through the park grounds. Open daily. Admission fee. Corstorphine Rd., Murrayfield (phone: 334-9171).

The Grassmarket – This wide and ancient street is flanked by a weird conglomeration of cozy eateries, elegant shops, and seedy-looking flophouses. It was the scene of the public hangings of Edinburgh commonfolk (the famous were hanged at the Mercat Cross) and of city fairs. Leading off Grassmarket are two streets of note: West Bow, which has some intriguing boutiques, and Cowgate, where stands the sixteenth-century Magdalen Chapel, a jewel of a church (you'll have to phone the caretaker to arrange to see it: 225-1836).

Dean Village – This 800-year-old grain milling town on the Water of Leith is a quiet haven over 100 feet below the level of much of the rest of the city. In summer the woodland walk along the river is popping with earth-loving bohemians who live in the next village downstream, Stockbridge. The whole area is a fine place to soak up local color, calm down, or cool off. End of Bell's Brae (turn left off Queensferry St. onto Bell's Brae as you approach Dean Bridge from the west end of Princes St.).

- **EXTRA SPECIAL:** The Edinburgh International Festival is held every year during the last 2 weeks in August and the first week in September. It features the best-known, most highly regarded performers of our time in opera, music, theater, and dance. Each year brings different orchestras, soloists, theater and opera companies — all are absolutely top-notch.

  Accompanying the festival proper is the phenomenal Edinburgh Festival Fringe, an orgy of over 300 productions by amateur and lesser-known professional companies from Europe, Britain, and the US who come to Edinburgh at their own expense to strike a blow for art and for themselves. Perhaps the most celebrated Fringe success story was Tom Stoppard's *Rosenkrantz and Guildenstern Are Dead.*

  And the Edinburgh Military Tattoo, a spectacular concert in full Highland dress by the massed pipe bands of Her Majesty's Scottish regiments, blasts forth most nights during the festival on the Castle Esplanade.

  Those interested are advised to reserve tickets — and hotel space — as far in advance as possible, especially for the most popular attractions such as the Tattoo. Bookings open January 1 for the Tattoo and in late April for the international festival — a detailed festival brochure is available by April from the BTA. You can reserve through a travel agent or write directly to the individual events. For the international festival, it's the Festival Box Office, 21 Market St., Edinburgh EH1 1BW (phone: 226-4001); for the Tattoo, the Tattoo Office, 1 Cockburn St., Edinburgh, EH1 1QB (phone: 225-1188); and the Edinburgh Festival Fringe Society is at 170 High St. (phone: 226-5257).

SOURCES AND RESOURCES

The Scottish Tourist Board, 5 Waverley Bridge (phone: 332-2433 or 226-6591), offers information, guidebooks, maps, leaflets, and all City of Edinburgh publications. On sale there is *Restaurants in Edinburgh* and the *Official Guide to the City and District*, updated annually. It's your best bet in local city guides. In it is a reasonable working map of downtown areas, with places of interest marked. A good, more detailed map is the Edinburgh number of the *Geographia Street Atlas and Index* series, on sale at most local bookshops. The pamphlets on Edinburgh history and legend at the *Camera Obscura* bookshop (see *Special Places*) will add greatly to your appreciation of what you see of the city. Each costs about $3.

For Local Coverage – The *Scotsman*, morning daily; the *Edinburgh Evening News*, evening daily; *What's On*, published monthly by the city, listing forthcoming happenings for every given day; another *What's On*, a free, privately owned monthly, available in most hotel lobbies; *Teletourist Service*, recorded daily telephone prospectus from April through September (phone: 246-8041). Also see the *Festival Times*, during the Edinburgh Festival.

GETTING AROUND: You can walk from the Royal Mile into the Grassmarket or to Princes Street and from there to Dean Village and the New Town.
Bus – City Transport Headquarters is at 14 Queen St. (phone: 554-4494), parallel to Princes St. two blocks away. Route maps and timetables are available from their information office at the Air Terminal on Waverly Bridge. You can go anywhere by bus from Princes Street — if you have exact fare. The Tourist Board office has details of bus tours of the city and countryside. Longer-distance buses go from St. Andrew's Square Bus Station, St. Andrew's Square (phone: 556-8231).

Taxi – There are cabstands at St. Andrew's Square Bus Station and in Waverley Station, off Princes St. Or phone City Cabs (phone: 228-1211) or Central Radio Taxis (phone: 229-5221).

Car Rental – All major national firms are represented.

MUSEUMS: The city runs three museums of local history: *Huntly House*, the Canongate (phone: 556-5813); *Canongate Tollbooth*, the Canongate (phone: 556-5813); and *Lady Stair's House* (a Burns, Scott, and Stevenson museum), Lawnmarket (phone: 225-8160). The *Scottish National Gallery* is described in *Special Places*. Other museums of note are:

The Scottish National Portrait Gallery/The National Museum of Antiquities – These museums are on two sides of one building. 1 Queen St. (phone: 556-8921).

The Scottish National Gallery of Modern Art – Matisse to Picasso, in the city's lovely Royal Botanical Gardens. Inverleith Row (phone: 332-3754).

The Royal Scottish Museum – A museum of natural history, science, and technology, great for kids. Chambers St. (phone: 225-7534).

The Edinburgh Wax Museum – With every notorious Scot from Macbeth to Billy Connolly. 142 High St. (phone: 226-4444).

Museum of Childhood – Antique toys, games, dolls, and costumes, all beautifully explained and arranged. 38 High St. (phone: 556-5447).

The DeMarco Gallery – Headquarters for avant-garde art. 32 High St. (phone: 557-0707).

Lauriston Castle – A sixteenth-century home entirely decorated with Edwardian antiques. Off Cramond Rd. S (phone: 336-1243).

EDINBURGH / Sources and Resources

SHOPPING: Princes Street is Edinburgh's main shopping street. The best buy by far is in clothes and fabrics, particularly Scottish tartans and woolens. Also worth at least a look are antiques — particularly Victoriana — in the area around St. Stephen's Street in Stockbridge. Bone china and Scottish crystal are attractive, and don't miss the shortbread, which is on sale just about everywhere. We especially recommend the following shops:

Jenner's Department Store – Sells everything, especially bone china and Scottish crystal. Princes and St. David's sts. (phone: 225-2442).

Janet Lumsden – Antique silver, jewelry, glass, and porcelain. 51A George St. (phone: 225-2911).

The Scotch House – This is the place for classy, expensive woolens such as kilts, sweaters, tweeds, scarves, shawls, and mohairs. 60 Princes St. (phone: 226-5271).

Jan Struther – Rare, pre-Victorian *objêts d'art*. 13 Randolph Pl. (phone: 225-7985).

The Woollen Mill – A good, inexpensive alternative to the Scotch House at 139 Princes St. (phone: 226-3840); 453 Lawnmarket (phone: 225-1525); and 51 High St. (phone: 556-9786).

Debenham's – A branch of the London firm, with clothes, accessories, cosmetics, and more. 105–107 Princes St. (phone: 225-1320).

Pitlochry Knitwear – Bargains in Scottish products, especially sweaters, kilts, and ladies' suits. 26 North Bridge (phone: 225-3893).

SPECIAL EVENTS: The *Edinburgh International Festival* and its overflow the *Edinburgh Festival Fringe* are held every year for three weeks starting in mid-August. (For details, see *Extra Special.*) The *Edinburgh Folk Festival*, an increasingly important annual event, occurs in March. (For details, contact the Folk Festival office, 170 High St., Edinburgh EH1 1QS; phone: 226-3645.)

SPORTS: Golfing – Golfing is Scotland's national mania. The game was invented in Edinburgh in 1457. A letter from your home club president or pro will get you into any of the city's 22 courses (you'll only need it for the posh ones like *Royal Burgess, Bruntsfield*, both in suburban Barnton, and *Muirfield* in nearby Gullane). Clubs can be rented. Full details on all courses are in a booklet called *Scotland: Home of Golf*, on sale at the Tourist Board office.

Skiing – *Hillend Ski Center* on the Pentland Hills is the largest artificial slope in Britain. Equipment for hire. Open daily 9:30 AM to 9 PM, weekends May through August 10 AM to 5 PM (phone: 445-4433).

Swimming – Have a dip in the luxurious *Royal Commonwealth Pool*, built for the 1970 Commonwealth Games. Open weekdays 9 AM to 9 PM, Saturdays and Sundays 10 AM to 4 PM. Dalkeith Rd. (phone: 667-7211). For other sports, consult your Edinburgh *Official Guide*.

THEATER: The *King's*, 2 Leven St. (phone: 229-4840), and the *Lyceum*, Grindlay St. (phone: 229-9697), are Edinburgh's two main venues. Most of their offerings could be described as mainstream mediocre. The *Playhouse*, 20 Greenside Pl. (phone: 557-2590), is a converted cinema where variety acts and musical productions are staged. *The Traverse*, 112 West Bow (phone: 226-2633), a private theater club with an avant-garde image and a much higher standard, sometimes opens its doors to the public. *The Netherbow*, 43 High St. (phone: 556-9579), and *Theatre Workshop*, 43 Hamilton Pl., mount small-scale, artistic productions. See the dailies for schedules.

MUSIC: Classical music is the city's overriding passion. High-brow musical events are held at Usher Hall, Lothian Rd. (phone: 228-1155), where the *Scottish National Orchestra* holds performances on Friday nights at 7:30. The *Scottish Opera Co.*, which has excellent standards, has frequent seasons at the *Playhouse* (see *Theater* for address) where other famous names in both classical and nonclassical music give concerts. Rock concerts are held at the *Playhouse* and the *Odeon Cinema*, 7 Clerk St. (phone: 667-7707). For chamber music try the *Queen's Hall*, Clerk St. (phone: 668-2117). At *St. Mary's Cathedral*, Palmerston Pl. (phone: 225-6293), evensong is sung on weekdays at 5:15 by a trained choir with boy sopranos. Also, countless amateur groups swell the city's halls and churches. For details on events, consult the dailies. Good jazz is on tap free at the popular pub *La Grenouille*, 24–28a Abercromby Pl. (phone: 556-8701), every evening but Sundays.

NIGHTCLUBS AND NIGHTLIFE: Edinburgh isn't exactly Las Vegas; it isn't even Philadelphia. Discos here are usually filled with a very young crowd, but you could risk the following if you're under 30: *Uptown* (it's classy and expensive), 25–27 Market St. (phone: 226-4224); *Millionaires*, 57 Frederick St. (phone: 225-3379); *Cinderellas Rockerfellas*, 99 St. Stephen St. (phone: 556-0266); *Valentino's* (for real local color), 3a E Fountainbridge (phone: 229-5151); and *Coasters Roller Disco* (teenagers leave at 11 PM so others can roll up to an after-hours bar), W Tollcross (phone: 229-5353). Jazz and folk music can be heard at bars and hotels around the city; check the *Evening News*'s "Nightlife" page or *What's On* magazine. *Calton Studios*, 24–26 Calton Rd. (phone: 556-7066), is a popular bar/snackery/cinema.

BEST IN TOWN

CHECKING IN: In Scotland it is practically impossible to get a room without an accompanying kippers-to-nuts Big Scottish Breakfast (you pay for it whether you eat it or not). Expect to shell out $90 and up for a double with breakfast in the hotels listed below as expensive; $70 to $90 for those in the moderate category; between $40 and $60 for the cheapies-but-goodies in the inexpensive range. Unless otherwise noted, hotels accept all major credit cards. Should you find it impossible to get into any of our selected hotels, the Scottish Tourist Board at the airport, and in town at 5 Waverley Bridge (phone: 226-6591), has an accommodations service covering all of Edinburgh and district.

The George – Indubitably the best in town. It is in the New Town between Charlotte and St. Andrew's squares and is known for its comfort. It has 212 bedrooms, two dining rooms, two bars. Phones in rooms. 19–21 George St. (phone: 225-1251). Expensive.

The Caledonian – An elephantine Edwardian railroad hotel with 212 rooms, three dining rooms, and three bars. Celebrities love it. Phones in rooms. West end of Princes St. (phone: 225-2433). Expensive.

Dalhousie Castle – Originally built in the twelfth century and added onto ever since (Queen Victoria once stayed here). Now it's a luxury country-house hotel with 25 rooms. About 8 miles south of Edinburgh (phone: Gorebridge 20153). Expensive.

The Post House – An ultramodern, all-conveniences affair, this is a good place to be if you have a car (it's beside the zoo, out of the city center). Its low-priced coffee house is less stuffily British than almost anywhere else. Breakfast optional. It has 208 rooms, all with phones. Corstorphine Rd. (phone: 334-8221). Expensive.

Braid Hills Hotel – Muriel Spark fans will remember that this is where Miss Jean Brodie, by then past her prime, took tea. An old established family-run hotel in the southern suburbs toward the Pentland Hills. 134 Braid Rd. (phone: 447-8888). Moderate.

The Howard – Its flower-filled window boxes are the last word in winsomeness. It has 26 rooms, with phones (and, surprisingly for a hotel this size, private baths). 32–36 Great King St. (phone: 556-1393). Moderate.

Melville Castle – This was the family seat of "King Harry the Ninth" or Henry Dundas, the first Viscount Melville, the Tory Lord Advocate who ruled Scotland from Westminster almost single-handedly by a system of patronage in the late eighteenth and early nineteenth centuries. It's superbly romantic and highly historic. It has 23 rooms, all with phones. No credit cards. In the village of Lasswade, about 6 miles south of Edinburgh (phone: 663-6634) — ask for directions. Moderate to inexpensive.

The Donmaree – This sweet little family hotel in a respectable suburb has 20 rooms. 21 Mayfield Gardens (phone: 667-3641). Moderate to inexpensive.

Galloway Guest House – Not as well equipped as the *Donmaree,* but more centrally located, just off the panoramic Dean Bridge. Guests have limited access to the kitchen; the nine rooms have no phones. No credit cards. 22 Dean Park Crescent (phone: 332-3672). Inexpensive.

EATING OUT: Reports on Scottish food vary from calling it a joke to claiming it is at least superior to the English. You might want to try some of the following specialties: cock-a-leekie soup (chicken and leek), salmon, haddock, trout, and Aberdeen Angus steak. Scones originated in Scotland, and shortbread shouldn't be missed. Only the restaurants in our inexpensive category serve food continuously throughout the day and evening; others keep the city's formal hours (lunch until 2:30, dinner anywhere from 6). Expect to pay $50 and up for dinner for two, excluding wine and tips, in establishments listed as expensive; $30 to $50 in moderate establishments; and $30 and under in inexpensive places.

Prestonfield House – A 300-year-old country estate within its own peacock-laden park grounds. Candlelit dinners in rooms with tapestries, paintings, and blazing open fires. French cooking. Reservations necessary. Off Priestfield Rd. (phone: 667-8000). Expensive.

Mermans – This small immensely popular seafood restaurant changes its menu seasonally. The décor is French provincial, but the crowd is a mixed bag — artists, tourists, and businesspeople. Reservations recommended. Closed Mondays and Saturday lunch; closed Sundays September to April. 8–10 Eyre Pl. (phone: 556-1177). Expensive.

Cosmo's – The nearest thing in the city to Rome since the Roman Catholic cathedral. Everybody who works here is sunnily Italian, as is the menu. Fabulous seafoods and veal, and a cocktail bar built of imported Italian marble. Reservations necessary. Closed Sundays and Mondays. 58A Castle St. (phone: 226-6743). Expensive.

The Howtowdie – White tablecloths and glass cases full of taxidermists' birds set the keynote at this Highland-style establishment long famed for its ritzy image and traditional Scottish cooking. Reservations necessary. Closed Sundays. 27a Stafford St. (phone: 225-6291). Expensive.

Beehive Inn – Among the fittings in this Old Town restaurant is a cell door from the very old town jail. Steaks and fish are served from an open charcoal grill and are followed by luscious puddings. Closed Sundays. 18 Grassmarket (phone: 225-7171). Expensive.

298 EDINBURGH / Best in Town

Denzler's – Swiss staff and cuisine, the finest wines, ultramodern decor, and droll menu (try their luscious Black Forest Gâteau — no, it isn't baked trolls with cream, it's chocolate cake). Reservations necessary. Closed Sundays. 80 Queen St. (phone: 226-5467). Expensive.

North British Hotel – Eat here for authentic Scottish cuisine, served up in a rustic basement called the *Cleikum Restaurant*. Try their "Edinburgh fog" for dessert, a sumptuous confection made of Drambuie and fresh cream. 1 Princes St. (phone: 556-2414). Moderate.

Shamiana – Tandoori (Indian) food at its finest. Everything is cooked fresh from scratch with a heady potpourri of delicate spices. Pale pink tablecloths, bone china, waitresses in saris give the place a rarefied air. Reservations necessary. Open evenings only, closed Sundays. 14A Brougham St. (phone: 229-5578). Moderate.

Edinburgh Rendezvous – Lovers of Chinese cooking should make for this pleasant, dimly lit dining parlor. Reservations necessary. 10A Queensferry St. (phone: 225-3777). Moderate.

Madog's – Here you'll find American fare (steaks, salads, baked potatoes) in a setting of wicker chairs, potted palms, pop music, and big glossy photos of Hollywood heroes, gangsters, and molls. Reservations necessary at lunchtime and Friday and Saturday nights. Closed Sundays October through May. 38a George St. (phone: 225-3408). Moderate to inexpensive.

Nimmo's – The bistro here serves homemade steak pies for lunch and has candlelit Continental meals at night. There's a charming wine bar for pub-lunchers, too. Reservations necessary for the bistro. Closed Sundays. 101 Shandwick Pl. (phone: 229-6119). Moderate to inexpensive.

Henderson's Salad Table – This cafeteria-style vegetarian's heaven-on-earth may keep you standing in line for as long as 15 minutes, but it's worth it. Piles of salads, hot pots, opulent desserts. Closed Sundays, except during Festival. 94 Hanover St. (phone: 225-3400). Inexpensive.

Duncan's Land – This salad bar, in a lovely seventeenth-century house, has light country-French cooking. On Sundays crêpe suzettes are served continuously from 11 AM to 5 PM. Closed Mondays. Gloucester St. (phone: 225-1037). Inexpensive.

Doric Tavern – Lots of traffic suffuses this busy little haven that has a tasty international menu, arguably the best value in town for the money. Reservations necessary. Closed Sundays. 15 Market St. (phone: 225-1084). Inexpensive.

The Arches – The dining room adjoining this bustling university-area bar has very good fresh breaded-fish lunches and suppers. Closed Sundays. 66–67 South Bridge (phone: 556-0200). Inexpensive.

SHARING A PINT: Until recently, boozing was restricted to puritanical hours. Now you can imbibe from 11 AM to 11 PM, and a few places have opened up where the taps keep flowing until the wee hours. Among the best pubs: *Bannerman's*, 53–57 Niddry St. (phone: 556-3254), in a newly excavated sixteenth-century stone house lined with plants and old brandy casks, has been the "in" place to drink since its splashy all-night launching party during the 1980 Edinburgh International Festival; the *Abbotsford*, 3 Rose St. (phone: 225-5276), is a haunt of Scotland's "Makars" (playwrights and poets) and journalists; *Bennett's*, Leven St. (phone: 229-5143), is a noisy but atmospheric theater-district pub with a Victorian hangover; the *Beau Brummel*, 99 Hanover St. (phone: 225-4680), is a neo-Regency plush artifact in mid-city; and the *Tilted Wig*, 3 Cumberland St. (phone: 556-1824), facetiously known as the "Wilted Twig," is notable for its uncompromising trendiness and has a clientele of bar-hogging English smoothies, whom you can scatter at a stroke by standing in the doorway shouting, "Nigel, your MG's on fire!"

GALWAY

The ancient port city of Galway hangs on to a romantic past that has been seasoned as much by myth as by reality. It isn't the glory of the early Gaelic kingdoms that haunts the local folk memory so much as the swashbuckling days of the Spanish Main. It was then that the prevailing sou'westerlies speeded tall ships toward Galway from the ports of Spain. In the fifteenth and sixteenth centuries, the two places were engaged in a rich, bustling commerce and the image of noble Spanish *hidalgos* swaggering through the cobbled streets of Galway still burns bright in the imagination.

Galway is proud of its medieval Spanish connection, almost to the point of forgetting that the really potent influence in shaping the city was Anglo-Norman. The citizenry sees the hand of Spain everywhere, and indeed some of the old back-street town houses and courtyards are faintly reminiscent of things *español*. Down near the docks, the celebrated Spanish Arch is an extension of the fortress walls that protected the old city and likely got its name from the Spanish sailors who once frequented the nearby alehouses.

Galway nurtures the fables of a colorful past in other ways. Its most famous legend is that of the mayor who hanged his own son. This archetype of the stern father was one James Lynch Fitzstephen who, in 1493, condemned his son Walter as a murderer. Apparently, Walter had killed a visiting Spaniard for stealing his girlfriend. So popular was Walter throughout Galway that no one could be found to hang him, so the father had to do it himself. A stone memorial window marks the execution spot today. Even though gray-bearded historians have debunked this story in modern times, the stone window still stands and most Galwegians are loyal to the legend.

There's a stronger ring of truth to another much-told story, that of Christopher Columbus discovering Galway before he ever clapped a weather eye on America. It is held that he called here and prayed in St. Nicholas's Church, en route to the uncharted western seas. It might be considered an auspicious stopping-off place for any would-be discoverer, because this particular St. Nicholas was the patron saint of sea voyagers. Whatever the truth of the Columbus story, it is hard to shake the faith of Galway people in their own notable explorer and saint, Brendan. They and many other Irish people believe St. Brendan discovered the New World centuries before the Italian upstart. Naturally, Brendan sailed from Galway port.

Galway's origins go back long before the sixth-century St. Brendan and Christian times. There were settlements on its river in pagan days. The Irish for Galway is *Gaillimh* (pronounced GOLL-iv) and there's a legend that the name comes from a princess, Gaillimh, who was drowned in the river. Nowadays, the river is called the Corrib and its surging waters rushing into Galway Bay are the pulsing soul and spirit of the city. In summertime, legions of silver salmon swarm in from the Atlantic feeding grounds in response to the immemorial mating call and fight their way upriver to the headwaters where they were spawned. That used to be one of the more uplifting sights in Galway, and it still is in a way, though the salmon have been thinned out by pollution and the genocidal nets of the factory ships.

It was the Normans, and not the Spaniards or anyone else, who developed Galway into a thriving mercantile city. In the thirteenth century they hopscotched from Britain to Ireland with the help of a Pope and a traitorous Irish prince, and when their armies reached Galway they quickly subdued the native tribes, taking over the city. They built stout walls around it to keep out the wild Irish, and then, in a matter of decades, became more Irish than the Irish themselves. Much later, in the mid-seventeenth century, Cromwell smashed his iron fist on the city and reinforced the chains of conquest.

Galway became known as the City of the Tribes because of the 14 dynastic merchant families that controlled its wealth and fortune for several centuries. Outside the walls, across the river, the relics of the ancient Irish civilization survived in the fishing village called the Claddagh, which spreads out from Nimmo's Pier at the estuary of Galway Bay. Its thatched cottages have been torn down and replaced by drab, utilitarian homes, but it still manages to hold on to its own identity and remain aloof from Galway City.

From the middle of the nineteenth century until quite recently, Galway was a port for passenger liners plying the Atlantic between the United States and Europe. The passage was not always comfortable. During the potato famine of the 1840s, thousands of starving Irish peasants sailed from Galway to the New World aboard vessels whose abysmal conditions won them the chilling name "coffin ships."

Only in recent years has Galway become industrialized. It has grown in size in the past two decades and has ventured warily into the era of affluence. Progress has altered the leisurely rhythm of life in the city and introduced a more frantic tempo, but it's still a small town, really. The old-time charm lingers on particularly in its back streets and alleyways. It is there that in fanciful moments you can almost hear the thrum of Spanish guitars and the clack of Castilian castinets.

Well, why not?

GALWAY AT-A-GLANCE

SEEING THE CITY: There are no really great vantage points from which to get an overall view of Galway City. The best bet for a bird's-eye reconnoiter is from atop the *Great Southern Hotel,* which is right in the middle of things in front of the railway station on Eyre Square. From the *Claddagh Bar and Grill* in the penthouse you can look across the rooftops of the city and get a general feel of what it might be like out there. An inquiry at reception will get you up to the rooftop almost anytime (phone: 64041).

GALWAY / At-a-Glance

SPECIAL PLACES: Galway is a small town (population 30,000), so you can see just about everything worth seeing in a single day. What's more, you can do it on foot. A walk through the city streets — making sure not to miss out on those history-haunted back lanes — is highly recommended. Galway weather is infuriatingly temperamental and rain clouds are never far off, but even in the gentle drizzle of the famous Irish "soft day," you can set off with a mac and cover the whole town without risk of drowning. You might even walk out to Salthill, the seaside resort that's about 1.5 miles from downtown and where, if the clouds have decamped, you can catch one of the best views of the sun going down on Galway Bay.

Eyre Square – This is the heart of the city and the place you'll probably see first. It once was the Fair Green (where livestock and produce were sold), and is now named after one of the ruling merchant tribes, the Eyres. (Charlotte Brontë got the title of her famous novel when she saw the name Jane Eyre on a gravestone during a visit to Galway.) The original pastoral appearance of the green was destroyed by local authorities in an outrageous act of philistinism during the 1960s when they poured concrete sidewalks along its edges. The park within the square is named after John F. Kennedy in memory of his Galway visit. There's a fascinating statue of a quirky gnome of an Irish writer called Padraic O Conaire at the northern end. A splendid cut stone doorway of a type seen in the better homes of long ago also stands in the park, this one from the home of another of the tribes, the Brownes.

St. Nicholas's Church – This is the place where Columbus is said to have prayed before sailing off to discover America. Originally built by the Anglo-Normans in 1320, it was greatly added to down the centuries. After the Reformation, the church became the prize in a tug-of-war between Protestants and Catholics and changed hands a number of times before Cromwell's forces finally secured it for the Protestants. Outside the church, you can also wander through the country market that is set up on Saturday mornings. Market St.

Lynch Memorial Window – Just up the street from the church, this stone window marks the spot where the mayor of the city, James Lynch Fitzstephen, is supposed to have hanged his son Walter for murder in 1493. It isn't the actual window through which the luckless lad exited into the next world — it was carved some 200 years later. The hanging story is a good one but almost certainly untrue. Market St.

Lynch's Castle – The ubiquitous Lynch tribe that gave so many mayors to the city originally lived in this sixteenth-century building, regarded as the finest town castle in all Ireland. It's now a bank but has been lovingly restored and preserved. Shop St. at the intersection called the Four Corners.

Salmon Weir – The centuries-old salmon fishery is below the Salmon Weir Bridge opposite the new Catholic Cathedral. This is a pleasant place to pass an hour in summer watching the salmon on their way up to the spawning grounds.

Catholic Cathedral – On the site of a former jailhouse opposite the Salmon Weir Bridge, this is new, though inspired by Renaissance and other church architecture of the past. It is a big building but not remarkably lovely. Earl's Island.

Spanish Arch – The best-known landmark in Galway. The arch was built in 1594 as an addition to the old town wall and as protection for Spanish ships docking nearby to unload their wines. There's a museum now attached to the Arch (see *Sources and Resources*) through which you can climb to the top and look across the Corrib to the Claddagh. Beside Wolfe Tone Bridge where the river enters the sea.

The Claddagh – This district was originally a fishing village where the native Irish clung to their old culture in defiance of the usurping Anglo-Normans within the walls. Claddagh people no longer fish nor speak Irish, but they still proudly maintain a sense of separateness from the city. The famous Claddagh ring — two hands clasping a heart surmounted by a crown — was fashioned by local goldsmiths and was the traditional wedding band. Cross the Corrib at Wolfe Tone Bridge and you're in the Claddagh.

Salthill – Galway's seaside resort is really a part of the city, a mere 1.5 miles from downtown. Salthill has three sandy beaches on Galway Bay but invariably the weather is hostile to sunbathing and surfing. When the weather is good, the swimming is safe and there's no crowding on the beaches. The Leisureland complex which dominates the seafront has a huge heated indoor swimming pool and Coney Island–style amusements for children and adults. Southwest of Galway, reachable by frequent buses from Eyre Sq.

Franciscan Abbey – Built in 1836, the abbey is on the site of a thirteenth-century friary that was founded by the De Burgos (Burkes), the first Norman lords of Galway. St. Francis St.

University College – The original building, completed in 1849, was modeled in neo-Gothic style on some of the colleges at Oxford. Built as a nondenominational institution, it was once condemned by the Catholic bishops as godless and Catholics were forbidden to attend, but they ignored the ban. Some interesting new buildings are going up on the part of the campus that adjoins the Corrib River. A small university, it has a friendly and unstuffy atmosphere — someone will always be glad to show you around. Main entrance to the campus is off University Rd. (phone: 7611).

■ **EXTRA SPECIAL:** Generally, Galway is a quiet place but it does have its moments. In the fall it lets down its hair and stages the closest approximation of *la dolce vita* you'll find in Ireland. This is the *Galway Oyster Festival,* held every year over a very long and vertiginous weekend in September. A most sybaritic occasion, it has many more temptations than the oysters everyone ostensibly comes to eat.

The organized events of the festival are rather expensive and must be booked in advance. It's also advisable to reserve a hotel room, especially if you plan to stay at the *Great Southern* — the center of the festival — or at any of the other better hotels in Galway. To attend all the events of the festival, from Friday night to Sunday morning, including a reception and dinner, festival banquet, lunch, oyster tasting, and recuperative Irish coffee "morning after," costs about $150 per sore head. This does not include hotel, nor does it include the heavy run on your pocket during a weekend of intensive socializing that involves much buying of booze. Count on an outlay of at least $350 for the weekend. For details, call the tourist office (phone: 63081) or write to Áras Fáilte, Eyre Sq., Galway.

Another festive occasion is *Galway Race Week,* beginning on the last Monday of July. This is a synonym for 6 days of heavy gambling on the ponies running at Ballybrit racetrack within walking distance of the city center. It also entails heroic drinking round the clock and heavy poker sessions in hotel bedrooms, all earthy and great fun even if you don't like horses.

Finally, don't leave Galway without visiting the Aran Islands (see *Connemara* tour, DIRECTIONS), and, oh, go ahead and take part in one of those medieval banquets in Dunguaire Castle (see *County Clare* tour, DIRECTIONS). Information on both of these is available from the tourist office.

SOURCES AND RESOURCES

For comprehensive information and advice, first go to the tourist office, Áras Fáilte, just south of the western side of Eyre Sq. During the summer, another office is open on the Promenade in Salthill (phone for either office: 63081). Pick up all of the free literature and maps including, when available, the Galway Junior Chamber of Commerce's listing of summer events in Galway and Salthill. A small booklet, *Tourist Trail of Old Galway,* describes a walking tour and costs 30p at the tourist office.

Hardiman's *History of Galway* is the definitive work on the city's past and can be

GALWAY / Sources and Resources

bought at the Connacht Tribune newspaper office on Market St. or at *Kenny's Bookshop,* High St. For more detailed sources, try the County Library in the Hynes Building, St. Augustine St.

For Local Coverage – Two weeklies, the *Connacht Tribune* and the *Connacht Sentinel,* and a giveaway, *The Galway Advertiser,* provide strictly local news.

GETTING AROUND: If the weather allows, you can walk all over the city without great stress.

Bus – The central departure point for all city buses is the west side of Eyre Sq. City bus service stops at 11:30 PM. Buses for points outside the city leave from the railway station behind the *Great Southern Hotel.* (The only trains leaving the station are for Dublin and intervening stops.) All buses and trains are run by CIE, which also operates touring coaches (phone: 62141).

Taxi – Plenty of cabs are available and they're not too costly. Go to the central cabstand on the north side of Eyre Sq. or phone 7888 or 66508.

Car Rental – It's best to pick up your car at the port of arrival in Ireland, usually Shannon or Dublin, where the major rental companies operate. *Avis* has a Galway office at the Áras Fáilte tourism office (phone: 68901).

MUSEUMS: Galway's only museum is the *Galway City Museum,* and though it's tiny, it houses a range of exhibits that highlight the city's past. A spiral staircase from the museum takes you onto the top of the Spanish Arch from which you can look across the Corrib to the Claddagh.

SHOPPING: Good values are to be found in native knitwear and homespun tweeds as well as Irish glass, bone china, Connemara marble, and other ornamental ware.

Blue Cloak Boutique – Fashions of the times at moderate cost. 31 Upper Abbeygate St. (phone: 7785).

Lydon Boutique – High-class, with-it fashions for smart young ladies. It's expensive, but you get value. Shop St. (phone: 66205).

Moon's Department Store – A large, American-style store stocking quality items. William St. (phone: 65254).

O'Maille's – Everything on view is wholesomely Irish — Aran sweaters, Donegal tweeds, and shapeless Connemara hats. Pricey but worth it. Dominick St. (phone: 62696).

Treasure Chest – Superior gift shop with many unusual things including classic Irish crocheted garments. Eglinton St. (phone: 63862).

SPECIAL EVENTS: The *Galway Oyster Festival* and *Galway Race Week* are held in September and July respectively. (See *Extra Special* for details.) The *Galway Arts Festival* takes place in May with classical music, poetry readings, art exhibitions, and theatrical happenings.

SPORTS: Boating and Sailing–Rowboats and outboards can be hired for trips up the Corrib River and into Lough Corrib, the big lake upstream. Contact *Frank Dolan,* 3 Riverside, Galway City (phone: 65841). In summer, Dolan also operates a water-bus from Woodquay, north of the courthouse, carrying passengers on daily, 3-hour sight-seeing tours of the lake. For all types of sailing on Galway Bay, contact the *Galway Bay Sailing Centre,* Rinville, Oranmore (phone: 84527).

Fishing – A license must be bought and a fee paid to fish for salmon at the weir, which has an international reputation among anglers. For details and booking, call the Galway Fishery (phone: 62388). There's free fishing for brown trout on Lough Corrib, but, again, you'll need a license if you're after salmon. Boats can be hired. Phone *Des Moran,* Knockferry Lodge, Knockferry, Rosscahill (phone: 80122), or the tourist office (phone: 63081). To go sea angling for shark, contact *Elmer Kavanagh,* 2 Victoria Pl., Galway City (phone: 64789).

Golfing – There's a challenging 18-hole course in Salthill where visitors are welcome (phone: 22169 or 21827).

Swimming – The beaches at Salthill are superb if the weather is good. If not, there's the indoor pool at *Leisureland* on the seafront in Salthill, open every day (phone: 21455).

THEATER: The *Druid Theatre,* Chapel La. (phone: 62212), stages traditional and avant-garde productions at irregular intervals, with both lunchtime and evening performances. Its summer season consists of plays by Irish writers, in English. There's an Irish-language theater — *An Taibhdhearc* (pronounced An THIGH-vark) — which has been producing plays in Irish for over 50 years. The emphasis during the tourist season is on traditional Irish music and dance interspersed with a short play in Irish, so heavily mimed that no knowledge of the language is needed. The theater is on Middle St. (phone: 62024) and performances take place on Mondays, Wednesdays, and Fridays during July and August.

MUSIC: There are no regular concerts apart from a classical season from late fall to early spring in the *Jesuit Hall* on Sea Rd. (phone: 65521). Jazz is hard to find but a not-bad Dixieland band blasts away some Sunday afternoons in the *Galway Bay Hotel,* Lower Salthill (phone: 64121). Traditional Irish music is heard in many pubs in Galway and Salthill and you'll have to consult local papers to keep track of these sessions.

NIGHTCLUBS AND NIGHTLIFE: The fact that there are no true nightclubs does not mean life ceases at midnight. Most hotels have drinking sessions until near dawn. Some bars, too, continue serving illegally after closing time (11:30 PM in summer, 11 PM in winter, except Sundays when it's an hour earlier) and discreet inquiry will gain you access to these. There are a number of late-night discos, mostly for young people (the generation gap has a higher threshold in Ireland and below 40 can be "young"), and again you'll have to check the local newspapers for what's happening where. The best permanent disco is *Fagins* in the basement of the *Great Southern Hotel,* Eyre Sq. (phone: 64041). In summer, most Salthill hotels have cabarets and discos.

SINS: Sin is acceptable in Galway as long as you don't take pleasure in it. A cautious step-by-step approach of considerable subtlety is advised in overtures to the opposite sex. Once you have won confidence, all is possible. Useful hint: A lot of drinking can be presumed in almost any social encounter in Galway, so if you can keep your alcohol level down, you will have a decided advantage over more drunken rivals. Galway has no red-light district.

BEST IN TOWN

CHECKING IN: The better hotels in Galway have become expensive though you still can find some moderately priced ones that are good. A few have adopted the American plan and no longer include breakfast in the room rate. Where breakfast is included, it's the gargantuan Irish meal of bacon, eggs, and sausages — usually very good and you pay for it whether you have it or not. In the following listing, assume that a private bath is included unless otherwise specified. Expensive means $55 to $75 a night for a double room; the moderate category is $30 to $45; and inexpensive rates range from $20 to $28.

Ardilaun House Hotel – Once the stately home of an aristocratic scion, building and grounds still retain a patrician aura. It's hidden away among trees and shrubs on Taylor's Hill, the best address in town (phone: 21433). Expensive.

Corrib Great Southern Hotel – This is a younger sister of the big Victorian hotel on Eyre Sq. and it aspires to similar standards. It's modern and comfortable. Dublin Rd. (phone: 65281). Expensive.

Great Southern Hotel – The superior hotel, with 120 of the most comfortable rooms you can get in Galway. Its elegant foyer is the center of social life in the city and an easy place to strike up new friendships. The food in the *Claddagh Grill* is great; a heated swimming pool and sauna are welcome bonuses. Eyre Sq. (phone: 64041). Expensive.

Anno Santo – For those who prefer the quiet life, here is a classy, intimate place with a relaxed atmosphere. Specify private bath. Threadneedle Rd., Salthill (phone: 22110). Moderate.

Skeffington Arms – This is a small and homey place where you get friendly attention. Specify bath here, too. Eyre Sq. (phone: 63173). Moderate.

EATING OUT: Strangers to Galway should not venture into any restaurant without having it *reliably* recommended; there are a few shoddy places best avoided. However, the city does have some exceptionally good eating places and some of the better ones are in hotels. Don't expect anything too adventurous because the cuisine generally is quite unsophisticated with simple unadorned dishes. Native beef and lamb are among the world's best, so you can't go wrong with straight steaks or chops. Surprisingly, perhaps, good seafood is hard to come by, though the places we list are all versatile with fish. In season, Galway salmon from the Corrib River is superlative, and during the "r" months the oysters from the bay are possibly the best of the entire globe. To eat well, stick to the expensive restaurants, though there are a number of commendable ones in the moderate range. Stay away altogether from the inexpensive joints. Expect to pay $45 and upward for dinner for two with wine in the expensive category and $40 to $45 in the moderate bracket. Credit cards are accepted. A service charge is included in all bills, but a tip is expected all the same! Note that most of the restaurants listed open briefly for lunch, then close and reopen for a 2- or 3-hour dinner period, usually from 7 PM on. Since several are out of town, it's a good idea to check on the hours they keep before you get in the car.

Ardilaun House Hotel – Although recently refurbished, with its decorous wood paneling and glass chandeliers, this restaurant retains a nineteenth-century ambience. The food is conventional but of very high order and it's a popular dining place for families. Fresh meats and fish are the specialties. Taylor's Hill (phone: 21433). Expensive.

Claddagh Grill – On the top floor of the *Great Southern Hotel* and the finest all-around restaurant in the city. Try the wonderful lamb from Connemara or the Corrib salmon. The Continental dishes are good, too. Great Southern Hotel, Eyre Sq. (phone: 64041). Expensive.

Moran's of the Weir – This lovely thatched pub on the edge of the water is the most famous place in Ireland for oysters, but at other times of the year there are smoked salmon, mussel soup, and other seafoods. Pub hours. On the road to Limerick, 10 miles out of the city; turn right just before the village of Kilcolgan (phone: 86113). Expensive.

Oranmore Lodge Hotel – The restaurant in this hotel confines itself to a few main dishes, all very good. Particularly toothsome is the Carpetbagger Steak — a sirloin crammed with prawns. Oranmore village, 6 miles from downtown on the Dublin Rd. (phone: 84175). Expensive.

Salthill Hotel – The food here is always good but especially so on Irish nights when the menu is planned around such native foodstuffs as lamb, salmon, oysters, and prawns. The Promenade, Salthill (phone: 22711). Expensive.

The Silver Teal – An Irish restaurant that has a way with French sauces. The seafood dishes are opulent; there are lobster and pheasant in season. Moycullen village, 7 miles north on the road to Oughterard (phone: 85109). Expensive.

Ty-ar-mor – You'll have to travel a few miles out of the city to get to this one, too. It's a Breton restaurant atmospheric with nets and lobster pots, in the seaside village of Barna. Seafood and crêpes are the specialties and the cuisine is *très bon*. Reservations recommended. Sea Point, Barna (phone: 69186). Expensive.

Eyre House Restaurant – Undistinctively modern but crisply fresh in appearance, this is the best place in the city center for quick snacks or full-course meals. Open all day. Eyre Sq. (phone: 62396). Moderate.

Skeffington Arms – The hotel's dining room serves the best steak in town but the scallops and duck are also memorable. It's delightfully informal and friendly. Eyre Sq. (phone: 63173). Moderate.

Lydon House Restaurant – Downstairs is a good, stand-up, fast-food eatery; upstairs is a more formal, sit-down restaurant with an orthodox but tasty menu. 5 Shop St. (phone: 61131). Moderate to inexpensive.

SHARING A PINT: Unfortunately, there are probably more bad pubs than good ones; the Irish don't seem to mind topering in uncomfortable, cheerless surroundings. The bars in our hotel listing are uniformly good, but don't be afraid of letting your instinct guide you into strange pubs. You often discover the nicest places that way. Some pubs have their own attractions. *McDonagh's Thatched Pub* on Main St. in the village of Oranmore (6 miles from downtown on the Dublin Rd.) is old-fashioned and very friendly, with plenty of atmosphere and an open fire on cold days. *Moran's of the Weir,* already mentioned in *Eating Out* for its famous oysters, is also a wonderful place for a "jar" (10 miles from downtown on the Limerick Rd.; turn right just before Kilcolgan village). In town, *Seagan Ua Neachtáin,* at the corner of Quay St. and Cross St., is the definitive Irish pub-cum-general-store, like they used to have 100 years ago. It's frequented by intellectuals and those who think they're intellectuals. There are snugs and a fireplace. *Freeney's* on High St. is another old-style pub where you'll find plenty of chat while standing at the bar and *The Yacht* on St. Francis St. is modern, clean, and comfortable but with an antique flavor.

the steps of the City Chambers. Rioting ensued, 50 people were injured, two important Red Clydesiders went to jail, and the next day armed troops and tanks blazened into the city. Yet somehow this token taste of blood had cleared the air, and within a few days most strikers returned to work and the tanks disappeared.

The Glasgow you visit today is a mass of contradictions. It has a greater variety of quality cultural events than Edinburgh (except during the Edinburgh Festival), yet it also has one of the highest crime rates in Europe. Right in its middle, near its most elegant buildings, are streets in a state of shameful dereliction. The Gorbals and other tenement areas have been bulldozed and refitted with faceless skyscraper apartments, yet the rumbustiousness and camaraderie of the days when 30 people shared one toilet, and every drink was a half of whisky knocked back with a pint of beer to chase it, linger on.

The Second City, however, is gone. Elevated motorways on concrete slabs thread their way over parts of Glasgow's once-majestic urban scene, and the Clyde, which sent the ringing din of riveting from its busy docks all over the city, is still. Population has declined from over a million to 809,000 and Birmingham has outstripped Glasgow as London's runner-up in size. Yet at least half of all Scots still live within 20 miles of Glasgow, and engineering and printing, to say nothing of textile, food, drink, tobacco, and chemical industries, soldier on, despite rising unemployment. Whither now? There are Scottish nationalists who believe that, given the failure of efforts to bring the country a degree of autonomy via less drastic means, Glasgow's best bet might be for Scotland to go for complete independence.

GLASGOW AT-A-GLANCE

SEEING THE CITY: Getting an overhead gander at Glasgow is almost like finding the Holy Grail. The city is devoid of rooftop restaurants and publicly accessible steeples. Make your way to Glasgow University (buses 10 and 59 leave frequently from the city center for University Avenue), and storm the front of the Gothic vaults of the main university building, architect Sir George Gilbert Scott's elephantine monstrosity built on Gilmorehill in 1870. Turn right and right again until you reach the lodge of the "Bedellus" who with his magic key will unlock a door that leads to the steps to the top of Glasgow University Tower. If you can stand the climb, the reward is spectacular: Just below you is lovely Kelvingrove Park, with the River Kelvin winding through. Across the river is Kelvingrove Art Gallery, on a hill above a wooded glade. South of you is the River Clyde, and southeast is downtown Glasgow. Be sure you arrive on a weekday, at either midmorning or midafternoon (around 11 AM or 3 PM), otherwise you'll wait a long time for the man with the key. As an alternative, you can take an elevator to the top of the nearby Glasgow University Library for a second-best view. University of Glasgow (phone: 339-8855).

SPECIAL PLACES: One way to see Glasgow is to take it period by period. But start in the middle of things, with Victorian Glasgow, because it is this era that is the essence of the city. Except for the Transport Museum, located well away from the center (and to which you may want to dedicate as much as half a day), the surviving Victoriana listed below is quite conveniently placed. The rest of the sights — Medieval Glasgow, the Old Merchants' City, Modern Glasgow, and Clydeside attractions — are not far afield either, but don't expect to cover everything the same day. If you visit from July through September, hop aboard the zany, 2-hour, 14-mile bus tour of the city that costs £2.20 for adults and departs at 2 PM daily from the Glasgow Travel Centre in St. Enoch Square (phone: 226-4958). It was designed by a professional scriptwriter for natives and tourists alike.

VICTORIAN GLASGOW

George Square – Also called "Glasgow's Valhalla," this intriguing mix of equal parts statues, flower plots, picnickers, and pigeons was originally laid out in 1781 and named after King George III. It came into its own in Victorian times, when most of the grandiose buildings now surrounding it were constructed. Since Bloody Friday it has been the undisputed central focal point of the city. The Glasgow Information Bureau, on the west side of the square, will give you a pamphlet explaining the statues.

City Chambers – William Young, a local boy who made good in London, designed Glasgow's Italian Renaissance–style city hall, and Queen Victoria officially opened it in 1888 to the roars of 600,000 spectators. Inside, the loggia, staircases, and grand banqueting hall, with their sumptuous interplay of granite, mosaics, marble, and stone, make a millionaire's mansion look like a log cabin. Guided tours begin at 10:30 AM and 2:30 PM weekdays (except Thursdays and when a banquet is in progress). George Sq. (phone: 221-9600).

Merchants' House – Opposite the information bureau is the Glasgow Chamber of Commerce building, built in 1877 by native architect John Burnet (the ungainly upper three stories spoiling the effect of the domed turret were added later). Glasgow invented chambers of commerce in 1659 when its Merchant Guild erected a house, unique at that time, from which to minister to the widowed and orphaned of the collective merchant poor. That building — and that institution — were this one's ancestors. (Glasgow's Trades Guild, not to be outdone by its archrival, followed suit with a similar institution and eventually built the elegant Trades House of 1794, designed by the renowned Scottish architect, Robert Adam. This is on nearby Glassford St. and is well worth a look.) Open weekdays May through September from 2 PM to 4 PM, unless a special meeting is taking place. 7 George St. (phone: 221-8272).

Buchanan Street, Gordon Street – For row after nonstop row of massive, public architectural Victoriana, nowhere in the world beats this!

Museum of Transport – In 1962, a huge turnout of Glaswegians wept openly as they watched a parade of trams from all eras make a farewell memorial run through the streets. The trams were then lovingly roundhoused and became the nucleus of this museum. Also present are vintage cars, trains, and fire engines of Scottish design, plus a bevy of brightly painted Victorian items: traction engines, craftsmen's carts, carriages, even a one-horse open sleigh. The oldest bicycle in the world is here, looking like a couple of mill wheels. There is also an extensive nautical exhibition — pictures and models only — at which you can brush up your Clydeside history. Open daily 10 AM to 5 PM; Sundays 2 PM to 5 PM. 25 Albert Dr. (phone: 423-8000).

The Necropolis – Every tombstone is a virtual Parthenon in this graveyard of Glasgow's wealthy Victorian industrialists. Save a few gasps for the *pièce de résistance*, the huge, round, double-decked Menteith Mausoleum (date: 1842; recipe: gingerbread) on the east side beside a bird's-eye view of a local brewery. The towering statue of John Knox was erected in 1833 (before the brewery). Keep clear of the place after 4:30 PM, when it fills up with imbibers, petty thieves, glue sniffers, and (possibly) resurrectionists. Open all day. Across the Bridge of Sighs off Cathedral Sq.

MEDIEVAL GLASGOW

Glasgow Cathedral – A perfect specimen of pre-Reformation Gothic architecture, this was the only church on the Scottish mainland to have its inner structure spared during pillaging by sixteenth-century Protestant zealots bent on destroying "monuments of idolatry." Its fifteenth-century carved stone choir screen, separating the aristocracy at the front of the building from the plebians at the back, was saved through petitioning by Glaswegian stonemasons: Such was the prestige of the Glasgow trade guilds. Have a look also at the remarkable fan vaulting in the crypt over the tomb of Glasgow's patron saint, St. Mungo, and at the chair Oliver Cromwell sat in when he visited Glasgow in 1650 (Glasgow was lucky because at most places he visited he was too busy burning and wrecking to sit down.) The chairs the Queen and Prince Philip sit in when they worship in Glasgow Cathedral can be seen (the Queen turns Presbyterian automatically when they hit the Scottish border). Open Sundays 1 PM to 6 PM; Mondays through Saturdays 10 AM to 7 PM April through September, and 10 AM to 5:30 PM October through March. Cathedral Sq. (phone: 552-0220).

Provand's Lordship – Just opposite the cathedral is the oldest house in Glasgow, built about 1471. It was the town house of the prebend, or provand, of a nearby country see. Imagine a colony of such buildings extending up and down the adjacent streets and you will have an idea of the Glasgow of Mary Queen of Scots's time. The house was closed in 1980 for restoration and repair and until work is completed (date unknown), visitors cannot go inside.

THE OLD MERCHANTS' CITY

Glasgow Cross – This was the heart of the city in the eighteenth century, before George Square took over. The large reproduction of an etching you saw on a wall of Merchants' House shows what it used to be like looking west down the Trongate. Today, the Tolbooth steeple (1626) and the Tron Church steeple (1636) are all that's left from earlier times. The Edinburgh stagecoach stopped in Glasgow Cross, carrying newspapers from the capital, and Glasgow's merchants conducted their morning business and sipped their "meridians," or noonday rums, in the Tontine Hotel, opposite the Tron Church. If you see the "scaffies," or city street sweepers, leaning on their brooms chatting garrulously together at 4:30 each afternoon, eating ice cream bought from a van beside the Tolbooth steeple, they are perhaps acting under the influence of a folk memory two centuries old. You can't see anything better than this for local color! Intersection of Gallowgate, Trongate, Saltmarket, and High St.

Royal Exchange Building – The main part of this structure, now a library, was the mansion of William Cunningham, the most famous tobacco lord of all. Ask at the front desk for the historical pamphlet. Closed Wednesdays and Sundays. Royal Exchange Sq., off Queen St. (phone: 221-1876).

Virginia Street – Nos. 37 to 53 are the best mid-eighteenth-century examples of street architecture still in the city. Explore the closes behind, where horses were stabled and Highland housemaids en route from the city wells stopped to dally with the grooms. Tobacco lords kept offices in these buildings, on a surprisingly modest scale. No. 33 was the tobacco auction hall. Step inside — it's just as it was in the 1700s.

MODERN GLASGOW

Glasgow School of Art – This is the most famous building in Glasgow and one of the most famous buildings of its period in the world — Charles Rennie Mackintosh's finest example of the style poet laureate John Betjeman called "Beardsley-esque baronial." Its east wing was completed in 1899, the rest, with additions to the east wing, in 1909. Ironically, Mackintosh, an architect, interior designer, and artist of the avant-avant-garde, won the competition for the design of the school because his plan was the cheapest to build! Today, few dispute his unqualified genius. The library especially, with its almost infinite attention to the tiniest decorative details, is exquisite. Open Mondays through Fridays 10 AM to noon and 2 PM to 4 PM. The porters conduct informal guided tours and relevant literature is for sale in the student shop in the basement. 167 Renfrew St. (phone: 332-9797).

John Logie Baird Plaque – You'll find it by the door of the room where Baird invented television (if he invented it — he is said to have been anticipated by an obscure Irish curate), in the main hall of the University of Strathclyde. The Scottish inventor demonstrated a true television system in 1926. Open weekdays 9 AM to 5 PM. George St., just east of George Sq. (phone: 552-4400).

BY CLYDESIDE

Custom House Quay – The Glasgow Corporation has fitted out its disused docksides with flower-decked walkways. Bands play here in summer, and discos blare at night, while the anchored *Carrick* casts a silent eye upon all. The *Carrick,* a contemporary of the famous clipper *Cutty Sark,* holds the world sailing-ship record of 65 days from Australia to London. Custom House Quay adjoins Clyde St.

Clyde Street – Continuing east, you'll see on your left the seventeenth-century, Dutch-style tower of Glasgow's *original* Merchants' House, preserved for its magnificence when the house itself was razed. At nos. 64 to 76 the world's most pretentious fishmarket, dated 1873, is dripping with sculpted rosettes and topped with winged horses. The building, though intact, is now derelict. At the end of Clyde Street, around the corner to the left along the Saltmarket, are the Doric-porched Justiciary Courthouses, where the last public hanging in Glasgow, that of the dashingly notorious conman and poisoner Dr. Pritchard, occurred in 1865.

Glasgow Green – This is the oldest public park in Europe, and it has certainly seen a lot of action! The heart-rending statue at the west entrance was erected in 1881 by temperance reformers, after which massive turnouts of public temperance pledgers were a common sight on the green for decades. During World War I, you couldn't see the grass for the sea of tweed caps at Red Clydesiders' rallies. The green was also for centuries the site of Glasgow's chief washhouse and bleaching lawn: Foreign visitors commented on the brazenness of the local washerwomen, who lifted their skirts about their thighs to dance barefoot on the dirty clothes stewing in their tubs. It was on Glasgow Green one fine Sunday afternoon in 1765 that James Watt, playing hookey from church, had a vision of the steam condenser that changed the history of the world. Open all day. The west entrance is opposite the Justiciary Courthouses in the Saltmarket.

The People's Palace – You never know what you'll find at this museum of local history, since the city owns more objects than it can possibly display at once and keeps changing the show. The place is impressionistic and fun, with everything from theatrical bills and political pamphlets to elaborate wrought-iron streetlights and fountains and the ridiculous pouting stone faces that once adorned the facade of the Tontine Hotel. There are exhibits from every century. Open daily 10 AM to 5 PM; Sundays 2 PM to 5 PM. East side of Glasgow Green (phone: 554-0223).

- **EXTRA SPECIAL:** How about a trip on the last seagoing paddle steamer in the world, the *Waverley?* From mid-June through September, the Paddle Steamer Preservation Society operates this charming Victorian craft on one-day round trips from Stobcross Quay, Glasgow, to Tighnabruaich, beyond the Firth of Clyde on the beauteous Dunoon Peninsula. As you cruise the Clyde you'll see the cranes and derricks in the dockyards that once supplied over half the world's tonnage of oceangoing ships. Have lunch in the restaurant (with bar) on board, or bring sandwiches. Sailings from Glasgow are on Fridays and Saturdays only. For full details, contact Waverley Excursions Ltd., New Waverley Terminal, Stobcross Quay (phone: 221-8152).

SOURCES AND RESOURCES

The Glasgow Information Bureau, George Sq., Glasgow G2 1ES (phone: 221-7371), has stacks of free leaflets recommending things to see and do not only in Glasgow but throughout Scotland. Ask at the desk for the official city guidebook, *Seeing Glasgow,* and its accompanying *Useful Information Supplement* (50p for the two); for *Wining and Dining in Glasgow,* a list of downtown restaurants giving address, phone number, type of food served, and opening hours; for *Glasgow Leisure,* a monthly pamphlet containing a comprehensive diary of local entertainment; and the small single-sheet map of the center of Glasgow (no charge for the last three items). Bartholomew publishes a complete map of Glasgow, available here for 85p. John Smith and Son, booksellers, 57–61 St. Vincent St. (phone: 226-3047), will provide you with a copy of *Glasgow at a Glance* (£2.50). This is your bible, chronologically wrapping up every important building in town with an erudite blurb and a stunning picture, so don't leave it behind in your hotel. Short historical paperbacks about Glasgow are on sale, too, plus a selection of touring and restaurant guides and maps.

For Local Coverage – The *Glasgow Herald* is Glasgow's one respectable morning daily; the evening daily is the *Evening Times.*

GETTING AROUND: Rule Number One is to use your feet in the George Square district — you can't view Victorian architecture properly unless you wallow in it. Buchanan, Gordon, and Sauchiehall streets are pedestrian zones.

Bus and Subway – Buses are frequent and well run, but you'll probably have to ask where to get the one you're looking for, since they have no single central rendezvous point. Exact change is required. The Glasgow Information Bureau has timetables and you can call the Transcentre, 103 St. Vincent St. (phone: 248-3371), for other information.

Subway trains run every 5 minutes (none on Sundays or after 7 PM). The system's central stops are marked on your single-sheet map: Hillhead Station is a good alighting point for west-end shops and restaurants.

Taxi – Fares are cheap (60p for the first mile, 10p for each additional ¼ mile). Taxis are hard to get at night, however, so try at Central Station.

Car Rental – Renting a car is recommended because there is plenty to lure you out of downtown Glasgow. All the major firms are in the Yellow Pages and parking places are listed on the single-sheet map and in the *Useful Information Supplement.*

Train – Railway trains leave Central Station on Gordon St. (phone: 204-2844) every 10 minutes for Glasgow's south side, calling at Pollokshields East (for the Transport Museum); every third train goes to Whitecraigs (for Rouken Glen Park — see *Sports* below) as well.

MUSEUMS: The *Transport Museum* and the *People's Palace,* described in *Special Places,* are high on the list of things to see. Below are some other museums of interest. Admission is free to all.

Art Gallery and Museum – British and European paintings including Rembrandt's *Man in Armor* and Dali's *Christ of St. John of the Cross* in addition to natural history, ethnography, and the decorative arts. Organ recitals take place in the promenade at 3 PM every Saturday. Closed Sunday mornings. Kelvingrove Park (opposite Kelvin Hall on Dumbarton Rd. (phone: 334-1134).

Hunterian Museum – Geological, anthropological, and historical collections, and Roman relics. Closed Saturday afternoons and Sundays. In the main building of Glasgow University, Gilmorehill, off University Ave. (phone: 339-8855, ext. 221).

Hunterian Art Gallery – Paintings, drawings, prints, and furniture by (among others) Whistler and Charles Rennie Mackintosh. Closed Saturday afternoons and Sundays. Hillhead St. (phone: 339-8855, ext. 7431).

Pollok House – Works by El Greco, Goya, Murillo, and William Blake, plus antique furniture, silver, porcelain, and glass, all displayed in a house designed by William Adam, the father of the famous family of Scottish architects, and completed in 1752 (later additions by Sir Rowand Anderson were begun in 1890). It is surrounded by extensive park grounds, so take your car, or take the bus tour to Pollok House that leaves from the Glasgow Travel Centre in St. Enoch Square. For details, call 226-4958. Closed Sunday mornings. 2060 Pollokshaws Rd. (phone: 632-0274).

Haggs Castle – An ornate castellated late-sixteenth-century structure containing the original kitchen with cauldrons, spits, and barrels, and a Victorian nursery. A children's activity workshop — butter-making, spinning, weaving and more — takes place on Saturday afternoons (reservations necessary on local holidays) in a nearby cottage, and the landscape includes a knot garden. Closed Sunday mornings. 100 St. Andrews Dr. (phone: 427-2725).

Royal Highland Fusiliers Museum – Three centuries of the Glasgow and Ayrshire Regiment: uniforms, weapons, medals, and pictures. Open Mondays through Fridays. 518 Sauchiehall St. (phone: 332-0961).

SHOPPING: Tuesday or Saturday is early closing day (1 PM) for some shops, though most city-center establishments remain open daily except Sunday. Local wares include woolens, pottery, crystal, Victorian bric-a-brac, jewelry, shortbread, and whisky. Here's what's where:

Fergusson's – High-class foodstuffs such as shortbreads, malt whiskies, and giant slices of cheesecake you can elope with and eat on a bench in George Square. 67 Union St. (phone: 221-0195).

Fraser's – This four-tiered, balconied, Victorian-vintage department store with central court, glass-paneled ceiling, and a couple of hundred feet of suspended chandelier offers English bone china, clothes, linens, Edinburgh crystal, or just a beautiful breath of rarified air. 21 Buchanan St. (phone: 221-3880).

Iona Shop – Specialists in Celtic jewelry, including hand-crafted pieces of silver and polished Scottish stone. Located in the Argyll Arcade, the L-shaped passage between Argyll and Buchanan streets that is Glasgow's famous diamond and jewelry center (phone: 221-9038).

Lawrie Renfrew's – Fishing equipment, free in-the-know advice to fishermen, and the-one-that-got-away sessions with the rest of Mr. Renfrew's clientele. Gone fishin' Thursdays. 514 Great Western Rd. (phone: 334-3635).

Lawrie's – The sort of place where the landowning milord buys his deerstalking "breeks" (breeches). Kilts, skirts, jackets, pure wool plaids, tweeds, mohairs, accessories, and souvenirs. Highland dress made to order and clan tartans traced for visitors unsure of their Scottish connections. 110 Buchanan St. (phone: 221-0217) and 38 Renfield St. (phone: 221-9047).

Saltoun Pottery – Hand-thrown mugs and jugs designed by talented Glaswegian Nancy Smillie. 24 Ruthven St. (phone: 334-4240).

Upstairs Downstairs – Eastern objects and imported Indian clothes for women, in joyous native designs. 625 Great Western Rd. (phone: 334-9623). Visit also *Eurasia Crafts,* 492 Great Western Rd. (phone: 339-3933), and *Koh-i-noor Crafts,* 611 Great Western Rd. (phone: 334-1569), or 173 Byres Rd. (phone: 339-2884).

Victorian Village – Antiques, roomfuls of ornaments and old lace. Beethoven's

Pastoral wafts through the adjoining corridors while you browse or dawdle in the charming tearoom. 57 W Regent St. (phone: 332-0808).

SPECIAL EVENTS: Parades, band concerts, sports competitions, beauty contests, and disco dancing are what goes on in summertime at community festivals, and every Glasgow district has one, usually in late May or June. Get the complete list from the Glasgow Information Bureau. During the last 2 weeks in June, the *Scottish National Orchestra (SNO) Proms* — 14 concerts with famous guest soloists and conductors — are held in Kelvin Hall. The Proms have nothing to do with dancing, but the final night is traditionally an orgy of well-known musical tours de force at which the audience sends up balloons and joins the chorus. For further information, contact the SNO, 3 La Belle Pl., Glasgow G3 7LH (phone: 332-7244). *The Glasgow International Folk Festival* takes place in early July; for details, contact Colin McAllister, 18 Teith Pl., Cambuslans (phone: 641-8112).

SPORTS: Boating – At *Rouken Glen Park,* Glasgow's 228-acre arcadia, weather permitting. Rowboats are about 50p a go. Try *Hogganfield Park* and *Queen's Park,* too.

Fishing – The Firth of Clyde, the ocean, and the upland waterways near Glasgow are all popular. The Glasgow Information Bureau has two booklets for sale, *Scotland for Fishing* (65p) and *Scotland for Sea Angling* (60p), and other pamphlets on the subject for free. Or ask Lawrie Renfrew (see *Shopping*).

Golf – Get *Strathclyde Golf,* a free leaflet, from the Glasgow Information Bureau. It supplies details of the championship courses along the Ayrshire coast as well as the Glasgow courses. Rent equipment from a pro shop and have ready an introductory letter from your home club secretary.

Hiking – Glasgow has 7,000 acres of municipal green space, much of it woodland, in over 70 parks. *Seeing Glasgow* describes attractions in the larger parks. The Glasgow Information Bureau has guides to the trails for 15p.

Horseback Riding – The *Kilmardinny Farm and Riding Establishment Ltd.,* Milngavie Rd., Bearsden (phone: 943-1310), is your best bet.

Soccer – It's called football here, and in Scotland, football is just about synonymous with two teams, Glasgow's *Celtic* and *Rangers.* Kickoff is 7:30 PM on Wednesdays and 3 PM on Saturdays, from August through May. Celtic Park, at 95 Kerrydale St., is the *Celtic* home stadium, and Ibrox Park, on Edmiston Dr., is the home of the *Rangers.* Get tickets from the turnstiles prior to the games and note that since Scottish women themselves are rarely in attendance at these cultural phenomena, foreign women would definitely feel out of place. League play-offs and cup finals are at Hampden Park on Somerville Dr.

THEATER: Since 1942, the *Glasgow Citizens Theatre,* in deepest Gorbals on Gorbals St. (phone: 429-0022), has been famous throughout Scotland for its vigorous experimentalism, high standard of performance, and lusty approach to what are usually considered highbrow classics. Closed June through August. The *Pavilion,* Renfield St. (phone: 332-0478), is the inheritor of the rich "Scotch comic" music hall tradition that Glasgow has given the world — *vide* Harry Lauder. Pre-London runs and large amateur-dramatic-society productions are at the *King's,* Bath St. (phone: 248-5153). *The Mitchell Theater,* Granville St. (phone: 221-3198), has variety acts and light musicals. There is also a handful of locales where the flower of upcoming young artistic Glasgow unfolds its petals: the *Glasgow Print Studio and Drama Centre,* 128 Ingram St. (phone: 552-0704); the *Athenaeum Theatre,* in the Royal Scottish Academy of Music and Drama building on Buchanan St. (phone: 332-5294); and the amazing *Third Eye Centre,* 350 Sauchiehall St. (phone:

332-7521), which publishes its own glossy monthly brochure describing events on its premises including plays, mime, dance, cabaret acts, jazz, films, talks, poetry readings, appearances by folk and rock groups, and workshops in dramatic arts for all ages. Open Tuesdays through Saturdays, 10 AM to 5:30 PM and 7 PM to 10:30 PM; while you're there, stop in at the bar, café, or trendy bookshop. The *Glasgow Film Theatre* (for art films) is at 12 Rose St. (phone: 332-6535).

MUSIC: The restored *Theatre Royal* on Hope St. (phone: 331-1234), originally built in 1882, is the elegant, new headquarters of the prestigious Scottish Opera Company. Other national opera companies perform there when Scottish Opera is on tour (as do professional theater groups). *City Hall,* Candleriggs (phone: 552-1850), *Henry Wood Hall,* Claremont St. (phone: 332-7244), are the places for important orchestral and classical concerts, supplemented by *Glasgow Cathedral,* which often hosts choral and sacred works, and *Kelvin Hall,* site of the SNO Proms, though normally an exhibition center. Also in Candleriggs is The Ticket Centre (phone: 552-5961), where you can reserve tickets for the *King's* and *Mitchell* theaters and *City* and *Kelvin* halls. Rock rolls in the *Apollo Theatre* on Renfield St. (phone: 332-9221). Bagpiping and Highland and Scottish country dancing must be traced to city parks and to small parish halls — have a look at your copy of *Glasgow Leisure.* As for jazz, Glasgow's jazz king is Frank Pantrini. His incomparable sextet plays the pub and restaurant circuit when its members get a night off from their regular orchestra jobs. Check the dailies for where. The City of Glasgow Municipal Club runs a Grand Ole Opry house Wednesday, Friday, Saturday, and Sunday nights at Paisley Road Toll (phone: 429-5396).

NIGHTCLUBS AND NIGHTLIFE: Your safest course is a theater evening with a restaurant meal afterward. This will steer you clear of the restless natives whose idea of a Big Night Out is a long crawl from one mobbed, fuming pub to another, the progression marked by rantings, singing, and battles of wit. Gambling halls and dance hangouts usually have an unadorned and, to a tourist, tawdry air. Oasis in the wilderness: *Charlie Parker's,* Royal Exchange Sq. (phone: 248-3040), specializing in drinks, dinner, and disco. Keep an eye out also for establishments with occasional cabaret acts, such as *Halibee's Design Studios,* 55 Ruthven La. (phone: 334-8560), which has jazz and folk nights, a vegetarian menu, and no bar (customers bring their own bottles).

Pubs clank shut at 11 PM. Consult your copy of *Wining and Dining in Glasgow* for restaurants that have extended-hours licenses to serve drinks with food after the pubs close. You can drink until 2 AM in the overnight-guests-only bar of your hotel without having to eat.

SINS: It's impossible to sin with panache in Glasgow, unless you invent your own methods. How about streaking naked across the top of the City Chambers' Jubilee Pediment, rolling a barrel of whisky to pour on the heads of the city police when they invite your descent? (The sin here would be in the waste of the whisky.) The red-light district is Blythswood Sq. (streetwalkers only) and the gay scene, known for its friendliness and crusading solidarity, pivots around the Scottish Homosexual Rights Group (SHRG), which runs a club with a bar and disco. The club, 4 Queen's Crescent (phone: 333-0749), is open most evenings. It has a members-and-guests-only policy (minimum age 18), so phone Roy Moseley, the manager, to arrange to get in. Glasgow's gay pub is currently *Vintner's,* 312 Clyde St. (phone: 221-2089.)

BEST IN TOWN

CHECKING IN: A well-known Scottish television executive recently defined a typical Glasgow hotel as a "reasonable, functional, bathroom's-got-a-bath, bedroom's-got-a-bed kind of place." Comfort you'll certainly get but don't expect to be overwhelmed by the picturesque. The price of a room includes breakfast whether you eat it or not, and top-class establishments will want you to show your mettle by guzzling prunes, porridge, herrings, eggs, bacon, sausages, tomatoes, coffee, and toast, all in one sitting. Private baths are available unless otherwise stated. Our hotels in the expensive range charge anywhere from $80 and more a night per double; moderate hotels charge $60 to $80 per double; and inexpensive hotels $45 to $60 per double. Guesthouses and bed-and-breakfasts are a lot cheaper. Lists of these for areas throughout Scotland are in two booklets, one for each type, published by the Scottish Tourist Board and sold (about £1 apiece) by the Glasgow Information Bureau in George Square.

The Albany – Where the visiting pop stars stay — this is a slick 251-room flat-topped box with a big-city image. Inside, it's soft lights, carpets, and chrome. One of the two dining rooms is a popular carvery serving Scottish fare. Bothwell St. (phone: 248-2656). Expensive.

The Grosvenor – This pure white 96-room Victorian showpiece in the West End, opposite the Botanic Gardens, is elegance incarnate. Grosvenor Terr. (phone: 339-8811). Expensive.

The Holiday Inn – Yes, it's one of *the* Holiday Inns and has everything from individual mini-bars in the 297 rooms to a heated indoor Jacuzzi whirlpool. Argyll St. (phone: 226-5577). Expensive.

The Central – An architecturally-distinguished railway hotel of the 1880s, the *Central* is next to Central Station. It's spacious and gracious in the Victorian mode, but it was built right over a streetful of slum houses, so it may be haunted by the home-loving ghosts of the dispossessed. Sumptuous bedrooms (211), a hairdresser, three dining rooms, including *The Malmaison* (see *Eating Out*). Gordon St. (phone: 221-9680). Expensive.

Beacon's Hotel – Consider it a bit of historic Glasgow in the form of a charming Victorian terraced house with 26 rooms and period decor. Edward VII once stayed here. The view across Kelvingrove Park to the town of Paisley and the hills beyond is glorious. 7 Park Ter. (phone: 332-9438). Expensive.

The Normandy – Here you'll find the smooth and efficient anonymous facelessness of any custom-built airport hotel. It's near Glasgow's Abbotsinch Airport and favored by businessmen for conferences. 142 rooms. Inchinnan Rd., Renfrew (phone: 886-4100). Moderate.

The North British – Life inside it revolves around the circular cocktail bar in the middle of its large lounge-cum-lobby. Some of the 130 rooms have lovely views of George Square and there is an excellent dining room with Scottish food. The hotel has a warm, old-fashioned, highly-civilized air. George Sq. (phone: 332-6711). Moderate.

The Pond – There are 137 rooms in this somewhat lethargic modern hotel in the west end. The name comes from the usable boating pond, which it overlooks, and it's a good place for kids. 2–4 Shelley Rd. (phone: 334-8161). Moderate.

The Sherbroke – The bar here is the neighborhood pub, ideal for helping you forget you're a tourist. This elegant old nine-bedroom mansion-house is on a knolltop on the city's south side. 11 Sherbroke Ave. (phone: 427-4227). Moderate to inexpensive.

The Marie Stuart – Bill Tennent, a local television personality, runs this grand old house with 23 rooms well south of the Clyde. Glaswegians like it for wakes and weddings. No private baths. 46–48 Queen Mary Ave. (phone: 423-6363). Inexpensive.

EATING OUT: Native food, dismissed with a laugh by the ignorant because of the names of some of its dishes ("haggis," "powsowdie," "cullen skink"), is actually delicious. Top of the Scottish gastronomic pops are Aberdeen Angus steak, lamb with rowanberry jelly, venison, moor grouse, salmon, and trout. For a meal for two expect to pay over $50 at restaurants listed as expensive; $30 to $50 at restaurants listed as moderate; and under $30 at restaurants listed as inexpensive. This selection does not include any of Glasgow's numerous pubs with catering facilities, fish and chips shops, and plastic-age fried chicken or burger joints. Time your hunger pangs carefully. Most restaurants are traditionally open for lunch from noon until 2:30 PM and for dinner from 5 PM or 7 PM until 11 PM or so. Few are open continuously throughout the day and few are open on Sundays.

La Bonne Auberge – French food, French waiters, French posters with pictures of early bicycles. This restaurant in *Beacon's Hotel* is the haunt of the peppy young go-ahead set. The wine bar is fun. Closed Sundays. 7 Park Ter. (phone: 332-9438). Expensive.

The Malmaison – Glasgow's best. Vast international menu, attentive service, old-fashioned elegance — everything is in the grand manner, including the small balcony with a pianist or consort of violinists. Closed Sundays. Central Hotel, Gordon St. (phone: 221-9680). Expensive.

Poacher's – The trendiest restaurant in town is in an old farmhouse off a narrow lane in the west end. Decor is dark green with matching shrubbery. The menu (Scottish fare — something different cooked fresh every day) is recited. Book ahead. Closed Sundays. 235 Byres Rd. (phone: 339-0932). Expensive.

L'Ariosto – High-backed pine chairs, tiled floor, dim lighting, soft music, and lots of lovers' nooks make this romantically and classily Italian. The bill of fare doesn't stop at spaghetti. Dancing Tuesday through Saturday nights. Closed Sundays. 92/94 Mitchell St. (phone: 221-8543). Expensive to moderate.

The Fountain – Small and unpretentious, this restaurant is in the London image, known for its expense-account lunches. Menu is international, with emphasis on charcoal grills. Closed Sundays. 2 Woodside Crescent, Charing Cross (phone: 332-6396). Expensive to moderate.

The Colonial – One big board in the middle of a large room groans with whole salmons and other rarities. Eat here and you'll see the unseen face of business Glasgow. Closed Sundays. 25 High St. (phone: 552-1923). Moderate.

La Parmigiana – Italian cuisine served here, by jolly Italian waiters. Striped awning outside, bijou-type intimacy within. Dining is accompanied by the strains of "O Sole Mio" and other gems sung to the tune of a small guitar. Closed Sundays. 447 Great Western Rd. (phone: 334-0686). Moderate.

The Rogano – Seafoods are a specialty and there's an oyster bar in this part pub, part restaurant, which media people and talkative about-towners have claimed as their own. Its antique fixtures include mirrors and glass paneling adorned with sea themes. Closed Sundays. 11 Exchange Pl. (phone: 221-5677). Moderate.

The Ubiquitous Chip – No, this is not a fish and french fries outlet. The menu caters to the discriminating palate, featuring local delicacies when they are in season. And the glassed-in courtyard with a fountain and an art deco water lily mural pleases the eye, too. Closed Sundays. 12 Ashton La. (phone: 334-5007). Moderate.

Trattoria Caruso – Food is Italian plus basic British. Across the street from the

Theatre Royal, this is popular with actors and theatergoers. An extension to the dining area is a chic new pizza parlor. Closed Sundays. 311/313 Hope St. (phone: 331-2607). Moderate to inexpensive.

The Danish Food Centre – Seafoods with sweet sauces and other Scandinavian delights upstage the somewhat antiseptic decor. By day, it's a good place to know for a quick lunch or coffee with pastry. By night — smorgasbord. Open Tuesdays through Saturdays 10 AM to 5 PM and 5:30 PM to 11 PM; closed Sundays. 56 St. Vincent St. (phone: 221-0518). Moderate to inexpensive.

The Ad Lib Mid Atlantic – Steaks and real-beef hamburgers, piped disco music, and posters of glamorous American celebrities are all part of the effort to make Yankees feel at home and Glaswegians feel they're not. Cocktails are a specialty. Open Mondays through Saturdays noon to 2 AM, Sundays 6 PM to 1 AM. 111 Hope St. (phone: 248-7102). Inexpensive.

The Shenaz – You'll be met by a venerable ancient in a turban and led to a candlelit table. Order lager, not wine, with your exotic Indian fare. Open for lunch and dinner weekdays; dinner only on Sundays. 17 Granville St. (phone: 248-4804). Inexpensive.

Moussaka House – The food and the owners are Greek, and there are lots of young patrons. Don't be surprised if the proprietors are seized by the bacchanalian whim to give you a free drink or a flower. Open for lunch and dinner weekdays and for dinner on Sundays. 36 Kelvingrove St. (phone: 332-2510). Inexpensive.

SHARING A PINT: The *Saracen's Head* or "Sarry Heid," at 209 the Gallowgate, has a fascinating history dating from the fourteenth century, when its patrons, the Knights of St. John, returned from the Crusades with Moorish heads mounted on sticks and stuck them in the turf outside as spoils of war. The *Pewter Pot,* 392 N Woodside Rd., is where the literati meet. *Curler's,* a megapub with eight separate bars at 256 Byres Rd., was once an old coaching inn; it has jazz nights and a painted mural with portraits of some of its famous former habitués.

KILKENNY

Ireland's best-preserved medieval town is the minute inland city of Kilkenny, 75 miles southwest of Dublin. Beginning as a tiny Gaelic settlement around the monastery of St. Canice (whence its Irish name, *Cill Chainnigh,* "the cell of Canice"), it came to prominence under the Normans when their leader, Strongbow, seized it in 1170 and built a fortification on the hill over the River Nore. The walled town was peopled with a purposeful community of Norman families, of whom ten in number — "Archdeakin, Archer, Cowley, Langton, Ley, Knaresborough, Lawless, Raggett, Rothe and Shee . . ." as an old list rhymes them off — distinguished themselves particularly and rose to power. Between the Gothic cathedral at one end and the strong castle at the other, the houses, inns, shops, new friaries, and the merchants' parish church crowded inside the city walls on the high bank of the river.

Its reputation as a stable and industrious market town thus established, Kilkenny then went on to achieve some notoriety. In the early fourteenth century, a formidable Norman woman named Dame Alice Kyteler, daughter of a banker, prosperous survivor of four husbands, and wealthy herself through moneylending (a practice, not incidentally, frowned upon by the church), was accused of witchcraft by Richard le Drede, bishop of Ossory, the local see. Dame Alice was supported by Arnold le Poer, the seneschal, and many powerful friends; the bishop, by the law and the commission he had from the Pope to extirpate heresy. A Kilkenny friar records the confrontation: "On Monday . . . the lady Alice Kyteler was tried, found guilty, condemned as a heretic for divers sorceries, manifold heresies, offering sacrifices to demons . . ." Though her powerful friends resisted and even imprisoned the bishop, he and the authority of the Church won that round. Dame Alice fled to Scotland, her maid Petronilla was burned at the stake in her stead, and Le Poer died in prison. The bishop did not get off scot-free either. He was accused of heresy and had to flee to the papal court in Avignon.

Several decades later, the name Kilkenny became associated with infamy. As elsewhere in Ireland, the Normans had been intermarrying with the Irish and "going native" in other ways, too. Such fraternization was perceived as a threat by the English king who by now feared being left with too few trustworthy settlers to rule the island on his behalf. Consequently, a parliament held in Kilkenny in 1366 (the city was important enough to be a regular meeting place, along with Dublin, of the Irish Parliament the Normans had instituted) passed the Statutes of Kilkenny. These forbade the Normans to marry the Irish, prohibited them from adopting the Irish language, customs, or dress, and segregated native Irish everywhere beyond the walls of towns.

From the end of the fourteenth century and for centuries thereafter, the castle of Kilkenny was occupied by the Butlers, earls of Ormonde, the most powerful family in medieval Ireland and long in the forefront of Irish history. They lived peaceably with the Gaelic chieftains, but at the same time were rich from royal favor. They married into the royal family, hosted royal visits, and acted frequently as the king's deputy in Ireland. Under their protection Kilkenny was spared the worst horrors of Henry VIII's Reformation and the devastating cycle of rebellion and repression that ensued during the reign of Elizabeth. The Butlers conformed to Protestantism and the city monasteries were silently suppressed, becoming civic property. John Bale, an English friar appointed the first conforming bishop of Ossory, smashed statues in the cathedral and wrote fiery sectarian pamphlets, but he is better remembered in Kilkenny for the morality plays he wrote and had performed at the Market Cross, which once stood near the center of High Street.

The city could not totally escape the racial and religious conflict of the times, however. When another revolt — the Ulster Rebellion, which would be brutally crushed by Oliver Cromwell — broke out in 1641, Kilkenny became the seat of the independent Irish Parliament set up by Anglo-Irish and Old Irish Catholics united for action in their common defense. It met from 1642 to 1648, presided over by Lord Mountgarrett, a member of a minor Catholic branch of the Butlers, while the earl, the king's man, sat on the fence. Though the confederation went so far as to establish a mint, manufacture weapons, raise an army, and receive ambassadors, it fell apart from within when its Norman and Irish factions began to disagree, and it disbanded in confusion. In 1660, Cromwell arrived to take Kilkenny for the English Parliament.

After the ritual window-breaking and statue-smashing in St. Canice's Cathedral, Cromwell's rule in Kilkenny was less bloody than elsewhere. Families involved in the parliament were banished west of the Shannon, "to Hell or Connaught," along with the rest of the propertied Catholics who had opposed the Protector. Those from Kilkenny never went, however; they secretly hung around the city until the Restoration brought back the king and a Butler again, now duke of Ormonde, as his viceroy. The duke managed to bring about a return of some of the lands confiscated from Kilkenny's leading citizens, but they and the city never quite recovered from the events of the century and never regained their former influence.

It is perhaps due to the long dark years of decline that followed that so much of Kilkenny's early architecture remains intact — the city was simply not prosperous enough to tear things down and rebuild them on a grand scale, nor was there any need to do so. The gloom began to lift with a cultural revival in the nineteenth century and dispersed completely in recent years, leaving only a lingering air of quaintness to temper the changes of a city now in expansion. The Butlers have been gone from the castle since the 1930s but they characteristically and munificently presented it to the people. Its beautiful gardens and park are there, the art gallery has a notable collection of portraits, and the dukes' fine stables have become the Kilkenny Design Workshops, a nursery of modern design talent. The Rothes' house has been restored as a museum and library; the Shees' almshouse has now been refurbished.

322 KILKENNY / At-a-Glance

Once a year, Kilkenny Arts Week has music resounding through castle and cathedral. The little medieval city that witnessed so much Irish history is still the integral core of a busy and modern, yet still traditional community.

KILKENNY AT-A-GLANCE

SEEING THE CITY: Kilkenny lies in two neat crescents on either side of a river valley basin and does not afford heights for the sweeping panoramic view. If you stand in the terraced rose garden in front of Kilkenny Castle, you can survey the city's limits from the castle behind you to the compact gray St. Canice's Cathedral in the distance, while the river below gives drama and movement. From here, though, you'll be looking *through* the town, catching its recurrences of church spire and Tholsel clock tower. The reverse view is from the top of the round tower at the cathedral (entrance 50p), but it is so high up that the city becomes a gray mass and the climb, because of the low parapet, is not to be recommended for those with vertigo.

SPECIAL PLACES: The street that straggles from the castle to the cathedral is Kilkenny's Royal Mile. It starts at the castle gates as the Parade, an oblong plaza with the castle's classical stables and a decorous row of Georgian houses on one side and a tree-lined promenade, the Mayor's Walk, along the garden wall on the other. High Street, Kilkenny's main commercial street, comes next, with the medieval just under the surface of its respectable Georgian face. The Tholsel, "the house of taxes," is the mid-point of High Street. Beyond it on the right a unique Kilkenny feature occurs at intervals — the slips, or arched, stepped alleyways giving access to the street at river level. Dashing down slips and side alleys is very much part of sight-seeing and shopping in Kilkenny. After High Street, the thoroughfare widens again as Parliament Street, and you see the restored Rothe House and the classical courthouse. Then it narrows to medieval size for Irishtown and leads you to St. Canice's Steps at the foot of the cathedral.

Kilkenny Castle – Kilkenny's most imposing monument looms grandly through trees over the river at the southeastern end of town. The Norman conqueror Strongbow had put up earthen fortifications here and his successor in the early thirteenth century, William the Earl Marshall, replaced them with an irregular quadrangle of curtain walls reinforced by a fat round tower at each of the four corners. The Butler family, Norman earls of Ormonde, bought it in 1391 and from then on it, and they, dominated the city. Though the family in residence remained the same for over five centuries, the castle itself underwent many changes. When the earls became dukes in the seventeenth century, it was rebuilt as a French château; it was re-Gothicized in another major reconstruction in the nineteenth century. Gardens and park are open to the public in daylight hours and the interior may be visited (guided tours are available). Particularly notable is the nineteenth-century Gothic-revival picture gallery. Designed by Benjamin Woodward, it has a painted hammer-beam roof by J. Hungerford Pollen and a fine collection of Butler family portraits. Open daily June through September; closed Mondays in winter. Admission fee. The Parade (phone: 21450).

Kilkenny Design Workshops – This cupola-crowned classical group of buildings with a semicircular courtyard once formed the castle's stables. The horses' stalls originally had decorated plaster ceilings, whereas the grooms occupied plainer and more cramped quarters upstairs. Since 1965 the buildings have housed the government-sponsored Kilkenny Design Workshops where subsidized craftsmen from many countries work in metal, wood, pottery, and cloth, pioneering new design standards for goods to be produced by private enterprise and teaching their art to Irish students. Visitors are not allowed in the workshops, but the splendid showroom and shop on the premises sells products designed or made here or simply inspired by the workshops' presence (see *Shopping*). Open daily. The Parade (phone: 22118).

Shee Alms House – One of the few surviving Tudor almshouses in Ireland was founded in 1582 by Sir Richard Shee "for the accommodation of 12 poor persons." The charity, thus begun by one of Kilkenny's leading families, endured for three centuries. After the adjoining St. Mary's Church became Protestant during the Reformation, a chapel in the almshouse was used for Catholic services. In the present century, the house has served as a storehouse, but it has been refurbished and now holds the city's tourist information office. Rose Inn St.

St. Mary's Church – Parts of this church are believed to date from the thirteenth century. A fine display of Tudor and Stuart grave monuments is housed in the north transept. St. Mary's La.

High Street – Kilkenny's main street has undergone considerable change through the centuries, but a pause here and there still helps to recall its earlier days. Nos. 17, 18, and 19 hide a Tudor house (built in 1582) that belonged to the Archers, another of the town's ten leading families, and you can see their crest above the door. Behind it are the remains of the "Hole in the Wall," a supper house famous enough in the late eighteenth and early nineteenth centuries to have merited a verse: "If you ever go to Kilkenny/Ask for the Hole in the Wall/You may there get blind drunk for a penny /And tipsy for nothing at all." Farther along, raise your eye above the red and gold sign of Woolworths, and you'll see a Tudor gable with the impaled arms of Henry Shee and his wife, Frances. He was a mayor of Kilkenny in the early seventeenth century and this was their town house.

The Tholsel – The Saxon word for "the house of taxes" is another name for Kilkenny's town hall. Built in the mid-eighteenth century, it has open arcades that provide a market below and support a fine Georgian council chamber above. High St.

Rothe House – John Rothe built this solid Tudor merchant's house — actually three houses around two courtyards, with room for shop, storage, and living quarters — in 1594. Rothe was a member of another of Kilkenny's important families, and his wife Rose was an Archer. After the Rothes lost the house in the seventeenth century because of their association with the Confederation of Kilkenny, it eventually became a school. Finally, the Kilkenny Archaeological Society bought it, restored it, and opened it in 1966 as a library and historical museum. Open weekdays and Sunday afternoons from April through October, Sunday afternoons only the rest of the year. Admission charge. Parliament St. (phone: 22893).

St. Francis Abbey – This one-time Franciscan friary is on the premises of the eighteenth-century Smithwicks Brewery, desolate among beer casks and empty crates but still worth seeing. It was founded in the thirteenth century by Richard the Marshall and suppressed, along with the rest of the Irish monasteries, in the sixteenth century. The seven-light east window and the bell tower with its unusual supporting figures are from the fourteenth century. Off Parliament St.

The Black Abbey – The church of the Dominicans, or Black Friars, is on high-walled Abbey Street just beyond Black Freren Gate, the last remaining gate in the city walls. Its history is similar to that of the Franciscan abbey; both were founded and suppressed at approximately the same time, though the Black Abbey survives today as an active Dominican priory. Immediately after suppression, however, townspeople built thatched huts within its walls and it was for a time used as a courthouse before being reclaimed, restored, and opened again for worship. Abbey St.

St. Canice's Cathedral – This building, raised in the thirteenth century by the first Norman bishop, Hugh de Rous, occupies the site of the early Irish monastery of St.

324 KILKENNY / Sources and Resources

Canice and a later Romanesque-style church. A plain cruciform structure, it is nevertheless impressive for its size — the second largest medieval cathedral in Ireland — and its simplicity. The Master of Gowran (a mason who also worked on a neighboring church at Gowran) contributed some vigorous stone carving, in the west doorway particularly, but the renowned stained glass of the east window survived the Reformation only to be smashed to bits by Cromwell's troops, who also left the cathedral roofless and did considerable damage to its many monuments. The church's collection of sixteenth- and seventeenth-century tomb sculptures, many by the O'Tunneys, a local family of sculptors, is still remarkably rich, however, and its hammer-beam roof (a product of a later restoration) is notable. Outside, the round tower predates the cathedral, though its roof is not the original one. St. Canice's Library, established 300 years ago, has 3,000 old volumes. Reached via St. Canice's Steps, which are linked to St. Canice's Pl. by Velvet La. Open 9 AM to 1 PM and 2 PM to 5 PM daily.

- **EXTRA SPECIAL:** *Kilkenny Arts Week* takes place at the end of August or the beginning of September. It is basically a music festival, with lunchtime recitals and grand evening concerts in the castle and cathedral, the classical music interspersed with programs of traditional music and folk song. Poetry readings — some well-known writers have read their work here — are another fundamental ingredient, as are art exhibitions and street theater. It is a friendly, all-join-in event that actually lasts for 9 days, each one ending at the Arts Week Club, where the social side of the festival goes on until the wee hours. For information, write the office at Butler House, Patrick St., Kilkenny.

SOURCES AND RESOURCES

In Kilkenny, the Tourist Information Office, Shee Alms House, Rose Inn St. (phone: 21755), has information, maps, and leaflets. The city map is free; a *Guide to Kilkenny and Heritage Area* costs £1.

For Local Coverage – Kilkenny has two weeklies, *The Kilkenny People* and *The Kilkenny Standard*, published on Wednesdays. The three Dublin morning dailies are also available. Local events are posted weekly in the Tholsel arcade on High St.; details on daily happenings are available at the tourist office.

GETTING AROUND: Kilkenny is a walkable city, and there is no city bus service. From castle to cathedral is just over a mile. You might need a taxi to get to the railway station, which is a little farther away.

Bus and Train – CIE buses and trains serve McDonagh Station, John St. Upper (phone: 22024).

Taxi – Cabs are available from *Delaney's*, John St. (phone: 21396); *Hennessy*, Castlecomer Rd. (phone: 21867); and *Martin*, Michael St. (phone: 22979).

Car Rental – The nearest rental point is *Tully's Travel Agency* in Carlow, 25 miles away (phone: 0503-31257).

Coach Tours – Guided historical tours, which include afternoon tea, leave from Kilkenny Castle at 2 PM on Saturdays in the summer, and cost about £3.50.

MUSEUMS: In addition to the Butler family's distinguished portrait collection, the *Kilkenny Castle* art gallery features occasional traveling exhibitions. The restored *Rothe House* contains the Kilkenny Archaeological Society's museum of local history. See *Special Places*.

KILKENNY / Sources and Resources

SHOPPING: The presence of the Kilkenny Design Workshops has led to a proliferation of choice craft shops in Kilkenny. The town also has literary associations (Jonathan Swift, among others, attended Kilkenny College) and two good bookshops. (Most shops are closed Thursday afternoons.)

Jody Cahill – Antiques veering to bric-a-brac. William St.

Callaghan and Connolly – Antique and period furniture. 14 St. Kieran's St. (phone: 21053).

Liam Costigan – Modern jewelry by a Kilkenny Design Workshop graduate. Colliers La.

Finds – Definitely bric-a-brac. St. Kieran's St.

Rudolf Heltzel – Exquisite modern jewelry, this time by a pioneer Kilkenny Design Workshop teacher. 10 Patrick St. (phone: 21497).

Hodges Figgis – An excellent modern bookshop, strong on Irish titles and local publications. High St. (phone: 22974).

Kilkenny Design Shop – An Aladdin's cave of modern Irish design in silver, glass, pottery, wood, and textiles, many items designed and some produced on the premises. Good bargains in household items. The Parade (phone: 22118).

The Monster House – A solid, traditional department store selling woolens, tweeds, glass, and all the rest. High St. (phone: 22016).

Don Roberts – Secondhand books, maps, and prints, especially Irish material and local authors. Issues catalog. St. Kieran's St. (phone: 0409-5054).

Rothe Crafts – The merchant's shop at Rothe House is stocked with knits, tweeds, glassware, and souvenirs. Parliament St.

Caroline's Boutique – The best of a recent wave of trendy clothes shops. The Parade.

SPECIAL EVENTS: *Kilkenny Arts Week* is held every year in late August or early September (see *Extra Special*). Other events are: the *International Air Rally* (phone: 22036) at the Kilkenny airstrip, held annually during the third weekend in June; the *National Hot-Air Balloon Championships* at Castle Park in late September; and *Heritage Weekends,* with historical and archaeological tours and entertainment, in late April and early October.

SPORTS: Fishing – There is good trout fishing in the rivers Nore and Dinan north of Kilkenny. Consult the Kilkenny Anglers Association, Secretary Paddy Troy (phone: 22148 or 22084).

Golfing – The *Kilkenny Golf Club* (phone: 22125) accepts guests at its pleasant 18-hole course about 1 mile from town.

Greyhound Racing – Races are held at St. James's Park every Wednesday and Friday evening (phone: 21214).

Horse Racing – The racecourse (phone: 26126) at lovely Gowran Park, 10 miles from the city, is the site of 8 meetings a year.

Hurling – Ireland's ancient and spectacular stick and ball game is played most stylishly in Kilkenny. There is usually a game on Sunday afternoon at Nowlan Park.

THEATER: The Kilkenny New Theatre group presents Summer Pub Theatre, a show of light plays, at the *Club House* hotel during the season. Other events occur in association with Kilkenny Arts Week. The national *Pub Theater Festival,* planned to be an annual event, was inaugurated in November 1981.

MUSIC: Except for traditional Irish music, regular musical performances are confined to Kilkenny Arts Week.

NIGHTCLUBS AND NIGHTLIFE: Pubs for the mature and discos for the young is the extent of the nightlife in Kilkenny as in most Irish towns. During the summer, special traditional Irish musical evenings are provided for visitors at the *Conradh na Gaeilge Rooms,* Rothe House, on Mondays and at the *Newpark Hotel* on Wednesdays, at the *Rose Hill House* on Saturdays and Sundays. The *Springhill Hotel* is given over to *céilí* (Irish dancing) on Wednesdays, to cabaret on Saturdays, and to disco on Sundays.

SINS: Repent for past sins or prepare for future ones. Dublin's Leeson Street is 75 miles away.

BEST IN TOWN

CHECKING IN: Despite its obvious attractions, Kilkenny has not been much of a hotel town, at least until recently. The tourist circuit of Ireland tends to go clockwise around the coast, ignoring the interior, and only lately have hotels in midland towns roused themselves from a rather dull state of commercial plainness. There are exceptions, however, and on the whole, Kilkenny's hotels offer good value. Most make it into a moderate bracket of $40 to $60 per double room with breakfast; inexpensive ones cost less than that. Should you find it impossible to get into the hotel you select, the Tourist Information Office will be happy to help out. Your alternative may be a town or country home or farmhouse, and you might enjoy the experience.

Newpark – A Victorian country house on the north edge of the city has been skillfully combined with modern extensions and converted into a comfortable 45-bedroom hotel (38 with bath). The service is friendly, the decor attractive, there are phones in the rooms, and all is set in spacious grounds. Castlecomer Rd. (phone: 22122). Moderate.

Rose Hill House – This is a Regency gem built as his own home by William Robertson, the architect who gave Kilkenny Castle its final Gothic trim. His touch here produced a fanciful structure in which the hotel's public rooms have retained some of their former domestic charm. The 20 bedrooms — ultramodern and spacious, with bath, phones, color TV, and video system — are in a separate block. College Rd. (phone: 22603). Moderate.

Springhill – Modern and of the motel type, this hotel provides 48 well-equipped rooms on the southern edge of the city. It is useful if you have a car. Phones in rooms. Waterford Rd. (phone: 21122). Moderate.

Club House – Full of atmosphere, with a cozy bar, old-fashioned dining room, and a fine collection of turn-of-the-century magazine cartoons. The *Club House* is downtown in a basically Georgian building and it's somewhat short on baths — four of the 30 bedrooms have them. High tea is served instead of dinner. Patrick St. (phone: 21994). Inexpensive.

KILKENNY / Best in Town

EATING OUT: Like the Midlands generally and for the reasons suggested in *Checking In,* Kilkenny is not a food adventure. A good rule to follow in smaller centers off the beaten tourist track is to go for the plainly cooked Irish staples, which can be excellent: bacon, eggs, and brown wholemeal bread for breakfast; roast beef, lamb, boiled bacon, or salmon at other meals, served with fresh vegetables and topped off with fruit tarts (tell them to hold the custard — usually out of a package — and they will probably add a dollop of fresh cream). Do not disdain eating in your hotel: It is often better than elsewhere and the locals also use it for eating out. As most likely you will be traveling by car, some worthwhile places in attractive spots at a distance have been included below. Expect dinner for two (without wine or tips) to cost from $20 to $35 in a restaurant listed as moderate; under $20 in an inexpensive one.

Lord Bagenal – You'll find this modern restaurant 15 miles from Kilkenny in a historic town at a crossing of the River Barrow. The menu features fresh fish and Dublin Bay prawns are a house specialty. Phone for reservations. Leighlinbridge (phone: 21668). Moderate.

The Maltings – Home cooking and an intimate atmosphere are the drawing cards here. The restaurant is by the riverside, 16 miles from Kilkenny, and it's open for dinner only, Tuesdays through Saturdays. Reservations are recommended. Inistioge (phone: 29484). Moderate.

Newpark Hotel – Good, straightforward Irish food, efficiently served, is the mainstay of this hotel restaurant, and a few Continental specialties provide variety. The wine list is reasonable. Castlecomer Rd. (phone: 22122). Moderate.

Kyteler's Inn – In a pleasantly decorated historic building, this restaurant serves plain but good food cooked over an open wood fire, as well as some more ambitious dishes. St. Kieran's St. (phone: 21064). Moderate.

Rose Hill House Restaurant – New decor in period style complements an already fine Regency villa built by architect William Robertson for himself. The enthusiastic young manager, trained on the Continent, has introduced seafood (crab, eel, prawns, scallops) as an unusual specialty for a restaurant in the Midlands. College Rd. (phone: 22603). Moderate.

Mulhall's Restaurant – A digression off High Street through a small arcade and into a medieval lane leads to this airy, modern restaurant of wood and stone. Excellent coffee and pastries baked on the premises are on the menu all day; light or regular lunches are offered; and dinner is served on Thursdays, Fridays, and Saturdays only (until 9:45 PM). Pudding La., off High St. (phone: 21329). Inexpensive.

SHARING A PINT: Smithwicks, a medium-tart ale-type beer, has been the local brew for well over 200 years. You may get a free sample if you take the guided brewery tour (Parliament St.) at 3 PM daily, May through September. To try it elsewhere, take your pick of the pubs. They range from the dark and cozy but spartan to the modern, well-lighted plastic. A list of the best includes *Tynans Bar,* 2 Horseleap Slip, a turn-of-the-century pub that has survived with its fittings — brass scales, grocery drawers, beer pumps, gilt mirrors — miraculously intact. Locals and cosmopolitans share its great atmosphere and honest drink. The exterior of *The Marble City Bar,* 66 High St., is a museum piece; the interior is less authentic, but its character has not been overwhelmed by modernization. *Kyteler's Inn,* St. Kieran's St., was once the house of the redoubtable Dame Alice. It now has a friendly nest of bars and a beer garden. The *Club House Bar* is a quiet oasis in the hotel on Patrick St., with sporting prints, cartoons, and cast-iron bar tables. *Fitzpatricks,* Parliament St., is a restored pub convenient for lunch after a visit to Rothe House next door. Also good for pub grub is *Langton's,* 69 John St., a lively, social pub favored by the young.

LIMERICK CITY

The fourth largest city in Ireland offers an appropriately engaging introduction to the country for those many, many visitors who begin journeys here after the short half-hour trip in from Shannon Airport. Limerick is a major port, an inevitable product of its enviable position on the River Shannon; and while the city has a reputation for industry, those it is most famous for are all amiably light: traditional Limerick lace, still produced here; wonderfully cured hams and bacon; salmon fishing; and flour milling.

Limerick is a city of narrow streets, handsome Georgian houses, and impressive public buildings such as the Custom House and the Town Hall. This gracious architecture hardly reflects its violent history. Invaded by the Danes in the early tenth century, the area suffered many long years of skirmishing, which ended only when the Vikings were finally crushed by the Irish chieftain, Brian Ború. He made Limerick (in Irish, *Luimneach*) the capital of Munster. In the twelfth century, the Anglo-Normans conquered the town, and settling on the island formed by the river Shannon and its tributary, the Abbey, they built stout walls to keep the natives at bay. This area became known as English Town, and the section across the river Irish Town.

Undeterred by walls, the Irish continued to make sallies into English Town, led by the king of Munster, Donal Mor O'Brien. Upon his death in 1194, however, the Normans consolidated their position, and in 1210 King John ordered a strong castle and fortified bridge built to control the crossing point of the River Shannon. In later years the city walls were extended for added security.

During the seventeenth century the city was torn between revolts by the Irish who seized the city and sieges by the English to bring them to their knees. The Treaty of Limerick in 1691 was to end hostilities and grant political and religious liberty to the Irish and the Catholics, but repeated violations of the treaty forced thousands into exile. Many of Limerick's most important landmarks — Thomond Bridge, the city walls, and St. Mary's Cathedral — have associations with these turbulent times.

But as befits a city that is the major western gateway to Ireland, contemporary Limerick has a great deal to offer besides its ancient history and sites. A roster of activities includes fishing, horseback riding, horse racing, golfing, and swimming and boating on the Shannon. The medieval banquets held at the nearby Bunratty and Knappogue castles as well as the *céilís* at the Folk Park offer a delightful — if somewhat rowdy — sampling of traditional Irish hospitality. The countryside surrounding Limerick has a quiet beauty, perfect for a peaceful day's rambling: Low hill ranges ruffle the plains; small towns rise here and there, each with its ruined castle, abbey, or bridge.

Unlike most Irish cities, Limerick does not have important literary connections. It is, however, the home of the *limerick,* that famous five-line rhyme derived from a round-game in which an individual extemporized a nonsense verse, followed by a chorus that included the words, "Will you come up to Limerick?" Over the years the term *limerick* became associated with the rhyme scheme *aabba* invented by the nineteenth-century nonsense poet Edward Lear. A typical limerick might go like this:

> There was a fair Irish city,
>   That lent its good name to a ditty;
> Though of dubious worth
>   The verse caused great mirth,
> Now the limerick outshines Limerick City.

LIMERICK AT-A-GLANCE

SEEING THE CITY: For the best view of this rather flat city, climb to the top of King John's Castle; the key to the building is available from Mrs. Mooney, who lives directly across the street from the main entrance to the castle. You can also view the city from the spire of St. Mary's Cathedral. Contact the caretaker to gain access to the tower.

SPECIAL PLACES: Limerick is very compact and most of the important sights are located in the same general area. As traffic is sometimes congested, the city is really best seen on foot.

CITY CENTER

Thomond Bridge – The present bridge, dating to 1840, was designed by Irish architect James Pain to replace the thirteenth-century structure erected by King John to defend the city. The original had a guard house and gate at the west end and a drawbridge at the east end near the castle. The Treaty Stone, on which the famous Treaty of Limerick was reputedly signed in 1691 after the Williamite Seige ended, is on the west side of the new bridge.

King John's Castle – This fortification at the east foot of Thomond Bridge was built in 1210 by King John to guard the city against invaders. It is one of the oldest examples of Norman architecture in Ireland, with rounded gate towers standing sentry over the curtain walls. In the eighteenth century a military barracks was installed within the walls, and, later, houses were built in the castle yard, some of which remain. The castle is in reasonably good condition and is open to the public during the summer months.

St. Mary's Cathedral – Established in 1172 by Donal Mor O'Brien, the last king of Munster, it has been restored and extended a number of times and combines features from many different centuries. Note especially the unusual (and unique in Ireland) fifteenth-century choir stalls whose misericords are carved with many medieval emblems, including those of Richard III. The cathedral is open daily in the summer, 9 AM to 1 PM and 2:30 to 6 PM; in the winter, 10 AM to 1 PM and 2:30 to 4 PM. Nicholas St. and Bridge St.

Baal's Bridge – The original structure on this location linked the turf of the conquerers — English Town — with that of the natives — Irish Town. In Irish *Baal* means "bald," that is, the bridge had no battlements, but rather supported a row of houses. These disappeared in 1830 when the present bridge was constructed.

Limerick Walls – Forming a rough diamond shape, the Limerick walls run east and southeast from Ball's Bridge, along Old Clare Street and Lelia Street to the grounds of St. John's Hospital. There were four main gates: East Watergate, John's Gate, Mungret Gate, and West Watergate. The largest remaining portion of the walls is behind Lelia Street. Traces of the Black Battery (so called because it successfully resisted the Williamites) are found on the hospital grounds, while a badly deteriorated bit can be seen looking from Pike's Row toward High Street. There are two other sections — one forming part of the building housing Sinnotts Joinery Works and the other standing in the Charlotte Quay parking lot.

St. John's Cathedral – Originally intended as a parish church, this Gothic revival cathedral built in the nineteenth century eventually became the see of the diocese. It houses two of Ireland's most remarkable ecclesiastical treasures, the magnificently carved mitre and crozier made by Cornelius O'Dea, who was one of Limerick's bishops in the fifteenth century. At 280 feet, St. John's spire is the highest in Ireland; it's rather more ornate than the rest of the structure. The memorial to Patrick Sarsfield, hero of the 1690–91 sieges, which is located on the cathedral grounds, was rendered by John Lawlor of Dublin in 1881.

St. John's Square – A few steps from the cathedral, this square constructed around 1751 was once lined with fashionable stone houses owned by the local gentry. The square declined slowly over the years until the twentieth century, when the houses were used less glamorously as offices, tenements, barracks, and a butcher shop. Eventually they fell into neglect and were abandoned, although interest in them has recently been revived and restoration undertaken.

Newtown Pery – Just 200 years old, this is the "new" part of Limerick — a grid of streets roughly extending between Sarsfield Street in the north and the Crescent on the south. Named after Edward Sexton Pery, a Speaker of the Irish House of Commons, under whose patronage the renovation was begun, the development was distinctly Georgian in character with town houses constructed of red brick. In the Crescent is a memorial to Daniel O'Connell, "the Liberator," rendered by Irish sculptor John Hogan in 1857. (O'Connell founded the movement for Catholic emancipation.)

ENVIRONS

Bunratty Castle and Folk Park – The original castle on this site was built in the fifteenth century by the McNamara family, but appropriated around 1500 by Conor O'Brien, earl of Thomond. Refurbished in the 1950s, it's now famous for the colorful medieval banquets presented in the great hall every evening (see *Nightlife*), but the castle also houses an incredible collection of European paintings, furniture, and tapestries dating from the fourteenth to seventeenth centuries. From the battlements, you have a splendid view — as did the Earl's warriors — of the surrounding countryside. Behind the castle is a model village, with cottages, workshops, and exhibits demonstrating how people in different regions of Ireland lived and labored years ago. The castle and Folk Park are both located on the main Ennis road. Across the street from them is the mustard-colored Bunratty Cottage, a shop noted for its clothing designed by the locally well-known Vonnie Reynolds.

Knappogue Castle – Built in 1467 by the McNamara family, this castle was recently bought by an American and restored to its original fifteenth-century elegance. Surrounded by lush green pastures and grazing cattle, Knappogue presents an imposing front. The interior is no less impressive, with its soaring ceilings and handsome antique furnishings. Ask to see the owners' magnificent private dining room. Open daily. About 12 miles northwest of Limerick, near Quin.

Quin Abbey – Although the Franciscan friary, dating to 1402, is now roofless and in ruins, you can still see the tombs of the founding McNamara clan. Quin.

Craggaunowen – This project, like Bunratty, was developed to document life-styles in Ireland long ago. The complex has both a ring fort dating from early Christian times and a *crannóg,* or lake dwelling (stone hut situated on an island), typical of the Bronze Age. The castle on the grounds is not a reproduction, but rather an actual fortress built by the McNamara family in the sixteenth century. In the intervening years it suffered neglect and changed hands several times, but is now restored and contains many medieval artifacts. Open daily. Quin.

Adare Manor – This stately neo-Gothic mansion located in Adare, generally considered the "prettiest village in Ireland," was commissioned in the nineteenth century by the earl of Dunraven. Various features of the house such as the minstrel's gallery, staircase, dining room, and fireplaces were designed by A. W. Pugin. (At press time it was temporarily closed to the public.) 10 miles southwest of Limerick on the Cork road.

Lough Gur – Around this lake are found a number of ancient ruins, including stone circles, cairns, dolmens, and crannógs. Human bones, weapons, and pottery have all been unearthed here and experts estimate earliest habitation of the site to be 2,000 BC. A guide to the area (£1.65) can be obtained from the Limerick Tourist Office. 12 miles south of Limerick on the Bruff road.

The Craggaunowen Museum – Donated by Celtic historian John Hunt, who also sponsored the Craggaunowen Project in Quin (see above), this is a collection of many artifacts found in Ireland dating to the Bronze and Early Iron ages. Open summers only, Mondays to Fridays, 9:30 AM to 5:30 PM. Located 3 miles east of Limerick, at the National Institute for Higher Education, off the Dublin Road.

■ **EXTRA SPECIAL:** An appropriate finale to a day's castle climbing would be an aromatic glass of mead and a chat with the flamboyant Ian O'Casey in his wine bar at Mountcashel Castle. Actually a towerhouse built in the fifteenth century by Conor O'Brien, earl of Thomond, it has been carefully restored and is now listed as a National Monument. Up the circular staircase on the top floor is the tiny, corbel-roofed dining room, where O'Casey serves candlelit evening dinners sometimes accompanied by traditional Irish music. On the road between Sixmilebridge and Quin (phone: 44777 for reservations).

SOURCES AND RESOURCES

For general information, brochures, and maps, visit the Tourist Information Office at 62 O'Connell St. (phone: 47522). The staff here will advise you on any problems or questions you may have, and will make hotel reservations anywhere in the country.

The *Official Guide to Limerick* ($3), *Shannonside* (free), and *Limerick and Tipperary* (15p) are all available at the tourist information office. *The Story of Limerick* by Robert Wyse Jackson will set you straight on the city's long history.

For Local Coverage – The *Limerick Chronicle* and the *Limerick Leader* are both published three times a week. The weekly tourist board's *What's On* guide gives information about local entertainment schedules.

GETTING AROUND: Bus – Service between Dublin, Limerick, and Shannon Airport is frequent and convenient. The terminal, Colbert Station, is on Parnell St.; call 48777 for departure and arrival schedules.

Taxi – There are cabstands on Thomas St., Cecil St., and at Colbert

Station. Or, you can order a taxi from one of the following: *Conway Cabs* (phone: 44070); *Renny Cabs* (phone: 77277); *Speedi Cabs* (phone: 48844); *Tara Cabs* (phone: 44070).

Car Rental – All the major Irish and international firms are represented at Shannon Airport. In the Limerick area, you can rent a car from *Bunratty Car Hire,* Coonagh Motors, Coonagh Cross, Caherdavin, Limerick (phone: 52781); *Dan Ryan Car Rentals,* Punch's Cross, Limerick (phone: 45566); *Andy Lacey Car Rentals,* Setright's Cross, Cratloe (phone: 97300); or *Treaty Car Rental,* 37 William St., Limerick (phone: 46512).

MUSEUMS: The *Limerick Art Gallery,* which exhibits modern Irish painting, is in People's Park on Pery Sq.; the *Limerick Civic Museum,* which documents local history, is on St. John's Sq.

SHOPPING: Along Limerick's main shopping street, O'Connell, are many knitwear, crystal, and crafts stores. If you're interested in antiques, you can find furniture, paintings, and prints in *George Stacpoole's* place at 35 Cecil St., and china and jewelry at *Once Upon a Time* on Ellen St. and *Grange Antiques* on O'Connell St. To buy famous Limerick lace go to the *Good Shepherd Convent* on Clare St. (phone: 45178).

SPECIAL EVENTS: Although there are various country fairs throughout the year, the most important event in this area is the annual *Limerick Civic Week* in late March, which features a St. Patrick's Day parade, a singing competition, a crafts exhibit, an international band competition, and a charity ball hosted by the mayor.

SPORTS: Boating – In Killaloe, about 12 miles north of Limerick, are several companies that rent cabin boats for cruising the Shannon and neighboring lakes: *Atlantis Marine Ltd.* (phone: 76281); *Cormacruisers Ltd.* (phone: 76251); and *Derg Line Cruisers* (phone: 76364).

Cycling – You can rent a bike from *Noel McMahon & Son,* 24 Roches St. (phone: 46718); *Nestor Brothers Ltd.,* 28 O'Connell St.; or *Limerick Sports Store,* 10 William St. From *Raleigh Rent-a-Bike* you can hire a bicycle, buy insurance, and obtain touring maps of the area. (Contact Irish Raleigh, Broomhill Rd., Tallaght, Co. Dublin.)

Fishing – To fish for salmon in the Shannon or for trout and grilse in the Mulcair or Bunratty rivers, you must request a permit from the Shannon Fisheries, c/o ESB Showrooms, O'Connell St., Limerick City (phone: 45599).

Golf – Both the *Limerick Golf Club* at Ballyclough (phone: 44083) and the *Castletroy Golf Club* on the Dublin Road (45261) are open to the public; you can rent equipment and use the clubhouse.

Horses – You can hire horses at the following stables: *Ashroe House,* Newport; *Ballylooby House,* Knocklong; *Balleyteigue House,* Bruree; and *The Stables,* Rathkeale.

Hunting – Hiring a horse for a day will run about $60 and the cap fee about $80. To make arrangements to join a hunt, write in advance to hunt secretary J. R. Sheehy, Foxfield, Patrickswell (phone: 96120).

NIGHTCLUBS AND NIGHTLIFE: The Limerick area offers a wide range of evening entertainment for every taste — from ballad sessions to disco dancing. During summer, King John's Castle is the setting for poetry readings, as well as *seisiún,* evenings of traditional Irish music and dance (Thomond St.). More formal, perhaps, is the *céilí* offered at Bunratty Folk Park, a program of singing, dancing, and storytelling accompanied by an Irish meal. In a similar vein are the banquets held at Bunratty and Knappogue castles — "medieval" feasts enlivened by traditional music and historical sketches. (Both located on the main Limerick/Ennis road; for reservations, call Shannon Castle Tours at 61788.) Irish cabaret, a dinner-plus-variety show, is offered by several hotels in the area, as are discos; check *What's On* for details. Finally, there are many singing pubs in Limerick and local papers provide information on these.

SINS: In this part of horse-crazy Ireland, playing the ponies is a most fitting sin. You can place your bet at one of Limerick City's many "turf accountant" offices or at the racetrack. Although the two main events, the Irish Derby and the Irish Grand National, are both held in County Kildare, the excitement is just as real at the smaller races held at Greenpark in the city and at Limerick Junction, about an hour's drive on Tipperary Road. At both courses you'll see 10 or 12 colorful "turf accountants" (bookies); lists of runners and the odds being offered are written on blackboards. "Punters" (gamblers) simply walk up to the bookie, hand him the money, name their choice of horse, and receive a betting slip with the man's name on it. If you win, return the slip to the bookie for your payoff — first allowing another race to lapse so that he can make up his cash.

BEST IN TOWN

CHECKING IN: Perhaps because of its proximity to Shannon Airport, Limerick City has several new modern, comfortable hotels, some of whose dining rooms are quite good. Expect to pay $90 and up for a double in a hotel listed as very expensive; between $65 and $80 in expensive; and between $40 and $60 in moderate. In addition to the large hotels we mention, there are numerous small guesthouses for which you can make reservations at the local tourist board.

Dromoland Castle – Unadulterated luxury prevails at this renovated and luxurious former O'Brien stronghold. Besides 67 large, comfortable bedrooms, it offers golf, riding, tennis, fishing, and shooting within its spacious grounds. The dining room is formal, as befits a palace, and its cuisine is excellent. Newmarket-on-Fergus (phone: 7-1144). Very expensive.

Jury's – Just over the bridge from the city center, this modern hotel offers efficient service and has 100 well-appointed rooms. Its restaurant, *The Copper Room*, is particularly good. Ennis Rd. (phone: 47266). Expensive.

Limerick Inn – This is a modern, comfortable motel with 133 rooms, a Continental restaurant that's very good, and well above average service. Ennis Rd. (phone: 51544). Moderate.

Limerick Ryan – Part of the dependable Ryan Hotel Chain, it has 184 rooms, a restaurant, and a bar in which ballad sessions are featured. Ennis Rd. (phone: 45922). Moderate.

Shannon Shamrock Inn – This Paddy Fitzpatrick hotel has 81 rooms, a heated indoor pool, a sauna, a French/Irish restaurant, and a bar. It's next to Bunratty Castle and Durty Nellie's pub. Bunratty (phone: 61177). Moderate.

EATING OUT: While the Limerick area is not known for its wealth of restaurants, you won't be disappointed with a meal at any of the places recommended below. Expect to pay $65 and up for dinner for two in places listed as expensive and between $30 and $55 in those mentioned as moderate.

The Copper Room – The best in the city, this rather small but attractive hotel restaurant offers excellently prepared French cuisine. Service is efficient and friendly. Open for dinner only. Ennis Rd. (phone: 55266). Expensive.

Merryman – Rather fussily decorated in mock Georgian style with red velvet seating and gold-painted window frames, this eatery has become a little run down in appearance of late. Service lacks polish — the staff is rather offhand — but this gives the place a certain charm. The menu offers such basics as roast duckling, beef, and lamb, or grilled salmon and steak. Open for lunch and dinner. 102 O'Connell St. (phone: 47412). Moderate.

Hi-Way – Easily overlooked because of its somewhat commercial atmosphere, this place has good food, fast service, and a friendly, interested staff. Open till 2 AM. Dooradoyle (phone: 27449). Moderate.

NOTE: For an inexpensive lunch costing between $5 and $10, try one of the following: *Punch's Pub,* at Punch's Cross and O'Connell St.; *The Cloister,* beside the Franciscan church on Henry St.; or *The Galleon Grill-Bistro,* on O'Connell St.

SHARING A PINT: *Nancy Blake's,* on Denmark St., is a quiet, friendly little pub where local working people drink. The oak-beamed *Lucky Lamp* at 9 Ellen St. used to be a wine store, and so the wines available range from the pedestrian to the extraordinary. The place also serves bar snacks — salads, soups, sandwiches — and attracts a youngish crowd in the late evening, when it can become crowded. The clientele at *The Courtyard,* a modern bar in Todds Bow, off William St., is mostly shoppers and office workers at lunch time and young people in the evening. The hamburgers and other light meals served here are inexpensive, and it's a good choice for parents with children. Not generally frequented by women, *Dick Devine's,* a traditional tavern on Nicholas St. across from St. Mary's Cathedral, has a good atmosphere nonetheless. *O'Farrell's Inn,* 1 Thomas St., is a cozy pub whose walls are decorated with various coats of arms and whose arched, wood-paneled ceiling echoes the shape of a *currach. Durty Nellie's,* which may be the best-known pub in Ireland, is about 10 miles from Limerick City, right next door to Bunratty Castle. Although often jammed with both tourists and locals, the place is quite attractive, and has a small restaurant called the *Oyster,* where you can have a light meal or sandwich. If you're lucky, you might also catch some music.

LONDON

British author and journalist V. S. Pritchett noted that the essence of London was contained in the very sound of its name: *Lon-don,* a weighty word, solid, monumental, dignified, even ponderous. London is a shapeless city without a center; it sprawls anarchically over 620 square miles and brims over with a variety of neighborhoods and people. One of its sharpest observers, Daniel Defoe, portrayed London in the eighteenth century much as it could be described today: "It is . . . stretched out in buildings, straggling, confused . . . out of all shape, uncompact and unequal; neither long nor broad, round or square."

London can best be understood not as one city but as a conglomeration of villages that were incorporated whole, one by one, as the monster expanded — Chelsea, Battersea, Paddington, and Hampstead are just a few. Fortunately, all of its important parks and squares have remained inviolate, but not without a struggle, for London's merchant class — its backbone and its pride — has always resisted and defeated town planners, ever since Parliament turned down Sir Christopher Wren's splendid plan to rebuild after the fire of 1666. It was royalty and aristocracy that created and preserved the parks — St. James's Park, Hyde Park, Kensington Gardens, Regent's Park, and Kew Gardens were all royal parks — and their enthusiasm became contagious. The passionate regard of Londoners for their green spots has been one of the city's saving graces as it grew so helplessly and recklessly, more in the spirit of commerce than of urban planning.

Today's London — though marred by soulless high-rise intruders of glass and concrete — boasts more greenery than any other metropolis can hope to display these days. Aside from its many garden squares and the meticulously tended gardens of so many Londoners' homes, the city is punctuated by a series of large parks and commons; besides those already mentioned, there are Wimbledon Common, Highgate Wood, Primrose Hill, Hampstead Heath — the list goes on and on. And to make even more certain that citification does not intrude too far into London life, a green belt, almost 100 square miles of forest and grassland, virtually encircles the city and, to the chagrin and impatience of "developers," is meticulously preserved by law.

London's other natural resource, the River Thames, has not been so fortunate. As any glance at a map will show, London follows the serpentine meanderings of the Thames, England's principal river. Nearly everything of interest in London is on or near the Thames, for London is London because it is a natural port. The river has always been London's mainstay, for centuries its only east-west road. But the Thames is a working river; it is no longer

— as it was in the heyday of Elizabeth I — also used for ornament or for pleasure. In miles of wharves and dockland, there is little beauty to behold. Yet it has rightly been said that "every drop of the Thames is liquid history." At the site of the Naval College in Greenwich, for example, there once stood a royal palace where Henry VIII and Elizabeth I were born — and where tournaments, pageants, and banquets were held.

A great river port and a city of gardens, London is also a city of stately squares and monuments, of royalty with its pomp and ceremony, a cosmopolitan city of the first rank. Until World War II, it was the capital of the mammoth and far-flung British Empire upon which, it was said, the sun never set. For many centuries, a powerful Britannia ruled a considerable section of the globe — the largest since Roman times — and the English language spread from the inconsiderable British Isles to become the dominant language all over the world, from North America to India.

If the British Empire is most certainly in decline, it is declining gracefully among memories of its great days; and if once-subject peoples hated their oppressor, they love London, and many have chosen to live there. London is still the center of the Commonwealth of independent nations that were once British colonies, and its cosmopolitan atmosphere owes a great deal to the ubiquity of former colonials. Their presence is felt in the substantial Indian-Pakistani community in the Southall district of West London; in the strong Caribbean flavor in Brixton; in Chinatown in and around Gerrard Street — a hop, skip, and a jump from Piccadilly Circus; in the Cypriot groceries and bakeries of Camden Town; and in the majestic new mosque on the fringe of Regent's Park.

A tantalizing diversity of accents flavors the English language here — accents from Australia and Barbados, Bangladesh and Nigeria, Canada and Malaysia, Kenya and South Africa, Sri Lanka and Ireland, Hong Kong and the US. And then the various inflections of Britain itself are also to be heard in the streets of London — the lilt and rasp of cockney, Oxford, Somerset, Yorkshire, the Scottish Highlands, and the Welsh mining towns.

London's somewhat onomatopoeic name derives from the Celtic term *Llyn-din,* meaning "river place," but little is known of London before it was renamed *Londinium* by the Romans in AD 43. The rather fantastical twelfth-century historian Geoffrey of Monmouth may have originated the myth widespread in Shakespeare's day — that London was founded by Brute, a direct descendant of Aeneas in 1108 BC, who named it Troynovant, new Troy, or Trenovant. Even in medieval times, London had grandiose notions of its own importance — a prideful self-image that has been amply justified by history.

The city was sufficiently prominent for the Norman invader William the Conqueror to make it his capital in 1066. During the Middle Ages, the expansion of trade, population growth, and the energetic activities of its guilds of merchants and craftsmen promoted London's prosperity. Indisputably, London's golden age was the English Renaissance, the sixteenth century, the time of Queen Elizabeth I, Shakespeare, and Drake's defeat of the Spanish Armada. The Tudor buildings of London were wiped out in the great fire of 1666. Christopher Wren, the architect of genius, undertook to rebuild many buildings and churches, the most outstanding of which is St. Paul's Cathedral.

The eighteenth century, a highly sophisticated age, saw the building of noble homes and stately squares, of which only Bedford Square and Fitzroy remain complete. In the early nineteenth century, interest continued in homes and squares; and only in the Victorian age, the height of the Empire, were public buildings like the Houses of Parliament redesigned, this time in grand and fanciful neo-Gothic style.

London has seen whole catalogues of heroes and villains, crises and conflagrations, come and go, sometimes swallowed whole in the passage of time, sometimes leaving relics. Still on elegant display is stately Hampton Court Palace, the most magnificent of England's palaces, where Henry VIII lived now and again with five of his six wives. There is a spot downtown — in front of the Banqueting House on Whitehall — where another king, Charles I, was beheaded by his subjects, who were calmly committing dreaded regicide 150 years before the more explosive French across the English Channel even contemplated such a gesture.

London has lived through the unbounded permissiveness of the flamboyantly royal Restoration period (1660–85), when even King Charles II frequented brothels and didn't care who knew it, and it has survived the stern moral puritanism of the Victorian era, when it was downright rude to refer to a *breast* of a chicken or a piano *leg*. And most recently, London stood up with exemplary courage under the devastating effects of the Nazi bombings, which destroyed a great many buildings and killed thousands of people.

Many of our images of London, taken from old movies, actually mirror its realities: Big Ben rises above the Houses of Parliament, somberly striking the hour; ramrod-straight scarlet-uniformed soldiers half hide their faces in towering black bearskin hats; waiters at the Bank of England still sport the kinds of top hats and tailcoats their predecessors wore for a century; lawyers in court still don wigs and black robes. A few images, however, are outdated: The bowler hat has been slipping steadily out of fashion for years, and rigidly enforced environmental regulations have made London's once-famous peasoup fogs rare.

London's nearly infinite variety of urban moods includes the sturdy edifices lining Whitehall, center of the British government, with Trafalgar Square at its head and Parliament at its foot; the elegant shopping areas of Knightsbridge, Bond Street, and the Burlington Arcade; suburban chic in Barnes and Blackheath; handsome squares in Bloomsbury; melancholy mystery in Victoria and Waterloo train stations with their spy-movie atmosphere; the vitality of East End street markets; and the riparian tranquillity of Thames-side towpaths in Putney and along Hammersmith Mall.

The British have a talent that amounts to genius for government — for democracy and political tolerance — a talent that has been developing ever since the Magna Carta was signed in 1215, and one that makes London's ambience easy and relaxed for individualists and eccentrics of all sorts. It is no wonder that the eccentric and inveterate Londoner of the eighteenth-century heyday, Dr. Samuel Johnson, once declared, "When a man is tired of London, he is tired of life, for there is in London all that life can afford."

Johnson's opinion, though somewhat overblown, was essentially shared by one of several modern American writers who chose to live in London.

Disillusioned with New York, Boston, and Paris, Henry James decided in favor of London in 1881. Somehow he concluded that London was a place eminently suited to human life: "It is not a pleasant place; it is not agreeable, or cheerful, or easy, or exempt from reproach. It is only magnificent. You can draw up a tremendous list of reasons why it should be unsupportable. The fogs, the smoke, the dirt, the darkness, the wet, the distances, the ugliness, the brutal size of the place, the horrible numerosity of society . . . but . . . London is on the whole the most possible form of life."

LONDON AT-A-GLANCE

SEEING THE CITY: London has, for the most part, resisted the temptation to build high. Aside from a handful of modest gestures toward sky-scraping, there aren't many towering structures to obscure panoramic overviews of the city from its higher vantage points, which include:

London Hilton Hotel – There were discreet noises of disapproval from Buckingham Palace when it was realized that the view from the roof bar of the *Hilton* included not only the palace grounds but, with high-powered binoculars, the insides of some of the royal chambers as well. In fact, the view over Mayfair, Hyde Park, and Westminster is breathtaking. Park La. (phone: 493-8000).

Westminster Cathedral – Not to be confused with Westminster Abbey. The top of the bell tower of London's Catholic cathedral looks down on a broad expanse of the inner city. There is an elevator to take you up for a token charge. Off Victoria St. near the station, at Ashley Pl. SW 1.

Hampstead Heath – Climb to the top of tree-studded Spaniards Row, on the northern rim of this "wilderness" in north London. On a clear day, the view south from the Heath makes the city look like a vast village.

South Bank Arts Center – On the south bank of Waterloo Bridge, the bunkerlike complex of cultural buildings is an attraction in itself, including as it does Royal Festival Hall, the National Theatre, the National Film Theatre, the Hayward Gallery, and other cultural attractions. And for a view of London, looking across the Thames — upriver to the Houses of Parliament, downriver to St. Paul's Cathedral — the whole area is something special.

The Monument – Only the most stalwart will climb the 311 steps to see a view somewhat blocked by new financial district buildings. It is just north of London Bridge on top of Fish St. Hill, 60 King William St. EC4 (phone: 626-2717).

St. Paul's Cathedral – The reward for climbing the 600 steps into the dome of this cathedral — the largest in the world after St. Peter's in Rome — is a panoramic view of London.

SPECIAL PLACES/ATTRACTIONS: Surveying London from the steps of St. Paul's Cathedral at the turn of the nineteenth century, a visiting Prussian general commented to his English host: "What a place to plunder!" Even those who are less rapacious will appreciate the extraordinary wealth of sights London displays for visitors to inspect. Though some are dispersed in various corners of this vast city, most are clustered reasonably close together in or near the inner districts of Westminster, the City, and Kensington.

London A-Z or *Nicholson's Street Finder,* inexpensive pocket-sized books of street maps (available in bookstores and from most "news agents"), are very useful for finding your way. Also helpful are maps of the subway system and bus routes — both available free from the London Transport information centers at several stations including

WESTMINSTER

Changing of the Guard – An American who lived in London once said, "There's just no better way to convince yourself that you're in London!" At 11:30 AM every day (every other day between autumn and spring) this famous ceremony takes place in the Buckingham Palace forecourt.

The Horse Guards – If you haven't had enough, you can see a new guard of 12 men troop in with trumpet and standard, daily at 11 AM; alternate days in winter; 10 AM on Sundays. On the west side of Whitehall.

Buckingham Palace – The royal standard flies from the roof when the monarch is in residence at her London home. Although George III bought the palace in 1762, no sovereign lived here until 1837, when Queen Victoria moved in. The palace, unfortunately, is open only to invited guests. Its interior contains magnificently decorated apartments, a superb picture gallery, and a throne room (66 feet long), where foreign ambassadors are received and knights are knighted. The palace grounds contain the largest private garden in London (40 acres). And the gate that was built for the entrance, too narrow for the coaches of George IV, now marks an entrance to Hyde Park and is known as Marble Arch. Buckingham Palace Rd.

State Visits – If you aren't going to be in London for the Queen's official birthday in June, you might want to see her greet a foreign dignitary in full regalia. This happens quite frequently; it is announced in the royal calendar in the London *Times* and on posters in the subway. The Queen meets her guest at Victoria Station, and they ride to Buckingham Palace in a procession of horse-drawn coaches, followed by colorful Horse Guards. Meanwhile, at Hyde Park Corner, the cannoneers on horseback perform elaborate maneuvers before their salute thunders through the whole city.

Queen's Gallery – Treasures from the royal art collection are on display to the public only in this room of the palace. Exhibitions change about once a year. It is open daily; closed Mondays. Admission charge. Buckingham Palace Rd. SW1.

Royal Mews – The mews is a palace alley where the magnificent state coaches and the horses that draw them are stabled. The public is admitted on Wednesdays and Thursdays, from 2 to 4 PM. Buckingham Palace Rd. SW1.

St. James's Park – Parks are everywhere in London and Londoners love them. This is one of the nicest, where at lunch hour on a sunny day you can see the impeccably dressed London businessmen lounging on the grass, their shoes and shirts off. With its sizable lake inhabited by pelicans and other wild fowl, St. James's was originally a royal park, laid out by Henry VIII in 1532.

The Mall – The wide avenue parallel to Pall Mall and lined with lime trees and Regency buildings leads from Trafalgar Square to Buckingham Palace. This is the principal ceremonial route used by Queen Elizabeth and her escort of Household Cavalry for the State Opening of Parliament (November) and the Trooping of the Color (June). It is closed to traffic on Sunday afternoons.

Trafalgar Square – One of London's most heavily trafficked squares is built around the towering Nelson Monument — a 145-foot column topped by a tall statue — which honors Lord Nelson, victor at the naval Battle of Trafalgar in 1805. At the base of the monument are four huge bronze lions and two fountains. Flanked by handsome buildings, including the National Gallery and the eighteenth-century church of St. Martin in the Fields, the square is a favorite gathering place for political demonstrations, tourists, and pigeons.

Piccadilly Circus – Downtown London finds its center here in the heart of the theater district and on the edge of Soho. The traffic island in the center of the busy "circus," or circle, serves as a meeting place for young people during the summer. The famous statue popularly known as Eros was actually designed in 1893 as *The Angel of*

Christian Charity, a memorial to the charitable earl of Shaftesbury — the archer and his bow were meant as a pun on his name.

The National Gallery – One of the world's great art museums, this is an inexhaustible feast for art lovers. In the vast collection on display are works by such masters as Uccello, Da Vinci, Titian, Rembrandt, Rubens, Cranach, Gainsborough, El Greco, Renoir, Cézanne, and Van Gogh. Trafalgar Sq. WC2 (phone: 839-3321).

The National Portrait Gallery – Right behind the National Gallery is this delightful museum. Nearly every British celebrity you have ever heard about is pictured here, with the earliest personalities at the top and the twentieth-century notables at the bottom. 2 St. Martin's Pl. WC2 (phone: 930-1552).

Whitehall – This broad boulevard stretches from Trafalgar Square to Parliament Square, lined most of the way by government ministries and such historic buildings as the Banqueting House (completed in 1622, with a ceiling painted by Rubens) and the Horse Guards (whose central archway is ceremonially guarded by mounted troopers).

Detective novel fans may be interested to know that Scotland Yard once occupied a building at the Trafalgar end of Whitehall; it now houses offices for members of Parliament. The Yard has moved to Victoria Street near St. James's Park.

Downing Street – Off Whitehall, a street of small, unpretentious Georgian houses includes the official residences of the most important figures in the British government, the Prime Minister at number 10 and the Chancellor of the Exchequer (secretary of the treasury) at number 11.

Westminster Abbey – You can easily get lost among the endlessly fascinating tombs and plaques and not even notice the Abbey's splendid architecture, so do look at the structure itself, and don't miss the cloisters, which display its Gothic design to advantage. Note also the fine Tudor chapel of Henry VII, with its tall windows and lovely fan-tracery vaulting, and the thirteenth-century chapel of St. Edward the Confessor, containing England's Coronation Chair.

Ever since William the Conqueror was crowned here in 1066, the Abbey has been the traditional place where English monarchs are crowned, married, and buried. You don't have to be an Anglophile to be moved by the numerous tombs and memorials with their fascinating inscriptions — here are honored (not necessarily buried) kings and queens, soldiers, statesmen, and many other prominent English men and women. Poets' Corner, in the south transept, contains the tombs of Chaucer, Ben Jonson, Tennyson, Browning, and many others — plus memorials to nearly every English poet of note and to some Americans, such as Longfellow and T. S. Eliot.

The Abbey is itself a lesson in English history. A church has stood on this site since at least AD 170; in the eighth century, it was a Benedictine monastery. The current early English Gothic edifice, begun in the thirteenth century, took almost 300 years to build.

Guided tours of the Abbey are offered twice daily in winter and four times a day in summer, except Sundays (phone: 222-5152). Broad Sanctuary SW1.

The Houses of Parliament – The imposing neo-Gothic, mid-nineteenth-century buildings of the Palace of Westminster, as it is sometimes called, look especially splendid from the opposite side of the river. There are separate chambers for the House of Commons and the House of Lords, and visitors are admitted to the strangers' galleries of both houses by lining up at St. Stephen's Entrance, opposite Westminster Abbey. Big Ben, the world-famous 13.5-ton bell in the clock tower of the palace, still strikes the hours. The buildings themselves are open to the public on Saturdays. Westminster Hall, with its magnificent hammer-beam roof, and the gold and scarlet House of Lords are well worth seeing. Parliament Sq. SW1.

The Tate Gallery – London's fine art museum includes an impressive collection of sculpture and art. It has recently been extended to include a permanent display of British modern art. Millbank SW1 (phone: 821-1313).

LONDON / At-a-Glance

Soho – This area of London is full of character; lively, bustling, and noisy by day; discreetly enticing by night. Its name comes from the ancient hunting cry used centuries ago when the area was parkland. The hunting, in a way, still goes on, but there's not much to shout about nowadays. Soho lacks the sophistication and glamour of its counterparts in Europe but, on the other hand, it is not sleazy either. The striptease clubs vie for customers with numerous restaurants serving inexpensive (mostly Italian) food. Soho offers a diversity of entertainments: Shaftsbury Avenue is lined with movie theaters. Gerrard Street abounds with Chinese restaurants, and it is the place to go for Chinese New Year celebrations. London's liveliest fruit and vegetable market is on Berwick Street (if you shop here, never touch the produce as the vendors will get furious). Old Compton Street has several good delicatessens, where you could buy a picnic lunch to take to — of course — Soho Square.

Covent Garden – Tucked away behind the Strand, Covent Garden was the site of London's main fruit, vegetable, and flower market for over 300 years. The area was immortalized in the musical *My Fair Lady* by the scene in which young Eliza Doolittle sold flowers to the ladies and gents emerging from the Royal Opera House. The Opera House is still there but the rest has gone. The market moved out in 1974 and the Garden has since undergone extensive redevelopment. The central market building has been converted into London's first permanent late-night shopping center with emphasis on all-British goods. In the former flower market is the London Transport Museum, whose exhibits include a replica of the first horse-drawn bus and a steam locomotive built in 1866. Boutiques selling good-quality clothes for men and women are springing up all over, along with discos, wine bars, and brasserie-style restaurants. On weekends the whole area is packed with young people. One nice touch: Just to remind everyone of the Old Covent Garden, there are about 40 of the original wrought-iron trading stands from which the home-produced wares of English craftsmen and women are sold.

Bloomsbury – Well-designed squares — Bloomsbury Square, Bedford Square, Russell Square, and others — surrounded by pretty, terraced houses, form this aristocratic district. Within its confines are the British Museum and the University of London, with its Courtauld Gallery, renowned for its impressionist collection. The Bloomsbury Group of writers and artists included Virginia Woolf, her husband Leonard Woolf, her sister Vanessa Bell and her husband Clive Bell, Lytton Strachey, E. M. Forster, Roger Fry, and Maynard Keynes. Living nearby and peripheral to this central group were D. H. Lawrence, Bertrand Russell, and others. Unfortunately, none of the original buildings in Bloomsbury Square has survived, but the garden is still there, and nearby Bedford Square remains complete. Virginia Woolf lived at 46 Gordon Square before her marriage.

The British Museum – One of the world's largest museums offers a dazzling array of permanent exhibitions — including the legendary Elgin Marbles (from the Parthenon) and the Rosetta Stone — and an equally impressive parade of temporary displays. The Egyptian and Mesopotamian galleries are especially stunning. The manuscript room of the British Library, within the museum, displays the original Magna Carta together with the signatures of a great many famous authors — Shakespeare, Dickens, and Joyce among them — and numerous original manuscripts, including *Alice in Wonderland*. To take a look at the gigantic Reading Room where so many books — Marx's *Das Kapital*, for example — were written, you must write to the library for tickets. Great Russell St. WC1 (phone: 636-1555).

Oxford Street – London's main shopping street includes large department stores *(Selfridges, Debenhams, John Lewis)*, chain stores offering good value in clothes *(Marks and Spencer, C & A, British Home Stores, Littlewood's)*. It has recently been widened for pedestrians, and one section is closed to traffic other than taxis and buses.

The Burlington Arcade – A charming covered shopping promenade dating from the Regency period (early nineteenth century), the arcade contains elegant, expensive shops selling cashmere sweaters, antique jewelry, and other costly items. Off Piccadilly (the street, not the circus) near Bond St. W1.

Hyde Park – London's most famous patch of greenery (361 acres) is particularly well known for its "Speakers' Corner" at Marble Arch, where crowds gather each Sunday afternoon to hear impromptu diatribes and debates. Among the park's other attractions are sculptures by Henry Moore; an extensive bridle path; a cycle path; the Serpentine lake, where boats for rowing and sailing can be rented and where there's swimming in the summer; a bird sanctuary; and vast expanses of lawn.

Madame Tussaud's – The popularity of this wax museum is undiminished by the persistent criticism that its effigies, besides being hideous, do not resemble the illustrious personalities they are supposed to imitate. Moved to London from Paris in 1802 when Madame was 74, the current museum includes her effigy and those of her contemporaries, many modern and historical personalities, and the gory Chamber of Horrors, with its murderers and hangmen. Marylebone Rd. (phone: 935-6861).

THE CITY

The difference between London and the City of London can be confusing to a visitor. They are, in fact, two different entities, one within the other. The City of London, usually called only the City, covers the original Roman London. It is now the "square mile" financial and commercial center of the great metropolis. With a lord mayor (who only serves in a ceremonial capacity), a police force of its own, and a resident population of 6,000 due to rapidly growing new developments — it is the core of Greater London. The latter, with its governing body, the Greater London Council, administers 32 boroughs including the City.

St. Paul's Cathedral – The cathedral church of the London Anglican diocese stands atop Ludgate Hill and is the largest church in London. This Renaissance masterpiece by Sir Christopher Wren took 35 years to build (1675–1710). Its domed exterior is majestic and its sparse decorations are gold and mosaic. The interior contains particularly splendid choir stalls, screens, and, inside the spectacular dome, the "whispering gallery," with its strange acoustics. Nelson and Wellington are buried below the main floor, and there is a fine statue of John Donne, metaphysical poet and dean of St. Paul's from 1621 to 1631 — he stands looking quite alive on an urn in an up-ended coffin which, typically, he bought during his lifetime and kept in his house. Wren himself was buried here in 1723, with his epitaph inscribed beneath the dome in Latin: "Reader, if you seek his monument, look around you."

A gorgeous monument it remains; though damaged by bombs during World War II, it became a rallying point for the flagging spirits of wartime Londoners. More recently, St. Paul's raised British spirits as the site for the royal wedding of Prince Charles and Lady Diana Spencer in July 1981. The Golden Gallery at the top of the dome, 542 steps from the ground, offers an excellent view of the city. St. Paul's Churchyard EC4.

Old Bailey – This is the colloquial name for London's Central Criminal Court, located on the site of the notorious Newgate Prison. Visitors are admitted to the court, on a space-available basis, to audit the proceedings and to see lawyers and judges clad in wigs and robes. Old Bailey EC4.

The Museum of London – Well-designed exhibits and displays depict London history from the Roman occupation to modern times. The museum is in the Barbican, the modern building complex that was constructed in a part of London devastated by bombers during World War II. London Wall EC2 (phone: 600-3699).

The Bank of England – Banker to the British government, holder of the country's gold reserves in its vaults, controller of Britain's banking and monetary affairs, "the Old Lady of Threadneedle Street" is the most famous bank in the world. Bathed in tradition as well as the mechanics of modern high finance, its porters and messengers are attired in traditional livery. Threadneedle St. EC2.

Mansion House – Right next to the bank is the official residence of the lord mayor of London, containing his private apartments, built in the eighteenth century in Renaissance style. Mansion House St. EC4.

Lloyd's – A palatial building houses the world's most important marketplace for international high-risk insurance. True to tradition, the Lutine Bell, salvaged from a sunken frigate, sounds out whenever a mishap occurs that is covered by Lloyd's insurers. Leadenhall St. EC3.

The Stock Exchange – The second largest exchange in the world can be seen from the viewing gallery on weekdays from 9:45 AM to 3:15 PM. Old Broad St. EC2 (phone: 588-2355).

The Monument – A fluted Doric column — topped by a flaming urn — was designed by Sir Christopher Wren to commemorate the Great Fire of London (1666) and stands 202 feet tall, allegedly 202 feet from the bakery on Pudding Lane where the fire began. The view from the top is partially obstructed by new buildings. Fish St. Hill EC4 (phone: 626-2717).

The Tower of London – The foundations of the infamous tower were built by William the Conqueror in the eleventh century. Originally conceived as a fortress to keep "fierce" Londoners at bay and to guard the river approaches, it has served as a palace, a prison, a mint, and an observatory as well. Today the main points of interest are the Crown Jewels; the White Tower (the oldest building), with its exhibition of ancient arms, armor, and torture implements; St. John's Chapel, the oldest church in London; the Bloody Tower, where the two little princes were murdered in 1485 and Sir Walter Raleigh languished from 1603 to 1615; and Tower Green, where two of Henry VIII's queens — and many others — were beheaded. The yeoman warders still wear historic uniforms. They also give excellent recitals of that segment of English history that was played out within the tower walls. You can see the wonderful Ceremony of the Keys here every night at 9:30 PM; you'll have to reserve tickets several months ahead. Write Resident Governor, Queen's House, HM Tower of London EC3N 4AB (phone: 709-0765).

Fleet Street – Most native and foreign newspapers and press associations have their offices here — in the center of London's active newspaper world. The street also boasts two seventeenth-century pubs, the *Cheshire Cheese* (number 145) and the *Cock Tavern* (number 22). The *Cheshire Cheese* is the tavern where Dr. Samuel Johnson held court for the literary giants of his day — Goldsmith, Boswell, and others.

Johnson's House – In nearby Gough Square is the house where Johnson wrote his famous *Dictionary;* the house is now a museum of Johnsoniana. Admission charge. 17 Gough Sq. (phone: 353-3745).

The Inns of Court – Quaint and quiet precincts house the ancient buildings, grounds, and gardens that mark the traditional center of Britain's legal profession. Only the four Inns of Court have the right to call would-be barristers to the bar to practice law. Especially charming is the still-Dickensian Lincoln's Inn, where young Dickens worked as an office boy. In its great hall the writer later set his fictional case of *Jarndyce v. Jarndyce* in *Bleak House.* John Donne once preached in the Lincoln's Inn chapel designed by Inigo Jones. Both hall and chapel can be seen if you apply at the Gatehouse in Chancery Lane. Also lovely are the gardens of Lincoln's Inn Fields, laid out in 1618 by Inigo Jones on the site of an old dueling ground.

Silver Vaults – An underground silver market contains rows of shops selling old and new silver objects, ranging in price from modest to extravagant. Chancery La. WC2.

OTHER LONDON ATTRACTIONS

Regent's Park – The sprawling 472-acre park just north of the city center has beautiful gardens, vast expanses of lawns, a pond with paddleboats, and one of the finest zoos in the world. Bordering the park are elegant terraced homes.

344 LONDON / At-a-Glance

Camden Passage – This quaint pedestrian alleyway lined with antique and specialty shops has an open-air market — pushcarts selling old jewelry, curios, and antiques — on Wednesday mornings and Saturdays. Islington, north of the city, N1.

Hampstead Heath – The north London bucolic paradise of wild heathland, meadows, and wooded dells is the highest point in London. Kenwood House, an eighteenth-century estate and garden on the heath, is home to the Iveagh Bequest, a collection of artworks (Gainsborough, Rembrandt, Turner, and others) assembled by the first earl of Iveagh.

Kew Gardens – Here are the Royal Botanic Gardens, with tens of thousands of plants and trees. The gardens' primary purpose is to serve the science of botany by researching, cultivating, experimenting, and identifying plants. The shaded walks, floral displays, and magnificent Victorian glass greenhouses — especially the Palm House with tropical trees — make even a winter visit worthwhile.

Portobello Road – West of Kensington Gardens, this area is famous for its antique shops, junk shops, and outdoor pushcarts; it is the largest street market in the world. The pushcarts are out only on Saturdays, which is the best and most crowded day for the market. Less well known is Bermondsey Market, Long Lane SE1, on Fridays from 7 AM on; this is where the antiques on Portobello Road or Camden Passage were probably purchased.

Victoria and Albert Museum – Born of the 1851 Exhibition, the museum contains a vast collection of fine and applied arts (probably the largest collection of the latter in the world) — an amalgam of the great, the odd, and the ugly. Especially delightful are the English period rooms. There are superb collections of paintings, prints, ceramics, metalwork, costumes, and armor in the museum, which also contains English miniatures and famous Raphael cartoons. Cromwell Rd. SW7 (phone: 589-6371).

Greenwich – This Thames-side borough is traditionally associated with British seapower, especially when Britain "ruled the waves"; it includes such notable sights as: the National Maritime Museum on Romney Rd. (phone: 858-4422), containing superb exhibits on Britain's illustrious nautical past; the Old Royal Observatory, with astronomical instruments; *Cutty Sark,* a superbly preserved nineteenth-century clipper ship that's open to visitors; Royal Naval College, with beautiful painted hall and chapel; and Greenwich Park, 200 acres of greenery sloping down toward the river.

Richmond Park – The largest urban park in Britain is one of the few with herds of deer roaming free. (Hunting them is illegal, though this was once a royal hunting preserve.) It also has large oaks and rhododendron gardens. From nearby Richmond Hill you can enjoy a magnificent view of the Thames Valley.

Manor Houses – Five beautifully maintained historic homes are located in the Greater London area. Notable for their architecture, antique furnishings, lovely grounds, and, in the case of Kenwood, an eighteenth-century art collection, these homes are all accessible by subway or bus. For directions, see listings of Kenwood, Ham, Chiswick, Syon, and Osterley on the back of the London map published by the British Tourist Authority.

Hampton Court Palace – Situated on the Thames, this sumptuous palace and gardens are in London's southwest corner. Begun by Cardinal Wolsey in 1515, the palace was appropriated by Henry VIII and was an occasional royal residence for two centuries. Its particular attractions include a picture gallery, tapestries, state apartments, Tudor kitchens, the original tennis court, a moat and drawbridge, a great vine (two centuries old), gardens, and a maze. You can go to Hampton Court by bus, by train, or, best of all, take the boat from Westminster Pier (3½ hours one way). Hampton Ct., E. Molesey, Surrey (phone: 977-8441).

■ **EXTRA SPECIAL:** *Windsor Castle* is the largest inhabited castle in the world. It is the Queen's official residence and was built by William the Conqueror in 1066 after his victory at the Battle of Hastings. Windsor looks like a fairy-tale castle in a child's picturebook: The huge Norman edifice looms majestically above the town; you feel awed and enchanted as you climb up the curving cobblestone street from the train station, past pubs and shops, toward Henry VIII's Gateway. The castle precincts are open daily and there's a regular changing of the guard. The State Apartments, which can be toured when they're not in use, are splendidly decorated with paintings, tapestries, furniture, and rugs. There is an exhibition of drawings by Leonardo da Vinci, Michelangelo, and Raphael, and a room displaying Queen Mary's dollhouse. Queen Victoria and her consort, Albert, are buried at Windsor. The castle is bordered by 4,800 acres of parkland on one side and the town on the other. While the town still has a certain charm, heavy tourism is beginning to have a deleterious effect. Across the river you can visit *Eton* — considered by some to be the more attractive town — which is famous as home to the exclusive boy's school founded by Henry IV in 1440. On hot summer afternoons you'll probably see some decidedly scruffy-looking boys playing on the river. Don't miss taking one of the many boat trips along the Thames to places like Marlow, Cookham, or Henley (where the first sailing regatta in the world was held in 1839). The *Royal Windsor Safari Park* is a few miles to the southwest. Once a royal hunting ground, it's now a drive-through zoo, whose residents include baboons, camels, rhinos, cheetahs, and Bengal tigers. Be forewarned: In summer the park is very popular and traffic is bumper-to-bumper. An alternative would be to take the safari bus. Admission: £2.50. A final attraction in the Windsor area, found 5 miles to the southwest, is *Savill Gardens* — 35 acres of flowering shrubs, rare flowers, and woodland. Open from March to December.

The train from Paddington takes you right into the center of Windsor, to Windsor and Eton Central (39 mins), or there's a Green Line coach from Victoria (1.5 hrs).

SOURCES AND RESOURCES

The London Tourist Board's main information center, at Victoria Station (phone: 730-0791), is the best local source of information on current happenings. A wide range of leaflets and brochures on the city's landmarks and events are available as well as a staff to answer questions on what to do, how to do it, and when. Suboffices are at Heathrow Travel Centre (open 7 days a week) and in *Selfridges* and *Harrods* department stores. The City of London Information Center is at St. Paul's Churchyard, London EC4 (phone: 606-3030). Information on Britain generally is available from the British Tourist Authority (BTA), 64 St. James's St. SW1 (phone: 499-9325). Particularly helpful is the BTA publication *London Week,* containing up-to-date details of events and diversions. For recorded information on the day's events, telephone 246-8041. One of the most comprehensive and useful guidebooks to London is the *Blue Guide to London* (Benn). The annual *Good Food Guide* ($16.95) and *Egon Ronay's* hotel and restaurant guide ($13.95) are available in most bookstores (prices slightly lower in Great Britain).

For Local Coverage – Of London's several newspapers, the *Guardian, The London Times,* and the *Daily Telegraph* are most useful. Also two weekly magazines, *What's On in London* and *Time Out,* are both published every Thursday.

GETTING AROUND: Bus and Subway – The London public transport system gets sluggish now and then but is still reasonably efficient. The network of underground train and bus lines covers the city pretty well, though buses suffer from big-city traffic congestion. The tops of London's famous, red double-decker buses do, however, offer some delightful views of the city and its people. The London underground train system is easy to understand and to use, with clear directions and poster maps in all stations. Pick up free bus and subway maps from tourist offices or train station ticket booths. The fares on both trains and buses are set according to length of the journey. On most buses, conductors take payment after you tell them where you're going; some require that you pay as you enter. Train tickets are bought on entering a station. Retain your ticket: You'll have to surrender it when you get off (or have to pay again), and bus inspectors make spot checks to see that no one's stealing a free ride. There are also Red Arrow express buses, but you'll have to check stops before you get on. With just a few exceptions, public transport comes to a halt in London around 11:30 PM, though it varies according to subway line and bus route. If you're going to be traveling late, check out available transport facilities.

A go-as-you-please ticket, which can be bought at the London Tourist Board or at any underground station — at about £8 for 3 days, £10 for 4 days, and £15 for 7 — gives the holder unlimited travel on bus and subway within a specified area.

The subway now links Heathrow, London's main airport, with downtown. The Piccadilly Line zips from Piccadilly Circus to the airport in about 45 minutes. For bus and subway information, call 222-1234.

Taxi – The fine old London cabs are extremely comfortable but increasingly expensive. It is customary to tell a London cabbie where you're going *before* entering the cab. When it rains or late at night, an empty cab (identifiable by its roof light being on) is often very difficult to find, so it is wise to carry the telephone number of one or more of the cab companies that respond to calls by phone. A 15% tip is customary. There are many "minicab" companies that do not use meters so you must fix the fare before you set off. Hotel porters or reception desks usually can make arrangements to have such a car pick you up at a specified time and place. You should also be aware that taxi rates are higher after 8 PM and on holidays.

Car Rental – Several agencies, including *Hertz*, at 35 Edgware Rd. W1 (phone: 402-4242), and *Avis*, Headfort Pl. SW1 (phone: 245-9862), are represented in London. *Swan National*, 305 Chiswick High Rd. (phone: 995-9463/4665), is cheaper, or try *Guy Salmon Car Rentals*, 7–23 Bryanston St., Marble Arch (phone: 408-1255), or *Godfrey Davis*, 129 Wilton Rd. SW1 (phone: 834-8484). And for riding in style, call *Avis Luxury Car Services* (phone: 235-3235) for chauffeur-driven Rolls-Royces and Daimlers.

Walking Tours – A trained guide can show you Shakespeare's London or that of Dickens or Jack the Ripper — many different tours are offered. These reasonably priced tours last up to 2 hours, generally in the afternoon or evening. *Time Out* magazine and city information centers have listings of tour companies.

Bus Tours – London Transport's 2-hour unconducted tour (leaflets describe the sights you pass) leaves every hour from three spots: Marble Arch, Piccadilly Circus, and Grosvenor Gardens (phone: 222-1234). It's the cheapest and most comprehensive tour of London. Among other good bus tours — some of them guided — are those run by American Express (phone: 930-4411), Thomas Cook (phone: 499-4000), and Frames' (phone: 837-3111).

Taxi Tours – Several firms and taxi drivers offer guided tours of London; details are available at information centers. You can make arrangements for the personal services of a member of London's Guild of Guides by phoning London Transport's Tour Department (phone: 222-5406).

Boat Excursions – See London from the Thames. Boats leave roughly every half-hour from Westminster Pier at the foot of Westminster Bridge and sail downriver to the Tower of London and Greenwich or upriver to Kew. Also available is a journey along Regent's Canal through north London (summer only). Jason's Trip, Little Venice W2 (phone: 286-3428). For further information about these and other boat trips, contact the London Tourist Board's River Information Service (phone: 730-4812).

SPECIAL EVENTS: Dates vary marginally from year to year and should be checked — together with details — with the London Tourist Board. In early June you can enjoy the annual *Trooping of the Color,* England's most elaborate display of pageantry — a Horse Guards' parade, with military music and much pomp and circumstance — all in celebration of the queen's official birthday. You can see some of the parade without a ticket, but for the ceremony you must book in February by writing to the Brigade Major, Headquarters, Horseguard Division, Horseguards, Whitehall, SW1. Ticket prices run between £2 and £5. Late June heralds the *Wimbledon Tennis Championship* — the world's most prestigious — complete with a member of the Royal Family presenting the prizes. The traditional fare is strawberry tea (strawberries and cream). The *Henley Royal Regatta,* which takes place in early July (at Henley-on-Thames, a 1-hour train ride from London), is an international rowing competition and one of the big social events of the year — it also features strawberry tea. At the end of July, horse lovers can enjoy the *Royal International Horse Show* at Wembley, London, with all manner of equestrian displays and gymnastics. The *Royal Tournament,* a military pageant, takes place at Earls Court for 3 weeks in July. November is the time for the *State Opening of Parliament; Guy Fawkes Day* is on November 5, when fireworks and bonfires mark the anniversary of the plot to blow up both houses of Parliament and King James I in 1605; and on the second Saturday in November, an inaugural procession for the new Lord Mayor, who rides in a golden carriage, followed by floats and bands.

MUSEUMS: Many of London's museums are described in *Special Places.* Other noteworthy museums include:

The Natural History Museum, Cromwell Rd. SW1 (phone: 589-6323).

Science Museum, Exhibition Rd. SW7 (phone: 589-3456).

Planetarium, Marylebone Rd. NW1 (phone: 486-1121).

Dickens's House, 48 Doughty St. WC1 (phone: 405-2127).

Jewish Museum, Woburn House, Upper Woburn Pl. WC1 (phone: 387-3081).

Wallace Collection, Sir Richard Wallace's fine collection of European paintings, sculpture, and armor, at Hertford House, Manchester Sq. W1 (phone: 935-0687).

Dulwich College Picture Gallery, works by European masters in one of England's most beautiful art galleries, College Rd. SE21 (phone: 693-5254).

Courtauld Institute Galleries, a remarkable collection of French Impressionist paintings, Woburn Sq. WC1 (phone: 580-1015).

Institute of Contemporary Arts, The Mall, SW1 (phone: 930-0493).

The Museum of Mankind, ethnographic exhibits, 6 Burlington Gardens W1 (phone: 437-2224).

Sir John Soane's Museum, as well known for its architecture as for its collection, which includes Hogarth's series, *The Rake's Progress,* 13 Lincoln's Inn Fields, WC2 (phone: 405-2107).

SHOPPING: Although London is one of the most expensive cities in the world, savvy shoppers can still find good buys. The current lure, however, is more for fine British workmanship and style than very low prices.

The favorite items on a tourist's shopping list in London are cashmere and Shetland woolen knitwear; fabric (tweeds, blends, men's suitings); riding gear; custom-made men's suits, shoes, and hats; shotguns; china and crystal; umbrellas; antiques; sporting goods; English food specialties (jams, marmalade, various blended teas, Stilton cheese, shortbread, and others). Books published by British houses, once a fine buy, are now sky high in price, and you'll do better to buy the US editions.

Devoted bargain hunters recognize that the best time to buy British is during the semiannual sales that occur around New Year's Day and again in early July. The Christmas/New Year's sales offer by far the best bargains in the city, and the crowds are the equal of the low prices. Much of the merchandise sold has been purchased especially for the sale period, though lots of standard merchandise is also included in the general price cutting. Many stores remain open on New Year's Day to accommodate the crowds, and the best publicized single sale is that offered at *Harrod's* for three weeks beginning the first Saturday in January. That opening day is an event in itself.

Be sure to bring your passport along when you shop and always inquire about the VAT application forms when you make a large (over $25) purchase. The VAT (Value Added Tax) is a 15% surcharge which you must pay at the sales counter, but for which you may be reimbursed when you return home. Though scattered about the city, shopping tends to center in Westminster, particularly along Bond Street, Oxford Street, South Moulton Street, Piccadilly, Regent Street, Brompton Road, and Jermyn Street. Other good shopping streets are Kings Road, Kensington High Street, and Kensington Church Street.

This is a city of markets; we have already described Portobello Road and Camden Passage in *Special Places*. Also worthy of note are Camden Lock Market, Camden High St. NW1, on Saturdays and Sundays, for far-out clothes, leather items, antiques, and trinkets and the very famous Petticoat Lane, Middlesex St. E1, on Sunday mornings for fruit, vegetables, cheap clothes, and crockery.

The following list of stores is only a sampling of London's treasure houses.

Anderson and Sheppard – A reputable "made-to-measure" tailor for men's clothes, 30 Savile Row W1.

Antiquarius – A good place for antiques. Flood St. SW3.

Aquascutum – Needs no introduction; famous for raincoats, jackets, and just about everything else for men. 100 Regent St. W1.

Laura Ashley – A relatively inexpensive women's boutique specializing in romantic styled skirts, dresses, and blouses. 7–9 Harriet St. SW1; four other branches along Sloane St.

Asprey – Fine jewelry and leather. 165 New Bond St. W1.

William Bedford – For beautiful but expensive antiques. 327 Upper St. N1.

Browns – Beautiful but expensive women's clothes. 27 S Molton St. W1

Burberry's – Superb but expensive men's and women's raincoats and traditional clothes, and home of the now nearly ubiquitous plaid that began life as a raincoat lining, at 18 Haymarket SW1; 161 Regent St. W1.

Church's – For fabled men's shoes. Burlington Arcade W1; New Bond St.

Crocodile – For chic and expensive women's clothes. 56 Beauchamp Pl. SW3.

Justin De Blank – For excellent quality specialty foods, especially cheese and take-out dishes. 42 Elizabeth St. SW1.

Dillon's – A good bookstore, London's most scholastic, partly owned by London University. 1 Malet St. WC1.

Fenwick – Sells trendy, moderately priced women's clothes. 63 New Bond St. W1.

Fortnum and Mason – Boasts designer originals (usually of the rather dowdy variety), an appealing soda fountain, and one of the most elegant grocery departments in the world (where the staff wears striped trousers and morning coats). 181 Piccadilly W1.

Foyle's – London's largest bookstore. 119 Charing Cross Rd. WC2.

Gidden's of London – For riding gear. 15 Clifford St. W1.

Thomas Goode and Company – London's best china and glass shop first opened in 1827. Even if you don't plan to buy anything, you may want to look at their beautiful 1876 showroom. 19 S Audley St. W1.

Grays Antique Market – The hundreds of stalls here and at the annex down the street sell everything from antique playing cards to sixteenth-century furniture. 1 Davies Mews, W1.

Habitat – Up-to-the-minute designs with realistic prices for furniture and household goods. 156 Tottenham Court Rd., W1 and 206 King's Rd. SW3.

Hamley's – One of the three largest toy shops in the world with 12 floors. 188 Regent St., W1.

Harrods – The ultimate department store, although it does tend to be quite expensive. It has everything, even a mortuary and a bank, and what it doesn't stock, it will get for you. The "food halls" particularly fascinate visitors, and traditional British merchandise is available in abundance. For those interested in trendy styles, it has the Way In boutique. 87/135 Brompton Rd., Knightsbridge SW1.

Harvie and Hudson – Men's shirts made to order. 77 Jermyn St. SW1.

Douglas Hayward – A reputable made-to-order tailor. 95 Mount St. W1.

Heal's – Furniture and fabrics in the best modern designs. 196 Tottenham Court Rd., W1.

Hobbs and Company – Gourmet and specialty foods. 3 Garrick St. WC2.

Jaeger – For tailored (and expensive) women's clothes. 204 Regent St. W1.

Herbert Johnson – Sells men's hats. 13 Old Burlington St. SW1.

Peter Jones – Another good, well-stocked department store, offering moderately priced, tasteful goods. Sloane Square, SW1.

John Keil – Lovely, expensive antiques. 25 Mount St. W1.

John Lewis – Yet another good, moderately priced department store, particularly noted for its fabrics department and household goods. Oxford St. W1.

Liberty – Famous for print fabrics. Scarves and ties a specialty. 210 Regent St. W1.

Lillywhites – For the whole gamut of sporting goods. Piccadilly Circus SW1.

John Lobb – World-famous for made-to-order shoes that will last ten years or more with proper care. 9 St. James's St. SW1.

Marks and Spencer – Locally nicknamed "Marks and Sparks," this is a chain of stores specializing in clothes for the whole family, made to high standards and sold at very reasonable prices. Its linens and sweaters (especially cashmere and Shetland) are among the best buys in Britain. 458 Oxford St. (and many other outlets).

Harvey Nichols – A luxury department store specializing in fashion and household goods. Knightsbridge SW1.

Partridge Ltd. – For fine (but expensive) antiques. 144 New Bond St. W1.

James Purdey and Sons – The place to go for shotguns and other shooting gear. 57 S Audley St. SW1.

Reject China Shop – Good buys in slightly irregular, name brand china are sometimes available here. For a fee, the shop will ship your purchases back home. 34 Beauchamp Pl. SW3.

Peter Robinson Top Shop – For young, trendy, moderately priced women's clothing. Oxford Circus W1.

Sandon & Co. Ltd. – Another good tailor for men's clothes. 7 Savile Row W1.

Scotch House – Famous for Scottish wools, sweaters, tartans — a wide selection of well-known labels. 2 Brompton Rd. SW1, and many other branches.

Selfridges – This famous department store offers somewhat less variety than *Harrods*, but it has just about everything too — only a little less expensive. The extensive china and crystal department carries most patterns available. Oxford St. W1.

Simpson – Has elegant garments for men and women. 205 Piccadilly W1.

James Smith and Sons – This is the oldest umbrella shop in Europe. 53 New Oxford St. WC1.

Smythson of Bond Street – The world's best place to buy diaries, note pads, calendars, and exotic ledgers in which to record odd data. 54 New Bond St. W1.

Sotheby and Company – The world's oldest art auctioneer, *Sotheby's* is interesting

350 LONDON / Sources and Resources

to look at even if you don't plan to buy. They auction books, porcelain, furniture, jewelry, and works of art; at times, even such odd items as vintage cars and wines. Viewing hours are between 9:30 AM and 4:30 PM on weekdays, at 34–35 New Bond St. W1 (phone: 493-8080).

Swaine, Adeney, Brigg, and Sons – For riding gear. 185 Piccadilly W1.

Turnbull and Asser – Marvelous men's shirts made to order. 71 Jermyn St. SW1.

Wedgwood – For porcelain, of course. 34 Wigmore St. W1.

Westaway and Westaway – A very good selection of cashmere and Shetland wool kilts, sweaters, scarves, and blankets. 65 Great Russell St. WC1.

SPORTS: Soccer (called football hereabouts) and cricket are the most popular spectator pastimes, but London offers a wide variety of other spectator and participatory sports.

Cricket – The season runs from mid-April to early September. The best places to watch it are at Lord's Cricket Ground, St. John's Wood Rd. NW8 (phone: 289-1615), and The Oval, Kennington SE11 (phone: 735-4911).

Fishing – Several public ponds right in London are accessible to the angler. A permit is required from Royal Parks Department, the Storeyard, Hyde Park W2 (phone: 262-5484). The department can also provide information on where to fish.

Golf – Aside from private clubs, for which membership is required, there are several municipal courses, some of which rent out clubs. Try *Pickett's Lock Center,* Pickett's Lock La. N9 (phone: 803-3611), *Addington Court,* Featherbed La., Croydon (phone: 657-0281), and *Twickenham,* Staines Rd., Twickenham, Middlesex (phone: 979-0032). *Wentworth* and *Sunningdale* are the best courses within driving distance of London, and a letter from your home club pro or president may give you access to their links.

Greyhound Racing – Empire Stadium, Wembley (phone: 902-8833); White City Stadium, Wood La. W12 (phone: 743-7220). There are evening races, so check the afternoon newspapers for details.

Horse Racing – Nine major racecourses are within easy reach of London, including Epsom, where the "Derby" (pronounced Darby) is run, and Ascot, where "Royal Ascot" takes place — both in June. The flat racing season is from March to November; steeplechasing, August to June. Call the Jockey Club, 42 Portman Sq., W1 (phone: 486-4921) for information.

Horseback Riding – Try *Bathurst Riding Stables,* 63 Bathurst Mews, W2 (phone: 723-2813), and *Ross Nye's Riding Establishment,* 8 Bathurst Mews, W2 (phone: 262-3791).

Ice Skating – There is the *Queen's Ice Skating Club,* 17 Queensway W2 (phone: 229-0172), and *Silver Blades Ice Rink,* 386 Streatham High Rd. SW16 (phone: 769-7861). Skates are for rent at both rinks.

Rugby – An autumn-through-spring spectacle at Rugby Football Ground, Whitton Way, Twickenham.

Soccer – *The* big sport in Britain. The local football season is autumn to spring and the most popular clubs are *Arsenal,* Highbury Stadium, Avenell Rd. N5 (phone: 359-0131); *Chelsea,* Stamford Bridge, Fulham Rd. SW6 (phone: 381-0111); *West Ham United,* Boleyn Ground Green E13 (phone: 470-1325).

Swimming – Several excellent indoor public pools include: *Swiss Cottage Center,* Adelaide Rd. NW3 (phone: 278-4444), *Putney Swimming Baths,* 376 Upper Richmond Rd. SW15 (phone: 789-1124), and *The Oasis,* 167 High Holborn, WC1 (phone: 836-9555). There is outdoor swimming in the Hyde Park Serpentine, and Hampstead Heath, in the summer.

Tennis – Aside from private clubs, more than 50 London public parks have tennis courts available to all. Get information from the London Tourist Board (phone: 730-0791).

THEATER: London remains the theater capital of the world, with about 50 theaters regularly putting on plays in and around its West End theater district and a vigorous collection of "fringe" theaters in various parts of town. Best known, and most accomplished, are the two main repertory theater companies — the *National Theatre Company* at the National Theatre, Waterloo Rd. SE1 (phone: 928-2252), and the *Royal Shakespeare Company*, which recently moved to the new Barbican Centre, The Barbican EC2 (phone: 628-8795), both equipped to present dazzling productions of both classics and new plays. Shakespearean plays are also performed in summer at the open-air theater in Regents Park.

In the West End, presentations include both first-class and second-rate drama and comedy, a fair sprinkling of farce (for which the British have a particular fondness), and the best of imports from the American stage. Visitors from the US often find attending theater in London easier — and somewhat cheaper — than it is at home. Except for the small handful of runaway box office successes, tickets are usually available for all performances. In most cases, you can reserve by telephone, but tickets must be picked up well before curtain time.

The quality of London's fringe theater varies from accomplished and imaginative to amateurish. Theaters in pubs are at the *King's Head* in Islington, 115 Upper St. N1 (phone: 226-1916), and at the *Bush* in Shepherd's Bush (phone: 743-3388); the *Riverside Studios* in Hammersmith, Crisp Rd. W6 (phone: 748-3354), and the *New End Theatre* in Hampstead, 27 New End NW3 (phone: 435-6054), have established reputations for the excellence of their productions, which often move on to the West End and sometimes even directly to Broadway. Lunchtime fringe theater presentations offer an alternative to sight-seeing on rainy days.

Check *Time Out* for comprehensive lists, plot summaries, and theater phone numbers. Daily papers list West End performances. If you don't have the time or inclination to go to the box office, you can buy theater tickets through a ticket broker, who will charge a fee for this service.

Show tours to London are very popular in season; if you are interested, see your travel agent for package deals. If you want to reserve individual tickets in advance, there's an agency that keeps a listing of what's on in London. For a service charge of between $4 and $9 per ticket, the agency will sell you the best seats only. Contact *Edwards & Edwards,* 226 W 47th St., New York, NY 10036 (phone: 212-944-0290; toll-free, 800-223-6108) or *KPI Tours & Travel,* 1290 Ave. of the Americas, New York, NY 10104 (phone: 212-397-3200). *Fourways Travel* also has a current schedule and sells London theater tickets at all prices for about a $3 service charge. 950 Third Ave., New York, NY 10022 (phone: toll-free, 800-223-7872).

If you're interested in what goes on behind the scenes, *Theatreland Tours* (phone: 240-0915) offers daytime tours of a number of theaters guided by actors.

MUSIC: Few cities offer a greater variety of musical performances — both classical music and the many varieties of popular music. For classical music, the focus of attention is the *South Banks Arts Center* with its three concert halls — Royal Festival Hall, Queen Elizabeth Hall, and the Purcell Room — (phone: 928-3191 for all three) and Royal Albert Hall, Kensington Gore SW7 (phone: 589-8212). The latter is the home of the Henry Wood Promenade Concerts, or, simply, the Proms, an 8-week series of orchestral concerts that has been a popular feature of the London summer scene (July to September) for decades. There are no seats and tickets are cheap, because the Proms came into being to give students and other nonaffluent members of the populace an opportunity to dress up and be part of a grand musical event. The performances are tops (some broadcast live by the BBC), and the standing-room-only audience is large and enthusiastic. *Wigmore Hall,* Wigmore St. W1 (phone: 935-2141), is best known for recitals of chamber music and performances

352 LONDON / Sources and Resources

by some of the world's most accomplished instrumental and vocal soloists. Concerts are also often held in the dignified, splendid setting of St. John's Church, Smith Square SW1 (phone: 222-1061). The *London Symphony Orchestra* performs in its own concert hall at Barbican Centre, The Barbican EC2. During the summer there are outdoor concerts given at Kenwood, Crystal Palace, and Holland Park, and bands play in many of London's parks.

Operas at Covent Garden opera house, Bow St. WC2 (phone: 240-1066), are internationally famous. The *English National Opera Company* offers its performances at the Coliseum, St. Martin's La. WC2 (phone: 836-3161). The best of London's ballet performances are presented at Covent Garden, the Coliseum and at Sadler's Wells, Roseberry Ave. EC1 (phone: 837-1672). Details about concert, recital, opera, and ballet performances can be found in the arts sections of the Sunday newspapers.

Although some superstar popular musicians and vocalists make occasional appearances in converted movie houses, parks, and even deserted airfields outside town, much good live popular music can be heard in London's music pubs. Among the best of them are the *Bull's Head,* Lonsdale Rd. SW13 (phone: 876-5241); *Two Brewers,* Clapham High St. SW14 (phone: 622-3621); *Nashville,* 171 North End Rd. W14 (phone: 603-6071); *Kensington,* 54 Russell Gardens, Holland Rd. W14 (phone: 603-3245); and *Hope and Anchor,* 207 Upper St. N1 (phone: 359-4510).

NIGHTCLUBS AND NIGHTLIFE: Not two decades ago, they virtually rolled up the sidewalks in London at 11 PM. Now there's a very lively and often wild nightlife, including nightclubs, jazz clubs, historical feast entertainments, and gambling casinos. Some wind up around midnight; most go on until well into the early morning hours. A few nightclubs with floor shows are *Talk of the Town,* Leicester Sq. W1 (phone: 734-5051); the *London Room,* Drury La. (phone: 831-8863); and *Omar Khayyam,* 177 Regent St. W1 (phone: 734-7675). There is dancing at all three. There's a show but no dancing at *Madisons,* Camden Lock, Chalk Farm Rd. NW1 (phone: 485-6044). The best jazz clubs are *Ronnie Scott's,* 47 Frith St. W1 (phone: 439-0747), and *The 100 Club,* 100 Oxford St. W1 (phone: 636-0933). *Dingwalls,* Camden Lock, Chalk Farm Rd. NW1 (phone: 267-4967), has a continually changing program of much-acclaimed performers of popular music.

A special nighttime treat is called a *historical feast entertainment,* complete with traditional meals served by costumed waiters and waitresses. Menus resemble those of traditional Elizabethan feasts, and there is period music, horseplay, occasional mock sword fights, Shakespearean playlets, and other light entertainment. Try *Tudor Rooms,* 80 St. Martin's La. WC2 (phone: 240-3978); *Beefeater,* St. Katherine Dock E1 (phone: 480-7017); *Shakespeare's Tavern,* Blackfriar's La. EC4 (phone: 408-1001); and *King Arthur's Court,* Northumberland Ave. WC2 (phone: 408-1001).

As for discos, the scene is a rapidly changing one, and many places—such as expensive and exclusive *Annabel's,* 44 Berkeley Square (phone: 629-3558)—are open only to members. At the moment, the three most popular discos are: the *Embassy,* 7 Old Bond St; *Maunkberry's,* 57 Jermyn St.; and *Legend's,* 29 Old Burlington St. *Tramps,* 40 Jermyn St. SW1 (phone: 734-0565), where up-and-coming starlets and the chic social set meet to disco, is open to members only.

Comedy based on female impersonation is a major theme in British popular humor, as reflected in the number of pubs where female impersonators regularly perform. These include: *Union Tavern,* 146 Camberwell New Rd. SE5 (phone: 735-3605), and *Black Cap,* 171 Camden High St. NW1 (phone: 485-1742). Phone for details.

Information on gay clubs and pubs is contained in the biweekly *Gay News,* sold at larger newsstands.

SINS: London has a reputation for free and easy gambling, but over the last year or so the Gaming Laws have been enforced more rigorously and many clubs have had to shut down. It is best to check the current situation at your hotel desk when you arrive. Gambling club membership is usually available within 48 hours upon presentation of your passport. Card games, roulette, and dice are featured in most of the clubs.

By reputation, Soho is the sin center of London, but being ripped off is often the only sin visitors experience there. Soho striptease clubs usually give very little or no value for the money. Some of the worst are touted by street barkers or men who sidle up to passersby in the street, promising exotic and erotic pleasures. Exceptions, which try to redeem the good name of striptease, are *Raymond's Revue Bar,* 8 Brewer St. W1 (phone: 734-1593), and *The Windmill Theatre,* Great Windmill St. W1 (phone: 437-6312).

Soho does, however, boast a goodly number of prostitutes, some walking the street looking for customers, some advertising their services discreetly on nameplate cards in doorways — "Celeste, French lessons, second floor" — that sort of thing. Street walkers are also much in evidence in the Shepherd's Market district at night, and when the police aren't cracking down, on Park Lane, near the *London Hilton* and *Dorchester* hotels. Many of the "massage parlours" that have sprouted in various parts of town (there are several in Soho) offer clients more than massages.

Blue movies are shown in many movie houses — advertisements for them appear in *What's On in London.* And the *Gay Switchboard* (phone: 837-7324) offers telephone information and advice to visiting gays of both sexes.

BEST IN TOWN

CHECKING IN: Visitors reaching London without hotel reservations between early spring and midautumn are in for an unpleasant adventure. For many years now, there has been a glaring shortage of hotel rooms in the British capital during the prime tourist season, which each year seems to begin earlier and end later. (For a small fee, the London Tourist Board at Victoria Station, platform 15, or at the underground station in Heathrow, will try to help you locate a room.) This, general inflation, and the difficulty of finding suitable hotel staff are largely responsible for often excessive hotel charges, generally out of keeping with other costs in Britain. As a rule, expensive hotels do not include any meals in their prices; moderate and inexpensive hotels generally include Continental breakfasts in theirs.

Prices — with bath, English breakfast, VAT, and a 10% service charge sometimes included — are $110 to $160 and up for a double room in an expensive hotel; $65 to $100 is moderate; and $40 to $60 is inexpensive.

Claridges – Even the bathrooms and clothes closets are immense in this lush outpost for visiting royalty, heads of state, and other distinguished and/or affluent foreigners. The line of chauffered limousines outside the main entrance sometimes makes traffic there impenetrable. Wrought-iron balconies and a sweeping foyer staircase help provide a stately setting for one of London's most elegant hostelries. Brook St. W1 (phone: 629-8860). Expensive.

Connaught – A touch too sober for high livers; a trifle too formal for the rough-and-ready crowd. But there aren't many hotels left in the world that can rival this old London fixture in providing welcome, elegance, and comfort — particularly in its luxurious suites. Carlos Pl. W1 (phone: 499-7070). Expensive.

Dorchester – Located right next to the *Hilton,* overlooking Hyde Park, this very luxurious hotel, now under Arab ownership, maintains its traditional British atmosphere, with Georgian and Regency furnishings and elegant service. Its restaurant serves fine food. Rooms are tastefully furnished, and there is 24-hour room service. The hotel is presently installing central air-conditioning, refurbishing some rooms, and adding a shopping arcade. Park La. W1 (phone: 629-8888). Expensive.

Montcalm – A smaller, elegant hotel with a lovely facade, a warm-toned and understated interior, and top-notch service. Its rooms have all the usual comforts, and many of its suites are especially luxurious. There's a bar and a small French restaurant. Great Cumberland Pl. W1 (phone: 402-4288). Expensive.

London Hilton – Well situated off Hyde Park corner, near shopping and theater, this contemporary high-rise hotel offers luxury accommodations and views of the park and the city. Special attention to business executives includes a multilingual switchboard, secretarial staff, office equipment, and private dining rooms. The rooms here have all the amenities plus space for reading and writing. There's every conceivable service plus a few more — the *Roof Restaurant* with a view, the *Polynesian Restaurant,* and a pub, disco, and snack bar. 22 Park La. (phone: 493-8000). Expensive.

Churchill – A turn-of-the-century palatial mood is reflected in the discreet, impressive decor and the slightly overbearing marble lobby. This is a well-run, efficient place, with a pleasant restaurant and a snack room that serves the best bacon and eggs in London. Very popular with Americans looking for accommodations somewhere between the old world and the new. Portman Sq. W1 (phone: 486-5800). Expensive.

Berkeley – Remarkably understated, this 150-room hotel manages to preserve its impeccably high standards while keeping a low profile. Soft-spoken service complements the tastefully lavish, traditional English decor. Wilton Pl. W1 (phone: 235-6000). Expensive.

Dukes – Despite the small size of its 42 rooms, this is an establishment where nobility and prestige shine through. It even extends to the rooms' being named for former peers. 35 St. James's Pl. SW1 (phone: 491-4840). Expensive.

Grosvenor House – Despite the drabness of its lobby, this 467-room grande dame has a swimming pool, solarium, sauna, and some interesting shops. Park La. W1 (phone: 499-6363). Expensive.

Park Lane – If you don't mind the noise of the city streets, the location of this 400-room hotel in the heart of London should appeal to you. All rooms have recently been redecorated, and some have views of Green Park across the street. Piccadilly W1 (phone: 499-6321). Expensive.

Inter-Continental – Smack-dab in the middle of town, right on Hyde Park Corner, with windows overlooking the route of the mounted troops as they go cantering off for the Changing of the Guard each morning. Its well-proportioned rooms are equipped with refrigerated bars. Modern, comfortable, but the location's the main allure. 1 Hamilton Pl., Hyde Park Corner W1 (phone: 409-3131). Expensive.

Ritz – The fellow who was heard to mutter snootily, "Nobody stays at the *Ritz* anymore," was off-base, especially since the recent renovation restored much of the old luster and certainly got the "bugs" out. While the fare offered in the *Ritz* dining room is just acceptable, the decor is splendid and the service impeccable. Piccadilly W1 (phone: 493-8181). Expensive.

Savoy – A favorite of film and theater performers, some of whom check in for months and have nothing but praise for the accommodations and service. Once one of London's top addresses, it is just coming back into vogue. It's a huge place (400 rooms) with armies of chambermaids and porters to keep things running, though the reputation of its once famous *Grill Room* has slipped lately. The Strand WC2 (phone: 836-4343). Expensive.

Brown's – As English as you can get, retaining pleasing, quaint, Victorian charm, and not at all marred by heavy, sturdy furniture or the somewhat hushed atmosphere. Strong on service. If it's an English tea you're after, this is the place. Dover St. W1 (phone: 493-6020). Expensive.

Europa – Conveniently close to the American Embassy and West End shopping is this modern and quite reasonably priced hotel. It's bright and busy, and it has everything — lounge, bar, restaurant, shops, very comfortable rooms, and good service. Grosvenor Sq. W1 (phone: 493-1232). Expensive.

Cavendish – Immortalized as the *Bentinck,* the hotel run by Louisa Trotta (in real life, Rosa Lewis) in the recent TV series *The Duchess of Duke Street,* this homely old place offers one of the most attractive locations in central London, near Bond Street. Its 255 rooms are comfortable, if not elegant. Jermyn St. SW1 (phone: 930-2111). Expensive.

Britannia – Mahogany furniture, velvet armchairs, rooms painted in colors you might choose at home — all very tasteful and solid, despite the anonymity of its spacious foyer with its pretentious chandeliers. This is where the American Embassy — also on the square — often puts up visiting middle-ranking State Department officials. Grosvenor Sq. W1 (phone: 629-9400). Expensive.

Stafford – In a surprisingly quiet side street in the city center, this is where many American television and newspaper organizations put up visiting correspondents to give them efficient, friendly, British small-hotel management at its best. Many visitors think of it as their own personal secret, but it's been out for some time. 16 St. James's Pl. SW1 (phone: 493-0111). Expensive.

Selfridges – Just behind the department store of the same name, this hotel is modern both in furnishings and tone, with a refreshing, unaffected courtesy that seems often to escape some of London's midtown establishments. Conveniently located for shopping. Orchard St. W1 (phone: 408-2080). Expensive.

St. James' Club – For about $180 you can become a member of this exclusive residential club in the heart of London. It's quite an experience: you have full use of club suites. The club's Rolls-Royce fetches you from the airport and the magnificent art deco dining room serves some of the best food available in London. 7 Park Pl., SW1 (phone: 629-7688). Expensive.

Chesterfield – In the heart of Mayfair and near Hyde Park, this small, recently rebuilt Georgian mansion has a certain exclusive elegance. Bedrooms are thoroughly modernized and well equipped. Amenities include an informal coffee shop and a small bar that opens onto a flower-filled patio. 35 Charles St. W1 (phone: 491-2622). Expensive.

Cadogan – Very comfortable older place, redolent of Edwardian England. Oscar Wilde was arrested here, and Lillie Langtry, who was having an affair with the Prince of Wales (later Edward VII), lived next door. The furniture and decor are original, but modern conveniences are offered as well — phone, TV, refrigerator in every room, bar, and restaurant. The hotel has 75 rooms. 75 Sloane St. SW1 (phone: 235-7141). Expensive to moderate.

Drury Lane Hotel – Convenient to the theater district and fashionable Covent Garden, this hotel is small and ultramodern with a cool, sophisticated decor. There's an elegant bar and you can have snacks on the terrace. 10 Drury La., High Holborn W2 (phone: 836-6666). Moderate.

Embassy House – Over a million pounds has just been spent on renovating this Edwardian-style building on a wide tree-lined street in Kensington. It is very near the Albert Hall and all the main museums, and an easy walk from Harrods and Hyde Park. Although the decor is modern, there are elaborate high ceilings and elegant staircases. No restaurant, but a coffee shop and bar. 31 Queensgate SW7 (phone: 584-7222). Moderate.

Gatwick Hilton International – Part of the airport's expansion program, this hotel has been built to provide much-needed accommodations for the ever-increasing number of visitors using the Gatwick gateway. Connected to the terminal by an enclosed walkway; amenities include many services for business travelers: bars, health club, 24-hour room service, and more. Gatwick Airport (phone: 51-80-80). Moderate.

Royal Horseguards – This is one of the few London hostelries that overlooks the Thames with views of the South Bank. Recently modernized, it is a good base for those interested in the changing of the Buckingham Palace guard, Westminster Abbey, and the Houses of Parliament. Riverside rooms have balconies and there's a pleasant terrace. 2 Whitehall Ct. SW1 (phone: 839-3400). Moderate.

White House – A very big hotel, converted from apartments, in a quiet spot near Regents Park. Modernized and efficiently run, its facilities include a coffee shop, wine bar, and fine restaurant. Albany St. NW1 (phone: 387-1200). Moderate.

Basil Street – A relic with a reputation for graceful, old-fashioned service and beautiful antique furnishings to match. It draws a faithful international clientele who, if they can get reservations, prefer staying here to patronizing any of the modern, impersonal, newer hotels. Down the street from *Harrods* department store. Basil St. SW3 (phone: 730-3411). Moderate.

Kensington Hilton – A bit out of the way, this modern hotel offers a great deal of comfort at prices cheaper than those of most Hiltons. Services include a restaurant, piano bar, medieval banquets on Saturdays in the summer, and a lavish brunch on Sundays. Rooms are well designed and well maintained, some with balconies and color TV. 179–199 Holland Park Ave. (phone: 603-3355). Moderate.

Durrants – This elegant Regency-style hotel has a splendid location behind the Wallace Collection and is only a few minutes' walk from the shopping on Oxford Street. It has been family-run for over 50 years and all the rooms have retained their character while being kept comfortably up-to-date. Ask for a room with brass bedsteads. George St. W1 (phone: 935-8131). Moderate.

Royal Court – Unassuming, clean, comfortable hotel with a courteous, helpful staff, at the head of London's fashionable Chelsea shopping and residential district and within quick, easy reach of the rest of the action in town. Sloane Sq. SW1 (phone: 730-9191). Moderate.

Ebury Court – A small hotel with smallish but cozy rooms. Its faithful clientele testifies to its comfort and suitability. Hard to beat — all things considered — in a town where hotel prices tend to be unreasonable. 26 Ebury St. SW1 (phone: 730-8147). Moderate.

Harewood Hotel – This small modern hotel is well maintained by a pleasant and efficient staff. Some of the rooms have private terraces. Restaurant and wine bar. Harewood Row (phone: 262-2707). Moderate to inexpensive.

Sloane Hall Hotel – This Victorian town house has been turned into a simple, clean, adequate place to bunk out in London without cutting too deeply into your financial resources. It has a resident proprietor and a helpful staff. 6 Sloane Gardens SW1 (phone: 730-9206). Inexpensive.

YMCA – This relatively new "Y" could be the best and most comfortable low-cost hotel in the middle of London. Adequate, tidy rooms, complemented by a series of facilities not often found in hotels — including squash courts, a gym, billiard room, swimming pool, and sauna. Close to the British Museum and Oxford Street shopping district. Men and women of all ages are accepted. 112 Great Russell St. WC1 (phone: 637-1333). Inexpensive.

Diplomat Hotel – Small, with no restaurant and only 26 rooms — all with baths

— it is nonetheless comfortable, friendly, and inexpensive. In Belgravia at 2 Chesham St. SW1 (phone: 235-1544). Inexpensive.

Pastoria Hotel – Located in the very center of the West End, near all theaters, this pleasant, comfortable little hotel has 52 rooms, most with baths and TV; it has a bar and a restaurant. St. Martin's St. WC2 (phone: 930-8641). Inexpensive.

Portobello Hotel – An unpretentious place, made up of two Victorian houses uniquely furnished in the military style of the Crimean War era. It has 26 rooms — all with baths, phones, and TV — a restaurant and a bar, both open 24 hours a day. Near the Portobello Market at 22 Stanley Gardens W11 (phone: 727-2777). Inexpensive.

EATING OUT: Few London restaurants were ever known for the excellence of their cuisine — and some visitors of times past might call that a charitable understatement. But there's been a notable transformation in recent years. While restaurants offering really good English cooking — and not simply "chips with everything" — are still not easy to find (some are listed below), there has been a veritable explosion of good foreign restaurants in town (some of which are also noted below).

A meal for two will cost about $100 at a restaurant listed as expensive; $50 to $75 is moderate; and $30 and under inexpensive. Prices do not include wine, tips, or drinks. Some London restaurants have developed the Continental habit of automatically adding a service charge to the bill, so make certain you're not tipping twice. Reservations are necessary in all restaurants below.

Carrier's – In the middle of the Camden Passage antiques market, this place resembles a French provincial house, with bright printed fabrics on walls and windows, and plain wooden chairs and tables. The simple setting belies the sophistication of the food; try the pheasant pâté (a mixture of pheasant, veal, pork, truffles, and pistachios) or the rack of lamb topped with crushed green peppercorns, parsley, and lemon-flavored breadcrumbs and more. Closed Sundays. 2 Camden Passage N1 (phone: 226-5353). Expensive.

Capital Hotel Restaurant – The elegant, comfortable, small dining room in this hotel near *Harrods* department store offers well-chosen and admirably prepared French dishes. It is considered by some discriminating Londoners to be the best place in town to eat. Avoids the aren't-you-lucky-to-get-a-table attitude flaunted by some other better London restaurants. Basil St. SW3 (phone: 589-5171). Expensive.

Tante Claire – Run by chef Pierre Koffman and his wife, Annie, this place has been awarded two Michelin stars. While fish dishes are the chef's specialty, everything — especially the duck, calves liver, and *Pied de Cochon farci aux Morilles* (pig's foot stuffed with foie gras and mushrooms) — is excellent. Reservations necessary. Closed Saturdays and Sundays. 68 Royal Hospital Rd SW3 (phone: 352-6045). Expensive.

Wilton's – Good food, skillfully prepared, elegantly served in a Victorian setting. Game, oxtail, steak and kidney pie — what the best of English cooking can be all about. Closed Friday nights, Saturdays, and Sundays. 27 Bury St. SW1 (phone: 930-8391). Expensive.

Le Gavroche – This French restaurant was recently awarded three Michelin stars —the first and only in the country to be so honored. It features classic Gallic cooking, with many dishes that qualify as genuine masterpieces. 43 Upper Brooke St. W1 (phone: 408-0881).

Connaught Hotel Restaurant – Very dignified and very proper, this distinguished restaurant, with merely two Michelen stars, retains its reputation for excellent cuisine and impeccable service. It's not a place for loud conversation or outlandish attire, but for appreciation of masterful culinary performance. The setting matches the distinction of the menu. Carlos Pl., W1 (phone: 499-7070). Expensive.

Leith's – A fine Continental restaurant in an out-of-the-way Victorian building northwest of Kensington Gardens, *Leith's* serves outstanding hors d'oeuvres and desserts as part of a fine prix fixe dinner. Its wine selection is also very good. 92 Kensington Park Rd. W11 (phone: 229-4481). Expensive.

The Guinea Grill – Down an alley off Berkeley Square, this unimposing restaurant serves the best beef in Britain. It also substitutes displays of its fresh food — steaks, chops, fresh vegetables, and fruit — for a menu. It's as good as it looks, cooked with care. Closed Sundays. 30 Bruton Pl. W1 (phone: 629-5613). Expensive.

Gay Hussar – Perhaps the best Hungarian restaurant this side of Budapest. Its substantial menu offers a varied selection; goulash, of course, but much else. The food here has the unfortunate distinction of being extremely filling as well as delicious. Informal atmosphere, with a regular clientele drawn from London's newspaper and publishing world. Make reservations early. Closed Sundays. 2 Greek St. W1 (phone: 437-0973). Moderate.

Sweetings – A special London experience, this fish restaurant is one of the great lunchtime attractions in London's financial district. You may have to sit at a counter with your lobster, brill, or haddock — but it will be fresh and perfectly prepared. Weekday lunchtime only. 39 Queen Victoria St. EC4 (phone: 248-3062). Moderate.

Hungry Horse – This is the place to discover what a properly made English meat pie should taste like, as well as other English goodies. Don't be put off by having to pass under an archway and climb down a flight of stairs to get there — if anything, the inside looks a touch too tidy. 196 Fulham Rd. SW10 (phone: 352-7757). Moderate.

Tate Gallery Restaurant – Who would expect one of London's better restaurants to be in a fine art museum? But there it is — a genuine culinary outpost (leaning toward French cuisine), not just another museum eat-and-run hangout. Lunch only. Closed Sundays. Tate Gallery. Millbank SW 1 (phone: 834-6754). Moderate.

Wheeler's – Of the chain of London seafood restaurants with the same name, this is the best. It's an old-fashioned establishment on three floors which specializes in the many ways of preparing Dover sole, most of them delicious. Closed Sundays. 19 Old Compton St. W1 (phone: 437-7661). Moderate.

Poons of Covent Garden – This Cantonese restaurant has built a reputation for good authentic cooking and specializes in wind-dried food. Unlike many Chinese restaurants in London whose kitchens are perhaps best not seen, here you can watch the chefs at work through a glass partition. Closed Sundays. 41 King's St. WC2 (phone: 240-1743). Moderate.

Tuttons – One of the few restaurants in London that serves food all day, it's a very popular and lively brasserie in a former Covent Garden warehouse and a handy snack spot for theatergoers. Open from 9 to 12:30 AM daily; Sundays, 12 to 11:30 PM. 11 Russell St. WC2 (phone: 836-1167). Moderate.

My Old Dutch – At this authentic Dutch pancake house, you'll be served endless varieties of sweet and savory pancakes off genuine blue Delft plates. Loud music. 132 High Holborn WC1 (phone: 242-5200). Moderate.

Flanagan's – The specialty here is traditional English food — mostly fish. The decor is Edwardian, with sawdust on the floors and much gaiety. Diners are invited to sing along with the pianist who does his best on an old honky-tonk piano. Two locations: 11 Kensington High St. W8 (phone: 937-4111) and 100 Baker St. W1 (phone: 935-0287). Moderate.

Le Routier – The English equivalent of a truck-stop diner, this place has an interesting location overlooking the craft workshops and canal at Camden Lock. Inside you'll find a brasserie atmosphere, with specialties of the day chalked up on a blackboard. Very popular for lunch on weekends. Commercial Place, Chalk Farm Rd. NW1 (phone: 485-0360). Moderate.

Kalamaras – A small and friendly taverna with authentic Greek food prepared under the watchful eye of the Greek owner. The menu here is more varied than in most of the other Greek/Cypriot restaurants in London. Bouzouki music is sometimes played in the evenings. Closed Sundays. Two locations: 66 and 76 Inverness Mews W2, off Queensway (phone: 727-5082 and 727-9122). Moderate.

Au Bon Accueil – Over the years this very busy if somewhat cramped French restaurant has kept up its reputation for good food and low prices. Efficient service in two small rooms plus a basement. Closed Saturday lunch and Sundays. 27 Elystan St. SW3 (phone: 589-3718). Moderate.

Shezan – This quiet, brick-and-tile restaurant is just below street level, and prepares some very fine Indian food. Specialties include marinated-in-yogurt *murch tikka lahori* (chicken cooked in *tandoori,* or clay ovens) and *kabab kabli* (minced spiced beef). An enthusiastic staff will explain the intricacies of tandoori cooking, help with your order, and lavish you with excellent service. Closed Sundays. 16 Cheval Place SW7 (phone: 589-0314). Moderate.

Anemos – You'll find this very lively Greek/Cypriot restaurant is always crowded. Music blares from loudspeakers, waiters sing and clap, and when things get particularly riotous there's dancing on the tables. Not the place for an intimate evening but very jolly for celebrations. Closed Sundays. 34 Charlotte St. W1 (phone: 636-2289). Moderate.

Bloom's – A large restaurant specializing in Jewish food, *Bloom's* has a bright and bustling atmosphere, a bit like the dining room of a large hotel, with waiters who almost — but not quite — throw the food at you. The popular take-out counter serves up hot salt beef (corned beef) sandwiches. Closed Friday evenings and Saturdays. 90 Whitechapel High St. E1 (phone: 247-6835). Moderate.

Chicago Pizza Pie Factory – A little while ago, an American advertising executive turned his back on the ad world to bring London deep-dish pizza Windy City style, along with Schlitz beer and chocolate cheesecake. Londoners beat a path to his door and haven't yet stopped clamoring to get in. Closed Sundays. 17 Hanover Sq. W1 (phone: 629-2669). Inexpensive.

Rugantino – Food rather than trimmings is the emphasis in this small, cosy Italian eatery in Soho, though some of the dishes are very delicately put together. With fresh ingredients from the market and tender culinary care in the kitchen, this restaurant understandably draws a faithful crowd of regulars, including personalities from the British theater district nearby. Closed Sundays. 26 Romilly St. W1 (phone: 437-5302). Inexpensive.

The Standard Indian Restaurant – Possibly the best Indian restaurant in London — and cheap, too — it tends to get crowded quickly. There are no reservations, so if you're headed here, dine early to beat the rush. 23 Westbourne Grove W2 (phone: 727-4818). Inexpensive.

Great American Disaster – This is a big and popular place, serving good hamburgers, southern fried chicken, and spare ribs to the tune of loud pop music. The service is very friendly. 335 Fulham Rd. SW10 (phone: 352-7555). Inexpensive.

Hard Rock Café – An American-style place, with a loud jukebox and good burgers. It's always crowded. 150 Old Park La. W1 (phone: 629-0382). Inexpensive.

The Widow Applebaum – Not an authentic "New York Jewish" delicatessen, but this place serves pretty good herring, cold cuts, chopped liver, potato salad, dill pickles, and apple pie. 46 S Molton St., W1 (phone: 629-4649). Inexpensive.

Wolfe's – If you begin to crave an all-American meal, stop by this little eatery for a satisfying cheeseburger and fries. 34 Park Lane (phone: 499-6897). Inexpensive.

Dumpling Inn – This Peking-style restaurant serves excellent Oriental dumplings, and most of the other dishes are equally good. Try the fried seaweed; it's got lots of vitamins and tastes terrific. The service, though efficient, is a little brisk. 15A Gerrard St. (phone: 437-2567). Inexpensive.

Calabash – West African cuisine gives this restaurant a unique position on London's restaurant map, especially since it's located in the bubbling Covent Garden district. The service is accommodating and helpful and the food is both good and different. Closed Sundays. Downstairs at London's "Africa Center," 38 King St. (phone: 836-1976). Inexpensive.

The Bangkok – Known for its *saté* — small tender slices of beef marinated in a curry and soy sauce and served with a palate-destroying hot peanut sauce. From your butcher block table you can watch your meal being prepared by chefs in the windowed kitchen. Closed Sundays. 9 Bute St. SW7 (phone: 584-8529). Inexpensive.

Geales' – This place in the western reaches of London serves up truly English — and fresh — fish and chips in a setting that looks like a 1930s tearoom. Go early, because *Geale's* is no secret. Closed Sundays and Mondays. 2 Farmer St. W8 (phone: 727-7969). Inexpensive.

Danish House Coffee Room – Located in the basement of a shop selling Danish goods, this place is a handy lunchtime stop for Knightsbridge shoppers. It's self-service and unlicensed with a counter offering delectable Danish open-face sandwiches and assorted tempting sweets. There is also afternoon tea and coffee. Open 9 AM to 5 PM; closed Sundays. 16 Sloane St. SW1. Inexpensive.

Cranks – There are three branches of this self-service vegetarian restaurant. All are popular and serve good homemade desserts as well as salads, quiches, and other hot food. Drop in for coffee or afternoon tea. Open 10 AM to 11 PM; closed Sundays. 8 Marshall St. W1 (phone: 437-9431); in Heal's on Tottenham Court Rd. (phone: 637-2230); or in Peter Robinson's at Oxford Circus. Inexpensive.

SHARING A PINT: There are several thousand pubs in London, the vast majority of which are owned by the six big brewers. Most of these pubs have two bars: the "public," which is for the working man who wants to get on with the business of drinking, and the "saloon," which makes an attempt at providing comfort and may serve good food and wine as well as beer. Liquor at the latter may cost more. Eating in a crowded pub is not always easy because the limited number of tables are barely large enough to hold all the empty beer glasses, let alone food. Pub food is hearty but not especially imaginative: a ploughman's lunch, which is a hunk of bread and cheese plus pickle; cottage pie, which is ground meat with mashed potato on top baked in the oven; sausages; and sandwiches.

Here are the names of some of the best pubs: *Dirty Dick's,* 202 Bishopsgate, is offbeat but popular, with fake bats and spiders hanging from the ceilings, sawdust on the floor, and good bar snacks; *The Mayflower,* 117 Rotherhithe, is hidden among wharves and warehouses on the Thames and named for the ship that sailed from here to Plymouth Rock; *Admiral Codrington,* 17 Mossop St. SW3, is large and Victorian, with brass beer pumps, engraved mirrors, and good food; *Dickens Inn* by the Tower, St. Katherine's Way E1, is a converted warehouse overlooking a colorful yacht marina and serving shellfish snacks; *George Inn,* 77 Borough High St. SE1, dates from 1676 and retains the original gallery for viewing Shakespearean plays in the summer; *Flask Tavern,* 77 Highgate West Hill N6, serves drinks at three wood-paneled bars and on its outside patio; *Lamb,* 94 Lambs Conduit St. WC1, is also wood paneled and hung with photos of past music-hall performers; *Museum Tavern,* 49 Great Russell St. WC1, is across the road from the British Museum and decorated with hanging flower baskets; *Princess Louise,* 208 High Holborn WC1, has live music, cabaret, and a wine bar upstairs with good food; *Salisbury,* 90 St. Martins La. WC2, is vintage late Victorian with ornate mirrors and a marble counter and has a gay clientele; *Old Bull and Bush,* North End Rd. NW3, dates to the seventeenth century and has a garden; *Prospect of Whitby,* 57 Wapping Wall El, was once the haunt of thieves and smugglers, as the oldest riverside pub in London (now it draws jazz-lovers); *Sherlock Holmes,* 10 Northumberland St. WC1, is dedicated to Holmesiana and excellent, made-to-order meat sandwiches; *Ye Olde Cheshire Cheese,* 145 Fleet St. EC4, is a seventeenth-century pub with paneled walls and sawdust floors popular with the Fleet Street set.

WINE BARS: A new innovation on the London scene, they serve wine by the glass or bottle, accompanied by such light fare as quiche and salad. You will find prices lower in wine bars than in restaurants and can often reserve tables in advance. Here's a selection of the finest: *Boos,* 1 Glentworth St. NW1, combines rustic decor with simple homemade food; *Cork and Bottle,* 44–46 Cranbourne St. WC2, is patronized by the London wine trade and has a classical guitarist providing background music; *Draycott's,* 114 Draycott Ave. SW3, has tables grouped outside on the pavement and is frequented by the smart London set; *Ebury Wine Bar,* 139 Ebury St., is in the heart of Belgravia and serves good food (try the English pudding), and offers live music nightly; *Loose Box,* 7 Cheval Pl. SW7, features home-cooked food and a roof garden; *Shampers,* 4 Kingly St. W1, is conveniently located near the famous *Liberty* department store for shoppers and sometimes has a classical guitarist in the evenings; *34 Baker Street,* at that address, is a sophisticated, late-night spot, where you can sip a drink and listen to the baby grand; *Russkies Wine Cellar,* 6 Wellington Ter., Bayswater Rd. W2, is elegant and Edwardian, with good food and jazz.

OXFORD

For 600 years, England had only two universities, and though more than 40 institutions of higher learning have opened their doors since the early nineteenth century, the two venerable ancients are still so embedded in the British psyche that they are often called by one name, Oxbridge, put asunder only by scholars debating questions of academic supremacy or by tourists comparing their visible merits. Although neither argument is likely to come to a conclusion soon, the casual visitor will notice a difference between Oxford and Cambridge. Whereas Cambridge, often described as a "city within a university," has the atmosphere of a small country town, Oxford is larger and bustling, not quite a metropolis, but transformed by a twentieth-century auto industry on its outskirts into a "university within a city."

Fortunately, Oxford University, though only part of present-day Oxford, remains its historic core, one of the great living architectural treasures of the world, where examples of every building style from the eleventh century on are preserved in less than one square mile. Oxford is Britain's oldest university, but age coupled with academe has not produced a dark, dreary collection of moss-covered monoliths. A much-quoted line by the nineteenth-century poet Matthew Arnold — "That sweet city with her dreaming spires" — aptly describes the university's towers, domes, and constant repetition of pinnacles when seen from afar or above. Close-up, as the visitor stands before a single facade of ribbed golden stone, limpid panes of glass, or alternating panels of the two, any sense of the laborious process of study fades and Oxford becomes the idea of learning incarnate, all light, clarity, and brilliance, even in the most inclement weather.

No one knows why scholars began to gather here. The city was probably in existence on the banks of the River Thames (called, in Oxford, the Isis) and its tributary, the Cherwell, long before the first reference to it appeared in the *Anglo-Saxon Chronicle* in 912. In 1121, the Priory of St. Frideswide was founded and it was possibly the presence of scholarly monks that drew English students to Oxford after a quarrel between Henry II and the French resulted in the closing of the Sorbonne to Englishmen in 1167. The university then developed quickly. By 1300, the first colleges had been established (University, Balliol, and Merton) and there were 1,500 students on hand.

Relations between town and gown were immediately antagonistic. Early students lived in lodging houses at the mercy of price-gouging townspeople; townspeople saw their city taken over by a young and boisterous occupying army. An outbreak of hostilities in 1209 caused some students to flee and set up a university at Cambridge. Even greater trouble in 1355, on St. Scholastica's Day, resulted in the death of 62 students and in the rest being driven from town. That the dispute was eventually resolved in favor of the university was a measure of its royal protection (because scholars became the basis of a king's loyal civil service, the gown-crown connection was strong). Thereafter, on every St. Scholastica's Day from 1357 to 1825, city dignitaries performed the humiliating penance of placing 62 pennies on the altar of the university church of St. Mary the Virgin and for nearly 500 years the university virtually ruled Oxford.

Rivalry between town and gown is now light-hearted, but the structure of the university has scarcely changed since the Middle Ages. By 1400, every student was required to be listed on the roll (matricula) of a master (or teacher — later to be called a don, from the Latin *dominus* for "master") responsible for him, and all were required to live in colleges or halls rather than in scattered lodging houses. The proliferating colleges became self-contained communities — behind the gates of each were living quarters, chapel, library, kitchen, dining hall, and even a brewery. This collegiate system in its modern guise continues to baffle visitors. Many an undergraduate popping out of Worcester or Wadham has been accosted by lost tourists looking for Oxford College, unaware that all 34 of Oxford's colleges are part of Oxford University. Young men and women (the first of five women's colleges opened in 1878, and most of the colleges are now open to both sexes) seeking admission to the university have to be accepted, usually after an examination, by individual colleges, and live in them or in lodgings approved by them. But the university arranges academic curricula, administers financial aid from the government, and awards degrees.

This medieval organization also accounts for the type of sight-seeing experience to be had in Oxford. More than 600 buildings in the city are considered of outstanding architectural merit and most belong to the university. Your time in Oxford will be spent wandering through gateways into "quadrangles," or courtyards (the students live up numbered staircases around the quads), discovering gardens, cloisters, and chapels, visiting the occasional open library or hall, following a passageway through still another arch and into one more quadrangle, often a spacious green lawn coaxed to perfection by centuries of loving care and hardly any pounding of feet — the sign will say who's allowed to walk on the grass and it's usually dons, sometimes postgraduates, occasionally undergraduates, never visitors.

Much of Oxford's history is brought to life by the anecdotes of local guides well versed in the city's folklore: How Dr. Johnson, a poor student at Pembroke College, was ashamed to walk into nearby Christ Church — always a grand college — because of his rundown shoes, yet threw away a pair of new ones left at his door by a rich scholar. Or how (the story everyone tells) one would-be undergraduate, up for an interview, was greeted superciliously by a don who turned from the awed youth, opened a copy of *The Times,* and said, "Right, impress me" — at which the boy took out a box of matches, set fire to the paper, and won a scholarship.

Oxford is, of course, its students (8,500 undergraduates, 3,000 postgraduates, plus 2,000 dons in a town population of 90,000) and they do use humor to relieve the weight of tradition that is everywhere. (At times, even on their backs. If exams are under way, visitors will see them going around in *subfusc* — dark suits or skirts with short black gowns on top and mortarboards on their heads, the age-old traditional dress for special occasions.) Some of the weightier traditions, in fact, seem actually born of silliness: "The Mallard Song" sung by the fellows of All Souls celebrates a duck that flew out of a drain when the college was built. The Boar's Head Ceremony held at Queen's College at Christmas honors a legendary scholar who saved himself from a wild boar's attack by stuffing a Latin book down the animal's throat.

None of this, however, changes the fact that Oxford's stock-in-trade is the pursuit of knowledge, and of this visitors tiptoeing around quadrangles are constantly reminded by the firm signs asking them to be quiet. Such a polite command is not hard to obey, especially if it's all the better to hear the choristers of Christ Church singing in the cathedral. But even without the background sound, the sight of the sun glinting off the exalted architectural complex of Radcliffe Square, or of the progression of college facades on High Street coalescing to a magnificent skyline, is an inspiration.

OXFORD AT-A-GLANCE

SEEING THE CITY: An initial bird's-eye view of Oxford is absolutely essential so that you can get a clear idea of the layout of the colleges. Two of the best vantage points for such a perspective are the gallery near the top of the spire of St. Mary's Church, in High Street — colloquially known as "The High" — and the cupola at the top of Christopher Wren's Sheldonian Theatre on Broad Street. From St. Mary's you see much of High Street, with its gentle curve that is fancifully said to reflect most people's natural stroll: All Souls College; University College; and the Radcliffe "Camera," or Library. From the Sheldonian you look onto Broad Street (better known as "The Broad"); across The Broad to Balliol and Trinity colleges; closer by, down at Exeter College, the Bodleian Library, the Radcliffe Camera, and the Clarendon Building — once the home of the university printers, later to become the Oxford University Press. For a traditional view of Oxford's "dreaming spires," find the slightly unkempt piece of free land called Port Meadow, between the River Thames and the railway line. Or, closer and more congenial, though slightly less panoramic, Christ Church Meadow, near the southernmost point of the city, to the east of St. Aldate's.

SPECIAL PLACES: Ask any but the most disenchanted Oxford graduate about special places and he or she will answer "my college." Virtually all of them are worth a visit, but happily the most impressive are the most central. Not one is too distant from Carfax (from the French *quatre voies,* "four ways," or from the Latin *quadrifurcus,* "four-forked" — where the four main streets of Oxford met in Saxon times and still do) to be visited on foot.

THE HEART OF OXFORD

Magdalen College (pronounced Mawdlin) – Magdalen Tower, guarding the eastern end of High Street, was called by King James I, "the most absolute building in Oxford." An anthem is sung from the top of the tower at dawn every May Day morning. The college was established in 1458, by William of Waynflete, a bishop of

Winchester, who was one of the first college founders to emphasize the importance of a chapel. There is a famous deer park, where the animals are fairly tame. Across High Street from Magdalen, also on the banks of the River Cherwell, are the Botanic Gardens, the oldest in Britain, laid out in 1621 with approximately £5,000 given by Henry Danvers, earl of Danby, primarily for the study of medicinal herbs. High St.

All Souls College – Founded 21 years before Magdalen by Henry Chichele, Archbishop of Canterbury, All Souls has a certain mystique: It does not have undergraduates, only 60 fellows engaged in research and teaching. Because of its great academic distinction and wealth, it has been called "the most exclusive club in Britain." (A member of the college once remarked that he never needed an encyclopedia; if he wanted to know anything he just had to ask a colleague over dinner.) Behind All Souls' small fifteenth-century front quadrangle is the eighteenth-century great quadrangle, with twin towers and the magnificent Codlington Library whose central adornment is a sundial made by Christopher Wren. High St.

University College – Across High Street from All Souls, "Univ," as it is known, is the oldest college in Oxford (1249). It used to be believed that it was founded by Alfred the Great, though the most telling comment on that occurred when one don — on being asked to a formal dinner to celebrate the millennium of Alfred's "foundation" — declined to come and sent two burned cakes instead. There are 435 undergraduates and postgraduates, about average for an Oxford college. High St.

Church of St. Mary the Virgin – The oldest university building of all is part of St. Mary's; it looks like an aisle of the church, because in the fifteenth century it was remodeled. St. Mary's fourteenth-century spire is one of the dominant features of the Oxford skyline, and the church is a fine example of Perpendicular Gothic. High St.

Radcliffe Camera – This building commemorates Oxford's most generous eighteenth-century benefactor, Dr. John Radcliffe. It's such a distinctive building that when seen from miles away under the right conditions and from the right viewpoint, it has been compared as a landmark with Cambridge's King's College Chapel. Designed by James Gibbs — influenced by plans for a projected mausoleum for Charles I at Windsor — and completed in 1749, it was originally called the Radcliffe Library and is now a reading room for the Bodleian, the university library. Radcliffe Sq., behind St. Mary's.

Bodleian Library – Ball games are not allowed on the grass between the Radcliffe Camera and the Bodleian Library, and strollers are discouraged, because the earth here is only a thin crust: Below it are massive stores of books, and underground railways that bring books, on request by readers, from their shelves. The creation of the Bodleian Library, only certain parts of which are open to visitors, was the outstanding achievement of seventeenth-century Oxford. It was founded by Thomas Bodley, born in 1545 and a fellow of Merton at 19. He chose the comparative obscurity of academic life and devoted himself to the library project. It is one of the great libraries of the world, and has the right, like the British Museum Library and the Cambridge University Library, to a copy of every book published in the country. Across the road from the Sheldonian Theatre is an extension to the Bodleian, the New Bodleian, built in all its ugliness in the late 1930s. Radcliffe Sq.

Sheldonian Theatre – The degree-giving ceremony is held in the Sheldonian, which was designed by Christopher Wren in 1669, then professor of Astronomy at the university. (As in the case of Sir John Vanbrugh and many other architects of the seventeenth and eighteenth centuries, interest in architecture was a hobby, rather than a profession.) Based on a classical amphitheater, it is enhanced by its own courtyard, entered from Broad Street, which it shares with the Clarendon Building. Its interior, also used for concerts and plays, is magnificent, and you can climb a wide wooden stairway, polished by generations of feet, to the cupola for a partial view of central Oxford's spires and gargoyles. Broad St.

New College – Its full name is St. Mary College of Winchester Oxenford, but when it was completed in 1386, the full effect was so stunning that the college, founded by William of Wykeham, bishop of Winchester, has always been known as New College. The front quadrangle is the original one (the first quadrangle built as such in Oxford, following the example of Merton's Mob Quad, which became a quad bit by bit), though the top story on three of its sides was added in the late seventeenth century. The other side is formed by the chapel, which should be seen inside, too, for various treasures including the bishop's crozier. New College's garden quad, also added in the late seventeenth century, incorporates a stretch of thirteenth- and fourteenth-century city wall. New College La.

Balliol College – Apart from All Souls, which does not admit undergraduates, Balliol is academically the most impressive college in the university, with a long list of distinguished graduates, particularly in the field of politics (Lord Curzon, Harold Macmillan, Edward Heath). The college originated in 1255 when the bishop of Durham levied a fine upon John de Balliol, a powerful landowner. He was to pay a sum of money for several years toward the support of poor Oxford scholars. After his death in 1269, his wife continued the project. Balliol, founded in approximately 1263, was actually a living quarters, not a college as we know it today. Outside Balliol, in the middle of Broad Street, a cross on the ground marks the spot where three Protestant martyrs, Thomas Cranmer, Nicholas Ridley, and Hugh Latimer, were burned at the stake during the reign of Mary Tudor in 1555. Broad St.

Exeter College – In the Fellow's Garden of Exeter is one of Oxford's most famous trees, a horse chestnut that reaches over the boundary wall toward Brasenose. It is said that when the branches of the tree *touch* Brasenose, Exeter will beat Brasenose on the river. The tradition is scoffed at, but Brasenose undergraduates are known to clip the branches just in case. The college is associated with the rise of the pre-Raphaelite movement: William Morris and Burne-Jones were fellow students and later close friends. There is a William Morris tapestry in the chapel. Broad St. at Turl St.

Christ Church – Lesson one: If you don't want to be taken for a complete country bumpkin, never say "Christ Church College," but simply "Christ Church." Lesson two (very subtle, this one): Contrary to usage at the other colleges, fellows, or dons, here are known as "students," but undergraduates never are. Christ Church was founded on the site of the Priory of St. Frideswide by Cardinal Wolsey in 1525, was refounded by Henry VIII in 1532 and 1546, and includes among its august alumni such names as Sir Philip Sidney, Richard Hakluyt, John Locke, John Wesley, John Ruskin, Lewis Carroll, W. H. Auden, and many others. Its exquisitely vaulted chapel is also Oxford's cathedral, one of the smallest cathedrals in England, while its sixteenth-century Great Quadrangle (or Tom Quad) is Oxford's largest. Great Tom, the imperious bell in Tom Tower, hangs right above the main Christ Church entrance and resounds 101 times at 9:05 each night, the original curfew time for the 101 undergraduates it summoned by its first peal. See, also, the paneled and gilded medieval dining hall and the eighteenth-century Palladian Peckwater Quad, behind Tom Quad. St. Aldate's.

Merton College – University College was founded in 1249, Balliol in 1263, but if it's a question of official papers, then Merton (founded in 1264, with final statutes dated 1274) can claim to be the oldest college in Oxford. It has, at any rate, Oxford's oldest quadrangle, Mob Quad (begun 1304), whose south and west sides are formed by England's oldest library — no lending library, some of the books are still chained to desks as they were for the early scholars. Merton also has Oxford's first collegiate chapel, containing original thirteenth-century stained glass. Intimate, quiet, and less neatly laid out than the other colleges, Merton's buildings only gradually assumed the familiar quadrangle form, but once this pattern was copied by New College, it was the model for all the colleges that followed. Merton St.

Ashmolean Museum – This collection of paintings, sculpture, musical instruments, artifacts of the Stone and Bronze ages, and other objets d'art originally belonged to John Tradescant (d. 1638), then his son, who in turn left it to Elias Ashmole, also a collector.

Among the treasures you can see here are Michelangelo and Raphael drawings, and the Pomfret and Arundel marbles. Perhaps the most famous item in the whole museum is the exquisite Alfred Jewel, found in a field in 1693 and marked with an old English inscription "Alfred Had Me Made." The Ashmolean's wealth of rarities and curiosities outgrew its original building in the nineteenth century and moved to new premises. The Old Ashmolean, next to the Sheldonian Theatre on Broad Street, is now the Museum of the History of Science. Beaumont St. (phone: 57522).

OFFBEAT OXFORD

The Covered Market – Built in the nineteenth century, this is a busy and charming if down-to-earth street market. In its maze of tiny lanes crammed with tiny shops, the aroma of just-ground coffee and fresh fish mingles with that of ripe cheese and blood-stained sawdust from the butcher's shops. After a colorful morning's stroll, drop by at the rough-and-ready but locally popular *George's Cafe,* 77 The Market (phone: 49527). Outwardly unprepossessing, this basic, unchic coffee and tea shop, where you can buy pies, sandwiches, or cakes, claims a cult following among undergraduates. The tables may be covered in crumbs, the service off-hand, the floor unswept, the other customers morose or argumentative, but the place has style.

Blackwells Bookshop – Virtually an Aladdin's cave filled with books, *Blackwells* is where tourists buying paperback guides to the city rub shoulders with fellows of All Souls collecting esoteric tomes ordered on their behalf and undergraduates dutifully gathering up texts recommended by their tutors. Broad St., opposite the Sheldonian Theatre; other branches are on Hythe Bridge St., Leckford Rd., and (for music) Holywell St.

■ **EXTRA SPECIAL:** Early summer sees Oxford at its best and brightest, and although most undergraduates have exams on their minds, that does not seem to obtrude — perhaps it even helps. Oxford has all kinds of activities and fetes during this season; check the *What's On* brochures as well as the college notice boards. There are open-air plays in college gardens; "commem" balls — grand, all-night black-tie affairs, to which you will have no trouble obtaining tickets; picnics and madrigals on the river; garden parties; church festivals, and much more. (*A word of caution:* Because hotel rooms are at a premium at this time, be prepared to accept hotel accommodations some distance from the city center or even in the surrounding countryside. Woodstock and Weston-on-the-Green, for example, have good hotels.)

SOURCES AND RESOURCES

The Thames and Chilterns Tourist Board, 8 The Market Pl., Abingdon, Oxfordshire, OX14 3UD (phone: 0235-22711), will provide essential background information, but will certainly direct you to the City of Oxford Tourist Information Centre, St. Aldate's (opposite the Town Hall, about 100 yards from Carfax; phone: 48707). It is excellent, and the staff is very helpful. (Unfortunately, the information center is only open during office hours, and on Sundays during the summer. Complain loudly about that; it might do some good.) The center stocks a massive amount of tourist literature, guides, and maps and *What's On* brochures. The inexpensive *Oxford Guide* and the *Oxford Vade Mecum,* on sale in most bookstores, are both useful and detailed; *Oxford, An Explorer's Guide,* has illustrated maps that are particularly successful in helping strangers identify the colleges as they come to them.

For Local Coverage – The *Oxford Mail* evening newspaper (whose editor, incidentally, is traditionally allowed to dine in All Souls when the mood takes him).

368 OXFORD / Sources and Resources

GETTING AROUND: Except for the trip from the train station, for which you will need a taxi or a bus, and unless you choose a hotel out of the center, you will not need transport. Everyone goes on foot or by bicycle.

Bike – These can be hired from *Penny Farthing*, 27 George St. (phone: 49368).

Taxi – Unfortunately, cabs in Oxford are not cheap, compared with most other cities. There are cabstands in several locations around the city; one such convenient spot is the taxi rank near the Randolph Hotel. To order a cab by phone, call *Radio Taxis* at 49743.

Bus – The *South Midlands Bus Company*, which provides very good service linking the city center with its outskirts, is located at 395 Cowley Rd. (phone: 774611).

Car Rental – You can rent a car from *Luxicars, Ltd.*, 265 Iffley Rd., Cowley (phone: 40101), or *Godfrey Davis*, Seacourt Tower, Botley Rd. (phone: 46373). Parking in Oxford is difficult to find, but day-trippers can take advantage of the "Park and Ride" scheme. Leave your car free of charge in the parking lots clearly marked as you enter Oxford, then take the blue and white buses that run frequently to the city center.

MUSEUMS: In addition to those mentioned in Special Places, other museums of note are:

Museum of Oxford – The history of the town from Norman times by means of photographs and models. Closed Mondays. St. Aldate's (phone: 815559).

University Museum – Mainly natural history, in what was once Oxford's most architecturally controversial building. Parks Rd. (phone: 57467).

Pitt Rivers Museum (access through the University Museum) – Ethnology, archaeology, musical instruments, weapons (phone: 54979).

Christ Church Picture Gallery – Old masters, glassware, antiques. In Canterbury Quad, Christ Church (phone: 42102).

Brass Rubbing Centre – Replicas of mainly local original brasses for that exceptional souvenir. University Church, Radcliffe Sq. (phone: 721200).

SHOPPING: Inspired by the groves of academe, you will probably want to buy books, and possibly paintings or prints too. Besides *Blackwells*, there are several other bookstores on Broad St., but the city's largest secondhand bookstore, *Robin Waterfield's*, is at 36 Park End St. Along High St., you'll find many antique and picture shops; the *Oxford Gallery* sells as well as exhibits paintings. Little Clarendon St., just north of the Ashmolean, has a couple of good crafts shops; two of these are *Gallery 57*, at No. 29, and *Playhood Toyshop*, at No. 22. For a picnic lunch or some jars of interesting comestibles to take home, you can't do better than to shop in the *Covered Market*, off High St. (A jug of wine to accompany that picnic can be found at *Oddbins*, 108 High St.)

SPECIAL EVENTS: Late May sees one of the biggest events of the Oxford calendar — *Eights Week*, when teams from each of the men's colleges compete for the coveted title of Head of the River. *Commencement* takes place in the Sheldonian Theatre, most spectacularly at the end of the summer term, when honorary degrees are awarded to distinguished men and women. Each September, the *St. Giles' Fair* is held in St. Giles', between the Randolph Hotel and the point at which the Woodstock and the Banbury roads fork off to the north. Traffic has to be diverted to accommodate this traditional, hundreds-of-years-old fun fair.

SPORTS: Boating – The sport most popularly associated with Oxford is rowing, especially in view of the Boat Race held every year against Cambridge. The river at Oxford is too narrow to accommodate teams racing side by side, so the colleges have devised "Bumps," or staged races in which crews try to bump each other's boats. But the best way for visitors to get properly acquainted with the river is to hire a punt (available at *Howards,* Madgalen Bridge, or *Hubbocks,* Folly Bridge). As long as you hang on to the pole at all times you cannot really come to grief. Motorboats can also be rented for longer excursions from *Medley Boat Station,* Port Meadow (phone: 511660), or *Salters,* Folly Bridge (phone: 43421).

Golf – The *Southfield Golf Club* on Hilltop Rd., Headington (phone: 42158), welcomes visitors weekdays only; no temporary membership is required.

Swimming – Take a dip at the *Ferry Pool,* near Ferry Centre, Summertown (phone: 50330).

THEATER: *The Playhouse,* Beaumont St. (phone: 47133), opposite the Ashmolean, is the university theater and features professionals on tour and amateurs from the university. The *Apollo,* George St. (phone: 44544), plays host to opera, ballet, pantomime, visiting pop groups, and jazz concerts. Production schedules for both are published in the *Oxford Mail.*

MUSIC: Virtually all the colleges have a chapel of considerable architectural interest, and many of these showcase concerts and recitals. The best Oxford music is church music, and *Christ Church, Magdalen College,* and *New College* all have choir schools — so standards are very high. The *Holywell Music Rooms,* said to be the oldest of their kind in Europe, are a delightful setting for small concerts, as is the *Sheldonian Theatre.* Just watch for advertisements in the local newspapers or on college notice boards.

NIGHTCLUBS AND NIGHTLIFE: During the school term Oxford is a young city, so it is not surprising to find a lot going on. *The Boozer,* Frewin St., off Cornmarket, provides rock music on Saturdays and Sundays; *Wellington Wine Bar,* Shoe La., has jazz on Thursdays, Fridays, and Saturdays; *Cape of Good Hope,* the Plain, features various disco groups; and *Blades,* Botley Rd., offers light meals and live music.

SINS: Despite the recent admission of women to the men's colleges and the presence of a few women's colleges, Oxford remains largely a male bastion. In such a setting, *lust* naturally flourishes. If *gluttony* is your secret vice, indulge in a meal and a bottle of claret at the wickedly excellent restaurant *Les Quat' Saisons* in Oxford or at the *Bear* in the nearby town of Woodstock.

BEST IN TOWN

CHECKING IN: Perhaps it is because members of the university (which includes anyone who has graduated from it) can always get a room in their old college, or perhaps it is because during the vacation there are so many university landladies whose merits are passed by word of mouth — whatever the reason, Oxford is short of top-grade hotels, and for the few that do exist, you will usually need to make reservations well ahead. You need never go without a bed however; if you are having trouble, consult the information center in St. Aldate's (phone: 48707). Expect to pay $60 and up for a double room in a hotel listed as expensive; $40 to $60 for a moderate; and under $40 for inexpensive.

Linton Lodge – A short bus or taxi ride from the city center, this modernized Edwardian town house has 73 bedrooms; an oak-paneled dining room with a Continental menu; and pleasant, peaceful gardens. 13 Linton Rd. (phone: 53461). Expensive.

The Randolph – The best in town, with Victorian Gothic charm, an efficient staff, and a very good location directly opposite the Ashmolean Museum and close to the Playhouse Theatre. Facilities include 110 rooms, all with phones and TVs; a comfortable restaurant that serves Continental food and offers a reasonable fixed-price dinner; a snack shop for quick meals; and a bar. Cream teas are served every afternoon in the lounge. Beaumont St. (phone: 47481). Expensive.

Eastgate – Not quite as luxurious as the first two, but it enjoys an excellent location fairly near Magdalen College. Although the rooms here are smallish, the staff is friendly. 73 High St. (phone: 48244). Moderate.

Oxford Europa Lodge – This modern, recently renovated hotel plays host to many conventions. For the casual tourist, however, it also offers sleek rooms and a convenient restaurant and pub. This is a good starting point for a Cotswolds journey, as the Lodge is located outside Oxford on the A40 Wolvercote Roundabout (phone: 59933). Moderate.

TraveLodge – It's one of those standardized, no-frills motels that offers efficient service, a 24-hour cafeteria, and a 24-hour gas station. Peartree Roundabout (phone: 54301). Moderate.

Turf Tavern – Well-known historic city-center pub close to the walls of New College, reached through a maze of pedestrian alleys. It's small (11 rooms), but has lots of atmosphere. 4–5 Bath Pl. (phone: 43235). Inexpensive.

Welsh Pony – A nineteenth-century pub near the bus station (but reasonably central). These are simple lodgings (only 9 rooms, no phones), but you can start your day with a good breakfast. 48 George St. (phone: 42998). Inexpensive.

EATING OUT: Oxford offers more in the way of restaurants than it does hotels. If you cannot secure an invitation to dine at High Table with a don in one of the colleges (gastronomically it may not be tops, but for atmosphere it's unbeatable), you can still eat very well indeed. This is, after all, a very sophisticated community, and fine food is much appreciated. Expect to pay $55 and up for dinner for two, excluding wine and tips, in establishments listed as expensive; $25 to $35 in moderate establishments; and $25 and under in inexpensive places.

Restaurant Elizabeth – Housed in one of Oxford's finest late-fifteenth-century buildings, this chic little restaurant has a good location, where you can enjoy a fine meal as a fitting end to a day or weekend exploring Oxford. The sophisticated menu features French cooking; house specialties include trout stuffed with shellfish soufflé, Châteaubriand, and *caneton à l'orange*. Reservations necessary. Open daily; closed Christmas, and most of August. 84 St. Aldate's (phone: 42230). Expensive.

Les Quat' Saisons – Ostensibly a simple bistro, it is situated in a row of shops. Inside, however, you'll find flickering candlelight and elegant cream-colored lace tablecloths; an extensive wine list; and skillfully handled haute cuisine, as well as game in season. The restaurant, opened only in 1977, was an immediate success and claims a strong local following. Service, however, can become slow on a busy evening. Reservations necessary. Closed Sundays, Mondays, Christmas, and July. 272 Banbury Rd. (phone: 53540). Expensive.

La Sorbonne – Occupying the second floor of a beautifully preserved half-timbered seventeenth-century house with overhanging caves, this place offers French fare in a friendly, informal atmosphere. The wine list, as well as the service, is very good. Reservations necessary. Closed Sundays, the last 2 weeks of August, and first week in September. 130a High St. (phone: 41320). Expensive.

Ristorante Saraceno – Handily located halfway between Oxford's New Theatre and the Playhouse, this modern, white-walled French/Italian restaurant is popular with theatergoers, who pause here for a taste of the warm south — be it scampi, scaloppine, or zabaglione. Closed Sundays. In the basement under the Jaegar's boutique at 15 Magdalen St. (phone: 49171). Expensive to moderate.

Cherwell Boathouse – Perched on the Cherwell, a tributary of the Thames, this restaurant is in a refurbished boathouse that rents punts and a gondola. Two imaginative and set menus of three courses are offered daily — a recent example included hot vichyssoise, West Indian deep-dish meat pie, and Caribbean apple and grape dessert. Reservations necessary. Open daily for dinner; also lunch Sundays. Off Bardwell Rd. (phone: 55978). Moderate.

Clements – Run by an Oxford alumnus, this double-fronted eatery offers carefully prepared food with a French accent. The ambience is relaxed and informal, but details such as candles and fresh flowers on the tables are not overlooked. Open daily for dinner; also lunch on Saturdays and Sundays. 37 St. Clements, near Magdalen College (phone: 41431). Moderate.

Brown's – This sprawling row house restaurant decorated with lots of mirrors and hanging plants is probably the most popular place in Oxford. It's always crowded so be prepared to wait in line and share tables. The entrées are wholesome and filling — spaghetti, steak and mushroom pie, hot sandwiches — and the desserts are homemade. No reservations. Open daily. 7–9 Woodstock Rd. (phone: 511995). Inexpensive.

Go Dutch – The pancakes served here are a meal in themselves — 10 inches in diameter and thick with a variety of fillings. Owner Rowena Greenwood recommends the bacon-and-apple. A fairly recent addition to Oxford's restaurant scene, *Go Dutch* looks rather like Grandma's dining room, with heavy gate-leg furniture and plant-filled windows. No reservations. Closed Mondays. Park End St. (phone: 40686). Inexpensive.

Lotus House – This suburban Chinese restaurant serves above-average Cantonese cooking; the house specialties are Crispy Duck and Sizzling Steak. Open daily for lunch and dinner. Reservations necessary. 197 Banbury Rd., Summertown (phone: 54239). Inexpensive.

Maxwell's – This faintly art deco, American-style diner is the place to go when you suffer a Big Mac attack. The menu features better-than-average hamburgers, milkshakes, and banana splits. Open daily. Queen St. (phone: 48833). Inexpensive.

The Nosebag – Oak-beamed ceilings, handmade pottery, and classical music make this eatery a pleasant respite in a busy sight-seeing day. The soups, salads, and daily hot and cold specials are all very reasonably priced. No reservations at lunchtime, when it's very crowded; reservations recommended at dinner. Open daily. 6–8 St. Michael's St. (phone: 721033). Inexpensive.

SHARING A PINT: The *Turf Tavern,* 4–5 Bath Pl., is a great favorite, snuggling close to the walls of New College; the *Bear,* in St. Aldate's, close to Christ Church, was once a coaching inn and is full of atmosphere; the *White Horse,* in Broad St. next door to Blackwells, is handy and historic, despite the recent addition of electronic games; and *The King's Arms,* close to Wadham, is a convenient spot for a little nip.

STRATFORD-UPON-AVON

Even without William Shakespeare's pervasive presence, Stratford-upon-Avon would be a very pleasant stopping point on a tour through the Warwickshire heart of England. It is a charming town, set congenially in the midst of peaceful green countryside, on a bend of the gentle River Avon. It is filled with the elegance of lovely, early-sixteenth-century half-timbered buildings. In its picture prettiness, swans glide by the spire of its riverside parish church, and trees, flowers, and gardens further soften its aspect. It is small enough to be seen in a day's stroll but large enough to have all the attributes of a busy market town — which it is and has been since receiving its first royal market charter in 1196, fully 368 years before William Shakespeare's birth ensured its enduring fame.

Stratford was first a Celtic settlement, then a small Roman town, its name — a mixture of the old Welsh for river and the Roman for street — meaning "the place where the street (or *straet*) fords the river *(afon).*" In the thirteenth century, the Guild of the Holy Cross, an Augustinian religious fraternity, was formed and it fostered the development of industries and crafts. It also maintained the grammar school and had almshouses and its own chapel, all of which were built by citizens of the town and are still among Stratford's most interesting buildings today.

The town has always been fortunate in the generosity of its citizens. John de Stratford, an Archbishop of Canterbury in the fourteenth century, is thought to have rebuilt Holy Trinity Church and to have established a college of priests to serve it. Later on, Hugh Clopton, who was to become Lord Mayor of London at the end of the fifteenth century, built the nave and tower of the Guild Chapel and the splendid 14-arch Clopton Bridge, which still takes the heavy traffic of the twentieth century into and out of town. More recent benefactors have been Charles Edward Flower, whose patronage made the first Shakespeare Memorial Theatre a reality in 1879, and his grandson Sir Archibald Flower, who was the major contributor to the present theater, opened in 1932.

Stratford's most illustrious citizen, of course, was William Shakespeare, son of John Shakespeare — "Gulielmus filius Johannes Shakespere" as the parish register puts it. Though he has been dead for more than three and a half centuries, his attraction is as strong as when he was a famous writer of plays in Elizabethan and Jacobean London. England's, and probably the world's, greatest playwright dominates the life of Stratford-upon-Avon: His houses and his children's houses are visited by hundreds of thousands of people every year; the big theater on the river, one of the world's most famous, bears his name and its actors perform his works; hotels and restaurants are named after him; and shopkeepers live on the sale of books, prints, portrait busts, trinkets, and souvenirs with a Shakespearean theme. The Shakespeare Connection is a lucrative one, and it is to the credit of Stratford's residents that they have not allowed it to overwhelm and cheapen their delightful town.

The Shakespeare Connection in a nutshell? Well, he was born here, on or about April 23, 1564, and he died here on April 23, 1616. In between, he grew up, went to school, moved to London to seek his fortune, and came back wealthy enough at 33 to buy a large house, New Place, in 1597, to which he retired in 1610, and where he died of a fever caused, it is said, by too strenuous an evening of eating, drinking, and being merry with friends a day or two beforehand.

Shakespeare's father was a glovemaker and his mother, Mary Arden, came from a respectable family of small landowners at Wilmcote, 3 miles from Stratford. The family house, from which John Shakespeare conducted his business, was on Henley Street, slightly to the north of the center of the busy little town. Young William went to school at the King Edward VI Grammar School on Church Street, and in 1582 married Anne Hathaway, a yeoman farmer's daughter 8 years older than himself. They had three children, Susanna and the twins, Judith and Hamnet (the latter died aged 11 in 1596). Then came the years of fame and glory in London, followed by a short period of happy retirement tending his garden in Stratford.

After his death, the town's interest in its brilliant native son subsided somewhat, though there was always a steady trickle of people to see his house and his garden with its famous mulberry tree. The turning point in the town's long-range fortunes came with David Garrick's Shakespeare Jubilee in 1769. The event could be called the original "Shakespeare Festival," and it grew out of Stratford's plans to decorate its rebuilt Town Hall.

Garrick was then England's foremost Shakespearean actor and as such was offered the honorary "Freedom" of the borough if he would provide a portrait or bust of Shakespeare to be hung in the Town Hall along with a portrait of himself. To no one's surprise, he accepted this opportunity to appear before an admiring posterity and organized his great jubilee — 3 days of celebration that, though marred by torrential rain, helped secure the future of Stratford as a great tourist attraction. The two portraits that were the occasion for the jubilee were both destroyed by fire in 1946, but a bust of Shakespeare that Garrick presented to Stratford can still be seen in the Town Hall.

The Shakespeare revival in Stratford grew apace during the nineteenth century, helped by interest from abroad and especially from the US. The first Shakespeare Memorial Theatre opened in 1879 to the sneers of the London theater establishment, but it was not long before they had to swallow their pride and take a serious interest in the little provincial theater, especially once the prominent producer Frank Benson began putting on Shakespeare there in 1886. His company remained for 30 years and established a performing tradition that became influential throughout the theater world.

Today Stratford-upon-Avon may be devoted to Shakespeare, but it has not been swamped by his cult. Its other side, its ancient existence as a very lively market town, continues unabated and almost undisturbed. Once a week, as has happened for centuries, Cotswold farmers bring their produce to market and shoppers come in from the surrounding villages. Branches of many of the large chain stores and a shopping mall blend with the Shakespearean sites, hotels, and restaurants. It's a comfortable mix of commerce and culture, of modern and medieval, that allows life to go on for its inhabitants while preserving for visitors the feel of countless generations that have gone before, and for the pilgrims who seek it, a shrine.

STRATFORD AT-A-GLANCE

SEEING THE CITY: The towers of Holy Trinity Church and the Guild Chapel are not open to visitors and there are no tall modern buildings from which to get a bird's-eye view of the town, but the layout of the center of Stratford is simple. Most visitors start their tour at Shakespeare's Birthplace on Henley Street, which runs diagonally down to intersect Wood Street/Bridge Street, one of the four main thoroughfares that cut east-west across Stratford. The other three are Ely Street/Sheep Street, Scholars Lane/Chapel Lane, and Chestnut Walk/Old Town. Running north to south starting at the river are Waterside/Southern Lane, High Street/Chapel Street, and Rother Street/Windsor Street/Shakespeare Street.

SPECIAL PLACES: The Shakespeare Birthplace Trust is the official body that, on behalf of the nation, owns the five most important buildings connected with William Shakespeare. These are the Birthplace itself, New Place (with Nash's House), Hall's Croft, Anne Hathaway's Cottage, and Mary Arden's House. The Shakespeare Centre, the Trust's headquarters on Henley St., is also an academic center, opened in 1964, for anyone wishing to study its splendid collection of books and documents relating to Shakespeare, including translations of his plays in 67 languages. There is usually an exhibition in the front hall, where the engraved glass panels by John Hutton (depicting characters from the plays) are well worth a look. The Shakespeare Centre is open daily except Sundays; admission is free to the library and records office but there is a charge for the exhibitions. There is an individual admission fee for each of the Birthplace Trust buildings, but it's possible to lower the cost by buying an inclusive ticket for entrance to all five. The phone number for the Shakespeare Centre and all Trust buildings is 4016.

Most of Stratford's special places, including the ones without Shakespearean connections, are in the center of town within easy walking distance of each other. In the course of a day's stroll, you can see everything listed here (with the exception of Anne Hathaway's Cottage and Mary Arden's House), as well as experience the everyday workings of a typical English market town.

THE SHAKESPEARE BIRTHPLACE TRUST

Shakespeare's Birthplace – The spiritual center of Stratford-upon-Avon lies in this modest, half-timbered and gabled Tudor building where William Shakespeare was born on or about April 23, 1564. The house, visited by more than half a million people of all nationalities every year, is beautifully maintained and furnished with objects typical of Shakespeare's period. The bedroom in which the Bard is assumed to have been born is upstairs, its window scratched with the signatures of famous people who have visited it, including those of Sir Walter Scott, Alfred, Lord Tennyson, and the actress Ellen Terry. The Birthplace also houses a museum of relics and records of

Shakespeare's day and a fine library. Don't miss the well-kept garden behind the house; in it grow many of the flowers, herbs, and plants Shakespeare knew. Open daily, except Good Friday morning and Christmas. Admission charge. Henley St. (phone: 4016).

New Place – Shakespeare's house stood on this site. The building passed out of the family's hands in 1670, and its last owner, constantly irritated by the numbers of admirers wanting to see it, demolished it in 1759. All you can see today are part of the foundations, and the once-extensive gardens. There is a replica of an Elizabethan knot garden — an elaborately laid-out formal garden typical of those times — and the Great Garden, which contains topiary work and a mulberry tree said to have been grown from a cutting from Shakespeare's original tree. The young mulberry in the center of the lawn was planted by Dame Peggy Ashcroft to mark the 200th anniversary of David Garrick's Jubilee. Nash's House, adjoining the gardens, was once owned by Thomas Nash, husband of Shakespeare's granddaughter Elizabeth Hall, and is furnished with items of their period. It also houses New Place Museum, devoted mainly to local archaeological material. Open daily, except Sunday mornings in winter, Good Friday morning, and Christmas. Admission charge. Chapel St. (phone: 4016).

Hall's Croft – A short walk from New Place to Old Town, a quietly elegant residential street, brings you to Hall's Croft. Shakespeare's elder daughter, Susanna, and her physician husband, Dr. John Hall, lived in this lovely house with its gabled front and overhanging upper floor from 1607 to 1616. Inside, it is the beautifully furnished house of a well-to-do Jacobean family, immaculately kept, with brass and copper glowing, and flowers in the living rooms. Don't miss the bedroom with its four-poster, and Dr. Hall's dispensary, stocked with pottery jars of herbs and potions, pestles and mortars, and surgical instruments. A large walled garden behind the house, again immaculate, provides an oasis of sweet-scented calm. Open daily, except Sunday in winter, Good Friday, and Christmas. Admission charge. Old Town (phone: 4016).

Anne Hathaway's Cottage – So many hundreds of drawings, prints, engravings, and plaques portray this pretty, thatched house, that it is something of a surprise to come across the building itself on the outskirts of Stratford. It's about a 2-mile walk from the center of town (shorter by a footpath from Evesham Place) but it can also be reached by bus from Bridge Street, or even by bicycle. The trip is worth it, because Anne's cottage retains a charming English country air, with roses, jasmine, and other scented flowers in the garden, and Tudor furnishings in the house. Open daily, except Sunday mornings in winter, Good Friday morning, and Christmas. Admission charge. Shottery village (phone: 4016).

Mary Arden's House – Shakespeare's mother lived in this lovely gabled farmhouse in Wilmcote village before her marriage. The house is set in a garden, and the barns in back house a museum devoted to rural life and farming. About 3 miles from Stratford, Wilmcote can be reached by road or even by boat along the canal. Open daily, except Sundays in winter, Good Friday morning, and Christmas. Admission charge. Wilmcote village (phone: 4016).

OTHER STRATFORD ATTRACTIONS

Holy Trinity Church – On the bank of the River Avon, this stately parish church dates from the thirteenth century. Shakespeare was baptized and buried here, and photocopies of the church register entries of both events are on display. On the north wall of the chancel is a bust of the poet carved by his contemporary Gerard Jannsen, a memorial erected by the Shakespeare family in 1623. Shakespeare's grave is below the bust, flanked by those of his wife and other members of his family. Open daily. Small admission charge to the chancel. Old Town.

Gower Memorial – An imaginative statue of William Shakespeare crowns this impressive memorial, which its creator, Lord Ronald Sutherland Gower, labored over for 12 years. Unveiled in 1888, it stands with its back to the Royal Shakespeare Theatre in Bancroft Gardens near Clopton Bridge. The four life-size bronzes at its base are of Hamlet, Lady Macbeth, Falstaff, and Prince Hal.

The King Edward VI Grammar School – This half-timbered building on Church Street can trace its origins back to the thirteenth century and it was here that Shakespeare learned his Latin and Greek. Since it is still a school, it can only be visited by special arrangement, but don't walk by without pausing for a glimpse through the gateway or without noticing the ancient almshouses that border it.

The Guild Chapel – The beautiful, gray stone tower of the Guild Chapel is one of the finest landmarks in Stratford. It rises above the austerely elegant chapel, which was rebuilt by Hugh Clopton about 1496, on the site of a building dating from the mid-thirteenth century. Today it is used by the grammar school, which holds a daily service there during the school term. Paintings that once covered the walls have mostly disappeared, except for one, *The Day of Judgment,* over the chancel arch. The Chapel adjoins the grammar school and almshouses on Church St. and is open daily.

Harvard House – The Stars and Stripes flying from a flagpole above the front door indicates the special importance of this old half-timbered building, dating from 1596. It was the home of a wealthy Stratford alderman, Thomas Rogers, whose daughter Katherine was the mother of John Harvard, founder of the university. The house now belongs to Harvard and is furnished in the style of the Elizabethan period. Open daily but closed Sundays through Wednesdays, November to March. Admission charge. High St.

Shrieve's House – If you find yourself on Sheep Street, stop for a moment outside this imposing late-sixteenth-century private house with its great studded door and gateway opposite the Town Hall. Shakespeare undoubtedly knew the owners of this Stratford town house, and may well have attended the wedding feast of their daughter there in 1613.

Stratford's Motor Museum – Nothing to do with Shakespeare at all, but it's worth a visit. The museum's specialty is cars from a bygone golden age, the 1920s. There are about 30 cars, and bicycles and motor bicycles as well. Open daily except Christmas. Admission charge. Shakespeare St. (phone: 69413).

Stratford Brass Rubbing Centre – Here is an opportunity to make your own souvenir of Stratford. The Centre has exact replicas of a large number of brasses, many from the Stratford area, and supplies paper and wax as part of the charge for doing a rubbing. Open daily. Royal Shakespeare Theatre Summer House, Avonbank Gardens (phone: 297671).

Louis Tussaud's Shakespearean Waxworks – This includes scenes from Shakespeare's plays, richly costumed and with sound effects. Open daily. Admission charge. 60 Henley St. (phone: 5880).

Drinking Fountain and Clock – The ornate fountain and clock in the center of Rothermarket was the gift of George W. Childs, a Philadelphian who presented it to the town in Queen Victoria's Jubilee year of 1887. It was unveiled by the famous actor Henry Irving.

■ **EXTRA SPECIAL:** A visit to the *Royal Shakespeare Theatre* at its imposing riverside location is a major event for theater and Shakespeare lovers from all over the world. You can be sure that the production you'll see will have been thought out in meticulous, often controversial, detail and will be excitingly staged and beautifully acted by the Royal Shakespeare Company. The season, during which at least six of Shakespeare's plays are presented, generally runs from the end of March or early April to the end of January. Tickets should be bought as far in advance as possible from the box office or through a ticket agency (bookings for the season are divided into three periods, with tickets for the first period going on sale in early March), though it is often possible to buy them at the last minute.

The theater holds back a few medium-priced tickets (maximum 2 per person) and some standing-room tickets for sale on the day of performance. Bona fide students (with identification to prove it) may chance upon an unsold ticket immediately before the performance. The theater has two restaurants, and a shop selling a good range of books and other items about the theater in general and Royal Shakespeare Company productions in particular. The attached Theatre Picture Gallery and Museum has interesting paintings, portraits, and relics of famous theater personalities. The Royal Shakespeare Theatre, Stratford-upon-Avon, Warwickshire CV37 6BB (phone: 292271 for booking; 69191 for 24-hour information on seat availability).

SOURCES AND RESOURCES

The Tourist Information Centre at Judith Shakespeare's House, 1 High St. (phone: 293127), offers maps of the town, leaflets, accommodations advice, and guidebooks including the *Official Guide to Stratford-upon-Avon District,* published by Stratford's District Council. Bookshops and newsagents are also well stocked with maps, guides, and other publications of interest to the visitor. The Stratford-upon-Avon Tourist (Telephone) Service (phone: 67522) gives prerecorded information such as opening times, telephone numbers, and other details of places of interest in and around the town. Short and long tours of the town and surrounding countryside are conducted daily by Guide Friday Ltd., 32 Henley St. (phone: 294466). Most departures are from the company office but they will also pick you up, by reservation only, at some of the major hotels. Guided tours by chauffeur-driven car can also be arranged.

For Local Coverage – *Focus,* a magazine published by the *Stratford-upon-Avon Herald,* is useful, while the newspaper itself is also helpful.

GETTING AROUND: The best way to see Stratford-upon-Avon is on foot. Most of its important streets are laid out in a simple grid pattern, so it's not easy to get lost.

Bus – *Midland Red Omnibus Company,* Warwick Rd. (phone: 4181), serves Stratford and the surrounding villages. The bus departure point is on Bridge St. near Clopton Bridge.

Taxi – Taxis are relatively expensive, and can't be flagged down on the street. Go to the cab stand at the intersection of Rother and Wood Sts. or call 69999. Your hotel can also get you a taxi.

Car Rental – Two local firms are *Arden Motors,* Arden St. (phone: 67446), and *Foster Motors,* Western Rd. (phone: 293532). *Guide Friday Ltd.,* 32 Henley St. (phone: 294466), will arrange rentals through the major national and international companies. The nearest *Hertz* and *Avis* locations are in Coventry.

Bike – Stratford and its surrounding countryside are ideally suited to exploration by bike. *Knotts Cycles,* 15 Western Rd. (phone: 5149) rents bicycles; another branch is located out-of-town at the Stratford Youth Hostel, Alveston (phone: 297093).

Boat – Short trips for an hour or so or a holiday lasting several weeks are both possible on the Avon and the historic, early-nineteenth-century Stratford Canal. Rowing boats, punts (propelled by poles), and canoes can be rented at the boathouse by Clopton Bridge. *Western Cruisers Ltd.,* Western Rd. (phone: 69636), and *Stratford-upon-Avon Marine Ltd.,* Clopton Bridge (phone: 69669), rent larger craft, including gaily decorated river barges.

SHOPPING: Stratford's shops stock some quite attractive items. Look for good-quality handicrafts — including pottery, stained glass, and carved woods — as well as English sheepskins and leather clothing, and the well-known makes of English china. Sheep Street has several elegant antique shops and an arcade with a dozen or so antique dealers' booths. Many of Stratford's shops carry the customs forms overseas visitors must fill in to obtain relief from the Value Added Tax (VAT); ask for them when making your purchase. Early closing is usually Thursday afternoon. A sample of interesting shops in Stratford:

Campbell's Croft – Knitting, embroidery, and crafts materials, including the shop's own needlepoint canvas of Anne Hathaway's Cottage. 31 Henley St. (phone: 4428).

Peter Dingley – Good quality British-made crafts, including pottery and carved wood. 16 Meer St. (phone: 5001).

Lamberts of Stratford – Comprehensive selection of English chinas and crystal. 1 Henley St. (phone: 293174).

Sentre Arts – Another shop where everything is handmade. The stained glass is unusual and attractive. Centre Craft Yard, off Henley St. (phone: 68731).

The Shakespeare Centre Bookshop – Specializes in Shakespearean books and other publications and sells gifts and souvenirs. Henley St. (phone: 4016).

The Sheepskin Shop – Leather jackets, coats, children's toys, and other items. 33 Sheep St. (phone: 293810).

The Tappit Hen – Broad range of English pewter. 57 Henley St. (phone: 69933).

SPECIAL EVENTS: Every spring, usually on the Saturday nearest April 23, Stratford and the world unite to honor Shakespeare. A procession that includes ambassadors from many countries walks from his Birthplace to Holy Trinity Church to lay floral tributes on his grave. Flags of the nations are unfurled on Bridge St. and there is a luncheon and special performance at the Royal Shakespeare Theatre.

The Boat Club holds its annual *Regatta* in June, and in October there's the *Mop Fair,* when stalls, sideshows, and amusements take over the streets of the town center. You may even see a pig roasted on a spit.

SPORTS: Stratford has facilities for many kinds of sports; ask at the information center for a complete list.

Fishing – Go to 37 Greenhill St. for daily and season fishing tickets; you can get the necessary Fishery Board license there also.

Golf – Visitors pay greens fees to play on the *Stratford-upon-Avon Golf Club*'s 18-hole course on Tiddington Rd. (phone: 297296).

Swimming – The District Council's modern pool at Bridgeway is open daily; there is a small admission charge (phone: 68826).

THEATER: In addition to the main *Royal Shakespeare Theatre* along the river, the Royal Shakespeare Company runs another, smaller theater, *The Other Place,* on Southern Lane where it performs plays by Shakespeare and others, including modern playwrights. The season starts in May. Information from the Royal Shakespeare Theatre (phone: 292271) or from The Other Place, Southern Lane, Stratford-upon-Avon CV37 6BB. *The Heritage Theatre,* Waterside (phone: 5709/69190), is the home of "The World of Shakespeare," an entertainment of sound, music, and tableaux, with continuous performances daily.

MUSIC: Stratford's tradition is drama rather than music, but the town plays host to orchestras, bands, and soloists throughout the year. During the winter season, when the Royal Shakespeare Company is on holiday, the Royal Shakespeare Theatre is devoted to visiting operatic and ballet companies, and to various concerts.

NIGHTCLUBS AND NIGHTLIFE: Evenings are fairly quiet in Stratford. Pubs close at 11 PM and young people complain about the lack of discos, but their elders are happy with the music and dancing offered over the weekend at good restaurants such as *Marlowe's,* 18 High St. (phone: 4999); *The Rheinland,* with music but no dancing, 13–14 Meer St. (phone: 69161); or *Christophi's Greek Restaurant,* 21 Sheep St. (phone: 293546). Several of the larger hotels also offer dinner dancing.

SINS: There is scope for indulging in a bit of *gluttony* in Stratford, which boasts a fine array of tea and cake shops. The well-stocked window of *Pargetter's Patisserie,* 3 Bridge St. (phone: 293182), is a nearly irresistible display of breads, cakes, pies, and pastries. The *Welcombe Hotel,* Warwick Rd. (phone: 295252), is famous for its Saturday and Sunday afternoon cream teas, replete with hot scones, pancakes, and other goodies.

BEST IN TOWN

CHECKING IN: If you intend staying in a modest bed-and-breakfast, there is no need to make reservations in advance; many of these worthy British establishments line the main roads leading into town. You should book ahead for a good hotel, however, especially at the height of the season, June to September. The Tourist Information Centre, 1 High St. (phone: 293127), supplies copies of the official *Accommodation Register* and can help you find somewhere to stay if you arrive in Stratford without reservations.

A B&B offers a comfortable room (no private bath) and a good breakfast for about $11 to $14 per person a night. For the same thing in an inexpensive hotel, you will pay about $14 to $25 per person per night. Moderately priced hotels — which may not have private bathrooms with all rooms but will at least have hot and cold water in all rooms — run about $25 to $50 per person per night. And expect to pay from $50 to $85 per person in the large, expensive hotels. All of these rates are based on single occupancy; rooms for two are normally less than twice the single rate, of course. Smaller hotels may not accept credit cards, while the larger ones usually will.

Falcon – One of those stunning, half-timbered buildings that make Stratford so picturesque, the 68-room Falcon overlooks the gardens of New Place, Shakespeare's house. Inside, it is less elegant than the Shakespeare hotel, but has a charm of its own. Chapel St. (phone: 5777). Expensive.

Shakespeare – A Stratford landmark, this gabled, timber-fronted sixteenth-century building is the place to stay if you want a taste of Elizabethan England. David Garrick stayed here in 1769, and since then most of its rooms have been named after Shakespeare's plays: You could find yourself sleeping in the *Midsummer Night's Dream* room and eating in the *As You Like It* restaurant. The 66-room hotel has been carefully modernized and its authentic atmosphere endures. Chapel St. (phone: 294771). Expensive.

Stratford Hilton – Behind the somewhat pedestrian facade lie all the comforts and services expected of a major hotel chain. Color TV, individual climate control, and a mini-bar are in all 250 rooms. It's a short walk or a 15-minute ride by private canal barge — the *My Lady Hilton* — to the Royal Shakespeare Theatre. Bridgefoot (phone: 67511). Expensive.

Welcombe – This elegant, 82-room hotel set in extensive parkland on the outskirts of Stratford was once a private mansion and retains the atmosphere of an English country house. The menu in its paneled restaurant is basically French. The park has room for an 18-hole golf course plus a heli-pad with connections to nearby Birmingham airport; the hotel's garage has car-servicing facilities and gas. Warwick Rd., 1¼ miles from town center (phone: 295252). Expensive.

Falstaff – A welcoming little hotel, it is well-placed in the center of town and its 6 double bedrooms have all the basic amenities. 27 Bridge St. (phone: 297223). Moderate.

Stratford House – Once a private Georgian home, this charming 9-room hotel has been recently modernized in delightful style. Sheep St. (phone: 68288). Moderate.

White Swan – There is a centuries-old mural of *Tobias and the Angel* in the lounge of this fifteenth-century hotel, which overlooks the American fountain in Rothermarket. Spacious restaurant, oak-beamed bar, and 55 rooms. Rother St. (phone: 297022). Moderate.

Coach House – On a main road out of town, this is a rambling hotel on several floors. Nine bedrooms, pleasant dining room, and a friendly atmosphere. 17 Warwick Rd. (phone: 4109/67331). Inexpensive.

Glenavon Private Hotel – Just up the road from Holy Trinity Church and Hall's Croft, this is a congenial, family-style hotel in a quiet part of town. 6 Chestnut Walk (phone: 292588). Inexpensive.

Payton – Another well-maintained little hotel with a homelike atmosphere, it, too, is in a quiet part of town, though only a short walk from the back gate of Shakespeare's Birthplace. 6 John St. (phone: 66442). Inexpensive.

EATING OUT: With the help of a range of fast-food and snack restaurants, Stratford manages to feed its hundreds of thousands of visitors pretty well. Those arriving just for the day find that the coffee houses and tearooms are generally good, and many of them stay open long enough to provide an evening meal. Pizzas, hamburgers, and the glass-of-wine-with-food have all found their way into town, and the sausage-egg-and-chip cafés offer good value for the money. At midday, there is the ploughman's lunch (bread, cheese, and pickle) to be sampled with a pint of beer in one of Stratford's typical pubs, many of which also offer an array of hot and cold food at the bar.

Those staying overnight can expect the full British breakfast — fruit juice, cereal, sausage, bacon and eggs, toast, and tea or coffee — in the morning, though a lighter Continental breakfast — usually fruit juice, croissants or toast, and coffee — is also available. Evening meals range from a standard "meat and three vegetables" to international cuisine. Prices for a three-course meal for two, without drinks but including VAT and service charge, work out at about $35 to $42 in the expensive category; $23 to $32 in the moderate category; and under — sometimes well under — $18 in the inexpensive category.

Christophi's – White stucco and blue awnings give this Greek restaurant an attractive air. For those whose tastes do not run to *taramasalata* or *moussaka*, there are more conventional grills, too. Dancing every evening, and a cabaret on Fridays and Saturdays. Open evenings only; closed Sundays. 21 Sheep St. (phone: 293546). Expensive.

Da Giovanni – A discreetly curtained front and restrained gold lettering hide a plush restaurant very much in the Italian grand manner, complete with leather sofas and chairs, flocked wallpaper, and bronze statues. Delicious Italian cooking. Closed Sundays. 8 Ely St. (phone: 297999). Expensive.

Marlowe's – Approached down a narrow alley off the High Street, Marlowe's is in a house that dates back to Shakespeare's time. Once an inn, it's now a restaurant with a distinguished air, where oak paneling and wood fires in winter add to the atmosphere. The food is standard international cuisine, and the wine list is good. Open daily. 18 High St. (phone: 4999). Expensive.

Stratford Hilton – The Warwick Grill was conceived on a luxury scale and has an impressive central buffet. Check the menu for re-creations of authentic Elizabethan dishes. Open daily. Bridgefoot (phone: 67511). Expensive.

Arden Hotel – The restaurant here draws theatergoers (the Royal Shakespeare is just across the road), and both restaurant and bar are good places to celebrity-spot. The food is simple, based on the best available fresh ingredients. Open daily. 44 Waterside (phone: 294949). Moderate.

Falstaff – Eye-catching red gingham curtains and red awnings attract visitors to this pretty restaurant attached to the Falstaff Hotel. They stay because the fare is also attractive. Delicious snacks and teas are served all day, and there is a good choice of main meals. Open daily. 27 Bridge St. (phone: 297223). Moderate.

Rheinland Restaurant – Rustic jollity is the keynote here, abetted by an accordionist who plays patrons' requests on Saturday and Sunday evenings. The menu is extensive, with many German dishes. Closed Mondays. 13–14 Meer St. (phone: 69161). Moderate.

Box Tree and River Terrace – Both are in the Royal Shakespeare Theatre building and both are open to nonplaygoers — if you can't get theater tickets, at least you can say you've been there. The Box Tree is open for lunch on matinee days and Sundays, and every evening before and after performances except Sundays; the River Terrace, on the ground floor with a view of the river, is open from midmorning for snacks and light meals. Waterside (phone: 293226). Moderate to inexpensive.

Chinalight – A big, efficient Chinese restaurant with a mainly Cantonese menu. This is the place for a filling meal, quickly served. Open daily. 4–5 Henley St. (phone: 297343). Inexpensive.

Cobweb – Above a cake and confectionary shop, in a building so old that both the floors and the beamed ceilings have distinct slopes, this charming restaurant offers omelets, grills, and salads, as well as a typically English afternoon tea. Open daily. 12 Sheep St. (phone: 292554). Inexpensive.

Centre Coffee House – A spotlessly clean, modern-style coffee shop where the salads are fresh and the pâté homemade. Conveniently situated opposite Shakespeare's Birthplace. Open daily (except Mondays in winter). Henley St. (phone: 297490). Inexpensive.

Old Tudor House Restaurant – Your basic English sausage, eggs, and chips with everything, but nicely prepared and presented. A good family place — they will even provide a highchair for the baby. Open daily. High and Ely sts. (phone: 297140). Inexpensive.

SHARING A PINT: Among Stratford's array of pubs, two are particularly worth raising an elbow in. The *Garrick Inn,* next to Harvard House on High St., dates back to late Elizabethan times, but its ambience is delightfully Dickensian, with several small bars (phone: 292186). The *Dirty Duck* is Stratford's theatrical pub, where actors and actresses come for their post-show pints and the atmosphere can become charged with the euphoria engendered by a good performance. Waterside (phone: 297312).

WATERFORD

Waterford is a gentle city of Georgian doorways and back streets with names like Lady Lane. It stretches for a bit more than half a mile along the southern bank of the River Suir, well up a long inlet from the sea, and during the seventeenth century its harbor was one of the busiest in the country. Meat, fish, and corn were exported to the Continent and wine came back. Ships bound for America were provisioned here. Today, one of the principal exports from its still-busy quays is beef, though Waterford crystal is the most famous.

The old Waterford Glass Factory was founded in 1783, at a time when the city — originally a Viking settlement — was undergoing a burst of development and beginning to outgrow its medieval dimensions. Graceful Georgian homes belonging to the merchant class began to appear along The Mall, and John Roberts, an architect responsible for many of the city's elegant structures, was at work designing the public buildings and churches that are among the city's most prominent landmarks — City Hall and the Catholic and Protestant cathedrals are all his. The latter, which was erected between 1773 and 1779 on the site of a much earlier church, is a stately testimony to Waterford's rich Protestant families, some of whom were carried up the slight incline into Cathedral Square in sedan chairs.

Waterford's most famous landmark, however, is a remnant of Viking times. Sitric the Dane is credited with fortifying the site of the city in the ninth century, and Reginald the Dane, who was a descendant of Sitric, is believed to have strengthened the fortifications by erecting (in 1003) what has since become known as Reginald's Tower. Along with the city walls and two other towers, Reginald's Tower protected the city from invasion first by the Celts and later, when the Norsemen and Celts put aside their differences to join forces against a common enemy, from invasion by the Normans. You can still see part of the old city wall inside the Reginald Lounge, adjacent to the tower.

The Normans finally did take Waterford in 1170, in the person of Richard de Clare, an emissary of Henry II of England. De Clare was better known as Strongbow, for the sureness of his weapons and tactics, and his victory over the city's defenders was both an easy and far-reaching one. The capture of Waterford was the beginning of the Anglo-Norman domination of Ireland. Strongbow's marriage shortly thereafter to Eva, the daughter of Dermot MacMurrough, the Irish king of Leinster, consolidated the position of the conquering Normans. This fateful event, too, took place in Waterford, reputedly in Reginald's Tower (though the original Viking cathedral, predecessor of Christ Church Cathedral, may have been the actual site).

King John granted the city its first charter in 1205 (his sword and several of the city's subsequent charters are in the Reginald's Tower museum), and for several centuries to come, Waterford would be intensely loyal to the English crown. Henry VII gave it its motto, "Unconquered City," in the fifteenth century, in gratitude for its successful efforts in fighting off attacks by two pretenders to his throne. But loyalty to the English king in temporal matters did not extend to recognition of the crown's supremacy in religious matters. The city remained Catholic in the sixteenth century, and because of this, its charter was eventually withdrawn and its Catholic citizens suffered much in the Cromwellian sieges of the mid-seventeenth century. Their churches were closed and confiscated and many were sent as slaves to the West Indies.

Several abbeys flourished in Waterford. The ruins of the once-extensive thirteenth-century Dominican Friary can be seen. Another large abbey, the Holy Ghost Friary of the Franciscans, or, as it is known locally, the French Church, was built a little later in the same century and is also now in ruins. Both were suppressed by Henry VIII's Dissolution of the Monasteries, the Franciscan friary to become a hospital and then a home to a colony of French Huguenot refugees.

Most visitors come to Waterford to tour the glass factory and concentrate on the gift shops around the quays. But there are revealing detours from the beaten path. You can walk out to Ballybricken Green, one of the oldest sections.

When the Normans controlled Waterford proper, this is where the Irish lived, outside the Patrick Street gate of the city walls. And the side streets and back lanes of this city of 40,000 people are worth discovering for their quaint houses, historic churches, and unexpected finds such as the ancient carvings on the friary wall in Lady Lane. Not much of the great abbeys may remain, but in these narrow passageways, Waterford's medieval atmosphere seems trapped forever like snow in a glass paperweight.

WATERFORD AT-A-GLANCE

SEEING THE CITY: Redmond Bridge spans the River Suir at the western end of the city. It can be a quiet spot from which to view the town, looking not unlike an eighteenth-century New England coastal village with its large buildings and many church spires.

SPECIAL PLACES: With the exception of the Waterford Glass Factory, about 1.5 miles from the center, most of the city's major points of interest are conveniently located in a central area between Redmond Bridge and Reginald's Tower, either along the quays or just a few blocks off them. Go to the glass factory by car, taxi, or bus; then see the rest of the sights on a walking tour to be taken at your own speed. You'll come across most of the city's shops, restaurants, pubs, and hotels in the same vicinity.

Waterford Glass Factory – It is said 3,000 people a week visit the Waterford Glass Factory to watch Ireland's most famous crystal being mixed, blown, and cut by hand from the raw ingredients of silica sand, potash, and red lead. Not only are the guided tours free, they are also interesting and enjoyable. The original plant opened in 1783 and continued in operation until 1851, when English law imposed heavy duties on the exported glass and made it an unprofitable operation. With the help of the Irish government, Waterford reopened on a small scale in 1947, and has since outgrown its buildings several times. The company now employs 2,700 people who cannot keep up with orders for their product, which is exported all over the world (the US is the biggest market). A Waterford chandelier hangs in Independence Hall in Philadelphia and 16 of them are in Westminster Abbey. The factory is closed on weekends and is usually closed for holidays during the first 3 weeks of August. Tours are given Mondays through Fridays at 10:15, 11, and 11:45 AM, and at 1:45, 2:30, and 2:50 PM. You can check on the times and reserve in advance — highly advisable in summer — by calling 73311, or you can make arrangements through the tourist office. No crystal is sold at the factory. About 1.5 miles from the center of Waterford on Cork Rd.

St. Saviour's Dominican Church – This handsome church was built in 1874. The solemn interior features Corinthian columns and lovely frescoes over the altar. Corner of Bridge and O'Connell sts.

Chamber of Commerce – Architect John Roberts designed this aristocratic building of 1795 as a home for the Morris family, which was prominent in the shipping trade. It was purchased by the Chamber of Commerce in 1815. A large fanlight graces the entrance, and it is worth a look inside to see the beautiful plasterwork and splendid oval staircase. Open weekdays. Georges St.

The Clock Tower – Nineteenth-century sea captains relied on this landmark along the quays to keep their ships on schedule. It once had troughs of water at its base from which horses could drink and was thus known as the Fountain Clock. Built in 1861, the original clock was replaced in 1954. The Quay.

Cathedral of the Most Holy Trinity – After the confiscation of their churches in the mid-seventeenth century, the Catholics of Waterford did not receive permission from the city's Protestant-controlled government to build another until 1792. Architect John Roberts designed it for them and it was completed in 1796. The cathedral has a beautifully carved oak pulpit. Barronstrand St.

Lady Lane – This little passage has been described as the best surviving example of a medieval street in Waterford. It is a charming lane with Georgian doorways on one side and two old stone carvings (one dated 1613) visible on the wall of the Franciscan Friary on the other side. Off upper Barronstrand St. (Broad St.).

Christ Church Cathedral – John Roberts also designed this Protestant church, which was completed in 1779 on the site of an earlier church erected by the Norsemen in 1050. The Norsemen had made Waterford a diocese of its own, and the old church grew in size and property through several centuries until Henry VIII's Dissolution of the Monasteries. Later, Cromwellian troops occupied the original church for a time. The present cathedral incorporates some monuments from the old church and a number of interesting tombs. Cathedral Sq.

The French Church – Founded as a Franciscan abbey in 1240, this once included six chambers, a kitchen with four cellars, and stables, in addition to the church whose ruined nave, choir, and Lady Chapel still remain. After it was dissolved by Henry VIII, the former friary saw use as a hospital, a burial place for some of Waterford's prominent families, and as a parish church for French Huguenot refugees. Architect Roberts is among those buried here. You can visit the church by obtaining the key from the house across the road; a notice on the door gives the address. Bailey's New St.

Reginald's Tower – This 70-foot stone tower on the quays was built for defense purposes by Reginald the Dane in 1003. It was captured by Strongbow in 1170, and has had use as a mint, a military storehouse, and an air-raid shelter. It now houses a historical and maritime museum, which can be visited for a nominal fee. Open Mondays through Fridays from 9:30 AM to 12:45 PM and from 2 to 5:30 PM; and Saturdays, 9:30

AM to 12:30 PM, from April through September; closed in winter. Corner of The Quay and The Mall.

Father Luke Wadding and The Mall – This statue just across the street from Reginald's Tower commemorates the birth in 1588 of one of Waterford's most distinguished sons. The Franciscan scholar was famous as a linguist and author of the annals of his order, and although he spent most of his life in Rome, he helped his Catholic countrymen both morally and financially in their attempts to establish their own constitution and government. The *Tower Hotel* on the left is on the site of the old bowling green. City Hall, completed in 1788 for the merchants of Waterford, now houses a museum (see *Museums*) and the Theatre Royal as well as administrative offices. Behind City Hall is the Bishop's Palace, designed in 1741 by Richard Castle, who also did Powerscourt, Westport House, and the Irish Parliament and the Rotunda Hospital in Dublin. It is now used by the city engineering staff.

- **EXTRA SPECIAL:** *The Waterford International Festival of Light Opera* has been taking place every September for over 20 years. For 2 weeks, amateur companies from England, Wales, Scotland, Northern Ireland, and the Republic compete to give the best performance of an operetta or musical, and for 2 weeks visitors to Waterford have a chance to see and hear again such popular productions as *The Merry Widow, Oliver, South Pacific,* or the like. Fringe events include a ball, band concerts, bridge tournaments, sports competitions, and singing competitions in the pubs which, as is usual during a festival in Ireland, are open until late. Tickets are reasonably priced and can be obtained along with specific information on programs and dates from the festival booking office in the Theatre Royal, The Mall, Waterford (phone: 74402).

SOURCES AND RESOURCES

The Tourist Information Office at 41 The Quay (phone: 75788) is open year-round. Hours from May through September are usually from 9 AM to 6 PM, Mondays through Saturdays; in winter it closes at 5:15 PM weekdays and 1 PM on Saturdays. One of the most helpful of the number of pamphlets and guides for sale is Patrick Mackey's *Selected Walks Through Old Waterford,* a handsomely illustrated paperback (£1), containing much information and history written in a style that is interesting and easy to follow. The Royal Life Saving Society's brochure *A Guide to Swimming in Waterford* gives information on sports (and, in addition, it carries advertising from restaurants within a 15-mile radius). The Tourist Information Office in nearby Tramore, the large seaside resort about 8 miles southwest of Waterford, is open during July and August in Railway Sq. (phone: 81572). The office puts out *All About Tramore,* an excellent guide to sports, entertainment, and restaurants in the area.

For Local Coverage – The *Munster Express* published Thursdays and Fridays and the *Waterford News and Star* published every Thursday give specific information on entertainment and special events in the city and vicinity.

GETTING AROUND: Waterford can be a busy turnstile for traffic. Both the Dublin-Cork and Wexford-Tipperary roads pass through here, but much of the traffic avoids the narrow streets of the old city, traveling instead along the quays and then out along The Mall. The city is easily explored on foot, and for a change of pace, you can hop aboard one of the afternoon cruises of the River Suir and take your tea en route.

Bus and Train – Local buses stop on The Quay. The CIE bus station (phone: 73403) is at 36 The Quay, a few doors from the tourist office. Trains for Dublin, Limerick, and Rosslare Harbour (and intervening points) leave from Plunkett Station (phone: 73401), located near Redmond Bridge on the north side of the River Suir. You can take a taxi into the city center for about $3, although it is a short walk if you are not burdened by luggage.

Taxi – Cabs wait at Plunkett Station only (until plans for a central taxi stand on the quays materialize). The tourist office will call a taxi for you, or you can call one yourself (phone: 75222). The minimum fare is about $3, with travel outside the city limits costing about 50¢ a mile.

Car Rental – There are a number of car rental agencies in Waterford including *Boland's Car Hire,* George St. (phone: 75308); *Tom Moloney,* O'Connell St. (phone: 72244); and *Murrays Rent a Car,* The Mall (phone: 31444).

MUSEUMS: Besides Reginald's Tower (described in *Special Places*), the City Hall contains several items worthy of inspection. During normal business hours, you can visit the Council Chamber of this spacious building to view its beautiful glass chandelier, made at the original Waterford factory, a replica of which hangs in Philadelphia's Independence Hall. There is also a complete dinner service of old Waterford glass, and a flag from the Irish Brigade that fought on the Union side in the American Civil War. The Mall.

SHOPPING: With the exception of some lovely gift and crystal shops along the quays, Waterford is a pleasant, but not an outstanding, place to make your purchases. You'll find several inviting boutiques and jewelry stores on the long shopping street that begins at Barronstrand. Smaller shops close on Thursdays and some shops stay open late on Friday evenings. Among the notable ones are:

George's Court Shopping Arcade – An attractive, skylit assemblage of late-model boutiques, food shops, and cookery and decor stores encircling a central café. Off George's St.

The Book Centre – Large, and with a good selection of works by Irish authors. 9 Michael St.

Joseph Knox – This lovely store behind a Victorian shopfront is a major distributor of Waterford crystal and English bone china, and it's often crowded. If you do more than browse — there are many handsome pieces of porcelain and cut glass on display — you can arrange for your booty to be mailed. 3 and 4 Barronstrand St.

Shaw & Sons – A homey department store. It sells a broad range of goods, from Aran sweaters to silver. 53 The Quay.

Midget, Ltd. – Stocked with stacks of appealing handcrafted baskets, crocks, stoneware, Kilkenny pottery, homespuns, and such. 85 The Quay.

Hennebry Camera – All the basics and accessories plus kindly expert sorts who will try to help when your shutter won't or the flash doesn't. 109 The Quay.

Quay's End – A grandmother's (or mum's or aunt's) delight of a shop full of handmade dresses, jumpers, half-pint jump suits, and other enchantments for the very young. Nice prices, especially considering the workmanship. Near Reginald's Tower on The Quay.

SPECIAL EVENTS: The city's *International Festival of Light Opera,* which occurs every September, provides the excuse for a host of fringe events. (For details, see *Extra Special.*)

WATERFORD / Sources and Resources

SPORTS: Waterford has a variety of sports facilities both within and just outside the city, and the seaside resort of Tramore has a 50-acre amusement complex. During the summer, buses to Tramore leave on the half-hour from The Quay. You can check *All About Tramore* for information on the sports and entertainment activities going on there.

Golf – The 18-hole course of the *Waterford Golf Club* (phone: 74182) is open to the public. It's located in a scenic setting about 1.5 miles outside the city. Visitors are also welcome at the 18-hole course of the *Tramore Golf Club* (phone: 81247), a mile from Tramore.

Greyhound Racing – The dogs race at *Kilcohan Park* on Tuesdays and Saturdays in June, and daily for a week in August. For specific information, call the *Waterford Greyhound Track* (phone: 74531).

Sailing – Details are available from the *Waterford Sailing Club* in Dunmore East, 9 miles southeast of the city (phone: 83230).

Squash – There are two courts at *Henry Downe's Pub,* 10 Thomas St. (phone: 74118). Other facilities are at the *Celtic Squash Club,* 71 Barrack St. (phone: 76541).

Swimming – The *Waterford Glass Swimming Pool* on the Cork Road is open to the public. You must arrive on the hour, and you may swim for a 45-minute session for a small fee. Hours vary, so it's probably a good idea to check in advance by calling Brian Williamson, pool manager, Waterford Glass Ltd. (phone: 73311, ext. 266). Tramore has a 3-mile beach, with lifeguards on duty during the summer. Surfboards and deck chairs can be rented at the beach.

Tennis – *St. Anne's Lawn Tennis Club* on St. John's Hill has both grass and hard courts (phone: 74350).

THEATER: Special productions take place during the summer at the *Theatre Royal,* housed in part of City Hall on The Mall (phone: 74402).

MUSIC: The high point of Waterford's musical season is the 2-week *International Festival of Light Opera* in the fall. In addition to the light opera on the program, there is also a singing pubs competition. (See *Extra Special.*) *Seisiún,* an evening of traditional Irish music and dance, takes place about once a week during July and August in Dunmore East. Check with the tourist office for exactly where and when the *Seisiún* musicians and dancers will be appearing and try to be present: The "sessions" are very authentic and the performers are among the best in Ireland.

NIGHTCLUBS AND NIGHTLIFE: There's a dinner dance every Saturday night at the *Granville Hotel* (phone: 55166), and the *Ardree Hotel* (phone: 32111) is a popular place for weekend disco; a number of other hotels and pubs—such as the *Hotel Metropole* (phone: 74195)—feature special appearances by popular and traditional singing groups. The best way to keep abreast of these and other regional festivities that might be going on is to consult the local papers.

SINS: Indulge yourself at the *Coffee and Cake Shop,* 47 Patrick St., where all the buttery cookies and pastries tempting you from behind the glass case are made on the premises.

BEST IN TOWN

CHECKING IN: Waterford's hotels are convenient to the city center, and they offer the visitor a nice choice between the modern and the old. There are also a number of bed-and-breakfast houses in the area. If you wish to stay in this type of accommodation, the tourist office will help you find a vacancy in a house that meets their approval. Expect to pay from $50 to $60 for a double room in an expensive hotel; from $35 to $50 in moderate; and under $35 in inexpensive.

The Ardree – In this modern hotel on a hill on the northern side of the River Suir, all 100 rooms have views that are especially striking at night when the lights of Waterford are twinkling. Amenities include private baths, air-conditioning and central heating, and use of an indoor swimming pool at a sister hotel in Tramore. Favored by bus tour groups. Ferrybank (phone: 32111). Expensive.

Granville – This Georgian mansion is probably Waterford's classiest hotel. It was once the home of Irish patriot Thomas Meagher and was the scene of some unruly political meetings. One unpopular politician escaped a mob out front by climbing through the building's skylight. These days the hotel exudes an air of graciousness and respectability, with 55 rooms, recently and appealingly redone, and a fine-looking paneled lounge bar, restaurant, and grill on the premises. The Quay (phone: 55166). Expensive.

Dooley's – According to the brochure of this old coaching inn in the quays, tired passengers used to alight here for "prime Waterford beef and a glass or two of tolerable claret." The hotel, now neatly and attractively modernized, retains a cozy charm and still has a reputation for good food. The atmosphere is friendly and the rooms comfortable. The Quay (phone: 73531). Moderate.

Tower Hotel – Centrally located on The Mall near Reginald's Tower, this 100-room hotel is in the process of being refurbished—with mixed success—as we go to press. Ask for one of the newly done rooms fitted out with good-looking Scandinavian furniture; all accommodations have private baths. A favorite for local functions, with an extremely helpful and pleasant staff. Food in the big dining room is quite good. The Mall (phone: 75801). Moderate.

EATING OUT: Waterford does not have a large selection of restaurants in town, but with the inclusion of a few hotel dining rooms, there are enough recommendable ones to keep visitors well fed. For anyone in a hurry or homesick for the US, there is *Chapman's Delicatessen* on the quays. Most pubs serve a lunch of soup and sandwiches or a special costing between $3 and $4. Dinner for two with house wine will cost between $20 and $30 in a moderate restaurant, and $40 in an expensive one.

Granville Hotel – The cheerfully elegant Sword Room, handsomest in-town place for lunch or dinner, offers à la carte and table d'hôte choices, nicely priced chef's specials and "mini dinners" (three courses plus beverage), plus a Candlelight Dinner Dance on Saturday night. The Quay (phone: 55111). Expensive to moderate.

Ballinakill House – George Gossip, whose mother's mother's home this was, has personally and determinedly restored the lovely manor house, outside and in (including the tall-windowed Georgian lounge with its stunning river view). Now his wife Suzie is chef, and he hosts dinners in the white-walled dining room ("part of a Norman tower with its top knocked off") with huge fireplace, polished floor, well-spaced gate-legged tables. The à la carte/table d'hôte menu, changed daily, is limited but delicious—from the carrot and orange soup and chicken with white wine vinegar through the almond soufflé and fresh grapefruit sorbet. Wine license only. About 15 minutes from Waterford on the Dunmore East Rd. (phone: 74138). Expensive.

Annestown House – This handsome country house, overlooking a wide lawn and dramatic sea, has been in John Gallowey's family for 150 years. In its homey lounge and small dining room, he and his wife, Pippa, offer nightly menus that blend style, the freshest ingredients, and home-cooked flavor in near-perfect proportions. À la carte dinners only, May through October. Delightful for a lingering summer evening. Reservations essential. About half an hour from Waterford on the coast road to Dungarvan (phone: 96160). Expensive.

Dooley's – This is an old hotel on the quays with a reputation for good lunches and dinners. The Quay (phone: 73531). Moderate.

Reginald Grill – With a varied menu, this grill is quite handy because it's open continuously from lunch until 10:45 PM. Next to Reginald's Tower. The Mall (phone: 55611). Moderate.

Stonecourt – It is difficult to imagine that this was once a department store. Wicker furniture, a fountain and a stream inhabited by plants and fish, and a skylight have transformed it into a tropical dining room. The emphasis is on "homecooking American style" with steak, fish, and liver on the menu in addition to, naturally, hamburgers and cheeseburgers. Closed Sundays. O'Connell St. (phone: 55145). Moderate.

Teaser's – An up-to-date, up-beat deli-café, pleasant for lunch, tea, snacks; also does Friday and Saturday dinners, with wine. 124 The Quay (phone: 55908). Inexpensive.

Galley Cruising Restaurants – Dine as you cruise past the sylvan beauties of the River Barrow or Nore or down toward the sea (depending on the state of the tide and the inclination of the skipper). The 3-hour dinner trip is fun, and the food — fresh and all home cooked — unusually good for the size of the galley. Cruises depart from New Ross (15 miles northeast of Waterford) Tuesday through Saturday from April through September. Reservations are essential. New Ross (phone: 051-21723). Expensive, but the boat trip is included in the price of the meal.

SHARING A PINT: *Egans,* 36/37 Barronstrand St., is a Tudor-style bar with plenty of room to stretch. It's a convenient place to pause in shopping, enjoy a pint, and listen to the locals discuss the business of the day. *T.&H. Doolan's* in George St. is a small, old-fashioned gem. At the *Reginald Lounge,* on The Mall, there is usually a lovely peat fire, and old armaments hang on a wall that is really a restored section of the original city wall dating from the twelfth century. If you like jazz, drop in on a Sunday afternoon when there's often a session by Waterford musicians. Whatever you do, don't leave town without looking in at *The Munster,* a 300-year-old inn, revived and added onto by the Fitzgerald family. The entrance to the mellowed though modern lounge, a favorite meeting and greeting spot for young Waterforders, is on The Mall; but walk around to the original Bailey's New St. door to see the men's bar on the right, and the tiny but grand antique-paneled Oak Room on the left, before you decide where to settle.

WEXFORD

You won't be long in Wexford Town before discovering that its people are its main attraction. Their Irishness is not of the mild, gentle folk strain. Here they are keen of mind and quick in discussion, and they often like their wit a bit on the saucy side. Spend a pleasant day browsing in the narrow-streeted and hilly town, then head for the nearest bar stool (an easy assignment as one local claims there are more than 50 pubs in Wexford), and you'll find that a friendly comment or two from you is likely to get things going, be it a recitation of the local history or a soliloquy on the praiseworthy local weather. If you happen to be a visiting Irish-American, expect a lively debate on the political fortunes of the Kennedy family, whose ancestors came from nearby Dunganstown in County Wexford.

It won't be difficult to engage the hardy ladies of the Country Market in conversation, either. They can tell you that from medieval times the market has been the heartbeat of the town, and that in the days of the schooners, the ships could dock quite close to unload their goods for sale. They'll also look you straight in the eye and tell you that long before the young people started their natural foods campaign, the wives of Wexford farmers knew the benefits of vegetables grown in chemical-free soil, and they never forsook their homemade breads and jams for commercial substitutes.

This boldness of spirit is not all talk. It produced such illustrious native sons as John Barry, regarded as the founder of the American navy, born 10 miles from Wexford at Ballysampson, and Sir Robert J. McClure, discoverer of the Northwest Passage. The boldest and proudest Wexford men of days gone by, however, were those who took part in the Rebellion of 1798. In that year, the United Irishmen were unsuccessful in planning a general uprising against the British, so Father John Murphy, a County Wexford priest, independently led his parishioners, armed with pitchforks, in revolt. The rebellion lasted a month before it was suppressed, but it has remained alive in folk memory through Irish ballads such as "The Wearing of the Green" and "The Boys of Wexford."

Wexford has a population of 14,000 people, with another several thousand living in the suburbs. Located where the River Slaney flows into the shallow Wexford Harbour, the town is old and has an impossibly narrow main street, a legacy of its Viking past. It is said that a settlement existed here as early as AD 150, but it was the Vikings who developed it, calling it *Waesfjord*, which means "harbor of mud flats." Initially, the Vikings used this as a base from which to plunder the countryside and later turned it into a major trading post.

The Anglo-Norman invasion led by Richard de Clare, earl of Pembroke, known as Strongbow, ousted the Vikings in 1169 and launched a new era of domination. The face of the town also changed. Selskar Abbey rose at its northwestern edge — Henry II came here in 1172 to do Lenten penance for the murder of Thomas à Becket and it was here that Strongbow's daughter was married — and Wexford soon became a walled town, with five fortified gateways and four castles. The only remains of these defenses are the West Gate, built in the fourteenth century and used until the end of the sixteenth century, and a portion of wall nearby.

Norman nobles used one of the town's squares for the bloody sport of bullbaiting and to this day the square is called the Bull Ring. The name stuck, despite the fact that the worst of a much bloodier slaughter, the massacre of Wexford's citizenry by Oliver Cromwell in 1649, took place in the Bull Ring. The townspeople erected no monument to remind them of this deed, but when they got around (in 1905) to commemorating the insurgency of 1798, in a stroke of independent-mindedness, they placed their statue of an Irish pikeman here. More of the same spirit lies behind the confusion of Wexford's street names. Many have two, one dating from the days of British rule, and the other from the founding of the Irish Republic in 1922, the latter likely to be the name of a rebel.

Wexford has not been immune to the recent recession, but the establishment of an industrial estate with German and American firms has brought needed jobs into the area in recent years. Lett & Company, which transplants small seed mussels into Wexford Harbour from less nourishing areas, is located in Wexford Town and is the biggest single employer in the Irish fishing industry.

Then there's the tourist industry, which Wexford comes by almost effortlessly, given its location in the sunniest part of Ireland, near the 6-mile beach of Rosslare, which draws Irish holidaymakers unsolicited as honeybees to clover. Not entirely effortlessly, however, because the local energy that goes into putting on the yearly Wexford Opera Festival and all its accompanying fringe events, cannot be discounted. At opera time, nearly every family in town has at least one member backstage sewing costumes or painting props, or elsewhere hanging pictures for an exhibition or setting up chairs for a lecture.

That the festival exists at all is the result of another stroke of boldness on the part of Wexford's people. Some 30 years ago, a group of residents tired of listening to phonograph records and resolved to hear the real thing, even if they had to produce it themselves. The orchestra was hired, singers were engaged, other professionals were called in, and what eventually was to become an acclaimed event on the international opera calendar was off to a brave beginning.

WEXFORD AT-A-GLANCE

SEEING THE CITY: The best way to see Wexford is on foot. If you begin at the Tourist Office on Crescent Quay and walk in a northerly direction, you'll enjoy the harbor and the sea air. Any street off the quays leads to Main Street, which runs parallel to the harbor and is the central shopping area, but if you turn left at the Bank of Ireland onto Common Quay Street (also known as O'Hanlon Walsh Street), you'll find yourself in a square known as the Bull Ring. This winds around to the right into the Cornmarket and Abbey Street, where you'll find *White's Hotel.* At this writing, the stone stairs in the tower of nearby Selskar Abbey are dangerous, and the footing at the top, precarious; but, for the daring, the view of town, harbor, and countryside is rewardingly superb.

SPECIAL PLACES: Discovering Wexford on your own is not a fatiguing undertaking. The town's memorials, churches, and abbey are all within a 5-minute walk of Main Street.

John Barry Memorial – In 1956, the US presented Ireland with this handsome statue of the founder of the American navy, who was born in County Wexford in 1745. Commodore Barry stands on Crescent Quay where two former American presidents, Dwight D. Eisenhower and John F. Kennedy, both laid wreaths on separate occasions. The inscriptions on the monument list a few of Barry's accomplishments during the American War of Independence. Walk up the street behind the monument for a lifelike view of the commodore looking out to sea with his mighty cape blowing in the wind. Crescent Quay.

Maritime Museum – A retired lighthouse ship — the *Guillemot* — on the quays is home to a museum devoted to Wexford's seafaring days. When the ship's flag is flying, the museum is open. Summer only from 10 AM to 9 PM. There is a small admission fee. Custom House Quay.

Bull Ring – The medieval practice of bullbaiting — killing bulls for sport — once took place in this small, historic square. This is also the place where on October 1, 1649, Oliver Cromwell had 2,000 Irish men, women, and children slaughtered. A statue to a pikeman, done by Oliver Sheppard and erected in 1905, now dominates the square in tribute to the peasants who took part in what came to be known as the Rebellion of 1798. Oscar Wilde's mother lived in the house that is now Diana Donnelly's boutique (legend says she was born in room 10 of the *Old Wexford Coaching Inn*). At the east side of the ring on Tuesdays, Fridays, and Saturdays from 9:30 AM to 12:30 PM, you'll find a number of Wexford women selling their vegetables, baked goods, jams, jellies, and honey in buildings dating from 1871. Sometimes there are crafts for sale, too.

St. Iberius Church – A Georgian gem (Church of Ireland) built in 1760, on land occupied by other houses of worship dating back to earliest Norse days. Handsome interior and superb acoustics make it a favorite Festival concert hall. South of the Bull Ring on Main St.

The Arts Center – Once the Market House, then Town Hall, recently restored as a cultural headquarters and special-events site. Its now-elegant second story boasts five Waterford chandeliers. Around the corner from the Bull Ring on the Corn Market.

The Twin Churches – The Roman Catholic Churches of the Immaculate Conception on Rowe St. and the Assumption on Bride St., both designed by Robert Pierce, were inaugurated on the same day in 1858 when Wexford's original nine parishes became two, thanks to the unflagging efforts of Fr. James Roche, who is buried in the Bride St. church.

Selskar Abbey – It is a pity the town has not done more in restoring and promoting this twelfth-century site. The abbey was once quite extensive although all that can be seen today are a fourteenth-century battlement tower and church. A long-covered passage runs underground to the far side of town. Tradition says Henry II did penance here for murdering Thomas à Becket, but historians now think St. Mary's, protected within the town walls, a more likely site for his acts of contrition. Some of the older people in town can remember when the church was still in use. You can explore the ruins by obtaining a key from a nearby house (there's a notice on the gate telling you where). Behind the abbey remain the old West Gate, the only one of Wexford's five original gateways still standing, and part of the town walls. Entrance at the intersection of Temperance Row, West Gate, and Slaney St.

Franciscan Friary – Built in the seventeenth century on the site of an earlier church destroyed during Cromwellian times, this was the parish church for Wexford Town until the twin churches of the Assumption and the Immaculate Conception were completed in 1858. The Franciscan Friary was extensively redecorated in the nineteenth century, when the vaulted ceiling, marbled columns, and organ were added. School St.

Johnstown Castle – This nineteenth-century turreted Gothic mansion incorporates an earlier castle and is the former home of the Esmonde, Grogan, and Fitzgerald families. It is now owned by the State Agricultural College, but you can visit the beautiful gardens, lakes, and nature trails that surround it. The grounds are open to the public without charge from 10 AM to 6 PM daily — take a picnic basket. Exhibits in the Irish Agricultural Museum in the castle's restored farm buildings include harness ware and antique farm machinery as well as a reconstructed farm kitchen and bedroom and a creamery. Open May through October, Mondays through Fridays from 9 AM to 12:30 PM and 1:30 to 5 PM, Sundays from 2 to 5 PM. Small admission fee. Off the Rosslare Harbour Rd., 2½ miles south of Wexford.

- **EXTRA SPECIAL:** If you feel like time in the outdoors, spend a day roaming the Saltee Islands, Ireland's largest and most famous bird sanctuary. During spring and early summer, the Great Saltee (which is 1 mile in length) and the Little Saltee are home to over 3 million gulls, puffins, and other feathered creatures that delight bird-watchers. The islands are a 45-minute boat trip off the coast of Kilmore Quay, about 20 miles southwest of Wexford. You can arrange the trip by calling fisherman Willie Bates there at 29644. Kilmore Quay itself is a quaint fishing village of thatched cottages and has the lovely, modern *Hotel Saltees,* where rooms are named after different species of birds found on the islands.

SOURCES AND RESOURCES

Wexford's Tourist Information Office on Crescent Quay is large and open all year, Mondays through Saturdays, from 9 AM to 12:45 PM and 2 to 6 PM (phone: 23111); winter hours may differ slightly. You can drop in for help or just to browse through the racks heavy with information on hotels and sights in the area. During the summer the Junior Chamber of Commerce puts out an excellent monthly guide that is available free from the tourist office as well as from most hotels. It contains names and phone numbers of doctors, dentists, and pharmacists as well as the timetable for buses and trains to Dublin and the ferries operating out of Rosslare Harbour. It also has two good maps of the town with a suggested walking tour. The Chamber of Commerce publishes a mini-brochure with some of the same information in a more condensed form along with a map.

For Local Coverage – *The Wexford People,* the town's weekly newspaper, comes out on Thursdays with the news and an entertainment listing for the area.

GETTING AROUND: If you've come to Wexford by car, park it and see the town on foot. Among the dozen or so parking lots, there's a convenient one near the tourist office — turn left onto Custom House Quay if you're entering via the bridge and you'll find it on the right, just before the statue of John Barry. (For others, see the detailed town map in the monthly Junior Chamber of Commerce guide.) Consider tagging along on an Old Wexford Society walking tour. Its members conduct them throughout the year at hours set to suit current visitor demand. Check starting times and places with your hotel or the tourist office.

Bus and Train – There is no in-town bus service — it's not necessary. When you're ready to leave, however, you'll find the bus and railway terminals in Redmond Pl., near the quays just north of the bridge. CIE operates both buses and trains between Wexford and Dublin and between Wexford and Rosslare Harbour, 13 miles southeast (not to be confused with Rosslare, or Rosslare Strand, the seaside resort between Wexford and Rosslare Harbour). Ferries leave Rosslare Harbour regularly for Wales and for LeHavre and Cherbourg in France. Irish trains and buses are not known for adhering to timetables so check with CIE for delays (phone: 22522 from 6:30 AM to 6 PM). For information on ferries to Wales, call British Rail at 33115.

Taxi – Cabs are expensive, but sometimes they're the quickest and most convenient way of reaching your destination. Phone 22485, 22949, or 24056 to get one.

Car Rental – There are a number of car rental companies in Wexford and in nearby Rosslare Harbour, where some have dropping-off stations for their vehicles rented elsewhere. *Boland's Car Hire* has offices in both Wexford (phone: 23329) and Rosslare Harbour (phone: 33288). *Murrays Rent a Car* (phone: 22122) is located near the railway station and bus depot at the north end of town.

Bicycle – *John Murphy,* 22A North Main St.; *Terrence Roche,* Spawell Rd., and *S.F. Bell,* Redmond Pl., all have bikes for rent.

SHOPPING: The best guide to shopping in Wexford is to walk along Main Street and let yourself be tempted by the storefronts. Most stores are open from 9 AM to 5:30 PM, with slightly later hours on Fridays and Saturdays. During fall and winter, many are closed on Thursdays.

Barker's, Joyce's, and Martin's – All three have extensive collections of Waterford crystal and Belleek and other chinas. S Main St.

The Casket – Hand-knit sweaters, tweeds, leather goods, gifts—all made in Ireland. 43 S Main St.

Hore's – A good place for Irish linens. 31–37 S Main St.

Laurence's – A jewelry shop with attractive rings at reasonable prices. Bull Ring.

Lowney Antiques, Ltd. – Intriguing browsing, town's best selection of beautiful old things, large and small. Shipping arranged. S Main St.

Mary Ormsby's – Irish designer knits, suits, accessories, lingerie. Anne St.

Papilio – Mary and Brian Byrne pride themselves on operating a clothing shop where nearly all of the goods are Irish-made. 45 S Main St.

The Wool Shop – Offers a large choice of Aran sweaters, woven belts, and rugs. 39–41 S Main St.

SPECIAL EVENTS: Since 1951, the *Wexford Opera Festival* has brought singers from all over the world to present rarely performed operas, usually to sold-out audiences who've waited long and come from afar for the pleasure. The operas, three of them per festival, can be obscure works of the seventeenth, eighteenth, and nineteenth centuries, or even contemporary ones, and the performers may be equally unknown, though many are "discovered" here and go on to international careers. The nineteenth-century Theatre Royal on High Street is the Georgian setting of these 12 days of music that begin in late October, and since it seats only 446 opera lovers, early booking is necessary — bookings by mail open in June. Write to the Wexford Festival Opera, Theatre Royal, Wexford (phone: 22240), but if you don't get seats, don't despair. Many other events, from concerts, art exhibitions, and lectures, to street theater, fashion shows, and fishing contests, take place around the opera core and there is no doubt that this is the liveliest time of the year to be in Wexford under any pretext.

The *Wexford Mussel Festival* threatens to become an annual affair, too. It was held for the first time in September of 1980 and featured 3 days of fun, including the selection of a Wexford "mussel" man.

SPORTS: The monthly guide published by the Junior Chamber of Commerce has detailed information on recreational activities. The leisure center in the *Talbot Hotel* on the quays is open to nonresidents and has a number of facilities including a heated indoor swimming pool, squash courts, and saunas.

Golf – The *Wexford Golf Club* has a 9-hole course. *The Rosslare Golf Club* (phone: 32113) has an 18-hole course at Rosslare, 11 miles southeast of Wexford.

Horse Racing – Flat racing is held 5 times a year in the small-town atmosphere of Wexford's *Bettyville Racecourse.*

Riding – At *Horetown House,* the Young family offers daily rides, all levels of instruction, indoor ring, cross-country course for experienced riders on seventeenth-century manor grounds. Picnic rides, riding holiday packages, wonderful home-cooked food too. 12 miles west on L160 Rd. at Foulksmills (phone: 055-21124). *Shelimar Stables* in Trinity (phone: 39251) also do lessons, skill-paced rides on woodland, mountain trails.

Swimming – Southeast Ireland is known for its comparative abundance of sunshine, which can be enjoyed at a number of beaches around Wexford including Curracloe, Rosslare, Carne, and Kilmore Quay.

THEATER: During the summer season, there is Irish cabaret several nights a week at the *Talbot Hotel* (phone: 22566). Special programs take place at the *Wexford Arts Centre,* located in the old Market House in the Cornmarket (phone: 23764).

MUSIC AND NIGHTLIFE: Wexford is a lively town at night with plenty of good singing pubs and cabaret and ballroom dancing at most of the larger hotels. If you're lucky, *Sonas,* a popular group of five young musicians, will be singing Irish ballads as well as a few humorous, modern tunes. There is Irish music most nights in *The Barn* of *White's Hotel* and in the *Tavern Bar* of the *Talbot Hotel.* On Thursday nights, there is jazz in *Old White's* on North Main Street; later in the evening there is a disco in the hotel's extension on Abbey Street. *Kelly's Strand Hotel* in Rosslare (phone: 32114) also has dancing and entertainment most evenings. Watch out for *Seisiún,* an evening — or session — of song and dance sponsored by Comhaltas Ceoltóirí Éireann, a national organization for the promotion of traditional Irish folk music. These very authentic sessions are held in some 30 cities and towns during the summer. In Wexford, they usually take place once a week in *White's Hotel.*

SINS: *Nangle's Coffee Shop,* 22 N Main St., serves some delicious pastry. For a less sinful treat, try the oat and honey squares at the *Natural Food Store* on Selskar St.

BEST IN TOWN

CHECKING IN: Wexford is a very hospitable town. There are several fine hotels in the area and plenty of bed and breakfast houses. During the summer months, an expensive hotel room will cost about $50 and up double (most hotels include breakfast in their rates), a moderate one about $40, and

396 WEXFORD / Best in Town

an inexpensive one $35 or less. A single B&B room will cost about $12, and a double about $20. Rates are lower December through March, but about $10 higher per room on bank holidays and during Opera and Mussel festivals.

White's Hotel – Modern exterior, but with a pleasant neo-Georgian warmth about its public rooms; guest rooms are neat and convenient; most have private bath and/or shower, color TV. With congenial lounge bar, first-class à la carte restaurant, a variety of entertainment in season. Very cordial management. Abbey St. (phone: 22311). Expensive.

Talbot Hotel – Modern and near the quays, the *Talbot* offers patrons a leisure center, two good restaurants, and several bars, including the *Bacchus Bar* overlooking the indoor swimming pool. Trinity St. (phone: 22566). Expensive.

Kelly's Strand Hotel – This modern resort hotel on Rosslare Strand is usually booked well in advance. It is a popular weekend retreat for the Irish and is known for its good food and recreation facilities (tennis and squash courts, indoor and outdoor pools, saunas, beach). Closed from mid-December to mid-February. Rosslare (phone: 32114). Expensive to moderate.

Kincone Motor Hotel – New, comfortable, and much smaller than *White's, Kelly's*, or the *Talbot*, this 18-room hotel is just across the bridge from Wexford. Dublin Rd. (phone: 23611). Moderate.

Old Wexford Coaching Inn – Formerly part of White's Hotel, recently redone in "old world" style and now run as a separate entity by the same management. It dates back to 1779 (says its brochure, "Any creaks are two hundred years old and harmless"). Neat, bright rooms, some with antique furnishings, with and without private baths (hall baths are closer, larger than most) at very reasonable rates. Coffee shop, bar with good pub grub, Captain White's Restaurant on premises. N Main St. (phone: 24002). Inexpensive.

County Hotel – Older but nicely furnished, this is a small hotel in the middle of town. Anne St. (phone: 24377). Inexpensive.

Killiane Castle – John Mernagh inherited this lovely 230-acre estate from his dad, and he and his wife, Kathleen, have converted it into a gracious guesthouse. They also have apartments to rent and hope to eventually restore the seventeenth-century tower on the grounds. Open March through October. Off the Rosslare Harbour Rd., Drinagh (phone: 22272). Inexpensive.

St. Aidan's Mews – This very old place near the Church of the Immaculate Conception is now a tidy guesthouse where you'll be tended to by Catherine and Martin Redmond. All rooms have hot and cold water. 25 Lower John's St. (phone: 22691). Inexpensive.

EATING OUT: Whether you wish to dine by candlelight or to have a tasty salad in relaxed surroundings, you're likely to find a restaurant to suit your appetite and billfold in Wexford. Dinner for two with house wine in an expensive restaurant will set you back $40 or more. In a moderate one, you'll probably pay between $20 and $35, and in an inexpensive one, the bill will be under $20.

Captain White's – Comfortably stylish seafood restaurant with cozy cocktail bar; has made the Irish Tourist Board's top ten listing for several years. Only freshest fish, seafood done with great skill and respect. Chowder, mussels, scallops, pink trout with walnut stuffing are commendable; trust maître d's daily suggestions. Some meat choices too. In Old Wexford Coaching Inn on N Main St. (phone: 24002). Expensive.

Esker Lodge – Inviting home setting for restaurant with reputation for finest and freshest of Irish/Continental food. Homemade soups, Kilmore crab, scallops, prawns, Slaney salmon, and trout. Wine license. Closed November through March. Within view of the beach near Curracloe about 15 minutes from Wexford (phone: 37171). Expensive.

Kelly's Strand Hotel – The hotel has an elegant restaurant where you can dine on such tempting dishes as fresh scallops in season and apricot soufflé. There is often entertainment to round out the evening. Closed from mid-December to mid-February. Rosslare (phone: 32114). Expensive.

Selskar Restaurant – Attractive dining room with excellent Irish/Continental menu, pleasing atmosphere, service. For a gracious splurge. In White's Hotel on Abbey St. (phone: 22311). Expensive.

Talbot Hotel – There are several choices in this hotel. The *Guillemot Restaurant* is the main dining room, the place for serious eating accompanied by a selection from the extensive wine list. For seafood, steaks, chops, and salads, go to the *Pike Room Grill,* and for soups and sandwiches (or some delicious mussels), it's the *Tavern Bar.* Trinity St. (phone: 22566). Expensive in the restaurant, moderate in the grill, and inexpensive in the bar.

Farmer's Kitchen – Informal atmosphere, friendly service, good local seafood, steaks. Lunches and dinners; closed Sundays. On Rosslare Rd. (phone: 23295). Moderate.

The Old Granary – Tables are in booths in this quiet, rustic restaurant with a beamed ceiling and wooden pillars. The reputation for good food is well established and the menu is varied. Westgate (phone: 23935). Moderate.

Tim's Tavern – Casual, folksy, recommended by locals for lunches, dinners, good steaks. 51 S Main St. (phone: 23861). Moderate to inexpensive.

Old Wexford Coaching Inn Coffee Shop – Breakfasts, morning coffee and cakes, teas, gratifying pub grub and seafood platters. N Main St. (phone: 24002). Moderate to inexpensive.

The Bohemian Girl – Homemade soups, salads, and appetizing specials make it a particularly good lunch stop. Kay and Seamus McMenamin run this colorful pub named after the opera by William Balfe, who lived in the corner building. N Main and Monck sts. (phone: 23596). Inexpensive.

Michael's Restaurant – This is pleasant and dimly lit, with aquariums and a nautical motif. 94 N Main St. (phone: 22196). Inexpensive.

SHARING A PINT: The *Crown Bar* on Monck St. is the oldest pub in Ireland still held by the original family. Fiona Kelly and her mother, Mrs. Annie Kelly, open for business in the late afternoon and they can help you recall the past when the *Crown* was a stagecoach inn popular with traveling judges and their assistants. You'll see why the *Crown* is also one of Ireland's best-known pubs (it's been on television in various European countries) if you sip your drink in the cozy back rooms. They're filled with antique prints, military gear, swords, and other arms — including two guns from the famous Howth gun-running incident of 1914 — that the proprietor's father, the late Aidan Kelly, collected from all over the world. Another stop for a drink and a chat is the *Thomas Moore Tavern* in the Cornmarket. The poet's mother was born here. *Tim's Tavern,* S Main St., has thatching over the bar and good snacks, and *Andy Kinsellas,* also on S Main St., is a handsome old place and a quiet refuge from the shopping traffic. *The Shambles,* Common Quay, has old-time dance music some evenings.

YORK

"The history of York," according to King George V, "is the history of England." In 1971, York celebrated its 1,900th birthday, and each successive epoch of the country's past is still legible in its ruin sites, buildings, and monuments. The Middle Ages are especially well represented, and for many visitors, it is this aspect of York that is the most interesting. Within the 3 miles of ancient defensive wall is perhaps the best-preserved medieval city in Great Britain, containing its largest medieval church, York Minster, and its best-preserved medieval street. The quirky, timbered, slightly akimbo buildings in the Shambles — once the butchers' quarters — may look like a stage set, but they are as authentic as the day they were built.

In AD 71, the Romans chose the meeting point of the rivers Ouse and Foss as the site of Eboracum, at first a temporary camp, then a permanent fort. From that it grew to become a major Roman city that the Emperor Hadrian (of Hadrian's Wall fame) used as a home base and where Constantine the Great was proclaimed Emperor. It flourished as a trade center at the hub of a network of roads and as a port for seagoing ships that navigated the 50-mile stretch up the River Ouse. The most inspiring physical legacy of those times is the surviving Multangular Tower in the museum gardens (though its upper stonework is "merely" medieval).

The Romans left to defend their own country in the early part of the fifth century and little is known of the next slice of history until the Saxons gained control of the city in the seventh century. They built a wooden church, the first York Minster, predecessor of the present building. The conquering Danes, arriving in the ninth century, further developed the city as an important port, called it Jorvik, and gave the name "gate," the Norse for street, to several of its thoroughfares. Some of Jorvik's original Viking buildings have been excavated recently, superbly preserved in the peaty earth. The Normans' eleventh-century presence is recorded in today's landscape as two humps of earth on which William the Conqueror raised two wooden castles. One hump remains as Baile Hill; the other supports Clifford's Tower, a later structure in stone.

It was in the thirteenth century, however, that the city began to assume its familiar shape. Though it had earlier been surrounded by an earth mound and a wooden stockade, these were now replaced by the actual limestone walls, together with the four principal gateways (called bars, just to confuse matters): Monk Bar, Micklegate Bar, Walmgate Bar, and Bootham Bar. Within the boundaries, several churches, friaries, nunneries, and an abbey established York as a cradle of European Christianity and as the country's second city.

The Minster, growing grander and grander over the 250 years of its construction, was finally completed in 1472, and has been York's crowning glory ever since.

Medieval city planners developed their roads along the main Roman streets. Stonegate was, for example, the Via Praetoria; Petergate, the Via Principalis; and Micklegate, meaning the Great Street, was the main route from London where the only bridge over the Ouse stood. The medievals then built connecting alleyways and the characteristic timber-framed buildings that overhang them, each story projecting farther than the one below. The Shambles is one such street; now restored not as a lifeless museum piece but as a still busy commercial artery.

The prosperity of medieval York stemmed from its thriving wool trade. With the slow decline of this industry, and in the wake of Henry VIII's purge against the power of the church, the city was doomed for some time to play only a minor role in English history until it became a fashionable social center in eighteenth-century Georgian Britain. The racecourse, Assembly Rooms, and many splendid town houses belonging to large, landowning families were part of this scene. Because it was widely favored by wealthy northerners as a refuge from the grime of early industrialization, York remained relatively factory-free, with candy works a notable exception. It did, however, spawn George Hudson, a railway inventor and entrepreneur who was largely responsible for making the city a keystone in Britain's expanding railway network. Today you can see a plaque to his life and work outside the Railway King Hotel on George Hudson Street (the house of Joseph Hansom, inventor of the first horse-drawn cab, is in Micklegate).

To absorb York's antiquated atmosphere, simply wander around, particularly in the labyrinth of streets and alleyways in the shadow of the Minster. Stroll along the gates — the activities that once took place in them are evident in their names: Colliergate was the street of the charcoal dealers, Spurriergate belonged to the spurmakers, and Stonegate was the route used to carry building materials to the Minster. Whip-ma-whop-ma-gate is the longest name for the shortest street, one named after a whipping post where criminals were punished.

Everywhere there are curiosities of the past. In Petergate, for example, there is a working gas lamp in front of the Minster South Door. At Nos. 5 and 7, and at several other points in town, you can see the original firemark signs put there in Georgian days when each insurance company had its own fire engine that would only go to the rescue of its own blazing customers.

York does have its shabbier, modern appendages, though it has managed more successfully than most cities to conserve its age-old character. Whether it can continue to resist pressures to keep up-to-date by widening streets and building taller buildings, remains to be seen. In the meantime, it is not unusual for over 2 million visitors a year to step into York's time capsule to enjoy its ancient airs and graces. You will not be alone in admiring this most historic of cities.

YORK AT-A-GLANCE

SEEING THE CITY: For those who need an aerial perspective before tackling some of York's inner alleyways, the city walls offer a 3-mile-long vantage point. The route along the crest of the barricades dates back to the 1200s and is still the traditional promenade for both natives and visitors. The path — 3 feet wide and often without handrails, so be careful — can be reached from the bars, or gateways, where the walls join the major roads (Bootham, Monk, Walmgate, Fishergate, Victoria, and Micklegate bars). The stretch between Bootham Bar and Monk Bar is particularly attractive and affords a good view of the spires and buttresses of York Minster. Allow at least 1½ hours, more if you want to drop down to inspect something you've spied at closer range. The walk, which is delightful in springtime when clouds of daffodils hug the grassy banks, is open daily from dawn till dusk.

SPECIAL PLACES: Nearly everything you'll want to see in York is in the medieval heart of the city. The only exception is the National Railway Museum on the west side of the Ouse near the railway station.

York Minster – York without the Minster's imposing skyline presence would be like Paris denied its Eiffel Tower. This grandiose church — the Cathedral of St. Peter — is the largest gothic cathedral north of the Alps. It was built over a period of 250 years, from 1220 to 1472, but even before that, there was a church on the spot, several in fact: The first was a wooden one built in the seventh century (the word *minster* is Anglo-Saxon for a mission from which the surrounding country was evangelized). York Minster contains the finest collection of medieval stained glass in England. Of the 130 windows (most removed at the outbreak of World War II and painstakingly put back together again), the thirteenth-century Five Sisters Window of delicate grisaille glass is the most famous, although the Rose Window commemorating the fifteenth-century Wars of the Roses and the West Window with its heart-shaped tracery are perhaps the most beautiful. Among the Minster's other proud features are the late-fifteenth-century choir screen with its sculpted kings of England, and the Undercroft. The church was in danger of collapsing until desperately needed renovations were begun in 1967. During the course of the repairs, the foundations of an early Norman cathedral were revealed and it was discovered that the medieval church had been raised right above the city's Roman headquarters. There is now an Undercroft Museum where visitors can see the massive twentieth-century concrete underpinnings as well as an exhibit on the history of the Minster and its site. The Minster is open daily, though sight-seeing is restricted during services. The choir is normally open, but not during services. It costs nothing to wander around the Minster itself, but there is an admission charge for the Undercroft Museum.

Treasurer's House – The official residence of the Treasurer of the Minster (until the post was abolished in 1547) is behind the Minster on the site of a Roman building. Though it dates back to the thirteenth century, most of what exists today is from the seventeenth century. The last owner, Frank Green, renovated the building and gave it to the National Trust in 1930. Visitors can see period furniture, tapestries, and a lively exhibition showing some of the personalities who have been associated with the house. Open daily from April through October. Admission charge. On some summer evenings (contact the TIC for details) you can enjoy coffee by candlelight in the main hall and music in the drawing room. Minster Yard (phone: 24247).

St. William's College – One of York's many picturesque half-timbered structures, this was built in 1453 to lodge the Minster's chantry priests and has been restored as a meeting place for church convocations. Its Georgian quadrangle is a particularly remarkable feature. Those interested in becoming more directly involved in the city's history, and possibly returning home with a fourteenth-century archbishop in tow, will find a wide selection of replicas in the York Brass Rubbing Centre here (phone: 52232), many taken from original brasses found in local churches. Admission is free; materials and advice, 50p. Open daily. College St. (phone: 34830).

The Shambles – Mentioned in the *Domesday Book*, this narrow cobble-stoned alleyway is one of the best-preserved medieval streets in Britain, if not in Europe. Originally it was a street of butcher shops, known as Fleshammels, but it is now lined with antique, craft, and gift shops (some still have the sloping wooden shelves in front that were used to display meat). People living in the upper stories of these typically medieval overhanging buildings can shake hands with their neighbors across the road if they lean out the windows far enough. The Shambles leads from King's Square (at the foot of Petergate) to The Pavement.

Castle Museum – The private collection of everyday "bygones" accumulated by a country doctor from Pickering, 25 miles northeast of York, and donated to the city in 1925, forms the basis of this museum which has become one of the most important folk museums in the country. Stars of the show are the reconstructed streets: a Victorian cobbled one complete with Hansom cab (the original taxi), candlemaker's, blacksmith's, and other shop fronts, and an Edwardian street with gaslighted pub. Among the other, diverse displays are a Victorian parlor, a Georgian dining room, snuffboxes, policemen's truncheons, old musical instruments, vintage candy bars that include sugar pigs and spice mice, firearms, and unintelligible tape recordings of the local Yorkshire dialect. All this is housed in a former eighteenth-century prison for women (conveniently located opposite the Assize Courts), with various craftsmen's workshops set up in the converted cells — except for one that remains untouched. In it Dick Turpin, the notorious highwayman who rode Black Bess and terrorized travelers in the early stagecoaches, was imprisoned before being executed in 1740. Open daily. Admission charge. Tower St. (phone: 53611).

Clifford's Tower – A confusing history is attached to this remnant of York Castle. William the Conqueror erected a wooden fortress on a man-made earth mound here in 1068 (and another across the river on a second mound on which nothing remains). In 1190, a rioting anti-Jewish mob burned it down, killing 150 of the Jews of York who had taken refuge inside. The existing quatrefoil stone tower, actually the medieval keep of the castle, was built in the thirteenth century, gutted by fire in the seventeenth century, and later restored and named after a Roger de Clifford who had been executed here in 1596. In the nineteenth century, the tower was used as a prison. Open daily. Admission charge. Tower St.

National Railway Museum – The only national museum outside London is packed with reminders of the days of steam and appropriately housed in the old depot where the locomotives went for maintenance and repairs. The most famous items are the Pacific Mallard loco, which still holds the world's steam speed record at 126 mph, and Queen Victoria's luxuriously appointed Pullman carriage. Many of the locomotives and carriages on display stand on two giant turntables in the 2-acre Great Hall, and lots of other aspects of railway history are covered by the exhibits in the museum galleries. There is a shop and an upstairs restaurant overlooking the main London-Edinburgh line. Open Mondays through Saturdays from 10 AM to 6 PM; Sundays from 2:30 PM to 6 PM. Leeman Rd. (phone: 21261).

Yorkshire Museum and Museum Gardens – The museum contains exhibits that date back 160 million years, but apart from the geological items, it is probably best known for its collection of archaeological remains, particularly finds from Roman York. In the gardens are the ruins of St. Mary's Abbey (founded ca. 1080), once the most important Benedictine monastery in the north of England. (It was suppressed by

Henry VIII's Dissolution of the Monasteries and thereafter lost many of its stones to local building projects.) The Multangular Tower and a section of the city walls, their lower portions Roman, are also in the gardens. Open daily. Admission charge for the museum. Museum St. (phone: 29745).

City Art Gallery – The collection includes old masters dating back to the fourteenth century, but works of nineteenth- and twentieth-century European painters tend to be the specialty. The building itself is Victorian. Open daily. Admission charge. Exhibition Sq. (phone: 23839).

The Assembly Rooms – Built in the 1730s, this was once the most fashionable social center in the north of England. It was *the* place to go in Georgian times to play cards and dice, drink tea, or attend a grand ball. Today dances are still held here, though exhibitions and conferences are more usual. The design of the building is Italian Palladian and the colonnaded Egyptian Hall is its chief interior feature. Open weekdays in August only. Blake St. (phone: 22848).

Holy Trinity Church – Completed before 1500, this picturesque church on a picturesque street contains eighteenth-century wooden box pews, each with its own door enabling it to be occupied by a single family. There is also a split-level pulpit. Goodramgate.

Merchant Adventurers' Hall – The wealthiest and most powerful of the city's trade guilds built this excellent example of a medieval guildhall in the fourteenth and fifteenth centuries. It has lovely timberwork inside and out. Open Mondays through Saturdays. Fossgate (phone: 54818).

The York Story – York from pre-Roman times to the present day is the subject of exhibits in the city's heritage center, housed in the former St. Mary's Church. Lots of lavishly constructed models, a slide show, and audio presentations are included in the center, which was designed as York's contribution to European Architectural Heritage Year in 1975. It's worth seeing first, to help put things into perspective, before you explore the real thing. Open daily. Admission charge. Castlegate (phone: 28632).

■ **EXTRA SPECIAL**: The oldest inhabitants of York are its ghosts — the city is widely reckoned to be the most haunted in Europe. Monks, black cats, a duke, a thirteenth-century mayoress, the headless earl of Northumberland, and marching Roman soldiers have all been seen by upstanding and sober members of the community. Several buildings are steeped in ghostly tales. The modern Theatre Royal, for example, stands on the ruins of St. Leonard's Hospital whose medieval crypt is now a theater club room inhabited by the Grey Lady, the ghost of a young nun said to have been buried alive in the walls for having an affair with a monk. You can see for yourself: A 2-hour walking tour, led by an expert guide, leaves the *Angler's Arms* in Goodramgate at 8 PM Mondays through Fridays from the end of May to the beginning of October in search of "haunted and historic York." The tour costs £1 and booking isn't necessary. Just turn up in body and spirit.

SOURCES AND RESOURCES

The Tourist Information Centre in the De Grey Rooms, Exhibition Sq. (phone: 21756), has lots of free or nominally priced pamphlets on the city and the surrounding area, including the *Official York Guide* (about 60p). A free 2-hour walking tour, led by members of the Association of Voluntary Guides, leaves here two or three times a day

YORK / Sources and Resources

from Easter through October. The TIC is open daily in summer, closed Sundays in winter. There is also a 24-hour recorded telephone message with up-to-date information on events (phone: 8041). Except for Venice and Florence, York has probably been the subject of more books and guides than any other single noncapital city in Europe. A broad selection is for sale at the York Minster Bookshop and at the bookstore in the Castle Museum. Among the shorter booklets worth reading are *The City of York and the Minster,* by A. L. Laishley; *Georgian Houses in York,* by the York Georgian Society; *Roman York from AD 71,* by the Yorkshire Architectural and York Archaeological societies; and *York Mystery Plays,* by Elizabeth Brunskill. Ronald Willis's *A Portrait of York* and the historical work called simply *York,* by George Benson, are meatier tomes.

For Local Coverage – The *Yorkshire Evening Press* is the city's daily newspaper, on sale at various newsstands and from street-corner venders (whose cry doesn't sound anything like *"Yorkshire Evening Press"*).

GETTING AROUND: York is to be explored on foot, especially since parking is virtually impossible on the street and most of the major car parks are outside the walls, away from where you really want to be. Because it is a compact city, with all places of interest within strolling distance, you won't be logging mammoth mileages. There are guided walking tours and bus tours if you don't feel like going it alone, even 15-minute clip-clops around the town on a horse-drawn carriage, with en route commentary by the driver. They leave from opposite the front of the Minster and cost 80p (phone: 769490).

Bus – The railway station is really the hub of the bus network. The *West Yorkshire Bus Company* sells a 2-day tourist ticket allowing unlimited travel on any of its city bus routes for £2.50. Buy it from the driver on the city tour bus, from the company's head office on Rougier St. (phone: 24161), or from the British Rail inquiry desk in the station. The company operates 1¼-hour city bus tours that cost £1.25 and leave from outside the station daily except Saturdays from the beginning of April to the end of October. Tickets for these can be bought from the bus driver.

Taxi – Centrally located cab stands are at St. Sampson's Sq. (phone: 22333), by the ABC Cinema on Piccadilly (phone: 54579), by the Odeon Cinema on Blossom St., next to the Windmill Hotel on Queen St., at the railway station, and at Bootham Bar.

Car Rental – You won't need a car to see the city but they are available if you plan an excursion into the countryside. Major firms represented include *Godfrey Davis,* Station Garage, Leeman Rd. (phone: 20394); and *Kenning,* Micklegate Bar (phone: 59326).

Bicycle – Not at all an unusual mode of transportation in York. You can rent one from the *York Cycle Works,* Lawrence St. (phone: 26664).

Boat – Several companies operate river tours. From mid-March through September, *Hills Boatyard,* Lendal Bridge (phone: 23752), has hour-long, 6-mile cruises up the Ouse to Bishopthorpe Palace, the thirteenth-century home of the Archbishop of York, and back (60p). Times of the sailings are posted on the notice board by the boatyard gates.

MUSEUMS: In addition to the museums described in *Special Places,* you may want to visit *Impressions.* When it opened in 1972, it was the first photographic gallery outside London and there still aren't many others. Apart from its changing exhibitions, there are cards, prints, and specialist books on sale. Open Tuesdays through Saturdays, plus Sundays in August and Mondays in August and December. 17 Colliergate (phone: 54724).

SHOPPING: York's Newgate marketplace has been the focal point of all trading activities since medieval times. The setting is beautiful and the variety of wares is bound to interest browsers of all dispositions. Among the stalls you'll find antiques, clothing, bric-a-brac, and homemade Yorkshire foods as well as fish, fowl, and vegetables. The market is in full swing every day except Sunday and Monday. More conventional shop premises range from Georgian frontages in the city's older thoroughfares to modern shopping center facilities, the latter of little interest to the tourist.

Antique shops abound. Most carry a wide selection of pieces and periods, though they may be known for a specialty. Among them are *Greenwoods* in Stonegate (jewelry), *Monk House* in Goodramgate (brass and copper), *York House* in Petergate (furniture and paintings), *Trinity* in Goodramgate (dolls), *Morrison* in The Mount (furniture), *Donald Butler* in Goodramgate (fine china), and several others. There are lots of antiquarian bookshops, too, including *Spelman's* in Micklegate, *K Books* in Fossgate, and *MacDowell and Stern* in Petergate.

Some better stores are listed below. Not all of them may stock goods you'd thought of buying, but they've been included as curiosities.

Cox – Sheepskin: Slippers, gloves, rugs, coats, hats, footmuffs, and powder puffs are among its variations on a theme. 19 The Shambles (phone: 37210).

Ralph Ellerker's – Famous since 1796, then as a saddler and harnessmaker, now as a store for the modern equestrian who rides for pleasure. Apart from its ancient beams and rich leathery fragrance, you'll also discover ropes and canvasses, a macrame or yachting enthusiast's dream. Lots of regular gift ideas, too. 25 Walmgate (phone: 54417).

Mulberry Hall – One of England's most respected porcelain shops. 17 Stonegate (phone: 20736).

Precious – A wonderful toy shop, the biggest in the city, and an exciting place to be for all children from 8 to 80. Lots of railway models. 87 Petergate (phone: 53751).

Alan Stuttle Gallery – Original oils, watercolors, and limited-edition and other prints, including many of York. 42 Stonegate (phone: 24907).

Wooden Horse – An interesting collection of diverse ethnic items ranging from African tribal rugs to Nepalese clothing, Chinese kites, and Mexican silver. 9 Goodramgate (phone: 26012).

York Insignia – Maintains records of nearly all known coats of arms and handpaints thousands of heraldic shields each year, from the bona fide personal arms of forebears to the emblems of professional bodies, schools, universities, ships and regiments, companies, and even hometowns. *York Insignia* can advise you on tracing your ancestors as well as make a shield to your own design. 1 Minster Gate (phone: 59762).

York Minster Gifts – Just about every conceivable souvenir of a stay in York, including exclusive and limited editions of quality giftware. 48 Low Petergate (phone: 27138).

Liberty – The famous London store now has a branch in York, with printed fabrics and a variety of gifts. 15 Davygate (phone: 33093).

SPECIAL EVENTS: The *York Races,* run a few days each month from May through October (the most important race, the Ebor Handicap, takes place in August), are usually the biggest events on the calendar. They are regularly upstaged, however, by the *York Cycle of Mystery Plays,* a reenactment that traditionally takes place every fourth year. The 48 plays — first performed in the mid-fourteenth century and repeated for about 200 years thereafter — tell the story of man from the Creation to the Last Judgment. Originally presented by the medieval guilds, each of which chose a Biblical story to illustrate, the revived plays are still performed by local citizens, 200 of them, along with a handful of professional actors.

Most of the plays are set dramatically against the ruins of St. Mary's Abbey, but some are presented on authentically built wagons drawn around the city as in medieval times. The performances (last held in June 1980) go on for 3 weeks and coincide with the *York Festival* of symphony, chamber, opera, and choral music, dance, art exhibits, and other entertainment including a bell ringing competition in York Minster. The next festival and plays will be held in 1984; for details, contact the York Festival Office, 1 Museum St., York Y01 2DT (phone: 26421).

SPORTS: **Boating** – Rowboats are rented by the hour at *Hills Boatyard*, Lendal Bridge (phone: 23752).

Cricket – To see a first-class match, go to Leeds, 25 miles away. Yorkshiremen have always been fanatical cricketers and the *Yorkshire County Cricket Club* is based at the *Headingley Cricket Ground*, St. Michael's La., Leeds (phone: 52865). When Yorkshire meets Lancashire, it's the Wars of the Roses all over again — check local papers for the date of the annual "battle."

Fishing – Licenses to fish the River Ouse and others can be bought at *Hookes*, 28–30 Coppergate (phone: 55073), *G. E. Hill*, 40 Clarence St. (phone: 24561), or *Bulmers* at Monk's Bar (phone: 54070).

Golf – There are more than 60 courses within an hour's drive of York, but four within easy reach of the city center are the *Fulford Golf Club*, Heslington La. (phone: 413212), the *Heworth Golf Club*, Muncastergate, Malton Rd. (phone: 24204), the *Railway Institute*, Pike Hills, Tadcaster Rd. (706566), and the *York Golf Club*, 6 miles out of town at Strensall (phone: 490304). All allow temporary visitor membership. There is also a driving range at Wiggington Rd.; open daily from 11 AM to 9 PM (phone: 59421).

Horse Racing – The *York Racecourse* is the most important racetrack in northern England. Entrance to the grounds costs about £1, but if you don't want to take advantage of the facilities inside, you can watch from the common land around the track, even stroll almost to the winning post, without payment. The races begin in May and reoccur for a few days each month through October. Peak of the season is the running of the Ebor Handicap in August. On the Knavesmire, 1 mile south of the city (phone: 22260).

Swimming – The *Barbican Baths* are the city's most modern, with three separate pools. Admission charge. Paragon St. (phone: 30266).

Tennis – Courts are available at Rowntree Park, Hull Rd. Park, Glen Gardens, Scarcroft Rd., and at the university. Book at the courts.

THEATER: The *Theatre Royal*, St. Leonard's Pl., was built in 1740 and became one of the country's leading theaters in Georgian times. Rebuilt by the Victorians, it is still York's main theater, offering a range of dramatic performances by both local groups and leading actors and actresses. The box office is open from Monday through Saturday (phone: 23568), and most performances begin at 7:30 PM or 8 PM. The *Arts Centre*, housed in a converted medieval church in Micklegate, has much more varied entertainments — films, exhibitions, music, and other events — in addition to plays (phone: 27129).

MUSIC: With the exception of the University of York Music Department, which gives twice weekly concerts during term time in *Lyons Concert Hall*, York is a generally poor city for all kinds of music. A few pubs and restaurants have live folk or jazz performances, and there are several discos, but lovers of classical music will be extremely fortunate if they hear any during their stay. The *Theatre Royal* and the *Arts Centre* are the most likely settings for musical events and the tourist information office will know of any others.

NIGHTCLUBS AND NIGHTLIFE: York is not a night town. If you crave action in the wee hours, your best bet is to drive to Leeds, which thrives on things happening when most of its respectable citizens are tucked into their beds. However, York does have a few discos worth visiting. Most require jackets and ties; some allow informal attire other than jeans. Entrance charges vary according to the DJ and night of the week but generally they are inexpensive and membership, if necessary, is nominal for the transient visitor. The *Old World Club,* Stonegate (phone: 22904), has two dance floors, six bars, a beer garden, and light meals, all enjoyed by a predominately young crowd. *Prince Consort,* Bootham (phone: 21002), offers dinner and dancing in a Georgian house from 10 PM on Mondays through Saturdays. *Barrons,* 71 Micklegate (phone: 20602), is a converted, bistrolike cellar discotheque that serves meals between 11 PM and 1:15 AM Mondays through Saturdays. The *Barge,* a floating pub near the Skeldergate Bridge, has live folk music and occasionally jazz on Friday and Saturday evenings. Call 32530 to find out who's on when.

SINS: York isn't a sexy town. You won't be able to hear, see, or indulge in outlandish practices, and if you ask a local where the red-light district is, he'll probably point to the nearest set of traffic lights. York is famous for one vicelike indulgence, however — Yorkshire pudding. Despite its name, it isn't a dessert but a traditional accompaniment to roast beef served at Sunday lunch. The secret of a successful "pud" lies in its lightness and everyone seems to have his or her own secret recipe to achieve the same end. To make yours, whisk one egg, add a little milk, and gradually work in 3 ounces of flour, beating well. Add the rest of a half-pint of milk, leave it for an hour, then heat up some beef drippings in a baking tin. When very hot, pour in the batter and cook in a hot oven (around 425°) till the pudding rises and turns crispy brown at the edges.

BEST IN TOWN

CHECKING IN: August is a hopeless time to visit York if you want to stay in the city center. Not only is it the peak time for tourists, but their numbers are swelled by racegoers, here for the most important meeting on the calendar. Rather than try to squeeze into too few city beds, car drivers are advised to travel out and find smaller hotels in the Vale of York, the flat band of land to the north of the city, or even to go to Harrogate, a half-hour ride to the west where there's bound to be a room, even at the height of the summer. The Tourist Information Centre can give on-the-spot advice about room availability from its extensive lists, and it operates a booking service for a small fee, for those who apply in person. A double room with breakfast costs $70 and up at hotels listed as expensive; from $45 to $70 at moderate ones, and less than $45 at inexpensive ones.

Abbey Park Hotel – A 5-minute wander away from the city center, the 84-room *Abbey Park* is a vintage Georgian brick building with updated bedrooms. The restaurant is known for its traditional Sunday lunch of roast beef with Yorkshire pudding and onion gravy, followed by typical English syllabub. The Mount (phone: 25481). Expensive.

Dean Court Hotel – This modernized, clean, bright Victorian house has 35 rooms, several of which overlook the Minster. Its coffee shop gives the hotel an American flavor. Duncombe Pl. (phone: 25082). Expensive.

Judges Lodging – The stone head above the doorway represents Aesculapius, the Greek god of healing, because the building was once the town residence of a well-known physician. Later it was the residence of the Assize Court judges, hence the name. Built about 1710 in Georgian style; you'll find four-poster beds in some rooms. Cuisine is French and the wines are personally imported by the proprietor. 9 Lendal (phone: 38733). Expensive.

Royal Station Hotel – The place to go to experience Victorian period charm at its most overwhelming. This magnificent railway hotel has been in operation just over 100 years and although necessary steps toward modernization have been taken, the traditional air remains, especially at teatime in the high-ceilinged lounge. Naturally, it's convenient to the station. Station Rd. (phone: 53681). Expensive.

Viking Hotel – Large (187 rooms), centrally located, and with excellent service, the *Viking* is an expanse of Scandinavian modernity on the banks of the River Ouse. The restaurant specializes in local dishes you will never have heard of, including Filey Cobble stew, which you can consume with some Theakston's Old Peculier ale and round off with a taste of Brontë liqueur. North St. (phone: 59822). Expensive.

Abbots Mews Hotel – Located in a quiet cul-de-sac a few minutes' walk from the city center, this was a coachman's cottage in Victorian times. 6 Marygate La., Bootham (phone: 34866). Moderate.

Chase Hotel – The building is nineteenth century with later additions and it overlooks the Knavesmire racecourse. This is a pleasant, traditional sort of hostelry, about 1.5 miles from the center. Tadcaster Rd. (phone: 707171). Moderate.

Coach House Hotel – The seventeenth-century origins of this guesthouse are still much in evidence, with oak-beamed ceilings throughout. It's located in the same, traffic-free cul-de-sac as the *Abbots Mews Hotel*. There are no private baths. 20/22 Marygate, Bootham (phone: 52780). Moderate.

The Post House – Large, modern, and built close to the ground, this is about 1.5 miles from the center. Part of it faces the racecourse; restaurant and other public rooms are arranged around a cedar of Lebanon tree planted in the garden of the manor house that used to occupy the site. There are 104 rooms and a sauna. Tadcaster Rd. (phone: 707921). Moderate.

Ashcroft Hotel – The 2.5-acre setting with a view of the River Ouse compensates for this hotel's distance from the city center (1 mile). Specify private bath. 294 Bishopthorpe Rd. (phone: 59286). Inexpensive.

Hill Hotel – This Georgian establishment is family run, and since it has only 14 rooms, staying here is like staying in a private home — with private bath or shower, use of a delightful garden, and cordon bleu cuisine. About 2 miles from city center. 60 York Rd., Acomb (phone: 790777). Inexpensive.

Jorvik Hotel – Small and modest — about half of the rooms have private bath. The *Jorvik* faces the Abbey Gate and the eleventh-century St. Olave's Church. 52 Marygate, Bootham (phone: 53511). Inexpensive.

Punch Bowl Hotel – Here's a coaching inn that became an almshouse that became a home before it became a home-away-from-home again. It's a charming old place next to Micklegate Bar, with a restaurant serving very English food, especially at Sunday lunch. Blossom St. (phone: 22619). Inexpensive.

EATING OUT: Yorkshire's reputation for mountainous portions of everything is as apparent in its major city as anywhere else in the county, although the more cosmopolitan restaurants are less likely to plump you out of all proportion than those that pride themselves on real Yorkshire kitchens. The most renowned local specialty, of course, is roast beef with Yorkshire pudding (see

Sins). And if you thought there was nothing as American as apple pie, be advised that — topped with a slice of Wensleydale cheese — this is just as much of an institution here as it is back home. Parkin, an oatmeal, molasses, and ginger-rich cake, is another Yorkshire institution, traditionally made for Guy Fawkes Day (see *Sharing a Pint*). From $7 to $13 per person will buy a full meal with coffee and dessert (but without wine) in a restaurant listed below as moderate. You'll pay less than $7 at those listed as inexpensive. In addition to its restaurants, several of York's pubs serve good quality bar snacks at lunchtime. The best of these are included in the listings.

Betty's Tea Room – There's nothing better than to come in from York's chilling winter air and wallow in the coziness of toasted, home-baked tea cakes and crumpets puddled in butter, Yorkshire parkin, Brontë-rich fruitcakes, and *Betty's* famous rarebit, made from farmhouse cheddar and Yorkshire ale, grilled on toast, and all according to a secret recipe. Open for main meals, too, either in the licensed restaurant or the cafeteria. Closed Sundays. St. Helen's Sq. (phone: 22323). Moderate.

Charlie's Bistro – The intimate atmosphere here is a favorite with the young set. Lots of steak-based dishes on the menu and Charlie Chaplin photos on the walls. Closed Sundays. Tanner Row (phone: 25120). Moderate.

Lew's Place – Good food, good beer, and good coffee are served in loud, bustling surroundings, and the menu is quite extensive. Closed Sundays. The Ship Inn, King's Staith, King St. (phone: 28167). Moderate.

Plunkets – With some very tasty food, *Plunkets* has a friendly ambience, good music in the background, lots of plants, and quality hamburgers. 9 High Petergate (phone: 37722). Moderate.

Thomas's Wine Bar – Pick your own lunchtime salads from a wide selection or dine in the upstairs bistro in the evening. 3 Museum St. (phone: 54494). Moderate.

Tigga – Some very English meals (roast beef with Yorkshire pudding, apple pie with cheese) are turned out in this Tudor-fronted building, along with some very American (ten varieties of hamburger) ones. There is also a gift shop selling ceramics and other crafts. 49 Goodramgate (phone: 33787).

The Baked Potato Wagon – Spuds to go, baked and blessed with a variety of fillings including mussel salad, curried rice, coleslaw, franks, and 20 others. Open daily until 11 PM. 33 Swinegate (phone: 35950). Inexpensive.

Bibi's Pizzeria – Enormous pizzas, baked in a brick oven, complete with pasta choices and a few other temptations besides. The atmosphere is lively. Closed Sundays at lunch and on Mondays. 115 Micklegate (phone: 34765). Inexpensive.

The Cross Keys – This pub has one of the best shepherd's pies in town (ground beef crowned by mashed potato and lightly grilled). Goodramgate (phone: 59408). Inexpensive.

King's Manor Restaurant – The historic Tudor setting of the York University refectory is open to the public for lunch from noon to 2 PM Mondays through Fridays. Both salads and hot meals are available. Exhibition Sq. (phone: 59861). Inexpensive.

St. William's Restaurant – Once a medieval house for chantry priests, now a luncheon spot for salads, quiche, teatime tea, and cakes. Stop in after visiting the nearby Minster or when you tire of brass rubbing. College St. (phone: 34830). Inexpensive.

York Wholefood Restaurant – The emphasis here is on unprocessed, additive-free, natural ingredients done up in various vegetarian dishes. Closed Friday and Saturday afternoons and Sundays. 98 Micklegate (phone: 56804). Inexpensive.

SHARING A PINT: York has an embarrassment of riches when it comes to pubs. There are some 150 all told, quite a few of them crammed with character and characters. The drink is beer, especially beer from the local breweries and especially the famous Theakston's Old Peculier. *Ye Old Starre Inn,* easily located at 40 Stonegate by the gallows right across the road, is York's oldest alehouse. Its name was first recorded in 1644 and it has been a popular lodging house both for actors from the Theatre Royal and for church dignitaries visiting the Minster. Today's interior is Victorian. The *Bay Horse* pub, 55 Blossom St., where you can try the locally brewed John Smith beer, and the tiny *Blue Bell,* Fossgate, are other places to imbibe in a Victorian setting. The *King's Arms,* on King's Staith, is still sometimes flooded in winter with waters from the adjacent embankment — a board records the various flood levels. At the *Roman Bath,* St. Sampson's Sq., customers can view genuine Roman steam baths, or rather their 2,000-year-old remains. General Wolfe, who lost his life winning Québec for the British, spent part of his youth in the *Black Swan Inn,* Peasholme Green. It was built as a merchant's house in the sixteenth century, and a room upstairs was used for illegal cockfighting. *Young's Hotel,* 25 High Petergate, is reputedly on the site of the birthplace of Guy Fawkes, the man who tried (unsuccessfully) to blow up the British Parliament in 1605, bequeathing to children all over England an annual (November 5) excuse to burn him in effigy to the accompaniment of firecrackers.

DIVERSIONS

For the Body

Great Golf

True golf devotees contend that the finest — and most authentic — golf courses in the world are found in Britain and Ireland. This is hardly surprising since the sandy land that runs along their coasts was the terrain that first spawned the game. It's hard to believe that less than a century ago golf was virtually unknown anywhere outside Scotland, though the Scots proved great apostles of the game, spreading the word from Perth (where the first recognizable 6-hole course is thought to have been constructed on the city's North Inch), St. Andrews, Prestwick, and Dornoch.

These are the icons of a game that has gripped the attention of an entire planet, and even now the courses found in Scotland, England, Northern Ireland, and the Irish Republic provide a very different sense of the game than can be acquired anywhere else on earth. These are the courses that owe the greatest debt to nature as golf course architect — relics of the old, totally natural links on which the game evolved. In the book *The World Atlas of Golf* the origin of the game is described with these words, "To this day nobody knows who laid them out . . . there were no fairways, no tees, and no greens, simply agreed starting and finishing points. The game had reached St. Andrews, Carnoustie, Leith, Dornoch, Montrose, North Berwick, and Musselburgh by the beginning of the sixteenth century. Golf thus became established on linksland . . . St. Andrews became — and still is — one long fairway, with nine holes out to a distant point, and nine holes back . . . designs incorporated stone walls, blind shots, hedges, irregularly-shaped mounds and greens in geometric shapes."

But it's more than history that lures generations of modern-day golfers to the game's breeding grounds. The intensity of the challenge found on these courses remains as vital as ever, and the chance to pit one's own skill against the achievements of golf's greatest historic figures is nearly irresistable. Not to play these courses at least once in a lifetime is not to know the real horizons of the game.

SUNNINGDALE, Sunningdale, Berkshire, England: While the Old Course is considered the championship layout here, the New is probably the harder of the two. When you play them, you will discover that the decision on difficulty is an arbitrary one at best. Fairways and greens are meticulously maintained, and this is perhaps the finest single brace of courses in England. Private but approachable. Information: Sunningdale Golf Club, Ridgemount Rd., Sunningdale, Berkshire, England (phone: 0990-21681).

WENTWORTH, Virginia Water, Surrey, England: The East Course at Wentworth is generally considered the prettiest of the three courses and can do wonders for a shaky backswing. (There's also a par 3 layout here.) But it's the West Course that is sometimes not so affectionately called the "Burma Road." For a high-handicap player, the West is not unlike putting an innocent's head into the mouth of an unfriendly lion, and especially from the back tees, the cry of "You can't get there from here!" is continually heard. Again, it's a private club that's likely to offer access to traveling players on weekdays with prior notice—upon presentation of your own club membership card and a letter from your club president. Information: Wentworth Golf Club, Virginia Water, Surrey GU25 4LF, England (phone: 09904-2201).

ROYAL LIVERPOOL, Hoylake, Merseyside, England: More properly called "Hoylake" after its location at the mouth of the Dee estuary, this is the site where the first British amateur championship was held. The first international competition was also played here between England and Scotland in 1902. The course contains one controversial aspect: It's possible to be out-of-bounds here and still lie within the course. At the seventh hole, it's possible to hit a perfect long iron directly at the heart of the green and see the ball hop over a bank to lie out-of-bounds, a scant few yards from the flag. This is not a course for the faint of heart. Information: Royal Liverpool Golf Club, Meols Dr., Hoylake, Merseyside, England (phone: 051-632-3101).

ROYAL LYTHAM & ST. ANNES, Lytham St. Annes, Lancashire, England: Possessed of little visual splendor and set in an essentially urban setting, the course remains one of the most difficult of all the tracks in Britain. Nerve and subtlety are both required here, and the course has maintained a special place on the British Open championship rota. Don't be deceived by the apparent tranquillity; the course is a test of golf that's among the finest in Britain. Information: Royal Lytham & St. Annes, Links Gate, Lytham St. Annes, Lancashire FY8 3LQ (phone: St. Annes 0253-724206).

ROYAL BIRKDALE GOLF CLUB, Southport, Lancashire, England: The site is one of England's most compelling, amid a stunning expanse of dunes on the Lancashire coast. This layout has hosted more championships and international competitions than any other course in Britain since the end of World War II, and is a layout of surpassing challenge. The final six holes cover almost 2.5 miles, and it takes supreme accuracy — rather than raw power — to avoid the proliferation of fairway bunkers. Information: Royal Birkdale Golf Club, Waterloo Rd., Southport, Lancashire, England (phone: Southport 0704-67920).

GANTON GOLF CLUB, Ganton, Yorkshire, England: The east coast of England is not well known for its golfing venues, but this course in Yorkshire is one of Britain's finest inland layouts. The holes are set on open heathland, more lush than the conventional seaside links. The prime hazards here are bunkers and gorse that have been set in the most diabolical positions, especially those placed alongside and amid fairway landing areas. Perhaps the greatest lure here is the variety of challenge that requires consummate concentration. Information: Ganton Golf Club, Ganton, North Yorkshire, England YO12 4PA (phone: 09444-329).

ROYAL ST. GEORGE'S GOLF CLUB, Sandwich, Kent, England: This corner of Kent is rich in history and no course has a more constant involvement with the evolution of English championship golf. It was here that the first American ever won the British Amateur championship, and where Walter Hagen became the first American to win the British Open. The course, often called "Sandwich," was also the site for the first Walker Cup matches ever held in England. It is a place where players interested in the heritage of the game will want to make their own mark. Information: Royal St. George's, Sandwich, Kent CT13 9PB England (phone: Sandwich 0304-613090).

ROYAL AND ANCIENT GOLF CLUB, St. Andrews, Fife, Scotland: This is the prime magnet that draws all of the world's golfers, for this course dates, they say, from the fifteenth century. Its aura is only slightly diminished by the bathers and strollers who consistently cross the first and eighteenth fairways of the Old Course — it's the shortest route to the beach — though once out on the course, its extreme difficulty and subtly careful design become more readily apparent. There are three other courses on the same site — the Eden, Jubilee, and New (which was *opened* in 1894) — but it's the Old that you must play. Make your plans carefully to play here on the right day, because there's no play on the Old Course on Sunday. Information: Links Management Committee, Golf Pl., St. Andrews, Fife K416 9JA Scotland (phone: 0334-75757).

GLENEAGLES, Auchterarder, Perthshire, Scotland: The Scots tend to denigrate the superb quartet of courses here because they do not conform to the treasured linksland tradition. But visiting golfers will fall prey to no such prejudice, and the King's Course in particular is an absolute joy to play. It's also consistently in the best condition of any Scottish course, and the extraordinary hotel here is reason enough for a visit. Information: Gleneagles Hotel Golf Course, Auchterarder, Perthshire PH3 1NF, Scotland (phone: 07646-3543).

CARNOUSTIE, Carnoustie, Tayside, Scotland: Just 5 miles from St. Andrews as the crow flies (or 25 miles by road) is this site of half a dozen British Open golf tournaments. If the Medal Course (the best of the trio of tracks here) is the least impressive of the championship Scottish courses at first glance, it takes only one round of play to appreciate its true value. It encompasses the very essence of what's best about playing golf in Scotland, and the back nine in particular — with the famous fourteenth hole called "Spectacles" — and the three backbreaking finishing holes will leave you with memories (not necessarily pleasant) that you will not soon forget. Information: Carnoustie Golf Links, Links Parade, Carnoustie, Tayside DD7 7JE, Scotland (phone: 0241-53249).

THE HONOURABLE COMPANY OF EDINBURGH GOLFERS, Gullane, East Lothian, Scotland: Most commonly called "Muirfield," this is probably the single best course in Scotland — and the most difficult to gain access to. If you'd like to confront a punishing kind of persecution, write ahead on your own club stationery and ask for a specific tee-off time. It is normally granted on weekdays, but *must* be arranged in advance. The status of Muirfield has grown with each decade since its founding in 1744, and it's the golf club with the longest continuous existence in the world. Tucked along the south shore of the Firth of Forth, Muirfield is both beautifully simple and totally challenging. Note that women are not admitted as members and are permitted on the course only when playing with a member of the opposite sex—and then only on weekdays. Information: The Honourable Company of Edinburgh Golfers, Muirfield, Gullane, East Lothian EH31 2EG, Scotland (phone: 0620-842123).

ROYAL DORNOCH, Dornoch, Highland, Scotland: No course in the world offers more wild beauty than this northernmost of the globe's great golf layouts. The course sweeps in a great curve along the shores of the Dornoch Firth, a site of splendid isolation. London is more than 600 miles away, and the wind can be a roaring gale. Still, there are few who have ever played here who have not felt a singular elation from the experience. Information: Royal Dornoch, Dornoch, Highland, Scotland (phone: 086-281-219).

PRESTWICK, Prestwick, Strathclyde, Scotland: This famed course was the site of the first twelve British Open Championships. It has recently been put off the British Open rota because of its limited facilities for handling crowds, but the historic associations in which this course is involved still make it worth playing. However, when the wind comes out of the east, you may need earplugs to drown out the din from neighboring Prestwick Airport. Information: Prestwick Golf Club, Links Rd., Prestwick KA9 19G, Ayrshire, Scotland (phone: 0292-77404).

ROYAL TROON, Troon, Strathclyde, Scotland: Laid out along the beach, with the outgoing nine heading virtually straight down the strand and the closing nine paralleling it only a few yards inland, the only distraction is that the course lies directly below the flight path into Prestwick Airport. So it sometimes seems as though players are about to be sucked up into the jet wash. Another classic British Open layout, it is one of the few important private clubs in Scotland, though playing privileges are usually made available to visitors who are members of clubs in the US (providing, that is, that they're men; women are admitted only to certain areas on certain days). Information: Royal Troon Golf Club, Craigend Rd., Troon, Strathclyde, Scotland (phone: 31-15-55).

TURNBERRY HOTEL GOLF COURSE, Turnberry, Strathclyde, Scotland: The two courses here, the Ailsa and the Arran, are quite close in quality, but it's the Ailsa on which the British Open was played in 1977. The wind blows in from the sea, and it sometimes takes an act of courage just to stand up on the craggy tees and hit out into the teeth of what occasionally seems like a major gale. The beautiful *Turnberry Hotel* provides some respite from the elements, but the golfing challenge is the real lure here. Information: Turnberry Hotel Golf Course, Turnberry, Strathclyde KA26 9LT, Scotland (phone: 06553-202).

ROYAL PORTHCAWL, Porthcawl, South Glamorgan, Wales: Not a links course in the strictest sense, though there are occasional sandhills. The main hazards, however, are gorse, hummocks, heather, and deep bunkers. The good news is that the lay of the land permits players to look across Bristol Channel to the long dark line of the Somerset coast. Founded in 1891, the course combines links and heathland play, and there's a particularly high premium on a golfer's ability to place shots accurately against often furious natural elements. Just trying to find the fairway here can be a humbling experience. Information: Royal Porthcawl Golf Club, Porthcawl, South Glamorgan CF36 3UW, Wales (phone: 065671-2251).

BALLYBUNION, Ballybunion, Co. Kerry, Irish Republic: No less an authority than Herbert Warren Wind calls this one of the ten toughest courses in the world, and you will have no reason to disagree. The course is laid out at the point where the Shannon River estuary meets the Atlantic Ocean, and you should be not the least concerned that the out-of-bounds area beside the fourteenth hole is a graveyard. Welcome to Ireland. Information: Ballybunion Golf Club, Co. Kerry, Irish Republic (phone: 068-27146).

KILLARNEY GOLF AND FISHING CLUB, Killarney, Co. Kerry, Irish Republic: There are now two courses here beside the legendary lakes, but it's the older course that is by far the better. The scenery is startling and dramatic in this fabled spot, and it may take an act of will to keep your head down, though it may not be worth the effort. The sight of the lakes framing the purple mountains is a once-in-a-lifetime experience. Information: Killarney Golf and Fishing Club, Mahoney's Point, Killarney, Co. Kerry, Irish Republic (phone: 064-31034).

PORTMARNOCK, Portmarnock, Co. Dublin, Irish Republic: This fabled layout (just outside Dublin) is perhaps the best single course in the Republic. The short flag sticks, which are set on springs to let them swing freely in the breeze, tell you something about the wind hazards here, though again the quality of the course — especially the greens — is superb. Be prepared for soaring scores but a bracing outing. Information: Portmarnock Golf Club, Portmarnock, Co. Dublin, Irish Republic (phone: 323082).

ROYAL DUBLIN, Dollymount, Co. Dublin, Irish Republic: The "other" Dublin area golfing magnet that, though second to Portmarnock, still deserves a place among Europe's best. Again, the winds blow here and the rough grows to a size not normally known in the New World. Information: Royal Dublin Golf Club, Dollymount, Dublin 3, Irish Republic (phone: 336-346).

LAHINCH, Lahinch, Co. Clare, Irish Republic: This extraordinary course has been known to inflict players with every plague save famine and flood. It has one short par 5 that has been lengthened a bit by putting something that looks like the Great Wall of China in the middle of the fairway, and to add a little extra spice to your round, there's a 145-yard par 3 that's completely blind. Would you like to guess how they managed that? Our pick for the best in the west of Ireland. Information: Lahinch Golf Club, Lahinch, Co. Clare, Irish Republic (phone: Lahinch 3).

COUNTY SLIGO GOLF CLUB, Rosses Point, Co. Sligo, Irish Republic: More popularly called "Rosses Point," this western Irish links maintains the conflict between golfer and the Atlantic ocean breezes. How you play here depends a lot on which way the prevailing hurricane happens to be blowing. Rosses Point is not quite as tight a course as the other Irish monsters, and some of its greens are even reachable by mere mortals in regulation figures. Chances are that this is the Irish golf course where your spirits (not your score) will soar. Information: County Sligo Golf Club, Rosses Point, Co. Sligo, Irish Republic (phone: 1071-77186).

WATERVILLE GOLF CLUB, Waterville, Co. Kerry, Irish Republic: A modern resort hotel adjoins this newest of the first-class Irish courses. But don't get the idea that this is a resort course, since the layout is as rugged as the surrounding countryside. The course plays between the Atlantic coast and an inland lake that's best known to trout fishermen. And this is the longest (7,116 yards) of the Irish tracks. Though long teeing areas allow the course to be shortened to under 6,000 yards, playing from the back tees here can make for a very exhausting afternoon. Information: Waterville Golf Club, Waterville Lake Hotel, Co. Kerry, Irish Republic (phone: Waterville 56-73-81).

ROYAL PORTRUSH, Portrush, Co. Antrim, Northern Ireland: Though the "troubles" in Northern Ireland persist, the golf remains above the internecine disputes. The Dunluce Course is the championship layout here and is named after the striking old castle that is perched on the white cliffs above the fairways. The wind off the North Sea is usually intense and constant. Information: Royal Portrush Golf Club, Dunluce Rd., Portrush, Co. Antrim BT56 8JQ, Northern Ireland (phone: 0265-2311).

ROYAL COUNTY DOWN, Newcastle, Co. Down, Northern Ireland: This is "where the Mountains of Mourne sweep down to the sea." The British Amateur championship was played here a few years ago, and there are hazards in certain places that can prove rather startling to weak-kneed players. The minutes of the founding club meeting in 1889 reported that "the Secretaries were empowered to employ Tom Morris to lay out the course at a cost not to exceed £4." God alone only knows how Old Tom hacked this course out of the rough sandhills for that price, but he sure made a beauty. Information: Royal County Down Golf Club, Newcastle, Co. Down, Northern Ireland (phone: 23314).

Tennis

Britain practically closes down in late June or early July during the fortnight of the Wimbledon Lawn Tennis Championships. Ticket touts do a brisk trade at the queues outside the gate (and even advertise in the personal columns of the newspapers), and those who aren't lucky enough to secure tickets stay home and watch the competition on their televisions.

This passion has definitely had its effect on the number of participants in the sport, and the population of courts, players, clubs, and cute little robin's-egg blue outfits has soared in the last few years; although tennis still has a long way to go before it becomes the national mania in Britain and Ireland that it is in the US, there are now hundreds of thousands of players, and courts are seldom hard to find. While you still wouldn't come here to play tennis, you should be sure to pack your racquet and your tennis whites, since a tennis match is a fine, rapid way to get off the standard tourist circuit and into local life (which, in the case of British tennis clubs, is most often that of the upwardly mobile middle classes). In these circles, playing well is considered important — but playing as if you mean to win at all costs isn't the style. If you pass muster, you may end the match with at least an invitation to tea.

WHERE TO PLAY

Municipal courts abound in both Britain and Ireland; tourist literature can provide their locations in the towns you'll be visiting. In addition, many hotels have their own courts. In Britain, the five-star establishments are most often your best bet, because instruction is usually available on the premises. In Ireland, Co. Kerry is something of a hotbed of tennis; Killarney alone has seven hotels with hard courts — *Aghadoe Heights, Cahernane, Dunloe Castle,* the *Europe,* the *Gleaneagle,* the *Great Southern,* and the *Torc Great Southern;* and there are courts at the *Sceilig* in Dingle, the *Hotel*

Glencar in Glencar, *Riversdale House* in Kenmare, the *Great Southern* in Parknasilla, the *Earl of Desmond* in Tralee, and the *Butler Arms* and the *Waterville Lake Hotel* in Waterville. Britain's Lawn Tennis Association (Baron's Court, West Kensington, London W14 9EG, England; phone: 01-385-2366) can supply lists of affiliated private tennis clubs where visiting players are almost certain to get a game; the Irish Tennis Association (15 Cill Eanna, Raheny, Dublin 5, Irish Republic; phone: 01-338916) can answer questions about playing around Ireland. For details about courts in Dublin, write to the Dublin Corporation, City Hall, Dublin 2.

If you want to spend more than just a casual hour a day on the courts, you may want to plan your trip around stops at a handful of resorts and tennis schools at which the game is given more than just a passing nod, such as the following.

Beaconsfield School of Lawn Tennis, Beaconsfield, Buckinghamshire, England (phone: 04946-4744). Individual and group courses at modest cost under the supervision of the president of the British Women's Tennis Association. Lodging is with local families; the setting is the rolling, wooded Chiltern Hills.

Fulcher School of Tennis, Thurleston Tennis Centre, Henley Rd., Ipswich, Suffolk IP1 6TD, England (phone: Ipswich 0473-210-903). This center sponsors summer tennis camps for adults and families nearby in Bildeston at Old Buckenham Hall, Brettenham Park.

Tennis Coaching International, Thurleigh Rd., Milton Ernest, near Bedford, Bedfordshire MK44 1RF, England (phone: Milton Ernest 02302-2914). An extensive program of courses at private and municipal clay, asphalt, and grass courts in the area. Videotape and ball machines and backboards are available.

Tennis Europa, 35 Cobden Ave., Bitterne Park, Southampton SO2 4FU, England (phone: 0703-556415). Residential junior and adult courses at every level, from beginner on up, at centers in Swanage and Guildford; videotapes record your efforts against ball machines.

Mount Olympus Country Leisure Estate and Hotel, Hartlebury Rd., Stourport-on-Severn DY13 9LT, England (phone: 02993-77333). Special tennis holiday programs May through September. Accommodation is on the premises and the atmosphere is about two parts country club and one part tennis — charming and purely British. Squash is also available.

Holbrook House Hotel, Holbrook, Wincanton, Somerset BA9 8BS, England (phone: 0963-323-77). No coaching is offered but an all-weather court and a grass court adjoining this charming centuries-old former country house are available to guests.

Kelly's Strand Hotel, Rosslare, Co. Wexford, Irish Republic (phone: 053-32114). Good tennis facilities, including indoor courts, plus a coach, at a family-run hotel that is famous for its food.

WHERE TO WATCH

The big deal is unquestionably the *Wimbledon Lawn Tennis Championships,* which take place in late June or early July at the All England Lawn Tennis and Croquet Club. Still a magnet to players good enough to compete for much bigger cash prizes elsewhere, this tourney is an experience even if you've never held a racquet. Grass courts, strawberry teas, and the legendary Centre Court make for such a spectacle that you may find the world-class matches that are going on quietly on all the outlying lawns to be hardly more than side shows. Good seats for late-round matches are completely sold out months in advance, as are many seats throughout the tourney; and there are long lines for the tickets that are available. However, patience is generally rewarded. Centre Court and Court Number One seats are allocated by lottery. Write for the allocation form in October and return it with a remittance by the application deadline, the following January 31. (The address is: All England Lawn Tennis and Croquet Club,

Church Rd., Wimbledon, London SW19 5AE, England.) If you've been successful, tickets arrive in May; otherwise, your money is returned. Vacation America (555 Fifth Ave., New York, NY 10017; phone: 212-490-3800) and Fourways Travel, Ltd. (950 Third Ave., New York, NY 10022; phone: 212-935-5180, and toll-free from outside New York State, 800-223-7872) both offer packages that include Wimbledon tickets as part of the deal.

In the Irish Republic, the *Irish Open* is the major event of the season. Although it's not now a major tournament, a number of up-and-coming players from the international circuit usually make the scene. For more information on other Irish tourneys, contact the Irish Tennis Association (above).

Horsing Around

Britain and Ireland are among the world's most horse-mad nations — as they have been practically ever since the Romans, and later the Normans, brought horses to Britain many centuries ago. There were races as early as the twelfth century at London's Smithfield Market. Period romances speak of races between knights and noblemen. Later, Henry VIII and James I kept stables (the latter's at Newmarket), and from James II on down, English monarchs have been horse fanciers. Elizabeth II, who keeps a stable and rides regularly, can be at her most animated when urging on her horse. Princess Anne, who ranks in the international class in the demanding game of three-day eventing, competes in shows all over the country with her husband, Captain Mark Phillips. In Ireland, "The Race" is a national passion, and the horses and their trainers are legendary among horse lovers all around the globe. Millions of pounds worth of Irish-bred horses are exported every year.

For travelers, the ubiquity of the mania for horses means that equestrians will never want for a common ground for conversation in the village pubs around Britain and Ireland; and that horse-oriented vacations abound in both nations.

MEETS, SHOWS, AND RACES

You'll be meeting Britons and the Irish on their favorite turf when you take in one of the dozen international shows and hundreds of national events held in both Britain and Ireland every year. Britain alone has some 60 racecourses — 17 devoted solely to flat racing (whose season runs from the third week in March to the first week in November), 24 solely to National Hunt racing (or steeplechasing, whose season begins early in August and ends in June), and the rest with facilities for both. Major courses include *Ascot,* near Windsor in Berkshire (see below); *Doncaster's Town Moor* course, in South Yorkshire (the successor to two other courses that flourished in the area as early as 1595), home of the William Hill Futurity, the former Observer Gold Cup, a mile-long contest for 2-year-olds, and of the St. Leger Stakes, a September race for 3-year-old colts and fillies and the last classic of the flat racing season and the third in Britain's Triple Crown; *Epsom,* in Surrey (see below); the lovely *Goodwood,* situated in Sussex in the Duke of Richmond's Park, especially noted for the 1-mile Sussex Stakes, held in late July; *Newmarket,* the celebrated old course in Cambridgeshire, England's flat-racing headquarters; and *Sandown Park,* founded in 1875, now the home of the Eclipse Stakes, a 1¼-miler run every July since 1886 and named to honor the eighteenth-century nonpareil from whom all of the world's thoroughbred race horses are said to be descended. (This animal, who prompted his owner's now apocryphal remark "Eclipse first, the rest nowhere" didn't compete until he was five — but placed first in every race he entered.) The Triple Crown of the British racing season goes to the horse

420 DIVERSIONS / Horsing Around

that wins Newmarket's Two Thousand Guineas, the Epsom Derby, and Doncaster's St. Leger. (Newmarket, the center of flat-track racing in England and the focal point of British training, is also the home of a number of stud farms, including the National Stud, open to the public on special days during August; Tattersalls, the celebrated English horse auctioneer founded in London in 1766, conducts a number of sales throughout the year, the most important being the two Yearling Sales held in fall.)

Tracks are always grass — rather than dirt or a synthetic surface as in many countries — so that meetings last only 4 or 5 days at a stretch (just 3 days in winter), and are spaced far enough apart to give the turf time to recover between meetings; the nationwide schedule is arranged so that there's always something going on in each region of the country. For dates and locations of upcoming weeks' fixtures (as racing events are called here), consult listings in newspapers such as *The Sporting Life*. A season-long fixtures calendar is available in booklet form from the Racing Information Bureau, Winkfield Rd., Ascot, Berkshire SL5 7HX, England (phone: 0990-25912). This organization's excellent *A Day at the Races: A Newcomer's Guide to Racing* — which describes, among other things, how to bet — is also worth getting.

Ireland's fixtures calendar includes some 280 race meetings at 27 racecourses, all of them wonderfully entertaining, with the brouhaha of bettors calling out the names of horses and "on course men" shouting the odds as they are posted on a board in the stands, wiped out, and reposted as the wagers are placed. At Fairyhouse and Punchestown, 14 and 20 miles from Dublin respectively, there are large enclosures where families picnic in the grass and watch the goings-on. At festival meetings in Punchestown in April, Killarney and Galway in July, Tramore in mid-August, Tralee in late August or early September, and Listowel in mid-September, all the inhabitants for miles around stop work to watch the races. (The Tralee event takes place at the same time as the *International Rose of Tralee Festival*, a nonstop, week-long wingding.) Things are more informal — a bit more unbridled — in Ireland than on the other side of the Irish Sea. Ireland's Newmarket is the Curragh, where racing has been going on ever since the third century AD; the main races nowadays are the *Irish Sweeps Derby*, the *Irish Guinness Oaks*, the *Irish St. Leger*, and the *One Thousand Guineas* and the *Two Thousand Guineas* (nicknamed, respectively, the One and Two Thousand Guinnesses). The *Irish National Stud*, adjacent to the Curragh, where you can see some of the nation's greatest stallions and mares, is open to the public for nothing more than payment of a small admission charge; the *Irish Horse Museum*, also on the grounds, has displays that tell about horses from prehistoric days until present, with good coverage of draft horses as well as racing, hunting, show jumping, and steeplechasing. (For details, contact the Manager, Irish National Stud, Tully, Co. Kildare, Irish Republic; phone: 045-21251). For a calendar of all races, and for the latest dates of those described below, contact the Irish Racing Board, 9 Merrion Sq., Dublin 2, Irish Republic (phone: 761171).

GRAND NATIONAL, Aintree, near Liverpool, England: The grueling steeplechase described in Enid Bagnold's *National Velvet* — the most famous race of its kind and the premiere event of the steeplechase season subjects competitors to 4½ lung-tearing miles over wickedly mischievous banks and ditches and extremely high fences reputed to be bigger than those of any other steeplechase course in the world; it's so tough that only a small percentage of competitors even finish, and only a half-dozen horses have won the competition even twice in more than a century. Fences such as the Chair, grim and formidable, and Becher's Brook, named after the brilliant jockey who fell there during the first Liverpool steeplechase in 1839, occasion thrills and spills that you'll remember for years to come: This is the sort of race that warms even those who don't know a Totalisator from a tic-tac man. At least, seeing it will help you understand the comment of the *Liverpool Courier* after the first race: "All men of ardent feelings love moderate danger for the very excitement it produces and the intrepidity it brings to

DIVERSIONS / Horsing Around 421

action." On the night before, be sure to stop in at the cavernous cocktail lounge of the immense, rococo *Adelphi Hotel* to see the jockeys who will prove the point on the morrow. The Grand National takes place annually at the end of March or early in April over a Thursday, Friday, and Saturday. (The main event is held on Saturday.) For details, contact the Aintree Racecourse, Aintree, Liverpool L9 5AS, England (phone: 051-523-2600).

ROYAL ASCOT, Ascot, Berkshire, England: The June meeting at this racecourse on the southern edge of Windsor Great Park, 25 miles west of London and just 5 miles from Windsor Park, has enjoyed royal patronage ever since Queen Anne drove over to watch the first races on the Ascot Common in 1711 — and it is still considered a high point of the London social season. Ascot is where Eliza Doolittle (of George Bernard Shaw's *Pygmalion* and Lerner and Loew's *My Fair Lady*) first encountered high society; things were oh-so-social then, and they still are today. In the Royal Enclosure — the pricey part of the seating area — men still wear top hats and morning coats, and women dresses of little-girl frilliness or exhibitionistic skimpiness (depending on the wearer's temperament). Models come here hoping to catch a photographer's eye — and launch a career; while yet other females, including more than one dowager oddball, show up in preposterous bonnets. The key race in the meeting is the Ascot Gold Cup — a 2½-miler that ranks as the most important of British flat racing's long-distance contests. The King George VI and the Queen Elizabeth Stakes, a 1½-miler first run in 1951 during the *Festival of Britain,* takes place at Ascot annually in July. Details: Ascot Racecourse, Ascot, Berkshire SL5 7JN, England (phone: Ascot 22211).

BADMINTON HORSE TRIALS, Badminton, Avon, England: Three-day eventing, Princess Anne's specialty, is one of the toughest tests that horse and rider can face; the trials held annually since 1949 at the Duke of Beaufort's lovely green park in Badminton — the small West Country village that has become something of a fox-hunting mecca because the duke's world-famous pack of foxhounds make their home here — are so important that they're regularly televised, and in prime time no less: Certainly, the trials are the world's longest running and most famous. Over 250,000 people attend. The first part of the event is given over to dressage, the third to the jumping test, and the second to tests of speed and endurance that include the Cross Country — more demanding than show jumping — with some 34 solid fences about 4 feet high and 6 feet wide — many of them brand-new that year; a few of them (such as the Jump into the Lake, the Normandy Bank, and the Quarry) hardy annuals that still manage to send riders' hearts into their throats. While the competitors are jumping over steep-sided ditches and large hedges, you'll follow the crowd of spectators from one large refreshment tent to the next, and toast the success of the brave with large glasses of brandy that are served there. It's also fun to visit the centuries-old stables where the horses are kept, next to the house; to see the Deer Park, full of red and fallow deer; and to browse through the veritable village of shops and exhibits — and not just devoted to sports — that goes up for the duration in the Badminton Park. The competition lasts 4 days and always takes place in April — the precise date depending on that of Easter and on the engagement schedule of the Queen, who always attends and hands out the prizes on the final day. General admission is always available; for grandstand seats for the final Jumping Test in the main arena and the awards presentation that follows, you need to write for tickets early in January. Details: Badminton Horse Trials Office, Badminton, Avon GL9 1DF, England (phone: Badminton 0454-21-272).

THE DERBY STAKES, Epsom, Surrey, England: The race after which the Kentucky Derby was named, first held in 1780 and named after one of its founders, the sporting twelfth earl of Derby, is a carnival as much as a 1½-mile speed trial for 3-year-old fillies and colts. All kinds of people turn up: ancient Gypsy families come to settle debts and arrange marriages; the top-hatted and tail-coated rich with Rolls-Royces and picnic hampers; families with children; Cockneys from the East End just

422 DIVERSIONS / Horsing Around

out for a good time; fortunetellers; gaudy tipsters predicting the winners; bookies with bulging Gladstones stuffed with fivers quoting the odds; their helpers peering through binoculars to the other side of the course, where white-gloved tic-tac men are using age-old hand movements to signal how the money is going. The spectacle of this national festivity — the event that Benjamin Disraeli himself called the Blue Riband of the Turf — has hardly changed a bit since the eighteenth-century English painter George Stubbs memorialized it on canvas. Ever since Sir Charles Bunbury's horse Diomed won the first race in 1780, the Derby Stakes has had a history punctuated with colorful characters, among them the early-nineteenth-century Jem Robinson, who won a thousand pounds on a bet that within a single week, he would win the Oaks and the Derby (the latter for a seventh time), and marry; and Miss Emily Davison, a suffragette who died in 1913 after hurling herself under the hoofs of King George V's Anmer. The meeting usually takes place during the first week in June; the Derby is staged on a Wednesday, and the Oaks — Epsom's other major contest, a 1½-miler for fillies named after the Earl of Derby's shooting box — 3 days later. Buy a grandstand ticket if you must, but it's more fun to watch the goings-on from the hill in the middle of the course. Details: United Racecourses, Ltd., Racecourse Paddock, Epsom, Surrey KT18 5NJ, England (phone: Epsom 26311).

HAMBRO LIFE JUMPING DERBY INTERNATIONAL, Hickstead, West Sussex, England: Incorporating the British Jumping Derby, this August event at the All England Jumping Course ranks as the nation's premiere show-jumping event. The fact that only just over a dozen horses have jumped clear rounds on the course since 1961 should give you an idea of its difficulty; the Derby Bank, one of several permanent obstacles in the International Arena here, is famous among horse folk. Novice jumping, showing classes, and dressage take place in other arenas. The Derby (or any of the other events held here during the year) is worth a visit if only for the look it gives you of Englishmen at play. The whole production is fast and easily understood. Details: The Secretary, All England Jumping Course, Hickstead, West Sussex RH17 5NU, England (phone: Hurstpierpoint 0273-834315).

HORSE OF THE YEAR SHOW, Wembley, near London, England: Hunters, hacks, and ponies show up in October for this important fixture of the British equestrian calendar. The Horse Personalities of the Year awards are always popular, but the whole event presents you with a wonderful display of horseflesh, an equine extravaganza if ever there was one. Details: Horse of the Year Show, Wembley Arena, Wembley, Middlesex HA9 ODW, England (phone: 01-902-1234).

ROYAL INTERNATIONAL HORSE SHOW, Wembley, near London, England: Even if you're among the ignorant folk who might sit in the stands and refer to the dressage display as "those circus horses who dance" — as more than one spectator has been known to do at this immensely popular July annual, over 60 years old and among the most prestigious shows in the international equestrian calendar — its magic will win your heart in a twinkling. You will see dressage, Arabians, hackney ponies in single harness, pairs of ponies, weight-carrying cobs, heavy horse turnouts, private and regimental coaches, and children's ponies ridden sidesaddle; small, lightweight, middleweight, and heavyweight hunters; small and large hacks, ladies' hacks; costers' turnouts, ponies, or donkeys; and more. Jumping competitions keep you on the edge of your seat from start to finish: Sometimes the outcome is in doubt right up until the last sleek animal has taken the last white fence. Midway through each evening's events, there are exhibition riding shows and performances by military bands. Details: Royal International Horse Show, Wembley Arena, Wembley, Middlesex HA9 ODW, England (phone: 01-902-1234).

CONNEMARA PONY SHOW, Clifden, Co. Galway, Irish Republic: These attractive creamy native ponies, the focus of an increasing degree of attention over the last decade, make fine pets — and excellent jumpers, as you'll see at this lively and friendly (but very professionally run) country show first organized over 60 years ago. Some 300 of the finest of Ireland's Connemaras are usually on hand; they are intelligent, full of stamina, versatile, and even-tempered, a real pleasure to see. Details: Connemara Pony Breeders Society, 73 Dalysfort Rd., Salthill, Galway, Co. Galway, Irish Republic (phone: 091-22909).

DUBLIN HORSE SHOW, Dublin, Irish Republic: Whereas other cities wilt during the warm days of summer and the citizens escape to the seaside and the mountains, Dublin is awhirl with activity from the Tuesday after the first Monday in August through the following Saturday, as horse lovers from Britain and the Continent converge on the city for this event, one of the best shows of its kind in the world, and certainly the high point of the year for Dublin society. It was first held in 1868. For Ladies' Day, the Thursday of Horse Show Week, citizens don their best bib and tucker, and every night, Dublin's plusher hostelries play host to elegant hunt balls. Hotel rooms are scarce as hen's teeth — so hard to find, in fact, that if you haven't booked well in advance, you may end up lodging with a family near the showgrounds. The main show-jumping event, held on Friday, is the Nations Cup for the Aga Khan Trophy. Stand tickets for this competition and other important ones are difficult to come by, but standing room is always available. Also in Dublin during Horse Show Week are a series of international polo matches, which take place about 3 miles from the city's center in Phoenix Park. In May, there's show jumping on the Horse Show grounds at the Spring Show. For more information, contact the Royal Dublin Society, PO Box 121, Ballsbridge, Dublin 4, Irish Republic (phone: 01-680645); for housing details, contact Dublin Tourism, 51 Dawson St., Dublin 2 (phone: 01-747733).

IRISH GRAND NATIONAL, Ratoath, Co. Meath, Irish Republic: Ireland's main steeplechase event takes place at Fairyhouse Racecourse annually on Easter Monday, Tuesday, and Wednesday. Everybody who is anybody attends. Details: Norman Colfer, 3 The Georgian Village, Castleknock, Co. Dublin, Irish Republic (phone: 01-214475).

IRISH SWEEPS DERBY, Kildare, Co. Kildare: Irish racing is world famous and Irish-bred horses regularly win the Continent's classic competitions; this event, a 1½-miler for 3-year-olds held at the Curragh annually in late June, is Ireland's star race. Among the other classic races that make this track so important are the One Thousand Guineas (1 mile for 3-year-old fillies, in May); the Two Thousand Guineas (1 mile for 3-year-olds, in May); the Guinness Oaks, founded in 1963 (1½ miles for 3-year-old fillies, in July); and the Irish St. Leger (1¾ miles for 3-year-olds, in October). Details: Irish Racing Board, 9 Merrion Sq., Dublin 2, Irish Republic (phone: 761171).

LIMERICK JUNCTION, Tipperary Town, Co. Tipperary, Irish Republic: If you're jaded by big meetings, this small racecourse named after the nearby railway station, 100 miles from Dublin, is for you. In the heart of racing Ireland — not far from the home of none other than Vincent O'Brien, one of the world's leading buyers, breeders, and trainers of racehorses — this racecourse has events regularly from March through November, and draws a crowd that is at least as interesting as the horses. If you note an equine aspect to the features of some of the onlookers, you're not imagining it: That's what comes of generations of looking after horses. In its own small way, the Limerick Junction course shows offer everything that is delightful about Irish racing — and Irish character. For more information, contact the Irish Racing Board, 9 Merrion Sq., Dublin 2, Irish Republic (phone: 761171).

RIDING HOLIDAYS AND PONY TREKKING

The British and the Irish flock to horse holidays with exactly the same enthusiasm that Americans flock to dude ranches — except that they are more likely to wear jodhpurs than jeans, swing into saddles without horns as well as with, and do their riding at a stable that doesn't always have anything more than a casual arrangement with their lodging place. Top-notch horses, delightful scenery, and the chance to join the natives in one of their favorite pastimes are the main attractions.

DIVERSIONS / Horsing Around

When you do begin to look into the possibilities of an equestrian holiday, you may at first find the lingo bewildering. The term *riding holiday,* for instance, refers to not just any vacation spent on horseback, but specifically to one where you'll trot, canter, occasionally even take small jumps, and get basic instruction either by a full-fledged instructor accredited by the British Horse Society (a BHSI), a British Horse Society–designated assistant instructor (BHSAI), or, in smaller establishments, horse folk who instruct as a summer job. The organizations that sponsor such activities, called "riding holiday centres," may also arrange for you to compete in local shows and contests — great fun — where you may find yourself making horse talk with anyone from a local farmer to the squire's lady. Some riding holiday centers — those termed residential — have accommodations on the premises; some arrange for you to lodge in nearby guesthouses, old coaching inns, quaint hotels, or with local families. Rank beginners and advanced equestrians alike can sign up for riding holidays, which are available year-round.

Pony trekking, on the other hand, involves day-long trips on the back of a sturdy native pony or cob (a stocky, short-legged horse), and has you traveling mainly at a walk — partly because most participants are inexperienced riders, partly because you do your riding across moors, through dense forests, and in steep mountain country mainly in Scotland, the Lake District, the north of England's Dales, and sections of Wales, along narrow trails and roads that don't lend themselves to a faster pace. Absolute novices may be provided with some instruction, but it will ordinarily be at a relatively elementary level (and if you want more than this, you'll want to sign up for a riding holiday). Also, pony trekking has a limited season — usually from about the middle of April until late September or, in some areas, early October. Note that Ponies of Britain, a nonprofit organization that inspects both trekking and riding holiday centers in Britain — an expert on the subjects — suggests that children under 12 will get tired and bored while pony trekking and are generally better off at a riding holiday center that specializes in youngsters. The real joy of pony trekking is the scenery en route, for on horseback, you can cover great sweeps of terrain — forests, fields, and meadows full of ferns or bracken, or spotted here and there with a clump of rosy heather or purplish foxglove and thistle — that may not otherwise be accessible to any but the most intrepid of Wordsworthian walkers. With your saddles squeaking, the horses' hooves pounding out a soothing rhythm, the smell of leather and sweat perfuming the sweet clean air, you'll pass through forest dells to wild clear streams with whitewater lacy as a Renaissance lady's collar; struggle up steep rocky hillsides; and then promenade across their flat summits, with the woods-and-farms countryside spread out at your feet like a piece of green velvet patchwork. It's a bit like taking a long hike — but with someone else doing the walking for you.

The following include some of the best of British and Irish centers offering riding holidays and pony trekking. A more comprehensive list of both types of establishments is available for about £1 plus postage from Ponies of Britain, Ascot Race Course, Ascot, Berkshire SL5 7JN, England (phone: Ascot 0990-26035/26925).

Moat House, Benenden, Kent, England (phone: 058-082-581), or, in the US, Patricia Grindle, 22 Pleasant St., South Natick, MA 01760 (phone: 617-655-7000). An English riding school in the traditional mold. Princess Anne took riding lessons here while a student at the well-known Benenden School nearby.

Earl Soham Lodge Training Centre, Earl Soham, Woodbridge, Suffolk IP13 7SA, England (phone: 072-882-249). General equitation in addition to a number of specialized courses and clinics featuring some of the luminaries of the British horse scene.

Gooseham Barton Stables, Gooseham, Morwenstow, near Bude, Cornwall, England (phone: 028-883204). Lovely riding through quiet, scenic countryside and forests, with a sandy beach nearby. Accommodation in a farmhouse or a self-catering four-berth trailer. For experienced riders and unaccompanied children aged 12 and older; beginners out of peak season only.

Silverdown Riding School, Harwell, Didcot, Oxfordshire OX11 0LU England (phone: 023-586-377). Riding holidays, with dressage courses and gymkhanas in addition to the more usual instruction.

Tarn Hows Hotel, Hawkshead, Ambleside, Cumbria, England (phone: 096-66330). Some riding experience is essential here, but for those who have it, participation is a delight: This is the Lake Country. The hotel boasts magnificent views and the famous tarn is less than a mile distant. March to November.

Porlock Vale Equitation Centre, Porlock, near Minehead, Somerset TA24 8NY, England (phone: Porlock 0643-862-338). Instruction in all branches of equitation at one of Britain's first residential riding establishments.

Ravenshill Trekking and Trail Riding Center, Kielder, Bellingham, Northumberland, England (phone: 0660-50251). Located in the upper reaches of the North Tyne Valley, surrounded on three sides by the Kielder forest, the largest man-made woodland in Europe, the Ravenshill country house is the center for riding holidays with all kinds of horses—well-bred hunters, sturdy Fells ponies, and Welsh ponies alike. Novices are accepted along with experienced riders.

Shilstone Rocks Stud, Widecombe-in-the-Moor, Newton Abbot, Devon TQ13 7TF, England (phone: Widecombe 036-42-281). A riding and trekking center and stud on a Dartmoor farm with a history that goes back to the Domesday Book.

North Wheddon Farm, Wheddon Cross, near Minehead, Somerset TA24 7EX, England (phone: 064-384-224). Riding in the wild moors of surrounding Exmoor National Park, with lodging in a fine, attractive, old Georgian farmhouse.

Crabbet Park Equitation Centre, Worth, near Crawley, West Sussex RH10 45T, England (phone: Crawley 0293-882601). A top-class English equitation center offering courses for riders of all skills and training for British Horse Society examinations.

Highland Riding Centre, Borlum Farm, Drumnadrochit, Highlands, Scotland (phone: 045-62220). This center is especially good for families. There is a donkey for small children to ride, and livelier mounts are available for the experienced. Instruction can be tailored to all levels. Long established and well run.

Blair Castle Trekking Centre, Blair Atholl, Pitlochry, Tayside, Scotland (phone: 079-681263). The Highland ponies here are owned by the Duke of Atholl, and guides from the Atholl estate lead half-day, day-long, and week-long treks. Instruction is available to those who want it.

Cwmyoy Pony Trekking Centre, Daren Farm, Cwmyoy, Gwent NP7 7NR, Wales (phone: Crucorney 087-382-306). Pony trekking through the heather-purpled Black Mountains and Brecon Beacons National Park.

Golden Pheasant Riding Centre, Tal y Garth Farm, Glyn Ceiriog, near Llangollen, Clwyd, Wales (phone: 069-172281). Accommodation is in a comfortable hotel. Instruction is available in stable management as well as riding; there's an enclosed outdoor manège and a cross-country course.

Cae Iago Trekking Centre, Farmers, Llanwrda, Dyfed SA19 8LZ, Wales (phone: 055-85303). Excellent trekking through beautiful wild country, with instruction for all levels of riders and trail rides for the experienced.

Lisderg Riding Centre, Belmont, Co. Offaly, Irish Republic (phone: Belmont 23).

Ashton Equestrian Centre, Castleknock, Co. Dublin, Irish Republic (phone: 01-301046 or 01-307611). Riding lessons for students at all levels.

Anner House Farm, Cloneen, Co. Tipperary, Irish Republic (phone: 052-31201). Private and group lessons.

Horetown House, Foulksmills, Co. Wexford, Irish Republic (phone: 051-63633). Week-long packages with riding lessons and trekking.

Castle Leslie Equestrian Centre, Glaslough, Co. Monaghan, Irish Republic (phone:

047-81700). Riding lessons, with five separate cross-country courses.

Assolas Country House, Kanturk, Co. Cork, Irish Republic (phone: Kanturk 15). Lovely spot with riding-teaching stables nearby.

Churchview Riding Stables, Kilglass, near Strokestown, Co. Roscommon, Irish Republic (phone: Strokestown 47). Rural riding.

Kellett Riding School, Kill, Co. Kildare, Irish Republic (phone: 045-97208). Training for equestrians of all levels by internationally known horsewoman Iris Kellett.

Renvyle House Hotel, Renvyle, Co. Galway, Irish Republic (phone: Renvyle 3).

Whitfield Court Polo School, Waterford, Co. Waterford, Irish Republic (phone: 051-84216). Europe's only residential polo school. Beginners and advanced players alike have attended from more than 25 countries; some call their polo vacation the most memorable of their lives.

Ashbrooke Riding School, Brookeborough, Co. Fermanagh, Northern Ireland (phone: Brookeborough 242). Instruction for riders of all levels; training includes dressage, show-jumping, and cross-country events. Restored housekeeping cottages available.

Newcastle Riding Centre, 35 Carncaville Rd., Castlewellan, Co. Down, Northern Ireland (phone: Newcastle 22694). Riding instruction for beginners upward and escorted pony treks.

POST TREKKING

There's nothing quite so delightful as seeing the country from the back of a horse or sure-footed native pony, heading from inn to inn along narrow trails, abandoned train beds, and down wide sandy beaches — and staying away from the trekking center for up to a week at a time. *Post trekking,* or *trail riding,* as this activity is called, is not widely available, and it is not generally recommended for riders without experience, as it usually involves good horses and a fast enough pace to cover about 25 miles a day. A warm camaraderie usually develops en route, so that you become one of a cohesive band of pilgrims straight out of *Canterbury Tales* as you traverse the miles. That's one reason for going. Post trekking is also a practically worry-free holiday: There are guides to keep you going at a reasonable pace, to make sure you don't get lost, and to arrange for your luggage to be transported from one hostelry to the next. And at the end of each day, there's always a hot bath, a rustic feast, a good night's sleep in a clean-sheeted bed, and one of those massive breakfasts (the kind that make you feel as if it's going to take an Act of Parliament to get you into the saddle) before you hit the trail once again. Two excellent post treks are described below. For information about others, contact the Irish Tourist Board and Ponies of Britain (Ascot Race Course, Ascot, Berkshire SL5 7JN, England; phone: Ascot 0990-26035/26925).

NORTHUMBERLAND, ENGLAND: You can begin either at the Solway Firth in the west or on the North Sea coast in the east for 5- or 6-day trips through the hills and the Scottish Borders country, site of the famous Roman Wall. Trips are available from June to October. Details: Kidlandlee Riding Centre, Harbottle, Morpeth, Northumberland, England (phone: 0669-50254).

ALONG THE CONNEMARA TRAIL, Irish Republic: The particular attraction of this route, beyond the wonderful landscape that unfolds as you travel along pretty hill roads and tracks, are your lodgings in luxurious establishments such as Galway's *Great Southern Hotel,* where the trip begins and ends, and the delightful *Abbeyglen House Hotel* in Clifden, Co. Galway. A highlight of the trip is the final day's romp down a glorious long beach. Your mounts are hunters or half-bred horses, and you can go from May through September. For details, contact: William Leahy, The Connemara Trail, Aille Cross, Loughrea, Co. Galway, Irish Republic (phone: 091-41216).

DINGLE PENINSULA TRAIL, Irish Republic: This adventurous 80-mile circle trip takes you along beaches, out-of-the-way bridle paths through mountain defiles, and lovely stretches of sand in this sea-washed expanse of rugged hills. Accommodation en route is in good guesthouses — and the food is both good and plentiful. Trips are offered from May to October. Details: William J. O'Connor, William J. Riding Stables, Ballyard, Tralee, Co. Kerry, Irish Republic (phone: 066-21840).

IN ROB ROY COUNTRY, SCOTLAND: This is post trekking at its best. You travel from Aberfoyle via The Trossachs, Strathyre, Balquhidder, Killin, Lochearnhead, and Callander on registered Highland ponies. The terrain is magnificent, and the views are superb. May and October. Details: Mr. Hugh McGregor, Baillie Nicol Jarvis Hotel, Ballinton, Thornhill, by Stirling, Scotland (phone: 078-685219).

FROM THE NORTH SEA TO THE ATLANTIC, SCOTLAND: The Scottish highlands are sparsely populated, wildlife-rich, wonderfully historic—and they go on and on and on, for hundreds of square miles. The lochs and glens in the remoter corners are accessible only on horseback and on foot—and that is the beauty of these trips. A 10-day expedition takes in 200 miles of some of Britain's grandest scenery, from the Moray Firth southeast across the Dava Moor, across the Spey River, over the Cromdale Hills, across the eastern flanks of the Cairngorm Mountains, to the western end of Loch Ness, and onward to the sea. A 5-day trip is also available. Details: Tony and Miranda Montgomery, Wester Golford, Moyness, Nairn, Highland, Scotland (phone: Brodie 203).

CARAVANNING

Meandering along a narrow lane flanked by billowing meadows and fields, in a horse-drawn wagon, with grand vistas stretching off toward a purple-hazed horizon, is one of the most relaxed ways you might find to spend a week — and Ireland is one of the few countries in the world where you can see just why. A number of regions of the country have agencies that rent out old-style Gypsy wagons, bright-painted on the outside, fitted out with berths inside; and the roads of the surrounding countryside are small and traffic-free — perfect for this kind of caravanning. The main centers are in counties Cork, Kerry, Leitrim, Limerick, Mayo, and Wicklow. Agents can suggest the most scenic routes; steer you to the beaches, overlooks, quaint old pubs, interesting restaurants, and historic sites in the areas you'll be passing through; and name the best overnighting spots, usually about 10 miles apart. The weekly cost for a caravan that will accommodate four is from £95 to £140, depending on the season. For a list of the half-dozen or so agencies, contact the Irish Tourist Board.

The principal operators include the following:

Blarney Romany Caravans, Blarney, Co. Cork (phone: 021-85700).

Dieter Clissmann Horse-Drawn Caravan Holidays, Carrigmore Farm, Co. Wicklow (phone: 0404-8188).

Slattery's Travel Agency, Tralee, Co. Kerry (phone: 066-21722).

Connemara Horse Caravans, Westport House Country Estate, Westport, Co. Mayo (phone: Westport 130).

Shannon Horse Caravans, Adare, Co. Limerick (phone: 061-43844).

HUNTING

In both Britain and Ireland, hunting — riding to the hounds (as distinct from shooting, which involves going after a quarry with firearms) — is an extremely popular pastime, and there are some 200 hunts each in Britain and Ireland meeting from November until spring. In Ireland alone, an ardent follower could hunt every day of the week

— out on Sunday with the *Bermingham and North Galway;* on Monday with the *County Limerick* or the *Duhallow* in County Cork, which dates from somewhere before 1745; on Tuesday with the *Ormond* in County Tipperary or the *Galway Blazers,* so called because during one convivial evening after the day's outing, the group accidentally set fire to the hotel at which its members were making merry. (John Huston, the famous film director and actor, is among the Blazers' past Masters of Fox Hounds.) On Wednesday, the avid hunter could ride with the *Tipperary,* and on Thursday with the *County Clare* or with County Tipperary's three-century-old *Scarteen Black and Tans,* whose distinctively colored dogs gave a name not only to the hunt but also to a section of the British forces that were in Ireland in 1920. Fridays and Saturdays give an even wider choice. The same situation prevails in Britain. And most hunts, on both sides of the Irish Sea, are delighted to receive guests.

Quite apart from the quality of the horses you will encounter (and the half-thoroughbred Irish hunters command high prices all over Europe for their bred-in ability to take their fences), there is some stupendous scenery awaiting the visitor, and a rider may be forgiven for taking a tumble if distracted by the view — say, over the rolling farmlands of Leicestershire, England's best hunting country, or, in Ireland, across the miles and miles of hand-built loose gray limestone walls, which give the Galway landscape a gritty character — and which make for excellent hunting. Besides Galway, Ireland's best hunt country is in Clare, Limerick, Tipperary, and North Cork, and in the South — Limerick and Cork — you encounter great double banks, one or two yards high and as wide, made of clay and stone.

You'll meet all sorts of hunting and all sorts of terrain in Ireland — and all sorts of people as well, since hunting is a very democratic sport here, with hunt memberships made up not only of the gentry, but also of priests and diplomats, innkeepers and farmers, and a variety of humbler horsemen; those who don't ride, follow the goings-on by bicycle, on foot, or in their cars and stand by for the chance to watch the hounds and the horses passing. From the stirrup cup that almost invariably precedes each meet to the rendezvous afterward in some favored hostelry, the atmosphere is at once efficient, orderly, friendly, and convivial; and the huntsman is judged not only on his skill in horsemanship but by his ability to mix with the hunt and share in the gaiety.

ENGLAND: The most favored hunt country centers on the town of Melton Mowbray in Leicestershire, which is renowned as much for its hunting as for its distinctive pork pies and well-known hunt cake, a rum-laced fruit mixture. The *Quorn, Cottesmore,* and *Belvoir* hunts (this last named for the duke of Rutland's splendid old castle nearby) are known throughout the country; to arrange for a hunt here, contact *Belvoir Vale Riding Centre, Ltd.,* Point Farm, Stathern, Melton Mowbray, Leicestershire, England. *Burrington Farm* (c/o J. S. Raymond Jones, Burrington, near Bristol) can arrange for its guests to hunt with the Mendip Farmers, or the Beaufort, Berkeley, and Quantock Staghounds. Catering to visitors' hunting holidays in Northumberland is the *Percy Arms* in Otterburn, Northumberland NE19 1NR (phone: 0830-20261). Other organizations that can arrange for or advise you on hunting holidays include *Best in Britain,* 48 Epple Rd., London SW6 4DH, England (phone: 01-731-1733), and *Savills Estate Agents,* 20 Grosvenor Hill, London W1 (phone: 01-499-8644). For advice on hunts in other parts of the country, contact The Masters of Foxhounds Association, Parsloes Cottage, Bagendon, Cirencester, Gloucestershire, England (phone: North Cerny 470).

IRISH REPUBLIC: Dedicated huntsmen will tell you that if you can hunt in only one place in Ireland, it should be around Galway, with one of the three Galway hunts: The *Bermingham and North Galway,* which you can contact through Lady Cusack-Smith, Bermingham House, Tuam, Co. Galway (phone: 093-24133); the *County Galway* (the aforementioned Blazers), whose secretary is Lt. Commdr. Stoney, The Kennels, Craughwell, Co. Galway (phone: Craughwell 37); and the *East Galway,* which you can get in touch with through its secretary, Mrs. J. R. North, Northbrook, Kilconnell, Co. Galway (phone: 0905-86617). *Bermingham House* is the place to stay for the Galway hunts; the *Great Southern Hotel* (Eyre Sq., Galway City; phone 091-64041) is also well-appointed and comfortable.

A handful of other hunts here are of special interest to visitors because of their variety of terrain and because of the availability of associated guesthouses and hotels — among them the *County Limerick* (c/o Michael Birchy, Fortgeorge, Rathkeale, Co. Limerick; phone: 061-40833), which is associated with the *Dunraven Arms* in Adare, Co. Limerick (phone: 061-94209); the *Duhallow* (c/o K. Thompson, Brook Lodge, Mallow, Co. Cork; phone: 022-21114), associated with the *Assolas Country House* in Kanturk, Co. Cork (phone: Kanturk 15); the *County Clare* (c/o Mrs. L. Hannon, Ardsolus, Quin, Co. Clare; phone: 065-25601), associated with the *Ballykilty Manor,* Quin, Co. Clare (phone: 065-25627).

Most fox hunt clubs hold cub meets from September to November, for training purposes; you can join these workmanlike affairs, usually held early in the morning, providing you're a proficient rider, by advance arrangement with the secretaries of the individual hunts.

Harrier hunting — the less glamorous sport of riding after the hare — is also done in Ireland at over 30 hunts. Near Dublin, there are three that are excellently run and take visitors by appointment: the *South County Dublin* (c/o Mrs. H. Kavanagh, Brittas Lodge, Brittas, Co. Dublin; phone: 01-582162); *Fingal Harriers* (c/o Mrs. C. J. Haughey, Abbeville, Kinsealy, Malahide, Co. Dublin; phone: 01-450879); and *Bray Harriers* (c/o C. J. Warren, 11 Whitethorn Rd., Dublin 14; phone: 01-694403).

NORTHERN IRELAND: There are 15 flourishing hunt clubs here, including the immensely popular *Iveagh Harriers* (c/o Mr. R. E. Boyd, 3 Mountainview Ter., Banbridge, Co. Down; phone: Banbridge 22468); the *County Down Staghounds* (c/o Mr. Minnis, 74 Ravara Rd., Ballygowan, Co. Down; phone: Ballygowan 316); and the *East Down Foxhounds* (c/o Sven Mackie, Ballydugan House, near Downpatrick, Co. Down; phone: Downpatrick 2048).

Wonderful Waterways and Coastal Cruises

Whether you're dangling your hand from a dinghy or slicing through the waves underneath a billowing sail, being on a boat is something special. People wave and sing and talk to each other, the winds whip at your hair, the waves rock you like a baby in a cradle. The pace seems closer to man's own than that of the Concorde, slowing you down rather than speeding you up, and when your foot touches shore again, you can't help but feel supremely relaxed.

Britain and Ireland, with their literally thousands of miles of shoreline and thousands of miles of inland waterways, offer myriad opportunities for just that kind of refreshment. The British and Irish have always had a love affair with water, and when their own vacations come around, they take to it in droves — and, in the process, support all manner of boat rental operations, sailing schools, and cruising establishments, so that when you come to the islands from abroad, you don't have to have your own craft to enjoy the nations' offshore pleasures.

SAILING

It's possible to sail in the English Channel. Many Britons do — and they savor the challenges posed by its changeable winds and the strong tides. Irish sailors looking for high adventure tackle the North Atlantic, off the exposed west coast. But both Britain and Ireland also offer more forgiving waters that don't, like these, require such stout seagoing yachts and solid sailing experience. In Britain, for instance, there are the sheltered bays along the notched Devon, Essex, and western Scotland coasts; the celebrated Solent, the 3-mile-wide arm of water between the north coast of the Isle of Wight and England's southern shore, south of Southampton, known as the cruising ground of the rich ever since the mid-nineteenth century when Queen Victoria started summering there in a palace-sized "cottage" designed by her husband, Prince Albert; and the coastal waters of East Anglia, where splendid gaff-rigged sailing barges — Thames barges once used for cargo and now revamped to accommodate up to 12 passengers at a time — are common sights. (For particulars on the sailing barge *Victor,* write the Ferry Boatyard, Dorothea Wharf, Lower Upnor, Rochester, Kent.) These popular cruising grounds' counterparts in Ireland are mainly on the east coast, where the waters are relatively calm and the concentration of yachting clubs is high, particularly around Dublin and Belfast; in Dun Laoghaire harbor alone, there are four clubs. Arklow, Bray, Carlingford, Malahide, Skerries, and Wexford are especially heavily used among small-boat sailors. The south and southwest coasts both offer sheltered bays and coves in quantities great enough to put them among most-favored cruising grounds; dinghy sailors congregate around the ports of Ballycotton, Baltimore, Crosshaven, Dunmore East, Kinsale, and Youghal in the south, and Bantry, Dingle Bay, and Tralee Bay (Fenit) in the southwest. Cork City boasts one of the largest natural harbors in the world and provides excellent facilities for cruising and racing; its yacht club was founded in 1720.

When you want suggestions for exactly where to sail in any given area, your best sources in both Britain and in Ireland are local yacht clubs and harbormasters. In Britain, you should also stop in at the pub patronized by the local branch of the Royal National Lifeboat Institution's members, who are apt to be experienced watermen whose families have fished in the area for hundreds of years; their advice will come salted with tales of shipwrecks, which you can contemplate over a pint of beer.

SAILBOAT CHARTERS: These are widely available in resort centers of the most popular sailing areas; experienced sailors can charter bareboats for cruises, while novices can hire their craft with crew. In Ireland, for instance, the latter service is provided by *Hugo du Plessis* (Ballylickey, Bantry, Co. Cork) for trips to Galway's Aran Islands. In Britain, the *Yacht Charter Association* (Lymington Yacht Haven, King Saltern Rd., Lymington, Hampshire SO4 9XY, England) can give details on its members, who have boats of all sizes for charter around the country. Also contact *Scotland Afloat* (Dochgazzoch, Inverness 1V3 6JX; phone: 0463-863202).

SAILING SCHOOLS: If you don't know how to sail and want to learn, you may sign up for a week's sailing course at one of the dozens of sailing schools around the countries. Two organizations see to it that certain minimum safety standards and levels of instruction are met — in Britain, the Royal Yachting Association (Victoria Way, Woking, Surrey GU21 1EQ, England; phone: Woking 04862-5022); and in Ireland, the Irish Association for Sail Training (c/o the Irish Federation of Marine Industries, Confederation House, Kildare St., Dublin 2, Irish Republic; phone: 01-779801). Complete lists of approved schools can be sent on request by the RYA and, for Ireland, by the Irish Yachting Association (87 Upper Georges St., Dun Laoghaire, Co. Dublin, Irish Republic; phone: 01-800239).

DIVERSIONS / Wonderful Waterways and Coastal Cruises

Among the noteworthy schools are the following:

Fowey Cruising School, 22A North St., Fowey, Cornwall PL23 1AQ, England (phone: Fowey 2129). In the Channel Islands, the Scilly Islands, and to all the south coast harbors from Torquay to Penzance.

Jersey Cruising School, Albion House, Gorey, Jersey, Channel Islands (phone: 0534-51983). Sailing in the breezy Channel Islands.

Ocean Youth Club, Ltd., 2 Stoke Gardens, Gosport, Hampshire PO12 1PD, England (phone: 070-17-83630). Some of Britain's finest sailing; mainly for young people aged 15 to 21.

Scimitar Sailing School, 5 Crowsport, Hamble, Hampshire, England (phone: Hamble 042-122-2219). Cruising courses in various locations.

Hayling Sailing School and Windsurfing Centre, Northney Marina, Hayling Island, Hampshire, England (phone: Hayling Island 070-16-67334).

Blue Water Sailing, 11 Saffron Park, Kingsbridge, South Devon, England (phone: 0548-3605).

John Sharp Sailing, Brockles Quay, St. Veep, Lostwithiel, Cornwall, England (phone: Bodmin 0208-872470).

Island Cruising Club, The Island, Salcombe, Devon TQ8 8DR, England (phone: 054-884-3481). Courses in handling cruisers, keelboats, and dinghies, with lodgings aboard the club's own floating hotel, a converted Mersey ferry.

Dolphin Sailing School, The Foreshore, Woodside, Wootton, Isle of Wight PO33 4JR, England (phone: 0983-882-246). Cruising in the Solent with beginners, and, with more experienced crew members, to the waters of the West Country and Brittany.

Tighnabruaich Sailing School, Tighnabruaich, Argyll, Strathclyde PA21 2BD, Scotland (phone: Tighnabruaich 070-081-396).

Lochearnhead Water Sports Centre, Lochearnhead, Tayside, Scotland (phone: Lochearnhead 05673-330).

Riversdale Sailing Centre, Riversdale Farmhouse, Ballinamore, Co. Leitrim, Irish Republic (phone: Ballinamore 122). Instruction on tranquil Lake Garadice, inland.

Baltimore Sailing School, Baltimore, Co. Cork, Irish Republic (phone: Baltimore 41).

International Sailing Centre, 5 East Beach, Cobh, Co. Cork, Irish Republic (phone: 021-811237). Based in Cork Harbor, where yachtsmen have been sailing as a sport for nearly three centuries; the world's first yacht club, the Cork Water Club, was founded here in 1720.

St. Brendan's School of Sailing and Navigation, Derrymore West, Tralee, Co. Kerry, Irish Republic (phone: 066-30132).

Dineen's Sailing Centre, 51 St. Brendan's Ave., Dublin 5, Irish Republic (phone: 01-310452). In the nearly always calm waters at Malahide.

Glenan's Irish Sailing Centres, 1 Kildare St., Dublin 2, Irish Republic (phone: 01-76775). An international institution that originated in France in 1947. Three centers in Ireland.

Dun Laoghaire Sailing School, 115 Lower Georges St., Dun Laoghaire, Co. Dublin, Irish Republic (phone: 01-806654). Cruising in the Irish Sea, to Wales and the Isle of Man. Wintertime navigation classes—and windsurfing as well.

Galway Sailing Centre, Rinville, Oranmore, Galway, Co. Galway, Irish Republic (phone: 091-63522). Sailing in lovely Galway Bay.

Ocean Youth Club, Maritime House, 103 Corporation St., Belfast, Northern Ireland (phone: 0232-32567). A branch of the school in Gosport, Hampshire.

Strangford Sailing School, 23 Killinchy St., Comber, Co. Down, Northern Ireland (phone: Comber 0247-872458). Courses for all ages in cruisers and dinghies.

Day trips around Strangford Lough and charter boats are also available. *Ulster Sailing School,* West Pier, Harbour, Carrickfergus, Co. Antrim BT38 7BQ, Northern Ireland (phone: Carrickfergus 65022). At the mouth of Belfast Lough opening to the Irish Sea.

EVENTS: Even if you don't compete, these can be fun to watch: Not only do all the sailing craft look postcard perfect against the blue sky and the blue water on a breezy summer's day, but the well-tanned yachting folk striding around in their Topsiders and toasting their victories at the local pub also make for an entertaining spectacle. One of the biggest of the British events is the *Cowes Week,* which takes place in the Solent and is sponsored by the Isle of Wight–based Royal Yacht Squadron, a club so exclusive that even royalty has been barred from membership. True, you don't see the 300-foot spectator craft — floating hotels, really — that once appeared at Cowes every year in August, or the grandiose racing yachts that used to accompany them; and the days are gone that you might see four bearded gentlemen promenading along the waterfront and later learn that all of them were kings — as you might have in Edwardian days. But the event still brings literally millions of pounds worth of yachts to the area, along with an equally high sum's worth of somebodies' rich uncles. The goings-on are as toney as ever, and the race is remarkably easy to see from shore, especially around the Royal Yacht Squadron's esplanade (best for viewing the start) and Egypt Point, where the racers come so close to land that you almost feel that you could swim out and touch them — if only you could catch up. The tough *Fastnet Race,* held every other year, is also important. During the meeting, yacht crews searching for volunteers to join them on this race to and from a sea-pounded rock offshore roam Cowes's cobbled streets rather like press gangs in the days of Nelson. In Ireland, where the racing is in full swing in May and June, one of the major events is the *Round Ireland Race,* which takes place biennially in June; the *Royal Cork Yacht Club's Sailing Race Week,* held in mid-month, is also important.

In Britain, the RYA (address above) governs sail racing; its Irish counterpart is the Irish Yachting Association (address above).

CRUISING THE INLAND WATERWAYS

Salt air isn't the only tonic that will make a vacation lively: While thousands of Britons and Irish descend on harbors along the coast, just as many more head for waters inland, and spend their holidays floating down narrow canals or streams, or navigating lakes and broads such as those described below. This extensive system of waterways, some 2,200 miles in England alone, takes in the most wonderful scenery — castles of kings and queens, universities renowned around the globe, exquisite gardens manicured to just this side of absolute perfection, nature preserves, and tranquil lakes and fens. While the noteworthy streams of other countries — Germany's Rhine and France's Seine, for instance — carry too much ship traffic to be enjoyable for pleasure boaters, many of Britain's canals are free of commercial craft, and are consequently ideal for recreation.

There are two ways to go — by self-skippered boat or on chartered cruises. The self-skippered arrangements work like this: You hire your craft, a cabin cruiser or a steel-hulled so-called narrowboat that is only about 7 feet wide (and even then it's a tight fit through the locks). Someone shows you how to work the thing and tells you whom to call if you break down. You buy a pile of groceries, some fishing tackle, and a book of folk songs — and cast off for a floating holiday that will take you along as many miles of waterways as you choose, at the rate of about 15 to 20 miles per day. There are plenty of places to moor, to walk and bicycle in the countryside, and to buy fresh supplies. If you fear you'll feel as if you're driving at Indy after only an hour of Driver's Ed., you can hire a skipper to do the piloting. And if you don't feel

DIVERSIONS / Wonderful Waterways and Coastal Cruises 433

like cooking, you can stop in restaurants along the way. Alternatively, you can join a group on one of the so-called hotelboats that can be found on some of the waterways. The cruising life is simple, idyllic, and restorative, any way you slice it. And everyone who does it goes home talking about next year. The British Waterways Board (Melbury House, Melbury Ter., London NW1 6JX, England; phone: 01-262-6711) can supply a great deal of general information about the cruising possibilities in Britain, as can the Irish Tourist Board and the Northern Ireland Tourist Board for opportunities across the Irish Sea. Bookings for a variety of types of craft on a wide assortment of British waterways can be arranged through *UK Waterways Holidays Ltd.* (Melbury House, Melbury Ter., London NW1 6JX, England; phone: 01-262-6711); *Blakes Holidays* (Wroxham, Norwich, Norfolk NR12 8DH, England; phone: 06053-3221/3); or their agents; *Bargain Boating* (Morgantown Travel Service, 127 High St., Morgantown, WV 26505, USA; phone: 304-292-8471); *Hoseasons Holidays Ltd.* (Sunway House, Lowestoft, Suffolk NR32 3LT, England; phone: 0502-62211); *Skipper Travel Services,* 210 California Ave., Ste. H, Palo Alto, CA 94306 (phone: 415-321-5658); *Boat Enquiries Ltd.,* (43 Botley Rd., Oxford, Oxfordshire OX2 0PT, England; phone: 0865-727288); the *Central Booking Agency for Inland Waterways Activities* (289 Main St., Thornton, Leicestershire LE6 1AJ, England; phone: Bagworth 053-021-230); and the *British Waterways Board* (address above). Be sure to review sales material thoroughly to see what is or is not included: Some firms offer a discount for two consecutive weekly bookings; and some include free linen, fuel, car parking, and VAT, for which others may charge, in their rates. Also make sure you know if there is a cancellation penalty.

THE NORFOLK BROADS, England: Described in a 1965 Nature Conservancy Report as "an extensive system of marshland, interconnected waterways and shallow lakes or Broads lying in the valleys of the Rivers Bure, Yare, and Waveney and their tributaries," this area—formed as a result of medieval peat digging—was discovered by vacationers at the end of the nineteenth century, and has been booming as a recreational center ever since, and the villages are full of establishments where you can park your car, have a meal and a good night's sleep, and rent or moor a boat. Thousands of British families come here every summer to do just that: Along with fishing, boating is the prime recreational activity in the Broads. They are the finest inland sailing waters in Europe with the exception of Holland; and the rivers and lakes teem with cruisers chugging along at about 5 miles an hour; when dusk falls, boats are tied up in force along the riverbanks, the pubs do a booming business as vacationers come in off the water for a pint and some talk, and the moorings take on an eerie blue glow as those who have stayed aboard switch on their televisions for another sort of evening's relaxation. Certainly, most Broads cruisers don't come here to get away from the crowds but to join them. But the months of April, May, June, September, and October are peaceful throughout the area; and even in season, there are a number of areas in this lacework of dykes and rivers where you can get off to yourself for a bit among the reedy swamps, scrubland, and occasional bits of forest; in all there are some 140 miles of navigable waterways. Acle, Potter Heigham, Horning, Stalham, and Wroxham are the centers for most commercial facilities. Most boats are floating bungalows, complete with television and central heating; prices vary according to the time of year and the size of the boat. For more information, contact the two major area liveries, *Blakes Holidays* (Wroxham, Norwich, Norfolk NR12 8DH, England; phone: 06053-3221/3), and *Hoseasons Holidays Ltd.* (Sunway House, Lowestoft, Suffolk NR32 3LT, England; phone: 0502-62211); or the company that operates the only hotel boat here, *Boat Enquiries Ltd.,* 43 Botley Rd., Oxford, Oxfordshire OX2 0PT, England; phone: 0865-727288).

THE ENGLISH RIVERS: Of all the nation's streams, there are three that warrant special attention because of their navigability and accessibility. The Thames, which stretches across the breadth of the southern part of the country and is navigable for about 125 miles, twists and winds its long way through pastoral green landscapes punctuated by villages so quaint you'll think you've stepped into a photograph from *National Geographic;* there are lovely estates, grand old houses, medieval churches, marvelously well-tended gardens — and even a few gray cities where the unceasing roar of traffic may almost make you forget the birdsongs that accompanied you along the rest of your trip. As Robert Burns once commented, "Father Thames is liquid history." Commercial traffic along most of the Thames's navigable length is light, and the current is almost nonexistent in most seasons.

Also delightful is the River Avon between Stratford and Tewkesbury, which takes you through a string of delicious sixteenth-century villages (including none other than Stratford-upon-Avon, where you can take in performances of the *Royal Shakespeare Company* when you tie up for the night); the river proper is linked to a system of narrow canals that give you the option of making loop cruises. The Severn, England's longest river, takes you through towns like Worcester, noted for its splendid old cathedral and its porcelain manufactory, and Upton, a market town full of houses dating to the Georgian era and earlier, as it meanders for 42 navigable miles from Stourport to ancient Gloucester. *UK Waterways Holidays Ltd., Hoseasons Holidays, Blakes Holidays,* and *Boat Enquiries Ltd.* (addresses above) can tell you about boat hires; for information on other boat hire firms operating in these waters, contact the BTA. Also consult the Upper Avon Navigation Trust, 10 Guild St., Stratford-upon-Avon, Warwickshire, England (regarding the River Avon between Stratford-upon-Avon and Evesham); the Lower Avon Navigation Trust, Ltd., Gable End, the Holloway, Pershore, Worcestershire WR10 1AW, England (phone: 0386-552517) — for information about the Avon below Evesham; and the Thames Water Authority, Nugent House, Vastern Rd., Reading, Berkshire RG1 8DB, England (regarding the Thames above Teddington; phone: 0734-593333).

BRITAIN'S CANALS: The Industrial Revolution brought many changes to Britain, not the least of them being the lacing together of the country by literally hundreds of miles of canals — canals that were abandoned not long afterward when the railroads began to prove their greater speed. Many of the canals continued to be used for freight for many years — but it has been only recently that they have seen anything approaching the traffic they did at first. Now, though, the boats that thread their way through the canals are transporting holidaymakers, and their primary concern is not commerce but leisurely enjoyment of the now-pastoral scene along the route — open countryside, towns, and cities. They take bikes along on the cabin tops to cycle into the villages along the way for a drink in the pub of an evening, or a foray to the local greengrocer's. Children enjoy working the locks by which the craft can sail uphill. All along the route, there are old buildings whose impressive size or construction testify to the canals' former importance. Some have been converted to contemporary uses: The canal-side granary on The Grand Union Canal at Stoke Bruerne in Northamptonshire now houses the Waterways Museum where you can see exhibits relating to the canals' heyday. A good publication to take along with you on any canal crawl is the British Waterways Board's *Canal Architecture in Britain.* To order a copy, and for more information about planning a cruise, contact British Waterways Board (address above). The British Tourist Authority can provide information on where to rent a craft.

THE RIVER SHANNON, Irish Republic: In a country where the rivers and canals are delightfully pollution-free, as well as relatively uncrowded even in the July and August peak season, this stream stands out. The longest river in Ireland, it is navigable for about 140 miles of its course from its headwaters in Derrylahan in County Cavan southward and slightly west to the Atlantic, with only six locks along the way, and commercial traffic has been banned entirely. You can cruise the stream in its entirety, beginning around Carrick-on-Shannon and, en route, taking in giant Loughs Derg and Ree — broad places in the river, which are inland seas, really, and so susceptible to storms and heavy waves that boaters are advised never to cross them alone. Or you can tackle a trip across Ireland, beginning in Dublin on the Grand Canal, heading due west through its 44 locks, and then covering only the lower portion of the Shannon from near Portumna to the Atlantic. Or you could make any number of shorter cruises along just portions of this route. Alternatively, you could begin on the Grand Canal at Dublin and turn southward near Robertstown to explore the River Barrow, which flows into the sea near Waterford. Wherever you go, you can expect to encounter lovely waterside villages, fascinating small towns, and unspoiled pastoral countryside littered with abbeys and castles and old fortifications. Amateur botanists, ornithologists, and peripatetic archaeologists alike should have a field day; photographers call these landscapes paradise. Good guides to the waters include the *Inland Waterways Association of Ireland Shannon Guide* (£5) and the *Guide to the River Barrow* (£1.65); they're available from Eason & Son, Ltd., 40–42 Lower O'Connell St., Dublin 1, Irish Republic. For a comprehensive list of the companies that will rent cabin cruisers for trips on the Shannon, contact the Irish Tourist Board; the Emerald Star Line, St. James's Gate, Dublin 8, Irish Republic (phone: 01-720244) has the largest selection, with some 200 well-maintained craft in its fleet and bases at both Carrick-on-Shannon and Portumna.

THE ERNE WATERWAY, Northern Ireland: Two huge island-studded lakes joined by narrows at the ancient island town of Enniskillen, the Erne Waterway in Co. Fermanagh is a paradise for birds, wild flowers, and anglers. Six miles wide in spots, and running 26 miles almost to the Atlantic, Lower Lough Erne has 154 islands where you can land to visit old churches, castles, and ruined monasteries, plus dozens of coves and inlets to explore, good hotels and tackle shops, and plenty of hire-cruiser operators. On the labyrinthine Upper Lough Erne, navigation can become something of a challenge, with waves of open-sea size when the winds blow. Below the lake, passing the little village of Belleek, where the world-famous lustrous Belleek pottery is made, the Erne river at last plunges into a gorge to meet the ocean. To find out more, contact the Erne Charter Boat Association, 40 Erne Marine, Bellanaleck Quay, Enniskillen, Co. Fermanagh, Northern Ireland (phone: 0365-82), for a copy of its free booklet *Holidays Afloat and Ashore on the Erne Waterway,* which lists all the association's members and their facilities. The Northern Ireland Tourist Board, 48 High St., Belfast BT1 2DS (phone: Belfast 46609), also keeps copies of this booklet and can provide details of cruising holidays around Strangford Lough and day cruises on Lough Neagh, the biggest lake in Britain and Ireland.

Gone Fishing

It's not hard to understand the overwhelming popularity of Izaak Walton's (called "the Father of Angling") sport when you consider just how much water there is on the islands, how pretty most of the angling hot spots are, and how good the fishing is. Though the day is long past that a monster 72-lb., 8-oz. salmon can be caught in the London section of the Thames — as it was in the early part of the nineteenth century — most of the streams and lakes in Britain are remarkably pollution-free; and conditions in a number of those which used to be, like England's Thames, are improving. The game fishing — that is, for salmon, sea trout, and brown trout — is some of the best in the world, and the sea fishing and coarse fishing — for bream, carp, chub, dace, perch, pike, roach, tench, eel, and other species — are excellent.

Each section of Britain and Ireland offers a different proportion of these three types

436 DIVERSIONS / Gone Fishing

of angling, and where you go will depend on what you're looking for. In Scotland and Wales, the rivers are thought of entirely as game fishing streams. Scottish rivers are world famous for their salmon (though other game species are taken), particularly because of the consistent excellence of the fishery; Britain's record salmon, a 64-pounder bagged in 1922, was caught in Scotland's Tay. In Welsh rivers, salmon, and to an almost equal extent sea trout (called sewin amongst the natives), are the big deal. English streams stand out for the sheer variety of angling offered: Some streams are consecrated primarily to game fishing; some entirely to coarse fishing; and some are mixed fisheries, offering both coarse and game species. There are many reservoirs, and many waters are stocked. The rivers of Northern Ireland are particularly productive — both for game fish and coarse fish; it's almost a situation of an embarrassment of riches, and a few streams seldom see a fisherman. The same situation prevails, but to an even greater degree, in the Irish Republic.

Game fishing is the glamour sport on the local angling scene, and while you might do some coarse fishing or some sea angling as a sidelight to a sight-seeing vacation here, game fishing is something that you will probably want to plan your entire trip around. In Britain, that's all the more true because of the existence of many quaint old fishing hotels, eminently comfortable places and the perfect answer to one pressing problem encountered by most avid fishermen hankering for an exciting angling vacation — that of the fed-up fishing widow. Attractively situated within a short drive of all the shops, ruins, and cathedrals an inveterate sight-seer could desire, the best of these hostelries offer spacious chambers with high ceilings, French doors, and a balcony entwined with wisteria, or similar features. Cucumber sandwiches and currant scones, fruitcakes and jam tarts may be standard fare at tea, and at dinner, you can discuss not just the best flies of the day but also where to get the best buy on a pair of sheepskin gloves or handmade tapestries.

Hotels and Inns with Fishing (free from the British Tourist Authority) lists many angling-oriented hostelries in England, Scotland, Wales, and Northern Ireland; the Angling Information Service of the well-organized Irish Tourist Board can tell you about their Irish counterparts. For further information about all types of fishing in all of Britain, consult the excellent *Where to Fish* (Harmsworth Press, Ltd., 8 Stratton St., London W1, England), or the *AA Guide to Angling in Great Britain,* edited by Colin Graham (published by the Automobile Association and available from the British Travel Bookshop, 680 Fifth Ave., New York, NY 10019, and British Gifts, PO Box 26558, Los Angeles, CA 90026, for $7.95 plus $1.50 for postage and handling). The latter describes not only the quality of the angling on British rivers, still waters, and canals but also tells you which Water Authority governs each, and where you can go to get permission to fish that stream. A number of publications covering angling in various regions of England are available, among them *Fishing in the North West* (available from the Rivers Division, North West Water Authority, PO Box 12, Warrington, Cheshire WA1 2QG, England); the *Birmingham Anglers Association Guide* (available from the Heart of England Tourist Board, PO Box 15, Worcester, Hereford & Worcester WR1 2OT, England), and the *North East Angling Guide* (available from the Northumbria Tourist Board, 9 Osborne Ter., Jesmond, Newcastle upon Tyne, Tyne & Wear NE2 1NT, England). The *Angling Guide* (published by the Department of Agriculture for Northern Ireland), gives you fairly comprehensive information about all kinds of angling here; copies are available from the Fisheries Division, Department of Agriculture, Castle Grounds, Stormont, Belfast BT4 3TA, Northern Ireland. For the same sort of information about Wales, consult the *Angling Guide to Wales* (published by the Wales Tourist Board and available for $5 postpaid from the British Travel Bookshop at the address above).

GAME FISHING

At their best, Britain and Ireland can show you such good fishing for salmon, trout, and sea trout, that you'll sound as if you're telling fish stories when you talk about it back home.

In England, hatchery-raised trout can be found almost everywhere except the east coast — in lakes, reservoirs, and a variety of rivers. Native brown trout proliferate in the famous chalk streams of the southeast — fast, clear-flowing, highly alkaline, and generally ideal for nurturing big ones that rise freely even when they reach 4 pounds or more; these streams offer some of the world's best dry fly trout fishing.

You might wait a decade for your turn to fish more famous rivers like the Itchen and the Test. But *Orvis (UK) Ltd.* (The Mill, Nether Wallop, Stockbridge, Hampshire SO20 8ES, England; phone: 026478-212) offers exceptional though inevitably expensive angling to a limited clientele on private stretches of these two legendary streams, which flow practically in the shadow of Winchester Cathedral, Izaak Walton's burial place. *Orvis* waters include a short stretch on the celebrated Itchen, which produces extra-wily wild trout; a further short beat on the Itchen, which includes a tributary stream; and yet another on the Test itself, good for large and exceptionally active trophy fish.

Other well-known area streams include the Derwent, an important, and especially scenic tributary of the immense Trent; the Dove, where Walton fished — though it's generally not the stream it once was; the Eden, famous for its January-to-May run of spring salmon; the Kennet; the Lune; the Ribble, especially in the middle reaches; and the Wharfe. The Camel and the Fowey are two of Cornwall's important sea trout rivers, and some hotels have good water on the Tamar, among southwest England's most important game fisheries; the Taw, a game river known for a March-to-May spring salmon run, with good sea trout action beginning in July, with some roach and dace downstream; and the Torridge, where the same salmon-in-spring, sea-trout-in-July patterns prevail. In the northwest, the Coquet and the Esk are the best-known salmon streams.

In Wales, the Wye is justly famous for salmon, and several hotels have water on the main river and on its tributaries. The Dee, which yields good-sized salmon and smaller browns and sea trout, and the swift Usk, which has produced some 800 salmon usually averaging 10 pounds and more every season for the last eight decades, are Wales's other important salmon rivers. The prolific Towy, and the Dovey and the Conwy, both of which hold numerous records, are the counterparts of the Dee and the Usk for sea trout sport. Offering good opportunities for both sea trout and salmon action, there's the Clwyd; the Glaslyn, which rises in Snowdon; the Mawddach; the Taf, which has its source on Mynydd Prescelly; and the important Teifi, which claims some of the Principality's top trout fly fishing. For a bit more information, consult the *Angling Guide to Wales* ($5), published by the Wales Tourist Board.

In Scotland, exclusiveness is the hallmark of the very finest angling — some streams are so closed that even rich folk and VIPs may find the door barred — but it does not prevail along all of the Tay, the king of Scotland's salmon rivers, or along the entire length of its rivals, the Aberdeenshire Dee, noted by some fly fishermen as Britain's best major salmon stream; the fast-flowing Spey, Scotland's most thrilling fishery; and the prolific Tweed. Also good are the aptly named Awe, which produced a record 57-lb. salmon in 1921 and a 21-lb. sea trout, the Scottish record holder, in 1980; the Cree, especially in summer; the Don, superb for dry fly trouting; the Northern Esk, which produces abundant numbers of medium-sized salmon; the Findhorn, among the more outstanding of the smaller Scottish salmon streams, with brown trout sport rivaling that of the nearby Spey and good sea trouting in summer; the fairly exclusive, fly-only Helmsdale; the good-quality Naver, especially for salmon and sea trout; and the 30-mile-long Ythan, an excellent sea trout fishery. *Scotland for Fishing,* a publication of the Scottish Tourist Board (65p), can provide some details.

The Irish Republic offers excellent angling for wild brown trout — which are not found in Britain except in streams like the Itchen and the Test, where rights are privately controlled and waiting lists for fishing holidays stretch years into the future. There is also good salmon fishing here. Like Scotland's, this one depends to a great extent on spate rivers — which can offer fine sport when a stretch of rainy weather produces the proper conditions; but, with the exception of the river Moy and the celebrated Blackwater, Ireland lacks the mighty streams that do not depend on precipitation to assure good fishing, and so the quality of your experience is less predictable than it would be in Scottish waters. But it will also be less expensive and more accessible — and if the success of your vacation does not hinge on the number of fish you take, an Irish angling holiday can be an excellent choice.

Angling for both salmon and sea trout (which make up an important part of the Irish Republic's fishing) can be done from the banks of rivers, or drifting in a boat on one of the many large lakes. Generally speaking, the best salmon and sea trout fishing is on the south and west coasts. But there's good fishing in the River Slaney, which goes into the sea at Wexford, on the east coast. Scenic Lough Currane, near the resort town of Waterville, Co. Kerry, has the distinction of having free salmon and trout fishing with the largest and earliest run of sea trout in Ireland. Near the village of Killorglin, Co. Kerry, Caragh Lake and its rivers — the Meelagh, Brida, Owenroe, and Caragh — have good fishing, good hotels, and good pubs. Even those who do not fish will enjoy the salmon at Galway City; the spectacle of the salmon nudging their way upstream from the Weir Bridge on the River Corrib, which drains Loughs Corrib and Mask, is one of the city's more remarkable sights. In June after rain, the stretch of water near Oughterard is as good a place as any to fish. In Connemara, where even the average fishing is above average, the Ballynahinch fishery, especially around Clifden, stands out, as does the nearby river Gowla. (Its adjoining lakes are also good for sea trout.) Kylemore Lake, near Leenane, Co. Galway, is lovely and, if anything, underfished; the River Moy vies with the Blackwater for the title of Ireland's premier salmon fishery. Brown trout are everywhere in Ireland, and any time during the open season, you should get enough action to keep you happy. There are small browns in the tiny lakes and rivers from Cork north to Donegal, larger ones in the great lakes of Mayo and Galway — Loughs Corrib, Mask, and Conn — and fish that are bigger yet again in the midland lakes of Arrow, Derravaragh, Owel, and Sheelin. The River Laune and the beautiful Killarney lakes are also good.

The season generally runs from February 15 to the end of September, but March, April, and September stand out — as does the period from mid-May to mid-June, during the mayfly hatch, when the fish rise high and fast, and many anglers call the action the season's best. Lough Derg on the Shannon and Lough Mask and Lough Carra in Co. Mayo are widely considered the best lakes for mayfly fishing; Lough Corrib has its proponents as well, though the hatch tends to be a bit unpredictable. At any rate, wet-fly fishing on these lakes at that time of year is usually excellent.

For abundant detail about centers, seasons, and such, on these streams and others, consult the Irish Tourist Board's fact-packed brochure *Game Fishing in Ireland.*

In Northern Ireland, you'll find an abundance of sea trout near the mouth of the Upper Bann and plenty of brown trout in the Lower Bann (also good for salmon), the Ballinderry, the Moyola and the Main (also good for salmon and a local species of very large trout known as the dollaghan), and the Blackwater (which also produces salmon in the upper reaches and big catches of coarse fish lower down — all rivers that feed giant 153-square-mile Lough Neagh, the island's largest expanse of still water, itself seldom fished with rod and line because the angling is so good on the feeder streams. The rivers in the narrow, picturesque valleys known as the Glens of Antrim —

among them the Glenshesk in Co. Antrim — have good runs of sea trout, as well as salmon, in July and August. On the north coast, the River Bush is world famous and the Foyle and its tributaries — the Derg, Finn, the Mourne, and the Strule — form one of the best mixed game and coarse fishing areas. Lough Melvin, in the west, which has a spectacular run of spring salmon, is worth a special visit since it also contains three unique trout species — the sonaghan, the gillaroo, and the ferox — and an Ice Age predecessor of the trout — the char. A detailed look at fishing in all of these areas is provided by *Game Fishing in Northern Ireland,* published by the Northern Ireland Tourist Board (free).

A large percentage of game fish waters in the Irish Republic can be fished at little or no cost, and in Northern Ireland, the Department of Agriculture has developed a large number of public fisheries. But nearly all game fishing waters in England, Wales, and Scotland are private, with the fishing rights controlled by clubs and associations, some of which permit no outsiders at all to fish their beats; some of which charge a fee high enough to effectively implement the same situation; and some of which sell day tickets, weekly tickets, or short-term association memberships at less prohibitive prices, rising — usually with the quality of the fishing — from the nominal to the expensive-but-still-not-exhorbitant range. These are generally available through the association's office in advance, or on the spot through hotels, pubs, and tackle shops. To find out who owns the fishing rights to any given stretch of stream in England and Wales, contact the local Water Authority; in Scotland, one of the District Fishing Boards, addresses of which can be obtained from local tackle shops. In Northern Ireland, the Tourist Board (48 High St., Belfast BT1 2DS), the Department of Agriculture (Fisheries Division, Stormont, Belfast BT4 3TA), and the Fisheries Conservancy Board (21 Church St., Portadown, Co. Armagh) can provide the necessary advice. For a list of Water Authority offices, contact the British Tourist Authority; the *AA Guide to Angling in Great Britain* (which also covers Northern Ireland) tells you which stream is under the supervision of which Water Authority. For information about the Irish Republic's trout waters, contact the Irish Tourist Board in Dublin.

In addition to permission, you also usually need, for salmon, sea trout, and brown trout, Water Authority–issued rod licenses, available through fishing hotels, post offices, pubs, and tackle shops. (But you don't need a rod license to fish for any game fish in Scotland, or for brown trout in the Irish Republic.) When you purchase your license, you should also inquire about local rules governing such matters as closed seasons and minimum sizes for each species, bait and tackle permitted, and Sunday fishing (prohibited in Scotland for salmon and sea trout and in some areas for brown trout and coarse fish as well).

COARSE FISHING

All the fish in freshwater rivers and lakes that are not trout or salmon — bream, carp, chub, dace, perch, pike, roach, rudd, eel, and tench — go by the name of coarse fish, and there are millions of anglers who have made this quarry their specialty. The almost total absence of coarse fish in the streams and still waters of Scotland and Wales is compensated for by the abundance in England and Northern Ireland. In England, there is an enormous range of possibilities particularly in the eastern and central regions: the giant and sluggish Great Ouse, where you'll find almost every species (although some stretches boast larger populations of a given species than others), with the town of Huntington among the most favored angling centers; the Nene, also primarily for bream and roach; the Norfolk Broads and the Broadland rivers like the Bure, the Waveney, the Yare, and their tributaries (except during the daytime in summer, when boat traffic makes the angling fairly slow), especially for bream and roach; and the Welland, another big important stream. In the Irish Republic, where the waters are freer from pollution than many in Europe, the coarse fishing can be exceptional and

440 DIVERSIONS / Gone Fishing

in fact most waters are greatly underfished. Recently, more and more anglers from abroad have discovered the joys of Ireland's long, slow, and deep rivers, its half-dozen great lakes up to 30 miles long, and its thousands of lesser lakes. Not many Irish fish, of course, are as heavy as the 42-pound pike caught in the river Barrow or the 38-pounder caught in Lough Corrib a few years back, but most Irishmen believe that plenty of far bigger fish, particularly pike, lurk in the depths of the rivers and that the present records will not last too long.

The River Erne, which runs into Northern Ireland, offers great coarse fishing, with the major centers to be found at lovely Lough Gowna, the source of the Erne, and the area near Belturbet, Co. Cavan, between the two lakes; at nearby Foley's Bridge and Drumlane Lake, the action is so lively that some locals will swear that everyone catches a fish. The river Barrow, flanked by the kind of supremely pastoral countryside that you expect when you go to Ireland, has its best fishing at Graiguenamanagh, Co. Kilkenny, an attractive village in the shadow of Mount Leinster, once a great monastic center. Best of all is the lordly River Shannon, with its three great lakes — lovely 25-mile-long Lough Derg, 17-mile-long Lough Ree, and 7-mile-long Lough Allen. Some of the best centers are at Mohill, Co. Leitrim, well-organized Carrick-on-Shannon, and Lanesborough, Co. Longford, in a famous "hot water" stretch, where catches running into the hundreds of pounds have been made.

For an abundance of detail about all of these streams and others, get a copy of the Irish Tourist Board's *Freshwater Coarse Angling Guide.*

Northern Ireland, though still best known for its game fishing, offers some of Europe's finest coarse fishing as well. On the Upper Bann, the section above Lough Neagh is a standout and has recently produced the world 5-hour coarse match record — 208 lb, 1 oz, 13 drams. The fact that most of the fish were weighing in at 4 to 6 ounces each gives some indication of the huge number of fish that are there for the catching. The Lower Bann, north of Lough Neagh, also has fine coarse angling, especially for perch. Also superb is Lough Erne, with its two gigantic loughs; the area around Enniskillen, where the world 5-hour match record was broken three times before it was won by the Bann, is particularly good. The Fairy Water, a tributary of the Foyle via the Strule, was the first of Northern Ireland's coarse fisheries to come into the public eye, and it still yields roach in immense quantities. Lough Creeve has proved to have a perch growth rate exceeding all other Irish waters. And the Quoile, which flows south from its source not far from Ballynahinch, has made a big splash with its rudd production. *Coarse Fishing in Northern Ireland,* published by the Northern Ireland Tourist Board, gives more details about angling there. Pike fishing, another of the province's attractions, is found at its best in both Lough Ernes, and the two Lough Macneans and in Lough Beg at the mouth of Lough Neagh.

In Northern Ireland you need a rod license (issued by the Fisheries Conservancy Board) for everywhere except the Foyle system. A coarse fishing permit is also required for waters controlled by the Department of Agriculture. In the Irish Republic, no rod license is required. There is no closed season in either part of the island.

SEA ANGLING

Britain has hundreds of miles of ragged coastline where you can catch anything from half-pound flounders off a sandy bottom to giant mako sharks in deep waters, or wrasse, pollack, and mackerel from the rocks. You don't need a license, and few advance arrangements are necessary; tackle can usually be hired; and the chef in your hotel or guesthouse will usually cook your prize on request. For trips out over the wrecks and sunken reefs where some of the bigger fish lurk, boats and professional skippers are readily available, and a day out with a group in a boat with a local who can rendezvous with fish on request can be a most rewarding (and reasonably priced) experience. All you need is a stomach strong enough to hold up through a day on the short choppy seas. Shore fishing for sea bass with a powerful rod and reel requires a little more equipment — namely good oilskins — since these delicious creatures favor "storm beaches" and the best fishing is done when there's a strong onshore wind that will drench you to the skin with salt spray. In England, the best areas include the Channel ports of Dover and Deal, in Kent; the small resorts of New Haven and Littlehampton, in Sussex; Salcombe, set in a many-branched estuary with wooded hills in rolling Devon; Fowey and Looe, among the rocky cliffs of Cornwall; and the mountainous Isle of Man in the middle of the Irish Sea between England and Ireland. The potential of the fishing in Scotland is largely unexploited. Shetland and Orkney have Britain's best common skate action, and the Pentland Firth, which separates Orkney and the mainland, produces large halibut. In the southeast, there's plenty of good shore fishing from the rocks and beaches. *Scotland for Sea Angling* (60p), published by the Scottish Tourist Board, gives further information. In Wales, the best shore fishing is found west of Cardiff, and the fishing offshore in the south can be superb. In the north and west, boat fishing is quite good. For the details, consult the *Angling Guide to Wales* ($5), published by the Wales Tourist Board.

In the Irish Republic, though sea angling has been organized only for the last quarter-century, there are some 200 sea angling clubs with headquarters at towns along the long coastline, and throughout the year, they sponsor about 250 fishing competitions. The big quarry include shark and skate — blue shark, which can weigh in at over 200 pounds and come in season around the south and west coast from mid-June to mid-October; porbeagle shark, of which the record 365-pound specimen was caught off the Mayo coast; the tough-fighting, hard-to-catch mako shark, which visits the south coast in summer; the common skate, a worthy adversary at its most plentiful around the south and west coasts in deep water from April to early October, growing to over 200 pounds; and the somewhat smaller white skate, which favors the western seaboard. Flatfish, halibut, conger, monkfish, mackerel, ling, cod, red sea bream, pollack, ray, turbot, plaice, brill, and flounder can be found around the coast. (Note that there is a conservation order on the common skate, and in order to preserve the species, anglers are asked to return to the water any skate caught alive.)

In Co. Cork, Kinsale is one of the many excellent places to fish (and, in fact, ranks among the best in the country): The angling is well-organized, the town is pretty, and there are numerous good lodging places and fine restaurants. You can go out for blue shark, skate, and conger with local boats and skippers. Also good is Fenit, in Co. Kerry, where you can catch monkfish, ray, conger, and skate right from the ocean pier, or arrange for a boat to take you out into the even more productive waters of Tralee Bay for larger specimens. In Co. Clare, a few miles west of Doonbeg, at Baltard, there is the 140-feet-deep Pool, just off the shore, whose waters teem with mackerel, pollack, and reportedly, porbeagle shark. In spite of its fame, it is extremely dangerous for fishing (many lives have been lost there) and anglers are best advised to go elsewhere. The surf fishing for bass and the flatfishing northward along the delightfully scenic Clare coast road is good, and Green Island at the south of Liscannor Bay is renowned for its rock fishing; porbeagle sharks of around 150 pounds have been landed here. Ballyvaughan and Liscannor (birthplace of the inventor of the submarine), further up the coast, have boats and tackle for hire. In Co. Mayo, there are many major sea-angling centers. Clew Bay, with its 365 islands in the shadow of Ireland's holy Croagh Patrick, has fast tides that give splendid opportunities for shore fishing, while Westport boasts a number of excellent charter boats that go out for the renowned shark and skate fishing; many Europeans come here. Lovely Achill Island, favored by English anglers to such an extent that the coastline fairly resounds with their clipped accents, has superb deep-sea fishing, and past creels have included a number of record-sized shark; the main centers are Purteen Harbour and Darby's Point. Belmullet, the peninsula on the northwest coast, is also famous for its deep-sea action and shore fishing, as are Newport and Kilalla. The brochure *Sea Fishing,* published by the Irish Tourist Board, provides a wealth of detail about what you can catch where and with what off the shores of the Irish Republic. It also includes information on tides, best times to fish, clubs, competition dates, and a list of Bord Fáilte–approved boats.

In Northern Ireland, good bass and sea trout action can be found at Portrush and Portstewart, in Co. Antrim. A record hake was caught in Belfast Lough, and Strangford Lough and Carlingford Lough in County Antrim have produced record skate (182 lb) and tope (66 lb, 8 oz), respectively. Wreck fishing from Portaferry at the mouth of Strangford Lough always guarantees good cod, ling, and conger. But almost everywhere you go along the coast, you'll find an abundance of rocky points, piers, estuaries, and storm beaches that don't get nearly the attention the good sea angling — among Britain's best — certainly warrants. The Northern Ireland Tourist Board publishes *Sea Fishing Off Northern Ireland,* a good guide to what you'll find.

For more information about sea angling around Britain, consult publications like *Sea Angler,* and *Sea Angling Monthly,* available on many newsstands. The National Federation of Sea Anglers (26 Downsview Crescent, Uckfield; Sussex TN22 1UB; phone: 0825-3589) sponsors a number of competitions and may be able to answer some specific questions.

FISHING SCHOOLS

CHARLES BINGHAM FISHING, LTD., Coryton, near Okehampton, Devon, England: Mr. Bingham, who offers courses from February to October, has held salmon, trout, and sea trout permits on many miles of the waters of the River Dart and its tributaries on Dartmoor for 20 years, so he knows the waters very well. The school, which emphasizes fly fishing, concentrates on teaching beginners the basics, but also provides good refresher courses for experienced anglers. Lodging is in the Fisherman's Wing of the comfortable family country house. Details: Charles Bingham Fishing, Ltd., The Rod Room, Broad Park, Coryton, near Okehampton, Devon, England (phone: Chillaton 082-286-281).

THE ARUNDELL ARMS HOTEL, Lifton, Devon, England: This traditional West Country hotel pioneered fishing courses many years ago and now offers them for beginning, intermediate, and advanced anglers. In addition, there are always two bailiffs on the property to advise visiting fishermen. Information: Arundell Arms Hotel, Lifton, Devon PL16, England (phone: 056684-244 or 056684-456).

OSPREY FISHING SCHOOL, Aviemore, Highland, Scotland: Introductory fly fishing courses, weekend-long crash courses in fly fishing, and salmon fishing courses are available, along with game fishing holiday packages, at this Scottish Highlands institution presided over by one Jim Cornfoot, an amiable Scotsman who has been fishing these waters since he was 10 — nearly 30 years. You'll learn casting; watercraft; fly tying; spinning; knots; entomology; and rod, reel, and line construction; you'll learn how to choose the right tackle and equipment for your needs, and how to use a landing net; you'll get in plenty of casting practice, both on the waters adjacent to the school and on the wide, shallow River Spey; and you may be invited by the locals to wash down a dram or two of famous Grouse whisky with a pint of good beer — the favored local method of raising good cheer and keeping out the damp. Details: Osprey Fishing School, The Fishing Centre at the Aviemore Centre, Aviemore, Highlands, Scotland (phone: 0479-810911).

PEEBLES ANGLING SCHOOL, Peebles, Borders, Scotland: This small county town in the beautiful rolling Border area is just 25 miles from Edinburgh. A popular center for fishing on the river Tweed, it offers Friday-through-Sunday trout fishing courses, presided over by former British Open casting champion Andy Dickison, in

April and May and Sunday-to-Sunday salmon week courses in November, when the large salmon, usually weighing in between 10 and 30 pounds, are running. Private instruction in both bait and fly casting techniques is also available, and Melrose Abbey (for more about which, see *Ancient Monuments and Ruins*) and Abbotsford, the former home of novelist Sir Walter Scott, are nearby. Accommodation is at the *Tontine Hotel*, a three-star Trusthouse Forte establishment. Details: Peebles Angling School, 15 Violet Bank, Peebles, Scotland (phone: Peebles 20782).

GAME FISHING HOTELS

The complicated process of arranging to fish in areas where the angling rights are privately held — that is, on most streams in Britain and on a few in Ireland, where access to almost all waters is free — can be much simplified when you base yourself at a special fishing hotel, which may either control a stretch of a nearby stream or be able to carry out the necessary negotiations with owners of local estates. Most of the following establishments are country house hotels, in attractive settings; waters to which they control rights are indicated. Hotels mentioned in areas where fishing is free are conveniently located with respect to the best local waters — and, like the rights-owning establishments, are exceptionally hospitable to anglers: When you want to haul out your tales of that day's triumphs, you'll be sure to find a willing ear.

Cavendish Hotel, Baslow, Derbyshire DE4 1SP, England (phone: 024688-2311). Rivers Derwent and Wye.

Red Lion Hotel, Bredwardine, Hereford & Worcester Wharfe, England (phone: 09817-303). River Wye.

Buck Inn, Buckden, North Yorkshire BD23 5JA, England (phone: 075676-277). River Wharfe.

Tillmouth Park Hotel, Cornhill-on-Tweed, Northumberland TD12 4UU, England (phone: 0890-2255). River Tweed.

Izaak Walton Hotel, Dovedale, Derbyshire DE6 2AY, England (phone: 033529-261). River Dove.

Bull Hotel, Downton, near Salisbury, Wiltshire SP5 3HH, England (phone: 0725-20374). Hampshire Avon River.

Carnarvon Arms Hotel, Dulverton, Somerset TA22 9AE, England (phone: 0398-23302). Rivers Exe and Barle.

Fox and Hounds Hotel, Eggesford, Chulmleigh, Devon EX18 7JZ, England (phone: 0769-80345). Rivers Taw and Little Dart.

Horse Shoe Hotel, Egton Bridge, Whitby, Yorkshire YO21 1XE, England (phone: 0947-87245). River Esk.

Bull Hotel, Fairford, Gloucestershire GL7 4AA, England (phone: 0285-712535). River Coln.

Green Man, Fownhope, Hereford & Worcester, England (phone: 043277-243). River Wye.

Hackness Grange Hotel, Hackness, near Scarborough, Yorkshire YO13 0JW, England (phone: 0723-69966). River Derwent. In North York Moors National Park.

Holne Chase, Holne Ashburton, Devon TQ13 7NS, England (phone: 03643-471). River Dart.

Deer Park Hotel, Honiton, Devon EX14 0PG, England (phone: 0404-2064). River Otter.

Arundell Arms, Lifton, Devon PL16 0AA, England (phone: 056684-244 or 456). Tamar River. (See also *Rural Retreats.*)

Edenhall Hotel, Penrith, Cumbria, England (phone: 076881-454). River Eden.

Anglers Arms Hotel, Weldon Bridge, Morpeth, Northumberland NE65 8AX, England (phone: 0665-70-271). River Coquet.

Crown Hotel, Wetheral, Carlisle CA4 8ES, Cumbria, England (phone: 0228-61888). River Eden.

Half Moon Inn, Sheepwash, Devon EX21 5NE, England (phone: 040923-232). River Torridge.

Rising Sun, Umberleigh, Devon EX37 9DU, England (phone: 0769-60447). River Taw.

Kenmore Hotel, by Aberfeldy, Tayside PH15 2NU, Scotland (phone: 08873-205). River Tay.

Ardoe House Hotel, Banchory Devenick, Aberdeen, Grampian AB1 5YP, Scotland (phone: 0224-47355). River Dee.

Banchory Lodge, Banchory, Grampian AB3 3HS, Scotland (phone: 03302-2625). River Dee.

County Hotel, Banff, Grampian AB4 1AE, Scotland (phone: 02612-5353). River Deveron.

Craigellachie Hotel, Craigellachie, Grampian AB5 9SS, Scotland (phone: 03404-204). River Spey.

Dunkeld House, Dunkeld, Tayside PH8 0HX, Scotland (phone: 03502-243). River Tay.

Seafield Lodge Hotel, Grantown-on-Spey, Woodside Ave., Highland PH26 3JN, Scotland (phone: 0479-2152). River Spey.

Ednam House Hotel, Kelso, Borders TD5 7HT, Scotland (phone: 05732-24168). River Tweed; trout only.

Invereshie House, Kincraig, Highland PH21 1NA, Scotland (phone: 05404-332). River Spey.

Grant Arms Hotel, Monymusk, Grampian, Scotland (phone: 04677-226). River Don.

Tweed Valley Hotel, Walkerburn, Borders EH43 6AA, Scotland (phone: 089687-220). River Tweed.

Gwydyr Hotel, Betws-y-Coed, Gwynedd LL24 0AB, Wales (phone: 06902-217). River Conwy.

Gliffaes Country House Hotel, near Crickhowell, Powys NP8 1RH, Wales (phone: 0874-730371). River Usk.

The Lake Hotel, Llangammarch Wells, Powys LD4 4BS, Wales (phone: 05912-202). Rivers Irfon and Wye.

Lake Vyrnwy Hotel, Llanwddyn, Powys SY10 0LY, Wales (phone: 069173-244). Lake Vyrnwy.

Emlyn Arms, Newcastle, Emlyn, Dyfed, Wales (phone: 0239-710317). River Teifi.

Tyn-y-Cornel, Talyllyn, Gwynedd, Wales (phone: 065477-282). Tal-y-llyn Lake.

Mount Falcon Castle Hotel, Ballina, Co. Mayo, Irish Republic (phone: 096-21172). Near the River Moy and Lough Conn.

Zetland Hotel, Cashel Bay, Co. Galway, Irish Republic (phone: Cashel 8). Near the Gowla River, Lough Gowla, Lough Inagh, and the Invermore fishery.

Ashford Castle Hotel, Cong, Co. Mayo, Irish Republic (phone: 094-22644).

Dunloe Castle Hotel, Gap of Dunloe, Co. Kerry, Irish Republic (phone: Killarney 32118).

Towers Hotel, Glenbeigh, Co. Kerry, Irish Republic (phone: Glenbeigh 12).

Glencar Hotel, Glencar, Co. Kerry, Irish Republic (phone: Glencar 102). Upper Caragh River and Cloon Lake.

Kylemore Pass Hotel, Kylemore, Co. Galway, Irish Republic (phone: Kylemore 10).

Sheelin Shamrock Hotel, Mountnugent, Co. Cavan, Irish Republic (phone: 049-32323).

Newport House Hotel, Newport, Co. Mayo, Irish Republic (phone: 098-41222). Newport River and Lough Beltra.

Dromoland Castle, Newmarket-on-Fergus, Co. Clare, Irish Republic (phone: 061-71144). Eight miles from Shannon Airport.

Corrib Hotel, Oughterard, Co. Galway, Irish Republic (phone: 091-82238). The proximity of Corrib River and Lake makes this town a popular destination for fishermen. See below.
Egan's Lake Hotel, Oughterard, Co. Galway, Irish Republic (phone: 091-82275). Lough Corrib.
Sweeney's Oughterard House Hotel, Oughterard, Co. Galway, Irish Republic (phone: 091-82007).
Pontoon Bridge Hotel, Pontoon, Co. Mayo, Irish Republic (phone: Foxford 20).
Blackwater Lodge Hotel, Upper Ballyduff, Co. Waterford, Irish Republic (phone: Ballyduff 35). Blackwater River.
Butler Arms, Waterville, Co. Kerry, Irish Republic (phone: 066-23100). Lough Currane.
Waterville Lake Hotel, Waterville, Co. Kerry, Irish Republic (phone: Waterville 7). Lough Currane.
Corralea Lodge, Belcoo, Co. Fermanagh, Northern Ireland (phone: Belcoo 325). Upper Lough McNean, Lough Erne.
Mahon's Hotel, Irvinestown, Co. Fermanagh, Northern Ireland (phone: 036-5621656 or 657). Lough Erne.
Manville House, Aughnablaney, Letter, Co. Fermanagh, Northern Ireland (phone: Kesh 31668). Loughs Melvin and Erne.
Everglades Hotel, Londonderry, Co. Londonderry BT47 2PA, Northern Ireland (phone: 46722). River Foyle.
Royal Arms Hotel, 51/53 High St., Omagh, Co. Tyrone BT78 1BA, Northern Ireland (phone: Omagh 3262). River Strule.
Beach Hotel, Portballintrae, Co. Antrim, Northern Ireland (phone: Bushmills 31214). River Bush.

Freewheeling by Two-Wheeler

The landscapes you see from the roads of Britain and Ireland unfold with such endless diversity at every bend and turn that traveling through as quickly as you might in a car seems a real shame: The villages full of ancient half-timbered houses; the heather-clad plateau country with its deep valleys and minuscule settlements; the rolling hills; the quaint seacoast towns; and the regions of moors and mountains all beg to be explored at bicycle-speed — that is, fast enough so that you can cover a fair amount of terrain, but slow enough that you can stop to inspect a wildflower or admire a view. You want to be able to pull over to the side of the road, or pop into a teashop with a minimum of fuss or bother. Cycling lets you do all that. And there's something quite special about the rhythm of your days on the road — the slow but steady ticking away of the miles, the lure of the unknown just over the next hill, the ready meetings with your fellow cyclists on the road or at pubs and hostels, and the special camaraderie that prevails.

The fact that Britain and Ireland offer not only a great variety of scenery in a relatively compact area, but also an abundance of well-surfaced, little-trafficked secondary roads, as well as many facilities for rental and repair and hundreds of small restaurants and informal hotels that are no less than delighted to welcome bedraggled pedalers, makes the countries well-nigh perfect candidates for cycle touring vacations — for beginning tourers and experts alike. Even if you're not particularly experienced, and even if you put off your planning until the last minute, you can still enjoy yourself on a two-wheeling vacation here: Just travel light, start out slowly, and don't give up just because you develop saddle-soreness and tender muscles.

Rentals are widely available in both Britain and Ireland. In Ireland, *Irish Raleigh* (Broomhill Rd., Tallaght, Co. Dublin, Irish Republic; phone: 01-521888) operates a rental scheme over all of the island; you can get three-speeds, ten-speeds, and tandems. For names of cycle hire firms in Britain, consult the yellow pages of the telephone book in the area you're visiting; the BTA publishes listings of bike rental agencies throughout Britain. Rental rates vary (as do the quality of the bikes available and the standard of maintenance), but you can expect to pay $25 to $30 for a week's rental of a good ten-speed model, or slightly more if you also need insurance, panniers, lights, and the like. You will find broader selections at large companies, usually based in cities — though basic machines can be had in rural towns for as little as $2 a day.

However, since the amount of pleasure you derive from your trip will at least partially depend on how well you like your bike, you may well want to bring your own. Airlines will generally transport bikes as part of passengers' personal baggage, but may insist that the whole machine be crated. If you don't have a bike and want to buy one, it may or may not make sense to wait until you reach Europe to get it, depending on the relative prices of bicycles and the exchange rates prevailing at the time. If you come with your own cycle, be sure to check your insurance coverage before you leave home. If you have none, consider joining the *Cyclists' Touring Club* (Cotterell House, 69 Meadrow, Godalming, Surrey GU7 3HS, England; phone: 04868-7217), which has a plan for its members. You will also need to bring a basic set of tools and spares, including tire pump, puncture repair kit, tire levers, spanners/wrench, spoke key, chain rivet extractor, chain links, inner brake cables, pliers, odd nuts and bolts, brake blocks, oil can, batteries and bulbs, freewheel block remover, rag, extra spokes, inner tubes and outer tires, and a small file for honing spokes. British law requires that your cycle have two independent brakes, and a red rear light and reflector as well as a white light in the front for night riding; since you'll be riding on the left here, it's a good idea to fix the front light onto the right-hand side. Not required by law — but certainly eminently practical — are a padlock and chain, though theft is not the problem in rural areas that it is in centers such as Birmingham, Glasgow, Liverpool, Manchester, Sheffield, and, of course, London — where you probably won't be doing much cycling anyway.

To get out of these cities without battling the traffic is a relatively simple matter, since you're allowed to take your bike with you when you travel by train — at no extra charge. The procedure is simple: You buy your ticket, take your bike onto the platform and ask the guard's permission to put your bicycle in the luggage van — a request that is seldom refused, and only then when the car is full of other goods. There are only a few exceptions: Charges are made for travel on the super-fast Inter-City 125 trains and for a few others; and bikes are prohibited altogether on some other lines. Be sure to label your bike with your name, address, and the station of origin and destination. And don't forget it when you arrive.

BEST CYCLING AREAS

Your touring possibilities are myriad. In England, for instance, you can travel on any number of "B" and unclassified roads connecting nearly every community in the country. In Wales, only the trunk routes in the southeast are too busy for cycling. In Scotland, their counterparts in the south are generally busy. In summer, Scotland's "A" routes in the north can be congested, more because of their narrow and winding nature than because of the quantity of traffic they carry, as can the north and west coast routes and some of the interior highways in Wales. Nearly all the roads in both Northern Ireland and the Republic (with the exception of trunk routes between the larger cities) offer cyclists not only smooth surfaces but also little traffic. In addition, both nations have unsurfaced tracks, cattle drovers' routes, bridleways, and woodland paths that lend themselves to two-wheeling (though the going can be a bit rough). Britain has, for instance, some 2,000 miles of towpath alongside the canals that ribbon the countryside, waterways constructed during the Industrial Revolution and now largely deserted by commercial transport. (If you decide to cycle here, you can get the necessary permits from the British Waterways Board, Willow Grange, Church Rd., Watford, Hertfordshire WD1 3QA; phone: Watford 26422. The London office is at Delamere Ter., Paddington, London W2; phone: 286-6101.)

Here are some of the best cycling areas in Britain and Ireland.

LONDON, England: Bicycling may not be everyone's idea of the best transportation here, and in fact, it can prove a nightmare to newcomers not forewarned about patterns of flow and congestion. But it's also true that there's no better way of seeing the real London — away from the main thoroughfares used by most buses and taxicabs. Traveling by bike, more than any other mode of transport, will give you a feel for the way London's villages all fit together. The London Cycling Campaign publishes the excellent booklet *On Your Bike* (80p, including postage), which is full of maps of central London on which are designated streets good for bicycling. Though it is really aimed at Londoners who use their bikes as transportation, it can be useful to sight-seers as well — and serves as an excellent primer on English laws pertaining to cyclists, and cycling safety, maintenance, and repairs. Cycling shops are also listed. A similar publication, *Bike It,* covers north and east London (70p, including postage). To order copies, contact London Cycling Campaign, Colombo Street Centre, London SE1, England (phone: 01-928-7220).

EAST ANGLIA, England: The generally low-lying terrain of Suffolk and Norfolk, which, along with parts of neighboring counties, used to be an old Saxon kingdom, seems made for cyclists — though there are enough gentle hills to keep the horizons constantly changing. East Anglia is a land of farms, isolated villages full of thatched houses, grand mansions, and inspiring Gothic churches. Where these flatlands slip gently into the sea, there are salt marshes and sand dunes, teeming with birds; deserted beaches; and The Broads. *Cycling in East Anglia* (£1.50, from Cycling World, Andrew House, 2a Granville Rd., Sidcup, Kent DA14 4BN, England) covers lodgings, routes, camping, and cycle hire in the area. For general information, contact the East Anglia Tourist Board, 14 Museum St., Ipswich, Suffolk IP1 1HU, England (phone: 0473-214211).

THE COTSWOLDS AND THE HEART OF ENGLAND: This region shows a number of faces to the world: There are the chalk hills known as the Chilterns, billowing up out of the valley of the Thames; the jagged blue-hazed Malvern Hills; the Avon valley, with Stratford, the Bard's hometown, and nearby villages full of thatched-roof cottages — not to mention the Cotswolds, where you'll roll past dotted pastures and shallow trout streams that look like ribbons of silver when you see them from on high, through placid hamlets (some almost *too* picture-postcard pretty), and alongside occasional fuzzy patches of beech trees that shimmer in the sunshine. Everywhere you see the limestone characteristic of the area — intricately fitted as cottage walls and stone fences, and colored the mellow hues of cream and honey and slate so that the structures seem to grow out of the earth itself. There are ups-and-downs enough that beginners may find themselves stretched to the limits; intermediate pedalers should find the challenges just about right. Details: Heart of England Tourist Board, PO Box 15, Worcester WR1 2JT, England (phone: Worcester 29511); and the Thames & Chilterns Tourist Board, 8 The Market Pl., Abingdon, Oxfordshire OX14 3HG, England (phone: 0235-22711).

NORTH YORK MOORS, England: This roughly oval moorland plateau, barren-looking until summer blossoming of heather makes it glow purple and blue, is broken up by inviting dales where cozy accommodations can be found. A 553-square-mile national park, bounded on the east by the North Sea, it is generally a country of sheep-dotted, stream-crossed pastures, with fine views in the uplands, and tiny villages. National Park Information Centres are located at Danby Lodge, not far from Grosmont; in the market town of Pickering, site of ruined Pickering Castle, and at Sutton Bank, on the western edge of the park, with magnificent views of the Vale of York. The roads between Pickering and Whitby and Whitby and Scarborough can be busy, but most other north-south routes over the moors are quiet enough, and dead-end valley lanes are idyllic. Details: Yorkshire & Humberside Tourist Board, 312 Tadcaster Rd., York YO2 2HF, England (phone: 0904-707961).

THE PEAK DISTRICT, England: The Pennine Hills, England's great backbone, begin in this wild upland practically within shouting distance of the great industrial centers of the Midlands. The more southerly area offers steep-sided valleys; in the north, the characteristic formations are the sharp-edged gritstone cliffs that inspired Daniel Defoe to dub them the nation's Andes. As you leave the Peak District and go farther north, the Pennines become wilder, more remote, and harder to cycle. Details: East Midlands Tourist Board, Exchequergate, Lincoln, Lincolnshire LN2 1PZ, England (phone: 0522-31521).

THE SOUTHEAST, England: Even as close as this area is to London, the countryside is still given over to orchards and hop fields, woods, and farmlands green and fertile enough to warrant the nickname the "Garden of England." You'll do your cycling on roads and country lanes through the ranges of low chalk hills known as the North and South Downs, which stretch eastward to the high cliffs on the shores of the English Channel, and are separated by The Weald — the farm- and village-dotted remains of a once-large regional forest. Practically wherever you go, the land is fine for beginning cyclists. Much of the area has been designated an "Area of Outstanding Natural Beauty"; Canterbury, Chichester, Winchester, and Salisbury Cathedrals and a number of seacoast castles and fortifications are among the points of interest. Details: South East England Tourist Board, Cheviot House, 4–6 Monson Rd., Tunbridge Wells, Kent TN1 1NH, England (phone: 0892-40766).

LAKE DISTRICT, England: Unquestionably one of England's grandest regions, this mountain mass, its valleys bejeweled with lakes, is a favorite among Britain's national parks — and with reason: The ravines and their sapphire tarns, and the volcanic peaks, stark and jagged, sometimes rising abruptly from just above sea level so that they seem even bigger than they really are, make for an effect of striking grandeur. When you consider the man-made landscape — the velvety pastures laced with lichen-splotched drystone walls, the antique farmhouses, and the lovely villages — it's not hard to see why William Wordsworth, a native son whose various cottages are preserved and open for tours, was so inspired (as were countless other poets and artists down through the years). The hills you encounter can be steep — but then, some of those whistle-fast descents from the tops rank among the country's most exhilarating. Despite the area's popularity, there are still plenty of quiet roads. The *Observer's Book of the Lake District* by John Parker (£1.80; Frederick Warne Publishers, Ltd., 40 Bedford Sq., London WC1B 3NE, England) contains excellent town-by-town coverage of the area *Cycling in the North West* (£1.50, from Cycling World, Andrew House, 2a Granville Rd., Sidcup, Kent DA14 4BN, England) covers routes, accommodations, lodgings, and cycle hire in the area. There are information offices in Ambleside, Bowness, Brockhole, and Windermere. For more information, write the Cumbria Tourist Board, Ellerthwaite, Windermere, Cumbria LA23 2AQ, England.

THE SOUTHWEST, England: From the cathedral cities and Stonehenge, on the Salisbury Plain, to the New Forest, through the peaceful towns of Dorset (Thomas Hardy's Wessex), and on to the Somerset and Devon uplands — among them Exmoor and Dartmoor — and rugged Cornwall, the southwest of England will challenge even expert cyclists, though less so along the coast than throughout the hilly inland areas. But as you work your way toward Land's End the scenery will reward you amply for your efforts. The villages are lovely, the vistas unfailingly grand or pastoral, the traditional cream teas scrumptious, and the seacoast wonderfully varied. There are desolate moors, prehistoric ruins (South Cadbury among them; see *Ancient Monuments and Ruins*), and medieval churches to see. Also see the new *Cycling in the West Country* (£1.50, from Cycling World, Andrew House, 2a Granville Rd., Sidcup, Kent DA14 4BN, England): it covers lodgings, camping, routes, and cycle hire. Traffic in coastal resort areas can be a problem in summer, particularly on weekends. Details: West Country Tourist Board, Trinity Ct., 37 Southernhay E, Exeter, Devon EX1 1QS, England (phone: 0392-76351).

YORKSHIRE DALES, England: Rivers flowing down from high in the Pennine Hills have cut out a wondrous landscape of steep mountains and deep valleys whose finer points are not well known even in Britain. Like Teesdale, the northernmost of the dales, most boast impressive waterfalls. Swaledale is generally ranked as one of the lovelier dales, but the others have their particular charms as well: Wensleydale, its local cheese; austere, lonely-looking Wharfedale; Nidderdale, with its impressive How Stean gorge; Airedale, with its spectacular Craven Country, Malham Cove's gigantic limestone bluffs, and the heavily-visited Gordale Scar gorge; and not-too-well-known Ribblesdale, in the center of the Pennines, where there are abundant potholes and waterfalls — to name only a few. Nearly 700 square miles of this water-carved wonderland have been designated as a national park. Details: Yorkshire & Humberside Tourist Board, 312 Tadcaster Rd., York YO2 2HF, England (phone: 0904-707961).

THE NORTHEAST, England: This quiet, sparsely populated area boasts more ancient remains and medieval castles than any other part of Britain; Hadrian's Wall and Scotland's Melrose, Jedburgh, and Kelso abbeys (described in *Ancient Monuments and Ruins*) are among the notable sites. The grass-covered Cheviot Hills offer particularly challenging cycling; the rest of the area, mainly given over to forests, farms, and beaches, is more rolling. Details: Northumbria Tourist Board, 9 Osborne Ter., Newcastle-upon-Tyne NE2 1NT, England (phone: 0632-817744).

WELSH MARCHES, England: In this area between Chepstow, on the Bristol Channel to the south, and Liverpool Bay, just north of Chester, the green and gentle hills of the valley of the meandering Wye and the country north of that offer some pleasant cycling. There's the Forest of Dean, the wild woods between the Rivers Severn and Wye; Hay-on-Wye, a town full of bookshops, including "the world's largest"; the Shropshire Hills; and historical towns like the ancient religious center of Hereford, picturesque Ludlow, and Shrewsbury, full of half-timbered houses. Castles and abbeys are abundant. Details: Heart of England Tourist Board, PO Box 15, Worcester WR1 2JT, England (phone: 0905-29511).

THE HIGHLANDS, Scotland: This region of ridges and glens, some loch-filled, are really restricted to cyclists with plenty of pedal power and a love of wilderness wandering: There are few roads; even the main routes tend to shrink to narrow tracks, particularly in the west, where they get crowded during the summer; and there are few bicycle shops, so you have to carry all spares. The rewards are many, however: The northwest coast, looking much like Norway with its fjords; the vistas of snow-capped peaks; Cawdor Castle at Nairn; and vast blue Lochs Ness and Lochy, to name only a few. *Cycling in Scotland* (£1.50, from Cycling World, Andrew House, 2a Granville Rd., Sidcup, Kent DA14 4BN, England) will fill you in on lodgings, camping facilities, and cycle-hire outfits. Also contact the Highlands & Islands Development Board, PO Box 7, Bridge House, Bank St., Inverness IV1 1QR, Scotland.

THE NORTH, Wales: Apart from the highway along the north coast, the roads here — as elsewhere in the country — are not at all heavily trafficked as they twist and climb into wild, mysterious mountains that are some of the most beautiful in all of Britain — slate-brown, full of foaming rivers, huge smooth lakes, castles, and prehistoric sites. The Isle of Anglesey, across a narrow channel to the north, is more rural than rugged, making for a pleasant contrast. For information on routes, accommodations, camping, and cycle hire, see *Cycling in Wales* (£1.50, from Cycling World, Andrew House, 2a Granville Rd., Sidcup, Kent DA14 4BN, England). For other details, contact the North Wales Tourism Council, Civic Centre, Colwyn Bay, Clwyd LL29 8AR, Wales (phone: 0492-56881).

MID AND SOUTH WALES: Inland, the terrain is peaceful. Farms are interspersed with patches of woods. Rolling hills climb out of pastoral valleys. The neat hamlets scattered here and there are laced together by country lanes and "rough stuff" tracks — unsurfaced but bikeable if you're adventurous. But in the south, the countryside is dramatic. You'll encounter the mountains of the Brecon Beacons, with their thundering cascades, lakes, forests, moorlands, passes, deeply incised valleys with their rich industrial and cultural heritage; and the Pembrokeshire coast, where mountains plunge to the sea and rocky headlands are interspersed with delightful sandy beaches and punctuated by historical towns such as Monmouth, Chepstow with its castle, and St. Davids with its historic cathedral. For intermediate cyclists, this is Wales's must — an experience of a lifetime, to boot. *Cycling in Wales* (£1.50, from Cycling World, Andrew House, 2a Granville Rd., Sidcup, Kent DA14 4BN, England) will tell you about area lodgings, camping, and cycle-hire facilities. For other information, contact the Mid Wales Tourism Council, The Owain Glyndwr Centre, Machynlleth, Powys SY20 8EE, Wales (phone: Machynlleth 2401); and the South Wales Tourism Council, Ty Croeso, Gloucester Pl., Swansea SA1 1TY, Wales (phone: 0792-465204).

THE DUBLIN ENVIRONS, Irish Republic: The wonderful thing about Ireland is that once you get about 20 miles outside Dublin or 10 miles from Cork, Derry, Galway, Limerick, or Waterford, all of the country's roads are virtually traffic-free. But even within these bounds, it's possible to find byroads that will delight you. In County Meath, practically from the doorstep of Dublin Airport, you can take on nearly ideal runs through villages like St. Margaret's, Ballyboghil, Naul, on to Duleek and into the remarkable Boyne Valley and the Hill of Tara (whose sites are described in *Ancient Monuments and Ruins*). Don't miss the giant tumuli and monastic remains at Slane and Navan. South of Dublin, if you like hill climbing, you can take the road from suburban Rathfarnham to the Sally Gap and Calary Bog and, within a half an hour, find yourself out of sight of human habitation, in lovely countryside where the lark rising is the only sound you hear. The small-but-lovely Wicklow Mountains, which extend from around Dublin in the north to as far south as Arklow, and inland for about 25 miles from the sandy shores of the Irish Sea, make for excellent cycling; the wide, long, dune-backed strand at Brittas Bay is one of the best places for a swim here, and Glendalough (described in *Ancient Monuments and Ruins*) is the local sight-seeing must. For cyclist-oriented information about lodging and camping facilities as well as for route information, consult *Cycling in Ireland* (£1.50, from *Cycling World,* Andrew House, 2a Granville Rd., Sidcup, Kent DA14 4BN, England). Also contact the Eastern Region Tourism Organisation, 1 Clarinda Park, N, Dun Laoghaire, Co. Dublin, Irish Republic (phone: 808571).

THE WEST, Irish Republic: The 700-foot Cliffs of Moher, which plunge into the foaming sea near the spa town of Lisdoonvarna and the Burren, bare and almost lunar in appearance, are two of the notable sites in not-too-often-visited County Clare, while in more-frequented County Galway, you'll want to explore the whole of the rocky, boggy, Gaelic-speaking region known as Connemara, with The Twelve Bens presiding over flatlands speckled with ruined rock-walled cottages. There are good beaches — and they're seldom busy; Loughs Corrib and Mask (see *Gone Fishing*) are not too far distant. Still farther north, small roads take you between pretty quiet villages scattered around the tranquil heather and rhododendron country of less-populated Mayo or hug a coastline as wild and lonesome as those tired of city life could ever desire. The routes from Newport and Mulrany by Lough Furnace, over the bridge at Achill Sound to Achill Island, and then around Achill Island, are pleasant. For route informa-

DIVERSIONS / Freewheeling by Two-Wheeler 451

tion and a rundown of lodging and camping facilities, see *Cycling in Ireland* (described above). Also contact Shannonside Tourism, 62 O'Connell St., Limerick, Irish Republic (phone: 061-47522); and the Western Region Tourism Organisation, Áras Fáilte, Galway, Irish Republic (phone: 091-63081).

THE SOUTHWEST, Irish Republic: Outside busy Cork City, counties Cork, Kerry, and Limerick are quite rural. There are mountains and steep gradients, but gently rolling hills and flat valleys are part of the cycling picture as well. Most dramatic scenery is along the coast, where you'll encounter lovely deep bays and cave-pocked cliffs and promontories. Blarney Castle is here, along with the remains of Mourne Abbey and Castlemore Barrett; the fishing town of Youghal; the pretty port of Kinsale; the remote district around Allihies on the coast; Georgian-era Bantry House; Killarney; *Durty Nellie's Inn* (see *Pub Crawling*); Ross Castle and the ruined remains of Muckross and Innisfallen Abbey; and the spectacular Gap of Dunloe that slashes through the countryside between Macgillycuddy's Reeks and the Purple Mountains. The Ring of Kerry and the Dingle Peninsula are particular standouts. For information about routes, campgrounds, and places to lodge, consult *Cycling in Ireland* (described above). Also contact the Cork/Kerry Region Tourism Organisation, PO Box 44, Tourist House, Grand Parade, Cork, Irish Republic (phone: 23251).

NORTHERN IRELAND: Ulster's 5,500 square miles encompass some of the most spectacular and varied scenery that one could imagine. Blue mountains and sandy beaches, open moorlands and clear lakes, small towns hidden away in the green places of the countryside, and fishing villages strung out along the rocky shores — and you are never more than an hour from the sea. The only heavy traffic you will meet on the excellent network of small, well-signposted roads is the occasional tractor, and the only traffic jams are caused by sheep and cattle changing fields. Perhaps the most rewarding outing for the cyclist is to take the 60-mile coast road from Larne up around the northeast corner of County Antrim to the resort of Portrush. The celebrated Antrim coast road, which passes countless villages, ruined Norman castles, and the nine green Glens of Antrim, is reminiscent of justly famous Californian Highway One, which runs south of Carmel. Ancient rocks jut out as cliffs in all their brilliant colors — bright red sandstones, white chalk, black basalt, and blue clays. As you pedal round the top of Ireland, you can see the beckoning hills of Scotland. Stop off at Ballycastle and take a boat across to Rathlin Island where Robert the Bruce once found sanctuary. There's a new guesthouse on the island and you can walk or cycle across to the bird sanctuary on the west side and explore the cliffs and caves. Once back on the mainland, pedal on to the strange and remarkable rock formation called the Giant's Causeway, an astonishing complex of basalt columns packed tightly together; the tops of the columns — 38,000 of them — form stepping stones leading from the cliff foot and disappearing under the sea. Details: Northern Ireland Tourist Board.

HOW TO PLAN A TOUR

After you've made up your mind about what region you want to explore, it's a fairly easy matter to sketch out an itinerary. First decide on exactly what you want to see and do: For ideas, consult local tourist literature; articles about touring in bicycling magazines such as the Cyclists' Touring Club's bi-monthly *Cycle Touring* (available from the club; address above) or *Cycling World* (published by Stone Industrial Publications, Ltd., 2a Granville Rd., Sidcup, Kent DA14 4BN, England; phone: 01-302-6150 or 01-302-6069), both widely available from bicycle stores and at larger newsstands, as well as from the publishers; and specialized bikers' books such as the *Cyclists' Touring Club's Route Guide to Cycling in Britain and Ireland* by Christa Gausden and Nicholas Crane (Oxford Illustrated Press, Sparkford, Yeovil, Somerset

452 DIVERSIONS / Freewheeling by Two-Wheeler

BA22 7JJ, England; phone: 0963-40653), which lists 365 interconnected routes based on minor roads and lanes throughout Britain, suitable for tours lasting anywhere from a single day to several months. *Cycling World* publishes a good series of books that outline routes and detail facilities for lodging, camping, and cycle hire (£1.50 each).

Once you have a general idea of where you want to go, plot out your tour on a large-scale highway map of the country — the sort of map that you can usually obtain at no charge from a national tourist office. Base your daily mileage on what you usually cover on the road at home, but be sure to allot time for en-route dawdling — chatting with the locals, long stops for admiring the panoramas from a picnic spot, walks through ruined abbeys, and the like. (Beginners may be able to tick off 10 miles, while experts who can manage 100 may call an intermediate's 50 just an easy morning's pedal.)

Then tackle detailed route finding with small-scale topographical maps that will not only tell you about the smallest country lanes, but also alert you to the contours of the land and the steepness of the hills throughout the area you've chosen to cover. The 1:100,000-scale maps published by Bartholomew & Son, Ltd. (Duncan St., Edinburgh EH9 1TA, Scotland) key contours to colors and are excellent; they can be ordered directly from the company; or, by members from the Cyclists' Touring Club (address above). These can be used in conjunction with lodging guides such as the BTA publications *Britain: Stay on a Farm, Britain: Stay at an Inn,* and *Britain: Hotels and Restaurants,* as well as the CTC's annual handbook for members, which lists not only some 3,000 inexpensive hotels and B&Bs that extend particularly warm welcomes to cyclists but also bicycle repair shops throughout the country. The CTC Touring Department also provides excellent trip-planning help to its members.

As you travel, of course, you just may not feel like pedaling as far as you've planned on any given day, or bad weather may militate against meeting your mileage. In such cases, you can either revise your route — or hop a bus or train to catch up.

CYCLING HOLIDAYS

Although there are no organized bike trips in the Irish Republic, there are several cycling holidays available in Britain and Northern Ireland. Among them are the following:

Youth Hostel Association Adventure Holidays, Trevelyan House, St. Albans, Hertfordshire AL1 2DY, England (phone: 0727-55215). Group trips to favored biking destinations in England and Wales.

Carefree Cotswold Holidays, The Mulberries, 3 Cudnall St., Cheltenham, Gloucestershire (phone: 024-28378). Bicycles and accommodations provided for tours of the Cotswolds.

East Anglia Cycling Holidays, The Bookshop, Yoxford, Suffolk IP17 3BR, England (phone: 072877-246). This organization, the largest cycle holiday company in Great Britain, offers go-as-you-please packages in thirteen areas in Britain, including the Cotswolds, The West Country, the Wye Valley, the Yorkshire Dales, Sussex, East Anglia, and the Scottish Highlands and Borders. You never travel in a group, but there are normally others following the same route at the same time, and at the end of each day, you can keep to yourself — or mingle at your lodging place with the others. Accommodations are in youth hostels, pubs, inns, and farmhouses. Cycles can be supplied if you don't want to bring your own.

Bike Tours, 66 Walcot St., Bath, Avon, England (phone: Bath 0225-65786). Tours in East Anglia, the Southwest, and Brittany, with tent camping and sag wagons.

Freewheeling, 9 Kandahar, Aldbourne, Marlborough, Wiltshire, England (phone:

Marlborough 40069). A half-dozen cycling holidays in the Cotswolds, Wessex, Dorset, the Isle of Wight, and the Mendips.

Cyclists' Touring Club, Cotterell House, 69 Meadrow, Godalming, Surrey GU7 3H7, England (phone: 04868-7217). Tours organized by club members in Britain and Ireland and on the Continent.

Scottish Cycling Holidays, Ballintuim Post Office, Blairgowrie, Tayside PH10 7NJ, Scotland (phone: 025086-201). Week-long holidays with accommodation in hotels and private guesthouses.

Stalking and Shooting

Men have been making sport of their search for game, both large and small, since the time of the Pharaohs (who were so enamored of the activity that they looked forward to continuing it in the afterlife) — and the sport's devotees in Britain and Ireland are no less enthusiastic. The Glorious Twelfth, which marks the opening of the shooting season for grouse, is something of a national day of festivity in Britain. But grouse are only one quarry. In both Britain and Ireland, you can go for a variety of game, from rabbits to pigeons to wildfowl to pheasants (which were first brought to Britain by the Romans). Britain is known all over the world for its red grouse shooting, and riflemen from the far corners of the globe come here to participate in shoots at which teams of beaters drive the birds over a line of camouflaged guns, or to flush them out with the aid of pointer or setter dogs. Woodcock, migratory birds that overfly the islands in the fall, are another favorite target, challenging because of their predilection for flying erratically between trees. Capercaillie, which inhabit pine and fir forests, are also sought after, as are snipe, which fly fast and unpredictably. Snipe, which favor boggy areas, are particularly numerous in Ireland because of its abundance of bogs. In Scotland, you can also stalk deer, taking advantage of all available cover as you creep up on the animal — often over a period of several hours and a distance of several miles, until you get within 80 to 200 yards of it. Though this is a very expensive proposition, it is also one of the most exciting of the sports that the United Kingdom has to offer, and — despite the fact that the red deer trophies taken here are not as large as those you might get on the Continent — many a sportsman prizes his Scottish trophies far more than larger ones taken more easily. Roe buck and Sika stag trophies compare favorably with Europe's. And the delights afforded by the scenery — everything from flat heather moors to mountainous rocky countryside and wooded farmland — may even outweigh the pleasures of the sport.

All shooting is done on private land, on estates managed specifically with the shooting in mind. (On some sections of grouse moors, for instance, the heather is burned at certain seasons, and in others the moorland left to grow to give protection to the birds at various stages in their development. Keepers and farm managers patrol the estates to prevent poaching.) Many of these are run in association with a booking agency specializing in shooting holidays, and when you decide to begin planning for a shooting holiday, these are your best contacts. Such agencies can send you the particulars of several estates; not only the details of the shooting but also fairly complete descriptions of the sort of accommodations available. Most shoots are organized in groups of six to eight, and it's common for friends to get together to form a shoot; if you can't make up a party on your own, the agents can usually fit you into someone else's (though, quite naturally, most groups are wary of having an inexperienced sportsman in their midst because of the danger of injury). The same organizations can advise you in advance about open seasons and license requirements.

454 DIVERSIONS / Stalking and Shooting

ENGLAND, SCOTLAND, WALES, and NORTHERN IRELAND: Here, you can go for red deer in the Scottish Highlands, almost always with the help of a professional stalker, or for roe buck throughout much of England, as well as southern and eastern Scotland. Pheasant, which are raised almost like chickens, can be found in nearly all shooting areas. Grouse are common quarry in the north of England and Scotland. Snipe can be found in the boggy country of the Hebrides, Wales, and Norfolk, while woodcock are most usually taken in western Scotland and in Cornwall.

Firearms certificates, which must be obtained by visitors from overseas, can be arranged through reputable agents such as the holiday tour organizer; a minimum of 1 month's notice is necessary. Game licenses, available from all main and branch post offices, are also required.

Organizations that can set up shooting holidays include the following:

Best in Britain, 48 Epple Rd., London SW6 4DH, England (phone: 01-731-1733).
Bill Nicholson Tourist Promotions, 36 Castle St., Edinburgh EH2 3BN, Scotland (phone: 031-226-6692).
John Birth Sporting Organisation, Greenlawalls Lodge, Duddo, Berwick-on-Tweed, Northumberland TD15 2PR, England (phone: 089-082-261).
Macsport Ltd., St. Nicholas House, Banchory, Grampian AB3 3YJ, Scotland (phone 03302-3411).
Major Neil Ramsay & Co., Farleyer, Aberfeldy, Perthshire PH15 7JE, Scotland (phone: 0887-20523 or 20540).
Peter Readman Sporting Agent, 10 Glamis Ave., Melton Park, Newcastle-upon-Tyne, Tyne and Wear, England (phone: 089-426-4719).
Sport in Scotland, 22 Market Brae, Inverness, Highland IV2 3AB, Scotland (phone: Inverness 0463-222757).
Travel Scotland, 10 Rutland Sq., Edinburgh EH1 2AE, Scotland (phone: 031-229-7366).
Irish Tourist Handling, Ltd., 13 Moss Rd., Banbridge, Co. Down, Northern Ireland (phone: 082-065-208).
Tourist Services Ireland, 15 Lombard St., Belfast BT1 1RB, Northern Ireland (phone: 0232-22454).
Game Services, Pinetree House, 32 Aughnatrick Rd., Hillsborough, Co. Down, Northern Ireland (phone: Hillsborough 682176).

In addition, a number of hotels can organize shooting holidays. Among the more pleasant are the following:

Whitton Farm House, Rothbury, Northumberland NE65 7RL, England (phone: 0669-208-11).
Cottage in the Wood Hotel, Holywell Road, Malvern Wells, Worcestershire, England (phone: 06845-3487).
Hollybush House Hotel, Hollybush, Strathclyde, Scotland (phone: 029-256-214).
Craig-y-Dderwen Country House Hotel, Betws-y-Coed, Gwynedd LL24 0AS, Wales (phone: 069-02-293).
The Golden Pheasant Hotel, Glynceiriog, near Chirk, Llangollen, Clwyd LL20 7BB, Wales (phone: 069-172-281).
Carlton Hotel, Belleek, Co. Fermanagh, Northern Ireland (phone: 036-565-282).
Lakeland Hotel, Bellanaleck Quay, Enniskillen, Co. Fermanagh, Northern Ireland (phone: 036-582-301).

For more information, contact the British Field Sports Society, 59 Kennington Rd., London SE1 7PZ, England (phone: 01-928-4742); the National Rifle Association, Bisley Camp, Broodwood, Woking, Surrey GU24 0BP, England (phone: 048-67-2213); and the Clay Pigeon Shooting Association, 107 Epping New Rd., Buckhurst Hill, Essex IG9 5TQ, England (phone: 01-505-6221). For more information on stalking and shooting in Northern Ireland, contact the Chief Wildlife Officer, Forest Service, Department of Agriculture, Belfast BT4 38B, Northern Ireland (phone: 0232-650111).

IRISH REPUBLIC: The main game species in Ireland are cock pheasant, wild duck, white-fronted geese, woodcock, and snipe. Grouse and partridge are scarce, but pheasants are reasonably plentiful (though not usually hunted by visitors).

A number of estates are available to visitors, among them the following:

Alpine Club Shoot, Inniscrone, Co. Sligo, Irish Republic (phone: 096-36252). Has 150,000 acres. Attached to the *Alpine Hotel.*
Ballyarthur Estate Shoot, Arklow, Co. Wicklow, Irish Republic (phone: 0402-5100).
Donegal Highlands Game Shoot, c/o Gilbert McCool, 20 The Willows, Glasnevin Rd., Dublin 11, Irish Republic (phone: 01-305530). Has 250,000 acres in Co. Donegal.
Shooting Days Youghal, c/o Tom Maloney Tours, 6 St. Patrick's Quay, Cork, Co. Cork, Irish Republic (phone: 021-507411). Accommodation at the simple *Hilltop Hotel* in Youghal.

A number of hotels feature shooting among their attractions. Some are:

Ashford Castle Hotel, Cong, Co. Mayo, Irish Republic (phone: 094-22644). One of the most luxurious establishments in the country; a sportsman's paradise, offering some of its best woodcock shooting.
Great Southern Hotel, Parknasilla, Co. Kerry, Irish Republic (phone: 064-45122). Miles of shooting over some outstandingly beautiful country.

All visitors wishing to shoot wild birds must be in possession of a current Irish firearm certificate and an Irish hunting license, which authorizes them to hunt game species during open seasons. These must be applied for well in advance (at least a month). Contact the Forest and Wildlife Service, Leeson La., Dublin 2, Irish Republic) for details. *Wildlife and the Law* (60p, from the Government Publications Sale Office, GPO Arcade, Dublin 1, Irish Republic) gives all the particulars.

Great Walks and Mountain Rambles

Almost any walker will tell you that it is the footpaths of a country — not its roadways — that show off the landscape to best advantage. You're closer to earth than you are when driving or even biking, and you notice details that might not otherwise come to your attention: incredibly tiny wildflowers blossoming cheerfully in a crack between limestone boulders, for instance, or a fox lurking in the shadows of the woods at dawn. And the scenery moves by you at a relatively slow speed: Hedgerows, fences, and the green velvet pastures can be contemplated at leisure; there's time to ponder the loveliness of the fluffy clouds scudding across a domelike sky as intensely, luminously blue as the shimmering island-jeweled waters at your feet. Churches and barns, old windmills and lichen-crusted stone walls, and farms and villages are seldom far out of sight as you follow in the footsteps of Neolithic man or Bronze Age gold traders, travel along Roman ways, or tracks first defined by smugglers, cattle drovers, abbots, or coffin carriers, whose ways would often be marked at the tops of passes by the stone piles where they rested their load. Many paths were literally walked into existence by generations of country folk traveling to work, market, church, or the local ale house, and in all, over 100,000 miles of public footpaths have been recorded and mapped (a number that swells still further when you consider those in Scotland, where the laws do not require that they be mapped and measured). In England and Wales, many are in the 10 national parks and 32 Areas of Outstanding Natural Beauty (AONB). The national parks, which cover some 5,256 square miles, about 9% of the total acreage of England and Wales, contain some of their most spectacular scenery, a blend of mountain and moor, down and heatherland, cliffs and seashore, and all offering plenty of relatively wild mileage for the pedestrian. The land is not owned by the state, as in some countries, but remains in private hands, so that you must stick to the right-of-way unless so-called access agreements exist, permitting you to do otherwise (as in over half of Dartmoor and the Lake District, for example). By custom and tradition, however, walkers are free to roam over open moorland. Local planning authorities, responsible for the parks' administration now, protect their landscape, clear away eyesores, lay out footpaths, regulate vehicular traffic, appoint wardens, and alert the public to their recreational potential. AONBs enjoy a looser measure of legal protection. The Countryside Commission, the body that is in part responsible for designating these especially scenic areas, has also created several official long-distance trails by creating new rights-of-way and linking them to established footpaths. The route of each of these trails is highlighted by *signposts* (which announce its beginning and its direction) and by *waymarkings* (acorn symbols placed at potentially confusing junctures).

In Scotland, you won't be walking in national parks as in England, because there are none, despite the fact that the scenery is some of Britain's loveliest and most varied — mountains and moors, lochs, grassy hills, forests and glens, cliffs and sandy beaches, and very few people. The law regarding rights-of-way is complex — and in principle you can't walk just anywhere. But in practice, you can roam more or less freely as long as you respect the obviously off-limits, and keep off the moors during the early-August-through-late-October grouse shooting and deer stalking season.

In the Irish Republic and Northern Ireland, the situation is similar. Though some hundred-odd forest parks — as well as national parks such as Killarney's Muckross Estate and Donegal's tranquil Glenveagh — exist throughout the country, the walks here are mainly short and relatively easy; for longer tramps, you've got to head into the wild high country, mainly along the coast, where your way leads along sheep trails and worn dirt tracks marked only occasionally by stone cairns, and where (as in Scotland) map and compass are essential companions. With summits that seldom rise above 3,000 feet, these mountains are no giants. But because the way up begins in valleys that are usually near sea level, the hikes turn out to be a good deal more demanding than you might at first expect. Your rewards are abundant, however: The sea-and-mountain views that keep you company as you go are awash in incredible blues and intense greens (thanks to the abundant rainfall). And chance encounters en route with fellow ramblers, or with tweed-hatted shepherds and their collies, can be a lot of fun.

That's true even when the weather turns rainy, as it may well do even at the height of the British summer (which King Charles II once gloomily described as "three fine days followed by a thunderstorm") — providing you come prepared. Stout walking shoes or boots are essential, as is a good rain parka, with leggings. And in addition to the usual walker's gear, you always need a spare sweater, even on a day hike — especially on the British hills, where conditions can turn literally arctic within a matter of hours. Both hiking and backpacking equipment are best bought in the US, where the selection is greater and prices are lower.

WHERE TO WALK

You don't have to dismiss the idea of walking in Britain just because you're not a hotshot mountaineer at home. Even novices can share the delights: Just find a hotel in the heart of good walking country, and use it as home base for daily expeditions; at the end of each day, you'll come back to a hot bath and a hearty meal.

Areas that offer these experiences are delightfully abundant. Among Areas of Outstanding Natural Beauty, a number are really good for walking: the path-crossed, beechwoods-dotted chalk uplands known as the Chilterns, which roll through parts of Bedfordshire, Buckinghamshire, Hertfordshire, and Oxfordshire (for details about which, contact the Thames & Chilterns Tourist Board, 8 The Market Pl., Abingdon, Oxfordshire OX14 3HG, England; phone: 0235-22711); the 582 square miles of the oh-so-English Cotswolds, full of cozy villages, extending through the counties of Avon, Gloucestershire, Hereford and Worcester, Oxfordshire, and Wiltshire (Heart of England Tourist Board, PO Box 15, Worcester WR1 2JT, England; phone: 0905-29511); rolling Dorset, with the "far from the madding crowd" scenery of novelist Thomas Hardy, and its fine seaside scenery (West Country Tourist Board, Trinity Ct., 37 Southernhay East, Exeter, Devon EX1 1QS, England; phone: 0392-76351); the distinctive Norfolk Coast, a delight to those whose souls resonate to its moody expanses of salt marshes and tidal creeks (East Anglia Tourist Board, 14 Museum St., Ipswich, Suffolk IP1 1HU, England; phone: 0473-214211); the meandering Wye Valley and the Forest of Dean, where you can explore woodlands and lovely cliffs-and-gorges river scenery (Heart of England Tourist Board, above); and, in Wales, the breezy Gower Peninsula, where you can tramp through the coastal dunes-and-beach country, or head inland up into the hills (South Wales Tourism Council, Ty Croeso, Gloucester Pl., Swansea SA1 1TY, Wales (phone: 0792-465204).

In addition, the national parks offer still better walking — and public transportation is good enough that you don't have to plan all your trips to end back at your starting point.

Ireland's mountain areas open up still further options. In the area around Clonmel alone, there are the Galtees, the location of one of Ireland's highest inland peaks — 3,018-foot Galtymore; the Comeraghs, with their flat summits and beautiful corries (blunt, cliff-backed valley ends known elsewhere as cirques); and the less-demanding Knockmealdowns to the west. You can hike around 1,722-foot Ben Bulben, in County Sligo, storied in the lore of the poet William Butler Yeats, who is buried not far away; or tackle County Mayo's isolated Nephins, with distances between possible overnight stops substantial enough to keep beginners away — and views, solitude, and scenery (magnificent moors and cliff-girt coastline) plentiful enough to make them a favorite among enthusiasts. Achill Island, off the coast, offers more of the same. In mountainous Donegal, both the rough Derryveagh Mountains in the north, and, in the south, the Slieve League's high cliffs near Carrick and the Blue Stack Mountains are also popular. For guidebooks covering these walks, contact the Federation of Mountaineering Clubs of Ireland (FMCI), 20 Leopardstown Gardens, Blackrock, Co. Dublin, Irish Republic.

Some of Britain and Ireland's most interesting walking country is detailed below:

LAKE DISTRICT NATIONAL PARK, Cumbria, England: This 866-square-mile preserve, the largest of all the parks, is also one of the most beautiful with its jewellike lakes; its steep mountains, rising precipitously from close to sea level so that they seem even higher than they actually are; and its dazzling colors, a function of the seasonal changes in vegetation. Poets and writers — among them Coleridge and Ruskin, Hugh Walpole and Beatrix Potter — have been inspired by the landscape for centuries; the area's fame has grown to such proportions that you can no longer expect to "wander lonely as a cloud" just everywhere — as did the nineteenth-century romantic poet William Wordsworth. To experience the real beauties of the Lake District, you must steer clear of the larger tourist centers such as Ambleside, Keswick, and Windermere; avoid weekends and public holidays; or go just a bit farther afield than everyone else — something that is not too difficult since there are hundreds of miles of footpaths here, ranging from nature trails and level walks along the lakeshore and in the valleys to the

458 DIVERSIONS / Great Walks and Mountain Rambles

strenuous routes that cross the mountains from valley to valley. By tradition, visitors can go almost anywhere, and with care, anyone can reach the summits of 3,206-foot Scafell, 3,054-foot Skiddaw, and 3,116-foot Helvellyn — three of the park's more noteworthy peaks. To familiarize yourself with the landscape, you might want to sign up for one of the park's short guided walks. A number of leaflets describing walks from various starting points are available from the park's information office, and for most purposes, these will suffice. The best general guidebook to the area is W. H. Pearsall's *The Lake District National Park* (£1.95, plus postage, from Her Majesty's Stationery Office [HMSO], PM1C, Atlantic House, Holborn Viaduct, London EC1P 1BN, England); the best footpath guides, which describe your way in illustrations and delightful commentary, are in Alfred W. Wainwright's five-volume *A Pictorial Guide to the Lakeland Fells* (Westmorland Gazette, 22 Strickland Gate, Kendal, Cumbria LA9 4ND, England). For general area information, contact the lake District National Park Information Office, Bank House, High St., Windermere, Cumbria LA23 1AF, England; and the Cumbria Tourist Board, Ellerthwaite, Windermere, Cumbria LA23 2AQ, England.

NORTH YORK MOORS NATIONAL PARK, Yorkshire, England: The site of the largest expanse of heather-covered moorland in England and Wales, this 553-square-mile park is a walker's paradise with its 1,130 miles of public footpaths and overall scenic splendor — rolling heather moors, which flower to even higher glory in August, as well as placid, rich green dales, and vale plains where you'll find market towns, villages, rows of cottages, and a peppering of distinctive farmhouses built of light gray or honey-colored stone, capped by red pantile or gray slate roofs and looking as solid as fortresses — in all, a naturally beautiful landscape that man's additions have only enhanced. Considering the additional visual rewards offered by the dramatic, cliff-lined coastline that edges the park on the east, it's not hard to understand why, each year, the area attracts some 137,000 visitors on an average summer Sunday. But when you step out onto the moors, except at Easter and during the summer, you'll see only the occasional sheep, staring contentedly at you through even the vilest weather. The 93-mile-long Cleveland Way, which skirts the coast and the park's inland boundaries on its way around most of the circumference of the park, and the Samaritan Way, which runs over the moors for 33 miles, are among the longer footpaths; but there are many others. General information about the park, as well as a number of leaflets describing the two long-distance walks and others, can be had from the park's Information Service (North York Moors National Park, The Old Vicarage, Bondgate, Helmsley, Yorkshire YO6 5BP, England; phone: 0439-70657).

NORTHUMBERLAND NATIONAL PARK, Northumberland, England: This long, skinny 398-square-mile region, one of England's least populated, extends southward from the Scottish border, through the lonely sheep-spotted Cheviot Hills and the heather- and bracken-clad Simonside Hills, to Hadrian's Wall — the most spectacular legacy of Britain's four-century-long Roman occupation, and one of the world's most important archaeological remains outside Greece and Italy (see *Ancient Ruins and Monuments*). The diversity of landscape results from a lively geological history whose players include an ancient volcano (which created the Cheviots), the sea (which subsequently inundated the land), monumental up-thrusting forces that created the highlands, and glaciers that carved the terrain into an approximation of its present shape. The Pennine Way, one of the most difficult of England's long-distance footpaths (described below), is among the especially scenic trails in the park. For more information, see John Philipson's *Northumberland National Park* (95p, plus postage, from HMSO, address above). Also contact the park's Information Service, Eastburn, South Park, Hexham, Northumberland NE46 1BS, England (phone: 0434-605555).

SNOWDONIA NATIONAL PARK, Gwynedd, Wales: Bordered on the west by beach-edged Cardigan Bay, this 838-square-mile expanse of mountains, glacier-scoured passes and valleys, lovely lakes, and white-foaming waterfalls is by no means the exclusive territory of climbers — who come here by the score to tackle 3,560-foot Snowdon (the loftiest summit in England and Wales) and the other 13 peaks over 900 meters in the still-wild Snowdon range. Hikers have their pick of all manner of trails through farmlands and forests, sheep pastures, and the rocky hills. In addition to a program of guided walks, there are a number of nature trails and other footpaths for which descriptive leaflets are available through the park's Information Service, Penrhyndendraeth, Gwynedd LL48 6LS, Wales; phone: 076-677-0274), which can also provide general information about the park. For details about places to stay, contact the North Wales Tourism Council, Civic Centre, Colwyn Bay, Clwyd, LL29 8AR, Wales (phone: 0492-56881); or the Mid Wales Tourism Council, The Owain Glyndwr Centre, Machynlleth, Powys SY20 8EE, Wales (phone: 0654-2401).

KERRY AND WEST CORK, Irish Republic: The republic's choice offering for walkers and scramblers, this region of relatively unexplored red sandstone country is known, first and foremost, for the Macgillycuddy Reeks, the high peaks that form the roof of Ireland; the main peak, 3,414-foot Carrantuohill, can provide a good day's workout with fine views as your reward; local guides are available. But the whole of the Iveragh Peninsula, the largest of Kerry's trio of peninsulas, whose eastern end the Reeks occupy, boasts enough equally good walking to keep you occupied for more than one vacation. East of the Reeks, and east of the Gap of Dunloe, there's 2,739-foot Purple Mountain; to the south, there's 2,756-foot Mangerton, whose summit is accessible via the deep lake known as the Devil's Punch Bowl. And in addition to the walks on the Iveragh Peninsula, there are those on the more southerly Beara Peninsula, backboned by the Caha Mountains, where you can climb 1,887-foot Sugarloaf and 2,251-foot Hungry Hill, or explore the deep valleys, as well as the treks on the Dingle Peninsula, the most northerly peninsula of the three, where the standout peak is 3,127-foot Brandon, a giant that drops almost straight into the sea on the north. For general information, consult the Irish Tourist Board; for the details, see the *Irish Walk Guide: South-West* by Sean O'Suillebhain and J. C. Coleman's *Mountains of Killarney* (£1.25 and 65p respectively, from Jean Boydell, 56A Rockville Drive, Blackrock, Co. Dublin, Irish Republic).

WICKLOW MOUNTAINS, Cos. Wicklow and Dublin, Irish Republic: Reaching southward from Dublin City, these thousand-odd square miles of granite domes and the deep valleys between them — Glencree, Glendalough, and Glenmalure, among them — can offer some pleasant days' walks. The 1,654-foot summit of Sugarloaf Mountain, which can be seen from many parts of the capital proper, stands out as just one example: In the center of an area where the mountains close in on small patches of rolling farmland, it offers fine views, at first out over the sea not far away, and beyond that, on a clear day, all the way to the Welsh mountains; the ascent begins near Rocky Valley, off the main Dublin-Glendalough Road, and the descent takes you through the wooded Glen of the Downs — a steep-banked, 800-foot-deep ravine that the novelist Sir Walter Scott once termed "the most beautiful view" he had ever seen. The Irish Tourist Board can provide general information; for particulars, consult *Dublin and Wicklow Mountains*, a detailed account of how to get up into these hills edited by members of the Irish Ramblers' Club and available at £1.25 from Jean Boydell, at the address above.

CONNEMARA, Co. Galway, Irish Republic: One of Ireland's most scenic and unspoiled regions, Connemara offers its share of the country's best walking. The quartzite pyramids known as the Twelve Bens, which are the most widely known of the peaks here and look like nothing more than minor hills, provide the quality of experience afforded by real mountains, because of their cliff-bound ridges and slopes of bare rock and scree. (In fact, the north face of 2,336-foot Bencorr offers some of the country's best rock-climbing.) The highest, 2,395-foot Benbaun, provides solid footing and fine views out over some of the other good Connemara hiking country — most notably the north-south running range known as the Maumturks, to the east; and, to the north, the Mweelreas, rising impressively out of the northern rim of Killary Harbour. Still farther north, not far from the southern shore of Clew Bay, Ireland's holy mountain, 2,510-foot Croagh Patrick, affords yet another good climb — among Ireland's more popular, and, consequently, well worn and easier to follow than most you'll encounter here (but still a challenge because of the loose shale at the top). Tens of thousands climb "the Reek," as the mountain is called, on the last Sunday in July as part of a great national pilgrimage; even out of season, you probably won't have the Pilgrim's Path to yourself, since the view from the top out over beach-ringed Clew Bay — boasting as many shades of blue as the Bahamian seacoast, and littered with landfalls — is worth gawking at any time of year. For further information of a general nature, contact the Irish Tourist Board; more detailed information about the walks themselves is contained in the *Irish Walk Guide: West* by Tony Whilde (£1.25) and *The Twelve Bens* by Joss Lynam (£1), both available from Jean Boydell (address above).

MOURNE MOUNTAINS, Co. Down, Northern Ireland: This granite range in the northeastern section of the island south of Belfast is not very large, but the scenery is especially lovely, with good views, sapphire lakes, and rugged gray rocks. The principal peak of the group, 2,796-foot Slieve Donard, stands out as one particularly good climb — both relatively easy and especially attractive as you approach it from the town of Newcastle; on fine clear days, you can see the Isle of Man, the peaks of the English Lake District, the mountains of Wales, and Scotland's islands. If you have a full day, you should walk along the ridge to 2,448-foot Slieve Bignian, to see the aptly named Silent Valley and its reservoir, and, beyond it, the lonely little Lough Shannagh. Other good hikes include the ascents of 2,394-foot Bearnagh and of 2,512-foot Commeragh. The once-a-year Mourne Wall Walk — a 22-mile group trek that takes place in June — covers the main peaks of the range (gaining an impressive 10,000 feet of altitude in all). For more information about the walk, contact the Youth Hostel Association of Northern Ireland, 56 Bradbury Pl., Belfast BT7 1RU, Northern Ireland. For details about hiking in this area at any other time of year, consult J. S. Doran's *Hill Walks in the Mournes,* which describes 17 good hikes (80p from Mourne Observer Press, Castlewellan Rd., Newcastle, Co. Down, Northern Ireland). On the spot, the personnel at the various mountaineering club huts can be helpful; for huts' locations, ask at the FMCI before you go.

STAR TREKS

If day-tripping strikes you as a bit tame, consider a walking tour along one of a number of several long-distance footpaths in England and Wales. Twelve of them have already been created by the Countryside Commission, by establishing new rights-of-way to link together previously existing trails to form continuous, multimile stretches of public footpath; each is signposted and, at shifts in directions and other potentially confusing points, waymarked with acorn symbols. In addition, there are over 60 other long-distance walks devised by local county councils, rambling groups, and even individual enthusiasts eager to share their love of a particular corner of the English landscape, sometimes their own rural backyard. The number of these long-distance delights, both officially and informally gotten together, is increasing all the time. In Ireland, hiking groups are also beginning work on two long-distance footpaths.

One of the pleasures of these routes is that, while they take you through some of the nation's loveliest countryside, they're close enough to civilization that you can overnight en route at small hotels, B&Bs, or huts and mountaineering hostels — that is, unless you prefer the independence and self-sufficiency that a tent, sleeping bag, and your own cookstove can bestow, in which case you've the option to backpack. Camping is occasionally permitted, though you should make a point of asking permission of the landowner before putting up your tent for the night, particularly where the surrounding land is cultivated — not only to avoid problems but also to make friends: More than one farmer has been known to show up in the morning bearing a pint of fresh milk for visiting campers to pour over their morning granola. For details on any of these trails, contact the Countryside Commission (Dept. CC, John Dower House, Crescent Pl., Cheltenham, Gloucestershire GL50 3RA, England), which publishes a free leaflet on long-distance footpaths, and the Ramblers' Association (1/5 Wandsworth Rd., London SW8 2LJ, England; phone: 01-582-6878). Ask for copies of the Fact Sheets (46p each, postpaid) covering the walking area in question. These contain comprehensive bibliographies and tell you which maps you'll require.

For information about other long-distance footpaths in other parts of the country, consult the following: Geoffrey Berry's *Across Northern Hills: Long-Distance Footpaths in the North of England* (£4.50; Westmorland Gazette, 22 Strickland Gate, Kendal, Cumbria LA9 4ND, England); D. G. Moir's *Scottish Hill Tracks*, which describes short paths that can be hiked in sequence over long distances (95p; John Bartholomew & Son, 12 Duncan St., Edinburgh EH9 1TA, Scotland); Barbara Blatchford's *The Long Distance Walker's Handbook* (available for £1.80 from the author at 11 Thorn Bank, Onslow, Guildford, Surrey, GU7 5PL, England (phone: 0483-60085); and Showell Styles's *Backpacking in Wales* (£3.95; Robert Hale, Ltd., Clerkenwell House, 45–47 Clerkenwell Green, London EC1R 0HT, England). Also contact the Sports Council for Northern Ireland, 2A Upper Malone Rd., Belfast BT9 5LA, Northern Ireland (phone: 0232-661222).

THE CLEVELAND WAY, from Helmsley to Filey, North Yorkshire, England: This horseshoe-shaped, 100-mile-long footpath takes you over moors and down dales, and then sweeps you along the tops of the cliffs of the county's stunning coastline. The going, while not particularly rough, does take more out of you than either the North and South Downs trails or the Ridgeway (all described below), and, though rain will probably not trouble you in this relatively dry corner of the nation, the occasionally chilly spells require that you be prepared with warm clothing. For details about this route in particular, get a copy of *The Cleveland Way* (£2.95, plus postage, from HMSO, address above).

THE COTSWOLD WAY, from Chipping Camden, Gloucestershire, to Bath, Avon, England: The attractions of this route along the crest of a limestone escarpment — one of those outside the purview of the Countryside Commission — include ever-changing skies, the panoramic views out over the wooded valleys and lush green fields, and frequent calls at the delightfully mellow yellow villages scattered here and there along the way. The pathway ends at the Roman baths themselves. *The Cotswold Way* by Mark B. Richards (85p; Thornhill Press, 24 Moorend Rd., Cheltenham, Gloucestershire, England) describes the route.

THE DALES WAY, from Ilkley, West Yorkshire, to Bowness-on-Windermere, Cumbria, England: Apart from a climb up and over the Pennines' watershed (where only fate determines whether a raindrop finds its way to the North Sea instead of the Irish), this 81-mile-long hike involves low-lying country along the banks of lovely clear rivers. For details, see Colin Speakman's *The Dales Way* (£1.75; Dalesman Publishing, Ltd., Clapham, Lancaster LA2 8EB, England).

THE LONDON COUNTRYWAY, around London, England: Even the metropolis has its rural back door: This 200-mile-long circular path shows it off. For details, see Keith Chesterton's *The London Countryway* (£5.50; Constable & Co., 10 Orange St., Leicester Sq., London WC2H 7EG, England).

NORTH DOWNS WAY, from Farnham, Surrey, to Dover, Kent, England: This

141-mile-long footpath takes you through the rolling Surrey Hills and Kent Downs, along the crest of the North Downs, and across several rivers and highways to its end at Shakespeare Cliff, where the panorama spread out before you is of the celebrated English Channel. In parts, the footpath follows the medieval Pilgrims' Way. The North Downs Way is similar to its cousin, the South Downs Way (described below), but with more nooks and crannies and fewer grand, obstacle-free stretches in which to develop a steady stride. But the going is relatively easy, as is access to London via train. (On weekends and in summer, the route can be rather crowded.) For details, consult Christopher John Wright's *A Guide to the Pilgrims' Way and the North Downs Way* (£3.50; from Constable at the address above), *North Downs Way* by Denis Herbstein (HMSO, address above), and *North Downs Way Maps* (£1.90; available from the Countryside Commission, John Dower House, Crescent Pl., Cheltenham, Gloucestershire GL50 3RA, England; phone: 0242-21381).

THE PENNINE WAY, from Edale, Derbyshire, England, to Kirk Yetholm, Borders, Scotland: The first of the official trails to be designated, "expressly for those who seek the call of the hills and the lonely places," this track takes you along 270 demanding, often extremely boggy miles, up the backbone of England to a point just north of the Scottish border, traversing the Pennines, the Peak District National Park, and the Cheviots; and traveling through eerie forests and over high peaks; down old pack horse and shepherds' tracks and old Roman roads; across several rivers; and along well-preserved portions of Hadrian's Wall to a point not far from the impressive fort at Housesteads. Waterfalls and peat bogs, fine views, limestone cliffs, ruined mines, and other landmarks all add still more variety to the pathway. But it's not for everyone: In all, you gain more altitude than you would climbing Everest, and the weather can be terrible (dangerous, at this latitude, at these altitudes); in addition, while there are plenty of B&Bs for some of the route, long sections of trail are empty enough that you'll need to carry camping gear. But for experienced walkers, this famous footpath is a delight. Of the handful of publications covering the route, one of the best is Alfred Wainwright's *A Pennine Way Companion* (£2.25; Westmorland Gazette, address above); also consult Tom Stephenson's *The Pennine Way* (£3.95; from HMSO, address above).

THE RIDGEWAY, from Overton Hill, near Avebury, Wiltshire, to Ivinghoe Beacon, Buckinghamshire, England: This 85-mile-long footpath follows the ancient Icknield Way and the Great Ridgeway, first trod by Neolithic man; and, consequently, ancient burial places, religious monuments, Iron Age hill forts, and other evidences of bygone days, are abundant along your route as it traverses farms, beech woods, and downlands. The section from Overton Hill to Goring has been designated a bridleway — and so can be used by cyclists and horseback riders as well as hikers; but at no point is the going particularly difficult. For details, consult Sean Jennett's *The Ridgeway Path* (£2.95; from HMSO, at the address above); and H. D. Westacott's *The Ridgeway Path* (£1.50; Penguin Books).

SOUTH DOWNS WAY, from Eastbourne, Sussex, to Harting, near Petersfield, Hampshire, England: It's true enough that in his *Natural History of Selbourne* Gilbert White referred to the South Downs as "majestic mountains"; and, indeed, when you stand on high and look southward toward the sea, or in the opposite direction, across the partly wooded Weald (the remains of an ancient forest), toward the North Downs, you do feel you're at the top of the world. Nonetheless, the 80-mile route through the range of chalk hills known as the South Downs offers relatively gentle walking. And there's no shortage of places to stay along the way. This is the country's only long-distance bridleway — you'll encounter cyclists and horseback riders on your journey. For details, consult Sean Jennett's *South Downs Way* (£2.95 from HMSO, address above), or the Eastbourne Rambling Club's *Along the South Downs Way*, which describes the route in both directions and on to Winchester (£1.50 from the Eastbourne

DIVERSIONS / Great Walks and Mountain Rambles

Rambling Club, 28 Kinfauns Ave., Eastbourne, Sussex BN22 8SS, England).

SOUTHWEST WAY, from Studland, Dorset, to Minehead, Somerset, England: For lovers of hours spent with the sea as a constant companion, this 550-mile track is not only England's longest long-distance footpath, but also its best — and, except for its considerable number of ups and downs, the going is not so difficult. There are four sections: the Dorset Coast Path, noted for its special quiet loveliness; the South Devon Coast Path, much of it through the South Devon and East Devon Areas of Outstanding Natural Beauty, where you'll find stunning headlands, broad rivers, busy resort towns, quiet bays, and lush greenery; the Cornwall Coast Path, which takes you around Land's End, past spectacular cliffs, lighthouses, stone circles, and more resorts; and the Somerset and North Devon Coast Path, which leads from Exmoor National Park into the North Devon Area of Outstanding Natural Beauty — full of stony beaches and high beautiful cliffs. Along the length of the path, accommodations and campsites are easy to find (but since this is a resort area, you need to reserve ahead for visits during school holidays). For more information, consult Mark Richards's *Walking the North Cornwall Coastal Footpath* (£1.80; Thornhill Press, address above); the Sou'West Way Association's *Complete Guide to the Coastal Path* (available from the Sou'West Way Association, 1 Orchard Dr., Kingskerwell, Newton Abbot, Devon TQ12 5DG, England); H. D. Westacott's *The Devon South Coast Path* (£1.50) and *The Dorset Coast Path* (£1.25), both from Penguin Books; *Cornwall Coast Path* by Edward Pyatt (£3.95, from HMSO); Brian Le Merries's *South Devon Coast Path* (£2.95, from HMSO); *Dorset Coast Path* by Brian Jackman (£2.95, from HMSO); and *Somerset and North Devon Coast Path* by Clive Grinnell (£3.95, from HMSO).

THE WOLDS WAY, from Filey, North Yorkshire, to North Ferriby, Humberside, England: The most recently approved of the official long-distance footpaths, this one traverses considerable agricultural land and follows the chalk hills and pretty valleys of the Yorkshire Wolds for 71 miles, from the eastern terminus of the Cleveland Way to the banks of the River Humber to the south. For details, consult David Rubinstein's *The Wold's Way* (£1.75; Dalesman, address above), or Roger Ratcliffe's *Wolds Way* (HMSO, address above).

OFFA'S DYKE PATH, from near Chepstow, Gwent, to Prestatyn, Clwyd, Wales: For 60 out of its total 168 miles, this Welsh track follows the distinctive earthwork built by King Offa of Mercia in the eighth century as a frontier between England and Wales. It takes you through the Shropshire Hills and Wye Valley Areas of Outstanding Natural Beauty; climbs up into the imposing Black Mountains; visits Hay-on-Wye, the town of books (see *Shopping*); and eventually takes you along a high ridge through the Clwydian Hills. The walking can be demanding in spots; the terrain is wonderfully varied, taking in everything from wild hills to wooded valleys and peaceful lowlands. For details, consult Christopher John Wright's *A Guide to Offa's Dyke Path* (£4.50; Constable, address above) and John B. Jones's *Offa's Dyke Path* (£2.95, plus postage, from HMSO, at the address above). For more information, contact the South Wales Tourism Council, Ty Croeso, Gloucester Pl., Swansea SA1 1TY, Wales (phone: 0792-465204).

PEMBROKESHIRE COAST PATH, from St. Dogmaels to Amroth, Dyfed, Wales: Despite the beauty of the wild seascapes of this southwestern part of the country, the area has remained unspoiled by visitors, and often you can walk for many hours along this 168-mile-long footpath without meeting a soul. That is only one of its special offerings, however: It also gives you a look at some wonderful scenery — sandstone cliffs, windswept headlands, jagged inlets and coves, and green and inviting, but icy, water. And the walking is easy. For details, consult John Barrett's *The Pembrokeshire Coast Path* (£2.95, plus postage, from HMSO, at the address above). Also: Pembrokeshire Coast National Park, County Offices, Haverford West, Swansea SA61 1Q2, Wales (phone: 0437-3131); or the South Wales Tourism Council (address above).

THE WICKLOW WAY, from Marlay Park, near Sandyford, Co. Dublin, to Moyne, Co. Wicklow, Irish Republic: So far, only 24 miles of this footpath have been completed, but they're worth noting for their proximity to Dublin — and for their sheer beauty and wildness: Though you're never more than a couple of miles from civilization, you're always out of calling distance from the settled lowlands, and when drastic weather changes occur, as they sometimes do, you can find yourself in serious trouble if you're not prepared with the proper clothing. The rewards are ample, especially in terms of views — which by turns take in the high Powerscourt Waterfall, the mountains of Wales, the Irish Sea, the Mourne range, and more. For general information, see *The Wicklow Way*, available from the Irish Tourist Board, and the Irish Ramblers' Club's *Dublin and Wicklow Mountains* (£1.25), or the *Irish Walk Guide: East* (£1.25), both available from Jean Boydell, at the address above.

MAPS AND MORE INFORMATION

When Daniel Boone was once asked whether he had ever been lost, he replied, "Nope, but I was a mite confused once for three days." To avoid that fate, and to help plan your wanderings, you'll need the proper maps and guidebooks.

Some of the most beautiful areas of Britain are covered by 1-inch-to-1-mile Tourist maps and by 1:25,000-scale Outdoor Leisure maps. For the several regions that these exist, they are your best choice. Elsewhere, consult the relevant 1:50,000 Ordnance Survey maps. Rights-of-way are indicated by red lines (the dotted lines referring to footpaths, the dashes to bridleways). These symbols and the many others are explained in an elaborate key, a brief study of which will have you reading these British plans as well as, if not better than, the far less colorful US Geological Survey maps.

In addition, virtually every defined trail in Britain is also covered by one or more step-by-step guidebooks. To find out exactly what's available and what you need, contact the Ramblers' Association (1/5 Wandsworth Rd., London SW8 2LJ, England; phone: 01-582-6878) for copies of the Fact Sheets (46p each, postpaid), which list relevant guidebooks and maps for the main walking areas of the country. Authoritative general books on walking in Britain such as H. D. Westacott's *Walking in Britain* (95p, Penguin) provide the same sort of information for footpaths, AONBs, and national parks throughout England, Scotland, and Wales; this publication also contains useful information about techniques and equipment that will serve you well when planning a walking trip in Britain. And the Countryside Commission (address above) publishes a free leaflet covering more than 60 recreational paths in England and Wales.

The best magazine for the hiking enthusiast is *The Great Outdoors,* published by Holmes McDougall, Ltd., Ravenstoft House, 302/304 St. Vincent St., Glaslgow G2 5RG, Scotland; phone: 041-221-7911), and available from most large news agents; in addition to both informative and descriptive articles on hiking, backpacking, and cycling, each issue includes a useful directory that lists stores that specialize in outdoor equipment, maps, books, and local guidebooks, plus advertisements for organizations that sponsor walking tours and equipment rental agencies.

As background reading, to put you in the proper frame of mind for your journey, try to locate a copy of John Hillaby's *A Walk through Britain* (Houghton Mifflin Co.; now out of print). Also see *Britain at Your Feet: A Backpacker's Handbook* by David Wickers and Art Pedersen (£5.95, from Kogan Page, 120 Pentonville Rd., London N1 9JN, England); and John Merrill's *Turn Right at Land's End,* which describes a man's journey around the entire British coastline (£6.95, from Oxford Illustrated Press, Sparkford, Yeovil, Somerset BA22 7J5, England).

Many of these books can be bought at *Stanford's* (12 Long Acre, London WC2E 9LP, England; phone: 836-1321).

For the Wicklow Way and several counties in the Irish Republic, it's possible to buy 1-inch-to-1-mile Ordnance Survey maps; for the rest of the country, ¼- and ½-inch

DIVERSIONS / Great Walks and Mountain Rambles

maps are available. All series are essentially accurate, but since cliffs are not always shown, you're best advised to check out your route locally before you head for the hills. To get maps, contact the Ordnance Survey Office, Phoenix Park, Dublin, Irish Republic; or the Government Publications Sale Office, GPO Arcade, Henry St., Dublin 1, Irish Republic. *Eason's* bookstore (O'Connell St., Dublin 1) stocks a good selection. C. W. Wall's *Mountaineering in Ireland* (£1.50, contact Jean Boydell) covers all mountain areas in Ireland, detailing huts and hostels among other things. *Irish Walk Guides* (£1.25 each), a few of which have been referred to in the preceding copy, are also available for the northeast, the northwest, the east, and the southeast, all of which may be ordered from Jean Boydell. Maps are included, but the paper quality is poor, and dedicated hill climbers will want to supplement them with the OS maps.

For maps covering Northern Ireland, write Her Majesty's Stationery Office, 80 Chichester St., Belfast BT1 4JY. The Mournes are now covered by an outdoor pursuits map called "Mourne Country," scaled to a generous 2½ inches per mile (produced by the Ordnance Survey of Northern Ireland, 83 Ladas Dr., Belfast BT6 9FJ, Northern Ireland). There are ¼- and ½-inch maps for the rest of the country. Be sure to check your route locally before setting out.

GROUP TRIPS

If you don't want to go it alone — or do all the requisite planning — contact the following organizations about group treks:

Edale Adventure Holidays, Warren Lodge, Edale, via Sheffield, Yorkshire S30 2ZD, England (phone: 0433-70256).

The Dales Centre, Grassington, near Skipton, North Yorkshire BD23 5AU, England (phone: 0756-752312).

Head for the Hills, 21 Pembroke Ave., Hove, East Sussex BN3 5DB, England (phone: 05912-388).

Earth & Sky Travel, Ltd., 37 Runley Rd., Luton, Bedfordshire, England.

Countrywide Holidays Association, 100 Cromwell Range, Manchester M14 6HU, England (phone: 061-225-1000).

YHA Adventure Holidays, Trevelyan House, 8 St. Stephen's Hill, St. Albans, Hertfordshire AL1 2DY, England (phone: 0727-55215).

Ramblers Holidays, Ltd., 13 Longcroft House, Fretherne Rd., Welwyn Garden City, Hertfordshire AL8 6PQ, England (phone: Welwyn Garden 31133).

Mountain Goat Holidays, Victoria St., Windermere, Cumbria LA23 1AD, England (phone: 09662-5161). Organized guided walking tours in the Lake District.

Earthwalk, Pen-y-wern, Kerry, Newtown, Powys, Wales (phone: 0686-28282). Six-day walks through the little-known hills of Montgomeryshire, with vehicles and trailers to carry your belongings.

John Noble Journeys and Expeditions, Llanddwyn, Ffordd Glyder, Port Dinorwic, near Caernarfon, Gwynedd, Wales (phone: 0248-670046). Walking adventures in Snowdonia, following ancient roads or going down to the sea.

Association for Adventure Sports (AFAS), c/o Tiglin Adventure Centre, Ashford, Co. Wicklow, Irish Republic (phone: 0404-4169). Mountaineering training courses and adventure holidays in Connemara, the Galtees, and Kerry.

Society of Irish Foresters, c/o Royal Dublin Society, Ballsbridge, Dublin 4, Irish Republic (phone: 01-866751). Organizes one walk annually in some part of the country, usually on the second Sunday in September.

For the Mind

Marvelous Museums

It may be true, as people often say, that in 1649 when King Charles I died and the Parliamentarians auctioned off his collection of paintings and other treasures, Britain lost a heritage. But the growth of the great national collections beginning as early as the seventeenth century with the founding of Oxford's Ashmolean Museum, and the collecting mania of the eighteenth and nineteenth centuries — when the rich were really rich and gentlemen made careers of their hobbies, accumulating not only the fine art of Western Europe, but also trifles and prizes from the farthest corners of the empire — more than made amends. As a result, Britain is home to a staggering agglomeration of works of art from all over the world. And although some small percentage of this remains in private hands, the better portion is on display in the nation's great museums, not to mention hundreds of country houses that are as noteworthy for the collections housed within as for their often stunning architecture. (England's National Portrait Gallery, for instance, maintains two collections outside London at Montacute, Somerset, and at Beningbrough, North Yorkshire.) The furnishings in such homes are often in mint condition, and seeing them displayed along with porcelain, silver, and tapestries is indeed a pleasure. You'd need a lifetime to go around to all these stately pleasure domes.

As for Britain's museums themselves, they are usually well conceived and well designed so that you don't often have problems seeing the pictures because of improper lighting or accumulated filth. And despite recent cutbacks in government support of the arts, most museums are free, and open every day except on principal holidays. Special lecture programs are usually offered as well, and they are designed as much for experts in the fields as for beginners seeking a greater appreciation of what they've seen and admired. Check the newspapers or a museum's events calendar for notices; they're almost always worth your while.

In Ireland, the picture is not so rosy. While the collections themselves were amassed much like England's, the institutions that house them have been continually plagued by shortages of funds, and for many decades, Ireland's antiquities have not been kept in the manner to which they should have become accustomed. The Natural Science Museum in Dublin, for instance, has a staff of less than a dozen, while its London counterpart employs nearly 800. But there are signs that the situation is improving: More money is being spent and many regional museums have been set up with some good results; the Monaghan County Museum is but one example. While it will always be important for scholars and researchers to have exhibits in one central place, facsimiles as well as material of local interest may eventually help enlarge these few and currently tiny regional museums — and certainly, this is a step in the right direction.

No matter where you are, your museum visits can be a great deal more pleasurable if you follow a few simple guidelines. First, make several short visits to a large museum rather than one long one. Stay just an hour, and take in no more than a dozen really fine works. There's no fatigue quite like aching, yawny museum fatigue — once described as the dread "Museum Foot" — and when it has set in, merely sitting for 3 minutes in front of a Rubens won't cure it. So plan to go when you're fresh — preferably as soon as the museum opens, before the crowds have arrived. If possible, know what you want to see before beginning your rounds, so that you don't clutter your senses with too many bleeding saints and blustery seascapes; most museums publish excellent pamphlets or booklets to steer you to the more noted works in their collections, and it's a good idea to buy a copy. At the very least, stop at the museum shop on your way *in* to thumb the catalogue or look at the postcards to get an idea of what there is to see and where you'll find it.

And visit a gallery or an auction house occasionally — just to remind yourself that once, it was *all* for sale.

AMERICAN MUSEUM IN BRITAIN, Bath, Avon, England: Oddly enough, this elegant and very English town is home to one of the country's best collections of things American — Hopi kachina dolls and Shaker furniture, patchwork quilts and Pueblo pots, and even a teepee and a Conestoga wagon. While British visitors (particularly children) are marveling at these oddments, munching gingerbread baked in historic ovens on the spot, and otherwise pondering how their colonies were getting along in the days before the big revolt, Americans admire the quality of the items on display and the thoughtful manner in which the several period rooms were put together. Claverton Manor, the Greek Revival mansion housing these exhibits, was where Sir Winston Churchill delivered his first political speech in 1897. Details: American Museum, Claverton Manor, Bath, Avon BA2 7BD, England (phone: 0225-60503).

CECIL HIGGINS ART GALLERY, Bedford, Bedfordshire, England: Installed in the fine old Victorian structure that was once the home of a local brewer and art lover named Cecil Higgins and in an adjacent annex built in 1974, this lively and especially hospitable museum boasts a distinguished collection of watercolors by artists such as Constable, Cotman, Gainsborough, and Turner, and fine displays of prints by Dürer, Picasso, Rembrandt, the Impressionists, and others; these are displayed in a succession of constantly changing exhibitions in the new building. The Victorian Mansion is set up to show you how a family might have lived about a century ago, and has a homey lived-in look: A fire winks on the hearth, clocks ticktock faithfully away, children's toys litter the floor next to a dollhouse, a letter lies half-written on the desk, and a woolly shawl hangs from the hatstand, just waiting for a Victorian lady to throw it on her shoulders and leave the house for a walk. As you walk through the house, a number of oddities stand out — but few more than the mahogany-edged chair-bed, a precursor of today's sofa beds. And throughout, the captioning helps you understand what you are seeing. Details: Cecil Higgins Art Gallery, Castle Close, Bedford, Bedfordshire MK40 3NY, England (phone: 0234-211222).

BIRMINGHAM MUSEUM AND ART GALLERY, Birmingham, West Midlands, England: Boasting one of the nation's most important art collections outside London, with good representations from the seventeenth through nineteenth century, this institution gives you an exceptionally good look at the work of the pre-Raphaelites, in an assemblage that is well-nigh without equal; English watercolorists from the eighteenth century onward are also particularly thoroughly represented, and there are outstanding collections of postage stamps and silver plate. In addition, the Department of Archaeology and Ethnography shows off objects from cultures around the world, the Department of Local History exhibits items from the Birmingham of bygone days, and the Department of Natural History displays, among other things, a life-size replica tyrannosaurus and Britain's finest fossilized triceratops skull. The associated Museum of Science and Industry in Newhall Street exhibits old steam engines, aircraft, cars, machine tools, scientific instruments, and the like — a large number of them actually in working order. You can see them in action at the Steam Weekends held in March and October, at the Traction Engine Rally in May, and at the Stationary Engine Rally in September. Details: Birmingham Museums and Art Gallery, Chamberlain Sq., Birmingham, West Midlands B3 3DH, England (phone: 021-235-2834).

BRIGHTON MUSEUM AND ART GALLERY, Brighton, East Sussex, England: Installed in the former stables of the Prince Regent's fantastic "Eastern" palace (now one of the world's great showpieces), the Museum and Art Gallery houses fine collections of old master paintings, watercolors, furniture, musical instruments, costumes, and English pottery and porcelain, as well as of archaeological and ethnographic items and displays relating to Brighton history; the collections of applied art of the art nouveau and art deco periods — in which the museum specializes — are particularly interesting. The unique Hove Amber Cup, found in 1857 in Hove, in a Bronze Age barrow carbon-dated to about 1500 BC, is another treasure. As part of the museum's lively program of special exhibitions, shows on the Jazz Age, British India, the Gothic Revival, Vanity, fairies, and other such subjects have been mounted in the past; check in advance to see what's on when you visit. Details: Royal Pavilion, Art Gallery and Museums, Brighton, East Sussex BN1 1UE, England (phone: 0273-603005).

FITZWILLIAM MUSEUM, Cambridge, Cambridgeshire, England: One of the nation's greatest and oldest public museums, the Fitzwilliam was founded in 1816 when Richard, the seventh viscount Fitzwilliam of Merrion, left his superb collections, his library, and a good endowment to his alma mater, the University of Cambridge; and the collections — not to mention the stature of the museum — have been growing ever since. Thanks to the innovative spirit of Sir Sydney Cockerell, the museum's fourth director, it is also especially charming, and a good deal less chilly and solemn (though every bit as grand) as its peers: Cockerell instituted the then-revolutionary policy of livening up the picture galleries with oriental rugs, sculpture, period furniture, and even flowers. When you visit, you'll want to pick up a copy of the museum's brochure-guide to lead you through the extensive collections of coins and medals, European applied arts, Islamic and Far Eastern treasures, manuscripts, paintings and drawings, portrait miniatures, prints, and west Asiatic, Egyptian, and Greek and Roman antiquities. Be sure to note the lovely Roman mosaic fountain niche from first century Baiae; the extensively illuminated thirteenth-century Peterborough Psalter; Rembrandt's *Portrait of a Man;* Delacroix's *Odalisque;* and Renoir's *Coup de Vent* (a favorite of even those who ordinarily find the artist's work a bit saccharine). The music collection, which includes autographed scores of Handel, Bach, Chopin, Britten, and Elgar, is one of Britain's finest, and the holdings of works by Blake and the members of his circle are without peer. Details: Fitzwilliam Museum, Trumpington St., Cambridge, Cambridgeshire CB2 1RB, England (phone: 0223-69501).

THE BRITISH MUSEUM, London, England: Founded in 1753 around the lifetime accumulations of Sir Hans Sloane, one of the earliest physicians to use the smallpox vaccine, this vast institution remains Britain's largest and most celebrated, and trying to knock it off in a single visit is like trying to master nuclear physics while in a barber's chair. The crown jewels of the collection, consecrated to the whole of human history, are the renowned Elgin Marbles, the massive sculpture and reliefs that once adorned the ruined Parthenon, bought for £57,000 from the Turkish sultan, and carted off to safe, civil England. But you'll also find the Rosetta Stone, the black basalt tablet that provided the key to Egyptian hieroglyphics; the Royal Gold Cup; the deep blue and white cameo-cut Portland Vase, a great marvel of the glassmaker's art dating from Roman times; the gold and silver treasures from the Sutton Hoo Burial Ship, found at an East Suffolk archaeological excavation; the Tomb of Mausolus from Halicarnassus, which brought the word *mausoleum* to the English language; the Temple of Diana from Ephesus; many mummies, among them the one that occasioned the legends of the curse of the mummy's tomb; and much more. The collections of Greek, Roman, and Egyptian antiquities are unrivaled anywhere else in the world, and a new permanent display is devoted entirely to Etruscan civilization. Man Before Metals gives you an enthralling look at the art and technology of the Stone Age. The Near and Far Eastern departments are magnificent reminders of the time when Britannia ruled the waves. In the Manuscript Saloon of the British Library (a separate institution since 1973, though still housed in the British Museum), you can see the original Magna Carta, plus the signatures of Shakespeare, Dickens, and Joyce; a Gutenberg Bible; sketchbooks of Dürer and da Vinci; manuscripts of Mozart and Bach; and the original copy of *Alice in Wonderland*. The British Library Reading Room, where Karl Marx wrote *Das Kapital*, is accessible only to those who come well recommended (preferably by a scholar of some note) and apply in advance for a ticket, or who pay £3 and join the National Art Collections Fund. The rest of the museum can be overwhelming; guidebooks to various sections of the collections, for sale in the main lobby, are good investments when you want to examine one aspect of its offerings in some detail. More information: British Museum, Great Russell St., London WC1B 3DG, England (phone: 01-636-1555, or, for the library, 01-636-1544).

COURTAULD INSTITUTE GALLERIES, London, England: When you learn that this institution was established in 1932 to teach art history to University of London students, you might not expect anything very special. Yet like a good many museums of its type, this one is approachable and enjoyable in ways that its far larger and more widely known confreres can never be. The setting, replete with oriental rugs and handsome furnishings, is lovely; beyond that are the collections, made up of the art bequests of industrialist Samuel Courtauld (whose generosity also benefited the Tate Gallery, below) as well as Lord Lee of Fareham and art critic Roger Fry (who organized London's first post-Impressionist exhibition in 1910): The excellent assemblage of Impressionist and post-Impressionist works includes Manet's *Bar at the Folies-Bergère* and *Le Déjeuner sur l'Herbe;* van Gogh's the *Artist with His Ear Cut Off* and *Peach Trees in Blossom;* Cézanne's *Lake of Annecy* and one rendering of the easily recognizable *Card Players;* Tahitian scenes by Gauguin; and wonderful works by Bonnard, Renoir, and Seurat. In addition, there are primitives, Flemish and Renaissance paintings, eighteenth-century portraits by English painters, pieces by two creative spirits of nearby Bloomsbury, Vanessa Bell and Duncan Grant, and the superb Princes Gate Collection of Flemish and Italian Old Master paintings and drawings. Details: Courtauld Institute, University of London, Woburn Sq., London WC1H 0AA, England (phone: 01-580-1015).

DULWICH PICTURE GALLERY, Dulwich, London, England: Tucked away in a quiet, leafy, almost rural suburb of southeast London, this gallery boasts a collection of old masters well worthy of a capital city anywhere. The nation's oldest public picture gallery, it contains works bequeathed by the great Shakespearean actor-manager Edward Alleyn, the founder of Dulwich College, plus nearly 400 others from the collection of the French-born art dealer Noël Joseph Desenfans; many of these had been collected at the behest of Poland's King Stanislaus, who abdicated before they could be delivered (or paid for). There are works by such Dutch painters as Rembrandt, Cuyp, and Hobbema; by seventeenth- and eighteenth-century British portraitists such as Gainsborough and Reynolds; by the Flemish painters Rubens and van Dyck; by Claude, Poussin, Watteau, and Charles LeBrun — all Frenchmen; and by Italians such as Raphael, Veronese, Tiepolo, and Canaletto, among others. The building itself — austere and, some think, a bit odd — was designed by Sir John Soane in 1811. Details: Dulwich Picture Gallery, College Rd., London SE21 7AD, England (phone: 01-693-5254).

THE IVEAGH BEQUEST, London, England: The collection here, assembled by the first Earl of Iveagh, includes works by Cuyp, Gainsborough, Hals, Rembrandt, Reynolds, Romney, Turner, Vermeer, and others, and would stand out in itself; what makes this institution particularly interesting is its setting, a late seventeenth-century house remodeled in 1764 by the Scottish architect Robert Adam, a marvelously stately structure that was scheduled for demolition until it was rescued in 1925 by the first Earl of Iveagh, who then presented the house together with the better part of his own collection to the nation. The mood is of an eighteenth-century English country house; the chamber recitals, poetry readings, and open-air concerts held here frequently in summer complete the effect. Details: The Iveagh Bequest, Hampstead La., London NW3 7JR, England (phone: 01-348-1286).

THE MUSEUM OF MANKIND, London, England: Only the collections of Berlin's Ethnographic Museum can rival those of the British Museum, which are housed in this structure behind the Burlington Arcade. By far the largest part of its holdings of items relating to tribal African, American, and Pacific cultures is brought out of the relative limbo of the reserve areas only seldom, for special theme exhibitions. However, the greatest treasures are always on display: lacy Javanese shadow puppets, devil masks from Sri Lanka, pre-Columbian gold pieces, a crystal skull made by the Aztecs, and New Guinean masks, among others. Details: Museum of Mankind, 6 Burlington Gardens, London W1X 2EX, England (phone: 01-437-2224).

NATIONAL GALLERY, London, England: Among the greatest art museums on earth, this was instituted in 1824 when the connoisseur Sir George Beaumont convinced the government to buy the three-dozen-plus paintings put up for sale after the death of the wealthy Russian-born merchant-collector John Julius Angerstein — among them Rembrandt's *The Woman Taken in Adultery* and *The Adoration of the Shepherds,* Rubens's *The Rape of the Sabine Women,* and Titian's *Venus and Adonis.* Subsequent gifts and acquisitions have endowed it with a collection that is remarkably balanced, showing off a cross-section of the chief schools of western European art through seven centuries. Leonardo da Vinci's great cartoon *The Virgin and Child with St. Anne and St. John the Baptist* has a dimly lit room all its own; and here and there masterpieces such as Botticelli's *Venus and Mars,* Holbein's *The Ambassadors,* Breughel's *The Adoration of the Kings,* van Eyck's *Arnolfini Wedding,* and Chardin's *The House of Cards* — over 2,000 jewels in all — glow at you from the walls. As the holdings are highly selective rather than comprehensive, the museum is not huge (though nearly every item it owns is on view at any given time), and seems especially inviting as a result. Homan Potterton's *A Guide to the National Gallery* (available at the museum) makes an erudite — and delightful — companion to your visit. Information: National Gallery, Trafalgar Sq., London WC2N 5DN, England (phone: 01-839-3321).

NATIONAL MARITIME MUSEUM, Greenwich, London, England: Installed in England's first Palladian building, a beautifully proportioned white structure designed in 1616 by Inigo Jones for James I's consort, Anne of Denmark, this institution tells the story of Britain's long involvement with the sea — a matter of no mean importance when you consider the history of the empire — in some 3 miles of galleries. To see it all in chronological order, begin in the Queen's House — the Palladian section of the structure, noted for the graceful spiraling Tulip Staircase, which took its name from the shape of the fleurs-de-lis decorating the wrought-iron banisters; the great paintings of marine battles, the maps, the scale models of ships, and the delicate-looking navigational instruments are worth noting. Then continue into the West Wing, where galleries devoted to Lord Nelson display, among other items, the uniform he wore during the Battle of Trafalgar, and then into the East Wing, which brings you up to the time of World War II. Also part of the museum are galleries devoted to fishing and whaling, the development of boats and steamships, and ships' figureheads. The Barge House shows off, among other craft, Mary II's intricately carved royal barge (1689). Also in Greenwich, don't miss seeing the *Cutty Sark,* once known as the fastest clipper in existence; the 53-foot ketch which, in 1966-67, bore the late Sir Francis Chichester — solo — around the world; the Christopher Wren–designed Old Royal Observatory, in whose courtyard a brass strip marks the Prime Meridian; and more. Details: National Maritime Museum, Romney Rd., Greenwich, London SE10 9NF, England (phone: 01-858-4422).

THE NATIONAL PORTRAIT GALLERY, London, England: Established in 1856, this gallery is devoted to the portraits of the most important figures in British arts, letters, history and politics, military life, science, and assorted other fields; and in all, over 7,000 of their likenesses, arranged chronologically, stare down at you from the walls. Elizabeth I is there as a young woman and a dowager, not far from Shakespeare, Mary Queen of Scots, Thomas More, Cardinal Wolsey, Essex, Leicester, and Raleigh. The list of authors portrayed reads like the table of contents in a college literature text — Pepys, Milton, Dryden, Pope, Swift, Boswell, Johnson, Tennyson, Dickens, the Brontë sisters, Wilde, Auden, Shaw, and more. There's too much to see in one visit, but it's difficult not to want to give it a try. Special exhibits on historical themes or individual artists are frequently mounted as well. Details: National Portrait Gallery, St. Martin's Pl., London WC2H 0HE, England (phone: 01-930-1552).

THE QUEEN'S GALLERY, London, England: The British Royal Collection — one of the world's greatest — remained outside the experience of the common man until 1962, when this gallery was created at Buckingham Palace, and even now, only a fraction is on view at any given time. But the exhibitions that are mounted here never fail to impress, whether they are devoted to a subject such as royal children, animal paintings, or British soldiers; to single pictures — da Vinci or Gainsborough, to name two from past shows; or to groups of painters — the Italians, or the Dutch, for instance. Exhibitions change about once a year; check the newspapers for up-to-the-minute information, or contact the Queen's Gallery, c/o the Lord Chamberlain's Office, St. James's Palace, London SW1, England (phone: 01-930-3007).

SIR JOHN SOANE'S MUSEUM, London, England: Located on the north side of central London's largest square (a haunt of lawyers since the eighteenth century), in two buildings specifically designed for the purpose by the great architect Sir John Soane (1753-1837), this museum is most probably like no other you'll ever encounter. The structures themselves are odd, their small rooms and narrow passages quirkily angled and always surprising (all the more so when seen in light of the plain and fairly straightforward exterior). In the Library, for instance, the spaces behind the flying arches are mirrored, so that you're left with the impression of more space than there actually is. The Monk's Yard, a "Gothick fantasy," is concocted of bits of masonry from the old Palace of Westminster; the Monk's Parlour houses Flemish woodcarvings, casts from medieval sculptures and buildings, and models for architectural features for some of Soane's own designs; the Sepulchral Chamber contains the alabaster sarcophagus discovered in the tomb of Seti I (d. 1290 BC) by G. B. Belzoni in 1817, purchased by Soane for £2,000 after British Museum authorities decided not to; and the shallow-domed Breakfast Room displays ingenious use of mirrors and indirect lighting. All in all, the place is a hodgepodge — but who ever said a house had to be otherwise? Don't miss Hogarth's famous series *The Rake's Progress*, recounting the life and hard times of one Tom Rakewell, and his four-part political satire *The Election*, both installed in an interesting double-walled room. Details: Sir John Soane's Museum, 13 Lincoln's Inn Fields, London WC2A 3BP, England (phone: 01-405-2107).

THE TATE GALLERY, London, England: Built in 1897 on the site of Millbank Prison, the gift of the sugar broker and art collector Sir Henry Tate, this national collection of modern painting and sculpture from the mid-nineteenth century to the present, and of British paintings from the sixteenth to nineteenth centuries, came into being less than half a century after the National Gallery, when bequests had swelled the size of the latter's collection to an extent that there was no longer room to house all the paintings — 282 oils and 19,000 watercolors by Turner, among them. Tate bequeathed his own collection plus £80,000 to house it, art dealer Sir Joseph Duveen gave additional funds, and the Gallery was on its way. A magnificent new wing was added in 1979. Often overlooked is the fact that the Tate is also home to one of the world's best collections of French post-Impressionist works; the sculpture collection offers excellent examples of the artistry of Rodin, Maillol, Mestrovic, Moore, and Epstein. The British Department is one of the country's best repositories of works by Blake, and there are modern works of conceptual, minimal, optical, kinetic, British figurative, pop, and abstract art. Rothko, Nevelson, Bacon, Ernst, and Picasso are all represented. Rex Whistler, the noted trompe l'oeil painter, is responsible for the decor of the excellent restaurant. Details: Tate Gallery, Millbank, London SW1P 4RG, England (phone: 01-821-1313).

VICTORIA AND ALBERT MUSEUM, London, England: An offspring of that celebration of the progress of human knowledge known as the Great Exhibition of 1851, this museum originally came into being in a roundabout fashion as a repository of the finest in craftsmanship from around the world, from ancient times onward, to lend inspiration to leatherworkers and ceramicists, furniture-makers and woodcarvers, architects and dressmakers, silver- and goldsmiths, and other artisans working in the applied arts in the nineteenth century. The original function has not been abandoned even today, though the collections are a bit more wide-ranging than perhaps was originally intended, encompassing as they do not only textiles and furniture but also watercolors and paintings — among them John Constable's *Salisbury Cathedral from the Bishop's Grounds;* the collections of British art (which include the Constable Collection, presented to the museum by the artist's daughter) stand out for their scope and comprehensiveness. Besides being very broad-ranging, the museum is also remarkably accessible, thanks to the organization of the displays into primary galleries that show off the finest examples of objects of a given era and style, and study collections devoted to a single discipline, such as ceramics, jewelry and metalwork, musical instruments, textiles and fashions, tapestries, theater, and the like. Of particular interest are the Raphael cartoons (designs for tapestries for the Sistine Chapel), the period rooms, Queen Elizabeth I's virginals, the world's first teapot, and the intricately carved, abundantly graffiti'd Great Bed of Ware, which Shakespeare's Sir Toby Belch mentioned in *Twelfth Night* and (measuring about 11 feet square) was said to be big enough to sleep a dozen couples, half of them at the head, the other half at the foot. The Chippendale furniture once owned by David Garrick, pieces by designer William Morris and his followers, Marie-Antoinette's music stand, Russian imperial jewels, patchwork quilts, medieval hangings, and tiles and stained glass are also on exhibit. For more information: Victoria and Albert Museum, Cromwell Rd., London SW7 2RL, England (phone: 01-589-6371).

THE WALLACE COLLECTION, London, England: The fourth marquess of Hertford, who died in 1870 after having lived most of his life in Paris, had one major criterion in collecting: "I only like pleasing paintings," he claimed. But what he called "pleasing" included works of many types — Italian, Dutch, French, Flemish, and Spanish, as well as British — as you'll see when you visit Hertford House, his former town house off Oxford Street, which now contains the collection he amassed and added to that was first put together by his great-grandfather in the eighteenth century and enlarged in the two succeeding generations. The museum's French furniture from the seventeenth and eighteenth centuries is very fine, as are the considerable numbers of eighteenth-century French clocks and the collections of miniatures, gold boxes, and Sèvres porcelain. Painters whose work is represented include Boucher, Canaletto, Fragonard, Gainsborough, Guardi, Hals, Rembrandt, Reynolds, Rubens, Titian, van Dyck, Velázquez, and Watteau. The famous collection of oriental and European armor was formed principally by Sir Richard Wallace, the illegitimate son of the fourth marquess of Hertford. His widow, Lady Wallace, bequeathed the vast collection to the nation in 1897. Details: Wallace Collection, Hertford House, Manchester Sq., London W1M 6BN, England (phone: 01-935-0687).

ASHMOLEAN MUSEUM, Oxford, Oxfordshire, England: As Oxford's Bodleian was Britain's first truly public library, so is the Ashmolean — opened in 1683 — its first public museum (possibly the first in Europe as well); it will be celebrating its tercentenary in May 1983. When you visit, you'll find many of the same scenes enjoyed by Oxford scholars over the years — among them, examples of items from Tradescant's Ark, the "closet of rarities" assembled by John Tradescant the Elder (d. 1638), which formed the nucleus of the collection, as well as odd lots such as Guy Fawkes's lantern, Powhatan's mantle, and the armor-plated hat that belonged to William Bradshaw, who was president of the court that passed sentence on Charles I. Medieval pieces, armorial porcelain, bronzes (Chinese, Greek, Roman, Etruscan, Italian Renaissance, later European), ceramics (Asian, English, and European), clocks and watches, coins and medals, antiquities (Cretan, Cypriot, Egyptian, Etruscan, Greek, near Eastern, and Tibetan), paintings (Dutch, English, Flemish, French, Impressionist, Italian, Venetian), and weapons (European prehistoric, Japanese, medieval English, middle Eastern, Greek, Roman, and Etruscan) are all represented in this omnium gatherum of a museum: There's something for everyone. Details: Ashmolean Museum, Beaumont St., Oxford, Oxfordshire OX1 2PH, England (phone: 0865-512651).

NATIONAL GALLERY OF SCOTLAND, Edinburgh, Scotland: One of a trio of National Galleries of Scotland located within walking distance of one another, this one, situated on a manmade embankment known as the Mound at the center of Princes Street Gardens, has a small but vital collection of European paintings, prints, and drawings that includes works by Verrocchio *(Madonna and Child),* Domenichino *(Adoration of the Shepherds),* Claude *(Landscape with Apollo and the Muses),* Poussin *(Mystic Marriage of St. Catherine),* Gauguin *(Vision of the Sermon),* Andrea del Sarto *(Self-Portrait),* Velázquez *(Old Woman Cooking Eggs),* Rembrandt *(Woman in Bed),* Vermeer *(Christ in the House of Martha and Mary),* Watteau *(Fêtes Vénitiennes),* Degas *(Diego Martelli),* van Gogh, Renoir, Cézanne, Monet, Goya, Gainsborough, Reynolds, Constable, Millais, Turner, and others. The collection of works by Scottish artists is particularly good; don't miss Henry Raeburn's the *Rev. Robert Walker,* ice-skating through a scene that looks almost luminous. Details: National Gallery of Scotland, The Mound, Edinburgh EH2 2EL, Scotland (phone: 031-556-8921).

ART GALLERY AND MUSEUM, Glasgow, Scotland: One of Britain's finest civic art collections, this one installed in fine red sandstone buildings near the banks of the River Kelvin in Kelvingrove Park includes a variety of works from many European schools (though the collections of Dutch art of the seventeenth century, French of the nineteenth and early twentieth centuries, and of Scottish works are particularly strong); Corot, Degas, Delacroix, Manet, Millet, Raeburn, Reynolds, Turner, Van Gogh, and Whistler are among those represented. Don't miss Rubens's *Nature Adorned by the Graces,* Giorgione's *The Woman Taken in Adultery,* Rembrandt's *A Man in Armour,* and Salvador Dali's *Christ of St. John of the Cross.* In addition, the building houses galleries devoted to natural history (and to British birds and geology in particular), and to Scottish prehistory and folk life, ethnographical materials from as far away as Africa and Polynesia, decorative arts from western Europe, and more. The collection of European arms and armor, housed in a striking glass-roofed hall, is particularly fine. For more information, contact Glasgow Museums & Art Galleries, Kelvingrove, Glasgow G3 8AG, Scotland (phone: 041-334-1134).

NATIONAL MUSEUM OF WALES, Cardiff, Wales: One of the largest museums in Britain, this institution, opened to the public in 1927, concentrates on things Welsh —its plants and animals, its industry past and present, its history and prehistory, its rocks and minerals, and its fine and applied arts. A Coal Mining Gallery illustrates mining techniques, an Iron and Steel Gallery treats the manufacture of tinplate, iron, and steel during the last three centuries, and a Shipping Gallery shows models of lighthouses and ships, plus figureheads. Among archaeological exhibits, the Caergwrle Bowl, noteworthy for its abundant gold embellishments, and the collection of stone monuments and casts thereof, representing the fifth through the ninth centuries, are particularly interesting. The collection of wax models of plants in the botany section ranks among the world's finest; and the displays of the Welsh countryside and the animal kingdom in the newest section of the museum are also musts. The fine arts galleries include many paintings from the rest of Europe as well; Welsh painting is represented by the eighteenth-century landscape artist Richard Wilson and the twentieth-century painters Augustus John, Gwen John, J. D. Innes, Frank Brangwyn, and David Jones. Antique buffs should be sure to explore the China Room, which contains good examples of Swansea and Nantgarw china and porcelain. Details: National Museum of Wales, Cardiff, South Glamorgan, Wales (phone: 0222-397951).

THE CHESTER BEATTY LIBRARY, Dublin, Irish Republic: The collection that copper millionaire Chester Beatty bequeathed to the Irish nation in 1968, housed near the Royal Dublin Society building in plush, embassy-belt Ballsbridge, evokes one superlative after another. Its Mogul collection is the world's very best, and collections of Persian, Turkish, and Arabic antiquities are considered among the world's best outside their countries of origin. The collection of Chinese jade books is the largest in the world; the Chinese snuffbox collection was among the first ever assembled. The collection of Japanese illuminated manuscripts *(nara-e)* ranks with the foremost in Europe, as does the collection of Japanese woodblock prints *(surimono)*. The important Biblical Papyri, 11 manuscript volumes of the Bible dating from the early second to the fourth century, are also in the Library's possession. And the Islamic collection is simply breathtaking. Naturally, it is only possible to exhibit a tiny fraction of the Library's possessions at any given time, but the permanent exhibits do show off a representative sampling, and there are major exhibitions a few times a year. The bus service from the center of Dublin to Ballsbridge is very good, and a visit here is a must. Details: Chester Beatty Library, 20 Shrewsbury Rd., Dublin 4, Irish Republic (phone: 692386).

THE NATIONAL MUSEUM, Dublin, Irish Republic: The massive Thomas Deane-designed building on Kildare Street into which the old Royal Dublin Society moved its collection in 1890 and the antiquities from the Royal Irish Academy a short time later has lost some of its territory over the years; its display space is inadequate, and many items are exhibited in ways that do not show them off to their best advantage. All the same, the museum should not be missed. It has priceless collections of prehistoric gold artifacts, such as solid gold dress fasteners, torques, and lunulae made by the skilled craftsmen of the Bronze and Iron Ages, as well as finds from the site of Viking Dublin. These, together with such early Christian treasures as the Ardagh Chalice and the Cross of Cong, may be viewed in a specially designed exhibition area opened in 1980. The Georgian silver, Waterford crystal, and Belleek pottery on display is equally captivating. And look for St. Patrick's Bell; the Book of Kells (on loan from Trinity College until 1983); and the Derrynaflan chalice, paten, and strainer, found in March 1980 at Kellenaule in Tipperary. They're worth inquiring about. Details: The National Museum, Kildare St., Dublin 2, Irish Republic (phone: 765521).

THE NATURAL HISTORY MUSEUM, Dublin, Irish Republic: Much loved for its refusal to change even one iota over the course of the past century, this museum, originally among the three major Royal Dublin Society collections, was moved over a century ago to a building designed by Thomas Clarendon and constructed on the south side of Leinster Lawn, with an entrance on Merrion Square. The first sight to greet a visitor's eye is that old favorite, the Basking Shark, ever popular with school parties, who also have soft spots for the Giant Irish Deer and the fine display of birds. On the ground floor, the Irish Room shows off Irish fauna and a new exhibition of Irish insects. Foreign collections — among them some stuffed giraffes and elephants — are displayed on the next floor and, above that, there's the priceless assemblage, dating back to the museum's earliest days, of glass models of the invertebrates. Since the museum's last period of vigorous acquisition — from the 1880s to 1914, when deep-sea explorations generated additions to the marine biology and zoology sections — there has been very little activity in the museum. The impressive geological collection has long languished unseen for want of a proper home (though plans to display it somewhere in Dublin are currently afoot). This evidence and others of a recent upsurge of interest are most welcome, as is the ecology-conscious generation's increasing use of the museum as a research tool and archive center. Details: Natural History Museum, Merrion St., Dublin 2, Irish Republic (phone: 765521).

WEXFORD COUNTY MUSEUM, Enniscorthy, Co. Wexford, Irish Republic: This town has a medieval air with its narrow streets winding down to the River Slaney on one side, and Vinegar Hill, where the Irish rebels were defeated in 1798, rising on the other. The museum, housed in a Norman castle for which the Elizabethan poet Edmund Spenser once held a lease (one of the few Irish castles not in ruins), contains muskets, pikes, and other relics of the battle, as well as objects from the 1916 Rising (during which this town was the last in the country to surrender). But the museum's contents are not restricted to military impedimenta: A kitchen at the back of the castle, and, behind that, a dairy, show off the traditional cooking utensils and tools of the period, and there are striking displays of figureheads salvaged from ships wrecked off the Wexford coast, a stone covered with Ogham script, ships' anchors, stone crosses, and chalices dating from the seventeenth century. Even apart from the varied collection, however, the view from the castle roof would make the museum well worth visiting. Details: Wexford County Museum, Castle Hill, Enniscorthy, Co. Wexford, Irish Republic.

MONAGHAN COUNTY MUSEUM, Monaghan, Co. Monaghan, Irish Republic: The Republic's first county museum, this institution — though situated in a bleak old court house with huge Doric columns that must have put the fear of God into prisoners during the last century — has a stunning and eclectic collection ranging from neolithic relics to folk items. You'll see china dinner sets, examples of lace made in nearby Carrickmacross and the cotton crochet known as Clones lace; the Cross of Clogher, which dates to the early fifteenth century; a cauldron (circa 800 BC), found in a bog in 1854; old photos; and, in an open-air exhibition area, a collection of querns (hand mills), milk churns, and milestones from the now-unused Ulster Canal. In a small way, this museum is one of Ireland's most progressive, and the collections are constantly improving. Details: Monaghan County Museum, Court House, Monaghan, Co. Monaghan, Irish Republic (phone: 047-82211).

MUCKROSS HOUSE FOLK MUSEUM, Muckross, Killarney, Co. Kerry, Irish Republic: Emphasis at this museum, one of the Republic's most forward-looking, is as much on making the objects on show interesting to visitors as on preserving them, and a great deal of thought and effort has been put into every display. In addition, you'll see potters and weavers at work, as well as other artisans toiling in the forge and the harness-making shop producing the kind of items displayed in the museum proper. When you've had your fill of these, you can go out for a stroll on one of the nature trails that meander across the vast grounds (which, together with the early-nineteenth-century house where exhibits are set up, were presented to the nation in 1932). The footpaths alone might warrant a visit here, encircling as they do, two of the lakes of Killarney; you'll also find a superb natural rock garden and an abundance of free-roaming red deer and rare flora. Kerry is one of the country's real beauty spots. Details: Muckross House Folk Museum, Muckross, Killarney, Co. Kerry, Irish Republic (phone: 064-31440).

IRISH AGRICULTURAL MUSEUM, Wexford, Co. Wexford, Irish Republic: Though still in its infancy, this museum in the fine, restored nineteenth-century farm buildings of Victorian Gothic Johnstown Castle, 4 miles southwest of Wexford town, gives an excellent picture of just how much Irish farming has changed in the last 50 years. On display are the hand flails, the pitchers, turnip pulpers, butter-making instruments, ploughs, harrows, sowers, mowing machines, harnesses, and carts and traps that were once among every Irish farmer's most important tools. A complete model of an old kitchen is on exhibit, along with a laundry, a creamery, a laborer's bedroom, and a stable. There is ample room for expansion, and already this museum is well on its way to becoming one of the nation's important folk museums. Yet it's already worth a browse, and the castle's ornamental grounds — with meandering pathways, artificial lakes, interesting shrubs and flowers, and fine picnic area — are a delight. The castle and surrounding farm are used for soils research by the Agricultural Institute. Details: Irish Agricultural Museum, Johnstown Castle, Wexford, Co. Wexford, Irish Republic (phone: 053-22888).

THE ULSTER MUSEUM, Belfast, Northern Ireland: Housed in a neoclassical building from the 1920s and a well-designed modern addition, in the city's delightful Botanic Gardens with their great Palm House and Tropical Ravine, the collections shown here are broad-ranging: There's an old and functioning water wheel (in the Industrial Archaeology section); a collection of contemporary painting and sculpture unrivaled in Ireland (in the Art Galleries); interesting prehistoric collections that include the only surviving pair of late Bronze Age trumpets that can still be played; a display of minerals and gemstones unique in the country (including the biggest group of quartz crystals in Britain and Ireland, an attractive display of fluorescent and phosphorescent minerals in a darkened central vault, and a full-sized cave); and, adding a touch of glitter, the fabulous collection of jewelry, coins, and other items from the *Girona,* a galleass of the Spanish Armada, which went down off the Antrim coast in 1588. In front of the entrance there's an enormous, now-extinct coelacanth, and in the museum store you can buy copies of the gold *No tengo mas que dar te* ring, the original of which was worn by a Spanish sailor as he went to his watery grave, mindful, no doubt, of the sweetheart who gave it to him. Details: The Ulster Museum, Botanic Gardens, Belfast BT9 5AB, Northern Ireland (phone: 0232-668251).

THE ULSTER FOLK AND TRANSPORT MUSEUM, Holywood, Co. Down, Northern Ireland: This is the place to see how Ulster folk lived back in the old days, in the city and the country alike. Town houses, including a terrace of six from Belfast, as well as traditional farmhouses, mills, a church, and schools, have been moved here brick by brick, stone by stone; then furnished with the everyday objects of the appropriate period, and landscaped as they might have been originally. A farm from mid-Antrim has been reconstructed right down to the walls and ditches around the fields. And, in addition, there's an assortment of galleries where you'll see vehicles used in Irish transport over the ages — from wheelless sledges and elegant horse-drawn carriages to automobiles and even a vertical take-off plane; rolling stock is kept in Belfast in Witham Street, off the Lower Newtownards Road. Details: Ulster Folk and Transport Museum, Cultra Manor, Holywood, Co. Down BT18 0EU, Northern Ireland (phone: Holywood 5411).

The Performing Arts

When the summer festival season ends, winter's cultural whirlwind begins. London has lately become something of a dance capital, hosting not just its own progeny — among them the Royal Ballet and the London Festival Ballet — but also visiting companies from home and abroad. The *Royal Opera House, Covent Garden,* ranks among the world's greats. And there's always music in the air, whether it's classical — and played by a symphony orchestra, a chamber group, or a soloist — jazz, or the most traditional folk work. And the theatri-

DIVERSIONS / The Performing Arts 477

cal tradition both in Britain and in Ireland runs deep and strong. London, for instance, is a hotbed of dramatic affairs, with literally hundreds of offerings in hundreds of playhouses. Alone, the West End (London's answer to Broadway) boasts some 50 theaters that regularly mount ostensibly commercial productions (although many, as a result of British theater's fondness for the experimental, have a long way to go before they make money), and the fare swings wildly: The tiny *Duchess,* for example, for years the host of *Oh! Calcutta,* gave itself over to a glistening *Private Lives* in 1980, and by now may be playing *Hamlet* for all one can forecast. The same tradition of eclecticism and experimentation has put the English theater — and great actors and actresses like John Gielgud, Laurence Olivier, Edith Evans, and so many others — at the forefront of world drama.

The Irish, for their part, tend to agree with theater critic Kenneth Tynan, who once noted "Ireland's sacred duty to send over, every few years, a playwright to save the English theatre from inarticulate glumness" — but you can't blame the attitude on sour grapes, because the contribution of this nation's writers is equally outstanding, and all out of proportion to the island's small population. The names of Sheridan, Goldsmith, Wilde, Shaw, Synge, O'Casey, Behan, and Beckett, for instance, inevitably crop up wherever great drama is under discussion — and with them, the names of actors and actresses such as Siobhan McKenna and Barry Fitzgerald. A current feature of the Irish theater scene is the series of bilingual (Irish-English) shows mounted each summer at Galway's usually all-Irish *Taibhdhearc na Gaillimhe* (Middle St., Galway; phone: 091-620-24). Also look out for the *Irish Theatre Company,* a national traveling troupe that continues the country's great tradition of itinerant players; for details of these "fit-ups," contact the group's Dublin headquarters at Marlborough Pl., Dublin 1 (phone: 72-34-33).

With all this going on, settling on an evening's entertainment (or an afternoon's, or even a morning's, for that matter) can pose some problems. When it comes to theater, one man's meat is another's moan, so before you settle on a play, ask a friend, if you have one in the area or, failing that, check newspapers — in London, for instance, the *Sunday Observer* or well-regarded tourist magazines such as *What's On* or *Where to Go.* Information about what's playing in Ireland can be found in the daily papers in Dublin, Cork, and Belfast; in Galway's weekly *Connacht Tribune;* and in the fortnightly events guides, *In Dublin* and *What's On in Belfast.*

But no matter where you go, some theaters fairly reliably turn up with productions and concerts that are more interesting or wonderful than others, and some are worth a visit in their own right — either because they are particularly beautiful, or unusually historic. A few are quite small, so that even the most remote corner (or "gods," as the heights of the balconies are called) affords a fine view of the activities on stage — and the prices are usually relatively low by stateside standards.

We've given a sampling of halls worth going out of your way to experience. It's usually possible to order tickets in advance directly through the individual box offices; and, for London shows, through *KPI Tours & Travel* (1290 Ave. of the Americas, New York, NY 10104; phone: 212-397-3200).

BIRMINGHAM REPERTORY THEATRE, Birmingham, West Midlands, England: A list of the past members of the nation's first repertory company, which makes its home here, reads like a *Who's Who* of British theater. Richard Chamberlain, Julie Christie, and Albert Finney played here; and so did Laurence Olivier, Paul Scofield, Ralph Richardson, and Edith Evans, among others, during the years after Sir Barry Jackson founded the organization in 1913 with his own money "to serve an art instead of making that art serve a commercial purpose." In addition to earning fame for its actors, the Rep also became known for its attention to modern work, particularly plays by George Bernard Shaw, back in the days when Shaw was considered a contemporary;

478 DIVERSIONS / The Performing Arts

for its successes in London; for Jackson's involvement with the origins of the *Malvern Festival (Feis and Fleadh: The Best Festivals);* and for its modern-dress productions of Shakespeare — all of whose works the company has performed at least once, in one form or another, over the years. Now in a spiffy new home, the Rep performs a season of plays that emphasizes the classics; one British premiere, in a 901-seat Main House, cunningly designed on a steep tilt so that no one ever sits more than 65 feet from the stage; and assorted new works and innovative restagings of golden oldies in the more flexible 50-by-30 Studio Theatre. At Christmastime, there's always a show meant to delight Britons of all ages (*The Wizard of Oz* and *Pinocchio* are past successes). And when the company is not in residence, the Main House hosts visiting troupes such as the National Theatre, Ballet Rambert, and others. An interesting sidelight is that the Theatre's Hire Department (in Oozells St.) rents out an extensive range of props and fancy dress, and sells stage make-up and accessories (call 021-643-6034 for details). For program information, contact the box office on Broad St., Birmingham, West Midlands B1 2EP, England (phone: 021-236-4455).

THEATRE ROYAL, Bristol, Avon, England: Peter O'Toole, Barbara Leigh-Hunt, Jane Lapotaire, and many other well-knowns of the British stage have started out on the boards of this splendid eighteenth-century playhouse, the oldest continuously active theater in Britain, and one of a pair that serve as home to the respected Bristol Old Vic Company. (The remaining theater is the New Vic, which opened in 1972 and is used for smaller productions.) No matter which you attend, you can count on a thrilling evening, whether you see one of the classics to which the Theatre Royal is so well suited, or a contemporary piece. A number of performances are given each year by the Bristol Old Vic Theatre School (Downside Rd.). Details: Theatre Royal, King St., Bristol, Avon, England (phone: 0272-24388).

THE COLISEUM, London, England: You have a sense of occasion when you visit this floridly Edwardian 2,358-seat hall, London's largest, at the foot of St. Martin's Lane not far from St. Martin-in-the-Fields and the National Gallery: The interiors are all alabaster and marble, bronze and splendid gleaming mahogany, as posh as those of the ships that crisscrossed the Atlantic during the years around 1904, when the hall was opened. Diaghilev's Ballet Russe performed here, as did Sarah Bernhardt, Mrs. Patrick Campbell, Ellen Terry, and a child star named Noel Coward; the impresario who conceived the place even staged tennis matches and rodeos to keep it filled. Since 1968, the English National Opera Company (formerly the Sadler's Wells Opera Company), which stages masterworks in English, has called it home, and is in residence during a late-July-through-May season. Details: Coliseum, St. Martin's La., London WC2N 4ES, England (phone: 01-836-3161).

THE NATIONAL THEATRE, London, England: When you visit one of the trio of houses in this handsome large Thames-side drama complex, you'll have plenty to talk about — even if you don't like what you see. That, however, is unlikely, for Albert Finney, John Gielgud, Ralph Richardson, Peggy Ashcroft, and Paul Scofield have all appeared here; and many another breath-stopping actor can be seen here, in parts ranging from the soul-stretching to the small, in a selection of plays that embraces the classics; translations of works by European dramatists such as Schnitzler, Horvath, Feydeau, or Brecht; revivals of contemporary plays; new pieces by living playwrights like Pinter, Stoppard, Brenton, Storey, or Bolt; and adaptations of books such as *Lark Rise* or *The World Turned Upside Down.*

The building itself is wonderful, with an interior that feels like a walk-through sculpture, a huge foyer with bars that seems to be London's answer to Paris's sidewalk cafés, and all manner of walks, terraces, restaurants (which you can visit even if you're not theater-going), with fine views of Somerset House and the river curving off toward St. Paul's.

Before performances ensembles and soloists play for free in the foyers, and you can browse through art exhibitions while you listen. There are also almost always so-called platform performances — brief plays, readings, poetry, music, and mime — in the 890-seat proscenium-arch Lyttelton and the 1,160-seat open-stage Olivier, the largest of the three theaters; thanks to the excellent design, both theaters feel almost as intimate as the 400-seat Cottesloe, the third in the complex, used for works that call for small-scale staging. Details: National Theatre, South Bank, London SE1 9PX, England (phone: 01-928-2252, or, for credit card bookings, 01-928-5933).

OPEN AIR THEATRE (REGENT'S PARK), London, England: It's hard to find a more pleasant way to spend a summer evening in London than to take in a performance of Shakespeare (or, occasionally, Shaw) in this lovely amphitheater-in-the-woods near Queen Mary's Rose Garden. Established in 1932 by Sydney Carroll and Robert Atkins, it quickly became an institution among London theater-goers, and actors from Vivien Leigh and Deborah Kerr to Jack Hawkins and Robert Helpmann have played here. Since 1962, the New Shakespeare Company has made it a home base. The new auditorium, which opened in 1975, provides plenty of space for a bar, a visit to which is an integral part of any experience here; Puck's Fizz and mulled wine, barbecue and the cold buffet are the big deals. Details: Open Air Theatre (Regent's Park), London NW1, England (phone: 01-486-2431).

THE ROUND HOUSE, London, England: This large space — a terminal for the London and Birmingham Railway until 1869, a warehouse until 1964, and an arts center until it was fitted out as a theater in 1967 — offers you a refreshingly different sort of theater: Stars like Vanessa Redgrave play roles they've always wanted to tackle here, and the best regional and foreign companies call the place home when they're in London. Generally speaking, the audience is very young and aware. And, though you may not be carried away by what's happening, you won't be bored. Details: The Round House, Chalk Farm Rd., London NW1 8BG, England (phone: 01-267-2564).

ROYAL ALBERT HALL, London, England: Designed in the Italian Renaissance style, and opened by Queen Victoria in 1871, this round house is truly splendid — a quarter of a mile around, and domed, with red brick and terra-cotta facades, an immense Great Organ, and three tiers of boxes with seats for thousands. All manner of musical concerts, from a Bach B Minor Mass to a spine-tingling, cannon-throttled "1812" Overture, will fill it up. Particularly special are the Henry Wood Promenade Concerts (The Proms, in local parlance), which attract hordes every year from July to September. Concerts feature the *BBC Symphony Orchestra* and visiting orchestras from Britain and the rest of the world in programs of composers from all eras; some pieces are specially commissioned for the occasion. Traditionally, the final concert closes with a program of British music that includes Elgar's "Pomp and Circumstance March." For this, and for other programs, prices are remarkably low. Box office: Royal Albert Hall, Kensington Gore, London SW7 2AP, England (phone: 01-589-8212).

ROYAL COURT THEATRE, London, England: One of the most famous of London's small theaters, this one has made theatrical history more than once — first in about 1904 with Harley Granville Barker's stagings of Arthur Pinero farces and George Bernard Shaw plays, and again in the late 1950s when George Devine's English Stage Company presented John Osborne's *Look Back in Anger*. Even today, the theater is associated with the contemporary, and works of dramatists like Wesker, Jellicoe, and Bond can often be seen. And, though chronic shortages of money are a fact of life, standards are always high. The Royal Court is a great place for talent-spotting, and the audience is lively. Most recently, *Bent* started here before heading for the West End and Broadway, and the latest *Hamlet* was pronounced revolutionary. Never a dull moment. Information: The Royal Court, Sloane Sq., London SW1, England (phone: 01-730-1745).

ROYAL FESTIVAL HALL, London, England: The city's premiere concert hall, which opened in 1951, occupies a site on the South Bank in the *South Bank Arts*

480 DIVERSIONS / The Performing Arts

Complex not far from the *National Theatre* (above), the *National Film Theatre,* the *Hayward Gallery,* and two smaller halls, the 1,100-seat *Queen Elizabeth Hall* and the 370-seat *Purcell Room.* The river views, the foyers, and the various facilities for concert-goers and other culture vultures are abundant, and there's almost always someone playing. Details: Royal Festival Hall, Belvedere Rd., London SE1 8XX, England (phone: 01-928-3191).

ROYAL OPERA HOUSE, COVENT GARDEN, London, England: Worth a look for its grandeur alone, this jewel of a 2,000-seat opera house, the third on the site, is splendidly Victorian, with its red plush, its shaded lights, its scarlet and gold tiers, its domed turquoise ceiling, and its sweeping horseshoe-shaped balconies. But the play's the thing, and some of the best singers in the world have performed here in the past — among them Dame Nellie Melba, Dame Joan Sutherland, Kirsten Flagstad, and Maria Callas. The traditions of excellence continue unabated, so that now the hall ranks among the world's half-dozen true greats of its kind, and newcomers believe that success here gives their careers the stamp of international greatness. The Royal Opera shares the house with the Royal Ballet, which, under noted choreographers such as Frederick Ashton and Kenneth MacMillan, with dancers like Antoinette Sibley and Margot Fonteyn, Rudolf Nureyev and Anthony Dowell, has become one of the world's most noted companies. Whether you visit the hall for opera or ballet, your experience is bound to be something special. Nearby, a silver casket on the south wall of St. Paul's, Covent Garden, contains the ashes of Ellen Terry, who died in 1928. Details: The Royal Opera House, Covent Garden, London WC2, England (phone: 01-240-1066).

SADLER'S WELLS THEATRE, London, England: Built on the site of a pair of mineral springs discovered in 1683 by one Richard Sadler, this member of the trio of the capital's oldest more or less continuously operating halls has seen its bawdy ballads, its jugglers and clowns, rope-dancers and performing animals, plays and pantomimes, and even roller-skaters and boxers; reopened after a brief closing during the war, it hosted the world premiere of Benjamin Britten's *Peter Grimes,* and, in its time, it has also been home to the Royal Ballet, the National Theatre, and the English Opera. Today, touring opera and dance companies from all over the world appear here — in past years, Merce Cunningham and the Mevlevi Dervishes, the Nederlands Dans Theater, the Irish Ballet, the Leipzig Opera, and the Sadler's Wells Royal Ballet, which annually comes home from its season-long tour for the holidays. The hall is a bit dank and dreary, but the young and with-it audience and the onstage goings-on make a stop here well worth your while. Details: Sadler's Wells Theatre, Rosebery Ave., London EC1R 4TN, England (phone: 01-278-6563).

THEATRE ROYAL (DRURY LANE), London, England: The productions may not be London's most innovative, but this 2,283-seat theater, with its beautiful symmetrical staircase and domed entranceway — "a tradition, national treasure" and "not just a theater" in the words of one past showman — is unarguably one of London's most historic. The fourth playhouse on the site, it was preceded by a theater where Charles II met Nell Gwyn, who once sold oranges at the entrance; by another designed by Christopher Wren, with John Dryden as chief playwright, and as manager, David Garrick and Richard Sheridan, whose 1777 *School for Scandal* was written upstairs while actors rehearsed completed sections below. The present house, designed by Benjamin Wyatt in 1812, has seen opera and drama, pantomime and film, and even musicals. Edmund Kean, whom many believe to be the greatest tragedian of all time, played here in 1814, and so did Sir Henry Irving, Ellen Terry, John Gielgud, and other famous actors. The theater has its tradition — the cutting of the so-called Baddeley Cake (named after the actor whose will supplied the funds) in the Grand Saloon after the performance every January 6 — and its ghost, a gray-cloaked, high-booted bewigged fellow who haunts the upper circle — in the daytime only, however. For a splurge, hire one of the two royal boxes, which come complete with tiny Regency or

Adamesque retiring rooms behind. Details: Theatre Royal (Drury Lane), Catherine St., London WC2, England (phone: 01-836-8108).

THEATRE ROYAL (HAYMARKET), London, England: Architect John Nash, who designed this small modish theater, gave it a wonderful Corinthian portico, which looks all the grander when floodlit, as it often is at night. Henry Fielding managed a predecessor on the site around 1737, and the present hall, built in 1821, has been the setting for plays by everyone from Ibsen to Wilde, T. S. Eliot and Tennessee Williams to Noel Coward, Barrie, and Rattigan; Sir Beerbohm Tree played here in the late nineteenth century. The hall itself, renovated at the beginning of this century, is all white, rich blue, and gold leaf; there's a wonderfully crafted royal arms above the stage, and a solemn round of "God Save the Queen" precedes every show, following a tradition that has been virtually abandoned elsewhere. Details: Theatre Royal (Haymarket), Haymarket, London SW1, England (phone: 01-930-9832).

WIGMORE HALL, London, England: Some performers, although well-enough known, never travel to the US — and it's those whom you'll often hear at this small, elegant Renaissance-style hall created in 1901 by Frederick Wilhelm Carl Bechstein (of piano fame), and full of alabaster and marble. A delight for recitals and chamber music, thanks to acoustics that are nearly perfect, it has hosted debuts by Artur Rubinstein (in 1912), Elisabeth Schwarzkopf (in 1948), and Daniel Barenboim (in 1958); and recitals by Julian Bream, Peter Pears, Andrés Segovia, and many others. Details: Wigmore Hall, 36 Wigmore St., London W1H 9DF, England (phone: 01-935-2141).

YOUNG VIC THEATRE, London, England: The theater, founded only about a decade ago, is relatively new by London standards, but the spirit of experimentation and the *joie de jouer* that go into the productions are as much a tradition in the British theater as is the Bard himself. Founder Frank Dunlop's adaptation of a Molière work, which went to Broadway as *Scapino!,* his production of Tom Stoppard's satire *Rosencrantz and Guildenstern Are Dead,* and his many lively productions of Shakespeare's works are typical fare in the boxy main hall, while children's pieces and the avant-garde are standard in a small studio theater. Details: Young Vic, The Cut, Waterloo, London SE1 8LP, England (phone: 01-928-6363).

ROYAL EXCHANGE THEATRE, Manchester, England: Installed in a former cotton exchange, the Royal Exchange Theatre Company, whose roots go back to 1959 and a group of actors who had trained at the Old Vic Theatre School, performs Sheridan, Chekhov, Coward, Ibsen, Eliot, and a variety of other works old and new, including an occasional world premiere. Several productions have gone on to London or Broadway, and audiences usually pack the unusual theater-in-the-round, Europe's largest, to 90% capacity. Concerts of classical and folk music and jazz are also held here, along with a host of other activities. Details: Royal Exchange Theatre, The Royal Exchange, Manchester M2 7DH, England (phone: 061-833-9333).

THEATRE ROYAL, Norfolk, Norwich, England: When you consider atmosphere, the sleek Theatre Royal, a 1970 update of a structure put up in the 1930s in the theater-and-cinema style of the day, the fourth theater on the site, doesn't hold a candle to those of the capital. Yet, as Europe's most successful provincial theater, it is that remarkable thing, an arts institution that manages to be totally self-supporting, and current management keeps things hopping with a continual and very lively procession of circus, grand opera, ice shows, ballet, pantomime, variety shows, vaudeville, classical music concerts, and programs from the touring companies of the National Theatre Company, Sadler's Wells Royal Ballet, the Glyndebourne Opera, the London Festival Ballet, and foreign dance companies. Charlie Chaplin, as the Lancashire Lad, performed in a previous hall on the site, back in 1904 when it was called the Norwich Hippodrome. Nowadays, the theater is open every day except Christmas, and if you're in the area, a visit here is not to be missed. Details: Theatre Royal, Theatre St., Norfolk, Norwich, NR2 1RL, England (phone: 0603-28205/28206/28207).

DIVERSIONS / The Performing Arts

ROYAL SHAKESPEARE THEATRE, Stratford-upon-Avon, Warwickshire, England: The senior of the United Kingdom's two national theaters, under the patronage of Her Majesty the Queen, this 1,500-seat hall opened on April 23, 1932, on the Bard's own birthday — appropriately enough, since it's Shakespeare that you'll see on these boards throughout the late-March-through-January season. The immense Royal Shakespeare Company — the association of actors, directors, and designers who name the place as one of their principal homes — has numbered almost all the greats of British theater among its members in the course of the last century, and the quality of the work is at least professional if not superb, and often innovative (witness one season's *Taming of the Shrew* with motorcycles). *The Other Place,* a small theater seating between 150 and 200 depending on the play, houses the company's small-scale productions of new British writings and classical works. And in London, where the 1,000-seat *Aldwych* and the smaller *Warehouse* theaters have been the group's longtime bases, the RSC moved to a new theater and attached studio space in the *Barbican Arts Centre* — a complex consisting of a concert hall, library, restaurants, gallery, and the like — in late 1982; the season here, almost continuous throughout the year, includes a mix of Shakespeare (transferred from the previous Stratford season) and new productions of modern and classical works. (Much to the dismay of many British producers, the *Aldwych* was purchased by the American Broadway magnate James Nederlander.) For details, contact the Royal Shakespeare Theatre, Waterside, Stratford-upon-Avon, Warwickshire CV37 6BB, England (phone: 0789-292271); or the Royal Shakespeare Company, Barbican Centre, Barbican, London EC2Y 8DS, England (phone: 01-628-8795).

CITIZENS' THEATRE, Glasgow, Scotland: The *Times* called it Britain's "most challenging theater," the *Observer* characterized it as "the most unusual and individual theater in the land," the *Daily Mail* noted that it "puts the West End in the shade," and the US's *After Dark* commented on its "outrageously adventurous nature" and its "perverse and avant-garde flair": The accolades for this first-rate regional theater just don't stop. The century-old playhouse-with-a-past has recently been renovated, and the house is now a stunning example of a traditional proscenium-arch Victorian theater. The company has performed over 120 British and foreign classics since its formation, and has acquired a reputation around the world; most of the actors have worked with the company for over a decade, and all are paid the same salary. During the summer months, when the company is not in residence, visiting troupes can be seen. Details: Citizens' Theatre, Gorbals, Glasgow G5 9DS, Scotland (phone: 041-429-0022).

THEATRE ROYAL, Glasgow, Scotland: Those who think that Edinburgh is home to anything cultural in Scotland are overlooking the fact that it is Glasgow that is home to the Scottish Opera, the Scottish National Orchestra, and the Scottish Ballet; and that Scotland's only opera house is here. The Theatre Royal, which lays claim to that distinction, is without question one of the more gorgeous relics of Victorian days in Britain. Now owned by the Scottish Opera, it has been recently and ingeniously restored — so that the most modern theatrical equipment is available but mainly hidden; when you visit, your main impression will be of the marvelous plaster work ornamenting the swooping balconies and the domed ceilings, of the overwhelming sumptuousness of the scheme of things. Unlike many refurbished opera houses, this one is not done in red and gold, but in various shades of cream and brown, highlighted here and there with blue and orange. The Scottish Opera subscription season runs from September through May; when the opera is not in residence, the hall welcomes performances by many other companies including the Scottish Ballet, Sadler's Wells Royal Ballet, Ballet Rambert, the Royal Shakespeare Company, the National Theatre, the English National Opera, and others. For more information, contact the Theatre Royal, Hope St., Glasgow G2 3QA, Scotland (phone: 041-331-1234, or, for credit card bookings, 041-332-9000).

IRISH BALLET COMPANY, Cork, Co. Cork, Irish Republic: In 1945, when Joan

DIVERSIONS / The Performing Arts

Denise Moriarty returned to Cork from her dance studies abroad and began her long battle for a national ballet company, she was condemned from the pulpit. No doubt, it was suspected that anything more sensual than the rigid, arms-at-the-sides traditional dancing, with its concentration on footwork to the exclusion of any other movement, would lead to dreadful depravities in theaters throughout the land. But Ms. Moriarty persevered, founding the amateur Cork Ballet Company in 1945, and was rewarded in 1973 when Ireland finally acquired its own national ballet, the state-subsidized and fully professional Irish Ballet Company. In addition to performing many of the standards from the classical repertoire, Ms. Moriarty and the company's artistic advisor, Domy Reiter-Soffer (who has also worked with the Back Door Company of Israel and American Ballet Theatre), have created many new works in contemporary styles. The company has also developed a unique blend of Irish traditional dancing and ballet that mixes the detailed steps of the former with the latter's physical expressiveness to produce a highly original form that reaches its peak in a version of John Millington Synge's *The Playboy of the Western World,* which was presented very successfully in both London and New York with the renowned Chieftains supplying the music. Much of the company's time is devoted to touring Ireland; you'll find them at the *Cork Opera House* in February; with the Cork Ballet Company in November; and at Dublin's *Abbey Theatre* in June. For program details and other information, contact the Irish Ballet Company, 1b Emmet Pl., Cork, Co. Cork, Irish Republic (phone: 021-20-112).

ABBEY THEATRE, Dublin, Irish Republic: The fine collection of portraits, including likenesses of W. B. Yeats, Lady Gregory, John Millington Synge, and Sean O'Casey, which graces the foyer of the Abbey Theatre, is a vivid reminder of those heady days when the premieres of O'Casey's *The Plough and the Stars* and Synge's *The Playboy of the Western World* were greeted by riot and disorder: Though audiences are less boisterous now and the company is less likely to be arrested, as in Philadelphia in 1912, for performing "immoral and indecent" plays, the Abbey still presents the best of contemporary Irish playwriting, and you'll see productions of works by Brian Friel, Hugh Leonard, and Tom Murphy, among others, as well as revivals of the classics that made the 75-year-old Abbey Players famous to begin with. Work by a younger generation of actors and writers is presented downstairs, in the *Peacock;* the opportunity to visit this wonderfully intimate auditorium should not be missed. After the show, slip across the road for a drink in *The Plough,* full of photographs of past *Abbey* successes, or *The Flowing Tide,* where you can admire the stained-glass panels set into the walls — and mingle with the actors whose efforts you have just applauded. Details: Abbey Theatre, Lower Abbey St., Dublin 1, Irish Republic (phone: 74-45-05).

FOCUS THEATRE, Dublin, Irish Republic: Dublin's smallest theater is also one of its most exciting. In 1963, when Deirdre O'Connell returned to Ireland after studying in New York at Lee Strasberg's Actors' Studio, she began to train some Dublin actors in Stanislavskian technique, and, by 1967, had formed the nucleus of a company and moved into a converted garage in a lane off Pembroke Street. An evening in this tiny, 72-seat auditorium is never disappointing, whether the play is a classic by Chekhov or the latest offering of a young Irish writer. Besides the resident *Focus Company,* there is a *Studio Company* of young actors-in-training who occasionally present their own improvised and very original adaptations of Irish legends and literature. It is no exaggeration to say that, along with some of the finest actors in Dublin (including Miss O'Connell herself), you are watching the stars of tomorrow. Details: Focus Theatre, 6 Pembroke Pl., Dublin 2, Irish Republic (phone: 76-30-71/68-29-93).

GAIETY THEATRE, Dublin, Irish Republic: The Gaiety is where many a Dublin child brought for a special occasion to a pantomime, perhaps, or a Gilbert and Sullivan musical, gets a first taste of the magic of theater. It was founded in 1871 by Michael Gunn and his brother John (a bust of whom can be seen on the staircase that leads to the Circle) and, although the original gallery, or "gods," was removed when the theater was renovated in 1955, the theater remains a very fine example of the typical nineteenth-century playhouse — marvelously opulent with its red carpets, dark pillars, golden draperies, and ornate pink cream plasterwork; the orchestra pit's brass surround adds its gleam to the total effect, and, when you sit in a private box, you feel like no less than visiting royalty. The Letters Patent issued at the theater's founding allows for the production of "any interlude, tragedy, comedy, prelude, opera, burletta, play, farce or pantomime," and today's repertoire remains just that broad. As a result, the list of the famous who have played at the Gaiety is formidable, including as it does, Lily Langtry, the D'Oyly Carte Opera Company, Burgess Meredith, Siobhan McKenna, Paulette Goddard, the Bolshoi Ballet, Peter O'Toole — and, of course, Dublin's own Jimmy O'Dea, who for nearly 30 years appeared in pantomime and musical and, in the character of Biddy Mulligan, captured the true spirit of the city. His delightful successor today is the diminutive and exuberant Maureen Potter. Details: Gaiety Theatre, South King St., Dublin 2, Irish Republic (phone: 77-17-17).

GATE THEATRE, Dublin, Co. Dublin, Irish Republic: The name of the Gate Theatre is synonymous with those of Michael MacLiammoir and Hilton Edwards, who organized the company in 1928 to present plays of unusual interest, irrespective of nationality or period, at a time when the *Abbey* devoted itself entirely to Irish work. The founders' tradition continues, and you're as likely to find at the Gate a play by Tennessee Williams as one by Brian Friel or a young unknown. The auditorium is quite small and, as you'd expect from a company with the Gate's reputation for excellence in stage design, beautifully decorated so that you may feel less like a modern play-goer than a spectator at some eighteenth-century aristocrat's court theater. The young Orson Welles was once employed by the Gate, after exaggerating his previous experience — but proved his talents there as, subsequently, elsewhere. Details: Gate Theatre, Cavendish Row, Dublin 1, Irish Republic (phone: 74-40-45).

OLYMPIA THEATRE, Dublin, Irish Republic: The Olympia occupies a very special place in the hearts of Dubliners, perhaps because of its connection with music hall, always the most popular form of theater here. Patrons on the 1879 opening night at Dan Lowrey's Star of Erin (as the playhouse was then called) enjoyed such wonders as Mademoiselle Miaco, the Boneless Wonder, and Signor Zula, who swung from a high trapeze by his feet, with weights suspended from his teeth. Part of the Olympia's charm may be gauged from the fact that the smaller stalls bar is named, not for some famous performer or patron, but for Kathleen Kelly, who served wit and kindness as well as drink from behind the counter for many decades. The Olympia is the only theater in Dublin that still retains its gallery, or gods, from whose dizzying heights one can see the tops of the performers' heads far below. Also notable are the Waterford cut-glass chandeliers and the two huge mirrors on either side of the circle in which the spectators can monitor their own reactions while watching the performance. And, though television has meant the end of theatrical variety, the Olympia still presents concerts and pantomimes as well as plays, both Irish and foreign, and hosts visiting performers such as mime king Marcel Marceau. After each show, the bars remain open for half an hour; the actors congregate in Kelly's Bar to drink to the memory of days gone by. Details: Olympia Theatre, Dame St., Dublin 2, Irish Republic (phone: 77-89-62).

ROYAL DUBLIN SOCIETY CONCERT HALL, Dublin, Irish Republic: While most people think of traditional Irish music when they think of Dublin, it's also true that high-quality classical music can be found here. This is at least in part thanks to the Royal Dublin Society, which stages recitals from November to March in its Members' Hall, also known as the RDS Concert Hall. Although the acoustics are not all that one might desire for the small chamber ensembles and soloists that make up the majority of the Society's recitals, the attractive book-lined walls add a touch of intimacy that you don't often encounter in concert halls nowadays. And a great many distinguished musicians have played at the RDS in recent years — among them the Smetana String Quartet, the Beaux Arts Trio, Emmanuel Ax, Yehudi Menuhin, and Shera Cherkassy (these last two during concerts of the prestigious John Player series, which is based here). Details: Royal Dublin Society, Ballsbridge, Dublin 4, Irish Republic (phone: 680645).

DRUID LANE THEATRE, Galway, Co. Galway, Irish Republic: Installed in a former grocery warehouse in the oldest part of the city, near the Spanish Arch, the quays, and the old city walls, the home of the Druid Theatre Company is perhaps the most attractive small theater in Ireland, its intimacy enhanced by the way in which the seating surrounds the stage on three sides. The company was founded in 1975 by Garry Hynes, still the artistic director, and in that astonishingly short time has become renowned for its productions of Irish classics such as John Millington Synge's *The Tinkers' Wedding* and Dion Boucicault's *The Colleen Bawn,* as well as contemporary Irish plays and works from abroad. There's good reason to believe that the lane on which the theater is built is haunted by the ghost of a faceless nun who walks slowly through the surrounding streets at night. But don't let this dissuade you from an evening with this exciting young company. Details: Druid Lane Theatre, Druid La. (also known as Chapel La.), Galway, Co. Galway, Irish Republic (phone: 091-68-617).

SIAMSA TÍRE, THE NATIONAL FOLK THEATRE OF IRELAND, Tralee, Co. Kerry, Irish Republic: In the evenings of the days before television, the country people of Ireland would gather around a turf fire to play music, sing songs, tell stories, and just recount the day's activities. Such an occasion was called a *siamsa* (pronounced shee-am-sah) and down in "The Kingdom," as Kerry is called, a Catholic priest has taken the spirit of those days of neighborly entertainment and translated it into a stage show that has been received with delight not only abroad but, proof of its faithfulness to tradition, in Ireland itself. The show *Siamsa* is a whirlwind of song, dance, and music in three acts, which recreates a time when life was simpler, certainly harder, but perhaps more rewarding in its closeness to nature. Watching it in Siamsa Tíre's fine new theater in Tralee, you have the feeling of sitting in a country kitchen long ago. *Siamsa* is not only a recreation of the past, but also a proof of the liveliness of those traditions. The company performs in Tralee from June through September. Information: Siamsa Tíre Theatre, Godfrey Pl., Tralee (phone: 066-230-55) or Siamsa Tíre, Finuge (phone: Finuge 943), both in Co. Kerry, Irish Republic.

GRAND OPERA HOUSE, Belfast, Northern Ireland: When architect Robert McKinstry first went into the deserted building of Belfast's Grand Opera House and Cirque in the summer of 1975, he found the house manager's black jacket still hanging on the back of his office door. Crates of bottled beer stood unopened behind the bar where 4 years of dust topped the dour liquids in the half empty glasses. An upturned chair floated in the orchestra pit. The ashtrays on the backs of the seats in the circle were stuffed with the detritus of chocolate box wrappings and butts of now unfashionable local cigarette brands. In a drawer in the projection room lay a single copy of a pamphlet entitled *How to Emigrate.* But now the Opera House — as much a victim of the decline in theater-going as of "the troubles" — has come back to life, in part under McKinstry's guidance. The brass rails that once reflected the footlights that illuminated Pavlova and the "Divine Sarah" (Bernhardt) glisten again, and the turn-of-the-century theater has been restored to its full plush and stucco glory. In November each year the Opera House is the star of The Belfast Festival at Queen's; at Christmas comes the pantomime and during the rest of the year the program ranges from the Abbey Players, the Irish Ballet Company, the Irish Theatre Company, and Scottish Opera to traveling troupes from London, Edinburgh, and — recently — as far away as Quebec. Opera performances, guest recitals (Carlo Bergonzi and Alec McCowen have been featured), and musicals all have their place in the house's varied repertoire. Note that if you visit Belfast in July and early August, you'll find the House closed. Details: Grand Opera House, Great Victoria St., Belfast BT2 7HR, Northern Ireland (phone: 0232-667687).

WHERE TO HEAR TRADITIONAL IRISH MUSIC

Though there are more concerts, folk festivals, folk clubs, and informal sessions of music-making in Ireland than ever before, those magical nights of wild sweet music and hilarity are still as elusive as the rainbow's end. You might hit upon the right pub on the wrong night, or settle yourself down beside a stack of musicians only to find that they're more of a mind to chat with each other than lash out the reels. Before you set out to fill your ears with concertinas and flutes, it's useful to have a pretty good idea about where you might expect to find them.

For Dublin, you'll find a thorough listing of the traditional goings-on in the fortnightly magazine *In Dublin* and in the ads in the *Evening Press*. The famous *Slattery's* of Capel Street and the creaking old *Brazenhead* on Lower Bridge Street are only two of your options.

For information about concerts, folk clubs, and festivals around the country, see the Folk Column in Friday's *Evening Press*. Also, before you leave Dublin, stop in at the elegant Belgrave Square headquarters of the Comhaltas Ceoltóirí Éireann (CCE; detailed in *Traditional Music and Dance,* PERSPECTIVES), or phone the office at 800295 to get a list of CCE branches and sessions "down the country."

The mountainous area of County Kerry known as Sliabh Luachra, with its bordering county of West Cork, the land of melodeons, polkas, and slides, is one of the few places in Ireland where people still dance to the music. In tiny Knocknagree, West Cork, the locals — including more than one sprightly octogenarian — have been tripping it out every Friday and Sunday night for over 2 decades at *Dan O'Connell's,* to the accordion music of Johnny O'Leary, widely reckoned among the most original and effective masters of the squeezebox in Britain and Ireland; he founded the sessions with the late Denis Murphy, one of the best pupils of that great fiddle master Padraig O'Keeffe. Similar dancing can be found at *Peggy O'Riordan's* in Cullen and the *Two Mile Inn* outside Killarney. Rath Mhor is known for its music pubs, as are Scartlaglen, Rathawaun, Ballydesmond, Knocknabower, and Kanturk, birthplace of the young accordionist Jackie Daly, who plays with the group De Danann. Traveling west through Kerry, you'll find traditional music in various pubs in Tralee and in Irish-speaking Dingle. Among the tough, hearty citizens of Dún Quin, on the wild tip of the Dingle peninsula, a favorite gathering place is *Kruger's* pub.

In Clare, which locals deem the home of the very best Irish music, the community of Miltown Malbay hosts the week-long *Scoil Samraidh Willie Clancy,* a traditional music school that draws the county's finest musicians for nonstop music sessions — in the pubs and hotels, on street corners, and in tents and under open skies all day and all night. In Ennis, *Kelly's* pub and the *Old Ground Hotel* keep things lively on weekends; the *Fleadh Nua,* a summer weekend of music and dancing, is worth planning for, as is Lisdoonvarna's July folk festival, the biggest in Ireland. Kilkee, Ennistymon, Feakle, and Tulla (home of the Tulla Céilí Band, still going strong now after some three decades) are good bets throughout the year. At *Gus O'Connor's,* a homey pub in Doolin with lobster pots hanging from the ceiling and photos of local musicians on the walls, Micho Russell can often be found (despite his recent celebrity) playing his tin whistle in the simple centuries-old style he learned over 50 years ago.

Galway city is known for its swans, its natives' soft speech, and *Cullens,* in whose cozy back room musicians can be found just about any night of the week. The *Quays* and the *Crane* also have music. In Salthill, within walking distance of the city center, the *Cottage Bar* and *Faherty's* pub occasionally resound to a few fiddles and banjos. Galway is also the gateway to rocky, desertlike, Irish-speaking Connemara, where the musical emphasis is not so much on instruments as on songs, which are sung in the *sean nós* style — solo, heavily ornamented, unaccompanied, and in Irish. Look for music at *An Droighnean Donn* and *Hughes* pubs, in the town of An Spideal; at the venues *Teach Furbo* and *An Poitin Stil,* farther into the country; and at the pub *An Cruiscin Lan* in the village of An Cheathru Rua. In tiny Cleggan, 10 miles from Clifden, Connemara's capital, you'll find sessions at *Coyne's* on Wednesdays and the *Pier Bar* on Fridays. On Inishbofin Island, musicians on some nights blast away at *Day's* pub until long after licensing hours — since no *gardai* live on the island, its pubs never have to close.

Donegal is fiddle country and you can't pass through it without hearing about the Fiddler King, Johnny Doherty, born in Fintown in 1895 into a family of traveling musicians and tinsmiths; until his recent death, this little town drew many musicians and listeners who came to hear him play. Now a noteworthy spot for great bowing (nightly), *Teach Hiudai Bhig* in Bunbeg in Gaoth Dobhair also has the traditional after-Mass get-together on Sunday mornings. *Teach Leo,* in the village of Dobhair, is also a good bet for music. The island of Arranmore — only a 30p boat ride from Burtonport, exists in another time and another world, and the sessions at its *Castle Hotel* and *Jimmy's* pub — stocked with visiting musicians from the mainland and from Belfast — go on into the wee hours. In August, don't miss the Festival of International Folk Music in Letterkenny.

Northern Ireland has a music all its own — a plaintive, almost eerie blend of fiddles and flutes, with long spare notes and little ornamentation — closer to that of the Shetland Islands or Sweden than to Kerry's frolicsome polkas and slides. Since the onset of the troubles, Belfast's traditional music has been taken up in the Catholic community and largely ignored among Protestants, and informal pub sessions in Belfast city center are a thing of the past; if you venture into the Catholic enclaves such as the Markets or Falls areas, however, you'll be rewarded by some fine sessions. Try the *American Bar* on Corporation Street on Wednesdays, *Kelley's Bar* on Short Strand on Saturdays, and *Pat's* bar on Princes Dock Street almost anytime. Also good are the *Casement Social Club* in Andersonstown, *Cumann Chluain Ard* on Hawthorne Street, or *Beacon's* at the corner of the Springfield Road, and clubs in the New Lodge and Surf Lodge areas. In County Antrim, Irish music is played enthusiastically by Catholics and Protestants alike; the town of Portglenone is noted for its fine sessions. Also highly recommended is the beautiful *Crosskeys Inn* outside Toomebridge, where, on a Saturday night, you might find as many as four sessions at once. In Cookestown, County Tyrone, look for music at *Raymond Conway's* bar on Fridays.

Feis and Fleadh: The Best Festivals

With their wealth of talents in so many fields it's hardly surprising that Britain and Ireland should be blossoming with festivals. What is surprising is that, not depending for a moment on the possibility of the summer being warm and sunny, they take place virtually year-round. From Scotland to the west of England, from Ireland's green shores to East Anglia's fens, the place is alive with festive celebrations lasting anywhere from a day or a week to a month or even a whole summer. Some are oddball festivals devoted to snuff-taking or pancake-racing; some are rooted in centuries-old tradition, with plenty of morris dancing, craft displays, and brass band music.

In Ireland, in addition, places that grow potatoes have potato festivals, towns that sell strawberries stage strawberry festivals. And all during the summer, when the evenings are long and the weather is warm, people stand around in their town's main square listening to bands and ballad singers and meeting neighbors they mightn't have had a proper chance to speak to since the previous year's event. There is a very good reason for this abundance of festivals: During festival times, the draconian Irish licensing laws that force the pubs to close at 11 PM in the winter and 11:30 in the summer ease up a bit, and all bars are allowed to stay open until 1 AM (though in the cities, late-night drinking — that great source of Irish joy — is confined to a single appointed place). Consequently, festivals whose raison d'être may be entirely ludicrous or inherently uninteresting can often be the best. The atmosphere is usually jolly, and there is generally a feeling that something is actually happening.

Just as many events throughout the area concern themselves with drama, music, and the visual arts; small specialized music festivals are increasingly abundant. In Ireland, for instance, Killarney holds an annual Bach Festival, Cork an International Jazz Festival, and Dublin a Festival of Twentieth-Century Music. Also, the number of Woodstock-style music festivals with acres of tents and dozens of superstars is growing. These are held mainly in June and July and can, if the weather is good, be very enjoyable. The same goes for the kind of event known in Ireland as a *fleadh cheoil* ("festival of music"), which you'll find almost every weekend in summer all over Ireland. The festivals manage an extraordinary combination of sixties bonhomie and the long-standing Irish tradition of playing music at fairs. Whether you take in the biggest of the breed, the all-Ireland *Fleadh Cheoil,* which generally takes place the third weekend in August in either Buncrana, County Donegal, or Listowel, County Kerry, or one of the smaller affairs, you'll find the experience fairly unbelievable. Thousands of people, young and old, take over the host town. Guesthouses and hotels don't have a bed to spare, ordinary homes turn into lodging places, and the young put up tents. Pubs stay open late, people drink in the streets, and day and night the music continues on and on. Many of the best interpreters of Irish traditional music and dance show up for performances and competitions alike (so it is not all just drinking and carousing). The size of the throngs who come to listen and take part demonstrates once again how Irish traditional music has grown in importance and popularity over the last decade. For dates, contact the central organizers in Dublin. Comhaltas Ceoltóirí Éireann, 32 Belgrave Sq., Monkstown, Co. Dublin (phone: 800298).

At the larger events of all types — in addition to all the listed offerings — you will still get, like a plum in a pie, the "fringe": The one at the Edinburgh festival is world-famous (and, to be truthful, sometimes more interesting than the main show, though recently installed director John Drummond has brought a whole new air of excitement to Edinburgh's annual junketings), but many other festivals also have their sideshow. Add to that the fact that host towns are often *en fête* too, with floral displays everywhere, and the fact that standards of British catering have been creeping upward enough that you'll almost always find one or two good restaurants for that all-important socializing over a meal or a drink before and after events — and you've got the makings of a fine vacation, especially when you combine it with a visit to a historic house or a splendid English, Scots, Welsh, or Irish garden. Check also with bodies such as the National Trust, the various Garden Schemes, and local tourist boards as to other area events.

No matter where you go, remember that even though festivals may be full of Serious Events they are also, in a word, fun — and it's likely that you'll get a chance to meet and talk with local people who will be delighted to welcome you as a foreign visitor to their hometown. Therein lies a good deal of the charm and pleasure of a country festival, and the memory may stay with you forever. The various countries' tourist boards, as well as the British Tourist Authority, can provide you with listings of festivals of all types. Meanwhile, here are some notes on a few of the best.

WORTH A LONG DETOUR

ALDEBURGH FESTIVAL, Aldeburgh, Suffolk, England: Beloved by musicians the world over for its warmth, intimacy, and exceptionally fine acoustics, the remarkable concert hall established by composer Benjamin Britten and tenor Peter Pears is the focal point for this quaint little sea town's annual festival of concerts, lectures, poetry readings, and exhibitions, which takes place for two weeks in mid-June. Details: Festival Office, High St., Aldeburgh, Suffolk 1P15 5AX, England (phone: 2935).

ARUNDEL FESTIVAL, Arundel, West Sussex, England: Held annually for 10 days in August, this festival is held in a charming South Downs resort dominated by a Norman castle owned by the premier duke of Great Britain; its panoramic tilting yard is used as an open-air theater for the festival goings-on — performances by the New Shakespeare Company and, each year, special emphasis on one other aspect of the arts. And there are many other events, ranging from concerts of classical music to gymkhanas. Details: Festival Office, Lyminster House, Lyminster, Littlehampton, West Sussex BN17 7QJ, England (phone: 0903-883284).

BATH INTERNATIONAL FESTIVAL OF MUSIC, Bath, Avon, England: For 2 weeks in late spring every year, this magnificent city, famous for its Roman baths and outstanding Georgian architecture, offers a catholic choice of concerts by top musicians; informative tours and lectures in historic buildings, houses, and gardens; performances of opera and dance by leading small companies; many art exhibitions; relaxed late-night musical shows; and a candlelight procession through the handsome streets. What sets this event apart are the concerts' settings. The performances of choral works and the organ recitals are presented in Bath Abbey or nearby Wells Cathedral, while you'll see concerts and operas in handsome halls that date from the late eighteenth or early nineteenth century — an *opera buffa,* for instance, in the city's *Theatre Royal,* an intimate hall rebuilt and refurbished more than once since its 1805 construction, or a recital or chamber music concert in the elegant circa-1771 Bath Assembly Rooms, the largest of which, the eggshell blue and gray Ball Room, is illuminated by no less than five 200-year-old chandeliers. During intermissions, you'll promenade through similarly stately, classically proportioned halls; and your route to your hotel will take you through streets that seem equally removed from the modern: The spell doesn't let up for a minute. Details: Bath Festival Office, Linley House, 1 Pierrepont Pl., Bath, Avon BA1 1JY, England (phone: 0225-62231).

BRIGHTON FESTIVAL, Brighton, East Sussex, England: Brighton, that strange mixture of the beautiful, with its Regency buildings, and the scruffiness typical of a popular seaside resort, is always a joy to visit — but never more than during the 2 weeks in May when the Brighton Festival fills up the town with music, both classical and popular, in recitals, chamber programs, orchestral concerts, and operas, as well as programs of dance and drama, art exhibitions, and seminars — many of which take place in the Prince Regent's magnificently bizarre and exotic Royal Pavilion. Usually, there's also a dramatic fireworks display, some sheepdog trials and guided walk, a bric-a-brac market, and open house at local artists' studios, plus a grand procession by the light of hundreds of real torches. Details: Festival Office, Marlborough House, 54 Old Steine, Brighton, East Sussex BN1 1EQ, England (phone: 0273-29801).

BUXTON FESTIVAL, Buxton, Derbyshire, England: The plays, operas, films, and lectures presented in this attractive Georgian spa town's elegant, exquisitely renovated opera house — the only Edwardian opera house outside London — and its fine concert hall as part of this young and still rapidly developing 2-week-long July-and-August event focus on a writer such as Sir Walter Scott or William Shakespeare, and the arts that influenced him. Buxton nestles amidst the rugged hills of central England's Derbyshire Peak District and is easily accessible from Manchester. Details: Festival Office,

Opera House, Buxton, Derbyshire SK17 6XN, England (phone: 0298-71010).

CHELTENHAM INTERNATIONAL FESTIVAL OF MUSIC, Cheltenham, Gloucestershire, England: This delightful Regency spa town's annual July festival (held for 2 weeks in some very historic local venues) presents a wide range of music, with a bias toward the contemporary and the British; some works are commissioned especially for the event. There are children's concerts, master classes, dance programs, opera, and more. The Cheltenham Festival of Literature, which runs for a week in November, includes a national poetry competition. Details about either: Town Hall, Cheltenham, Gloucestershire GL50 1QA, England (phone: 0242-21621).

CHICHESTER FESTIVAL THEATRE, Chichester, West Sussex, England: The repertory for this extremely popular theater festival, which runs from May through September, includes a mixture of the old (including Shakespeare) and the new: The emphasis is on entertaining rather than experimenting, and the most successful plays usually end up in London. During its two decades of existence, the roster of performers has grown into a veritable *Who's Who* of the English-speaking theater, and the festival has come to be the most important annual theatrical event outside London, Edinburgh, and Stratford. The theater that houses the goings-on is attractively modern, hexagonally shaped, and set in a lovely parkland; every seat is a good one. Another plus: Chichester itself, a magical place in some of the most enchanting country in Sussex, is sophisticated enough that restaurants keep late hours and chefs serve lobster thermidor as well as steak-and-kidney pie. Details: Chichester Festival Theatre, Oaklands Park, Chichester, West Sussex PO19 4AP, England (phone: 0243-781312).

THREE CHOIRS FESTIVAL, Gloucester, Gloucestershire, and Hereford and Worcester, Herefordshire and Worcestershire, England: This event, whose home rotates among the three towns and lasts for a week in August each year, emphasizes the great English tradition of choral singing in joint performances by the three renowned cathedral choirs of works both classical and modern, including a few commissioned especially for the occasion. The surrounding Welsh border country is wonderfully scenic and full of beautiful old buildings, and the hospitality is a delight. Details: Festival Office, Deansway, Worcester WR1 2JG, England (phone: 0905-26494).

GLYNDEBOURNE FESTIVAL OPERA, Glyndebourne, East Sussex, England: Founded in 1934 by John Christie and his wife, the singer Audrey Mildmay, and held on their ancient Sussex country estate some 50 miles south of London, this festival, which runs from the third week in May to the first week in August, is top-drawer musically — with artists coming from all over the world — and socially as well: The splendid program of opera (five productions each summer) is garnished with a 75-minute supper interval — perfect for a meal in one of the restaurants, or for champagne picnics in the gardens and on the velvety English lawns. Details: Glyndebourne Festival, Lewes, East Sussex BN8 5UU, England (phone: 0273-812321).

HAXEY HOOD GAME, Haxey, Humberside, England: One of dozens of English festivals rooted in age-old tradition, this one got started on Old Christmas Day long ago when a lady lost her hood to a sudden gust of wind, and thanked the 13 men who rescued it by awarding them each a piece of land on the simple condition that they invent a game based on the incident, and then compete in it annually forevermore. As played today every Epiphany by the descendants of those men along with an assortment of other villagers, the contest involves a Lord, 13 Boggins, and a Fool, in many speeches, a bonfire, a no-holds-barred free-for-all in which writhing and grunting masses of humanity struggle for long hours over a piece of leather, and equally drawn-out victory celebrations in the local pubs. Details: Tourist Information Centre, Doncaster Central Library, Waterdale, Doncaster, South Yorkshire DN1 3JE, England (phone: 0302-69123), and the British Tourist Authority, 680 Fifth Ave., New York, NY 10019 (phone: 212-581-4700).

DIVERSIONS / Feis and Fleadh: The Best Festivals 491

GREENWICH FESTIVAL, London, England: The events of this annual 2-week-long June festival include operas; mime and dance performances; poetry readings; concerts of jazz and classical and folk music; as well as many children's events. Internationally known artists such as Janet Baker, Claudio Arrau, James Galway, Alfred Brendel, and others perform alongside amateurs and local groups: The Greenwich Festival began as a purely community-oriented affair. Greenwich itself is a historic town on the banks of the river Thames and the magnificence and variety of its concert locations make its festival very special indeed. Details: Greenwich Festival Office, 25 Woolwich New Rd., London SE18, England (phone: 01-317-8687).

ANNUAL BOTTLE KICKING AND HARE PIE SCRAMBLE, Hallaton, Leicestershire, England: When the *Guardian* described this small village's 700-year-old Easter Monday event, the high point on the village calendar, as being "unsurpassed for sheer animal ferocity," it wasn't far from wrong: As the opposing two teams from neighboring villages scramble to maneuver two out of three small wooden beer kegs across a goal line, the field is sheer anarchy — a situation that may have something to do with the fact that every now and again each player drops out to have another pint (earlier drafts having been consumed in some local pub). Details: East Midlands Tourist Board, Exchequergate, Lincoln, Lincolnshire LN2 1PZ, England (phone: 0522-31521), and the British Tourist Authority (above).

HARROGATE INTERNATIONAL FESTIVAL, Harrogate, North Yorkshire, England: Elegant buildings stand alongside modern facilities in this renowned Victorian spa town. Its 2-week-long festival, which takes place in July and August, and aims to bring British and international artists of the highest quality to an area that sees relatively little of them the rest of the year, features orchestral and chamber music, celebrity recitals, middle-of-the-road plays, late-night shows, literary events, and programs for children. Details: Festival Office, Royal Baths, Harrogate, North Yorkshire HG1 2RR, England (phone: 0423-62303).

CITY OF LONDON FESTIVAL, London, England: London's own festival, held in July within the old city's square mile, utilizes the area's many fine halls and churches — including St. Paul's itself — for concerts of serious music, often featuring choirs and leading soloists. There is also a parallel Fringe program of day- and nighttime events, both out of doors and in, including street theater, poetry readings, and jazz. Details: City of London Festival, 64 West Smithfield, London EC1A 9DY, England (phone: 01-606-1973).

THE LONDON-TO-BRIGHTON VETERAN CAR RUN, London, England: Until 1896, one now-amusing British law prohibited the operation of a car unless it was preceded by a man on foot carrying a red flag (so as not to scare other people's horses). Its repeal is the raison d'être for this 50-mile drive — held annually in November — full of shiny antique autos. Details: RAC Motor Sports Division, 31 Belgrave Sq., London SW1, England (phone: 01-235-8601).

LORD MAYOR'S PROCESSION, London, England: For this November event honoring the newly inaugurated Lord Mayor and the profession that he is leaving for the duration of his term, one group marches in seventeenth-century armor, and the honoree is transported in a 3-ton coach. The parade is wonderfully colorful and well worth a look if timing is right. Details: City of London Public Relations Office, Guildhall, London EC2P 2EJ, England (phone: 01-606-3030).

MALVERN FESTIVAL, Malvern, Worcestershire, England: At this event emphasis is given to the music of Edward Elgar (who was born in Malvern), the plays of his great friend George Bernard Shaw, and the work of their contemporaries: Drama and music are about equally important here. The plays are presented in the Festival Theatre, and the chamber concerts in historic houses scattered throughout the picturesque Malvern Hills of the area, within easy reach of the Cotswolds and Wales. And there's a varied fringe program. Details: Malvern Festival Theatre, Malvern, Worcestershire WR14 3HB, England (phone: 06845-3377).

KING'S LYNN FESTIVAL, King's Lynn, Norfolk, England: The Queen Mother is the patron of this late July week of art exhibitions and classical music, both serious and light, plus jazz and folk events, puppetry, magic shows, and children's theater — and she usually attends. Street shows and fireworks round out the program. The site, an ancient market town riddled with quaint streets, curious churches, and historic buildings, is also a delight. Details: King's Lynn Festival, 27 King St., King's Lynn, Norfolk PE30 1HA, England (phone: 0553-4725).

HOBBY HORSE CELEBRATIONS, Padstow, Cornwall, England: Among Europe's oldest festivals, this annual May Day event brings this sleepy seaport town to life. Caroling and carousing go on all night, but the real highlight of the affair is a long parade in which the Hobby Horse — a fabulous creature with a fierce-looking cone-shaped head protruding through a black, sailcloth-covered hoop — acts out a skit in which he dies and is revived over and over and over, then, at day's end, prances around a Maypole. Details: West Country Tourist Board, Trinity Ct., 37 Southernhay E, Exeter, Devon EX1 1QS, England (phone: 0392-76351), and the British Tourist Authority (above).

SALISBURY FESTIVAL, Salisbury, Wiltshire, England: This September event, one of the leading cultural affairs in the South of England, includes lovely concerts by candlelight in the cathedral, operas and plays, a variety of late-evening shows, and assorted outdoor events. There are many points of interest in the region — mysterious prehistoric Stonehenge and Wilton House among them — and Salisbury itself is a fine old town. Details: Salisbury Festivities, The King's House, 65 The Close, Salisbury, Wiltshire SP1 2EN, England (phone: 23883).

YORK FESTIVAL, York, North Yorkshire, England: During most of June (but not every year), this historic city gives itself over to one of the country's largest festivals: An average of ten events are presented daily in the magnificent old minster as well as in churches, theaters, and colleges. Concerts, dance performances, plays, exhibitions, lectures, and outdoor spectaculars are all part of the goings-on. Details: York Festival Office, 1 Museum St., York, North Yorkshire YO1 2DT, England (phone: 0904-26421).

SCOTLAND'S HERITAGE FESTIVAL, countrywide, Scotland: This wonderful event, which takes place in about 50 different sites throughout the nation, includes lectures on, tours through, and musical and literary events and art exhibitions in Scotland's castles, country houses, cathedrals, and private homes. Sometimes these elegant structures are the settings for superb banquets, and sometimes you can buy an all-inclusive package that features an overnight stay in one of the stately homes. Details: Scottish Tourist Board, 23 Ravelston Ter., Edinburgh EH 4 3EU, Scotland (phone: 031-332-2433).

EDINBURGH FESTIVAL, Edinburgh, Scotland: During its 3-week run in late August and early September, this grande dame of festivals offers you a positive cornucopia of activities. Most of Edinburgh's bigger public buildings, as well as many smaller ones, are taken over for exhibitions, performances, and other cultural affairs of global significance, or for nearly 400 more experimental presentations of the Festival Fringe, which the *Guinness Book of World Records* lists as the largest arts festival in the world. The fringe gives particular encouragement to comics; past performers have included Dudley Moore, and Michael Palin and Terry Jones, later of the Monty Python team. There, as at the festival proper, you'll also find music, dance, theater, opera, and the visual arts representatives; there are many world premieres. The artists are the best in the world, and the audiences are big and international. The colorful Tattoo that takes place at the castle every night is almost as popular as the musical goings-on. Details: Festival Society, 21 Market St., Edinburgh EH1 1BW, Scotland (phone: 031-226-4001), and the Festival Fringe Society, 170 High St., Edinburgh EH1 1QS, Scotland (phone: 031-226-5257).

UP-HELLY-AA, Lerwick, Shetland Isles, Scotland: Early January, when this traditional event rooted in pagan ceremony takes place, is a season of gales and snowstorms and of long nights and blink-and-you-miss-them days in this little town at Latitude 60° North (the same as Greenland and Siberia). But that doesn't daunt Shetlanders, who don Viking regalia to parade behind a replica of an ancient war galley to the town park, where they set the thing aflame with hundreds of torches that redden a sky already bright with the Aurora, then set out for hotels and halls for merrymaking wild enough to warm the coldest hearts. Shetlanders living all over the world come home for this event. Details: Shetland Tourist Organisation, Market Cross, Lerwick, Shetland, Scotland (phone: 3434), and the British Tourist Authority (address above).

THE ROYAL NATIONAL EISTEDDFOD, varying sites in Wales: Held for a week in August in different locations every year, this colossal event in celebration of Welsh language and culture, established in 1176, includes some of Europe's biggest choral, vocal, and instrumental competitions in classical, folk, and pop genres; plus concerts, plays, lectures, and craft exhibitions. Most festivities take place in a vast mobile pavilion — and there are some spectacular ones. The official language is Welsh, but translation facilities are free. Details: British Tourist Authority (address above).

FISHGUARD MUSIC FESTIVAL, Fishguard, Dyfed, Wales: The renowned Welsh choral tradition has generated this week-long July annual. The music is mainly classical, but new works are commissioned for performance by visiting musicians from home and abroad; and there's also jazz, poetry, film, and art. The festival ends with the presentation of a large choral work. Many concerts take place in ancient St. David's Cathedral. Fishguard itself, the location for the 1971 filming of Dylan Thomas's *Under Milk Wood,* starring Richard Burton, is a beautiful place — backed by cliffs and partially edged by a shingled beach. Details: Mrs. Marion Butler, Fishguard Music Festival, Summerhill, Penbanc, Fishguard, Pembrokeshire, Dyfed, Wales (phone: 873612).

INTERNATIONAL MUSICAL EISTEDDFOD, Llangollen, Clwyd, Wales: Music and friendship abound here for a week in mid-July as over 10,000 competitors from 30 countries from Hungary and Bulgaria to Norway, Italy, South Africa, the USA, and others compete in folk song and dance competitions and choir contests. Evening concerts are given by choirs and dance groups and renowned singers and instrumentalists. The colors and the costumes and the sounds are dazzling, and there's always a special moment — as, for instance, the time a group of Zulu dancers swept onstage, interrupting the national anthems, to present the festival's music director W. S. Gwynn Williams with their tribe's highest honor. Details: Eisteddfod Office, Llangollen, Clwyd LL20 8NG, Wales (phone: 0978-860236).

ST. PATRICK'S WEEK, countrywide, Irish Republic: Irishmen from around the world come to the Auld Sod to celebrate the feast day of the nation's patron saint. In Dublin, the week beforehand means concerts of music and dancing on St. Stephen's Green, Gaelic football and hurling, and horse racing; and there's a mammoth St. Paddy's Day parade, with military bands, accordion bands, fife and drum bands, flute bands, marching bands, pipe bands, and show bands from all over the world, not to mention the crowd of a quarter of a million. It goes without saying that all the pubs and cabarets are jammed (though you won't find the green beer so beloved in stateside bars) and that citizens of Cork, Galway, Limerick, and Sligo are almost as wild and woolly. Details: Irish Tourist Board, 590 Fifth Ave., New York, NY 10036 (phone: 212-246-7400).

CORK FILM FESTIVAL, Cork, Co. Cork, Irish Republic: This fall (September or October) event, held in the pleasant, hilly, and Italianate city that Corkmen like to think of as Ireland's true capital, annually features the work of a single director and the films of a particular country, and offers many European premieres. Special emphasis is put on short films, and awards are given for these according to traditions begun by the man

494 DIVERSIONS / Feis and Fleadh: The Best Festivals

who founded the event in 1956 and then went on to become the Irish Film Censor. At night locals head for the Film Festival Club, to join visitors, the assembled critics, and assorted other personalities involved in the growing Irish film industry. Details: Cork Film Festival, 38 MacCurtain St., Cork, Irish Republic (phone: 021-502221).

DUBLIN THEATRE FESTIVAL, Dublin, Irish Republic: For the first 2 weeks of October, the Irish theater goes mad. Plays open daily — new plays by contemporary Irish authors, old plays by dead Irish authors, productions by visiting theater companies, late-night revues, mime shows. Actors get work, directors get work, would-be theater critics get work. Theater people are all very happy. And so are visitors. Those who like light comedies will be as gleeful as those who swear by experimental theater. Anyone with stamina and eclectic tastes could spend 2 entire weeks watching plays and then rounding off each night in a special Festival Club where all the casts usually congregate, along with directors and critics, whose discussions have been known to degenerate to a physical level. Increasingly the festival seems to be functioning as a showcase for new works by Irishmen like Hugh Leonard, Stewart Parker, Brian Friel, and J. Graham Reid — and visitors should be pleasantly surprised by the quality of the productions. Details: Dublin Theatre Festival, 47 Nassau St., Dublin 2, Irish Republic (phone: 778439).

DUN LAOGHAIRE SUMMER FESTIVAL, Dun Laoghaire, Co. Dublin, Irish Republic: During the last week in June, this old, prosperous, well-kept borough 6 miles from Dublin, which, although increasingly a bedroom community, continues to retain its own essentially Victorian style, goes culture-mad. There are loads of exhibits of old photographs and paintings; art shows and musical soirées in the Maritime Institute on High Street; tours of the area and trips to pretty Dalkey Island; balls; regattas; lectures; concerts of all types and descriptions featuring everything from light classical fare to sea chanteys and other traditional music, and even opera; and, for children, afternoon Punch and Judy shows, theater workshops, and windsurfing exhibitions — in short, a little something for everyone. Dun Laoghaire also has a good harbor, which on fine summer days fills up with lovely boats and yachts, and favorite swimming holes like Killiney, Seapoint, and the Forty-Foot are just down the road. Details: Dun Laoghaire Summer Festival, Box 9, Dun Laoghaire, Co. Dublin, Irish Republic (phone: 822054).

GALWAY OYSTER FESTIVAL, Galway, Co. Galway, Irish Republic: This city on Ireland's western seaboard, colonized in the sixteenth century by Elizabethan planters, and the surrounding bays have always been famous for their oysters and scallops. In recent years local agencies and fishing cooperatives have actually farmed them. So it's only appropriate that the big annual wingding here, traditionally held in late September just as the shellfish come back into season after a succession of R-less months, is devoted to the succulent creature; after you've been to all the cultural festivals, this is the place to come and relax. The festival begins with the Irish Oyster-Opening Championship; people come from around the globe to take part in the World Oyster-Opening Championship that takes place 2 days later; and, throughout the festival, there are yacht races, golf competitions, and other festivities. If you exhaust these activities, head for the pubs of Clarenbridge, where many a tasty bivalve slips down an eager throat on a stream of foaming stout. Or take a boat or plane to the Aran Islands. Or go out and explore the city: Some of the Tudor doorways and coats of arms are still visible in Shop Street. Details: Áras Fáilte, Victoria Pl., Galway, Irish Republic (phone: 091-63081).

GOREY ARTS FESTIVAL, Gorey, Co. Wexford, Irish Republic: For the first 2 weeks in August anything can happen in Gorey. One night there's jazz, the next a puppet show or a performance by Ireland's newest rock band or perhaps mainstream theater. When you include the major exhibitions of painting and photography that take place at the same time, the readings, the writing workshops, and the master classes in both classical and Irish traditional music that are part of the goings-on here, it seems that there is, literally, something for everyone. Paul Funge, the Irish painter who designed and built the exhibition area and theater where most of these events take place, is, in the words of Irish art critic Adrian Dunne, "the mercurial superstar of the Irish art scene." Though Funge is still only in his midthirties, what happens in Gorey is a reflection of his many talents. The festival, and indeed the town, are served by two wonderful hostelries — friendly, efficient, and cavernlike *French's Bar* on Main Street, and across the road, the *Railway Hotel,* which, since nothing has been touched for years, has the feeling of the Ireland of 40 years ago. When you've had it with culture, you can head for the beaches at nearby Courtown and Ardamine. Another delight: the train ride down from Dublin, right along the shore and then into some of the nation's lushest countryside. Details: Gorey Arts Festival, Rafter St., Gorey, Co. Wexford, Irish Republic (phone: 055-21470).

KILKENNY ARTS WEEK, Kilkenny, Co. Kilkenny, Irish Republic: Now old and established enough to have acquired a fringe, this event held at the end of August or the beginning of September benefits greatly from being held in one of the most pleasant and prosperous of Irish towns, not to mention from the presence there of a group of very comfortable hotels, and a location which makes it feasible to drive down from Dublin (a matter of 2 hours), have a drink in *The Marble City* or *Tynan's Bar,* catch a lunchtime concert, see the city's many interesting sights, attend an evening concert in acoustically excellent St. Canice's Cathedral, stop in at the Arts Week Club to make merry until all hours of the night — and then, if you're not worn out, drive back to Dublin. Many writers — poets Robert Lowell and Ted Hughes among them — have read their work there; but music is the main thing, and many of the performers are internationally known. Traditional music and folk songs are on the program along with classical works. Details: Kilkenny Arts Week, Butler House, Patrick St., Kilkenny, Co. Kilkenny, Irish Republic.

LISDOONVARNA MUSIC FESTIVAL, Lisdoonvarna, Co. Clare, Irish Republic: During the second weekend in July, tens of thousands show up in this community in the southwest part of the country for the biggest and best of all the new-style festivals held over the summer in Ireland — 3 days of nonstop rock, folk, country, reggae, blues, and traditional music. If the weather is good — and it often can be — everybody has a ball; if not, the show still goes on. Over the years, such international stars as Richard and Linda Thompson, John Sebastian, Country Joe McDonald, and Emmylou Harris have appeared. Lisdoonvarna is near the town of Doolin, famous for its traditional musicians (see *The Performing Arts*), and not far from a stunningly beautiful district called the Burren, full of caves that can be visited and limestone outcrops that take on different hues with the changing of the light. If you're not the type to sleep in tents (as many festival-goers do), you can lodge in any number of local hotels, guesthouses, and farmhouses — but you will need reservations. If you don't have a car, you can go with a bus group from Dublin. Details: Zenith Promotions, Lisdoonvarna, Co. Clare, Irish Republic (phone: Lisdoonvarna 152 or 153).

LISTOWEL WRITERS' WEEK, Listowel, Co. Kerry, Irish Republic: Locally born playwright John B. Keane, who runs a pub here, and the writer Brian MacMahon, another resident, are the presiding spirits of this increasingly popular and enjoyable festival held during the first week in July. They hold workshops in drama, poetry, and fiction for aspiring writers; produce plays by young Irish writers; launch books; and stage lectures on many aspects of contemporary Irish writing. Yet, the atmosphere is anything but academic. People are interested in enjoying themselves, and have been known to go on doing so all night. The writers who attend may talk plenty of shop, but they're apt to give equal time to the outcome of tennis finals at Wimbledon, which occur at the same time, or to the previous night's hoopla. The pubs, mostly old-fashioned and very friendly, stay open late, and often, a musician in the crowd will suddenly bring out his instrument for a round of something traditional and Irish. There's also an official club where a band plays dance music, and the assembled writers, aspiring writers, and locals, together with assorted hangers-on — when not drinking

— leap about the floor. Details: The Secretary, Listowel Writers' Week, St. Patrick's Hall, Listowel, Co. Kerry, Irish Republic (phone: 068-21074).

THE ROSE OF TRALEE INTERNATIONAL FESTIVAL, Tralee, Co. Kerry, Irish Republic: Nowadays, nobody takes the competitive element of this beauty-contest-with-a-difference too seriously. But girls still come from all over the world at the end of August or the first of September to vie for a Waterford crystal trophy and the title "Rose of Tralee," first made famous by tenor John McCormack: "She was lovely and fair/Like a Rose of the summer/Yet it was not her beauty alone that won me/O no it was the truth in her eyes ever dawning/That made me love Mary, the Rose of Tralee." But this 6-day event goes beyond McCormack and, as a sort of Irish Mardi gras, provides an extraordinary range of entertainment, from donkey and greyhound races and tugs-of-war, to fireworks, brass band concerts, performances of traditional music, cabarets, and much more. At any given moment you could find four or five acts going on in different parts of the town, and people roam the streets from early morning until late at night. There's always something happening, and most of it is free. Nearly 100,000 attend. Details: Festival of Kerry, Ltd., 5 Lower Castle St., Tralee, Co. Kerry, Irish Republic (phone: 066-21322).

NATIONAL PILGRIMAGE TO CROAGH PATRICK, Westport, Co. Mayo, Irish Republic: Annually on the last Sunday in July, thousands of pilgrims follow in the footsteps of Patrick, the good saint who had what some might call a masochist's knack for concocting ways of doing penance. Barefooted, sometimes crawling on his knees, he would make his way over thorns and jagged rocks, through mud and water, to the summit of this mountain. As he did then, his followers do today — and, once at the top, they circle the chapel there fifteen times. It's a sight to see — often quite moving. Details: Tourist Office, The Mall, Westport, Co. Mayo, Irish Republic (phone: Westport 269).

WEXFORD FESTIVAL OPERA, Wexford, Co. Wexford, Irish Republic: In the latter half of October when the nights get long and cold, this harbor town comes alive with an event that, from a social point of view alone, is probably one of the most enjoyable in Ireland, and the town's narrow winding streets fill with opera lovers from all over the world. The festival's long drawing card is the opera — usually two seldom-performed works by well-known composers and one contemporary opus. Ticket prices are low even by European standards, and performance quality is very high, as it has been since the festival's inception in 1951. Talented newcomers often use Wexford to launch their careers, and many well-known singers (among them Frederica von Stade) have sung there. Much of the backstage work, the ushering, and ticket selling is done by volunteers, and at least one member of most local families is directly involved in the festival — as a result, this otherwise very elite event has become a very public and popular one. What makes it really special, though, is the productions' setting — a tiny opera house that seats only 446, situated down a capillary of a side street — plus a general feeling of style and opulence at all the events, which also include concerts and recitals, and exhibitions and readings at the local arts center. All of Wexford's public buildings — several of which were designed by Pugin — are floodlit for the duration. And, of course, the pubs keep late hours. Details: Theatre Royal, Wexford, Co. Wexford, Irish Republic (phone: 053-22240).

BELFAST FESTIVAL AT QUEEN'S, Belfast, Northern Ireland: One of the three biggest arts festivals in Britain and Ireland, this event, held in November, has, since its beginnings in the early 1960s, created excitement and controversy on the cultural scene that even "the troubles" have not been able to undermine. Although it covers the entire spectrum of the arts, there traditionally has been an emphasis on classical music. But the jazz and film programs are excellent; the world of graphics is well represented; and there is plenty going on in drama as well, with visiting companies from the Republic and the rest of Europe. Artists from all over the world, superstars like Cleo Laine and Dietrich Fischer-Dieskau, have performed here. And there is a tremendously healthy fringe, fed with generous amounts of undergraduate zest by students of Queen's University (on whose Victorian campus most festival events take place); and, as usual, it is the smallest and least expected events that one remembers with particular affection. In short, a visit here would be a rare and extraordinary introduction to what is good and enjoyable in Belfast. Details: Festival House, 8 Malone Rd., Belfast BT9 5BN, Northern Ireland (phone: 0232-667687).

IF YOU'RE NEARBY

WINDSOR FESTIVAL, Windsor Castle, Surrey, England: Concerts, lectures, walks, and exhibitions that take place in or near Windsor Castle and Eton College occupy this community annually for 2 weeks in September or October. Details: Dial House, Englefield Green, Surrey TW20 0DU, England (phone: Egham 32618).

CAMDEN FESTIVAL, London, England: Rare and early opera, dance, and jazz are featured in the concert halls, churches, and playhouses of this London borough every year for 2 weeks in March. Details: St. Pancras Library, 100 Euston Rd., London NW1 2AJ, England (phone: 01-388-7727).

ARBROATH ABBEY PAGEANT, Arbroath, Tayside, Scotland: The abbey in question, built in the thirteenth century, was dedicated to St. Thomas à Becket. The festival takes place annually for a week in September. Details: Festival Office, 105 High St., Arbroath, Tayside DD11 1DP, Scotland (phone: 72609).

EDINBURGH FOLK FESTIVAL, Edinburgh, Scotland: Folk music, dance, crafts activities, children's events, lectures, conferences, *ceilidhs*, and poetry readings fill up the schedule for this festival, which takes place for a week every March. Details: Festival Office, 170 High St., Edinburgh EH1 1QS, Scotland (phone: 031-226-3645).

PITLOCHRY FESTIVAL, Pitlochry, Perthshire, Scotland: Plays, concerts, and art exhibitions are presented in Scotland's Theatre in the Hills, from April through mid-October. Details: Pitlochry Festival Theatre, Pitlochry, Perthshire PH16 5DR, Scotland (phone: 0796-2680).

NORTH WALES MUSIC FESTIVAL, St. Asaph, Clywd, Wales: New and old music is presented in this quiet town's fifteenth-century cathedral, the smallest in England and Wales, annually for a week in late September. Details: North Wales Music Festival, High St., St. Asaph, Clywd, Wales (phone: 583429).

ST. DAVID'S CATHEDRAL BACH FESTIVAL, St. David's, Dyfed, Wales: Her Majesty the Queen is the patron of this small, new festival held in Wales's largest cathedral, the shrine of the nation's patron saint, St. David, which comes as a surprise, because the surrounding area is rural and isolated. But so will the cathedral's interior, which is far more ornate than the rather plain exterior, and the quality of the music — not only traditional music but also newly commissioned pieces. Details: Yr Oriel Fach Bookshop, St. David's, Dyfed, Wales (phone: 0437-788-480).

SWANSEA FESTIVAL, Swansea, West Glamorgan, Wales: Annually for 3 weeks in October, Wales's most important arts festival is held here, where Dylan Thomas grew up and wrote *Under Milk Wood*. There's ballet, drama, poetry, art, and a week of opera featuring the Welsh National Opera Company. But orchestral music is the main feature, and, in fact, the quantity of it offered is second only to that of the Edinburgh Festival. You'll always find an orchestra from London, another from the Continent, and another from Wales, and the list of past soloists has included the likes of Ashkenazy and Abbado. Details: Swansea Festival, The Guildhall, Swansea, West Glamorgan SA1 4PA, Wales (phone: 0792-50821).

CORK INTERNATIONAL CHORAL AND FOLK DANCE FESTIVAL, Cork, Co. Cork, Irish Republic: This event takes place annually for a week in April or May. Details: Festival Office, 38 McCurtain St., Cork, Co. Cork, Irish Republic (phone: 021-502221).

Antiques and Auctions

Acquiring an antique is always a special pleasure — in Britain and Ireland, where such items are among your best buys, no less than at home. The antique business is livelier in London than almost anywhere else in the world, and good pieces can be found all over the rest of Britain and Ireland as well — in antique shops and at antique fairs, and at flea markets and in auction houses. Prices are finely tuned throughout both countries, and the price you pay for an item does not usually bear any relation to the size of the town you buy it in. Even the owners of small shops in obscure villages are likely to have all the latest market figures. (Occasionally, you'll find that certain locally popular pieces cost less outside the area where most collectors do their buying, but you can't count on it. Irish things sell well in Ireland — but they also move briskly in London; and the same is true just about everywhere else you go.)

Of course, you'll never know a good buy even when it's right under your nose unless you know your merchandise. If you don't, you're wise to stick to the most reputable shops (many of which belong to one or another of Britain and Ireland's several regional and national dealers' associations) — especially for major purchases. Antique shops are abundant and well distributed; and, often, the presence of a lovely small establishment will give you an excuse to stop for a while in a picturesque town that you'd otherwise pass right through. For a comprehensive round-up of operations in England, Scotland, and Wales, consult the annual *Guide to the Antique Shops of Britain* (£5.95, from the Antique Collectors Club, 5 Church St., Woodbridge, Suffolk). Or see the Address Book section of the monthly magazine *The Connoisseur*, which lists specialist shops and dealers. As many dealers keep limited hours, be sure to phone ahead to make sure someone will be there when you arrive.

Auction houses, found all over England and Wales, can also yield rich treasures — and occasionally at very good prices as well. But here, as at flea markets, you've got to know your merchandise. Though you may pay less for any given item than you would in a shop, it's only too easy to end up paying more by allowing yourself to get carried away in the heat of the bidding.

Seasoned auction-goers know better, and set themselves a limit before the bidding begins. They also visit the exhibition of merchandise that takes place a few days or more before the sale. ("If you can't be at the sale, you can leave a commission bid with the auctioneer, or even place an order by telephone — but if you can't be at the exhibition, you have no business buying," noted one aficionado.) Only there will you have the chance to examine the lots at close range, to inspect for nicks, cracks, and other flaws that can affect their value, and for signs that what you're paying for is what you're getting. Caveat emptor is the order of the day.

Reputable houses, of course, make every effort to help their customers avoid mistakes, and publish lists of prices they estimate the lots will fetch — and, often, whole illustrated catalogues full of carefully worded descriptions that can give you a great deal of information about the house's opinion of an item's age and authenticity. "Style of the eighteenth dynasty" in a sale of Egyptian statuary denotes a fake, whereas a simple "eighteenth dynasty" identifies the real McCoy. "Signed" means the house believes that the signature on the painting is the artist's own, while "bears signature" indicates only the possibility. "Dated" means that the lot bears a date and that the date may be accurate. A work of art identified by the artist's full name is believed to be genuine, while the use of only the surname and initials points toward the possibility of a fake, and the use of only the artist's last name suggests that a follower probably did the work.

Whatever you buy and wherever you buy it, note that antiques produced at least 100 years before the date you bring them into the US are not subject to customs duty; be sure to get a proof of antiquity when you hand over your money. If your purchase is so large it has to be shipped back to the US, the dealer may be able to supply names of reputable shippers.

ENGLAND

England's thriving middle class ensured a constant demand, over the centuries, for all manner of lovely china and crystal, knickknacks and furniture, silver, jewelry, and other treasures. Now, with hard times at the doorstep, these treasures — having acquired a patina and the additional distinction that only age can confer — are coming into the marketplace once again, and London, where much of the activity is centered, has become something of a grand souk — full of "collectibles" of undistinguished origins as well as the kind of high-priced items with impeccable pedigrees for which the British antiques trade has always been known. The nation is the world's center for trade in the offbeat — autographs, books and bookplates, ephemera, model soldiers and model steam engines, scientific instruments, and typewriters — in addition to the traditionally collectible such as silver and jewelry, brass and pewter, guns and pistols, glass and furniture, and more. You'll find clocks and watches, of which Britain has produced some of the world's finest examples, particularly from the mid-seventeenth to the mid-eighteenth century. Firemarks, the plaques that used to be tacked up on the outside of a building to announce that it was insured against fire, are another hot item, as are bottles. Well worth planning a visit around, particularly to get an overview of the market, are the nation's antiques fairs. Most important is the *Burlington House Fair*, which combines the long-standing *Burlington Fine Art Fair* and the *Antique Dealers' Fair* held for many years at the *Grosvenor House Hotel;* this new event is planned to fill up the Royal Academy annually in March. But for lovers of finely bound books and old parchment pages, the *Antiquarian Book Fair,* which takes over the *Europa Hotel* in Grosvenor Square every June, is a must. And the well-established *Chelsea Antiques Fair,* which fills the Chelsea Old Town Hall (King's Rd.) every September and March; the *Fine Art & Antique Fair of Great Britain,* a June event; and the new *Antiques Fair* that takes place in October at the *Park Lane Hotel* can also turn up a treasure. Outside London, the important gatherings include the one at Southampton's *Polygon Hotel* in April; the *Lincoln Annual Antiques Fair,* which has antiquers in the town of Lincoln abuzz in mid-July; and Bury St. Edmunds's *East Anglia Annual Antiques Fair* in early September.

For extensive listings of dealers around the country, a representative sampling of which follows, consult the annuals mentioned above, and write for the membership lists of the British Antique Dealers' Association (20 Rutland Gate, London SW7 1BD), and the London and Provincial Antique Dealers' Association (112 Brompton Rd., London SW3 1JJ); enclose a stamped, self-addressed envelope with your request.

BATH, Avon: Among this charming spa town's 5 dozen shops, you'll find one leading British silver dealer — *Mallory* (5 Old Bond St. and 1-4 Bridge St.). There are over 40 dealers (twice that many on Wednesdays) at *Great Western Antique Centre* (Bartlett St.; open daily except Sundays) and at the *Guinea Lane* antique market (Wednesdays). *Phillips & Jollys Auction Rooms* (1 Old King St.) regularly holds specialist sales, which are something of a rarity outside London.

BIRMINGHAM, West Midlands: The *Birmingham Thursday Antique Fayre* (141 Bromsgrove St.) sells arms, militaria, furniture, clocks, and small objects ranging from porcelain to Victoriana every Thursday. Also, *Weller and Dufty Ltd.* (also at 141 Bromsgrove St.) are leading auctioneers of modern and antique arms, armor, and militaria; *World Wide Arms Ltd.* (next door at 140 Bromsgrove St.) is another source for the same sort of merchandise.

BOURNEMOUTH, Dorset: *R. E. Porter* (2–4 Post Office Rd.) is one of the nation's leading specialists in antique spoons; the store also carries antique silver tea sets, coffee pots, salvers, casters, cream jugs, and cutlery, as well as antique jewelry and Baxter prints.

BRIGHTON, East Sussex: This old fishing town, which became a famous resort under the patronage of the Prince Regent, now boasts some 500 antique shops, concentrated in the crannied area known as The Lanes. The *Original Pianola Shop* (102a North Rd.) stocks a truly amazing assortment of reconditioned pianolas, gramophones, and piano rolls. Also visit *David Hawkins* (15b and 15c Prince Albert St., The Lanes) for items of all descriptions and prices; and *B. J. and G. H. Smith* (39–40 Meeting House La.) for silver, silverplate, and various small well-priced items. *Holleyman and Treacher Ltd.* (21a–22 Duke St.) has all kinds of secondhand and antiquarian books, maps, prints, and music; and *Fisher Nautical* (157 Sackville Rd.) offers one of Britain's largest stock of nautical books. There are 18 stallholders selling dolls, furniture, and a good assortment of other items at the *Brighton Antiques Gallery* (41 Meeting House La.); *Meads* of Brighton (St. Nicholas Rd.) sells art and antiques every fourth Thursday; and *Raymond Inman Auction Galleries* (35–40 Temple St.) puts collections on the block once a month, and silver and jewelry every 3 months.

BROADWAY, Worcestershire: The large showrooms of *H. W. Keil* stock a good selection of merchandise from the seventeenth and eighteenth centuries, as well as some of the best walnut in the country.

CAMBRIDGE, Cambridgeshire: *Hammond & Co.* (The Auction Rooms, Cambridge Pl.) has sales of antique and general goods.

CHELTENHAM SPA, Gloucestershire: There are over 5 dozen antique shops in this eighteenth-century spa town. Don't miss *H. W. Keil* (129–131 The Promenade), for mahogany and oak furniture of the seventeenth, eighteenth, and early nineteenth centuries, as well as Persian rugs, brass chandeliers, and cut glass. A branch is located in Broadway, Worcestershire.

CHESTER, Cheshire: The *Chester Antiques Hypermarket* (41 Lower Bridge St.) has nearly 40 dealers selling all kinds of rarities.

DATCHET (near Eton), Berkshire: *Charles and Jane Toller* (20 High St.) rank as Britain's leading dealers in treen — small wooden articles made for domestic and decorative functions; pewter, English delft, brass, and copper items are also available.

EXETER, Devon: *William Bruford* (Bedford St.) is renowned for silver, an expert in spoons.

HENLEY-ON-THAMES, Oxon: The *Antique Galleries* (18 Hart St.) has 6,000 square feet of showrooms full of antiques, Georgian and Victorian furniture, silver, and the like.

LONDON: Auction Houses – One of Europe's great antiques market centers, London is also the focus for Britain's antiques trade. Anything can be bought here, and everything has a market value and instant liquidity — thanks, in part, to the presence in the city of a handful of auction houses so impressive that they're worth a visit even if you don't want to buy. At *Sotheby's* main rooms at 34–5 New Bond St., for instance, Britons parade an assortment of bundles — wrapped in blankets or newspapers and cradled in market baskets — before the house's experts in the hopes of discovering Great-Aunt Charlotte's favorite goblet to be a valuable bit of late-eighteenth-century Bristol glass. Meanwhile, upstairs, prospective buyers equipped with notepads and even magnifying glasses are leaning and bending, poking and peering at items on exhibit, looking very much like characters in a period etching; nearby chandeliers glitter alongside a computer board that translates bids into dollars, yen, marks, lire, and Swiss and French francs, while antiquities, arms and armor, paintings and prints, furniture and rugs, wine, and even antique cars are knocked down at near-lightning pace. *Sotheby's*

DIVERSIONS / Antiques and Auctions

started out as rare books specialists, but the better part of the house's current antiquarian books trade is now handled by the Bloomfield Place salesroom of New Bond Street at regularly scheduled sales; *Sotheby's Belgravia* (19 Motcomb St.) devotes itself to collectibles from the Victorian era to the 1930s — not only paintings and prints but also porcelain, furniture, and silver. *Christie's* (8 King St., St. James's), founded in 1766 when the Grand Tour was in its full flower, has even finer showrooms and offers a feast for lovers of ceramics, silver, jewelry, books, paintings and drawings, coins and antiquities, wine, and a handful of other fashionable collectibles; the smaller *Christie's South Kensington* branch (85 Old Brompton Rd.) specializes in newer collecting fields. Up-and-coming *Phillips,* London's number three firm (7 Blenheim St.), puts on the block the kind of items that its specialists consider good hedges against inflation — Lalique crystal, nineteenth-century color-plate sporting books, English paintings from the late 1800s, and the like; one of several Phillips branches, *Phillips West 2* (10 Salem Rd.), attracts Londoners on the lookout for secondhand furniture, books, and assorted small items. *Bonham* (Montpelier St.), which made headlines in April 1978 by knocking down a pair of Queen Victoria's knickers, is London's only family-owned auction house; you'll find fine art and antiques, generally in the medium price range, plus wine and jewelry; dealers make up a good percentage of the clientele. Cat Stevens's musical equipment and Sir Francis Chichester's yacht, *Gypsy Moth III,* also fell to the hammer here. Visit *Gibbons* (Drury House, Russell St.) and the *City of London Philatelic Auctions* (170 Bishopsgate) for stamps, and *Spink* (5–7 King St.) for coins.

Markets – At any given time, you'll find the best range of wares at good prices in one place at the city's various permanent markets, including the *Chelsea Antique Market* (245A–253 King's Rd.), the oldest in the group; the extensive *Gray's Antique Market* (Davies St.); and the *Knightsbridge Pavilion of Antiques* (112 Brompton Rd.). You'll find knowledgeable and generally helpful stallkeepers and a wide variety of all kinds of antiques. At the relatively new *Antiquarius* (15 Flood St., entrance on King's Rd.), there are some 200 stalls crowded with Victorian clothes, art nouveau items, and other curiosities, and at the attractive antiques center in Camden Passage (Islington), you do your browsing in over fourscore shops and boutiques, and (on Wednesday morning and all day on Saturday) in a lively open-air market. Other open-air markets flourish all over the city, and for ferreting out curios, they can't be beat. On Saturday, *Portobello Road,* near Notting Hill, draws antiques lovers from all over the world trying to buy up bits and pieces of England at a couple of thousand stalls; the activity is simply astonishing. (However, the crowds that make for such a great show here also mean that you can't expect to turn up a treasure at a good price except occasionally in winter, when the weather is so blustery that only the most intrepid antique hounds venture out-of-doors.) The *Bermondsey-New Caledonia Market* complex, where several hundred dealers hold forth every Friday in a good-sized open space at the end of Long Lane and in an erstwhile factory nearby, is known for being something of a dealers' market. Fresh shipments from the country go on sale here first and, in fact, many of the goods you'll see in Portobello Road were probably purchased here. However, if you arrive after 9 AM, the best will be long gone; regulars try to arrive not much later than 5 AM. The selection ranges from china and breadboards to silver candlesticks and Victorian glass — a little bit of everything under the sun.

Shops and Specialists – If you don't like auction action, and weary at the thought of the madding market mobs, you needn't give up on experiencing the London antiques scene. Shops along Bond St., Mount St., and Kensington Church St. can provide all sorts of delights — a red lacquer Queen Anne bureau, an ornate ebony-veneered clock, a lovely pair of George II candlesticks, for instance. Some dealers stock a variety of kinds of goods, but just as many more have evolved specialties. In their so-called specialty shops, bargains are almost nonexistent because the dealer always knows his wares. But if you're a collector yourself, or you aspire to be, or you're willing to pay the going rate in return for the assurance that comes from buying from a connoisseur,

DIVERSIONS / Antiques and Auctions

these stores can prove your happiest hunting ground. That's true even if your funds are limited, because — though some stock only the crème de la crème of the genre — many try to display items to appeal to all budgets. For antiquities, *Charles Ede Ltd.* (37 Brook St.) has the best range of Greek, Roman, and Egyptian work in a variety of price ranges.

Stores selling books abound. In addition to the handful in Cecil Ct., there's *Dawson's* (16 Pall Mall), which boasts good selections in the fields of economics, English literature, medicine, music, science, theater, and travel; five-floored *Francis Edwards* (83 Marylebone High St.), the oldest purpose-built bookshop in the world, whose specialties include manuscripts, autographs, and books on travel, naval and military works, and histories of technology and transport; the famous firm of *Maggs Brothers* (50 Berkeley Sq.), founded in 1853, run by the same family ever since, and now occupying a stately old Georgian building; and *Bernard Quaritch* (5–8 Lower John St., Golden Sq.), old and established, stocking books of the sixteenth century and earlier, plus manuscripts, and works on literature, medicine, natural history, and science. Other antiquarian booksellers are even more specialized. *Heraldry Today* (10 Beauchamp Pl.) concentrates on heraldry and genealogy; *Travis & Emery* (17 Cecil Ct., near Charing Cross Rd.), in music, including scores; *Wildy & Sons* (Lincoln's Inn Archway, Carey St.), in old documents of law and criminology; the *Meridian Bookshop* (2 Nelson Rd., Greenwich), in ships and the sea.

You'll find a number of shops purveying antique ceramic ware in York St. and its continuation, Harcourt St., and Kensington Church St. In addition, don't miss *Jellinek & Sampson* (156 Brompton Rd.), which stands out for its stock of early English pottery (plus needlework, early oak, naive paintings, and the like); and *Earle D. Vandekar of Knightsbridge* (138 Brompton Rd.). His selection of pre-1830 ceramics ranks among Europe's largest, and you'll also find Chinese export porcelain, English and continental porcelain, pottery, early glass, chandeliers, candelabras, and always, some furniture as well. *Richard Dennis* (144 Kensington Church St.) deals only in English studio pottery between 1870 and 1950, particularly *Doulton, Wedgwood, Martin* and *Moorcroft. Haslam and Whiteway* (105 Kensington Church St.) has a bit more of the same; *Oliver-Sutton* (34c Kensington Church St.), a Staffordshire figurines specialist, is home to the world's largest collection. Anthony Oliver has authored two books which are considered the standard reference works on the subject, and, with his partner, Peter Sutton, advises several major museums on Staffordshire pottery. *John Creed* (5A Camden Passage) has blue-and-white Staffordshire.

Specialists in clocks and watches often also stock barometers — an oh-so-English item to take home with you, given Britain's concern for the weather. You can buy eighteenth- and early-nineteenth-century English long-case and bracket clocks at *Aubrey Brocklehurst* (124 Cromwell Rd.) and *E. Hollander* (80 Fulham Rd.); the latter also has good stocks of eighteenth- and early-nineteenth-century barometers. *Camerer Cuss* (54–6 New Oxford St.) also offers French carriage clocks and antique watches. For other French clocks, see *Philip and Bernard Dombey* (174 Kensington Church St.). You'll find the best in scientific instruments at *Harriet Wynter* (50 Redcliffe Rd.; it's not a shop, so phone ahead to 352-6494 to make sure she's in). *E. Dent* (Glider House, Claremont Rd.) made Big Ben; the shop also sells reproductions of eighteenth- and nineteenth-century clocks.

In a country with a history as long as Britain's, coins and medals are especially fascinating. They're the focus at *Spink* (5–7 King St.), as they have been since 1666 when the establishment was founded, and at *A. H. Baldwin* (11 Adelphi Ter.), founded in 1872.

For dolls and toys, visit *Kaye Desmond* (17 Kensington Church Walk), an amazing place. Also stop at *Pat Walker* (139 King's Rd. in the *Antiquarius Market*), where antique dollhouse furniture is also available.

For ephemera — that is, printed items such as advertisements, signs, and posters — *Dodo* (185 Westbourne Grove) is a must; Victorian and Edwardian lingerie and assorted jackets and dresses from the twenties and thirties round out the stock.

If you like firearms and weaponry, don't miss *Peter Dale* (11–12 Royal Opera Arcade, Pall Mall), a specialist in antique guns, edged weapons, and armor dating from the sixteenth century to the nineteenth.

The production of glass boomed in Britain beginning with the lead crystal work of George Ravenscroft, and it is currently very popular among British collectors. Leading shops include *Denton Antiques* (87 Marylebone High St.), good for Victorian decanters, glasses, and cut glass; and the important *Howard Phillips* (11a Henrietta Pl.), which offers an outstanding, worldwide selection of glass from pre-Roman days through the 1830s.

The jewelry market, particularly Victorian pieces, is also booming in Britain. Aside from the street markets, which abound in stalls selling only jewelry, you'll find the most desirable pieces at *Collingwood* (46 Conduit St.), jewelers to the Queen, and the old, established *Hennell* (1 Davies St., Berkeley Sq.). The latter, founded in 1736, is the oldest firm of silversmiths in London, and has been selling jewelry as well since 1833. See *Richard Ogden* (28–29 Burlington Arcade) for antique rings and other jewelry; and *Wartski* (14 Grafton St.), London's most important dealer in Fabergé items. Antique jewelry, silver, and snuff boxes are also available. *Graus Antiques* (125 New Bond St.) offers watches, objets d'art, vertu, and jewelry.

For music boxes, *Keith Harding* (93 Hornsey Rd.) is tops, since the 17 specialist craftsmen whose work has made the place famous as a center for restoration also overhaul every item before it goes up for sale. Horological books and books on music boxes and automatons are also available. For all kinds of antique musical instruments and music, visit *Tony Bingham* (11 Pond St.). *John & Arthur Beare* (7 Broadwick St.) restore, sell, and generally look after the best violins and other instruments in the family, including those belonging to leading musicians passing through town.

Antique pewter is the specialty at *Richard Mundey* (19 Chiltern St.; phone 935-5613 for appointment). For silver, the big Chancery Lane *Silver Vaults* at nos. 53–64 are well known for the crush of glittering items on sale; equally good hunting is to be found, however, at the *Bond Street Silver Galleries* (111–112 New Bond St.). Big, important dealers — where you'll occasionally find that wonderful high-quality, reasonably-priced small item — include *S. J. Phillips* (139 New Bond St.), home of London's most extensive stock of English and Continental silver of the nineteenth century or before; *How* (2–3 Pickering Pl., phone 930-7140 for an appointment), the city's leading specialist in early silver from Scotland and Ireland, with early English silver on hand as well; and *Thomas Lumley* (on the third floor at Standbrook House, 2 Old Bond St., phone 629-2493), who offers very special pieces from England and the Continent, some of them quite unusual and some in the Victorian and art nouveau styles. Also good: *J. H. Bourdon-Smith* (24 Mason's Yard, Duke St., St. James's) for pieces dating from 1680, and *M. J. Christie* (26 Burlington Arcade) for eighteenth-century and animalier bronzes.

Stamp collectors make pilgrimages to world-famous *Stanley Gibbons* at 399 Strand; an auction company is located at Drury House, Russell St. Also don't miss *A. Constantine* (124 Grand Blds. in Trafalgar Sq.), *W. E. Lea* (1 The Adelphi, John Adam St., Strand), and *H. A. Wallace* (94 Old Broad St.).

MANCHESTER: The 3-decade-old firm *The Connoisseur* (528 Wilmslow Rd., Withington) has paintings and eighteenth- and nineteenth-century English and French furniture, plus Sèvres and Meissen porcelain. For silver and silverplate, visit *Koopman & Son* (4 John Dalton St.). *James Cook Antiques, Ltd.* (213–215 Slade La., Burnage) has church furnishings such as pews and other architectural fittings. For foraging, the *Butter Lane Antiques Centre* (40A King St. W) is good.

PENZANCE, Cornwall: *Taylor Lane & Creber* (67 Morrab Rd.) has 2-day sales of art and antiques every other month or so, plus a number of annual sales of antiquarian books, pictures, and coins and medals; occasionally, there are also treasure trove sales in which pieces of eight and other finds from old wrecks are put on the block.

READING, Berkshire: *Bracher & Sydenham* (24 Queen Victoria St.) ranks with Britain's top silver dealers.

TETBURY, Gloucestershire: *Michael G. Cox* (16 Market Pl.) displays a fine collection of clocks and barometers, and also one or two pieces of seventeenth- and early-eighteenth-century walnut furniture.

WORTHING, West Sussex: *Geoffrey Godden,* who has authored many books about pottery and porcelain, has special exhibitions of exceptional specimens of the kind of ceramic items that he also sells in his showrooms at 17–19 Crescent Rd.; he also runs popular study-meetings on English pottery and porcelain. Call before you pay a visit (phone: 093-3598).

YORK, North Yorkshire: *W. F. Greenwood & Sons* (37 Stonegate) has a good selection of furniture dating back to 1660, plus ceramics dating from 1740 and jewelry from 1720. *Henry Hardcastle Ltd.* (51 Stonegate) is good for period English silver and silverplate.

SCOTLAND

Because of Scotland's relative remoteness from the antique trade's London hotbed, the books and coins, firearms and weaponry, glass and jewelry, paintings and pewter, pottery, silver, and other items that skillful native artisans once turned out apace have not yet been emptied out of the old Scottish great houses. As a result, antiquing in Scotland can be very good. Edinburgh is Britain's second city when it comes to the antiquarian book trade. Scottish-made duelling pistols, though primarily traded in England now, are particularly beautiful, crafted as they were from combinations of steel and brass with stocks often gracefully contoured like hearts or fish tails and embellished with Celtic designs. And Scottish silver, from both the eighteenth and the nineteenth centuries, is justly famous. An overview of the Scottish market can be had at the *Edinburgh Annual Antiques Fair,* which takes place at the *Roxburghe Hotel* every August. If you miss it, just browse through the shops — extensive listings of which can be found in the *Guide to the Antique Shops of Britain* (above); many of the most reputable Scottish dealers belong to BADA or LAPADA (above). Some of the better include the following:

ABERDEEN, Grampian: *William Young* (1 Belmont St.) and *John Bell* (56 Bridge St.) offer good selections of china, silver, furniture, and the like; both are members of BADA.

AYR, Strathclyde: One of Scotland's several noteworthy outdoor markets takes place in this Ayrshire town on Tuesdays from 10 AM to 4 PM. You could combine your visit here with a stop at *Afflecks' Auction Rooms* (Nile Court, off High St.), where sales begin at 10 AM.

EDINBURGH: Thistle and Dundas streets, West Bow, Randolph Place, St. Stephen's Street, and Grassmarket are full of antique shops purveying everything from furniture and Sheffield plate to Scottish paintings and leather-bound books. Both *Christie's* and *Sotheby's* have offices in town — the former at 5 Wemyss Pl., the latter at 112 George St. *Lyon & Turnbull* (51 George St.) is the local auctioneer. *Phillips* holds weekly sales at 65 George St. At the *Greyfriars Market* (Forrest Rd.), you can buy everything from posters to secondhand clothes. On Sundays, the day's major market takes place from 10 AM to 4 PM, on the city's outskirts at Ingliston. *Mrs. Iris Fox* (West Bow) specializes in Wemyss ware, brightly colored pottery turned out in the town of Kircaldy in the late nineteenth and early twentieth centuries; prices are generally high because this is an exceptionally popular local collectible. *James Thin* (opposite the Old Quad of the university at 53–9 South Bridge) is also good for antique volumes as well as for new and secondhand academic and general books. Other booksellers are scattered all over the New Town.

GLASGOW: Glasgow's answer to London's *Petticoat Lane* is *The Barrows* (at 244 Gallowgate), which holds forth on Saturdays and Sundays from 8 AM to 5 PM. Pronounced "th' Barras," it's a good bet for bargains — as many thousands of antique lovers discover every year. *John Smith & Son* (57–61 Vincent St.) is good for secondhand and antiquarian books; the fourth floor is particularly Scottish. BADA member *Muirhead, Moffat & Co.* (182 W Regent St.) stocks silver, china, and fine-quality period furniture; *Thornton Taylor Antiques* (2 Fernleigh Rd.) stocks porcelain, jewelry, glass, silver, and the like. *Golightly Antiques* (36 Gibson St., by Glasgow University) stocks Edwardian and Victorian furniture, china, silver, and the like. *Christie's* Glasgow saleroom is located at 164–166 Bath St., and *Phillips in Scotland* holds sales at 98 Sauchiehall St.

WALES

Wales was never a wealthy country to begin with, and it didn't have an extensive landed gentry to promote the creation of the kind of fine old objects that later generations have come to covet as antiques. Couple that situation with the industriousness of London dealers, who have been nosing around Wales for years, and you've got fairly slim pickings. Even indigenous early-nineteenth-century porcelains like Swansea, sturdy and greenish, and Nantgarw, translucent and fragile-looking, and the carved wooden "love spoons" once used to announce an engagement can be hard to find. But the market is a bit more flush than it used to be, and the kind of relatively simple oak furniture that Welshmen counted among their specialties is fairly abundant — you'll see when you take a turn through the stalls at the *Welsh Annual Antiques Fair*, which takes place at the Hotel Metropol in Llandrindod every July, or browse through any of a number of good shops scattered around the country. Here, too, the two British antiques annuals and the directories of BADA and LAPADA can steer you to interesting establishments — a number of which follow.

CARDIFF: *Peter Philp* (77 Kimberly Rd.) is good for Welsh oak, English and Continental furniture and pottery.

HAY-ON-WYE, Powys: This pretty town, full of brick and stucco houses and narrow hilly streets, has become famous as the home of *Richard Booth*, who likes to boast that he is the world's largest secondhand and antiquarian bookseller; as a result, he claims, Hay-on-Wye has "more books for sale per head of population than any other town in the world." Whether or not that's true, the business — which now occupies a former cinema, fire station, and pub, not to mention a couple of houses — is something to see; and whether or not you manage to ferret out a bargain, you're sure to find something of interest.

NEWPORT, Gwent: The world's leading specialist in Welsh-made Nantgarw and Swansea porcelain is *D. S. Hutchings* (210 Chepstow Rd.).

IRISH REPUBLIC

When your thoughts turn to Ireland and antiques, you probably think of Irish silver, which was produced in quantity in Dublin during the eighteenth century, when the capital's output rivaled that of any other in Europe, as well as in provincial towns such as Cork and Limerick (whose products have today become rare and highly collectible).

But Waterford glass, made for only 50 years beginning about 1780 before the factory closed for just over a century, is also popular. Paintings are also important, although it was not until recently that an Irish school of painting was recognized; pieces from the nineteenth century are most common. Irish coins and firearms hold a great deal of interest for some, while other collectors covet Irish pewter, generally made around Cork. Irish furniture is another matter altogether: The fine craftsmanship of country-house woodworking ought to give you an idea of the standards of the past centuries, but there is not much documentation of the field and beyond the superabundance of carvings of masks, acanthus, scrollwork, paws, shells, and the like, there is little to differentiate it from the English. The simple pine settles, chairs, and tables of Irish cottage days, which were once trashed or burned when the owner's finances improved, are increasingly sought-after. And in all fields, work of the eighteenth century attracts more attention than it did some years back; and it's now so pricey that you may want to look at other eras (though in general, Irish collectors have shied away from the kind of trendy collectibles that have taken the English market by storm in the last few years).

Irish antique shops are widely scattered all over the country. Most offer a general selection, though a few specialists do exist. The Irish Antique Dealers' Association is the local trade group; for a list of members, write the Secretary, 27 S Anne St., Dublin 2. If the dealer you contact doesn't have what you want, chances are he'll tell you where to go to get it. For times and venues of auctions, consult the Saturday edition of the *Irish Times*. The *Irish Antiques Fair* — Ireland's main event of its type, sponsored by the Irish Antique Dealers' Association at the Mansion House during the first full week of August (to coincide with the Dublin Horse Show) — manages to derive even a bit more gloss from its timing at the height of Dublin's biggest social season. But the events held in Cork during the month of April, and in Limerick during the month of November, both attract major dealers and classy wares. For dates and details, contact Louis O'Sullivan, 31 Killiney Rd., Killiney, Co. Dublin.

Here are some good bets for year-round shopping.

COUNTY CLARE: *Davoc Rynne* runs what must be the most westerly antique shop in Ireland. Right beside the Atlantic at Spanish Point, it has a broad offering that includes a preponderance of country items. In Ennis, *Tony Honan* runs a fascinating shop where the china and bric-a-brac is heaped and piled all over the place; there's an enormous stock of small things, and many clocks. Close to Bunratty Castle, *Mike McGlynn* has stocked a traditional Irish cottage with plenty of good-quality eighteenth- and nineteenth-century furniture, some paintings, and a smattering of oriental pieces.

COUNTY CORK: Cork City has only a few shops but they are interesting and varied. The large and rambling *C. O'Connell Ltd.* (5 Lavitts Quay), now famous for the reproduction Cork chairs that cabinetmakers manufacture on the premises, always has a good selection of furniture that is — thanks to the efforts of the firm's craftsmen — always in excellent condition. *Regency Antiques* (8 Winthrop St.) makes a specialty of Georgian and Victorian English and Irish silver, antique jewelry, and other pieces, and *Presents Ltd.* (Oliver Plunkett St.), which looks as if it stocks only reproductions, will turn up a section full of really interesting antique pieces on closer inspection; the shop has been run by the same family for four generations. Not far away on Lower Oliver Plunkett St., *Victoria* is not to be missed if you're out for the unusual, especially dolls and vintage clothing, and *Gerry O'Hanlon* deals primarily in bric-a-brac. *Marlboro Antiques* (Marlboro St.) has antique jewelry and gold and silver watches. Also check the papers for announcements of auctions held regularly in the *Joseph Woodward & Sons* salerooms (Cook St). Outside Cork, *Mary Lombard* sells a fine range of furniture in a disused church, The Manse, in Fermoy, a little town full of ruins that is primarily known for its fine salmon fishing; and, in Buttevant, Mrs. O'Driscoll has filled the sheds at her *St. Josephs Store* full of furniture in all conditions. Near Mallow,

DIVERSIONS / Antiques and Auctions

a once-fashionable spa town in the pretty Blackwater River valley, *Carrigacunna Castle Antiques,* which occupies the castle of that name in Killavullen — on really wonderful grounds — stocks a fine range of paintings and furniture.

COUNTY DONEGAL: In Donegal Town, *Sean Thomas* has packed a shop in the Diamond — an architectural curiosity in its own right — with really fine jewelry and other pieces of Irish interest. Old Belleek is a specialty.

COUNTY DUBLIN: The capital is the true center for the Irish antiques trade, and if you were pressed to name a single location here, the new restoration of the Earl of Powerscourt's house on South William Street and Clarendon Streets would be the standout. Imaginatively developed into a shopping center, with its courtyard roofed in glass, it is now home to some of the city's best dealers, including *Malcolm Alexander, David Allen, Courtville Antiques,* the *Emerald Butterfly, Ian Haslam, Inigo Jones, Gerald Kenyon, Lucius Antiques, Melvin Samuels,* and *Scott Antiques.* The quays along the Liffey, an antique-hunting ground where you could once turn up treasures for shillings, are a sad sight nowadays, with their semiderelict buildings. But a few dealers still do trade there, and even though much of what you'll turn up is "junque" or reproductions, a good browse still makes for a pleasant Saturday morning, thanks to the fine evocative panoramas of those reddish facades with their fading lettering, and the odd assortment of dusty prints and used furniture that turn up in the area's secondhand shops. In central Dublin, shops are close enough together that it's easy and fun to walk from one to the next. One of the longest established dealers in the country, in business since the early 1800s, is *Edward Butler* (14 Bachelors Walk); the family, formerly cabinetmakers whose marked furniture is much sought-after by collectors, stocks the same fine quality pieces in much the same atmosphere that it did generations ago. Farther down the street on Ormond Quay, *Lawlor Briscoe* operates a large well-put-together shop stocked with fine furniture in superb condition, and *Ormond Antiques* next door specializes in smaller items in brass and porcelain, including some Belleek, plus decorative furniture. Uninteresting-looking *Balfe's,* farther down the quay, will surprise you with its nice stocks of unusual items. *Kevin O'Kelly* — across the river via the pedestrians-only Liffey Bridge and down Wellington Quay — specializes in coins of Irish interest and silver. Nearby, under Merchants Arch, you'll find *Patrick Oman,* who will pack and ship any purchase you make to any part of the world. *Lionel Mitchell,* not far from Grafton Street at 40 Clarendon St., has made a specialty of mantelpieces from Irish houses, but also stocks brassware and furniture; *Antiqcurios,* a few doors away, is tiny but packed with interesting and unusual pieces — always something different. The elegant *Saskia Antiques,* at number 43 S. William St., always has a good selection of oak and English pieces, while the *Neptune Gallery,* next door (at number 42), has a fine range of Irish prints and paintings. *Hibernian Antiques,* back off Grafton St., at 27 S Anne St., recently moved to this location and is stuffed with things of Irish interest and good English furniture. Nearby at number 24, *Phyllis Jackson* crams her small *Rembrandt Antiques* and its basement and shelves with pretty items from all periods; if you collect porcelain, you're in for a real treat here, as she's one of Ireland's experts. Across the street at number 10, *Hyman Danker* deals in fine silver and jewelry; this is a real family business, and if you don't see what you're looking for, be sure and ask, since the Danker brothers and their daughters, who run the place, can be extremely helpful. *J. W. Weldon,* a tiny shop full of silver, antique jewelry, and related pieces, at 18 Anne St., is nearby. Into Duke St., look for *Irene Antiques,* a specialist in silver and jewelry, on the ground floor at number 17; there's no shop window, so look for the sign on the door. The *Grace Pym Gallery,* farther down the street on the first floor at number 15, specializes in Irish paintings. *Anthony Antiques,* run by the Dell family at 7 Molesworth St. (off Dawson St.) is actually two shops joined together; the specialty is opulent furniture. Farther down the street at number 20, *James Gorry,* a specialist in pictures and restoration, holds regular exhibitions of Irish paintings that are such an event that people queue up to get in and buy up the majority of the pictures within the first quarter of an hour. On Kildare St., the *Cynthia O'Connor Gallery* at number 35a always carries a stock of very interesting Irish paintings and often holds special exhibitions; Norah Breen's *Kildare Antiques,* at number 19, offers very fine Regency furniture, quality Irish paintings, and some silver, and, at number 16, *Ronald McDonnell,* one of Dublin's great dealers, stocks furniture and paintings, glass and silver, and assorted curios that are almost as wonderful as the very beautiful old house he sells them from. In Lower Pembroke St., Marianne Newman runs her *Pembroke Antiques,* a charming shop full of pretty things at number 1, and, next door at number 1a, *T. J. Mitchell* sells and restores antique furniture.

A handful of other shops are scattered around the city. Increasing numbers of dealers are setting up business along Francis St., in the Liberties, near St. Patrick's Cathedral and the Guinness brewery. *Paul Cooke,* who in fact lives above his shop at number 59, runs an extensive business, selling from his rapidly changing stock, and doing custom upholstery as a sideline. Nearby at number 78, *Bits and Pieces,* whose proprietors also will re-leather desktops, is also good for unusual, out-of-the-ordinary items. The *City Brass Company,* located at the bottom of the street, restores as well as sells. Also in the area is Clanbrassil St., well worth a wander for the assortment of shops you'll find there dealing in a motley lot of secondhand wares that are often displayed out on the sidewalk, and Mill St., where the delightful *Orken Brothers* have installed an incredible range of merchandise in a large old warehouse. At 14 Harcourt Rd., *Denis Cusack* runs a small, idiosyncratic shop where you'll often find the oddity of interest, and not far away at 6 Claremount St., his brother *P.J. Cusack* stocks furniture of quality, including many Continental pieces. *Sean McGahan,* at 57 Prussia St., stocks furniture in varying states of repair.

You can also find antiques in Dublin at auction. *James Adam & Sons* (on St. Stephen's Green beside the *Shelburne Hotel*), Ireland's major regular auction room, has good general sales as well as an occasional specialist gathering; and *Allen and Townsend* holds monthly sales at the Mansion House. *Keane Mahony Smith* auctions Irish paintings and other fine art every six weeks in their salesrooms at 35 Molesworth St., and stages occasional special sales as well. On the quays, *Tormey Bros.* (26–27 Lower Ormond Quay) has regular sales of mainly household items where you'll also turn up a fine piece every so often.

In Dun Laoghaire, very close to the terminal for the ferry to Holyhead, on Salthill Pl., *Roxane Moorhead* operates a small establishment that offers many small decorative pieces of furniture, nice china, and an assortment of other items; *Elizabeth Antiques,* the shop at 11 Patrick St., sells an even larger variety of goods. And in Stillorgan (Woodlands Ave., in Beaufield Mews) *Jill Cox* runs a restaurant-cum-antique shop, open nightly, that is very good on both counts.

COUNTY GALWAY: In Galway City, *Cobwebs,* down near the Spanish Arch, is small but fascinating, full of the unusual and the beautiful — facsimiles now, as well as antiques. For prints and books, visit *Kennys* on High St., one of the nation's most important dealers in the field, and so eminently browsable that you can spend literally hours poking through the extensive stock. Contemporary Irish paintings are also sold here.

COUNTY KERRY: *Henry Dodd* stocks various small items of quality, including many relating to nineteenth-century Kerry, in his two shops here — one on Plunkett St., Killarney; the other in the Square in Killorglin (a town otherwise mainly famous for its big Puck Fair).

COUNTY KILDARE: In Prosperous — on weekends only — *Hugh Cash* and his son Hughie do a big business on a large assorted stock at their business behind their home — primarily, but not entirely, to dealers.

COUNTY KILKENNY: *Clive Nunn,* at the Mill Ballyduff in Thomastown, is your

DIVERSIONS / Antiques and Auctions 509

man if you've taken a fancy to the pine furniture of the type found in Irish cottages.

COUNTY LIMERICK: Limerick City, on the banks of the Shannon, has *Abbey Antiques* at Lock Quay with its fine range of good-quality furniture and clocks of all descriptions (a specialty); *Castle Antiques* (Castle St., opposite the Castle) stocks a nice range of period furniture, antique clocks and watches, gold and silver coins, medals, jewelry, paintings, antique bottles, glass, oil lamps, scales, and old instruments. For china and jewelry, visit *Once Upon a Time* (Ellen St.) and *Grange Antiques* (on O'Connell St. below the *Royal George Hotel*). The shop run by George Stacpoole (35 Cecil St. here; he runs another shop in the town of Adare) looks small, but in actuality is positively crammed with furniture, paintings, prints, silver, china, and unusual decorative items. Across the road from Stacpoole's Adare shop, there's *Simon Quilligan*, a widely known character who — when he's there on Saturdays — hauls piles and piles of merchandise out into the street, without seeming appreciably to reduce the clutter that fills the house to the ceilings; in the words of another local dealer, Quilligan "could probably buy and sell every one of us," and since the talk is as good as the merchandise, a visit here can be a real experience. Close by Adare, in Rathkeale, there are yet other traders, who deal mainly in Victoriana, from their warehouses behind the main street, and hold forth primarily on weekends; be prepared to haggle over prices.

COUNTY LOUTH: In Drogheda, a flourishing industrial center, *Greene's Antique Galleries* (The Mall) stocks superb silver, fine Irish pictures, and good-quality furniture, while *Salt House Antiques* (Wellington Quay) has fine furniture plus old prints, maps, old books, and bric-a-brac.

COUNTY MAYO: In Westport, the *Earl of Altamont* sells from a fine varied stock installed in the basement of his Westport House.

COUNTY OFFALY: The Hoctor family sells fine-quality eighteenth- and nineteenth-century furniture, silver, porcelain, pictures, and glass from *Ivy Hall* here.

COUNTY TIPPERARY: In Tipperary Town, there's *The Antiquarian* (Church St.), a large shop that stocks good-quality furniture and clocks; *Courtville Antiques* (St. Michaels St.), good for fine jewelry, silver, and small pieces of furniture; *Laurence O'Toole*, who has filled an old barn almost next door with brass, china, silver, and, amongst it all, feathers. Just outside Roscrea, *Victor Mitchell* has barns full of furniture, with a good selection of pine pieces, which he sells at retail and at monthly auctions.

NORTHERN IRELAND

The antiques scene here is much the same as in the Republic: the wares are similar and the shops are equally evenly distributed; many of the dealers here also belong to the Irish Antique Dealers Association, and look to Dublin's big *Irish Antiques Fair* with anticipation. Among fairs of more regional interest, there's the *Culloden Fair* (held annually at the *Culloden Hotel*, Bangor Rd., Craigavad, Holywood, Co. Down), and the *Ballygally Antique Fair* (Ballygally, Co. Down); for dates, contact the local tourist offices.

Meanwhile, here are some good bets for a browse.

COUNTY ANTRIM: There are a number of shops in Belfast. *Fortwilliam Lodge Antiques* in Fortwilliam Park, named for the rustic quarters it occupies, is good for Victoriana, silver, and jewelry. *John and Charlotte Lamb* (on Shore Rd.; by appointment) sell superb eighteenth- and nineteenth-century furniture, pictures, and silver — much of it from the Continent and most of great quality. *Sinclair's Antique Gallery* (26 Arthur St.) specializes in fine jewelry and silver, while the *Tom Caldwell Gallery* (at 40/42 Bradbury Pl.) is not to be missed if you're interested in Irish paintings; glass, ceramics, oriental carpets, and kilims can also be found. Outside Belfast, the *Antique Shop* on Antrim Rd., in Templepatrick, stocks small country items; *Ballinderry An-*

tiques (Ballinderry Upper, Lisburn) sells jewelry, silver, silverplate, and some furniture; *Glynn Park Antiques* (Glynn Park, Carrickfergus) stocks English and Continental furniture, silver, and objets d'art — many of them quite large. In Newtownabbey, Anne MacHenry stocks lovely items in excellent condition — eighteenth- and nineteenth-century furniture as well as silver and high-quality bric-a-brac — at her shop *New Abbey Antiques* (Glen Rd., Jordanstown); and in Ballymena, *Scott McKeown Antiques* (75 Shankbridge Rd.) stocks furniture, silver, and pine. *Brian R. Bolt* at Ballaghmore Rd., Portballintrae, a district of the town of Bushmills, specializes in small items such as treen and silver (by appointment only; phone: 02657-31129).

COUNTY ARMAGH: In Armagh, *Hole in the Wall* (Market St.) won't disappoint you with its wide-ranging stock of antiques, and in Loughall, *Hueys Antiques* (Main St.) carries antique furniture, porcelain, and silver.

COUNTY DERRY: *Forge Antiques* occupies a handsome old forge on the main road midway between Coleraine and Portstewart; there's a branch at 24 Long Common in Coleraine.

COUNTY DOWN: In Banbridge, *Jeremy Cahill* (Church St.) sells furniture, though mainly to the trade, while *Cameo Antiques* (Bridge St.) has interesting Victorian jewelry, silver, and porcelain. *Richmond Antiques* at 10 Bridge St., Banbridge, has Victorian and modern jewelry, porcelain, reproduction furniture, paintings, and bric-a-brac.

COUNTY FERMANAGH: *Mahon Antiques* (Lisnarick Rd.) in Irvinestown has furniture and bric-a-brac.

Ancient Monuments and Ruins

Britain and Ireland have been inhabited for thousands of years, and scarcely a single one of the population groups who have settled here has disappeared without leaving a trace. The countryside is littered with their remains: stone walls, tombs and burial chambers, barrows and henges, hilltop forts, castles, abbeys, crosses, churches, and towers. Ruined and crumbling, they stand as reminders to a turbulent and fascinating past.

Prehistoric monuments are fairly evenly distributed throughout the area, although the Irish Republic has the richest group of early Christian monuments, round towers, and high crosses. Romanesque and Gothic cathedrals are particularly well represented in England, and to a certain extent in Scotland and Wales.

Fairly comprehensive books on these historic places include *Early Ireland: A Field Guide* by Anthony Weir (£7.95; Blackstaff Press Ltd., 144 University St., Belfast BT7 1HH, Northern Ireland); the *Guide to the National Monuments in the Republic of Ireland* by Peter Harbison (£5.40; Gill and Macmillan Ltd., Goldenbridge, Inchicore, Dublin 8, Irish Republic); and *The Past All Around Us: An Illustrated Guide to the Ruins, Relics, Monuments, Castles, Cathedrals, Historic Buildings and Industrial Landmarks of Britain* (£10.95; Reader's Digest Association Ltd., 25 Berkeley Sq., London W1X 6AB, England).

AVEBURY STONE CIRCLE, Avebury, Wiltshire, England: Eighteen miles from Stonehenge, the map explodes with prehistory. Not only will you find here Silbury Hill (Europe's most massive artificial earth mound), but also an abundance of long barrows, standing stones, and stone circles — among them, just off the A4 between Marlborough and Calne, the Avebury stone circle. One of the largest in the world, and certainly the greatest among Britain's some 900 megalithic rings, it encloses approximately 28 acres, at the center of which are traces of two smaller stone circles; the whole is ringed by an earthen bank that stands 20 feet high in spots, and, abutting it, a ditch up to 30 feet deep. About 200,000 tons of earth were moved to create the ditch and bank; some of the heaviest of the 25 stones that remain from the group of 100 that once completed the ring weigh over 40 tons and would have required about 200 people to raise. It has been estimated that if 750 people worked here for 10 hours a day for 2 months of every year (after the harvest was in), then the enclosure would have taken about 4 years to complete. And this was during the second millennium BC, a time when the population of the surrounding region, according to some estimates, numbered only about 1,500. Why such a whole society of small farmers was prepared to take time off to create such a place in an age when merely subsisting was a struggle is not known; nor is the nature of the ceremonies that took place there, or the type of beliefs that governed them, or even, for that matter, the ring's exact function, though speculation suggests that it was probably used as a meeting place or a temple, or to fulfill some astronomical function. As is the case with most stone circles, there is no evidence of human sacrifice. Yet Christians who sought to eliminate all records of their pagan past attempted in the fourteenth century to break up and bury many of the stones (and at least one of their number, a man whose trade as a barber was identified by a pair of scissors found alongside him, was crushed to death in the effort, when a pillar toppled over on him). More early efforts at destroying the great stone circle never entirely succeeded, and, though it probably ceased to serve its original purpose in the first millennium BC, the tradition of its importance persisted, and it continued in use as late as the nineteenth century, when maypoles were erected within the circle and children frolicked there, as their ancestors, waiting for the midsummer sun to appear, might possibly have done. The stones here are smaller than those at Stonehenge and in a natural state rather than hewn; Avebury exceeds the more widely known circle, in the words of one seventeenth-century observer, "as a cathedral doeth a parish church." For information about the region, contact the West Country Tourist Board, Trinity Ct., 37 Southernhay E, Exeter, Devon EX1 1QS, England (phone: 0392-76351).

GLASTONBURY ABBEY, Glastonbury, Somerset, England: Romance and tradition cling to this historic site like ivy to the walls of a Harvard dormitory; and no matter where you look in British history, particularly British ecclesiastical history, Glastonbury will turn up. The site itself was probably sacred in pre-Christian days; later, progressively larger churches were built as the abbey became increasingly wealthier. At one point, one of Britain's more irreverent observers noted that the first son born of a marriage between the abbot of Glastonbury and the abbess of Shaftesbury would own more land than the king. Under Dunstan, who introduced the Benedictine rule after he was chosen as abbot in the year 940, the abbey became a center of learning, producing many great ecclesiastics; and for many years, England's premier abbot was Glastonbury's. Its greatness endured for centuries afterward, and its importance diminished only with the Dissolution of the Monasteries in 1539 under Henry VIII, when Thomas Cromwell (later executed at the Tower of London) ordered the elderly abbot Richard Whiting, the sixtieth abbot of Glastonbury, hanged on the Tor. In the words of the eighteenth-century writer William Stukely: "For every week a pillar or buttress, a window jamb or an angle of fine hewn stone is sold to the best bidder . . . they were excoriating St. Joseph's Chapel for that purpose, and the squared stones were laid up by lots in the Abbot's Kitchen; the rest goes to paving yards and stalls for cattle, or to the highway." Lead stripped from the roofs was melted down in fires fueled by priceless manuscripts and carved wooden screens that were antique even then.

Legend has elaborately embellished the known history of the millennium before this debacle. One story says that Christ came here as a child in the company of Joseph of Arimathea, the wealthy trader in whose garden tomb Christ's body was placed when it was taken from the cross. According to another story, Joseph of Arimathea came

512 DIVERSIONS / Ancient Monuments and Ruins

alone; landing here in the winter, and, wearily, planting his staff into the ground, he saw it sending up leaves and blossoms. It was he who, as legend would have it, brought to England the Holy Grail, which Arthur's knights sought so avidly in later years. Traditions also record that King Arthur was buried at Glastonbury; and it is widely told that toward the end of the twelfth century, when Henry II had excavations made here, monks found a stone inlaid with a leaden cross that had been inscribed according to Gerald the Welshman, "Here lies buried the renowned King Arthur in the isle of Avalon with Guinevere his second wife"; there were two skeletons, one of a man of gigantic size, and one of a woman with a bit of golden hair that crumbled at the touch. The bones were reburied at Glastonbury's high altar, but the tomb was broken up at the dissolution and the bones were dispersed; the leaden cross no longer exists, but a drawing made at the beginning of the seventeenth century does. As to the ultimate truth of the whole story, no one can say. But Cadbury Castle, believed to be Arthur's Camelot, is not far away; and roads can still be traced between the two sites. As historians keep busy speculating, you can visit the impressively large ruins of the abbey, which are surrounded by manicured lawns ringed by a stone wall; walk down into an ancient crypt; take in a performance of a play or pageant (in summer); buy a book at the local bookstall; climb the 525-foot Tor for a view out over Wiltshire Downs and the Mendips all the way to Bristol (on a clear day); poke around at the Chalice Well where the Holy Grail is supposed to be lost; see a thorn tree grown from a cutting of the one that sprouted from Joseph of Arimathea's staff; and tour the Somerset Rural Life Museum, installed in the massive Abbot's Barn, where cheese-making equipment and other odd-looking nineteenth-century agricultural impedimenta are on display. Glastonbury proper is not too exciting a town, filled as it is (like Stratford-upon-Avon and other towns-with-a-past) with souvenir shops and the like; but the Glastonbury Thorn still flowers in the middle of the winter. The abbey now belongs to the Church of England, the Tor to the National Trust. The historic George and Pilgrim's Inn, an establishment that first opened its doors to travelers in 1475, is nearby. For details, contact the West Country Tourist Board (address above).

TOWER OF LONDON, London, England: The Tower—known in some quarters as the world's most famous castle—is actually a complex of buildings. Begun during the days of William the Conquerer and expanded many times over the years, it has figured in British history for nearly a millennium as palace, fortress, treasury, mint, bank, arsenal, munitions factory, garrison, library, museum, observatory, and even zoo. Its most famous function, however, has been that of prison, and many came through the so-called Traitor's Gate hoping to be ransomed or pardoned and thereby avoid the fate —endless incarceration or, worse, death—of those who had passed that way before them. Many hoped in vain. The stories of the executions, murders, and suicides within these walls are legion. Henry VI, imprisoned during the Wars of the Roses, was stabbed to death during his prayers, allegedly by Richard, Duke of Gloucester, the "usurper of the realm" who became Richard III when he murdered the about-to-be-crowned Edward V and his brother the Duke of York. (The youngsters disappeared from public view in 1483 while lodged in the Tower; the next trace of them was two sets of bones found under a staircase in Charles II's time.) Henry VIII hustled wives, dissidents, and possible claimants to the throne into the Tower's depths, the first step in the journey that usually ended at the executioner's block. Among those who made that journey were Anne Boleyn and Catherine Howard, the monarch's second and fifth wives, who were executed on the Tower Green and buried in the chapel of St. Peter ad Vincula; Sir Thomas More, who met his end after rejecting his sovereign's claim to the leadership of the English church ("the king's good servant but God's first," he explained); and Thomas Cromwell, the not-always-so-jolly king's chief administrator. Later, Lady Jane Grey was beheaded on Tower Green after the Duke of Northumberland, the father of her husband Lord Guilford Dudley, persuaded her young cousin Edward VI to pass his crown to the 15-year-old Jane rather than to Elizabeth's sister Mary, the rightful heir to the throne; she reigned for 9 days, beginning on July 10, 1553, until the English rallied around Mary I. In the days of Elizabeth I (who herself had been imprisoned in one of the Tower's grim cells on the orders of her sister Mary), the Earl of Essex was executed at the age of 34 after the discovery of a plot to kidnap the aging queen —once his lover. James I dispatched Sir Walter Raleigh to the Tower in 1603; he passed the time of day writing *A History of the World* until 1615, when the monarch finally had him beheaded. In modern times, German spies were executed in the courtyards during the two world wars, and in 1941, Rudolf Hess, Hitler's deputy, was imprisoned there. Such colorful episodes of the Tower's history are hard to imagine when you're confronted with the multitudes of tourists and guides milling about, as they do most of the year; it's most atmospheric when other people don't go—on a rainy day, for instance, or at night for the Ceremony of the Keys. (Book ahead by writing to the Resident Governor, Queen's House, HM Tower of London EC3N 4AB.) Rapiers, clubs, maces and flails, long-bows and cross-bows, cannon and muskets, shields, daggers, and all manner of other weapons, as well as glittering armor and, appropriately enough, fearsome-looking instruments of torture are displayed in the White Tower, the 100-foot-high structure begun by William the Conqueror in 1077 as the Keep and renamed in the mid-thirteenth century when Henry III had the structure whitewashed; the collections are among the finest of their kind in the world. In the Jewel House, a later addition to the complex, you'll see the Crown Jewels—the splendid St. Edward's crown worn only during coronations; the Imperial State, which contains over 3,000 precious stones, including four large pearls that Elizabeth I used as earrings; the ancient Black Prince's Ruby, which Henry V wore at Agincourt; the storied Stuart Sapphire; and the 317-carat Second Star of Africa, the second largest of the four gigantesque stones cut from the 3,106-carat Cullinan. The largest Star, a 530-carat, pear-shaped bit of glitter, which is not only the world's biggest cut diamond but also, according to some experts, its most perfect, embellishes the Royal Sceptre, which is also in the Jewel House, along with countless swords, bracelets, ewers, dishes, and their dazzling company. Don't fail to look for the Tower's group of ravens, whose eventual demise, legend has it, means that the Tower will fall.

HADRIAN'S WALL, near Newcastle-upon-Tyne, Northumberland, England: Take any road west of Newcastle-upon-Tyne and abruptly the place names are all Latin: This is the country of Hadrian's Wall, that phenomenal fortification put up by the Romans in the second century AD, some 40 years after the Roman general Agricola had penetrated into northern Scotland, when it seemed as though the Roman conquest was about to be extended over the whole island and it looked as if even Ireland might be conquered by a single legion. But even in this climate of optimism, the Picts, who painted themselves blue, posed a difficult case, and the Romans cast about for a means of protecting themselves from the strange wild men to the north. Hadrian's Wall was the result. A standout even in an empire full of impressive fortifications, it stretches over 70 miles across the neck of England, from what is now Bowness-on-Solway, on Solway Firth, in the west, to Wallsend, at the mouth of the River Tyne, in the east; it consists of a broad V-shaped ditch (the vallum) and a stone barrier 15 feet high, up to 9 feet thick (enough to drive a chariot along), and punctuated at regular intervals by so many guard towers, massive forts, and "milecastles" that some 5,500 cavalry and over half that many infantry were required to man it. Surprisingly enough, considering the wars and skirmishes that have taken place on and around it in the centuries since the Romans abandoned the country, many of these fortifications are still standing. The ditch is almost entirely intact; the wall itself can be seen from the Military Road, and the ruins are particularly extensive in the area between Sewingshields and Greenhead (where the wall runs along the border of Northumberland National Park for some 15 miles). There are fine views into the hills, and, at Housesteads, site of the most impressive remains of the 17 forts that once punctuated the wall, you'll see what's left of the barracks, the commandant's offices, the granaries, and a latrine. Similarly well preserved are the ruins west of Housesteads at Peel Crag and Walltown Crags. At Vindoland, near Bardon Mill, and farther west near Greenhead, there are two fine new museums which depict life on Hadrian's Wall during the Roman Army's occupation. Scale models and exhibits at Newcastle University's Museum of Antiquities, at Newcastle-upon-Tyne, provide a good introduction to what you'll see on the wall itself. Details: Northumbria Tourist Board, 9 Osborne Ter., Newcastle-upon-Tyne, Northumberland NE2 1NT, England (phone: 0632-81744).

CADBURY CASTLE, South Cadbury, Somerset, England: A century ago, when a party of Oxford archaeologists climbed the hill above this village 2 miles from the Wincanton-to-Ilchester A303, an old man met them at its foot and asked tearfully whether they had come to take the old king away. He was referring to Arthur. For this hill fort, one of the many occupied by a farming community since the eighth century BC and stormed by Vespasian, is thought by some to have been Camelot. Fortified for over five centuries, it was defended on the eve of the Roman invasion by four massive earth banks that the Romans partially dismantled before slaughtering the inhabitants and leaving the settlement to lie derelict for the next 200 years. Then, in the late third or early fourth century, activity here — perhaps in the form of pilgrimages — resumed, and, toward the end of the fifth century, the innermost of the four ancient banks was greatly strengthened by the addition of a new rampart held together with timber framing, a new gateway was built, and a small wooden tower was created above it, in building styles that reflected the manners of the Celts and the Romans. When men moved back into the old forts, it was usually to take advantage of the abandoned defenses to provide themselves with an attack-proof homestead. But the prehistoric ramparts here enclose some 18 acres — enough space, suggests archaeologist Leslie Alcock, to have accommodated an army as large as Arthur's. If he was truly the military leader for several small kingdoms, as some historians have surmised, this isolated hill near South Cadbury would have made an ideal base, situated as it was high enough to send signals by lantern to distant Glastonbury, where allies could then, in turn, summon armored horsemen from the hill forts of South Wales. Even the traditions of the Round Table find their corroboration at South Cadbury, with the excavation of a great hall, 63 feet by 34 feet, wooden and thatched. During the digging, fragments of imported pottery and broken wine pitchers were found, and it's easy to imagine these early Britons carousing in the days of darkness brought down around them during these years of warfare. For local tourist information, contact the West Country Tourist Board (address above).

STONEHENGE, Wiltshire, England: It's hard to appreciate this fantastic monument, not far from magnificently spired, equally celebrated Salisbury Cathedral, surrounded as it is by fences and gates — and all the more so when tour buses are disgorging masses of tourists on day trips from London, a common sight. Yet the mysterious pull exerted by England's most famous prehistoric monument — two concentric circles of stones, some over 20 feet high, ringed by a ditch 300 feet in diameter — is so strong that it's hard not to sense the rightness of myths that explain its origins in terms of Merlin and magic: Certainly the fiction is only a little stranger than the fact — that it was constructed in stages beginning in about 2750 BC, with stones that were rafted and dragged for many long miles (some from as far away as southwestern Wales), and then raised with wooden levers and rollers and ropes made of leather thongs. Its function is similarly unknown; some archaeologists — remarking on the way in which various stones are aligned with midsummer sunrise and midwinter moonrise — point out the possibility that it served as a sort of vast open-air observatory. Or perhaps that it was used for worship. Today, in midsummer, English druids still come here to celebrate their antique rites: Dressed in hooded white robes and carrying mistletoe and

DIVERSIONS / Ancient Monuments and Ruins 515

holly and banners emblazoned with mystical signs, they sing their hymns and chant strange runes as they march in procession amongst the megaliths and so await the coming of the dawn. For details about the region, contact the West Country Tourist Board (address above).

GLENELG BROCHS, Glenelg, Highland, Scotland: The fact that the name of this hamlet-by-the-sea, the county town of the old Inverness-shire, is a palindrome ranks with the lovely rocky mountain scenery as one of the more fascinating aspects to the place. Archaeologists and lovers of antiquities, however, are most drawn by the presence of two of the best preserved of Scotland's 500 or so defensive stone towers known as brochs. Many now are little more than piles of rubble; the ones at Glenelg are not too much different than they were when the Picts built them all over the country during the Iron Age, with their 30-foot-high dry-stone inner and outer walls, hollow between; their stone lintels; and their center courtyard. Nearby Dun Grugaig, another broch, occupies a lovely site close by a roiling cascade and fine views southward toward Ben Sgriol. For local information, contact the Highlands and Islands Development Board, Bridge House, 27 Bank St., Inverness IV1 1QR, Scotland (phone: 0463-34171).

MELROSE ABBEY, Melrose, Borders, Scotland: "If thou would see fair Melrose aright/Go visit it by the pale moonlight," wrote Sir Walter Scott in his *Lay of the Last Minstrel* about the ruins here. Among the finest and best preserved in Scotland, they move present-day visitors just as they did that celebrated nineteenth-century Scottish poet, who spent the last two decades of his life at nearby Abbotsford in a turreted, baronial sort of manse that is open to the public for tours. Melrose Abbey, one of four Border abbeys founded for a group of Cistercian monks by David I in 1136 just after the return of Roman Christianity to Scotland, was destroyed during English raids in 1322, restored by Robert Bruce in 1326, battered again in 1385, and ultimately destroyed in invasions in 1543 and 1544 — that is, all but the few sections that stand today in mute testimony to its past beauty. Particularly lovely is the reddish stonework in parts of the nave: the large five-light window in the south transept, the elaborately carved foliage embellishing the capitals nearby, the flying buttresses, and the porcine gargoyle playing bagpipes on the roof. According to tradition, the heart of Robert Bruce — which Sir James Douglas was taking to the Holy Land when he was killed — was buried under the east window, and Tom Purdie, the forester for Scott's estate, and Peter Matheson, the writer's coachman, are interred in the abbey cemetery. The choir is believed to be the resting place of Douglas himself as well as Alexander II and Michael Scott, the wizard of the *Lay of the Last Minstrel*. Melrose town, described as Kennaquhair in Scott's *Monastery* and *The Abbot*, is at one corner of what is widely known as the Scott Country, whose boundaries are also delimited by the towns of Galashiels, Selkirk, and Dryburgh. The latter is the site of Dryburgh Abbey, where Sir Walter Scott, Earl Haig (commander-in-chief of the British Army during World War I), and members of their families are buried. The ruins of its cloister are remarkably preserved — far better than those at the ruins of the remaining pair of David I's Border abbeys, not-far-distant Kelso and Jedburgh. Both of these are also worth visiting; at Jedburgh, you can tour the house where Queen Mary stayed for a short while and visit imposing, nineteenth-century Jedburgh Castle, which now houses a museum devoted to the penal system of the period. Details: Borders Regional Council, Tourism Division, Newtown St., Boswells, Borders TD6 0SA, Scotland (phone: 0835-23301).

SKARA BRAE and MAES HOWE, Mainland, Orkney, Scotland: This 70-island group across the Pentland Firth from John O'Groats on the Scottish mainland has Britain's densest concentration of prehistoric monuments — an average of about three recorded sites of archaeological note per square mile; those on the large island known as Mainland are particularly notable. Maes Howe (or "greatest mound"), for instance, is Europe's best example of a Stone Age circular chambered cairn — and it has no rivals on the mainland. Constructed as the tomb of a very important chieftain and measuring over 110 feet across and over 300 feet around, this hollow 24-foot-high mound of rock and clay is entered through a low, stone passageway, which gives access to a vaulted chamber 14 feet square flanked by a trio of burial niches walled and paved in huge single stones embellished in what some authorities believe to be the single richest group of Runic inscriptions to be found in any one place in the world. The carvings left by Norsemen who raided the grave in about 2,500 BC, describe how the grave goods were taken away by night, hint of a hiding place nearby, and tell of the problems that resulted when two members of a band that had sought refuge here during a storm went crazy. You can see the kind of village where the same Stone Age men, whose deaths are so widely memorialized, lived at Skara Brae, which was constructed at about the same time as Maes Howe, lived in for perhaps six centuries, and then inexplicably buried with sand for the almost four millennia that followed, until unearthed by another storm around 1850. Most of the pottery, beads, tools, and implements found on the site are now displayed in the National Museum of Antiquities in Edinburgh; but the site as you see it today — a group of small squared lane-linked huts clustered around a central courtyard in a field just about 20 feet above sea level — is impressive enough. The flagstone blocks with which the structures were built, the slate shale with which they were paved, the shelves and built-in boxes and cubbyholes, stone beds, drains, and other impedimenta of the life of the three dozen souls who called this home so long ago are still remarkably well preserved. Other antique sites are nearby: the four remaining Standing Stones of Stenness, a henge dating from about 2,300 BC; the great Ring of Brogar, where more than two dozen stones can be seen inside a ditch on a 2.5-acre site; the Gurness Broch, Orkney Mainland's best representation of this type of structure, situated amidst a group of other stone buildings of assorted ages; the Onstan Chambered Cairn, dated about 2,500 BC; and many more — on this island and on the others. Cliff-bound Hoy, for instance, boasts two martello towers constructed as defenses against American privateers. The islands are particularly lovely during the twilight nights of late summer, when the sun never quite rests. Not all archaeological sites can be seen at all times, and some are relatively inaccessible; so it's wise to plan your visit well before you arrive. For details, contact the Orkney Tourist Organization, Kirkwall, Orkney KW15 1NX, Scotland (phone: 0856-2856).

CAERNARVON, Gwynedd, Wales: Though little remains of this castle but its walls, it is easy to imagine the grandeur that Edward I planned when he began construction in the late thirteenth and early fourteenth centuries. He was building not only a military fortress, but also a symbol of his sovereignty over Wales and, accordingly, he had it executed very much in the style of the Romans who had ruled Wales centuries earlier from this site on the Menai Strait, with stonework much like that he had seen during the Crusades on the fifth-century Roman wall at Constantinople. The cost of such monumentality was immense—the equivalent of nearly £2 million by today's standards at the halfway point. There were shooting galleries both high and low, courtyards and drawbridges, portcullises, arrow loops and spyholes—many of which, or remnants thereof, can still be seen. With the turrets and towers to explore, vaulted chambers to poke around in, and walls and lawns to walk upon, this is understandably a popular destination in Wales. Dr. Samuel Johnson, on visiting the castle two centuries ago, allowed as how he had not thought that there had been such buildings, that it surpassed all his ideas. You may well agree. The future Edward VIII was invested here in 1911, and the present Prince Charles in 1969—only appropriate since Edward I called himself the first Prince of Wales, and his son Edward II was born here. For more information about the area, contact the North Wales Tourism Council, Civic Centre, Colwyn Bay, Clwyd LL29 8AR, Wales (phone: 0492-56881).

CONWY CASTLE, Conwy, Gwynedd, Wales: Counted among Europe's greatest fortresses when taken together with the town's walls, and once one of its most powerful fortifications, this magnificent piece of medieval architecture, one of ten castles built by Edward I in his efforts to control the Welsh, must have been all the more striking in its early years when its walls—whitewashed at the time—gleamed brightly from afar. But even now the structure is altogether impressive. Built in the main between 1283 and 1287 after designs by the king's castle engineer, one James of St. George, it required the work of some 1,500 men and the expenditure of some £20,000 before its completion. The eight towers, each with walls 15 feet thick, rise to a height of 70 feet; they are not, as they seem, perpendicular to the ground, but instead taper gradually toward the top. The Northwest Tower has a fine view over the river, and the Prison Tower has a concealed dungeon as fearsomely dark and close as the imposing 38-by-125-foot Great Hall just above is spacious and airy, with its grand north- and east-facing windows. In the part of the castle known as the Inner Bailey, which lies to the east of the Great Hall, you can view the elegantly detailed Queen Eleanor's Chapel, the best-preserved part of the structure; the name is odd, because it wasn't finished during her lifetime. The most important battle fought within the castle's walls took place in 1294, during a rebellion led by Prince Madog ap Llywelyn; Edward I took refuge there and, when trapped without proper food and water by the rising waters of the river, was almost beaten. The castle's subsequent history was marked by a visit by Richard II at the end of the fourteenth century; occupation by Royalist forces during the seventeenth century; and plundering, dismantling, and damage during the nineteenth century. For more information about the area, contact the North Wales Tourism Council (address above).

BALLINTUBBER ABBEY, Ballintubber, Co. Mayo, Irish Republic: The site of this Augustinian community has long been an important one; tradition tells us that St. Patrick baptized local peasants with water from its well. Later, the monastery became the departure point for pilgrimages to Croagh Patrick. Now it is noted for the fact that Mass has been said in its church ever since the community's founding by Cathal Crovdearg O'Conor, the king of Connacht, for the Canons Regular of St. Augustine in 1216 — despite the suppression of the abbey under Henry VIII and the depredations of the Cromwellians in 1653. The fact that there has been no interruption in religious rites for over 760 years makes the church unique in the English-speaking world. It is an exceptionally handsome structure. Thanks to sensitive restoration work begun on the initiative of a former priest, Father Egan, finished in 1966, a new wooden roof was constructed for the nave and the interior walls whitewashed in the ancient fashion, so that the church looks much as it must have upon its completion. The carving around the three lancet windows in the gable and on the capitals of the chancel exemplifies the best work of a school of talented late Romanesque carvers who worked in the province of Connacht in the early thirteenth century after the rest of the country had gone over to the Gothic style; the Augustinians, who were more permissive in their rules than some other orders, allowed the artists more latitude in their designs — and the results reflect the fact. The wonderfully monstrous snakes twined around each other on the capitals between the triple round-headed window in the front of the church (which you'll be able to see in those distant gloomy recesses only if you've brought along field glasses) and the grotesque creatures creeping along the corbels that uphold the chancel's ribbed vaulting are just two examples. Nearby, you can see the well where St. Patrick did his baptizing and the attractive cloisters, reconstructed from the ruins of the fifteenth-century originals with the aid of fragments that came to light in the course of archaeological excavations in the 1960s. For local information, contact Áras Fáilte, Galway, Irish Republic (phone: 091-63081).

ROCK OF CASHEL, Cashel, Co. Tipperary, Irish Republic: Even in Ireland's earliest days, before any fortresses or cathedrals or castles were built atop this chunk of carboniferous limestone, the Rock must have looked a bit unreal, rising precipitously, as it does — a block of slate gray — above the rocky green plains all around; now, capped by the spare and broken remains of structures once frequented by saints, kings, and bishops, the Rock provides a visual experience that is, quite simply, one of Ireland's most stupendous. The longtime capital of the kings of Munster, the Rock was visited in 450 by St. Patrick, who baptized King Aengus and his brothers. (During the baptism ceremony, St. Patrick accidentally put the point of his crozier through the king's foot; the king, thinking the action part of the ceremony, bore the pain with fortitude.) Later, Brian Ború, who defeated the Norsemen who overran Munster in the tenth century, was crowned king here, and, though it stayed in the hands of his descendants, its importance declined; in 1101, it was presented by Brian's grandson, King Muirchertach, to the church, which is responsible for most of the buildings in the tightly grouped complex you see on the Rock today. These are as impressive when you see them at close range as they are from afar. Dominating the scene is the cathedral, begun in the thirteenth century and abandoned in 1749 when the then-archbishop (too laggardly, perhaps, to trek to his church) removed the lead roof; the central tower offers fine views into the distant mountains and to the Devil's Bit — the mountain pass said to have been created when the Dark Angel took a large bite. (The size of the Rock is said to match the void in the mountain exactly.) A very well preserved round tower, probably twelfth century, stands at the corner of the cathedral's north transept; and the massive rectangular, three-storied archbishop's palace, honeycombed with passageways to explore, adjoins the west end of the cathedral's nave, which was never completed. The twelfth-century Cross of St. Patrick is nearby, along with the remains of the fifteenth-century Hall of the Vicars Choral, used to house laymen who participated in the chanting of the cathedral's services. Tiny Cormac's Chapel, wedged into a corner between the cathedral's choir and its south transept, is especially interesting. Built in 1134 by Cormac MacCarthy, the bishop of Cashel and the king of Desmond (in the realm created after a defeat by the king of Connaught divided Munster in half), it is well known as the nation's best example of the Irish Romanesque style; volumes have been written tracing its origins. You will probably be most impressed by the elaborate carvings, the ribbed vaulting, twisted capitals, and richly embellished blind arcades; the tympana (the surfaces between the arch and the lintels) surmounting the south door by which you enter today, and the far grander north door, through which worshipers gained access to the nave until the construction of the cathedral, are beautiful. The lions and centaurs you see here are even more exotic than the human heads that peer out at you from around the chancel. After you've completed your tour, don't fail to see some of the older structures in Cashel proper — among them the fifteenth-century Quirke's Castle and the eighteenth-century Palace of Protestant Archbishops — both now used as hotels. Also worth noting are the ruins of the thirteenth-century Dominican monastery close to the center of town, and the eighteenth-century Church of Ireland St. John the Baptist Cathedral. For local information, contact the South Eastern Region Tourist Information Office, 41 The Quay, Waterford, Co. Waterford, Irish Republic (phone: 051-75823).

GLENDALOUGH, Co. Wicklow, Irish Republic: Nestled in a valley deep in the Wicklow Mountains about 30 miles south of Dublin, this "valley of the two lakes" is the most beautifully situated of Ireland's important early Christian monasteries, particularly when the gorse blooms in May. This monastery grew up around the site where St. Kevin settled to renounce human love and live as a hermit during the sixth century, and like many other Irish monasteries, was pillaged and sacked many times by the Vikings and assorted other marauders; like Clonmacnoise, it was particularly vulnerable because of its fame as a seat of learning. And, as at Clonmacnoise, the ruins are extensive: better than half a dozen churches, crosses, grave slabs, a priest's house, a round tower, and old wells. The stone of which most are constructed, granite and mica-schist, has chipped and crumbled over the centuries, giving the walls a rough texture and providing a fine medium for the growth of the pale soft local lichen; the buildings at Glendalough have that particularly antique look that you may imagine all ruins will have until you find out otherwise. It's certainly pleasant to spend a day here, poking around among the broken walls, wandering along the pathways between them, and admiring the glass-smooth waters of Upper and Lower lakes. Especially noteworthy are the seventh-century cathedral, Ireland's largest pre-Romanesque church; St. Kevin's Church (generally known as St. Kevin's Kitchen) with its round-tower-like belfry rising up above a stone roof; the small, twelfth-century Priest's House, perhaps originally a mortuary chapel or even the saint's shrine; the Reefert Church, around whose walls sleep many Leinster kings; and, farther down the valley, accessible via a narrow sylvan path, St. Saviour's Monastery, a twelfth-century church probably built by Laurence O'Toole, former abbot of Glendalough, archbishop of Dublin, and Ireland's first canonized saint. There are especially fine walks around the Upper Lake, which is picturesquely backed by the steep cliffs of Camaderry and Lugduff mountains, ribboned by the rushing Glenealo Stream and a waterfall; the stand of firs on the north side is quite lovely. Local information: Eastern Region Tourism Organisation, 1 Clarinda Park N, Dun Laoghaire, Co. Dublin, Irish Republic (phone: 808571).

GRIANÁN OF AILEACH, Burt, Co. Donegal, Irish Republic: Ulster cannot boast megalithic monuments of the scope of Leinster's Boyne Valley cemeteries (although there do exist several structures with elaborate entranceways that have earned them the name "court graves," as well as standing stones and stone circles and dolmens). Here, however, the most characteristic and striking ruins are those of circle-shaped ring forts, which protected farmhouses up until AD 1000 (and which you'll find today scattered here and there by the thousands throughout Ulster's fields), and, even more striking, stone *cashels* (a circular wall enclosing a group of ecclesiastical buildings). The Grianán of Aileach (the sunny place in the territory of Aileach), one of the most important antiquities in the northern part of the island, is among the most striking. Situated atop 800-foot high Grianán Mountain not far from Londonderry, this fortification measures about 77 feet across; the 13-foot-thick walls, restored in the 1870s by the bishop of Derry to their original height of 17 feet, contain galleries and guard chambers, and enclose a series of stairway-connected terraces. The views afforded by the topmost of these, out over the blue reaches of Loughs Foyle and Swilly, are glorious — fully worthy of the O'Neills, the kings of Ulster, whose northern branch made this fortification its base from approximately the fifth century AD through the twelfth, when Muirchertach O'Brien, the king of Munster, avenging the pillaging of his own residence, completed the destruction of this structure, which had already been badly battered during a 676 attack by the southern O'Neills under Finechta the Festive: The Munster king instructed each of his men to carry away a single stone of the fort. The exact date of construction is unknown, since no excavations have been made here; in their Annals of the Kingdom of Ireland, the Four Masters put its origins back in the Iron Age, while other scholars suggest that it was probably built within a few centuries either way of the lifetime of St. Patrick — that is, in the fifth century AD. The round shape has inspired the church nestling at the foot of the mountain at Burt, one of Ireland's most interesting modern structures. It was built in 1967 after designs by Liam MacCormick and Una Madden. Similar, and equally impressive, fortifications include Dun Aengus on the Aran Islands, and Staigue Fort in County Kerry. Details about the area are available from the Donegal/Leitrim/Sligo Region Tourist Information Office, Temple St., Sligo, Co. Sligo, Irish Republic (phone: 071-61201).

HILL OF TARA, near Navan, Co. Meath, Irish Republic: Little but legend and a handful of earthworks and stones remains of the glories of Tara — but of legend and conjecture there is plenty, and this 512-foot hill about 25 miles from Dublin, commanding a fine view of a vast expanse of lush meadows, is well worth a visit. Already a significant burial place two millennia before Christ (as revealed by the excavation of one of the site's most notable monuments, the Mound of the Hostages), it ranked among Ireland's most important political and religious sites for almost 2,000 years all told; it became the center of priestly rulers even before St. Patrick came to Ireland in the fifth century, and long served as a residence for anyone strong enough to make himself at least nominally high king of Ireland. One of Tara's most glorious periods came in the first centuries after Christ, when the celebrated Cormac the Wise constructed the wooden palaces that you can read about in some of Ireland's early literature. (It was his daughter who, though betrothed to Finn MacCool, eloped with Diarmuid O'Duibhne, and gave rise to the wonderful stories about the lovers' flight from one end of Ireland to the other.) Later, after St. Patrick triumphed in a contest of feats with the druids of High King Laoghaire, whose authority the saint had challenged, the king allowed his subjects to be converted to Christianity (although he himself remained a pagan until his death). Tara's importance declined until its abandonment in 1022. Relics of all of these eras can be seen today. The Mound of the Hostages (*Dumha na nGiall*), an early passage grave (ca. 1800 BC) with a 17-foot-long corridor, covered by a mound that measures 72 feet in diameter, is at one edge of the large circular Iron Age ring fort called the Royal Enclosure (*Rath na Ríogh*), at whose center are two other earthworks — the Royal Seat (*Forradh*) and Cormac's House (*Teach Cormaic*), where you'll see a modern statue of St. Patrick and the 5-foot-long chunk of granite known as the Stone of Destiny (*Lia Fáil*), which, according to tradition, would roar when the king being crowned upon it was acceptable. Just south of the Royal Enclosure is *Rath Laoghaire*, which is said to be near the above-mentioned king's burial place. To the north, you'll find the Rath of the Synods (*Rath na Seanaid*), an erstwhile fortress and burial place; the Banquet Hall (*Teach Miodchuarta*), where festivities are reported in the twelfth-century *Book of Leinster*, and where each class of society had its own compartment; the circular *Rath Gráinne*, named for the fugitive king's daughter; and the odd-shaped Sloping Trenches (*Claoin Fhearta*), which probably had a ceremonial function of some sort. Also interesting is Adamnán's Stone, a 6-foot-high chunk of sandstone bearing the incised likeness of a human figure — perhaps the horned Celtic Cernunnos or a type of fertility figure known as a *sheila-na-gig*. For local information, contact the Eastern Region Tourism Organisation (address above).

NEWGRANGE, Newgrange, Co. Meath, Irish Republic: Very few relics of the daily life of the people of the Neolithic Age (ca. 3700–2000 BC) survive in Ireland today; it seems as if all the creative energies of the communities of this period were directed toward the construction not of homes for the living, but of monumental repositories for the remains of the dead, and the whole valley of the river Boyne, about 30 miles north of Dublin, is scattered with cairns, standing stones, and earthworks both large and small. Of these, Newgrange is the most impressive by far. In fact, this so-called passage grave ranks among the most important of its type in Europe, and scholars have spent centuries studying it. Literature of the ancient Irish links it to a mysterious personage who is sometimes called Oengus an Brogha (Oengus of the Palace) and sometimes dubbed Oengus mac an Dagda (Oengus son of the good god); some archaeologists have suggested that Newgrange and similar tombs on the Continent were constructed for the important personages in groups of traders and prospectors who first migrated from Spain or Portugal around 4000 BC. Certainly, they had a civilization far more highly organized than the widespread belief in our "primitive ancestors" credits them — at least if they are to be judged from the sophistication of the building and decorative techniques evidenced here. The earth mound that is the most immediately obvious feature of Newgrange, entirely man-made using alternate layers of turf and stones, is unusually large — 40 feet high and 300 feet in diameter; estimates put the quantity of stones required for the whole undertaking at 180,000 tons. Now covered with grass, the mound was originally paved with white quartz pebbles so that it glistened brightly enough in the sun to be seen from afar. Inside, leading into the depth of the hill from the entrance on the southeastern frontage, is a 62-foot-long, yard-wide passage. High enough to let you walk upright and lined with a series of orthostats, or upright stones, 5 to 8 feet high, it ends at a generally circular burial chamber, whose notable features include its beehive-shaped ceiling paved with overlapping stones (following a method of construction found over and over again at Irish ruins of this period), and, adjoining the main chamber — and giving the tomb's interior a roughly cruciform shape — three recesses contain stone troughs or basins probably once used to contain the ashes of the dead. On the morning of the shortest day of the year, rays of sun shine directly up the passageway to the center of the burial chamber — a design that required some sort of calendar to calculate. The decoration throughout further confirms that sophisticated minds were at work. The ceiling of the north recess, covered with carved spirals, lozenges, triangles, zigzags, diamonds, and other shapes, is particularly noteworthy, as are the gigantic threshhold stone, at the entrance to the tomb, and many of the orthostats. Similar motifs appear on many other megalithic stones (and on Mycenean tombs as well); it's thought that far from being mere ornament, the designs, probably rooted in the pre-Mycenean civilization of the third millennium BC, are magnificent abstract representations of gods, goddesses, and human beings. A museum and tourist information office at Newgrange can give you details about Newgrange as well as about nearby Dowth and Knowth, the two other major monuments in this area, which is often called Brugh na Boinne (Palace of the Boyne). Details: Eastern Region Tourism Organisation (address above).

CARRICKFERGUS CASTLE, Co. Antrim, Northern Ireland: Along with Trim Castle in County Meath, Carrickfergus Castle remains the mightiest symbol of the presence of the Normans in Ireland after the invasion of 1169. Situated strategically on the shores of Belfast Lough, it is one of Ireland's strongest castles, and its story continues through a number of important eras in Irish history. Founded in 1180 by John de Courcey, the first Norman Lord of Ulster, it was besieged in 1210 by King John of England, who feared the rising independence of his Norman barons. After some resistance, the castle fell to Robert Bruce, whose brother Edward had invaded Ireland from Scotland in 1315. In 1690, William of Orange landed here during his campaign to defeat the Stuart kings and to take possession of Ireland; some 70 years later, it was taken by a French expeditionary force. The American John Paul Jones, captaining the *Ranger*, defeated the HMS *Drake*, which was moored beneath the castle, in 1778; and from 1796 until 1798, Irish patriots were incarcerated there. You enter the impressive structure through a gate flanked by two rounded towers, then proceed through the Outer Ward past a handful of sixteenth-century storehouses into the Middle Ward; the Inner Ward, which is adjacent, is dominated by the squarish Keep—five stories or about 90 feet high, 56 feet across, and 58 feet deep. A stairway, which climbs inside the 8-foot-thick walls, takes you upward from the ground level (where you'll see an early-twentieth-century steam engine and an antique wood canoe) to a group of military exhibits on the floor above, and into the Great Chamber, a spacious room with good-sized windows and a spiral staircase that climbs to yet another level, which offers still better views over the harbor and the town. The city's handsome late-eighteenth-century Town Hall, and its Church of St. Nicholas, which dates from the twelfth and seventeenth centuries, are also worth visiting; don't miss the monument there to Sir Arthur Chichester, who figured importantly in the establishment of the Ulster we know today. For more information, contact the Northern Ireland Tourist Board.

For the Experience

Pub Crawling

Everywhere you go in Britain and Ireland, there's a pub, and in most places there are many pubs. In Ireland there are 11,000 licenses to sell intoxicating liquor, and even if every eligible adult were a drinker, there would still be more pubs per head than any place else on earth; towns like Listowel seem to have more pubs than dwelling houses. In Britain, London alone has 5,000 pubs; in the country, there are so many that during World War II, when road signs were removed, people could give directions in terms of the local watering hole: "Turn left at the *Dog and Duck,* go for half a mile as far as the *King's Arms,* then . . ." Those English villages that have lost their last remaining pub have won some degree of celebrity as a result, being very unusual indeed. There are pubs in the city and in the country, pubs in the theater district, pubs patronized heavily by journalists, pubs with gardens, and pubs where you can listen to music or catch a striptease show.

Yet only a fraction of them have the kind of decor and atmosphere that would measure up to most Americans' idea of what British and Irish pubs are like. Dark paneling, a long mahogany bar, and an abundance of engraved glass mirrors and gleaming brass fittings are occasionally to be found — but they're the exception rather than the rule, both in Britain and in Ireland. Most offerings are less remarkable.

In Ireland, for instance, there are hundreds of pubs which, though reasonably well run, are functional, unpretentious — and instantly forgotten; there are thousands of "lounge bars," where you will find soft seats, soft lighting, soft Muzak, and soft carpets — just like home; and there are the so-called singing pubs, which are well advertised and known to all taxi drivers. (Contrary to popular belief, singing is greatly discouraged in most Irish pubs, particularly in the cities, and only in the singing pubs is one guaranteed music — but even then, the quality is variable, the crowds enormous, and the comfort minimal.) Then there are a few pubs like the city-center establishment in the west of Ireland, where there are flush toilets for men but none at all for women; where the glasses are doused only infrequently in cold water; and where the only ice is in the voice of the owner at closing time. The Guinness draft is a danger to public health; there are few stools and only one table; and the fire, when lit, is carefully covered in case the habitués might derive a jot of warmth from it. The most timorous suggestion that there might be room for improvement causes the proprietor to purse his lips in profound disapproval: Any improvement would "spoil the place." As for the above noted west of Ireland pub, before you tumble to the floor in spasms of mirth, you should know that in this pub, and *only* in this pub, are you likely to hear a heady discourse on the relative merits of Eliot, Pound, and Auden, intermingled with passionate discussion of the forthcoming All-Ireland Hurling Final and the chronically bad state of the country's industrial relations, while you sip 15-year-old whiskey from the barrel and listen to music, which comes from an ancient wireless and is usually classical. To round off the picture, one corner of the bar is gay.

Character is the word that the Irish use to describe premises like these, and it doesn't have anything to do with whether the walls are paneled in mahogany and polished or plastered and badly in need of a paint job. The true joy of Irish pubs is chat, banter, repartee. The physical shortcomings of the premises are more often than not made up for by the spiritual and mental experiences that are to be enjoyed.

Your average British pub, while far less primitive, may be no more wonderful to look at: Beset by Formica and other plastics, a loud juke box, a regular battery of electronic games that blip and bleep and squeal above whatever noises of good cheer a draft from the pressurized aluminum keg has managed to encourage, the garden-variety, British pub reflects many of the most obnoxious intrusions of twentieth-century civilization.

Yet, paradoxically enough, it doesn't seem to matter. Just as an American neighborhood tavern can manage to entertain even when the floor is ugly green tile, its bar stools covered plastic, and its lighting murky, the pub is a centerpiece of social life here. (In Ireland, in fact, the melancholy truth is that very few people choose a pub for comfort. Masochism being a national malaise, the more stuffy, smoky, noisy, pokey, and uncomfortable a pub is, the more likely you are to have people tell you how much they are enjoying it.)

Before you set off on that most convivial of pleasures, the pub crawl, there are a number of facts you'll find useful.

Pubs are also for eating in, but only at lunchtime. You will receive looks of horrified incredulity if you ask for food in the evenings: These are devoted to "serious" drinking. "Pub grub" is usually fairly simple fare: In Britain, the choices most often are sandwiches; a *ploughman's lunch,* a hunk of bread and cheese plus pickle; or *cottage pie,* ground meat topped with mashed potato and baked in the oven. In Ireland, the selection consists mostly of soup or sandwiches (although delicious exceptions such as those noted below do exist). An exception: In London, many pubs serve food into the evenings.

Pub crowds vary. British pubs usually attract a motley crowd of all ages — silver-haired ladies clutching shopping bags and bolting shots of gin; workmen in stained overalls arguing politics and draining pints of beer; tourists juggling plates of Scotch eggs and pints of lager. In Ireland, until recently it was not only considered improper for ladies to drink in bars, but they would often be refused a pint. Although the clientele in countryside pubs tends to be mostly male, those in the city draw an equal number of women. And if you look carefully, you'll notice that the snugs — cubicles traditionally reserved for genteel ladies — may now be occupied by men seeking privacy or quiet amid the clamor.

Pub hours differ widely from area to area and occasionally also from pub to pub. Most pubs in England, Scotland, and Wales open in the late morning, do a booming business through the lunch hour, shut down for the afternoon, then start serving again at the end of the working day or around the dinner hour; closing is generally around 10:30 or 11 PM. But local variations are legion. Pubs in market areas may begin business with the sun; country pubs may stay open later than city pubs; pubs in Edinburgh and Glasgow are generally open throughout the day. Pubs in other parts of the country, particularly in the islands and in certain corners of Wales, are generally closed all day Sunday.

In Ireland, all pubs open at 10:30 AM and close at 11:30 PM on weekdays, except in winter, when they close at 11 PM. In Dublin, Cork, Limerick, and Waterford, the pubs close from 2:30 to 3:30 PM for a hiatus known to all as the "holy hour." On Sundays, pubs in Northern Ireland are closed; in the Republic, they are open from 12:30 to 2 PM and again from 4 to 10 PM. Pubs in the countryside are usually quiet during the day, since people still eat a noon dinner at home; you should visit in the evening if you want to catch these bars at their liveliest. Pubs in the cities do a bustling day-long business, as people flock in at lunchtime for a snack and perhaps in the late afternoon for a drink.

Beer is not the only brew. The sheer variety of drafts can perplex newcomers. You can drink ale, bitter, mild, stout, and lager — whose varying tastes derive from varying proportions and types of malt, hops, sugar, yeast, and water. Lager — a brew like Denmark's or Holland's, which a good many British drinkers don't consider beer at all — is made from a yeast that sinks to the bottom of the brewing tank during the fermentation process (rather than rising to the top, as does the yeast used in more traditional British brews). It is also activated at a lower temperature — resulting in a product that stays clear instead of turning cloudy when cooled. Bitter, usually served on draft, has a good strong brown color and a frothy head, and a taste that tends toward the sharp or the earthy (thanks to a large proportion of hops in the brew). The terms "special" and "best," applied to bitters, refer not to quality but to strength. So-called pale and light ales are the bottled versions of bitter; pale is apt to be the stronger of the two. Brown ale, also bottled, tends to be a bit sweeter and a bit darker than bitter. Mild is the result of a second fermentation after the drawing off of the bitter. Served on draft, it is usually sweeter in taste, and (except in the Midlands, where the milds look almost like bitter) usually dark brown to black in color. Stouts — brews made of a malt that has been roasted — are all very dark and sometimes sweet; Guinness, Ireland's most famous drink, is thick and rich like all stout, but not at all sweet. Guinness, particularly, seems to be an acquired taste; to sample it at its best, stop in at the factory, the world's largest exporting brewery, on the shores of the Liffey at St. James Gate, where, after a film describing the brewing process, you can sip a pint, or — more likely after you've tasted the super-fresh brew — two or three.

In the last few years, Britain has seen an increasingly large number of pubs serving so-called real ales, brews that are still fermenting when they are delivered to the pub (in a wood — or, more usually, a metal — cask). Unlike keg beers, which have been filtered and even pasteurized at the brewery and then packed under pressure, real ales require careful handling — but the taste warrants the effort: You'll want to see for yourself. The *Good Beer Guide,* published under the aegis of the active Campaign for Real Ale (CAMRA) and available for £3.95 from its offices at 34 Alma Rd., St. Albans, Hertfordshire AL1 3BW, England, lists over 6,000 pubs that serve the better brews; or CAMRA's *Scottish Real Ale Guide* (£1 from Ken Garden, 107 Broughton St., Edinburgh, Scotland); together with *Egon Ronay's Pub Guide* (published by the Egon Ronay Organisation Ltd., Greencoat House, Francis St., London SW1P 1DH, England), are the best guides to pubs worth your time. In Edinburgh, consult the *Complete Edinburgh Pub Guide* (available from Edinburgh University Student Publications, 1 Buccleuch Pl., Edinburgh EH8 9LW, Scotland) as well as the city's own *Pub and Restaurant Guide* (available for 25p at tourist information offices). The following selection, which includes some of the very best, most unusual, and those with the most atmosphere, shows off the variety of pubs you'll turn up when you prowl farther afield.

MINER'S INN, Acomb, Northumberland, England: Only 2 miles from Hexham, a busy but largely unspoiled market town with a beautiful ancient abbey, this cozy eighteenth-century coaching inn, comfortable if a bit garish in its plushness, has thick stone walls, immense and impressive original oak beams, brass ornaments that suggest antiquity, a garden where children are welcome, and — perhaps best of all — a pleasantly mixed clientele that includes not only locals but also bankers and plastics manufacturers who drive out from 20-mile-distant Newcastle, long-distance hikers heading for the Roman Wall or the Northumbria National Park, and campers from a nearby caravan park. Local venison, halibut, and steaks are among the dishes available in the restaurant at moderate prices. Phone: Hexham 603909.

THE EAGLE, Cambridge, Cambridgeshire, England: One of the oldest of dozens of pubs in this ancient university city, this former coaching inn in sequestered Eagle Yard, near King's College Chapel and just off Bene't Street, is a favorite among undergraduates — but there's generally an agreeable assortment of young townspeople on hand as well; the excellent lunchtime salad buffet is popular with both groups. Architecturally important, and therefore "listed" so that the building can't be tampered with, the *Eagle* has been little altered over the years — and certainly not prettified — since it was used by stagecoaches on the route between Huntingdon, Hertford, and London; and both of its wood paneled bars, one much larger than the other, are fairly spartan, with their bare floors and uncushioned seating, but they're rich in atmosphere as a result. You can still see, running outside the windows of the upper story, an old gallery, which, in the absence of interior passages to connect the upstairs rooms, performed the same function as corridors do nowadays. Phone: Cambridge 353782.

ROYAL OAK, King's Bromley, Staffordshire, England: The public bar section of this half-timbered erstwhile farmhouse, originally part of a big estate, is basic if congenial; but the lounge bar is wonderfully comfortable with its red carpet, button-backed plush seats, and when the weather warrants, open fires: It's just the place to while away a long winter's eve. The dining room is just as attractive: The long oak beams there and in the bars — said to have come from early-seventeenth-century sailing ships — give the place that old world look that you expect when you travel in England; there's no question but that the place really does date from 1610, as local historians assert. The venison and the omelets are worth a detour, and the scenery in the surrounding country is exceptionally pretty in places, and highly underrated. Burton-on-Trent is the nearest town of any size. Phone: Yoxall 472289.

ANGEL HOTEL, Lavenham, Suffolk, England: Even in a superbly preserved medieval town like Lavenham, where scarcely a dwelling seems less than a few centuries old, this pub on the marketplace overlooking the historic gray-and-white half-timbered guildhall — itself barely changed for hundreds of years — is very old, dating in part from the fifteenth century and built atop the much older remains of a dormitory for a religious order. There are now two bars — one, the public, catering to the needs of locals; the other, oak-beamed and thickly carpeted, more attuned to the requirements of the many tourists who flock to Lavenham and, after much rubbernecking around the rural corners of Suffolk, want to put their feet up. The games room, where children are welcome, is complete with a pool table, an electronic Outer Space game, and a dart board. At midday, excellent meals of spaghetti, roast beef and Yorkshire pudding, and ploughman's lunches are always available; evening meals can be had by arrangement. Phone: Lavenham 247388.

DIRTY DICKS, London, England: Abandoned by his fiancée on the eve of his wedding day, the Dirty Dick in question, one Nathaniel Bentley, went into seclusion and lived out his life in isolation and ever-increasing squalor in the apartments that now make up the downstairs section of this pub. The spiders and bats you see nowadays swinging from the ceilings and attached to the walls as reminders of the weird, Dickensian story, are fake — but the offbeat decor makes a visit to this otherwise fairly touristy establishment a pleasant enough way to begin an evening. The area above, rebuilt in 1870, lends itself to other functions: Galleried and spacious, with wood everywhere and sawdust-sprinkled floors, it's plain rather than plush (much like the East End surrounding it), and, in its dark and clubby way, it's a supremely restful place to quench your thirst after a hectic Sunday morning's bargaining along nearby Petticoat Lane. The lunchtime bar snacks are very good. The address is 202 Bishopsgate. Phone: 283-5888.

EL VINO, London, England: Though it's a wine bar rather than a pub, this establishment deserves special mention as a bastion of City tradition. Women may not stand at the bar, men must wear ties, and the bartenders sport stiff white collars and tails. When you add the magnificently polished Victorian setting, you could hardly imagine a more Dickensian scene. Savoring the varied offerings of wine—both plain and fortified—is a tony Fleet Street crowd, not so much the hard-working newsmongers but the publishers and feature writers, plus an occasional lawyer. Located at 47 Fleet Street. Phone: 01-353-6786.

THE MAYFLOWER, London, England: This pub at 117 Rotherhithe Street —

in an area full of old warehouses and wharves on the south side of the Thames in the heart of London's East End — is rather hard to find, but well worth seeking out. Though partly rebuilt in the mid-eighteenth century, bombed during the war, and then restored, it retains a strong flavor of the sixteenth and seventeenth centuries, when it was new; it even has a license to sell British *and* American postage stamps, a courtesy originally provided as a service to passing sailors. Previously known as the Spreadeagle and Crown, it was renamed about 20 years ago to commemorate the sailing of the celebrated *Mayflower*, which was fitted out near this point and sailed from here on the first leg of its famous voyage to Plymouth Rock. An old copy of the passenger list (on parchment, no less) is on display inside; outdoors, there's a model of the Pilgrim Fathers and a milestone that indicates the distance to London Bridge (2 miles). The river is best seen at low tide, when children scramble to their hearts' delight among the driftwood and seawrack.

SHERLOCK HOLMES, London, England: Forget about Baker Street; This Northumberland Street pub, which Conan Doyle used to frequent when it was called the Northumberland Arms (and which he mentioned in his *Hound of the Baskervilles*), is the nearest you will come to the great man. Drawings and photographs of actors playing Holmes and of scenes from Holmes and all manner of other Holmesiana adorn the downstairs bar; upstairs, on the way to a first-floor restaurant, there's a replica of Holmes's Baker Street study, cleverly walled off by glass. The collection of memorabilia was assembled in 1951 by the Sherlock Holmes Society of London for the Festival of Britain, and this smart and congenial pub — whose clientele, appropriately enough, includes policemen from nearby Scotland Yard — provides it with an excellent home. Phone: 930-2644.

THE PIKE AND EEL, Needingworth, Cambridgeshire, England: Pubs where fishermen congregate tend to be clubby places, however humble, and ordinary visitors may not feel welcome. This establishment, built of brick in the sixteenth century and much extended during Oliver Cromwell's time, is an exception — yet there's no mistaking where its loyalties lie: In front, a large garden, with lawns and umbrella-shaded tables, runs down to the river Ouse, where yachts and cabin cruisers are moored in summer. And inside, glass cases show off stuffed pike and eels (not particularly agreeable to look at, but a favorite quarry of nighttime fishermen hereabouts). The flat, windswept, and mysterious fens that surround this low-ceilinged, oak-beamed pub make it all the cozier, and it's pleasant to spend the night in one of the handful of rooms available to overnight lodgers. The restaurant has a fine local reputation, particularly for Dover sole and halibut dishes; bar snacks are also good. Needingworth is not far from St. Ives. Phone: St. Ives 63336.

PLOUGH AND SAIL, Paglesham, Essex, England: This clapboard-walled pub is better known by yachtsmen than by passing motorists: The location — not far from the town of Rochford, near the Essex marshes within sniffing distance of the North Sea — is wonderfully remote, and cars just do not pass. Yet the pub itself is remarkably lively thanks to the vivacious family of broad-speaking former East Enders who run the place. It is also quite comfortable — but charming and very much of the period. Summer weekends bring crowds; at other times, things are quieter, and in chilly weather, there's always a log fire crackling on the hearth. The bar snacks are great. Phone: Canewdon 242.

BLACK SWAN, Stratford-upon-Avon, Warwickshire, England: Sir John Gielgud, Albert Finney, Peter O'Toole, and Glenda Jackson have all frequented this place at one time or another: The "Dirty Duck," as it's informally known, is very much the actors' hangout. That is due in part to a location conveniently down the street from Stratford's Shakespeare Memorial Theatre, but in equal part, perhaps, to a certain attitude on the part of the management that rates the comforts of its thespian patrons as a high priority. No matter that less illustrious visitors may have to try a little harder to order some of that wonderful steak and kidney pie—there's always someone interesting to look at while waiting. An added benefit is that while normal pub hours are kept in principle, it's usually possible to have a pint or two a bit beyond the time that establishments in the rest of England have closed down. Phone: Stratford-upon-Avon 297312.

ROSE AND CROWN, Tewin, Hertfordshire, England: Overlooking the village green, in a part of the Home Counties whose peaceful aspect belies its relative nearness to London (about 25 miles) and its even greater proximity to the new town of Welwyn Garden City, the *Rose and Crown* is a typical country local, with a mixed clientele — deadly serious darts players, who monopolize the boards in the public bar for matches with representatives from neighboring towns' watering spots; village elders, playing cribbage or dominoes; children, who frolic out in the garden in summer; and stylish young people, who favor the comfortable pile-carpeted lounge. The bar snacks are good, and the warm, pleasant, candlelit restaurant serves up traditional English food like roast beef, steak-and-kidney pie, and jugged hare, at modest prices. Phone: Tewin 7257.

HOLE IN THE WALL, Tunbridge Wells, Kent, England: From the mid-seventeenth century until the early 1970s, this red-brick structure known in Victorian times as the Central Smoking Divan and believed to date back to the Restoration, housed a tobacconist's shop; the snug in the rear was virtually unknown. The establishment that now occupies the premises is still a bit off the beaten track, tucked away as it is at 9 High Street. But it's otherwise transformed. The interior space has been divided into two tiers, one overlooking the other; and both areas are full of red flocked wallpaper and comfortable furniture with upholstery to match. There's a separate restaurant, but the homemade pies and pasties and assorted other bar snacks served in the single bar are quite tasty. The variety of beer available is also good, since this is a so-called free house — not owned by a brewery like most in England. Phone: 0892-26550.

ROYAL OAK, Winsford, Somerset, England: There are other pubs that claim to be 300 years older than this archetypically pretty West Country village inn adorned outside by hanging flower baskets. But, as it dates from the fourteenth century, it still ranks among the nation's oldest, and it is certainly one of the most imposing properties in the area, with its whitewashed stone walls, its thick thatched roof, and its interesting sign — an oak surrounding the head of Charles I. (Such a tree, which supposedly sheltered the king during his flight from Cromwellian troops, functions in English lore much like the beds in which George Washington slept: There are whole galaxies of communities which, in search of a claim to fame, have managed to come up with one.) The *Royal Oak,* which is popular with passing tourists, has two bars, both heavily beamed — a traditionally spartan public, with a dart board; and a comfortable lounge. Good snacks are served, including a fine steak-and-kidney pie. Minehead is the closest good-sized town. Phone: Winsford 232.

GLOBE INN, Dumfries, Dumfries and Galloway, Scotland: To most Scots, the poet Robert Burns is Shakespeare, Tolstoy, Mozart, and Beethoven all rolled into one; and so, the fact that this pub on a narrow alley near 56 High Street was his "favourite howff" makes it very important indeed — even though it was old even before he knew it, and even though only one room of the building where Burns lodged is really part of today's *Globe.* Certainly, it's an exceptionally charming place — and would be even if you couldn't see verses that the poet inscribed onto glass with a diamond stylus, sleep in the room where Burns slept (albeit on rare occasions), and sit in his favorite chair. The *Globe* has as its signpost not a globe, but Burns's head. Meals served at lunchtime — on the order of soups, roast beef, Yorkshire pudding, and sweets — are good and inexpensive. Phone: 0387-2335.

THE TILTED WIG, Edinburgh, Scotland: This locally famous city pub at 1 Cumberland St., in elegant, classically inspired New Town, names among its distinctions a garden where, in summer, you can sit under umbrellas and order from a waitress; a good selection of beers (real ale among them); and a clientele that, as the name suggests, includes a disproportionate number of lawyers and solicitors, especially at lunchtime. You might well think you'd walked in on some private club: The walls are hung with all manner of etchings and engravings on juridical subjects, elegant French wallpaper adorns the ceiling, and there's oak paneling to complete the cozy effect. Among the assortment of good bar snacks, there's haggis. Phone: 031-556-9409.

OWAIN GLYNDWR HOTEL, Corwen, Clwyd, Wales: Here's a place with real local character. Used by townspeople more often than by tourists, this establishment on the town square occupies a plaster-over-stone building that was partly built in the thirteenth century, used to be a monastery's outbuilding, and is said to be haunted by the ghost of the fifteenth-century Welsh freedom fighter Owen Glendower. There are three bars — among them an unpretentious old-style public bar with a dart board and a juke box; another — rather plush and cozy with its red carpet, original oak beams, decorative horse brasses, and old saddles; and yet another, a small one attached to the restaurant. And on tap, you won't find the aerated (and even gassy) pressurized brews, but instead a good range of real ales. Bar snacks like scampi or steak and chips are provided as well as complete meals. Phone: Corwen 2115.

GROES HOTEL, Ty'n-y-Groes, near Conwy, Gwynedd, Wales: The oldest pub in Wales, as many believe, is installed in a building that was already old when the license was issued in 1573. Whitewashed and pleasantly tree-shaded, with thick walls constructed from locally quarried Conwy stone, which may date from an Ice Age, the pub is full of charming antique settles — the kind of high-backed wooden benches traditionally used for sitting in front of the fire on a cold night because of the protection they afforded from cold drafts. Here, the fireplace conceals a locally famous "priest hole," the hideaway for many a devout Roman Catholic during Elizabeth I's reign. The views — out over the Conwy valley and distant Snowdon, Wales's highest mountain — are outstanding, and the bar and restaurant specialties, among them fish and homemade steak pie, are worth saving your appetite for. Phone: Ty'n-y-Groes 249.

DURTY NELLIE'S, Bunratty, Co. Clare, Irish Republic: In the opinion of some experts, this is the finest pub in Ireland. Situated on the main road within 10 miles of Limerick City and Shannon Airport, it is next door to Bunratty Castle, where the buses disgorge great clumps of tourists bound for the medieval banquets (see *Mead and Meat Pies: Historical Banquets*); and so the pub is never without its share of rubberneckers, mostly American. Nonetheless, the large majority of people in the vast and almost always crowded premises are Irish — and very intent on enjoying themselves in the lounge, where the tourists go; in the local bar, where they do not; or in the piano room, separating the two, from which the highest volume of music comes. Upstairs is what the management terms the "quiet bar"; and sure enough, it's an oasis of stillness, where the murmuring of the two dozen white doves kept by owner Roger Porritt is about the only sound. The *Oyster*, the restaurant on the premises, which has a small stand-up bar, is also pleasant; you may sit at the tables only if you are ordering a meal. The fare is good, the prices reasonable, and the restaurant is popular with locals on a night out. If you are not of a mind for a full meal, try the roasted corned-beef-cheese-and-onion sandwiches, which are available in the bars. Music and song may erupt in *Durty Nellie's* at any time; it's welcomed and even encouraged by the enlightened management. Phone: 061-74861 or 061-74072.

HENCHY'S, Cork, Co. Cork, Irish Republic: Cork City is a kind of independent nation within the Republic, and the rest of the Irish are often made to feel that they should show their passports when they enter the environs. This has much to do with the distinctive singsong local accent, whose subtle variations may be heard at *Henchy's* — at least by those with an ear fine-tuned to linguistic distinctions. If yours isn't, you'll enjoy the spectacle anyway. All levels of Cork society are represented — even to the odd poet, a regular, who is very odd indeed. The pub, a night place if ever there was one with a fine snug, is owned and almost entirely run by women (a not uncommon situation, with the husband usually holding another job). The pub is at 40 St. Luke's.

THE OYSTER TAVERN, Cork, Co. Cork, Irish Republic: While *Henchy's* is splendid for *drinking* and listening, this not-to-be-missed wonder, tucked away off Patrick Street in a small arcade opposite *Bolger's*, is delightful for *eating* and listening. The food, particularly the fish, is fine: The whitebait is delicious enough, and the portion generous enough, to make a main dish in itself when it's on the menu. But the real joy is hearing the maitre d' sing out, "Your table will be ready in five more minutes, *Professor*" (or *"Doctor,"* or even, bless the mark, *"Surgeon,"* as the case may be — Cork people are very high on titles). Phone: 021-22716.

THE BAILEY OF DUKE STREET, Dublin, Irish Republic: The watering place for generations of Dublin's writers and artists directly across the street from *Davy Byrne's* (below) has been preempted by ubiquitous youth, and the clientele is now what can only be described as androgynous, with not a writer or artist in sight. At night, it's definitely for the young and pretty of all sexes, but at other times, there is peace, and time to admire the handsome iron-and-marble tables. The best way to use the pub is to meet for drinks at noon, and, at about one (having reserved a table), climb the stairs to the restaurant overhead, where the food is quite good and the service faultless; on your way up or down, be sure to study the original door of Bloom's house at 7 Eccles Street, lovingly preserved by the Bailey's former owner, artist and patron John Ryan. Phone: 773055/770600.

THE BRAZENHEAD, Dublin, Irish Republic: Here, legend has it, the winsome Robert Emmet plotted the ragged and abortive little rebellion of 1803. Although only a few hundred yards from *Guinness's* famous brewery, the Brazenhead hubristically disdains to serve draft stout. It is a dark and very intimate place, with hallways leading off in all directions, one of them into the little room where the poetry and music sessions are held. The poetry readings have a charmingly inverted nature: One gets the impression that the people are listening to poetry while drinking, rather than the opposite. Outside on the quays and not too far away is the church immortalized by James Joyce in the opening line of *Finnegans Wake:* "riverrun, past Eve and Adam's, from swerve of shore to bend of bay, brings us by a commodious vicus of recirculation back to Howth Castle and environs." You may pause a while and watch the seagulls swoop and screech above Anna Livia Plurabella. This seventeenth-century "hotel" on Bridge St. is not easily found: Better ask a taxi driver. Phone: 779549.

DAVY BYRNE'S OF DUKE STREET, Dublin, Irish Republic: Nothing remains of the pub where, on June 16, 1904, Leopold Bloom had Gorgonzola cheese and his glass of Burgundy, and, nowadays, you may have to settle for Irish Brie and a bottle of claret. This causes consternation to some avid Joyceans. The story goes that a fervent one from Seattle, having saved his money for 20 years, at last had salted away enough to visit Ireland. He stepped inside the "moral pub" that Joyce had described, took in the "renovation" in one horrified glance, and headed straight back to Seattle — obviously, not one of the Beautiful People. They converge here; look each other over; converse in high, self-conscious voices; and sometimes find new partners. Sandwiches, salads, and cheese (including the above-mentioned Brie, which is surprisingly good) constitute the unassuming lunch fare, and the walls are decorated with what one nonbeautiful Dubliner called "muriels." Phone: 711298.

DOHENY & NESBITT'S, Dublin, Irish Republic: This Lower Baggot Street establishment, owned and run by Ned Doheny and Tom Nesbitt, who served their time in New York and returned 20 years ago to buy the place and leave it mercifully unrenovated, is very small, and late at night, especially on weekends, it's almost impossible to breathe for the heaving mass of trainee architects, students from the College of Art around the corner, and tired political pundits taking time off from reporting the proceedings in the Dail (parliament), also around the corner. So come early, or, better still, sidle in at noontime, when you will have breathing space and an opportunity to munch on hot beef sandwiches, medium, well-done, or (rare treat in Ireland) rare. The bar is close to the National Museum, National Library, National Gallery of Art, and St. Stephen's Green, that wonderful city-center oasis of quietude, ponds, and trees. Phone: 762945.

MULLIGAN'S OF POOLBEG STREET, Dublin, Irish Republic: This very old pub, which has been in existence since the 1750s, serves nothing but plain drink. But what it does, it does well, and the pint of Guinness draft you get here is probably the most consistently good, if not the best, in the country. (A constant flow throughout the day is the secret.) The curates — that is to say, the barkeeps — have abandoned their charming aprons, but it is still possible to visualize what it was like to drink here 100 years ago. There are three rooms in constant use, and, since the pub is situated between the harbor, the *Irish Press*, and Trinity College, the patrons include journalists, dockworkers, and students. In these frantically egalitarian days, part of the fun of drinking in *Mulligan's* is guessing whether that long-haired melancholic in the corner is a longshoreman, a music critic, or an aspiring Lionel Trilling. Phone: 775582.

NEARY'S OF CHATHAM STREET, Dublin, Irish Republic: The back door of this pub opens directly opposite the stage door of the *Gaiety*, the capital's principal variety theater, so the noises here are made mostly by actors, musicians, and the sort of pallid cohorts that these two professions attract. Visiting celebrities from both professions drop in here from time to time, so you may find yourself rubbing shoulders with the great. When this happens, the place is full and there is little comfort, but at lunchtime, it's easy to find consolation in the sandwiches, or, in season, fresh oysters. Four beautiful gas lamps stand on the marble counter, the seating is plush and bouncy, and there is usually a young "lounge boy" running his feet off trying to serve everybody at once. Phone: 777371.

THE STAG'S HEAD, Dublin, Irish Republic: Nowadays, this classic on Dame Lane (off Dame Street), gorgeously fitted out right down to its stained-glass windows, generally draws a clientele from all strata of society, but at lunchtime on weekdays you will note a preponderance of the pinstripe vests, fob watches, and cold noses of members of the legal profession as they dig into their hot meat-and-two-veg meals. You never know whom you'll meet, because the pub is awkward to get to. (But the conservationists who yelped with dismay at a recent threat to pull it down are seldom moved to actually visit the place.) Phone: 779307.

MORAN'S OYSTER COTTAGE, The Weir, Kilcolgan, Co. Galway, Irish Republic: A family-run, thatch-roofed pub over 100 years old, hard by the tidal river, *Moran's*, which started serving oysters and crab in a small way back in the 1960s, is now a thriving and much-extended bar and seafood restaurant. If you are a party of four, six, or eight, this is the perfect place for a lunch in one of the comfortable snugs or, if the weather is fine, outside in the sunshine, at the tables in front of the pub. Galway oysters are served with homemade brown bread — which sends most Americans into a swoon — butter, and Guinness. Or you may have smoked salmon, dressed crab, or any of a number of soups. There is never much to choose from, but what little there is is always delicious, and the wine list is adequate to the fare. *Moran's* is an important part of the Galway Oyster Festival (see *Festivals*), a jolly gathering much beloved of Ireland's nouveau riche crowd, which descends on the town in force every year in mid-September. Phone: 091-8613.

SEAGAN UA NEACHTÁIN, TABHARNEOIR, Galway, Co. Galway, Irish Republic: Ireland's western capital has a number of comfortable and well-run pubs, but none as authentic and little-changed as this family house at the corner of Cross and Quay streets, which is still (as almost all pubs once were) a grocery shop as well. Some nights the main door of the pub (above which the name of the owner is written out in Irish) will not open, and you must go around to the side door (on Quay Street), and give a knock. You will be quietly ushered into a small room, the pub's one-and-only, where someone may be singing a lament or playing a tune on the tin whistle. And if you make too much noise, you may be shushed. The pub is the antithesis of *Durty Nellie's:* Voices are never raised, Irish is often spoken, and potential patrons are carefully screened. The typical, quiet, Irish pub of old. Maybe the last of them. No phone.

THE TOWERS HOTEL, Glenbeigh, Co. Kerry, Irish Republic: Hotel bars are much of a muchness — with a few noble exceptions — among them the *Horseshoe Bar* of Dublin's *Shelbourne* and this one, which is really an annex to a justly famous seafood restaurant. To a tiny extent, the *Towers* is famous for being famous, and the bar walls are lined with pictures of the Burl Ivesean former proprietor, Ernie Evans, in the company of the dozens of international celebrities who have enjoyed his largesse. Françoise Sagan and her ilk (if there be such) come and while away the time here, for instance — and understandably, since Glenbeigh is the perfect base for exploring the Ring of Kerry. There is music here every night, much of it of the inspired amateur variety and some of it even very enjoyable. The *Glenbeigh Hotel* down the road has delightful rooms; ideally, you'll stay there, and eat, drink, and be very merry at the *Towers.* Phone: Glenbeigh 12.

AHERNE'S PUB & SEAFOOD BAR, North Main Street, Youghal, Co. Cork, Irish Republic: For complex historical reasons, the Irish are, at best, indifferent to fish and only very gradually is the prejudice (ludicrous in an island people) being abandoned; this establishment owned and managed by former army captain Gerry Fitzgibbon, his wife Betty, and their family — perhaps the best and most unpretentious pub restaurant in the south — is in the vanguard of the movement to dissipate it. In the bar, you can get smoked mackerel, smoked salmon, oysters, and dressed crab, in addition to chicken liver pâté, vegetarian salad, and all kinds of succulent sandwiches; and in the restaurant, lobster, scallops, prawns, mussels, black sole, fresh trout, and salmon from the River Blackwater, which enters the sea here, are served, as well as a number of nonpiscine dishes. A wine bar was added not long ago. Youghal (pronounced yawl) is worth visiting anyway: An attractive Victorian seaside resort, it is the location for the house where, legend has it, Sir Walter Raleigh grew the first potatoes in Europe. The bar food at *Aherne's* is available all day, but it is advisable to call for reservations to eat in the restaurant. Phone: 024-2424.

CROWN SALOON, Belfast, Northern Ireland: This venerable establishment on Great Victoria Street, opposite the *Europa Hotel,* has recently been marked for preservation by the National Trust — as it well deserves. The windows are stained glass, the floor is of mosaic tiles, the stone fireplace is immense, the walls are covered with brocade, and the snugs — where serious drinkers can hoist their pints in contented privacy — are in the same good condition you might have found them when the place was built back in Victorian days. Next door, and notable, is *Robinson's,* which has ornate papered walls, a mahogany bar, polished wooden snugs, and a men's room dubbed "Adamant."

BLAKE'S OF THE HOLLOW, Enniskillen, Co. Fermanagh, Northern Ireland: Noted for its handmade lace, its attractive knit sweaters, and its Belleek china, Enniskillen is also home to this handsome old pub, tucked away in a rabbit's warren of streets and alleys not far from St. Macarton's Cathedral. The bar is long, made of solid mahogany with a top of solid marble; the snugs, made of pine, are attractive enough to warrant praise from Ulster Heritage Societies publications; and the alcoholic specialty of the house is 10- and 15-year-old Dublin pot-still Irish whiskey, so rare in Ireland as to be almost a collector's item. As for the mood, it is always subdued, and television intrudes on the drinkers' solitude only for major sporting events. The entrance on Church St. is easiest to find.

Rural Retreats

To travelers from abroad, the most striking features of the British and Irish countrysides are the absence of billboards, the almost total lack of motels — and the abundance of homey inns, guesthouses, and country-manors-turned-hotels. The tradition of inn-keeping, particularly in England, goes back for centuries, and you can tell: Wooden stair treads are worn to concavity by the footsteps of travelers down over the ages; and walls are half-timbered, ceilings beamed. In northern England, the lodging places tend toward the rickety-and-quaint; in the south, there is an excellent assortment of charming, country house hotels. Ireland, which for a long time demonstrated a notable lack of such hostelries-with-personality, has been catching up fast.

As for the food, establishments in both Britain and Ireland are in varying states of emergence from the age of soggy sprouts and overcooked plaice, meat roasted to a fare-thee-well, and vegetables that would make the army's steamtable offerings look crisp. A whole generation of young Irish chefs, trained on the Continent and, in a surprising number of cases, at the hotel school at Shannon, have brought the kind of new look to the nation's menus that England, Scotland, and Wales began to see a few years ago. This means a respect for the freshness of ingredients so intense that some masters of the new cuisine don't just go out and buy the best that the local market has to offer, they also work with local farmers to have vegetables planted and grown to their specifications. The undeniably positive by-products are no longer destroyed through overcooking. And unlike some of the practitioners of the nouvelle cuisine in France, the new chefs here are seldom overly fussy about their presentations, but instead (particularly in Ireland), delightfully straightforward and unpretentious.

In both Britain and Ireland, some of these special establishments are more noteworthy than others — either because of their decor, the friendliness of their management (more often than not a whole family), or their setting or food. Here is an assortment of some of the best castle-hotels, inns, country houses, and restaurants the rural region has to offer. Some warrant a stop when you're in the area; a handful of others, perhaps a shade more wonderful on one or more counts, are worth planning a whole holiday around.

WORTH A LONG DETOUR

ELMS HOTEL, Abberley, near Worcester, Hereford and Worcester, England: Built primarily during the early eighteenth century after designs by a student of Sir Christopher Wren, then added to during a neo-Classical 1927, this grand country house has a magnificent tree-lined drive and gardens as clipped and formal as they come; the scene suggests morning suits and garden-party hats, white gloves and flouncy dresses. The interiors are just as elegant, from the sumptuously carpeted oak staircase to the public rooms full of tufted settees and velvet-upholstered chairs and the fine Library Bar, still boasting its original mahogany bookcases; the guest rooms boast oil paintings, interesting knickknacks, spacious bathrooms, antique furnishings (one room is graced by a four-poster bed), and—not the least important—fine views over the surrounding park. But despite the luxury of the setting, the Elms is never stuffy, and it's easy to spend days on end strolling across the grounds, batting tennis balls on the hotel's courts, and practicing your putting on its green. Details: The Elms Hotel, Abberley, Hereford and Worcester WR6 6AT, England (phone: Great Witley 666).

EASTWELL MANOR, Ashford, Kent, England: Set in some 3,000 acres of parkland picturesquely speckled with fluffy white sheep, this elegant, rambling stone country house was opened as a hotel just in 1980, but, though the present house was rebuilt in 1926, its history can be traced back to the Norman Conquest; over the years it has had 20 owners, and Queen Victoria once made a visit here. (You can see a picture of her, seated in a chair on the manor's frozen lake, surrounded by the other members of her skating party, when you arrive for a stay). In 1977, the estate was bought as a working farm and shooting preserve by the Bates family, renovated by the elder Bates's construction company, decorated by his wife, and turned over to their son Matthew to manage, and has been earning hearty kudos ever since, for a lavish use of space and splendid service that reminds guests of an earlier, grander age: One visitor called it "the world's best twenty-room hotel." Though the rooms are absolutely huge, they are so cleverly decorated with sitting areas, soft colors, and pretty fabrics, that they seem positively inviting; all of the bathrooms are vast, but some are sumptuous as well. Among public rooms, there's an oak-paneled bar to lure guests down for drinks before dinner, which is served in a baronial dining room. The menu is French, with an emphasis on nouvelle cuisine; you can order such delicacies as *aspèrges feuilletées au beurre fondu* and *fricassée de fruits de mer*. Since the young chef is English, there is also a short menu of local specialties — among them smoked eel and roast English lamb (which, like the beef, comes from the estate). A very extensive wine list, which includes two English wines, complements the offerings. Details: Eastwell Manor, Eastwell Park, Ashford, Kent TN25 4HR, England (phone: 0233-35751).

BELL INN, Aston Clinton, Buckinghamshire, England: Once a favorite of Evelyn Waugh, this former coaching post of the Duke of Buckinghamshire has been welcoming guests since about 1650. But seldom during the last three centuries has it looked quite as lovely as it does today, with its cozy bar—the ceiling beamed, the floor paved in flagstones, the air warmed by the fire blazing away on the hearth—and its scattering of antiques. Fresh flowers are a common sight, both in the public rooms and in the guest quarters, which are located in former stables and malt houses ranged around a small, cobbled courtyard. Bath salts, bathroom scales, and thick terry robes, refrigerators stocked to answer post-midnight thirsts, and other amenities complete the picture. The setting, on A41 a few miles east of Aylesbury and not far distant from Heathrow, is not the nation's most pastoral, but when one is cosseted in that fashion, it almost doesn't matter. And the food is good enough to warrant a special mention. While you will find traditional English fare such as tipsy cake and poached salmon, it's also possible to savor wondrous French specialties such as *caneton ballottine*, a savory, crisp-skinned boned duckling; the wine list is especially fine. Details: Bell Inn, Aston Clinton, Buckinghamshire HP22 5HP, England (phone: Aylesbury 0296-630252).

WATERSIDE INN, Bray-on-Thames, Berkshire, England: Two Michelin stars have been awarded to only a very few restaurants in England, yet the fact that the *Waterside Inn* can claim this distinction is only part of the reason to make a detour to the village of Bray, not far from Windsor and 34 miles west of London. Owners Albert Roux and his brother Michael Roux (French chefs with embassy experience and service *chez* the best private families before they opened *Le Gavroche* in London, now a Michelin three-star winner) chose to open their country restaurant on the banks of the Thames in a setting that provides a feast for the eyes before the feast for the palate begins. In spring, enormous red tulips are in bloom all around the outside windows, flowering cherry trees line the river, and swans circle past almost as though summoned by a magic wand. In summer, you can move out into this backdrop and enjoy a before-dinner drink on the terrace, letting the sight of weeping willows and boats on the water distract you — momentarily — from the extraordinary menu. The Roux brothers are ceaselessly inventive, but among their enduring specialties are a fish mousse appetizer, enclosed in a crêpe, decorated with a stripe of spinach mousse flavored with Pernod, tarragon, and leek; *tournedos Arlette*, a fine piece of beef, cooked to perfection and lightly sauced with butter and Dijon mustard; and *sablé aux poires,* a dessert of fresh pears on a shortcake topped with light custard and a fresh strawberry sauce. The wine list is first rate and some of the restaurant's personal touches are charming. Tiny hot tomato hors d'oeuvres, served with cocktails, are unabashedly described as tiny pizzas; finger bowls are masculine and feminine, i.e., flowers for the lady, a slice of lemon for the gentlemen. The cost of all this is "rather dear," as the typically understated British would say, but less than what its equivalent would come to in Paris and well worth it for a special and memorable dining occasion. Closed Mondays, Sunday dinners from October through Easter, and for about four weeks from December 25. Note that the inn does not have rooms. Details: Waterside Inn, Bray-on-Thames, Berkshire SL6 2AT, England (phone: 0628-20691).

LYGON ARMS, Broadway, Hereford and Worcester, England: The *Lygon Arms* wasn't founded nearly as long ago as some houses and public buildings in the Cotswolds, but 1532 seems a respectable enough birthdate; that makes it old enough to have frequently welcomed Charles I as a guest and to have harbored Oliver Cromwell on the eve of the battle of Worcester. But there are indications that the building itself is much older: A stone fireplace set into one 4-foot-thick wall, for instance, which appears to have been crafted in the fourteenth century; and the front doorway and the rear courtyard door date from the fifteenth century. All of the rooms are furnished with antiques of similarly remarkable vintage, and a few pieces are of quality substantial enough to be illustrated in *The Dictionary of English Furniture.* The nine rooms in what is called the old wing are particularly charming — a study in Tudor, with beams, charmingly tilted oak floors, and dozens of blue Spode dishes on the fireplace mantels; the Great Chamber — one of the hotel's most famous rooms, for its vaulted timber-crossed ceiling and its massive canopied bed — is number 20. The rooms in the new wing, only a shade less charming, boast plumbing that is a bit more dependable. All this is as you might expect in the inn that is probably Britain's most photographed. What may surprise you is the quality of the service. For example, if you ordered Foster's Lager on your previous visit, and you arrive late on a hot, sunny afternoon, along with your tea will be a Foster's. As for meals, they are elegant, and though the Great Hall, with its barrel-vaulted ceiling, great fireplace, and fine wood paneling, has never been one of the area's best restaurants (and you were well advised to stick to English standbys like roast beef and Yorkshire pudding, steak and kidney pie, or saddle of lamb), this situation may well change with the arrival of a talented young chef named Shaun Hall. At any rate, the after-theater suppers — consisting of smoked salmon, cold chicken, roast beef, salad, and fresh strawberries — can be a joy, as are the game dishes, served in season. The wide, mile-long street on which the inn fronts, is almost as pretty as the cream-colored stone hotel itself, and Stratford-upon-Avon is just 20 miles away. Details: The Lygon Arms, Broadway, Hereford and Worcester WR12 7DU, England (phone: 0386-852255).

THE GEORGE HOTEL, Chollerford, Northumberland, England: On the banks of the romantic River Tyne near Humshaugh and Hexham, not far from the Roman camp of Chester, this creeper-clad establishment is equipped with most creature comforts — yet it never relinquishes the coziness that has always made it one of Northumberland's outstanding hotels. You'll find both a public bar and a hotel bar (where drinks are more expensive), charming riverside gardens where you can arrange to have your afternoon tea on a warm summer's afternoon, plus fishing and putting on the hotel grounds and superb hiking in the surrounding countryside. There are some 54 rooms here in all; those in the new annex are the larger. Details: George Hotel, Chollerford, Northumberland NE46 4EW, England (phone: 043481-611).

GRAVETYE MANOR, near East Grinstead, West Sussex, England: Located about halfway between London and Brighton, at the end of a meandering country road some 4 miles from East Grinstead, this ivy-covered Elizabethan manor house, built by one Roger Infield for his bride, Katherine Compton, in 1598 and enlarged in the same style over the centuries since, has become one of rural England's most impressive hostelries since it was converted to use as a hotel in 1958; it's now internationally known. One point of fame is its gardens, created by *Gravetye*'s most famous owner, the great English horticulturalist William Robinson, who eschewed the formalized style that had been favored until then for a more natural look. In the years after his death in 1935, the gardens suffered badly, and it was left to the present owners to restore them to their former glory; whether you see them during a stroll along the garden paths, or through your mullioned windows, they never cease to give pleasure. Robinson's influence is felt inside as well. The rooms are paneled with the estate's oak, bouquets of flowers he planted brighten the corners of all the rooms, and the 15 guest rooms are named for English trees such as bay, holly, beech, and ash. Many of these rooms have fireplaces; all have thick carpets, soothing decor, and such extras as a fruit basket, an ice-water thermos, books, a hair dryer, and a special red telephone for emergencies. Touches like these have earned the hotel its membership in the prestigious Relais et Chateaux group. Its restaurant's Michelin star is equally well-deserved. Current owner Peter Herbert takes justifiable pride in his wine list, one of the most extensive in the country, and in his menu, which changes with the season. Among the highlights: a velvety chicken liver pâté, *sole de Douvre Victoria* (grilled Dover sole garnished with langoustine, avocado, and tomato), the tenderest Scotch beef, and a selection of fresh vegetables from *Gravetye*'s own kitchen garden, cooked to crisp perfection. A separate dessert menu lists some 20 sweets (including homemade sorbets and ice creams) plus savories and cheeses. There are ways to work off a bit of excess: playing croquet on the lawn, fishing in the well-stocked trout pond, or sight-seeing in the neighborhood, where there are several other gardens of note. Details: Gravetye Manor, East Grinstead, West Sussex RH19 4LJ, England (phone: 0342-810567).

COMBE HOUSE, Gittisham, Devon, England: It takes a long time to wend your way down the winding drive to *Combe House,* a cream-colored Elizabethan mansion that dates back to the fourteenth century; but it doesn't particularly matter because the lush emerald parkland that rolls around you on all sides, studded with rhododendrons, magnolias, and cherry trees, is so lovely. The mansion, owned by a descendant of Dr. Johnson's biographer James Boswell, is roomy, elegant, and furnished throughout with antiques, but not too formal; and almost every room has something that catches your eye: the ornate plaster ceiling and gleaming paneling in the main hall, full of squashy chintz-covered chairs, for instance; or the pink dining room's rococo fireplace, attributed to Chippendale, depicting the fable of the fox and the crow; or the bar (the kind of place solitary travelers might enter and find friendly and gregarious faces), hung with old hunting and coaching prints. Most guest rooms are exceptionally large and — a rare and therefore notable bonus — very quiet. And the food is good, thanks to Cordon Bleu–trained Therese Boswell, the chef and co-owner. The hotel has fishing rights to 1.5 miles of the south bank of the river Otter, which can produce some good creels of brown trout, and the establishment makes an excellent base for tours of East Devon, and for visits to nearby golf courses or to the ocean only 7 miles away. Details: Combe House Hotel, Gittisham, near Honiton, Devon EX14 OAD, England (phone: 0404-2756).

THE BOX TREE, Ilkley, West Yorkshire, England: This small restaurant may just be the chief industry of the small town of Ilkley, 16 miles northwest of Leeds. When Englishmen Malcolm Reid and Colin Long opened it in a 300-year-old cottage nearly 20 years ago, they served afternoon teas only, because they were entirely unschooled in the gastronomic arts and the operation of a restaurant. Over the years, as they taught themselves and business grew, they graduated from teas to lunches to dinners, and finally to a two-star rating by the august *Michelin Guide,* an honor shared by only a few other restaurants in their native land. This extraordinary increase in stature, however, has not been accompanied by a comparable increase in size. The *Box Tree* still seats about 50 diners and, given its reputation, you can now hardly get in the door. Even with reservations, you may spend a bit of time in a waiting room attractively stocked with the owners' collection of antique English porcelain. The rest of the restaurant is decorated with more antiques and genuine objets d'art, replacements for the reproductions that were good enough for tea but not for grand cuisine. The menu is not overly long, though there is certainly enough to choose from: The *coquilles Saint-Jacques* and the *dariole de champignons et truffes,* for starters, have been praised in the past; the *marquise au chocolat et cognac* is a popular dessert. In between, any number of entrées are worthy and the wine list is weighty — some 200 selections, including "native" wines. The *Box Tree* is open for dinner only (lunches and teas were dropped years ago). It's closed Sundays, Mondays, the first week in February, and 2 weeks in August. Details: The Box Tree, Ilkley, West Yorkshire LS29 9DR, England (phone: 0943-608484).

ARUNDELL ARMS, Lifton, Devon, England: This former coaching inn, covered with Virginia creeper, would be pleasant enough by anyone's standards: Log fires blaze away on the hearths downstairs, the floors are laid with locally quarried dark blue slate, and the culinary offerings (which include an excellent Tamar salmon cooked in pastry with tarragon butter) are of international standard. But it really stands out for its fishing; for half-a-century now, it has owned the fishing rights on 20 miles of the Tamar, the stream that forms the boundary with Cornwall and ranks as the best of the West Country salmon streams, and four of its tributaries, so-called spate rivers, which rise on the moors and deepen and widen as they come down through woods and farming country into the valleys. Some of the smaller streams run knee-deep over pebbly beds, down long riffles of rough white water, sometimes forming deep pools that are especially lovely when dappled with sun and shadow from the leaves of the alder trees whose branches meet overhead. In the course of the last decade or so, the season's salmon take has averaged around 80 (in 1980, 100 were bagged), and there's an abundance of beautifully colored, wild and wily brown trout — small, but scrappy enough to take a dry or wet fly with a great slash and then fight like tigers. Also worth noting is the big run of salmon and sea trout for which the Tamar is famous; the first spring salmon usually have entered *Arundell Arms* waters by mid-May, and the fishing for them, mostly by fly only, runs right through to mid-October. Sea trout fishing runs from July to early September, by fly only, and since the best of the sea trout are taken at night, guests usually go out for them after dinner and fish until midnight or after, sometimes all night. If that's not enough, the great sea- and shark-fishing centers of Looe, Plymouth, and Padstow are not far away. Details: Arundell Arms Hotel, Lifton, Devon PL16 OAA, England (phone: 056684-244 or 056684-456).

COTTAGE IN THE WOOD, Malvern Wells, Malvern, Worcestershire, England: Much more than a cottage, this Georgian mansion — rambling but beautifully proportioned — occupies 7 acres of its own woodlands, and enjoys wonderful views over the Severn Valley. The style is very English and very traditional; both in the main building and in the more modern coach house annex, the rooms are superbly appointed, and the level of maintenance is high. One of the 20 guest rooms boasts a four-poster. The cozy and intimate restaurant is ideal for special meals; English dishes predominate on the menu, and the wine list is excellent. Note that Malvern Wells is distinct from the larger, better-known former spa town just to the north, Great Malvern. But both places are famed for mineral water, and during your stay, you should be sure to try a bottle of the locally produced Malvern Water — sold in London in the 1780s for a princely shilling a bottle. Details: Cottage in the Wood, Holywell Rd., Malvern Wells, Malvern, Worcestershire WR14 4LG, England (phone: 06845-3487).

CHEWTON GLEN HOTEL, New Milton, Hampshire, England: The New Forest, which William the Conqueror claimed as a royal hunting ground in 1079, was already old when this brick mansion went up on 30 acres of peaceful parkland near its fringes. It must have looked a bit raw in contrast at first, but the years have mellowed it and it now seems almost as old as the forest. Since 1967, managing director Martin Skan has renovated the rooms, built new kitchens, completed a modern wing, converted the coach barn and the stable into suites, added a swimming pool and a tennis court, and, along the way, won an Egon Ronay Hotel of the Year award, a Michelin star (albeit only one), and membership in the exclusive Leading Hotels of the World and Relais et Chateaux associations. That those kudos were well-deserved is immediately evident when you see the rooms. Named for characters from *The Children of the New Forest,* whose author Captain Frederick Marryat spent some time in the house during the nineteenth century, they are done up with pretty flowered fabrics that are constantly replaced to keep things looking fresh, and the televisions (color, yet) have been equipped to show a feature film every evening; a bottle of sherry is set out to greet you when you arrive; and the bathrooms come furnished with fragrant bars of Roger & Gallet soap and little packets of Badedas. The same perfectionism pervades the hotel's restaurant, the *Marryat Room,* from the fresh bouquets of flowers and the Villeroy & Boch dinner plates to the exquisite food produced by a 25-year-old French chef and his staff of 12. Though the raw materials are English, the cooking is nouvelle, with sublime specialties such as *coquilles St. Jacques au gingembre; fresh salmon marinated in olive oil, coriander, and lemon juice; canard aux framboises;* roast rib of Scotch filet stuffed with foie gras, baked in pastry, and served with a Périgourdine sauce; chicken cooked in a mint-flavored cream sauce; and more. The wine list offers nearly 200 selections ranging from an inexpensive Moselle to a Château Lafite-Rothschild 1952. There are function rooms and small conference rooms, and your stay may indeed coincide with a very superior seminar of government ministers and senior Whitehall officials or of foreign dignitaries. However, even *Chewton Glen* has its critics, who say that it lacks heart; that it is, perhaps, *too* smooth and *too* professional. You'll appreciate it most if you recognize high standards and are irritated by equally expensive establishments that don't quite measure up. Details: Chewton Glen Hotel, New Milton, Hampshire BH25 6QS, England (phone: 04252-5341).

THE DUCK INN, Pett Bottom, Kent, England: Housed in an unpretentious little sixteenth-century country cottage and patronized by minor royalty and West End stars, this is widely regarded as the best and most exclusive restaurant in southeastern England. Fine French cuisine is painstakingly prepared by Ulla Laina, the only female chef in England to be awarded a Michelin star. Try the *brandade parisienne* (a fresh fish pâté). The *Duck* is not easy to find, but well worth the effort; it's about 5 miles outside Canterbury, near the village of Bridge on the road to Dover. Closed Mondays and Tuesdays, and 2 weeks each in March and October. Details: The Duck Inn, Pett Bottom, Kent CT4 5PB, England (phone: 830354).

SHARROW BAY HOTEL, Pooley Bridge, Cumbria, England: For over three decades, Francis Coulson — an actor who wanted to get away from the London theater — has been cooking up some of Great Britain's best food for guests at this establishment, a member of the Relais et Chateaux group installed in a late seventeenth-century house that had been enlarged over the years to comfortable size, and in a quartet of other buildings nearby. You might have avocado mousse topped with tiny cooked prawns and unsweetened whipped cream; roast pork loin with fresh rosemary, stuffed with sage-and-onion dressing, and served with apple sauce and cracklings; and an egg-custard flan and a coffee soufflé, served with petits fours. Or end with sticky toffee sponge, or almond meringue *gâteau dacquoise* with strawberries, or lemon flummery, or any number of other equally wonderful sweets; the *gâteau Alcazar,* a cake made with almonds and kirsch, is a standout. Considering that the menu's other offerings are equally mouth-watering, it's not surprising that some people motor up from London, 300 miles distant, just to lunch here. What makes *Sharrow Bay* particularly wonderful, however, is that the care that makes every meal such a treat also is accorded the workings of the hotel. The guest rooms are beautifully decorated in the English style, furnished with antiques here and there, plus books, parlor games to amuse, and opera glasses with which to scan the waters of Lake Ullswater, on whose shores the main house fairly floats. Thick carpets everywhere make for a quiet more intense than even the country setting alone could afford, and the efficient central heating system keeps the old house beautifully warm when the weather is chill. The proprietors, Francis Coulson and Brian Sack (who joined Coulson in 1952), try to welcome all their guests personally on arrival, and the feeling is very much of visiting someone's very elegant country home. There are 29 bedrooms altogether, 19 of them with private bathrooms or showers; just under half are in the main house, with the others scattered among a cottage and a gatehouse on the grounds, a converted farmhouse a mile away, and a seventeenth-century cottage in the village of Tirril 4 miles distant. Closed December through February. Details: Sharrow Bay Hotel, Penrith, Cumbria CA10 2LZ, England (phone: 08536-301/483).

KING'S HEAD HOTEL, Richmond, Yorkshire, England: This 23-room establishment on the edge of the impressive cobbled marketplace has hardly changed at all since the eighteenth century — at least on the outside. Inside, however, it's plush, warm, and welcoming. The wide main staircase, the sort that ladies *glide* down on their way to the bar, makes it a real pleasure to travel to and fro from the guest rooms, which are full of eighteenth-century features — sash windows, elaborate moldings, high ceilings, decorative paneled doors — and carpeted with red or rich patterns to set off the white or cream walls. The restaurant is comfortable and the service solicitous; the best tables overlook the marketplace. Details: King's Head Hotel, Richmond, Yorkshire D40 4H5, England (phone: 0748-2311).

THE GEORGE OF STAMFORD, Stamford, Lincolnshire, England: The gallows sign originally put up to scare away highwaymen still hangs in front of the inn, and you can almost hear the London and Edinburgh stagecoaches clattering to a stop when you have a drink in the still-preserved cobbled yard behind the hotel. The entranceway has floors of stone, the ceiling in the bar is beamed, and, throughout the establishment, you'll find paneling and rough stone walls. All in all, it's very comfortable, with good food available both in the restaurant and the bar. Of the close to 50 rooms in the hotel, most have baths; the ones in the front can be a bit noisy because of the passing traffic. Stamford itself, a study in gray stone, is a gem. Details: The George, St. Martin's High St., Stamford, Lincolnshire, England (phone: 0780-55171).

ALVESTON MANOR HOTEL, Stratford-upon-Avon, Warwickshire, England: Whether or not *Midsummer Night's Dream* actually received its first performance here, as some longtime Stratford residents like to suggest, this establishment fairly oozes with the English atmosphere that most people travel to England to find. From the warm oak-paneled entryway to the fine lounge, it is the kind of place you feel you could stay for hours. The atmospheric Manor Bar is remarkable for its attractive paneling and beamed ceiling. Of the 112 guest rooms, those in the main building are the most interesting; those in the new wing tend toward the standard-British-modern. Best of all, the Alveston is a mere 5-minute walk from the theater. Details: Alveston Manor Hotel, Clopton Bridge, Stratford-upon-Avon, Warwickshire CV37 7HP, England (phone: 0789-4581).

MILLER HOWE, Windermere, Cumbria, England: If you tire of looking at the ever-changing light and shade over Lake Windermere in this lovely Wordsworth country hotel, you can play Scrabble, read a book from your private bookshelf, or just browse through any number of knickknacks you may find in your bedroom. There is something very personal about the rooms at the *Miller Howe,* as though you have borrowed someone else's private domain for a day or two. If you want, you can wander into the kitchen to watch the friendly cooks prepare roast loin of lamb with five fresh herbs; pea, pear, and watercress soup; or any number of other goodies that appear on the interesting menu. These eventually wind up on your table in the charmingly autumnal yellow and brown dining room that looks out on to a beautiful flagstone terrace and flower-bordered lawns, which in turn slope gently to the lake. The bathrooms here are basically sybaritic. Step out from your scented shower and you will find morning tea waiting for you in pretty floral pots with homemade bread and marmalade to satisfy hunger pangs before a substantial breakfast downstairs. Dinner specialties include loin of Lakeland lamb and smoked salmon and avocado roulade. Details: Miller Howe, Windermere, Cumbria, England (phone: 09662-2536).

GLENEAGLES HOTEL, Auchterarder, Perthshire, Scotland: *"Heich abune the heich"* — better than the best — might seem a grandiose claim to make about a hotel. But once you've experienced this 210-room Scottish Versailles of a hotel — Britain's finest luxury resort — you will have very little quarrel with the decades of hoteliers who have believed in the truth of their boast, from the early days when a chief point of pride was the fact that every room had its own bath — at a time when no other hotel outside London could say the same — and on through the years, as crowned heads, aristocrats, and millionaires flocked to the establishment by the score. Nowadays, the first thing most visitors rave about are the golf courses — four of them, since the new Glendeven course opened in September 1980. But nongolfers never want for things to do, either: On the 610-acre grounds, there are facilities for fishing, croquet, lawn bowling, miniature golf, Ping-Pong, tennis, squash, dancing, billiards; plus a sauna, hairdressing salons, whirlpool, swimming pool, and Turkish bath. The gardens alone, spotted with bright-colored flowers, are a joy. The rooms are high-ceilinged and spacious enough that you don't trip over each other when room service sets up your tea things; the windows are big enough to give you an eyeful of the lonely Scottish hills beyond the gardens; and the service can't be faulted, thanks to a better than one-to-one staff-to-guest ratio. When pipe bands set up on the velvety lawns, the sound is enough to give you goose bumps. Open year-round. Details: Gleneagles Hotel, Auchterarder, Perthshire PH3 1NF, Scotland (phone: 07646-2231).

INVERLOCHY CASTLE, near Fort William, Highland, Scotland: When Queen Victoria came to visit this baronial granite mansion a decade after Lord Abinger built it in 1863, she noted in her diary that she had never seen "a lovelier or more romantic spot." She wasn't the only visitor to express those sentiments. Outside there are the terraced gardens, the rhododendron bushes bigger than a child's playhouse, the emerald lawns, and, beyond them, the great mass of Ben Nevis and the Western Highlands rising in the distance; inside, there are antiques enough to do justice to a museum — carved mahogany sideboards, gleaming oak chests, portraits by Sir Benjamin West, and such — and wonderful carved paneling, elaborate moldings, frescoes: Almost everyone who comes for just a night regrets not having planned to stay longer. The dozen guest rooms are spacious and quiet, and the food is particularly good; the chef is Mr. Ken Mac Phee. Dinner, always at 8, consists of locally caught game and fish, and the wine list is outstanding. Closed November through April. Details: Inverlochy Castle, Fort William, Highland PH33 6SN, Scotland (phone: Fort William 0397-2177).

SKEABOST HOUSE HOTEL, Skeabost Bridge, Isle of Skye, Scotland: Built in Victorian times, and beautifully situated at the southernmost tip of a sea loch, this 22-room hostelry — one of the finest hotels on "the islands" (as Scotland's Inner and Outer Hebrides are widely known) — incorporates all that is best in Scottish country hotels, without being exorbitantly expensive. Particularly in the old part of the hotel, the ceilings are high, the furniture old-fashioned (or antique), and the armchairs and sofas plush and comfortable; when it's cool, log fires blaze on the hearth. The restaurant is perhaps more functional than you might expect, but a genuine attempt is made to serve interesting local dishes, and at relatively modest prices. Closed November to mid-April. Details: Skeabost House Hotel, Skeabost Bridge, Isle of Skye IV51 9NP, Scotland (phone: 047-032-202).

PLAS GLANSEVIN, Llangadog, Dyfed, Wales: A *gemütlich* place, this eight-room establishment known for the evenings of traditional Welsh entertainment presented in a combined dining room and concert hall at the back of the house has a very lived-in feel, and you should not expect to find everything just so: There may be a pair of dusty Wellingtons lying in the corner of the entrance hall, and some corners of the fine old building (parts of which date from the eighteenth century) are due for redecoration. But this relaxing and informal hostelry — the kind of place where children feel welcome — is delightfully warm and not only because log fires are lit when the weather turns chilly. As for the Welsh evenings, they are — being as authentic as can be — much less awful than they sound. (See *Mead and Meat Pies: Historical Banquets*). Details: Plas Glansevin, Llangadog, Dyfed SA19 9HY, Wales (phone: 05503-238).

PORTMEIRION HOTEL, Portmeirion, Gwynedd, Wales: The only lodging place in the bizarre Italianate village created by the architect Clough Williams-Ellis, who died in the late 1970s, this is a really out-of-the-ordinary establishment. The main building, which had a superb view over a river estuary and housed the restaurant and a number of public rooms, recently burned. However, most guests stay in a scattering of cottages around the pastel-colored, ornately decorated, and altogether fantastic village — overlooking the famous decorative fountain or the estuary, or set atop a hill above it all; and these are still open for business. Closed November to Easter. Details: Portmeirion Hotel, Portmeirion, near Penrhyndeudraeth, Gwynedd, Wales (phone: 0766-770228).

PADDY BURKE'S, Clarenbridge, Co. Galway, Irish Republic: *Burke's* was strictly a pub till the bar food got so good that it started winning awards. Now locals still gather at dusk for a jar at the bar, but the large room to the left has been turned into a proper restaurant with tapestried chairs and all that. The bar food is still exemplary (big Galway oysters in season, smoked salmon, the rich house pâté, smoked mackerel salad from the cold buffet); it's ideal for a drop-in lunch provided you can remember to get rolling again. The dining room food is excellent too. If they're on the menu when you arrive, sample the scampi bisque, the sea trout stuffed with cucumber, or the roast lamb with forcemeat and brandy; then, if you can still find room, apple and blackberry pie for dessert. There's draft beer and Guinness, of course, plus house wine and a limited wine list. Meals are served during all pub hours (phone: 091-86107).

ASHFORD CASTLE HOTEL, Cong, Co. Mayo, Irish Republic: It looks like an extended Magic Kingdom lining the shore of Lough Corrib, complete with green demesne and velvet lawns, drawbridge and portcullis, gothic-arched entry and an oak-paneled great hall handsomer in its reality than any Disney architects could dream up. The fact is that although Ashford is often called a "fantasy" place, in its ramble of buildings the present hotel incorporates not one, but three real-life castles: the ruins of the de Burgos's thirteenth-century stronghold, the original Ashford House (an eighteenth-century French-style château), and Sir Benjamin Guinness's splendid nineteenth-century Victorian addition — all so deftly linked to later guest-room wings you can scarcely tell where one ends and the next begins. A hotel since 1939 and unstintingly refurbished in 1972 by its new Irish-American owner, John Mulcahy (who also owns County Kerry's *Waterville Lake Hotel*), Ashford's sense of luxury is genuine: fine paintings, sculpture, and antique armor are artfully deployed around its public rooms; gilt-framed mirrors reflect the sparkle of its Waterford chandeliers; thick oriental-toned carpeting hushes footsteps in salons and corridors. And at least one real-life king has stayed and played here: Edward VII of England, for whom, they say, the billiard room was built. The fishing (salmon, trout, pike, and perch) and shooting (pheasant, woodcock, snipe, and duck) attract sportsmen from all over the world; there are also a 9-hole golf course (guests only), tennis, croquet, boating, picnicking on the Lough's wooded islets; and miles of walks wander through the rose gardens and into the trees. The dining room serves unremarkable lunches; dinners are expertly done with matching wines from an extensive cellar. All 77 guest rooms are poshly, if sparingly, furnished; those in older wings tend to be smaller than those in the new; all have private baths, but not always showers. Closed January to mid-April. Information: Ashford Castle, Cong, Co. Mayo, Irish Republic (phone: 094-22644).

ARBUTUS LODGE, Cork, Co. Cork, Irish Republic: Next to the *Mirabeau,* it's Ireland's most talked-about restaurant, having garnered three Egon Ronay stars (plus an "Outstanding" for its cellar), a Gault Millau toque, two Automobile Association rosettes, and — an Irish rarity — a Michelin star. Declan Ryan's apprenticeships in the Isles and on the Continent included stints with the Frères Troisgrois at Roanne with whom his kitchen still makes an informal exchange (a Troisgrois fils recently served as his sauce chef). Now elegantly established in the ballroom of his family's small hotel in suburban Montenotte, he offers a menu of classic and "sensibly nouvelle" French cuisine based on the best of locally grown foods ("no flying stuff halfway round the world"). The emphasis is on style with integrity ("if you doll a dish up to the point where you don't know what it is, you've made a mistake"); case in point: his *mosaique des légumes* — an intricate terrine of vegetables in ham aspic in which each ingredient maintains its own bright identity. Also notable: the sea bass with fresh ginger, escalope of salmon in sorrel sauce, breast of pheasant with three purées, a most interesting board of local cheeses. The seven-course Tasters Menu is an excellent introduction. Lunch 1 to 2, dinner 7 to 9:15. Closed a week at Christmas and on Sundays to nonresidents (phone: 021-501237).

DOYLE'S SEAFOOD BAR, Dingle, County Kerry, Irish Republic: Tucked away in a narrow old house at the back of town, John and Stella Doyle's place has a scrubbed, rustic look (butcher-block tables, rush-seated chairs, flagstone floor) and a menu that's gathered all sorts of good-guide stars. You can lunch from the bar's blackboard (a Saturday choice included kedgeree; quiche; open smoked salmon sandwiches on Stella's crusty brown bread; and house salad, nicely dressed). Or step to the rear and order something more substantial: Don't miss the subtle smoked mackerel pâté, piquant crab bisque, scallop and chicken pie (steeped in wine sauce, wrapped in puff pastry). Or indulge in lobster or crayfish served with pots of garlic butter, then almond meringue or kiwi fruit for a light, happy ending. Lunch 12:30 to 2:15, dinner 6 to 9. Closed Sundays and November through February (phone: Dingle 144).

TOWERS HOTEL, Glenbeigh, Co. Kerry, Irish Republic: Photographs of famous guests — Charlie Chaplin, Burl Ives, Robert Mitchum, and others — and sketches of now-no-more Kirarery, the village built for the filming of *Ryan's Daughter,* line the walls of the publike bar. Good soup smells waft from the kitchen, and the expansive hospitality that is proprietor Ernie Evans's trademark enfolds you and makes you feel at home. In this anglers' hotel by the sea, the best dishes are naturally from the sea too: fresh-made smoked mackerel salad and fresh salmon mousse; rich cockle and mussel soup (make a lunch of it with brown bread, sweet butter, and crisp cucumbers); a medley of baked scallops with prawns and crab mornay. You can have poached fresh salmon steak with a choice of cucumber and lemon sauce or splurge on hollandaise made to order; or lobster in season. Desserts seem rather an afterthought; better Irish coffee in the lounge. Don't book on Saturday — which is Candlelight Dinner Dance night — unless you feel like a party. Otherwise, make this a "must" stop on any Dingle drive. Dinner 7:30 to 9; lunch, tea, and sandwiches all day. Closed November and December (phone: Glenbeigh 12).

THE VINTAGE, Kinsale, Co. Cork, Irish Republic: The arbor with plastic grapes pendant, the brown cloths and flickering red candles that have always constituted this restaurant's decor were never all that memorable. But a change is in the offing, and in any case, the food has always been outstanding. Every evening, in a kitchen that is, by restaurant standards, minuscule, Gerry Galvin, who started at Shannon, and his young crew conjure up a menu remarkable for its freshness (that word again) of ingredients and approach. Once-tired appetizers have new zest (fruit salad is topped with sweet vinaigrette and a twirl of tomato sorbet). Or try curried apple soup. Quenelles — sometimes chicken, sometimes smoked salmon — are light and lovely; soufflé Atlantique is flecked with seafood; brill is baked with mushroom pâté and cream. Duckling and herbed loin of lamb are other choices; banana soufflé or homemade fruit ice for dessert. Dinner only, 7 to 10. Closed Tuesdays, Wednesdays, and November through February (phone: 021-72502).

LONGUEVILLE HOUSE AND PRESIDENT'S RESTAURANT, Mallow, Co. Cork, Irish Republic: There's a lovely formality about this cream-white Georgian manor house on a hill and its fine interior detail (inlaid mahogany doors, a marble Adam fireplace, Italian plasterwork ceilings). There's also inviting color and clutter: bowls of flowers, chairs to sink into, paintings, a Victorian whirligig stand stacked with paperbacks as well as room-high shelves of rare editions. In the valley of the Blackwater River below, the massive ruins of Domineen attest to the fact that this has been O'Callaghan soil since the start of Irish time. The castle was tumbled and the land commandeered by Cromwellian forces in the 1600s. A full 300 years later, it is back in family hands. Now Michael O'Callaghan and his wife, Jane, are hosts in a handsome house famous for its food. On any given evening, the gooseberry chutney, the cream of tomato and vegetable soups, the chicken, the lamb, and the pink trout are lovingly home-cooked with sophisticated simplicity and consumate skill by Jane. The sweets — soufflé cake, fresh fruit tarts, homemade ice cream — are good enough to swoon over. The O'Callaghans care a lot — enough to spend their "off" months (from mid-October to Easter) "refreshing" — Jane at London's Cordon Bleu or with one of France's great chefs, Michael traveling in search of wines for his impressive cellar. Between meals, guests lodged in *Longueville*'s 20 pretty rooms (all with private baths) fish in the Blackwater's pools, ride from nearby stables, play the free Mallow golf course, or sun in the palm-lined Victorian conservatory. Outside guests are welcome for dinner only. Information: Longueville Country House, Mallow, Co. Cork, Irish Republic (phone: 022-27156).

BALLYMALOE HOUSE, Midleton, Co. Cork, Irish Republic: Ballymaloe House dates from the seventeenth century with extensions and a chunky stone keep that survives from a fourteenth-century castle of the Fitzgeralds. It beckons across fields where ponies graze and grassy lawns where plump sheep crop away as you drive up. You park under the big chestnut tree by the flagstone terrace with its tubs of flowers. A breeze ruffles the ivy walls, the door swings open, and you're home — even if it's your first visit. As the Allens, Ivan and Myrtle, whose 400-acre farm this is, put it, Ballymaloe is an "old family home, with the family still in it, children and grandchildren come and go, guests become friends." There are usually children around, but they don't get underfoot and there's plenty for them to do: swim, ride the ponies, play croquet. Early children's meals are served, and in summer, a counselor is laid on. Meanwhile, grownups occupy themselves at the swimming pool, on the tennis court, 9-hole golf course, or trout pond — all free to guests (there's a charge for riding and deep-sea fishing trips). And they gather in the lounge to wait for Myrtle's meals, famed through all Ireland. The food is simple and marvelous — even at breakfast: "muisli" cereal is grated apple, oatmeal, syrup, a squeeze of lemon; the marmalade is homemade. But then almost everything is; and, with rare exceptions, everything is grown on the family farm as well. Lunch is a cold buffet; the dinner menu is short, straightforward: perhaps crudités with garlic mayonnaise (so perfectly fresh that a cucumber wedge is like nothing you've ever tasted) or watercress soup to start; then locally smoked mackerel, "little pots of hot mussels," or homemade Danish pâté; summer turkey baked in butter and fresh herbs, roast rib of beef with three sauces, or French casserole of roast pork with Normandy mustard sauce; and the board of local cheeses, fruit tarts, cake, and — finally — coffee with Ballymaloe chocolates. Of 25 guestrooms (21 with bath/shower), those in the main house are most comfortable; the recently upgraded courtyard rooms are just as good, if not better. Alternative gatehouse, gate lodge, and rooms at son Timothy's farm home are also available. Outside guests are welcome for lunch or dinner. Information: Ballymaloe House, Shanagarry, Midleton, Co. Cork, Irish Republic (phone: 021-62531).

DROMOLAND CASTLE, Newmarket-on-Fergus, Co. Clare, Irish Republic: It sits, gray and graceful, turreted and towered, in the heart of a 400-acre park whose green velvet lawns roll away into dark green woods. Ireland's banner flies from the battlements mirrored in the small lake. And if *Dromoland* looks like a fantasy come true, it's because it is — for guests who roam its garden, golf on its 9-hole course, fish and boat on its lake and streams, ride horseback over neighboring hills, and call it temporary home. More especially it is home to Bernard McDonough, a West Virginia gentleman who'd always wanted a castle to call his own and finally realized his impossible dream when he bought this sixteenth-century seat of the bold O'Briens and restored it as a hotel. A regal job he's done too. Inside, antique O'Brien portraits line halls that glow with rich wood paneling, silken fabrics, and sunlight. Through the tall dining room windows, you can watch deer on the distant morning grass (the breakfast buffet is piled with fresh fruits, croissants, fresh-baked pastries); at night its damask walls and polished silver gleam in the chandelier light, and the food is very good. Its 67 rooms — all with bath — are airy and bright with flowered papers and flower colors. The occasional Irish purist harumphs and finds it "all a bit too grand." But its many repeat guests and Mr. McDonough, who flies over for a visit now and again, wouldn't have it any other way. Information: Dromoland Castle, Newmarket-on-Fergus, Co. Clare, Irish Republic (phone: 061-71144).

RESTAURANT MIRABEAU, Sandycove, Co. Dublin, Irish Republic: Widely touted as one of the best and the most expensive restaurant in Ireland, the *Mirabeau* comes as a surprise: The small house near the quay is easily overlooked, and guests are personally welcomed at the front door by owner and chef Sean Kinsella. Similarly unassuming are the decor and ambience inside — simple oaken tables and chairs grouped around a fireplace, with assorted lanterns, ship clocks, and other nautical artifacts hung from the ceiling. Don't be deceived, however: Kinsella, a County Clare man who served his apprenticeship at the *Gresham Hotel* in Dublin and then spent several years as a chef aboard a luxury passenger liner, is a master showman — before being ushered into the dining room, his guests relax quietly in the bar with a glass of wine, listening to recorded classical music, and watching as the day's fresh catch and choice meats are paraded by on large platters. Dinner is a leisurely and sensual affair, with each individually prepared course more attractive, aromatic, and delicious than the last. The portions are remarkably generous, and most guests will be hard pressed to rise from the table afterward, let alone finish the meal. You'll find the bill singular, but then so is the experience (phone: 01-809873).

IF YOU'RE NEARBY

THE PRIORY HOTEL, Bath, Avon, England: A Gothic-style, Georgian-built residence converted to a small hotel; country-house atmosphere, antique furnishings, heated swimming pool in the English garden, and highly praised French cuisine in the dining room. All of the 15 rooms have private baths or showers (phone: 0225-331922).

GARDEN HOUSE HOTEL, Cambridge, Cambridgeshire, England: Modern, luxurious hotel with lawn stretching to the edge of the Cam. Many of the 117 rooms have balconies overlooking the riverside, all have private baths or showers (phone: 0223-63421).

HOTEL TRESANTON, St. Mawes, Cornwall, England: Three buildings with the look of an oversized whitewashed cottage on a hillside; scenic views, terraced gardens, very good restaurant. Closed mid-November through mid-February. Of the 26 rooms, all have private baths (phone: 0326-270544).

THE CASTLE HOTEL, Taunton, Somerset, England: A Norman fortress made welcoming by its peaceful garden, 40 luxurious bedrooms (no two furnished alike), fine dining room, and polished English manner (phone: 0823-72671).

THE CLOSE, Tetbury, Gloucestershire, England: A sixteenth-century wool merchant's home of Cotswold stone. Beamed bedrooms with antiques, some with four-poster beds; walled garden with pool, croquet, dining room known for its French touch. All of the 12 rooms have baths or showers (phone: 0666-52272).

ISLAND HOTEL, Tresco, Isles of Scilly, Cornwall, England: Old and new architecture together in this resort hotel on a car-free island; private beach, heated outdoor pool. Fishing charters arranged, sailing and rowing available. Closed mid-October through February. Of the 36 rooms, most have private baths (phone: 0720-22883).

CULLODEN HOUSE, Inverness, Highland, Scotland: An eighteenth-century mansion whose guest rooms and public rooms are stuffed with antiques; the dining room is by Adam, and there's a sauna. All of the 21 rooms have baths or showers (phone: 0463-790461).

RUTHIN CASTLE, Ruthin, Clwyd, Wales: A large nineteenth-century mansion on the grounds of a ruined medieval castle; fine dining and medieval banquets, Welsh-style. Extensive parkland, fishing. All of the 64 rooms have baths or showers (phone: 08242-2664).

BALLYLICKEY HOUSE, Ballylickey, Co. Cork, Irish Republic: Former hunting lodge with Bantry Bay view, gardens, pool; famed for French cuisine. All of the 23 rooms have baths; 3 chalets. May to October (phone: 027-50071).

CAHERNANE HOTEL, Killarney, Co. Kerry, Irish Republic: Elegant Victorian vacation-home-turned-inn on 100-acre estate; many nearby and on-site sports facilities including private river fishing. All 35 rooms have baths (the high-ceilinged and antique-furnished bedrooms in the original mansion are more romantic than those in the modern annex). Mid-April to October (phone: 064-31895).

CROCNARAW COUNTRY HOUSE, Moyard, Co. Galway, Irish Republic: Inviting and homey Georgian house on 20-acre Atlantic shore estate; tasty meals with fish, fresh seafood, fresh-from-the-garden vegetables, dairy products. Of the 10 rooms, 6 have baths. April to October (phone: Moyard 9).

RATHMULLAN HOUSE, Rathmullan, Co. Donegal, Irish Republic: Extended country house on 50-acre grounds with sandy beach; self-contained family beach chalets. Of the 21 rooms, 16 have baths. Easter to October (phone: Rathmullan 4).

LISS ARD HOUSE, Skibbereen, Co. Cork, Irish Republic: Impressive 150-year-old manor house, converted with fine sense of style, color; handsome antiques. Worthy bar, good Irish food. Country riding, instruction, jaunting car rides featured; other sports arranged. Of the 10 rooms, 5 have baths (phone: 028-21511).

NUTGROVE, Annadorn, Downpatrick, Co. Down, Northern Ireland: An early Victorian mill house situated deep in leafy Ulster and full of idiosyncrasies and a reassuring grace. Potted tongue, leg of lamb *en croûte* with spiced oranges, seafood pancakes, and blueberry crisp are the specialties of the kitchen. When you drift off to sleep at night, you do it between pure Irish linen sheets (phone: Seaforde 275).

LONDONDERRY ARMS, Carnlough, Co. Antrim, Northern Ireland: An old coaching inn built in 1854, this hostelry boasts a fine front verandah with a view of the harbor and, because the proprietor had a passion for the beloved Irish steeplechaser Arkle, a miniature museum devoted to the steed (phone: Carnlough 85255).

CULLODEN HOTEL, Craigavad, Holywood, Co. Down, Northern Ireland: Splendid neo-Gothic bishop's palace, grandly appointed, overlooking Belfast Lough; gardens, tennis, and squash. All 80 rooms have baths (phone: Holywood 5223).

OLD INN, Crawfordsburn, Co. Down, Northern Ireland: Part-thatched, antique-furnished Jacobean inn in town. Four noteworthy suites; 26 rooms, 14 with bath/shower (phone: Helen's Bay 853255).

Teashops and Tea Gardens

That great British institution, afternoon tea, had been given up for lost a few years ago: The cost of the ingredients and the extensive labor required had soared, just as weight-watchers had begun to question the healthfulness of the scones-and-pastries habit that their parents and grandparents always took for granted. But like that other great British institution, fish and chips — which was also, for a brief moment, put down as a thing of the past — afternoon tea has survived and has actually enjoyed something of a resurgence in popularity as harried Londoners have given up the rat race, moved to the country, and converted cow barns and old cottages into quainter-than-quaint teashops where you can get the kind of set teas that dreams are made of — those archetypically wonderful teas whose passing was so vigorously lamented until just recently.

The reasons for the revival of interest in the institution are hard to gauge. Simple economy may be among them: As the prices of full meals climb, tea becomes increasingly attractive since most vacationers know that they can get by on nothing more than a full breakfast in their hotels and a relatively inexpensive tea in some country café. But nostalgia, in the form of a stubborn refusal to abandon tradition in the face of stern realities, may also figure. Tea as an afternoon meal, first served in the late eighteenth century by the duchess of Bedford to entertain her guests between the early lunches and late dinners at her house parties, soon became an integral part of everybody's everyday life. A whole industry grew up around the manufacture of teacups and saucers, cake stands, tea forks for the cakes, silver teapots, sugar bowls and tiny silver tongs, linens, and the like. Less aristocratic families developed elaborate teatime rituals around the new meal in Victorian days; at a time when, it sometimes appeared, Britons lived to eat rather than the other way around, it seemed quite natural to nosh away the otherwise gustatorily empty late afternoon hours. "Everything stops for tea" became an English saying, and the World War I poet Rupert Brooke wrote about it in a poem, referring to a tea garden at Grantchester, near Cambridge (which still exists after all these years, in a sun-dappled meadow close to where the undergraduates leave their punts).

In days gone by, beginning around the turn of the century when one Miss Cranston established the nation's first tearoom in Sauchiehall Street, Glasgow, running such tea gardens and tea shops was considered one respectable occupation for spinsters, and the foods you find at tea still reflect their genteel touch. Honey and country preserves, particularly strawberry jam, show up on the tea tables, along with biscuitlike scones. In Devon and Cornwall, thick clotted cream — too stiff for pouring — invariably accompanies the cakes; strawberry teas, a summertime specialty, include a bowl of the luscious red fruit. In country districts, especially in Shropshire, you'll often encounter "farm teas," made up of enough salad, ham, fish, and other fairly substantial edibles that you can skip your evening meal and still not go to bed with a rumbling stomach. During high tea, as served in its most elaborate form at some London hotels — the Ritz among them — it may take you a couple of hours or more to make your way through the endless procession of comestibles — thin sandwiches filled with cucumbers, watercress, or smoked salmon, and delicate pastries; not to mention the good selections of fine China and India brews. High teas such as the Scots love so well — still found in many seaside cafés around Britain — consist of a salad or "something on toast" in addition to the usual spread of buns and cakes. That may include, depending on where you are and when, Victoria spongecakes, gateaux (cream cakes), rock cakes, fairy cakes, Battenberg and Madeira cakes, buns, scones, flans and egg dishes,

DIVERSIONS / Teashops and Tea Gardens

savouries (meat pies), Bakewell puddings, meringues, cheesecakes, lemon meringue pies, lemon curd tarts, and more. In Scotland, fruitcakes, soda bread, and tea breads (a sort of cake-and-bread hybrid) show up on the tea table. In Wales, you can expect bacon, fish, pancakes, and Bara Brith (speckled bread). Many of the food specialties of the south appear most frequently at teatime: brandy snaps doused with fresh cream, custard tarts smoothed with red currant jelly and slathered with more cream, Chelsea buns, and above all, crumpets — a wintertime delight that resembles America's English muffin, but with a hole.

The settings for tea are as varied as the food. In Scotland, with few exceptions, you'll have to take your chances in big hotels. (Those of the British Transport Hotels Group are recommended.) And in Wales, except in a few towns that are more frequented by tourists, it's in a café that you'll find the best teas. In England, teashops are most numerous in the south and the west; cream teas, originally a West Country specialty, have become equally popular in other areas. You might pause for one in some unpretentious shop — or you might find yourself pouring your Earl Grey in the orangery, the dairy, or the stable of one of England's stately homes (especially if the house is owned and run by the National Trust). You can munch your teacakes in a battlefield, old almshouses, a castle, Sally Lunn's original shop, or the Pump Room in Bath. Or in a nursery full of cacti (*The Cactus Nursery*, Brandy La., Rosudgeon, Penzance, Cornwall). Or in the shop where the lace for Queen Victoria's wedding dress was made (*The Old Lace Shop*, Fore St., Beer, Devon). Or in an old coaching hostelry (*Greyhound Inn*, Folkingham, Lincolnshire). Or in a Gypsy caravan (*Stone Cross Cottage*, Godshill) or in a thatched hut half covered in creepers and rambling roses (*Dunnose Cottage*, Luccombe) — both on the Isle of Wight, an exceptionally good location for summertime tea seekers. Local tourist offices can generally tell you what's good when you arrive in their area.

Here, then, a representative sampling:

WORTH A LONG DETOUR

SHIP'S LIGHTS TEAROOM, near Bridport, Dorset: Eype, a pretty hamlet a mile or so southwest of Bridport and only half that from the sea, is so tiny that you might not expect to find anything in the way of a teashop amongst its handful of little houses — but there it is, in one of those archetypically whitewashed two-story cottages that are scattered so picturesquely along the winding lanes of this part of England. Inside, there's a little parlor where you can sit when the weather is poor, and modest overnight accommodation is available. But the best thing about the *Ship's Lights* is the garden, a glorious enclosure that in summer fills up with emerald green and scarlet, brilliant yellow and orange — and, next to an old stone wall, there really is an old ship's light. You can take tea here, and savor scones slathered with Devon clotted cream and jams as sweet and full of fruit as any you'll ever taste; and if you're really hungry, you can sample some of the establishment's own home-baked pastries or fancy cakes and sandwiches — all the tastier for the fresh sea air that comes with the package. Lunches available in summer. Phone: Bridport 23059.

THE OLD FIRE ENGINE HOUSE, Ely, Cambridgeshire: If you have ever been to a first-class restaurant, got as far as dessert, and wished you could come back the next day for that, then you'll like this well-established restaurant, locally well known as a teashop, not far from Ely's lovely, stark, and cool cathedral, a landmark in this flat, low-lying part of eastern England. Some of the gateaux, pastries, and flans served here are worthy of any groaning sweets trolley. Scones are served warm, if you wish, and there's local honey and homemade shortbread. A good example of the kind of place

DIVERSIONS / Teashops and Tea Gardens 547

best known as a restaurant but also operating, on a more modest and certainly more inexpensive scale, as a teashop, it's especially handsome with its shady, well-tended garden, large windows and chintz curtains, warm-looking flagstone floor, and solid wooden furniture. Open daily (phone: Ely 2582).

THE GATEWAY CAKESHOP, Evesham, Worcestershire: Aside from the fairly uninspiring snack bars in bread shops and in shopping areas, and plastic and functional establishments run by chains, it's increasingly difficult to find a pleasant spot for tea in a town; most teashops are such small operations that rising rents have been lethal to them. But every country market town has its cake shop, and many of them serve tea on the side. The *Gateway,* installed in a pretty Tudor town house, is a good example. Dark and cozy and full of plain old-fashioned furniture, with ancient oak beams overhead, and round panes of Georgian bottle glass in many of the windows, the establishment is great for afternoon teas (and it's for these that the place is locally best known — even though morning coffee and cakes and light lunches are also served). John and James Miller, who do the baking, are famous for their fruit pies and gooey cream-and-liqueur cake. People in the town swear by their bread — and it makes an exceptionally fine addition to any picnic. The *Gateway* is located at 7 Market Pl., in the oldest part of this historic town, and when you've finished with your tea, you can go out and explore two old churches nearby — one from the twelfth century, the other from the sixteenth — and the square high stone bell tower in between, once a part of a Benedictine abbey. Open daily, but only in the afternoon on Sundays (phone: Evesham 2249).

THE SETTLE, Frome, Somerset: Situated in the most charming part of the oldest corner of this old town, an area of cobbled streets and half-timbered houses, this small Cheap Street establishment is warm and homey looking with its red brick walls and black and white paintwork. Inside, there are vases of flowers to brighten the windowsills, and pressed wild flowers to decorate the menus; and an autumnal color scheme — all russets, grays, and golds — makes things more appealing still. Best of all is the immense variety of imaginative yet inexpensive food: scones made from whole wheat flour, soups, salads, baked potatoes with all manner of unusual fillings, sandwiches stuffed with cucumbers and other goodies, plus savory dishes like cottage pie, potato-and-cheese pie, and — the specialty — Frome bobbins, a delicious confection of apricots and sultanas which have been steeped in local cider. Open every day, but only after 3 PM on Sundays (phone: Frome 5975).

KEEPERS RESTAURANT, Haworth, West Yorkshire: The Brontë sisters' hometown, which is generally overrun by visitors, suffers no shortage of places to eat. But at this relatively new restaurant and teashop off High Street in a tiny cul-de-sac near the top of the hill, the proprietors have not let the regular supply of transient customers make them complacent. The mid-eighteenth-century building in which the establishment was installed in the early 1970s is exceptionally comfortable and attractive with its dark blue flowered wallpaper, the wooden or navy plush seats, and wallfulls of prints and paintings (not, alas, for sale); white tablecloths give the place a Victorian flavor. Homemade cakes and scones and cream teas are always available at teatime, as are sugary homemade meringues and a rich chocolate brandy cake; and curries are a specialty at lunch. Open daily (phone: 0535-42919).

THE ORIGINAL MAIDS OF HONOUR SHOP, Kew Gardens, Surrey: Directly opposite one of outer London's most famous public gardens, the eighteenth-century Royal Botanic Gardens at Kew — and accordingly so busy during the tourist season that you need to go as early as 3 PM to enjoy your tea in a leisurely fashion — this shop has been serving up Maids of Honour (a curd tartlike sweet first mentioned in a fifteenth-century manuscript and said to have been enjoyed by Henry VIII) for over a century now — and it's as pretty as ever, part whitewashed, with a handsome brick-and-tile roof and broad eaves. The impression of *rus in urbe* is enhanced by the wrought ironwork and Victorian lampposts outside and an old-fashioned interior. The waitresses are as attentive as they can be, and, with the help of a handful of young girls, fuss over orders of pots of tea and toast, scones and fancy cakes, like so many English nannies. Closed Sundays and Monday afternoons. 288 Kew Rd. (phone: 01-940-2752).

THE BARN, Sidmouth, Devon: Installed in a fifteenth-century cottage, this pretty stucco-walled establishment looks almost like an antiques-and-bric-a-brac shop with its walls hung with handsome old prints and paintings, its pretty cupboardlike Welsh dresser, its shelves chockablock with old cottage china, vases, miniatures, and assorted other fascinating bygones. You sit at rustic old tables, set with vases of flowers from the garden, and enjoy homemade cakes or hams cured on the premises, or salads made of vegetables straight from the garden. Things are very chic here, and friendly besides. Lunches are served as well as teas and accommodation is sometimes available (phone: Sidmouth 3613).

IF YOU'RE NEARBY

THE OLD ORIGINAL BAKEWELL PUDDING SHOP, Bakewell, Derbyshire: Bakewell puddings are said to have been invented here by mistake when an original recipe was misunderstood, and the place has become a tourist attraction in its own right. On the square. Phone: 062-981-2193.

THE OLD LACE SHOP, Beer, Devon: The lace for Queen Victoria's wedding dress was made here, on these fairly unpretentious premises. Evening meals are available as well as cream teas. Fore St.

ROSE OF TORRIDGE CAFÉ, Bideford, Devon: Once a hotel (Charles Kingsley wrote part of *Westward Ho!* here), this old-fashioned establishment now serves good cream teas. On the quay. Closed Sundays.

BANTAM TEA ROOMS, Chipping Campden, Gloucestershire: An extra-friendly staff serves up fine homemade cakes plus salads and hot dishes on High St. in the middle of this exquisite and, though much visited, unspoiled Cotswold village. Closed Mondays.

HORSE WITH THE RED UMBRELLA, Dorchester, Dorset: This establishment at 10 High West St. offers a very good selection of cakes, pastries, gateaux, and savouries, and it's a great place to stock up for a picnic. Closed Sundays and bank holidays. Phone: 035-62019.

GREYHOUND INN, Folkingham, Lincolnshire: The teas served in this former coaching inn are substantial enough to replace a meal. The village itself — an important place in the eighteenth century — is large but charming and wonderfully tranquil. Phone: 05297-301.

BAY TREE, Stamford, Lincolnshire: In one of England's loveliest and most historic market towns, this tiny tearoom at 10 St. Paul's St. maintains a strong reputation for top-quality gateaux and lunchtime snacks. Closed Mondays. Phone: 0780-51219.

STONE CROSS COTTAGE, Godshill, Isle of Wight: A Gypsy caravan stands in the garden where you can have your tea — and homemade cakes and fresh strawberries — when the sun shines. If it rains, there's lots of room indoors.

DUNNOSE COTTAGE, Luccombe, Isle of Wight: Tucked away in a thatched cottage half covered in creepers and rambling roses, this bright and sunny tearoom serves lovely homemade cakes and gateaux, and, on Sundays, a fine hearty roast for lunch. Phone: Shanklin 2585.

EDITH'S CAFÉ, Marlborough, Wiltshire: Installed in three old cottages on London Rd., Edith Coplestone's tearooms have a far-flung reputation for their light and delicate spongecakes, shortbreads, flapjacks, and even hot savouries. Closed Wednesdays and part of September.

THE STABLE DOOR, Middleham, Yorkshire: Light lunches are available, but this

Market Place establishment is best known around this famous racehorse training center for its wonderful cream teas and delicious fat scones and fruitcake. The service is friendly, too. Phone: 0969-23568.

WHEATSHEAF COFFEE SHOPPE, Morpeth, Northumberland: This establishment at 1 Newgate Street has a really fine sandwich bar, as well as good whole wheat bread and an interesting range of sweets. Closed Sundays and bank holidays. Wheatsheaf Yard. Phone: 0670-519414.

ASSEMBLY HOUSE, Norwich, Norfolk: The arrangement here is unpretentious, but the eighteenth-century building on Theatre St. where this tearoom makes its home is as elegant as can be; its homemade scones and cakes are as delicious as its hot snacks and honey-cured hams — an East Anglian specialty. Closed Sundays and bank holidays. Theatre St. Phone: 0603-27526.

THE COFFEE POT, Paignton, Devon: This friendly family-run place situated by the harbor at 47 Roundham Rd. serves great homemade scones, and better-than-average cakes and cream teas. Phone: 0803-550178.

THE CACTUS NURSERY, Rosudgeon, Penzance, Cornwall: You'll find cream teas with homemade scones and cakes, specialties for children, and, yes, cacti (and many other green things) — for sale, though not to eat. Brandy La.

SUTHERLAND HOUSE, Southwold, Suffolk: In an offbeat little seaside holiday town, this well-established and slightly genteel place at 56 High St. is a good bet for hot meals as well as scones and pastries. Closed Mondays, open bank holidays.

COTTAGE TEASHOP, Tintagel, Devon: The homemade bread and cakes and the toasted tea cakes at this cozy place are good enough to draw constant crowds to this 500-year-old cottage, and you may have to wait. Phone: Camelford 770639.

MAWNEY'S KITCHEN, Woodstock, Oxfordshire: The old-fashioned pies and pastries confected here include a wonderfully mild bread pudding, and mouth-watering whole-meal and date scones. 52 Oxford St. Closed Mondays and Tuesdays.

OLD BAKERY, Woolpit, Bury St. Edmonds, Suffolk: This bakery and teashop off the busy Midlands-to-Felixstowe A45 trunk road offers many treats like locally cured ham, as well as pies and cakes; you can get an evening meal here, too. Closed Sundays and Mondays in winter. Phone: Emswell 40255.

COFFEE SHOP, Yarm, Cleveland: The savouries and the sweets served here at 44 High St. are not the least of the charms of this lovely — and underrated — town, once an important coaching stop. Closed Sundays and bank holidays. Phone: 0642-782017.

Mead and Meat Pies: Historical Banquets

It would be hard to find a more touristy way to pass an evening than one of the period banquets held in some six dozen hotels, castles, and other historic buildings throughout England, Wales, Scotland, and, to a lesser degree, Ireland. Yet, like a good Gothic novel, these entertainments are a painless way to absorb a bit of history, and the chance they give you to slurp down a five-course feast in the best Tom Jones fashion — that is, with a knife as your only utensil — can be a lot of fun besides. Knights and ladies in satins and velvets, jesters, and maybe a king or queen, provide entertainment as you sup, while a Henry VIII, a Queen Bess, a William Shakespeare, or some other figure out of the distant past acts as master of the ceremonies.

These usually begin in a foyer where a bit of bread is served with salt "to ward away

550 DIVERSIONS / Mead and Meat Pies: Historical Banquets

evil spirits" and your health is toasted with mead — a heady concoction of fermented honey, apples, and spices, "to be drunk for virility and fertility," as your hosts tell you by way of explaining the origins of the word *honeymoon,* "one month, or moon, after a wedding" — and then continue, after the mead has taken effect, in a banqueting hall full of long oak trestle tables set with pewter plates, mugs, and the knife with which you're to shovel in your supper. (Most people find this progressively less difficult as the evening wears on — perhaps thanks to the copious quantities of wine and beer that are poured with each remove, as banqueting parlance names your courses). Serving wenches keep the food coming, and between removes, the singers and jesters and harpists keep you smiling — or at least they try, and actually succeed with some people (and not always the same ones who have swallowed wine and beer enough to put Henry VIII himself under the table). You may or may not find the entertainers appealing, depending on your tolerance for the occasionally forgettable. What you find does depend on where you go: In the country, the music can be sublime by any lights; city banquet leaders' proclivity for *Oklahoma* and other all-American favorites meant to please the bus groups may drive you to fury. As for the food, it varies too. Along with reminders to "Belch . . . near no man's face with corrupt fumosity," your menu will list a number of removes in appropriate lingo. There is "Ye Potted Spiced Mete," for example, the making of which is also described: "Take: Item — Finest Gammons and choicest parts. Boyle them until ye mete so tendre leaves ye bones. Ye whole pounded in a marble mortar to smoothest paste. Strewe over it: Item — Freshly ground Herbes and Spices and Item — Liquor from ye hocks — Then when perfectly mixed, set all into Potting pans." The idea is nice, but in practice, the meat may taste like nothing more nor less than your local deli's second-best corned beef — and if you're in an urban area, you're doing well if it's even that good. Often, you will be glad for the distractions of the entertainment and the palate-numbing effects of the wine or beer; sometimes even the terminally hungry traveler may find himself picking at the plain roast chicken.

But on the other hand, it's seldom that you're served something that's totally inedible, and there's usually no shortage of food. Moreover, times will come when you'll toss down the food with the relish of the famous Tudor himself; sometimes you'll find yourself belly-laughing at one of the jester's corny jokes; and sometimes, too, a song will turn out to be so beautiful and even ethereal that it brings tears unbidden to your eyes. The best banquets — a few of which are listed here — may surprise you in just that way.

Some operate nightly, others only on weekends, and still others on a seasonal basis. Reservations are required, and most banquet managers demand a deposit when the booking is made (usually about $4.50) and full payment of the fee, usually from about $18 in more remote areas, to about $35 in a city, no later than a month in advance. For listings of other feasts, some of them from periods other than the medieval, contact the British Tourist Authority and the Irish Tourist Board.

BEEFEATER BY THE TOWER OF LONDON, London, England: In the historic vaults of a former ivory warehouse, within cannon shot of the Tower in picturesque St. Katherine's Dock, Henry VIII lords over a crowd that can number 450. The entertainment borders on the vaudevillian, and the food on the banal, but the atmosphere is lively and bawdy, and the setting is impressive. Open nightly. Details: Beefeater by the Tower of London, Ivory House, St. Katharine's Dock, London El, England (phone: 01-408-1001).

SHAKESPEARE'S TAVERN AND PLAYHOUSE, London, England: In the sixteenth century, the area known as Blackfriars played a large part in Shakespeare's life, being both his home and place of work. Today, a former wine cellar here is the setting for an Elizabethan banquet whose creators have paid homage to the Bard by hanging up murals that depict scenes from his plays and by filling up the "Bill of Fayre" with dishes like "Puck's Pâté." If Shakespeare were around to see the entertainment, he doubtless would put down his pen in disgust. The puppet and magic shows are insipid, and the staging of the fight scene from *Macbeth* manages to be dull; and in between times, members of the audience, invited to jig to Scottish reels, weave between the tables in a valiant attempt to work off the five removes. You can't help but wonder what Will would have made of it. Nonetheless, the food is a cut above the *Beefeater's*, and you may enjoy the supper-clubby atmosphere. Open nightly. Details: Shakespeare's Tavern, Blackfriars La., London EC4V 6ER, England (phone: 01-408-1001).

THE SALSTON TAVERN, Ottery St. Mary, Devon, England: Beautifully situated in the heart of Devon, the old manor house that the Coleridge family once called home, now a comfortable hotel, regularly hosts special "Medieval Banquet Weekends," where you can join the court of Henry VIII on Friday night and work off the feast in the indoor swimming pool, sauna, and squash courts on Saturday. Banquets are also held on Thursday nights. Details: The Salston Tavern, Ottery St. Mary, Devon EX11 1RQ, England (phone: 040-481-2310).

ADAMTON COURTE, Monkton (near Prestwick), Ayrshire, Scotland: There's a corny quip to the effect that the haggis is a three-legged beastie that hops around the mountaintops; in reality it's a delectable concoction of not-so-sweet-sounding sheep's pluck, and at this true north-of-the-border banquet, held at Adamton Courte near Prestwick Airport in "Robbie Burns Country," the haggis is played in by bagpipers and served, as custom goes, with potatoes and turnips, locally called "champit tatties and neeps." Details: Adamton Courte, Monkton, Ayrshire, KA9 2SQ, Scotland (phone: 0292-70678).

CAMBUSNETHAN PRIORY, Wishaw, Strathclyde, Scotland: After the banquet is over, the hall turns into a disco — but otherwise, everything at this home of King Robert and his royal household, past a set of gallows and down a hill, is remarkably authentic, from your welcome, which comes with the admonition that "weapons and hourses (sic) are to be left in the forecourt," to the last remove. Hotel open daily; banquets by appointment. Details: Cambusnethan Priory Hotel, Wishaw, Strathclyde ML2 0RW, Scotland (phone: 069-83-72101).

PLAS GLANSEVIN, Llangadog, Dyfed, Wales: Held in a refurbished stone barn in south Wales, this entertainment is not so much a medieval banquet as a Welsh evening or *hwyrnos* (literally "late night"). It's informal, not touristy, and reminiscent of the days before electricity and easy transportation, when rural people used to gather at their neighbor's place to sing along to melodies of the sweet Welsh harp, and to dance, play games, tell stories, and recite poems. Your meal — hearty fare like roast leg of lamb and the traditional Welsh stew known as cawl, followed by a traditional pudding with fresh cream — is served in front of a huge walk-in fireplace. Inevitably, all the banquets are attempting to show off the twentieth century's idea of life in historical period — but because the Welsh commonly enjoyed just such evenings as the Glansevin's until very recently, what you find here has an extra bit of authenticity and that much more immediacy. Open weekends throughout the year, Wednesdays through Saturdays in summer, and other evenings if demand warrants. Details: Plas Glansevin, Llangadog, Dyfed SA19 9HY, Wales (phone: 055-03-238).

RUTHIN CASTLE, Ruthin, Clwyd, Wales: Although history says that Ruthin Castle came to be in 1296, when Reginald de Grey enlarged the original wood-and-stone fortress on the site, legend has it that the castle was created by two giants throwing stones at each other from opposite mountaintops. True or not, the castle's subsequent stormy history — full of changes of ownership, and death and destruction that left the castle a near-total ruin more than once — needs no embellishment. Today's offerings are equally wonderful, from the food — among the best in Britain and certainly the best of the banquets' — to the entertainment, which features a jester who is actually funny and minstrels (local housewives rather than the usual moonlighting pros) who sing their beautiful Welsh ballads to the accompaniment of harps, like angels. And the setting, in a wonderfully pastoral corner of northern Wales, full of rolling hills dotted with peaceful cattle and scattered here and there with quaint old farmhouses and pretty villages, can't be beat. Details: Ruthin Castle, Ruthin, Clywd LL15 2NU, Wales (phone: 082-42-2664).

BUNRATTY CASTLE, Bunratty, Co. Clare, Irish Republic: After you climb the narrow circular stone stairway to the dining hall and quaff your first goblet of mead, you can stroll around for a close look at this fifteenth-century castle's remarkable collection of art and antiques; traditional songs and harp music sustain a pleasantly medieval mood during the banquet. The meal itself is less impressive — spareribs and chicken (unadorned and, curmudgeons say, not all that appetizing), wine, and spongecake. Open nightly. Details: Shannon Tourist Office, Shannon International Free Airport, Co. Clare, Irish Republic (phone: 061-61664).

KNAPPOGUE CASTLE, Quin, Co. Clare, Irish Republic: Served in a huge stone dining hall lit by candles and hung with tapestries, the banquet here is very hearty, if not especially medieval: salad, soup, steak, vegetables, cheese, and fruit. While the evening's program includes some forgettably silly comic skits and sing-alongs, it also features snippets of Irish history and some very fine music performed on the harp and sung by the "ladies of the castle." As for the castle itself, it deserves a daytime visit as well so that you can explore its several elegantly furnished rooms and walk around its verdant and undulating grounds. Open nightly. Details: Shannon Tourist Office, Shannon International Free Airport, Co. Clare, Irish Republic (phone: 061-61664).

Shopping Spree

Shopping and Europe used to go hand in hand. You could buy things in Europe that you couldn't buy at home — or at least at prices far lower than you paid stateside. Nowadays, waltzing currencies have made things a bit more expensive, but the quality and selection that have always characterized the shopping in Britain and Ireland are still to be found, and a shopping spree doesn't always end up costing you an arm and a leg. You may even find some bargains.

In using the following sections — which describe just what you'll find where — you'll notice that our discussion of shopping in Ireland seems disproportionately long when compared with that of Great Britain. This is because the most tempting British shopping is found in the cities and is discussed in depth in the individual city reports. If, however, you restrict your shopping in Ireland to the cities, you'll miss much of the best the island has to offer, which is scattered throughout the countryside. For this reason, we have organized the Irish shopping sections county-by-county.

ENGLAND

Even the English Tourist Board concedes that the shopping is more or less uniform all across the nation: Most towns have their *Marks & Spencer,* their *Boots,* their *W.H. Smith,* or their local variations thereof. But whether you shop here or in London boutiques and department stores or any of scores of small one-of-a-kind shops scattered throughout the countryside, you'll find the workmanship nearly as good as ever, and selections that can't be beat: cashmere and Shetland woolens; tweeds and men's suitings; riding gear; custom-made men's suits, shoes, and hats; shotguns; umbrellas; sporting goods; English food specialties such as jams and marmalade, blended teas, Stilton cheese, and shortbread; and more. The antiques market is booming, and paintings and sculpture can be found in galleries all over the country (see *Antiques and*

Auctions). Handcrafted items abound. Books published by British houses, once a fine buy, have gone sky high, and you'll do better to buy the US editions; but rare and secondhand volumes are easy to find and well priced. Shops in the nation's stately homes, particularly those belonging to the National Trust, often stock quality merchandise commissioned especially for sale there. Engravings, paintings, and brass rubbings are frequently sold in the churches and cathedrals you'll visit. China and crystal are such an important British specialty that the British Tourist Authority has issued a booklet that includes information about seconds shops, museums, and factories. And while the days that England played bargain basement to Europe are almost as far past as the era when the sun never set on the British Empire, it's still possible for savvy shoppers to do well pricewise in Britain. The "jumble sale," the nation's answer to the basement or yard sale, is one very happy hunting ground: You can buy secondhand items and even a few unsung antiques at rock-bottom prices. Check ads in the local papers for announcements. New merchandise may also come cheap. True, the outlets on the premises of the *Royal Doulton, Spode, Minton,* and *Wedgwood* factories at Stoke-on-Trent do not offer first-quality goods at a discount, but those at *Wedgwood* and *Spode* do sell seconds — that is, china with slight imperfections — at half the retail price, as do a number of other shops around the country. London's by-now-legendary Christmas/New Year's sales (as well as their somewhat less sweeping July versions) are every bit as thrilling as they're cracked up to be. Londoners — not to mention the rest of the British, and hordes of shoppers from the Continent — wait breathlessly for them, and British reserve is left in shreds when the doors are flung open for the first bargain hunters of the day. Many items have been purchased especially for the event, but prices are also slashed on goods in stock. Remember that marked prices on everything except children's clothing and books (which are tax-exempt) include a 15% VAT, which can be refunded to you in many instances. For information about the procedure, see *Shopping,* GETTING READY TO GO. The BTA's *Shopping in London* ($4 postpaid, from the British Travel Bookshop, 680 Fifth Ave., New York, NY 10019) is an excellent guide.

Even if you don't buy anything when you prowl through Britain's shops, you'll have a great time chitchatting with the friendly local folk whether you shop in busy, bustling London, or at the memorable emporiums scattered around smaller English towns and cities detailed below.

BATH, Avon: This most elegant of Britain's cities is a treasure house for antiques lovers; see *Antiques.* For other details, contact the West Country Tourist Board (address above).

BRIGHTON, East Sussex: Shops in this cosmopolitan "London-by-the-Sea" stock nearly everything offered by the establishments of the fashionable quarters of the capital. Those in East Street and around George Street in the nearby community of Hove are particularly chic—great for window shopping and buying sprees alike. The nook-and-crannied Lanes area, full of brick-paved alleyways, has almost as many antique shops as pubs and teahouses. See the chapter on Brighton; for other details, contact the South East England Tourist Board, The Cheviot House, 4–6 Monson Rd., Tunbridge Wells, Kent TN1 1NH, England (phone: 0892-33066).

BUNGAY, Suffolk: *Nursey's* at 12 Upper Olland St. has been famous for its sheepskin coats, hats, gloves, slippers, rugs, and other items for almost all of the 200 years since its founding; the company likes to call itself the pioneers of the sheepskin coat.

CAMBRIDGE, Cambridgeshire: This is the town for books. *Heffer's* at 20 Trinity St. still supplies many undergraduates with their books; branches are at 30 Trinity St. (works for children), and at 13 Trinity St. and 31 St. Andrews St. (paperbacks). You can find Penguin books at the company's bookstore at 51 Trumpington Street, rare and fine books at *Deighton, Bell* at 13 Trinity St., and secondhand books at *G. David,* a

Cambridge institution at 16 St. Edward's Passage. *Bowes and Bowes* has been on the corner of Trinity and Market for four centuries now. Also distinctive is *Friar's House*, located in Bene't St. behind King's Parade—with the finest selection of collectors' paperweights in East Anglia. Cambridge badges, plaques, cuff links, and college rugby shirts are for sale at *Ryder and Amies* (27 King's Parade), while *W. & G. Taylor*, the tailors at 5 Trinity St., also offer tweeds and tartans, deerstalker hats, and 6-foot-long college scarves. For more information, see the chapter on Cambridge, and contact the East Anglia Tourist Board, 14 Museum St., Ipswich, Suffolk IP1 1HU, England (phone: 0473-214211).

CASTLETON, near Buxton, Derbyshire: The well-known semiprecious yellow and blue decorative stone called Blue John comes from ancient mines in this Peak District town not far from Sheffield; you can buy jewelry and other ornaments at the entrance to the mines as well as in local shops. Details: Tourist Information Centre, The Crescent, Buxton, Derbyshire, England (phone: 0298-5106).

CHANNEL ISLANDS: There used to be plenty of craftswomen on Jersey who spent their time knitting the island's distinctive navy blue, oiled wool pullovers; and on neighboring Guernsey, woman's organizations used to turn out similar models in white as well—but now they only hand-finish what machines have made. You can buy the product at shops along cobblestone-paved byways such as the Arcades, High St., and The Pollet in St. Peter Port. For a unique souvenir, pick up one of the narrow-necked milk cans sold all over Jersey and Guernsey in different sizes. Jersey's other claim to fame is a handsome pottery made and sold near Gorey village. Cabbage walking sticks also make a distinctive and unusual souvenir. And luxury goods cost considerably less on both islands than in England thanks to the absence of high import duties and of the VAT. Details: Jersey Tourism, Weighbridge, St. Helier, Jersey, Channel Islands.

CHELTENHAM, Gloucestershire: This is a good base for shopping in the Cotswolds. For antiques, unspoiled Chipping Campden, Northleach, and Stow-on-the-Wold are good. The village of Broadway attracts throngs to its array of shops. Area information: Heart of England Tourist Board, PO Box 15, Worcester WR1 2JT, England (phone: Worcester 0905-29511).

CHESTER, Cheshire: Of all provincial cities, this old community of medieval, half-timbered houses offers what is most certainly the most charming atmosphere for shopping in the country. The many boutiques installed in the several levels of the ancient structures in The Rows always seem to be full of trifles and treasures you simply can't live without—antiques and silver, clothing in a range of prices, wallpaper, and more. See the chapter on Chester for further information, and contact the North West Tourist Board, The Last Drop Village, Bromley Cross, Bolton BL7 9PZ, England (phone: 0204-591511).

DARTINGTON, Devon: The shop at the Dartington Hall complex sells the woven willow baskets that are handcrafted all over the West Country. Dartington glass in simple modern shapes can be had at the Torrington factory in North Devon. Pottery and weaving here are also first-rate. Local information: West Country Tourist Board, Trinity Court, 37 Southornbay E, Exeter, Devon EX1 1D5 England (phone: 0392-76351).

DERBY, Derbyshire: The cathedral here has a workshop where you can commission church embroidery and heraldic work, and you can visit the factory that makes *Royal Crown Derby* bone china—and, afterward, the reject shop opens to four guests. Details: Derbyshire County Council, Derby Reference Library, The Wardwick, Derbyshire DE4 3AG, England (phone: 31111).

MINEHEAD, Somerset: The Exmoor area is a wonderful place for woolens and sheepskin products, and this town, along with nearby Porloch and Dunster, is a prime center. For local information, contact the West Country Tourist Board (address above).

HERSTMONCEUX, East Sussex: Trugs — shallow, bent-willow baskets — are this town's claim to fame, and you can get them in some two dozen sizes at the workshop of *Thomas Smith*, manufacturer to Her Late Majesty Queen Victoria (established over 150 years ago). Each one is individually finished and made from locally grown woods—pliable sweet chestnut for the rims and handles and split-resistant willow for the body—to produce a product that is light in weight and incredibly durable. The wide, shallow flower trugs, the strong, deep fireside log trugs, and the shallow round bowls are particularly handsome. For local information, contact the South East England Tourist Board (address above).

KENDAL, Cumbria: Not far from this delightful town, on Danes Rd. in Staveley, is *Peter Hall Woodcraft*, which turns out traditional English furniture; small gift items are generally for sale as well (phone: 0539-821633).

KILBURN, Yorkshire: The woodcrafting traditions begun by the late Robert Thompson, who won fame for carving a tiny mouse on each one of his works, are upheld at *Robert Thompson Craftsmen Ltd.*, where you'll find small items such as ash trays, fruit bowls, and cheese boards — and watch artisans at work on English oak furniture (phone: Coxwold 218).

LONDON: One of the finest shopping centers in the world, London offers you the ultimate in things traditional and fantastic alike. The variety evident in the selection of women's clothing—everything from tweed hacking jackets and cashmere sweaters to silk-and-lace lingerie and evening gowns confected of billowing yards of chiffon—prevails for most other items as well, no matter where you go. Bond Street and progressively more expensive New Bond and Old Bond streets would leave even an oil sheikh's number-one wife yearning for more of the kinds of luxury items that these places make their specialty. Ditto for pedestrians-only South Molton Street. Regent Street, running parallel to Bond Street between Oxford and Piccadilly circuses, is as elegant as its shops' facades. Piccadilly and St. James's Street boast many stores holding royal patents. Turning north off Piccadilly, the circa-1819, roofed-over Burlington Arcade is fine for a rainy day; south of Piccadilly and parallel to it, Jermyn Street is *the* place for blue-ribbon custom tailoring. Knightsbridge is known for its fairly expensive, eminently window-shoppable emporiums—and for the department store *Harrod's*. The greatest department store in London, if not in the world, it occupies 4½ acres and five selling floors, and no one questions whether it lives up to its motto *Omnia Omnibus Ubique* (Everyone, Everything, Everywhere); the bacon and the butter that you can buy in the astonishing food halls are the city's least expensive, and that's only the beginning. What's not in the house can be ordered.

Beauchamp Place is full of interesting shops purveying fashions, china, and jewelry —as is Sloane Street, which begins at the Knightsbridge underground station. King's Road, the continuation of Sloane Street, which made its fame in "Swinging London" days, is mostly sad and tatty; but the people-watching is great there on Saturday mornings. Nearby Fulham Road has a good range of shops as well. Carnaby Street, another holdover from the sixties, is a tourist trap. Covent Garden, on the other hand, has been bustling since the removal of the vegetable market in 1974; alone, the wonderfully restored Covent Garden Market has three floors of shops, and there are dozens more all over the area.

London is also known for its street markets. Berwick Street in Soho has been bustling with fruit and vegetable hawkers for over a century now (Mondays to Saturdays). Electric Avenue in Brixton, where you'll find exotic food and secondhand clothes, has a Caribbean flavor (Mondays through Saturdays, half-days on Wednesdays). Camden Lock, where Chalk Farm crosses Regent's Canal, stocks bric-a-brac, junk, and crafts (Saturdays and Sundays). The Kensington Market, off Kensington High Street, is a maze of lanes and stalls selling offbeat clothing, jewelry, antiques, and knickknacks (Mondays through Saturdays). Petticoat Lane, which radiates from Middlesex Street, overflows with wares that are mostly rubbish, but browsing is always fun (Sunday mornings). The world-renowned Portobello Road flea market near Notting Hill, a *Harrod's* among street markets, shouldn't be missed. And an early-morning visit to the vast halls where London's meat is distributed, the Smithfield Market, shows off yet another side of fascinating London (Mondays through Fridays).

For more information, see the chapter on London, *Antiques and Auctions,* and the BTA's *Shopping in London,* described above.

OXFORD, Oxfordshire: Another good town for books. *B. H. Blackwell, Ltd.,* stands out for sheer size; its Norrington Room is famous for the largest single collection of books housed in one room anywhere in the world. Competitors are ranged along Broad Street. Oxford is also home to the impressive *Stanton King Model Shop* (17 High St.), chockablock with miniature steam engines, trains, boats, and vintage cars. For details, see the chapter on Oxford and contact the Thames and Chilterns Tourist Board, 8 The Market Place, Abingdon, Oxfordshire OX14 3HG, England (phone: 0235-22711).

SOUTHWOLD, Suffolk: This seaside resort has a good assortment of boutiques; most interesting is the *Amber Shop* devoted solely to the fossilized resin for which Suffolk is famous; jewelry and carvings come in a variety of designs and price ranges. For area information: East Anglia Tourist Board, 14 Museum St., Ipswich, England (phone: 0473-214211).

STOKE-ON-TRENT, Staffordshire: This has been Britain's pottery-producing center since the eighteenth century, and the selection of Wedgwood, Spode, Minton, and Royal Doulton here is the best in the country. There are seven seconds and firsts shops in The Potter's Acre district near Gladstone Working Pottery Museum, Longton; the museum itself sells its own factory's products, which include both craft pottery and white wares. Details: Gladstone Working Pottery Museum, Uttoxeter Rd., Longton, Stoke-on-Trent, Staffordshire ST3 1PQ, England (phone: 0782-319232 or 311378).

STREET, Somerset: If you're a nut about *Clark's* shoes, you'll want to look for low-priced seconds in this town near Glastonbury, home of the company's 150-year-old headquarters and a fascinating museum that displays the queer-looking footgear of ages past. More Somerset shopping information: West Country Tourist Board (address above).

WHITSTABLE, Kent: The old section of this town is jammed with secondhand shops selling everything from books and bric-a-brac to old clothes and even a few valuable antiques. Details: Tourist Information Centre, 1 Tankerton Rd., Whitstable, Kent CT5 2AB, England (phone: Whitstable 272233).

SCOTLAND

The green and windswept land of castles and links has given rise to one of the world's finest woolen industries, and if you've planned to invest in new sweaters, skirts, jackets, or trousers this year, the selection here warrants waiting until your arrival to do it. The subtly patterned and colored Harris tweeds woven by hand in the Outer Hebrides come from Scotland. So do Shetland and Fair Isle sweaters, plus most of the world's best-quality lambswool and cashmere pullovers and cardigans. Tartans are Scottish, and there are some 500 patterns — most of which you can buy by the yard or have stitched up into a kilt — or, for ladies, a "kilted skirt" — if the impulse strikes you. Sheepskin coats are a good buy — as are books, particularly antiquarian volumes (details about which can be found in *Antiques and Auctions*). Scottish jewelry is wonderful and distinctive: round silver bowls called *quaiches,* used in Gaelic ceremonies; Armada plates, based on designs captured from the Spanish Armada; Celtic crosses set with luminous pearls from the River Tay; Luckenbooth brooches representing two entwined hearts surmounted by a crown; paperweights, clan brooches and kilt pins, and other treasures set with quartz, amethyst, cairngorm stones, and other semiprecious jewels. Scottish crystal is well crafted and plentiful, as is fishing and shooting equipment. Whisky, while not inexpensive, comes in a selection you don't find stateside. And you can always take home a set of bagpipes.

As in England, prices on first-quality items do not vary from one place to the next

DIVERSIONS / Shopping Spree

— but journeys into the countryside will often lead to an outlet where you can buy seconds, remnants, or discontinued styles at less-than-retail prices.

ABERDEEN, Grampian: *Messrs. Fishing Tackle Ltd.* (35 Belmont St.) is famous for its rods and reels; *John Dickson & Son,* the venerable sporting goods store, has a branch here. Area information: Grampian Regional Council, The Leisure, Recreation, and Tourism Department, Woodhill House, Ashgrove Rd., W, Aberdeen AB9 2LU, Scotland (phone: Aberdeen 0224-23401).

EDINBURGH: It's in this city that you can get the best overview of things Scottish, and mile-long Princes Street, Edinburgh's Fifth Avenue, is the best place to do it. Side streets, where less-expensive goods are to be found, and Georges Street are also good. In addition to department stores such as *Jenner's, R. W. Forsyth, Ltd.,* and *Hamilton & Inches,* don't miss *Kinloch Anderson* (16 Georges St.), Kilt Makers for the Royal Family; you can buy kilts and kilted skirts, either ready-made or bespoke, in some 400 of the 500 tartans in existence, from Abercrombie, Balmoral, Black Watch, and Culloden to Urquhart and Wallace, and if you need a sporran, a tweed jacket to match the plaid, a tie, stockings, garters, or any other accessory to complete your outfit, the store can supply that, too. For bagpipes — some with gold, ivory, or silver fittings — see *J. & R. Glen* (497 Lawnmarket); *William Sinclair & Son,* a few miles away; and *Hugh MacPherson* (Maitland St.), who sells both bagpipes and Highland costumes handmade by local women. For more information, see the chapter on Edinburgh, and contact the Lothian Regional Council, Department of Recreation and Leisure, 40 Torpichen St., Edinburgh EH3 8JJ, Scotland.

ELGIN, Grampian: This old market town, known for the impressive ruins of the thirteenth-century Elgin Cathedral, is the center for the manufacture of several varieties of malt whisky (*Gordon & MacPhail,* South St., Elgin) — all of which are readily available here. For local tweeds and tartans, visit the *Johnston's Mill Shop.* Details: Grampian Regional Council (address above).

GALASHIELS, Borders: Not far from Hawick and the home of the Scottish College of Textiles, this town is well known for its woolens, and the roadsides of the surrounding area are scattered with discount mill outlet stores. Details: Borders Regional Council, Newtown St., Boswells, Borders TD6 0SA, Scotland (phone: 0835-23301).

HAWICK, Borders: Famous for knitwear, this old market town is full of mills with outlets where you can get second-quality goods at a fraction of the retail price. Details: Borders Regional Council (address above).

LOCH LOMOND, Strathclyde: The *Antartex Factory,* with wonderful sheepskin goods at factory prices, is about half an hour's drive from Glasgow (phone: Alexandria 52393 or 56638).

OUTER HEBRIDES, Western Isles: The wool cloth bearing the distinctive trademark of the Harris tweed, a circle and a Celtic cross, is handwoven by islanders following age-old methods; the yard goods are for sale in shops throughout the islands. Stornoway, the largest town of the Lewis-Harris landmass, has a mill that sells tweeds at competitive prices. Sweaters knit from Harris wool are available at all the local craft shops. On Eriskay, island women produce the distinctive patterned local fisherman's sweaters. For more information, contact the tourist office at 4 South Beach Quay, Stornoway, Isle of Lewis.

PERTH, Tayside: The rare freshwater Scottish pearls from the Tay, Spey, and other rivers are the specialty at *A.&G. Cairncross,* 18 St. John St. (phone: 0738-2436). For more shopping information, contact the Perth Tourist Association, the Round House, Marshall Pl., Perth, Tayside PH2 8NU, Scotland.

ST. ANDREWS, Fife: This is home to the *St. Andrews Woollen Mill,* one of the nation's biggest and best outlets for knitted and woven woolens and cashmeres — first quality, seconds, discontinued lines, and remnants. For details: St. Andrews Woollen Mill, The Golf Links, St. Andrews, Fife, Scotland.

WALES

Wrought iron, leatherwork, basketry, and carved wood are but a few of this area's specialties. Woolen weaving is still important, and you can visit workshops at various mills to see the weaving process for yourself; the Wales Tourist Board will point you on your route.

Meanwhile, handicrafts are flourishing so beautifully that the same organization now publishes the leaflet *Wales — Crafts and Rural Industries* (available for about 30p from the Board at Brunel House, 2 Fitzalean Rd., Cardiff, South Glamorgan CF2 1UY, Wales) explaining current goings-on and describing some 200 craft enterprises, mills, potteries, and retail shops. It's well worth a look. A few notable take-home items include those found in the following towns:

CARDIFF, South Glamorgan: The center for the marketing of things Welsh, Cardiff has dozens of shops—some intriguingly set into shopping arcades, some in big department stores such as *Howells of Cardiff* (St. Mary St.) and *David Morgan* (The Hayes). Best bets for traditional Welsh rural crafts—bedspreads, pottery, woodwork, carved Welsh love spoons, and the like—include *Things Welsh* (Duke St. Arcade), *Welsh Rural Crafts* (Royal Arcade), and *Pethau Cain* (Pontcanna Pl., Llandaff Fields). For more information, see the chapter on Cardiff and contact the South Wales Tourism Board, Darkgate, Carmarthen, Dyfed, Wales (phone: Carmarthen 0267-7557).

ISLE OF ANGLESEY: The *Bodeilio Centre* near Llangefni has a museum tracing the history of Wales's most important domestic crafts—spinning and weaving. Details: Bodeilio Weaving Centre, Talwrn, Llangefni, Anglesey, Gwynedd LL77 7AT, Wales. and sells locally made pottery, silverware, and woven goods.

BLAENAU, FFESTINIOG, Gwynedd: This great old slate-mining town has a gift shop at the mines where you can buy souvenirs carved before your eyes. For more information, contact the Mid Wales Tourism Council, Owain Glyndwr Institute, Maengwyn St., Machynlleth, Powys SY20 8EE, Wales.

HAY-ON-WYE, Powys: *Richard Booth (Bookseller), Ltd.*, listed in the *Guinness Book of World Records* as the largest secondhand bookshop on earth, displays about a million books on nearly 11 miles of shelves in its many buildings. The selection at this shop alone would warrant a trip to the town. But the droves of bibliophiles who have discovered the town have spurred the establishment of yet other bookshops—bringing the total to a dozen—so that Hay-on-Wye now calls itself the "Town of Books."

LLANWRTYD, Wells, Powys: The *Royal British Legion Cambrian Factory*, a short walk from the center of town, sells yarn spun from a locally made wool as well as Welsh tweeds and knitwear made from it. Details: Royal British Legion Cambrian Factory, Llanwrtyd, Wells, Powys LD5 45D, Wales (phone: 05913-211).

IRISH REPUBLIC

Among the best purchases you can make are Irish food items — smoked salmon, which can be found conveniently plastic-wrapped in airports and shops; heather honey from the Boyne Valley; Irish cheddar; Molly O'Rourke's fruitcakes; W. H. Mosse–brand mix for Irish brown soda bread; and Bewley's cakes and coffees. Most of these items are available at the big Shannon Airport shop. Machine-made, heather-toned knits by Gaeltarra Eireann, Glenabbey, and Carberry Knitwear are also lovely. Books are a big business. And you'll find a wider selection of Irish whiskeys than you might readily locate at home. Power, Jameson, Paddy, Tullamore Dew, and others — no longer produced in small, scattered family distilleries but under the same roof at the Midleton Distillery in Midleton, County Cork — are usually expensive because of heavy taxes;

look for special offers at supermarkets and specialist wine shops, or make your purchases at a car ferry or the duty-free shop.

But it would be a mistake to leave Ireland without one of the nation's distinctive handmade items in your suitcase. That the nation escaped the worst of the Industrial Revolution has meant that many traditional crafts never died out; the last few years' surge of interest in tradition has seen them flourishing as never before. Attracted by Ireland's wide-open spaces and the mobility permitted by the EEC, Dutch, French, German, and Swedish emigrés have brought new ideas and increased sophistication to rural craftsmen, and craft shops, workshops, and stores throughout the country now stock handmade goods in both traditional and contemporary styles — the kind of treasures that you would never turn up in Manhattan or Missouri let alone Manchester or Milan. Shillelaghs and blackthorn walking sticks are still to be found, and briar pipes are world-famous. There are hand-turned tableware and platters, salt and pepper shakers, and tables and chairs with rustic-looking seats made of twisted hay or straw. Pottery — a craft indigenous only to Youghal in County Cork, Carley's Bridge in County Wexford, and Coalisland in County Tyrone — is being produced in an increasing number of studios all over the island, especially in Clare, West Cork, Dublin, Kerry, and Kilkenny; it comes in simple sculptural shapes and earthy colors. Metalsmiths produce bowls and bracelets, chains and earrings, pendants and rings, and tea and coffee sets in silver, gold, or copper. Sometimes jewelry is inset with semiprecious stones or half-moons of Connemara marble; sometimes the designs derive from the Book of Kells. Glassmaking — an Irish tradition that goes back to the early seventeenth century — is also important; the Waterford crystal enterprise, having closed in 1851, began turning out its glittering hand-cut crystal wares once again 101 years later — and business is booming. Galway crystal is also lovely. A tablecloth of real Irish linen makes a perfect companion, and linens decorated with "sprigging" (scattered hand embroidery in white or colors, by a method developed in east Donegal during the 1840s famine) can also be found. Fine cotton Irish lace, the crafting of which was introduced for the same reasons at about the same time, can make an everyday wearable fit a special occasion: The Clones knot, rose, and shamrock patterns are the most common, but the convent teachers who produce most of Ireland's lacework nowadays have dozens of others. Basketmakers turn the rushes and sallies that grow along the country's slow-flowing rivers and lakes into sturdy shallow baskets, shopping baskets, table mats, St. Brigid crosses, harvest knots, and other items. Graphic artists fill engravings and woodcuts, screen prints, and lithographs with wonderful images; still others who have adopted as their medium the Indonesian art of batik, a form of wax-resist dying, turn out wall hangings, scarves, and cushions filled with faces and owls and Celtic scrolls. Clare, Cork, Dublin, and Kilkenny are the main centers. Leatherworkers, whose studios are concentrated in County Kildare, the main horse-breeding and training center, turn out some of the world's finest saddles and riding whips, boots, coats, shoes, handbags, and belts — as you'd expect from a nation that has always been so dominated by livestock; the traditional goatskin drum known as a *bodhrán* makes an especially interesting souvenir. Weavers no longer give the world the kind of homespun, handwoven tweeds that differed from one part of the country to the next because of regional variations in the wool and dyes — but tweed from Donegal, which comes from Ireland's northwest coast in weights that vary from the nearly chiffonlike to the heavy and rugged, is still one of Ireland's best buys — as are bags, cushions, gloves, hats, scarves, sportswear, table mats, wall hangings, and other items made from it. Packaged lengths of tweed, sometimes accompanied by skeins of matching yarn, are also a good bet, and a hacking jacket of Donegal tweed could be one of the most durable — and beautiful — you've ever owned. Equally renowned are fishermen's sweaters hand-knit from heavy oiled or scoured off-white wool, in the tree of life, crooked road, tobacco, carrageen moss, castle, and popcornlike bobaleen stitches, combined in almost sculptural patterns that sometimes resemble the carvings on Celtic crosses. There's a special meaning to each pattern (e.g., God bless, good luck, or good fishing). Originally, they were made on the Aran Islands; but now, cottage knitters throughout the west and north produce them for sale across the nation (and, indeed, around the world). The selection is usually best not on the Aran Isles but in the cities — particularly Galway and Dublin — and no two are quite alike. Stained glass, musical instruments, patchwork quilts, cut stones, candles, handmade carpets and rugs, that will last lifetimes, and soft toys and quaint rag dolls clad in fisherman's sweaters and Donegal tweeds also can dazzle you; hand-tied fishing flies are also important (though less so than in Scotland).

Every county usually has its specialty and its assortment of little shops, some of which keep company with workshops in craft centers ("craft clusters" in the local English) where you can watch the artisan as he beats out a silver bowl or weaves a stripe into a fluffy bedspread. Details can be found in the *Craft Hunter's Pocket Guide,* available free from Irish Tourist Board offices in the US. Note that except at sales, seconds are rarely available.

The Republic's VAT, ranging from 18% to 30% on most things other than clothing and footwear, can be avoided by having your purchases delivered directly to your departing plane, or mailed to your home (in which case you'll pay US customs duty).

Shopping hours are usually 9:30 AM to 5:30 PM Mondays through Saturdays (with one early closing day in rural areas, usually Wednesdays or Thursdays)—and never on Sundays.

Here's a survey of some of the best — arranged county-by-county to help you map out a shopping trip.

COUNTY CAVAN: *Cavan Crystal Ireland Ltd.* makes fine glassware on Dublin Rd., Cavan; seconds are available in the factory shop. Area information: Midland Region Tourist Information Office, Dublin Rd., Mullingar, Co. Westmeath, Irish Republic (phone: 044-8761).

COUNTY CLARE: In Ballyvaughan, the *Manus Walsh Craft Workshop* produces lovely enamelware. At *Bunratty Cottage Fashion Shop,* opposite Bunratty Castle, Vonnie Reynolds creates dramatic, highly individual clothing for both men and women; lace made by local handworkers adds drama to her ballgowns. Classic tweed coats, suits, and capes are also available there, along with crocheted blouses in cotton, knit suits, and more. Brian Mooney, who studied the art of distilling perfumes with the monks, and his wife, Nora, operate *Vincent Craft Fragrances* in The Burren, bottling their fragrances in cut-glass flagons, some encased in rushwork baskets or ornamented with a bit of Irish linen or lace. In Ennis, *Denis Maurer* makes standout jewelry. In Shannon, in the craft cluster known as *Ballycasey House*, Alison Erridge and Michele Hughes of *Ballycar Design* make and sell quilts, cushions, scarves, and panels—hand- and machine-embroidered—in silks and fine cottons, beautifully designed and colored; in the same complex, you can also buy Aran sweaters, silver jewelry, handwovens, souvenirs, and other items from all over County Clare, County Limerick, and North Tipperary. County information: Mid-Western Region Tourist Information Office, The Granary, Michael St., Limerick, Irish Republic (phone: 061-47522).

COUNTY CORK: At Ballydehob, an artists' colony of sorts, *Norah Golden* (Main St.) produces fine colorful batik, and other artisans work in pottery, graphics, and handweaving. In Dripsey, the *Tweed Mill Shop* at the Dripsey Woollen Mills is good, and in Durrus, *Wilf Stock* produces interesting figurines in metal. *Macroom Carpets* of Macroom has a standout factory shop. At Shanagarry, *Stephen Pearce* creates distinctive pottery in a single lovely pattern using white glaze on red clay; his tall, narrow-necked Irish stewpots make a delectable soup indeed. The *Shanagarry Pottery,* run by Pearce's father, Phillip, makes pots that are glossy black with a milky white interior that spills over the rim to form a border against the black. And the *Fastnet Co-Operative Society,* headquartered in Skibbereen, produces some of the nation's most interesting candles; you may even be able to watch them being made. Local particulars: Cork/Kerry Region Tourist Information Office, Tourist House, Grand Parade, Cork, Irish Republic (phone: 021-23251).

COUNTY DONEGAL: The birthplace of the tweeds for which Ireland is so famous, this county does a thriving business in woolens, especially tweeds — colored like the bluebells and gorse, hawthorn and heather of the landscape itself — in herringbones and houndstooth checks. In some places, you'll see whole bales of the stuff stacked alongside the road outside the cottages of the weavers, waiting for finishers' trucks to come pick it up. The town of Ardara is justly famous for its homespun tweeds, which, though occasionally colored with synthetics as well as vegetable dyes, exist in the most subtle and luscious of hues. Particularly noteworthy are those at the *John Molloy (Ardara) Ltd. Factory Shop,* situated on the outskirts of Ardara on the Killybegs Rd. Don't miss the *Campbell's Tweed Shop, J. F. Heron,* and the *Tweed Shop* for fine hand-embroidery and hand-knitting. Local knitters send their work to *G. Kennedy & Sons Ltd.,* where you'll see fascinating demonstrations, and *C. Bonner & Sons Ltd.* Outside Ardara, *Rogan of Donegal* in Ballyshannon does fishing flies. At *Teresa's Cottage Industries* at Church View, Bruckless, you can watch the girls cutting out fine, pure white Irish linen, making it into cloths and napkins, embroidering it, and edging it with crochet for the firm's thriving mail-order business. *John Shiels* turns out exquisitely designed spinning wheels at Bridge St., Cardonagh, and *Fred Hanna,* in Donegal Town, is the place for Irish tweed hats and caps. *Scott McNutt* of Downings produces fine handwoven tweeds. In Killybegs, *Donegal Carpets* (whose products can be seen in Dublin Castle, the White House in Washington, DC, and Buckingham Palace) makes hand-knotted rugs and wall hangings. For area information: Donegal/Leitrim/Sligo Region Tourist Information Office, Temple St., Sligo, Co. Sligo, Irish Republic (phone: 071-61201).

COUNTY DUBLIN: Blackrock is home to a good many interesting craftworkers, most notably the *Crock of Gold* (Newtownpark Ave.), where gossamer stoles and scarves are woven in fairy colors; *Dublin Crystal Glass Company* (Avondale, Carysfort Ave.), where you'll find good values on engraved and hand-cut baubles produced on the premises. On Leslie Ave. in Dalkey, the *Cuala Press* makes wonderful hand-painted prints from the drawings of Jack B. Yeats, plus hand-printed books. In Dollymount, at the *Royal Dublin Golf Club,* Fred Smyth golf clubs have been made since 1898; you can get a 15% reduction if you visit the pro. In Dun Laoghaire, at 71 York Rd., *John Murphy* sells jewelry from his workshop. *Hills* at Lucan produces good tweeds. In Rathfarnham, artisans in the workshops at *Marley Park Craft Courtyard* make and repair guitars and harps, among other things, and Muriel Beckett designs and weaves rugs and wall hangings. *Wynne's Pottery,* in Sandyford, is worth a look if only to meet proprietors Ron and Pat Wynne. For more county information, contact the Eastern Region Tourist Information Office, 1 Clarinda Park N, Dun Laoghaire, Co. Dublin, Irish Republic (phone: 01-808571).

COUNTY GALWAY: In Clifden, *Millars* is one of the best for the Irish tweed hats and fabric. *Joe Hogan* at Loch na Fooey, Clonbur, makes and sells baskets of willow —or sally, in local parlance—traditional baskets, including the low potato basket known as the sciob and a full range of turf and log baskets. *James Jocelyn* makes small, interesting pieces in marble, in a traditional Connemara cottage at Glinsk (between Carne and Cashel). *Connemara Handicrafts* at Letterfrack, perhaps the finest crafts shop in the nation, has a wonderfully comprehensive selection of handmade Irish products. At Moycullen, you can watch Ambrose Joyce hew marble at *Connemara Marble Products.* In Oughterard, *V'Soske-Joyce* turns out the crème de la crème of Ireland's hand-carved carpets in enormously varied designs — you can even order one made to resemble your backyard garden. In Spiddal, *Mairtin Standun* offers fishermen's sweaters in Bainin wool, as well as linens, tweeds, claddagh rings, and sheepskin rugs. Al O'Dea of *Corrib Crafts* in the town of Tuam makes and sells rustic furniture in uniquely Irish designs. Local information: Áras Fáilte, Galway, Irish Republic (phone: 091-63081).

COUNTY KERRY: Killarney is full of crafts shops and in Kenmare you'll also see a variety of local crafts. Dingle Town is home to one of Ireland's more interesting candlemakers, *Celtic Craft Candles*. While driving around the Dingle peninsula, you'll see signposts for many potteries. One of these, *Louis Muleahy Pottery*, at Ballyferriter, turns out some very elegant ceramics; potters will be interested in seeing the large waste-oil-fired kiln. Rugs and blankets woven from plant-dyed wools are also for sale here. In Beaufort, the *Kerry Woollen Mills* makes travel rugs and other woolen fabrics. Local information: Cork/Kerry Region Tourist Information Office (address above).

COUNTY KILDARE: *Berney Brothers* of Kilcullen makes saddles of all types, while in nearby Naas, *Tutty's*, famous for footwear, will make shoes or boots to fit two left feet, if need be. In tiny Prosperous, *Brid ni Rinn* makes and sells woodcarvings and sculpture. In Timolin, you'll find lovely pewter holloware and jewelry at the *Irish Pewtermill*. Area information: Eastern Region Tourist Information Office (address above).

COUNTY KILKENNY: In Cuffsgrange, at *Desart Lodge*, Peter Wenger turns out superb batiks. In Tintine, The Rower, *Peter and Marjorie Clark* produce fine copper work. *Legan Castle Pottery* in the Golden Vale village of Thomastown is an enduring ceramics workshop; visitors have the freedom of the workshop and may even have a go at the potter's wheel. Other area information: South Eastern Region Tourist Information Office, 41 The Quay, Waterford, Co. Waterford, Irish Republic (phone: 051-75823).

COUNTY LAOIS: Patrick Dunne at *George Galbraith Woodturners*, Corbally, is known for his woodturned pieces; an assortment of crafts is available at the shop on the Abbeyleix Estate beside the town of Abbeyleix. Other area information: Midland Region Tourist Information Office, Dublin Rd., Mullingar, Co. Westmeath, Irish Republic (phone: 044-8761).

COUNTY LEITRIM: *Cyril Cullen* has a shop and studio in a handsome Georgian house in Carrick-on-Shannon; the knitted and crocheted styles that he and some 1,400 women working in their homes with wool, linen, and cotton yarns produce are very haute, and the shop is overflowing with treasures, for sale and not, including a lovely Irish harp. For local particulars, contact the Donegal/Leitrim/Sligo Region Tourist Information Office (address above).

COUNTY LIMERICK: In Limerick City, at the *Good Shepherd Convent* on Clare St. you can watch three women—one of whom has been at her craft for half a century—creating the delicate Carrickmacross lace, and buy bits of the well-known local lace at very attractive prices. The Shannon airport nearby has a huge duty-free shop where you can buy cigarettes, liquor, French perfumes, Swiss watches, and English and Irish goods — linen tablecloths, Connemara wool rugs, Aran sweaters, smoked salmon, fresh-baked brown soda bread, and more. Prices are not always Ireland's lowest, but you can't beat the convenience: china and crystal can be packed on the spot, and there's a money-back or replacement guarantee against breakage. At the *Orchard Pottery* in Castleconnell, you'll find attractive pots and wares. In the village of Adare, west of Limerick, *Michelina Stacpoole's* shop carries fine high-fashion knits for women in pure wool. Other Limerick information: Mid-Western Region Tourist Information Office (address above).

COUNTY LONGFORD: *Michael Casey* in Barley Harbour, Newtowncashel, far off the beaten track, is known for the free-form carvings he does in subfossilized oak, yew, and deal wood that he digs from the bogs that have preserved it for some 6,000 years. Other Longford information: Midland Region Tourist Information Office (address above).

COUNTY LOUTH: *Michael Madden*, who works at Feede, Mountpleasant, in Dundalk, produces handsome carpets. Local particulars: Eastern Region Tourist Information Office (address above).

COUNTY MAYO: *Providence Mills,* in Foxford, produces lovely tweeds; you can watch the spinning, dyeing, and weaving on tours of the mill. The town of Westport is a good bet for craft-hunting, whether you're looking for a pair of lambskin slippers or some more traditional handmade item; don't miss the art center on the grounds of stately Westport House, a handsome Irish country home. Local details: Western Region Tourist Information Office (address above).

COUNTY ROSCOMMON: The *Slieve Bawn Co-Operative Market* in Strokestown has a variety of crafts, and is especially good for basketry, rushwork, and attractive Lumra rugs, made from unspun, undyed wool. A variety of other craft makers work at the *Strokestown Craft Cluster;* visitors can see the artisans plying their trades. For other area shopping information, contact the Midland Region Tourist Information Office (address above).

COUNTY TIPPERARY: The town of Cashel has a number of studios and shops. *Pádraig Ó Mathúna* will delight you with his fine work in silver, gold, and enamels in a style that is visibly influenced by his 2-decade-long study of old Irish metalwork and stone carvings. Nenagh is home to another of the country's good tweed-producers, *John Hanly & Co. Ltd.;* the retail shop is on Clare St. In Puckane, *Puckane Community Crafts* is known for wooden wall plaques carved with typical Irish scenes. In Tipperary, *McInerney's of the Irish House* sells some of Eire's most attractive fishing flies. For other local shopping information, contact the South Eastern Region Tourist Information Office and the Mid-Western Region Tourist Information Office (addresses above).

COUNTY WATERFORD: Ireland's most prestigious product, world-famous Waterford crystal, is produced here for sale in top Irish stores and around the world. The Waterford factory is open for tours that show off the dramatic process, from the blowing of the glass to the cutting, by which the stunning goblets, vases, bowls, and other items on display in a palatial marble exhibit hall nearby are produced. (Note that the factory is closed for 3 weeks annually, usually in July or August.) You can do your buying elsewhere — in Waterford or at gift shops in other parts of the island. For details about other shopping in Waterford, contact the South Eastern Region Tourist Information Office (address above).

COUNTY WESTMEATH: Mullingar, an important cattle marketing center, has a good crafts center as well as a scattering of other shops, including *Mullingar Pewter.*

COUNTY WICKLOW: *John Tyrell* of Arklow builds sailing boats for important races and famous people. Avoca is a favorite place of artists and craftsmen, a number of whom have established studios there; *Avoca Handweavers* do particularly outstanding work—lovely and soft. In Bray, *Jan and Carlo Zanoni* turn out enameled pieces and metal sculpture at their studio on Violet Hill, while other shops nearby offer an assortment of other typically Irish wares. At *Stitchers of Enniskerry* in Enniskerry you can get patchwork quilts, rugs, cushions, and the like. For other shopping hints for the area, contact the Eastern Region Tourist Information Office (address above).

NORTHERN IRELAND

The spiderweb-fine Carrickmacross lace is made in towns in the southern part of the province, and creamy wafer-thin Belleek china is made in County Fermanagh. Irish linen, the making of which once kept the flax ponds going in Cork, Donegal, and other parts of the Republic, is now produced only in Northern Ireland. If you're looking for something in particular, refer to *A Guide to Northern Ireland Crafts & Craftsmen,* published by the Local Enterprise Development Unit, 19 Linenhall St., Belfast BT2 8B5, Northern Ireland. Comprehensive shopping information about all six counties can be provided by the Northern Ireland Tourist Board.

COUNTY ANTRIM: In Belfast, *Smyth's Irish Linen,* 20 Wellington Pl., and *Simpson Brothers Ltd.,* 6 Callender St., stock quality Irish linens, Irish crochet, and lace, together with a wide selection of Irish-made souvenirs.

COUNTY ARMAGH: The celebrated Carrickmacross lace is made and sold by *Rose Feeney* of Crossmaglen, just across the border from Carrickmacross proper.

COUNTY DOWN: In Bangor, *Terry Magowan* (The Forge) produces fine woodcarvings and *George Lowden* at 6A High St. makes classic and folk guitars. In Gilford, *Shane's Leather* has bags, belts, and the like in the finest saddlery leather — many of them embossed with Celtic motifs. In Newtownards, the *James Hanna Workshops* (Glenford Way), is known for copper items and the *Design Workshops* produces handsome traditionally styled patchwork quilts. In Rostrevor, Mrs. Gerd Hay-Edie and her daughter Karen do striking woven items at *Mourne Textiles;* the rugs of unspun natural pure wool and the Irish tweeds will have you reaching for your wallet before you know what you're about.

COUNTY FERMANAGH: The famous *Belleek Pottery* in Belleek conducts tours of its premises (phone: Belleek 501).

COUNTY LONDONDERRY: On Main St., in Swatragh, *Glenshane Cottage Industries* stocks all the traditional knits.

COUNTY TYRONE: The *Mill Pottery* at Dunamanagh produces a wide assortment of stoneware pottery, while Dungannon is home to *Kenneth Black* (139 Drumenney Rd.) who makes lovely jewelry to order, on individual designs, and to the factory where fine Tyrone crystal is produced (phone: 08687-25335).

DIRECTIONS

Great Britain

Southeast England

For better or worse, geography conspired to make Kent and Sussex — the broad heel of land that opens out below London to form the bluff-lined and beach-speckled coast of southeast England — the only welcoming mat England has ever extended to the Continent. It is country suited to landing parties: Kent's rich orchards, hop fields, thatched barns, and high-hedged roads giving way to Sussex's high South Downs, from which one can see for miles in all directions. To the north is the wide estuary of the Thames; to the south, the English Channel; and to the east, where England and France are only some 20 miles apart, the Straits of Dover.

Such an invitation has been hard for European warlords to resist, and for 2,000 years attempts have been made to enter England through the southeast. Some have been successful. The Romans established an administrative center in London, and the Normans conquered all of England after their decisive victory at the Battle of Hastings in 1066, a date no English schoolchild ever forgets. Other attempts have failed. From August to October 1940, Britain stood virtually alone against the full weight of the Nazi war machine as the Battle of Britain raged over Kent. But each of these efforts has left some mark on this extraordinarily rich part of England. Kent, the Garden of England, nurtures as much history as fruit and hops in its fertile countryside.

Much of the southeast is dominated and influenced by London. Hundreds of thousands of those who live in this region commute daily to and from the capital. The region, too, is London's principal playground, and on good summer weekends its beaches and country resorts fill with hosts of fugitives from town. But the countryside and the coast have proved surprisingly tenacious despite their proximity to a city of 8 million inhabitants. Once you realize that this area, and especially the northern part of Kent, is Britain's main thoroughfare to Europe, and that it is one of the most densely populated parts of the country, you will be prepared not to find vast tracts of it in virgin condition. But having said that, you will be surprised at how much of it is unspoiled and rarely visited and at how well it has held on to its past.

Along the south shore of the Thames as far as Gravesend, major industries dominate the waterfront before the Kent countryside comes into view and Thameside busyness gives way to the first of several holiday resorts that round the northeast coast of the county. Below the river and the coast, parallel to them, lie the North Downs, a range of low chalkland hills that run east from

Surrey to meet the sea spectacularly as the white cliffs of Dover. Impossible to cultivate, they are either forested or left to grazing. Still farther south lies the Weald, the central region of the southeast. The Weald takes its name from the Anglo-Saxon *Wold,* meaning "a wood." Throughout the later Middle Ages, the woods of this region were cleared, and the fertile soil turned to agricultural use. The result was a prosperous area of substantial villages and market towns, and to this day it is quite possible to find them still full of sixteenth- and seventeenth-century houses and farms, and to sense in them a strong continuity with their isolated past.

Up and over the South Downs that run through Sussex and Hampshire below the Weald, you come to a coast given over largely to pleasure. Like the Kent coast, the Sussex coast abounds with resorts. They are a little less fashionable now than in their Victorian and Edwardian heydays, but perhaps more attractive for that very reason. In the little ones especially, you will find clear signs of the elegance that transformed these watering places from the fishing villages that they once were.

The major sights of England's southeast — Canterbury, Dover, Hastings and Battle, and Brighton — can all be visited on a day trip from London. Travelers with little time should certainly choose the most appealing destinations and make the journey by car or, even more simply, by train. But more rewarding is a perambulation through the countryside, following the coast as a rough guide, and taking in both the large, obviously popular spots along the beaten path and the smaller, quieter places off it.

The route outlined below begins in Rochester, familiar to readers of Charles Dickens, then takes the less-traveled road to Canterbury through hop-growing country, the town of Faversham, and the old-fashioned seaside resorts of Whitstable and Herne Bay. From Canterbury the route returns to the coast at Sandwich, one of the five Cinque Ports that banded together in the Middle Ages to furnish ships to a previously nonexistent English navy. Next along the coast is the historic port of Deal, and Dover and Hythe, two more of the Cinque Ports, are a short drive farther south. The route then crosses the Romney Marsh — a bleak peninsula once known to smugglers, now livened by a string of tiny, traditional beach towns — on its way to Rye and Winchelsea and to Hastings and Battle, where a new era began for England. Next comes a fork in the road: You can detour into the Kent and Sussex Weald, where the essential character of this part of England can still be felt, or you can head straight for the hurly-burly of Brighton. The route ends in Southampton, but not before visits to Arundel and Chichester and, if you wish, a sojourn on the Isle of Wight.

The southeastern region is a very popular vacation spot, so make hotel reservations far in advance. Expect to pay around $60 and up for a double in those places listed as expensive; from $40 to $60 in moderate; and under $40 in inexpensive. A meal for two, excluding wine, tips, or drinks, will run about $35 to $50 in places listed as expensive; $25 to $35 in moderate; and under $20 in inexpensive.

ROCHESTER: The River Medway forms a natural barrier between London and the Channel, neatly dividing Kent in two, and Rochester is primarily a bridge town for the river. It can be easily overlooked now that the M2 motorway from London to Dover rushes by it 2 miles upriver, but if you take the turning before the Medway bridge, you will soon find yourself in the center of the city. The Romans recognized Rochester's strategic importance early and built a bridge (the London to Dover extension of Watling Street, England's ancient Roman highway, crossed the river here), and after they left, a succession of bridges followed. The Normans, too, saw the importance of the crossing and late in the eleventh century began a magnificent castle to defend it. The enormous square keep, 120 feet high with 12-foot-thick walls, was built in the twelfth century and is still standing, open to adventurous visitors prepared to climb its steep spiral staircases and be rewarded by a marvelous view of the Medway estuary, the North Downs, and, best of all, Rochester Cathedral. This is adjacent to the castle, set on a seventh-century foundation, with a plain Norman nave and many features gradually added between the twelfth and fourteenth centuries. The Norman doorway at the west entrance, the walled choir, and many of the tombs are noteworthy.

Castle and cathedral share the summit of Boley Hill, the center of the old city and an area that boasts many ancient and interesting buildings. They catch the rare flavor of a Victorian city, a flavor enhanced by their close associations with Charles Dickens, who lived in nearby Chatham as a boy and came back near the end of his life to Gad's Hill, 7 miles west. Many of the scenes of his novels take place in Rochester and the surrounding countryside, and each year, in May or June, the city stages a rich festival in his honor. Dickens's favorite inn, *The Leather Bottle* (in Cobham, 3 miles west), figures in the *Pickwick Papers* and still dispenses food, drink, and atmosphere. The *Royal Victoria and Bull Hotel* on Rochester's High Street, near the bridge and Boley Hill, is both the Bull Inn of the same novel and the Blue Boar Inn of *Great Expectations,* and many of the shops around it are readily identifiable as Dickensian settings. The sixteenth-century Restoration House on Maidstone Road is Miss Havisham's Satis House in *Great Expectations* (not open to the public), and if you have the time to go about 6 miles north to the village of Cooling you'll find the original setting of Joe Gargery's forge and the graveyard where Pip first met Magwitch. Both are on the edge of an alluringly bleak marshland. Thinly disguised, Rochester is also the Cloisterham of Dickens's last, unfinished, work *The Mystery of Edwin Drood.* This strange novel gives a good picture of Victorian Rochester, but much can also be seen in the marvelous Dickens Centre in Eastgate House on High Street (open daily). The house itself is Elizabethan and appears in *Edwin Drood* as the Nuns' House. Dickens's Gad's Hill home is not open to the public, but the Swiss chalet in which he wrote has now been moved to the garden of Eastgate House.

CHECKING IN: *Royal Victoria and Bull Hotel* – In fact, a 400-year-old coach house, and in fiction, the scene of Dickensian revels — the novelist thought it was a "good house" with "nice beds." Food is plain English fare, well cooked and well served. (High St., Rochester; phone: 0634-46266; moderate.)

En Route – Before proceeding to Faversham, you may want to make an 8-mile detour to Maidstone, the bustling agricultural center of Kent, with a long history in the brewing industry. Many old buildings line its streets, several of which have been closed to traffic to preserve these fine examples of early architecture. Near the town's fourteenth-century Church of All Saints is a medieval building with an Elizabethan front, the Archbishop's Palace, open by special arrangement only. What may have been the palace stable or a tithe barn now houses the Tyrwhitt Drake Museum of Carriages, a collection of ornate, horse-drawn vehicles (open weekdays year-round, plus Sundays in summer). Chillington Manor, an Elizabethan mansion on St. Faith's Street, is the home of the Museum and Art Gallery, which contains the memorabilia of essayist William Hazlitt, a native of Maidstone (closed Sundays). Leeds Castle, built in the middle of a lake in the 1200s, is 4 miles east of Maidstone. This former residence of Henry VIII and Lord Culpepper (governor of Virginia, 1680–83) is often the object of a day trip from London.

Returning to Rochester, you'll find Allington Castle, an imposing, moated, thirteenth-century castle, and the Friars, a Carmelite retreat at Aylesford, both off Route A229. The Order controls the structures and conducts afternoon tours daily.

FAVERSHAM: If you are in a hurry or the weather is dull, the motorway will whisk you from Rochester to Faversham in half an hour. The old main road (A2), however, winds through Gillingham, then Sittingbourne, where there is a museum of sailing barges at the Dolphin Yard (open Sundays, Easter through October, and public holidays), and some Kent countryside that is especially lovely when the apple blossoms are out or the hops are fully grown. Faversham is at the center of hop-growing country, and the cone-shaped structures seen frequently in this region, called oasthouses, are used to dry the hops. Most people bypass the town, a pity that perhaps adds to its attractions for those who do stop. Another Roman site, it received its first charter in 811 and developed after that into a fine medieval city, not least because it was once a small port on the quiet River Swale, which divides the Isle of Sheppey from the Kent mainland. The whole town is beautifully redolent of a thriving brewing industry: Tours of Shepherd Neame Ltd., which has been brewing ale here since the late sixteenth century, can be arranged, but only with a month's written notice.

The best place to sample Faversham's past is on Preston Street in the Fleur de Lis Heritage Centre, a well-illustrated guide to the town's 1,000 years of history housed in a converted fifteenth-century inn (closed Sundays and Thursday afternoons). In the Market Place at the center of town, where three of its oldest streets meet, is the Guildhall, a nineteenth-century rebuilding of a sixteenth-century market hall, raised on pillars. At the north end of the Market Place is Court Street, containing many seventeenth- and eighteenth-century houses. Joining it is Market Street where, at number 12, James II was held prisoner by local fishermen as he tried to escape to the Continent. The many sixteenth- and seventeenth-century houses jostling together on West Street, however, make it the loveliest street of all. Faversham Creek, about 3 miles north of town, has medieval warehouses and a delightful pub, the *Coal Exchange Inn,* while the little harbor of Conyer Creek, a few miles to the west, is a favorite spot for artists and sailors. None of these places is much known, except by locals who, quite understandably, have kept them to themselves.

CHECKING IN: *Ship Hotel* – Sited in an eighteenth-century coaching house with many Tudor features, it's the perfect place in which to get the feel of this pleasant town. (West St., Faversham; phone: 079582-2179; moderate.)

WHITSTABLE AND HERNE BAY: From Faversham, the direct route into Canterbury follows the M2 motorway, but a slower, winding route along the Thames estuary coast will bring you, after about 10 miles, to the small seaside towns of Whitstable and Herne Bay. Like Faversham and Rochester, these places are usually bypassed by overseas visitors, although they are quite popular with the English holidaymakers who have had the luck to discover their quiet charms. For centuries, Whitstable thrived as a fishing port involved principally in the production of oysters, the famous "Whitstable Natives." But by the 1950s, the Thames had become so polluted that the trade declined almost to nothing. The good news for both environmentalists and gourmets is that the river is now so much cleaner than before that the oysters have returned, and so have the restaurants selling them. (For two especially good ones, see *Eating Out.*) The nicest part of the old town still clusters around the old harbor. Here weatherboarded houses perch right on the edge of the shingle beach, and in the narrow streets you'll find a host of small pubs selling local ale and offering a very friendly welcome to the visitor. Another of Whitstable's attractions is the huge number of secondhand or "junk" shops, more per hundred yards than in almost any other town in the southeast. Stroll along High Street from the harbor to the town center and you'll find books, old clothes, antiques, and all sorts of bric-a-brac every few steps of the way. The prices aren't

London prices, so you could pass a whole day in these shops, looking for bargains.

Herne Bay, the small town next to Whitstable, could be the nearest thing to a Victorian seaside resort in England. Primarily a retirement town with a predominantly elderly population, it has a general air of sedateness that is very attractive. Like its saltier neighbor, however, it abounds in friendly pubs and in good secondhand shops, too. The holiday resorts of Margate, Broadstairs, and Ramsgate lie along the coast beyond Herne Bay, but our route takes us south along the pleasant country road leading from Whitstable directly into Canterbury.

EATING OUT: Le Pousse Bedaine – In a suburb that joins Whitstable (on the way to Herne Bay), this is a well-known French restaurant. It's quite expensive but worth it for a special evening out. Closed Sunday evenings. (101 Tankerton Rd., Tankerton; phone: 0227-272056; expensive.) **Pearson's Oyster Bar** – Don't leave Whitstable without sampling the locally caught seafood at Pearson's on the seafront, and watch out for the local Fremlin's ale — it's strong. You'll probably have to reserve a table to eat in the restaurant above rather than the pub below, but if you do you'll be able to see out over the Thames estuary to the Isle of Sheppey. Sunsets there are so spectacular that the painter Turner used to sketch them for future use. (Sea Wall, Whitstable; phone: 0227-272005; moderate.)

CANTERBURY: This is the spiritual center of the Anglican faith and Britain's cathedral city par excellence. It was from Canterbury that St. Augustine converted the English to Christianity, founding both an abbey and a church in AD 602. St. Augustine's Abbey survives in ruins, but the first cathedral was lost to fire and replaced by the massive eleventh-century masterpiece that today dominates the red-roofed, still medieval town around it. The murder of Archbishop Thomas à Becket in 1170 and his canonization 2 years later elevated the cathedral to its status as a shrine and since then Canterbury has been the goal of pilgrims, including Chaucer's group, who wended their way to the scene of Becket's martyrdom telling tales. Modern visitors should allow plenty of time to explore the cathedral — it's marked in every nook and corner with nine centuries of English history — and the many other ancient buildings that are "must see's." Afterward, you'll find several inns, such as the sixteenth-century *White Hart* near the cathedral, the half-timbered *Seven Stars* on Orange Street, or the bow-windowed *Olive Branch* on Burgate Street, inviting places to stop and rest. For a full report on the city's sights, hotels, and restaurants, see *Canterbury,* THE CITIES.

En Route – Part of Canterbury's prosperity grew from its role as a market center for the many villages and agricultural communities of East Kent, and it still serves the same purpose for the region. If you have time, these small villages are well worth visiting. Particularly nice ones are Chilham, 10 miles to the southwest, which has the magnificent Chilham Castle (open to the public only when Elizabethan banquets are held in the Norman keep); Barham, which nestles below the Downs just off the Dover Road, 5 miles southeast of Canterbury; and Westbere, tucked away off the main Margate Road, 3 miles northeast of the city. Westbere has kept its almost medieval character intact, and in the middle of the village you'll find the *Yew Tree,* a delightful inn in a medieval house.

EATING OUT: Wife of Bath – Five miles south of Chilham is Wye, a village that would escape notice altogether if it weren't for this very fine restaurant with English and French cuisine. Weekly menus change with the season to ensure as much absolutely fresh food as possible and English wine is served. Make reservations. (4 Upper Bridge St., Wye; phone: 0233-812540; expensive.)

SANDWICH: Route A257 leads due east from Canterbury to the medieval port of Sandwich, one of the original five Cinque Ports (see *En Route* after Deal). As Sandwich's harbor became clogged with silt in the sixteenth century, the city lost importance and it is now 2 miles from the sea. Sandwich gained lasting fame, however, when the fourth earl of Sandwich invented the world's most popular and enduring meal. According to legend, the earl was loath to leave the gaming tables to eat and asked that a concoction of bread and meat be made for him. Since he was a dissolute man — and infamous for having been in charge of the admiralty when Britain lost its North American colony — the story has something of the ring of truth about it. Two inns, the *Bell* and the *King's Arms,* will be glad to provide a sample of this handy bar snack and something with which to wash it down. Richborough Castle, just off Route A257 a mile and a half outside of Sandwich, was established by the Romans in about AD 43 and added to by the Saxons during the third century. Route A258 leads to Deal, about 6 miles south along the coast.

CHECKING IN: *Fleur De Lis Hotel* – This is a small (5-bedroom) house in the center of Sandwich. The hotel's oak-paneled restaurant has been converted from the old Corn Exchange. (Delf St., Sandwich; phone: 0304-611131; moderate.)

DEAL: Deal was an important shipping center through the early nineteenth century. Under Henry VIII, three castles were erected here: Deal Castle, designed in the shape of a six-petaled rosette (open daily); Walmer Castle, more like a four-leaf clover and located a mile south of the city (open daily); and Sandown Castle, since washed away and nothing more than a pile of stones at the northern end of the seafront. There is a good possibility that Caesar's forces landed along this shore when the Romans invaded Britain, and Henry VIII feared a repeat Roman invasion, this time in the form of a Holy War that the pope might launch against him as the self-proclaimed head of the Church of England. Off the coast of Deal are the Goodwin Sands, a dangerous and complicated series of sandbanks that are exposed at low tide. Lighthouses and lightships illuminate the area after dark, but maritime accidents persist even though Deal is no longer the swaggering seaport it once was. Before the coming of steamships, the narrow stretch of shallow water between Goodwin Sands and the shore, popularly known as the Downs and not the safest anchorage, was filled with cargo vessels and men-of-war. The Time Ball Tower on the seafront, a late-eighteenth-century structure, used to give the correct Greenwich time to ships in the Downs (the ball dropped every day at 1 PM).

CHECKING IN: *Royal Hotel* – The best feature of this comfortable hotel are the balconies of the rooms facing the English Channel. The hotel is decorated with Georgian antiques, and its restaurant serves quite good fresh fish. (Beach St., Deal; phone: 03045-5555; moderate.)

En Route – Traveling south on A258 toward the busy port of Dover, Walmer Castle is only 1 mile from Deal. Built as a fortress by Henry VIII, the castle became the official residence of the Lord Warden of the Cinque Ports in the mid-1700s. This association of seaports began in the eleventh century, when five principal ports (Hastings, Romney — now New Romney — Hythe, Dover, and Sandwich) banded together to provide England with a makeshift navy. Later this was formalized by a charter that granted certain privileges in exchange for the pledge of supplying ships and men for the country's defense. Other ports along the southeast foot of England, the part closest to France, became involved in this arrangement during the dangerous period from the thirteenth to the sixteenth century. Following the establishment of the Royal Navy, the importance of the association and the post of its highest officer, the Lord Warden, declined drastically, and though there is still such a title today, it is largely without power. Two of the most prominent Lord Wardens to live in the castle have been William Pitt the Younger and the first duke of Wellington. The castle is open to visitors except when the present Lord Warden is in residence (usually in August). Dover, the Gateway of England, is only 7 miles farther south on A258.

DOVER: The chalky white cliffs of Dover have been a strategic landmark ever since the early Iron Age, when a settlement was established here. Roman invaders quickly erected a fortress and an octagonal lighthouse, or pharos, and an extension of the ancient Roman roadway called Watling Street ran between Dover and London via Canterbury. The Romans' pharos still stands within the walls of the more recent Dover Castle, an imposing Norman stronghold on the eastern cliffs of the city. Its huge, square keep was built by Henry II in the 1180s around a 240-foot-deep well — the keep had a lead-piped water supply, a surprising amenity for so old a structure. You can easily spend several hours wandering throughout the towers, gateways, and chambers, outer bailey, inner bailey, and keep of the enormous fortification, and even the underground works, where passages lead into the cliffs, are open to the public. On clear days, France is easily visible across the Straits of Dover, roughly 20 miles away, and the view from the battlements of Dover Castle atop the 400-foot bluff overlooking the city and sea is magnificent. Dover is one of Britain's main embarkation points for ferries to France (Calais, Dunkirk, and Boulogne) and Belgium (Oostende and Zeebrugge), and talk of a channel tunnel has yet to threaten its activity.

During both world wars, Dover again rose to prominence as a point of departure for troops bound for the Continent and as the goal of planes straggling back from the fighting. The city was pounded by long-range artillery during World War II, and the thick castle walls sheltered the population through the 4-year bombardment.

CHECKING IN: *Holiday Inn* – This is large, luxurious, and convenient to the ferry terminals, so it's popular with overnighters on their way to and from the Continent. It has a restaurant and a heated indoor swimming pool. (Townwall St., Dover; phone: 0304-203270; expensive.)

En Route – The famous cliffs extend southwest toward Folkestone, neatly trimming the coastline with a tall white chalk seawall for almost 7 miles. Beyond this point the cliffs fall away, exposing the shore. Stretching westward is a line of defenses constructed in the early nineteenth century against the threat of an invasion by Napoleon: a series of 74 small coastal fortresses — circular martello towers from Folkestone around Beachy Head to Seaford. The towers are reinforced a short distance inland by the Royal Military Canal, dug in the same period, from Hythe to Rye. Additional defenses were erected in 1940 when Hitler massed his forces along the French coast. Take Route A20 southwest along the coast from Dover to Folkestone before picking up Route A259 for the additional 4 miles to Hythe.

If you're favored with good weather in Folkestone, take a stroll on the Leas — a broad, mile-long, grassy walkway on the crest of the cliffs just west of the harbor. From here the coast of France unfolds in a beautiful panorama 22 miles distant. On the east side of the harbor is the Warren, where a section of the chalk cliff has crumbled and fallen on the beach — a great hunting ground for fossils. Folkestone has a plentiful supply of good, reasonably priced family hotels, many of them on the seafront.

CHECKING IN: *Eastwell Manor* – Set in some 3,000 acres of parkland, this is an elegant and rambling stone Jacobean-style country house with huge rooms that are positively inviting. There's also an oak-paneled bar to lure guests down for drinks before dinner, which is served in a baronial dining room. The menu is mostly French nouvelle cuisine, but there are some local specialties. (Eastwell Park, Ashford; phone: 0233-35751; expensive.)

HYTHE: Three martello towers still guard the one-time Cinque Port of Hythe, although the harbor has long since silted up and the sea receded. There are also fortifications from other periods, including the ruins of a Roman castrum, Stutfall Castle, about 2.5 miles west of Hythe along the banks of the Royal Military Canal that bisects the city. Above Stutfall is Lympne Castle (pronounced Lim), a residence of the archdeacons of Canterbury until the mid-1800s. It incorporates a square twelfth-century Norman tower into its otherwise fourteenth- and fifteenth-century construction and though it is not impressively fortresslike, its sweeping views as far as the sea would have satisfied any ancient watchman (open daily June to September). Saltwood Castle, about a mile north of town, was used as a meetingplace by Thomas à Becket's murderers before their trip to Canterbury (open Sundays from the end of May through July, and daily in August except Saturdays and Mondays). Hythe itself is a pleasant seaside town, a mixture of old houses, inns, and antique shops on narrow streets. The presence of over 1,500 human skulls in the medieval church has never been satisfactorily explained. Hythe is also the place to catch a ride on the Romney, Hythe, and Dymchurch Light Railway (open Easter and during the summer months). Miniature engines hauling real passengers for modest fares puff back and forth along the sea edge of Romney Marsh, the remote, sparsely populated lowland stretching southwest of Hythe.

En Route – Route A259 takes you into Romney Marsh, first following both the coast and the railway as far as New Romney (like Hythe, also a closed port, having lost its harbor in the thirteenth century), then bearing inland toward the ancient towns of Rye and Winchelsea. If you stopped for the view from Lympne Castle, you will have seen a great deal of this flat, sometimes bleak expanse of low-lying fields and marsh grass full of grazing Romney Marsh sheep and full of memories of the old smuggling days when untaxed (and often illegal) cargoes were unloaded here. In deep winter, the marsh can seem utterly detached from the present century. In summer, however, there are many attractions. The coast is flat, sandy, and ideal for bathing, frequented far more by English vacationers than by overseas visitors. If you want to see the English doing all the traditional seaside things, then Dymchurch, St. Mary's Bay, or Littlestone-on-Sea, New Romney's seaside suburb, are the places to go. Dymchurch, a popular weekend resort with a 5-mile beach, lies in the shelter of a 3-mile fortified seawall built by the Romans to prevent the marshes from flooding. The wall has been continuously improved, and the fortifications were added in 1940. Inland, the hamlets and villages of Romney Marsh proper are less frequented than the coastal towns and well worth seeing. These are quiet spots with ancient and historic churches — some of which, at some period in their past, served as caches for smugglers' contraband. Burmarsh, Newchurch, St. Mary in the Marsh, Ivychurch, Snargate, and Fairfield (all off Route A259), and Old Romney, Brenzett, and Brookland (on A259) are all typical. After Brookland, Route A259 crosses the border of Kent and heads into Rye (21 miles from Hythe) in neighboring East Sussex.

CHECKING IN: *Chantry Hotel* – This is a friendly half-timbered hotel next to fine sandy beaches. (Sycamore Gardens, Dymchurch; phone: 030382-3137; moderate.) ***Red Tiles Hotel*** – A pleasant country hotel, it's located in 2 acres of lawns and gardens only half a mile away from good beaches. (Warren Rd., Littlestone-on-Sea, New Romney; phone: 06793-2155; moderate.)

RYE: Along with Winchelsea, Rye is one of the two "Ancient Towns" added to the original Cinque Ports, though the receding sea and centuries of silt buildup have obstructed its port, limiting traffic to small coastal vessels and fishing boats. Now the harbor is no more than a narrow creek winding its way to town and Rye, essentially a medieval seaport stranded 2 miles from shore, combines the flavor of a large fishing village with that of a remote country settlement. The effect is an alluring one that draws nearly as many visitors as Canterbury. Rye stands on an almost conical sandstone hill, its red roofs piled up to the point of the parish church on top, the whole fairy-tale conception circled by a crumbling fourteenth-century wall. The town was razed by the French in 1377 and again in 1448, destroying the most historic buildings, but many of the houses erected during the late fifteenth century still grace the narrow, cobblestone streets. Gabled and half-timbered, Rye is quite simply a lovely town, and it retains the atmosphere of medieval times along with a measure of its former bustling activity.

Both the *Mermaid Inn,* rebuilt during the fifteenth century and rumored to have been a smugglers' rendezvous, and the timbered *Flushing Inn* (fifteenth century) are excellent haunts for travelers. The works of the great clock (ca. 1560) in the twelfth-century Church of St. Mary are thought to be among the oldest still functioning in England. Lamb House, a Georgian building on West Street, was the residence of novelist Henry James from 1898 until his death in 1916 (open afternoons Wednesdays and Saturdays, April to October). Fletcher's House, now a teashop near Lion and Market streets, is thought to be the birthplace of the sixteenth-century dramatist John Fletcher. The thirteenth-century Ypres Tower (here pronounced Wipers) was purchased by the de Ypres family in the early fourteenth century; it is now a museum housing exhibits pertinent to the Cinque Ports and some local pottery. Rye specializes in pottery and it's easy to pick up some good bargains in the many shops and workshops tucked just off the High Street area.

Winchelsea, also added to the Cinque Ports alliance before the changing coastline ruined its harbor, was completely relocated to its present site in 1283 by Edward I. The church, begun soon afterward, is dedicated to St. Thomas à Becket. Parts of William Thackeray's *Denis Duval* are set in the two towns.

CHECKING IN: *George Hotel* – The tiled facade is a Georgian addition, but behind that is a 400-year-old inn in Tudor style, with oak beams and fireplaces. Centrally located. (High St., Rye; phone: 07973-2114; expensive.) *Mermaid Inn* – When Queen Elizabeth visited Rye in 1573, she stayed here. Even older than the *George,* this beautifully preserved inn was rebuilt in 1420 and is one of the most charming old hotels in England. Its walls still conceal the priest holes and secret staircase used to avoid arrest in the old days of pirates and smugglers. (Mermaid St., Rye; phone: 07973-3065; moderate.) *Mariners' Hotel* – The reception and service are exceptionally warm in this lovely seventeenth-century house, now a 16-room guesthouse. (High St., Rye; phone: 07973-3480; moderate.)

EATING OUT: *Taylor's* – This very good restaurant is superbly set in a seventeenth-century house. Cuisine is both English and French and the service is friendly. (68 The Mint, Rye; moderate.) *Flackley Ash* – This cosy hotel has a well-deserved reputation for its food prepared by owner-chef Clive Bennett, who also holds several "gourmet weekends" during the year. (London Rd., Peasmarsh; phone: 079721-381; moderate.)

HASTINGS (ST. LEONARDS and BATTLE): Nine miles from Rye, Route A259 meets the coast at Hastings and adjoining St. Leonards. The small town of Battle is 6 miles inland. This area is of immense strategic and psychological importance to England, as becomes clear when its history is reviewed: It was here that the last successful invasion of the British Isles began.

Following the death of Edward the Confessor in January 1066, Harold of Wessex, the son of Edward's adviser, ascended to the throne of England. His claim to the monarchy was weak, however, and Duke William of Normandy felt his own to be more justified, since Edward had been a distant cousin and Harold himself, he said, had previously sworn to support his right to wear the crown on Edward's death.

It was just a few miles west of Hastings, at Pevensey Bay, that William landed his forces on September 28, 1066.

King Harold and his men were busy fighting his brother Tostig and the invading king of Norway (another claimant to the throne) in the north, and after defeating them at the Battle of Stamford Bridge, Harold and his tired army marched southward. They gathered support en route but it was not until the morning of October 14 that Harold's men, perhaps 10,000 ax- and spear-carrying foot soldiers, formed a shield wall along a ridge just north of Hastings. William's force was composed of a few thousand archers and several thousand mounted knights and armed men. Norman arrows rained on the defenders, and cavalry charges broke on the wall of spears and shields. In the late afternoon William faked a retreat, drawing many of the inexperienced English militiamen from their positions, and decimated them with his cavalry. King Harold and the remainder of his army were soon slaughtered. On the spot where Harold planted the Royal Standard, where he and his closest followers actually died, William the Conquerer erected Battle Abbey. By Christmas, William was crowned king of England in Westminster Abbey.

Hastings today is a popular resort much loved by the British for its wonderful setting between the hilly South Downs and the Channel coast. The original Cinque Port city stagnated after the harbor became clogged with silt during the late twelfth century, and the 600-year sleep that followed kept the Old Town beautifully intact. This is at the east end of Hastings, where the town began as a fishing village. Narrow streets and age-old houses characterize this area, and two medieval churches survive, the fourteenth-century St. Clement's and the fifteenth-century All Saints'. Even the tall, skinny, tarred-wood sheds, or "net shops," built in the sixteenth century and used to store fishermen's nets, have survived along a part of the beach called the Stade. Near them, the Fishermen's Church is now a museum (open daily except Fridays, Easter through September). The ruins of Hastings Castle, erected around the time of William's invasion, overlook the 3-mile beach area. The magnificent homes in this section of town reflect the resurgence of Hastings as a resort during the late eighteenth and nineteenth centuries when sea bathing became popular among the English. Eventually, the town grew westward to meet St. Leonards, a planned Regency "new" town laid out and developed by architects James and Decimus Burton in the 1830s. By the 1870s, the two had coalesced into one resort, with St. Leonards as its stylish western end. Hastings has all the usual seaside entertainments, and an amusement pier and pavilions plus a model railway add to the gaiety of its beachfront. The most beautiful aspect of the town, however, is natural — St. Clement's Caves (below the castle), once used by smugglers, and the cliffwalks to the east of Hastings.

The nearby small town of Battle, which derives its name from the famous Battle of Hastings, includes the abbey founded by William the Conquerer. The battle site, from the ridge where Harold formed his lines to the heights of Senlac and Telham on the far side of the valley, where William's forces gathered, is just southwest of the town. The abbey gatehouse is on Market Square, and the ruins of the abbey church (destroyed in about 1540) center on the spot where Harold fell. Those sections of the abbey that survived intact and those added in later years are now used as a school. (The Abbey ruins are open throughout the year excluding Sunday mornings from October to March.)

CHECKING IN: *Beauport Park Hotel* – Set off in a beautiful park area, this stately Georgian hotel has a formal garden to add to the timeless atmosphere. The service is in keeping with that feeling of another age, and the outdoor pool is a bonus during the summer. (Battle Rd., Hastings; phone: 0424-51222; expensive to moderate.)

En Route – From Hastings, Route A259 continues along the coast and rounds Beachy Head, 20 miles westward and just beyond the seaside town of Eastbourne. This chalk headland is one of the highest coastal peaks in Sussex, 575 feet above the Channel, and the views out to sea or back over the South Downs make it a favorite lookout point. The coastal road then continues to the large and busy resort of Brighton, another 20 miles or so away. In summer, however, the coastal road is often clogged with traffic, and to avoid it you may want to forgo Beachy Head and take the inland route to Brighton, A27, which veers off from A259 at Pevensey. If time permits, you may even want to leave the sea and salt air behind temporarily and detour inland directly from Hastings to visit the Weald, the prosperous band of farmland that stretches between the North and South Downs as far west as Hampshire.

THE WEALD: Hawkhurst, reached from Hastings via A21, then A229, is not only a splendid and typical large village in the Weald but also an excellent base from which to explore the countryside. Hawkhurst grew in association with ancient iron and cloth industries, the wealth of which, together with agriculture, fashioned an elegant village of many weatherboarded, substantial houses. In the early eighteenth century, the town was also famous as the home of the notorious Hawkhurst Gang of smugglers who terrorized the region — their delinquent faces were well known at the *Mermaid Inn* in Rye.

The Harris Craft Centre is worth a visit and there are several local places of interest, each within 15 miles of town. Northeast (along A229 as far as Sissinghurst) is Sissinghurst Castle, a beautiful Tudor house once owned by writers Victoria Sackville-West and Harold Nicolson, who laid out some of the loveliest formal gardens in the country, all contained within the red-brick walls and open to the public from April to mid-October. Bodiam Castle, southeast of Hawkhurst (off A229), is a spectacular moated ruin, one of the best examples of medieval military architecture in Britain (open daily April through October; closed Sundays the rest of the year). Southwest (along A265, outside the town of Burwash) is Bateman's, a seventeenth-century stone ironmaster's house that became the home of Rudyard Kipling and now hosts a museum of his life and work (open afternoons daily except Fridays, March through October). Heathfield, west of Burwash, is a small country town where an interesting market is held on Sunday mornings. Northwest (follow the A268 out of Hawkhurst, then the A21) is Scotney Castle, a mile southeast of the village of Lamberhurst. This is a particularly romantic ruin, part fourteenth and part seventeenth century, surrounded by a moat and a picturesque garden (open afternoons except Mondays and Tuesdays, April through October). Two miles west of Lamberhurst is Bayham Abbey, one of the finest monastic ruins in the southeast.

Bayham Abbey is just north of B2169, 4 miles east of Royal Tunbridge Wells, the health resort that has been extremely popular since the discovery of the "healing powers" of its mineral waters in 1606. A promenade called The Pantiles, designed as a shopping and visitor area in 1638, is just as popular today. The mineral waters can be sampled from the springs at the far end of the walkway, and the *Duke of York* pub serves those looking for something a little stronger at tables outside its Victorian building on the promenade. Royal Tunbridge Wells, a relatively new town for this region, was at the height of its glory in the eighteenth century, until sniffing sea air and bathing in saltwater became the socially and physiologically proper thing to do and the smart set transferred its allegiance to the upstart Brighton on the coast. Queen Victoria spent time here as a princess and because of this and other royal visits the town — once simply Tunbridge Wells — was permitted by Edward VII to add "Royal" to its name in 1909.

Royal Tunbridge Wells is only 36 miles from London and if you decide to cut short your tour of southeast England and return to the capital, you can easily do so by taking Route A21, which passes just east of town. A slight detour along the way would allow you to visit Knole, one of the largest and most magnificent baronial mansions in England, located outside the village of Sevenoaks on Route A225. The building, referred to by Virginia Woolf as "a town rather than a house" in her novel *Orlando,* sprawls over 3 acres and includes (according to legend) 7 courtyards corresponding to the days of the week, 52 staircases for the weeks, and 365 rooms — one for each day in the year. The house was begun in the mid-fifteenth century by an archbishop of Canterbury, then belonged in turn to Henry VIII and Queen Elizabeth I, who gave it to the Sackville-West family. The furnishings are virtually as they were in Elizabethan

DIRECTIONS / Southeast England

times and there is an impressive art collection (open Wednesdays through Sundays, April through November).

The southeast route continues with a visit to Brighton. To get back to the coast from Royal Tunbridge Wells, take Route A267 to the quiet B2192, which wanders through woods down to Lewes. From there, A27 crosses the South Downs to the seaside city.

CHECKING IN: *Justins* – This lovely, half-timbered country house is convenient to Bodiam and the many other castles in the area. A hearty breakfast, tea, and dinner are included in the room rate and the service is warm and friendly. (Bodiam; phone: 058083-372; moderate.) ***Calverley Hotel*** – An elegant eighteenth-century stone mansion set in a delightful garden, the *Calverley* overlooks the lower town. There are antiques throughout the hotel, but the chintz coverings detract more from the style than they add to the countrified atmosphere. (Crescent Rd., Royal Tunbridge Wells; phone: 0892-26455; moderate.) ***Gravetye Manor*** – Just west of Royal Tunbridge Wells is this ivy-covered Elizabethan manor house surrounded by glorious gardens. One of England's most impressive hostelries, its rooms are paneled with the estate's oak and brightened by bouquets of flowers. The restaurant's Michelin star is well-deserved with a menu featuring *sole de Douvre Victoria* (grilled Dover sole garnished with langoustine, avocado, and tomato), the very tenderest of Scotch beef, and velvety chicken liver pâté. (4 miles from East Grinstead; phone: Sharpthorne 0342-810567; expensive.) ***Royal Oak Hotel*** – This is a small, eighteenth-century weatherboarded inn with 12 rooms to let. The food is good and accommodations are very reasonable. (Rye Rd., Hawkhurst; phone: 05805-2184; inexpensive.)

BRIGHTON: The popularity of England's most famous resort began in the late eighteenth century and developed hugely during the early nineteenth century, leaving a wonderful architectural legacy for the modern visitor. Chief among the attractions — the heirloom, you might say — is the Royal Pavilion, the seaside home of the eccentric Prince Regent who became King George IV. The Pavilion was begun in 1786, then transformed between 1815 and 1821 into the exotic Mogul palace that exists today. Inside, its rooms are crammed with gorgeous chinoiserie and fully furnished in the original grand style, a sight to see especially during the summer when they are the setting for the Regency Exhibition. Brighton's seafront — King's Road — is chockablock with fish and chip cafés, cotton candy stalls, and amusement arcades, and the Victorian Palace Pier adds to the carnival atmosphere. Another attraction is the Old Town, known as the Lanes, a picturesque area of narrow, brick-paved alleyways full of good teashops, pubs, and antique shops. It's traffic-free and it will give you an idea of what Brighton was like before the fairy godmother touched her magic wand and turned the fishing village of Brighthelmstone first fashionable, then flossy. For a full report on the sights, hotels, and restaurants of this seaside resort, see *Brighton,* THE CITIES.

ARUNDEL: From Brighton, Route A27 hurries through a not particularly pleasing bit of coast, but the reward for the 20-mile drive is this small, medieval-looking town on the River Arun, spectacularly dominated by its massive castle and an equally large-scale cathedral. The castle, family seat of the dukes of Norfolk, dates from the eleventh century, though most of what is seen today — except for the Norman keep — was rebuilt in the old style in the eighteenth and nineteenth centuries. The picture gallery contains the dukes' collection, including paintings by Van Dyck, Gainsborough, and Reynolds, and on the grounds is the Roman Catholic Fitzalan Chapel, occupying a quarter of the town's fourteenth-century Anglican parish Church of St. Nicholas. The dual allegiance is explained by the fact that the dukes of Norfolk, who own the chapel, are Catholic — in the 1880s the fifteenth duke had a wall built to divide chapel from church and they still have separate entrances. The same duke had previously built the imposing, Gothic-style Roman Catholic cathedral Church of St. Philip Neri. Around these two monoliths of castle and cathedral, the town also has many old houses and small inns, Potter's Museum of Curiosity (containing the work of a Victorian taxidermist and naturalist who set animals in nursery rhyme tableaux), and a cheerful Saturday morning market.

Less than a mile to the north is the 55-acre Wildfowl Trust, where you can watch a sampling of the world's waterfowl from observation hides. North again, situated in a nineteenth-century quarry and limeworks, is the Chalk Pits Museum at Amberley. On display in this large open-air museum of industrial history are the original lime kilns, plus a blacksmith's shop, locomotive shed, a narrow-gauge railway, and much more.

CHICHESTER: The cathedral city of Chichester is 10 miles from Arundel. The original town was Roman and walled, and the city plan still reflects Roman beginnings in the two long, straight main streets that intersect at right angles at the sixteenth-century Market Cross. Portions of the walls, both Roman and medieval ones, remain, but Chichester today is predominantly a Georgian market town with many quiet corners and the lovely cathedral at its heart. The cathedral spire, visible from a distance, is a Victorian replacement of one that collapsed over a century ago, but the rest of the cathedral, built between 1091 and 1199, is largely Norman. The fifteenth-century bell tower is the only example of a detached belfry still surviving in England. The most attractive buildings of Georgian Chichester are close by on North Street and in an area called the Pallant, a city-within-a-city southeast of Market Cross, while the best of Roman Chichester is 1.5 miles west of town. In 1960, workmen laying a water pipe at Fishbourne discovered the remains of a magnificent Roman palace built in AD 70. When fully excavated, it turned out to be the largest Roman palace yet found in Britain. Twelve of the mosaic floors can be seen and there is a museum telling the history of the site up to AD 280 (closed December through February). In mid-July, Chichester stages the Chichester Festivities, a varied festival of the arts, which includes concerts in the cathedral. Better known is the top-flight Chichester Festival Theatre season, four plays running from May through September at a strikingly modern theater in the middle of a 40-acre parkland.

The nearby harbor is one of Britain's prettiest — it's a natural center for sailors with small boats. On its far shores, small resorts such as Bosham, West Itchenor, Emsworth, and Hayling Island are all quietly attractive. Goodwood House, 3 miles north on A286, is the historic home of the dukes of Richmond (open Sundays and Mondays, May through September) and the park around it is the site of the racecourse where the "glorious" Goodwood Week of racing takes place at the end of July. Six miles north of the city, at Singleton, the Weald and Downland Open Air Museum is set high on the South Downs and is especially worth a visit. Typical old buildings have been saved from destruction elsewhere in southeast England and transferred here, among them a fourteenth-century Kentish farmhouse, a fifteenth-century Wealdian hall house, and others (open daily except Mondays, April through October).

En Route – From Chichester, Route A27 continues west to the bustling naval town of Portsmouth where you can board a car or passenger ferry that will cross the Spithead — a body of water no more than 4 miles wide — and deposit you 30 to 45 minutes later at Ryde or Fishbourne on the holiday Isle of Wight. The hovercraft from Southsea, a residential suburb of Portsmouth, makes the trip even faster — in 10 minutes. Farther west, other ferry, hydrofoil, and hovercraft services leave from Southampton and Lymington and cross the Solent, again a maximum 4 miles wide, to arrive on the island at Cowes or Yarmouth.

CHECKING IN: *Ship Hotel* – This was originally a private house, built in 1790 for George Murray, one of Nelson's admirals. It is large and wonderfully old-fashioned in the Georgian manner. In April 1944, General Eisenhower dined here prior to D-day. (North St., Chichester; phone: 0243-782028; moderate.)

Ship Inn – Very small (6 rooms) and friendly, it overlooks the harbor. The buffet specializes in local Selsey crabs and oysters. (West Itchenor; phone: 0243-512284; moderate.)

EATING OUT: ***Hole in the Wall*** – This is an informal pub-restaurant that's popular among Festival Theatre–goers. (1 St. Martin's St., Chichester; phone: 0243-782555; inexpensive.)

ISLE OF WIGHT: Though it was once part of the mainland, it's a mistake to think of the Isle of Wight as a small (23 miles by 13 miles) piece of England cast adrift in the Channel, because it has a flavor of its own, at once pastoral and nautical. The island's northern end is flat, but its steep cliffs to the south are spectacular and draw the majority of visitors. Besides the seaside activity, walking is a major pastime here, and any of the local information centers can provide descriptive literature on the network of footpaths that lead nearly everywhere, including the circumference of the entire island. For most visitors, Ryde, one of the major resort towns and the main shopping center, is the gateway to the Isle of Wight. On the southeast coast, Sandown, Shanklin, and Ventnor are strictly resorts, busy and particularly sunny ones, and they clearly reflect the Victorian popularity that established and expanded them. Of the three, Ventnor, terraced up to the highest point of the island, is the oldest and perhaps the most interesting. Inland, there are many small villages, doubly remote for their island setting: Godshill has many thatched cottages and — rare sight — a working smithy; Calbourne, too, has thatched cottages and a fine crafts center that sells the work of over 80 local craftsmen at surprisingly reasonable prices. Newport, in the center on the River Medina, is the capital, and it's strangely the least hurried town on the island. A mile southwest, Charles I was once held prisoner in Carisbrooke Castle, parts of which date back to the twelfth century (open daily year-round). On the north coast, Yarmouth is an ancient town and an important yachting center, but Cowes, divided in two by the Medina, is the headquarters of British yachting, internationally famous. Highlight of the regatta season is Cowes Week, the first week in August, when ocean racers from all over the world compete in the blue Solent. Cowes is not all ocean yachting, however — there are plenty of facilities for smaller boats. Osborne House, Queen Victoria's palatial Italianate retreat (she used it for over 50 years and died here in 1901), is just outside of Cowes. The perfectly preserved state apartments and a museum are open to the public from Easter to mid-October.

CHECKING IN: ***Bugle Hotel*** – A small (24-room) brick-fronted hotel whose elegant paneled dining room specializes in beef filet stuffed with chicken livers and topped with sour cream. (High St., Newport; phone: 0983-522800; moderate.) ***King Charles I Hotel*** – Also small (29 rooms), parts of this hotel are hundreds of years old. King Charles is supposed to have stayed here several times when allowed out of his prison at Carisbrooke Castle. The hand-painted dining room and the lounge are captivatingly ornate and the service is friendly. (Grove Rd., Ventnor; phone: 0983-852161; moderate.)

En Route – Car ferries, hydrofoils, and hovercraft depart daily year-round from Cowes to Southampton, a major seaport favored by a double high tide, from the Solent and the Spithead. The city suffered heavy damage during World War II and as a result, it is largely modern, though there are some medieval remains, including parts of the ancient walls and the Bargate, once the north gate of the old town. Southampton was already an important port in the Middle Ages, trading with Venice up to the early sixteenth century, but a setback in its fortunes came when the port of Bristol captured the tobacco and sugar trade with the New World — and the black slave trade. Thousands of early American settlers sailed from Bristol, but Southampton has the honor of having waved good-bye to the *May-*

flower in 1620, and there is a Pilgrim Fathers' Memorial commemorating that voyage near the Royal Pier. When the day of the large transatlantic liners dawned, Southampton became Britain's chief port for the Atlantic crossing, bar none. Today, the last luxury liner making anything resembling a regularly scheduled transatlantic run is the *Queen Elizabeth 2*, and its home port is Southampton. Southampton is also an important embarkation point for cross-Channel ferries to Cherbourg and Le Havre, in France.

The cathedral city of Winchester, the starting point of our *Southwest England* route, is only 12 miles north of Southampton via Route A33. If you won't be touring Wiltshire, Devon, and Cornwall, you can visit Winchester, then proceed out of town on the A33, which meets the M3 motorway some 10 miles north and will speed you back to London. The distance from Winchester to London is 66 miles.

Channel Islands

Geographically the Channel Islands, lying as little as 8 miles off the coastline of Normandy and Brittany, are part of France. But historically the islands — Jersey, Guernsey, Alderney, Sark, Herm, Jethou, and a smattering of islets — have been connected with the British Crown for more than 1,000 years. They were part of the Duchy of Normandy when William the Conqueror invaded England in 1066 and became its king, and they remained part of Britain when Normandy was subsequently reunited with the rest of France.

This heritage has given the Channel Islands a curiously mixed identity — they are a sort of halfway house between England and France stuck out in the English Channel. Partly self-governing, and with a hodgepodge of English and French laws, they retain French as their official language yet universally speak English. They issue their own banknotes, coinage, and stamps, yet British currency is accepted. The food is French, but habits and manners are English.

The Channel Islands attract upward of 2 million tourists every year. Their popularity is partly due to the feeling of being "abroad" that the blend of cultures gives to both British and French visitors, partly due to their enviable sunshine record (situated about 100 miles south of the English mainland, they get the best of the weather), and partly due to the fact that no two of the islands are the same, and so offer visitors the opportunity to have one or several kinds of holiday. Jersey, the most southerly of the islands and also the largest (although it only measures 9 by 5 miles), has a reputation as a "swinging" holiday resort with a wide choice of hotels, restaurants, and entertainments. Quieter, centrally situated Guernsey, the other main island, is only now turning from agriculture to tourism as its principal livelihood. And on the smaller islands there is little to do except eat, sleep, walk, and admire some stunning seascapes and cliff scenery.

The islanders have been molded both by history and by the surroundings in which they live. Calm, unhurried, contemplative, yet with a sharp sense of humor, they also have remarkably sophisticated taste when it comes to food and wine — the development of smart restaurants on wealthy Jersey or even the smuggling of fine wines and spirits, which is still said to flourish, may be due to the close proximity of France.

They couple this with an enthusiasm for their own language — a Norman-French patois that differs from island to island and can still be heard in the countryside and markets — and with an equal enthusiasm for their ancient traditions, the most famous of which is a legal oddity dating from the Norman period and is known as the *Clameur de Haro.* There's no need to call an attorney if you feel that you are being legally wronged in Jersey or Guernsey — you just drop to your knees and shout: *"Haro! Haro! Haro! à l'aide, mon Prince, on me fait tort."* ("Help, my Prince, they are wronging me.") This has the same effect as a court injunction, but nowadays it is only used in cases of interference with real property. The penalties for ridiculing or abusing this ancient law are heavy.

Other island oddities include the ormer, a rubbery-fleshed shellfish related to the abalone but unique to the Channel Islands, which has a particularly attractive mother-of-pearl-like shell; and giant cabbages with stalks so long that walking sticks can be made from them. More practically, for souvenir hunters, there are the heavy-knit oiled wool sweaters known as "jerseys" and "guernseys," which have given their names to knitwear all over the world.

In recent years, Jersey and Guernsey have both made strenuous attempts to extend their tourist seasons. Both offer discount-priced, inclusive winter holidays at major hotels, and provide year-round entertainment that often comes up to London standards. This trend is likely to continue because, as the islanders point out, the climate is similar to that of Bermuda and thus offers an escape from British winters.

Prospective visitors should also note, however, that because the islands are exposed to the Atlantic, the sea is colder than you might expect and swimming is comfortable only between June and late September. The islands are also subject to dense sea mists that can disrupt air traffic. Such disadvantages, however, are easily outweighed by the exceptionally clean air.

Jersey has led the way in introducing new attractions such as spring and gastronomic festivals. But the most popular carnival on both Jersey and Guernsey is one that dates back to the 1902 coronation, the annual Battle of Flowers. This colorful and picturesque event, involving processions of floats decorated with flowers as well as other, less formal, celebrations, takes place in August and is the high spot of any visit.

JERSEY

Jersey, the largest of the Channel Islands, got its name from the Normans, who called it *Gersey* ("the grassy isle"). Between the two world wars it acquired the nickname of "the honeymoon isle," because of its popularity with newlyweds holidaying there from the mainland. (Traditionally, March was the most popular time for honeymooning because couples who married at the end of the fiscal year could claim full tax allowances for the preceding year. Now, however, honeymooning is a year-round activity and newlyweds even get a small gift from the local tourism department!)

It was in this interwar period that Jersey began the transition from isolated farming community to modern holiday resort. The main attraction then was the big, safe, sandy beaches, and the cheap accommodations. Today the beaches are unchanged, but now the island also boasts a sparkling nightlife as well as many fine shops, hotels, and restaurants. It also manages to pack into its tiny land area some glorious woodland walks, lots of quiet countryside where Jersey cattle graze, historic castles, and interesting sight-seeing trips.

The island's capital is the south coast port of St. Helier, which contains about half of Jersey's population. It is built around the rather ugly harbor, and is divided by a massive rock on which stands the Napoleonic Fort Regent — now converted into a comprehensive, all-weather entertainment, leisure, and sports complex. The town itself is a maze of narrow streets, some of them pedestrianized and many having French names, with a big range of shops specializing in low-duty luxury goods.

St. Helier is situated on one of Jersey's best beaches, St. Aubin's Bay, and out in the bay stands Elizabeth Castle, built on rocks in the sixteenth century and named after Queen Elizabeth I by Sir Walter Raleigh when he was governor of the island. At low tide the castle can be reached on foot by causeway, but there are boat services at other times. It is attractively floodlit on summer nights.

There is another fine castle 5 miles out of St. Helier on the east coast at Gorey: Mont Orgueil Castle. Built to defend Jersey against attacks from neighboring France in the twelfth to fifteenth centuries, it is beautifully preserved and, again, floodlit. Below the castle, the tiny fishing village of Gorey is worth exploring, and is a good place to stop and eat. Pub lunches are popular, and are an excellent value.

The north coast of the island is composed mostly of cliffs, which hide many small, sheltered beaches and tiny harbors. You'll do some excellent walking here, since there are fine views of the other islands as well as of France.

The west coast of the rectangular-shaped island consists almost entirely of one huge bay, St. Ouen's Bay, backed by sand dunes. Winter seas here, rolling in from the Atlantic, can be awesome, but in summer St. Ouen's is a popular beach too large to ever get crowded.

In addition to St. Aubin's Bay, the south coast has the island's most attractive bay, St. Brelade's, which has good recreational facilities as well as miles of sand. The nearby Portelet Bay is also popular, and is very sheltered. Those who tire of the beach will find an interesting little structure hidden beside St. Brelade's Church called the Fishermen's Chapel; it is an ancient monastic chapel dating back in parts to the sixth century, and has some recently discovered fourteenth-century murals on the walls (they are seen at their best in damp weather conditions).

Visits to the island's chapels, old Norman churches, and more modern churches (the "glass church," at Millbrook, is lavishly decorated with glass by the Parisian artist René Lalique) are, of course, free. But even the island's organized excursions are relatively cheap, and three of them are particularly worthwhile.

The first of these is to St. Peter's Bunker, in the center of the island. This museum of the German occupation of the Channel Islands during World War

II is housed in a seven-room German bunker. It provides a fascinating insight into how both occupiers and occupied lived during the war years.

Far more ancient history is to be found at La Hougue Bie, one of Jersey's two best-preserved Neolithic tombs. Visitors to the site, at Grouville, can creep down the 33-foot-long tunnel entrance to the tomb itself, where the temperature remains constant whatever the weather. The tomb is covered by a 40-foot-high mound on which two medieval chapels were constructed under a single roof. There are other historical exhibits on the grounds as well.

Finally, one of Europe's most interesting zoos has been set up in the grounds of Les Augrés Manor in the northeast of the island by author and naturalist Gerald Durrell. Jersey Zoo is not dedicated to the display of animals, or to entertainment, but to the preservation and rearing of some of the world's rarer species. Watch for the families of lowland gorillas, orangutans, Tibetan white-eared pheasants, and Egyptian bare-faced ibis, all very rare.

Jersey has direct airline links with most British airports, and there are daily services to and from London — Heathrow and Gatwick — taking only 25 minutes. There are also airline connections with France. Car ferries link Jersey both with France and with the British ports of Weymouth and Portsmouth (Sealink: Continental Ticket and Information Office, PO Box 29, Victoria Station, London SW1V 1JX). A number of firms specialize in inclusive holidays to the Channel Islands from Britain, and these include Preston Travel (4 Dollis Park, London N3) and Modernline Travel (Globegate House, Pound La., London NW10).

CHECKING IN: *Longueville Manor* – A magnificently restored manor house, with elegant furnishings in its public rooms and 37 bedrooms. There is also a pool and riding stables on the grounds. (St. Helier; phone: 0534-25501.) *Water's Edge* – At the bottom of a steep hill, beside the sea on the north coast, this handsome hotel is well away from the crowds. Swimming pool. 56 rooms. (Bouley Bay; phone: 0534-62777.) *L'Horizon* – On the beach at popular St. Brelade's Bay, the hotel has its own indoor pool and 104 rooms. (St. Brelade's Bay; phone: 0534-43101.

EATING OUT: *La Capannina* – Much favored by local residents, this place specializes in Italian dishes. (Halkett Pl., St. Helier; phone: 0534-34602.) *Mauro's* – Here you'll find traditional French and Italian food. (La Motte St., St. Helier; phone: 0534-20147.)

GUERNSEY

The second largest of the Channel Islands, Guernsey is roughly triangular in shape; its 5-mile-long east coast contains its two towns: the industrial port of St. Sampson, and the island's capital of St. Peter Port. The latter is a pretty town, built on a hillside overlooking the large harbor and the smaller islands of Sark, Herm, and Jethou. Like the other islands, Guernsey enjoys tax advantages, which makes shopping in the narrow, winding streets of St. Peter Port doubly appealing.

St. Peter Port is dominated by the town church, a granite building known as "the Cathedral of the Channel Islands," and by the medieval fortress of Castle Cornet, which overlooks the harbor. Castle Cornet saw action in the English Civil War, when the Royalist governor held it throughout a 9-year siege against a predominantly Cromwellian populace (the castle finally fell to the Parliamentary forces in 1651).

In addition to the castle and the church, St. Peter Port's most interesting building is Hauteville House, the nineteenth-century home of exiled French writer Victor Hugo who lived in Guernsey from 1855 to 1870; it now belongs to the City of Paris, and is furnished and maintained just as it was in the eccentric Hugo's day. Hugo chose the house because of the fine views that it has of the French coast.

With beaches on all three of its coasts, Guernsey can provide a sheltered bay whatever the direction of the wind. In good weather, the big, sandy beaches of the west coast are the best, particularly Cobo and Vazon, although swimmers should beware of the strong currents in places marked with danger flags. Children will like Portelet, a little harbor forming a tiny beach of its own within Rocquaine Bay. Lihou, an uninhabited islet, is offshore, as are the dangerous rocks of the Hanois, marked with a tall lighthouse.

There are several lovely walks along the picturesque south coast, which has a number of rocky headlands, towering cliffs, and good, sandy beaches — of these, Moulin Huet, Petit Bôt, Petit Port, and Saints Bay are the most popular. Visitors can stroll down to the beach along wooded paths beside streams known as "water lanes."

Although it's the beaches and cliffs that draw tourists, this is still predominantly an agricultural island, and much of the interior is given over to greenhouses in which early tomatoes and flowers are cultivated.

Many of the islanders' houses are notable for having "kitchen stones" sticking out from their chimneys. Guernsey was, and still is, a superstitious island, and legend says that passing witches will not curse a house if they can stop and warm themselves by the chimney.

Most of the parish churches on the island are Norman in origin. The sloping aisle of one of these, St. Pierre du Bois (St. Peter-in-the-Wood), has lead to a popular local joke that any bridegroom leaving the church after a wedding is already going downhill. Outside St. Martin's Church stands Guernsey's most famous resident, a prehistoric stone figure known as La Grandmère de Chimquiere or, more simply, La Grandmère. Locals do not pass La Grandmère without saying good morning to her.

Excursions on Guernsey are not particularly exciting — although the circular coach tour of the island is interesting. You can get anywhere on the bus services radiating from St. Peter Port. But do not miss seeing the grim German Underground Hospital, a relic of the World War II occupation, or the shell-dotted Little Chapel at Les Vauxbelets, an 18-by-10-foot model of Our Lady of Lourdes shrine in France — big enough only for a priest and a congregation of two.

Guernsey has direct airline links with most British airports, and there are daily services to and from London (Heathrow and Gatwick) and Southampton. The islands' own Aurigny Airlines (based at Alderney Airport on Alderney island) provides a regular interisland service as well as connections to Southampton and France. Car ferries run between Weymouth, Portsmouth, and Guernsey (Sealink). For package tours to Guernsey, contact the firms listed for Jersey.

CHECKING IN: *Old Government House* – Once the town's principal hotel, and still striving to retain that position by combining old-fashioned courtesy with 74 modern rooms and a pool. (St. Peter Port; phone: 0481-24921.) ***La Frégate*** – This restored eighteenth-century manor house has a good restaurant and 13 modern rooms, some of which overlook the sea. (St. Peter Port; phone: 0481-24624.) ***Le Chalet*** – A mile outside St. Peter Port, above a sheltered but stony beach, Le Chalet offers a peaceful atmosphere, fine sea views, and a good restaurant. 44 rooms. (Fermain Bay; phone: 0481-35716.) ***Cobo Bay Hotel*** – This modern hotel on the west coast overlooks the beach and has 29 rooms. (Cobo Bay; phone: 0481-57102.)

EATING OUT: *Steak and Stilton* – A popular seafront lunch spot, it's also nice in the evenings. The menu combines local fish dishes with those suggested by its name. (Esplanade, St. Peter Port.)

ALDERNEY

Besides being the most northerly and the most barren of the Channel Islands, Alderney is the least attractive to tourists. It's only about 4 miles long and a mile wide, and although it has a massive breakwater built as part of a Napoleonic military harbor, the port itself is a tiny one. Most of the population of only 1,700 live in or around the centrally situated town of St. Anne.

Hotel accommodation is sparse, heavily booked, and expensive in terms of what you get for your money. There is not much to do either — unless you enjoy walking alongside or swimming in one of the safe and sandy (and usually deserted) south coast bays.

Aurigny Airlines provides several flights a day from and to Southampton, and has frequent interisland flights from Guernsey and Jersey. There are also flights and a summer hydrofoil service to France, 8 miles away. There are no interisland boats; you have to hire a fishing boat.

SARK

An unspoiled atmosphere and an extraordinary individuality are the hallmarks of the feudal island of Sark — a rocky plateau of an island 9 miles off the coast of Guernsey. Its constitution dates back to Elizabethan times, and it still has a hereditary ruler, called the Seigneur, who today is Mr. Michael Beaumont, son of the famous Dame of Sark and her American husband. Cars, divorce, adoption, and income tax are banned on the island, and the Seigneur retains such ancient feudal rights as that of being the only person on Sark who may keep pigeons (a rule designed years ago to protect seed corn).

Sark is, in fact, the smallest state in Europe, which no doubt adds to its attraction for visitors. But it is not an island for swimming, sunbathing, or shopping — the beaches are all fairly inaccessible, and there is no town. Most tourists travel around by horse-drawn carriage (expensive) or hired bicycle (cheap), and visit tiny Creux Harbour; the sixteenth-century Seigneurie with its walled gardens; the two-man prison, which is Sark's only other noteworthy building; and the precipitous path known as La Coupée, where only 10 feet of soft rock and clay stops Sark from dividing itself into two islands.

There is a daily ferry service from Guernsey, weather permitting, and summer excursions also run from Jersey.

HERM

The attractive little island of Herm, 3 miles off Guernsey's capital of St. Peter Port, belongs to "King" Peter Wood, an ex-Army officer who leases and farms it. Roughly one and a half miles long and half a mile wide, it is a Channel Island in miniature, with cliffs on its northern tip and long, sandy beaches to the south.

It's a very popular destination for day-trippers from Guernsey, but some visitors like to stay overnight because of the island's solitude. A pub, some shops, and the island's only hotel cluster around the harbor, and footpaths lead from there to the common, the beaches (Belvoir Bay, on the east coast, is the best), and the farm. Shell Beach, also on the east coast, is the most famous beach in the Channel Islands: Instead of sand, it is made up of millions of tiny shells washed up by the Gulf Stream — many of them originating in the Caribbean.

A frequent launch service operates from St. Peter Port, Guernsey, in summer; winter visitors are met by arrangement.

CHECKING IN: *The White House Hotel* – A quiet, comfortable hotel, offering an unexpectedly high standard of service on so small an island. Its 38 rooms are heavily in demand with regular guests. (Phone: Herm 83, via Guernsey.)

JETHOU

This island, once the home of the English writer Sir Compton Mackenzie, is privately owned and cannot be visited.

Southwest England

That the legendary Arthur should spring from this distant corner of England isn't surprising. For here, where the island narrows down to a horny point separating the English Channel from the Atlantic, the boundaries between the natural and supernatural are very indistinct. It doesn't take long to notice it — a constant tug on your imagination, the sense that the low green hills and languorous rivers simmer with an animation barely and only intermittently apparent to human senses. This, after all, is a land where walking sticks sprout into flowering hawthorns, where dancing maidens turn to stone, and where a baby delivered to an old magician on the crest of a fiery wave becomes a warrior, a king, a superhuman mortal who unites and gives identity to the English people. Even today, when modern sensibilities are so ruthlessly rational, there are quite sane folk who claim that fairies dance on the Dorset coast and pixies bedevil Dartmoor travelers.

The land itself conspires to enchant. To the east, Dorset's rich dairyland folds and unfolds in a continuous succession of hills and vales, while Somerset's miles of meadows and orchards are cradled in a basin protected on all sides by hills and the sea. In the heart of Devon, the county occupying the broad square of the peninsula, is Dartmoor, a solitary and taciturn landscape of bare hills bristling with strange winds. Beyond, and to the end of England, lie the neat, stone-walled fields and lanes of Cornwall. But nowhere does the magic seduce as powerfully as where land meets the sea, and the southwest has more miles of coastline than any other part of England. Here are long strands of beach that disappear with the tide, steep coves nearly obscured by their dense foliage, headlands shrouded in mist, and towering black cliffs that meet the crashing sea in an Olympian test of wills.

For all its wildness, though, the southwest is essentially a human landscape. Thousands of years of habitation by man has shaped the countryside as surely and as gradually as the elements. The soft, sculpted shape of the hills is the result of centuries of plowing and grazing, and the high-hedged roads that have carried countless generations from village to village are etched deeply on the land. It's the cluster of thatched cottages covered with primroses, the isolated church standing on an open knoll above the sea, that please the eye as much as the grandeur of the setting.

Everywhere are reminders of the successive occupants of the land, from paleolithic drawings in the Mendip caves to a deserted World War II air force base near Bodmin Moor. Bronze Age circles, Iron Age villages, Celtic hill towns, Roman roads, Saxon farms, Norman churches and cathedrals, Tudor coastal fortifications, grand Georgian mansions, and Victorian resorts all combine to make this part of the country a visible record of English history. Some sites, like Stonehenge or the Normans' magnificent cathedrals, are well known, but others, perhaps the most rewarding, are those you come across yourself — an enigmatic formation of stones in the middle of a sheep pasture, or a fanciful church carving done by a nameless artisan of the Middle Ages.

The southwest is hardly an undiscovered paradise. Britons come by the droves to enjoy Cornwall's and Devon's fine beaches and warm weather. But apart from tourism, people make their livings much as they have for centuries, by sheep herding, dairy farming, fishing, and sea trade. There is now a good deal of mining for china clay around St. Austell, but tin mining, which for many hundreds of years brought wealth to Cornwall (or at least to some of its families), is almost a thing of the past. Plymouth and Exeter, both ports, plus Truro, Salisbury, and Wells, are the only cities the region can claim, and although the population in resort towns swells with summer visitors, the rest of the year you'd have to search a bit to find a crowd.

The route we suggest starts in Winchester and heads west to Sherborne — two Saxon towns that have arrived at the twentieth century with their vitality and charm intact — before plunging south through Dorset's rolling green countryside, then following the Dorset coast to Exeter, the gateway to Devon and Cornwall. The route then meanders through Dartmoor and heads back to the coast at the south Devon sea towns of Dartmouth and Plymouth. Crossing the River Tamar into Cornwall, the route hugs the coast all the way to the Lizard and Land's End before turning north. Then it climbs up the spectacular west coast of Cornwall, makes a loop through Bodmin Moor, and returns to the coast to stop at Tintagel, the legendary birthplace of Arthur. From here the route follows the steep and wooded north coast of Devon, passes into Somerset and Exmoor Forest, then cuts across the Somerset levels to the historic town of Glastonbury and the Cheddar Caves.

Take your time through this country. Much of its beauty and charm is to be found down exasperatingly narrow lanes that can't be taken at more than 20 miles an hour or along public footpaths that link village to village. There is also an extensive system of splendid coastal footpaths that even at the height of the tourist season are quiet, private retreats. (The National Trust, which maintains some of these paths, along with scores of historic sites, isn't supported by government funds, as most people think. So don't pass up its contribution boxes without expressing — in cash, that is — your appreciation for the fine job it does.) One last tip: Most towns and villages with tourist attractions have large car parks located near the center of town. Do use them. You'll save yourself the aggravation of trying to park on streets built for foot traffic — and possibly a dented fender.

There are so many excellent small hotels in this neck of the woods that you'll be tempted to extend your stay just to sample them all. Most are also well known for their food and open their restaurants to nonresidents. These hotels aren't cheap, but they are good value for the money. For a double room with breakfast, expect to pay between $70 and $90 at places we list as expensive; $45 to $70 for those in the moderate range; and between $25 and $45 for those listed as inexpensive.

WINCHESTER: Although Winchester lies slightly to the east of the center of England, it is, nonetheless, an excellent place to start a tour of the southwest. Here one meets the various people who overran, then settled, that part of England: Celts founded the town, Romans took it over, Saxons made it their capital, Danes besieged it, and Normans built the cathedral that presides majestically over it.

Sheltered between the green hills of the Hampshire downs and fed by the gentle River Itchen, Winchester takes its physical character primarily from the eighteenth century — Great Minster Street near the cathedral is a charming example of the graceful architecture that period produced. But it is the harmonious mix of buildings from every era, including low brick structures from the last few decades, and the welcome lack of quaint trappings that give Winchester its air of vitality.

The main tourist area, also the town's business and shopping district, runs along High Street, from the statue of Alfred the Great, the Saxon king who in 871 made this the capital of Wessex, at the east end, to Westgate, one of two gates remaining from the old city walls, at the west end. Westgate, which from the sixteenth century on was the town's prison (Charles I was among its inmates), is now a small museum. Prisoners' graffiti cover the walls and floors, and among the artifacts on display is the City Coffer, a sixteenth-century oak- and iron-bound casket at least 6 feet long, 4 feet wide, and 3 feet deep, a relic from the days when a city's coffer was something more substantial than the bottom line of an annual report. (Open daily.)

Just south of Westgate, and adjacent to the new Crown Court building, is the Great Hall, all that remains of the Norman castle that was a royal residence until destroyed by Oliver Cromwell's Parliamentarians in 1645 and considered to be one of the finest examples of a medieval hall in England. The Great Hall's most famous possession is King Arthur's Round Table. No one claims this great oak table 18 feet in diameter is *the* legendary table of Arthur's court, since it dates from only the fourteenth century. But such was the continuing power of Arthur's legend that nearly 1,000 years after his death, a shrewd King Henry VIII, wanting to strengthen his family's fairly recent claim to the throne, had the table painted with Arthur seated above a Tudor rose. (Open daily.)

At the center of Winchester, physically and spiritually, stands its magnificent cathedral. The massive transepts are Norman, but the long nave, with its intricate web of

590 DIRECTIONS / Southwest England

fan vaulting, is the work of William of Wykeham, a fourteenth-century bishop who also founded Winchester College (southeast of the cathedral), one of the oldest schools in England (open daily). The *Wessex Hotel,* whose cozy modern dining room faces the cathedral across the green expanse of the close, is a perfect place for afternoon tea. If time permits, take a walk along the Weirs, which follow the Itchen through town, past lovely gardens and the ruins of the Bishop's Castle (also a victim of the Civil War). Continue on the footpath beside the river for another mile or so and you'll come to the Hospital of St. Cross, founded in the early twelfth century for indigent men. (Open weekdays.)

CHECKING IN: *Fifehead Manor* – On the site of Saxon Earl Harold's and Lady Godiva's estate, this small hotel offers large, comfortably furnished rooms and a warm country ambience. The mullioned-windowed and oak-paneled dining room is especially pleasant. (Middle Wallop, about 15 miles west of Winchester; phone: 026478-565; expensive to moderate.)

SALISBURY: Compared to Winchester, Salisbury is a mere pup of a city. It wasn't until the thirteenth century that the church, exasperated by constant quarrels with its military neighbors and tired of the harsh weather it suffered from its exposed position on top of the hill at Old Sarum, decided to move the cathedral to the low-lying meadows beside the River Avon. The very elegant cathedral is crowned by the highest spire (404 feet) and houses the oldest clock (ca. 1386) in the country. Many other buildings in town present fine examples of medieval and Georgian architecture: Mompesson House, built in 1701, retains much of its original plasterwork and paneling; part of Malmesbury House dates back to the fourteenth century. A colorful market has been held in Salisbury every Tuesday (now also Saturday), ever since the king gave permission in 1227.

About 10 miles away, standing silently on the bleak Salisbury Plain, is Stonehenge, a wonder of the world that attracts about three quarters of a million visitors a year. The site (which measures about 100 feet in diameter) consists of several earthen banks and barrows; concentric circles of standing stones, some capped in pairs with lintels; and an avenue leading away from the site (originally toward the River Avon). Erected in three stages, beginning in about 3,000 BC, some of the stones are aligned with astronomical events (the position of the sun at summer solstice, for example). As a result, it is thought that the site may have had some primitive religious significance. Although the area is surrounded by wire fencing to deter latter-day druids from performing occult rituals, there is none of the usual touristy clutter and the surrounding rolling, grassy countryside is devoid of twentieth-century intrusions. (For more about Stonehenge, see *Ancient Monuments and Ruins,* DIVERSIONS.)

The broad plain north of Salisbury probably contains more prehistoric monuments per square mile than any other part of England. There are literally dozens of other relics left behind by men and women who worked the plain as early as 6,000 years ago. Woodhenge, a few miles to the northeast of Stonehenge, consists of six concentric rings of post holes whose timbers probably supported a circular temple. Durrington Walls, a 30-acre earthwork with a circular structure near the town of Durrington, is probably another temple. Then there are the numerous barrows (burial mounds): long barrows, round barrows, bowl-shaped, disc-shaped, and bell-shaped barrows. The *Official Guide to Stonehenge* by the Department of the Environment shows the location of many of the barrows and temples near Stonehenge.

CHECKING IN: *Rose and Crown Hotel* – Right on the bank of the Avon, it's a happy amalgam of ancient inn and modern hotel. There are four-poster beds in the half-timbered old inn and comfortable modern rooms in the new annex. (Harnham Rd., near Salisbury; phone: 0722-27908; moderate.)

EATING OUT: Salisbury's bustling downtown is full of pubs, and you could hardly go wrong stopping at any for a tasty pub lunch. If you're not deterred by convivial lunchtime crowds, try the *Haunch of Venison,* a venerable old pub smack in the center of things with a reputation for good food, or the *New Inn,* a cosy fifteenth-century pub near the cathedral. **Mayor Ivie** – This small, pleasant restaurant is one of a growing number devoted to old English cuisine. Smoked mackerel with horseradish sauce, beef in beer, and homemade breads are some of its specialties, but the menu changes every 3 months. Open for dinner only, closed Sundays. (2–4 Ivy St.; phone: 0722-3948; moderate.)

En Route – Avoid the major roads on the trek south from Salisbury Plain and take the unnumbered road that follows the Avon into Salisbury. This will take you through a string of pretty villages — Wilsford, Durnford (Greater and Little), and Woodford (Upper, Middle, and Lower). About half a mile beyond Lower Woodford, veer off to the right toward Wilton.

Wilton was once the capital of King Egbert's Wessex and Kent, and for many years its abbey was Salisbury's ecclesiastical rival. The abbey was dissolved by Henry VIII and the land given to the Earl of Pembroke. The opulent house that now stands on the abbey grounds was designed by Inigo Jones and contains a superb collection of art and furnishings and enough gilt to blind (open Tuesdays to Saturdays and Sunday afternoons from late March to October). Wilton also boasts what is probably the only Italianate basilica in the neighborhood and is the home of Wilton Carpets, which has been turning out fine wool carpets since the seventeenth century. (Factory tours by appointment.)

Although in this countryside of tidy villages tucked in the folds of green hills it is usually advisable to stick to secondary roads, take the main road, A30, from Salisbury to Sherborne. After you pass the town of Shaftesbury, once one of the wealthiest cities in England until its powerful abbey was destroyed by Henry VIII, there's a stretch of road that affords some of the most scenic driving in the country. To your left, a 15-mile-long escarpment rises dramatically over the gentle rolling pastures of Blackmoor Vale. Objectively, it's not very high, perhaps 400 to 500 feet. But it comes on so suddenly that Thomas Hardy described it as the "green sea of Blackmoor Vale washing up to the foot of the bare chalk uplands."

For Hardy fans, there is an obligatory stop nearby. About 5 miles outside Shaftesbury, turn left onto B3092 for another 5 miles to the pretty, prosperous village of Marnhull, transformed by Hardy into Marlott, the birthplace of the fictional Tess of the d'Urbervilles. Tess Cottage, supposedly the cottage Hardy had in mind when creating the Derbyfields, stands about a mile from the village church. It's a private residence, but can be viewed from the road. Head back to A30 via Fifehead Magdalen, the location of which above the Stour River is as pretty as its name is melodious.

SHERBORNE: Even before you reach Sherborne, you catch a glimpse of its powerful past. Standing on a knoll to the southeast of town are the ruins of Sherborne Castle, a magnificent fortified palace built in the early twelfth century by Roger de Caen, bishop of Sarum and, at his height, second in power only to Henry I. Even the remains are impressive: A grassy moat 30 feet deep encircles the site, and the thick walls and gracefully vaulted hallways still standing catch the late afternoon sun with a special brilliance. The castle passed back and forth between the monarchy and the church, and then to Sir Walter Raleigh. Eventually it was razed by Parliamentarian troops in the Civil War. (Open daily.) From the southeast corner of the castle keep you can see "new" Sherborne Castle, an Elizabethan house built by Raleigh after he despaired of ever modernizing Bishop Roger's castle. In the Digby family since 1617, the house contains an impressive collection of paintings, furniture, and porcelain. Sherborne

Castle and the grounds, landscaped by Capability Brown, are open Thursdays, Saturdays, and Sundays from Easter to September.

Like Winchester, Sherborne was a power long before the Normans came. It was chosen as one of two cathedral cities in Wessex in 707, and for the next 400 years the Saxon bishop-warriors consolidated the city's power and prestige. When the Normans moved the See to Sarum in the eleventh century, the church became an abbey, and when Henry VIII dissolved the monasteries, the townsfolk bought it for £300 and made it their parish church. Much of the splendid Norman church, built of golden-colored Ham Hill stone, remains, and there's even a door on the west front that dates from the Saxon cathedral.

Sherborne has long since passed into graceful old age. It's a charming town, compact and self-possessed, with an attractive high street. Its main industry these days is education. There are 10 private schools in Sherborne (a town of 9,000 people), and on weekday afternoons the streets are awash with blue-uniformed schoolchildren. The *Three Wishes Restaurant,* on Cheap St., does a delicious tea of clotted cream, scones, and jam.

En Route – Quiet, agricultural Dorset is a collection of villages, each prettier than the next, linked together by fields, hills and valleys, rivers, and spring-fed meadows of unparalleled beauty. While you can shoot straight down to Dorchester on A37 (pick it up at Yeovil, 5 miles west of Sherborne), you'd be missing the best of this county. Here's a route that will take you through a handful of Dorset villages and some of the loveliest countryside. The roads are sometimes little more than cowpaths, so don't expect to make time.

Start at Melbury Osmond, about 6 miles south of Yeovil, just off A37, a village of stone houses jumbled together in some of the greenest hills man ever laid eyes on. From here there's a public footpath (a little over a mile long) through Melbury Park, a lovely and peaceful private estate, to Evershot, a perfect gem of a village — one street long, one street wide — that looks like Melbury Osmond would if its cottages were laid side by side. (You can also reach Evershot by road.) The cottage just beyond Evershot's parish church is supposedly Hardy's model for the one where Tess rested on her travels.

From Evershot, take an unnumbered road to Minterne Magna, which will take you along the top of Batcombe Hill. It is hard to imagine a more beautiful drive. From the ridge of the escarpment, the land falls away to soft green pastures, hedged fields, and houses and farm buildings built of mellowed Ham Hill stone. This is a human landscape, sculpted by centuries of man's careful and continuous husbandry. It's a short stretch of road — perhaps 5 miles — but you'll be tempted to make it last much longer.

When this road runs into A352, turn south and proceed to Cerne Abbas. Once an abbey and market town, Cerne Abbas is now a pretty triangle of pubs, inns, and handsome merchant houses sitting in a little valley among the rolling upland hills of Dorset. Cerne's other claim to fame is the Cerne Giant, a 180-foot-tall man with prominently exposed genitalia carved into the chalk hillside overlooking the old abbey. There's some disagreement over the identity of the original sculptors, although it's safe to say the giant dates back to at least the Romans. For an especially good pub lunch, head for the *Brace of Pheasants* in Plush, a delightful village at the end of a coombe about 5 miles from Cerne Abbas.

Pick up B3143 at Piddletrenthide and follow the road through the other Piddle River villages to Puddletown, which for many years also took its name from the river until delicate Victorian tastes demanded the name be changed.

You're in the heart of Thomas Hardy country now. So many of his fictional characters crisscross this corner of Dorset that there is hardly a village, manor house, farm, or hill that doesn't have literary associations. Hardy himself was born a few miles west of Puddletown (Weatherbury in *Far from the Madding Crowd*) at Higher Bockhampton, on the edge of what he calls Edgon Heath, the brooding backdrop for *The Return of the Native*. His cottage is now in the hands of the National Trust and can be visited by prior appointment with the occupant (phone: 0305-2366). The gardens are open daily from March to October. A mile or so east of Puddletown is Athelhampton Hall, which Hardy calls Athel Hall, a fifteenth-century Tudor manor house with a remarkably well preserved dovecote from the same period. Athelhampton is a private home, but is open on Wednesdays, Thursdays, and Sundays from April to October, and from Tuesdays to Fridays and Sundays in August.

CHECKING IN: Summer Lodge – Everything about this small hotel speaks of care and thoughtfulness: bouquets of flowers everywhere; homemade shortbread on the tea tray; the quiet, good taste of the decor. The food — traditional English fare cooked with a French feeling for sauces and an oriental respect for vegetables — is excellent. (Fore St., Evershot; phone: 093583-424; moderate.)
Plumber Manor – Another small jewel set in the Dorset countryside, it's best — and deservedly — known for its food, which is elegantly and imaginatively English. But its six attractive bedrooms are easily equal to the food. (Sturminster Newton; phone: 0258-72507; moderate.)

DORCHESTER: Dorchester is Thomas Hardy's town. He lived here, wrote here, and made it live for thousands of readers who have never set eyes on its ancient cobbled streets or dour stone and brick facades. There's an excellent collection of Hardy material at the Dorset County Museum on High West St., which includes the original manuscript of *The Mayor of Casterbridge* (Hardy's name for Dorchester) and a reconstruction of the author's study. The museum also contains Roman mosaics and other artifacts from the time the town was known as Durnovaria. The Roman city boundaries are still visible in the Walks that ring the city center.

There's a relic of even older inhabitants just a mile or so southwest of town. Maiden Castle, an earth fort believed to be about 4,000 years old, is an astounding piece of work. Sprawling over 120 acres, wave after wave of earth ramparts lap up to an elevated enclosure that could hold 5,000 people. The last occupants of Maiden Castle were forcibly evicted by the vastly superior army of the Romans, who then abandoned the site for Dorchester. (Open all year.)

ABBOTSBURY: The straightest shot from Dorchester to the seaside village of Abbotsbury also happens to be the most scenic. Head out of Dorchester west on A35. About a mile from town turn left on an unnumbered road to Martinstown, then follow signs to Abbotsbury, and for the next 6 miles you'll watch the green Dorset hills tumble down to the coast. (Hardy Monument, about midway to your left, commemorates Thomas Masterman Hardy, a captain who served under Nelson at Trafalgar, not the novelist.) Abbotsbury is an exquisite village of thatched and stone cottages lining a single winding street. All that remains of the eleventh-century Benedictine Abbey is the tithe barn, although the abbey has survived, in a manner of speaking, since much of it was used to build many of the village's cottages. The Abbotsbury Swannery, which shelters many species of wild fowl, is open weekdays from May to mid-September, and a subtropical garden, open daily from March to September, flourishes in a coombe east of the village. Just outside Abbotsbury, going southwest on B3157, stop for a lofty look at Chesil Beach, a 10-mile-long pebble beach that separates Lyme Bay from a freshwater lagoon known as Fleet. The church standing lonely on a hill in the middle distance is St. Catherine's Church, the parish church of Abbotsbury.

LYME REGIS: Lyme Regis is probably best known for the Cobb, "a long claw of old gray wall that flexes itself against the sea," as the town's most famous citizen, John Fowles, describes it. (It was from the Cobb that Fowles's heroine, Sarah, the French lieutenant's woman, stared for sad hours at the sea.) Built over 700 years ago to create an artificial harbor, it has probably cost the good folk of Lyme Regis more to repair than it ever brought in in trade. Still, the attachment to it is long and unshakable, and today it harbors scores of pleasure craft and lobster boats.

This is the quintessential seaside town — whitewashed and salty, built up the steep hillsides over the harbor. In summer, Lyme Regis is a very popular resort, but at any other time of year, the seagulls make the most racket. Fossil hunting in the sheer sea cliffs near town is a local sport, but there is also a collection of fossils at the Lyme Regis Museum for those who aren't paleontologically adventurous. (Open daily Easter to September.)

CHECKING IN: *Combe House* – A slight detour inland from Lyme Regis will bring you to this cream-colored Elizabethan mansion run by James Boswell, a descendant of Dr. Johnson's biographer. It's an elegant and roomy hotel, furnished throughout with antiques but retaining an air of informality. And the food is good thanks to Cordon Bleu–trained Therese Boswell. (Gittisham, near Honiton; phone: Honiton 0404-2756; expensive.)

EXETER: In 1282, Isabella de Fortibus, countess of Devon, in a fit of pique with the citizens of Exeter, built a dam across the River Exe below the city in order to deprive it of its access to the sea and the rich trade it brought to Exeter's doorstep. The townsfolk were furious and vowed to undo the countess's work. They did — by building a canal to circumvent the Wear (called Countess Wear in its builder's honor) — and if it took 300 years to accomplish, it's just an indication of Exeter's determination to remain the preeminent city in the region. Exeter is still a thriving commercial center. But it is also a cathedral and university city, a government center, and the gateway to Devon and Cornwall for thousands of vacationers.

At the center of the city sits its grand cathedral, a Norman and Gothic work of great beauty. The cathedral is exceptionally rich in carvings, although you need binoculars to really enjoy the often fanciful creatures carved on the roof bosses. The Minstrels' Gallery on the north side, which shows an entire angel orchestra, is utterly charming.

Not far from the cathedral is *Mol's Coffee House,* a sixteenth-century inn, now an art shop. Across High Street from the cathedral close is the Guildhall, a municipal building built between 1330 and 1593 and in continuous use since then. (Open Mondays to Saturdays all year.) North of the Guildhall is the ruins of Rougemont Castle, a Norman fortification (open Tuesdays to Saturdays all year), and to the south is St. Nicholas Priory, a restored monastic house with a cavernous eleventh-century wine cellar that is the envy of all oeno-philes (open Tuesdays to Saturdays all year, but the ruins can be seen anytime). No boating enthusiast should miss the Maritime Museum on the Quay. With over 100 vessels from around the world, this is considered to be one of the finest collections extant. (Open daily all year.)

Five miles north of Exeter is Killerton, an eighteenth-century mansion housing a fascinating collection of costumes displayed in rooms decorated in different periods. Killerton's superb garden, with rhododendrons, azaleas, magnolias, and stately oak and beech trees, is a beautiful spot, and near here, at Killerton Clump, herons nest from March to July. Killerton House is open daily from April to October, and the garden is open all year.

DARTMOOR: Such is its reputation, Dartmoor's name alone evokes a vivid description: treeless brown hills covered with heather and gorse and pockmarked with treacherous boggy pits, a place where shaggy ponies run wild and the black hounds of hell collect the souls of the damned, a spot so god-forsaken and bleak that even desperate prisoners prefer the dank gloom of their cells to the inhospitable hills outside. And, in fact, the moors are startlingly severe, especially after the cultivated beauty of most English countryside. The B3212 road from Exeter to Plymouth will speed you through this wild landscape, but that would be a pity, since Dartmoor is far more than the barren, though incontestably beautiful, face it shows the passer-through. More than a dozen rivers rise in the upland moors, and as they make their way to the sea, they carve deep wooded valleys that are as lush and green as the moors are barren. Chagford, a picture-perfect village near the River Teign, has for years attracted artists, writers, and fashionable folk, as has Moretonhampstead, the village at the junction of the two main Dartmoor roads.

Scattered throughout Dartmoor are tors, rocky hills as high as 2,000 feet, that offer superb views of the surrounding countryside. One especially accessible tor is Hay Tor, not far from Widecombe in the Moor, one of the most picturesque villages in England and also, in summer, one of the most crowded. There are also numerous relics from prehistoric times — hill forts, stone circles, and barrows. Grimspound, about 3 miles from Manaton, is a Bronze Age settlement consisting of 24 hut circles and a stone enclosure that was probably used for livestock. And everywhere are the sheep, black-faced and woolly, pursuing scrubby moor grasses up steep hillsides, crowding onto narrow Devon roads through a break in the hedge.

Dartmoor is marvelous hiking country. Before you set out, though, stop at the National Park Information Center at Postbridge (much of Dartmoor is now national park land) to pick up maps and advice. Although the days when the moors seemed to mysteriously swallow up hapless travelers are gone, it would be foolhardy to misjudge them.

CHECKING IN: *Gidleigh Park* – Take 30 acres of secluded Devon woodlands, add a turn-of-the-century mansion built for comfort and elegance, furnish it in impeccable good taste, and you have Gidleigh Park. And as if that isn't enough, there's the food, nouvelle cuisine and certainly deserving of its Michelin star, and the wine list, mostly Californian and distinguished. (Chagford; phone: 0647-2367; expensive.)

En Route – Take B3357 southeast out of Dartmoor to Buckfastleigh. Buckfast Abbey, built by French Benedictine monks in the late 1800s, is open daily all year. Buckfastleigh is also the starting point for the Dart Valley Railway, a delightful steam railway that follows the River Dart down to the ancient city of Totnes, a trip of about 6 miles. (Open Sundays to Fridays, May to October.)

TOTNES: Totnes looks every bit as medieval as its name suggests. Its steep narrow streets curl up and around themselves, and the timbered and slate-shingled buildings that overhang the main street lean and sag like clowns in a Shakespearean comedy. If you climb the narrow passageway to the church and guildhall, a wonderful old building with columned porch and frightfully low oak doors, you'll find yourself peering down on the roofs of buildings. Totnes Castle, one of the first to be erected by the conquering Normans, stands near the center of town (open daily), and Totnes Museum, in one of the Elizabethan merchant houses, has an interesting collection of local costumes and household goods (open Mondays to Saturdays, March to October).

DARTMOUTH: In 1147, 164 ships sailed from here on the Second Crusade. Eight hundred years later, a fleet of 485 American ships left Dartmouth's snug harbor on another crusade, this time to the beaches of Normandy. In between the two events, the town grew and prospered, first from wine trade with Burgundy, later from cod fishing off the coast of Newfoundland, and whenever it could, from piracy and privateering.

It was the Elizabethans who really left their stamp on this thoroughly and wonderfully nautical town on the estuary of the Dart River. The crooked, elaborately decorated half-timbered buildings in the harbor area make Dartmouth look much the way it must have when Sir Walter Raleigh brought his royally sanctioned booty here. Occupying a commanding position above the harbor is the Royal Naval College, Britain's main naval training center since 1905, while right on the town quay is the Royal Avenue Gardens, a charming reminder of the town's present popularity as a resort. Its amusement park entrance, a blue and white iron gate strung with colored lights and topped with a crown done in lights, doesn't lead you to expect the beautifully kept garden where primroses, crocuses, and daffodils bloom as early as March. Just outside town is Dartmouth Castle, one of Henry VIII's many coastal fortifications. (Open daily all year.) Not much is left of its twin across the mouth of the river, Kingswear Castle (a private residence).

EATING OUT: *The Carved Angel* – The seafood in this bright and airy restaurant on the quay is outstanding, and no one has been heard to complain about the other dishes on its imaginatively French menu. Closed January. (2 South Embankment; phone: 08043-2465; expensive.)

En Route – Slapton Sands, about 5 miles south of Dartmouth on A379, is where American troops practiced for the invasion of Normandy. In the middle of the 5-mile-long stretch of sand is a monument erected by the US government, thanking the local people for the use of their beach.

PLYMOUTH: Driving into Plymouth from the east, you come across a curious sight — the ruins of a church in the middle of a traffic roundabout. The church, Charles Church, was destroyed during a Nazi raid on the city during the spring of 1941. Over 1,000 people died, 70,000 were left homeless, and most of the city center was devastated in that attack. The shell of Charles Church was left as a memorial to those who lost their lives, and if at first it seems irreverent to surround a memorial with traffic, on second thought, it seems entirely appropriate that it is there in the daily flow of life.

The raid irrevocably changed the face of this vigorous old port, the largest city in Britain's southwest. The postwar center is an excellent shopping area that draws people from all over the region, although, unfortunately, it isn't very handsome. But a lot of Plymouth was miraculously spared damage. The Barbican, on an indent of the sea called Sutton Harbor, is where rich Elizabethan merchants built their houses and is now a lively spot full of antique shops, art galleries, restaurants, and pubs. Elizabethan House on New St., with fine furnishings from that period, is open Mondays to Saturdays in winter and daily during the summer. Near here, too, is Mayflower Steps, a monument commemorating the sailing of the *Mayflower* in 1620. At the edge of the Barbican is Prysten House, a fifteenth-century priory that survived both Henry's purge of the monasteries and Hitler's terrible assault. (Open Mondays to Saturdays all year.)

In contrast to the amiable bustle of the Barbican, the face Plymouth shows the sea is a formidable one. The Citadel, a low gray stone fortress built in the late 1600s by Charles II and still used by the military, sits brooding on the high ground above the Sound. Its strength has never been tested, perhaps because the sight of it alone is enough to deter any would-be invaders. Sharing the commanding position over the Sound is Plymouth's famous Hoe, the broad green where Sir Francis Drake unhurriedly finished his game of bowls before dealing an ignominious defeat to the Spanish Armada. There's a statue of Sir Francis near the bowling green. At the center of the Hoe is another monument, this one to the thousands of sailors, British and Commonwealth, who were killed in the two world wars. It's a moving tribute, especially apt in this city whose namesakes in the far flung reaches of the Empire number no less than 40. Before leaving the Hoe, walk to the edge of the seaward side. Built into the rocky cliffs of the headland is a series of steps and platforms that lead down to an open-air bathing pool that juts out into the sound, a surprising retreat hidden away from the city that buzzes above it.

En Route – There are a wealth of historic homes near Plymouth. Just outside the city to the east is Saltram, a classic Georgian mansion containing Chippendale furniture, portraits by Sir Joshua Reynolds, and interiors by Robert Adam. The house is open Tuesdays to Sundays from April to October, but the gardens are open all year. About 10 miles north of Plymouth on high ground with a clear view of distant Plymouth Harbor is Buckland Abbey, Sir Francis Drake's house. It contains plenty of Drake memorabilia, as well as a Naval and Devon Folk Museum. (Open Wednesdays, Saturdays, and Sundays in winter; daily from Easter to September.)

Across the Tamar River (the border between Cornwall and Devon) and a bit to the north of Buckland Abbey is Cotehele, an especially lovely Tudor house in an exquisite setting of wildflowers and meadows on the Tamar River. There's also a working eighteenth-century watermill on the grounds. (Open daily, April to October.) Also across the Tamar, but just outside Plymouth, is Anthony House, a graceful Queen Anne mansion long — and still — the home of the powerful Carew family. (Open Tuesdays to Thursdays, April to October.) As you cross the Tamar to Saltash, look to your left for the Royal Albert Bridge, one of the engineering masterpieces by Isambard Kingdom Brunel, who has proudly signed this work in high, clear letters: "I. K. Brunel, Engineer, 1859."

ST. MAWES: Its mild climate isn't all that prompts comparisons between St. Mawes and the French Riviera. It has the same easygoing charm and the same air of a perpetual party. Sitting on the tip of a peninsula in a large sheltered bay, St. Mawes is a perfect yachting and fishing town. Add to this, stunning coast walks, secluded beaches, and subtropical gardens where, as one long-time resident says, "there's nothing as *common* as a palm tree," and it is easy to understand why the mood is so buoyant. Don't look for countrified charm here, although charm exists by the bushel in this village of whitewashed cottages ranging along the town quay. Well-to-do Britons with a yen for the sea and soft climate make St. Mawes a sophisticated outpost: Good food and gracious hotels are expected, not just hoped for.

Across the Carrick Roads, as the wide estuary of the Fal River is known, and linked by a pedestrian ferry to St. Mawes is Falmouth, once a port and now also a resort town. From here you can take a steamer up the Fal to the ancient high tide port of Truro, Cornwall's cathedral city, or south, down along the coast, then up the Helford River. Falmouth and St. Mawes share a pair of Henry VIII castles. St. Mawes Castle, its central tower surrounded by three battlemented semicircles, sits prettily on a knoll outside the village. Unlike Pendennis, its twin at Falmouth, which held out against Parliamentarian troops for 5 months, St. Mawes was never the site of any action and thus is in near-perfect repair. (Both castles are open daily all year.)

The gardens that flourish around the Carrick Roads are so wildly exotic partly because the climate is mild but also because Falmouth was the first port of call for water for English ships returning from long voyages, and for hundreds of years sailors brought back plants from the farthest flung reaches of the world. When the English turned their considerable gardening talents to these rare plants, they developed a dizzying number of subspecies. The church grounds of St. Just in Roseland, 4 miles outside St. Mawes and linked by coastal and inland footpaths, is a splendid garden where date palms, bamboo, camellias, rhododendrons, azaleas, Chilian fire bushes, and magnolias flourish alongside England's own bluebells, snowdrops, and primroses. North of St. Mawes is Trelissick Gardens, a beautifully tended woodland on the River Fal (open daily from March to October); to the west is Penjerrick Gardens (open Wednesdays and Sundays from March to September) and Glendurgan, on the Helford River (open Mondays, Wednesdays, and Fridays from March to October), each with enough varieties of subtropical and indigenous plants to satisfy the most avid gardener.

CHECKING IN: *Rising Sun* – It's hard to imagine a quainter, cosier, more gracious hotel than this one. The front terrace, which fills with the overflow of its congenial pub in warm weather, faces the town quay, and if you get a room in the front, you'll go to sleep to the sound of the tide slapping against the harbor wall. From the *Rising Sun*'s justly renowned kitchen comes crème brulée, a creamy custardy confection that to have once is to yearn for forever. (St. Mawes; phone: 0326-270233; expensive.) ***Tresanton Hotel*** – This lovably overgrown, white-painted and vine-covered cottage combines the sophistication and the country charm of St.

Mawes in one delightful package. On the coastal road, it has subtropical gardens spilling down its hillside toward the bay and a private beach. Sailing and water skiing are possible. All the 26 bedrooms have private baths; breakfast and dinner are included in the room price; and the food is delicious. Closed mid-November to April 1. (St. Mawes; phone: 0326-270544; expensive.)

THE LIZARD AND WEST PENWITH: It takes a jaded traveler indeed to resist the urge to travel to the ends of the earth, and in England the earth ends most spectacularly at the tips of a broad stirrup of land called the Lizard and West Penwith. Despite the summer crowds that converge on these popular spots, they are, nonetheless, impressive examples of nature's handiwork. The Lizard ends in cliffs of brilliant serpentine — olive green rock veined with red and purple and polished by the sea and wind — while Land's End meets the sea with granite cliffs and a wash of shiny black boulders. Go early in the morning or at sunset to avoid the crowds. Or better yet, park your car a mile or so away and approach the spots on foot via one of the coastal paths.

Just 10 miles from the cliffs of Lizard Point in the northern part of the peninsula is scenery of a different, but equally pleasing, order — wooded coves leading down to the River Helford. Helford village is a completely charming place on one of these sylvan inlets. The *Shipwrights Inn,* a pretty pub with sunny terraces jutting out over a brook, is a perfect spot to while away a summer afternoon.

On the main road from the Lizard to West Penwith, A394, is Helston, a pleasant market town best known for its Flora Day celebration, when the whole town turns out, flower bedecked and beribboned, to "furry" dance through the streets to a 1,500-year-old processional tune. The date, May 8, is well before the annual influx of vacationers, so the holiday is still mostly an event for townsfolk.

Midway between the two peninsulas is Godolphin House, built in the sixteenth century by one of the most powerful families in England whose fortune came from the rich tin veins in Cornwall. (Open Thursdays from May to June and Tuesdays and Thursdays from July to September.) The castle that seems to rise out of the water like a vision as you approach West Penwith is real enough. It's St. Michael's Mount, once a monastery, later a fortress, and for the last 300 years the home of the St Aubyn family. It's now owned by the National Trust and can be visited on Mondays, Wednesdays, and Fridays all year, and additionally on Tuesdays from June to October.

Land's End and the splendor of the Cornish coast is only part of West Penwith's attraction. This westernmost nub of England is an open-air museum of ancient Britons. There are dozens of stone circles (most, for some arcane reason, having nine or nineteen stones), hut circles, and burial mounds. Near Lamorna is a fascinating formation called the Pipers and the Merry Maidens — two tall upright stones and a circle of nineteen stones. Local legend has it that the village girls were caught dancing on the Sabbath, and they and their musicians were turned to stone as a punishment. Carn Euny, near Crows an Wra (Witches' Cross), and Chysauster, 5 miles from Penzance, are two well-preserved Iron Age villages.

If you want to see the source of much Cornish wealth, head for Pendeen, on the west coast, where you can visit Geevor Mine, a working tin mine that gives guided tours. You can also get a look at Cornwall's other mainstay — fishing — at Mousehole, a granity fishing village about 5 miles south of Penzance, or at Newlyn, once a Victorian artists' colony and now the largest fishing port in the southwest. Much of the delicious fish you get in this part of the country comes from there. A bit farther down the coast is Minack Theatre, an amphitheater built into the granite cliffs overlooking the sea. The season, which runs from June to September, includes a variety of theater productions — from Gilbert and Sullivan to Maxim Gorki — by different repertory groups. The setting is nothing short of spectacular, but be sure to wear warm clothes.

Penzance and St. Ives guard West Penwith like a pair of Henry's castles. Both are near excellent broad swaths of beach, and for that reason are crammed with the less appealing sights of tourism — acres of small, drab hotels, cheap cafés, and tacky souvenir shops. The Barbara Hepworth museum at the artist's home in St. Ives is, however, well worth a visit. (Open Mondays and Saturdays from September to June and daily in July and August.)

CHECKING IN: *Lamorna Cove Hotel* – This hotel takes its name from the tranquil wooded cove over which it perches. Although the modern additions don't do justice to the original granite house or the setting, the hotel is very comfortable, and the ambience relaxed and friendly. Fresh fish, of which there is an unending supply from nearby Newlyn, is a specialty. (Lamorna; phone: 073673-294; moderate.)

ISLES OF SCILLY: The often rough 2½-hour boat passage from Penzance to the Isles of Scilly prompted one wag to describe the islands as paradise which can only be reached through purgatory. Now, thanks to the 20-minute helicopter flight, you can go straight to heaven, in this case a group of 150-plus islands 30 miles off the Cornish coast. Connected by shallow straits treacherously studded with outcroppings of rock and reef, the islands have a schizophrenic nature. The northwestern side of the islands is usually bleak, windswept plains of gorse and heather. But the sheltered southern side supports vast fields of flowers — daffodils, jonquils, narcissus, anemones, iris, tulips, and lilies. Flowers are the main business of the 2,000 people who live in the Scillies: Over 1,000 tons of cut flowers are exported from here every year.

Only five of the islands are inhabited by man. The rest are home to seals, puffins, gannets, kittiwakes, and other ocean birds. (The rent for the entire island chain in the fifteenth century was six and eightpence — or 50 puffins.) Their quiet sandy beaches are perfect for a day of picnicking or sunbathing. No wonder ex–prime minister Harold Wilson chose these islands as a refuge from the political hurly-burly of 10 Downing Street.

St. Mary's is the largest island in the chain and has the distinction of having what is probably the cheapest and most quickly constructed castle in Britain — Star Castle, built by Sir Francis Godolphin in 1593 for under £1,000. The island of Tresco draws the most visitors. The gardens at Tresco Abbey contain a staggering variety of plants — between 3,000 and 4,000 — the lifetime achievement of botanical zealot Augustus Smith, whose descendants still hold the lease of the island. (Open Mondays to Saturdays all year.) Also on Tresco is the Valhalla Maritime Museum, which has a fascinating collection of figureheads from shipwrecks, relics of the days when Scilly islanders made their living scavenging from the many ships that went aground on Scilly's dangerous reefs. (Open Mondays to Saturdays all year.)

En Route – It's best to meander up the rocky north coast of Cornwall. No single road follows the coastline, but there are secondary roads that loop off the main road (the A30, which runs about 5 miles inland) to hug the coast for 5 to 10 miles before rejoining it. Just past Newquay, a popular and congested summer resort with a fine stretch of beach, take B3276 to Bedruthan Steps. Here, mammoth chunks of the cliff have tumbled onto the wide strand of beach below, forming steps for the Cornish giant, Bedruthan. When the tide is in, Bedruthan's Steps jut out from the white agitation of the sea like bits of black coral strung on a necklace, but when the tide is out, you can explore the rock pools and caverns cut into the cliffs by the sea. Continue on B3276 another 8 miles to Padstow.

PADSTOW: From June to September, Padstow, with its compact horseshoe of a harbor and pleasant tangle of streets, rings with the holiday fun of summer folk who come to fish, swim, and sail in the waters of the north Cornish coast and the Camel River. But on May 1, before the season gets under way, the town holds its own celebration, the Hobby Horse or, as it is locally known, 'Obby 'Oss, a day when a huge, fierce hobby horse prances through the streets in the midst of singing and dancing villagers. According to one story, the 'Obby 'Oss started when the village women, whose husbands were off fighting the French in one of the numerous wars between the English and their channel neighbors, fashioned an enormous stallion to scare away enemy raiders. However, most think the raucous celebration has its roots in earlier pagan times. Clearly, there is a strain of unrepentant wit — pagan or otherwise — in Padstow: One of the bench ends in the thirteenth- and fourteenth-century church shows the devil disguised as a fox, preaching to a flock of geese.

En Route – A few miles south of the town of Bodmin on B3268 is Lanhydrock, a grandiose Tudor-style house built in the late 1800s and set in meticulously tended grounds and rolling parkland. Never were the fruits of the Empire more impressively displayed. The elaborate kitchens — with numerous larders — and lavish baths are especially fascinating insights into that incredibly wealthy time. The house is open daily from April to October and the gardens daily throughout the year.

BODMIN MOOR: Bodmin Moor reverberates with almost as many legends as the more famous moor in neighboring Devon. Dozmary Pool, a shallow tarn nearly dead center of Bodmin Moor, is supposedly the pool (one of three) into which Arthur flung Excalibur. Nearby at Bolventor is Jamaica Inn, the scene of Daphne du Maurier's tale of smugglers and pirates. And there are holy wells — at St. Neot on the southern edge, and, on the northern edge, at St. Clether and Altarnun, whose well is reputed to cure madness by the near drowning of the sufferer.

Driving across the bare brown hills broken only by tors, it is easy to see how legends attach themselves to these spots. There are a few minor roads that penetrate the southeast corner of the moor, but to get to Rough Tor (pronounce Rough to rhyme with now) and Brown Willy, where the best views can be had, you have to circle the moor and come up behind it at Camelford, on its northwestern edge. From here you can drive to a car park at the foot of Rough Tor and climb up or hike on to Brown Willy, a mile away. There's a turnoff to the left just before you get to Rough Tor that takes you to an eerie relic of modern times — the ruins of a World War II Royal Air Force base at Davidstow. It could be a scene straight out of any number of contemporary doomsday stories: abandoned runways, control towers, all the paraphernalia of modern technology left to decay along with the crude barrows and hut circles of ancient Britons. Just to balance the vision of life left by the opulence of Lanhydrock, stop in at the North Cornwall Museum at Camelford, which has a reconstruction of a Cornish cottage. (Open Monday to Saturday, April to September.)

CHECKING IN: *Arundell Arms* – This former coaching inn covered with Virginia creeper is well worth a slight detour (about 15 miles east of Altarnun via A30): Log fires blaze away, the floors are laid with dark blue slate, and the culinary offerings are of international standard. But it really stands out for its salmon fishing, since it owns the fishing rights to 20 miles of the Tamar River. (In Lifton; phone: 056684–244 or 456; moderate.)

NORTH CORNWALL COAST: It would be a Herculean task to find any part of the Cornish coast not worth seeing. But there is a stretch of coast north of the Camel River that in 20 miles contains dramatic cliffs, surfing beaches, sand dunes, historic spots, and exquisite villages.

From Wadebridge, at the mouth of the Camel River estuary, take B3314 about 2 miles till you see a turnoff to Rock. Another 3 miles along this unnumbered road will take you past this not terribly attractive resort town to a car park at Daymer Bay. The dunes here are marvelous, covered with clumps of coarse grass and just the place to find dog-walkers and families on weekend outings. There is a golf course along the coast, and in the middle of one of the fairways stands St. Enodoc Church, less curious now, even given its fairly odd surroundings, than it was 100 years ago when it was half buried in sand and the vicar was forced to crawl in through the roof to deliver the sermon. It is hard to imagine who was there to hear it.

Stick to the unnumbered coast road by following signs to Trebetherick, Polzeath (a surfing beach), Pentireglaze, and Port Quin. According to local lore, all the men of Port Quin were lost at sea in one accident, and shortly after the women mysteriously disappeared as well. True or half-true, the abandoned village — four stone cottages that sit precariously over the water at the end of a steep cove and an old stone barn next to a tumbling stream — is now in the hands of the National Trust and is as lovely and quiet a spot as you'd ever hope to find.

Just a few miles from Port Quin is Port Isaac, an old corn port and modern-day fishing village that you literally descend into. Leave your car at the car park above town and walk down to the village. The *Golden Lion* pub sits right on the harbor wall and is a congenial spot from which to watch the tide slowly creep up the harbor. At the end of another steep valley about 10 miles up the coast is Trebarwith Strand, a truly magnificent meeting of land and water, where massive fingers of sculpted black rock, pink-veined and highly polished, lead down to a broad swath of beach that in high tide is completely covered.

From here it is just a mile or so to Tintagel, possibly the most visited spot in Cornwall. The town itself is unlovely and crowded most of the year. What draws such crowds is Tintagel Castle, the ruins of a twelfth-century castle and sixth-century monastery where, according to some folk, King Arthur, who has fascinated and inspired the English soul for fourteen centuries, was born. Even if you don't subscribe to that story, Tintagel is well worth a stop. Right on the edge of a rocky promontory, the castle ruins are dramatically beautiful. And if you follow the causeway to the castle and stand on the ramparts looking out to sea, it is hard not to feel a shiver of magic and history come together.

What Tintagel town lacks in charm, Boscastle, just 3 miles on, offers in spades. Boscastle is a cozy village sheltered in a deep valley that you enter from a ridge running along the valley wall. The dark stone buildings and the snug harbor give the village a serious, settled mien, not likely to be altered by the excesses of tourism. And as a conservation area, Boscastle will probably remain that way.

CHECKING IN: *Tredethy Country Hotel* – In a spacious manor house facing an expansive patchwork of fields, sheep pastures, and woods, this friendly hotel has large, pleasant rooms and 9 acres of grounds — including a swimming pool and redwood solarium — in which to wander. (Helland Bridge, near Bodmin; phone: 020884-262; moderate.) ***Bridge House*** – This seventeenth-century stone house on Boscastle Harbor offers small attractive rooms, a cheerful ambience, and a most charming location. Bed and breakfast only. (Boscastle; phone: 08405-477; inexpensive.)

CLOVELLY: Clovelly is so perfectly picturesque — an unbroken line of shuttered and flower-bedecked cottages down a steep, cobbled street to the harbor — you can't quite believe anything so quaint and charming isn't contrived. But Clovelly isn't, and despite the fact that it is on the map for every tourist bus coming to the Devon coast (the Cornwall-Devon border is less than 10 miles south), it remains stubbornly unaffected. No cars are allowed in Clovelly; visitors and villagers alike have to leave them at a car park at the top of the hill. And except for *Gladys Friend's* tearoom with six, maybe eight, tables there is nothing to *do* in Clovelly — no souvenir shops, ice cream vendors, amusements, or diversions — except to stroll down to the quay and make the arduous climb — for it is steep — back up. Because it is so popular, it is probably best to avoid it during the day in July or August. But if you go in the early morning or evening, you'll find simply a beautiful village going about its business.

NORTH DEVON COAST: Start a tour of the North Devon coast at Ilfracombe, long a port and shipyard, now a popular resort. With its ranks upon ranks of small hotels all with similar sounding names — Golden Sands, Sandy Cove, Cove Haven — and imposing Victorian hotels daringly perched on the city's magnificent cliffs, Ilfracombe has a certain period charm.

602 DIRECTIONS / Southwest England

Leaving Ilfracombe, take A399 east, a road that for about 8 miles follows a beautiful stretch of coast. Just past Combe Martin, a not very pretty resort town, take an unnumbered road to *Hunter's Inn* and Trentishoe. The variety of landscapes this road covers in a few short miles will make your head spin. First it follows a ridge above gentle green downs dotted with prosperous-looking farms. Then, suddenly, you're on the loneliest coast road in the world — wild moorland, raw to the sea wind, stretches on either side of you. Press on, for within another mile or so, the road runs along the top of a deep, wooded combe. When you reach the bottom of this serene valley, you'll be at the door of *Hunter's Inn*, a gabled and Alpinesque inn popular with tourists and a gathering spot for the hunt. Nonetheless, the spot is unarguably beautiful and a cool beer on the inn's terrace, in the company of the resident peacocks, is almost mandatory.

Lynmouth, about 5 miles on, is a pretty resort village hedged in by the sheer cliffs of the Lyn River Valley. You need steady nerves and reliable brakes on your car to take the direct road from Lynton, a larger town which literally hovers 500 feet above Lynmouth. It is a vertiginous drop, and the three sand-filled offshoots along the road — escape roads for runaway cars — probably see their share of business. Percy Bysshe Shelley lived here for a while, although the cottage he occupied was washed away in a 1952 flood that devastated much of the town.

There are two absolutely spectacular drives out of Lynmouth. One is along B3223 inland, which follows the high curving ridge of the East Lyn River Valley to Watersmeet, where the East Lyn and the Hoar Oak Water meet. Much of this land is owned by the National Trust, which has marked several nature trails through the dense woods of the valleys. The other drive is along the coast on A39, up Countisbury Hill (as demanding of your car's engine as the road into Lynton was of its brakes). Superlatives only suffice to describe the view. Bracken- and gorse-covered hills break suddenly at black cliffs, and in the distance looms Foreland Point, at 900 feet the tallest cliffs in England.

Porlock, about 12 miles east of Lynmouth and across the Somerset border, is utterly unlike most southwest sea towns that either cling to the edge of cliffs or shelter in narrow coves. Occupying a broad, sea level plain that opens up in the Exmoor Hills, it's a sweet little place whose efforts to cater to the tourist trade still don't detract from its sleepy, satisfied air. Porlock Weir, about 2.5 miles from town, is a pretty collection of hotels and harbor buildings, and the long curve of white beach with luxuriant subtropical flowers blooming in the distance looks positively Caribbean.

CHECKING IN: *Yeoldon House* – This rambling Victorian house on the edge of Bideford has been very ably converted to an attractive hotel. The rooms are bright and comfortable with plenty of thoughtful small touches, and the Cordon Bleu cooking certainly does justice to local produce and fresh fish. (Durrant La., Northam, near Bideford; phone: 02372-4400; expensive to moderate.) *Heddon's Gate Hotel* – Perfectly poised close to the sea in the midst of the national park, this large country house has a well-deserved reputation for good food and lodging and is popular with wildlife lovers. (Heddon's Mouth, Parracombe; phone: 05983-313; moderate.)

EXMOOR FOREST: Anyone expecting dense woods is likely to be disappointed by Exmoor Forest, as the parcel of hills in northeast Devon and west Somerset is known. It is a forest in the ancient English sense — land owned by the king and subject to his hunting laws. In fact, at one time early in the nineteenth century, a royal commission found only 37 trees in all of Exmoor. There are more trees than that now, but Exmoor is still more moor than forest, full of ancient relics, tors, wild red deer, and its famous ponies. Exford, at the center of Exmoor, is a pretty spot and a good center for fishing, hiking, or horseback riding. Oare, near the Somerset-Devon border, is at the head of Doone Valley, the setting for R. D. Blackmore's story, *Lorna Doone*. Doone Valley and the surrounding area are indeed lovely, but, sadly, have been commercialized.

DIRECTIONS / Southwest England

En Route – Around the town of Dunster, the moors give way to soft green meadows backed by even softer hills where clusters of houses linked by ivy-draped walls smugly sit. Dunster itself is a lovely town in a peerless setting, but it is very crowded in summer and is best seen off season. Dunster Castle, occupying a knoll on the edge of town, has been the home of the Luttrell family for 600 years and was the object of both Royalist and Parliamentarian attacks in the Civil War. (Open Sundays to Thursdays from April to September, and Tuesdays, Wednesdays, and Sundays in October.)

Five miles east of Dunster on A39 in a tranquil setting called Flowery Valley is Cleeve Abbey, built by Cistercian monks in the twelfth century. It was spared the full wrath of Henry VIII at the Dissolution of the Monasteries, and although the church no longer exists, the gatehouse, refectory, and dormitory are beautifully intact. (Open daily all year.) Continue on A39 another 10 miles or so to Nether Stowey, a village nestling on the eastern slopes of the Quantock Hills, where Samuel Taylor Coleridge wrote *The Rime of the Ancient Mariner*. (For a time William Wordsworth and his sister Dorothy lived about 4 miles away at Holford.) Coleridge's cottage, now owned by the National Trust, opens its parlor doors Sunday through Thursday afternoons from late March to September.

The A39 cuts across a broad basin of land between the Quantock and Mendip hills called the Somerset levels, low marshy land reclaimed from the sea over the centuries. Somerton and Glastonbury, about 15 miles inland, were, until the seventeenth century, islands, and the sea, at high wind and high tide, can still flood these towns. Indeed, it's thought that Somerset takes its name — summer settlers or settlers by the sea lakes — from this region. For during this season the lagoons would dry up, leaving behind fertile tidal land for grazing. Early inhabitants would drive cattle and sheep down to the plain in summer and then return to the hills when winter brought more flooding.

GLASTONBURY: About 20 miles east of Nether Stowey is Glastonbury, fabled island of Avalon where the strands of early Christianity and English national identity meet and intertwine. Christ himself is said to have built the church that later became the most powerful abbey in the country, and it was to this sacred spot that Arthur and Queen Guinevere were brought to be buried. The long and rich history of Glastonbury and nearby South Cadbury, thought to be Arthur's Camelot, is discussed in *Ancient Monuments and Ruins,* DIVERSIONS.

CHECKING IN: *George and Pilgrims* – Many a pilgrim has bedded down for the night at this venerable old hotel, and although it hasn't lost an ounce of the character it has acquired over the years, it has managed to incorporate all the comforts a modern traveler demands. For a real treat, ask for a room with a four-poster bed. (1 High St.; phone: 0458-31146; moderate.)

WELLS: What makes this little town basking on the sunny side of the Mendip Hills a city is its cathedral, an early-English-style church whose elaborately carved west front has been awing visitors for centuries. Inside, of less divine purpose perhaps but of spirited inspiration, is the Wells Clock, an enchanting timepiece made by a Glastonbury monk, Peter Lightfoot, in the fourteenth century. A carved figure of a man announces the quarter hour by kicking his heels against two bells, and four mounted knights, who charge out and knock each other off their steeds, bring in the hour.

The cathedral celebrates its 800th birthday this year, and in addition to numerous religious events, it will host a 9-month festival — from March to November — when choirs, opera companies, ballet troupes, and orchestras from all over the country will come to the cathedral to perform. For information on the festival calendar, write Canon Leslie Ward, Celebration Director, 23 Vicar's Close, Wells, Somerset BA5 2UJ.

CHEDDAR CAVES: Under the Mendip Hills that tower over the Somerset levels is a labyrinth of caves eaten out of the soft limestone hills by constant flooding. For thousands of years, and until as late as the mid-nineteenth century, many of these caves were inhabited by people. Adventurous spelunkers still explore the underground streams and roads, and thousands of tourists visit the larger caves, Cheddar Caves, near Cheddar, and Wookey Hole, near Wells. Cheddar Gorge, a deep limestone cleft through the Mendips, makes for a scenic drive, but is terribly congested in July and August. The town of Cheddar, home of the most famous English cheese, more recently has become the center of a thriving industry growing strawberries and anemones, which flourish on the sunny sheltered slopes of the Mendips.

From the Cheddar Caves, it's just a short ride to Bristol. (For a complete description of the city, its sights, hotels, and restaurants, see *Bristol,* THE CITIES.)

The Cotswolds

Less than 100 miles west of London is the region known as the Cotswolds. It encompasses about 450 square miles of rolling limestone upland of the Cotswold Hills, punctuated by charming, carefully preserved medieval towns and villages built from the honey-colored stone, quarried from the hills, which gives the region its character. The Cotswolds themselves stretch northeast in a curving 60-mile arc from Bath to the vicinity of Stratford-upon-Avon. Along their western edge they form a steep ridge of solid limestone, and their crest is the Thames-Severn watershed. But the overall character of the countryside is tranquil and picturesque, like a rich tapestry. Much of this land is a great, sweeping pasture for the famous Cotswold sheep, with their heavy ringlets of fleece that once upon a time brought wealth to the area.

This is the England of the imagination: rolling hills covered by copses of ancient oak and surviving elm, a landscape scaled to size for country walks and bird-watching. Towns are tied to one another by twisting country lanes that carry a constant commerce of farmers and shepherds, postmen, parsons, and pubgoers. The vista from any hill is as apt to include the square tower of a Norman church as a far field of cropping sheep, and any church is likely to be surrounded by the stone-tiled roofs of a tiny village, now no longer populated by farm workers but by retired folk, weekenders, and commuters to the larger towns. Village cemeteries are shaded by yews and village streams guarded by weeping willows. Nothing is very far from anything else, but privacy and protective isolation are accentuated by the quiet and country peace that settles over all. Village names are remnants of an earlier language and a younger England: Wyck Rissington, Upper and Lower Slaughter, Oddington, Guiting Power, Clapton-on-Hill, Bourton-on-the-Water, Moreton-in-Marsh.

The Cotswolds provided a rich agricultural center for the Romans until the fifth century, and the Roman presence is still visible in many places, such as the roads out of Cirencester and the baths in Bath. The Saxons routed the Romans; the Normans routed the Saxons; and they all left their mark. But when the Cotswold sheep began to pay off, it was the wool merchants of the Middle Ages who built the enduring symbols of the area — magnificent churches like the fifteenth-century one at Northleach and the fourteenth-century one to St. John the Baptist at Cirencester.

Our route through the Cotswolds is long, lazy, and serpentine. We begin in Oxford and end in Bath, both important and fascinating cities that border the Cotswolds area. In between we savor most of those golden towns that are quintessentially Cotswold in flavor: Northleach, Chedworth, Burford, Bourton-on-the-Water, Stow-on-the-Wold, Moreton-on-Marsh, Chipping Campden, Broadway, Winchcombe, Cheltenham, Cirencester, and Malmesbury.

An eminently English way to see the Cotswolds is to take to shank's pony and walk all or part of the 100-mile Cotswold Way, a trail that links a series of well-marked and easily negotiated paths that follow the crests of the Cotswold hills from Bath to Chipping Campden in the north. These ancient routes, first used by Neolithic travelers 3,000 years ago, were well worn by medieval pilgrims and traders moving from village to village, the same villages that dot the course today. One need not be an accomplished hiker to follow the Way for a distance, and the weak of spirit can take heart from the thought that village and pub are never far apart. The benefits are multiple: Immersed in the countryside, you have a walking-pace view of the villages, buildings, cottages, churches, Roman ruins, and barrows — Stone Age burial mounds — that dot the region (the barrow at Belas Knap, between Cheltenham and Winchcombe, is thought to be the most impressive specimen in England). The Way is maintained by the Gloucestershire County Council, which marks its course with large yellow arrows to make hiking easier. Thornhill Press publishes *The Cotswold Way,* an excellent guide by Mark Richards, available throughout the area.

A detailed guidebook entitled *The Cotswolds* is available from the Heart of England Tourist Board, Old Bank House, Bank St., Worcester WR1 2EW (phone: 0905–29511).

OXFORD: A visit to this beautiful city is the perfect start to a tour of the Cotswolds. For a detailed report on the city, its sights, hotels, and restaurants, see *Oxford,* THE CITIES.

To begin the Cotswold tour, take the A40 west from Oxford to Northleach.

NORTHLEACH: In the fifteenth century Northleach was one of the busiest wool towns in the Cotswolds. During this period prosperous wool traders built the church of St. Peter and St. Paul, which is designed in the Perpendicular style and constructed of local stone. Note especially how the South Porch is richly decorated with statuary and carved stone. It is perhaps best known, however, for its numerous brasses representing the wool merchants. The church has undergone and survived much recent restoration, including work by Sir Basil Spence, architect of Coventry Cathedral.

Because the River Leach did not provide sufficient power to drive the watermills that were speeding up the manufacturing process in other parts of the region, the wool trade declined after the sixteenth century and Northleach suffered. But the town came into its own again when stagecoaches began to run between London and Gloucester, and several coaching inns opened their doors to travelers. Today, unfortunately, heavy through-traffic on the A40 detracts somewhat from Northleach's charm.

Take the A429 south from Northleach and follow signs for Chedworth.

606 DIRECTIONS / The Cotswolds

CHEDWORTH: This quiet town has a fine Norman church worth a look inside for its carved stone pulpit. About 2 miles outside Chedworth in a pretty wooded part of the Coln Valley is a partly reconstructed Roman villa. Here you can see some very well preserved examples of Roman mosaic floors and bathhouses.

BIBURY: This picturesque village, through which the River Coln flows, is one of Britain's most photographed. The avid shutterbug will find yet another perfect composition everywhere he looks: Bibury's partly thirteenth-century church contains many of the earlier Saxon features, as well as some Norman additions. Then there's Arlington Row, a group of early-seventeenth-century stone cottages huddled together on a terraced hillside near the Coln, and Arlington Mill, a former seventeenth-century corn mill, which houses a craft museum.

En Route – An interesting side trip from Bibury would be to Quenington and Fairford; to reach these towns follow an unclassified road toward Coln St. Aldwyne.

At roughly the southernmost extreme of the Cotswolds proper, Quenington, in the Coln Valley, is notable for its well-restored seventeenth-century buildings, some of which open their gardens to the public in the summer. The best house is Quenington House, a nineteenth-century building on the site of what was a Preceptory, or lesser and subsidiary property, of the Knights Hospitalers, dating from about 1190. But the best gardens are probably those of Barnsley House. The Norman church was built in about 1170 and later restored in 1882 by the architect of Gloucester Cathedral. It's particularly famous for the stone carvings around the north and south doors.

Fairford, a little town perched on the edge of the Cotswolds, boasts a jewel of a parish church — built in the Perpendicular style by fifteenth-century wool merchants and lit by 28 brilliant stained-glass windows. As was then the custom, the windows were not simply decorative but also educational — they illustrated Bible stories for parishioners who couldn't read.

The English poet and clergyman John Keble was born in Fairford in 1792. He was one of the leaders of the Oxford Movement, which among other things made church services more formal and sought to reduce secular power over the church. Keble College, Oxford, was founded in his memory, partly with money left over from sales of Keble's poetical best seller, *The Christian Year,* which went into no fewer than 92 editions.

Fairford's main square, the Market Place, is lined with ancient trees and stone houses; there are several inviting old pubs, the best of which are probably *The Bull* and *The George.*

CHECKING IN: *Swan Hotel* – Crouched low by the River Coln (where you can cast a line for trout), this ivy-covered inn has just 24 rooms. (Off A453; phone: 028574–204; expensive.) *Bibury Court* – Run by the Collier family, this rambling hotel, set in 6 acres of gardens, is furnished in antiques; trout fishing is available. (Off A433; phone: 028574–337; moderate.)

BURFORD: From Bibury, take the A433 to Burford. Although on the edge of the Cotswolds, Burford is a typical Cotswold community — its steep main street, stippled with ancient stone houses and shops, rolls down a hill to meet the River Windrush. In the eighteenth century, Burford was an important coaching stop. Now, in the twentieth century, it's an antiquer's delight; Burford is full of antique shops — some of the most expensive in the country.

A number of Burford's buildings are antiques themselves, notably the almshouses built in 1457; The Grammar School for Boys founded in 1571; the Priory, an Elizabethan house; The Great House, built in 1690; and the Tolsey (or Toll House), now a town museum. The spired church is Perpendicular in style and has an old Norman tower. One of the houses in Sheep Street is known as "Kit's Quarry," built by Christopher Kempster, who was the master mason commissioned by Christopher Wren to provide stone from local quarries for St. Paul's Cathedral. Tours of Burford take place every Sunday afternoon in summer, conducted by members of the Burford and District Society.

Drive from Burford to Great Barrington, turning left on to an unclassified road just north of the bridge over the Windrush (approximately 4 miles).

THE BARRINGTONS AND WINDRUSH: From the fourteenth to the nineteenth centuries, the quarries of Great Barrington and Little Barrington produced some of the best Cotswold stone. Many of England's more impressive buildings were constructed using the stone, including sections of St. Paul's Cathedral in London and several Oxford colleges.

Great Barrington consists mainly of a double row of cottages partly surrounded by a country estate called Barrington Park. The centerpiece of the estate is a Palladian mansion which dates to 1736–38. Close to the house is a mostly Norman church that underwent complete restoration in 1815.

Little Barrington, across the River Windrush (which meanders rather than rushes), is the prettier of the two villages; it is centered around a triangular green, which was supposedly built over old quarry workings. The pub now called the *Inn for All Seasons* was popular with quarrymen, and it is said that its cellars are on the same level and have access to the quarry's underground passages. Little Barrington's houses are of different shapes, sizes, and periods and present a varied but harmonious composition.

The village of Windrush is also on this side of the river. From the pleasant tree-shaded lane that links it with Little Barrington there are lovely views across to Great Barrington. But the real reason for stopping in Windrush is to visit St. Peter's Church, a Norman building decorated with much fine carving, especially around the south doorway.

CHECKING IN: *Bay Tree* – This is a cozy, oak-paneled, fireplace-lit inn with 24 rooms. (Sheep St.; phone: 099382-3137; moderate.) *Lamb Inn* – Built of Cotswold stone and dating to the fifteenth century, this hotel also serves two meals and has a garden. (Sheep St.; phone: 099382-3155; moderate.)

BOURTON-ON-THE-WATER: This village is very pretty, with the River Windrush running right through it, crossed by unusual and attractive stone bridges that link rows of shops and small hotels set back behind greenswards where people picnic and children play. Be sure to visit St. Lawrence Church, which has a late-eighteenth-century spire and a fourteenth-century chancel; it was heavily restored in Victorian times — although more successfully than many. Next to the *Old New Inn* on High St. is a famous model village of Bourton; across the river on A429 is Birdland Zoo Gardens, a 4-acre preserve where many species of exotic birds reside.

A note of warning: Almost too popular, Bourton has allowed itself to become very commercialized and is jammed with tourists in the summertime.

En Route – Stow-on-the-Wold is about 4 miles north of Bourton-on-the-Water via A429; a pleasant detour would be a left turn toward the Slaughters. This lane leads first to Lower Slaughter, named after the Norman De Sclotre family; it's a rather self-consciously pretty village as yet unspoiled by tourist traffic. You may see artists at work on the green banks of the river. Upper Slaughter is on higher ground, as the name suggests, and is reached by winding leafy lanes. This village is more interesting than its sister. *The Lords of the Manor Hotel* at Upper Slaughter was originally the village rectory, and it was enlarged by one incumbent, the Reverend F. E. Witts, also known as the author of the *Diary of a Cotswold Parson*. Upper Slaughter also boasts the oldest and most impressive dovecote in Gloucestershire, dating from the sixteenth century. Also of note is *The Manor House,* an interesting Elizabethan building that incorporates the remains of a fifteenth-century priory and has an outstanding Jacobean porch. Open afternoons from May through September. And so strong is local pride that even some of the council houses are roofed in Cotswold stone slates. (Council houses are subsidized low-income residences.)

CHECKING IN: ***Lords of the Manor*** – If Upper Slaughter didn't have a beautifully preserved seventeenth-century manor house and surrounding grounds as a hostelry for visitors, it would be necessary to build one. Luckily it was done some 300 years ago, and we need only call for reservations. Just outside town. (Phone: 0451-20243; expensive.)

STOW-ON-THE-WOLD: This town sits squarely on the Fosse Way, one of the Roman trunk routes that cuts a swathe through southern Britain. (The name is not Roman but Saxon; and the road was used later by Normans as well.) Stow was another important wool market town in medieval times; there were two annual fairs, with merchants dickering over the sale of thousands of sheep. Many hotels, shops, and restaurants sprang up around the famous Market Square designed by the lord of the manor, the abbot of Evesham, in the eleventh century. The *King's Arms,* an old inn on the square, was once a lodging house for household servants of Edward VI, son of Henry VIII; in late March 1646, after what was to be the last battle of the Civil War, Cromwell incarcerated Royalist troops in the church that stands on one corner of the square.

En Route – From Stow-on-the-Wold it's about 1 mile to Upper Swell via the B4077; Lower Swell lies on the A436.

Upper Swell is a charming eighteenth-century village known for its handsome early-seventeenth-century manor house, arched stone bridge over the River Dikler, and early-nineteenth-century watermill capped with a Welsh slate roof. Stop for a moment at the parish church for a look at its exceptional Perpendicular-style font. Close to the village is the Donnington Brewery, once a corn mill, and now one of the last privately owned breweries. It's been producing beer since about 1865.

A mineral spring was discovered in Lower Swell in 1807, and for a while it was thought that the Swells might develop into another Cheltenham. All that remains of those fine dreams today, however, is a row of curiously decorated and rather exotic houses optimistically known as the "Spa Cottages." Despite this setback, Lower Swell regained its reputation with the success of another kind of watering hole — the *Golden Ball Inn,* which has for many years greeted travelers with food, drink (including Donnington beer), and a warm welcome. Treat yourself to lunch here.

Another sidetrip from Stow-on-the-Wold is in the opposite direction, to Chipping Norton, about 9 miles via A436 and A44.

"Chipping" may be a corruption of "cheapening," meaning "market." Chipping Norton, perched high on a hill near the Evenlode, was a busy market town for centuries. Today its wide streets are no longer filled with medieval wool merchants and its imposing Victorian tweed mill has been closed down. Instead, the market square now bustles with tourists sampling Chipping Norton's many cafés, pubs, restaurants, and hotels. The parish church, built in the Perpendicular style by wool merchants in the fourteenth and fifteenth centuries, is one of the largest in Oxfordshire and is especially noteworthy for its several fine medieval brasses.

Four miles north of Chipping Norton off A34 are the Rollright Stones, a circle of about 70 stones that date from between 1800 and 500 BC. To one side stand 5 other stones, said to represent a king and his knights. The name of these stones derives, it is believed, from *Rollanriht,* or "the jurisdiction of Roland the Brave." The name appears in the Domesday Book as *Rollandri.*

You'll have to get back on the A429 to proceed to Moreton-in-Marsh.

DIRECTIONS / The Cotswolds 609

CHECKING IN: *Fosse Manor* – This ivy-covered manor house has 21 spacious rooms and a restaurant. (Fosseway, Stow; phone: 0451-30354; moderate.) ***The King's Arms*** – This 500-year-old inn offers simple lodgings and a hearty breakfast. (Market Sq., Stow; phone: 0451-30364; inexpensive.)

MORETON-IN-MARSH: This town lies on the railway, and therefore has a more workaday atmosphere than most other Cotswold communities. It is another old market town that can be fun to explore on foot. Main Street, which follows the route of the Fosse Way, is unusually wide and contains many antique shops. On High Street is found the Market Hall, built in Victorian Tudor style in 1887. Note the Curfew Tower on Oxford Street; it dates to the seventeenth century and its bell was rung daily until the nineteenth century. About 1 mile west of town is the Batsford Park Arboretum with 50 acres of rare trees (open daily throughout the summer).

En Route – A worthwhile sidetrip from Moreton-in-Marsh is to Chastleton House; take A44 to the southeast, then turn right on to an unclassified road for Chastleton (approximately 5 miles). Chastleton House was built in 1603 by Walter Jones, a Witney wool merchant who bought the land on which the house stands from one of the "Gunpowder Plot" conspirators. Walter Jones spent half his fortune improving the house in 1603, and the other half — unfortunately for him — on the Royalist cause during the Civil War. He was a man of taste, as is shown by the richly carved wood paneling and the furniture. Among the items in the house are Charles I's Bible, used by him on the morning of his execution; valuable tapestries; and rare china. The topiary garden is one of the best in Britain: There are good views of it from the windows of the Long Gallery in the house. The idea of such gardens was imported from the Continent by William of Orange, and although the representation of birds and animals has altered over the years, the layout has remained the same. The house and gardens are open daily, except Wednesdays, all year round.

From Moreton-in-Marsh, take the A44 west for about 6 miles as far as the B4081. Turn right for Chipping Campden.

CHECKING IN: *White Hart Royal Hotel* – If you stay here, you will have shared a place with royalty — Charles I spent the night in this half-timbered posting inn in 1644. Cobbles more than 300 years old have been carefully preserved, and old hunting trophies and weapons adorn the Cotswold-stone bar. The hotel has 27 rooms and a small timbered dining room. (High St.; phone: 0608-50731; moderate.)

CHIPPING CAMPDEN: This town was restored carefully by the Campden Trust, a group of people mindful of the past; as a result, it is remarkably well preserved. If you can ignore the traffic — mostly visitors looking for somewhere to park — the main street looks just as it did hundreds of years ago. And Chipping Campden's many fine old buildings are a delight. The church, though heavily restored by the Victorians, is one of the best in the Cotswolds. Built in the Perpendicular style by the town's wool merchants in the fifteenth century, it is unusually large and contains several fine brasses. Near the church are almshouses dating to 1612. All along High Street, you'll see many houses crafted from warm Cotswold stone; also stop for a look at the handsome bow-windowed Grevel House (former home of a wealthy woolman) on Church Street. Across the way is a Woolstapler's Hall, a fourteenth-century house where wool merchants traded; it's now a museum of the town's history that also houses an important car collection. The Market Hall, a solid yet graceful structure composed of fourteen stone arches built in 1627, was where the area's farmers sold their dairy products.

En Route – From Chipping Campden take the B4081 north to Mickleton, then follow signs for Hidcote Manor Gardens, opposite which are Kifsgate Court

610 DIRECTIONS / The Cotswolds

Gardens. Note that while Hidcote Gardens are open 5 days a week during spring, summer, and autumn, Kifsgate Gardens are open only twice a week. Hidcote Manor Gardens are formal, with impressive and varied hedges, rare trees, and shrubs. The gardens were laid out in the first few years of this century by Laurence Johnston, and it was here that he originated the mixed or "harlequin" hedge. There are small individual gardens with pools, rare plants, and gazebos. As the poet Vita Sackville-West said of Major Johnston, "He spilled his cornucopia everywhere." Kifsgate Court Gardens are steeper, less formal, and like Hidcote, are enhanced by the presence of an impressive house, Mickleton Manor.

Pick up the A46 and proceed south to Broadway.

CHECKING IN: *Cottage In The Wood* – A few miles off the driving route, but worthy of a detour. Much more than a cottage, this mansion occupies 7 acres of woodlands and has wonderful views of the fertile Vale of Evesham. The style is very English and very traditional and guest rooms are superbly appointed. The intimate restaurant features English dishes and has an excellent wine list. Closed late-December and January. (Holywell Rd., Malvern Wells, Malvern; phone: 06845–3487; expensive.) *Cotswold House Hotel* – It's an elegant eighteenth-century house with 25 rooms. (The Square; phone: 0386–840330; moderate.) *King's Arms Hotel* – These two converted stone houses have a total of 17 rooms, a good restaurant, and quiet gardens. (The Square; phone: 0386–840256; moderate.) *Noel Arms Hotel* – You'll find a publike atmosphere at this former coaching inn — lots of oak beams, armor-hung walls, and a cheering fireplace. (High St.; phone: 0386–840317; moderate.)

EATING OUT: *Bantam Tea Rooms* – This cozy, traditional tearoom is the perfect spot for a cup. (High St.; inexpensive.)

BROADWAY: Henry James once described Broadway thus: "The place has so much character that it rubs off on the visitor . . . it is delicious to be at Broadway." Many people would agree with James, judging from the traffic and numbers of tourists who throng here to shop for antiques and to stroll among the seventeenth- and eighteenth-century golden Cotswold stone houses. (Partly due to heavy tourism and partly just to preserve the old stone — which is highly vulnerable to even the comparatively mild Cotswold weather — there has recently been some renovation and new building. But it has been done well, and stone facing rather than complete razing is the general rule.)

The *Lygon Arms* is probably Broadway's main attraction; the hotel's elegance is only exceeded by its history. The main building dates from 1530, though parts of it are more than 600 years old. It was frequented by Charles I and Oliver Cromwell, and rooms named after each have been carefully preserved or restored.

Some of Broadway's other notable structures include Middle Hill, the estate of Sir Thomas Phillips, the eccentric and wealthy book collector; St. Eadburgha's, a Norman-style church; and Broadway Beacon, an eighteenth-century, 65-foot-high, stern stone edifice on Broadway Hill, all of which are within Broadway Tower Country Park. You can climb the tower for a view of the countryside, spread your picnic lunch in one of the designated areas, or visit the 150-year-old barn that houses an exhibit on the geology of the hill.

En Route – Near the western end of Broadway, *before* you reach the A46 to Winchcombe, turn left for Snowshill Manor — about 3 miles. The manor house, a fine example of Tudor and Georgian architecture, was part of Catherine Parr's dowry (she was Henry VIII's last wife). It contains an eclectic collection of antiques and trivia accumulated by Charles Wade, who subsidized his mania with an income from West Indian sugar plantations. He was so devoted to his collection that he actually lived in the adjoining cottage in order to give it more space. Both are open to the public.

Another interesting sidetrip is to the Cotswold Farm Park, a survival center for rare breeds of British farm animals, including shire horses; Soay and Orkney sheep (the former originally from St. Kilda, a now uninhabited Scottish island far off the mainland in the Atlantic); and examples of the breed of sheep upon which the medieval wool trade depended. To get here, follow the unclassified road from Snowshill toward Bourton-on-the-Water, which joins the B4077 directly east of Temple Guiting. The park is just before that junction.

You must get back on the A46 to drive south to Winchcombe.

CHECKING IN: *The Lygon Arms* – Both Charles I and Oliver Cromwell slept in this elegant, sixteenth-century, ivy-covered inn. There are 70 antique-furnished rooms and an award-winning dining room. (High St.; phone: 0386-852255; expensive.)

EATING OUT: *Dormy House* – High on a hillside above the village, this former farmhouse with oak beams and a stone fireplace serves French-inspired cuisine. (Willersey Hill; phone: 0386-852711; expensive.)

WINCHCOMBE: Though it suffers a little from through-traffic, not all of Winchcombe is on the main road, and it is a good example of a genuine Cotswold town going about its business as it has done for several hundred years. Before the Norman Conquest this was the capital of Winchcombeshire, and here you will see half-timbering among the stone houses. For example, the *George Inn*, which once provided lodgings for pilgrims visiting nearby Hailes Abbey, has a half-timbered coaching yard. Hailes Abbey was built between 1245 and 1253 and prospered for some 300 years before Henry VIII's Dissolution of the Monasteries, at which time it was razed. (The order to surrender was actually given on Christmas Eve 1539.) Now only the ruins remain. The site is 3 miles northeast of Winchcombe, clearly signed off the A46. Winchcombe's nineteenth-century town hall, which contains the original stocks, now houses a folk museum. The parish church is mainly remarkable for the gargoyles that decorate its exterior — at least 40 of them; inside there is an altar cloth believed to have been woven by Catherine of Aragon, Henry VIII's first queen.

Half a mile southeast of the town center, clearly signed, lies Sudeley Castle, open to the public during the summer. Now the private home of the Dent family, its interior is quite labyrinthine. The castle has been home to several of England's queens: Catherine Parr, Anne Boleyn, and Elizabeth I all spent time here. During the Civil War that affected so much of this now tranquil part of England, Sudeley Castle was extensively damaged, and it was virtually abandoned for nearly 200 years. But with the help of Sir George Gilbert Scott, responsible for, among other things, London's Albert Memorial, the castle was restored. The restoration work went on until the 1930s; tantalizing traces remain of the original buildings, including a few dating to the fifteenth century, and some very old stained glass.

From Winchcombe follow the A46 to Cheltenham.

CHELTENHAM: Popularly regarded as a genteel place largely inhabited by geriatrics, Cheltenham is more lively than many think. For example, it's practically impossible to find accommodations within a 30-mile radius during Cheltenham Gold Cup Week, a national horse race held every March. (For information, write to Racing Information Bureau, 42 Portman Sq., London W1.) In addition, there is the Festival of Music and Drama in May and the International Festival of Music in July (for information, write Town Hall Box Office, Imperial Sq., Cheltenham, Gloucestershire). While here, try the waters that made Cheltenham famous — at both the Pittville Pump Room (named after local MP Joseph Pitt, who served in the House of Commons from 1825–30) and the town hall. The medicinal properties of these waters are said to derive from the magnesium and sodium sulphates and the sodium bicarbonate they contain. Before you leave Cheltenham, be sure to take a stroll along the famous Promenade, made lovely by its rows of great horse-chestnut trees. Along one side are shops and along the other beautifully preserved Regency terraced buildings. The town also has many spacious and colorful gardens, the best of which is the Imperial Gardens, adjoining the town hall on Imperial Sq.

The A435 will take you from Cheltenham to Cirencester.

CHECKING IN: *Malvern View Hotel* – This slightly out-of-town hotel with modern, comfortable rooms with lovely views and a rather good restaurant could be a pleasant home base for visitors to Cheltenham's races or festivals. (Off A46, Cleeve Hill; phone: 024267–2017; moderate.)

EATING OUT: *Forrest's Wine House* – Hearty German cuisine and wines are the specialty here. (Imperial La.; phone: 0242–38001; inexpensive.) *That Sandwich Place* – Stop here for a tasty lunch of salad or sandwiches. (69 Regent St.; phone: 0242–29575; inexpensive.)

CIRENCESTER: Established by the Romans at the junction at which their vital trunk route Fosse Way met five other roads, Cirencester (or Corinium) was a strategic link in their defenses. As a result, Corinium grew to be second in size only to London. In the sixth century it was destroyed by the invading Saxons, so little of the Roman occupation remains in the town itself. However, mosaic floors, sculpture, and pottery recovered from excavations now form the extensive collection of Roman relics in the Corinium Museum on Park St. You can also see the ruins of a Roman amphitheater on Cotswold Ave. Periods of English history seem piled one atop another by a profligate hand in Cirencester. The parish church, St. John the Baptist, built by wool merchants in the fourteenth century, is a fine example of the Perpendicular style. One of the largest churches in England, it is not to be missed for its rich stone carvings, magnificent array of medieval stained glass, and many fine brasses. On Stroud Rd. is Cirencester Park, the 3,000-acre estate of the earl of Bathurst; although the house is not open to the public, the grounds are. Also interesting are the Cirencester Workshops in the center of town. The craft gallery and workshops are open daily except Sundays.

Take the A423 from Cirencester to Malmesbury.

CHECKING IN: *The Fleece* – Outside is a handsome black and white half-timbered facade; inside are Cotswold-stone walls, fine open fireplaces, and low-beamed ceilings. The hotel's restaurant specializes in English meals and real ales — try Donnington Ale, the local brew. (Market Pl.; phone: 0285–2680; moderate.) *King's Head* – Opposite the famous parish church, this fourteenth-century coaching inn with 70 rooms has been completely modernized without destroying its charm. (Market Pl.; phone: 0285–3322; expensive.)

MALMESBURY: This pleasant little town high above the Wiltshire Avon is the site of a magnificent Norman abbey with a most unusual history: During the Dissolution under King Henry VIII in the sixteenth century, the building was sold to a clothier for £1,500. The man promptly brought in his weaving machinery and converted it into a factory. It was not until 1823 that a restoration effort was begun. Despite the many years of decay, the restoration was eminently successful, and today the abbey is considered one of the finest examples of Norman building remaining in Britain. The richly carved south porch and the musicians' gallery are especially impressive.

The town has two special connections with aviation. The first was established at Malmesbury Abbey in the eleventh century, when Brother Oliver attempted to defy gravity by leaping from the tower wearing a pair of homemade wings. He survived the leap but was lame ever after. And at Kemble, 6 miles north of Malmesbury, the Royal Air Force aerobatic team, the Red Arrows, practice their aerial formations.

Malmesbury is one of the oldest boroughs in England and a very well planned medieval city; it was already an important town before the Norman invasion. Some medieval remains are still extant, including fragments of walls and ruins of a twelfth-century castle that can be seen today at the *Old Bell Hotel.* Six bridges lead to the Market Square, at whose center is an impressive octagonal Tudor market cross. There are several lovely seventeenth- and eighteenth-century houses built by rich weavers on the adjoining streets. George Washington's ancestors appear to have come from the region, since at least five Washington predecessors are buried in a churchyard in Garsdon, 2 miles east of Malmesbury.

En Route – Southwest of Malmesbury are several noteworthy stops: Badminton House, off the B4040; Dodington House, off the A46; and Dyrham Park, farther south and also off the A46.

The Badminton estate has been in the same family, the Beauforts, for over 300 years, and is the magnificent setting each April of the Badminton Horse Trials, an international competition. For information, write: Box Office, Badminton Horse Trials, Badminton, Avon, G19 1DF. The house itself is open only on rare occasions during the summer months. (A note of fascinating trivia: the game of Badminton was invented here by house guests in the 1860s.)

Dodington House is an impressive neoclassical structure built between 1796 and 1817 for Sir Christopher Codrington, the wealthy owner of a West Indian sugar plantation. In the stable wing of the house is a carriage museum with hansom cabs, a pony phaeton, a funeral hearse, and a Black Maria.

Stop for tea served in the orangery of the elegant, low-lying mansion in Dyrham Park. Afterward, stroll around; the house, built between 1692 and 1704, shows considerable Dutch influence, perhaps because its owner, William Blathwayt, was a representative at the Hague.

From Malmesbury, you can follow the A46 to Bath.

CHECKING IN: *Old Bell Hotel* – This is a fabulous old inn, a wisteria-clad gabled building on the site of twelfth-century Malmesbury Castle. It still retains a medieval spiral staircase and part of the castle wall. There are 18 rooms, a garden, a good restaurant, and the charming *Castle Bar.* (Abbey Row; phone: 06662–2344; expensive.)

BATH: This city was once one of Europe's greatest spas. Originally founded by the Romans, who in AD 54 built an elaborate system of baths, it was named Aquae Sulis, after Sulis Minerva, a Roman goddess. In succeeding centuries Bath lost and regained its reputation; at one point in the seventeenth century, it became so popular with royalty and gentry that diarist Samuel Pepys wondered how the water could be sanitary with so many bodies jammed into it. For a detailed report on the city, its sights, hotels, and restaurants, see *Bath,* THE CITIES.

The Lake District

The most efficient bridging of the gap between London and Scotland passes perforce through the western Midlands, an area whose concentration of heavy-duty industrial cities is particularly high and whose interest to visitors is, consequently, supposedly low. Stoke-on-Trent, Sheffield, Manchester, Liverpool — these names reverberate with the crash of the steel mill and the roar of the factory. Well-meaning Londoners will most likely urge you to stay steadfastly to the east, ensuring that you encounter the bucolic pleasures of Cambridge, Lincoln, York, and Northumberland. Indeed, so splendid are those towns and the country around them that it is hard to argue with such advice unless you are fortified by a familiarity with the less obvious satisfac-

614 DIRECTIONS / The Lake District

tions to be had in the birthplace of the Industrial Revolution. Or unless bearing east means forgoing forever that crumpled, rumpled, well-watered mountain country known as the Lake District.

Only 25 miles across in any direction, there is a special intensity in the beauty of the Lake District — tarn, mere, beck, and fell, scoured and sculpted by the Ice Age and squeezed into the tiny county of Cumbria; just an hour or so north of Manchester. It is as though nature were offering a consolation for the sprawling rigors of the industrial belt, much too near-at-hand. No part of England is so universally loved by Britons — for the purity of its clearwater mountain lakes (meres); its almost vertical fields filled with grazing sheep, each field carefully delineated by painstakingly maintained stone walls; its sharp rocky peaks; and the thousands of tiny lakes (tarns) fed year in and year out by innumerable waterfalls and streams (becks). Its traditional industry has always been hill farming, which gives a steady rhythm to the lakeland year from lambing time onward, but increasingly the area's livelihood is tourism. For over 3 decades the Lake District has been a national park and visitors — hill walkers, rock climbers, historians, artists, ornithologists, or those seeking simply a bit of peace and quiet — number in the millions annually.

What is earth-loving and ancient in the English spirit is drawn irresistibly to the Lake District's uncompromising beauty. Small wonder that J. M. W. Turner, the famous English landscape painter, spent time here sketching it. The Lake District is primarily associated, however, with a group of his contemporaries, poets of the late eighteenth and early nineteenth centuries who not only celebrated the beauty of the region in words, but discovered here values to stand against the encroaching horrors of the industrial age. Chief among these poets was William Wordsworth, who lived here for most of his life, but others are equally well known: Robert Southey, Samuel Taylor Coleridge, and writers John Ruskin and Thomas De Quincey. Much of what you see and do in the region is associated with the Lake Poets.

One of the most surprising things about the Lake District is how small this famous area really is. You can drive right through it in less than an hour and yet spend a month without ever seeing half of what time and nature have created here. Looking at a map, you see that the principal lakes — Derwentwater, Ullswater, Windermere, wild Wastwater, Buttermere, Crummock Water, Grasmere, and Rydal Water — radiate from the central mass of the Cumbrian Mountains like the spokes of a wheel. A few of them, such as Thirlmere and Haweswater, are reservoirs slaking the thirst and industry of northern cities, but the living lakes are busy with sails and some of them with stately steamers. The distances between these postcard-perfect bodies of water are short, but each of the larger lakes provides a good base for exploring the neighboring area. Allowing time for some hiking as well as exploration of towns and villages, you could easily spend 2 days around each major lake — Windermere, Derwentwater, and Ullswater especially — before moving on.

The route described below begins in the southeastern corner of the Lake District at the town of Kendal, takes the back road to Lake Windermere, and crosses the water on the ferry to Near Sawrey, Hawkshead, and Coniston. The next leg of the trip, north from Windermere, crosses the paths of the Lake

Poets. For the last 37 years of his life Wordsworth lived at Rydal Mount, just a few miles from Ambleside. Dove Cottage, the home he had occupied previously, is a few miles farther north, at Grasmere. Thomas De Quincey, author of *Confessions of an English Opium-Eater,* took over the cottage after Wordsworth left for Rydal Mount. The route then proceeds north from Grasmere and passes Thirlmere from where there is easy access to the challenging 3,118-foot mountain peak, Helvellyn. At the end of this leg is Derwentwater — perhaps the most beautiful of all the lakes. Robert Southey made his home here, in the town of Keswick, where he frequently was joined by Percy Bysshe Shelley and Coleridge. The twins, Buttermere and Crummock Water, are just a short drive southwest of Keswick, and beyond them, in the northwest corner of the Lake District, is Cockermouth. Wordsworth and his sister Dorothy were both born and raised in Cockermouth, and the family home and nearby fields became part of the joyous imagery of the poetry that introduced this area to readers everywhere. From Cockermouth, two choices present themselves. One possibility is to follow the western boundary of the Lake District, heading south, from where numerous small roads lead into the heart of the mountains and the area's best climbing, a prospect particularly appealing for experienced and properly equipped backpackers and hill walkers. Another is to return to Keswick, drop south off the main road for a visit to the lovely lake of Ullswater, and complete the tour at the town of Penrith, conveniently located at the northeastern flank of the Lake District at the intersection of several main north-south and east-west routes.

The Lake District offers a wide range of accommodations from small but comfortable inns to some of the best hotels in the country, and plenty of guesthouses offering bed and breakfast *and* an evening meal for as little as $20 per person. Expect to pay between $60 and $120 for a double in those places listed as expensive; from $40 to $60 in moderate; and under $40 in inexpensive. A meal for two, excluding wine, tips, or drinks, will run about $35 to $50 in places listed as expensive; $25 to $35 in moderate; and under $20 in inexpensive.

KENDAL: Holiday traffic threads constantly through the one-way streets of this old market town, the gateway to the southern part of the Lake District. Because it is busily engaged in the manufacture of shoes, snuff, and Kendal mint cake (after six centuries in the wool industry), the town pays less attention to visitors than many another place in Cumbria. Visitors, in turn, in a headlong dash to begin lakeside vacations, often give short shrift to everything but the large local shopping center. But the old part of this town on the River Kent is an attractive huddle of slate-roofed buildings separated by small alleyways, yards, and courts, and there are several buildings of particular interest. The ruined Kendal Castle, on a hill east of town, dates back to Norman times and was later the birthplace of Catherine Parr, the last of King Henry VIII's six wives. The thirteenth-century parish church near the center of town is unusual for its five aisles and its brasses. Abbot Hall, a Georgian house beside the river, is now an art gallery with modern collections and eighteenth-century period rooms displaying furniture and paintings, including one by Turner and one by the famous portrait artist George Romney, who spent his youth in Kendal. The Museum of Lakeland Life and Industry, installed in what was once the stables of Abbot Hall, gives an interesting backward look at the social and economic life of the area. The Tourist Information Centre in Kendal's

616 DIRECTIONS / The Lake District

town hall has a mass of leaflets and hotel lists for the southern Lake District.

The main road west out of town climbs a long hill and, after about 2 miles, comes to a large traffic circle. Turn off the A591 here and head down the B5284 through countryside typical of the edge of the Lake District: neat fields, thick woodland, and a landscape that is all mounds and hummocks building up to the larger hills beyond. The village of Crook is along the way 5 miles from Kendal, and after another 5 miles the route crosses two roads skirting the eastern side of Lake Windermere and comes to a stop at the terminal of the car ferry. Bowness-on-Windermere and Windermere itself are a mile or so north of the terminal.

CHECKING IN: *Wild Boar Hotel* – This pleasant country hotel in a converted seventeenth-century house is a quiet, comfortable staging post. Gardens outside and a beamed bar and fireplaces inside add to its traditional charm. The dining room is highly rated. (Crook; phone: 09662-5225; expensive to moderate.)

WINDERMERE AND BOWNESS: These adjoining resort areas on Lake Windermere make up one town that is the focal point of tourism in the Lake District. Bowness is the actual port on the water and Windermere is just above Bowness, inland from the lake. Between the two, virtually every recreational activity — fishing, boating, sailing, golf, tennis, windsurfing, hiking, and even pony trekking — is available.

It is difficult to actually see Lake Windermere or the surrounding mountains from the town, but a 20-minute walk up Orrest Head hill (to the north of the railroad station) reveals all in a good view of the lake and the hills beyond. Scenic outlooks are a particular attraction of the Windermere countryside and some other notable ones include Queen Adelaide's Hill, an ideal picnic spot between Bowness and the main Ambleside Road; Millerground, a little farther along the same footpath; Biskey Howe, reached from Helm Road, Bowness; and School Knott, which has an easy, winding path to its summit east of Windermere. The information centers at Windermere and Bowness have details of these and other walks.

Lake Windermere, the largest of the lakes in the district (10.5 miles long), has a much softer aspect than most, the happy product of its luxuriantly wooded banks, filled with rhododendrons that burst into flaming color each June. The waterfront of Bowness has been attractively developed with restaurants overlooking the lake, chandleries, and shops. During the holiday season (May through October) pleasure cruises operate from the pier nearby along the length of Windermere between Lakeside at its southern end, Bowness, and Waterhead at its northern end. These services connect with the Lakeside and Haverthwaite Steam Railway, a private line running 3.5 miles south of Lakeside through the attractive valley of the River Leven. There are several small islands in the lake, and on one of them, Belle Isle, stands an eighteenth-century mansion that was the first completely round house built in England. It is one of the more unusual stately homes in the Lake District, and among its contents are portraits by Romney and lake views by the French landscape painter, Philippe de Loutherbourg (open May through September; ferry from Bowness). The Windermere Steamboat Museum just north of Bowness has a wonderful collection of Victorian and Edwardian steam launches, including *Dolly,* the oldest mechanically propelled boat in the world, built in 1850 (open Easter through September). The museum pieces are afloat and in working order and you may occasionally see them steaming about on the lake. Other boats illustrate the history of Windermere from the earliest times. Races are held on the lake on summer weekends, and the biggest, the annual power boat Grand Prix and Record Attempts Week, takes place in October. In late summer there is the Windermere Swim, when well-greased long-distance swimmers brave the chill length of the lake.

Midway between Windermere and Ambleside off the A591 is the Brockhole National Park Centre, a country house set in beautiful gardens and grounds that reach down to the lake. The center (phone: 09662–2231) has a constant program of lectures, films, and exhibitions covering crafts, natural history, farming, industrial archaeology, the ubiquitous Wordsworths, and other aspects of past and present life in the Lake District, and is open daily from 10 AM, late March to early November.

CHECKING IN: *Belsfield Hotel* – This is a magnificent Georgian house overlooking Lake Windermere and decorated with an interesting blend of period pieces and modern furnishings. A new wing (in the garden) has been added, making a total of 67 rooms. (Bowness-on-Windermere; phone: 09662-2448; expensive.) *Miller Howe Hotel* – Is it the beautiful view of the placid, tree-lined lake that makes this small (13-room) hotel seem such a bastion of calm or is it the impeccable service? In either case, there is hardly a better headquarters for touring the area and the restaurant is excellent, too. Closed mid-December until mid-March. (Rayrigg Rd., Windermere; phone: 09662-2536; expensive.) *Old England Hotel* – The standards of service and comfort are high in this Victorian mansion by the water. There are 90 rooms. (Bowness-on-Windermere; phone: 09662-2444; expensive.)

NEAR SAWREY: The ferry to the other side of Lake Windermere deposits travelers on a road leading to the village of Far Sawrey, then on to the village of Near Sawrey, the site of a Lake District literary connection more important to children than to adults. This is Hill Top Farm, the home of a Mrs. Heelis, better known as the author Beatrix Potter, whose Peter Rabbit classics, illustrated with drawings and watercolors of the hills and lakes around the village, have been staple reading for generations of youngsters. The quaint seventeenth-century farmhouse she lived in is open to the public (April through October) and while you are admiring the drawings on display, there may well be some small child searching earnestly through the garden for a glimpse of Peter, Jemima Puddleduck, Tom Kitten, or other old friends. When Mrs. Heelis died in 1943, she left the whole of her property, including 4,000 acres of land, to Britain's National Trust, a bequest that has done much to preserve the surrounding countryside.

CHECKING IN: *Tower Bank Arms* – There are only three double rooms in this cozy inn owned by the National Trust and they are a favorite with hikers. Good bar and food. (Near Sawrey; phone: 09666-334; inexpensive.)

HAWKSHEAD: Just beyond the head of Esthwaite Water, a small lake about 2 miles long, the road threads its way through a picturesque row of buildings. This is the quiet little village of Hawkshead and it offers an introductory course in Lake District life that begins at the seventeenth-century *Queen's Head Inn,* where you can get a pint of ale to fortify you for a stroll through the stone cottages of the town. Start at the Hawkshead Grammar School, founded in 1585 by native son Edwin Sandys, archbishop of York, and attended by Wordsworth between 1779 and 1783. He left a lasting impression there by carving his name in one of the original desks. While a student, Wordsworth may have lodged at Ann Tyson's cottage, on a lane off Red Lion Square, before moving to Green End Cottage in the hamlet of Colthouse, east of Hawkshead. Years later, he recalled the Esthwaite area where he spent his schooldays as "that belovèd Vale."

From Hawkshead, follow the signs over Hawkshead Hill directly to Coniston or detour via a steep byroad that leads to Tarn Hows, a small fir-fringed lake high in the hills that has the best views of the surrounding countryside, especially of Coniston Water to the south and of the mountain called the "Old Man of Coniston," which lords it over the lake.

CONISTON: Approaching from Hawkshead, Coniston is about half a mile around the northwest tip of Coniston Water. It is another charming village with strong artistic associations. A Turner masterpiece, now hanging in the Tate Gallery in London, was based on studies done at dawn from the crags above the village. Wordsworth wrote lovingly of the place and Alfred Lord Tennyson spent his honeymoon at Tent Lodge at the head of the lake. John Ruskin, the writer, painter, critic, social reformer, and scientist, moved here in 1871, producing some of his finest work at his home, Brantwood (open Easter to mid-October), on the lake's eastern shore. He is buried in the Coniston churchyard and there is a Ruskin Museum (also open Easter to October) in the village. It was on Coniston Water that Sir Malcolm Campbell set a world waterspeed record of 141 mph in his boat *Bluebird* in 1939, and his son, Donald, later set four world records here. The local history section of the Ruskin Museum has photographs of the younger Campbell's last (and fatal) attempt, in 1967, to set a new speedboat record on Coniston Water.

En Route – The A593 winds north from Coniston village into the junction of the Great Langdale and Little Langdale valleys. A side trip due west from this point follows a narrow road over two high passes in the mountains. The first, Wrynose Pass, is a long but straightforward climb. The second, Hard Knott Pass, is reckoned to be the toughest in Britain, a tortuous snake of a road climbing the fellside by hairpin curves and descending in the same style into Eskdale, the valley of the River Esk. The reward of the route is a series of wonderful views, but unless you're ready for some rigorous, adventurous driving, ignore the turn-off and follow the main road to Ambleside, Rydal, and Grasmere. Another alternative would be to take the cut-off to Elterwater, which has an excellent hotel, the *Britannia Inn,* then proceed directly and spectacularly into Grasmere via the narrow road over High Close, dropping steeply into Grasmere down a hill called Red Bank.

AMBLESIDE: Just less than a mile from the north end of Lake Windermere, Ambleside is an excellent touring base for climbers eager to explore lakeland's hills and forests. Wordsworth's famed Scafell Pike (3,210 feet, the highest peak in England) is a considerable hike from Ambleside, but other peaks are more accessible. Be sure to obtain detailed maps of trails and to make proper arrangements before starting any trek. The local information center is in Ambleside's old Court House in Market Square. A short distance away, up the lane past the *Royal Yachtsman Hotel,* is Stockghyll Force, a beautiful waterfall cascading 70 feet to rocks below. St. Mary's Church, erected in 1854 by Sir Gilbert Scott, has a memorial to Wordsworth and a mural of the village's rush-bearing festival, when flowers and rushes are carried through the streets to the church. The festival is thought to descend from a Roman harvest ceremony and is still held yearly on the first Saturday in July. Waterhead, the northern terminus of the Lake Windermere pleasure cruises (they can also be boarded at Bowness and at Lakeside) is just south of Ambleside on A591. Just 2 miles north is Rydal.

CHECKING IN: *Rothay Manor* – Near Ambleside at the head of Lake Windermere, this is a small, elegant hotel with its own croquet lawn. The country house feeling extends to the restaurant where the cuisine is imaginative. Closed mid-January to early February. (Rothay Bridge; phone: 09663-3605; expensive.)

RYDAL: William Wordsworth, with his wife, three children, sister, and sister-in-law, moved to this village in 1813 and lived here until his death 37 years later. His home, Rydal Mount, is an interesting, rambling old house, open to visitors from March to mid-January. It contains a large collection of memorabilia, including several portraits of his family and friends, and his personal library. His love of nature is reflected in the 4.5-acre garden he grew around Rydal Mount, as attentively cared for today as by the poet himself. Wordsworth drew heavily on the surrounding countryside for inspiration and poetic images, and the mute crags and flowered hillsides around his home appear repeatedly in his work. But the golden daffodils in Dora's Field, a plot of land below the garden, are not the descendants of the golden host he came upon unexpectedly while wandering "lonely as a cloud." The lake referred to in that poem is Ullswater and the poem predates Wordsworth's move to Rydal.

Just a short distance up the road is Nab Cottage, occupied briefly by Thomas De Quincey (1806) and later by Samuel Taylor Coleridge's eldest son, Hartley. The roadway continues to the village of Grasmere along the north bank of Rydal Water, which is one of the smallest lakes in the district and which, together with the River Rothay, links Lake Windermere to Grasmere Lake.

GRASMERE: The main route north from Rydal Water skirts Grasmere Lake, just a mile long and half as wide and, with an emerald green island in its center, almost too perfect for words. Farther on, off the highway to the right, is Dove Cottage, another of Wordsworth's homes, perhaps the one where his finest work was written. Then, at the heart of the Lake District, lies the beautiful and easily accessible village of Grasmere set against a backdrop of high hills. The road winds through town, its path dictated by the haphazard scattering of houses of somber, blue-green lakeland stone.

Wordsworth and his sister Dorothy lived at Dove Cottage from 1799 until 1808. Before their arrival, the house had been a small inn called the Dove and Olive Branch. While they lived there, it became a stopping-off place for a stream of eminent literary figures such as Coleridge, William Hazlitt, Charles Lamb, and Sir Walter Scott. After Wordsworth married (and fathered three children), he and his family moved, turning the cottage over to their friends Thomas De Quincey and his wife. A new Wordsworth exhibition building has been constructed in the Dove Cottage complex to replace the former museum that was just across the road. It contains manuscripts of letters and poems and a remarkable collection of portraits on loan from the National Portrait Gallery. Both the museum and the cottage are open to the public from Easter through September. Wordsworth lived in two more houses in Grasmere, first at Allan Bank where Coleridge was his house guest, then at the old rectory, before moving to Rydal Mount where he spent the rest of his life. Now the squat, foursquare walls of the Church of St. Oswald (parts of which may be thirteenth century) preside over his grave and those of his wife, his sister, and Hartley Coleridge, buried in a corner of the churchyard within earshot of the River Rothay.

Although August is the most crowded month in which to visit the Lake District, it is also the month of the Grasmere Sports Games, usually held on the third Thursday of the month. Begun in the mid-nineteenth century with the purpose of encouraging the sport of Cumberland and Westmorland wrestling, the event has been widened to include other traditional lakeland sports such as fell running and hound trailing. Until Cumberland and Westmorland were combined into Cumbria County (1974), competition between these rivals was intense, and the administrative alteration hasn't changed anything. The wrestling, especially, is a curious sport to watch. Competitors stand chest to chest and grasp one another by locking arms behind each other's back. The aim of this subtle combat is to throw the opponent to the ground and toward this goal the weighty and well-balanced wrestlers may struggle all day while other events take place elsewhere. Fell running or racing, an all-out dash to the top of the nearest mountain and back, is another spectacle at the Grasmere games. The Guides' Race directly up the steep sides of Butter Crags is undertaken by lean, narrow-chested athletes who move with astonishing speed up the fell to the turning point and then bound back down again with the agility of mountain goats. Other events are the hound trail competitions, which reflect the Lake District's importance as a center for fox hunting, done here on foot with packs of hardy hounds that ripple across the fells after their prey. (Caldbeck, in the far north of the Lake District, was the home of the celebrated huntsman John Peel, about whom John Woodcock Graves wrote the song "D'ye ken John Peel?" that practically became the Cumbrian anthem.)

Grasmere, like Ambleside, also has an annual rush-bearing ceremony, held on the Saturday nearest August 5, St. Oswald's Day. If you want to sample the tasty gingerbread that is distributed to the bearers, stop by the *Old Gingerbread Shop* — the local specialty will make a great snack while driving the rest of the route. There are some other distinctive shops in town, among them *English Lakes Perfumes,* offering such fragrances as Grasmere Rose and Keswick Gardenia, and the *Studio,* with the work of W. Heaton Cooper, best known of the Lake District watercolor artists. The sound of industrious clattering comes from the shop of *Chris Reekie,* weaver, who has a nice display of woolen wear, some of it produced on the original loom on which he served his apprenticeship in Scotland.

CHECKING IN: *Michael's Nook* – A charming Victorian country home furnished by the proprietor, Reginald Gifford, with many beautiful antiques. Some of the bathrooms have been "modernized," but the older ones are more fun. Reservations are necessary for the restaurant. (Grasmere; phone: 09665-496; expensive.) *Red Lion Inn* – This is an old coaching inn in the center of the village. Closed December through February. (Grasmere; phone: 09665-456; expensive.) **White Moss House** – Originally two separate cottages, Mr. and Mrs. Butterworth have made this 7-room hotel (converted in the late 1800s) into a pleasant place to stay. It overlooks Rydal Water, and there's usually a roaring fire to welcome hikers in from the dampness. No choice of entrees in the dining room where some uncommon English dishes are served and reservations are essential. Closed November through March. (Rydal Water; phone: 09665-295; expensive.)

En Route – Continuing north on A591, the road climbs Dunmail Raise. Over the summit, Thirlmere comes into view, a long, lifeless-looking lake from which water runs helped only by gravity to the taps and factories of Manchester, 100 miles to the south. In 1876, the lake level was raised artificially by the construction of a 100-foot-high dam intended to meet the needs of the industrial revolution in urban Lancashire. The unintended result was one of the earliest environmental battles in Britain and because of it, seeds were sown that eventually brought about the National Trust and, ultimately, the national parks. The village of Wythburn, at the foot of the lake, was lost in the flooding that occurred in the creation of Manchester's reservoir, but the tiny seventeenth-century chapel at Wythburn was on high enough ground to survive. It's worth a visit and its parking lot is the starting point of a climbing trail to the peak of Helvellyn, the 3,118-foot mountain that rises to the right of A591. Helvellyn offers spectacular views and can be climbed easily from the Thirlmere side. But the climb is more interesting from the east side where long, lateral ridges fall into Patterdale, a village on Ullswater. There are few more exhilarating scrambles in the whole of Britain than along Striding Edge to Helvellyn summit and back to Patterdale via Swirral Edge.

Keswick, 13 miles from Grasmere, is just a few miles beyond the north end of Thirlmere (the parking lot at this end is the start of a gentle forest trail). You'll get an excellent view of the area from the crest of Castlerigg, and a road on the right leads to the prehistoric Castlerigg Stone Circle.

KESWICK: Sheltered by the towering Skiddaw (3,053 feet), this ancient and prosperous market town sits close to the north shore of Derwentwater, 3 miles long and a mile wide, surrounded by a delightful mixture of bare rock, grassy banks, and forested glens. It is one of the loveliest (some say *the* loveliest) of lakeland's lakes, and there are rowboats and cruising craft that can be rented to explore its variety, troll for trout and pike, or visit some of the many tiny islands that dot its surface. One of these, Floating Island, is no more than a tangled mass of lake weeds riding on a bubble of swamp gas. The others, however, are more substantial, and several support beautiful homes. The remains of a seventh-century retreat are on the island of St. Herbert.

Many poets, including Shelley, Southey, Wordsworth, and Coleridge, were drawn to this area and Keswick's Fitz Park Museum displays some of their manuscripts, letters, and personal effects (open daily, Easter through October). Hugh Walpole, who lived on the shore of Derwentwater and set his powerful "Herries" series of novels in this valley, is also represented in the collection. Wordsworth's memory slips in again at Old Windebrowe, a sixteenth-century farmhouse lent to the poet and his sister in 1794. The kitchen and parlor are restored to their early condition and an exhibition illustrates the house's links to a number of other leading literary figures. Southey's home, Greta Hall (Coleridge lived in it for 3 years before the Southey family took over), has become Keswick School, and his body lies in the Crosthwaite churchyard. Southey, Wordsworth, and Coleridge all patronized the bar at the *George Hotel,* which claims to be the oldest structure in town. Judging by the crude stone masonry and faded walls, it may well be. Walpole is buried in St. John's churchyard.

Keswick earns its living from visitors and caters to them with a long list of hotels and boarding houses; the ubiquitous bed-and-breakfast sign is nowhere more evident than here. The information center, located during the summer in Moot Hall, Market Sq. (its winter address is Council Offices, Main St.), can advise you on accommodations, walks, and current happenings.

Two of the best points for viewing Derwentwater and its environs are at Castle Head (529 feet), just south of Keswick, and at Friar's Crag, a rocky headland on the lake. John Ruskin was particularly enamored of the latter, and there is a memorial to him here. Southey favored the view from the hill near Greta Bridge.

CHECKING IN: *Lodore Swiss Hotel* – On the edge of Derwentwater, 3 miles south of Keswick, with glorious views of the lake and Lodore Falls. Though the building is fairly large (72 rooms) and very grand in appearance, it is run by a family (the Englands) and their high standards are readily apparent. The restaurant features international, including Swiss, dishes. Closed November through March. (Borrowdale; phone: 059684-285; expensive.) ***Mary Mount Country House Hotel*** – Also on the shores of Derwentwater and owned by the Englands, this cozy 15-room hotel is set in beautiful woodlands. Paneled bar. Open all year. (Borrowdale; phone: 059684-223; expensive to moderate.) ***Royal Oak*** – This famous lakeland inn is old, rambling, and comfortable, and it's located in the center of town. (Keswick; phone: 0596-72965; moderate.)

En Route – Drive south on B5289 to the quite beautiful Borrowdale valley. The road runs between the east shore of Derwentwater and high gray cliffs that are immensely popular with climbers. Before the village of Rosthwaite, the Bowder Stone, a huge boulder that tumbled from some nearby height, stands precariously on edge near Castle Crag, a 900-foot-tall rock cone that can be climbed without too much effort in under half an hour. Great Gable, a little farther along the route, is a more challenging target — 2,949 feet of tough climbing. It takes about 3 hours to ascend this monster, but the view is well worth the effort: The entire area from Skiddaw to Windermere, and even the Isle of Man are visible from the crest.

Continue on B5289, crossing over Honister Pass, which rises well over 1,000 feet. From the summit there is an impressive view toward Buttermere Lake, with Fleetwith Pike and the steep face of Honister Crag dominating the road. A quarry operated by the Buttermere and Westmorland Green Slate Company is near the youth hostel here and visitors are welcome to watch the splitters (called "rivers") and dressers at work preparing the attractive olive-green slate for export all over the world. Beyond the pass, the road drops through rough territory before reaching Gatesgarth farm at the foot of the long, winding descent. The farm specializes in raising Herdwick sheep, a tough breed that is able to survive the often harsh conditions of the Lake District fells. They are thought to be either the original native sheep of Britain or to have been introduced by enterprising Norsemen who settled in this region a thousand years ago. (At the well-known Lakeland Sheepskin stores in Bowness, Ambleside, and Keswick, you can buy clothing made from Herdwick wool.)

The placid waters of Buttermere come into view as the roadway curves in a giant U, first west and then north. Buttermere's twin, Crummock Water, lies just beyond to the northwest. The flat mile of valley floor separating the two lakes suggests that they were once one, but each now has its own distinct character. In olden days, the village of Loweswater, off the north end of Crummock Water, was the metropolis of these parts and the pretty village of Buttermere lay tucked between the two lakes, nothing more than a huddle of houses and a small click-mill to grind rye and oats. The local balance shifted with the coming of the road across Honister Pass. The Lake Poets discovered and wrote about Buttermere and its charms, Turner painted the lake and Honister Crag, and gradually the number of visitors increased. Today the village has more than one hotel, including the *Fish Hotel,* a typical lakeland inn whose name reflects Buttermere's excellence as a place for trout fishing, particularly in April, May, and September. The village is also another popular base for climbers and not far from it, Scale Force, a lively waterfall with a drop of over 120 feet, is the object of a short, muddy excursion. The easiest access is by crossing the stream between the two lakes and following the path on the far side, but by all means, wear boots or hiking shoes.

A few miles farther north, B5289 intersects B5292; you can either take B5292 east over Whinlatter Pass (not as steep as Honister Pass) toward A66, Keswick, and Penrith, or extend your trip by heading west toward Cockermouth.

COCKERMOUTH: An attractive market town with a number of good antique shops, Cockermouth is famous as Wordsworth's birthplace (1770). It is strategically placed at the junction of the Cocker and Derwent rivers and though its origins date to pre-Roman times, little remains from its earliest period. Even its twelfth-century castle was destroyed during the Civil War violence of the mid-1600s. Wordsworth House (open daily except Sundays and Thursday afternoons from April to October) was built in 1745. This house, in which Dorothy and William were born and grew up, is a fairly simple, countrified example of Georgian architecture that has survived intact. The furnishings used by the Wordsworth family, however, are long gone. William's father is buried in the churchyard. Fletcher Christian, leader of the mutiny on the *Bounty,* was born in 1764 at Moorland Close, a nearby farmhouse.

CHECKING IN: *The Pheasant Inn* – This old coaching inn that still retains its traditional atmosphere is situated on Bassenthwaite Lake near Thornthwaite Forest. Food in the pub restaurant is simple and English. (Bassenthwaite Lake, off A66, near Cockermouth; phone: 059681-234; moderate.)

En Route – From Cockermouth, you can take A5086 south, explore the western fringe of the Lake District, and leave the area the same way you came in, via Kendal. Or you can return east through Keswick, detour from the main road onto A5091 to the shore of Ullswater, and leave the district via its northern gateway, Penrith.

If you choose A5086 south, Ennerdale Water, perhaps the least visited of the larger lakes, lies about 10 miles away, on a secondary roadway to the east. A similar turnoff about 10 miles beyond leads to Wastwater, the deepest of the lakes, set among stern and savage-faced mountains in marked contrast to the gentle placement of Windermere. The village of Wasdale Head, a mile beyond the lake, is an excellent climbing center, but these mountains are strictly for experts. Return to the main road (A5086 becomes A595 near Ennerdale Water) and drive to Ravenglass, a port at the mouth of the River Esk about 25 miles from Cockermouth. The Eskdale valley can be explored either by road or on the narrow-gauge, steam-powered Ravenglass and Eskdale Railway (narrow is an understatement — 15 inches make it positively skinny), which runs between Ravenglass and Dalegarth Station near the village of Boot year-round, although there's limited service in winter. Just beyond Ravenglass, Muncaster Castle, the seat of the Pennington family for 700 years, overlooks the Esk (open Easter to early October except on Mondays, Fridays, and Saturdays). Farther on, at Broughton, another secondary road (A593) leads up the Duddon Valley toward Coniston. Just east of Broughton, A595 bears south along the coast, and A5092 continues east toward A590, A6, the market town of Kendal, and the M4 motorway.

If you choose to visit Ullswater, return to Keswick (either on the main A66 road or on B5292 across Whinlatter Pass). Follow the main road east out of town for 9 miles, then turn south onto A5091, which leads to the second largest of the region's lakes, a lovely winding stretch of water cradled by high fells. The best way to explore Ullswater is to set out on it. Boats are for hire and cruises start at Glenridding pier at the head of the lake, and at its northern end, Pooley Bridge, with a pier to match, is another place to arrange a day's outing. The lake is only 7.5 miles long (and an average .5 mile wide) but the distance between the two towns by road is 13 miles, along a stretch of A592 that skirts the northern bank of Ullswater, bypassing Gowbarrow Park. This grassy fell comes alive with daffodils each year and traveling poets can, as Wordsworth did, pause beneath the trees to write about the yellow blooms that may be "fluttering and dancing in the breeze" just as they were when he saw them. On the lake's western shore, the pretty Aira Force waterfall is a pleasant place to stop. A worthwhile diversion from Pooley Bridge is the secondary road along the southern shore of the lake past the *Sharrow Bay Hotel,* which surveys the most scenic views in the district; the road leads ultimately to the peaceful valley of Martindale.

Route A592 continues northeast of Ullswater toward Penrith. (South of Glenridding at the opposite end of the lake it heads toward Windermere, crossing the Helvellyn mountain range through Kirkstone Pass, at the summit of which is the *Kirkstone Pass Inn,* one of the highest taverns in England. On the far side of the pass are the Troutbeck Valley, the village of Troutbeck, and the seventeenth-century Townend House, once the residence of a yeoman's family. The interior, furnishings, and timbered barn remain intact and can be visited daily except Mondays and Saturdays, from April to October.)

CHECKING IN: ***Leeming House Hotel*** – Commanding fine views over Ullswater, this is a gracious, porticoed country house in Georgian style. It's on the northern shore of the lake, not far from the site of the famous daffodils. The restaurant is rather grand. Closed December until mid-March. (Watermillock; phone: 08536-444; expensive.) ***Sharrow Bay Hotel*** – Partners Francis Coulson and Brian Sack have spent 30 years making the Sharrow Bay one of the most respected and attractive hotels in the area. This stone country house is on the southern shore of Ullswater, about 2 miles from Pooley Bridge, and rooms in a farmhouse addition are another mile down the road. The restaurant's fixed-menu dinners are a pleasure. Closed December until early March. (Pooley Bridge; phone: 08536-301; expensive.) ***Queen's Head Hotel*** – Though the exterior is a little faded, this eighteenth-century inn is as clean as could be and quite comfortable. It's located in a village southwest of Penrith. (Tirril; phone: 0768-63219; inexpensive.)

PENRITH: This charming town was burned twice during the fourteenth century by bands of marauding Scots from across the border, but since then it has withstood time and the onslaught of travelers comfortably. Its oldest section grew up around the thirteenth-century Church of St. Andrew (rebuilt in the 1700s) and the nearby sixteenth-century schoolhouse. Several conflicting legends surround the presence of the two stone formations on the church grounds, known as Giant's Grave and Giant's Thumb: One version holds that this is the burial place of an ancient king. The ruins of Penrith Castle are now a town park, but two fine sixteenth-century inns, the *Gloucester Arms* and the *Two Lions,* are still thriving.

Penrith is located at the convergence of several main roads. From here you can take the M6 just west of town, pick up the A74, and follow the A75 into Dumfries to connect with the *Scottish Lowlands* route.

Scottish Lowlands

No tourist should tread the hallowed ground of the Lowlands without first wedging a few rudiments of the history of Scottish Presbyterianism into his head. Here's an emergency grab bag of key religious events from the sixteenth century to the present, as well as brief profiles of the two major players:

John Knox, a brilliant and incendiary preacher fired by the theology of John Calvin, came to St. Giles's Cathedral, Edinburgh, in 1559. Many of the Norman-blooded Scottish nobility, looking to siphon off riches like those enjoyed by their counterparts in England under Henry VIII's Dissolution of the Monasteries, hopped on Knox's bandwagon against a corrupt Catholic Church and the Catholic Royal House of Stuart. This was the takeoff point for the Protestant Reformation in Scotland. With fifteen 4-hour sermons a week on the democratization of Christian worship rumbling from his pulpit, Knox soon gathered the rabble to his bosom. His reforms were implemented in every corner of the Lowlands amid the wrecking of church interiors and ravaging of altars. Yet contrary to generations of popular opinion, Knox was no puritan; he could enjoy a good belly laugh and freely sanctioned his fellow citizens to drink, dance, and be merry. Killjoy-ism closed in on the Presbyterian faith much later, in the wake of Royal persecution from London.

Charles II, successor in 1660 to a disagreeable Cromwellian interlude (which had however allowed Presbyterianism to flourish), continued his executed father's bad habit of ramming Episcopacy down Scotland's throat, backed by an obsequious and dissolute Scottish Parliament. Groups of worshipers called Covenanters (because of two written oaths they had signed, some in blood, proclaiming their inalienable anti-Episcopal beliefs) gathered on open hillsides, away from the churches, flouting a Parliamentary Act. Charles's troops zeroed in for a series of massacres. The Lowlands, especially Scotland's southwest, are full of Covenanting martyrs' graves.

In 1712 a new act was passed by England's and Scotland's now unified Parliaments, which instituted lay patronage; this was a system revoking the right of congregations to choose their own ministers, and granting the task instead to each parish's local "laird" (lord or resident aristocrat). Often tyrannical, these handpicked ministers tightly controlled life in the Lowland towns and villages, banning music, dancing, theatrical performances, and country walks on Sundays. Scotland's national bard, Robert Burns, was one of many who were forced at the hands of church elders to appease God's wrath by standing publicly in a wooden dock protractedly confessing to fornication.

With the coming of the Industrial Revolution, economic and social conditions in the Lowlands, especially Glasgow and Edinburgh, became appalling. In comparison to their working-class congregations, men of the cloth were fat cats. In 1843, 450 ministers with sorely tried consciences walked bravely out of their manses, their livings, and the annual General Assembly of the Church of Scotland to form a new movement, the Free Presbyterian Church. This breach was not healed until 1929, after lay patronage had been abolished within the Kirk (as the established Presbyterian Church was called). Attendant upon the tireless and dedicated slum-based social work of the new Free Church was a harsh (but possibly necessary) list of "don'ts" for its followers: no uncleanliness; no laziness; no bankruptcy; no "Sabbath breaking"; no drinking and gambling; no loud, indelicate behavior. As you'll quickly discover, these cast-iron virtues are tightly woven into the fabric of Scottish life today, especially on Sundays, when the world stops.

The language spoken by Lowlanders derives from "La'lands," an old form of Norman-infused Anglo-Saxon once known as "Inglis." It's full of dialect words, rolled *r*'s, and unexpected pronunciations: *guid* for "good," *doon* for "down," *fitba* for "football." La'lands is sometimes droll, often pithy, and — with the help of great poets like William Dunbar, Robert Burns, or Hugh MacDiarmid — sweepingly majestic. It's worth reading a bit of Burns or MacDiarmid (Dunbar is unfathomable at first sight, like Chaucer) to get a sense of Lowland Scotland's people, speech, and concept of nationhood.

Have a look also at the English-language Lowland poetry of Sir Walter Scott, who set *Marmion* and *The Lay of the Last Minstrel* among the Border Country's rolling, variegated, green-and-brown brackeny hills. The Borders, Scott's home for many years, are the Lowlands' most intriguing district: It's a moorish land interspersed with lush farms and prosperous mill-spangled towns. Ruined abbeys sit like sad marooned kings above gladed loops in the River Tweed. Picturesque villages dot its valleys. Its folklore is widely known, especially its ballads, from *Thomas the Rhymer and the Queen of Elfland* (on which the English poet John Keats may have based *La Belle Dame Sans Merci*), to narrative poetry that recounts the dramatic cattle-rustling Border Raids of the fourteenth, fifteenth, and sixteenth centuries. Under this Scottish version of the chivalric code, knights called "moss troopers" or "reivers" gathered their families and retainers and forayed into each other's territory, burying their differences only when England reared its grim marauding head. British ex–prime minister Sir Alec Douglas-Home is descended from at least two of these families. The Riding of the Marches, an ancient way of delineating jealously guarded boundaries by tracing them in assembled companies on horseback, is ritually practiced on a festival day every summer by each of the main Border towns. Catch one if you can!

The Lowlands route begins at Edinburgh and runs east along the Firth of Forth, dips south into the Borders, veers southwest to the southern shore, then returns north to Glasgow via Galloway Forest Park and the Atlantic coast. The entire distance is about 335 miles. Be sure to buy the Scottish Tourist Board's kit called *Enjoy Scotland* (£1.80), which includes a very detailed touring map and a booklet of 1001 things to see. Keep scones (biscuits) or sandwiches, bought from bakeries in the towns, in your car for when lunchtime rolls around and you find you're still in the wilds. Don't pass a gas station assuming you'll see another one. If you're traveling in the Lowlands from May through September, you must book your hotels in advance.

The price categories for the hotels listed in this route are expensive, $80 and up for two for bed and breakfast; moderate, $60 to $80; and inexpensive, $45 to $60. Dinner for two in an expensive restaurant will run $50 and up; in moderate, $30 to $50; and in inexpensive, under $30.

EDINBURGH: For a detailed report on the city, its sights, hotels, and restaurants, see *Edinburgh,* THE CITIES.

En Route – On the B1348 is the Prestongrange Mining Museum, an 800-year-old colliery, which has as its showpiece a massive 5-story-high beam pump dating from 1874. Photographs and artifacts, a winding engine, and two real steam locomotives are on display too. Open weekdays till 4 PM; Saturdays by arrangement (phone: 661-2718).

GULLANE: Despite strong winds in winter, rich Edinburghers maintain a posh suburban existence here. Gullane gets more sun than anywhere else in Scotland. Tourists throng here in late spring and in summer because of its four incomparable golf courses. Muirfield, the finest (the site of the 1980 Open Championship), is the home of the Honourable Company of Edinburgh Golfers; to play it you'll need a letter of introduction from your home club secretary, submitted a day in advance. Gullane also has wide, luxurious sandy beaches.

CHECKING IN: *Greywalls Hotel* – Gullane's most exclusive place to stay, this is a lavishly appointed 24-bedroom golfers' retreat. (Just beside Muirfield Golf Course; phone: 842144; expensive.)

EATING OUT: *La Potinière* – The French cooking at this small and unassuming restaurant is so good that one of its recipes — *soufflé aux courgettes* — appears in the Good Food Guide's *Second Dinner Party Book.* Reservations a must. Lunches only, except Saturday, when there is dinner but no lunch. Closed Wednesdays and all of October. (On the main route through Gullane; phone: 843214; moderate.)

DIRLETON: This charming little village, with its spectacular castle and busy yew-encircled bowling green, is reputedly the prettiest in Scotland. The castle, entered dramatically by a long ramp leading sharply upward to a gate in its stark and stony heights, was built in 1225. Additions were made in the fifteenth and seventeenth centuries, but the whole was sacked by Oliver Cromwell's troops in 1650. The castle shares with clusters of seventeenth- and eighteenth-century cottages the borders of the Village Common. If you feel like taking a walk, trees and springy turf line the lovely Yellowcraig Nature Trail for 2 miles from Dirleton to the sea.

CHECKING IN: *The Open Arms Hotel* – This country-style hostelry with only 7 bedrooms is famed for its restaurant, which is included on the Scottish Tourist Board's Taste of Scotland roster. Decorated in peach and green, its candlelit tables are graced by such slowly-to-be-savored delicacies as salmon, venison, and Cranachan pudding — cream, toasted oatmeal, and rum, topped with fresh berries! (On the main route through Dirleton; phone: 241; expensive.)

NORTH BERWICK: The farming folk who inhabit the surrounding countryside habitually converge on this holiday spot, making the most of its sands, shops, and two fine golf courses. North Berwick has the kind of natural topography that proves God must be British: The middle-class beach is divided from the lower-class beach by the harbor, and each gives onto its own separate bay. The sun at east coast resorts like this one has a striking, harsh brilliance, unbroken by the soft air and purple-hilled isles that characterize the Atlantic coast to the west. You may offend the natives' old-fashioned priorities if you venture onto the middle-class beach without a hat!

A mile or so south of the center of town is North Berwick Law, a grassy rise decked with a whalebone arch, from which to enjoy a magnificent view. Motorboat trips from North Berwick go in summer to the nearby island of Fidra, and also to the fascinating Bass Rock, which every Edinburgh schoolchild is whisked off by at least one teacher in the course of his or her career to see. The rock's steep, straight sides make it look much higher than its 350 feet. It's part of a chain of volcanic masses, made of especially hard stone, that withstood glacial pressure in the last Ice Age (the Castle Rock, which

Edinburgh Castle sits on, is another). The Bass Rock is totally inaccessible except at one point, which made it irresistible to hermits in early Christian times; to prison wardens detaining Covenanting ministers at the time of King Charles II; and to soldiers rallying round the flag of the exiled Stuarts who needed a safe fortress in the reign of William of Orange. Today the Bass Rock is "held," as is Fidra, by the keepers of its lighthouse and scores of swirling silvery gannets. For boat trips, contact Fred Marr (phone: 2838).

En Route – About 3 miles farther on is Tantallon Castle, on a cliff overlooking the North Sea. An extensive rose-colored ruin that once was a stronghold of the famous Border family named Douglas, it has captured the Scottish popular imagination and worked its way into the native patois. Any feat of the impossible is said to be as hard as to "ding doon" Tantallon Castle. You can go inside during daylight hours only.

DUNBAR: This quiet town, in sailing-ship days the only safe port between Edinburgh and the English city of Berwick, is now a golfing and sailing haven for vacationers seeking a rest. But it wasn't always restful. The earl of Hertford attacked it by land in 1544, during the so-called Rough Wooing by which King Henry VIII tried to force Scotland to bind the young Mary Queen of Scots to his son Edward in a treaty of marriage. Years later Mary stayed in Dunbar Castle (today a mere shred) with her husband-and-cousin Lord Darnley, and again with her lover Lord Bothwell who carried her off there, fairytale-style, after the murder of Lord Darnley. Cromwell laid waste the town in 1650. The Castle was destroyed in 1567, after Mary and Bothwell had fled for their lives.

At West Barns on the coast road just east of Dunbar are the *Doris and Bryan Green* leathercraft workshops, located in an old schoolhouse. Here you can buy attractive hand-tooled bags and other goods of original design (call beforehand: 63463).

EATING OUT: *Café Greco* – Soups, omelettes, curries, Continental entrees, salads, and pie are specialties at this culinary oasis within the old stone walls of a tall, gray Dunbar house. The modern decor in black, white, and orange has a startling elegance. Open noon to 10 PM during the tourist season. (88 High St.; phone: 62749; inexpensive.)

En Route – When you have left the Great North Road (the A1) by turning south on the A6112, you will come to Edinshall Broch, about 4 miles above the town of Duns. A *broch* is an Iron Age castle that is circular and has galleries within the thickness of its walls. Edinshall Broch is one of ten of these in the Lowlands. It's larger than most and was used as a place of retreat until well into Roman times.

Continue on into Duns, where you'll find the Jim Clark Memorial Trophy Room, full of the late world motor-racing champion's spoils of victory. It's in the Burgh Chambers, Newton St.; open Easter through September. The *George Nitsche Pottery,* 57 Castle St., the first of a dazzling array of small craft workshops and potteries along your way through the Lowlands, is here too. Duns became the county town of Berwickshire when Scotland lost Berwick once and for all to the English in 1482.

COLDSTREAM: You now reach (not for the last time) the trout-laden waters of the River Tweed. The 300-foot Tweed Bridge across the river into England was built in 1776, after which it rapidly became notorious for heavy traffic in eloping couples heading for the Old Marriage House beside its northern entrance. (Scotland's relatively lax marriage laws made Coldstream the British equivalent of Maryland.) The town is famous too as the starting point of the 1660 march of the Coldstream Guards to London, where they effected the restoration of Charles II. Their original headquarters is on the north side of the main square.

En Route – About 2 miles northwest on the A697 is The Hirsel, Sir Alec Douglas-

Home's ancestral home where he resides today. The house itself is closed to the public, but the magnificent gardens are open and include rhododendrons, woodlands, and a small lake chockablock with wildfowl. BBC Radio at its most precious has been known to fill an idle minute or two with live choruses of Hirsel birdsong.

KELSO: Site of one of the four Border Abbeys of the incomparable Scott Country, this small bastion of what could almost be French civilization (its center looks like an enormous *grande place*) is nonetheless your first taste of the netherworld between past and present, legend and reality, which suffuses this part of Scotland. The town, like the abbey, is situated on the rivers Tweed and Teviot. Its five-arched bridge, begun in 1800, was an exact model for the later Waterloo Bridge across the Thames, demolished in 1934. The lamp standards you see at the bridge's south end were salvaged and brought here from London after the demolition.

Kelso Abbey, founded in 1128 by King David I (son of the King Malcolm who succeeded Macbeth, and ancestor of King Robert the Bruce) was destroyed by the earl of Hertford in 1545. What remains of it shows a Norman-Transitional style unique in Scotland. In the main Kelso car park behind the abbey is *The Kelso Pottery*, where you can watch the making and glazing of stoneware and buy some of the products (phone in advance: 2027). The mid-September Kelso Ram Sales in Springwood Park are a fascinating event indigenous to Border life, and Civic Week, the third in July, is full of colorful equestrian pageants based on local folklore and tradition.

En Route – Some 2 miles northwest of Kelso on the B6089 is Floors Castle, seat of the dukes of Roxburgh, said to be the largest inhabited mansion in Britain. It has 365 windows, one for every day in the year. Built by William Adam in 1721, it underwent various additions and remodelings until it became spectacularly grandiose — a kind of fantastic Brobdingnag dollhouse, with its battlements, water spouts, and pepper-pot towers, its amphitheater, and its golden gates. The furniture, porcelain, tapestries, and paintings are all superb. The fine grounds include a holly tree supposedly marking the spot where King James II (of Scotland) was killed in 1460 firing one of his own cannons. Open May 2 through September 30. Pipe band displays on certain days in summer.

A 20-mile detour north to Hume Castle, Mellerstain House, and Smailholm Tower is a must (these places are clearly marked on your *Enjoy Scotland* touring map: the route between them from Kelso and back — the B6364, some unnumbered roads, and then the B6397 — forms the shape of a fan). Thirteenth-century Hume Castle preceded The Hirsel as seat of the earls of Home. Cromwell wrecked it in 1651. The view from its parapets (these were reconstructed in the eighteenth century) is glorious. If you're lucky, you'll have the whole castle to yourself; it's been unoccupied since the seventeenth century.

Mellerstain House is, architecturally speaking, an Adam pie — begun in 1725 by William and finished in 1778 by his famous son, Robert. Despite this, it is proportionally perfect. No finer meringue exists anywhere than the plasterwork ceilings inside; Mellerstain is one of the great Georgian houses of Scotland. There are outstanding collections of eighteenth-century furniture too, and paintings by old masters. Open daily except Saturdays, May through September. (Mellerstain House takes part in the annual Springtime in the Borders Festival in early June, mounting an exhibition of its vintage car collection.)

Sir Walter Scott used to sit like a medieval princess in the top of Smailholm Tower concocting romantic novels. The best extant example of a sixteenth-century Border keep, its 57-foot summit overlooks vast expanses of country, English and Scottish, that sweeps your breath away! Strategically placed stone fortresses like Smailholm, into which Border reivers herded women, children, and cattle as enemies approached, had roofs fitted out with pans of pitch and peat for kindling; on a clear night it was said to take only 2 minutes for a chain of danger signals to reach Edinburgh Castle from the English borderline.

CHECKING IN: *Cross Keys Hotel* – Well known as Kelso's best, this 23-bedroomed, newly renovated old inn has Taste of Scotland cooking and a charming bar decorated with horse and wagon motifs. (The Square; phone: 3303; moderate.) *Ednam House* – This historic hotel with an arresting facade, built in 1761 as the abode of a prominent Kelso merchant, still has its original Italian ceilings. A key to one of its 32 bedrooms secures you exclusive fishing rights on a nearby stretch of the Tweed. (Bridge St.; phone: 24168; moderate.)

JEDBURGH: Although the priory section of Jedburgh Abbey was leveled during the Rough Wooing, the church is amazingly well preserved. The elegant rose window is nicknamed St. Catherine's Wheel (a Catherine Wheel is a circular-acting firework). There was a church here as early as the ninth century, but the abbey dates from 1138, when David I brought Augustinians to Scotland from Beauvais in France. It enjoys a lovely setting above Jed Water, a tributary of the Teviot. In certain evening lights it appears to be made of solid gold.

The great and wise King Alexander III, the first king of a truly unified Scotland, was married in Jedburgh in 1285 to a young and beautiful second wife. His love for her seems to have spurred him to foolish and hotheaded passion: It is said that the spectral figure of Death was seen among the dancing guests at the wedding reception in Jedburgh Castle, now the site of the Jail Museum — and sure enough, Alexander was killed when his horse fell over a cliff as he rode out 6 months later on a stormy night, against the advice of all his aides, from Edinburgh Castle to join his bride in Dunfermline. The museum, in the Castlegate, is as it was in 1823 when erected as an experimental "modern" jail. Open daily April through September.

Jedburgh was once surrounded for protection by a series of "bastel houses," one of which, on Queen St., was a residence of Mary Queen of Scots. Today it is open to the public (March through October) and is fascinating chiefly for the number of portraits it contains of that enigmatic lady, each looking less like the next than the last. In the unlikely event you are in Jedburgh in mid-February, you can enter the spirit of Mary's troubled times by watching the annual Ba' Game, played in the sixteenth century with Jedburgh citizens' slain enemies' heads! The "Uppies" (those born above the Mercat Cross) and the "Doonies" (those born below) have to get a ball into its goal (the goals are the Jail Museum grounds and the Townfoot) by fair means or foul in a space of 2 hours.

The Friday after the second Saturday in July sees the start of the 3-day Jethart Callants' Festival, in which the Riding of the Marches takes the form of mounted ceremonial dashes to historically important places, the Jedburgh flag to the fore. A "callant" is a gallant, or youngblood. Also part of the festival are the Jedburgh Border Games, held on the Saturday in Riverside Park from 10 AM to teatime.

En Route – About 2 miles north of Jedburgh on the A68 is the *Borders Craft Centre*, purveying a full range of goods made in the Border area (open afternoons only except in summer). The *Bongate Studio Pottery* is in Jedburgh's Bongate; the *Oxnam Pottery* is in Camptown, 4 miles south on the A68 along the Jed Water; *Monteviot Woodcraft*, 3 miles north of Jedburgh, is at Harestane's Mill, Monteviot. The town is short on restaurants and hotels but you can have coffee and home-baked goodies at the *Mercat Café*, 5 Bongate, and the *Border Coffee Shop*, 3.5 miles south on the A68. On sale at *Millar's*, 10 High St., are "Jethart snails," a traditional Jedburgh mint-flavored hard candy of escargotian color and shape.

HAWICK (pronounced Hoyk): The largest of the Border burghs, this busy farm market and knitwear and electronics capital rings the junction of the Teviot and Slitrig rivers. It has contributed many a famous player to internationally known rugby teams and its citizens are inveterate rugby nuts. Its home team, the Greens, plays Saturdays at Mansfield Park.

In the leafy shades of the 107-acre municipal Wilton Lodge Park is Hawick Museum and Art Gallery, bursting with Border relics. The Riding of the Marches is at its most full-blooded in Hawick, where it is called the Common Riding and takes place around the second week in June. It is led by an unmarried callant elected months in advance, the "Cornet," who trains his men beforehand through a series of death-defying cavalry charges, culminating in their promotion to the Ancient Order of Mosstroopers. Three days of festivities include the Mosstroopers' all-important private performance at breakfast of ancient druidic rites in preparation for the Riding; the thrilling equestrian chases that constitute the Riding; additional horse races (at which you can place official bets) on Hawick Moor; athletic matches in Volunteer Park between top British professionals; all-night dinners and dances; and the singing, on the town heights at dawn, of the Hawick battle song "Teribus," which begins in Latin, lurches into Old Norse, and then plunges into Scots. The whole experience is the ultimate in Scottish machismo, if you can stay the course!

SELKIRK: To get here drive north on the A7 from Hawick to the Ettrick Water. Halliwell's House, in the main square, is an interesting museum of ironmongery (open afternoons June through September, except Thursdays and Sundays). Sir Walter Scott was sheriff of Selkirkshire from 1799 to 1832; the courthouse, on High St., displays some of his letters. If you're here at teatime, try a slice of "Selkirk bannock," the richest raisin bread in the world.

En Route – From Selkirk a 20-mile circular detour via the A699, A68, A6091, B6360, and A7 takes in Dryburgh Abbey, Melrose Abbey, and Abbotsford House.

Across the Tweed from the village of St. Boswell's is majestic Dryburgh Abbey; many think its setting the most beautiful of all. It too was founded in the reign of David I and later sacked by English raiders. Only the transepts remain of the church, but the cloister is nearly complete. Sir Walter Scott is buried here, as is Earl Haig, Britain's chief World War I general.

Another of David I's now ruined monasteries, Melrose Abbey graces the central square of the lovely little town of Melrose. Notice that the abbey's exquisite fifteenth-century traceried stonework features a pig on the roof playing bagpipes! According to legend the heart of Robert the Bruce is buried in the abbey; another legend has it that the Eildon Hills, which loom to the southeast, are shaped as they are (two pointed, one shorter and flat-topped) because the devil was so piqued by the dawn chanting of the abbey monks that he thrust three mountains between them and the rising sun — but dropped and broke one mountain in transit. Sir Walter Scott used to gaze across the Tweed at the Eildon Hills from a point above Melrose now known as Scott's View (it's on the B6356 a couple of miles east of town; see your *Enjoy Scotland* touring map).

If you'd like to go riding or pony trekking in the Eildon Hills, contact Elspeth McDonald at the Ellwyn Glen Riding Centre, Pavilion Estate, Melrose (phone: 2908). Hikers can do the Eildon Walk, with the aid of nature-trail leaflets available (free) at the tourist information bureau next to Melrose Abbey.

Built to Sir Walter Scott's own specifications in 1812–24, his fascinating country home, Abbotsford House, broods in stately somnolence by the Tweed. A trip here gives a vivid picture of Scott's personality. He could carry his starry-eyed antiquarianism to laughable lengths, as when he made off with the door to Edinburgh's just-razed, fifteenth-century "Heart of Midlothian" (the county jail), and had it installed in a wall at Abbotsford. He later wrote a not-so-laughable book about the Heart of Midlothian. There are historic relics he carefully collected, impressive armories, a 9,000-volume library, and the study in which he wrote the Waverly novels trying to reduce a £117,000 debt. The effort eventually killed him; he died at the age of 61. Open daily from the last week in March through October.

Returning to Selkirk and proceeding 3 miles to the west on A708, you'll find Philiphaugh, the field where the army of the noble Scottish Cavalier poet-soldier the Marquis of Montrose lost a key battle to Puritan forces in 1645. Near the Yarrow Water is Bowhill, home of the dukes of Buccleuch and Queensberry (one dukedom), another of the Borders' ancestral palaces. This one has early-nineteenth-century silk brocades and hand-painted Chinese wallpapers, sumptuous art treasures, lush woods and gardens, an elaborately inventive jungle-playground-type Tarzan complex for kids, and pony trekking. Open Mondays, Wednesdays, and weekends in May, June, and September; daily, except Fridays, in July and August. Adjacent to Bowhill is Newark Castle, a 5-story oblong towerhouse where the "Last Minstrel" recited his "Lay" to the duchess of Buccleuch. It was a royal hunting seat for the Forest of Ettrick in the Middle Ages. Another 4 miles along is picturesque Yarrow Kirk, dating from 1640.

Continuing along the Yarrow you reach the wild, godforsaken country over which the merlinhawks fly. These small ferocious birds are said to embody by magic the spirit of Merlin the wizard. Near desolate St. Mary's Loch and its sibling the Loch of the Lowes are two historic inns where Scott met literary friends — the *Gordon Arms* and *Tibbie Shiels* (both are on your *Enjoy Scotland* touring map, albeit in tiny print). Across the main road from St. Mary's Loch you can see the remains of Dryhope Tower, which, like Smailholm, is a medieval watch or "peel" tower.

Stay on the A708. On your right, about 8 miles before Moffat, is the Grey Mare's Tail, a magnificent 200-foot waterfall formed as the Tail Burn drops from Loch Skeen to meet the Moffat Water (you lose the Yarrow at St. Mary's Loch). The whole area is resplendent with wildflowers. Covenanters used to hide out here. The hollow below the falls is the "Giant's Grave," which figures in Scott's poem *Marmion*.

CHECKING IN: *Dryburgh Abbey Hotel* – A good place to leave your car while you cross the Tweed by foot on pilgrimage to Dryburgh Abbey, this nineteenth-century house à la baronial mode has all the swagger of the horse-and-hound set that patronizes it. It has 29 bedrooms, serves elegant afternoon teas, and its restaurant is the last word in Taste of Scotland cooking. Closed November through March. (On the banks of the Tweed; phone: 22261; expensive.) ***Phillipburn House Hotel*** – Families are positively coddled in this slickly modernized old house overlooking the famous battlefield of Philiphaugh. There are 17 bedrooms, gardens and woodlands, a heated swimming pool, a well-equipped playground, riding and fishing facilities, and real log fires. (On the A708, 2.5 miles west of Selkirk; phone: 20747; moderate.) ***Burt's Hotel*** – In addition to full-fledged restaurant meals this bustling hostelry with 22 bedrooms provides substantial and delicious bar snacks. Gleaming everywhere under its wooden roofbeams are pieces of polished copper and brass. (Market Sq., Melrose; phone: 2285; inexpensive.)

EATING OUT: *The Queenshead* – Robert Burns once slept in this friendly coaching inn during a stint as an exciseman. Although no bedrooms are available today, the bar has tasty food including homemade soups. (West Port, Selkirk; phone: 21782; inexpensive.)

MOFFAT: The pride of the town is Colvin Fountain, erected in 1875; the huge bronze ram on top symbolizes the importance of sheep farming in the surrounding districts. Moffat was for two centuries also a fashionable spa, and among the eighteenth-century greats to case the place were James Boswell, Robert Burns, and the James Macpherson of *Ossianic Ballads*. Today it's a touring base, flush with hotels and Italian cafés. But it retains a days-gone-by image and seems unlikely ever to shed its air of pleasant pokiness.

A good pottery with a retail showroom is the *Moffat Pottery,* Ladyknowe (in the town center beside the telephone exchange). Also at Ladyknowe are the *Moffat Weav-*

ers, who exhibit antique looms as well as demonstrate the art of skirtmaking. They keep a shop with a wide choice of Scottish products including their own.

A detour 6 miles north on the A701 brings you to the Devil's Beef Tub, famous in literature and lore. An astonishing feature of Dumfriesshire's natural geography, its vast smooth basinlike recess has a rotund regularity more believable in classical art than in nature. As its name suggests, Border reivers herded pilfered steers into the Devil's Beef Tub for purposes of concealment. If your family name is Armstrong or Douglas, your ancestors were the scourge of this part of Scotland.

CHECKING IN: *Beechwood Country House Hotel* – A comfortable haven on a Moffat hill, this 8-bedroom home-away-from-home sets a tempting Taste of Scotland table including beetroot soup, venison casserole, and the best Orkney cheeses. Restaurant reservations necessary on weekends and for dinner. (Harthope Pl.; phone: 20210; moderate to inexpensive.)

DUMFRIES: The A701 brings you to this quaint but sonorous symphony in red sandstone. Although its written history begins in 1186 with its legal recognition by King William the Lion, it is in fact much older; excavations have yielded Bronze Age relics. In Dumfries you are out of the bewitched furze-ridden Borders; here in the gentle dale of the River Nith you'll find, as all over the surrounding area of Galloway, hillocked meadows flecked with buttercups, peacefully grazing cattle, and grass as green as any in Ireland. Spring comes earlier to Dumfries and Galloway than elsewhere in Scotland and the climate stays comparatively warm.

In summer Dumfries is a-bubble with Burns freaks visiting Burns House on Mill Vennel (now called Burns St.), where he died in 1796. His tomb in nearby St. Michael's Churchyard is augmented by an unintentionally humorous sculpture showing him at his plough (Scotland knows him as "the Ploughman Poet") somewhat hampered by Coila, the muse of Scottish poetry, who flings o'er his shoulders a voluminous mantle as cumbersome as a tent. *The Globe Inn,* Burns's "favourite howff" in a narrow alley off High St., is exactly as it was in his day, furnishings and all, and is still in the bartending business. Then there is Ellisland Farm, 6½ miles north of Dumfries on the A76. Here Burns lived from 1788 to 1791, trying to make a living by the new agricultural methods (such as drainage) being introduced then. He failed, partly because he was also at the time a Dumfries exciseman traveling on horseback up to 200 miles a week. Several of his poems were written at Ellisland; these are commemorated by plaques at points where inspiration came to him.

A saunter through Dumfries takes you past some other not-to-be-missed high spots: Greyfriars Church on High St., whose monastery (now a supermarket) was the scene in 1306 of the murder by Robert the Bruce of his cousin and heir to the Scottish throne, John "the Red" Comyn; the Burns Statue opposite this church; the Mid Steeple of 1707, which is the remains of the central square's old Town Hall; and Dumfries Academy on Academy St., where a teenaged J. M. Barrie, a pupil there, first conceived the characters Peter Pan and Wendy while exploring the garden of the Moat Brae Nursing Home in the lane behind. The River Nith is spanned by the six-arched Devorguilla's Bridge, a thirteenth-century gift from Devorguilla Balliol, founder of Balliol College at Oxford (and ancestral cousin-in-law of the Bruce and the Red Comyn). The expansive "caul," or weir, by the bridge is a salmon leap and was once the power supply for the town's many grain mills. The path through the 2-mile wood along the Nith bank is Burns's Walk.

Blacklock, Farrie and Sons, 16–18 Church Crescent, is considered by many the best bookseller north of Oxford. A delectable trove of antiques has filtered into Dumfries's multitudinous curiosity shops. A side step down Friars' Vennel to Whitesands by the Nith brings you to an interesting farmers' market, held Wednesdays on a former site of horse and hiring fairs.

The Burgh Museum, Observatory Rd., housed in an eighteenth-century windmill, has local archaeological and other exhibits and a camera obscura (closed Tuesdays and Sundays October through March). There's also a folk museum, in Old Bridge House, Mill Rd., adjacent to Devorguilla's Bridge. Lincluden College, on the A76 a mile north of town, is an ecclesiastical edifice remarkable for its fifteenth-century heraldic stone adornments. Dumfries has an excellent municipal indoor swimming pool on Greensands by the Nith, and canoes for hire along the quays.

The Theatre Royal on Shakespeare St. bolsters its usual pop-vein fripperies with occasional plays by the likes of Ibsen and Coward. Gracefield Arts Centre on Langlands St. is a showcase for works by Scottish artists; it also sponsors the Dumfries and Galloway Arts Festival every year around the last week in May, providing military, rock, and folk bands, a serious guest orchestra, puppet shows, and exhibitions. *Guid Nychburris* (Good Neighbors) Week, in late June, is a sort of Milk Run of the Marches that offers concerts, parades, baby and beauty shows, the cavalcaded "stobbing and nogging" of Dumfries's boundaries, and the "kirking" (public promenading to church) of a newly elected Cornet.

Worth a jaunt into the countryside are Shambellie House, at the village of New Abbey, 7 miles south of Dumfries on the A710, and twelfth-century Caerlaverock Castle, 9 miles south of Dumfries on the B725. Shambellie House, approached through an avenue of tall gracious pines, opened in 1982 for the first time as Scotland's foremost museum of costumes. Caerlaverock Castle is a striking triangular ruin with round turrets and a real moat. Try to visit it at sunset. The castle was a prime target in the fourteenth century for Edward I's wars against Scotland and its weak king, John Balliol (Devorguilla's son, known to his subjects as *Toom Tabard,* which means "empty coat"). Next to the castle is Caerlaverock National Nature Reserve, on the Nith estuary and the Solway Firth: Here you can see the exhilarating spectacle of 9,000 barnacle geese in open flight (East Park observation towers open September to mid-May only). Also at New Abbey near Shambellie House is Sweetheart Abbey, built in 1273, the last pre-Reformation Cistercian foundation in Scotland and one of the nation's most beautiful. Devorguilla, who established it, is buried here; her husband's heart, encased in an ivory casket, sits in the tomb upon her bosom — hence the abbey's name.

CHECKING IN: *Cairndale Hotel* – This rouge-hued stone inn is what passes in these parts for a *bon viveur's* retreat. Its 60-car parking lot is handy (there are only 44 bedrooms) and its food — local produce cooked fresh — is Grade A. (English St.; phone: 4111; moderate.) *Station Hotel* – Owned by one of Dumfriesshire's rich dairy magnates, this overblown chocolate box with Hansel-and-Gretel portals has 30 bedrooms, a hearty array of Taste of Scotland delights, and several bars offering more than just milk. (49 Lovers Walk; phone: 4316; inexpensive.) **The County Hotel** – Prince Charles Edward Stuart, the "Bonnie Prince Charlie" of story and song, was a "guest" here in 1745 (failing to win Dumfries's support, he took the mayor hostage). His bedroom, one of 50, is preserved in Highland decor. The chef keeps a well-stocked Taste of Scotland pot. (79 High St.; phone: 5401; moderate to inexpensive.)

EATING OUT: *Bruno's* – In this ritzy Italian sanctum thoughts of salmons and haggises vanish at the flick of a canellone. The red-plush banquettes have at one time or another seated most of the posteriors in Caledonian gourmetdom. No lunches; closed Tuesdays. (3 Balmoral Rd.; phone: 5757; expensive.)

En Route – Follow the A75 southwest from Dumfries to Castle Douglas, an unassuming little town with an idyllic setting on Carlingwark Loch, a-sprinkle with brightly painted boats. *Galloway Gems* at 5a Church St. sells handmade silver jewelry, set with Galloway stones. At Bridge of Dee where the road crosses the

Dee River is *Whitehill of Balmaghie,* cabinetmakers and woodturners, who host prearranged tours (phone: 233).

KIRKCUDBRIGHT (pronounced Ker-coo-bree): About 6 miles south on the A711, this town, long famous as an artists' haunt, was used by the late-nineteenth-century Glasgow School as a base from which to work on their characteristic "kail-yard" (farmyard) scenes of the surrounding countryside. Its flowery lanes, elm-lined streets, and enchanting knots of whitewashed eighteenth-century cottages appeal no less to present-day palettes; all summer the place supports a steady stream of painters, pupils, and patrons. Broughton House on High St. was once the home of A.E. Hornel and contains many of his canvases. Adjacent to the much-photographed picturesque harbor is an exhibition gallery.

Dominating the harbor is jagged MacLellan's Castle, built in 1582. The town's impressive Mercat Cross dates from 1610 and the late-sixteenth- or early-seventeenth-century tollbooth once imprisoned the American naval hero John Paul Jones. The Stewartry Museum on St. Mary St. houses, among other features of Kirkcudbright history, a John Paul Jones display (open Easter to October only).

The fascinating process of copperwheel engraving on glass can be viewed at *David Gulland's,* 6 Barrhill Rd. (phone first: 31072).

CHECKING IN: *The Selkirk Arms* – This charming, comfortable 27-bedroom hotel where Robert Burns wrote the popular *Selkirk Grace* has wood paneling with some of Burns's verses, carved by a local artist. (Old High St.; phone: 30402; inexpensive.)

EATING OUT: *The Coffee Pot* – This cheerful bow-windowed snuggery across from the castle caters to everybody from snackers to three-course gorgers. Try fried trout, with baba au rhum for dessert. Open in summer only. (5 Castle St.; phone: 30569; inexpensive.)

En Route – Follow the A755 west from Kirkcudbright to rejoin the A75. Gatehouse-of-Fleet is a scenic spot renowned for its archaeological remains and its forest trails leading to lovely little Fleet Bay. Among the ancient sites in the district are Anworth Church on Gatehouse-of-Fleet's northwest outskirts, which contains a Dark Ages' cross; Palace Yard at Enrick, which is a medieval moated manor with the foundations of a palace of the Bishops of Galloway destroyed in the Reformation; and a first-century Roman fort just north of town beside the Water-of-Fleet. Relics of the not-so-distant past are the disused early-nineteenth-century cotton mill covered in ivy above Fleet Bridge and the soaring 75-foot castellated clock tower (ca. 1871) in mid-village. As in Kirkcudbright, artists of all kinds live in Gatehouse-of-Fleet. A good potter is *Bridget Drakeford,* the Drill Hall, Castramont Rd., who also makes porcelain.

The road from Gatehouse-of-Fleet to Creetown is full of delightful picnic places and the views along this stretch are terrific; you follow the eastern shore of Wigtown Bay to the Cree River estuary, looking across to the Wigtown peninsula. Cardoness Castle, a mile after Gatehouse-of-Fleet, is a well-preserved fifteenth-century stronghold with an original staircase. Carsluith Castle, 6 miles from Cardoness Castle, is a roofless sixteenth-century structure in the shape of an *L.* Between the two is Dirk Hatteraick's Cave (see your *Enjoy Scotland* touring map), a voracious crevice in the rocks where pigeonholes were cut to hide that dashing bandit's smuggled brandy. Kirkdale, a wooded glen near the cave, is the entrance to Cairn Holy, a neolithic graveyard.

The Gemrock Museum on the main road here in Creetown, with its fine collection of rocks, minerals, and semiprecious stones from all over the world, testifies to Galloway's preeminence in stone-building and jewelry-making. The Mersey Docks and part of the Thames Embankment are made of Creetown granite. *John*

Prince, jeweler and silversmith, is well worth a look-in at 93 St. John St. (phone first: 396).

GALLOWAY FOREST PARK: A glorious, gargantuan green space entered off the A714 a few miles beyond Newton Stewart, this majestic wilderness's chief fascinations are detailed on your *Enjoy Scotland* touring map. Rocky glens and mountain lakes have won it the title "The Highlands of the Lowlands."

Bruce's Stone on Loch Trool records an important victory there of Robert the Bruce over England in 1307, which helped secure Scotland's independence. A short walk away the Galloway Deer Museum has a tank full of live trout as well as other exhibits about indigenous Galloway species (open April through September only). But you don't need a museum to take in the native wildlife: red deer, roe deer, foxes, otters, red squirrels, and wild goats abound on the park's many miles of secluded woodland footpaths, and the wild geese and ducks, pheasants and grouse, falcons, owls, ravens, and golden eagles are an ornithologist's orgy.

En Route – Pick up the B734 at Barr off the northwest tip of Galloway Forest Park. This takes you to the Atlantic coast, where you can gaze at the regal heights of Ailsa Craig, rearing up out of the sea. Stay on the coast road until you reach Turnberry, the site of the internationally famous Ailsa championship golf course. You can visit Turnberry Lighthouse next to "Bruce's Castle" (the ninth hole); get there between 2 PM and 1 hour before sunset (phone the lightkeeper first: 225). Nearby Turnberry Castle is the real Bruce's Castle, said to be the birthplace of Robert the Bruce in 1274 (you'll have to look closely to spy its scant remains).

CHECKING IN: *Turnberry Hotel* – This lavish 124-bedroom resort looks like a landlocked ocean liner. It has a tennis court, hairdresser, indoor swimming pool, and reduced rates for residents on the Ailsa course as well as its other 18-hole course, the Arran. (Off the A719; phone: 202; expensive.)

CULZEAN CASTLE: About 12 miles south of Ayr is Scotland's most visited castle, Culzean (pronounced Koo-lane), situated within a remarkable 560-acre country park. Designed around an ancient tower of the Kennedy family (the earls of Cassillis) by Robert Adam in 1777, its turrets flank the Atlantic. General Dwight D. Eisenhower became its chief denizen in 1946, using it as a golfing base on frequent trips to Scotland. Note the drum-shaped drawing rooms in which even the fireplaces curve. Go in the morning to avoid the tourist buses that pour in after lunch, and ask for the head guide, Isabelle Mullin, a foremost authority on Culzean's contents and history.

The castle grounds include a walled garden, aviary, swan pond, camellia house, and orangery. There are palm trees everywhere, picnic tables, a seashore trail, and a tearoom. Farm buildings also designed by Robert Adam are now a lecture and exhibition theater and are (in summer) the starting point for conducted nature walks. The park grounds are always open; the castle, exhibition theater, and tearoom are open April through October only.

En Route – On the road beyond Culzean you'll see a sign marking the *Croy Brae,* also called "Electric Brae" because when its fantastic properties first became apparent, Ayrshiremen thought the cause could only be electricity. Now they think it's optical illusion: Switch off your motor and you'll coast uphill! (That however is nothing compared to your descent down the brae's other side, when you can coast uphill backward.) Along this route are some of the most beautiful views imaginable, often augmented by extraordinary weather effects creating ethereal lights. The shoreline gleams with watery inlets and wild red poppies, and the ghostly shell of Danure Castle, standing like a stony wraith against the sky, assails you as you start around the Heads of Ayr to meet the Firth of Clyde.

AYR: Ayrshire is Burns country the way the Borders are Scott country — a focal point for adulation. But where it's often foreigners who adulate Scott, it's the Scots themselves who revel in "Rabbie." Burns Night, every January 25, is a nationally observed occasion for dusk-to-dawn rituals of a kind that must have Scotland's Presbyterian forefathers bucketing up and down in their graves.

Burns was born in 1759 in the "auld clay biggin" built by his father, which is now the Burns Cottage Museum at Alloway, 2 miles south of Ayr on the B7024. Also on the site are the Land O' Burns Centre with its audiovisual program, book and crafts shop, cafeteria, and picnic tables; the Burns Monument, a rococo stone folly on a leafy hill; and the 700-year-old Brig O' Doon, where the witch in Burns's famous narrative poem, *Tam O' Shanter,* catches hold of Tam's mare's tail. Spooky-looking Auld Alloway Kirk, a ruin even in Burns's day, has an empty window through which Tam sees "Warlocks and Witches in a dance." Burns's father lies in Auld Alloway Kirkyard.

The Land O' Burns Centre has leaflets about a Burns Heritage Trail you can follow through two counties. A week-long Robert Burns Festival held every June in the Ayrshire district is administered from Alloway and includes music, poetry, exhibitions, dinners, and dances.

Back in Ayr, the Tam O' Shanter Museum on High St. was once a brewery to which Douglas Graham of Shanter (the real-life Tam) supplied the malted grain. Also to be seen in this busy dairy farmers' market town are its large harbor; the thirteenth-century Tower of St. John at Citadel Place; the fifteenth-century Auld Brig over the River Ayr; the sixteenth-century Loudon Hall, house of the hereditary sheriffs of Ayrshire, in Boat Vennel; and the seventeenth-century Auld Kirk built by Cromwell, where Burns was baptised, just off the High St. Ayr is celebrated too for its racetrack on Whitletts Rd., and its panoramic beach with a view of the Isle of Arran. Belleisle Park on the south side has a zoo, nature trail, lush gardens, and a championship golf course.

CHECKING IN: *Belleisle House* – An aristocrat's home before it became a hotel, this delightful place with 18 bedrooms retains such personal embellishments as engraved fireplaces. Elegant Taste of Scotland dishes are available. (Inside Belleisle Park grounds on Doonfoot Rd.; phone: 42331; moderate.) *The Pickwick Hotel* – This is one of the best of a seafront string of Victorian villas specializing in pure malt whiskies and Taste of Scotland foods. It has 15 bedrooms, each with a bath. (19 Racecourse Rd.; phone: 265990; moderate.)

En Route – Actually a continuation of Ayr, Prestwick is Scotland's main transatlantic airport. It also has a fine beach and a rather whimsical championship golf course, where the first-ever Open was played in 1860. *Adamton Courte,* an eighteenth-century castle of modest size, offers medieval banquets on weekends. It's located off the main road around Monkton, just north of Prestwick (phone: 70696; moderate).

Take the A77 from Monkton to Kilmarnock, a city in the heart of industrial West Scotland; from here to Glasgow are factories and smelting works, coalfields, and railroads. Burns's first poems were published in Kilmarnock; a Burns monument in Kay Park has good views of the surrounding countryside, and the Kay Park Museum has stacks of important Burnsiana including a large library. Museum open afternoons daily May through September; weekends only October through April. Also in Kilmarnock are Deen Castle, on Deen Rd., containing a fine collection of European arms and armor, as well as early musical instruments (open mid-May to mid-September only); and the Dick Institute, on Elmbank Ave., with archaeological exhibits, including fossils of international importance (closed weekends).

CHECKING IN: *Chapeltoun House Hotel* – A new antique-style cocktail bar in this posh early-twentieth-century mansion matches the original paneling. There are 5 bedrooms. Wonderful food is produced by the marriage (literally) of the chefs, who met in France at a Cordon Bleu cookery course. (On the A735 through Stewarton, 8 miles north of Kilmarnock; phone: 82696; expensive.)

Scottish Highlands

The Highlands of Scotland: The very words evoke romantic visions of hill and glen, bagpipe and drum, purple heather and curling mist. But behind the picture-postcard Highlands of every visitor from Queen Victoria to Pope John Paul II is a real Highlands that, though scenically among the most glorious places on earth, was for centuries a land of harsh living conditions, brutal internecine clan warfare, and rank exploitation by aristocratic power. It is a kind of divine wilderness suffering from depopulation even today.

That however only makes it more attractive to travelers, who can still steal a march on Paradise for two weeks or three in a Highland hotel away from the grime and confusion of modern city life. Just driving through the mountains, with their ancient Gaelic names *(Beinn Nevis, Beinn Bheag, Beinn à Chrulaiste)* and their plethora of interlinking waterways, is a soul-binding experience. Even better is to get out and walk — hillwalking, as it's called (it's really mountain climbing) is one of the great Scots pastimes; or just stroll down the glens and look up! If you do climb make sure you have a compass, warm clothes, and the right sort of boots. (You'll have a foot in everything from bogs to "scree," that is, loose slaty rubble.) And beware of hidden treacheries: A hike to a seemingly low peak from a warm sunlit valley could precipitate you suddenly into snow, thick fog, and a loss of your sense of direction. Every year people die on Scottish mountains from lack of knowledge, equipment, and judgment.

Historically, where the Lowlands came under English, French, Norman, and Scandinavian influence, the Highlands were dominated by the Irish, so that a true Highlander, one with Celtic blood, is very like his cousins in the Emerald Isle (always excepting Dublin). He is socially conservative, community conscious, and hostile to cosmopolitan ideas. He is courteously hospitable and as a rule no longer speaks Gaelic, but an English of old-fashioned phrasing. While Lowlanders got on with the business of urbanization, farming, trading, and general moneymaking in the seventeenth and eighteenth centuries, Highlanders remained cut off, nomadic, warlike, and idealistic. Loyalty to clan chiefs held good almost to a man. Cattle rustling, raiding, and feuds were rife. A Highlander's home, a bleakly appointed thatched-roofed stone cottage called a "black house," contained only one room — with a smoky fire on an earthen floor in its middle and wooden shelves for beds — and one stable, joined to family quarters by a large and gaping doorway.

Religion in the Highlands was, as the historian and essayist T. B. Macaulay put it, "a rude mixture of Popery and paganism." But after the Glorious Revolution of 1688–89 (by which the Roman Catholic James II was deposed from the British throne in favor of Protestants William and Mary), Episcopalianism and Presbyterianism both began to penetrate behind the Plaid

Curtain. The powerful Clan Campbell, dukes of Argyll, became Presbyterians and others followed, especially during the late eighteenth century, when Episcopalianism in its turn declined. For 3 centuries from 1700 a series of schisms rocked Presbyterian Highland Scotland, throwing up movements faster than people could count them and leaving large parts of the West Highlands today under the rod of the archaic sect, the "Wee Frees." A Wee Free Sabbath makes an ordinary Lowland Sunday look like a chapter in the life of Sodom and Gomorrah, so if you're anywhere west of Inverness on the Day of Rest, don't try to buy anything, including gasoline. Nor will it do you any harm to walk funereally, wear black, and make sure the proprietor of your chosen hotel sees you in church.

Not only religious but social shake-ups in the Highlands occurred on a massive scale. The late eighteenth and early nineteenth centuries saw the Clearances, the cruelly inhuman spectacle of landowners driving tenants from their homes in order to replace them with sheep, financially a more profitable venture. Thousands of Highlanders teemed south into Glasgow's slums and points more distant, never to return. Next came the era of the deer park, when a coterie of London-based aristocrats, the 7% of the Scottish population who owned 84% of the land, evicted another wave of Highlanders in order to create holiday playgrounds in the shape of private shooting and fishing preserves. Queen Victoria's love affair with her Highland castle at Balmoral inadvertently provided these plunderers with a fashionable impetus. Now the Highlands are undergoing another change: The Highlands and Islands Development Board, seeking to lure tourists and to take advantage of the North Sea oil boom that began in the early 1970s, has aided new wealth in parts of the Highlands but has increased the isolation of other parts, especially where fishing has suffered from oil operations or railway lines have been cut.

Customs and preoccupations that would long ago have vanished in less remote districts continue in the Highlands and these form no small part of Scotland's tourist delights. Apart from obvious examples such as kilt-wearing, bagpiping, and the drinking of pure malt whiskies tasting of smoked peat (*never* water them!), there are Highland games (contests of strength featuring such marathon events as "tossing the caber" — a caber is a full-grown de-branched tree); the National Mod (Scotland's peripatetic annual orgy of Gaeldom in which Gaelic singers and reciters compete for prizes — the Scottish Eisteddfod) and other folk and musical happenings; and "Nessie-Watching" (a sport begun by St. Columba of Iona, the sixth-century Christianizer of Scotland, who sighted a prehistoric monster in Loch Ness's mysterious deep).

Battlefields, too, are a big draw, not only for tourists but for a number of Scots in whose minds antiquity's shroud has never fallen across the annals of history. The Scottish National Party, still hoping for total severance from England, makes a yearly pilgrimage to Bannockburn where, in 1314, Robert the Bruce, Scotland's king from 1306 to 1329, definitively routed the invading army of England's King Edward II in one of the world's most dazzling and crucial military victories. Culloden Moor, near Inverness, is another focal point. Here Jacobitism, primarily a Highland movement seeking to restore the Stuart descendants of King James VI and I to the British throne, met a dire end in 1746 at the hands of the duke of Cumberland, second son of the

Hanoverian king George II. Whole clans were wiped out under the inadequate generalship of "Bonnie" Prince Charles Edward Stuart, the Jacobite royal heir, who fled in defeat to France whence he had come. All signs of Highland culture, including the kilt and the Gaelic language, were proscribed for a long time afterward, and the Culloden legend swelled the characteristic ethereal glooms of Celtic composers and poets in both Scotland and Ireland for generations.

This tour route begins at Stirling, "Gateway to the Highlands," and leads north through Glencoe, Fort William, and the "Great Glen" by Loch Ness to Inverness, a distance of some 160 miles. Two outings from Inverness are also suggested: one to Gairloch on the Wester Ross Atlantic seaboard, one to Balmoral at Braemar along Royal Deeside. As when touring the Lowlands, book hotels in advance from May through September; keep sandwiches in your car and be opportunistic about petrol pumps, which are harder to find than Brigadoon! Remote areas have paved-over cattle tracks as roads — if you meet a vehicle head on you'll have to back into one of the lay-bys provided at several-hundred-yard intervals. Carry the Scottish Tourist Board's *Enjoy Scotland* road map, which shows information centers, picnic tables, and woodland and nature trails in abundance. Hotels listed as expensive will charge $80 to $85 and up for bed and breakfast for two; moderate ones, from $60 to $80; and inexpensive ones, from $45 to $60. A meal for two in an expensive restaurant will cost $50 or more; in a moderate one, $30 to $50; in an inexpensive one, less than $30.

STIRLING: Like Edinburgh, Stirling began on an exalted crag and spread out downward; unlike Edinburgh, it failed to develop points of interest outside its ancient zones. You should zero in on Stirling Hill where you'll find Stirling Castle garnished by a subsidiary handful of aged buildings and intriguing ruins. The castle is the most famous in Scottish history, not only for its dramatic 250-foot drop to Stirling Plain and its eye-boggling view, but also for its strategic position controlling lands to the north during the Middle Ages, its associations with Robert the Bruce and his predecessor, William Wallace, and its magnificent Renaissance architecture, lavishly elaborated during its heyday as one of the four royal residences of the Stuart kings. Representations of Baccanalian-looking characters such as Love and Lust on the facade, the work of stonemasons from France employed by Mary of Guise, wife of James V, have been confused (but not obliterated) by centuries of irate Presbyterian rains. A guidebook bought at the castle entrance will heighten your enjoyment of the towers built by James III, the fine fifteenth-century hall, James V's palace, the Parliament Hall, the Chapel Royal of 1594, and the Argyll and Sutherland Highlanders' Regimental Museum (this prestigious company was quartered in Stirling Castle from 1850 until its partial disbandment in 1962). The Landmark Visitor Centre on the castle esplanade revives Stirling's past through an imaginative picture gallery and multiscreen show (there's a bookshop, crafts shop, and tea garden, too).

Mar's Wark, beside the castle, was built in about 1570 by the first earl of Mar, Regent of Scotland, and was the home of his descendants until 1715, when the sixth earl had to flee the country after leading an unsuccessful major Jacobite rebellion. It became a barracks, then a workhouse (hence its name). Bonnie Prince Charlie's army sacked and ruined it in 1746, but some of its exquisite embellishments remain. Also by the castle are the still-used Church of the Holy Rude, dating from 1414, where John Knox preached the sermon when James VI, aged 13 months, was crowned (open daily May through September); the Guildhall, south of the church, founded in 1639 by the then

Deal of Guild for the support of twelve "decayed Guild Breithers"; and the impressive seventeenth-century town house, Argyll's Lodging, now a youth hostel but once the residence of Sir William Alexander of Menstrie, the founder of Nova Scotia. An exhibition displaying the coats of arms of 107 Nova Scotian baronetcies is at sixteenth-century Menstrie Castle, Sir William's birthplace 5 miles to the east on the A91 (open 2:30 to 5:00 PM Wednesdays and weekends May through September). Cambuskenneth Abbey, on the River Forth a mile northeast of Stirling, was founded in the twelfth century by the Scottish king David I, and was the scene in 1326 of King Robert the Bruce's first formal Parliament. The church and conventual buildings are rubble but a detached 67-foot thirteenth-century bell tower survives intact.

The Scottish Wars of Independence, which took place in the years around the turn of the thirteenth century, were distinguished for the valor not only of the aristocrat King Robert the Bruce ("Robert de Brus" in his native Norman tongue) but also of William Wallace, the People's Hero, who drove back an English army in 1297 at the Battle of Stirling Bridge, a mile north of the castle. Wallace's control over Scotland was short-lived — he was defeated at Falkirk in 1298 by a massive avenging force, imprisoned in London, and hacked limb from limb in 1305 — but his memory is sacred in Scottish hearts. The grandly towering Wallace Monument near the site of his triumph (off Hillfoots Rd., 1.5 miles north-northeastward of town) is a famous landmark, erected in 1861. Inside, the Stirling District Council offers an audiovisual historical crash course. Views are heavenly from its 220-foot top.

Bannockburn, off the M80 just south of Stirling, is a must. Beside the Battlefield is a film theater where you can catch up with the full story of the Wars of Independence (open mid-spring to September 30). Bruce was not eager to fight the English at the time and place now so famous for his victory, but his hand had been forced by his brother, who made a deal in 1313 with the governor of Stirling Castle — in English hands since soon after the defeat of Wallace — securing the castle's return to Scotland if the English did not relieve it by St. John the Baptist's Day (Midsummer Day) of the following year (the Bruces had the castle under siege). On Midsummer Day, 1314, 20,000 English troops, commanded by King Edward II himself, marched on the castle. Bruce's tactics were brilliant: He let the English come within 2 hair-raising miles of the target and then attacked — on the only piece of ground in the English route north where his mere 5,500 spearmen could hope to hold out — at first light, before the king's cavalry could see to charge. Finding themselves cut off to left and right by unexpected and treacherous marshes, Edward's stalwarts fell back in confusion and flight. A magnificent 20-foot-high equestrian statue of Robert the Bruce in shining armor, unveiled by Queen Elizabeth on the battle's 650th anniversary, stands today on the spot reputed to have been the Scottish royal headquarters during the fighting.

Also to be seen in Stirling are its old Mercat Cross and its eighteenth-century tollbooth, on Broad St.; the bastion, or jail, within the original fortified town wall, just inside the Port St. entrance to the Thistle Shopping Centre; the fifteenth-century Auld Brig still used by pedestrians at Stirling Bridge (north of city center off the A9); and the Smith Art Gallery and Museum on Albert Pl., housing, among other treasures, objects from early local history. The MacRobert Arts Centre, one of Scotland's foremost music, film, and theater venues, is located on the grounds of Stirling University off the A9, 2 miles north of town. During the Stirling District Festival, held around the last week of May and first week of June, the center hosts Scottish dancing and other ethnic events while nearby great houses are used as concert halls. The Stirling Gallery, 7 Baker St., sells crafts and modern paintings.

CHECKING IN: *Royal Hotel* – Robert Louis Stevenson stayed in this impressive 32-bedroom mansion house as a boy, when his family visited the nearby spa. Its Taste of Scotland menu is much in local demand. (Henderson St. in the town of Bridge of Allan, 4 miles north of Stirling; phone: 832284; moderate.) ***The***

Golden Lion – Though now clinging for dear life to its immaculate historic pedigree, this 75-room hotel is nonetheless the best of Stirling's lately rather dubious center-city bets. Robert Burns, the royal family, Billy Graham, and a host of film stars have all stayed here. (8 King St., Stirling; phone: 5351; moderate to inexpensive.) **King's Gate Hotel** – Decorated like a house, the pleasant, down-to-earth atmosphere of this individualistic 15-room establishment takes its cue from the mounted zebra skins brought from East Africa by the proprietors. The food is cheap and good. (5 King St., Stirling; phone: 3944; inexpensive.)

EATING OUT: *The Lion and the Unicorn* – Dinner at this tiny, old-fashioned country inn (it has 4 bedrooms) is worth the 9-mile run from town. (Main St., Thornhill — take the A84 followed by the A873 northwest from Stirling; phone: 204; inexpensive.)

En Route – Take the A84 northwest. Between Stirling and Doune is Blair Drummond African Safari Park, full of free-roaming wild animals. Performing seals and parrots are an added attraction in summer (open from mid-March to the end of October only; £4.10 per car).

DOUNE: The dark fastnesses of fourteenth-century Doune Castle, ancestral seat of the earls of Moray, have lasted unscathed. Not so some of its owners: the "Bonnie Earl" of Moray, who was the "Queen's love" in the famous murder ballad (actually he was her nephew; the queen was Mary Queen of Scots), was killed by the earl of Huntly in a clan feud in 1592. Doune Castle is beautifully set in a wooded clearing at the junction of the Teith and Ardoch rivers, approached just south of Doune village by a side road off the A84 (open April through October only; closed Thursdays in April and October). Monty Python and his Flying Circus filmed *The Holy Grail* here.

Doune village has a sixteenth-century bridge, built originally by James IV's tailor to spite a ferryman who had refused him passage. A mile north of the village is the Doune Motor Museum, showing off the present earl of Moray's collection of vintage cars; next door are the resplendent 60-acre Doune Park Gardens (both are open April through October).

CALLANDER: A very long street with mountains to either side, this bustling gateway to Sir Walter Scott's beloved Trossachs, the "bristly country," just misses being a typical Highland town — the Teith flows through it too complacently for that, and its fields are too prosperously green. In former times it was a cattle drovers' stopping-place. If you give a day's notice to John Virando, proprietor of the *Callander Pottery*, 120 Main St. (phone: 30487), you can watch him hand-throw pots and decorate them.

CHECKING IN: *Roman Camp Hotel* – Peacocks on the lawn and lordly old-world hospitality are keynotes here. There are 15 bedrooms and the excellent Taste of Scotland dishes include beef, salmon, and venison. Closed November through March. (Off Main St., Callander; phone: 30003; expensive to moderate.) **Auchendoune** – This lovely private home full of antique furniture has a breathtaking view of Doune Castle and the Doune valley. Your hosts will make you feel like one of the family, serving American waffles for breakfast. (On the A84 at Doune's southern boundary — look for the Scottish flag flying from the roof; phone: 217; inexpensive.) **Dreadnought Hotel** – A crowning jewel adorning an almost uninterrupted fan of hostelries, this well-appointed 69-bedroom affair was built during the tourist boom in the early nineteenth century. It has since acquired modern private baths and official Taste of Scotland status. (Main St., Callander; phone: 30184; inexpensive.)

En Route – The A84 leads north of Callander through the Pass of Leny, noted for its waterfall, dwarfed oaks, and wild primroses. Four miles north of town, 2,875-foot Ben Ledi (Hill of God), overlooking Loch Lubnaig, is an easily manageable, highly rewarding 3.5-hour climb. The road skirts the edge of the lake to the picturesque hamlet of Strathyre, once a crofting settlement. Rob Roy's Grave is located along an unnamed side road turning west 2 miles farther north. The fabled outlaw lies in a setting of seraphic peace in the Macgregor family plot in Balquhidder Churchyard, beneath the lovely Braes of Balquhidder at the head of Loch Voil. The church itself contains an eighth-century carved tombstone and some old Gaelic bibles.

LOCHEARNHEAD: Famous throughout Scotland for its water skiing facilities, this resort on the west shore of Loch Earn is also an excellent spot for boating. *Lochearnhead Water Sports Center* and *Clachan Cottage Marina,* beside the lake on the A85, will cater to your sporting needs. *Bran Clay Pottery,* on the main road through town, has a workshop and showroom open daily from Easter through October. The road around Loch Earn makes a pleasant 10-mile detour, including views of two aristocrat-owned, fairy-tale mansions on the south shore. In July, Lochearnhead hosts the Balquhidder-Lochearnhead-Strathyre Highland Games.

CHECKING IN: *Clachan Cottage Hotel* – This row of white one-story cottages, halfway up a hill, winks at Loch Earn with its prettily lamp-lighted windows. There are 33 bedrooms. (On the A85 along the loch's north shore; phone: 247; inexpensive.) *Lochearnhead Hotel* – An atmospheric bar with natural stone nooks plus decorative armories and leather enhances this 42-room period piece. The splendid cooking includes Taste of Scotland selections. (On the A84 through Lochearnhead; phone: 237; moderate to inexpensive.) *Kingshouse Hotel* – Once the hunting abode of the "Bonnie Earl" of Moray, this small white edifice with 9 bedrooms outdoes most exponents of Highland decor with its tartans, oil paintings, stuffed stags' heads, and pheasants. The bar attracts "shepherds and gamekeepers" and there's a crafts shop in the byre. (On the A84, 2 miles north of Strathyre; phone: 646; inexpensive.)

EATING OUT: *Ledcreich Hotel* – Much patronized by surrounding districts, this captivating 4-bedroom country lodge is famous for its dinners, served en casserole in the manner of the provincial French. The restaurant, converted from a stable, has candlelight, red Regency chairs, and old wooden ceiling beams. Reservations. (On the north side of Loch Voil, 2 miles west of Balquhidder village; phone: 230; expensive.)

En Route – Glen Ogle, on the A85 immediately to the north of Lochearnhead, is a gloomy mountain pass with towering rock masses to left and right. It leads to Glen Dochart, once a place of ruthless bloodletting among the clans Campbell, Macnab, Macgregor, and Maclaren. Crianlarich, located in a pretty, tree-speckled hollow in an otherwise austere territory, is more a crossroads than a village: It fuses two routes north, one from Stirling and one from Loch Lomond. The road above it leading to Tyndrum (the A82) is the King's Road of 200 years ago — widened and paved over, of course! — linking Stirling Castle and Fort William. It was at Tyndrum that Robert the Bruce barely escaped with his life 8 years before the Battle of Bannockburn when he was ambushed by his enemies, the Clan Macdougall. (The Macdougalls still have the pearl-and-crystal brooch he lost in the struggle.) North of Tyndrum, in the vicinity of Bridge of Orchy, the cone-shaped wonder on your right is Beinn Dorain, a subject of praise in Gaelic poetry. Just to the north on the shore of Loch Tulla is a smattering of ancient trees, once part of the medieval Caledonian Forest. The road hits the barren edge of Rannoch Moor before bearing west to Glencoe.

GLENCOE: More famous than any city, town, or village for miles around, this most portentous and claustrophobic of glens was the scene, in 1692, of the massacre of the Clan Macdonald by the Clan Campbell. The Campbells were guests of the Macdonalds and murdered their hosts — on orders from King William III, to whom the Macdonalds had failed to pledge allegiance — in their beds. The horrible double-dealing nature of the deed has set it apart from the run-of-the-mill massacres, and if your name is Campbell, you'd better sign into Glencoe hotels under a false one, or you may be tarred, feathered, and run out of town on a *skean dhu* (the dagger a Highlander wears in the top of his sock).

Bald mountains on both sides of the glen make modern Glencoe a haunt of hillwalkers and skiers. The view from the top of the ski runs (there's a chair lift) is terrific — in spring anyway, when the clouds that usually sulk over the scenery disperse (skiing is available on weekends, New Year's, and Easter only). Popular foot-trails and climbs — some too tough for amateurs — are on your *Enjoy Scotland* map; beside them are the romantic names of topographical features such as Ossian's Cave, the Devil's Staircase, and Signal Rock (from which went forth the signal for the massacre). Wildcats, golden eagles, deer, and ptarmigans patrol the upper reaches of Glencoe's pinnacled heights. A visitor center giving geographical information is on the A82 (open mid-April to mid-October) and the Glencoe and North Lorn Folk Museum, containing historic relics and antique local domestic implements, is at the end of the glen beside Loch Leven (open May through September).

CHECKING IN: *Clachaig Inn* – Dramatically set in a deep rocky gorge, this 10-bedroom climbers' retreat has long been a Glencoe landmark. Its friendly, colossal public bar is a garrulous sea of beards and boots. (On the unmarked road north of the River Coe near Signal Rock; phone: 252; inexpensive.) *The King's House* – A medieval hunting lodge that became a barracks and later a staging post, this venerable octopus with sprawling public rooms and 22 bedchambers today harbors skiers (the Glencoe chair lift is just across the road). (On the A82 at Glencoe's east head; phone: 259; inexpensive.)

En Route – Until very recently, the small village of Ballachulish at the west head of Glencoe was a port for ferries crossing Loch Leven to North Ballachulish. It now boasts a bridge which, like the ferry, saves travelers bound for Fort William the long detour around the lake. At Onich, views across Loch Linnhe, a sea arm of the Firth of Lorn, are exceptionally stunning — Loch Linnhe stretches 32.5 miles from Fort William south to the Sound of Mull, encompassing the Hebridean island of Lismore. From Ballachulish and Onich northward, the route follows the Great Glen, an extraordinary 66-mile geographical fault that slices Scotland diagonally in two and leads all the way to Inverness.

FORT WILLIAM: A stone fort erected to quell unrest among turbulent Highlanders marked this site from the time of William of Orange until 1864. Then the fort was demolished to make way for a railroad, and the town you see here mushroomed up around the newly laid tracks. Fort William today is a hub not only for tourists but for campers, youth hostelers, conference-goers, and climbers. Snow-trimmed Ben Nevis (4,408 feet), Scotland's highest mountain, looms nearby looking (somewhat disappointingly) like a megalithic iced bun. Below it is the glen of the same name — narrow, lush, overpowered by the rocky monarchs of the mighty Mamore range.

The West Highland Museum in Cameron Square stockpiles objects that once belonged to Bonnie Prince Charlie, including his breeks and a lock of his hair. There's an antique "secret portrait" in which a smeared half-moon of paint turns into his likeness when viewed through a special cylinder (closed Sundays). The A82 just north of Fort William brings you to Old Inverlochy Castle, a thirteenth-century ruin with soaring circular towers. Also just above town, on the A830, the eight locks of Neptune's Staircase are a remarkable feat of engineering. Constructed between 1805 and 1822, they raise barges a total of 64 feet at the entrance to Thomas Telford's famed Caledonian Canal linking Loch Linnhe, Loch Lochy, Loch Oich, and Loch Ness.

644 DIRECTIONS / Scottish Highlands

For the most fun of all, take "Concrete Bob" McAlpine's 42-mile (84 miles round trip) scenic railway, parallel to the "Road to the Isles" (the A830, which you can also do — as a detour — by car) between Fort William and the Atlantic port of Mallaig opposite the Isle of Skye. The route, administered by British Rail ("Concrete Bob" was its builder), crosses the Caledonian Canal by a swing bridge, passes Loch Eil buttressed by 17 sea walls, and swoops above the Glenfinnan Monument at the head of Loch Shiel on a curving white viaduct of 21 pillared arches 100 feet high! The Glenfinnan Monument stands where Bonnie Prince Charlie unfurled the Jacobite flag to a roll of drums in 1745. If you have your own transportation, you can catch up on the Bonnie Prince's career at the Glenfinnan Monument Visitor Centre, open Good Friday to mid-October. The famous sands at Morar just before you reach Mallaig are so silvery they look as if they've been lifted wholesale from beside the Indian Ocean.

CHECKING IN: *Alexandra Hotel* – This attractive alternative to Fort William's chronic chromium blight has 89 bedrooms, red carpets, an open fire in the drawing room, and plain beige walls hung with paintings. The dining room is known for its English breakfasts. (Opposite the station, Fort William; phone: 2241; moderate.) ***The Moorings*** – Set on Loch Eil near the tiny papermill town of Corpach (the best place from which to view Ben Nevis), this delightful stone dwelling has 16 bedrooms and good Taste of Scotland home cooking by resident proprietors. (On the B8004 off the A830 near Neptune's Staircase; phone: 550; moderate to inexpensive.)

EATING OUT: *Inverlochy Castle* – Thought by many to contain the finest restaurant in Britain, this opulently furnished nineteenth-century mansion has 13 bedrooms, castellated wings and turrets, painted ceilings, and vulcanic blazes in huge marble fireplaces. Delicacies such as game pâté and spinach soup are exquisite curtain raisers for the ravishing entrées. Closed November to Easter. Reservations. (On the A82 just north of Fort William; phone: 2177; expensive.) ***Stag's Head Hotel*** – Bar lunches here are a knockout; for a couple of pounds you can get roast haunch of venison in port sauce or fresh salmon salad. There's a restaurant too with elegant dark oak furniture, and a drying-room for rain-drenched climbers' gear. Bedrooms total 41. (High St., Fort William; phone: 4144; moderate to inexpensive.)

En Route – Spean Bridge is 10 miles northeast of Fort William on A82. An impressive Commando Memorial, erected in 1952 just north of the bridge over the cauldronlike River Spean, honors World War II commandos who trained in this area. A 9-mile detour east (18 miles round trip) by the A86 and then the first left takes you to that geologists' dream, the Parallel Roads, a group of evenly graduated earthen terraces marking levels of lakes dammed by Ice Age glaciers. There's nothing quite like them in all of Europe. Return to the A82 and continue north through Invergarry, where the River Garry meets Loch Oich and where *Garry Crafts* produces and sells handmade gifts (open Monday through Saturdays, with specially arranged talks on summer evenings). A 20-mile civilization-haters' detour (40 miles round trip) at Invergarry — onto the A87 followed by the unmarked road to your left — fetches you up on the wildest, most untrammeled corner of Scotland, the shores of Loch Hourn (Lake of Hell), along a road thick with wild deer.

CHECKING IN: *Invergarry Hotel* – The pretty parlors and cheerful log fires at this stunning 15-bedroom inn are widely renowned. Newly culled local produce graces its tables. Dinner and breakfast both come with the price of your room. (On the A82, Invergarry; phone: 206; moderate.)

FORT AUGUSTUS: This fishermen's paradise at the base of Loch Ness will give you your first glimpse of the world-famous 22-mile waterway; while the Great Glen Exhibition, a museum by the Caledonian Canal in the center of town, has an audiovisual historical show to acquaint you with the monster (open June to mid-September only).

The fort that gave rise to the town was established (1730) on the site of a barracks set up after the 1715 Jacobite rising and was named after William Augustus, the son of King George II, who later erased Jacobitism forever at Culloden. Ironically, one of the fort's Protestant walls eventually became part of Fort Augustus Abbey, a lavishly designed Benedictine priory and school (on the main road) begun in 1876. The present community of monks gives guided tours of the abbey five times a day.

DRUMNADROCHIT: The A82 continues north along the edge of Loch Ness to this attractive hamlet at the head of Glen Urquhart. The ruins of pre-fourteenth-century Urquhart Castle, one of the largest in Scotland until it was blown up by Williamite forces in 1692, can be seen jutting into the water just south of the village. This is the point from which "Nessie" has most often been seen: Waters here are deeper than the North Sea and perfect for prehistoric inhabitors, but hunts by midget submarine, tungsten TV lamp, strobe light, time-lapse camera, and SX70 Polaroid have so far proven nothing.

Pony trekkers at Drumnadrochit should apply to the *Highland Riding Centre,* Borlum Farm (phone: 220); there's a plethora of beautiful glens nearby to be explored, gentler than the ones farther south. Glen Urquhart holds Corrimony Cairn, a neolithic structure with a circle of standing stones. The glens can be toured by car, too — consult your *Enjoy Scotland* map, which prints their names next to the roads that serve them.

CHECKING IN: *Drumnadrochit Hotel and Motor Inn* – A revamped Victorian hostelry with extensive contemporary additions, this popular 46-room resort has sailing facilities, take-away picnics (by arrangement), and a superb Loch Ness Monster exhibition (open also to nonresidents). (On the A82, Drumnadrochit center; phone: 218; moderate.) *Inchnacardoch Lodge* – Fishing, sailing, and water skiing are organized from this charming 17-bedroom country mansion house still retaining its original paneling. The tasty cooking is unwaveringly Scottish. (On Loch Ness off the A82 a mile north of Fort Augustus; phone: 6258; inexpensive.)

INVERNESS: Despite its flat location — a shock after previous scenic grandeurs — and the Plain Jane look of its streets, the "Capital of the Highlands" is an exhilarating place to be. It has a population of 32,000 and is the commercial and administrative hub of a vast surrounding region, overseen by the Highlands and Islands Development Board, which is stationed here. The River Ness winds a courtly path through the city's center beside high-spired churches, and the sun never quite goes down in midsummer, but bathes the shining water in an exquisitely lyric gold half-light.

Civilization is very old at Inverness, dating from at least as far back as the fourth century BC. Pictish kings ruled from here; it was for here that St. Columba of Iona was making, to convert King Brudei, when in 565 he spied the Loch Ness Monster. In the twelfth century, Inverness became a Royal Burgh under the patronage of King David I, who erected a castle on Castlehill. Jacobites sacked this castle in 1745 but it was eventually replaced by the present lovely pink one, housing the City Sheriff Court.

Not much remains of the Inverness of yore, though an amble down Church Street takes you past Dunbar's Hospital of 1668, the old High Church of 1772 (it has an earlier tower and spire), and the Steeple of 1791. Queen Mary's House on Bridge Street, now unrecognizably changed, is where Mary Queen of Scots stayed when she visited Inverness in 1562. A clock tower on Ness bank is all that's left of Oliver Cromwell's "Pentagon" (a 5-sided fort blown up at the time of the Restoration); but the Gothic Town House on High St. where Lloyd George and his cabinet met to discuss the 1921 Irish Treaty is alive and well. A minor nugget of preserved Victoriana is the area comprising Union Street, Queensgate, Station Square, and the adjacent part of Academy St. Tomnahurich Cemetery, on a cyprus ridge above the river, has a delightful view that contributes to its fame as the handsomest graveyard in Scotland.

But Inverness's best sights aren't urban. Culloden Battlefield, with its clan graves,

Well of the Dead, Memorial Cairn, and Old Leanach Farmhouse (a small war museum), lies 5 miles outside town on the B9006. Bonnie Prince Charlie's mournful fiasco here in 1746 was the last land battle on British soil. (For a guided tour of Culloden Battlefield, call 790607.) Near Culloden are the Clava Cairns, an extensive group of Bronze Age standing stones and graves. Cawdor Castle, the seat of the Thanes of Cawdor for 600 years, is 13 miles northeast of Inverness on the B9090. Within its walls, according to Shakespeare, Macbeth stabbed King Duncan. The castle has everything: a drawbridge, a tower built around a tree, a freshwater well inside the house; gardens, nature trails, a pitch-and-putt course; a picnic area, snack bar, licensed restaurant, and gift shop (castle and grounds open May through September only). Nearby, on the B9006 is Fort George, begun in 1748 to prevent another Jacobite rebellion. It's one of the finest late artillery bastions in Europe. Adjacent is the Regimental Museum of the Queen's Own Highlanders. The 7-foot Boar Stone at Knocknagael, 2 miles south of Inverness on the B861, is a striking, pig-decked ancient carved slab; equally hoary is the vitrified fort along the Craig Phadrick Forest Trail off the A9 to Inverness's west.

Throughout the year the Inverness Museum and Art Gallery in Castle Wynd mounts a dazzling barrage of learned lectures and special exhibitions; it also has a permanent display of Highland silver from the seventeenth century on, and a large natural history wing. Of utmost importance to local cultural life is the Eden Court Theatre on Bishop's Rd., opened in 1976. Designed with contemporary panache around part of an old ecclesiastical palace, its glass-gabled anterooms look out on the river while its high-walled auditorium hosts everything from ballet, opera, symphonic recitals, drama, films, and pop and rock concerts to *ceilidhs*. Abertarff House on Church St., the oldest building in town, has an illustrated history of Scottish Gaels from Iron Age Europe to the present day (closed Sundays).

Bught Park, off Glenurquhart Rd., is the rendezvous in summer for colorful Highland play-offs such as the MacTavish Cup Final North-of-Scotland Shinty Championships, the Highland Tug of War Championships, and the Inverness Highland Games. Northern Meeting Park on Ardross St. is the scene of summer tattoos, tartan shows for tourists, and piping competitions. From mid-May to mid-September a "Welcome Piper" struts his stuff on Castlehill, and to top all this there's a Music Festival and a Folk Festival in spring. You can pick up a comprehensive activities sheet at the tourist board office on Church St.

Cruises down Loch Ness on the *MV Scott II* (phone: 33140) and the *Jacobite Lady* (phone: 33999) operate from mid-April to September; and the breathtaking 3-hour train trip from Inverness south to Kyle of Lochalsh has been on BBC Television's "Great Railway Journeys of the World." *Holm Woollen Mills,* 1.5 miles outside town on Dores Rd., is owned by the famous Pringle Company and has tours as well as extensive showrooms.

CHECKING IN: *Culloden House Hotel* – Residents feel like kings in the light, spacious rooms of this beautiful eighteenth-century palace full of ornate plasterwork and priceless antique furniture. There are 21 bedchambers, carpets in the bathrooms, extensive park grounds, enchanting views, and a sauna. (On Culloden Moor; phone: 461; expensive.) *Station Hotel* – The comfortably plush Victorian grandeur of this central 63-room relic contradicts its scruffy exterior. The restaurant has good Taste of Scotland fare. (Academy St., Inverness; phone: 31926; expensive to moderate.) *Beaufort Hotel* – Half of Inverness is laid out before you at this glorious 21-bedroom hilltop mansion in a first-class residential area. All the charms of the past combine with private showers and color TVs. Enormous steaks are the chef's specialty. (11 Culduthel Rd., Inverness; phone: 222897; moderate.) *Caledonian Hotel* – This popular modern riverfront all-rounder zings inside with decorator colors. It has a bouncy local clientele, convivial staff, 120 bedrooms, a Laundromat, cabarets, and dancing. (Church St., Inverness; phone: 35181; moderate.) **Cummings Hotel** – The complete ordinariness of this 38-bedroom rectangle somehow manages to be endearing. Nightly Scottish cabarets here have been wowing audiences April through September for years. (Church St., Inverness; phone: 32531; moderate to inexpensive.) **Kingsmills Hotel** – Ten minutes walk from downtown, this striking white 200-year-old time capsule with its front door in an architraved turret has 54 bedrooms (some in recently built extensions), private squash courts, and 2 acres of gardens. (Culcabock Rd., Inverness; phone: 37166; expensive in summer, inexpensive in winter.)

EATING OUT: Dunain Park Hotel – Guests of this family-owned country house are treated to sumptuous breakfasts, snack lunches in the garden, teas with homemade jams, and outstanding, imaginatively prepared dinners. Nonresidents with the necessary reservation may partake of the latter — and if you insist on risking gout in this oasis with a hint of sniffy respectability, spend the week. There are six bedrooms. Closed December through February. (On the A82, 2.5 miles south of Inverness; phone: 30512; expensive.) **Dickens** – The decor in this fashionable midcity restaurant — a classic medley of browns and whites — is glossily smart. Its Chinese proprietors are equally adept at Chinese and European cooking. (77–79 Church St., Inverness; phone: 224450; moderate.)

Two possible mini-tours beyond Inverness will give you a taste of the amazing variations in typical Highland scenery — from the wild, rocky splendors and salty sea lochs of regions in the west to the heather-covered braes (hills), freshwater streams, and gentle pine forests of the Grampian Mountains in the east. Each is an approximately 150-mile round trip.

For the first, start out on the A9 west, switching to the A832 at Muir of Ord. This crossroads is at the southwest tip of Black Isle, a verdant peninsula full of whitewashed crofters' cottages between the Moray and Cromarty firths. Farther west, a detour via the A834 will take you to Strathpeffer, at its height as a fashionable spa in the late Victorian era. (The wedding cake architecture in the central square alone is worth the 6-mile round trip.) The A832 parallels the Inverness-Kyle of Lochalsh railway as far as Achnasheen, and a few miles beyond this romantic outpost is a sudden, spectacular view of Loch Maree, thought by many to be Scotland's loveliest lake. You'll skirt part of it later, just before the journey west ends at Gairloch in a triumph of scenic majesty opposite the Torridon peaks and the Outer Hebrides. Gair Loch, the sea inlet on which the village of Gairloch stands, is famous for sailing, deep-sea fishing and diving, and heavenly sand beaches. Six miles northeast, Poolewe is renowned throughout Britain for Inverewe Gardens, a sheltered subtropical spot where heather blooms with Himalayan lilies and huge South Pacific forget-me-nots. Flowers that survive only under glass at Kew Gardens in London grow here in the open air! There's an Inverewe Gardens Visitor Centre (open April to mid-October only).

The second mini-tour sets out on the A9 eastward, with the first stop at Tomatin by the River Findhorn for a demonstration of the process through which Uisge Beatha, "The Water of Life," comes into existence. Tours of the Tomatin Distillery take place at 3 PM on weekday afternoons and include a free sample of one of the 23 pure malt whiskies made in the Highlands east of Inverness (phone before you go: 234; closed first of July and August). Continue to the fun-loving Spey Valley town of Carrbridge, a microcosm of Scotland at leisure, bursting with anglers, skiers, climbers, ponytrekkers, and folk singers. The nearby Spey is one of Scotland's best salmon rivers, and the *Carrbridge Ski School* is a Strathspey legend. Do not, under any circumstances, bypass the Landmark Visitor Centre at Carrbridge, a parent of the Landmark at Stirling. It has a multiscreen theater, bookshop, crafts shop, bar, restaurant, nature trail, sculpture park, and picnic tables in a pine wood. Displays evoking Spey Valley through the ages are whimsically intriguing; they include the sound of artificial arctic winds, a hand quern in which you can grind your own oatmeal, and more. Live bagpipe and fiddle music rings out at Landmark on summer evenings.

Boat of Garten, where a ferry once whisked travelers across the River Spey, has a ski school, too, as well as considerable popularity with fishermen and an 18-hole golf course said to be a miniature Gleneagles. The Strathspey Railway offers a 6.5-mile journey to Aviemore (13 miles round trip) on a real-McCoy Victorian steam train on weekends from mid-May to mid-October and Mondays through Wednesdays during the summer months. (The holiday complex at Aviemore is a major winter sports center, with skating and curling rinks and several buses daily taking skiers to the nearby Cairngorm Mountain slopes during the November through April season.) Leaving Boat of Garten, an access road from the B970 carries you into Loch Garten Nature Reserve where you can watch those lordly fishhawks, the ospreys, back in Scotland after a long extinction. On the B970 beyond Nethybridge is thirteenth-century Castle Roy, a massive red ruin said to be the oldest castle in the country; an unclassified road east of Nethybridge eventually joins the A939 and leads on to Tomintoul, the highest village (1,160 feet) in the Highlands. Regally set on a ridge overlooking the glen of the River Avon and the vale of the Water of Conglass, Tomintoul has only one long street, but Scotland's largest collection of whiskies is in its shops. Between Tomintoul and Cock Bridge, the Lecht Pass road climbs to a height of over 2,000 feet across a seemingly trackless waste that looks like the surface of the moon.

The junction of the A939 with the A93 at Bridge of Gairn brings you finally to Royal Deeside, that magic valley of laughing water and soughing birch and pine, cosseted by blue hills. Crathie Church, where the Royal Family worships when staying at Balmoral Castle just across the River Dee, is a major sight here. The 11,000-acre Balmoral estate was bought by Prince Albert in 1852 and its existing castle was then widened for Queen Victoria to the present leviathan proportions. You can visit the castle ballroom (unless the Queen is in residence) daily except Sundays from May through July. A little farther along the A93 is Braemar, where Robert Louis Stevenson wrote *Treasure Island,* and another castle, Braemar Castle, a turreted seventeenth-century stronghold. *The* time of the year to drop into the festive little pocket of Braemar is the first Saturday in September, when the queen and 20,000 other people attend the 900-year-old Royal Highland Gathering (or Games) in the Princess Royal and Duke of Fife Memorial Park at Invercauld. Massed piped bands at the Braemer Games are the most sensational in all Scotland, and the number of local aristocratic mansions that disgorge their owners for the event — plus an international audience bent on wining and dining, mirth, and song — make it truly a Scottish day of days. Advance booking, a necessity, is possible from April 1. Write to the Bookings Secretary, Braemar Royal Highland Gathering, c/o Bank of Scotland, Braemar, Grampian, Scotland.

Scottish Islands

Scotland has 787 islands, including uninhabited stone dollops like Ailsa Craig and the Bass Rock (see the *Lowlands* route). These vary in size, topography, history, climate, racial mix, and ethos. Of the ones included here, however — Orkney and Shetland plus the Hebridean Arran, Skye, Harris, and Lewis — there are common denominators. All have a remote other-worldliness, a sense of infinite time; all but Arran reflect antiquity both in archaeological riches and in the natives' ardent stubborn tribalisms; all have vivid, unusual flora and fauna, colonies of seals, seabirds, and wildlife; all possess multicolored skies and magic, luminous air. All are sparsely populated. Winds can be incredible (a gale is recorded at the Butt of Lewis one day in every six) and on Shetland, Orkney, Harris, and Lewis there are almost no trees. Skye, Orkney, Arran, and Harris have fantastic gnomic rock formations, whipped perhaps from briny deeps by the gnarled wand of some primeval wizard. All but Arran and Orkney live by fishing and crofting, and all but Orkney and Shetland show a dangerous dependence on Highlands and Islands Development Board projects, and on tourism. So far tourists continue to roll in.

And not just tourists! Also drawn to the Islands are artists, craftsmen, poets, scholars, and dreamers, who set up shop in deserted thatched-roofed cottages and hag peat, write books, throw pots, and weave caftans. You'll have access to the wares of this entrepreneurial yeomanry as well as to Shetland sweaters and Harris tweeds. Don't miss reading the fascinating *West Highland Free Press,* a radical weekly published Fridays by immigrant intellectuals, from an old schoolhouse on Skye. Hugh MacDiarmid, the greatest Scottish poet of the twentieth century, lived for a time in Shetland; the composer Peter Maxwell Davies finds inspiration in the sounds around his Orkney home; Sorley Maclean, chief among contemporary bards of the Gaelic tongue, dwells in Skye. In addition to works by giants like these you should try a page or two by Orkney's delightful favorite sons, George Mackay Brown and Eric Linklater, and the Outer Hebrides's Compton Mackenzie (Mackenzie's novel *Whisky Galore* is especially delicious).

Two centuries of Viking invasions lasting from 800 to 1000 left all the islands under Norse control, linked with the also-vanquished city of Dublin and Isle of Man. In the Hebrides, Scottish Gaelic leadership gradually re-emerged though the Gaelic Lordship of the Isles was not absorbed into the Scottish crown until the reign of James IV. But Orkney and Shetland continued under Scandinavian occupation through the end of the Middle Ages. Their inhabitants today are still primarily Nordic; they keep up special friendship societies with Iceland and the Faroes, and surnames — a break from Scandinavian custom — have existed in Shetland only for the last 100 years. Orcadians and Shetlanders are a down-to-earth, straightforward people — Celtic Twilights and such mystiques have no place among them. Until recently they spoke Norn, a Viking dialect that has fostered a pleasing singsong quality in their English. Shetland fisherfolk employ many "haaf" words from Norn even now (there's a handy selection of 10 different nouns for "wind" and 19 for "sea").

The Western Isles preserve both the Highland culture now lost on the mainland (Gaelic is still spoken in parts of Harris, Lewis, and Skye) and the old-time Presbyterianism gone from the Lowlands. Many guesthouse owners eschew cooking, TV-watching, etc., on the Sabbath so mind when you wash your socks. A duality of the public and private man exists in the Hebrides, epitomized by areas that vote themselves dry before dotting the moors with illegal makeshift drinking *bothans* ("cabins"). The satiric tradition of the ancient Gaelic bards — in which verses were thought to wield witch-doctor-style curses — may have reinforced in Hebrideans their unquenchable love of invective; their mellifluous lilts promise Paradise but shoot wide of the mark, delivering the sentiments of hex-men in accents of angels.

Despite drawbacks like high prices, frequent wet weather, summer midges, and occasional roadside views of gargantuan rubbish dumps, the Scottish Islands are unsurpassed as holiday spots. Their romance is legendary. It's said there are peat fires in Hebridean houses alight continuously for over a hundred years, and that you can spy faeries in Skye's unearthly kaleidoscopes of sunbeams, mists, and rainbows. In Orkney and Shetland, where the land is so flat it scarcely breaks the sky's endless embrace, the moon, stars, and aurora borealis are dazzling. Fiddling and dancing swell all the village halls. Even the food tastes different; for example "bere bannocks" are made from a grain grown only in Orkney, and lamb in Harris and Lewis has a special sweetness caused by the heather in the sheep-feed. Best of all are the island people, who welcome you into their lives unquestioningly.

Airports in Lewis, Skye, Orkney, and Shetland are a thrill to set down at because of the comprehensive overviews you get of famous landscapes. Rentable cars get snapped up fast, so make sure you book yours before touchdown. Sea and air links are detailed below for each island individually under the name of the island. So are addresses of main tourist offices, where you should go for additional sight-seeing advice. Hotels listed as expensive will charge $80 to $85 and up for bed and breakfast for two; moderate ones, from $60 to $80; and inexpensive ones, from $45 to $60. A meal for two in an expensive restaurant will cost $50 or more; in a moderate one, $30 to $50; in an inexpensive one, less than $30.

ARRAN

Located 1¼ miles off Ayrshire's shore, Arran has 14 charming villages, no towns, and only 3 roads, one of which skirts in a circle a ravishing 60-mile coastline. A schizophrenic terrain, full of craggy Highland hills in the north but lush lowland farms and winsome little resorts in the south, makes the island a miniature Scotland. Arran's climate is comparatively dry and warm (here and there palm trees kiss the breeze) and every summer happy families arrive for idyllic low-key holidays. Juke boxes, cheap casinos, and chromium chip-shops are rare, but 2-year-olds on beaches with buckets and spades are prolific.

The chief villages, all by the sea, are Whiting Bay, Lamlash, Corrie, Lochranza, and Brodick. From Whiting Bay you can walk inland to the beautiful 140-foot Glenashdale Falls. Lamlash was a naval base till World War I and is now an educational and administrative center. Corrie with its adorable dinky harbor is the prettiest hamlet on Arran, while northerly Lochranza, dwarfed by a semicircle of most of Arran's spectacular over-2,000-foot peaks, is dramatically stark. Brodick is the island's main port and biggest tourist haunt; it's guarded by the soaring presence of (Mount) Goatfell and has an entrancing *cladach* (old fishing wharf).

Brodick Castle and Gardens are owned by the National Trust for Scotland, which also owns 7,000 acres nearby, including the lovely Glen Rosa. The Castle is an ancestral seat of the dukes of Hamilton and contains fine silver, porcelain, pictures, and trophies. The duchess of Montrose founded its opulent rhododendron garden in 1923 and its formal garden dates from 1710 (1.5 miles north of Brodick Pier; open May through September, plus some April afternoons). Lochranza Castle in Lochranza is a picturesque sixteenth-century ruin with two square towers (the key is with the custodian at his house, Croft Bank). It's only one of three places on Arran visited by Robert the Bruce — the others are King's Cross by Whiting Bay, where he embarked for the mainland in 1307 on the slow-boat to Scottish independence, and King's Cave, 2 miles north of Blackwaterfoot on the west coast (you have to walk it), a possible site of the legendary spider incident.

Rosaburn Heritage Museum, in an eighteenth-century croft on Brodick's northern edge, includes a smithy that demonstrates the art of horseshoeing (in summer). The Arran Nature Centre is owned and run by Brodick locals with a refreshing approach to natural history. Near Kilmory village on the south coast are the neolithic Kilmory Cairns, while the Standing Stones of Machrie Moor, a complex of six 15-foot Bronze Age megalithic circles, rise skyward on Moss Farm Road just south of westerly Machrie Bay — try to see them at sunset. Folklore maintains they supported the giant Fingal's cooking-pot.

Details of fishing, sailing, deep-sea diving, golf, swimming, pony trekking, hiking, and hill-walking are available from the Tourist Information Centre on Brodick Pier (phone: 2401). The center also publishes a comprehensive guide to Arran's crafts shops (most are in Whiting Bay). Boat trips to Holy Island across Lamlash Bay (daily Easter through October) give you a gander at a twelfth-century fort, St. Molios's Well (St. Molios was an Irish missionary), and herds of wild goats. You can watch the manufacture and packaging of Arran cheeses at the Torrylinn Creamery near Kilmory if you notify them 3 days in advance (phone: 240).

Festivals are Arran's long suit: there's a Music Festival (at the end of March), a Sea Angling Festival (in May), the Goatfell Race and Fiddlers' Rally (May), a program of events at Brodick Castle during Scotland's Heritage Festival (May–June), the Brodick Sheepdog Trials (June), the Heather Queen Gala (in July), the Lamlash Horticultural and Agricultural Shows (in August), the Corrie Capers, with family events like puppet and dog shows (August), and the Brodick Highland Games (August).

Several car-ferries go daily from Ardrossan on the mainland to Brodick. These should be reserved on summer weekends. During the tourist season, there's a route (about 8 sailings a day) from Claonaig on Kintyre to Lochranza. Further information from Caledonian MacBrayne Ltd., Ferry Terminal, Gourock, Scotland (phone: Gourock 33755). Ask Caledonian MacBrayne about their special deals called Hebridean Drive-Away, Island Hopscotch, and Car Rover Tickets — these could save you money.

CHECKING IN: *Kingsley Hotel* – Real beer in the bar makes this modest 29-bedroom seafront affair a worthy bet. Taste of Scotland menu. (Brodick; phone: 2226; inexpensive.)

EATING OUT: *Carraig Mhor Eating House* – Converted from a dwelling, this popular bay-side restaurant has a homey air. It serves omelettes and seafood at lunch, full dinners at night. (Lamlash; phone: 453; moderate.)

SKYE

Skye is a large island with 6 peninsulas, a coastline of sparkling sea lochs, and countless fabulous panoramas. Traditionally it has belonged to the clans

Macdonald and Macleod. Set very close to the most isolated parts of the West Highlands (herdsmen used to swim cattle across the narrow strait of Kyle Rhea from Skye to the mainland at low tide), it has a population of only 7,000.

On Skye's south shore are the legendary, oft-climbed Cuillins, a high mountain range whose tops Sorley Maclean described rhapsodically as "exact and serrated blue ramparts." In some lights they look black — like the teeth of a black saw blade. Their strange shape is the result of basalt dykes seeping into a hard underlayer of gabbro. Just west of the Cuillins is the lovely loch-side campsite Glen Brittle; northeast is Glen Sligachan, visited in 1773 by James Boswell and Samuel Johnson, guests at its inn (see *Checking In*). Bonnie Prince Charlie had popularized Skye by fleeing to it after Culloden in company with Flora Macdonald, a brave Skye native, disguised as Flora's maid; Boswell and Johnson met Flora 27 years later and wrote a tribute to her, enshrined today on a Celtic cross in Kilmuir Churchyard near the island's north tip.

Oak, birch, willow, and hazel grace most of Sleat, Skye's southernmost peninsula. The Aird of Sleat, below the village of Ardvasar, is barren, but its view across Sleat Sound to Mallaig is a wow! Lava flows and landslips have caused the phantasmagoric moss-dappled marvels on the basaltic northern peninsula of Trotternish, including the Old Man of Storr, a 160-foot obelisk well over 2,000 feet above the sea (a 3 to 4 hour climb from your car); the Kilt Rock; and the weird, pinnacled Quirang. Don't miss traveling the small corkscrew road from the Quirang to the Trotternish west coast.

Give equal time to castles and villages: Knock Castle on Sleat, with a vista across Knock Bay to the mainland territory of Knoydart, is a ruined Macdonald stronghold; so is Dunsgiath Castle at blissful Tokavaig on Sleat's opposite side, and Duntulm Castle near the tip of Trotternish. Castle Maoil ("The Roofless Castle"), a welcoming beacon for voyagers by ferry to the Skye pier at Kyleakin, was a keep of the Mackinnon Clan. Armadale Castle north of Ardvasar was a nineteenth-century Gothic mansion and family seat of the Macdonald chiefs, Lords of the Isles; nowadays, in summer, it's a clan Donald museum, congenial tearoom, and bookshop loaded with stuff about Skye. Dunvegan Castle on northwesterly Loch Dunvegan is the island's only remaining stately home, the 700-year-old abode of the Macleods (open Easter to mid-October; check out the castle guidebook for the story of the "fairy flag"). Villages to see are Skye's harbor and capital Portree, where you can shop and mail postcards (have a bun in *Mackenzie's Bakery* in the main square, too); Stein, a dreamy shell of an eighteenth-century fishing settlement on the Vaternish peninsula beside lavish fields of sweet wild orchids; Carbost, fermenting-ground of the incomparable Talisker whisky, on a forgotten corner of the Minginish peninsula; and Broadford and Elgol, at opposite ends of the majestic A881 past the Red Hills and (Mount) Blaven on the island's lower wing. Beautiful Elgol, from which Bonnie Prince Charlie left Scotland forever, has boat trips across Loch Scavaig into Loch Coruisk, a favorite subject of Romantic painters, hemmed in like a mighty well by the Cuillins.

Kilmuir Croft Museum near Kilmuir Churchyard is one of three folk museums on Skye; another is the Skye Water Mill and Black House on Loch Dunvegan (both open April through October). Glendale, not far from the

Black House, has a tempting line-up of crafts shops. There's a permanent display on the history of the bagpipes at Boreraig, also near Dunvegan.

Tourist Board offices in Broadford (phone: 361) and Meall House, Portree (phone: 2137) have information about climbing and hiking, swimming, fishing, golf, pony trekking, bird-watching, sailing, cruising, and dinghy excursions. En route to the neighboring island of Raasay you can see seals, porpoises, and (with luck) bottle-nosed whales. The Portree Highland Games and Dunvegan Piping Competition both take place in August.

Ferries leave the mainland for Skye from Mallaig, from near Glenelg (in summer), and from Kyle of Lochalsh. Details from Caledonian MacBrayne (except for the Glenelg run, owned by M.A. Mackenzie — phone: Glenelg 224). Loganair operates weekday flights around noontime from Glasgow to Broadford (phone for details: Glasgow 889-3181).

CHECKING IN: *Sligachan Hotel* – Travelers, aristocrats, painters, anglers, and climbers have been packing out this famous 23-bedroom landmark for over 200 years. A fascinating logbook documenting first ascents of the Cuillins is on show. Closed November through April (junction of the A850 and A863 at Glen Sligachan; phone: 204; moderate.) *Broadford Hotel* – Also in business over 200 years, the dining room at this serviceable old favorite exhibits a 4-foot Drambuie bottle honoring a past chef who invented the stuff for the Bonnie Prince. There are 28 bedrooms. Closed November through March. (Broadford; phone: 205; moderate.) *Macdonald Hotel* – Incomparable Scottish delicacies from the kitchens here bring gourmets running from 7-mile-distant Portree. There are 11 bedrooms. (Kensaleyre, north of Portree on the A856; phone: 339; inexpensive.) *Skeabost House Hotel* – Built in Victorian times, and beautifully situated at the southernmost tip of a sea loch, this 22-room hostelry is one of the finest on Scotland's islands. The furniture is antique, log fires blaze on the hearth, and the restaurant serves interesting local dishes. Closed mid-October to mid-April. (Skeabost Bridge; phone: Skeabost Bridge 202; moderate.) *Tigh Osda Eilean Iarmain* – Unique in its Gaelic-ness — there's a Gaelic-speaking staff, and Gaelic menus — this 13-bedroom hotel, owned and run by an Edinburgh banker who has also established on Skye a thriving Gaelic college, makes its own whisky, *Té Bheag*. Guests are allowed both to speak English and to sample the whisky. (Isle Ornsay; phone: 266; moderate to inexpensive.) *Stein Inn* – Situated right by Loch Bay, this quaint and beckoning 6-bedroom edifice at the outer edge of civilization is one of the most romantic hostelries on Skye. (Stein, on the Vaternish peninsula; phone: 208; inexpensive.)

EATING OUT: *The Three Chimneys* – Scallops, crab, salmon, and trout are specialties at this whitewashed cottage restaurant decorated with propped-up wagon wheels. (Colbost, beside the Black House Museum; phone: 258; moderate.) *The Three Rowans* – Also a candlemaker's shop, this inviting hilltop dining-cum-tearoom has a native Skye cook (an increasing rarity in Skye tourism) and three aged rowans outside to ward off evil (planted in the days when rowan trees had magic powers). (Kildonan, near Edinbane on the Portree-Dunvegan road; phone: 286; inexpensive.)

HARRIS

So unspoiled and deserted is Harris, 40 miles off Scotland's northwest coast, that the Scottish Tourist Board lists only one Harris entry in its booklet

Scotland: 1001 Things to See. That entry is St. Clement's Church, a cruciform building dating from about 1500 (restored in 1873) at Rodel on the island's southern tip. The exquisite carved stonework behind a Macleod chief's tomb shows the Twelve Apostles, a stag hunt, and an angel and devil weighing souls of the dead. The *Rodel Hotel* (see *Checking In*) has the key. Rodel itself is a tiny hamlet with clean-looking cottages and a pond ringed by slopes of mushrooms and wild blue irises.

North Harris is full of mountains, 8 of which exceed 2,000 feet; according to geologists these peaks are so old they antedate the separation of the continental land mass from Britain and Ireland and make parvenus of the Alps. Also on Harris are gleaming beaches, green seas, and, on lucky days, a still, clear air bright with the songs of birds. There are ranging moors with no roads; the whole atmosphere is primitive; the only real village — a one-streeter — is Tarbert. On the east coast are rocky shores verdant with "lazy beds," thin half-arable plots once tilled by crofters driven off richer lands in the west. The west coast has the almost Mediterranean sands of Luskentyre and Hushinish.

Your Harris survival kit should contain ordnance maps, sandwiches, dubbined boots, midge repellent, whisky, binoculars, your own angling equipment if you fish (fishing tackle is hard to come by on Harris). Bathing suits will be useful only if you like swimming in temperatures not usually exceeding 55°.

Tarbert is a picturebook townlet with general stores, a harbor, and a vast public vegetable patch full of strutting roosters. The Harris tourist office is in Tarbert (phone: 2011). Harris Tweed jackets for sale dangle from hangers on the outer walls of brightly painted corrugated-iron Tarbert sheds (you can also buy Harris Tweeds in Stornoway, or by the yard — about £4 per yard — from the weavers themselves in Drinishader on the coast farther south). Hard-wearing, made from the wool of Harris sheep, this world-famous fabric is hand-spun, hand-dyed, and handwoven on antiquated looms producing — sadly for those who'd like Harris Tweed blankets or swirling, seamless Harris Tweed capes — only an old-fashioned, narrow cloth length. Harris weavers have gone to court to protect their name on occasions when cheap imitators have usurped it.

Toe Head, the outermost point of the small peninsula northwest of Rodel (served by a sand track), is a wilderness full of golden eagles, sheep, and the distinctive and beautiful *machair,* a beach grass vibrant with a species of pale wild flower found only on Hebridean dunes. The trail from the B887 past (Mount) Uisgnaval More to Loch Voshimid, about 12 miles round trip, is in some weathers very eerie: it's the setting for J.M. Barrie's play *Mary Rose,* about a mysterious, mist-enshrouded, disappearing maid.

Ferries dock at Tarbert from Skye's port of Uig. Details from Caledonian MacBrayne.

CHECKING IN: *Scarista House* – Once a manse, this delightful 4-bedroom hotel near Scarista beach still has a fine library (open to residents) and no bar (but they don't charge you for corkage at table). (15 miles southwest of Tarbert on the A859; phone: 238; moderate.) *Harris Hotel* – This faithful standby lacks the refinement of *Scarista House* but is a reasonable (and more accessible) eatery, drinkery, and sleepery. It has 20 bedrooms. (Tarbert; phone: 2154; inexpensive.)

Rodel Hotel – – Unmodernized since the seventeenth century (there are fascinating antiques everywhere including, in the boudoirs, wee wooden washbasins), this former great house has passed from an aristocratic family to Jock McCallum, host extraordinaire and distiller of Royal Household, the smooth-as-silk house whisky. He's never counted his bedrooms but says he can put up 25 people. (Rodel; phone: 210; inexpensive.)

LEWIS

Lewis adjoins Harris, making the combined island 95 miles in length. Lewis is the upper partner. It consists of marshy peat bogs and a coastline dappled with 25 beaches.

Its center is Stornoway, the only actual town in the Outer Isles. Stornoway has a charming landlocked harbor with a large, tame colony of inquisitive gray seals — you can watch them from the pier along with the nostalgic spectacle of colorful homeward-bound fishing boats. Churches are everywhere, as befits a locale so Sabbath-conscious you can't even buy cigarettes from a machine on Sundays — neither shall ye drink in hotels ye aren't staying at. There's a pleasant square with an attractive town hall and a huddle of gracious houses on a hill. The *Stornoway Gazette,* with news of local events, comes out on Thursdays. Key shops are *Loch Erisort Woollens* on Cromwell St., *Lewis Crofters* (for outdoor gear) just opposite, and *The Corner Shop* (a delicatessen) on Kenneth St.

The A858 west from Stornoway has Lewis's main attractions including the Standing Stones of Callanish, an elaborate setting of megaliths, unique in Scotland, running Stonehenge a close second; Dun Carloway Broch, a well-preserved 30-foot Iron Age tower; the Shawbost Museum and Mill illustrating old Lewis folkways (open April through October, except Sundays); and the Lewis Black House, a clachan, or adjoining series of traditional thatched-roofed huts, now operated as a tourism gimmick — these were inhabited till 1960! Lews Castle Gardens on the west side of Stornoway harbor are worth a visit; so is St. Moluag's, a restored twelfth-century Episcopal church with regular Sunday services at the village of Eoropie, near the Butt of Lewis, the island's north tip (apply to "McLeod's" in the village for the key). On the Eye Peninsula to Stornoway's east is Ui Chapel, a picturesque ruin of a former priory in the burying ground of the Lewis Mcleod chiefs.

The Lewis tourist office is at 4 South Beach St., Stornoway (phone: 3088); here you can get advice on sailing, fishing, golf, hiking (the remote western parish of Uig is a good place), and bird-watching (Tiumpan Head on the Eye Peninsula has a burgeoning rabble of petrels and kittiwakes). The tourist office bookstall (the best in the Outer Isles) features a leaflet detailing Hebridean crafts and craftshops: you might want to buy a handmade set of Lewis Chessmen, modeled on four ancient sets discovered under Uig sands in 1831. Scandinavian in design, carved from walrus tusks and stained red on one side, the originals are thought to have been buried in the twelfth century by a shepherd after he murdered a merchant sailor whose ship, carrying the chessmen, ran aground. Museums in London and Edinburgh have the originals today.

Sea-angling competitions are a highlight of Stornoway summers, with the

Western Isles and the Highlands and Islands Open Boat Championships in August and the EFSA European Boat Championship in September.

Ferries to Stornoway are from Ullapool on the northwest Scottish mainland: for further information contact Caledonian MacBrayne (don't forget you can drive right into Lewis from Harris). British Airways fly to Stornoway from London, Glasgow, and Inverness.

CHECKING IN: *Caberfeidh Hotel* – Stornoway's finest, this custom-built haunt of tourists and businessmen on the edge of town has a garden, attractive tartan-and-mock-Viking furnishings, frequent *ceilidhs,* 2 bars and 40 bedrooms. The dining room specializes in seafood. (Percival Road South; phone: 2604; moderate to inexpensive.) *Uig Lodge* – Distance-wise the nearest hotel to New York, this comfortable 10-bedroom country house on the far west coast has wonderful food, an old-fashioned huntin'-shootin' air, and access to heavenly beaches. Closed December. (Uig; phone: 286; moderate to inexpensive.)

ORKNEY

Orkney comprises 68 islands, some 29 of which are inhabited. Throughout the whole cluster lie chambered cairns, traces of 78 brochs, rings of standing stones, and vestiges of prehistoric villages. Many are extensive survivals, making Orkney the archaeological treasure house of Great Britain.

Several pre-Pictish peoples lived on Orkney, then Picts, then Vikings. Strangely none of the races they conquered are mentioned by the Vikings in their remarkable medieval epic and folk-history, the *Orkneyinga Saga,* a product of Orkney's Golden Age. A fine long literary tradition of which the *Saga* is part stretches even to America: Washington Irving's father was an Orkney sailor and James Russell Lowell's forebears included two Orcadian clans.

More sunshine bathes Orkney (and Shetland) than almost anywhere else in Britain, and there are bright-hued farmhouses, green fields, primroses, violets, golden sands, and clifftop sea-pinks. Fulmars, cormorants, Manx shearwaters, petrels, gulls, kittiwakes, guillemots, puffins, and gannets abound. On country strolls watch out for bulls. Hotels should be booked several months in advance; so far Orkney seems oblivious to the lucrative potential of tourism, and accommodations are few.

Orkney's two centers of civilization are Stromness and Kirkwall on the largest island, the so-called Mainland. Stromness, in the west (Kirkwall is in the east), is a small eighteenth-century port that hasn't changed since its founding; it's full of charm and has a main street that snakes along the sea. The Pier Arts Center on Victoria St. in Stromness contains an internationally famous display of works by Ben Nicolson and Barbara Hepworth; the Stromness Museum, 52 Albert St., has a curio collection from local history. *Stromness Books and Prints* is well worth a browse.

Kirkwall is Orkney's capital, site of St. Magnus Cathedral, Orkney's pride. The cathedral is an impressive twelfth-century pink sandstone Norman building still in use, the burial place of St. Magnus, Orkney's patron saint. Easy-does-it in Kirkwall's ancient streets, which wind narrowly and look illusively like pedestrian precincts — till cars belt down them full throttle! A thriving stone-built town with crow-stepped gabled houses and magnificently old-fashioned shops painted berry and peach, Kirkwall also encompasses Earl Patrick's Palace, the imposing remains of an accomplished piece of Renaissance architecture belonging originally to a wicked Stewart earl, a nephew of Mary Queen of Scots; the Bishop's Palace, a thirteenth-century ruin with an ascendable sixteenth-century round tower; Tankerness House, a sixteenth-century merchant-laird's mansion and museum — sometimes with guest exhibitions — of 4,000 years of Orkney life; the Highland Park Distillery, which gives tours of its nearly 200-year-old special processes (and free sips of its whisky); and *Robert Towers's Workshop* at Rosegarth, St. Ola (phone: 3521), a manufactory of traditional Orcadian tall-backed, straw-weave chairs. Behind Kirkwall on Wideford Hill the view is a superb pastiche of bays and islets.

In a knot in mid-Mainland near the Harray and Stenness lochs are three venerable marvels, Maeshowe, the Standing Stones of Stenness, and the Ring of Brodgar. Maeshowe, the finest chambered cairn in western Europe, was constructed around 1800 BC, and is entered on hands and knees by a narrow downward-sloping tunnel. Viking marauders wrote the runic inscriptions in the cells. In midwinter, dusk's last shaft of sunlight strikes one of the dark entombing walls, as it has done for untold centuries, a deeply moving sight with a mystic suggestion of resurrection. The Standing Stones of Stenness — four are still upright — are part of a circle of 3000 BC; the Ring of Brodgar, 340 feet in diameter, boasts 36 stones of its original 60. Also on the Mainland are: Skara Brae, a neolithic complex with a paved courtyard, covered passages, and 10 one-room houses full of "built-in" stone furniture (life here came to an end when a sandstorm blanketed all, sometime after 4500 BC); Gurness Broch, over 10 feet high, surrounded by stone huts and inhabited well into Viking times; Click Mill, the only operative example of old-style horizontal-wheeled Orkney water power (wear rubber boots, it's in a bog); Corrigall Farm Museum showing old Orkney folkways (open April through September only); and Birsay, a quaint village with another ruined palace of the Stewart earls. Opposite Birsay is the Brough of Birsay, an adorable island and beachcombers' delight accessible only at low tide, where you'll find the remains of a Romanesque church and of Pictish and Nordic settlements.

Hoy, Orkney's most romantic island, is famous for its strange offshore rock formation, the Old Man of Hoy, a supreme test for rockclimbers. Hoy has hills, gaunt high cliffs, and wild unpopulated valleys. There's only one road, along the east coast, passing the martello towers built in 1812 against attack by American ships. Attainable by tramping inland is panoramic Ward Hill, Orkney's highest point at 1,565 feet, near the site of a supposedly haunted neolithic sepulcher called the Dwarfie Stone — this overlooks the beautiful half-deserted hamlet of Rackwick, Peter Maxwell Davies's home. If you go to Hoy, take a picnic; there's almost nowhere to buy food.

The island of South Ronaldsay is another good place to go, completely different from Hoy; you can drive to it from near Kirkwall via the island-hopping Churchill Causeway, erected in 1939–40 to protect the adjacent waterway of Scapa Flow, then a naval base. En route at the island of Lamb Holm is the lovely Italian Chapel, built in ornate Italianate style from a mere

Nissen hut by Italian World War II prisoners and affectionately preserved to this day by admiring Orcadians. It was in Scapa Flow in 1916 that Lord Kitchener's ship, the *Hampshire,* was blown up with him on board, and there 3 years later that the German Fleet of World War I heroically scuttled itself. Hoxa Head, the entrance to Scapa Flow, is a fascinating surreal jumble of half-sunk hulks and wartime concrete barriers. Also on South Ronaldsay is St. Margaret's Hope, an idyllic coastal settlement popular with artists and craftsmen, an excellent place to shop for handmade goods.

Other islands are alluring, too: northerly Westray has Noltland Castle, a prepossessing sixteenth-century relic; Wyre near the Mainland has twelfth-century Cobbie Row's Castle, the earliest authenticated castle in Scotland (it's mentioned in the *Orkneyinga Saga*), and nearby St. Mary's Chapel of the same date; ruin-rich Rousay, the "Egypt of the North" beyond Wyre, has bicycles and ponies and traps for hire and boat trips to Egilsay, another island, where St. Magnus was murdered (there's part of a fine medieval church on Egilsay). Sanday, well north of the Mainland near Westray, is seal country, a beachy place to take kids and has sellouts in *The Wool Hall* (every other Wednesday evening) of "seconds" made by the Sanday Knitters, a women's cooperative.

Tourist Board offices in Broad St., Kirkwall (phone: 2856) and the Ferry Terminal Building, Stromness (phone: 850716) have data on the rest of Orkney's islands and archaeology and on interesting natural features you can explore — most of the latter have intriguing names (Yesnaby Cliffs, Brinkie's Brae, St. John's Head, the Gloup of Deerness, the Barrel of Butter). Also available are tips on fishing, golf, deep-sea diving, crafts (potters are plentiful), walks, sailing, swimming, and bird-watching. Many British seafowl nest in Orkney (the season is May–July); their favorite places include the deserted islands of Copinsay and Eynhallow, the Mainland cliffs at Marwick, and the bird reserve on Westray at Noup Head. Information about local events is in *The Orcadian,* published Thursdays. The tourist offices give advice on getting from island to island.

Twice a winter Kirkwall's annual Ba' Games are played (they're just like the Jedburgh ones — see the *Lowlands* route). Other orgies are the internationally important St. Magnus Festival of the Arts in June; Kirkwall's County Show, a major agricultural fair in August; and Stromness Shopping Week in July, when all Orkney comes to Stromness for 7 days of fêtes, dances, and general merriment.

A 2-hour ferry route links Stromness with Scrabster, near Thurso on the Scottish mainland. For details: P&O Ferries Terminal, Pierhead, Stromness (phone: 850655); P&O Ferries, Portland Terrace, Southampton SO9 4AE (phone: 623-1505); or P&O Ferries Terminal, Jamieson's Quay, Aberdeen (phone: 572615). As well as regular services, P&O offers a special 4-day motorists' package tour. British Airways flies daily (except Sundays) from Aberdeen to Kirkwall; details of other flights, including inter-island Orcadian puddle-jumps, are at Kirkwall Airport (phone: 2233). Summer coach tours of major Orkney sights are organized by James Peace, Junction Rd., Kirkwall (phone: 2866).

CHECKING IN: *Balfour Castle* – The Polish Zavadski family who live in this late-nineteenth-century fantasy have only just started taking paying guests: you must stay 3 nights minimum and can book through the *Foveran Hotel* (see below). A real find, the place has all the trimmings of Victorian romanticism — dark paneling, a huge staircase, big rooms with gold-etched period floral wallpapers, intriguing outbuildings, and an island setting by a storm-lashed sea. (On Shapinsay across Shapinsay Sound from the Orkney Mainland; phone: 282; expensive.) *Foveran Hotel* – This comfortable, modern 8-bedroom oasis near Kirkwall operates a special scheme, in addition to its ordinary trade, with natives of the small island of Papa Westray: For a set price you get 5 days on the Orkney Mainland plus 5 in a Papa Westray farmhouse with personal guided trips to points of local interest. (St. Ola, overlooking Scapa Flow; phone: 2389; moderate to inexpensive.)

EATING OUT: *Creel Restaurant* – This little nook, near an old-world harbor filled with boats, is a memorable way to enjoy the sea's proximity. Order scallops, crab, or lobster when you phone for reservations. (St. Margaret's Hope, South Ronaldsay; phone: 311; moderate.) *Richan's Restaurant* – The delicious traditional Orcadian home cooking here complements the cheerful, typically Stromnessian decor. (Stromness; phone: 850039; inexpensive.)

SHETLAND

"Ultima Thule" sounds like the name of a fashionable debutante, but in fact it's what the Romans called Shetland. Nothing lies between Shetland and the Arctic Circle. Lerwick, Shetland's capital, is much farther from Edinburgh than Edinburgh is from London; it's breached even from Kirkwall by a distance of over 60 miles. The famous north Shetland outpost, the Muckle Flugga Lighthouse, a remarkable feat of engineering poised on faces of sheer, almost vertical rock, is Britain's last window on the world (alas, it's not open to the public, but you get a good view of it from the coast).

Shetland's 100 islands (only 3 are of any size) are chilly even in summer. Winters are very dark but May, June, and July nights are aglow with the "simmer dim," a beautiful horizontal twilight lasting several hours, the next thing to a midnight sun — everything under its luminous rays looks phosphorescent. There are no rivers on Shetland, but sparkling streamlets, lily-bright lochans, and bays jeweled with waving sea-pinks. The sea is inescapable, for you can always see or hear it; Lerwick rises right out of it as if in a fairy tale — houses, stone steps, ramp-shaped flagstone alleys, and all; nets and fishing boats are everywhere and the raucous cry of seabirds splits the air (300 bird species nest in Shetland, lining up colony-by-colony on rock-cliff shelves in a surreal cross between a supermarket and an aviary).

Traditionally it's said that an Orcadian is a farmer with a boat, whereas a Shetlander is a fisherman with a croft. This is still true, but North Sea oil has given Shetland an added dimension: coffers are bulging, Portakabin villages full of roustabouts have sprung up overnight, and there are symptoms of boomtown-ism like prostitution and black-marketeering. Sullom Voe, a waterway along the north Mainland (as in Orkney, the chief island is called the Mainland) serves a massive oil terminal covering a whole neck of land from sea to sea; helicopters carrying shiftmen whizz back and forth between offshore sites and Sumburgh Airport; tourists must battle riggers for rooms in Shetland's precious few hotels (reservations are vital). But around all this, life on the islands goes on as it has for generations, with great tracts of land given over to grazing the special small sheep that provide the wool for Shetlanders' famous sweaters.

Vikings dominated Shetland as long as 13 centuries ago, though other settlers were on the scene 1,000 years before that, as you'll see on the Mainland's south tip at Jarlshof, a fascinating sunken city with overlayers from three prehistoric civilizations. Orkney's archaeological treasures are older, but it's Shetland that clings to primitive forms: Shetland ponies are still reared on common landholdings, and Lerwick is in a way another Jarlshof with its arrow-thin streets, enclosing wharves, and snuggling clusters of stone-walled homes and warehouses. Commercial Street, Lerwick's main thoroughfare, is anything but a boulevard — yet it has its own glamour.

In pre-Victorian days when half the fishing fleet of Holland put in at Shetland after sailing the North Sea, Lerwick was a smugglers' nest and an almost European city. Explore Shetland's history at the Shetland Museum, Lower Hillhead, Lerwick (the exhibits cover prehistory to the present). Other Lerwick attractions are Fort Charlotte, built in 1665 to protect the Sound of Bressay from the Dutch; the Lerwick Town Hall, a Scots-baronial building with stained-glass windows and a climbable tower; and Clickhimin Broch, an ancient 17-foot stronghold within the remains of an Iron Age stone fort. *The Shetland Workshop Gallery,* 4–6 Burns La., Lerwick, has native crafts for sale: sealskin handbags, silver-and-polished-stone jewelry, sweaters, and Shetland shawls (the last, though large, warm, and sturdy, are so fine they can be drawn through a wedding ring). *John Tulloch (Wool Products) Ltd.,* Montfield Factory, Gilbertson Rd. (phone: 3150), now functions mostly as a collection point but still exhibits some finishing processes, and sells garments at cut-rate prices.

Yell and Unst are the next-biggest islands after the Mainland; they continue north from the Mainland in that order and are easily accessible. On Unst is Mu Ness Castle, constructed from rubble in the sixteenth century with an amazing eye for architectural detail. The prettiest Shetland islands are Bressay, Whalsay, Noss, Fetlar, Foula, the Out Skerries and Muckle Roe. Foula, 30 miles west of the Mainland, is the most isolated and therefore perhaps most exciting — it's served by a regular passenger line (no cars). But close your eyes, touch your map, and go where your finger falls! The islands are *all* pretty and there's no place you can't get by hiring a boatman, unless the weather's too rough — ask at the Lerwick tourist office, Alexandra Wharf (phone: 3434), or in outlying coastal pubs.

The tiny seal-haunted island of Mousa opposite Sandwick on the east Mainland (7 miles south of Lerwick) holds Mousa Broch, a princely 40 feet high, some say the best broch in Britain. St. Ninian's Isle, not an island but a small south Mainland peninsula, is famous for white sands and the priceless fifth-century silver plate unearthed there on a Dark Age church site in 1958. Other Mainland must-sees are the Croft Museum of nineteenth-century Shetland life on the A970 at South Voe; the Tingwall Valley Agricultural Museum of crofters' tools and implements, on the same road 5 miles north of Lerwick (open May through September); the Ness of Burgi, an Iron Age defensive stone structure near the southern town of Sumburgh; and Stanleydale, a neolithic heel-shaped edifice containing an oval chamber, at the western hamlet of Walls. Ruined Scalloway Castle, a building dating from 1600 in a flamboyant corbel-turreted medieval style, overlooks Scalloway, the unbelievably picturesque west coast Mainland fishing village that once was Shetland's capital (the castle belonged at that time to the wicked Stewart earls prominent also in Orkney).

Geological wonders of Shetland, visitable by boat, include "Orkneymen's caves," narrow of entrance but inside grand like cathedrals (the best is the stalactited Cave of Bressay, and there are lots along the coast of the island of Papa Stour); the sea-filled, once natural-bridged Holes of Scrada on the Mainland's northwesterly Esha Ness peninsula (you view these on foot); the Grind of the Navir, also at Esha Ness, where waves have ripped off huge cube-shaped rock hunks and carried them 180 feet; and the Bressay Giant's Leg (his other leg is said to be in Orkney and his body above you somewhere midway).

The Shetland tourist office (the one in Lerwick) has information on fishing, golf, deep-sea diving, hiking, crafts, and bird-watching. Unst is a good place to see Icelandic owls. Fetlar is now a 1,400-acre Statutory Bird Reserve; other ornithological havens are the islands of Foula, Noss, and Haaf Gruney, the Pool of Virkie on the Mainland's south tip, and Hermaness on Unst opposite the Muckle Flugga Lighthouse.

"Up Helly Aa," a dramatic boat-burning ceremony celebrating the return of the sun, dates from pagan times and is still performed in Shetland every January using traditional Viking costumes and boats; the Viking International Festival at Lerwick in September is a major sea-angling competition; and there's a Shetland Folk Festival at the end of April that gives full rein to Shetland fiddlers, a breed admired and envied by all of musical Scotland. The *Shetland Times,* published Fridays, has news of other events.

P&O Ferries runs an overnight route three times a week between Aberdeen and Lerwick. Details from P&O. There's no ferry to Shetland from Orkney. Flights into Shetland are frequent; British Airways goes from any major British airport (there are at least four flights every weekday from Aberdeen alone) and from Kirkwall, and Loganair zooms direct to a small landing strip at Tingwall from Edinburgh.

CHECKING IN: *Baltasound Hotel* – This 10-bedroom hybrid is, on the whole, more modern extension than grand old Victorian abode. There's a big bar with attractive local-interest posters. (Baltasound, Unst; phone: 334; expensive to moderate.) *Westings Hotel* – Another contemporary hostelry based on an old building, it has a distinctly Scandinavian appeal and 10 bedrooms. There is no bar, but the service is friendly, the food good, and the proprietors organize pony treks. (Wormadale, near Whiteness, Mainland; phone: 242; inexpensive.)

Wales

It doesn't take long to understand why Wales is to many Welshmen a song and an inspiration. It has been so for many centuries. From the earliest times — and Welsh has been written since the seventh century AD — bards have expressed their love of their land. And what an enchanting and enthralling land it is.

Wales is small. So you can get to know quite a lot of it even in a short time. It is 8,000 square miles, about half the size of Switzerland, has about 2.8 million people — and about 6 million sheep. It is about 200 miles in length and it takes about 6 hours to travel from north to south in a car in normal conditions. But don't: It would be like bolting down a gourmet meal.

Wales is special. From its seabird-haunted islets and seal-sentried rocks reaching out into the Irish Sea, to its mountains where Everest teams train, Wales mixes sudden drama with soft stillness. There is a grandeur about it, a sense of stubbornness. It is brightly pastoral, offset here and there with dark smudges of industry.

While Cardiff, the capital city, can be reached by the new 125-mph supertrains in less than 2 hours from London, there is a sense in which Wales remains England's unknown neighbor. It is, as it has always been, a mountainous stronghold in the west. The land and the people somehow keep their separate character. And a fifth of the people still use the Welsh language, rich in literature and color, older than English, the tongue of the original Britons. It is therefore a great vehicle for legends: Perhaps the legendary King Arthur himself roamed the hills of Wales in noble defiance of the encroaching Saxons.

Indeed, it was the Saxons who gave Wales its name. They called the fiercely defiant people who lived there the *wealas,* meaning "foreigners." The Welsh, however, gave their land a different name: Cymru (pronounced Kum-ree), meaning the "land of brothers." You'll see the word on the signs as you cross the border: *"Croeso i Gymru* — Welcome to Wales." (Don't be worried by the fact the Cymru changes to Gymru. Welsh is a language in which certain initial letters change depending on the words preceding them).

Bear in mind, as you travel around, that the story of the language is a considerable part of the story of Wales. It is one of the oldest languages and literatures in Europe. It is flowing and musical. And lovely Welsh first (given) names remain very popular. Females have names like Lowri, Menna, Megan, and Rhiannon. Males are called Idris, Owen, and Rhys.

In the sixth and seventh centuries Wales became a largely Christian country through the work of St. David and his followers. And St. David, the patron saint, is one of the prime figures of Welsh history. Between the sixth and thirteenth centuries Wales was divided into kingdoms and princedoms. The rulers sometimes fought amongst themselves as well as battling the English on the border. But there were exceptions, like the tenth-century King Hywel Dda (Hywel the Good) who framed laws for an orderly way of life. Hywel was not blind to human problems: He was a pioneer supporter of women's equality and decreed that a woman could get a divorce if her husband were impotent and had halitosis! Under men like Hywel, culture flourished and the *eisteddfod* (pronounced eye-steth-vod), a competitive festival of poetry and song, became part of the Welsh tradition. There are numerous *eisteddfodau* in Wales today, and the biggest is the National Eisteddfod held in the first week of August, which attracts huge crowds. This festival is traditionally a nomadic one, held alternately in north and south Wales. In 1982 it's scheduled to take place in Swansea. The bardic ceremonies were invented in the last century to provide pageantry (but no one takes them *too* seriously), and the winning poets are treated like pop stars, feted by crowds, blinking in the TV lights. What other country has, as national hero and king-for-a-day, a poet?

During the twelfth and thirteenth centuries the rulers of England sought to bring the troublesome Welsh under their control. The most striking reminders of this period are the great castles that dot the land. There are scores of them, many of them the finest in Europe, majestic residue of war and conquest. They look splendid against their backdrops of coast or mountains and reflect the wild land they were built to defend and subdue. Among the best are the eight built by King Edward I of England to complete and sustain his conquest. Hugely expensive, they brought the king to fiscal crisis, bankrupting some of his financiers. But warrior Edward was determined to defeat Llywelyn, Prince of Wales, and bring the country to heel. Llywelyn's head ended up on a pike in London, and Wales came under English control.

In the 1530s, during the reign of King Henry VIII, Wales and England were formally joined together and made equal under the law. In the same century the Bible was translated into Welsh, the most single important influence on the language's survival. It made the Welsh a literate people in their own language. And in the nineteenth century, when Wales embraced the nonconformist form of worship, the Welsh Bible was a keystone of education. During this century the Welsh language has declined in numerical strength. Some fear that it will eventually die out, and there have been many campaigns to strengthen it. Threatened as it is, it nevertheless remains strong and lively in certain respects. It is the domestic language of many people (there are more than half a million who speak it) and it lives in books, songs, comics, radio, and television.

Much of Wales is rural. It is a farming country. In the mountains you can see the tough little hill farms and hear shepherds whistling for their scruffy, intelligent, black and white dogs. A good Welsh sheepdog is worth hundreds of pounds.

The southeast of the country is heavily industrialized (coal mining, steel making, and manufacturing), and this is where most people live. The coal-mining belt stretches from Ebbw Vale in the east to Ammanford in the west, an area known as The Valleys. The narrow and tortuous valleys were once peaceful and wooded gorges, but the coal age changed everything. South Wales became an industrial powerhouse, one of the keys to British economic expansion. A century ago this part of Wales was the most intensively mined area of the world, and during the coal rush thousands of workers poured in from rural Wales, England, Ireland, Italy, Greece, and Spain. They made an exciting mixture, creating a varied and fascinating community, renowned for its spirit, its politics, and its culture. Coal's heyday has passed, but the valley towns, with their neat rows of houses slotted into the steep hillsides and the huge chapels standing guard, remain alluring.

While Welsh coal was warming the world, Welsh slate was roofing it. The great slate quarries and caverns of north Wales were the heart of a big industry. But that industry has shrunk dramatically and vast heaps of slate waste are monuments to an epoch.

Thus Wales is a place of contrasts. You don't have to be there long before you realize how it is weathered by history's storms. Its patches of industrial ugliness are honorable scars. And it has some of the loveliest scenery you are ever likely to see. As for the people, they are proud of their land, aware of its difference, and immensely hospitable. Their accents are distinctive (you will soon tell a South Welshman from a North Welshman) and their humor is delightful.

It is no wonder that Wales intrigues. It has a certain magic about it, an intangible something in the Celtic air.

Our route gives travelers the essential flavor, starting in the southeast and traversing the Brecon Beacons to lovely Carmarthen. It is all dramatic hills, soft pools, rushing waterfalls, and stately rivers. The route heads northwest across old Cardiganshire and to the pleasant and softer land of mid-Wales. Farther on it forges into sublime Snowdonia with its darkly handsome peaks and robust and defiant cottages and farms. It will be hard to resist the temptation to take diversions from the route. Why resist? Off the beaten track are many small pubs, guesthouses, farmhouses, and restaurants where you can get a night's stay and a decent meal at very reasonable prices.

Expect to pay $60 and up for a double room in those places we've listed as expensive; $40 to $60 in the moderate category; and under $40 in the inexpensive range. You'll find that a good majority of the hotels we list in the Welsh countryside are inexpensive — usually small inns with few rooms and delightful surroundings. But even expensive Welsh hotels aren't *too* expensive considering the experience that awaits. No matter where you stay, and even if it's off-season, book your room well in advance. This is especially crucial in summer months when the national music festivals are held throughout the country. There are few restaurants of note in Wales — the best are usually found in the better hotels.

MONMOUTH: The Romans saw at once that this site had an important strategic position at the junction of the rivers Monnow and Wye and built a fort here that they called Blestium. There is not much left of the later Norman fortifications except the remarkable bridge and gate house over the Monnow, dating from the thirteenth century. And, almost nothing remains of the castle where King Henry V was born. Today, Monmouth is an easygoing market town content with its role. There is an eighteenth-century shire hall in Agincourt Square with statues of Henry V and Charles Rolls, founder of Rolls-Royce, who was born nearby. The bottom of the hall is now a cluster of market stalls and parts of the interior, though not original, are interesting and attractive, especially the staircase and dome. Behind the hall is the Nelson Museum with some of the sea hero's memorabilia.

The countryside surrounding Monmouth is delightful, particularly the Wye valley. And you can take a meandering side trip to Tintern by driving 7 miles south on the

A466 road. The abbey, a lovely thirteenth- and fourteenth-century ruin in a tranquil setting beside the River Wye, was founded by a Baron Walter de Clare in 1131. The building fell victim to Henry VIII's Dissolution of the Monasteries in 1539. But though roofless and ruined, it's still romantic and inspiring. William Wordsworth, who wrote the famous poem about the abbey, commented, "No poem of mine was composed under circumstances more pleasant than this."

CHECKING IN: *The King's Head Hotel* – King Charles I of England, beheaded at the end of England's seventeenth-century civil war, is said to have stayed in this handsome place; and there is a fine plaster casting of this sad-end monarch for guests to ponder. A bar, and a restaurant, and 24 comfortable bedrooms. (Agincourt Sq.; phone: 0600-2177; moderate.) *Beaufort Arms Hotel* – Behind its charming Regency facade, the Beaufort offers 26 comfortable rooms, a convenient restaurant, and parking facilities. (Agincourt Sq.; phone: 0600-2411; moderate to inexpensive.) *White Swan Hotel* – This is a pleasant, friendly place with 18 bedrooms and a restaurant. (Priory St.; phone: 0600-2045; moderate to inexpensive.)

EATING OUT: *Charisma* – At this licensed bistro owned and run by Avril Pegram, Moroccan, Italian, French, and Greek dishes are served, as well as vegetarian food and inexpensive lunches (about 65p) of soup and garlic bread. (Shaftesbury House, 67 Monnow St.; phone: 0600-4388.)

En Route – In Gwent, 8 miles from Monmouth, on the main A40, is Raglan castle, built in the 1430s. It's central feature of the little town, and one of the best examples of late medieval castle-building. Henry VII was imprisoned here; and Charles I stayed at the castle after his army lost the battle of Naseby in the civil war. Note especially the large hall, the six-sided keep, and the long, surrounding wall.

Six miles south of Raglan, off the A449 road to Newport, is the meadowy little borough of Usk built on the bank of the river from which it derives its name. Taste Usk salmon while you're here; it's justly famous. The history-minded will enjoy the thirteenth-century Church of St. Mary's and the ruins of the castle dating from the days when barons ruled the border country in the twelfth century.

The A40 west from Raglan will take you to Abergavenny.

ABERGAVENNY: Gateway to the Brecon Beacons National Park, bustling market town, soaked in history, Abergavenny stands beside the River Usk guarded by four mountains: Sugar Loaf, Blorenge, Skerrid, and Little Skerrid. The streets of Abergavenny are lined with Tudor, Georgian, and Victorian buildings, and canny trading takes place in the marketplace where weatherbeaten farmers sell their sheep, pigs, cattle, and horses. Romans and Normans occupied the site of the town because of its strategic location, and the frontier Clan De Braose made it their base in the battles against the Welsh. Tough William De Braose invited Welsh chiefs to a Christmas dinner at Abergavenny castle in the twelfth century and had them murdered while they supped. The treacherous baron had his comeuppance years later: The king stripped his lands from him and William died a beggar. The castle ruins are worth exploring and from here you can get a great view over the rolling hills. Inside the castle is the Abergavenny and District Museum. Abergavenny is a good center for tourists: Hill-walking, fishing, and pony trekking are excellent and you can rent canal cruisers on the west side of town. Red Line Boats (Goytre Wharf, Llanover; phone: 0873-880516) has half-day (£10) and full-day (£17) rentals, but also provides cruisers by the week (from £90 to £230). Road House Holiday Hire (Main Rd., Gilwern, Gwent; phone: Gilwern 830240) rents narrowboats (traditional canal boats never more than 6 feet 10 inches wide) on a weekly basis only. Rates fluctuate between £100 and £195, depending on the time of year. There is a tourist information center on Monk Street with an exhibition on Brecon Beacons National Park.

En Route – The A40 toward Brecon is a delightful stretch through the Usk valley, with the Black Mountains to the right and the outriders of the Brecon Beacons to the left. There are pubs and small cottages, and little towns like Crickhowell that welcome fishermen and pony trekkers. Many travelers speak highly of the *Nant-y-ffin Cider Mill* in Crickhowell where you can get hearty homemade food — terrines, pies, cheesecake, and (in season) local salmon. All along this road are interesting narrow lanes turning off into the hills and anyone with the time and inclination to roam is advised to do just that: Turn off and explore. For example, at Llansantffraid you can turn left toward Talybont and drive for 9 miles through forest and hills to Talybont and Taf-fechan reservoirs: This is lovely walking and picnicking country. Another pleasant diversion on the road from Abergavenny to Brecon is to Hay-on-Wye — although you will need the best part of a day to enjoy it. Turn right onto the A479 just after Crickhowell, coast through the hills for about 20 miles to Talgarth, and pick up the A438 north to the B4350 to Hay-on-Wye. Hay is a picturesque little border town, whose main industry is secondhand books; it is absolutely bulging with books, a paradise for bibliophiles, and is reckoned to be the world's largest secondhand bookshop. From here, get back on the A438 southwest to Brecon.

CHECKING IN: *Angel Hotel* – In the center of town is this handsome old coaching inn with 29 comfortable rooms and a restaurant. It's convenient to the many attractions in the area. (Cross St.; phone: 0873-7121; moderate.)
Abergavenny Hotel – This inn may be smallish, but its welcome is very big. There are 11 rooms, a nightclub, and a restaurant. (21 Monmouth Rd.; phone: 0873-3802; inexpensive.)

BRECON: Still called by the old name of Brecknock, as you will see on some maps, Brecon is known in the Welsh language as *Aberhonddu.* Its English name is derived from *Brychan,* the vigorous Celtic chieftain (sire of 36 children, the story goes) who ruled this region in the fifth century. The Welsh name is taken from the River Honddu which runs into the Usk. Brecon has narrow streets, a cathedral, a busy livestock market, good shops and pubs, and a peaceful air. It's also a convenient home base for exploring Brecon Beacons National Park. The thirteenth-century cathedral, built first as a fortified priory, overlooks the River Honddu. The town's castle, built by the half-brother of William the Conqueror, was dismantled by the townsfolk during the seventeenth-century civil war in an attempt to avoid the bloodshed necessary to defend it. The remaining parts of the castle are now in the garden of the *Castle of Brecon Hotel.*

The Brecknock Museum, in the old Country Hall in Glamorgan Street, displays interesting examples of Welsh folk art and local crafts, such as the hand-carved wooden "love spoons" young Welshmen used in bygone days to plight their troth.

En Route – Take A470 south toward Merthyr Tydfil, for grand views of the Beacons' red sandstone peaks. Turn right after Libanus along A4215 to Defynnog and you will soon pick up signs directing you to the Mountain Centre of Brecon Beacons National Park. The park covers 519 square miles, running east to west, in the heart of the Black Mountains. The center is out in the wilds and a friendly, informal place where the park's staff is keen to help in your exploration of the mountains. You can use the center as a base for walking, for picnicking, for light meals, or for just sitting and staring (highly recommended). Join up with the A40 trunk road at Sennybridge, a pleasant town, and head west for Trecastle, with its engaging landscape. It used to be an important stop in the old coaching days, and its coaching inns deserve a visit. It is worth pausing here, anyway, to decide on your route to Llandeilo. You can continue on the A40 road, through the village of Halfway, and then go on to Llandovery — in Welsh *Llanymddyfri* ("the church among the waters"). Llandovery is a pleasant town where you can eat well and stay comfortably. It stands by the Tywi (Towy) river, the longest of Welsh rivers and famous for its salmon. The alternative route to Llandeilo needs more careful navigation. From Trecastle, turn left along a little-used country road toward Llanddeusant and thread your way through Twynllanan and up the A4069 to Llangadock, a quiet market town. Stop here to sample some traditional Welsh food and song, at nearby *Plas Glansevin* hotel (phone: 05503-238; moderate.) The attractive, quiet village of Bethlehem, off the A4069, is also worth a visit.

CHECKING IN: *Mountains Hotel* – Only 3 miles from town and tucked inside Brecon Beacons National Park, this modern hotel is convenient for park explorations and has 26 rooms, a restaurant, cafeteria, bar-lounge (with dancing on Saturday nights), and a salon. (In Libanus; phone: 0874-2939 or 4242; moderate.) ***Bishops Meadow Motel*** – Most people stay here for the great views of the Beacons. It's a modern hotel with 26 rooms, bar, cafeteria, and gas station. (On the A438, also called Hay Rd.; phone: 0874-2051; moderate to inexpensive.) ***Nythfa House Hotel*** – Another Georgian house nicely set on 4 acres, it has 15 guestrooms, squash, and sauna. (Phone: 0874-4287; moderate to inexpensive.) ***Landsdowne Hotel*** – In this handsome Georgian building are 11 pleasant rooms — one with a four-poster bed — and a good restaurant. (The Watton; phone: 0874-3321; inexpensive.) ***Wellington Hotel*** – This old, established centerpiece of Brecon Beacons National Park has 20 comfortable rooms, a restaurant, and 2 bars that serve a good variety of beers. (The Bulwark; phone: 0874-2506; moderate to inexpensive.)

LLANDEILO: Near this small riverside town are several interesting castles. Dynevor Castle (*Dinefwr* in Welsh) was built in AD 876 by Rhodri the Great, who divided the kingdom of Wales among his three sons so as to strengthen its defenses against invaders. Dynevor — given to son Cadell — was the stronghold of South Wales. The castle also featured in the wars between the Welsh and the English in medieval times, and was improved by members of the great Rhys family. After the English conquest, Dryslwyn Castle was the center of a Welsh uprising led by Lord Rhys in 1287. It failed — and Lord Rhys was beheaded. Carreg Cennen Castle stands impressively atop a cliff, naturally fortified and a hard nut for those warring medieval chiefs to crack. Dating from about the thirteenth century, it commands a marvelous view of the Black Mountain.

CHECKING IN: *Cawdor Arms Hotel* – In the center of town with 18 rooms, it's a convenient base for touring West Wales. (Rhosmaen St.; phone: 0558-823500; moderate.)

EATING OUT: *Angel Inn* – This small place is memorable for its homemade breads, desserts, and soups. (Heol Galed, Salem; phone: 0558-823394; inexpensive.)

CARMARTHEN: King Arthur's magician, Merlin, was said to have been born hereabouts and that's how this most pleasant of towns gets its name. In Welsh it is called *Caerfyrddin*, or "Merlin's City." In ancient times, as now, it occupied an important and strategic position above the Tywi (Towy) River. The Romans had a base here as the deteriorated amphitheater testifies, and the ruins of the Norman castle can still be seen. During the early part of the twelfth century, monks collected and wrote poems in the *Black Book of Carmarthen*, the oldest known Welsh manuscript, which can be seen in the National Library of Wales in Aberystwyth on the west coast. Carmarthen is one of the few places where you may still see coracles in use. (A *coracle* is a little basket-shaped boat made from tarred cloth stretched over a frail wooden frame, and it's been used in Wales for 2,000 years.) Coracle fishermen work in pairs, drifting down the river with a net suspended between their boats to catch salmon and sewin, a delicious sea trout. After drifting for a while, the fishermen climb onto the riverbank, hump their coracles onto their backs and, looking rather like upright turtles, walk back up the river to start all over again. During the nineteenth century, there were thousands of coracles on Welsh rivers, but laws framed to conserve fish and protect the sport of salmon fishing steadily squeezed the coracle men out. Today there are only about a dozen left, and most are on the rivers Teifi and Tywi around Carmarthen.

Carmarthen is also the administrative hub of the southwestern corner of Wales. Its large covered market draws crowds every Wednesday and Saturday, and behind it the cattle market holds sales each Monday, Wednesday, and Thursday.

In Nott Square stands a monument to Dr. Robert Ferrar, bishop of St. David's, who was burned at the stake on this site in 1555. Also of interest are the Dyfed County Museum in Quay Street and Merlin's Oak in Priory Street. Legend says than when the oak falls, so will the town; to make sure it does not topple, the townspeople have propped it up with concrete.

Incidentally, an interesting 13-mile side trip from Carmarthen is to Laugharne (pronounced Larn) where the Welsh poet Dylan Thomas lived and wrote many of his famous works. You can visit his home, called the Boathouse (now a Dylan Thomas museum), Brown's Hotel where he drank, and the churchyard where he is buried. Laugharne is reached by driving along the A48 to St. Clear's and turning left onto the A4066. Six miles farther along the road is Pendine with its romantic stretch of sands, on which 1930s heroes smashed world speed records in their roaring cars.

En Route – The A484 winds for 5 miles through pleasant wooded country to little Cynwyl Elfed with its white- and color-washed cottages, a genuine piece of old Carmarthenshire calm and beauty. Seven miles north of here the road branches northwest to Cenarth, noted for its waterfalls and the last of the coracle men on this stretch of River Teifi. But if you branch right, on the A486, you will soon be in charming Llandysul, with its late Norman church and bridge spanning the river rapids. Here you can pick up the A475 to Lampeter. If you have time, however, pick your way through the lanes and little roads to Llanybydder, a Teifi-side market town with a continuing tradition of weaving. Factories such as the Siwan Woollen Mills (Llansawel Rd.; phone: 0570-480722), welcome visitors. Try to be in town on the last Thursday of any month for the horse fairs, which attract prospective buyers from all over the world. And from Llanybydder it is only 7 miles into Lampeter.

CHECKING IN: *Ivy Bush Royal Hotel* – With more than 80 rooms, this is certainly one of the best hotels in Wales in terms of atmosphere, design, service, and cuisine. (Spilman St.; phone: 0267-5111; moderate.)

LAMPETER: Lampeter in Welsh is *Llanbedr Pont Steffan*. It's a busy place, where farming folk meet, set in the lush land of the upper Teifi valley. The most famous landmark is St. David's College, part of the University of Wales since 1971, but founded in 1822. Its buildings are open to visitors.

En Route – You have a choice of roads to Tregaron: The main A485 is quicker, but the B4343 on the eastern side of the Teifi is more attractive. The latter passes through Llanfair Clydogau, where the Romans mined silver, no doubt with the labor of indigenous slaves. The lure of Welsh gold and silver was one reason why the Romans conquered and colonized Britain. Four miles on is Llanddewi Brefi where St. David, patron saint of Wales, preached in 519. Stop for a look at the thirteenth-century church, supposedly built on the spot where David delivered an inspirational sermon.

Tregaron is 3 miles from Llanddewl Brefi. It's a friendly market town with some welcoming inns. In the square is a statue of the town's most famous son, Henry Richards (1812–88), dubbed the Apostle of Peace for his espousal of international arbitration and founding of the Peace Union, a forerunner of the United Nations.

Twm Shon Catti, a sixteenth-century Robin Hood–like character, rogue, and poet, was born and roamed near here. Just north of the town is the 4-mile-long Bog of Tregaron, said to be the largest peat bog in Britain and now the Cors Tregaron Nature Reserve. Tregaron earns part of its living as a pony trekking holiday center, and the land here is just right for riding: wild and remote. The central agency to contact for information on pony trekking is the Tregaron Pony Trekking Association, Tregaron (phone: 364). It will cost about £8 for a full day of riding.

Not many people know the road from Tregaron to Llanwrtyd Wells (20 miles away), but it is a thrilling journey over a narrow and winding mountain pass. Once in Llanwrtyd, you can pay a visit to the Cambrian Welsh Tweed Factory where yarn, spun from locally made wool, is sold. Our main route, however, continues up the B4343 to Pontrhydfendigaid and the abbey at Strata Florida, known in Welsh as *Ystrad Fflur,* or "the flowery way." The abbey, built by Cistercian monks in the twelfth and thirteenth centuries, is ruined now. It suffered in the fighting between the Welsh and English in medieval days, and received a final blow when Henry VIII ordered the destruction of monasteries. Although crumbled, it's worth a look. Beneath a yew is the grave of Dafydd ap Gwilym, one of the leading medieval poets of Europe, who divided his time between making verse and love.

In this district of old Cardiganshire there were once many lead mines, and the narrow-gauge steam railway, which runs from Devil's Bridge to Aberystwyth on the coast, started life as an ore-carrying line. It's a romantic ride today.

CHECKING IN: *Black Lion Royal Hotel* – This hostelry has 17 comfortable rooms and a restaurant. (High St.; phone: 0570-422172; moderate to inexpensive.)

ABERYSTWYTH: A popular seaside resort with both sand and pebble bathing beaches, Aberystwyth is also the seat of the University of Wales and the administrative center for Cardigan Bay. Its lively seafront promenade is lined with hotels and has a bandstand and the ruins of a castle, which stand sentinel on the headland.

History is carefully preserved at the National Museum of Wales (Penglais Hill), which houses some of the earliest Welsh manuscripts; and the past is still very much alive at Alexandra Road Station, where British Railways' last steam-powered service departs for the spectacular falls at Devil's Bridge, high in the Vale of Rheidol, which according to legend was built by the devil himself. Closer to home, the town's cliff railway carries visitors to the peak of Constitution Hill, where they have a splendid view of the bay and town.

Concerts and evening shows are regular features along the promenade, and at the university (King St.), the Arts Centre holds frequent exhibitions and the University Theatre presents a summer season of plays. Nearby is the Nanteos Stately Home, a Georgian mansion with an imposing oak staircase, some fine plasterwork, and Italian marble.

CHECKING IN: *Belle Vue Royal Hotel* – Striped window awnings lend a nice touch to this hotel on Cardigan Bay, which has a large restaurant, 48 comfortable rooms, and an 18-hole golf course nearby where guests can play for free Mondays through Fridays. (Marine Ter.; phone: 0970-617558; moderate.) *Bay Hotel* – Also facing the sea, the *Bay Hotel* has 41 rooms and a restaurant. (Marine Ter.; phone: 0970-617356; moderate to inexpensive.) *Marine Hotel* – It's next to the shopping district and has two bars, a restaurant, and lounges. (Marine Parade; phone: 0970-612444; moderate to inexpensive.) *The University College of Wales* – For something rather different, you can stay in one of over 1,300 rooms when students are away. The college is delightfully situated near Cardigan Bay and guests can take advantage of on-campus sports facilities. (For information, write The University College of Wales, Dept. H.A., King St., Aberystwyth; phone: 0970-3757; inexpensive.)

EATING OUT: Julia's – There have been many good reports about this pleasant restaurant; soups (especially the chilled sort), pâté, and syllabub are specialties. (17 Bridge St.; phone: 0970-617090; moderate.) **Blue Bell Inn** – On the A470 to Aberystwyth, in Llangurig village by the River Wye, is this attractive sixteenth-century country inn with good, reasonably priced meals and accommodations. (Phone: 05515-254; inexpensive.)

DEVIL'S BRIDGE: Monks built the first bridge over the Mynach River ravine, but two modern bridges have been built above the original. It is an attractive spot, and for a small fee you can take the steps down into the gorge and walk the winding paths to admire the river's waterfalls.

En Route – By now you will have decided whether to go to Aberystwyth and the coast. Our route branches inland on the A44 from Ponterwyd. On the right you'll see the sweep of the Ystwyth forest and on the left the rolling hills of the Plynlimon range, where the Wye and Severn rivers rise. It is worth penetrating this area on foot if you can. It's wild and haunting, with rushing streams, old caved-in farmhouses, and a few birds circling overhead. The road goes on to Llangurig, which has a handful of inns and shops and is a good place to stop for refreshment. The A470 forks toward Llanidloes.

CHECKING IN: Devil's Bridge Hotel – Built in 1787 as a hunting lodge, the hotel has an unusual Swiss-style appearance. There are 22 rooms and a restaurant. (In Devil's Bridge; phone: 097085-232; moderate to inexpensive.) **Woodlands Hotel** – This attractive stone house above the gorge at Devil's Bridge has 10 cozy bedrooms as well as a relaxing sitting room with fireplace and a good restaurant. (In Devil's Bridge; phone: 097085-666; inexpensive.)

LLANIDLOES: The central feature of the town, and you have to drive slowly to negotiate it, is the half-timbered market hall built in 1609. Llanidloes has a long tradition of wool weaving and trade, but the town was not always as calm as it looks today. In the 1830s the Chartist workmen's reform movement (a political organization popular in Britain then) began to have some impact on Llanidloes's discontented weavers, resulting in the Chartist riots of 1839. The museum in the market hall has some exhibits devoted to this episode in the town's history.

From Llanidloes, you can take several pleasant sidetrips into the country lanes of the district. One in particular starts on the eastern edge of the town, on the B4518, and leads out to Staylittle and Llanbrynmair. Six miles out from Llanidloes you'll come upon a lovely view over Llyn Clywedog reservoir, and everywhere you look in this area, there are equally pretty vistas.

En Route – The A470 follows the Severn River northeast and passes through Llandinam. Near the bridge you'll see a statue of the village's most famous son, Lord David Davies, the civil engineer, railroad builder, and developer of coal mining in the Rhondda valleys of South Wales. The town of Caersws above Llandinam is typical of the small settlements in this area, planted in the green and open land. It is worth making an 8-mile diversion here along the A492 east to Newtown, a busy and growing place with a mixture of many old and new architectural styles. Newtown is a hub of economic growth in this part of rural Wales, and industrial development here is designed to stop the drift of young people out of the countryside into the bigger towns of England. Newton's past prominence as a weaving industry giant is chronicled at the Textile Museum. There is also a museum devoted to Robert Owen, the social philosopher, who was born and buried in Newtown. Owen's many theories finally resulted in an experiment in communal living at New Harmony, Indiana.

The route from Caersws, slightly northwest of Llandinam, goes through Clatter and Carno, Commins Coch, and Cemmas Road along A470. From here you can take a 6-mile side trip down the A489 to Machynlleth, a market town with a tall clock tower as its signature, standing on the Dovey *(Dyfi)* River. The Welsh hero, Owain Glyndwr, who fought a doomed war of independence against the English in the years around 1400, chose Machynlleth for his capital and he was proclaimed king of Wales. Machynlleth is a busy meeting and trading place, and a good town for strolling.

The main route winds through the Dovey valley by way of the A470 to Mallwyd and Dinas Mawddwy, set in alpine countryside.

CHECKING IN: *Angel Hotel* – Congenial and very small with only 2 rooms. (High St.; phone: 05512-2381; inexpensive.) *Trewythen Arms* – An attractive Georgian house with 11 rooms, 2 bars, and a dining room that offers good country cooking. (Town center; phone: 05512-2214; inexpensive.) *Severn View Guest House* – This is a pleasant inn with a friendly atmosphere, and 10 nice rooms. (China St.; phone: 05512-2207; inexpensive.)

DINAS MAWDDWY – It looks hard to say, but pluck up some courage and say Deenass Mouth-oo-ee. It's a rather special place. The landscape is singular, with steeply sloped hills, and the soaring peaks of the Arans close by, to the north. The people here were once known for their red hair and independent nature. And 400-odd years ago travelers feared a gang of them known as the Red Robbers. They ambushed and killed a judge during Henry VIII's reign and for that they were finally hunted down and dispersed. Even today you might see flame-haired people in Dinas Mawddwy. But the visitors today need not worry that the spirit of the Red Robbers lives on: Dinas people are as friendly as the little town they inhabit. It is a restful place, with good fishing for salmon and trout or just for walking. The weaving industry has been revived with some success; the Meirion Mill is open to visitors and wools are available for purchase. You can also take a most enjoyable side trip for 15 miles or so along the narrow road to Llanymawddwy and up to Llanuwchllyn, an off-the-beaten-track ride leading to Bala Lake. The largest natural lake in Wales — almost 4 miles long — Bala is the home of the little gwyniad, a fish found nowhere in the world but here. The lake is also a center for sailing, canoeing, and swimming, and the Bala Lake narrow gauge railway runs alongside it. The town, at the lake's eastern end, has plenty of places to eat, drink, and stay. The whole area makes a worthwhile day out from Dinas Mawddwy.

CHECKING IN: *White Lion Royal Hotel* – A large and charming old post house, it's right in the center of town with a good restaurant and 22 rooms. (High St., Bala; phone: 0678-520314; moderate to inexpensive.) *Plas Coch Hotel* – This is a comfortable, centrally located hotel with a restaurant and 10 rooms. (High St., Bala; phone: 0678-520309; inexpensive.) *The Buckley Arms* – The amenities here include 14 comfortable rooms, 2 with private bath; central heating; a restaurant; and parking facilities. (Phone: 06504-261; inexpensive.) *Red Lion Hotel* – A bit smaller, but just as cozy as the *Buckley,* it has 6 rooms, all sharing a common bath. Central heating, parking, and a restaurant are other features. (Phone: 06504-247; inexpensive.)

DOLGELLAU: Pronounced Dol-geth-lee, this is the chief town of the old shire of Merioneth, now incorporated into the county of Gwynedd, which also includes Caernarfonshire and the island of Anglesey. Dolgellau is solidly built in dark, local stone and is a sturdy, foursquare town perfectly in tune with its surroundings. It lies under the bulk of Cader Idris mountain (the name means "Idris's Chair") and is an important marketplace for the many small mountain villages in the vicinity. It has ancient origins: The Romans were here, as were Cistercian monks who left Cymmer Abbey, founded in 1199. The church, built in 1726, has an interesting barrel roof, and its graveyard has a fascinating mixture of tombstones with Welsh and English inscriptions. The Welsh *Er Cof* means "In Memory." Dolgellau's bridge, built in 1638, is now protected as a historical structure and an old tollhouse also remains.

In the midst of Snowdonia National Park, Dolgellau is naturally an excellent place for touring by foot. Several paths lead up the slopes of Cader Idris ranging from easy walks to hard climbs. Two miles out of town, on the A494 Bala road, there is a turnoff to the left clearly signposted "Precipice Walk." This is a scenic walk, not difficult, and takes about 2 hours. Information on all trails winding up to the summit of Cader Idris is available from the park information center at Bridgend (phone: 0656-422888).

The Snowdon Sherpa bus service is an efficient way to get to and around Snowdonia National Park. You catch the bus at designated pick-up points in the area and it drops you off at major walking and hiking paths and trails leading to Mount Snowdon. A brochure with a map of the bus route is available from the BTA.

Gold found at Llanelltyd and nearby Bontddu transformed Dolgellau into a gold rush town for the last part of the nineteenth century. Traditionally, Welsh gold has been used for royal wedding rings, and you can see some displayed in the little jewelry shop in Dolgellau Square. Although the gold rush days are gone, a little prospecting still goes on.

En Route – An English poet once mused that there was only one thing better than going from Dolgellau to Barmouth, and that was going from Barmouth to Dolgellau. This route follows the estuary of the River Mawddach, with its fine scenery. You can go direct by the A496, or go to Penmaenpool on the A493 and cross the river by the narrow wooden toll bridges. It is a drive worth doing at an easy pace so you can enjoy the grand views.

And just around the corner, so to speak, is jolly little Barmouth, a resort tucked in under the mountainside and edging the waters of the Mawddach estuary. It is a good stopping place with beaches and a variety of sports and entertainment. For a few pence, you can walk across the rail and footbridge that spans the Mawddach. The view is sublime: sands, sea, and mountains. For more active outings, Barmouth has swimming, golf, climbing, fishing, and rough shooting. And, as you would expect in a seaside town like this, there are numerous hotels, guesthouses, and restaurants. It's ideal for those on a modest budget.

The A496 road runs northward to Llanbedr. On the left is the haunting stretch of dunes and marsh known as Morfa Dyffryn and to the right are the rather fearsome mountains called the Rhinogs, said to have been created by God while in a bad temper. Llanbedr is a quiet village and nearby is Mochras Island, or Shell Island, a shingly peninsula famed for the variety of shells on its shores. If you press inland from Llanbedr you will pick up the signs to Cwm Bychan, a remote lake, peaceful and still.

A few miles north of Llanbedr on the A496 is Harlech, one of the romantic names of Wales. Still a small village, Harlech's historic heart and motif is the castle, standing high upon the rocks and defying all who come. It's one of the most photogenic of Welsh castles, and provided the inspiration for "Men of Harlech," one of the best-known traditional Welsh songs. Completed in 1289, the castle was one of the many fortifications built by King Edward I during his campaign to subdue the Welsh in the thirteenth century. The rebel Owain Glyndwr (freedom fighter for the Welsh) captured it in 1404, but his war of independence came to an end shortly after the castle was stormed and taken by Henry of Monmouth. In 1468, Harlech was the last castle to fall to the Yorkists in the Wars of the Roses. It was also the last castle to hold out on the Royalist side in the seventeenth-century civil war. Thus, Harlech has its battle scars. Those with no fear of heights can walk all around the castle on its unfenced, 10-feet-thick walls and climb the 143 steps to the top of its gate house. Look toward the sea, half a mile away, and recall that when the castle was built it actually stood on the shore. Since that time, however, the sea has receded.

From here the road winds toward Talsarnau. On your left there is a good view of Tremadog Bay and the glistening Glaslyn estuary. Follow the signs to Penrhyndeudraeth and cross the river by toll bridge. *Penrhyndeudraeth* is a mouthful but actually, it's Welsh shorthand for "top of the hill overlooking two stretches of sand." It is a solid and amiable village, with lots of ships and pubs. But no doubt it is rather overshadowed by Portmeirion, just up the road on the A487.

CHECKING IN: *King George III Hotel* – Gerard Manley Hopkins once wrote a poem telling those "who pine for peace and pleasure" to "taste the treats of Penmaenpool." And many say he was referring to the *King George III,* a 300-year-old hotel and restaurant delightfully situated at the head of the Mawddach estuary. Freshly caught fish is the specialty in summer, and in winter, the menu turns to local game. All 12 guest rooms have views of the Mawddach estuary and the mountains. (Just out of town on the A493 in Penmaenpool; phone: 0341-422525; moderate.) *Golden Lion Royal Hotel* – The decor here ranges from casual to formal, with 28 comfortable, antique-furnished rooms. (Lion St., Dolgellau; phone: 0341-422579; moderate.) *Dolserau Hall Hotel* – A warm welcome, 12 lovely rooms, and a good restaurant await you here. (Just outside of Dolgellau on the Bala road; phone: 0341-422522; moderate to inexpensive.) *Gwernan Lake Hotel* – On the sweeping slopes of Cader Idris, this hotel has 11 simple, attractive rooms. There's also a bar with lakeside view and a restaurant. (Cader Idris Rd., Gwernan Lake; phone: 0341-422488; inexpensive.) *Cross Foxes Inn* – Snug, small, and situated within Snowdonia National Park. 5 rooms. (Brithdir, A470; phone: 0341-422487; inexpensive.)

PORTMEIRION: This is an enchanting corner of Wales, a village and hotel created by the distinguished, lovable, and fun-loving architect the late Sir Clough Williams-Ellis. He started work on it in the 1920s and today it is an established, picturesque, and rather Italianate waterside village. It has views of the mountains, the sea, and the river, and is accented by rhododendron, shrubs, trees, and flowers. It has been called the Welsh Xanadu. There is a campanile, a dome and a town hall, pools, and statuary. Of course, its character and vistas have made it ideal for film settings. And it was used as the set for the television series *The Prisoner.* Unfortunately, the lovely hotel here burned down, but accommodations are available in cottages in the village. There is an entrance fee for day visitors, which is on a sliding scale depending on the number of people already admitted. The larger the number of visitors, the larger the fee — a sort of crowd control. But usually you can get in for under £1. A delightful experience.

En Route – Just outside Portmeirion, on the main road, is the hamlet of Minffordd, where the philosopher Bertrand Russell lived for some years. He loved this part of Wales and it was one of his pleasures in his declining years to lie in bed and watch the sun go down over Tremadog Bay. The A487 leads westward into Porthmadog, often rendered as Portmadoc, which is reached by crossing a causeway for a small toll. The causeway is part of the harbor construction, planned by William Madocks in the 1820s, which led to the town's economic success as a port. He also built the town of Tremadog (*tre* means town) nearby, which was one of the first planned towns in Britain. It was also the birthplace of Lawrence of Arabia. Porthmadog is a busy holiday and business center, a good base for sailing and for exploring the local countryside.

Leaving Porthmadog, take the main road (A487) to Tremadog and turn right onto the Beddgelert road (A498). After 3 miles, turn right to Garreg and Tanybwlch. Incidentally, an interesting and rather spectacular side trip is to Tanybwlch by train, on the narrow-gauge railway from Porthmadog. This is a former slate railway that used to bring the stone down from Blaenau Ffestiniog for shipping from Porthmadog quay. It fell into disrepair, but has been successfully restored. Its gleaming steam engines are an impressive and picturesque sight as they wind through the gorges of Snowdonia. The railroad is now being refurbished all the way to Blaenau.

Back on the road, join the A487 near Maentwrog and from here go through Ffestiniog and pick up the A470 north to Blaenau Ffestiniog, 3 miles farther on. Blaenau, one of the great old slate towns, seems to be entirely grayish-blue, since buildings, roofs, garden fences, and other items are made from the slate that made Blaenau. The vast slate mines are today a kind of monument to the heyday that straddled the nineteenth and twentieth centuries. Slate is still worked on a smaller scale, and you can visit the enormous caverns hollowed out of the mountains at the Llechwedd Slate Caverns here. It is worth doing, for slate has a fascinating history, which is related as you explore the underground maze of mines. They are open daily from 10 AM to 6 PM (March through October only), but we recommend getting there early since there are attractions above ground as well: the Slate Heritage Theatre, which presents a short narrative on slate's importance to Wales; the craft shop where you can see workers carve souvenirs from slate and a gift shop where you can buy them; and a tramway exhibit of the old carriers that transported the slate from the mines. Llechwedd Slate Caverns are a popular attraction so it's a good idea to reserve tickets at least a day ahead (phone: 076681-306). You can also stop at the Goddfa Ganol Mountain Centre, where there's another mine open to visitors.

The landscape is dramatic in this area and remains so all along the A470 north to Betws-y-Coed. It is a noted beauty spot, resting in a narrow valley, and its famous Swallow Falls are close by, to the north, and worth seeing.

BETWS-Y-COED: (Pronounce it Betsy-Coyd to please the locals who have gamely suffered the mangling of their town's name.) Because it is at a major crossroads with easy access to Snowdonia National Park and Gwydir Forest, you'll find crowds here during the height of summer, especially on weekends. A midweek visit would be more enjoyable during the season. The town has ancient origins and a very old church with parts dating from the twelfth to sixteenth centuries. Its gray stone buildings are typical of this region. There is a good choice of craft shops; Welsh woolens are of high quality and Betws has a large selection. The *Anna Davies Welsh Wool Shop* (phone: 06902-292) sells tapestry garments, wools, tweeds, quilts, rugs, pottery, sheepskin, perfume, and knitwear. It's open 7 days a week, except Sundays in January and February.

En Route – At this point you may choose either of two side trips depending on how much time you have. First, you can make an expedition into deeper Snowdonia (known in Welsh as *Eryri*, "the land of eagles"). A reliable guide through the Snowdonia area is David Siviter at the Mountaineering Club in Bethesda (northwest from Betws-y-Coed, via the A5; phone: 0248-600612). Mr. Siviter, Secretary of the North Wales Guides Association, acts as a go-between for all guides in the area. Or, you can head westward to Capel Curig, Llanberis, Caernarvon, and the Isle of Anglesey.

It is a nice 8-mile drive along the A5 from Betws-y-Coed to Capel Curig, and you can circle Mount Snowdon itself by going 5 miles down to Pen-y-Gwrd and continuing on the A4086 to Llyn Peris and Llyn Padarn (two pretty lakes), passing through Llanberis, a Snowdonia town of mountains and quarries. The North Wales Quarrying Museum at Dinorwic, near Llanberis, is worth seeing and gives a good insight into the slate industry, once the great industry of this region. The Llanberis Lake Railway (1 ft. 11½ in. in gauge) runs alongside Lake Padarn for 2 miles from Padarn Park to Penllyn. The original railway transported slate from the Dinorwic quarries (the world's largest) to Port Dinorwic on the Menai Strait.

From Llanberis, it's a short trip to Caernarvon and the Isle of Anglesey — a trip worth considering. Some say Caernarvon is one of Wales's most remarkable cities and Anglesey one of its most scenic stretches of countryside. From Llanberis, take the A4086 to Caernarvon.

CHECKING IN: *Royal Oak Hotel* – Huddled in Snowdonia National Park and set beside the River Conway, the hotel is charming in an old-fashioned sort of way. The food is good and the service dependable. Fishing for trout and salmon in the river is convenient and permits can be had without much ado. (Holyhead Rd., Betws-y-Coed; phone: 06902-219; moderate to inexpensive.) *Craig-y-Dderwen Country House Hotel* – Snuggled in a cluster of trees right on the banks of the River Conway, the hotel has 22 rooms, 16 with private bath. Nine-hole golf is free for guests. (Betws-y-Coed; phone: 06902-293; moderate to inexpensive.) *Fairy Glen Hotel* – This seventeenth-century house — more of a B&B than a hotel — is conveniently situated near the entrance of Snowdonia National Park and the Lledr Valley, and also overlooks the River Conway. Some of the 10 rooms have private baths and there is central heating. A bar is available to guests; beef, trout cooked in butter with almonds, and roast duckling are the chef's best for dinner. (On Dolwyddelan Rd. in Betws-y-Coed; phone: 06902-269; inexpensive.) *Glan Aber Hotel* – Located on the A5, a backdrop of hilly woodlands makes this old stone mansion look quite attractive. There are 26 comfortable rooms (some with private bath), a restaurant serving traditional English and Welsh fare, and two bars. (Betws-y-Coed; phone: 06902-325; inexpensive.) *Henllys Hotel* – *Henllys* is the Welsh word for courthouse, and in 1975 Pete and Joan Smart transformed this old courthouse on the River Conway into a comfortable hotel. There are cushy chairs, beamed ceilings, a bar, and the bright, split-level dining room is the former courtroom. Next door to the hotel is a 9-hole golf course and there's also fishing and pony trekking nearby. (Betws-y-Coed; phone: 06902-534; inexpensive.) *Waterloo Motor Inn* – More modern in design than the other hotels mentioned, the *Waterloo* has three bars, a gas station, and free golf for guests. All 25 rooms have private bath; there's a grill for snacking, and a restaurant for more leisurely meals. (Betws-y-Coed; phone: 06902-411; moderate to inexpensive.)

CAERNARVON: Rendered in Welsh as Caernarfon (there's no *v* in the Welsh language and *f* is pronounced like *v*), the city's magnificence lies in its castle and its setting. Caernarvon Castle is one of Europe's greatest, built in the late thirteenth and early fourteenth centuries. Like some other grand castles in Wales, its construction was ordered by King Edward I of England as part of his successful effort to keep the rebellious Welsh in order. From this strategic site on the Menai Strait, beside the River Seiont, the English could control a huge stretch of the Snowdonia wilds.

Although the castle's interior was never fully completed, there are still many turreted towers and narrow passageways to explore. The Queens Tower holds the Museum of the Royal Welsh Fusiliers with a collection of regimental memorabilia; the Northeast Tower has an exhibit on the Prince of Wales investiture ceremony (Prince Charles was invested here in 1969); and the Eagle Tower has a display of medieval armor. The latter gets its name from three statuettes of eagles that were once perched on the tower's turrets; today, only one is left guarding it. Caernarvon Castle is open almost every day of the year (there's a small admission charge) and the staff is a jolly lot who are delighted to answer questions.

From the castle's ramparts, you can see the town walls. Built at the same time as the castle, the walls still surround the oldest section of the city. Inside the walls are fascinating narrow streets with little pubs and shops. In the main square (Castle Square) there is a statue of David Lloyd George, who rose from humble beginnings in the tiny village of Llanystumdwy, near Criccieth, to become MP for Caernarvon Boroughs, and, of course, prime minister of Britain and one of the twentieth century's greatest statesmen.

The shopping in Caernarvon includes crafts, and there is a branch of the Craftcentre Cymru group that sells tweeds, woolens, pottery, and items made from metal and wood. In addition, there's a market on Saturdays in Castle Square. For sporting activities, Caernarvon boasts two yacht clubs, tennis, and golf facilities, and good river and sea fishing.

Near town is the Roman fort of Segontium, a military center founded in AD 78. Some buildings date back only to the second century and some were rebuilt in the fourth century. Although there aren't a great many ruins left to explore, the museum here has interesting exhibits on the history of the Roman takeover of Wales, archaeological finds from the period, and displays on the Roman military system and culture.

CHECKING IN: *Royal Hotel* – A modernized coaching inn with 58 rooms and two well-regarded restaurants. One specializes in steak and fish; the other has a more varied menu. (North Rd.; phone: 0286-3184; moderate.) *The Black Boy Inn* – Dating back to the fourteenth century and located inside the old walled section of Caernarvon, this inn has charming wood beams, crooked floors, and low ceilings. Good breakfasts, lunches, and dinners are served in the attractive restaurant, and colorful locals frequent the bar. (North Gate St.; phone: 0286-3023; inexpensive.)

ISLE OF ANGLESEY: From Caernarvon, it's about 10 miles along the A487 road to Bangor, where you take a bridge over to the Isle of Anglesey. A lovely stone suspension bridge built in 1826 by Thomas Telford (a Scottish engineer) spans the Menai Strait. The bridge is not only handsome, but a tribute to its designer's skill, since it has no problem coping with the traffic loads of the present century. However, to alleviate congestion, the new Brittania Road Bridge has recently been opened.

These bridges cross over the swirling strait to the island of Anglesey, a corner of Wales that doesn't see many overseas travelers because it's rather off the beaten track. But it repays the trouble. Anglesey is a place for quiet, personal discoveries: a place to wander down narrow side roads and find charming, unspoiled hamlets and pubs.

You can cut diagonally across the island on the A5 to Holyhead, a distance of about 20 miles; or northeast to Beaumaris, a 9-mile drive; or, if you have the time, it's very rewarding to drive all the way around the island via the A5025 and the A4080.

Holyhead is bustling with a number of hotels, small restaurants, and pubs. Most likely, the reason for the bustle is the ferry service between here and Dun Laoghaire, Ireland, 3¼ hours away.

The cliff scenery around Holyhead is striking. South Stack, a tiny, rocky island brightened by a lighthouse, is justly famous for its pounding surf, shrieking seabirds, and strong sea breezes.

If you decide to cover the entire coast of Anglesey, there are all sorts of delightful, relaxing places with good beaches: Red Wharf Bay, Moelfre, Amlwch, Bull Bay, Cemaes Bay, and Rhosneigr. Sailing, fishing, walking, swimming, and sunbathing are the order of the day, and you can surf at Rhosneigr.

If you can't travel all the way to Holyhead, you can take the short drive (from the bridge) out to Beaumaris.

BEAUMARIS: The town of Beaumaris (pronounced Bew-marris) proudly harbors the last castle Edward I built in Wales, and many say he saved the best for last. Built at the end of the thirteenth century, the moated castle guards the entrance to the Menai Strait, and looks particularly fine against a backdrop of sea and mountains. Its beauty, however, is secondary to its strength: It has impenetrable fortifications. The castle was simply a milestone in medieval fortress building. The ingenious design includes two defense walls encircling the castle. The inner wall is square, while the outer wall seems square but actually has bowed sides. This roundedness permitted virtually no corner to go unseen by the castle's keepers. Also interesting is the angle at which the entryways meet the gate houses. Instead of a direct alignment, they're off-center to force a slanted approach by aggressors, making them almost certainly visible to the heavily armed guards.

Back on the main route, from Betws-y-Coed, the A470 winds attractively through the Conwy valley north to Llanrwst, a picturesque little market town beside the river with an interesting church and a most striking bridge across the Conwy, built in 1636, thought to have been the work of the noted architect Inigo Jones. From Llanrwst, take the A548 and watch, after about 5 miles, for signs pointing to Llansannan on your right. The road winds through wild and spacious country — hills, moors, and river valleys. From Llansannan, turn southeast onto A544 to Bylchau and look for signs for the A543 to Denbigh. It's a lovely run over the moors.

CHECKING IN: Henllys Hall Hotel – A former Franciscan monastery, set on forested acreage with superb Snowdonian views, it has tennis facilities, a good restaurant, and 21 rooms. (Beaumaris; phone: 0248-810412; expensive to moderate.) **Ye Old Bulls Head Hotel** – This establishment has been around since 1472, which makes it something of a historical landmark. Copper ornaments dangling from ceiling beams and snapping fires in the hearths warm up the place and the mood quite a bit. There are 17 pleasant rooms, some with private bath. (Castle St., Beaumaris; phone: 0248-810329; moderate.) **Plas Llanfaes Country House** – This small, comfortable establishment set in 7 acres of pretty grounds is renowned for its warm welcome. (Beaumaris; phone: 0248-810480; inexpensive.)

DENBIGH: Called *Dinbych* in Welsh, this town looks out over the Vale of Clwyd, the river that gives the county its name. This is true border country, so it has seen its share of battle-axing, swordplay, and the zizz of arrows. The castle, which stands on a hill, was first built by William the Conqueror as part of his effort to annex this region. It was greatly extended and improved during King Edward I's reign, and along with Edward's other castles — Harlech, Beaumaris, Conwy, Caernarvon, and Criccieth — it played a large part in bringing the Welsh under the king's rule in the thirteenth century. Later, the castle was sold by Queen Elizabeth I to Robert Dudley, her favorite courtier. And it was a focal point of the great civil war in the following century. Action against King Charles's supporters was directed from Denbigh and Sir John Owen, leader of a determined Royalist army, was captured and kept in the castle. It is worth visiting: Note its unusual octagonal towers. The Elizabethan town hall is just one of many interesting corners of Denbigh. The steep streets make for some memorable snapshots. Perhaps Denbigh's most famous son was H. M. Stanley, the poor local boy who made good; he emigrated to the US, became a newspaper man, explored Africa, and found Dr. Livingstone, he presumed.

En Route – Eight miles south on the A525 lies Ruthin (pronounced Rithin), a handsome town whose market square is fringed by sixteenth- and seventeenth-century houses. It was once a wool trade center, but its history goes much farther back. It was here that Owain Glyndwr started his uprising against English rule in 1400. Glyndwr and his men burned the town but failed to capture the castle. The medieval castle is now a ruin, but the big mansion on the site is a fine hotel, expensive as Welsh hostelries go, but with good facilities and fine dining. It is called, naturally enough, the *Ruthin Castle,* and you cannot mistake its imposing redstone appearance. The castle offers medieval banquets with ale, mead, roasts and the like done in what is thought to be a medieval style. It makes a jolly evening and you need to go with an empty stomach.

The route from Ruthin winds across the Vale of Clwyd and across the Clwydian range of mountains by way of the A494. But a side trip 15 miles along the A525 to the A542 to Llangollen is well worth any effort. It stands beside the rushing River Dee, and words simply cannot do it justice. The four-arched bridge across the Dee is traditionally one of the seven wonders of Wales and was built in the twelfth century. Later, it was widened. Llangollen is deeply embedded in the history and lore of Wales, and the town is featured in many legends of love, jealousy, rivalry, and blood and thunder. It takes its name from Collen, a saint of the ancient Celtic church. The Valle Crucis Abbey, 2 miles out along the canal, was ruined on Henry VIII's orders when he was stamping out monasteries, but it is still imposing. Any visit to this town must include the home of the "Ladies of Llangollen." These women were two eccentrics who played host to such literary lights as Wordsworth, Browning, Hazlitt, and Sir Walter Scott. The cottage, called Plas Newydd, is open to visitors.

Nearby, on the Corwen road, is Plas-yn-Ial. This is the ancient seat of the Ial family, whose name, pronounced "Yal" was corrupted to "Yale," and one of whose sons founded the American university. Llangollen is abundantly endowed with pubs, hotels, and cafés, and every July it rings to the sound of music, when the International Musical Eisteddfod, founded to bring the world's people together in peace, has the town bulging. People come from all over the world to compete in song and dance and instrument-playing, so that the town is a mass of color and a happy babble of tongues. Evening concerts are given by renowned singers and instrumentalists. Information: Eisteddfod Office, Llangollen, North Wales LL20 8NG (phone: 0978-860236).

CHECKING IN: *Bryn Morfydd Hotel* – Set on 36 acres, this hotel has 25 comfortable rooms with private bath and great views, tennis courts, a new golf course, and a swimming pool. But the jewel of the estate is a sixteenth-century manor house, which has 11 guest rooms and a banquet hall where breakfast is served. (3 miles south of Denbigh on A525 in Llanrhaeadr; phone: Llanynys 074578-280; expensive to moderate.)

Northern Ireland

Antrim Coast

In many ways reminiscent of the California coast as seen from Highway 1, the stretch of coastline between Larne and Portrush is an exceptionally beautiful one, offering spectacular views of the sea at every twist and turn. And along the eastern part of the Antrim Coast, as far as Ballycastle, drivers will be tempted to turn inland and explore the Glens of Antrim, a series of nine lovely valleys formed some 20,000 years ago by retreating glaciers. Of great interest to scientists, the coastline is a veritable textbook illustration of the geological history of the earth, with its rock layers of red sandstone, white chalk, black basalt, and blue clay jutting out from beneath ancient lava flows.

Antrim has been inhabited for at least 5,000 years and probably for a great deal longer than that. In Glenballyeamon, near Cushendall, stone "axe factories" dating from the Neolithic period have been discovered, and it is known that some of the tools made here of the local stone, diorite, were "exported" to countries outside Ireland. A Harvard University archaeological expedition has uncovered several layers of flint tools in a cliff face at Cushendun; they think they may have found the key to the Irish Stone Age. And Danish archaeologists believe this area to be a prime example of post–Ice Age developing society.

Although not part of the Roman Empire, Antrim was visited by the Romans from time to time and some trade developed with Britannia. Upon the decline of the empire and the weakening of its defense, Irish kings launched raiding parties to steal booty and capture slaves. One of the most famous slaves, Patrick, spent 6 years as a shepherd, then escaped to Gaul. Here he underwent monastic training and (legend says) had a holy vision recalling him to Ireland to convert the country to Christianity. He returned in AD 432 and proselytized from then until his death in about 457; he was later canonized. Throughout this region you'll hear lots of anecdotes about the saint's activities, and for centuries Slemish Mountain (1,437 feet) has been a place of pilgrimage on St. Patrick's Day.

Many Irish missionaries that set out to convert Europe hailed from the north of Ireland, most notably Saint Columbanus and Saint Gall who went to Germany, Switzerland, and Italy, and St. Columcille (or Columba) who went to Scotland. Because of the proximity of Ireland and Scotland, there had always been much traffic between the two countries. Besides Christianity Ireland gave Scotland its Gaelic language (which replaced Pictish from the fifth century onward); shared the game of hurling (called shinny or shinty in Scotland); and even sent over the famous bagpipes (there's a joke hereabouts that the Irish exported the bagpipes to Scotland and the Scots haven't seen the joke yet!).

The patriarch of the Scottish Royal House, Fergus, was Irish and the town of Carrickfergus is named in his honor. Two Scotsmen, Robert the Bruce and his brother Edward, who had freed their country from English rule, attempted to do the same for Ireland, but succeeded only briefly — Edward was declared king of Ireland in 1316, but his death 2 years later threw Ireland back into its feud with the English crown. The wars continued until the end of the sixteenth century, culminating in the conquest of the north by the soldiers of Queen Elizabeth I. To tighten English control, a new policy — the "plantation of Ireland" — was devised; this was a plan for introducing Scottish and English Protestant settlers into the area. The scheme was quite effective. Many plantation manor houses still exist today and can be seen along this route in Ballygalley, on Rathlin Island, and other places.

Whatever their roots, the people in the Antrim area are quite exceptionally friendly; in the countryside visitors will be bidden the time of day and perhaps engaged in a conversation. After all, the Irish say, "When God made time, he made plenty of it."

Our Antrim Coast route starts at Carrickfergus on the east coast, about 9 miles above Belfast, tracing the northeastern corner of Ireland. Its magnificent east coast curves around the base of steep headlands between which the beautiful nine glens of Antrim open to the sea. Almost every bay along the coast is a link in a chain of fine holiday resorts. Near the northernmost point, Torr Head is only 13 miles from Scotland. On the northwestern end of Antrim's coast is the Giant's Causeway, a curious basalt rock formation that's a celebrated natural wonder. The River Bann and Lough Neagh, the largest lake in Ireland and Britain, form the western boundary. The tour ends in Londonderry, the ancient walled city.

Generally speaking, hotels in Northern Ireland are not first-class by international standards, but they are always clean and usually reasonably priced. Most hotels have a dining room, where the food served is fresh and hearty, if not haute cuisine. The hotels mentioned in this chapter are all moderate, which means that a double room with bath will run between $45 and $55.

CARRICKFERGUS: Said to be one of the oldest towns in Northern Ireland, Carrickfergus was the north's main port until Belfast began to expand in the seventeenth century. Its proud history is personified by the grand castle built on a spit of basaltic rock and standing watch over the harbor. The castle has been carefully restored and is in an excellent state of preservation. Note especially the fourteenth-century portcullis and the machinery that operates it. Sections of the castle were begun by John de Courcey, earl of Ulster, in about 1180 and it was completed by his successor, Hugh de Lacy, by about 1205, although renovations were made as late as the seventeenth century to accommodate newly developed artillery. The stronghold's central feature is the rectangular keep. Ninety feet high and sixty feet square, its five stories are linked by a spiral stone staircase that winds up to the roof and ramparts. From here sentries could survey the sea for hostile ships and troops could defend the fortress. Carrickfergus has seen many aggressors: King John in 1210, who attempted to subordinate the

DIRECTIONS / Antrim Coast

earl of Ulster; Robert the Bruce of Scotland and his brother Edward in 1315, who took the castle (in an unsuccessful attempt to drive the English from Ireland); and the French under General Thurst in 1710, who merely wanted to steal food. On other floors of the castle, you can marvel at the 40-square-foot banqueting hall, inspect the old castle well, and of course, sneak down into the dungeon. The castle also houses the Regimental Museum, a collection of armor, artillery, cavalry uniforms, and other military artifacts.

St. Nicholas Church, first built in 1185, retains some of the original twelfth-century arcades and other features added in the fourteenth century, but most of the present structure dates from the seventeenth and eighteenth. The chancel, renovated in 1305, has just one original window, and the spire was only recently built in 1778. The church has a memorial to Sir Arthur Chichester, first English governor of Ulster and earl of Belfast. The four stained-glass windows were designed by Irish artists.

Sections of Carrickfergus's town wall remain, particularly the North Gate, which was the strongest due to restoration work in 1911. The four walls of the old County Antrim Courthouse on High St., which date from 1613, are now the exterior walls of the town hall. Also on High Street are some attractive eighteenth-century houses.

For those who wish to retrace the footsteps of the famous, Carrickfergus offers two interesting possibilities: Just east of town is Boneybefore, where the grandparents of Andrew Jackson (seventh president of the US) lived. A monument marks the site of their home. And, 2 miles along the coast road toward Larne, a right turn will lead you to Kilroot. Here you'll find the ruins of the church where Jonathan Swift began his clerical career. It was in Kilroot that he wrote his *Tale of a Tub*. (An aside to Swift fans: Cave Hill, which is near Belfast, supposedly inspired Swift to write *Gulliver's Travels*.)

Continue up the A2 to Larne.

CHECKING IN: *Dobbins Inn Hotel* – Near the castle and just off the coast road, this small hotel has 14 bedrooms. Its coffee lounge is warmed by a huge old stone fireplace; the nautical-styled restaurant offers dinner dances on Saturday evenings during the winter. (68 High St.; phone: Carrickfergus 63905; moderate.)

LARNE: Second only to Belfast in its importance as a port, Larne is the closest point in Ireland to Britain and the ferry trip to Scotland takes just a bit over an hour. Huge freight ships as well as smaller pleasure craft rock in her harbor.

A 95-foot tower is the first thing you'll see as you approach Larne. Modeled after the traditional Irish round tower, it was built to honor James Claine, a member of Parliament who so loved the harbor's view that he was buried upright so he "would never lose sight of it." Nearby you'll find lots of recreation facilities: You can swim in the pool, lie on the beach, take a boat ride, or play tennis. But if you'd like to tap Larne's historical vein, start with the Curran, a curved strip of land in the harbor and site of much excavation. At the end of the Curran are the ruins of Olderfleet Castle where many flint implements were unearthed. So many ancient artifacts have been found around here that fragments from Ireland's Stone Age are termed "Larnian." This is also where Edward the Bruce landed in 1315 with hopes of becoming king of Ireland. (He stayed only 2 years, then was killed near Dundalk.) St. Cedma's parish church is also worth a look for its stained-glass windows executed by Irish artist Wilhemina Geddes.

Island Magee, only a short ferry ride from Larne, is actually a peninsula. Most of its acreage is given over to farming, but there are plenty of spots for exploring and picnicking. The 250-foot high basaltic cliffs on the eastern coast of the island are called "The Gobbins" and are inhabited by flocks of singing seabirds. (Be careful on the cliffside walkways; they can be dangerous.) At Portmuck, north of the Gobbins, you'll find the ruins of a castle believed to have been the home of a Scottish family, the

Magees, from whom the snip of land takes its name. On the island's northern tip, near Brown's Bay is the 9-hole Island Magee Golf Course.

En Route – On the way to Ballygalley you'll pass Ballygalley Head, a cluster of irregular rock pillars formed by lava that burbled to the surface in the Cenezoic era. Ballygalley Castle, really a plantation manor house, was built in 1625 by a Scottish landowner, James Shaw. Although occupied by the Shaw family until the early nineteenth century, it was turned into a luxury hotel by Major Ian Gordon in 1948. It's a fine place to stop for dinner.

A bit farther up the road is Glenarm Castle, set near a forest park and glen. Built for Sir Randal MacDonnell, the first earl of Antrim, in 1636, it's been altered and added to over the years and is now largely eighteenth century in appearance, with minarets, Tudor windows, and cupolas. Near St. Patrick's Church is the grave of Shane O'Neill, leader of the sixteenth-century Irish revolt against the English. He was decapitated by the MacDonnells in Cushendun in 1567, and his head sent to Dublin where it was put on macabre display.

Just a few miles past Glenarm you'll come upon Carnlough, an old limestone quarrying town that's today a summer vacation spot. You're now entering Glencloy (one of the nine glens of Antrim), a valley crosscut by streams and splashed by numerous waterfalls. About 5 miles farther is Garron Point, a hub of land jutting into the North Channel presided over by Garron Tower. Originally a mansion and now converted to a school, it was built by Lady Londonderry between 1848 and 1850; visits are by appointment only.

Continuing on from Garron Point, you'll soon see Red Bay, which takes its name from the red sandstone cliffs that slope into it and which lies at the foot of one of the most scenic of Antrim glens, Glenariff. The cliffs are punctured in two places by tunnels through which the road passes. (The sandstone cut from the cliff was used to build Cushendall's courthouse.)

CHECKING IN: *Ballygalley Castle Hotel* – This hotel — a seventeenth-century manor house with a twentieth-century addition — has lovely views of Ballygalley Bay and 30 modern, comfortable bedrooms. The sleek, picture-windowed dining room serves fine, fresh fish. (274 Coast Rd.; phone: Ballygalley 212; moderate.)

CUSHENDALL/CUSHENDUN: Cushendall is a tiny but pretty town whose streets are lined with stately Georgian and Regency style houses. In the village center is a structure called Curfew Tower, a sort of gaol built by Frances Turnley in 1809. Cushendall is a holiday center, and you could stop here to do some swimming, boating, or fishing.

A few miles west of Cushendall you'll see signs for "Ossian's Grave," a court cairn or burial mound made of stones. The Ossian in question was a poet warrior in the third century AD and supposedly the son of that mythological Irish hero, Finn MacCool. Be forewarned that it's not an easy climb up the lower slopes of Tievebulliagh Hill to the grave.

Cushendun is regarded by some as one of the most attractive Irish villages; threaded by the Glendun River, it occupies a lovely sandy crescent of shore washed by the bay and anchored by sandstone cliffs at either end. The cottages on the north side of the river were designed by Clough William Ellis, an imaginative and innovative architect whose most famous work is at Portmeirion in Wales. The whitewashed stone cottages and the surrounding countryside are now maintained by the National Trust. This area has been much painted by artists and during the summer you'll often see them there busy at work. Cushendun is a pleasant spot for a sojourn. Despite some traffic, the village is delightfully tranquil; boats are available for hire; and you can explore the many caves in the sandstone cliffs. One of these is 20 miles deep and leads to Cave

House, the former vacation residence of poet John Masefield, which is now owned by the Catholic Church. The famous Irish chieftain Shane O'Neill (Shane the Proud), an opponent of Queen Elizabeth and a leader of an Ulster revolt against England, was assassinated in Cushendun in 1567.

En route – For a pleasant side trip head slightly east, then north over the Glendun Viaduct, an 82-foot-high bridge that crosses the Glendun river and offers an impressive panorama of the area. Across the bridge the road continues to Loughareema, called locally the "vanishing lake": When there is a downpour, the lake overflows, then almost immediately dries up because of the permeable chalk bed underneath it. Near Loughareema is Balleypatrick Forest with a 4.5-mile-long scenic drive. It's also a good spot for picnicking, pony trekking, or for just walking along the Corratary River.

At Cushendall you can take the Torr Road along the coast up to Fair Head.

FAIR HEAD: This impressive 636-foot-high cliff rising from huge sandstone blocks and towering over Murlough Bay is the northeasternmost point in Ireland. The terrain across the mouth of the bay and opposite the head is gentler, with lush green vegetation carpeting the slope right down to the sandy beach. This area was much loved by Roger Casement, the Irish patriot and international philanthropist, and there's a monument to him here.

BALLYCASTLE: At the mouth of the Glenshesk River and overlooked by the 1,696-foot-high Knocklayd Hill, Ballycastle is actually two towns linked together by Quay Road, a pretty avenue lined with trees and Georgian and Victorian homes. Lower Town is a seaside resort with facilities for swimming, tennis, boating, golf, and fishing. Upper Town, the older of the two, has restaurants, shops, and many fine houses. The center of upper town is called the Diamond; here you'll find the Greek-style Holy Trinity Church built in 1756, as well as a memorial to George O'Connor, one of the town's patrons. The Diamond is also the scene of the annual Ould Lammas Fair, a kind of flea market at which all manner of new and used articles are sold. Along the sidestreets leading from the Diamond are a few shops *(D. Donnelly & Co.* and *The Irish Shop)* that feature paintings by local artists.

On the outskirts of town is the Franciscan Bonamargy Friary, founded by the MacQuillan family in 1500. Damaged by fire in 1589, it was refurbished and occupied until 1642, after which it gradually went into decay; in 1931 the friary underwent final restoration. Note the earls of Antrim (MacDonnell) family tomb.

The town has mythological as well as religious associations, for it was in the nearby Sea of Moyle that the tragic Children of Lir, who were changed into swans by their jealous stepmother, had to spend 300 of their 900 years' transmutation.

Before you leave Ballycastle, be sure to visit Ballycastle Forest park and Knocklayd Hill, where there are camping sites and picnic grounds. Several scenic walks are also signposted in the Glenshesk valley, near the forest park.

RATHLIN ISLAND: A visit to Rathlin can be a delightful interlude in your driving journey, for you must leave your car behind and explore the island on foot. The 6-mile crossing takes 50 minutes by motorboat and should be undertaken only in good weather, as the Rathlin Sound can be treacherous when rough. (Long ago the sound was called the "Cauldron of Brecain" because it was in these stormy waters that Brecain — grandson of the legendary king of Ireland, Niall of the Nine Hostages — perished with his fleet.)

As you approach the harbor in Church Bay, you'll get a good view of Rathlin's steep, 200-foot-high white limestone cliffs that surround almost all of the island. Fishing is the main occupation on the island; lobster, conger eel, and many varieties of fish are all found in Church Bay; if you want to go fishing, talk to one of the local fishermen about arranging an outing.

With a population of only about 100, people are a minority here. The island is really owned and occupied by the thousands of seabirds that nest on Rathlin's crags and cliffs. The best vantage point for bird-watching is West Lighthouse, situated on the western end of the island. And the nearby vicinity of Kebble is a breeding ground for the island's puffin, guillemot, and razorbill population.

Although tiny, Rathlin has seen much history. The most famous landmark of all is Bruce's Cave, on the eastern end, to which Robert the Bruce retreated in 1306 after he was outlawed in Scotland. At Knockans, you'll see ruins of an Irish sweathouse, a primitive version of the sauna, for which steam was produced by pouring water on heated stones. (Remember Tomas Larkin purging his soul — and sweating off a drunk — in *Trinity?*) In the center of the island, Brockley is the location of a Stone Age "axe factory," and slightly north, Doonmore once was the site of an ancient hill fort. Near the harbor is an eighteenth-century manor house built by Viscount Gage.

CHECKING IN: *Rathlin Guest House* – Down on the harbor a few minutes' walk from Tony McCuaig's pub is a small (5 rooms) guest house with a reputation for hearty breakfasts. (The Quay; phone: 71216; inexpensive.)

THE GIANT'S CAUSEWAY: Most people would disagree with English writer Samuel Johnson's opinion that the Giant's Causeway is "worth seeing but not going to see." In fact, the rock formation is so remarkable that it's often called the eighth wonder of the world. Legend has it that Finn MacCool threw the polygonal rocks to the ground to begin a road of conquest to Scotland. The more prosaic explanation for the causeway's existence is that it was formed by the slow cooling of lava that burst to the earth's surface in the Cenozoic era about 70 million years ago. Altogether there are about 40,000 basaltic columns packed together in a shape so regular they seem man-made. Some sections of the lava were naturally molded into unique designs that have been nicknamed Lady's Fan, Lord Antrim's Parlour, the Giant's Horseshoe, and the Giant's Coffin. Another, called the Giant's Organ, is an astonishing 60-yard series of pillars of incredible regularity. Providing a backdrop to the causeway are large basalt pillars called "The Chimney Tops"; in 1588, the retreating Spanish Armada aimed an attack on these columns thinking they were part of Dunluce Castle. Past these stacks is Port Na Spania Bay where one of the Spanish ships, the *Girona,* was destroyed. In recent years, the wreckage of the sunken ship was explored and the items that were recovered are on display at Ulster Museum in Belfast. The collection consists of Renaissance jewelry, including a Cross of the Knight of Malta belonging to Captain Fabricio Spinola, some tableware, and artillery.

The adventurous can hire a boat and a boatman to wander through the nearby caves of the Causeway; one called the Runkerry is 700 feet long.

En route – Bushmills, a pleasant hamlet slightly southwest of the Giant's Causeway, is the location of the well-known Bushmills Distillery Company, the oldest distillery in the world, established by Thomas Phillips in 1608 and still in operation today. Visitors are welcome from 10:30 AM to 2:30 PM, Mondays through Fridays. The tour takes about an hour, and afterward you can sample the whiskies. Since the company is small, visits are by appointment only, but a day's notice is sufficient (phone: Bushmills 31521).

A few miles past Bushmills is Dunluce Castle, built by Richard de Burgh, earl of Ulster, in about 1300. Awesomely placed on a basaltic rock jutting from the sea, the structure is reached by a wooden walkway and has five towers linked by a curtain wall. Since its builders thought — with some justification — the fortress was impregnable, the castle is odd in that it doesn't have a keep. Dunluce was held for centuries by the de Mandevilles (also called the MacQuillans), but was taken from them by the MacDonnells during the sixteenth century, and they occupied it for the next hundred years. In 1639 the castle kitchen collapsed into the sea, killing eight servants; the buildings on the mainland, adjacent to the castle, are thought to be the rebuilt and safer kitchen and servant quarters.

PORTRUSH: This resort town has long sandy beaches and facilities for tennis, boating, and fishing. It's most famous, however, for the outstanding course at Royal Portrush Golf Club. The first Irish club to host the British Open, the Royal Portrush has two 18-hole courses and a 9-hole course. One of these is so scenic that it's hard to keep your eyes on the ball; this course, called the Dunluce, is the championship layout and is named after the striking old castle perched on the white cliffs above the fairways. (For more information on the Royal Portrush Golf Club, see *Great Golf*, DIVERSIONS.)

For the first time along this route, we veer inland from Portrush to Coleraine via the A29.

CHECKING IN: *The Links* – Small (14 rooms) but comfortable, this hostelry is a short 3-mile drive from the Royal Portrush Golf Club. (Strand Rd.; phone: Portstewart 2580; moderate.)

COLERAINE: A seventeenth-century plantation town at the head of the River Bann estuary, Coleraine was established by the London Company on land granted by James I in 1613. Since then Coleraine has become a bustling industrial center engaged in the distilling of whiskey and the linen trade. Some say that Coleraine's roots stretch far beyond the seventeenth century to prehistoric times, and indeed nearby archaeological excavations have indicated that there were settlements here as early as about 7000 BC.

Whatever Coleraine's ancient origins, you'll notice that most of its architecture is fairly recent. This is because many of the earlier structures were either washed away, burned out, pillaged, or rebuilt. Of the town's churches, St. Patrick's is most noteworthy despite changes and additions to its old framework and interior. First built in the seventeenth century, it was almost completely reconstructed in 1883 and bears little resemblance to the original. Aside from the church, Coleraine's most interesting structure is Charles Lanyon's stucco railway station constructed in the mid-nineteenth century. The newest development in Coleraine's architectural face is the modern concrete-and-brick buildings of the University of Ulster, which opened in 1968 and is located a few miles north of town off Portrush Road.

About a mile south of Coleraine is Mountsandel, the ruin of a fort once held by an early king of Ulster and later by the de Courceys. This is also where the Mesolithic artifacts thought to be the earliest traces of civilization in Ireland were discovered.

From Coleraine, take the coast road to Limavady; the signposts leading to this road are marked "Downhill."

DOWNHILL: Most historians consider Downhill the private domain of the colorful — and eccentric — Bishop Frederick Augustus Hervey, fourth earl of Bristol who in 1779 began his reign in Derry, one of the wealthiest of Ireland's church districts. Hervey was a man of extremes: He lived extravagantly, collected art avidly, and traveled extensively. Hervey always took a large group of attendants on his journeys and hotel owners were so anxious for his business that they sometimes named their establishments in his honor — hence, the many Bristol Hotels throughout Europe. Hervey's ostentatious life-style even included running horse races for the pleasure of his clergymen at Magilligan Strand, the 6-mile-long beach below the castle. Hervey, however, was not all frivolity. His more serious accomplishments include putting into practice the Catholic Relief Act of 1791; leading a private army on horseback to the Volunteer Convention in Dublin; and supporting demands and rallies for an Irish Parliament.

No fewer than four different architects were employed in designing the bishop's splendid estate. The castle's interior was destroyed by fire in 1851 and refurbished in 1876, but the restoration bore little resemblance to the original. Parts of the estate still standing are: the Bishop's Gate, an arched portal with Doric columns; the Lion Gate, a sandstone structure carved with the two animals that are on the Bristol coat-of-arms; and the Mussenden Temple, a circular, Corinthian-columned structure built by Michael Shanahan and modeled after the Italian temples of Vesta. Established as a memorial to Hervey's cousin — some say mistress — the temple was also used as the bishop's library. It's now open to visitors in the afternoons. At Magilligan Point (the west end of Magilligan Strand), there is a martello tower, one of the many early-nineteenth-century fortresses built in response to Napoleonic invasions. From Magilligan Point you can take a ferry over to Greencastle on the Inishowen Peninsula; it's a 1-mile trip across Lough Foyle.

En route – Take the Bishop's Road (yet another creation of Frederick Hervey's) from Downhill — it's a pretty jaunt through Eagle Hill and Binevenagh. Here you can stop to enjoy lovely vistas of Scotland and the mountains across Lough Foyle. Continuing along you'll see Hell's Hole, deep gorges that were carved into the cliffs by glaciers centuries ago.

LIMAVADY: This delightful old Georgian town set in the valley of the River Roe is perhaps best known as the place where William Thackeray wrote the poem, "Sweet Peg of Limavady"; he met his muse, a barmaid, at an inn on Ballyclose Street (the inn is now a private residence). It's also in Limavady that Miss Jane Ross heard and transcribed in 1851 that traditional Irish song, "The Londonderry Air," as it was played by a wandering fiddler named MacCormick. (The original composer is believed to have been Rory O'Caghan, a blind sixteenth-century harpist.)

When you visit Limavady's parish church, note its finely crafted woodwork and tapestried kneelers. Each of the latter has a different design, but all were rendered by local women.

Limavady actually means "dog's leap" and refers to the legendary dog who leaped over a wide crevice to deliver an important message to the chieftain of North Derry, Rory Dall O'Caghan. The parish church contains a carving of the "Dog of Limavady," and a spot in Roe Valley Country Park is designated "Dog's Leap" in commemoration. Also in the park are picnic and camp sites, walking trails, and a memorial called O'Caghan's Rock, which marks the site where O'Caghan's castle once stood.

In 1896 some valuable Celtic gold objects were found in the marsh area near Limavady called Broighter. Although it is thought that these items — a miniature boat and pieces of jewelry — date back to early Christian times, no one has ever determined to whom they belonged or whether they were hidden or lost. They are now on display at the National Museum in Dublin.

EN ROUTE – On the way from Limavady to Londonderry is Ballykelly Forest. Sometimes called Walworth Wood, it was planted in the seventeenth century to honor Sir William Walworth, head of the London Fishmongers' Company in the late fourteenth century. Walworth House, also part of the grounds, is now in ruins except for a few of its towers.

Continue along the A2 to Londonderry.

LONDONDERRY (also called Derry): Most often bypassed by travelers en route to Donegal or Belfast, this hardworking city astride the River Foyle deserves a visit as well. It's quite compact and all the major sites can be easily covered in a day's walk. Most of the special places are on the west side of the river within and just outside the old walls. For the official guide to Derry, contact the City Council's Amenities and Leisure Department, 5 Guildhall St., 2nd floor (phone: 65151).

Derived from the Irish word, *Doire,* the city's name means "oak grove." The site was a densely wooded hilltop when St. Columcille (or Columba) arrived in AD 546 to establish a monastery, and in the ensuing centuries the religious settlement became known as "Derry Columcille." The abbey was burned down by piratical Danes in 1812; this was just the first in a succession of invasions Derry was to endure. The city, however, continued to grow in size and importance, and in about 1164, the famous church, Templemore, was built.

Like other Irish cities, Derry came under English control when King Henry II claimed Ireland in the twelfth century. The skirmishes that ensued did not seriously damage the city until the rebellion in 1566 led by Ulster chieftain Shane O'Neill, during which Templemore was destroyed. Queen Elizabeth sent a small army to fortify Derry, but it failed and withdrew. In 1600 an English army led by Sir Henry Dowcra besieged and took possession of the city.

Dowcra called for the erection of huge earthen bullwarks to protect Derry against further invasions, but in 1608 another Irish chieftain, Cahir O'Doherty, raided the city and once again it was ruthlessly sacked. O'Doherty was later killed and his lands confiscated. With the accession of James I to the English throne in 1603, Derry was made a satellite of the City of London. As a result, its name was changed to Londonderry and — more important — it fell subject to the new policy of "plantation." The lands forfeited by vanquished Irish leaders were distributed among English and Scottish colonists. Estates went for a nickel an acre, and the newly created hereditary title of baronet sold for $2,500.

Between 1617 and 1619 the city was rebuilt and stone walls constructed in place of the earthworks. Derry successfully withstood three more sieges: In 1641 the Irish rose yet again against the English, and in 1648 during the English Civil War, Derry underwent a 4-month-long attack by Royalist forces. But it is the third siege that is most memorable.

In April 1689, in an attempt to gain a foothold in Ireland from which to resume the English throne, the deposed Catholic King James II marched on Londonderry. His troops shelled the city and blockaded the River Foyle to thwart rescue and to starve its citizens into submission. The garrison's commander, Colonel Lundy, something of a traitor, advised surrender and fled. A Reverend George Walker was then elected governor, and under his leadership Derry's population of 30,000 held out for 105 days until the relief ship *Mountjoy* broke through the barrier. Two days after the siege was over, James was defeated by "King Billy" (William III) at the famous Battle of the Boyne.

Though battered by these sieges, Derry's walls remain intact; they're about 1 mile in circumference and between 14 to 30 feet thick and 20 to 25 feet high. The four original gates — Shipquay, Butcher's, Bishop's, and Ferryquay — have all been restored. Guarding the walls is the famous "Roaring Meg," a cannon named for the thunder and fear it created in the Great Siege of 1689; you might also take a look at the flintstone watchtowers at Church Bastion and New Gate. (The former is better preserved.) The memorial to Reverend George Walker at Lord Dowcra's Bastion was damaged by a bomb in 1972.

From on top of the old city walls, you get a fine view of all Derry: Inside the walls is St. Columb's Cathedral and the Court House; to the northeast is the Guildhall; to the east drifts the languid River Foyle; to the south is Columba's Church; and to the northwest is St. Eugene's Cathedral. The city within the walls retains its original seventeenth-century layout, with four main streets leading from the central square (called the Diamond) to the gates.

Construction of St. Columb's — the Church of Ireland cathedral on London St. — was begun in 1628 and finished in 1633; since then it has undergone much restoration and alteration, although its facade remains basically austere "Planter's Gothic" in appearance. The original spire was built in 1778 by Frederick Hervey, bishop of Derry; the present 171-foot spire was added in the early nineteenth century. Its porch bears the telling inscription, "If stones could speak then London's prayse should sounde./Who built this church and cittie from the grounde," and its eighteenth-century chapter house displays the locks and keys to the original Derry gates.

The nearby Courthouse (Bishop St.) is presided over by statues of Justice and Peace, sculpted by Edward Smyth, who also worked on the Four Courts of Justice in Dublin.

688 DIRECTIONS / Antrim Coast

Designed in the Greek revival style, its handsome colonnade resembles the Temple of Erechtheus in Athens.

Follow Bishop Street to the Diamond, then pick up Shipquay. Leading down to Derry Quay, Shipquay is the main street of Derry, and in some stretches where the modern macadam paving is worn thin, the original cobblestones show through. (Often referred to as the steepest street in Ireland, Shipquay can be treacherous to walk down in leather-soled shoes on a damp or drizzly day.) Note the original red-brick eighteenth-century Custom House at No. 33, a well preserved example of Georgian design.

Just outside the gate at the foot of Shipquay Street, the fussy yet impressive Guildhall — with pinnacles, spire, and clock — was built in 1890 of local Antrim red sandstone. It houses the sword said to have belonged to the Irish chieftain Cahir O'Doherty, who led an attack on Derry in 1608. It was badly damaged by bombs in 1972, and most of the interior had to be reconstructed and its stained-glass windows replaced. Concerts and plays are sometimes held in the main hall.

From the Guildhall, you can proceed either north along Strand Road toward St. Eugene's or south along Foyle, Orchard, and Fountain streets toward St. Columba's Church.

St. Eugene's, a Catholic cathedral begun in 1851 and finished in 1873, was built in the Gothic revival style — tall and airy in proportion, yet scrupulously unadorned except for its fine stained-glass windows depicting the Crucifixion. It is located in the Catholic district called the Bogside and is reached from Strand Rd. along Great St. James St.

In striking contrast to St. Eugene's is St. Columba's, the many-gabled and marble-columned church built on the site of the original tenth-century church. It is sometimes called the Long Tower Church, which refers to the cylindrical shape typical of Irish fortresses built in the medieval period. Long Tower St.

Derry's location on the doorstep of Donegal means that the famous tweeds are in plentiful supply; try *The Donegal Shop*, 8 Shipquay St.; *Austin's*, a department store on the Diamond; and *Hill's*, Spencer Rd. If you're interested in pottery, stop at the *Ulster Ceramics* factory outlet at the Springtown Industrial Estate. For information about where to find other handcrafts, ask for the free booklet *A Guide to Northern Ireland Crafts and Craftsmen*, which provides the names, addresses, and specialties of Irish artisans in the Derry area. Write to: Local Enterprise Development Unit, Lamont House, Purdy's La., Newtownbreda, Belfast BT8 4TB.

The Derry area has several "leisure centers," which are open to the public and house pool, squash courts, sauna, and other facilities. These include: *Brook Park Activity Centre*, Rosemount Ave., Rosemount (phone: 62637); *Lisnagelvin Leisure Centre*, Richill Park (phone: 57695); *St. Columb's Park Activity Centre*, Limavady Rd., Waterside (phone: 43941); and *Templemore Sports Complex*, Buncrana Rd. (phone: 65521). The fishing in the River Foyle and its tributaries is legendary; a license may be bought from the Foyle Fisheries Commission at 8 Victoria Rd. (phone: 42100). The City of Derry Golf Club, an 18-hole golf course at Prehen, 2 miles south on Strabane Rd., is open to the public (phone: 42610).

Derry offers little in the way of nightlife, although a pleasant evening might be spent at the *Gate Inn*, 17 Butcher St. (phone: 63427), or at *New York, New York*, a nightclub on Strand Rd. (phone: 67123). The *Gweedore Bar* on Waterloo St. has traditional Irish music. There is no established theater, but concerts are often given in the Guildhall on Shipquay Pl. (phone: 65151), and plays staged in the Little Theatre on Orchard St. (phone: 62880).

CHECKING IN: *Everglades* – Probably the best place to stay in Derry, this modern hotel sports the seal of Florida on its brick exterior and a "tropical" decor inside because the owner, C. V. Armstrong, liked Tampa. It has 40 bedrooms, dining room, heated swimming pool, and sauna. Dinner dances are offered on Saturday nights. (Prehen Rd., Waterside; phone: 46722; moderate.) **Broomhill House Hotel** – Patronized mostly by traveling businesspeople and conventioneers, it has modern bedrooms and overlooks the Foyle. (Limavady Rd., Waterside; phone: 44854; moderate.)

EATING OUT: The two best choices for dinner in the Derry area are both just out of town on the road to Limavady. They are: the **White Horse Inn,** 68 Clooney Rd., Campsie (phone: 860606), and the **Glenhouse Hotel,** 9 Main St., Eglinton (phone: 810527).

Irish Republic

Southeast Ireland: Dublin to New Ross

This route will take you through only three Irish counties — Dublin, Wicklow, and Wexford — and it will keep you close to shore most of the time, yet the changing mood and character of the land along the way will still surprise you. It may seem impossible, but a mere half-hour's drive from the city center of Dublin brings you to the splendid isolation of the Wicklow Mountains. Here, great valleys with melodious names such as Glendalough, Clara, and Avoca, wind through the hills, and uncrowded roads pass unforgettable sights — a high waterfall, an ancient monastic settlement, a proud estate. Several miles out of Glencree, the boggy terrain, flaked with granite and crusted in late summer with purple heather, seems primitive, still awaiting the arrival of man, whereas the wooded glens met later seem more soothing in their ageless beauty, not quite as lonely.

To the south lies the friendlier, less dramatic landscape of County Wexford, where fertile farmland is served by picturesque villages and the historic town of Wexford itself. The coast is lined with inviting beaches — if you are ever going to make use of one in Ireland, it will probably be here in this sunniest, driest corner of the country. You'll find busy seaside resorts with shooting galleries, amusement rides, and golf courses, but you'll also find the secluded and tiny fishing village of Kilmore Quay, its traditional thatched cottages all freshly painted and still very much occupied.

En route, you'll come across urban exiles who have fled the congestion and pace of London and Dublin for the tranquillity of the Wicklow Mountains, weavers and potters with skilled hands musing away in modern bungalows and old cottages, and families cutting and collecting peat throughout the summer along the Military Road through Sally Gap. You'll meet the people of Wexford in singing pubs and good restaurants, while outside the town, time will seem to recede with the sight of older men in black suits rambling down country lanes, the postman delivering his parcels by bicycle, or women placing statues wrapped in rosary beads at the pilgrim shrines of Lady's Island.

The route heads south through the suburbs of Dublin to the residential and resort town of Dun Laoghaire and keeps to the coast as far as Bray. It then turns inland to the village of Enniskerry and Powerscourt Estate, continues west to Glencree, and turns south again over the Military Road to Laragh, the gateway to the monastic site of Glendalough. The route next passes through the vales of Clara and Avoca and returns to the coast at Arklow, from where a succession of smaller and larger beachside resorts and villages leads south and then west to Kilmore Quay, interrupted only by the county town of Wexford on Wexford Harbour. At Kilmore Quay, it is possible to backtrack to Rosslare Harbour (terminal for ferries to Wales and France) or to proceed to New Ross, from which neither Kilkenny nor Waterford is very distant.

A hotel listed as expensive will cost $60 or more for a double room; a moderate one, from $40; an inexpensive one, less than $40. Dinner for two without wine or tips will come to $40 or more in an expensive restaurant; $20 to $35 in moderate, under $20 in inexpensive.

DUBLIN: For a full report on the city, its sights, restaurants, and hotels, see *Dublin,* THE CITIES.

En Route – Leave Dublin by traveling south on O'Connell Street and turning left on to Nassau Street just after Trinity College. Follow the signs to Ballsbridge, passing Merrion Square with its Georgian houses, the American Embassy, and the grounds of the Royal Dublin Society (location of the famous horse show every August), and continue until Dublin Bay is visible on the left. This coastal road will take you by the Booterstown Bird Sanctuary and through the small towns of Blackrock and Monkstown, and then, 7 miles south of Dublin, into Dun Laoghaire.

DUN LAOGHAIRE: As the terminus of the cross-Channel ferry route from Holyhead, Wales, this busy residential town, holiday resort, and yachting center is one of the main gateways into Ireland. It has grown considerably as a suburb of Dublin in recent years and has innumerable hotels and restaurants, but it still has Victorian charm below its modern surface and you could as easily stay a few days as a few hours. Dun Laoghaire (pronounced dun leary) was named after a fifth-century Irish king (O'Leary in English) who established a fort, or *dún,* here to protect the lands of the High Kings of Tara from their rivals. In the sixteenth century, the area figured in the fighting between the English, who had their main port at neighboring Dalkey, and the Irish, who opposed the English from the nearby Wicklow Mountains. (Traces of the ditch marking the Pale, that area under English control, can still be found around Booterstown.) Dun Laoghaire remained primarily a small fishing village until the present harbor was built in 1817, opening the way for mailboat and ferry services with Wales. George IV came to christen the harbor in 1821 (after which the town was renamed Kingston and known thus for the next 99 years), the railway line from Dublin arrived in 1834, and Dun Laoghaire rapidly became a fashionable resort for the wealthy — many of the streets with their big Victorian houses are named after English royalty.

If you are just passing through town, head down to the harbor and walk the mile-long east pier, with Howth Head stretching in the distance. In summer, band concerts are sometimes held here, and not too long ago, people brought chairs to sit and watch the sunset. On a nice night, much of the town with spouses, children, and dogs in tow still parades the pier to watch the departure of the evening ferry. Nearby People's Park, which has swings and lovely flowers landscaped beneath shady trees, is the place to see next, perhaps after a stop for an ice cream cone at *Teddy's.* George's Street is the main shopping area, and at the corner of Royal Marine Road, you'll find one of the most modern shopping malls in Ireland, with three floors of boutiques and gift shops, and a tempting delicatessen in the basement. St. Michael's church across from the mall is worth a visit. Its striking modern design incorporates a nineteenth-century bell tower from an earlier church destroyed by fire. Farther down Royal Marine Road are the Post Office and Town Hall, built in 1878. If you feel like a pause in your sight-seeing, *Ann's*

Hot Bread Shop, where the apple squares sell out quickly, is on George's Street just around the corner from St. Michael's Church. Or walk up Patrick Street and try the *Austrian Pastry Shop,* where the sandwiches are fresh and the coffee strong. *Ursula's,* down on the waterfront, is also good for homemade food.

An enjoyable evening can be spent near Dun Laoghaire at Culturlann na hÉireann, the headquarters of the national organization for the promotion of traditional Irish music, song, and dance known as Comhaltas Ceoltóirí Éireann. The same group that sponsors sessions of authentic music and dance *(seisiún)* throughout the country during the summer has here converted a large house into a cultural center, transforming the basement into an Irish kitchen complete with peat fire. There is something going on most evenings from early June to early September: either *seisiún; céilí* dancing; *fonntrai,* a show spotlighting Irish traditions; or informal sessions of music and talk. Admission is charged, there is a nice bar area with tables for socializing, and there are off-season programs, too. The building is at 32 Belgrave Sq., Monkstown (phone: 800295), about 20 minutes on foot from Dun Laoghaire or a short drive by car (it's off the main road, so ask directions for Belgrave Square).

En Route – The coastal road southeast of town leads to a district known as Sandycove, the site of a martello tower built as protection against a possible Napoleonic invasion and now a museum dedicated to James Joyce. The author lived in the tower briefly with Oliver St. John Gogarty, and in the opening scene of *Ulysses,* the character Stephen Dedalus lives there with Buck Mulligan. The museum, which currently has a small collection of Joyce's letters, books, and other memorabilia, is the starting point of many a Bloomsday tour taken by Joyce fans every June 16, the day in 1904 on which the events of *Ulysses* take place. There is a small admission fee and visitors can climb to the top of the handsomely restored tower for a great view of the harbor and the Irish Sea as Joyce saw it. The museum is open May through September and by appointment at other times.

A short distance down the coastal road is Bullock Castle, at one time a powerful abbey and inn run by Cistercian monks who exacted tolls from ships entering Bullock Harbour and now owned by American Carmelite nuns who staff the adjoining nursing home. The castle has been restored, and the tiny prayer cells of the monks, the large dining hall, and the Victorian toy museum make it an interesting stop when open during the summer. (Note the carved head on the corner of the western wall, which dates the castle about 1150.) Bullock Castle is at the northern approach to the small resort village of Dalkey. A major port when Dublin was yet developing, it was once guarded by no fewer than seven castles, two of which remain on Castle Street (one has been reconstructed as the Town Hall). Continue following signs for the "Coast Road," which will take you around Sorrento Point and then, via the Vico Road, high over Killiney Hill for a view of Killiney Bay. A local saying, "See Killiney Bay and die," compares the view to that of the Bay of Naples. You can judge for yourself by parking your car and enjoying the beautiful stretch of ocean as far as Bray Head to the south and Dalkey Island to the north — the tiny flecks of black against the blue-gray surface of the water are fishing boats. At the end of Vico Road, follow the signs to Bray, in County Wicklow, a short 12 miles from Dublin and one of Ireland's most popular seaside resorts. Bray has a mile-long beach (a shingly one, compared to those farther south along the coast), with a mile-long esplanade running its length to Bray Head. A cable car rides to the top of this nearly 800-foot-high cliff, which rises sheer from the sea at the end of the esplanade.

After Bray, turn inland and drive the short 3-mile distance to Enniskerry.

CHECKING IN: *Dalkey Island Hotel* – This is an attractive hotel on the waterfront with a large restaurant and bar. (Coliemore Harbour, Dalkey; phone: 850377; expensive.) *Royal Marine Hotel* – This elegant, older hotel set back from the waterfront by a gracious lawn and gardens is a lovely setting for a drink and dinner followed by a romantic stroll down to the harbor. Amenities for guests include sauna baths, a beauty salon, and a large parking lot just behind the shopping mall on George's Street. (Royal Marine Rd., Dun Laoghaire; phone: 801911; expensive.) **Elphin Hotel** – Convenient to the harbor, this hotel has a bar and restaurant, but no rooms with private bath. (Royal Marine Rd., Dun Laoghaire; phone: 801663; inexpensive.)

EATING OUT: *Restaurant Creole* – This is a popular restaurant featuring steaks, seafood, and veal cooked in the French style. (20a Adelaide St., Dun Laoghaire; phone: 806706; expensive.) ***Digby's*** – On the seafront, this is an elegant place with a reputation for fine food. (5 Windsor Terr., Dun Laoghaire; phone: 804600; expensive.) ***Mirabeau*** – This restaurant is said to be the most expensive in Ireland. Owner and chef Sean Kinsella regards every night as opening night and offers a large selection of freshly made soups, fish, and curry dishes as well as inviting desserts. (Marine Parade, Sandycove; phone: 809873; expensive.) ***Restaurant na Mara*** – This restaurant in a former train station is known for its good seafood. (1 Harbour Rd., Dun Laoghaire; phone: 806767; expensive.) ***Salty Dog*** – Brian Rowan and Tony Hannigan opened this pleasant restaurant a few years ago, decorating it with the Persian rugs and wall hangings a roaming salty dog might have brought home from his travels. The daily menu features dishes such as boneless stuffed duckling, while on Sundays, you can partake of the special Indonesian rice table of 18 different dishes including deep fried chicken and spiced lamb. (3A Haddington Ter., Dun Laoghaire; phone: 808015; expensive.) ***Barrels*** – This home restaurant is hidden down a side street and named for the barrels propping up the bar. The specialty is steak. (Mews 61, Lower George's St., entrance from Convent Rd., Dun Laoghaire; phone: 809136; moderate.) ***Lotus House*** – There is good Chinese food here, at reasonable prices, and it's open Sundays. (54 Upper George's St., Dun Laoghaire; phone: 804103; inexpensive.) ***The Tree of Idleness*** – Chef Akis Courtellas has some of the ingredients needed for his lovely waterfront restaurant flown in from home. Born in Cyprus, he says that every Cypriot village has a tree of idleness under which the natives drink coffee and play backgammon. Under this one, you can dine in a romantic setting on moussaka made with a special Cypriot cheese and baklava chock-full of almonds. Be sure to try the Cypriot liqueur at meal's end. Reservations recommended. (Seafront, Bray; phone: 863498; inexpensive.)

ENNISKERRY: Though this tiny village is a very pretty one, its main attraction is the 14,000-acre Powerscourt Estate on its southern outskirts. A fire in 1974 destroyed the interior of the lovely eighteenth-century mansion, whose substantial skeleton still attests to its grandness, but the wonderful formal terraced gardens with pebble-paved ramps, statuary, and ironwork are still intact in a heady location looking out over the Wicklow hills to Sugar Loaf Mountain. There are also pleasant Japanese gardens on the grounds as well as a 400-foot waterfall, the highest in Great Britain and Ireland. The gardens are open from Easter to October; the waterfall area is open year-round. You can also browse through the two shops on the estate's grounds.

En Route – Head west out of Enniskerry, following signposts for Glencree. The road now climbs into the splendid Wicklow Mountains on a winding course hugged by trees that now and again give way to views of white cottages planted in the midst of brown fields. At Glencree, follow the signs south to Sally Gap over the Military Road, so called because it was built by the British after the rebellion of 1798 and used to flush out Irish rebels hiding in the glens of the Wicklows. This stretch of the route is a winding one, too, passing peat bogs, glacial lakes, and a landscape somber and unyielding in its flatness till it reaches the crossroads of Sally Gap (1,631 feet) and begins to descend toward Laragh through the valley of

Glenmacnass. At the northern end of the glen, where the road joins the course of the Glenmacnass River, there is a parking lot. Be sure to stop and walk down to the waterfall, pristine and powerful in its simple beauty as it tumbles over silent slabs of stone into the deep valley below. At the southern end, where the Glenmacnass River meets the Avonmore, there is the village of Laragh. Browse for a while in the large crafts shop run by Joe O'Neill and Jerry John, who are in the process of transforming a collection of old stone buildings into an arts center, then drive the mile west to the entrance to Glendalough.

GLENDALOUGH: This deep glen, set between two lakes amid the towering wooded slopes and granite hills of the Wicklow Mountains, is at once a place of great natural beauty and immense historical interest. Glendalough means "the valley of the two lakes," and in the sixth century, when St. Kevin came to Wicklow in search of tranquillity, he found it here. But the hermit's sanctity attracted so many disciples that, almost unwittingly, he founded a great monastery that eventually became one of the most renowned centers of learning in Europe. It was sacked by the Danes in the ninth and tenth centuries, and later (1398) by the English, although some of the buildings remained in use until Henry VIII dissolved the monasteries in the sixteenth century. Today the ruins of the monastic city are scattered over 1.5 miles of a valley that insulates visitors from the present the minute they step through the aged arched gateway at its entrance. It was in the solitude of the Upper Lake at the base of 2,296-foot Camaderry and 2,154-foot Lugduff that St. Kevin first prayed in his stone beehive hut. In the same area, with its gravestones and crosses, is Reefert Church, which was the burial ground of the O'Tooles and other local chiefs. You can walk (or drive) to the Upper Lake, make use of the picnic grounds there, and (for a small fee) hire a boat to take you out for some splendid views of the valley and a closer look at St. Kevin's Bed, an excavation in the cliff-face about 25 feet above water level, said to have been used as a retreat by the saint. As it grew, the settlement spread toward the Lower Lake and the entrance, and the ruins in this area include the Cathedral, the largest church on the site; St. Kevin's Church, with its sturdy stone ceiling; and the much-photographed Round Tower, over 100 feet high. Built in the ninth century, this was probably a bell tower, lookout point, and place of refuge all in one — the only door is fully 10 feet above the ground. Glendalough's walks and ruins are marked by plaques for easy exploration, and after steeping themselves in this ancient beauty made mellow by human habitation, visitors can stop at one of the many teashops in the vicinity. The *Royal Hotel* offers moderately priced accommodation, and there are also a number of bed-and-breakfast houses nearby.

En Route – Leaving Laragh by the road to Arklow (T61), the route once again parallels the course of a river, this time the Avonmore, and passes through the wooded Vale of Clara before reaching the town of Rathdrum, 8 miles south of Laragh. Here it is possible to interrupt the route for an interesting diversion at the nearby trout farm of Peter Morphew. For a few dollars you can rent a pole and spend the afternoon fishing for rainbow trout (paying about $2 for every pound you catch), then — for a bit more — have the staff cook it up for you with salad and chips, and eat it at the picnic tables around the pond.

About a 1.5 miles southeast of Rathdrum is Avondale, the lovely birthplace and home of the Irish patriot Charles Stewart Parnell, a member of a Protestant land-owning family who became a leader in the fight for Catholic emancipation and land reform in the nineteenth century. The house was built in 1777 by Parnell's cousin, Samuel Hayes, who was much interested in forestation and wrote the first book on tree-planting in Ireland in 1794. Now the 530-acre estate which the Parnell family inherited from Hayes in 1795 belongs to the Forest and Wildlife Service and is used as a forestry school. The guidebook on sale at the estate discusses the wildlife and trees found on the grounds as well as the recommended

DIRECTIONS / Southeast Ireland: Dublin to New Ross 695

walks, but for the tourist budgeting time, the house with its lovely furnishings and moldings is the main interest. Note the poster from the day Parnell addressed the US House of Representatives in 1880 (Parnell's mother was American, the daughter of Admiral Charles Stewart who fought the British in the War of 1812). The house is open to the public Fridays through Mondays from 2 to 6 PM, from May to the end of September; a nature trail on the grounds is open year-round.

From Avondale, return to Rathdrum and pick up the main road (T7) south toward Woodenbridge. The approximately 8-mile distance between the two towns is known as the Vale of Avoca, a beauty spot immortalized in verse ("There is not in this wide world a valley so sweet/As that vale in whose bosom the bright waters meet") by Ireland's national poet, Thomas Moore. The Meeting of the Waters, where the rivers Avonmore and Avonbeg join to form the River Avoca, is about 3.5 miles south of Rathdrum, and the tree under which Moore is supposed to have sat to contemplate the beauty he saw is marked by a plaque. Michael O'Sullivan's pub-restaurant overlooks this pastoral junction, standing on the site of a cottage where Moore once lived. (You can have an Irish coffee here and listen to the hearty publican, an amateur Moore scholar, discuss the poet's works — he owns an 1889 edition of the poems with the noted tribute to the vale on page 200.) If time permits, visit the Motte Stone, signposted near the meeting. The large boulder marks the halfway point between Dublin and Wexford, and you can sit on its top and enjoy a fine view of the countryside. Legend has it that the boulder was the hurling stone of the giant Finn MacCool.

Also near the meeting is the craft shop of the *Avoca Handweavers*. You can stop here or watch the actual weaving process in the small but friendly village of Avoca, about 3 miles south of the Meeting of the Waters (turn left at the sign for Avoca on the main road, and then left again after the bridge). The operation, in a cluster of stone buildings that was once a flour mill, employs about 30 people who prepare, roll, and weave the wool, about 75% of it for export. The remainder, as capes, jackets, bedspreads based on patterns supplied by the Kilkenny Design Workshops, or just yards of the soft material dyed in rich colors, can be bought in the mill shop. Besides the handweavers, Avoca has a short main street that seems like a stage set with its three or four buildings, a few of them pubs, and several bed-and-breakfast houses on the main road near the bridge, including *Riverview*, a lovely one run by May Byrne, a retired schoolteacher and fluent speaker of Irish. Another craft shop, *Glenwood Crafts*, adjoins the gas station near the bridge, and sells a surprisingly good selection of gifts.

About 2 miles south of Avoca, the Aughrim and Avoca rivers form a second "meeting of the waters" at Woodenbridge, and though no poets have sung its praises, many travelers find it more beautiful than the first. The main road then bears eastward toward the coast and in 5 miles arrives at Arklow.

ARKLOW: This busy town at the mouth of the River Avoca has long been a fishing and shipping port and a boatbuilding center: *The Gypsy Moth II*, the yacht that took Sir Francis Chichester around the world, was built in an Arklow shipyard. The town is also a popular seaside resort, with beaches to the north and south of it, and it is the home of *Arklow Pottery*, the largest pottery manufacturer in Ireland. Arklow was founded by the Norsemen, and when they gave way to the Normans, it became the property of the Fitzwalters, ancestors of the Butlers, one of the most powerful families in Irish history. The decisive battle of the Wexford Rebellion of 1798 was fought here; the insurgent leader, Father Michael Murphy (not the same Father Murphy who led the pikemen in Wexford), lost his life in the battle and a statue of him, the 1798 Memorial, now commemorates his bravery. The town's main attraction, however, is the *Arklow Pottery*, which employs 480 people and has been making domestic earthenware since 1935. During the summer, you can get a fascinating look at the process of turning the raw materials of flint, china stone, and water into clay, and the operation of machines that throw clay into plates in the wink of an eye. The conducted tours (from mid-June through August) take place every day of the week at 9 AM, 12, 2, and 3:45 PM, but it's best to check on the schedule before you go (phone: 0402-2134). The tours last about 30 minutes — and there is a shop on the premises where you can buy seconds at discount prices. Golf, tennis, fishing, and boating are all possible in the Arklow vicinity, but the major attraction outside of town is about 10 miles north, at Brittas Bay. The 3-mile stretch of silver strand and sand dunes can be crowded with picnickers and bathers from Dublin on sunny weekends, but normally it hosts only a modest crowd.

En Route – While the main road south follows the railway line to Wexford, the coastal road, a pleasant, quiet drive of about 40 miles, runs along a succession of sandy beaches located in the sunniest and driest part of Ireland. Courtown is a lively resort during the summer; besides its 2 miles of beach, it has an 18-hole golf course, typical seaside amusements, and entertainment — Irish nights, *seisiún*, and dancing — at the Tara Ballroom and the *Oulart Hotel.* In August, the nearby town of Gorey, 3.5 miles inland, hosts an arts festival that includes art exhibits, films, theater, and a variety of music from traditional Irish to jazz and rock. (The Church of St. Michael and Christ Church are among the things to see at other times of the year.) Farther south along the coast, the beaches continue almost uninterruptedly to Wexford, including especially good ones at Cahore, Kilmuckridge, Blackwater, and Curracloe, all backed by picturesque villages. South of Curracloe, where the River Slaney runs out to sea, the road crosses the bridge into Wexford.

CHECKING IN: *Marfield House* – This eighteenth-century mansion was once part of the extensive Courtown estate and has been handsomely restored by proprietor and chef Mary Bowe. Some of the furniture belonged to the original estate, and the 11 bedrooms are elegantly decorated. There are beautiful staircases, marble fireplaces, and long windows that look out onto the spacious grounds and gardens. Vegetables and herbs grown on the premises appear in the dining room where the dinner menu can include such fare as crab salad, beef Wellington, and chocolate whiskey cake. (On the Gorey to Courtown road, Gorey; phone: 055-21124; expensive.)
Arklow Bay Hotel – This is one of the nicest hotels in the area. Located just outside town on the coastal road to Dublin, it is a modern, single-story building with an appealing restaurant. (Arklow; phone: 0402-2289; moderate.) ***Courtown Hotel*** – Amenities at this attractive hotel include a heated indoor pool, sauna, and hair salon. (Courtown Harbour; phone: 055-25108; moderate.) *Royal Hotel* – The *Royal* is pleasant, in the center of Arklow, and it has a good restaurant. No private baths. (Arklow; phone: 0402-2451; moderate.) ***Taravie Hotel*** – This is a clean, comfortable hotel on the Courtown waterfront. (Courtown Harbour; phone: 055-25208; moderate.) ***Harbour House*** – This is a large bed-and-breakfast house in Courtown. (Courtown; phone: 055-25117; inexpensive.)

Eating Out: *Esker Lodge* – This is a lovely family-run restaurant less than a mile from the village of Curracloe. Closed mid-January through February. (Ballinesker, Curracloe; phone: 053-37171; expensive.)

WEXFORD: This town combines city sophistication with village warmth. Built on the River Slaney, its narrow streets date from medieval times, so leave your car outside the town proper or in the parking lot on the quays near the tourist office. Wexford was founded by the Vikings, taken by the Normans, suffered terrible destruction at the hands of Oliver Cromwell, then rose up in the Rebellion of 1798, when a local priest led his parishioners against the English armed only with pikes. Wexford has good singing pubs, restaurants, and hotels, but it is best known for its annual Wexford Opera Festival. For 12 days every October, rarely performed operas, new and old, are performed in the restored nineteenth-century Theatre Royal, sung by highly regarded, though not yet famous, opera singers from around the world. Wexford's normal population of 14,000 swells by about 6,000 at this time, and the whole town celebrates: There are singing pubs competitions, theater presentations, and other festival events. Be sure to have a drink at the intriguing *Crown Bar* on Monck Street, and at the *Thomas Moore Tavern* (the poet's mother was born in this house) in the Cornmarket. *The Bohemian Girl* at North Main and Monck streets is a good spot for lunch or an Irish coffee. For a full report on Wexford, its sights, restaurants, and hotels, see *Wexford,* THE CITIES.

En Route – If you wish to visit Johnstown Castle, a nineteenth-century Gothic-style mansion now owned by the State Agricultural College, proceed south of Wexford for about 3 miles via a country road. The grounds have lovely ornamental gardens, walks around artificial lakes, a picnic area, and the Irish Agricultural Museum, an interesting exhibit on farming and rural life. If not, start out on the road to Rosslare Harbour (T8 or N25). On a fine summer's day, this area southeast of Wexford is the stuff of poetry: Clean sea air sweeps over green hedges and down country roads little changed by the twentieth century. Turn left at Killinick and head for Rosslare (branching left when the T8 bears right for Rosslare Harbour). Rosslare, or Rosslare Strand, is a seaside resort in the middle of a wonderful 6-mile beach, which is not its only attraction. Besides the beach, there are public tennis courts, an 18-hole golf course, a playground, fishing and boating, and *Kelly's Strand Hotel,* which is a center of activity and a popular retreat for the Irish on weekends.

The road south from Rosslare leads to the village of Tagoat and two possibilities. A left turn onto the T8 will take you to a selection of good hotels and restaurants in Rosslare Harbour, the departure point for ferries to Fishguard, Wales, and Le Havre and Cherbourg, France (but don't follow the road to the end, since it leads directly onto the boats). Go straight through Tagoat, and you will come to the tiny village of Broadway, with an enormous tavern and thatched cottages. Broadway is at the head of Lady's Island Lake, actually a sea inlet, and Lady's Island is in the lake, connected to land by a causeway. The ruins of an Augustinian priory dedicated to the Virgin Mary and a Norman castle with a curiously leaning limestone tower are on the island, which has been the object of pilgrimages for centuries and still is in August and September.

From Lady's Island, you can continue east to Carne Harbour, where there is more beach and a very good seafood restaurant, the *Bakehouse,* or return to Broadway and turn left for Kilmore Quay, one of the most delightful villages in Ireland. Kilmore Quay is a fishing village whose main street is no more than a cozy row of thatched cottages with a fisherman's cooperative at one end. You can hire a boat here to visit the great bird sanctuary of the Saltee Islands (phone Willie Bates at 29644), a 45-minute trip off the south coast of County Wexford. Birdwatchers should note that about three quarters of the total Irish bird species have been seen in the county, and most of these frequent either Great or Little Saltee, where they rub feathers with many rare migrant birds. Great Saltee (only a mile in length) was once inhabited and caves in its rugged, rocky cliffs were used as hideaways by insurgents after the Rebellion of 1798 was crushed. If you want to stay in the area, the small, modern *Hotel Saltees* in Kilmore Quay has a restaurant and pleasant accommodations, with rooms named after the various species of birds found on the Saltees.

Less than 20 miles northwest of Kilmore Quay is the town of New Ross, built on a steep hill of the River Barrow. You can spend an enjoyable 3 hours dining on the water aboard the *Galley Cruising Restaurants* (phone: 051-21723) whose dinner cruises depart from New Ross at 7 PM Tuesdays through Saturdays during the summer. Five miles south of New Ross, on L159, is the John Fitzgerald

Kennedy Memorial Park, a splendid 480-acre arboretum commemorating President Kennedy, whose ancestors came from nearby Dunganstown. The park covers the lower slopes of Slieve Coillte, and if you drive to the top on a nice day, you'll see much of the counties of Wexford and Waterford. The city of Waterford is 15 miles southwest of New Ross and Kilkenny is 26 miles northwest.

Southcentral Ireland

Despite the recent influx of industry and factories, Ireland is still very much a rural and agricultural country, and this journey will take you through some of the island's best farmland. Tipperary Town is in the midst of the Golden Vale, fertile acreage extending from the valley of the River Suir, east of town, across the border into County Limerick, west of town. The rich pastureland rolls down to Mitchelstown, County Cork, where the vast creamery of the Mitchelstown Cooperative Agricultural Society gathers in its bounty, and then on to the valley of the River Blackwater, no less known for bounty of another sort. The Blackwater, which cuts across County Cork on its way into the Celtic Sea, is popular with sportsmen, especially fishermen keen on the trout, perch, roach, dace, rudd, and, above all, salmon, in it and its tributaries.

Mountain scenery is not missing: South of Tipperary Town, the Glen of Aherlow is a romantic drive through the mighty Galtee Mountains — you might meet a donkey cart or two along the road. Farther south, two other ranges, the Knockmealdowns and the Comeraghs, become a palette of greens in the afternoon light. The route goes around these two, but a detour, a hairpin scenic drive called "The Vee," will take you through the former if you have the time. Nor is seascape missing: The route also leads along the Celtic Sea from Cobh, where the great passenger liners once docked, into Youghal, where a version of *Moby Dick* was filmed, past cliffs and miles of beach into quaint Annestown, the seaside resort of Tramore, and, finally, Waterford. The route turns inland again after Waterford to enter a landscape where historic castles guarding river banks are commonplace, then terminates at Cashel, one of Ireland's greatest historic sites. If you're lucky, you'll have bad weather for your explorations here. A little fog and mist add a dimension of mystery to the imposing Rock of Cashel, and you will almost be able to hear the old heroes of Erin clanging their armor as you pass through the ruins.

The southcentral route forms a triangular loop that begins in Tipperary, goes south to the sea at Cobh, up the seacoast to Waterford, and then inland almost back to Tipperary, but turns north for Cashel at the town of Cahir. There are areas along the way where few tourists tread and hence they provide a glimpse of Ireland without make-up — raw and beautiful. These quiet stretches are interspersed with the liveliness of good pubs, restaurants, and lodgings that are plentiful from Tipperary right back around to Cashel. The shingles of artists and craftsmen working at studios and kilns in tiny villages will suggest impromptu breaks in the itinerary from time to time, and the organized tour of the Waterford Glass Factory, where you'll see how the classic crystal is made, should not be missed. You'll visit a remote Irish-speaking area, one of the few pockets of Irish not on the west coast, and you'll see a castle you've probably seen before — in film. The route is one that blends the pleasure and hospitality of Ireland with the tranquillity and beauty that once made it the land of saints and scholars.

Hotels listed as expensive will cost $60 or more for a double; those listed as moderate will range from $40 to $60; and inexpensive ones will be under $40 — well under in the case of the bed-and-breakfast houses included. Dinner for two (without wine) will cost $35 and up in an expensive restaurant; from $20 to $35 in a moderate one; and less than $20 in an inexpensive one.

TIPPERARY: "It's a long way to Tipperary," goes the famous World War I song, but this cozy town in the Golden Vale has developed a personality and prosperity in the last 10 years that makes the journey worth the distance. Viewed from the footpaths of the hills just outside town, "Tip," as it is called by the locals, resembles a quiet New England village bordered by the green back of the Slievenamuck Mountains. But Main Street is a busy place lined with pleasant shops, entertaining pubs, and good restaurants. This is prime farmland and many in the area are employed in the Tipperary Cooperative Creamery at the end of Bridge Street. Fenian leader John O'Leary was born in Tipperary, and the town was famous during the Land League Plan of Campaign of the 1880s, when residents refused to pay property rents to landlord Smith Barry and established a "New Tipperary" just outside the town borders. The shops and timber houses of Emmet and Dillon streets are still inhabited, although the plan eventually failed, especially when Smith Barry discovered he owned the land on which a new butter market had been erected by the rebels and tore it down. Kiely's Breads now stands on the site of the butter market, near the town well. Tipperary has had a long history (it grew around a castle built here by King John in the late twelfth century), but one which contrived to leave it with few very ancient or notable buildings (it was laid waste during the course of the Desmond Wars in the late sixteenth century). It is a friendly place, however, and to sample its hospitality stop at the Irish House on Main Street. Once a millinery, later a technical school, it has now been converted by Noel and Alice McInerney into a mini–shopping mall, with an American-donated, 6-foot Irish flag hanging from the handsome Georgian facade. The mall contains a large crafts shop, tourist information booth, a boutique, and a hair salon, but the pride of Irish House is its self-service coffee shop, which resembles the inside of a spacious, old-fashioned farmhouse. The tables are student desks, lantern-shaped lights by local craftsman James McEvoy hang overhead; blackened kettles swing from the crane in the fireplace, and the antiques on the mantel include an old top hat done in the original millinery. The sandwiches and pastries are made by Mrs. McInerney, who also gives demonstrations in the tying of fishing flies, a skill inherited from her father. Have a look at the guestbook, which includes the signatures of World War I veterans, lured to Tipperary by the Pied Piperish sound of its name. On Wednesday nights, there is a session of traditional music and dance at the Irish House. Elsewhere in town you can sip a pint of beer underneath a thatched roof in the *King's Well* across the street, or have a quiet drink at *Sloane's* near the Maid of Aran statue at the end of Main Street. The *Premier Club* has disco and cabaret entertainment, and there is a singing pubs contest every summer in Tipperary.

CHECKING IN: *Glen Hotel* – This inviting hotel is on the drive through the Glen of Aherlow a few miles outside Tipperary. 24 rooms. (Glen of Aherlow, Tipperary; phone: 062-56146; moderate.) ***Royal Hotel*** – Conveniently located right off Main Street, this older hotel has 20 rooms, only two with private bath. (Bridge St., Tipperary; phone: 062-51204; inexpensive.) ***Clonmore*** – Many visitors come back a second time to this popular bed-and-breakfast house in an attractive bungalow run by Mary Quinn. Four rooms with hot and cold running water and regular B&B rates. (Cork-Galbally Rd., Tipperary; phone: 062-51637; inexpensive.)

EATING OUT: ***Knocknagow*** – This country-style restaurant is housed in the renovated basement of *Kickham Lounge* and named after a novel by author Charles Kickham, who was born in County Tipperary. Run by Helen and Ted Dunworth, it is open for lunch and dinner. (50 Main St., Tipperary; phone: 062-51420; moderate.) ***Brown Trout*** – Long established and known for its inexpensive but good fare. The *Brown Trout* is light on atmosphere but generous on portions. (Bridge St., Tipperary; phone: 062-51912; inexpensive.)

En Route – Leave Tip by Bridge Street and follow the signs south for the "Glen of Aherlow," a lovely valley between the Slievenamuck Hills and the Galtee Mountains, and a wending, scenic drive. Stop at the car park before the statue of Christ the King, from where there is a vast view of the valley into which time does not seem to have intruded. Two-story farmhouses are more common than modern bungalows, and donkey carts pulling containers of milk still travel the roads. Follow the signs to Galbally and then on to Mitchelstown, just over the County Cork border.

MITCHELSTOWN: This butter- and cheese-producing town is an interesting mixture of the old and the new. The Catholic Church of the Blessed Virgin Mary with its window-slashed brick interior overlooks Mitchelstown from Convent Hill and was opened in 1980. In contrast, Kingston College was erected in 1761 by the earl of Kingston, whose family laid out much of the town. The establishment is a collection of attached stone houses that open onto College Square. Originally built as almshouses for "decayed gentlefolk" as well as some of the families who worked for the Kingstons, it is now home to about 30 retired couples. Each of the Georgian houses has a back garden and one house is set aside for community affairs, although daily life at the Kingston College once had its unharmonious moments. The houses used to share common entrances but this gave way long ago to individual doorways so that feuding families would not have to meet. The extensive creamery run by the Mitchelstown Cooperative Agricultural Society can be toured (stop in at the communications office in New Square). The Society, which began in 1917 and grew as small cooperatives merged with it, has 4,500 shareholders, all of whom are farmers, and employs about 2,300 people. Before leaving Mitchelstown, try the pastries at *Toren's* on Cork Street, and perhaps visit *Doran's,* the yarn and sweater shop nearby. Mitchelstown Caves, two long, complex caves with large halls and interesting formations that can be visited with a guide, are 6 miles northeast, off the Cahir Road.

En Route – Drive due south 10 miles to Fermoy, a fairly large and busy town that was once prosperous as a garrison for the British Army and is now popular with sport fishermen. The town straddles the River Blackwater, one of the better-known salmon-fishing rivers in Ireland. The Blackwater rises on the Cork/Kerry border and flows 85 miles out to sea at Youghal, and the stretch of the river around Fermoy is the part that is best for salmon. The river is also coarse fishing competition water with Fermoy as the fishing center that has hosted most of the championships. The genial tourist office run by Pat O'Mahoney (in a shop called *Sullivans* near the bridge) will inform you on other activities available in the area — there are numerous sports associations including five hunt clubs. Castle Hyde House, the beautiful Georgian home of Douglas Hyde, the first president of Ireland, is just outside town, but it is privately owned and not open to the public. About 3 miles northwest of town (off the Glanworth Road) and worth a visit is

Labbacallee or the Hag's Bed, one of the largest wedge-shaped gallery graves in the country. It looks like a pile of stones from the roadside, but closer inspection (climb over the steps in the stone wall at the side) reveals the massive shape of the two burial chambers covered by three immense capstones. It is guarded by several standing stones and dates from about 1500 BC.

From Fermoy, head south to Midleton and there turn west onto the T12 (N25), dropping down to the T12A at the turnoff for Cobh. The route leads across a strip of water to Great Island (approximately 17 miles by 2 miles) and curves down and around its southern side to where Cobh (pronounced Cove) stands facing the greater part of Cork Harbour.

COBH: One of the nicest times of the year to enjoy this one-time port of call for the great transatlantic passenger liners is during the annual International Folk Dance Festival, a week of dancing, concerts, fireworks, and parades each July. The blue haze of a summer's evening settles over the harbor and the graceful tower of St. Colman's Cathedral high on the hill above gives it a medieval character that is heightened by the presence of European dancers mingled on the waterfront in traditional costume, singing Irish songs in foreign accents, and waving the flags of their country. The cathedral, though not medieval (it was built between 1868 and 1915), is Cobh's most striking feature. It tops off the hill of old houses built shoulder to shoulder in ascending height and looks, from the harbor, like a guardian angel hovering over so many members of a family posing for their picture. During the famine years, the harbor at Cobh was the last image of Ireland impressed on the minds of thousands and thousands of Irish emigrants leaving their native soil on ships that all too often were not seaworthy enough to carry them to their destinations. The view then was without the cathedral, but those who survived the "coffin ships" to do well in the New World sent back money to help build this crowning touch to the town's skyline. Its exterior of Dublin granite is covered with statues and gargoyles, its interior features stained-glass windows and a 43-foot-high marble altar alive with carvings, and there are weekly concerts on the 47-bell carillon.

Until the eighteenth century, Cobh was a small fishing village accessible only by ferry and known simply as the Cove of Cork. In medieval times, it had belonged to an Irish chieftain whose son fought with Brian Ború against the Danes in the Battle of Clontarf (1014). Later, it became the home of Anglo-Irish families such as the Barrys, the Hodnetts, and the Roches, one of whose castles (the fourteenth-century Belvelly Castle) can be seen near the bridge on the way into town. The British began to develop the fishing village as a strategic naval base during the war with the American colonies. They erected a military barracks on the site of an ancient monastery across from Cobh on Spike Island (later used as a prison for Irish rebels and now an Irish army coastal defense station), and a naval station west of Spike Island on Haulbowline Island (now the site of a huge steel complex and headquarters of the Irish navy). Many of the town's streets were laid out during the 1800s, as Georgian and Victorian homes for British officers rose along Harbour Row. In 1838, the first transatlantic steamship sailed from Cobh, initiating an era of prominence for the town as an international passenger port, and in 1849, the Cove of Cork became Queenstown, renamed in commemoration of a visit by Queen Victoria. During World War I, both the British and the Americans used Queenstown's port facilities — when a German submarine sank the *Lusitania* off Kinsale in May 1915, it was from here that ships sailed to rescue the survivors.

Today, with its own name, Cobh is a holiday resort focused on its attractive harbor. The International Sailing Center, headquartered near the town hall in an old house where equipment lies in colorful disarray, offers courses in sailing. Sea angling can be arranged through the Cobh Sea Angling Club. The Royal Cork Yacht Club across the harbor at Crosshaven dates to 1720 and is the oldest in the world. The Lusitania

Memorial is in Roger Casement Square, where there are also some restored Italianate shops. A local museum is housed in a converted church on High Road. The rest of Great Island can be explored. Victims of the *Lusitania* disaster are buried in the Old Church Cemetery, about a mile north. The 20-acre gardens of the Fota estate, the grand home of the Smith Barrys and now owned by University College, Cork, are open on weekends. The college is restoring the house and developing a wildlife center on the grounds.

CHECKING IN: *Commodore Hotel* – This elegant hotel overlooks the waterfront. It has an old-world atmosphere, modernized facilities (about half the 42 rooms have private baths), a lovely dining room serving excellent meals, and a heated indoor swimming pool. Deep-sea fishing trips can be arranged. (Cobh; phone: 021-811277; expensive.)

En Route – The main Cork-to-Waterford road (N25) leads east to Youghal. But there are several reasons to turn off the road at Castlemartyr and follow the signs to Ballycotton, stopping 3 miles short of the coast at the tiny village of Shanagarry. One is a meal or an overnight stay at *Ballymaloe House*, a small guesthouse and family-run restaurant that is one of Ireland's most delightful country hotels. Another is a stop and perhaps some shopping at the pottery studios of Stephen Pearce and his father, Philip. Stephen Pearce, whose brown pottery with frosty white glaze is his trademark, built a studio for himself deep in the Shanagarry woodland a few years ago and has ever since been turning out a distinctive line sold in stores around the world. Philip Pearce, working in a complex of farmhouses, turns out pottery in handsome blacks and whites. (A third member of the talented family, Stephen's glassmaker brother, Simon Pearce, has a studio in County Kilkenny and a shop in Dublin.) Before leaving the area, drive down to the cliffs at Ballycotton for a breath of sea air, then return to the main road for the drive east into Youghal.

CHECKING IN: *Ballymaloe House* – Myrtle and Ivan Allen opened a restaurant in their stone farmhouse in 1964, and a year later began taking overnight guests. Now travelers from all over the world have stayed at this 400-acre rural retreat, an experience something like paying a visit to country cousins. The high ceilings and spacious rooms of the farmhouse, actually part of an old Geraldine castle, have been handsomely renovated, and other buildings such as the gatehouse and lodge have been modernized to make a total of 25 bedrooms. Tennis, golf (a 9-hole course), horseback riding, and deep-sea fishing (at nearby Ballycotton) are among the activities possible here. After years of cooking for a large family, Mrs. Allen now does so for her guests, using locally grown products, and her reputation has traveled far beyond quiet Shanagarry. The restaurant, where guests can buy a copy of her *Ballymaloe Cookbook*, is open 7 nights a week, with a cold buffet on Sunday. Reservations recommended. (Shanagarry, Midleton; phone: 021-652531; expensive.)

YOUGHAL: Pronounced "yawl," this is a pleasant resort town with an old quarter and a 5-mile beach situated where the River Blackwater pours into Youghal Bay. The tourist office on South Main Street in the eighteenth-century Clock Gate (which once served as a prison where inmates were flogged and often hung from the windows for their rebellious plots) can supply you with a *Tourist Trail* booklet describing a signposted walking tour of the town. The trail will take you up (Youghal is built on a hill) and around the old town walls, which date back to the fifteenth century and are among the best preserved in Ireland. St. Mary's Collegiate Church, dating from the thirteenth century, was damaged in 1579 when the town was sacked during the Desmond Rebellion, but it has been restored and is still in use. Nearby Myrtle Grove, an Elizabethan mansion (not open to the public but visible from the church), belonged to Sir Walter

Raleigh who helped put down the rebellion and was granted Irish lands by Elizabeth I for his effort. Raleigh, fresh from Virginia, is supposed to have planted Ireland's first potatoes on the property (and to have smoked the country's first pipe of tobacco here, too), but he probably never lived in the house, though he was the mayor, or warden, of Youghal for a time in 1588 and 1589. He sold the estate to Sir Richard Boyle, who rose from poverty to great wealth during Elizabeth's reign and became the first earl of Cork — a monument to him and his family is in St. Mary's. The tourist trail leads past the remains of Tynte's Castle, a tower house built by the English in the fifteenth century, and by the Benedictine Priory, which was Oliver Cromwell's headquarters during his Munster campaign of 1649 and is now partly converted into a teashop. Stop for a rest here or have a snack at the *Coffee Dock* nearby, if not a drink in the *Moby Dick* lounge around the corner from the Clock Gate. The lounge gets its name from the film, starring Gregory Peck, made in Youghal some years back, and it is appropriately decorated. *Youghal Carpets* is a long-established industry in town, and there are several potteries, including the *Youghal Pottery* on Quarry Road, where you can browse or buy in the showroom.

CHECKING IN: *Devonshire Arms* – This is a friendly, older guesthouse convenient to town. Eight of the 10 rooms have private bath. Open year-round. (Youghal; phone: 024-2827; moderate.) ***Hilltop Hotel*** – This modern hotel just outside Youghal has a stone ice house dating from the 1800s on its premises. All 50 rooms have private bath. Closed November through March. (Youghal; phone: 024-2911; moderate.)

EATING OUT: *The Bush Courtyard Restaurant* and *Wine Bar* – For a bit of romance, you might try this candlelit restaurant in the former stables of an old country house. (Quarry Rd., Youghal; phone: 024-2178; expensive.) ***Salmon Cellar*** – In the cellar of the *Youghal Inn* and known for its seafood. Open May through September. (*Youghal Inn,* Youghal; phone: 024-2592; expensive.) ***Aherne's Pub and Seafood Bar*** – Another spot popular for its seafood and for its award-winning bar food. (162/163 N Main St., Youghal; phone: 024-2424; moderate.)

En Route – Waterford is 48 miles from Youghal via the main (N25) route, but if you have time, explore some of the side roads along the way. Just north of Youghal, the road crosses the line into County Waterford, and a few miles farther along you'll come to a turn-off for Ardmore, a quaint village with impressive cliffs on Ardmore Bay (Ardmore means "the great height") and the site of many a shipwreck. There used to be an Irish college here whose students included Eamon de Valera and Maud Gonne MacBride. Ardmore is famous for the ruins of a monastery founded by St. Declan in the seventh century, though the buildings that remain are not quite that old. The twelfth-century round tower is one of the tallest and best-preserved examples of this type of structure in Ireland. Near it is St. Declan's Church (or Cathedral), Romanesque style, also of the twelfth century. St. Declan's Oratory (or Tomb) is a small church traditionally held to be the saint's grave.

Return to the main route and continue north toward Dungarvan, but turn off again before you get there and drive down to Ring, near Helvick Head. This is an especially beautiful spot in the evening, when you can sit on benches in the tall grass along the elevated waterfront and watch the sun set slowly behind the mountains as golden washes of light linger on Dungarvan Bay. Ring is a fishing village in the midst of the Waterford Gaeltacht, one of the few — and scattered — Irish-speaking areas left in Ireland. The Irish college here is half a century old and in the summer it is full of students learning the language and studying traditional music and dance. (If you wish to spend the night in Ring, a sign near the harbor will direct you — in Irish — to a friendly bed-and-breakfast house run by Mrs. Whalen, a fluent Irish speaker.) Ring is only 5 miles south of Dungarvan, an administrative center for part of County Waterford and a town that comes alive with a market on Thursdays. North of Dungarvan, leave the main route again and take the coastal route, following signs for Stradbally. The road goes inland for a distance and then follows the sea coast through a somewhat isolated region where the wind sweeps over grassy cliffs. Just before Annestown, stop at *Waterford Woodcraft,* a woodworking studio turning out functional and ornamental pieces in native woods including yew, gathered in the nearby Comeragh Mountains. Annestown has a small beach and the distinction of being just about the only village in Ireland without a pub. Its name comes from Anna De La Pore, a Catholic relation of Lord Waterford, who is said to have given Cromwell only buttermilk to drink when he sought accommodation for the night. The coastal route leads next to Tramore, a lively seaside resort whose population nearly doubles in July and August. Tramore has a 3-mile beach with lifeguards on duty in summer (you can rent surfboards on the beach), a 50-acre amusement park, 18-hole golf course, horse racing (the most important meeting is in August), and many hotels. The tourist office in Railway Square (open July and August) is well stocked with literature about sports, entertainment, and restaurants in town. From Tramore, it is only 8 miles north on the T63 to Waterford.

EATING OUT: *Annestown House Restaurant* – John and Pippa Gallowey run this elegant restaurant in their own home, but it's no ordinary home. John is a descendant of the Pallisers, and portraits of the illustrious family, including the archbishop of Cashel, hang in the parlor and dining room. The Galloweys do the cooking, and reservations are essential. Open for dinner from 7:30 to 10:30 PM. Closed November; from December to February, dinner is served on Sundays only. (Annestown; phone: 051-96160; moderate.) *Seanachie* – The name of this thatched-cottage restaurant is Irish for "storyteller." Brother and sister Michael and Laurann Casey, he with an interest in Irish culture, she a graduate of Cordon Bleu in London, have converted old farm buildings into an intimate dining room and a rustic bar where locals lift a few jars while raising their voices in ballads. The barnyard is now a courtyard for dancing. Open for lunch and dinner, and the food is varied. (5 miles south of Dungarvan on the main road, Dungarvan; phone: 058-41738; moderate.) *Katie Reilly's Kitchen* – There is no Katie Reilly, but a Peg Power ran a pub here for years. (Before that — as far back as 1870 — the place was an illegal drinking house called a "shebeen.") The Brennans, who own the pub, have expanded it into what was Peg's kitchen and bedroom and decorated every inch with antiques. Seafood and steaks are the specialties. Open for lunch and dinner; during the summer there is cabaret every night. (Tramore Rd., Waterford; phone: 051-75608; inexpensive.)

WATERFORD: Ireland's fourth largest city is a busy port on the banks of the River Suir. Reginald's Tower, built by Reginald the Dane in 1003, protected the small Viking settlement from invasion for a time, but in 1170, the Normans captured Waterford anyway, and the centuries of Anglo-Norman domination in Ireland began. The tower, now a museum, is Waterford's most prominent landmark, but the city also has several eighteenth-century churches and public buildings and the remains of once-extensive medieval abbeys. Waterford is best known, however, for the crystal that bears its name, and you can watch it being blown and cut as you tour the Waterford Glass Factory, about 1.5 miles from the center of town on the Cork Road. Tours take place on weekdays, except for the first 3 weeks in August. No crystal is sold at the factory, but you can buy it in town. For more information on the city's sights, accommodations, restaurants, and entertainment, see *Waterford,* THE CITIES.

En Route – The town of Carrick-on-Suir is 17 miles northwest of Waterford via the T13 (N24). On both sides of the river, partly in County Waterford, and partly in County Tipperary, the town was another of the seats of the Butler family of Kilkenny Castle. The Elizabethan manor house built (around 1600) by "Black Tom Butler," the tenth earl of Ormonde, is in a style uncommon in Ireland, probably because Black Tom had spent time in England and built it hoping to entice his cousin, Queen Elizabeth I, for a visit. What remains of a fifteenth-century Butler castle, much damaged by Cromwell, is behind the manor house. Be sure to stop at *Shanahan Willow Craft* on Chapel Street in Carrick-on-Suir. John Shanahan learned to make baskets from his father, who learned it from his father, who opened the shop in 1886. The nimble fingers of John and his brother, Michael, have woven some most unusual things — 10-foot goal posts for polo games and passenger baskets for hot air balloons — but their most popular items these days are linen baskets and baby cradles, and the prices are quite low for such skillfully crafted, handmade goods. After Carrick-on-Suir, continue on the T13 to Clonmel, another 13 miles.

CLONMEL: According to legend, ancient settlers were led to this town — "meadow of honey" in Irish — by a swarm of bees. It is the chief town of County Tipperary, an administrative, horse-breeding, and cider-making center. St. Patrick is said to have visited the area, which eventually passed into the hands of the powerful Anglo-Norman Butler family. In 1650, the town fell to Cromwell, but only after a very stiff resistance led by Hugh Dubh O'Neill. Clonmel runs along the River Suir, with wide O'Connell Street as its major thoroughfare. The Main Guard, a seventeenth-century building at the eastern end of the street, is said to have been designed by Christopher Wren and has been used as a courthouse, prison, and military headquarters. At the other end is West Gate, a nineteenth-century rebuilding of one of the town's original gates (you can see a portion of the old fourteenth-century town wall in the graveyard of St. Mary's Church of Ireland on Mary Street). A plaque on one side of West Gate commemorates Laurence Sterne, author of *Tristram Shandy* and a native of Clonmel. Be sure to stop by the nineteenth-century St. Mary's Catholic Church on O'Connell Street to see the ceiling and the ornate altar with statues; the latter is supposed to have been made for a church in Rome but mysteriously ended up here. The Franciscan Friary on Abbey Street has a thirteenth-century choir wall, a fifteenth-century tower, and a tiny chapel to St. Francis that is a beauty when the sun shines through the reds and oranges of its modern stained-glass windows. Near the entrance is a tomb of the Butler family. (Press the light switch on the wall at the side for a better look at the knight and lady carved on it.) The library on Parnell Street houses a museum of local interest. Also on Parnell Street is *Hearn's Hotel*, which at one time was the base of operations for the first Irish passenger transport system. In 1815, Charles Bianconi, an Italian-born resident of Clonmel, sent a horse-drawn carriage to Cahir. The number of vehicles and his network grew, and until the coming of the railways, "Bianconi cars" carried people all over the south of Ireland.

Clonmel has regular horse-racing meetings, weekly greyhound racing, good fishing in the Suir, and pony trekking into the Comeragh Mountains from Ballymacarbry (about 9 miles south of Clonmel). If time permits a detour, there is a magnificently scenic drive through the Knockmealdown Mountains southwest of town. Take the road to Ardfinnan and then on to Clogheen, where a left turn leads to a height of 1,700 feet and the hairpin curve known as "The Vee." The descent brings you into Lismore, a town on the River Blackwater, and the site of Lismore Castle. Built in the twelfth century and remodeled in the last century, it is not open to the public though its gardens are. The village of Cappoquin is 4 miles east of Lismore, also on the river, and the stretch of valley between the two is especially beautiful. From Cappoquin, you can return to the route by following the main Dungarvan road (T30) east as far as the turnoff to the T27, then driving the 20 miles north to Clonmel. Slievenamon, the "mountain of the women," rises to a height of 2,368 feet northeast of Clonmel; it is said the legendary giant Finn MacCool watched while girls raced up to its summit to win him as a husband.

CHECKING IN: *Clonmel Arms Hotel* – This is a comfortable and nicely furnished hotel in town. About half of the 37 rooms have private bath. (Sarsfield St., Clonmel; phone: 052-21233; expensive to moderate.) ***Hearn's Hotel*** – The starting point of Charles Bianconi's transport system still has the clock he used to keep the cars on schedule. This is a pleasant establishment with 31 rooms, again about half with bath. (Parnell St., Clonmel; phone: 052-21611; moderate.) ***Inislounaght House*** – Located a mile west of Clonmel, this is a lovely Georgian house with guest rooms and a restaurant much praised for its cuisine. All six rooms have private baths, and there are quiet grounds and wooden paths for strolling. Evie Reilly grows all her own produce, which ends up on the table in delicious dishes accompanied by a good selection of wines. She'll pack you a lunch if you are off for a day of exploring. (Marlfield, Clonmel; phone: 052-22847; moderate.)

En Route – From Clonmel, take the N24 west for 10 miles to Cahir. The lands of the Butlers also extended to Cahir (meaning "stone fort" and pronounced Care), where the family served as the earls of Glengall. Richard, the second earl of Glengall, helped plan much of the town, somewhat to his financial ruin. He commissioned John Nash to design the local Church of Ireland (1817) and also the Swiss Cottage Fishing Lodge in Cahir Park. The wallpaper, which can still be seen on the cottage walls, was imported from Paris. The town is small but pleasant and it prospers from what seems to be an annual influx of film makers to Cahir Castle, one of the largest and most splendid medieval castles in Ireland. Parts of *Barry Lyndon* were made here as were scenes of several other recent films. Built on a rocky inlet in the River Suir where an ancient ring-fort may once have stood, the castle dates mainly from the fifteenth century. It was thought to be impregnable, but it was captured by Robert Devereux, earl of Essex and Queen Elizabeth's favorite, in 1599, and by Cromwell in 1650, though each time it returned to the hands of the Butlers. It is now restored and open to the public year-round. Cashel is 11 miles north of Cahir via the N8.

CHECKING IN: *Kilcoran Lodge* – A few miles outside Cahir, on the right side of the Mitchelstown Road, this former shooting lodge is a charming country hotel on the slope of the Galtee Mountains. It has 22 rooms, 14 with bath. The cuisine in the airy dining room is good. (Cahir; phone: Cahir 261; expensive to moderate.) ***Carrigeen Castle*** – If you're up for a night in a cell, stop by this unusual bed-and-breakfast house run by Peggy Butler on the road to Cork. Built solidly in stone, it used to be a jail and Peggy and her husband have turned the seven cells into cozy guest rooms decorated with antiques. Hot and cold running water in all rooms; bed-and-breakfast rates. (Cork Rd., Cahir; phone: Cahir 370; inexpensive.)

EATING OUT: *Earl of Glengall* – This restaurant serves tasty pub lunches and more formal dinners at very reasonable prices. Irish and Continental cuisine. (The Square, Cahir; phone: Cahir 205; moderate.)

CASHEL: Dominating the market town that bears its name is the Rock of Cashel — Cashel of the Kings — the history of which spans sixteen centuries. From the fourth century, the kings of the province of Munster were crowned on this limestone rock rising proudly from the surrounding plain and they had their palace here. St. Patrick preached Christianity on the site in the fifth century and BrianBorú was crowned here in the tenth century. In 1101, his grandson, King Muirchertach O'Brien, gave the Rock to the Church and a period of great ecclesiastical building began. Even the roofless buildings retain their grandeur, but tiny Cormac's Chapel, still roofed, is a gem of Irish Romanesque architecture. Built between 1127 and 1134 by Cormac MacCarthy, both a king and a bishop, it is now wedged into an angle formed by the choir and the south transept of the sprawling cruciform cathedral, the largest building on the Rock, added in the thirteenth century. The 3-story archbishop's castle, actually a fortified residential palace, was added to the western end of the cathedral in the fourteenth or early fifteenth century. The oldest structure on the Rock is the twelfth-century round tower outside the north transept of the cathedral (as is usual for these watch towers, storehouses, and refuges in time of danger, the door is well above the ground). One of the first monuments to greet the visitor entering the top of the Rock is the twelfth-century Cross of St. Patrick. Its base is traditionally said to have been the seat of the king whom St. Patrick baptized here. Also in the grouping is the fifteenth-century Hall of the Vicars Choral, which housed laymen who participated in the cathedral services. The Rock is floodlit at night in the summer — an impressive sight, and there are guided tours, after which you can explore the town itself. On John Street, the Cathedral of St. John the Baptist, Church of Ireland, is a fine eighteenth-century classical building, which became the cathedral when the one on the Rock was abandoned. The building adjacent to it houses the Diocesan Library, an extensive collection of sixteenth- and seventeenth-century books. *Grant's Hotel* on Main Street was formerly Quirke's Palace, and parts of it date back to the fifteenth century. The *Cashel Palace Hotel,* also on Main Street, was the Palace of the Protestant Archbishops when it was built in the eighteenth century in lovely Queen Anne style. The ruins of a medieval Dominican Priory are also near the center of town. Before you leave, be sure to visit some of Cashel's craft shops: *Rossa Studio Pottery* and *Shanagarry Weavers* are two good ones on Cahir Road.

CHECKING IN: *Cashel Palace* – Edward Lovett Pearce, who designed the Parliament House in Dublin, designed this red-brick building (about 1730) as a residence for Protestant archbishops. It sits back off Main Street with lovely gardens behind it. Paneling, columns, and handsome marble fireplaces grace its interior. There are 20 old-fashioned, comfortable rooms with private bath. (Cashel; phone: 062-61411; expensive.) ***Cashel Kings Hotel*** – This is a modern, 40-room hotel set nearby on a hill just outside Cashel. The lounge in its interior is enhanced by a skylight and is the core from which rooms radiate, including the attractive bar and the restaurant, which is particularly noted for its fish and fresh vegetables. (Ballypadeen, Cashel; phone: 062-61477; moderate.) ***Longfield House*** – Another hotel with a pedigree, this beautiful Georgian home, just outside Cashel, once belonged to Charles Bianconi, organizer of Ireland's first transport system. It now has 10 guest rooms and is also a nice place for lunch or dinner (reservations are requested). Closed November through February. (Goold's Cross, Cashel; phone: 0504-42261; moderate.)

EATING OUT: *Chez Hans* – This is a high-quality restaurant with lots of atmosphere. It's housed in a small gothic chapel at the foot of the Rock of Cashel. High-backed chairs and choral background music further the theme. (Rockside, Cashel; phone: 062-61177; expensive.) ***Pepper's Restaurant*** – Tom Egan's restaurant, which opened in the summer of 1980, has been growing in popularity. Steaks are the specialty. The building itself, one of the oldest in Cashel, dates from the seventeenth century and was once a blacksmith's shop. It's now painted a pretty powder blue and is open for lunch and dinner as well as tea. (23 Main St., Cashel; moderate.)

West Cork

Although often overlooked in favor of its more famous neighbor, Kerry, West Cork is a very special part of Ireland. Here the landscape is a palette of infinitely changing colors, and the terrain varies from the soft shoulders of the inland Shehy Mountains to the sandy coves along the southern coast. Around Bantry Bay — an area kissed by the warm and gentle Gulf Stream current — you'll see lush palm trees and much other subtropical foliage. Pointing to several soaring 80-foot eucalyptus trees, one Corkman boasted: "The trees in this part of Ireland grow as tall as those in Disney cartoons!"

But scenic beauty is by no means Cork's sole attraction. Its fine bathing strands, climbable peaks, excellent fishing waters, and busy marinas make the area a paradise for sports-lovers. In addition, there are many lively, cheerful villages where pub regulars have formed singing groups; small mountain towns where the lilt of the ancient Irish tongue is on most lips; remote and lovely places where time has stood still. Even on the road, visitors will feel warmly welcomed. Everybody waves: The child on a bicycle beams; the farmer in the field looks up to lift an arm in salute, and conversations at cottage gates pause as heads turn and a chorus of hands are raised in greeting.

Our route, which begins and ends in Cork City, traces a leisurely circuit around West Cork. First stops are the Irish-speaking towns of Macroom and Ballingeary, and next is the historic, lovely lake of Gougane Barra. We continue west to balmy Bantry Bay, then south and east to the picturesque fishing villages of Skibbereen, Clonakilty, and Kinsale. The entire route is about 130 miles and can be covered easily in 2 days.

Except perhaps in high season, it's fairly safe to ramble along without reservations. A wide selection of accommodations is possible, from bed and breakfast in a simple bungalow to a gourmet meal and elegant room in a mansion-turned-hotel. Expect to pay around $60 and up per night for a double in those places listed as expensive; from $40 to $60 in moderate; and under $40 in inexpensive. A meal for two will cost about $35 to $50 in a restaurant listed as expensive; between $20 and $30 in moderate; and under $30 in inexpensive. Prices don't include wine, tips, or drinks.

CORK: For a detailed report on the city, its sights, hotels, and restaurants, see *Cork*, THE CITIES.

En Route – Route T29 takes you along the north bank of the River Lee and passes through the charming villages of Dripsey, with its woolen mills, and Coachford.

MACROOM: This small Irish town is interesting to Americans because it's the birthplace of William Penn, the founder of Pennsylvania. Macroom castle at the center of the town was granted to his father, Admiral William Penn, by Oliver Cromwell in 1654. While growing up here, the boy William was influenced by one of his father's frequent guests, Thomas Loe, a Quaker minister from Cork. Over the years the castle underwent much strife and was burned for the final time in the Irish Civil War in the early 1920s. The ruins have been declared a monument and partly restored. There's a nine-hole golf course nearby on a steep slope overlooking the Soullane River.

Macroom owes its existence to its location near the confluence of three rivers — Lee, Laine, and Soullane — where people have gathered to barter and swap food and produce for centuries. It's still a thriving market town, with an annual agricultural show in summer. Posters for this show advertise competitions for "horses, cakes, sheep, and honey" — a compelling collage of images and flavors!

En Route – Go back 1 mile on the Cork road, T64, and turn left for Inchigeelagh. Past Inchigeelagh the road hugs the north bank of the long and lovely Lough Allua. But the minor road along the south bank is even more beautiful, so that's the one you should take.

BALLINGEARY: This village is in the heart of the Gaeltacht — an Irish-speaking district — in West Cork, and every summer young people flock here from all over the country to study in school-sponsored Irish-language programs. Villagers, however, will greet you in a perfect and often mellifluous English; some language experts aver that the English spoken here is very similar to that used in Elizabethan times. There's a very good craft shop in the village, run by the Quill family, which produces and sells handsome garments made from the skins of sheep and goats. Just two doors from this shop is the birthplace of Cardinal Manning, the archbishop of Los Angeles.

Make a right turn 3.7 miles beyond Ballingeary, where the sign reads: Gougane Barra. The fork in the road is marked by a large crucifixion tableau, a memorial to local poet Máire Bhuí Ní Laoghaire.

GOUGANE BARRA: The mountain-encircled lake of Gougane Barra, source of the River Lee, is where St. Finbarre, the founder of Cork, had his hermitage in the sixth century. Joined to the lakeshore by a causeway is an island on which there's a replica of the original, now ruined oratory. The isolation and serenity of the place makes it immediately apparent why this valley was chosen for monastic contemplation. The surrounding area is a beautiful forest park with picnic areas and hiking trails. Fishing is free, although you may not catch anything; as one local put it, "St. Finbarre let everybody fish free, and that was about a thousand years ago, so I don't expect there's much left to catch."

Return to T64. Continue southwest as the road descends via Keimaneigh Pass and the Ouvane Valley to Ballylickey and Bantry.

CHECKING IN: *Gougane Barra Hotel* – The dining room at this small (34-room) hotel has lovely views of the lake and hills. If given notice, the owner will lend you a boat. Open April to October. (Gougane Barra; phone: Ballingeary 69; inexpensive.)

BANTRY: This is the home of the spectacular, mostly Georgian-style Bantry House. Now a national museum, but formerly the seat of the earls of Bantry, the house is open daily 10 AM to 6 PM and is furnished with antiques, tapestries, and paintings chosen by the second earl of Bantry during his travels in Europe in the eighteenth century. The mansion is surrounded by elegant terraces and gardens and looks out over beautiful Bantry Bay. Admission charge.

Bantry is the perfect homebase for those interested in water sports; there's a fine beach and facilities for skin diving and water skiing (*Vickery's Inn,* New St.; phone: 6). Bay cruises are run regularly from April through September; contact Michael Carroll at Bantry Bay Cruises (phone: 275).

En Route – Continue along the eastern shore of Bantry Bay; soon the road leaves the sea, and the landscape becomes a great patchwork of farm fields, with colors changing every mile. This region has enjoyed a great surge of affluence in the past decade and the prosperity is reflected in freshly painted farmhouses and neatly kept yards. In West Cork, as elsewhere in Ireland, cattle are the mainstay of the economy. (The human population of the entire Republic is just over 3 million, while the cattle population often reaches 9 million.) On the road, you will often have to stop your car to give way to lumbering herds, although the Cork farmer may not be leading his cattle on foot, but instead nudging them along with his Mercedes-Benz. One local wit remarked, "Americans can grumble all they like about oil sheiks, but here in Ireland we have milk sheiks!"

From Ballydehob you can drive directly to Skibbereen or try a scenic side trip westward down the peninsula. First on the detour is Schull, a little village popular with fishermen and sailors; a deep sea angling competition is held here in July and a regatta in August. Follow the road to Goleen, where you can sunbathe on the fine strand, then press on to Crookhaven, a pretty harbor town with some small beaches. A few miles farther are the dramatic cliffs of Mizenhead, the southernmost point in Ireland. You can go back to Schull and Ballydehob via the northern route across the peninsula, which passes Mt. Gabriel (1,339 feet).

CHECKING IN: *Ballylickey House Hotel* – This Georgian mansion set in its own lovely gardens offers elegant accommodations in 24 rooms with bath. Heated outdoor swimming pool. The atmosphere is coolly formal. The dining room sometimes rises to great heights with superb cuisine, but the quality of meals is uneven. (Ballylickey; phone: 027-50071; expensive.) *Westlodge* – A 60-room modern hotel, it has a restaurant that overlooks the mountains, an indoor pool, tennis courts, a sauna, and other amenities. (About 1 mile outside Bantry on the Cork to Killarney road; phone: 027-50360; moderate.)

SKIBBEREEN: This town offers some very good fishing in the nearby Shepperton, Ballinlough, Lissard, and Ballyalla lakes (tackle and boats may be rented). It's also a convenient jumping-off point for exploring the shores and islands of the quaintly named Roaring Water Bay. Eight miles to the southwest, the little town of Baltimore has been for hundreds of years one of Ireland's more popular ports of call due to its sheltered harbor. You can go fishing and boating here or take the Cape Clear Island ferry over to see Dunamore Castle or to photograph the great colonies of seabirds. There's also a ferry to Sherkin Island, which has an Outdoor Pursuits Centre for the hyperactive, with facilities for hiking, skin diving, riding, and boating.

En Route – It's a very pretty and relaxing drive along the coast road from Skibbereen to Kinsale; each small town is worth a look for its particular attraction. There's a ruined castle and prehistoric stone fort at Castletownshend; two old castles in Union Hall (where Jonathan Swift wrote the poem "Carberiae Rupes"); Glandore offers fine beaches and good fishing; Rosscarbery is the site of a monastery established by Saint Fachtna in the sixth century; Clonakilty is the home of the West Cork Regional Museum; and the Franciscan abbey found in Timoleague dates to the fourteenth century.

CHECKING IN: *Lissard House* – Only the freshest vegetables, meat, and fish are served in the dining room of this recently renovated Georgian mansion surrounded by its own lovely estate. The 10 luxurious bedrooms, half of which have private bath, are furnished with antiques. (Skibbereen; phone: 028-21109; moderate.)

KINSALE: Clinging to a hill overlooking the Bandon River estuary, Kinsale is an appealing little town whose tall, whitewashed houses huddle together along narrow, twisting lanes. A morning's stroll along the signposted walking tour will take you through the town's most charming streets and past St. Multose Church, an impressive stone structure dating to the thirteenth century. The wide and sheltered harbor at Kinsale is one of the most scenic in Ireland, and since the building of a modern marina in 1979, it has become a favorite port with British and European yachtsmen. Deep-sea fishing, off the Old Head of Kinsale, can be arranged (try the Kinsale Angling Centre, phone: 72611; or the Trident Hotel Angling Centre, phone: 72301), and the swimming and sunning are very fine on the neighboring strands at Summer Cove and Charles Fort. Another — but no less essential — attraction is the town's growing reputation as the "culinary capital of Ireland." There is, for the town's size, an extraordinary range of really top-class restaurants whose proprietors sponsor an annual Gourmet Festival in October.

Kinsale is also an important footnote in Irish history, for it was here in 1601 that the Irish forces, led by the earls of Tyrone and Tyrconnel, suffered final defeat at the hands of Queen Elizabeth I's army.

From Kinsale, it's just 18 miles back to Cork city.

CHECKING IN: Acton's Hotel – This member of the Trusthouse Forte hotel chain has a terrific location facing the harbor and a restaurant that specializes in fresh fish. The hostelry's 59 bedrooms, while fairly large, can be dismal and chilly. Pool. (Cork Road; phone: 72135; moderate.) **The Blue Haven Hotel** – This is a small, cozy hotel, with 12 rooms, 1 with bath. Here again, the dining room is the big attraction. Fresh produce and seafood dishes are the specialty of the house. The wood-paneled bar has log fires going; emphasis is on personal service. (Pearce St.; phone: 72209; moderate.) **White Lady Inn Hotel** – The hotel has only 10 rooms, none with bath. But its restaurant in this restaurant town is great. A member of the Good Food Circle, it has an excellent choice of fish and steaks. During high season there is nightly entertainment. (Lower O'Connell St.; phone: 72381; moderate.)

EATING OUT: The Vintage – This vine-covered, beamed little restaurant stands in a winding street near the harbor. The cooking is French, with particular emphasis on local produce. (Main St.; phone: 72381, 72530; expensive to moderate.) **Man Friday** – Beautifully situated in its own garden, this friendly restaurant specializes in seafood. (Scilly, Kinsale; phone: 72204; moderate.) **The Skippers Restaurant** – Another member of the Kinsale Good Food Circle, this small, intimate restaurant also specializes in seafood. (Near the pier on Lower O'Connell St.; phone: 72664; moderate.) **Max's Wine Bar** – It's a tiny but busy bistro that serves simple meals — salads, soups, and slices of lasagne. (Main St.; phone: 72443; inexpensive.)

Ring of Kerry and the Beara Peninsula

Artists and writers have for centuries celebrated the beauty of the Kingdom of Kerry, where the majesty of Ireland's highest mountains contrasts starkly with romantic glens, and the splendor of the rugged coastline gives way to glorious lakes and luxurious forests. It is a landscape of great variety, with the sea and ever-changing patterns in the sky as much a part of it as the primordial shapes of solid ground or the seasonal come-and-go of blossoming bushes and trees or the green ground cover. A good portion of this southwestern county is made up of two and a half peninsulas that constitute Kerry at its picturesque best: Dingle, Iveragh, and Beara, the latter shared with County Cork.

The best known of these mountainous projections into the Atlantic is the middlemost one, the Iveragh Peninsula, circled by a famed scenic route known as the Ring of Kerry. Browse through a brochure of bus tours of the Emerald Isle and a day trip around the Ring will rarely be missing. Nor will a stop in Killarney, both the gateway to the Iveragh Peninsula and the focal point of an enchanting district of mountains, lakes, and valleys that would put it on the map even if the Ring happened to be nowhere handy. Because Killarney is definitely on the beaten path and takes advantage of it, the town has its detractors who will point out that it is more of a tourist center than a representative Irish city and none the prettier for this transformation. Its fans will answer that Killarney has long been a tourist attraction and that there is no denying the beauty of the surroundings that made it so.

DIRECTIONS / Ring of Kerry and the Beara Peninsula

In truth, Killarney has relied heavily on tourism since the mid-eighteenth century when the local magnate, Lord Kenmare, developed the trade and four major roads were opened to the outside world. In the nineteenth century, Victorian travelers became the most enthusiastic of visitors. Killarney's purple glens, silent glades, ruined castles, and fairy isles afloat on misty lakes appealed to the Victorian imagination, and the journals of their travels are breathless with wonderment at what they saw and replete with apologies for their inability to convey its magic on their pages. Twentieth-century visitors can take heart. The enthralling scenery around Killarney hasn't changed at all, and if the parking lots of the town's hotels are filled with tour buses, its streets are also lined with pony traps and jaunting cars. Just as the Victorians would be swaddled in lap robes and stashed in the back of a horse-drawn carriage, so, too, will today's jet-age traveler be tucked in and trotted out of town in the turf-scented morning, off to affront the Gap of Dunloe.

Even back then there was disdain for the traveler on too tight a schedule. William Makepiece Thackeray, in his *Irish Sketch Book* of 1843, had little good to say of the "man coming from his desk in London or Dublin and seeing 'the whole lakes in a day.'" But many visitors today choose to do just that, to have time to push farther west to more open vistas on the wilder peninsulas. Out on the edge of Europe, these provide unforgettable sights of mountains and bare headlands meeting water in a splash of surf, of sandy coves, of offshore islands spotting the distant sea.

The Iveragh Peninsula is the most traveled, but an air of remoteness clings to it still in tiny fishing villages where Irish is spoken and in ancient stones left behind by forgotten peoples. Ascetic monks who withdrew as far as they could from the world built their retreat on Skellig Michael, and the deserted site can be visited today. According to George Bernard Shaw, "No experience that the conventional tourist travel can bring you will stick in your memory so strangely; for Skellig Michael is not after the fashion of this world."

This route begins in Killarney and explores the lakes around it, then proceeds around the Ring of Kerry in a counterclockwise direction from Killorglin to Kenmare. From Kenmare, it turns south to Glengarriff (a fair number of palm trees will linger in your mind along with pictures of peat bogs; the warm Gulf Stream causes Mediterranean flora to prosper in this corner of Ireland with the conviction of converts). Glengarriff is the starting point for a loop around the least traveled peninsula, Beara. (Dingle, the most northerly of the three Kerry peninsulas, is treated in a separate tour route.) Hotels encountered along the way are rated as in the rest of our Irish listings: $60 and up for a double room in an expensive hotel; from $40 in a moderate one; and under $40 in an inexpensive one. A meal for two in a moderate restaurant will range from $20 to $35, not necessarily with wine, while prices in expensive and inexpensive restaurants will naturally fall above and below that.

KILLARNEY: This lively marketing town is on the itinerary of almost every visitor to Ireland not so much for itself as for what lies around it. The lakes of Killarney and the mountains that hold them are in a boulder-and-rock strewn location of unrivaled natural beauty sculpted by the Ice Age and trimmed with woods of oak, cedar, mountain ash, juniper, holly, hawthorn, and the arbutus — or strawberry tree — the special botanic glory of the area recognizable by its small, glossy dark green leaves, white flowers in spring, and brilliant red berries in autumn and winter.

The three main lakes stretch through a valley in the mountains south of the town, with Killarney located on the largest, the Lower Lake, or Lough Leane. The Muckross peninsula separates the Lower Lake from the Middle Lake (also known as Muckross Lake), which is in turn connected to the Upper Lake by a narrow strait called the Long Range. The district includes the 11,000-acre Bourne Vincent Memorial Park, once a private estate whose owners presented it to the Irish government, which promptly turned it into a national park. Do not miss Muckross House, the focal point of the park, 3.5 miles from Killarney on the road to Kenmare (open daily Easter through October; closed Mondays the rest of the year). The nineteenth-century manor house of the estate contains furnished period rooms upstairs and a folk museum in the basement where a working weaver, potter, and blacksmith bring the display to life. Around the house, Muckross Gardens are especially glorious in May and June when the azaleas are in bloom and giant clumps of rhododendrons are ablaze with color.

Killarney's scenic mountains and lakes can be explored by car, taxi, bicycle, boat, pony, or on foot, but the most traditional way is by jaunting car — a horse-drawn wagon on which you and your companions sit back to back behind the driver and face the roadside. Visitors with the time for a leisurely exploration will not be at a loss to fill it, but those without that luxury will find that the standard tour routes set up by jaunting car and taxi drivers (at standardized rates — check with your hotel or at the tourist office) do cover the highlights.

The first, most comprehensive, and most spectacular route (a full-day tour available from May to October) is the trip through the Gap of Dunloe, a 4-mile long gorge between Macgillycuddy's Reeks and Purple and Tomies mountains, southwest of Killarney. You'll leave town by the Killorglin Road, passing the ruins of Dunloe Castle perched on a bend of the River Laune. Dating from 1207, the castle was a Gaelic stronghold for 400 years until temporarily rendered uninhabitable by Cromwellian forces. In the eighteenth century, one Donal O'Mahony, although a Catholic, maintained a feudal state here with a private militia of 4,000 men, and as far as Dublin Castle was concerned, he was as ungovernable as any medieval baron. At *Kate Kearney's Cottage,* a former coaching inn turned snack bar, pub, and souvenir shop at the entrance to the Gap of Dunloe, you'll transfer to the back of a pony or to a pony and trap (another of the traditional carts carrying visitors through the lake area) for the trip through the gap itself. (If you've driven your own car, you can park it here, but you'll have to come back for it later by taxi or jaunting car, which you might want to do anyway. *Gap of Dunloe Industries,* run by Michael Moriarity, is just about 100 yards short of the cottage, and is a good place to shop for jackets, capes, sweaters, scarves, blankets, and other Irish goods you might not want to take with you on horseback.) For the next 4 miles, you'll pass through an extraordinarily remote and gloomy scene, with massive rocks on either side and an accompanying narrow stream widening here and there into sullen lakes. One of them — Black Lough, or Serpent Lake — is where St. Patrick is supposed to have drowned the last snake in Ireland and to this day it is without fish. Emerging from the gap, the wooded Upper Lake, still 3 miles away, comes into view and Black Valley stretches off in the distance to the right. You'll stop for a picnic lunch (bring your own) when you reach Brandon's Cottage near the lake shore, then board a boat for the trip down the lakes: From the Upper Lake, considered to be the most beautiful of the three, the boat turns into the Long Range, which grows progressively swifter until the boatman "shoots the rapids" at the Old Weir Bridge into a beautiful calm spot called the Meeting of the Waters. After a look at Dinis Island, rife with shrubs and arbutus, you'll cross the Middle Lake (the mountain rising steeply above is Torc Mountain and it will be covered with rhododendrons in late spring) and row under Brickeen Bridge into the Lower Lake. Among its 30 islands, the most noteworthy is Innisfallen Island, with remains of a small church and an Augustinian priory of the eleventh and twelfth centuries. Innisfallen was the site of a monastery and important educational center for 1,000 years beginning in the seventh century — one of its students may have been Brian Ború himself. A major Irish historical source, the *Annals of Innisfallen,* compiled here from the tenth to the fourteenth centuries, is now in the Bodleian Library in Oxford. The tour ends at the now-ruined fifteenth-century Ross Castle, the last stronghold in Ireland to stand against Cromwellian troops. From here, a jaunting car returns visitors to town. Note that it is possible to drive through the Gap of Dunloe, but if you do, the recommended route is in the opposite direction, coming down from Moll's Gap, and then not until the late afternoon when the last of the ponies will have gone by.

The second standard itinerary is the half-day jaunting car tour of the Muckross estate to Muckross Abbey, Muckross House, and the Torc Waterfall. The entrance to Bourne Vincent Memorial Park is 3 miles from Killarney, and once inside, it is another ½-mile trot through the greenery and past herds of grazing Kerry cattle, an old Irish breed, to the remarkably well-preserved Muckross Abbey. Founded in 1448 by the Irish chieftain MacCarthy Mor and completed 50 years later, the abbey is mainly, but not entirely, Gothic, as is evident from the cloister: Two sides have pointed arches and two have rounded arches, indicating a change in style during the course of its construction. See the yew tree in the middle of the cloister (it is supposed to be as old as the abbey, but probably isn't), then go upstairs to see where the friars lived until the abbey was suppressed by the Cromwellians in 1652. The tour next takes in Muckross House and Gardens and then proceeds to Dinis Island and to the Torc Waterfall, where the waters of the Devil's Punch Bowl fall 60 feet into a leafy glen and a winding path leads above the fall for a view over the lakes. Motorists can do this route, too, by following the Kenmare Road, though some walking will be necessary to see Muckross Abbey, since only pedestrians, bicycles, and jaunting cars are allowed into the section of the park where it is located. Muckross House has its own entrance farther along the Kenmare Road where cars may drive in as far as the parking lot.

The third standard jaunting car itinerary, the half-day trip to Aghadoe Hill, can also be done by car. Start out on the Tralee Road, following the signs for Aghadoe, which may have been a pagan religious site prior to becoming a Christian settlement even before the time of St. Patrick. The ruins here include the stump of an eleventh-century round tower, a stone church of the same period, and a later, much truncated castle, but it is the Viewing Point just beyond the *Aghadoe Heights* hotel that is the main attraction. The entire Killarney area, from the spire of Killarney Cathedral on the left, clear across to Macgillycuddy's Reeks and the Iveragh Mountains beyond, is visible in one sweeping panoramic view.

Killarney town has hotels, restaurants, lively singing pubs (try *The Laurels* on Main Street), a racecourse, two beautifully situated golf courses, and ample opportunity for fishing — the catch is trout or salmon and you'll see fishing boats tucked away everywhere around the lakes. Few buildings are of architectural merit, though St. Mary's Cathedral on New Street, designed by Pugin and built between 1842 and 1914, is ranked among the finest examples of the Gothic revival in Ireland. Each July, the major choral work of the Killarney Bach Festival is performed in this superb setting. Killarney also hosts Pan Celtic Week in May, a week of song, dance, and sport by gathered Celts from Scotland, Wales, Cornwall, Brittany, the Isle of Man, and, of course, Ireland.

CHECKING IN: *Dunloe Castle* – This is not an old Irish fortress but a modern, German-owned hotel near the Gap of Dunloe. (The actual Dunloe Castle is on its grounds, however.) All 140 rooms have private bath, and other amenities include a heated indoor pool and sauna. Open April through October. (Beaufort, Killarney; phone: 064-32118; expensive.) ***The Europe*** – A sister hotel to the

Dunloe Castle, with the same German owner, it has a marvelous location on the shore of the Lower Lake and it, too, has a heated indoor pool and sauna. The 168 rooms vary in size and degree of luxury; many have balconies. There are two restaurants: The main dining room and a more intimate second room are good but not wildly exciting. Closed December, January, and February. (Fossa, Killarney; phone: 064-31900; expensive.)
Killarney Great Southern – The exterior of this mid-nineteenth-century railway hotel is stern and ivy-covered, but step inside and the tone is one of domesticated Victorian swank. The lobby is a mix of regally patterned carpets, overstuffed plush furniture, very high ceilings, and crystal chandeliers. The dining room is elegant, domed and pillared, and as large as a ballroom, but there is a smaller, equally elegant, restaurant, the *Malton Room,* beside it. Off the rambling corridors are 180 rooms, some spacious and traditionally decorated, some (in the new wing) modern and smallish. All have private bath. (Killarney; phone: 064-31262; expensive.) **Aghadoe Heights** – This modern hotel is small — 46 rooms that are less than luxurious but make up for it with fine, panoramic views of the lakes. The service is friendly and the restaurant is quite good. (Aghadoe, Killarney; phone: 064-31766; moderate.) **Castlerosse** – Also beautifully situated, this is a low, motel-style hotel adjoining one of Killarney's championship golf courses. It has 40 rooms with bath. (Killarney; phone: 064-31144; moderate.) **Ross** – In the town center, this hotel is warm, friendly, and family owned and run. The restaurant is simple but tasteful, with very good service. 42 rooms, 35 with bath. (Killarney; phone: 064-31359; moderate.)

EATING OUT: Deenach Restaurant – This nightclublike restaurant offers good food and dancing with the dining. (College St., Killarney; phone: 064-31656; expensive.) **Gaby's** – The Flemish couple who run this good seafood restaurant also offer some cooking from their homeland. The atmosphere is bright and nautical with light knotty pine wood and blue-and-white and red-and-white checkered tablecloths; there's a lobster tank at the entrance where you can pick your own. Closed mid-November through mid-March. (17 High St., Killarney; phone: 064-32519; moderate.)

En Route – The coastal road around the Iveragh Peninsula, known as the Ring of Kerry, is one of Ireland's most famous scenic drives. The complete circuit of the peninsula — which extends nearly 40 miles southwest of Killarney and has an average breadth of 15 miles — is an approximately 110-mile round trip that will take most of one day to see in a leisurely way. It is possible to do it counterclockwise as described below (from Killarney to Killorglin and around) or clockwise (from Killarney to Kenmare and around), but the former route is suggested because some of the scenery is seen to best advantage in that direction. (Tour buses take the same route, but they do it to be on the inside of the sharp curves in the often narrow road.) Do not attempt this scenic run if there is a sea mist, because you will see little, or during heavy and continuous rain — though the latter seldom lasts more than half a day. If in doubt, you should be able to get a weather report by phoning the Valentia Meteorological Station (phone: Cahirciveen 27).

From Killarney, take Route T67 for Killorglin. The jagged mountains to the left of the road are Macgillycuddy's Reeks, reduced to stumps by 200 million years of ruthless erosion but crowned, nonetheless, by the highest peak in Ireland, Carrantuohill (3,414 feet). Eight miles from Killarney, take the signposted turn left for Ballymalis Castle, on the banks of the Laune. This is one of a line of castles originally built by the Anglo-Normans when they overran the area in the early thirteenth century. The present castle — recently partly restored — is a typical sixteenth-century tower house of four stories: the ground floor for storage; the second for defense; the third for sleeping; and the top, a single, splendid living room. Return to the road and continue the remaining 5 miles into Killorglin.

KILLORGLIN: The presence of another Anglo-Norman castle, now almost totally ruined, gave rise to this small town on the River Laune. Killorglin is famous for its Puck Fair, actually a 3-day horse, sheep, and cattle sale accompanied by unrestricted merrymaking. Held every year from the 10th to the 12th of August, it is the area's greatest festival and draws people from all over County Kerry. On the first day, called Gathering Day, men of the town go into the mountains and capture the "puck," or wild male goat, who is then decorated with ribbons and enthroned on a platform above the town square from where he presides over the festivities until Scattering Day, the end of the fair. In the meantime, shops are open day and night. The Puck Fair has been going on for a long time but its origins are uncertain. It may date from the worship of the Celtic god Lúg or it may be an upstart from the seventeenth century when a herd of wild goats stampeded the town ahead of approaching Cromwellian soldiers and thereby saved many lives.

En Route – From Killorglin, continue southwest on T66 (N70) for the 9 miles to Glenbeigh. Along the way, you will pass Caragh Lake inland on the left, and if you detour to it, you will find it surrounded by magnificent scenery (the parking place up the rough road is one viewing point and another is at the end of the pathway leading to the top of the hill).

GLENBEIGH: This tiny holiday and fishing resort is situated at the foot of Seefin Mountain (1,621 feet), not far from where the River Behy flows out into Dingle Bay. The Glenbeigh Horseshoe, a semicircle of hills from Seefin to Drung Hill, is known to nature lovers as one of the county's most scenic mountain walks. At the end of the village are the gaunt — and burnt — ruins of Glenbeigh Towers, built by the local landlord, Lord Headley, in the 1870s. His architect was an Englishman who kept the famous actress, Ellen Terry, as a mistress during the years of construction, and had the bailiffs as constant visitors after Lord Headley took local action against him for cost overruns, leaking walls, and a leaking roof. A right turn onto an unclassified road beyond Glenbeigh leads, in 1.5 miles, to Rossbeigh Strand, a long spit of land reaching into Dingle Bay to nearly meet its counterpart, Inch Strand, coming across the water from the Dingle Peninsula. The 2 miles of sand beach are backed by dunes and at the end of the spit is a nineteenth-century stone tower built to guide ships into Castlemaine Harbour. In the eighteenth century, many transatlantic ships, driven by terrifying southwest storms, met their end at Rossbeigh, sometimes helped, it is said, by shipwreckers greedy for their cargo. Also remembered in the area are some much more remote incidents that occurred here — those connected with the Fenian cycle of Irish legends. Ossian, the son of Finn MacCool (who was the leader of the Fianna, a sort of standing army of the Iron Age), had met the beautiful, golden-haired Niamh, who persuaded him to return with her to her own kingdom. Together the pair mounted the girl's white horse and galloped out along the Rossbeigh spit into the western ocean to the paradisal Land of Youth. Ossian came back, 300 years later, but once off the horse, he immediately turned into a very old man. Another famous story is that of Diarmuid and Grainne, daughter of the king of Ireland, who was betrothed to Finn, whom she found too old. Instead, she forced Diarmuid, a handsome young Kerryman, to elope with her. With a gang of murderous desperadoes (hired by Finn) in hot pursuit, they fled — first to a cave at Glenbeigh. The chase lasted 7 years and eventually Diarmuid was killed (by a magic boar) and Grainne did marry Finn, but in popular speech, many Irish prehistoric tombs are still called "beds of Diarmuid and Grainne."

CHECKING IN: ***Ard na Sidhe*** – Elegant, quiet, and beautifully secluded in the forest at Caragh Lake, this was formerly a private home. Half of the 22 rooms have private bath. To find *Ard na Sidhe*, "hill of the fairies" in Irish, look for the signs on Route N70 between Killorglin and Glenbeigh. Open May through September. (Killorglin; phone: Caragh Lake 5; expensive.) ***Glenbeigh Hotel*** – Here the beauty is in the gardens. There are 21 old-world rooms, 7 with bath, and the restaurant is good.

Open March through October. (Glenbeigh; phone: Glenbeigh 4; expensive to moderate.)

EATING OUT: *Towers Hotel* – Not only is the *Towers* a famous hotel and restaurant, it is also the social center of town. It is expected that the high standards of the former owner, Ernie Evans, will be maintained by Brendan Sweeney—to whom it was sold in 1981—who has considerable experience in the trade. The specialty here is seafood, and the wine list is impressive. The hotel has 21 fairly comfortable rooms (4 with bath), but with all the singsong in the bar, there's not much sleep to be had. Closed November and December. (Glenbeigh; phone: Glenbeigh 12; expensive.)

En Route – The main road from Glenbeigh to Cahirciveen, a distance of 17 miles, encompasses some of the most memorable scenery of the Ring of Kerry. The road rises to Mountain Stage, so-called because it was once a station for stagecoaches, and hugs the side of Drung Hill (2,104 feet), providing wonderful views of Dingle Bay and the mountains of the Dingle Peninsula beyond. A cairn near the top of Drung Hill is reputed to be the grave of St. Finian, a major leader of the great religious movement of the sixth and seventh centuries. The road continues high over the sea to Kells, a small resort on Kells Bay, where it descends to a broad valley running on to Cahirciveen. A mile short of the town, just beyond the sharp turn left indicated by a series of striking yellow arrows, the ruins of Carhan House can be seen. Daniel O'Connell, the national leader — known as the Liberator — who achieved emancipation for Irish Catholics, was born here in 1875.

CAHIRCIVEEN: Set on the Valentia River at the head of Valentia Harbour, Cahirciveen grew up in the early nineteenth century. Its most notable building is the O'Connell Memorial Church on Main Street, meant to honor the centenary of Daniel O'Connell's birth in 1875, but only begun in 1888 when the cornerstone, sent by Pope Leo XIII from the catacombs in Rome, was laid. Across the bridge, about 2.5 miles northwest of town, are the remains of Ballycarbery Castle, which had been, in the fifteenth century, the magnificent castle of MacCarthy Mor, guarded by the old Gaelic O'Connell family as seneschals. Cromwell's forces destroyed the castle in 1652 and drove the O'Connells to County Clare, though they later returned to the area (a junior member eventually moved to Derrynane). The ruins of an ancient stone fort, Cahergal, are nearby, and another, Leacanabuaile, is a few hundred yards away. The latter, dating to the ninth or tenth centuries, is one of very few of these stone forts to have been excavated. Inside, the remains of three stone beehive houses, once occupied by a very poor farming community, were found, along with a square house apparently added later. Note the souterrain, originally an escape hatch, a place of refuge, and also a place for storage.

Valentia Harbour (you'll get a good view of it at the bridge) was well known in the eighteenth century as a smuggling port and hiding place for privateers. British naval vessels often anchored here, too, but the smugglers earned their tolerance with judicious gifts of brandy. Valentia Island, 7 miles by 2 miles, is in the harbor, joined to the mainland by a bridge at Portmagee. Its inhabitants live by fishing, farming, and some tourism — the sea fishing is especially good and so are the views from its steep cliffs. The island is one of the most westerly points in Europe, and the first transatlantic telegraph cable, which came to Valentia in 1866, was in use for 100 years.

En Route – The Ring of Kerry route (N70) turns inland across the tip of the Iveragh Peninsula to Waterville, 11 miles from Cahirciveen. Three detours along the way are possible, however: to Valentia Island (where there's good deep-sea fishing), to the offshore monastic site of Skellig Michael, and to the tiny village of Ballinskelligs on Ballinskelligs Bay. The turnoff for Portmagee and the bridge to Valentia Island is 4 miles southwest of Cahirciveen on N70 and the turnoff for

Ballinskelligs is 2 miles beyond that, also on N70. Skellig Michael, one of the Skellig Rocks, can be reached by boat from Portmagee or Valentia Island, but only when the weather permits.

VALENTIA ISLAND: Seven miles long and 2 to 3 miles wide, this tiny island is now connected to the mainland by a newly constructed bridge. Knightstown, at Valencia's eastern end, consists of one main street, a lovely harbor and waterfront, and is a popular holiday resort renowned for its deep-sea fishing. Also in Knightstown is the old Western Union cable office, the receiving station for the first messages sent across the Atlantic in 1858. Accommodations at the *Royal Hotel* (phone: Valentia Island 44; moderate) are comfortable, the food is good, and there's regular, name live entertainment; open April through October.

SKELLIG ROCKS: These two small islands, pyramids of rock actually, are 7 and 8.5 miles off the coast of Bolus Head. Little Skellig (445 feet high), the smaller of the two and all but inaccessible by boat, is a bird sanctuary with thousands of seabirds, especially gannets, nesting on its precipitous stone peaks. Bird life — puffins, razorbills, kittiwakes, gannets, and more — is abundant on Great Skellig (714 feet), or Skellig Michael, as well, but this island is better known for the remains of the simple monastic settlement that existed here for six centuries. Founded, according to tradition, by St. Finian and occupied by hermit monks between the sixth and twelfth centuries, the monastery has survived in almost perfect condition, probably because of the absence of frost in this mild westerly climate. Six beehive huts, intact and of advanced construction; two oratories evolving into the boat-shaped style that would be used at Gallarus on the Dingle Peninsula; a ruined medieval church; crosses and graves; even tiny patches of imported earth behind retaining walls where the monks may have attempted to grow something to vary their diet of seaweed, birds, and fish, are located on a rock shelf 550 feet above the sea. Three steep stone stairways, corresponding to the three separate landing places whose use once varied according to weather conditions, lead to the settlement. Boats for Skellig Michael leave only if the weather is suitable — a calm day when the wind is not coming from the east. The trip takes 1.5 hours one way from Portmagee, the point of departure closest to the island (the trip can also be made from Knightstown on Valentia Island and from Bunavalla, below Coomakista, farther along the Ring of Kerry). Allow at least 3 hours for exploration. The climb to the monastery by the most commonly used route consists of more than 600 steps, but once there, the site — which must have been terrifying in fierce Atlantic storms — is extraordinarily evocative and beautiful.

BALLINSKELLIGS: The blessing of a 4-mile beach along the western shore of Ballinskelligs Bay has made this tiny, partly Irish-speaking village a seaside resort. It is part of the Kerry Gaeltacht and in the summer a language school for children is conducted here. The ruins of a sixteenth-century MacCarthy castle are west of town, not far from the remains of an Augustinian monastery that was probably founded in the twelfth or thirteenth centuries by monks returning from the monastic settlement of Skellig Michael. The ruins date from the fifteenth century and are much eroded by the sea.

From Ballinskelligs, follow the signposts for Waterville; when you turn right onto the main route 6 miles northeast of Ballinskelligs, you'll be just above the bridge over the River Inny, 2 miles north of Waterville.

WATERVILLE: This small unspoiled village lies on a strip of land between the Atlantic Ocean and beautiful Lough Currane, on the eastern shore of Ballinskelligs Bay. Mountains rise from the east and south of the lake, several islands float in it, and in addition to Lough Currane, there are many smaller lakes in the vicinity. With all this water, Waterville is a famous angling center almost by default. Fishing for salmon, sea trout, and brown trout is free on Lough Currane and some of the smaller lakes, and by permit (available from hotels) on still others and the River Inny. No aquatic

DIRECTIONS / Ring of Kerry and the Beara Peninsula 719

pursuit is ignored: There is boating, bathing from the fine sandy beach on the bay shore, and, for resolute landlubbers, golfing on a championship course. Many early Christian remains — stone forts, religious settlements, beehive huts, and old roadways — are scattered around Lough Currane and the ruins of a twelfth-century Romanesque church are on a small island, Church Island, in the lake (you can hire a boat in Waterville if you wish to make the excursion). Waterville and Ballinskelligs Bay figure in many legends. According to one, Noah's son and granddaughter landed here after having been excluded from the Ark. According to another, the alignment of four stones on the skyline to the left of the road 1 mile south of town is the burial place of Scéné, wife of one of the eight leaders of the Milesians in the last, and greatest, of the legendary invasions of Ireland.

CHECKING IN: *Waterville Lake Hotel* – This deluxe modern hotel is just south of Waterville in a setting of unparalleled beauty on the shores of lovely Lough Currane, within a stone's throw of the sea, and it makes the most of the panorama around it. The 95 rooms are well-designed (8 penthouse suites have views of both the sea and the lake); the public rooms are beautiful (traditionally furnished with many antiques); and the restaurant is excellent. A motor cruiser will take you out to the Skellig Rocks; fishing trips can be arranged; and if you catch a salmon, the restaurant staff will smoke it for you to take back home. Open April through October. (Waterville; phone: Waterville 7; expensive.) *Royal* – This is a comfortable place with 47 rooms (25 with bath) and a dining room that has good food. There is also live entertainment regularly. Open April through October only. (Knightstown, Valencia Island; phone: 44; moderate.) *Butler Arms* – A well-known fishing hotel in town, this rambling, crenellated white house has been run by the same family for three generations and was a favorite haunt of Charlie Chaplin and his family. The 43 rooms, 21 with bath, are open April through October. (Waterville; phone: Waterville 5; moderate to inexpensive.)

EATING OUT: *The Huntsman* – Furnished with dark oak priory tables and chairs and offering lovely seaviews, this chef-owned restaurant specializes in seafood. Open for lunch, dinner, plus light snacks from 12 to 10 PM, daily. Closed November through March. (Waterville; phone: Waterville 11; expensive to moderate.) *Smuggler's Restaurant* – A renovated farmhouse with panoramic views all round, this, too, is chef-owned — by the brother of the *Huntsman*'s proprietor. Seafood specialties such as Valentia scallops St. Jacques, meat and poultry dishes, and selections from an extensive bar menu are offered 7 days a week, noon to 11:30 PM. (Cliff Rd., Waterville; expensive to moderate.)

En Route – Traveling south from Waterville on Route N70, the road winds up to a height of 700 feet at the pass of Coomakista and offers superb views. While the inland mountains rise sharply — to 1,600 feet — on one side, the lonely Skellig Rocks can be seen beyond the mouth of the bay on the other side, out in the open Atlantic. The road descends in the direction of Derrynane Bay, separated from Ballinskelligs Bay by a point of land called Hog's Head, and from the Kenmare River (even though this arm of the sea extending inland as far as Kenmare is in places as much as 5 and 6 miles wide, you'll only occasionally see it called Kenmare Bay) by another point called Lamb's Head. Before the village of Caherdaniel, a signposted road to the right leads to Derrynane House, ancestral home of the O'Connell family, with a magnificent beach to the front of it and a more sheltered one at the side. The O'Connells were a shrewd Irish family who lived by smuggling, importing embargoed goods, and exporting young Catholic Irishmen to European educations and jobs denied them at home. Daniel O'Connell, the first Irish Catholic member of Britain's Parliament, inherited the Derrynane property from an uncle and lived here during his political life, often holding consultations on the lawn with troubled constituents who would gather from miles around to speak to him. The house has now been restored and is open daily year-round as a museum with O'Connell's personal possessions and furniture. It is part of Derrynane National Historic Park, which also includes a nature trail through lovely scenery.

Next along the route, Caherdaniel, near the shore of Derrynane Bay, takes its name from a stone fort or *caher*, possibly of the sixth century, located a short distance outside the village. Near it are the ruins of a much older fort and what would seem to be an ancient road system used some 4,000 years ago to link copper mines in the mountains above with the harbor at Derrynane. The route then continues along the coast toward the small resort of Castlecove. Just short of the village a signposted left turn points the way to Staigue Fort, 2.5 miles off the main road, beautifully positioned at the top of a valley that stretches to the sea.

STAIGUE FORT: Nothing is known of the history of this circular stone fort, which could date as far back as 1,000 BC. Though such forts are plentiful in the area, Staigue is one of the largest and most sophisticated, a masterly example of drystone building held together without mortar. It is also one of the best preserved of all ancient Irish structures. Little has been lost of the wall, which is up to 18 feet high on the north and west sides, 13 feet thick at the base, and is scaled by sets of steps up to a long-gone rampart. The area enclosed is 90 feet in diameter, but contains no signs of houses, as at Leacanabuaile, leading to speculation that the fort — which has yet to be excavated — may have been occupied by nobility. In Iron Age times, the poor lived in stone houses; royalty and aristocracy rated perishable wooden ones. Admire the quality of the fort's stonework, the sloping back of the walls, the massive lintels, and, especially, the architectural flourish of the steps inside; and on your way back to Castlecove, look for a stone bridge with two spans on the left — apparently in a field going nowhere — part of an old road system. Close by is an exposed rock with copperworkers' scribings.

En Route – About half a mile beyond Castlecove village, a road branches off the main route to White Strand, a particularly pleasant beach with beautiful views and good bathing. The route then bends inland to Sneem, 13 miles from Caherdaniel, climbing through a low pass where there is a fine panorama of the Sneem valley with its great backdrop of mountains stretching as far — just dimly to be seen — as Macgillycuddy's Reeks beside Killarney. The glacial basins or corries in the mountains on the left were scooped out by the Ice Age, and antiquities of the Bronze and Iron ages — old fields, roads, settlements, standing and scribed stones — are scattered around them.

SNEEM: With its pink, green, bright red, robin's-egg blue, and even checked houses freshly painted each year, this is a very colorful and pretty village at the head of the Sneem River estuary. The town is divided in two by the river and it has two village greens. Just before the narrow bridge between them, note the tiny Protestant church on the left, with its curiously Elizabethan air, a piece of eighteenth-century antiquarianism. Because Sneem is in fishing country (brown trout, salmon, and sea trout abound in the river and nearby mountain lakes), the church's weathervane sports a salmon. Stop after the bridge to look at the river tumbling over the rocks below, quite gently usually, but spectacular after a heavy rain. Just beyond is the very attractive Italianate, nineteenth-century Catholic church on the right. You'll also want to stop at the *Blue Bull* — a pleasant country pub and restaurant — if only for a quick drink to see its collection of art by contemporary Irish artists. An anomaly in the collection is the death mask of James Joyce.

En Route – Outside Sneem, the Ring of Kerry route turns southeast toward the shore of the Kenmare River. A mile down the road a detour signposted "Oyster Bed" (so called because oysters grow here) leads down to a pier where you can

DIRECTIONS / Ring of Kerry and the Beara Peninsula

savor the calm of the approaching garden spot before returning to the main road and driving the remaining mile to Parknasilla. Known for its lush trees, shrubs, and beautiful seascape, Parknasilla owes its subtropical vegetation to its position in a sheltered curve of coastline backed by the 895-foot Knockanamadane Hill. *The Great Southern Hotel,* situated on the grounds of the one-time summer home of Charles Graves, Protestant bishop of Limerick and grandfather of the poet Robert Graves, was a favorite holiday place of George Bernard Shaw. From Parknasilla, the Ring of Kerry road runs east toward the upper end of the Kenmare River. Beyond Blackwater Bridge, in a forest on the right, is Dromore Castle, the seat of an old Gaelic family, the O'Mahonys, and the subject of a haunting lullaby. Also on the right, on a rock 2 miles out of Kenmare, are the ruins of Dunkerron Castle, a stronghold of the O'Sullivan family, branches of which occupied both sides of the Kenmare River from the early thirteenth century until they were driven out by the Cromwellians in the seventeenth century.

CHECKING IN: *Great Southern Hotel* – George Bernard Shaw stayed here at least twice annually for a period of almost 15 years; more recently, Queen Juliana of the Netherlands has been a guest. This luxury hotel, built on the verdant grounds of a former private estate in 1896, is carefully and splendidly done in Victorian style, while amenities are up to the minute. There are 60 rooms with private bath, a private (9-hole) golf course for guests, a heated indoor swimming pool, and fishing or boating on the bay. The cuisine is superb. (Parknasilla; phone: 064-45122; expensive.)

EATING OUT: *The Blue Bull* – A combination pub and restaurant, the place serves good food wherever you eat it, but the pub grub is extra good, and that's rare. The restaurant's food is French provincial. The premises also serve as a kind of art gallery, specializing in modern art by Irish artists. (Sneem; phone: 064-45231; moderate.)

KENMARE: This attractive town sits in a limestone niche surrounded by old red sandstone at the point where the River Roughty runs into the head of the sea inlet known as the Kenmare River. The location makes it an ideal base for touring either the Iveragh Peninsula to the north or the Beara Peninsula to the south. Kenmare is a planned, landlord's town, laid out according to the instructions of the first marquess of Lansdowne in 1775. A number of houses are built of the local limestone and there is a fine Roman Catholic church with striking roof timbers. Next to it is the Convent of the Poor Clares, founded in 1861 and well known because of its lacemaking school; the famous point lace and other types produced here are on display daily. The town's oldest monument, the Druid's Circle, is beautifully placed on the banks of the River Finnihy on Kenmare's outskirts and dates back to the Beaker folk, copper miners who arrived from Spain 4,000 years ago. This is a circle of 15 stones with a large boulder in the center, an example of a form frequent in and mainly confined to this peninsula. Such circles were places of worship, but may also have had secular, ceremonial use as well as astronomical significance — and there is some evidence that human sacrifice was practiced in them.

Kenmare shares the mild climate common to the south coast and the subtropical foliage evident at Parknasilla is to be seen here, too. There is bathing in the sheltered coves west of the town, extensive salmon and trout fishing, and opportunity for deep-sea fishing. The annual Fruits de Mer Festival, usually held in September, underscores all this aquatic abundance with lots of deep-sea fishing, seafood exhibitions and banquets, and a wide range of entertainment.

CHECKING IN: *Park Hotel* – Well situated on extensive grounds, this old-fashioned railway hotel of the 1890s has emerged from an extensive renovation with a fine new finish to its former elegance. Choice antiques have been in-

722 DIRECTIONS / Ring of Kerry and the Beara Peninsula

stalled in the public rooms — guests register at an early Georgian partner desk in the entryway, for instance — and in some of the bedrooms, six of which are master suites with period four-posters. All 50 rooms have modern, private baths. The hotel's French chef specializes in seafood, especially a tasty salmon à la menthe. (Kenmare; phone: 064-41200; expensive.) **Kenmare Bay Hotel** – This hotel has 68 airy and modern rooms, a pleasant bar, and a good restaurant. During the Fruits de Mer Festival, it can be very crowded. Closed January and February. (Sneem Rd., Kenmare; phone: 064-41300; moderate.) **Riversdale House** – The 40 rooms here (30 with bath) are large but sparsely furnished. The premises are modern. Dining room fare is good, including a wide range of dishes. (Kenmare; phone: 064-41299; expensive.)

EATING OUT: *The Purple Heather Bistro* – Seafood is the specialty of the house, with meals served in the comfortable bar. Closed from the end of October to Easter. (Henry St., Kenmare; phone: 064-41016; moderate.)

En Route – By the time you reach Kenmare, you will have covered 90 miles of the Ring of Kerry route, excluding detours. From here, the most direct road back to Killarney is Route T65 (N71) north, a distance of 21 miles. This will take you over the mountains through Moll's Gap and via Ladies View, a lookout point with a panorama of the wonderful lakes of Killarney that is supposed to have gotten its name because it particularly pleased Queen Victoria's ladies-in-waiting.

Route N71 south leads across the Beara Peninsula to Glengarriff (17 miles) and Bantry (29 miles from Kenmare). If pressed for time, it is possible to head directly to Bantry and pick up the West Cork route there (or at Ballylickey, 3 miles north of Bantry). Otherwise, extend your tour to take in the Beara Peninsula, a thinly populated, very under-developed region that is also very beautiful and the least frequented of the three great southwestern peninsulas. The full circuit can fill at least a day, but it can be shortened by cutting across the center of the peninsula on the spectacular Healy Pass Road. Leaving Kenmare on Route N71, you'll have fine views of the Kenmare River, adrift with swans, and of the surrounding mountains. The road follows the valley of the River Sheen for several miles, then crosses the River Baurearagh and begins to climb through a series of tunnels, the longest one passing under the border between County Cork and County Kerry. Beyond the main tunnel, far to the right, is Barley Lake, a striking glacial corrie filled with water, with an improbable road snaking up to it. The tortured Caha Mountains are on the right and the great stretch of Bantry Bay is visible below, with the tip of Whiddy Island barely discernible. The road then descends through a valley into Glengarriff.

GLENGARRIFF: Its name means "rough glen," a description that is only partially true of this lovely village snuggled into a deeply wooded glen at the southeastern corner of the Beara Peninsula. There is nothing rough about it, and sheltered as it is from any harsh winds by mountains on three sides, the village has a justly famous reputation for mild weather and luxuriant vegetation. Arbutus, eucalyptus, fuchsia, rhododendron, and blue-eyed grass are among the plants and trees that flourish in the glen, and on Garinish Island in Glengarriff Harbour, the growth is subtropical. Until the early part of this century, the island was bare, but its owners then began to transform it with an extraordinary richness of flowers and foliage laid out in beautiful, Italian-style formal gardens. At the highest point of the island is a martello tower, the first of many to be built around Britain and Ireland against the expected Napoleonic invasion of 1804–05. The island, which was given as a gift to the nation, is now open to the public (admission charge for the gardens). Boats leave Glengarriff daily from 9:45 AM to 5:30 PM (Sundays from 12:45 to 6 PM) from March through October. There is excellent sea and river fishing in and around the village and bathing is good along the nearby coves, one of which, Poulgorm ("blue pool") is an extremely picturesque spot just a 2-minute walk from the post office. Glengarriff also has tennis courts, a golf course, and unlimited terrain for riding and walking.

CHECKING IN: *Casey's* – This is a small and pleasant family-owned and -operated place with 20 rooms (only four with bath), and a dining room serving fine food. Open April through October (Glengariff; phone: Glengariff 10; moderate).

En Route – From Glengarriff, Route L61 twists west into poor and rocky country along the south coast of the peninsula. When you reach Adrigole village, 12 miles from Glengarriff, take the signposted road to the right for the Healy Pass.

HEALY PASS: Work on this road began as a relief project during the famine years of the mid-nineteenth century but stopped shortly thereafter. It was resumed in 1928 at the direction of Tim Healy, the first governor-general of the Irish Free State (a native of Bantry), and finished 3 years later. The road climbs to a height of 1,084 feet as it crosses the Caha Mountains (and, again, the border between County Cork and County Kerry) to provide rewarding views over Mizen Head and Sheep's Head to the south, and Derreen, Kilmakilloge Harbour, the Kenmare River, and the mountains of the Iveragh Peninsula to the north. In early summer the soft ground beside the pass will be spattered with the blooms of the pinguicula grandiflora, the large-flowered butterwort. The road descends to Lauragh on the northern coast of the peninsula but if you wish to extend your exploration of the isolated region farther west, turn back, admiring the splendid sight of Bantry Bay as you drop down to Adrigole.

En Route – Proceed west from Adrigole on L61. The route to Castletownbere is dominated by the lean, well-named Hungry Hill (2,251 feet), while Bere Island, with its two martello towers, emerges to the left in Bantry Bay. The island was named for Beara, a Spanish princess married to Eogan, a partly legendary and partly historical figure who landed here during the course of an invasion of Ireland. Eventually, the whole peninsula was named for the princess. Despite the spare countryside, note that holly and sally trees flourish and fuchsia is rampant; in early summer, great drifts of white lilies make a stunning show.

CASTLETOWNBERE: This village — no more than a string of houses along both sides of the street — grew up at the beginning of the nineteenth century when the copper mines at Allihies, west of town, were opened. Its sheltered natural harbor continued to earn it a living as the site of a British naval base until 1938, and it is now becoming one of Ireland's main fishing centers, with tourism increasing. Look at the seven dormer windows, like elegant ships' portholes, over the three houses facing the pier — they are a feature of the area. The ruins of the fifteenth-century Dunboy Castle, the stronghold of the branch of the O'Sullivans who were lords of this peninsula (the main branch occupied most of the Iveragh Peninsula) are about 2 miles west of town.

En Route – Continue on Route L61 west of Castletownbere for about 6 miles. When the road divides, with a sign pointing each way to Allihies, take the road to the right. There are good views of the two Skellig Rocks and of Scariff and Deenish islands at the end of the Kenmare River. The road passes the abandoned Allihies copper mines, first worked by Iberian miners some 4,000 years ago and reopened during the Napoleonic wars by the Puxley family, who made a great fortune. The Puxleys employed no fewer than 1,200 people at a time before the operation succumbed to competition in 1886, and when Daphne du Maurier wrote her book about the mines, *Hungry Hill,* she used Puxley family papers to research it, though naming it for a mountain some miles away. After skirting the little village of Allihies, now a shadow of its former self, follow the signs to Eyeries, then on to Ardgroom and to Lauragh, at the head of Kilmakillage Harbour. On a good day this stretch of the route will provide some of the most striking scenery in all of West Cork and Kerry.

LAURAGH: The Healy Pass road across the peninsula joins the scenic sea road, L62, at Lauragh. Close to the village is the estate of Derreen House, whose beautiful subtropical gardens are open to visitors three afternoons a week (Sundays, Tuesdays, and Thursdays) from early April through September. The gardens — much less formal than those of Garinish Island or Muckross House — are remarkable for rhododendrons, camellias, tree ferns, bamboos, and eucalyptus.

En Route – Route L62 passes the Cloonie lakes and Lough Inchiquin — well stocked with salmon and sea and brown trout — as it continues east along the coast to Kenmare.

Dingle Peninsula

The Dingle Peninsula is the northernmost of the mountainous promontories that stick out into the Atlantic from Ireland's southwest coast like toes extended to test the water. It is a jumble of old and varied peaks and cliffs, glacial valleys and lakes, headlands and bays, islands, strands, and great sand dunes stretching 30 miles west from the lowlying country around Tralee through mountains that turn to wild hills and meet the sea in splendid coastlines. The peninsula is blessed with a remoteness that has been an inspiration to poets and religious ascetics alike. It was on Dingle that John Millington Synge wondered why anyone was left in Dublin or London or Paris, and whether it wouldn't be better to live "with this magnificent sea and sky, and to breathe this wonderful air, which is like wine in one's teeth."

Dingle's dramatic rendering of nature's bare essentials never ceases to delight visitors. On a clear day there are stunning views: great panoramic expanses of green stopped by shimmering ribbons of water in the distance, then the farther gray-blue outline of the next peninsula, island, or rocky point, itself backlit by the phosphorescence of fine, silver-edged cloudings. On a less clear day when the depth of the scene diminishes, the eye is drawn to the hedgerows by the roadside, made up in spring of white hawthorn or yellow-flowering furze bushes, of languorous drapings of honeysuckle or purplish fuchsia just burst into bloom. Where they part, they reveal the patchwork of fields beyond, and an ample sampling of Ireland's green.

Dingle's topography is mountainous, but not in the alpine way. It rises — from the eastern Slieve Mish Mountains to the western Brandon Mountains — to rounded and treeless peaks, the effect the same as if some primordial giant had thrown down a heavy carpet to soften the contours and soothe his aching feet. This possibility is not entirely implausible because Dingle is alive with legend and folklore, its remote fastnesses the stamping ground of mythological heroes such as Cu Chulainn, its ports guarded by the larger-than-life Finn MacCool and his warrior army, the Fianna. Visitors may see only innumerable sheep ranging down valleys and over the distant hills, but to locals with longer memories, the land is the home of giants as tall as the tales.

The peninsula is also particularly rich in antiquities, especially prehistoric and early Christian remains, among them *galláns,* or standing stones; *ogham* stones, or pillars inscribed with the earliest form of Irish writing; and *clo-*

cháns, or circular beehive huts. The latter may be the most suggestive. Grouped in fraternal clusters or alone as solitary cells, monks isolated themselves in these stone huts on Ireland's lonely western fringes in the early days of Irish Christianity. The eremitical offshoot of Irish monasticism was nowhere stronger than it was in Kerry, and it's not hard for visitors to see why. Perched on the ledge of a wave-pounded rock or on the quieter summit of a deserted hill, the hermit monks could ponder at length both the awesome and the gentle face of God and perhaps, in a radiant flash of sun on sea, witness their own immortality.

Not all beehive huts are ancient, however. Farmers continue to copy the technique for modern animal shelters and sheds, one of many ways Dingle's timeless appearance endures to confound seekers of authenticity. A little over a decade ago, when scouts were searching for a spot to film *Ryan's Daughter,* a story that was supposed to have taken place in 1916, the peninsula was chosen because it looked as though it hadn't progressed much beyond that date, though none of its tiny villages had quite the look of abject poverty required (a model village was built).

Time has also stood still on Dingle in the matter of language. Its western reaches are part of the Gaeltacht, the collective name for the few surviving Irish-speaking areas of Ireland where geography protected what was lost elsewhere under British rule. The native Irish tongue can be heard in villages such as Dunquin and Ballyferriter, whose people use it daily, though they also speak English. During the summer, students come from all over the country to attend the Irish language schools here.

The scenic route around the peninsula is roughly in the shape of a figure eight, with the town of Dingle at the crossing. Roads are narrow and twisting but they're easy to negotiate just the same, and you'll have no trouble with traffic — though you may round a bend and come upon a traveling bank truck or a collie herding the cattle home. The drive is best on a very bright (not necessarily dry) day and to be avoided, if possible, in mist or continuous rain. You can see it all in a long day trip of approximately 100 miles from Tralee and back, including time for lunch in Dingle Town, through which the route passes twice. Though Tralee, where our route begins, is the usual gateway to Dingle, you could stay out on the peninsula itself — there are plenty of bed-and-breakfast houses and farms, plus small hotels and guesthouses and, in Dingle town, a modern A-category hotel.

As elsewhere in our Irish listings, a double room in an expensive hotel will cost $60 and up; in a moderate one, from $40; and in an inexpensive one, under $40. A meal for two in an expensive restaurant will cost $40 and up; in a moderate one, from $20 to $35; and in an inexpensive one, under $20.

TRALEE: This friendly, busy trading center of 18,000 people is the chief town of County Kerry and one of the most active in southern Ireland. It grew up around the thirteenth-century Desmond Castle, but because the town was destroyed at the end of the seventeenth century, its remains — such as the Georgian terraces on Denny Street and in Day Place and St. John's Cathedral Church — are mainly from the eighteenth and nineteenth centuries. Its major antiquity is the ruined Rathass Church, about a mile east, dating from the ninth and tenth centuries. Inside there is a stone commemorating an eighth-century notable in ogham, the earliest form of Irish writing. Ogham consists of groups of strokes and dots related to a spinal line and it arose, probably in this peninsula, about the beginning of the Christian era.

Tralee has a racecourse and a good golf course, plus salmon and trout fishing in its rivers, excellent deep-sea fishing, a choice of beaches, sailing, skin diving, and riding. Tralee is also the home of Siamsa tíre (pronounced Shee-am-sah teer), the National Folk Theatre of Ireland, which brings to life the customs of the Irish countryside through a program of music, singing, dancing, and mime several nights weekly from June through September. Its greatest attraction, however, is the Rose of Tralee International Festival, otherwise known as the Festival of Kerry, a week of carnivallike pageantry at the end of August or the beginning of September. This is Ireland's biggest bash and its highlight is the crowning of the Rose, the loveliest young woman of Irish descent in the world and the one who best exemplifies the qualities of the original Rose of Tralee from the song by William Mulchinock, who was born and died here.

En Route – The road to Dingle (T68) runs along the nineteenth-century ship canal to Blennerville, which is unusual for its ruined windmill and famous among bird-watchers for its mudflats in Tralee Bay. Less than a mile farther on where a roadway comes from the left, the twelfth- to thirteenth-century Annagh church is hidden on the right on a site claimed to be the birthplace of the sixth-century St. Brendan the Navigator, reputed to have discovered America even before the Vikings. (Fenit, across Tralee Bay, is the more likely birthplace.) Continuing out onto the peninsula, along its northern edge, there are wonderfully scenic views. The Slieve Mish Mountains are inland to the left and to the right a sweep of green tilts gently down to magnificent beaches on the bay, the green scattered with grazing cattle and sheep to the very edge of the pale gold sand.

The remains of the old Tralee and Dingle railway are along the route, now on one side, now on the other. Where the road divides just before Camp, going right for Castlegregory and left for Dingle, take the left fork and then turn left again under the broken arch of the old railway line and head straight across the peninsula toward Aughils. The mountain to the left of this road is Caherconree and, near its summit, the curious rock formation with cliffs on three sides and a narrow approach cut off by a substantial wall is a promontory fort dating from the Iron Age (which began in Ireland about 500 BC and lasted till the arrival of St. Patrick in the fifth century AD). It is notable not only because it is inland, while the many other promontory forts on the peninsula are on the coast, but also because it was the home of Cu Roi Mac Daire, a figure from a cycle of legends dealing with Iron Age heroes. Cu Roi was killed by Cu Chulainn, a small, fierce, brave man and a womanizer, after the former had stolen the beautiful Blathnaid, a woman for whom Cu Chulainn had set his cap. There are breathtaking views from the fort, reached via a marked trail that begins some distance farther along the road, and there are equally memorable views — of Dingle Bay and the Iveragh Peninsula — as the road descends to Aughils and Inch. When you reach the sea road at Aughils, turn right and Inch is only another 4 miles away.

CHECKING IN: *Mount Brandon Hotel* – One of the largest hotels in County Kerry, this is standard modern in style, but genial in its operation. All 162 rooms have private bath. Its two pub lounges, one large and one cozy, provide either nightly entertainment or quiet relaxation. (Tralee; phone: 21311; expensive.)
Ballyseede Castle – This lovely old hotel is 3 miles east of Tralee, set in parkland befitting a fifteenth-century castle. It has 13 rooms, 10 with bath. A medieval banquet and entertainment are provided in the seventeenth-century wing. (Tralee; phone: 21959; moderate.)

EATING OUT: *Cordon Bleu* – The menu at this casual and unhurried eatery offers a surprising range of well-prepared dishes, from (of course) veal cordon bleu to spaghetti to curried prawns. (The Square, Tralee; phone: 21596; moderate.) ***Oyster Tavern*** – Visit this pub for all kinds of seafood cooked in a straightforward manner and served in huge portions. The mixed seafood platter is heaped with everything but a lucky penny. Located about 3 miles west of Tralee at Spa, where there was a famous watering place in the eighteenth century. (Spa; phone: 36102; moderate.) ***Slatts*** – For lunch or dinner, try this comfortable lounge and bar with an open-hearth fire and delightful staff. Background piano music in the evenings is a pleasant accompaniment. (Boherbee, Tralee; phone: 066-21161; moderate.) ***The Brogue Inn*** – This big barn of a pub — strewn with agricultural instruments, too — is a good place for a light lunch. (Rock St., Tralee; phone: 22126; inexpensive.)

INCH: This sheltered seaside resort is at the base of the Inch Peninsula. Its name to the contrary, the peninsula provides a 4-mile strip of firm, golden sand that is excellent for bathing and was the setting for some of the beach scenes in the film *Ryan's Daughter*. The beach is backed by high dunes that have yielded evidence of mysterious sandhill dwellers who lived here in Iron Age times and perhaps earlier. In the eighteenth century, this same sandy spit stretching out into Dingle Bay was used to wreck ships from the West Indies. A lantern on the head of a moving horse would fool captains into thinking there was another ship ahead, not a sand bar.

ANASCAUL: Four miles west of Inch, the inland village of Anascaul is known as the location of the *South Pole Inn*. Now a pub where you can stop for a drink (no food served), this was once the home of Thomas Crean, who was a member of Robert Falcon Scott's last and fatal expedition to Antarctica (1910–1912). A signposted detour north from the town leads, in about 2 miles, to the beautiful Anascaul Lake in a boulder-scattered valley about which there is another Cu Chulainn story. A giant was carrying off a girl, Scál, but Cu Chulainn came to her rescue. From the mountains on either side of the lake each threw great stones at the other. Cu Chulainn was wounded and Scál, thinking him dead, drowned herself in the water.

En Route – The main Tralee-to-Dingle road (T68) is rejoined at Anascaul. Continuing west, it next passes through Lispole. Less than a mile beyond Lispole, look left for the standing stone, or gallán, of Ballineetig, about 100 yards from the road. This Bronze Age gravestone is the largest in the peninsula. The roughly pointed tip shows that it was a monument for a man — for women the tips were scooped out.

Farther along the road, where there is a good view of Dingle Harbour, turn left after a sign for an accident blackspot (a place with a bad record for auto accidents), then again sharp left at a house. A third of a mile beyond this in a field on the left, is the little burial place of Ballintaggart, an important site for the study of ogham stones. Inside the circular wall are nine of them, rounded, with the base, or spinal, line unusually omitted. The inscription of one stone commemorates the "three sons of Mailagnos," the next has a long Latin cross, and two others have short Greek ones, possibly added later as Christianity began to take over from paganism. Before leaving Ballintaggart, take a moment to enjoy the splendid sight of the Skellig Rocks off the coast of the Iveragh Peninsula in the distance. Then return to the main road and drive the remaining 1.5 miles into Dingle.

DINGLE: The peninsula's chief town lies at the foot of a steep slope on the north side of the harbor and is bounded on three sides by hills. It was the main port of Kerry in the old Spanish trading days, and in the reign of Queen Elizabeth I it was important enough as an outpost to merit a protective wall. In the eighteenth century, Dingle became a smuggling center, and during the French Revolution, a local man, Colonel

James Rice, was the linchpin of a plot to rescue Marie Antoinette and spirit her to "the highest house on the hill," located on Main Street. She refused when she learned her family would not come with her and the house has since been replaced by the Catholic presbytery. Today Dingle's population of 1,400 is dependent on fishing and tourism. Deep-sea fishing facilities are excellent, there is good bathing at various beaches in the vicinity, and there is pony trekking into the surrounding hills. You may be able to catch traditional Irish music sessions at the rough-hewn and barnlike *O'Flaherty's Pub* on Bridge Street; order a Guinness, pull up an orange crate, and sit down and listen. Dingle is also the gateway to the West Kerry Gaeltacht, the Irish-speaking district, as well as a good base for extended exploration of the archaeological antiquities of this rich area. Begin with the enormous rock called a *bullaun* on Main Street. It has holes in it and seems to have been used for grinding hard wheat in early Christian times.

CHECKING IN: *Sceilig Hotel* – Modern and not particularly distinguished in its outside appearance, this is, in fact, as traditionally Irish as a thatched cottage, complete with peat fires burning when the weather warrants it. There are 80 rooms, all with bath, and a heated outdoor swimming pool. The staff speaks Irish and English. Closed mid-December to mid-March. (Dingle; phone: 104; moderate.)

EATING OUT: *Doyle's Seafood Bar* – The Doyles moved from Dublin in the early 1970s, remodeled premises that until 1925 were the warehouse of the local Guinness distributor, and opened a rustically simple pub-restaurant with flagstone floor, stone walls, wood-paneled bar, and delicious, award-winning food. The cassoulet of crab claws is scrumptious. Closed Sundays and November through February. (John St., Dingle; phone: 144; moderate.) *Half-Door Restaurant* – On the same street as Doyle's, this restaurant run by John and Celeste Slye is not as renowned as its neighbor but it's a satisfying alternative. The menu features the best of the local catch — cooked simply, very easy on the sauces — but there is always one meat dish among the main courses for those who insist. Closed Tuesdays and later November to early March. (John St., Dingle; phone: 300; moderate.)

En Route – Head west out of town, and when you come to a junction, take the road in the direction of Slea Head. Just beyond a modern cemetery at Milltown there is an interesting set of antiquities inside a gate on the right. The site, an ancient burial ground referred to as the "gates of glory," consists of a great gallán, along with two others that have fallen and broken pieces of more stones. The mysterious scribings on top of one of the fallen galláns were made by early metal workers who came to Ireland from Spain some 4,000 years ago. The scooped-out hollows are called cup marks, and there are other complex markings on the rock. Many such stones can be found in Kerry, but no one has yet given an adequate interpretation of them.

VENTRY: About 4 miles from Dingle, this little village has a delightful beach. In Irish legend, Ventry Harbour was the scene of a great battle won by the hero Finn MacCool and his warriors, the Fianna, against the forces of the "king of the world," Daire Donn, who crammed the harbor with his ships and was held off for a year and a day before being wiped out to the last man. Beyond the harbor, the road continues to Slea Head on the lower slopes of Mt. Eagle, providing lovely coastal views of Dingle Bay. This cliff-hugging part of the route is particularly scenic and will, again, be familiar to filmgoers who have seen *Ryan's Daughter*. The village of Kirrary, which appeared in the film, was located along the coast west of Ventry, but don't look for it, because it was built from scratch for the filming and destroyed afterward to preserve the landscape as nature made it. The area from Ventry to Slea Head is also particularly rich in archaeological remains.

DUNBEG AND FAHAN: Just under 4 miles from Ventry, an Iron Age promontory

DIRECTIONS / Dingle Peninsula

fort, Dunbeg, can be seen below the road to the left. In addition to the wall that cuts off the triangular promontory, there are four earthen defensive rings, an underground escape passage (or souterrain) at the entrance, and remains of an inner house. Dunbeg may have been the first bridgehead established by the people who built the ancient town of Fahan, the greatest collection of antiquities in all Ireland. Fahan consists of over 400 *clocháns* (circular beehive huts constructed without mortar of overlapped or corbeled stones), cave dwellings, standing and inscribed stones and crosses, souterrains, forts, and a church — more than 500 remains in all — strewn along an old road above the main road for a distance of about 3 miles. To best see this settlement, which was possibly a full-fledged community between the sixth and tenth centuries, as large then as Dingle is now, keep to the main road until you've passed the small ford at Glenfahan, after which there is a sign indicating beehive huts. These are among the most interesting and convenient, but the owners of the property expect a small payment from visitors.

SLEA HEAD: The road from Dingle continues to Slea Head at the tip of the peninsula, where the view of the Blasket Islands, the westernmost point in Europe (except for Iceland), is spectacular. In September 1588, four ships of the Spanish Armada were driven by storms through Blasket Sound. Two reached shelter, but a third, the *Santa Maria de la Rosa,* came flying through the sound with its sails in tatters, crashed onto a rock, and sank, as did the fourth, the *San Juan de Ragusa.* (The remains of the *Santa Maria de la Rosa* were located at the bottom of Blasket Sound in the late 1960s.) The beach between Slea Head and the next promontory, Dunmore Head, is Coumeenole strand, attractive but dangerous.

THE BLASKETS: This is a group of seven islands, inhabited by an Irish-speaking community from prehistoric times but now deserted. The largest, Great Blasket (4 miles long and ¾ mile wide), was "the next parish to America" until 1953 when the remaining population of barely 100 could no longer support itself after several disastrous fishing seasons and was resettled on the mainland. Blasket islanders were adept at the art of storytelling and produced a number of books. The best-selling *Twenty Years A-growing* by Maurice O'Sullivan, *The Islander,* a masterpiece by Thomas O'Crohan, and *Peig* by Peig Sayers were all written by island natives. Boats to the Blaskets can be hired in Dunquin, north of Slea Head.

En Route – The road leaves the seacoast to cut across Dunmore Head, then continues north to Dunquin along a coast where many forms of fossils can be found. At Dunquin Harbour, the colored silurian rocks in the cliffs date from 400 million years ago. From Dunquin there are fairly regular sailings in summer to the Blaskets. Typically, the boat is a *curragh,* a light, canvas-covered canoe painted with tar which, if properly handled, is an extraordinarily seaworthy revival of the ancient boat originally made of skins. After Dunquin, the route passes Clogher Head and turns inland toward the village of Ballyferriter. Watch for the pottery at Clogher *(Potadóireacht na Caolóige).* You can stop and see the potters at work here, as well as buy some of the simple, cleanly decorated pieces they produce.

BALLYFERRITER: This is a small, mostly Irish-speaking village whose population is increased in summer by students taking part in Irish language schools. The ruined Castle Sybil, the home of the Anglo-Norman Ferriter family, is about 2 miles northwest of the village just above Ferriter's Cove. The castle was the birthplace of Kerry poet and patriot Piaras Ferriter, an insurgent leader who was hanged by the Cromwellians in 1653. Castle Sybil is said to be named after Sybil Lynch of Galway who eloped with a Ferriter. When her father sought her out she was hidden in the cave beneath the castle and was drowned by the rising tide.

Smerwick Harbour is about a mile north of Ballyferriter. There is a pleasant hotel, the *Dún An Óir,* here, named for the small, long-gone fort of Dún An Óir, the "golden" fort which used to stand on a promontory in the harbor. In 1580, an expedition of some 600 men financed by the Pope — mainly Italians, but also Spanish, Irish, and English

730 DIRECTIONS / Dingle Peninsula

— entrenched at the fort to support the cause of the Catholic Irish against the Protestant English in what was the first significant invasion of the British Isles for many centuries. The English (led by Lord Grey and including Edmund Spenser and, possibly, Sir Walter Raleigh) bombarded the fort from land and sea and soon its defenders capitulated. Once disarmed, they were slaughtered and the massacre of Smerwick rang throughout Europe, a warning to anyone who might again attempt to invade the Queen's territory.

En Route – Follow the main road east out of Ballyferriter, keeping to the left (avoid the narrow road that bears right up a hill). Turn right over the bridge at a gasoline pump, and, almost immediately, right again. The recently excavated eremitical and monastic site of Reask is a short distance farther along (about ¾ mile east of Ballyferriter). This gives a good idea of the layout of an early, perhaps seventh- or eighth-century monastery — the beehive huts, the oblong foundation of a boat-shaped oratory (a small church), the cross-pillars (upright stones incised with crosses), and the wall separating the upper, or consecrated, part of the monastery from the rest. Then go back down the road, turn right, and follow the signposts for the Gallarus Oratory, about 4 miles northwest of Dingle.

GALLARUS ORATORY: This small, rectangular church in the shape of an upturned boat is the best example of dry-rubble masonry in Ireland and probably the most perfect piece of early Irish architecture extant. Oratories are standard in monastic sites, but everywhere except here and on the remote Skellig Rocks, the unmortared roofs have fallen in from the great weight of their stones. Gallarus is still completely watertight and may date from as early as the eighth century, though the mastery of the corbel technique used in its building suggests a later date to some of the experts — perhaps as late as the eleventh or twelfth centuries. Besides a cross-pillar, signs of an early monastic settlement around it have yet to be found.

KILMALKEDAR: At the crossroads above Gallarus, turn sharp left for the remains of Kilmalkedar Church, a fine example of Irish Romanesque. The nave was built in the mid-twelfth century, the chancel a little later, and it once had a corbeled stone roof, a development of the Gallarus style. Even before the church was built, there was a Christian settlement here, dating back to the late sixth and early seventh centuries. Look inside the church for the "alphabet" stone, crudely carved with a Latin cross and the Latin alphabet, used for instruction in an early-seventh-century school. There must have been an even earlier, pagan, settlement on the site, too. A holed stone inside and another with ogham outside recall Indian yoni stones through which worshipers would have to pass to achieve regeneration. Reminiscent of these practices, the east window of the medieval church is known as the "eye of the needle," through which the faithful must pass to be saved. A well-carved pre-Christian sundial, and a large, crudely cut cross, one of the few in Kerry, are also outside.

Just north of the church is a roadway and, where it forks, the fifteenth-century St. Brendan's house is on the left. This was probably a presbytery for the church and had nothing to do with St. Brendan. The old Saints' Road, which ran through this area bisecting the fork, however, did. It led to the top of Mt. Brandon, named after St. Brendan, who is said to have had his retreat there. After his death, it was used for pilgrimages to his shrine, a practice which has since died out except for occasional revivals.

En Route – Continue on the road beyond Kilmalkedar and, at the T-junction, turn right and follow the signposts for Brandon Creek. It was from this spot that St. Brendan is reputed to have set out on his sixth-century voyages searching for the Land of Promise and, it seems, discovering America. Two ninth-century manuscripts, one recounting the story of his life and the other the story of his travels, were immensely popular in early medieval Europe and an inspiration for many voyagers, including Columbus, though at least as far as his travels are concerned, there may have been some confusion between the name of St. Brendan and that of the hero of an Irish pagan story, *The Voyage of Bran*. Bran and his Kerrymen companions traveled to magical western islands and, returning from one voyage, put ashore at Brandon Point, northeast of here. By this account, it was Bran, and not St. Brendan, who gave his name to the great Mt. Brandon.

From Brandon Creek, turn back in the direction of Dingle. Just 2 miles along you'll cross the Saints' Road again. If you turn left and drive up as far as you can, you will reach the spot from which the 3,127-foot summit of Mt. Brandon, Ireland's second-highest peak, is most easily accessible. It's about a 3.5-mile walk to the top and on a clear day, the views are magnificent. If you're not up to this strenuous trek — which thousands of pilgrims before you have made — return to Dingle and take the Connor Pass road out of town.

CONNOR PASS: Driving this road demands great care and it should be avoided in bad weather. Leave Dingle by the unclassified road marked Connor (or Conair) Pass, climbing northeasterly between the Brandon and the central Dingle groups of mountains. At the summit (1,500 feet), there are magnificent views in both directions, south over Dingle town and Dingle Bay, north to the bays of Brandon and Tralee, the great beaches of north Kerry, and on to the mouth of the Shannon. The road descends between cliffs and valleys and then, below the pass, continues east running parallel to beautiful beaches on Brandon Bay. At Stradbally, take the left fork for Castlegregory.

CASTLEGREGORY: The castle from which this tiny village got its name is now gone. It was built in the sixteenth century by a local chief, Gregory Hoare, whose daughter-in-law came to grief in 1580 when she poured out all the castle's wine rather than offer it to her country's enemies in the person of Lord Grey and a party of English troops lodging at the castle on their way to attack the fort at Smerwick Harbour. Her husband killed her in a fit of rage and the next day he, himself, died suddenly. The village is located at the neck of a sandy spit of land that separates the Tralee and Brandon bays. Beyond the limestone tip of the spit are the Maharee Islands, also known as the Seven Hogs. On one of these, Illauntannig, as on nearly every remote outcropping of rock in western Kerry, remains of an early Christian monastic settlement have been found. It is possible only with difficulty to arrange a boat to the island (and the ruins are in poor condition), so content yourself with a drive out along the spit from Castlegregory or a visit to Lough Gill, west of the village, an attractive lake noted for its waterfowl including a species of swan that comes all the way from Siberia to winter here.

En Route – Continue east, and at the town of Camp, take T68 back to Tralee, from where you are only 20 miles north of Killarney, the gateway to the *Ring of Kerry and the Beara Peninsula* route.

Clare

Clare, in the middle of the west coast of Ireland, is an "island" county; the Atlantic washes its north and west shores, the encircling River Shannon guards it on the east and south. What is left unwashed in the northeastern quadrant is guarded by a chain of hills. In its isolation Clare has retained much of the past — a sturdy political and economic independence, a music livelier and more varied than that of other parts of Ireland, a tenacious grasp of folk traditions, a speech dotted with the remnants of Irish language forms.

Clare landscape is varied, a microcosm of the Irish west coast generally, but with features that give it an original twist. Heading inward from the coast,

Clare terrain changes strikingly, from the wild rocky seacliffs to the marshy uplands behind them, to the central limestone plain dotted with lakes, to the great brown hills of the east. In the very north is the Burren country, a stony moonscape plateau.

History has left many interesting remains in Clare. Scattered over the northern hills are more than 150 dolmens, or Stone Age tombs, of the farmers who migrated here from France 5,000 years ago. There are nearly 3,000 circular forts in earth and stone, the fortified settlements of their Celtic successors. And over 200 castles are still extant, the earliest ones built by the Normans, the later by the Irish. Traces of the early Catholic church are found in Clare. Most "churches" are of the eremitical type; a collection of them is on St. Senan's monastic island in the mouth of the Shannon, and they dot the islets and the hillsides up the coast. Such ruins are particularly plentiful in the Burren where the early hermits found the isolation they desired; here the stony desert is dotted with oratories, "saints' beds" or shrines, wells, and stone crosses.

Claremen are mature and practiced politicians who sum up a situation and pragmatically choose a leader. In the tenth century they picked Brian Ború, head of an obscure clan called the Dal gCais. They fought for him until he became first king of Munster and then High King of Ireland; they died with him as he defeated the Vikings on the coast of Dublin Bay. At the great upsurge of Irish democracy in the nineteenth century they voted in Daniel O'Connell as Member of Parliament for Clare, and they supported Charles Stewart Parnell in the Land League Movement. In this century they elected Eamon de Valera, who was prime minister and president of an independent Ireland.

Although most Clare folk still pursue a rural lifestyle on small dairy farms, they are gradually adapting to a new world. Many country market towns are beginning to expand with factories, and more people are working in the transport, tourism, and service industries. The international airport at Shannon has not only established a duty-free zone and nurtured an industrial park with many welcome new jobs, but has also made County Clare the major western gateway to Ireland.

The route suggested below begins in Limerick City, which is where most people spend their first night after landing at Shannon. From here, you'll travel to Ennis, capital of Clare, then along the Shannon River through numerous little towns out to the lonely peninsula of Loop Head. From this wild Atlantic seascape, the road turns north to the resort towns of Kilkee and Lahinch, and on to the great Cliffs of Moher. An eastern leg explores the wonderland of the Burren with its unusual rock formations, caves, flora, and ruins.

Although the Limerick City area has many new large hotels, accommodations in Clare tend to be small hotels or B&Bs. You can expect to pay $65 and up for a double in those places listed as expensive; from $35 to $65 in moderate; and under $30 in inexpensive. A meal for two, excluding wine, tips, or drinks, will cost about $30 and up in places listed as expensive; $15 to $30 in moderate; and under $15 in inexpensive.

LIMERICK CITY: For a detailed report on the city, its hotels and restaurants, see *Limerick,* THE CITIES.

En Route – About 12 miles down the main Limerick-Ennis road is the tiny village, Newmarket-on-Fergus, which owes its name to a track-crazy eighteenth-century landlord who renamed it after the great center of English horse racing. The long demesne wall beyond the town encloses Dromoland Castle, well worth a look. It was once the home of the O'Briens, earls of Inchiquin, descendants of the high king, Brian Ború, and is now the deluxe *Dromoland Castle Hotel.*

ENNIS: This county seat of Clare (pop. 8,000), with its narrow winding main street intersected by even narrower lanes, has a lively medieval charm. Off Francis St. are the ruins of a Franciscan Friary founded about 1240 by Donough Mor O'Brien. A monument to Liberator Daniel O'Connell, who secured Catholic emancipation and sat in parliament for Clare, is located in O'Connell Sq. The modern De Valera Library and Museum, which was ingeniously adapted from a disused church, is on Harmony Row. Outside town on the Limerick road, you'll see signposts to Clare Abbey, the now undistinguished and abandoned ruins of an Augustinian monastery established in 1189 by Donal Mor O'Brien, King of Munster.

CHECKING IN: *Old Ground Hotel* – This ivy-clad, centrally located hotel is gracious and old-fashioned, with antique-furnished public rooms. It has 63 rather small and sometimes chilly bedrooms and a competent restaurant. (O'Connell St.; phone: 21127; moderate.) **West County Inn** – This large, modern hotel has 72 rooms with private bath, a coffee shop, a restaurant, and a sauna. Dinner dances are held every Saturday evening. (Clare Rd.; phone: 21421; moderate.)

EATING OUT: *Brogan's* – At this quiet old pub you can have a steak, smoked salmon, or soup and sandwich. (O'Connell St.; moderate.) **The Cloister** – Handsomely reconstructed with a view of the Franciscan friary, it serves good pub grub. (Francis St.; inexpensive.) **T.P.'s** – This traditional pub where soup, sandwiches, and political conversation are served is beside the O'Connell monument. (O'Connell Sq.; inexpensive.)

En Route – The L51 travels from Ennis along the bank of the Shannon estuary all the way to Kilrush. The landscape is gentle and pastoral and there are fine views across "the Shannon spreading like a sea" of the little wooded harbor town of Foynes, of Glin with its Regency castle, and of Tarbert with its lighthouse and electric power station. At Killimer a car ferry crosses every half-hour to Tarbert on the Kerry shore.

KILRUSH: The chief market town of southwest Clare, it has a number of small industries, including a factory for processing seaweed. Just outside Kilrush is Cappagh Pier, formerly the terminus for the river steamers that plied the Shannon from Limerick. From here you can take a boat to Scattery Island, the monastic retreat founded in the sixth century by St. Senan. On the island are five early churches dating from the ninth to eleventh centuries and a 120-foot round tower, the tallest in Ireland.

EATING OUT: *Saddle Room Steak House* – This restaurant serves Irish and Continental cuisine. (Vandaleur St.; moderate.) **Grotty's** – It's a favorite with traditional musicians. (At the corner of the square; inexpensive.) **Haven Arms** – This bar specializes in salads and other light meals. (Henry St.; inexpensive.)

En Route – Taking T41 out of Kilrush toward Kilkee, you pass through the rushy, windswept landscape typical of south Clare. About 6 miles out there's a sign for a holy well; turn left and in 2.5 miles you'll see a tidily kept holy well dedicated to St. Martin. Turning back from the well, go straight east parallel to the estuary.

Doonaha, the first hamlet you pass through, was the birthplace of Eugene O'Curry, a pioneer nineteenth-century Irish scholar and topographer. When the road hits the estuary again, you'll come to Carrigaholt, a picturesque village wrapped around a crescent of beach with a tall O'Brien castle guarding the little harbor. Another 8 miles farther down the spine of the peninsula is the last village, Kilbaha, and 4.5 miles beyond that is the lonely lighthouse of Loop Head. From the headland there are superb views to the south of the mountains of Kerry — the Macgillycuddy Reeks crowned by Carrantuohill, the highest point in Ireland, and Mount Brandon at the west end of the Dingle Peninsula. To the north you can see the whale-backed Aran Islands in Galway Bay and the saw-toothed peaks of Connemara. Below the lighthouse are some rocks separated from the shore by a deep chasm. Across this, legend has it, the Irish hero Cu Chulainn made a bold leap when pursued by a persistent female.

On the return journey from the head, branch left at the village of Killbaha for a mile to Moneen church. In a baptistery chapel on the left of the altar is a fascinating relic of the period of anti-Catholic discrimination in Ireland. What looks like an old-fashioned bathing machine, a little wooden hut with a canvas roof and windows, is in fact the only church allowed in this area in the first half of the nineteenth century. A bigoted local landlord refused to allow a church to be built, so the parish priest — lifting the idea from a horse-drawn carriage in which he had traveled from Kilrush to Ennis — had this structure built. Each Sunday it was drawn onto the beach, where he said Mass and his congregation knelt in the open. Known as "The Little Ark," the wooden chapel is still an object of veneration and the incident is illustrated in stained glass over the church door.

Just beyond the church there is a storm beach of huge rounded boulders; a half-mile farther on, a signpost directs you to the parking lot for the Bridges of Ross. These are curious rock formations carved out by the sea.

Another half-mile beyond the village of Cross, take a right turn on a narrow road, which after 2 miles reaches the coast and the top of Oldtown hill and gives you a view of miles of rugged cliffs ahead. The road soon begins to hug the cliff tops and the next 5 miles into Kilkee are a dramatic unfolding panorama of rock stacks and precipices. Occasionally you'll see remains of castle towers and stone forts in inaccessible places in the rock. The most striking phenomenon of all is Bishop's Island, a sheer stack of rock that's been cut off from the mainland but retains a beehive oratory and house associated with St. Senan.

KILKEE: This little resort town, with its charming rows of Regency-Gothic houses, has been a popular vacation spot for well-to-do people from Limerick since they came by Shannon steamer in the early nineteenth century. Its powdery, horseshoe-shaped strand is protected from the full force of the Atlantic by two bold headlands and offers safe bathing and boating. Because most of Kilkee's visitors rent houses, there are very few hotels. It's best to stop here for a dip and a drink at *Scott's* or *Marrinan's,* two pubs with good conversation.

En Route – The road to Lahinch runs inland for the next 20 miles, but if you have time, detour to see the high cliffs of Ballard Bay guarded by an O'Brien tower or the White Strand beyond the village of Doonbeg. In the small fishing village of Quilty, one of the pubs, the *Leon,* is named after the Spanish Armada ship that was wrecked off nearby Mutton Island. The distinctive stone walls you will see on the beach here are for drying seaweed — a valued crop.

MILTOWN MALBAY: This village is a strong traditional music center that hosts each July the Willie Clancy School of Piping (named after a beloved local piper). Featured here are the *uilleann* pipes — the Irish type played with a bellows under the elbow. They have a wide melodic variation and none of the shrieking shrillness of their cousins, the Scottish warpipes. On a Sunday or a holiday, and particularly during the school term, almost any of the bars in Miltown Malbay will have traditional music, as will those in nearby villages such as Mullagh, the Crosses of Annagh, or Quilty. Be forewarned, however: Traditional music happens rather than is planned, and you have to stalk it.

The nearby resort of Spanish Point commemorates sailors of the Spanish Armada who drowned here in September 1588. Those whom the sea did not claim were butchered by the followers of Loyalist Sir Turlough O'Brien of Liscannor.

LAHINCH: Prettily situated on the shores of Liscannor Bay, Lahinch is a cubistic composition of pastel-colored houses perched on a cliff; it has a somewhat exotic Mediterranean look. The visitor will find much to do here: There's a good beach, at which surfboards may be rented; bicycles can be hired from T. O'Sullivan, on Main St. (phone: Lahinch 12); boats are available, both for deep-sea and freshwater fishing; and an 18-hole championship golf course is open to guests (phone: Lahinch 3).

CHECKING IN: *Abderdeen Arms* – This hostelry is an oasis of comfort: Most of its 55 rooms have baths; the bar serves periwinkles rather than peanuts; and the restaurant offers some very fine seafood — try the Clahane lobster broth or the poached Inagh salmon. (Phone: Lahinch 20; moderate.)

> **En Route** – Take the coast road past the ruined tower house of Dough set among the golf greens on the left; on the right in the sandhills are the "tiger" holes of the golf course. Legend has it that fairy king Donn of the Sandhills rides his horse here on moonlit nights.
>
> The ruined medieval church of Kilmacrehy is about one mile on, to your left. Its founder, St. Mac Creiche, fought dragons, cured plagues, and was buried between high and low tide at a spot called "Mac Creiche's bed."

LISCANNOR: An ancient O'Brien tower guards this fishing village and birthplace of John P. Holland, inventor of the submarine and founder of the Electric Boat Company (which became General Dynamics). There is a small museum and library of memorabilia. The road climbs steadily out of Liscannor and at one point you come abreast of a tall urn-crowned column on the left. This is a good stopping point. Below you is Liscannor Bay, and all the billowy coast toward Miltown Malbay. The column was built to honor local hero Cornelius O'Brien. Beside it is *Dabhac Bhrighde,* St. Bridget's Well, a vernacular folk shrine still much visited by pilgrims. Its rushing waters, its quaint whitewashed courtyard surrounded by scarlet fuchsia, even the ex-voto offerings of pictures, rosary beads, and a pair of crutches attest to an abiding religious feeling that dates to pre-Christian times when this was a spring sacred to an ancient Celtic goddess.

CLIFFS OF MOHER: Two miles from the well, you turn right into the parking lot for the Cliffs of Moher. Follow the path up the hillside to the little tower, built by Cornelius O'Brien, a Clare landlord and patron, who intended it as a teahouse "for the entertainment and refreshment of lady visitors." Now it's just a giftshop and lookout, but the view from the top is spectacular: You look north to the Aran Islands and the Connemara mountains and south toward the Cliffs of Moher, a great curtain of sheer cliff face, rippling 5 miles along the coast and hanging over 600 feet above the sea.

> **En Route** – Back on the road and past the Cliffs of Moher, you'll again catch some marvelous vistas out toward the Aran Islands. On Inisheer, the nearest, you'll see an O'Brien Castle and a lighthouse to the left, and a village to the right. The inhabitants of Inisheer speak Irish, farm and fish for a living, and retain many of the customs described in the plays and essays of John M. Synge and in the novels of Liam O'Flaherty.
>
> The hills on the right of the road produce a slate flag — called Liscannor or Moher flag — which is used for roofing stables and outhouses and for decorative work in architecture. About 5 miles from the Cliffs of Moher is a detour 2 miles to the left to the village and harbor of Doolin. The village is a single row of

thatched fishermen's houses. Beside them is a pub, *O'Connell's,* which is famous for traditional music. From Doolin Harbor you can cross by motor launch (or in a curragh, if you want to go hazardously native) to Inisheer.

EATING OUT: ***McCann's*** **and** ***Bruach na hAille*** – Both serve simple but satisfying meals — fresh mackerel, scallops, crab, and other seafood. (Doolin; inexpensive.)

LISDOONVARNA: This town of beach hotels and boarding houses has been a spa resort since the eighteenth century due to its curative sulphur and iron springs. Lisdoonvarna is much patronized by local people in the autumn, when in addition to taking the waters, they play music, dance, and generally enjoy themselves. The Spa Wells Health Centre (phone: Lisdoonvarna 23) is open from June to October. Lisdoonvarna also plays host to a folk festival during the second weekend in July, a nonstop music event — folk, rock, traditional, and country. (Information: Zenith Promotions, Lisdoonvarna, Co. Clare, Irish Republic)

CHECKING IN: Lisdoonvarna hotels are simple to the point of primitive, but guesthouses are uniformly good. The best of the lot is ***Keane's,*** which has 12 rooms, most of which have a bath. The owner is a botanist and Burren enthusiast and usually caters to a distinguished clientele. (Phone: Lisdoonvarna 11; inexpensive.)

En Route – You may take either of two routes to Ballyvaughan, either the scenic coast road to Black Head or the Corkscrew Road through the Burren country.

About a mile out on the former, you'll see the fifteenth-century O'Brien castle, Ballynalacken, a roofless but walled ruin. From the castle's parapets you have a great view west across the bay to the Aran Islands and east over the gray hills of the Burren. Continuing north from Ballynalacken, the road runs along a shelf between the sea and overhanging limestone terraces. It's about 10 miles to the lighthouse at Black Head, from which you have fine views across Galway Bay to the mountains of Mayo and Connemara. Another 5 miles takes you into Ballyvaughan.

The aptly named Corkscrew Road is a narrow, tortuous lane clinging to the Burren hillsides. The vistas are nothing short of breathtaking, with soft mists rising prismlike from the neighboring valleys. The Burren takes its name from the Irish word *boireann,* meaning "rocky." It is literally a rocky desert of silvery gray limestone. General Ludlow, a commander of Cromwell's, returned after a reconnaissance to report that it had "not enough wood to hang a man, earth to bury a man, or water to drown a man!"

The Burren arrived at its present denuded state through the actions of ice, water, air, and frost over scores of centuries. The final effect is unique, and not by any means depressing. The color of the rock ranges from a somber pewter to a light silver and it has been rubbed and carved into marvelous shapes. Long fingers of green reach between the crags to provide relief for the eye and summer grazing for cattle.

Because of the absence of trees or of heavy vegetation the Burren is open to broad untrammeled light, the combination of which with all the other weather factors produces the Burren's final glory — its wild flowers. In late Spring, at the end of May, this desert blooms. The sparse patches of earth and grass on the bare rock-face suddenly become bejeweled with as exotic a collection of flora as can be seen anywhere in the world. Clumps of creamy gold mountain avens from the Arctic grow side by side with tall red and white orchids or the scarlet splash of bloody cranesbill from the Mediterranean. Beside these are the intense blue stars of the spring flowering gentian, which also grow in the alps. Small wonder that the monks of nearby Corcomroe named their abbey St. Mary's of the Fertile Rock.

BALLYVAUGHAN: This little coastal village nestles in one of the green valleys that slope down from the Burren hills. Two miles southeast of town is Aillwee Cave, the only one in the burren that is accessible to the visitor. Its remarkable stalagmites and stalactites and mysterious bear pits are worth seeing. Open daily, from April to October; for information, call Ballyvaughan 36, Kilfenora 26, or Lahinch 150.

CHECKING IN: *Hyland's* – This place is clean, cheerful, and small (13 rooms, most with bath). Seafood is the emphasis in the dining room. (Phone: Ballyvaughan 15; inexpensive.) *Gregan's Castle* – There's a charming homey feeling about this antique-filled castle perched on Corkscrew Hill and overlooking the Burren country and Galway Bay. There are 16 cozy bedrooms, 12 with bath. (Phone: Ballyvaughan 5; moderate.)

EATING OUT: *Manus Walsh's Gallery and Restaurant* – At this jewel of a restaurant, Morris sells paintings and crafts and his wife, Claire, serves up scrumptious lobster, crab, mackerel, and homebaked breads and cakes. (Phone: Ballyvaughan 9; moderate.) Some atmospheric pubs in town include: *Collins,* which offers folk music and talk; *Greene's,* a traditional pub that also serves solid food; *MacNeill O'Loughlin's,* another tiny and traditional pub; and *O'Loughlin's,* a place at the pier with seafood and music.

En Route – About 3 miles on is a spectacular tomb, the Poulnabrone Portal dolmen, well worth stopping your car and walking across the field to view. A few miles farther are signposts to the right for Caherconnell, a well-preserved *caher,* or stone ring fort, which protected four Iron Age and early Christian settlements. At the next crossroad stands Leamaneh Castle, a tower house built by the O'Briens in the fifteenth century, enlarged and fortified in the seventeenth century, and abandoned in the eighteenth century in favor of Dromoland Castle. Features of Leamaneh — a fireplace and gateway — were subsequently moved to Dromoland.

A 4-mile digression into the village of Kilfenora is recommended for a look at the remains of its twelfth-century cathedral whose chancel has some very good stone carving. In the cemetery are the three Irish high crosses carved with Bible scenes and Celtic and Scandinavian interlace ornamentation. The crosses are very typical of Irish art. The Kilfenora Burren Display Centre is a very worthwhile stop. Here, the unusual and fascinating flora of the Burren is reproduced in wax and silk, with special lighting and models to help explain what is special about the area and how it came to be. It's open daily from Easter through to October (phone: Kilfenora 30).

Return to the crossroads and turn south on the main road toward Corofin; from here it's 13 miles back to Ennis.

An alternative to returning to Ennis would be to continue southeast from Ballyvaughan toward Gort and Thoor Ballylee, after which you could connect with the *Connemara* tour route.

Continue along the coast road from Ballyvaughan for 9 miles and turn right at Bell Harbour, where there is a green monument signpost for Corcomroe Abbey. The abbey is reached by a narrow lane (signposted) just beyond the post office. Corcomroe, or St. Mary of the Fertile Rock, was founded in 1196 for the Cistercians by Donal Mor O'Brien, king of Munster. The church is distinguished by some vigorous Irish Romanesque carving on its columns, and there is an important tomb of Conor O'Brien, grandson of the founder.

Some 15 miles farther is Kinvara, home of the fifteenth-century Dun Gaire Castle, which overlooks Galway Bay and offers delightful medieval banquets on summer evenings. (For information or reservations, call 61788).

Take a sharp right turn along the road signposted for Gort, which is about 11 miles distant. Then, about a mile outside Gort, on the Galway road, turn left following signposts into Coole Park, the estate of Lady Augusta Gregory, the playwright and founder of the Abbey Theatre, and hostess to such literary lights as W. B. Yeats, George Bernard Shaw, John M. Synge, and Sean O'Casey. The house has been demolished, but the garden, with its autograph tree, survives. Walk by the lake and through the woods so often described by Yeats in his verse.

After Coole Park, continue along the Galway road for another mile and turn right at the signpost for Thoor Ballylee; follow the narrow country road for a mile or so.

Thoor Ballylee, a sixteenth-century tower house built by the De Burgo family, was Yeats's home from 1917 to 1929 and a frequent symbol in his poetry. It's open daily during the summer; for information, call Peterswell 8. Stop in the bookshop for a look and in the teashop for a cup and a slice of "barm brack" — raisin cake.

From here, it's just 21 miles on the main road to Galway City.

Connemara

There's scarcely any other part of Ireland where you come so intimately in touch with the past as in Connemara. That ancient Gaelic kingdom of bogland and mountain stretches across west Galway to the rocky rim of the wild Atlantic. It lies many removes from the modern world, a haunted mystical land where some kind of time warp seems to have made the centuries come to a halt.

Most Connemara people still speak the ancient Erse language. Now called Irish, it is the mother tongue that has become stilled throughout other parts of Ireland. In Connemara, you will find the biggest Gaeltacht — a region where Irish is the everyday language — in Ireland. But the reality nowadays is that most of the population, particularly the young, is bilingual, fluent in both Irish and English. And, with English emerging as the international medium of communication, Irish is increasingly threatened by extinction. However, the mother tongue *does* live and any visitor going into Connemara who has taken the trouble to learn a few Irish phrases will win an appreciative and warm welcome and won't go short of a drink.

It isn't merely the language that causes the echoes of other days to ring plangently through the glens and mountains of Connemara. This rugged and tempestuous land is a rich repository of many facets of the Celtic past. Everywhere there is a brooding sense of Ireland's ancient culture and tradition. And also to be found are vestiges of a way of life that was common to all European peasant societies many centuries ago.

Since those great mountains were sculpted against the western Irish sky and those glens were chiseled deep into the earth, the Connemara landscape has hardly changed and man has barely fixed his stamp on it. It is a stark and unyielding place that has shaped its people into strong and independent individuals with a stoic and earthy eye to the rest of the world.

The land was always begrudging to yield its beggarly substance, but the Connemara peasants farmed every crevice of its flinty earth. In the old days they lived off potatoes, and when the horrendous potato blight fell upon

Ireland in the 1840s, they suffered more than most others from the famine that followed. Thousands died in their thatched hovels or out in the stony fields and wild bogs, and thousands more fled westward to the shores of "Amerikay." Since then the region has been sparsely populated, the drain on its people continuing through emigration until today, when industrialization has slowed the flight from the land.

The sea is the other mighty element Connemara people have to wrestle with, and their battles have inspired such writers as John Millington Synge and Liam O'Flaherty to powerful prose and poetry. Until recent times, Connemara fisherfolk rode the Atlantic breakers in fragile curraghs to farm the sea. (The *curragh* is a boat of immemorial vintage, which originally was made from hides but now is sheathed in tarred canvas.) You can still see curraghs, powered by sinew and oar, off the Connemara coast today. They look like black scimitar blades knifing through the waves, seemingly frail and vulnerable but, in fact, ingeniously crafted to ride out the angriest of storms. They are widely used yet by the Aran Islanders.

Nobody should ever go to Connemara without also visiting the Aran Islands. They lie west of the mainland, facing the open mouth of Galway Bay, three rocky islands stripped bare of all trees by the Atlantic winds. Their isolation helps to preserve ancient traditions even more perfectly than in Connemara. Much of the primeval peasant life-style remains intact on the islands — even down to the dress worn by the old people. The biggest island, Inishmore, which attracts the preponderance of outside visitors, is developing beady-eyed commercial instincts, but the other two, Inishmaan and Inisheer, still almost totally maintain the ambience of another age.

The rapidly developing technologies of the twentieth century are only now beginning to come into Connemara. There are at last factories for the young people to work in instead of being forced onto the emigrant ship. The fishing industry is gradually being taken out of the curragh age. A measure of affluence has come upon the land. The old thatch cottages with their limewashed stonewalls are coming down to be replaced by rather alien-looking "mod-con" (concrete) bungalows.

But in Connemara the elemental link between man, the earth, and the sea is still a force. The old ways still survive and man faces nature with tools that are not much more advanced than those used at the dawn of civilization. And man somehow seems inconsequential out there on the Connemara landscape with its great gnarled mountains rearing into the sky, lone and level bogs spreading out toward desolate horizons, rivers racing toward the freedom of the sea, and valleys that have been lost to the outside world.

Our route starts in Galway City and heads northwest from there into Connemara territory. The road coils in a serpentine circle through valleys and mountains, at times verging the Atlantic and going through most of the untamed and rugged areas of unsurpassed beauty that have made Connemara famous. We travel along the edge of Galway Bay to get back into Galway City and then we take off for the Aran Islands.

An opening word of utmost caution: The roads you will be traveling over are for the most part narrow, winding, and poorly surfaced, in addition to which Irish drivers display an unnervingly cavalier attitude at the wheel. So, drive slowly, keep very much to the *left,* and at all times be prepared to encounter flocks of sheep or herds of cattle around that next bend.

A double room in a hotel listed as expensive will cost $55 to $75 a night; moderate means $30 to $45. Dinner for two (with wine) in the moderate category will run $40 to $45; expensive, more.

GALWAY CITY: For a complete report on the city, its sights, restaurants, and hotels, see *Galway,* THE CITIES.

En Route – Take N59 from Galway City to the village of Oughterard, 17 miles away. This road runs almost parallel with Lough Corrib, a marvelous fishing lake that is on your right all the way to Oughterard (pronounced OOKTHER-ARD). Most of the side roads to the right will take you to the shores of the lake, and it is easy enough to hire rowing or powered boats for pleasure trips on the lough or for fishing. (See *Sources and Resources,* GALWAY.)

OUGHTERARD: When you get to Oughterard it is worth visiting the sixteenth-century Aughnanure Castle, which is signposted and 2 miles southeast of the town. It was the redoubt of the ferocious O'Flaherty tribe who exhibited sanguinary instincts similar to the Borgias, once dispatching a dinner guest through a flagstone trap door into the river beneath the banquet hall. The castle has been restored.

But angling is the life and soul of Oughterard. Wander into any of the pubs or hotels and you will quickly find yourself immersed in the great terminological inexactitudes of fishing lore. Angling tourists from all over Europe come here to pursue the trout and salmon of Lough Corrib and the fish landed sometimes have been known to be even more immense than the ones that got away. Wander into *Keogh's* emporium on the main street (phone: 091-82212) and arm yourself with a rod bought or rented and get onto the lake for great thrills.

One period of the year, around about mid-May, is known as the time of the "carnival of the trout." That is when great clouds of newly hatched mayflies hover over the lake, and the trout go mad for them. Anglers capture masses of the mayfly, impale them on hooks, and "dap" them on the surface of the water with the aid of a special fishing line; the trout come out with their hands up.

CHECKING IN: *Cloonabinnia House Hotel* – Built on the lines of a Swiss chalet, this hotel is right on the shores of Lough Corrib and is much frequented by anglers from Europe. It has 18 comfortable rooms and fine food. Dinner reservations are recommended from June to August. (8 miles from Galway City on the road to Oughterard, signposted right turn; phone: 091-85187; moderate). *Currarevagh House* – This old aristocratic home on Lough Corrib is now a peaceful and relaxing guesthouse. Open only from April to October. Reservations necessary. (Second right turn on entering Oughterard, signposted for the 4 miles to the lakeside; phone: 091-82313; moderate). *Sweeney's Oughterard House Hotel* – Delightful ivy-smothered Georgian house with a deserved international reputation, this family-run hotel offers superb cuisine. Its sumptuous dinners are exclusively for guests staying in the hotel, but casual visitors can feast on a rich range of unusual fare in the lounge-bar. (Through the town, turn right over the bridge beside the church, left again, and you're there; phone: 091-82207; expensive.)

EATING OUT: *The Silver Teal* – The seafood is the specialty here; try the fresh salmon. (Moycullen village, 7 miles north on the road to Oughterard; phone: 85109; expensive.)

En Route – Still traveling northwest as you leave Oughterard, you are beginning to move into Connemara, but in this particular area the Irish language is rarely heard and you must travel much farther to reach the Gaeltacht areas. The land beyond Oughterard is desolate and bare, though in a valley to the left there are a number of small lakes. Ten miles out, you reach Maam Cross, an intersection where you turn right onto L100, a very precarious road where you carefully — *very* carefully — make your way into the lonely valley of Maam.

When Orson Welles passed this way at the age of 17 — long before becoming the *enfant terrible* of American radio, stage, and screen — he came riding on a donkey, probably the very best way to travel here. Motorists should stop often and get out and sit on a rock or a stone bridge, just to immerse themselves in the atmosphere or maybe to talk to a passing farmer. There is also much to see *above* the land itself. Look upward because artists have come from many lands to do just that in Connemara. Unless there is heavy sea mist or fog or impenetrable overcast, the sky above Connemara is a living mural of constantly changing cloud patterns with an astonishing interplay of light, color, and shadow, never for a moment the same and always a source of impassioned inspiration and agonizing frustration for painters.

Five miles farther on, you reach Maam Bridge and turn left to head toward the village of Leenane, 9 miles away. You are now deep in the Maam Valley, with the craggy Maamturk Mountains that dominate the Joyce Country on your left and the hills of south Mayo to your right. Two diversions might be worth venturing on here. From Maam Bridge you can take a road south into the Joyce Country until you come to the hill of Maumeen where legend says St. Patrick slept and where a sacred well named after him is still a place of pilgrimage. It is just 10 miles away amid magnificent mountain country. Or, 5 miles along the road to Leenane, you can turn right at the signpost for Lake Nafooey, which lies 5 miles away in a sequestered valley of bogland grandeur. You won't find anything closer to Shangri-La than Nafooey, outside the pages of a book.

LEENANE: This lovely village is lost at the bottom of a bowl of mountains, one of whose peaks is called "The Devil's Mother." Leenane also lies close to Killary Harbour, the only true Scandinavian-style fjord to be found in Ireland. The long arm of water reaches deeply in between giant mountains for 10 miles, and roads lining each side of the inlet provide dramatic panoramas of land and sea. The road north from Leenane goes into Mayo; walk 3 miles up this road for a view of the Aasleagh Falls on the Erriff River, and maybe to fish for salmon there, too.

CHECKING IN: *Leenane Hotel* – Run by one of a famous family of Irish hoteliers, the Foyles, this splendid hostelry is still redolent of Edwardian days (indeed, *that* particular Edward did once stay here). It is right on the shores of Killary Harbour so not surprisingly, the seafood is very good. Open only May 14 to September 30. (Just as you leave the village on the road to Clifden; phone: Leenane 4; moderate.) ***Peacocke's*** – A sort of Celtic bazaar located at Maam Cross, but offering a valuable service to tourists. There's a big bar for booze and fast grub; a more sedate sit-down restaurant with good fare; a shop with the whole bag of stereotypical Emerald Isle souvenirs — tweeds, wools, pottery; a small supermarket; a car-accessories shop; and a filling station. You can even stay overnight. (Maam Cross; phone: 091-82307; moderate.)

En Route – Leaving Leenane, you now head west on the road to Clifden, which runs along the shore of the Killary fjord. But there is much to view in between and a few byways to explore. Ten miles down the road you pass by Kylemore Abbey, a modern gothic building across a lake on your right. This was built by a doctor in the nineteenth century as an adoring and lasting monument to his wife, and is now a high-toned school for girls run by Benedictine nuns. They'll show you around the castle library, church, and pottery. They also serve the daintiest of teas.

RENVYLE: About 1 mile farther on from Kylemore, you'll see a signpost on the right for Renvyle, 6 miles away. This will take you to the precarious verge of the Atlantic ocean, where the rocky headland juts defiantly out into the ocean. Locals say that if while standing there you look directly west and squint hard, you'll see the next parish — Brooklyn! Out on the promontory is yet another ruined castle of those terrible O'Flahertys. All round this area are some very lovely and safe beaches. On the way into Renvyle you will have passed through another traditional village called Tullycross and here you can see modern versions of the traditional thatched Irish cottages that have been fitted with comforts and conveniences unknown to the peasantry of yore. These cottages can be rented at moderate rates though reservations far in advance are essential. (For information, call Áras Fáilte at 091-63081.)

CHECKING IN: *Renvyle House Hotel* – At this elegant hotel perched above the sea, the decor is of another age and an air of graciousness prevails. It once was the country residence of the great Irish wit, Oliver St. John Gogarty, the prototype of the character Buck Mulligan in Joyce's *Ulysses*. Closed January, February, and most of March. (Signposted on the right, 1.5 miles past Tully Cross; phone: Renvyle 3; moderate.)

LETTERFRACK: It's about 8 miles from Renvyle through Tullycross into Letterfrack village, back to the main road from Leenane to Clifden again. Letterfrack is a crossroads village of great charm. Visit most any of the pubs in the evening and you'll hear some of the best genuine Irish music played on fiddle and tin whistle. The village also lies in the shadow of the towering range of mountains called "The Twelve Bens." Just recently, the Irish government has taken over 3,800 acres of this wild mountainous terrain and turned it into a national park. Though still only in the early stages of development, it shouldn't be missed. The entrance is only about 100 yards south of the main street of Letterfrack. There are wide-open spaces in which to pitch camp and Diamond Mountain — reaching heavenward in the middle of the park — just begs to be climbed. While at the national park, you can also get a close look at the famous Connemara ponies. Indeed, these sturdy and tough little horses, renowned for their endurance, jumping powers, and amiability, can be found roaming all over Connemara. Some people believe that they are descended from Spanish horses that swam to the safety of the Connemara coast from ships wrecked in the Spanish Armada and interbred with local strains. Others say they have Egyptian bloodlines. Whatever the true story, the Connemara pony is now a breed of international celebrity, and there are Connemara pony societies all over the world, including the US.

CHECKING IN: *Kylemore House Guesthouse* – Not to be confused with the Kylemore Pass Hotel, the *Kylemore House Guesthouse* is a truly superior place to stay, one of a number in this area. It's worth a visit if only to see the precious antique furniture and paintings that adorn it. Absolute luxury, 7 acres of woods, 3 private fishing lakes with salmon and trout, and a table par excellence. A real find. Reservations essential. (3 miles east of Kylemore Abbey on the main Leenane-Clifden road; phone: Kylemore 3; moderate.) ***Rosleague Manor Hotel*** – Run by two more of the famous Foyle family, this gracious Georgian manor overlooks a quiet bay. Unusually good food. Open Easter to end of October. (2 miles west of Letterfrack on main road to Clifden; phone: Moyard 7; moderate.) ***Crocnaraw Country House*** – Another Georgian country home set in 20 acres of gardens and woods on the shores of the Atlantic, known for its cosseting of guests, free trout fishing, vegetables fresh from the garden, and tasty home cooking. (3 miles west of Letterfrack on main Clifden road; phone: Moyard 9; moderate.) ***Doon*** – This place is hidden behind hedges so you can easily miss it, but pray that you don't. Another great find — fresh-squeezed orange juice, lobster salads, chocolate cream slices, same-day fish, and more served at lunchtime only, from 12:30 to 3 PM. (4 miles west of Letterfrack, watch carefully for a tiny notice that says "Doon" stuck in the hedge, and turn right; phone: Moyard 21; moderate.)

CLIFDEN: This town, on the main road 9 miles from Letterfrack, is cradled in a glen at the head of an Atlantic inlet into which a river rushes. Though it only has a population of little more than 1,000, Clifden is called the capital of Connemara, a label that might be challenged by people in southern Connemara where scarcely anything but Irish is spoken. Clifden is an English-speaking town, a legacy of the days when Clifden was a favorite seaside summer resort of the British gentry. Many army officers from Dublin Castle (the former seat of British rule in Ireland) built or bought landed manors in and around Clifden, and some of those splendid residences are among the better hotels we have cited in this chapter.

Almost forgotten now is the fact that the first wireless messages from Europe to America were sent from Clifden. The inventor of radio, Marconi, set up a station in Derrygimlagh Bog, 4 miles south of the town. Marconi himself spent much time in Clifden. The buildings that housed the transatlantic wireless station were destroyed during the Irish civil war of the early 1920s, but some of the transmitting masts are still standing. The same bog has claim to another historic distinction. It was on its peaty surface in 1919 that the aviators John William Alcock and Arthur Whitten Brown landed their biplane, after having flown from Newfoundland to complete the first nonstop transatlantic flight. A pile of stones marks the spot today and nearby there's a more imposing limestone monument of a tailplane commemorating the event. These sites are well marked; travel about 4 miles out of the Ballyconneely road to get to them.

Anyone visiting Clifden must ascend the dizzying heights of the Sky Road, well named because when you're toiling up its steep slope you feel you may well reach the sky. The road is signposted from the town's central square; it's narrow and heart-stoppingly sheer and requires skilled gear-shifting if you're in a car. As you ascend, a fabulous view of Clifden Bay and the savage rocky west coast spreads out beneath you; farther out, you can see the small islands nestled like humpbacked whales in the Atlantic. At the highest point there's a walled-in car park where you can rest to take in the view at leisure and maybe have a picnic.

The fishing village of Cleggan, 7 miles to the northwest, should also be visited when you're in Clifden. Double back on the main road to Leenane and at Streamstown turn left. Cleggan is the embarkation point for Inishbofin Island, which in recent times has become a haunt of poets, philosophers, and artists from many lands. The mail boat that leaves Cleggan every noon — the temperamental Atlantic permitting — will carry you to the island. If a really bad storm brews up, though, you may be marooned on the island for days or even weeks, but in view of the hospitality and friendliness of the islanders, you could meet worse fates. The ruins of a monastery founded by St. Colman in the seventh century are still there, and the island also was once in the possession of those terrible O'Flahertys. The daring sea queen of the western waters, Grainne Ui Mhaille (pronounced GRAWN-ya ee WHAL-ya and translated as "Grace O'Malley"), also found shelter for her warships here in the days when she rebelled against the sovereignty of Queen Elizabeth. The iron gauntlet of Cromwell fell on the island in 1652 and the barracks where his Roundheads were billeted stands at the harbor entrance.

CHECKING IN: *Clifden Bay Hotel* – The original hostelry founded by the Foyle family already mentioned, and a place of warm informality, with music sessions on many evenings, lovely rooms, and fine food. (On Main St.; phone: Clifden 128; moderate.) *Alcock and Brown Hotel* – Very modern, very comfortable, very plush with an accomplished dining room. (Top of Main St.; phone: Clifden 134; moderate.) *Celtic Hotel* – Exceptionally friendly house where management and staff go out of their way to ensure your comfort. Pleasant rooms and a good restaurant. (Main St.; phone: Clifden 115; moderate.)

EATING OUT: *D'Arcy Inn* – Charming pub and eating place. Downstairs for the drink and the singing; upstairs for the toothsome delicacies, many of Continental inspiration. (Main St.; phone: Clifden 202; moderate.)

En Route – Leaving Clifden, you now start heading roughly southeast toward Galway City on the "low road," which hugs the jagged northern coast of the bay almost the whole way. It takes you quickly into the Gaeltacht area where most of the signposts are in Irish, but you're not likely to get lost for any great length of time and most people can speak English anyway to get you back on the track. Besides, it's a nice place to get lost in.

ROUNDSTONE: This is one of the loveliest sea villages in Connemara and in summertime it is crowded with tourists from across the globe. Its Irish name is *Cloch nah Ron,* which means "Rock of the Seals," and in the evening you can indeed see the whiskered heads of seals bobbing in the bay. Two granite piers built in the nineteenth century jut into the bay to protect the fishing boats. Rising almost directly behind the main street is Errisbeg Mountain, which is easy to ascend and from its summit you can see just about all of the west coast. The two finest beaches in Connemara are off the main road, less than 2 miles west of the village.

CHECKING IN: *Erriseask House Hotel* – One of those old rambling houses that reek of antique charm. Good food. (At Ballyconneely, 6 miles out from Clifden on the road to Roundstone; phone: Ballyconneely 6; moderate.)

EATING OUT: *Restaurant Francaise* – Authentic, very good French cuisine. (2 miles out from Clifden at Salt Lake Bridge on the road to Roundstone; phone: Clifden 206; moderate.) *The Fishery* – Superb seafood, particularly lobster, served up in a homey stone cottage. (4 miles beyond Ballyconneely on the road to Roundstone; phone: Ballyconneely 31; moderate.)

BALLYNAHINCH: Continue on the coast road from Roundstone for 10 miles to Ballynahinch, which is signposted and where you'll find the splendid Castle of Ballynahinch amid woodlands behind turreted gates. In a way, this is the true capital of ancient Connemara, because here resided the powerful albeit eccentric Martin family who were simply granted just about all of Connemara by an English king in the eighteenth century. (One of the Martins had a very nimble intuition: He pledged the right allegiance to the right royal house at the right time.) The dispossessed O'Flahertys (yes, those wild ones again) hated the Martins and put to the sword any that crossed their path, though the Martins themselves were no mean swordsmen. One of them, Dick Martin, won notoriety as a duelist, but redeemed his reputation by founding the Society for the Prevention of Cruelty to Animals, thus earning the name "Humanity Dick." The castle, now a hotel, has a magnificent setting among mountains, lakes, and woods. The Ballynahinch Fishery is world famous for salmon angling.

Leaving Ballynahinch Castle, double back on the road until you reach the signpost for Cashel and continue southeast along the coast once more. Cashel is lush with vegetation and shrubbery and provides a warm contrast with the stonier and starker face of the Connemara landscape. The view seaward is breathtaking.

CHECKING IN: *Ballynahinch Castle Hotel* – Ancestral home of the Martin dynasty and now a hotel that echoes with history. Much striking scenery and some of the best salmon fishing anywhere. Much frequented by American visitors. Open June 1 to October 12. (10 miles from Roundstone as you head for Galway City; phone: Clifden 135; expensive.) *Cashel House Hotel* – Often cited as one of Ireland's best hotels. Charles de Gaulle stayed here. Sheltered gardens, monastic quiet, and delicious food. Book well in advance. (On the coast road from Roundstone to Galway City, 14 miles from Roundstone; phone: Cashel, Co. Galway 9; expensive.) *N.B.: Make sure you specify Co. Galway because there's the other Cashel in Co. Tipperary.*

CARNA: About 10 miles south of Cashel, this sea village is in the heart of the Irish-speaking district. July, when there are a number of festivals of a maritime flavor, is a good time to be in Carna. The old-time sailing boats called "hookers" and "pucauns," along with the curraghs already mentioned, gather off Carna for regattas and races. Carna is also a marvelous place for traditional Irish music. You'll be welcome to join the informal sessions in the pubs or to go to an Irish dance which is known as a *ceili* (pronounced KAY-lee). It's also worth taking a trip out to MacDara's Island, the resting place of St. MacDara, protector of fishermen who still dip their oars in salute as they sail past the island. From Carna continue along the meandering coast road through Kilkieran to Gortmore and turn right here at the signpost to Rosmuc.

ROSMUC: This isolated area is a venerated place in modern Irish history. It was in a cottage here that the mystic poet and philosopher Padraig Pearse, who led the 1916 Rising against the British in Dublin, sought seclusion to contemplate Ireland's Celtic past and to dream of revolution and a free nation. Many leading political figures of those times joined him in the cottage to ponder Ireland's destiny. After the rising, Pearse and the other leaders were shot, but their action led to independence for the southern part of Ireland within 5 years. The cottage is a national monument open to the public. Returning to Gortmore, turn right as far as Screeb, 3 miles away, then right again until you come to Costelloe. Detour northwest here following the signpost to Carraroe.

CARRAROE: This village set amid furze-clad hills and stony fields is a place where the lingering charm of the past is at its strongest. Irish is the lingua franca and in the small farms, the old traditional ways of cultivating the land are still used. Children from all over Ireland come here in summer to gain fluency in speaking Irish. There are a number of pristine beaches tucked away in niches along the rugged shoreline, including a small coral strand less than 2 miles from the village. Return now to Costelloe and head southeast towards Galway City. Just before the village of Inverin, the road straightens out and runs directly east to the city, 16 miles away, and for the entire run you have Galway Bay on your right.

CHECKING IN: *Ostan Cheathru Rua* – (Pronounced OH-shtawn kah-roo roo-ah, which means "Hotel Carraroe.") This is the only hostelry that can, with an easy conscience, be recommended in this locality. It is up-to-date and most comfortable and the cuisine is good. Very often there are enjoyable sessions of Irish music. Open May 29 to October 2. (A highly visible signpost on the village's main street points the way; phone: 091-75116; moderate.)

THE ARAN ISLANDS: Galway City is the best jumping off spot for the Aran Islands and you can travel either by sea or plane. In summertime when the weather is good, the sea voyage in the motor vessels that sail from Galway harbor is the most enjoyable way to go as you get a chance to mingle and maybe share a pint with some of the islanders.

All three of the Aran Islands seem like geographical relics of the stone age abandoned in the Atlantic. They are hewn out of solid rock with a penurious layer of soil in some places, while in others there is no grass, only great slabs of stone. When the celebrated American film maker Robert Flaherty made a documentary of life on Aran in the thirties, one sequence showed a farmer grinding rock to dust and sprinkling it over his fields as topsoil. That was Flaherty indulging in undue artistic license to highlight the hardship of island life; such things never happened, but, still, the rigors of wresting a subsistence from the land and the sea around were heartbreaking.

The islands are named Inishmore, or the big island; Inishmaan, the middle island; and Inisheer, the eastern island, which is the smallest. All three have their own charms and their barren isolation has impregnably immured them in the past. They keep extant a way of life that has long since passed away in almost every other part of Europe. The big island, Inishmore, which has more constant and active contact with the mainland and attracts most of the tourists, is slipping more rapidly into the modern age than its two sister isles. The influx of free-spending tourists on Inishmore has uncovered a mercenary streak there. But the two smaller islands, Inishmaan and Inisheer, are the more fascinating ones for any visitor. On both of those many of the older inhabitants still dress in the colorful garb worn by their forefathers centuries ago.

The islands were inhabited in prehistoric times, possibly by the race known as the Fir Bolgs, and on Inishmore is the spectacular remains of an ancient civilization — the great fort called Dun Aengus. It is a savage symphony in stone spread over 12 acres on a cliff high above the Atlantic. There is another massive fort called Dun Chonchuir (pronounced Doon Krah-hoor) on Inishmaan and exploration of both those fortresses is quite rewarding.

On Inishmaan and Inisheer it would be almost sacrilegious to move around other than on foot — not that there's much choice as the automobile is still alien to these places. You can ride around on a horse-drawn jaunting car or on bicycles. Inishmore has a few taxis and one or two mini-buses. But walking also allows you to get closer to the pre-Christian and early Christian ruins that are everywhere to be found. The islands were a stronghold of the very special Irish monasticism of the sixth and seventh centuries.

Apart from safaris back into the Celtic past, there are many other intriguing things to see and do on the island. The tiny little pubs, some of them roofed in thatch, are scenes of boisterous merriment and song. You can fish off the coastal rocks or get a fisherman to take you out for a ride in a curragh, which can be quite a thrill. Some propitious fate has decreed that the waters washing the beaches of Inishmore be a little warmer than off the mainland, so the swimming can be good on hot summer days. The sheer cliffs rising from the ocean will test the nerve of anyone with a mountaineering spirit.

To get to Aran by plane, call Aer Arann at Áras Fáilte (the tourism office) off Eyre Square in Galway City; phone: 091-65119. There are several flights each day from Carnmore Airport, 5 miles north of the city off the Monivea Road.

The sea trips to the island are run by Córas Iompair Éireann (CIE), the national transport agency. During summer they sail daily with the tide to Inishmore, with stopoffs at the other two islands. At other times of the year, there are sailings only twice a week. For details contact CIE at the Railway Station, Eyre Sq., Galway City; phone: 091-62141.

There is an alternative daily sea route from Rossaveal Harbour in Connemara, serving the three islands. Arrangements for these trips can be made by contacting the Áras Fáilte office, off Eyre Sq., Galway City; phone: 091-63081.

Southern Mayo

Above brooding Connemara, the Mweelrea and Partry Mountains and the Sheeffrey Hills of southern County Mayo give way to a gentler landscape that wraps its way around the beautiful, island-studded Clew Bay. Croagh Patrick, the stately mountain where St. Patrick is said to have prayed and fasted for forty days for the salvation of the Irish people, is the predominant feature of the bay's southern shore, while Achill Island, Ireland's largest offshore island, guards the northwestern reaches of the bay. Inland, a series of lakes, most notably Lough Mask, which feeds into Lough Corrib near Mayo's border with County Galway, offer anglers excellent trout fishing. Southern Mayo's natural amenities and leisure facilities present traditional Ireland at its best, and many names associated with its heritage are famed in song and story.

The coastline, which presents a succession of sandy beaches, rugged headlands, and dramatic cliffs, is steeped in the legends of Grace O'Malley (Grainne Ui Mhaille), the sixteenth-century warrior sea-queen who made herself ruler of the district that surrounds Clew Bay and its islands after the death of her father. While some doubt the veracity of her legendary exploits, they have been handed down in the spoken tradition of the islanders and in the historical novel *Queen of Men* by William O'Brien. One of the most interesting tales concerns a marriage contract she made with her second husband, MacWilliam Oughter. They agreed that either party could dissolve the union after one year merely by saying, "I dismiss you!" Grace O'Malley took advantage of the escape clause at the end of the year, but not before she had garrisoned all of Oughter's coastal castles with her own followers to make her position as ruler of the area even stronger.

And while the authenticity of Irish history reaches back no farther than the seventh century, the plain of Southern Moytura near Cong is said to have been the scene of the first battle between two mythical tribes that ruled this area 3,000 years ago, the Fir Bolg, a race of small dark men, and the fair Tuatha De Denaan, said to be a race of magicians. Though the Denaan were victorious here they were later overcome in the Celtic conquest. Legend says the defeated Denaan changed themselves into fairies and ever since have inhabited the hills, forts, and caves of Ireland. Beneath the rocks of Cong, there are more than forty dark, unearthly looking caves, and not a few locals will tell you that it is likely that many of the "little people" went to live there.

There is more historical certainty about the role that Mayo men played in the agitations of the Land League, formed to help tenant farmers resist tyrannical and rent-racking landlords. Michael Davit, one of the founders of the league, was born at Straid, near Castlebar, and Captain Charles Boycott, one of the league's targets, lived at Lough Mask House on the shores of the southern Mayo lake.

This route begins at Cong, just over the border from County Galway and a pleasant 20-mile drive from Galway City, and skirts the western edges of Lough Mask beneath the Partry Mountains, heading north to Castlebar. From this busy town in the heart of the limestone plain country, the route goes west to take in Achill Island and south again around Clew Bay to the lovely planned town of Westport and along the curving bay to Louisburgh. From here the road leads south to Killary Harbour and dips into Joyce Country before following the northern shore of Lough Corrib back to Cong.

Expect to pay upward of $84 for a double room at an expensive hotel, and from $24 to $66 at a moderate one. Dinner for two at *Ashford Castle* will cost a minimum of $52; at moderately priced restaurants, two can dine well for from $25 to $50.

CONG: This tiny village on an isthmus between Lough Mask and Lough Corrib is best known for the ruins of the twelfth-century Cong Abbey and the luxury hotel, *Ashford Castle.* It may also be familiar to Americans as the setting for that quintessential Irish-American movie *The Quiet Man,* which was filmed in these precincts.

Cong Abbey, founded for Irish Augustinians by Turlough O'Connor, king of Ireland, is considered one of the finest examples of early architecture in Ireland. The ruins preserve several doorways and windows of a type transitional between Romanesque and Gothic and are best seen from the cloisters garth. Behind the west end of the abbey garth is a small stone house constructed so that the Cong River flows through a gully beneath the floor. The structure is known as the Monks' Fishing House because monks from the abbey supposedly fished through a trap door in its floor.

The ruins of the abbey are beside one of the entrance gates to the lovely grounds of Ashford Castle, which commands some of the finest acreage along Lough Corrib. The oldest part of the castle was built in the eighteenth century, but the castellated towers and a bridge on the river's edge were added later by Sir Benjamin Guinness. There are some 25 miles of landscaped walks through the demesne of the castle, which was converted into a hotel in 1939. Parts of the grounds are open to the public.

Besides the abbey there are several interesting historic artifacts and monuments connected with Cong and its environs. The celebrated Cross of Cong (now in the National Museum in Dublin) was discovered in a chest in the village early in the last century. Made of oak plated with copper and decorated with beautiful gold filigree work of Celtic pattern, it is a masterpiece of religious art. The little ruined church and the ancient Stone of Lunga on the low wooded island of Inchagoill in Lough Corrib belong to the age of St. Patrick. The stone is a 2.5-foot-high obelisk that bears ancient Roman characters thought to be the oldest Christian inscription in Europe outside the Catacombs.

The stream connecting Lough Mask and Lough Corrib has three parts of its short course underground at Cong and the subterranean channel is accessible from a number of caves that honeycomb the plateau of cavernous limestone between the lakes. The Pigeon Hole is the most accessible of the caves of Cong. It is reached by turning right onto New Saw Mill, a mile west of the village. At the first cottage on the right there is an iron gate that opens to a field and a short way from the gate, 61 stone steps lead down to the underground chamber.

Another underground curiosity is the Dry Canal, which was built as a relief scheme during the Great Famine of 1846 with the idea of connecting Lough Corrib and Lough Mask to extend navigation. When it was completed, however, it was discovered that despite the cut-stone banks and locks, the canal was incapable of holding water because of the porous limestone bed.

About a half mile from the village on all three approach roads to Cong, the visitor may notice small mounds of wooden crosses, called *crusheens*. For centuries it has been the practice of funeral corteges to stop at these spots to say a prayer and add another cross to the pile.

About 4 miles north of Cong, the ruins of a castle that belonged to Captain Charles Boycott can be seen on a minor road along the shores of Lough Mask. The name of Boycott, a retired British army officer who was unpopular with his tenants, came to stand for ostracism and isolation because workers refused to help him during the harvest season during the Land League agitation in the 1880s.

Cong is a center for hunting and fishing. Lough Mask is noted for large trout and pike; Lough Corrib — Ireland's second largest lake — is renowned for brown trout, pike, and salmon. The season for salmon and trout fishing in the lakes runs from February 15 to September 30 and on the rivers from March 1 to September 30. Fishing is free on both lakes with the exception of part of the Cong River within Ashford Castle grounds. Horses can be hired for riding in the area from the Cong Riding Centre (phone: Cong 29), and there is a secluded sandy cove for bathers that can be reached from an approach road off the Cong-Clonbur Road, 1 mile west of the village.

CHECKING IN: *Ashford Castle* – One of the finest castle hotels in Europe, its public rooms have paneled ceilings and impressive woodcarvings and stonework, set off by period furniture, Waterford chandeliers, and military memorabilia. Each of the 77 guestrooms has a view of the lake or the hotel's formal gardens and wide lawns, and there is a nine-hole golf course on the grounds. The dining room, which is walled in mirrors and looks out over the lake, serves elaborate French cuisine. Although it is possible to dine at the castle even if you aren't staying there, reservations must be made well in advance. (On Highway 98A just east of the village; phone: 094-22644; expensive.)

En Route – The route north from Cong to Castlebar follows a minor road along the western bank of Lough Mask beside the Partry Mountains, passing through Tourmakeady, a small Irish-speaking village. At the village of Partry, take the T40 about 3.5 miles north, where a road on the right leads to the largely restored Ballintubber Abbey, which has been in almost uninterrupted use as a place of worship since it was founded for members of the order of St. Augustine in 1216. The abbey consists of a cruciform church with nave transepts and choir. Three blocked windows of Norman design with double dog-tooth moulding are over the altar. The monastic buildings are at the end of the south transept, and in a chapel to the south of the choir there is an elaborate altar tomb with a row of figures on the pediment.

CASTLEBAR: The administrative capital of County Mayo, Castlebar is a thriving commercial center that began as a settlement where a castle was built by the de Barra family. It became famous during the 1798 Rebellion because a joint Irish-French force defeated the British army here in a battle known as the Races of Castlebar. The remains of John Moore, president of the Republic of Connaught that was proclaimed after the battle, are buried in the town's pleasant tree-lined Mall. The Castlebar Tourist Information Office (phone: 094-21207) is open only during the summer season.

In the pretty village of Turlough, 3 miles northeast of Castlebar, there is a well-preserved round tower beside the ruins of a seventeenth-century church.

CHECKING IN: *Breaffy House Hotel* – An elegant Georgian mansion with modern additions, it's set in 60 acres of wooded parkland. There are 43 pleasantly appointed guestrooms and the entire operation bears the personal touch of Mrs. Una Lee, the manager. (2 miles from Castlebar on the Castlebar-Claremorris road — N60; phone: 094-22033; moderate.)

En Route – Newport, an angling center on the northeast corner of Clew Bay beneath the Nephin and Nephin Beg Mountains, is 12 miles northwest of Castlebar on the L138. Two miles beyond Newport, a road to the left leads to the well-preserved Burrishole church of the Burrishole Friary, built in 1450 by Richard Burke. The central tower of the cruciform church remains and there are some good examples of pointed arches. About 2 miles farther west on the highway, an unpaved road on the left leads to the square tower of Grace O'Malley's castle of Rockfleet, where the warrior queen dismissed her husband after a year of marriage. Mulrany, a picturesque resort with a good bathing beach on the margin of Clew Bay, lies on the narrow isthmus that joins the mountainous Curraun Peninsula to the mainland. The main route to Achill Island follows the north shore of the peninsula, but the road along the southern rim of the peninsula is recommended for its fine seascapes.

CHECKING IN: *Newport House* – This white Georgian house set on the edge of the bay is a pleasant hotel with regency decor and 24 rooms. It has a French chef and a reputation for superb food, serving fresh produce from its own gardens, farm, and fishery. (Newport; phone: 098-41121; moderate.) *Great Western Hotel* – Surrounded by rhododendron, fuchsia, and trees on a hillside above the main road (N59), it dates from the days when the Irish railroad system stretched as far as Achill Island. The hotel, which has 71 rooms, has been modernized and offers guests a swimming pool and tennis court, as well as music and dancing on some Saturday nights during the summer. (Mulrany; phone: Mulrany 3; moderate.)

ACHILL ISLAND: The largest of Ireland's offshore islands, Achill is a popular holiday center, though little known to foreign visitors. It is dominated by three mountains, and its coast is marked by dramatic cliffs, as well as several charming resort villages with long, broad sandy beaches. Achill Sound, just across the bridge from the mainland, is the island's principal shopping center and has facilities for bathing, boating, and fishing. Beyond the town, the Atlantic Highway bears right off L148, the island's main road, and passes a keep of the O'Malleys. As it traverses the windswept tracts of peat bog that cover much of the island and supply fuel to the islanders, black-faced sheep dot the rolling bogs and occasionally block the winding road. Dooega, a small village at the mouth of a valley on the west side of the Minaun Mountain, is a convenient place from which to climb the mountain or the Minaun Cliffs, which rise to 800 feet.

Just before reaching Keel, the island's main resort town, you pass the spectacular Cathedral Rocks, water-carved cliffs that resemble a Gothic cathedral jutting up from the ocean. Keel, on a curving bay sheltered by Slievemore Mountain on the north and Croghun Mountain on the west, has a 3-mile-long sandy beach, a nine-hole golf course, and tennis courts, and is a center for surfing and underwater sports.

Two miles farther on are the whitewashed cottages of Dooagh, on a bay famous for salmon netting. Keem Bay, which has a wide beach of fine sand, sheltered by the steeply rising Moyteoge Head, is 3 miles farther west. Basking sharks frequent Achill waters in spring and are trapped in nets at Keem Bay and then killed with lances by island crews working from small canvas-covered curraghs. A steep road leads from Keem Bay to the summit of Croghun Mountain, with its 4-mile line of superb cliffs reaching as high as 2,000 feet above the ocean.

Heading back through Keem Bay, a road to the left leads north across the island to Dugort, a north shore village from which boatmen take visitors to the Seal Caves that extend far into the cliffs under Slievemore Mountain, a mass of quartzite rock and mica that rises to 2,204 feet.

In addition to sea angling, there is fishing for trout in Achill's lakes and the Dooega River, and in recent years the island has become a popular hang gliding center. There are numerous small hotels and guesthouses on the island open to visitors in summer. May and June are the best months to visit Achill, but Tourist Information Offices are open at Achill Sound (phone: Achill Sound 51) and Keel (phone: Keel 27) throughout the summer.

En Route – The N59 follows the curve of Clew Bay south from Mulrany to Westport, 8 miles below Newport.

WESTPORT: This charming seigneurial town in a hollow on the arm of Clew Bay was planned for the marquess of Sligo by James Wyatt, a famous British architect of the Georgian period. Its main street, known as The Mall, runs along both sides of the gentle Carrowbeg River, which is crossed by several picturesque stone bridges and is sheltered by a colonnade of lime trees. Westport is an important center for sea angling and was the scene of a meeting at which the Irish Land League was formed in 1879. The town also provided the setting for a number of novels by George A. Birmingham, the pen name of James Owen Hannay who was rector of the Church of Ireland here from 1893 to 1913. A mile and a half west of the town center in a lovely demesne overlooking Clew Bay and the Atlantic Ocean is Westport House, a fine Georgian mansion that was the home of the marquess of Sligo and is open to the public April 1 through October 5 (phone: Westport 171 or 130). Designed by the German architect Richard Cassels in 1730 and altered 50 years later by Wyatt, it houses fine collections of Old English and Irish silver; paintings by Sir Joshua Reynolds and James O'Connor, perhaps the best of Irish landscape painters; Waterford crystal; and fine old furniture. The attractive marble staircase was built by Italian artisans brought here specifically for that purpose. In a basement area, there is a warren of shops, an amusement arcade, and a teashop. Ireland's first zoo park is situated on the grounds, and Westport House Country Estates has holiday homes, horse caravans, and campers for hire.

Just outside the gates to the grounds of Westport House is Westport Quay, where boats may be rented for boating and fishing on Clew Bay. On Collanmore Island in the bay, there is a sail-training center for beginners and intermediates. (For information, contact Glenans Irish Sailing Centres, 1 Kildare St., Dublin 2; phone: 76775, 760938, or Carrowholly 728). The Westport Golf Club (phone: Westport 546), 3 miles from town, has an 18-hole, par-73 championship course that winds around the precipitous slopes of Croagh Patrick. One of its most interesting holes is the par-5, 15th hole with a carry from the tee across Clew Bay.

There is a 4-day international sea angling festival held here each June, and the Westport Horse Show, a 3-day event that is one of Ireland's important horse shows, is also held in June. In August, the Cailin Deas Festival includes sporting events, art displays, and a variety of musical entertainment and dancing. Westport has three dance halls and ballad sessions are held in some hotels and pubs during the summer. The Westport Tourist Information Office is located on The Mall (phone: 269).

CHECKING IN: *Westport Ryan's* – The largest (56 rooms) of Westport's six hotels, it offers cheerful and modern accommodations. (On the road from town to the quay; phone: Westport 333; moderate.) ***Hotel Westport*** – This modern, 49-room hotel maintains the best standards in town, is exceedingly friendly, and has a cuisine of estimable quality. (Cross the bridge at the bottom of James St., entering Newport Rd., and take the first left turn; phone: Westport 351; moderate.)

EATING OUT: *Ardmore House* – It's a small, intimate candlelit restaurant overlooking Clew Bay that specializes in fresh seafood. Owner-chef Pat Hoban prepares excellent Continental and Irish dishes, and his wife, Noreen, gives her personal attention to the dining room. Reservations recommended in summer months. (Rosbeg, Westport, 1 mile from the town center; phone: Westport 636; moderate.)

En Route – The graceful Croagh Patrick, Ireland's holy mountain 5 miles west of Westport, is one of the most impressive landmarks in the west of Ireland. From its 2,510-foot summit, there is an inspiring view of the island-dotted bay, making the 2-hour climb worth the effort. St. Patrick is said to have spent 40 days and 40 nights in prayer and fasting atop the mountain in 441, and each year Catholics make national pilgrimages to the mountain on the last Sunday in July. The route up the mountain begins near the Murrisk Abbey, which was built in the fourteenth century for the Augustinians and has a notable east window.

Eight miles farther west is Louisburgh, a pleasant fishing village at the mouth of the Bunowen River. There are several good sandy beaches nearby at Old Head, Carramore, Berta, Carrowniskey, and Thallabawn. In addition to several small hotels and guesthouses, there are ten self-catering cottages available through Rent an Irish Cottage Ltd.; for details, write to Shannon Airport House, Shannon International Airport, Co. Clare, Irish Republic; phone: 61580/61588. The local Tourist Information Office (phone: Louisburgh 50) is only open during summer months. A minor road west from Louisburgh leads to Roonah Quay where boats are available for trips to Clare Island.

CLARE ISLAND: Steeped in the legends of the sixteenth-century sea-queen Grace O'Malley, Clare Island guards the entrance to Clew Bay and offers the visitor a sense of peace and remoteness. Grace O'Malley's massive square castle on the east coast of the island above the harbor was converted into a coast guard station over 150 years ago and is not particularly interesting. Tradition says that the ferocious Grace was interred in Clare Abbey, a small fifteenth-century church about a mile and a half southwest of the harbor, but even if this is untrue it is worth seeing for its frescoes. There is only one small hotel on the island, but day-trippers can take advantage of several good beaches for bathing or picnics. There is a colorful regatta held at Clare Island every year in July.

En Route – Back on the mainland, the route south from Louisburgh crosses a desolate moor and climbs past Cregganbaum before descending to the Delphi Valley, which has a series of lakes and is flanked by the Sheeffrey Hills (2,504 feet) on the left. A sharp turn south brings you to the northern shore of Killary Harbour (see the *Connemara* route) and to the handsome waterfall where the Erriff River comes down from the mountain. At Leenane, a sparse fishing village at a bend in the Killary, the road to the right (L101) leads back to Cong through Joyce Country and along the northern banks of Lough Corrib.

Donegal

Donegal seems forever haunted by its history — harking back to the days when it was a proud and independent enclave ruled by its own kings and chieftains. Spiritually remote from the rest of Ireland, the area retains a strong individuality and an awareness of its former glory.

The sense of isolation is emphasized by the towering mountains that hem in the county. They are part of the same earth folds that make up the Scottish Highlands, a fact that may help explain the close affinity that exists between Donegal people and the Scots. All this is not to suggest that the Donegal people are not Irish; they are, but they are Irish in their own way.

There are those who say the Donegal people even look different from everybody else in Ireland and that you can spot them easily. Remarkable hair color — sandy to flaming red — cleanly chiseled features, penetrating blue eyes, and lips curled on the brink of whimsicality are some of the giveaway characteristics. Their speech has been set to music in the Ulster mode, more easily understood in the northern capital of Belfast than in the southern one of Dublin. The skirling lilt of the Scots brogue sometimes creeps in, too, because so many Donegal people have spent so much time in Scotland, forced there not only by hard times but by a kinship that goes back centuries.

The word *Dún na nGall* (Donegal) means "the fort of the foreigners," and is believed to refer to the Vikings who constantly raided Irish coastal areas during the ninth and tenth centuries. They may have established the fort that existed where Donegal Town now stands on the River Eske. There's also convincing evidence that this northwestern region of Ireland was settled long before the Norsemen came. The migrant races of the ancient world made successive incursions into Ireland, and traces of some of them have been found in Donegal including crude Stone Age weapons and tools.

Originally, Donegal was known as *Tirconnaill* (pronounced Cheer KUHN il) or the "Land of Conall." The name comes from Conall Gulban, son of an Irish king known as Niall (Neil) of the Nine Hostages because he always took prisoners when he raided foreign lands. This piratical king endowed his favorite son, Conall, with the wild territory of Donegal, and it was Conall who founded the Kingdom of Tir Connaill in the fifth century. A line of kings reigned until 1071.

The most glorious era in Donegal's history began with the emergence of the O'Donnell dynasty around 1200. The mighty O'Donnells held sway over Tirconnaill for four centuries, wielding powerful influence not only in Donegal but throughout Ireland. At a time when the old Gaelic chiefs were feuding among themselves, the O'Donnells maintained their independence in Tirconnaill by virtue of their superior war skills and with no little help from the "gallowglasses" — mercenary soldiers from the Scottish Isles.

In 1587, one of the clan, young Red Hugh O'Donnell, was kidnapped by an agent of Queen Elizabeth and held hostage in Dublin Castle to extort loyalty to the Queen from his father. When Red Hugh escaped after 5 years, he became the hero of Gaelic Ireland. He and another great chieftain, Hugh O'Neill of Tyrone, combined with a Spanish invading force in a final effort to defeat the armies of Elizabeth. Instead, they were themselves crushed at the disastrous Battle of Kinsale on Christmas Day 1601. This was the final death rattle of the old Irish chiefs. O'Donnell fled to Spain where he died, apparently by poisoning. His brother and successor, Rory O'Donnell, along with O'Neill, sailed in exile from the Donegal port of Rathmullan in 1607, an event known as "the Flight of the Earls." With their departure, all hopes of a revival of Gaelic dominance were quenched forever.

These stirring events of a past age are a vital part of the folk-memory of Donegal and have helped shape the character and personality of its people. The O'Donnells may be gone but their splendid empire of mountain and glen and wild coast is in the good keeping of their descendents. Most of these people live off the land or the sea, and some still make a living weaving the Donegal tweeds that find their way to the fashion salons of the world. There are parts of the county where Irish is spoken as it was in the time of Red Hugh.

Our tour, which starts at the most natural departure point, namely, Donegal Town, covers about 200 miles and could be driven comfortably in 4 days. We'll head northeast from here to make a huge straggling circle, girdling the entire county and returning at the end to Donegal Town. The greater part of the tour is along the sea coast that has some of the most dramatic scenery in Ireland, but it also takes in Donegal's magnificent mountains and valleys and lonesome bogs. The roads are not great at any time and in some stretches would unnerve a stunt driver, so ease off the gas pedal.

The price categories for the hotels listed in this route are expensive, $55 to $75 a night for a double room; moderate, $30 to $45; and inexpensive, $20 to $30. Dinner for two with wine in an expensive restaurant will run $45 and up; in moderate, $30 to $45; and in inexpensive, under $30.

DONEGAL TOWN: This is the town from which the entire county got its name. It is thought that the Vikings built a fort here and on that site the O'Donnell chieftains erected their own stronghold toward the end of the fifteenth century. That castle still stands though not in its original state; it was greatly added to in the seventeenth century by the Brookes, the English ruling family who supplanted the O'Donnells. The castle is now a national monument and open to the public daily. Bridge St. beside the stone bridge that spans the River Eske.

Donegal is a small town with a population of only 1,500 so it is easy to see all in a day. The obvious starting point is the Tourist Information Office on Quay St. (phone: Donegal 148), which is open from May to September and where you can get all the advice and literature you need about the entire northwestern area of Ireland.

On the quay beside the tourist office you'll see mounted on a block a huge anchor from a French ship that was part of an expedition sent by Napoleon in 1798 in an abortive bid to help the Irish in a rising against the British. Local legend says the anchor was cut from the frigate *Romaine* as she fled from Donegal Bay back to France.

Farther along the quay toward the sea are the ruins of a Franciscan friary built by one of the O'Donnells in the fifteenth century and repeatedly plundered after the fall of the clan so that little remains today. Some of the monks of this friary, led by lay brother Michael O'Cleary, compiled the great historical work on Celtic Ireland called *The Annals of the Four Masters.*

A few steps north of the tourist office is the Diamond, the central point of the town. (Diamonds, rather than the commonplace town squares, are distinctive architectural features of many towns in the northern part of Ireland.) The Donegal Diamond was laid out by British colonist Sir Basil Brooke when he took over the town in 1603. There is a red granite obelisk in the Diamond that commemorates the friars who compiled the *Annals.* Here also is one of the most notable stores in Ireland, *Magees,* the home of the handwoven Donegal tweed, which carries the work of weavers from all over the county. A demonstration of hand-weaving is usually in progress at the *Magee* store, and there are morning and afternoon tours of the factory every weekday (phone: Donegal 5).

From Donegal Town take the road northeast toward Letterkenny. Just 7 miles out you'll enter the Barnesmore Gap, which is a passageway through the Blue Stack Mountains and joins the southern and northern parts of the county. In olden days the gap was a lucrative hunting ground for highwaymen and other assorted brigands who preyed on travelers making their way through the mountains. The road also passes through the twin towns of Ballybofey and Stranorlar through which runs the Finn River, excellent for salmon and trout. Just before Letterkenny turn right at the signpost for Ramelton and from that village go on to Rathmullan.

CHECKING IN: *Hyland Central Hotel* – The best hotel in Donegal Town, its staff is friendly, courteous, and efficient. On top of that, it has very good food and comfortable rooms. (The Diamond, Donegal Town; phone: Donegal 27; moderate.) *Kee's Hotel* – A fine, homey hostelry where the cuisine is simple but of a high order. (Main St., Stranorlar, 18 miles north of Donegal Town on the road to Letterkenny; phone: Ballybofey 18; moderate.) *Gallagher's Hotel* – A small, old-fashioned, and very comfortable place to stay; meals include extra large helpings of fresh foodstuffs. (Main St., Letterkenny; phone: 074-22570; moderate.)

EATING OUT: *Biddy's O' Barnes* – A most unusual and quaint pub at the entrance to the Barnesmore Gap, it's an old-style Irish cottage where you sit in the kitchen beside a turf fire to quaff your libation. The women of the house will also serve you homemade brown bread and a mug of tea for nothing — all you have to do is ask. (Barnesmore Gap, 7 miles north of Donegal town on road to Letterkenny; inexpensive.)

RATHMULLAN: There is scarcely a lovelier seaside village than Rathmullan in all of Ireland — certainly, there's no other tiny spot so richly awash in history. It was here in 1587 that the young Red Hugh O'Donnell was kidnapped at the behest of Queen Elizabeth; the youngster was lured aboard a British ship anchored off Rathmullan, chained in the hold, and taken to Dublin where he was held for 5 years before he escaped and made his way back to Tirconnaill to rally his warriors against Elizabeth.

This was also the scene of one of the most tragic events in Irish history: the Flight of the Earls, when the great chieftains O'Donnell and O'Neill, attended by a retinue of followers, boarded a ship to sail in exile to Europe in 1607. They were the last of the Gaelic chiefs and their departure cleared the way for the final phase of the English conquest of Ireland.

History swept up on Rathmullan's shores again in 1798, when the French fleet planning to invade Ireland and aid a native rebellion against the British came to grief in Lough Swilly. Aboard one of the captured French ships was the leading insurrectionist, Wolfe Tone, a revered Irish patriot. Tone died, possibly by his own hand, while in prison awaiting execution.

The bay of Lough Swilly on which Rathmullan is located is one of the deepest sea anchorages in Europe. Although men o' war no longer sail into the long, deep harbor, in summertime hundreds of yachts, speed boats, and motor launches knife through the sheltered waters. There's great fishing offshore and every June fishermen from many lands gather in Rathmullan for the sea-angling festival.

You can walk for miles unhindered along the sandy shore of Lough Swilly, or you could get into your car and go north toward Fanad Head, taking the Knockalla Coast Road. Follow the signposts to Portsalon, 8 miles away. It's a precipitous and thrilling drive, for the road first climbs a coastal cliff towering above the Atlantic and then suddenly dips and sweeps downward to Ballymastocker Bay, a crescent of golden sands. As a spectacle, it's something of a heart-stopper. North of Portsalon, the road turns really mean but it's worth chancing the final 3 miles to Fanad Head just to take in the view from the top of the cliffs there. Then turn south and drive to the village of Tamney and continue down along the eastern fringe of beautiful Mulroy Bay to Kerrykeel and from there to the town of Milford.

CHECKING IN: *Rathmullan House Hotel* – This magnificent, rambling old mansion hidden away amid trees and close to the shores of Lough Swilly is one of the loveliest hotels in Ireland; very good food. (About ½ mile from Rathmullan on the road to Portsalon, watch for sign on gates at right; phone: Rathmullan 4; expensive.) *Fort Royal Hotel* – A delightful country house with its own beach on Lough Swilly, riding stables, tennis courts, and fine food. (About ½ mile from Rathmullan on the Portsalon road, immediately beyond the gates of Rathmullan House, with a sign indicating the narrow road that leads to it; phone: Rathmullan 11; moderate.) *Portsalon Hotel* – Beautifully situated overlooking Ballymastocker Bay, it's a comfortable hotel with good dining and riding stables on the grounds. (A signposted road to the right as you enter Portsalon leads to the hotel; phone: Portsalon 11; expensive.)

EATING OUT: *Moore's Inn* – Flavorsome nineteenth-century pub where the welcome is warm. Good drink and snacks. (Main St., Milford; phone: 074-53123; inexpensive.)

En Route – From Milford town we travel north along the western edge of Mulroy Bay toward Carrigart, 10 miles away. The bay is a narrow, elongated inlet like a Scandinavian fjord, and with trees edging its shore, is a lovely sight. Three miles out from Milford, the road winds by Cratlagh Wood, where in 1878 one of the most hated landlords in Ireland, the third earl of Leitrim, was murdered along with two of his servants. Follow the road up into the Rosguill Peninsula, one of the many Gaeltacht pockets of Donegal where Irish is still a living language, spoken mostly by the old people. When you get to Carrigart, turn left, and then just on the edge of town, turn right at the signpost for Rosapenna. This takes you onto the headland of Rosguill, where another spectacular seascape unfolds along the circular Atlantic Drive (signposted). The drive goes through an ecologically devastated "desert" where not a blade of grass grows and around lovely Dooagh Bay. As you leave the Rosguill headland, turn right on the road to Creeslough.

CHECKING IN: *Carrigart Hotel* – Noted for its conviviality and warm informality, this hotel also serves good food. (Top of the Main St. in Carrigart; phone: Carrigart 6; moderate.) *Rosapenna Golf Hotel* – Its 18-hole golf course is a great attraction; a splendid table. (Signposted right turn on the edge of Carrigart, 1 mile in on the Rosguill headland; phone: Downings 4; expensive.)

DOE CASTLE/CREESLOUGH: About 6 miles farther at Cashel, turn right at the signpost to Doe Castle; it's 1 mile down the side road. Perched on the edge of the sea, Doe Castle is one of the finest fortresses left in Ireland; to explore it, ask for the key in the second house up from the entrance. In the early sixteenth century, Doe Castle was the stronghold of the MacSweeneys, a clan of "gallowglasses" from Scotland who came to Donegal to fight for the O'Donnell chieftains and gained a foothold in the county themselves. Before he was kidnapped, Red Hugh O'Donnell lived here briefly under the fosterage of the MacSweeneys. Survivors of the Spanish Armada who swam from their wrecked ships to the Donegal coast found a haven in this castle.

Get back on the main road, turn right, and drive into Creeslough.

EATING OUT: *Corncutters' Rest* – One of the few pub-cum-fast-food eateries in Donegal that can be relied on for cleanliness and efficiency. Snacks downstairs during the day and an a la carte menu upstairs in the evening. (Main St., Creeslough; phone: Creeslough 67; moderate to inexpensive.)

En Route – Some 3 miles north of Creeslough on the road to Port-na-Blagh and Dunfanaghy, the texture of the landscape changes suddenly and dramatically, the stark, rugged barrenness giving way to a soft, green-wooded peninsula that juts into Sheep Haven Bay. This is the Ards Forest Park, which is open year-round to everybody. It is a relaxing shaded idyll where you can cut yourself off from the outside world amid ancient trees that stand sentinel above the bay. There are walks that wander through the woods and clearings that make perfect picnic places. At the edge of the forest there are white strands running down to the sea, where you can swim on those rare days when the sun brings the water up to a bearable temperature.

Port-na-Blagh and Dunfanaghy are delightfully unspoiled seaside resorts surrounded by beaches. Again, sadly it must be noted that while the whole jagged coast of Donegal is a treasure trove of beaches, they are hardly ever used because the rainy and windy weather discourages all but the most valiant of spirit. Just beyond Dunfanaghy, swing right to take the signposted road to Horn Head for another of those drives around the cliffs above the Atlantic. For Horn Head, you need a strong heart and a steady hand on the steering wheel, because up at the very top, at the brink of the ocean, you can look down those cliffs and get a glimpse of eternity. The massive cathedral cliffs also provide a nesting haven for thousands of seabirds in midsummer; this event attracts bird-watchers from many countries.

Back on the main road again, head southwest to Falcarragh, which is 7 miles away and part of the Gortahork Gaeltacht. Falcarragh has much of a Gaelic flavor because Irish is still widely used and many students come here every summer to study the native tongue. It is worth making a diversion at the crossroads in the village and turning left to travel the side road down to Muckish Mountain, 6 miles away. Muckish must be climbed because it's there, and from its peak 2,000 feet up, you can look down on all of the north of Ireland — a magnificent sight.

DIRECTIONS / Donegal 757

CHECKING IN: *Port-na-Blagh Hotel* – The dining room at this large, modern hotel perched on a cliff looking out over Sheep Haven Bay is particularly good on fish. (On your left as you drive in from Creeslough; phone: 074-36129; moderate.)

TORY ISLAND: Just 9 miles off the coast in the Falcarragh area lies Tory Island about which there are many legends. One dating back to antiquity tells of an ancient race of giants known as the Formorians inhabiting the island. Their chief was the feared "Balor of the Evil Eye," who was said to have supernatural powers and the remains of whose castle still stand on the cliffs at the eastern side of the island. More civilized influences prevailed after the arrival of Christianity, and there are some ruins where Donegal's most famous saint, Columcille, once presided over a settlement of monks.

Today there are only about 250 Tory islanders left and their life-style is much the same as that of their ancestors. They speak an Irish that has undertones of Scots Gaelic because of the age-old connection between Tory and Scotland. The islanders live in small, thatched cottages and cultivate the meager soil on their tiny holdings, raising oats and potatoes in those parts of the island protected from the fierce Atlantic storms. No trees grow on the island at all, but some wild flowers manage to bloom in the stony soil. The menfolk still go to sea on fishing expeditions in frail curraghs — the tarred-canvas-covered boats used for centuries in Ireland.

To relieve this hard and bitter life, there are some rather fascinating compensations. For instance, you'll find no rats whatever on Tory Island. The reason for this — according to the islanders — is that St. Columcille banished rats from Tory and blessed the soil so they daren't return. Even better — and perhaps more pertinent today — the islanders don't have to pay any taxes.

While on the island, try to scale the two *tors* (steep hills) from which it gets its name; the view is splendid. On top of one there's a holy stone upon which, it is said, if you stand and turn around to the right three times you'll be granted any wish that you make.

If you don't want to get marooned on Tory, make sure that no bad weather is in the offing on the day you make your trip. Wild Atlantic storms are frequent and Tory is often cut off from the mainland for 2 or 3 weeks at a time. But the people are extraordinarily kind and hospitable, so that an enforced stay can be a happy experience.

There are a number of ports from which you can sail to Tory, and Falcarragh is as convenient a one as any. Contact James Ferry, phone: Falcarragh 37.

En Route – Returning to the mainland, we get back on the principal road in Falcarragh and head southwest to Gortahork. At this point take the signposted road to Meenaclady that runs along the northern coast toward the promontory known as Bloody Foreland. Again, there are magnificent seascapes all along this stretch. Bloody Foreland is at the extreme northwestern tip of the Gaeltacht region known as Gweedore, and got its name from the blood-red color of the rocks as they are struck by the setting sun. Painters and photographers come to Bloody Foreland in summer hoping to catch one of these remarkable sunsets. The road swings around the headland and then heads south through the seaside resorts of Derrybeg and Bunbeg. The latter is a particularly attractive village, tucked away beneath tall cliffs and has one outstanding curiosity: the smallest harbor in the world. There is also a beautiful and very safe sandy beach here surrounded by sand dunes and crags that invite exploration.

Turn left in Bunbeg and follow the signpost to Gweedore village; that brings you back to the main route. From Gweedore, it's 2 miles east to Dunlewy, and Errigal is immediately north of the village.

CHECKING IN: *McFadden's Hotel* – A venerable and classy family-run hotel where friendliness and personal attention are the winning points. The food can be recommended too. (Main St., Gortahork; phone: 35267; inexpensive.) *The Gweedore Hotel* – Perched dizzyingly on the brink of a cliff way above a golden beach, this is a smart, ultramodern hostelry with all the creature comforts. Good food. (A signpost on Bunbeg's main street points the way to the hotel; phone: Bunbeg 85; moderate.)

MT. ERRIGAL/DUNLEWY: People unskilled in mountain-climbing should not attempt Errigal unless they are accompanied by a local guide. From the summit of this 2,466-foot mountain you can see as far away as the Scottish highlands. While in Dunlewy, you should also take the opportunity to walk south of the village into a strange exotic valley called the "Poisoned Glen." Poisonous weeds known as spurge grow prolifically in the glen and they have contaminated a lake making it unsafe to drink the water. Another peculiarity is that there are no birds in the valley, so that when the weather turns hot in summer all sorts of creeping and flying insects infest the place, making it feel uncomfortably like a rainforest, only without the trees!

Return to the main road to continue on to the Rosses.

THE ROSSES: This area, called "the Rosses," meaning the promontories or headlands of which there are countless numbers hereabouts, has large and lonely stretches of uninhabited bogland. Its very bleakness has an appeal of its own and it draws many tourists every summer.

About 3 miles south of Gweedore is the village of Crolly, which is famous for doll making and exports Crolly Dolls all over the world. You can visit the doll factory and buy a doll at cut rates. If you walk south of Crolly on the Dungloe road, be prepared for a deafening crash as you pass by a giant glacial boulder. This is the "Big Stone of the Leaping Fox" and legend says it will come tumbling down when an honest person passes it — so you've been warned. Instead of taking this road from Crolly to Dungloe, however, turn right at the signposted road to Annagary, which will lead you in a circle around the coast through Kincasslagh, Burtonport, and Dungloe, the real heart of the Rosses.

Turn right at the signpost for Burtonport, one of the busiest fishing ports in Ireland, landing more salmon and lobster than anywhere else. At the height of the fishing season, it is fun to watch the activity on the pier as the trawlers come in from the Atlantic to unload their catches. Also from Burtonport, you can take a boat out to the island of Arranmore, 3 miles offshore. Boats depart frequently from 10:30 AM; for information, call Arranmore 5. If you want to relax and do a bit of fishing you can catch rainbow trout in Lough Shure; contact Philip Boyle, phone: Arranmore 8. If you're fit you can try the 4-mile walk to Rinrawros Point, crossing a small mountain as you go. The point is a lovely spot dominated by a lighthouse.

Although it's considered the capital of the Rosses, Dungloe is an unremarkable town of 900 people. There's some very good trout fishing in the lakes and rivers around the town.

CHECKING IN: *Ostan Na Rosann* – It's a good, modern hotel with an indoor pool; the dining room serves wholesome food in enormous portions. (Just outside the town of Dungloe on the road to Burtonport; phone: Dungloe 91; moderate.)

EATING OUT: *Viking House* – The accent here is on seafood fresh from the Atlantic outside the door. Very popular in summertime so you need to book in advance, preferably the day before. (7 miles from Crolly on the coast road, watch for prominent sign on left-hand side of road once you've passed village of Kincasslagh; phone: Kincasslagh 3; moderate. Note: This is also an inexpensive guesthouse with eight rooms, a fine place to stay — if you can get a reservation.)

En Route – From Dungloe take the road south to Maas, 13 miles away, and turn right to travel into the pretty villages of Narin and Portnoo, both situated high above Gweebarra Bay. You can find real solitude in this area because it has not yet been overrun by tourists, and there are a number of secluded beaches and coves along the coast. When the tide is out, you can walk across the sands from Narin to the island of Iniskeel on which there are the ruins of a sixth-century church.

Travel around the circular road from Portnoo through Rosbeg until you come to a junction and turn right for Ardara, a village that just might well be the loveliest in all of Donegal. Ardara is tucked away in a deep valley where the Owentocker River races over rocks and boulders into Loughros More Bay. It is an area renowned for the weaving of Donegal tweed and there are many shops in the village where real bargains are to be had in tweed goods. For the more adventurous, signposts point the way to the Maghera sea caves where moonshiners used to ply their illicit art in olden days. Exploring these caves is an exciting experience, but first check the tidal schedules or you could be in great danger. Make sure to visit the Church of the Holy Family, which contains a very fine work in stained glass by the artist Evie Hone.

Two miles south of Ardara on the main road, turn right at the signpost for Glencolumbkille and when you reach Crobane 3 miles farther on, take the right fork of the road. This runs through the Glengesh Pass, a thrilling drive as the road climbs 900 feet into the clouds and then plunges dizzily down to the valley below. When the landscape flattens out, you're in Glencolumbkille.

EATING OUT: *Portnoo Hotel* – This fine hotel commanding a majestic view of the sea has a gracious, old-world air about it. The cuisine is admirable, particularly the fish. (On the seafront in Portnoo; phone: Clooney 10; moderate.) *Nesbitt Arms Hotel* – A traditional inn where the comfort of the guests is always in mind. Great food and a good buy. (Main St., Ardara; phone: Ardara 51; inexpensive.)

GLENCOLUMBKILLE: This is the lost valley where the patron saint of Donegal, Columcille (also known as St. Columba), came in retreat from the world. He built a monastic prayer house here in the sixth century and even today there are relics and reminders of his presence scattered around the glen. The whole place has a timelessness about it, as well as a slower tempo. The outside world scarcely intrudes.

On St. Columcille's feast day, June 9, hundreds of people make a 3-mile pilgrims' tour of the glen, stopping to pray at ancient stone crosses along the way. At one of those crosses, beside the Protestant Church, the pilgrims kiss the stone and then peer through an opening in the top in pursuit of a belief that if they are without sin they may be given a glimpse of the next world.

But it isn't only Christian memorabilia and artifacts that are to be found in Glencolumbkille. There's also much evidence of an earlier presence. Something close to 50 monuments traceable to pre-Christian times are scattered throughout the glen, including underground passages and burial places.

Some years back, in order to provide employment and halt emigration from the glen, the local people formed a cooperative to develop home crafts and industries and to attract more tourists. The results have been one of the more encouraging success stories of rural Ireland. One such enterprise was the building of a village of traditional thatched cottages. Visitors can rent these for any length of time at costs that run from inexpensive in off season to moderate during high season. Information about this community, which is not related to the Rent-An-Irish-Cottage scheme, can be obtained from the Glencolumbkille Cooperative Society, Glencolumbkille, Co. Donegal (phone: 5 or 24). If you want to see what life was really like beneath the thatched roofs of Irish cottages in other eras, there's a folk village close by where the past has been reconstructed in fine detail, well worth a visit.

760 DIRECTIONS / Donegal

To complete the tour circuit back to Donegal Town, take the road from Glencolumbkille to Carrick, Kilcar, and Killybegs. From here it's a 17-mile run into the town. Killybegs is of interest because it's Ireland's most important fishing port, and one of the great spectacles is to see the fishing fleet coming home in the evening with thousands of sea gulls shrieking above it.

CHECKING IN: *Glenbay Hotel* – An informal, warm-hearted place with a fine view over the Atlantic. Very good food. (At Malinmore, about 1.5 miles southwest of Glencolumbkille; phone: Glencolumbkille 3; inexpensive.)

INDEX

Index

Abbey Theatre (Dublin, Irish Republic), 483
Abbotsbury, England, 593
Aberdeen, Scotland, 504, 557
Abergavenny, Wales, 665, 666
Aberystwyth, Wales, 669–70
Achill Island, Irish Republic, 750
Adamton Courte (Monkton, near Prestwick, Scotland), 551
Aherne's Pub & Seafood Bar (Youghal, Irish Republic), 531
Airplane travel, 18–27
  on arrival, 26–27
  charter flight(s), 24–26
    bookings, 25–26
    cancellation insurance, 63
    consumer information, 26
  handicapped travelers, 66
  scheduled flights, 18–24
    baggage, 24
    fares, 18–22
    flying with children, 23
    gateways, 18
    getting bumped, 23–24
    meals, 23
    reservations, 22–23
    seating, 23
    seat size, 23
    smoking, 23
Aldeburgh Festival (Aldeburgh, England), 489
Alderney, Channel Islands, England, 586
Alveston Manor Hotel (Stratford-upon-Avon, England), 538
Ambleside, England, 618
American Museum in Britain (Bath, England), 467
Anascaul, Irish Republic, 727
Angel Hotel (Lavenham, England), 525
Anglesey, Isle of, *see* Isle of Anglesey
Annual Bottle Kicking and Hare Pie Scramble (Hallaton, England), 491
Antiques and auctions, 498–510
  England, 499–504
  Irish Republic, 505–9
  Northern Ireland, 509–10
  Scotland, 504–5
  Wales, 505
Antrim Coast, Northern Ireland, tour, 679–89
Antrim (County), Northern Ireland, 509–10, 564
Aran Islands, Irish Republic, 745–46
Arbroath Abbey Pageant (Arbroath, Scotland), 497
Arbutus Lodge (Cork, Irish Republic), 541
Architecture
  Britain, 140–44
  Ireland, 172–74
Arklow, Irish Republic, 695–96
Armagh (County), Northern Ireland, 510, 564
Arran Island, Scotland, 650–51
Art Gallery and Museum (Glasgow, Scotland), 473
Arts, performing, 476–87
  England, 477–82
  Irish Republic, 482–85
  Northern Ireland, 485
  Scotland, 482
  traditional Irish music, 486–87
Arundel, England, 578–79
Arundel Festival (Arundel, England), 489
Arundell Arms Hotel (Lifton, England), 442, 536
Ashford Castle Hotel (Cong, Irish Republic), 540–41
Ashmolean Museum (Oxford, England), 472–73
Assembly House (Norwich, England), 549
Auctions, *see* Antiques and auctions
Automobile insurance, 64
Avebury Stone Circle (Avebury, England), 510–11
Avon River (England), 434
Ayr, Scotland, 504, 635–36

764 INDEX

Badminton Horse Trials (Badminton, England), 421
Bailey of Duke Street (Dublin, Irish Republic), 529
Ballingeary, Irish Republic, 709
Ballinskelligs, Irish Republic, 718
Ballintubber Abbey (Ballintubber, Irish Republic), 517
Ballybunion Golf Club (Ballybunion, Irish Republic), 416
Ballycastle, Northern Ireland, 683
Ballyferriter, Irish Republic, 729-30
Ballylickey House (Ballylickey, Irish Republic), 544
Ballymaloe House (Midleton, Irish Republic), 542-43
Ballynahinch, Irish Republic, 744
Ballyvaughan, Irish Republic, 737
Banquets, historical, 549-52
　England, 550-51
　Irish Republic, 552
　Scotland, 551
　Wales, 551-52
Bantam Tea Rooms (Chipping Campden, England), 548
Bantry, Irish Republic, 709, 710
Barn (Sidmouth, England), 548
Barringtons, see Great Barrington; Little Barrington
Bath, England, 183-93, 613
　antiques and auctions, 499
　essay, 183-84
　hotels, 190-91
　local transportation, 187-88
　museums, 186, 187, 188
　music, 190
　nightclubs and nightlife, 190
　pubs, 193
　restaurants, 191-93
　shopping, 188-89, 553
　sights and activities, 185-87
　sins, 190
　special events, 189
　sports, 189-90
　theater, 190
　tourist information, 187
Bath International Festival of Music (Bath, England), 489
Battle, England, 575, 576
Bayham Abbey, England, 577
Bay Tree (Stamford, England), 548
Beara Peninsula, Ring of Kerry and, Irish Republic, tour, 711-24

Beaumaris, Wales, 676-77
Bed-and-breakfast (B&B), see under Hotel(s)
Beefeater by the Tower of London (London, England), 550
Belfast, Northern Ireland, 194-200
　antiques and auctions, 509
　essay, 194-95
　hotels, 199
　local transportation, 197
　museums, 196, 198
　music, 199
　nightclubs and nightlife, 199
　pubs, 200
　restaurants, 199-200
　shopping, 197
　sights and activities, 195-96
　　city center, 195-96
　　environs, 196
　special events, 197-98
　sports, 198
　theater, 198-99
　tourist information, 197
Belfast Festival at Queen's (Belfast, Northern Ireland), 496-97
Bell Inn (Aston Clinton, England), 533
Betws-y-Coed, Wales, 674, 675
Bibury, England, 606
Biking, 49-51, 445-53
　best areas for, 446-51
　holidays, 452-53
　tour, planning, 451-52
Birmingham, England, 499-500
Birmingham Museum and Art Gallery (Birmingham, England), 467-68
Birmingham Repertory Theatre (Birmingham, England), 477-78
Black Swan (Stratford-upon-Avon, England), 526-27
Blaenau Ffestiniog, Wales, 558
Blake's of the Hollow (Enniskillen, Northern Ireland), 531
Blaskets, Irish Republic, 729
Bodmin Moor, England, 600
Books and magazines, recommended, 110-11
Bournemouth, England, 500
Bourton-on-the-Water, England, 607
Bowness, England, 616-17
Box Tree (Ilkley, England), 535-36
Brazenhead (Dublin, Irish Republic), 529
Brecon, Wales, 666, 667

Brighton, England, 201–11, 578
  antiques and auctions, 500
  essay, 201–3
  hotels, 209–10
  local transportation, 206
  museums, 203–4, 205, 206
  music, 208
  nightclubs and nightlife, 208
  pubs, 211
  restaurants, 210–11
  shopping, 207, 553
  sights and activities, 203–6
    central city, 203–5
    environs, 205
  sins, 209
  special events, 207
  sports, 207–8
  theater, 208
  tourist information, 206
Brighton Festival (Brighton, England), 489
Brighton Museum and Art Gallery (Brighton, England), 468
Bristol, England, 212–22
  essay, 212–14
  hotels, 220–21
  local transportation, 217
  museums, 214–15, 216, 217–18
  music, 219
  nightclubs and nightlife, 220
  pubs, 222
  restaurants, 221–22
  shopping, 218
  sights and activities, 214–16
    central city, 214–15
    Clifton, 216
    docks, 215–16
    environs, 216
  special events, 218
  sports, 219
  theater, 219
  tourist information, 217
Britain, 115–55
  architecture, 140–44
  food and drink, 149–55
  history, 115–31
  literature, 131–39
  music and dance, 144–49
  See also England; Northern Ireland; Scotland; Wales
British Museum (London, England), 468–69
Broadway, England, 500, 610

Bungay, England, 553
Bunratty Castle (Bunratty, Irish Republic), 552
Burford, England, 606–7
Bus, touring by, 39–41
  handicapped travelers, 66
  passes, 40–41
Business hours, 96
Buxton Festival (Buxton, England), 489

Cactus Nursery (Rosudgeon, Penzance, England), 549
Cadbury Castle (South Cadbury, England), 514
Caernarvon (castle) (Gwynedd, Wales), 516
Caernarvon, Wales, 675–76
Cahernane Hotel (Killarney, Irish Republic), 544
Cahirciveen, Irish Republic, 717
Callander, Scotland, 641
Cambridge, England, 223–35
  antiques and auctions, 500
  essay, 223–24
  hotels, 233–34
  local transportation, 230
  museums, 228, 229, 230
  music, 232
  nightclubs and nightlife, 233
  pubs, 235
  restaurants, 234–35
  shopping, 231, 553–54
  sights and activities, 225–29
    colleges, 225–28
    other sights, 228–29
  sins, 233
  special events, 231–32
  sports, 232
  theater, 232
  tourist information, 229–30
Cambusnethan Priory (Wishaw, Scotland), 551
Camden Festival (London, England), 497
Camera and equipment, 104–6
Camping, 47–49
Canals, Britain's, 434
Canterbury, England, 236–43, 571
  essay, 236–37
  hotels, 242
  local transportation, 241
  museums, 239, 241
  nightclubs and nightlife, 242
  pubs, 243

Canterbury, England (*cont.*)
  restaurants, 243
  shopping, 241
  sights and activities, 237–40
    Canterbury Cathedral, 238–39
    environs, 240
    within old city walls, 239–40
    outside perimeter, 240
  sins, 242
  sports, 241–42
  theater, 242
  tourist information, 240–41
Car, driving own, 32–34
  gasoline, 33–34
  handicapped travelers, 66
  insurance, 64
Caravans, 47–49
  horse-drawn, 49, 427
Cardiff, Wales, 244–52
  antiques and auctions, 505
  essay, 244–45
  hotels, 250–51
  local transportation, 248–49
  museums, 246, 247, 248, 249
  music, 250
  nightclubs and nightlife, 250
  pubs, 252
  restaurants, 251–52
  shopping, 249, 558
  sights and activities, 246–48
    city center, 246–47
    environs, 247
  sins, 250
  special events, 249
  sports, 249–50
  theater, 250
  tourist information, 248
Carmarthen, Wales, 667–68
Carna, Irish Republic, 745
Carnoustie Golf Links (Carnoustie, Scotland), 415
Carraroe, Irish Republic, 745
Car rentals, 31–32
  fly/drive, 31
  handicapped travelers, 66
  local, 32
  from US, 31–32
Carrickfergus, Northern Ireland, 680–81
Carrickfergus Castle (Co. Antrim, Northern Ireland), 521
Cashel, Irish Republic, 706–7
  See also Rock of Cashel
Castlebar, Irish Republic, 749

Castlegregory, Irish Republic, 731
Castle Hotel (Taunton, England), 543–44
Castle hotels, *see under* Hotel(s)
Castleton (near Buxton, England), 554
Castletownbere, Irish Republic, 723
Cavan (County), Irish Republic, 560
Cecil Higgins Art Gallery (Bedford, England), 467
Channel Islands, England, tour, 554, 581–87
  Alderney, 586
  Guernsey, 584–86
  Herm, 587
  Jersey, 582–84
  Jethou, 587
  Sark, 586
Charles Bingham Fishing, Ltd. (Coryton, near Okehampton, England), 442
Cheddar Caves, England, 603–4
Chedworth, England, 606
Cheltenham, England, 554, 611–12
Cheltenham International Festival of Music (Cheltenham, England), 490
Cheltenham Spa, England, 500
Chester, England, 253–62
  antiques and auctions, 500
  essay, 253–54
  hotels, 259–60
  local transportation, 257
  museums, 257–58
  music, 259
  nightclubs and nightlife, 259
  pubs, 262
  restaurants, 260–61
  shopping, 258, 554
  sights and activities, 255–57
  sins, 259
  special events, 258
  sports, 258–59
  theater, 259
  tourist information, 257
Chester Beatty Library (Dublin, Irish Republic), 474
Chewton Glen Hotel (New Milton, England), 536–37
Chichester, England, 579–80
Chichester Festival Theatre (Chichester, England), 490
Children, hints for traveling with, 67–70
  accommodations and meals, 69
  on airplanes, 23

getting there and getting around, 69
packing, 68
planning, 68–69
what to see and do, 69–70
Chipping Campden, England, 609
Cirencester, England, 612
Citizens' Theatre (Glasgow, Scotland), 482
City of London Festival (London, England), 491
Clare, Irish Republic, tour, 731–38
Clare (County), Irish Republic, 506, 560
Clare Island, Irish Republic, 751–52
Cleveland Way (from Helmsley to Filey, England), 461
Clifden, Irish Republic, 743–44
Clifton, England, 216
Climate, 12–13
and clothes, 59–60
Clonmel, Irish Republic, 705–6
Close (Tetbury, England), 544
Clovelly, England, 601
Cobh, Irish Republic, 701–2
Cockermouth, England, 622
Coffee Pot (Paignton, England), 549
Coffee Shop (Yarm, England), 549
Coldstream, Scotland, 627
Coleraine, Northern Ireland, 685
Coliseum (London, England), 478
Combe House (Gittisham, England), 535
Cong, Irish Republic, 747–49
Coniston, England, 617–18
Connemara, Irish Republic, tour, 459–60, 738–46
Connemara Pony Show (Clifden, Irish Republic), 422–23
Connemara Trail, Irish Republic, 426
Connor Pass, Irish Republic, 731
Consular services, 77–78
Conwy Castle (Conwy, Wales), 516–17
Cork, West, Irish Republic, tour, 459, 707–11
Cork (city), Irish Republic, 263–71
antiques and auctions, 506
essay, 263–64
hotels, 270–71
local transportation, 268
museums, 265, 268
music, 270
nightclubs and nightlife, 270
pubs, 271
restaurants, 271
shopping, 268–69

sights and activities, 264–67
flat of the city, 265–66
north bank, 266
south bank, 267
sins, 270
special events, 269
sports, 269
theater, 269
tourist information, 268
Cork (County), Irish Republic, 506–7, 560–61
Cork Film Festival (Cork, Irish Republic), 493–94
Cork International Choral and Folk Dance Festival (Cork, Irish Republic), 497
Cornwall coast, North, England, 600–601
Costs, calculating, 53–56
accommodations, 54–55
food, 55
local taxes, 55–56
service charges, 56
transportation, 54
Cotswolds, England, tour, 447, 604–13
Cotswold Way (from Chipping Campden to Bath, England), 461
Cottage Teashop (Tintagel, England), 549
Cottage in the Wood (Malvern Wells, Malvern, England), 536
County Sligo Golf Club (Rosses Point, Irish Republic), 416
Courtauld Institute Galleries (London, England), 469
Credit cards, 80–81
Creeslough, Irish Republic, 756, 757
Crocnaraw Country House (Moyard, Irish Republic), 544
Crown Saloon (Belfast, Northern Ireland), 531
Cruises, waterways and coastal, 429–35
Culloden Hotel (Craigavad, Holywood, Northern Ireland), 544
Culloden House (Inverness, Scotland), 544
Culzean Castle, Scotland, 635
Cushendall, Northern Ireland, 682–83
Cushendun, Northern Ireland, 682–83
Customs and returning to US, 98–100
Cycling, *see* Biking

Dales Way (from Ilkley to Bowness-on-Windermere, England), 461

768 INDEX

Dance, *see* Music and dance, traditional
Dartington, England, 554
Dartmoor, England, 594-95
Dartmouth, England, 595-96
Datchet, England, 500
Davy Byrne's of Duke Street (Dublin, Irish Republic), 529
Deal, England, 572
Denbigh, Wales, 677, 678
Derby, England, 554
Derby Stakes (Epsom, England), 421-22
Derry, *see* Londonderry
Devil's Bridge, Wales, 670
Devon coast, North, England, 601-2
Dinas Mawddwy, Wales, 671
Dingle, Irish Republic, 727-28
Dingle Peninsula, Irish Republic, tour, 724-31
Dingle Peninsula Trail, Irish Republic, 427
Dirleton, Scotland, 626
Dirty Dicks (London, England), 525
Documents, entry requirements and, 56-57
Doe Castle (Creeslough, Irish Republic), 756
Doheny & Nesbitt's (Dublin, Irish Republic), 529-30
Dolgellau, Wales, 671-72, 673
Donegal (County), Irish Republic, 507, 561
Donegal, Irish Republic, tour, 752-60
Donegal Town, Irish Republic, 753-54
Dorchester, England, 593
Doune, Scotland, 641
Dover, England, 573
Down (County), Northern Ireland, 510, 564
Downhill, Northern Ireland, 685-86
Doyle's Seafood Bar (Dingle, Irish Republic), 541
Drinking, 97-98
Dromoland Castle (Newmarket-on-Fergus, Irish Republic), 543
Drugs, 98
Druid Lane Theatre (Galway, Irish Republic), 485
Drumnadrochit, Scotland, 645
Dublin (city), Irish Republic, 272-87, 450-51
  antiques and auctions, 507-8
  essay, 272-74
  hotels, 283-84
  local transportation, 280
  museums, 275, 277, 280
  music, 282
  nightclubs and nightlife, 282-83
  pubs, 286-87
  restaurants, 284-86
  shopping, 280-81
  sights and activities, 274-79
    north downtown, 274-79
    south downtown, 275-77
    suburbs, 278
  sins, 283
  special events, 281
  sports, 281-82
  theater, 282
  tourist information, 279
  wine bars, 287
Dublin (County), Irish Republic, 507-8, 561
Dublin Horse Show (Dublin, Irish Republic), 423
Dublin to New Ross, Southeast Ireland, tour, 690-98
Dublin Theatre Festival (Dublin, Irish Republic), 494
Duck Inn (Pett Bottom, England), 537
Dulwich Picture Gallery (Dulwich, London, England), 469
Dumfries, Scotland, 632-33
Dunbar, Scotland, 627
Dunbeg, Irish Republic, 728-29
Dun Laoghaire, Irish Republic, 691-93
Dun Laoghaire Summer Festival (Dun Laoghaire, Irish Republic), 494
Dunlewy, Irish Republic, 758
Dunnose Cottage (Luccombe, Isle of Wight, England), 548
Durty Nellie's (Bunratty, Irish Republic), 528

Eagle (Cambridge, England), 524-25
East Anglia, England, 447
Eastwell Manor (Ashford, England), 532-33
Edinburgh, Scotland, 288-98
  antiques and auctions, 504-5
  essay, 288-90
  hotels, 296-97
  local transportation, 294
  museums, 292, 294
  music, 296
  nightclubs and nightlife, 296
  pubs, 298

restaurants, 297–98
shopping, 295, 557
sights and activities, 290–93
  beyond Royal Mile, 292–98
  Royal Mile, 290–92
special events, 295
sports, 295
theater, 295
tourist information, 294
Edinburgh Festival (Edinburgh, Scotland), 492
Edinburgh Folk Festival (Edinburgh, Scotland), 497
Edith's Café (Marlborough, England), 548
Electricity, 97
Elgin, Scotland, 557
Elms Hotel (Abberley, England), 532
El Vino (London, England), 525
England, 9–10, 447–49
England, Lake District, tour, 448, 613–23
England, Southeast, tour, 448, 567–81
England, Southwest, tour, 448–49, 587–604
Ennis, Irish Republic, 733
Enniskerry, Irish Republic, 693
Entry requirements and documents, 56–57
Erne Waterway, Northern Ireland, 435
Exeter, England, 500, 594
Exmoor Forest, England, 602

Fahan, Irish Republic, 728–29
Fair Head, Northern Ireland, 683
Farmhouses, *see under* Hotel(s)
Faversham, England, 570
Fermanagh (County), Northern Ireland, 510, 564
Festivals, 487–97
  England, 489–92, 497
  Irish Republic, 493–96, 497
  Northern Ireland, 496–97
  Scotland, 492–93, 497
  Wales, 493, 497
Fishguard Music Festival (Fishguard, Wales), 493
Fishing, 435–45
  coarse, 439–40
  game, 437–39
    hotels, 443–45
  schools, 442–43
  sea angling, 440–42

Fitzwilliam Museum (Cambridge, England), 468
Flight insurance, 63–64
Focus Theatre (Dublin, Irish Republic), 483
Food and drink
  Britain, 149–55
  Ireland, 177–79
Foreign exchange, 81–82
Fort Augustus, Scotland, 644–45
Fort William, Scotland, 643–44

Gaiety Theatre (Dublin, Irish Republic), 483–84
Galashiels, Scotland, 557
Gallarus Oratory, Irish Republic, 730
Galloway Forest Park, Scotland, 635
Galway (city), Irish Republic, 299–306
  antiques and auctions, 508
  essay, 299–300
  hotels, 305
  local transportation, 303
  museums, 303
  music, 304
  nightclubs and nightlife, 304
  pubs, 306
  restaurants, 305–6
  shopping, 303
  sights and activities, 300–302
  sins, 304
  special events, 303
  sports, 303–4
  theater, 304
  tourist information, 302–3
Galway (County), Irish Republic, 508, 561–62
Galway Oyster Festival (Galway, Irish Republic), 494
Ganton Golf Club (Ganton, England), 414
Garden House Hotel (Cambridge, England), 543
Gate Theatre (Dublin, Irish Republic), 484
Gateway Cakeshop (Evesham, England), 547
Genealogy hunts, 106–10
  England and Wales, 106–8
  Republic and Northern Ireland, 108–9
  Scotland, 108
  special problems, 109–10

George Hotel (Chollerford, England), 534
George of Stamford (Stamford, England), 538
Giant's Causeway, Northern Ireland, 684
Glasgow, Scotland, 307–19
  antiques and auctions, 505
  essay, 307–9
  hotels, 317–18
  local transportation, 313
  museums, 310, 312, 313–14
  music, 316
  nightclubs and nightlife, 316
  pubs, 319
  restaurants, 318–19
  shopping, 314–15
  sights and activities, 309–12
    by Clydeside, 312
    Medieval Glasgow, 310–11
    Modern Glasgow, 311–12
    Old Merchants' City, 311
    Victorian Glasgow, 310
  sins, 316
  special events, 315
  sports, 315
  theater, 315–16
  tourist information, 313
Glastonbury, England, 603
Glastonbury Abbey (Glastonbury, England), 511–12
Glenbeigh, Irish Republic, 716–17
Glencoe, Scotland, 642–43
Glencolumbkille, Irish Republic, 759–60
Glendalough, Irish Republic, 518–19, 694
Gleneagles Hotel (Auchterarder, Scotland), 539
Gleneagles Hotel Golf Course (Auchterarder, Scotland), 414–15
Glenelg Brochs (Glenelg, Scotland), 515
Glengarriff, Irish Republic, 722–23
Globe Inn (Dumfries, Scotland), 527
Glyndebourne Festival Opera (Glyndebourne, England), 490
Golf courses, 413–17
Gorey Arts Festival (Gorey, Irish Republic), 494–95
Gougane Barra, Irish Republic, 709
Grand National (Aintree, near Liverpool, England), 420–21
Grand Opera House (Belfast, Northern Ireland), 485
Grasmere, England, 619–20

Gravetye Manor (near East Grinstead, England), 534–35
Great Barrington, England, 607
Greenwich Festival (London, England), 491
Greyhound Inn (Folkingham, England), 548
Grianán of Aileach (Burt, Irish Republic), 519
Groes Hotel (Ty'n-y-Groes, near Conwy, Wales), 528
Guernsey, Channel Islands, England, 584–86
Guesthouses, *see under* Hotel(s)
Gullane, Scotland, 626

Hadrian's Wall (near Newcastle-upon-Tyne, England), 513–14
Hambro Life Jumping Derby International (Hickstead, England), 422
Handicapped travelers, hints for, 64–67
  on airplanes, 66
  by car, bus, or train, 66–67
  planning, 66
  by ship, 66
  tours, 67
Harris Island, Scotland, 653–55
Harrogate International Festival (Harrogate, England), 491
Hastings, England, 575–76
Hawick, Scotland, 557, 629–30
Hawkhurst, England, 577
Hawkshead, England, 617
Haxey Hood Game (Haxey, England), 490
Hay-on-Wye, Wales, 505, 558
Healy Pass, Irish Republic, 723
Henchy's (Cork, Irish Republic), 528–29
Henley-on-Thames, England, 500
Herm, Channel Islands, England, 587
Herne Bay, England, 570–71
Herstmonceux, England, 554–55
Highlands, Scotland, *see* **Scottish Highlands, tour**
Hiking, 51–52, 455–65
  group trips, 465
  locations, 456–60
  long-distance footpaths, 460–64
  maps and more information, 464–65
History
  Britain, 115–31
  Ireland, 156–64

INDEX 771

Hobby Horse Celebrations (Padstow, England), 492
Hole in the Wall (Tunbridge Wells, England), 527
Honourable Company of Edinburgh Golfers (Gullane, Scotland), 415
Horse(s), 419–29
-drawn caravans, 49, 427
and hunting, 427–29
meets, shows, and races, 419–23
post trekking, 426–27
riding holidays and pony trekking, 423–26
Horse with the Red Umbrella (Dorchester, England), 548
Horse of the Year Show (Wembley, near London, England), 422
Hotel(s), 82–89
B&Bs (bed-and-breakfast), 84
castle, 84
costs, 54–55
farmhouses, 84–85
flats, homes, and cottages, 85–86
game fishing, 443–45
guesthouses and inns, 82–84
home exchanges, 85
home stays, 86–87
reservations, 87–89
rural retreats, 532–44
England, 532–39, 543–44
Irish Republic, 540–43, 544
Northern Ireland, 544
Scotland, 539, 544
Wales, 539–40, 544
See also hotels *entry under names of individual cities*
Hunting, 427–29, 453–55
England, 428, 454
Irish Republic, 428–29, 455
Northern Ireland, 429, 454–55
Scotland, 454
Wales, 454
Hythe, England, 573–74

Inch, Irish Republic, 727
Inns, *see under* Hotel(s)
Insurance, 62–64
automobile, 64
baggage and personal effects, 62–63
charter flight cancellation, 63
combination policies, 64
flight, 63–64
personal accident and sickness, 63
warning about, 63
International Musical Eisteddfod (Llangollen, Wales), 493
Inverlochy Castle (near Fort William, Scotland), 539
Inverness, Scotland, 645–47
Ireland, 11, 156, 450–51
architecture, 172–74
food and drink, 177–79
history, 156–64
literature, 164–72
music and dance, traditional, 174–76, 486–87
Ireland, Southcentral, tour, 698–707
Ireland, Southeast (Dublin to New Ross), tour, 690–98
Irish Agricultural Museum (Wexford, Irish Republic), 475–76
Irish Ballet Company (Cork, Irish Republic), 482–83
Irish Grand National (Ratoath, Irish Republic), 423
Irish Sweeps Derby (Kildare, Irish Republic), 423
Island Hotel (Tresco, Isles of Scilly, England), 544
Isle of Anglesey, Wales, 558, 676
Isle of Wight, England, 590
Isles of Scilly, England, 599
Iveagh Bequest (London, England), 469–70

Jedburgh, Scotland, 629
Jersey, Channel Islands, England, 582–84
Jethou, Channel Islands, England, 587

Keepers Restaurant (Haworth, England), 547
Kelso, Scotland, 628, 629
Kendal, England, 555, 615–16
Kenmare, Irish Republic, 721–22
Kerry (County), Irish Republic, 459, 508, 562
Kerry, Ring of, and Beara Peninsula, Irish Republic, tour, 711–24
Keswick, England, 620–21
Kilburn, England, 555
Kildare (County), Irish Republic, 508, 562
Kilkee, Irish Republic, 734

Kilkenny Arts Week (Kilkenny, Irish Republic), 495
Kilkenny (city), Irish Republic, 320–27
  essay, 320–22
  hotels, 326
  local transportation, 324
  museums, 322, 323, 324
  music, 326
  nightclubs and nightlife, 326
  pubs, 327
  restaurants, 327
  shopping, 325
  sights and activities, 322–24
  sins, 326
  special events, 325
  sports, 325
  theater, 325
  tourist information, 324
Kilkenny (County), Irish Republic, 508–9, 562
Killarney, Irish Republic, 712–15
Killarney Golf and Fishing Club (Killarney, Irish Republic), 416
Killorglin, Irish Republic, 716
Kilmalkedar, Irish Republic, 730
Kilrush, Irish Republic, 733
King's Head Hotel (Richmond, England), 538
King's Lynn Festival (King's Lynn, England), 492
Kinsale, Irish Republic, 710–11
Kirkcudbright, Scotland, 634
Knappogue Castle (Quin, Irish Republic), 552

Lahinch, Irish Republic, 735
Lahinch Golf Club (Lahinch, Irish Republic), 416
Lake District, England, tour, 448, 613–23
Lake District National Park (Cumbria, England), 457–58
Lampeter, Wales, 668
Laois (County), Irish Republic, 562
Larne, Northern Ireland, 681–82
Lauragh, Irish Republic, 723–24
Leenane, Irish Republic, 741
Legal aid, 77
Leitrim (County), Irish Republic, 562
Letterfrack, Irish Republic, 742
Lewis Island, Scotland, 655–56
Limavady, Northern Ireland, 686
Limerick City, Irish Republic, 328–34
  essay, 328–29
  hotels, 333
  local transportation, 331–32
  museums, 332
  nightclubs and nightlife, 332–33
  pubs, 334
  restaurants, 333–34
  shopping, 332
  sights and activities, 329–31
    city center, 329–30
    environs, 330–31
  sins, 333
  special events, 332
  sports, 332
  tourist information, 331
Limerick (County), Irish Republic, 509, 562
Limerick Junction (Tipperary Town, Irish Republic), 423
Liscannor, Irish Republic, 735
Lisdoonvarna, Irish Republic, 736
Lisdoonvarna Music Festival (Lisdoonvarna, Irish Republic), 495
Liss Ard House (Skibbereen, Irish Republic), 544
Listowel Writers' Week (Listowel, Irish Republic), 495–96
Literature
  Britain, 131–39
  Ireland, 164–72
Little Barrington, England, 607
Lizard, England, 598–99
Llandeilo, Wales, 667
Llanidloes, Wales, 670
Llanwrtyd, Wales, 558
Lochearnhead, Scotland, 642
Loch Lomond, Scotland, 557
London, England, 335–61
  antiques and auctions, 500–503
  biking, 447
  essay, 335–38
  hotels, 353–57
  local transportation, 345–46
  museums, 339, 340, 341, 342, 343, 344, 347
  music, 351–52
  nightclubs and nightlife, 352
  pubs, 360–61
  restaurants, 357–60
  shopping, 347–50, 555–56
  sights and activities, 338–45
    city, 342–43

other attractions, 343-44
Westminster, 339-42
sins, 353
special events, 347
sports, 350
theater, 351
tourist information, 345
wine bars, 361
London-to-Brighton Veteran Car Run (London, England), 491
London Countryway (around London, England), 461
Londonderry (city, also called Derry), Northern Ireland, 686-89
Londonderry (County, also called Derry), Northern Ireland, 510, 564
Londonderry Arms (Carnlough, Northern Ireland), 544
Longford (County), Irish Republic, 562
Longueville House and President's Restaurant (Mallow, Irish Republic), 542
Lord Mayor's Procession (London, England), 491
Louth (County), Irish Republic, 509, 562-63
Lowlands, Scotland, *see* **Scottish Lowlands, tour**
Lygon Arms (Broadway, England), 534
Lyme Regis, England, 593-94

Macroom, Irish Republic, 708
Maes Howe, *see* Skara Brae and Maes Howe
Magazines and books, recommended, 110-11
Mail, 96
Malmesbury, England, 612-13
Malvern Festival (Malvern, England), 491
Manchester, England, 503
Mawney's Kitchen (Woodstock, England), 549
Mayflower (London, England), 525-26
Mayo (County), Irish Republic, 509, 563
Mayo, Southern, Irish Republic, tour, 746-52
Medical aid, 75-77
Melrose Abbey (Melrose, Scotland), 515
Miller Howe (Windermere, England), 538-39
Miltown Malbay, Irish Republic, 734-35

Minehead, England, 554
Miner's Inn (Acomb, England), 524
Mirabeau, Restaurant (Sandycove, Irish Republic), 543
Mitchelstown, Irish Republic, 700
Moffat, Scotland, 631-32
Moher, Cliffs of, Irish Republic, 735
Monaghan County Museum (Monaghan, Irish Republic), 475
Money, 81-82
Monmouth, Wales, 664-65
Monuments and ruins, ancient, 510-21
England, 510-15
Irish Republic, 517-21
Northern Ireland, 521
Scotland, 515-16
Wales, 516-17
Moran's Oyster Cottage (The Weir, Kilcolgan, Irish Republic), 530
Moreton-in-Marsh, England, 609
Mt. Errigal, Irish Republic, 758
Mourne Mountains (Co. Down, Northern Ireland), 460
Muckross House Folk Museum (Muckross, Killarney, Irish Republic), 475
Mulligan's of Poolbeg Street (Dublin, Irish Republic), 530
Museum of Mankind (London, England), 470
Museums, 466-76
England, 467-73
Irish Republic, 474-76
Northern Ireland, 476
Scotland, 473
Wales, 473-74
See also museums *entry under names of individual cities*
Music and dance, traditional
Britain, 144-49
Irish Republic, 174-76, 486-87
See also music *entry under names of individual cities*

National Folk Theatre of Ireland, Siamsa Tíre (Tralee, Irish Republic), 485
National Gallery (London, England), 470
National Gallery of Scotland (Edinburgh, Scotland), 473
National Maritime Museum (Greenwich, London, England), 470-71
National Museum (Dublin, Irish Republic), 474

National Museum of Wales (Cardiff, Wales), 473–74
National parks, 457–59
National Pilgrimage to Croagh Patrick (Westport, Irish Republic), 496
National Portrait Gallery (London, England), 471
National Theatre (London, England), 478–79
Natural History Museum (Dublin, Irish Republic), 474–75
Near Sawrey, England, 617
Neary's of Chatham Street (Dublin, Irish Republic), 530
Newgrange (Newgrange, Irish Republic), 520–21
Newport, Wales, 505
New Ross, Dublin to, Southeast Ireland, tour, 690–98
Nightclubs and nightlife, *see* nightclubs and nightlife *entry under names of individual cities*
Norfolk Broads, England, 433
North Berwick, Scotland, 626–27
North Downs Way (from Farnham to Dover, England), 461–62
Northern Ireland, 11, 451
  See also **Antrim Coast, Northern Ireland, tour**
Northleach, England, 605
North Sea to the Atlantic, Scotland, 427
Northumberland, England, 426
Northumberland National Park (Northumberland, England), 458
North Wales Music Festival (St. Asaph, Wales), 497
North York Moors, England, 447–48
North York Moors National Park (Yorkshire, England), 458
Nutgrove (Annadorn, Northern Ireland), 544

Offaly (County), Irish Republic, 509
Offa's Dyke Path (from near Chepstow to Prestatyn, Wales), 463
Old Bakery (Woolpit, Bury St. Edmonds, England), 549
Older travelers, hints for, 73–74
  discounts, 72
  planning, 73–74
Old Fire Engine House (Ely, England), 546–47

Old Inn (Crawfordsburn, Northern Ireland), 544
Old Lace Shop (Beer, England), 548
Old Original Bakewell Pudding Shop (Bakewell, England), 548
Olympia Theatre (Dublin, Irish Republic), 484
Open Air Theatre (Regent's Park, London, England), 479
Opera houses, 480, 485
Original Maids of Honour Shop (Kew Gardens, England), 547–48
Orkney Islands, Scotland, 656–59
Osprey Fishing School (Aviemore, Scotland), 442
Oughterard, Irish Republic, 740
Outer Hebrides, Western Isles, Scotland, 557
Owain Glyndwr Hotel (Corwen, Wales), 528
Oxford, England, 362–71, 605
  essay, 362–64
  hotels, 369–70
  local transportation, 368
  museums, 366–67, 368
  music, 369
  nightclubs and nightlife, 369
  pubs, 371
  restaurants, 370–71
  shopping, 368, 556
  sights and activities, 364–67
    heart of Oxford, 364–67
    offbeat Oxford, 367
  sins, 369
  special events, 368
  sports, 369
  theater, 369
  tourist information, 367
Oyster Tavern (Cork, Irish Republic), 529

Package tours, 41–47
  European, booked in Britain, 45–47
  for handicapped travelers, 67
  sample, to Great Britain and Ireland, 43–45
Packing hints, 59–60
Paddy Burke's (Clarenbridge, Irish Republic), 540
Padstow, England, 599–600
Parks, national, 457–59
Passports, 56–57
  lost abroad, 57

INDEX 775

Peak District, England, 448
Peebles Angling School (Peebles, Scotland), 442–43
Pembrokeshire Coast Path (from St. Dogmaels to Amroth, Wales), 463
Pennine Way (from Edale, England, to Kirk Yetholm, Scotland), 462
Penrith, England, 623
Penzance, England, 504
Perth, Scotland, 557
Pike and Eel (Needingworth, England), 526
Pitlochry Festival (Pitlochry, Scotland), 497
Planning a trip, 57–59
Plas Glansevin (Llangadock, Wales), 539–40, 551
Plough and Sail (Paglesham, England), 526
Plymouth, England, 596
Portmarnock Golf Club (Portmarnock, Irish Republic), 416
Portmeirion, Wales, 673
Portmeirion Hotel (Portmeirion, Wales), 540
Portrush, Northern Ireland, 685
Prestwick Golf Club (Prestwick, Scotland), 415
Priory Hotel (Bath, England), 543
Pub crawling, 522–31
  England, 524–27
  Irish Republic, 528–31
  Northern Ireland, 531
  Scotland, 527–28
  Wales, 528
  See also pubs *entry under names of individual cities*

Queen's Gallery (London, England), 471

Rathlin Island, Northern Ireland, 683–84
Rathmullan, Irish Republic, 754–55
Rathmullan House (Rathmullan, Irish Republic), 544
Reading, England, 504
Renvyle, Irish Republic, 741–42
Restaurant costs, 55
  See also restaurants *entry under names of individual cities*
Retreats, rural, *see under* Hotel(s)

Ridgeway (from Overton Hill, near Avebury, to Ivinghoe Beacon, England), 462
Rivers
  England, 433–34
  Irish Republic, 434–35
  Northern Ireland, 435
Rob Roy Country, Scotland, 427
Rochester, England, 568–69
Rock of Cashel (Cashel, Irish Republic), 517–18
Roscommon (County), Irish Republic, 563
Rose and Crown (Tewin, England), 527
Rose of Torridge Café (Bideford, England), 548
Rose of Tralee International Festival (Tralee, Irish Republic), 496
Rosmuc, Irish Republic, 745
Rosses, Irish Republic, 758
Round House (London, England), 579
Roundstone, Irish Republic, 744
Royal Albert Hall (London, England), 479
Royal and Ancient Golf Club (St. Andrews, Scotland), 414
Royal Ascot (Ascot, England), 421
Royal Birkdale Golf Club (Southport, England), 414
Royal County Down Golf Club (Newcastle, Northern Ireland), 417
Royal Court Theatre (London, England), 479
Royal Dornoch (Dornoch, Scotland), 415
Royal Dublin Golf Club (Dollymount, Irish Republic), 416
Royal Dublin Society Concert Hall (Dublin, Irish Republic), 484–85
Royal Exchange Theatre (Manchester, England), 481
Royal Festival Hall (London, England), 479–80
Royal International Horse Show (Wembley, England), 422
Royal Liverpool Golf Club (Hoylake, England), 414
Royal Lytham & St. Annes (Lytham St. Annes, England), 414
Royal National Eisteddfod (varying sites in Wales), 493
Royal Oak (King's Bromley, England), 525
Royal Oak (Winsford, England), 527

776 INDEX

Royal Opera House (Covent Garden, London, England), 480
Royal Porthcawl Golf Club (Porthcawl, Wales), 416
Royal Portrush Golf Club (Portrush, Northern Ireland), 417
Royal St. George's Golf Club (Sandwich, England), 414
Royal Shakespeare Theatre (Stratford-upon-Avon, England), 482
Royal Troon Golf Club (Troon, Scotland), 415
Royal Tunbridge Wells, England, 577–78
Ruins, *see* Monuments and ruins, ancient
Rural retreats, *see under* Hotel(s)
Ruthin Castle (Ruthin, Wales), 544, 551–52
Rydal, England, 618–19
Rye, England, 574–75

Sadler's Wells Theatre (London, England), 480
Sailing, 430–32
 charters, 430
 events, 432
 schools, 430–32
St. Andrews, Scotland, 557
St. David's Cathedral Bach Festival (St. David's, Wales), 497
St. Leonards, England, 575, 576
St. Mawes, England, 597–98
St. Patrick's Week (country-wide, Irish Republic), 493
Salisbury, England, 590–91
Salisbury Festival (Salisbury, England), 492
Salston Tavern (Ottery St. Mary, England), 551
Sandwich, England, 571–72
Sark, Channel Islands, England, 586
Scilly, Isles of, *see* Isles of Scilly
Scotland, 10
Scotland's Heritage Festival (country-wide, Scotland), 492
Scottish Highlands, tour, 449, 637–48
Scottish Islands, tour, 648–61
Scottish Lowlands, tour, 624–37
Seagan ua Neachtáin, Tabharneoir (Galway, Irish Republic), 530–31
Selkirk, Scotland, 630, 631
Settle (Frome, England), 547
Severn River (England), 434

Shakespeare's Tavern and Playhouse (London, England), 550–51
Shannon River (Irish Republic), 434–35
Sharrow Bay Hotel (Pooley Bridge, England), 537–38
Sherborne, England, 591–92
Sherlock Holmes (London, England), 526
Shetland Isles, Scotland, 659–61
Ship, traveling by, 27–30
 ferries, 29–30
 freighters, 28
 handicapped travelers, 66
 inland waterways, 28–29
Ship's Lights Tearoom (near Bridport, England), 546
Shooting and stalking, *see* Hunting
Shopping, 90–93, 552–64
 duty-free shops, 92
 England, 552–56
 how to shop abroad, 91–92
 Irish Republic, 558–63
 Northern Ireland, 563–64
 Scotland, 556–57
 value added tax (VAT), 92–93
 Wales, 558
 what to buy, 90–91
 See also shopping *entry under names of individual cities*
Siamsa Tíre, National Folk Theatre of Ireland (Tralee, Irish Republic), 485
Single travelers, hints for, 70–73
Sins, *see* sins *entry under names of individual cities*
Sir John Soane's Museum (London, England), 471
Skara Brae and Maes Howe (Mainland, Scotland), 515–16
Skeabost House Hotel (Skeabost Bridge, Isle of Skye, Scotland), 539
Skellig Rocks, Irish Republic, 718
Skibbereen, Irish Republic, 710
Skye, Isle of, Scotland, 651–53
Slea Head, Irish Republic, 729
Sneem, Irish Republic, 720, 721
Snowdonia National Park (Gwynedd, Wales), 458–59
South Downs Way (from Eastbourne to Harting, near Petersfield, England), 462–63
Southwest Way (from Studland to Minehead, England), 563
Southwold, England, 556

INDEX

Special events, 13–18
  Great Britain, 14–16
  Irish Republic and Northern Ireland, 16–18
  tickets for, 104
  See also special events *entry under names of individual cities*
Sports, 93–95
  biking, 49–51, 445–53
  cricket, 94
  curling, 94–95
  fishing, 435–45
  Gaelic football, 95
  golf, 413–17
  Highland games, 95
  hiking, 51–52, 455–65
  horses, 419–29
  hunting, 427–29, 453–55
  hurling, 95
  polo, 94
  rugby, 93–94
  sailing, 430–32
  soccer, 93
  tennis, 417–19
  See also sports *entry under names of individual cities*
Stable Door (Middleham, England), 548–49
Stag's Head (Dublin, Irish Republic), 530
Staigue Fort, Irish Republic, 720
Stalking and shooting, *see* Hunting
Stirling, Scotland, 639–41
Stoke-on-Trent, England, 556
Stone Cross Cottage (Godshill, Isle of Wight, England), 548
Stonehenge (Wiltshire, England), 514–15
Stow-on-the-Wold, England, 607, 608, 609
Stratford-upon-Avon, England, 372–81
  essay, 372–74
  hotels, 379–80
  local transportation, 377
  museums, 375, 376
  music, 379
  nightclubs and nightlife, 379
  pubs, 381
  restaurants, 380–81
  shopping, 378
  sights and activities, 374–77
    other attractions, 375–76
    Shakespeare Birthplace Trust, 374–75
  sins, 379
  special events, 378
  sports, 378
  theater, 378
  tourist information, 377
Street, England, 556
Sunningdale Golf Club (Sunningdale, England), 413
Sutherland House (Southwold, England), 549
Swansea Festival (Swansea, Wales), 497

Tara, Hill of (near Navan, Irish Republic), 519–20
Tate Gallery (London, England), 471–72
Teashops/tea gardens, 545–49
Telephone, 96–97
Tennis, 417–19
Terms, British and Irish, and American translations, 111–12
Tetbury, England, 504
Thames River (England), 434
Theater(s), 477–85
  tickets, 104
  See also theater *entry under names of individual cities*
Theatre Royal (Bristol, England), 478
Theatre Royal (Glasgow, Scotland), 482
Theatre Royal (London, England)
  Drury Lane, 480–81
  Haymarket, 481
Theatre Royal (Norfolk, England), 481
Three Choirs Festival (Gloucester, Hereford, and Worcester, England), 490
Tilted Wig (Edinburgh, Scotland), 527–28
Time zones, 95–96
Tipperary (city), Irish Republic, 699–700
Tipperary (County), Irish Republic, 509, 563
Tipping, 89–90
Tory Island, Irish Republic, 757
Totnes, England, 595
Tourist information offices, 101–3
  Channel Islands, 102
  England, 101–2
  Irish Republic, 103
  Isle of Man, 102
  Isle of Wight, 102
  Northern Ireland, 103
  Scotland, 102–3
  US, 101
  Wales, 103

tourist information offices (*cont.*)
See also tourist information *entry under names of individual cities*
Tours, see Package tours
Tower of London (London, England), 512–13
Towers Hotel (Glenbeigh, Irish Republic), 531, 541
Train, touring by, 34–38
 further information, 38
 Great Britain, 34–36
 handicapped travelers, 67
 Ireland, 36–37
 passes, 37–38
Tralee, Irish Republic, 725–27
Transportation, local, see local transportation *entry under names of individual cities*
Transportation costs, 54
 See also Airplane travel; Bus, touring by; Car, driving own; Car rentals; Ship, traveling by; Train, touring by
Travel agents, how to use, 60–62
Traveler's checks, 79–80
Tresanton, Hotel (St. Mawes, England), 543
Turnberry Hotel Golf Course (Turnberry, Scotland), 415–16
Tyrone (County), Northern Ireland, 564

Ulster Folk and Transport Museum (Holywood, Northern Ireland), 476
Up-Helly-Aa (Lerwick, Shetland Isles, Scotland), 492–93
Upper Slaughter, England, 607–8

Valentia Island, Irish Republic, 718
Ventry, Irish Republic, 728
Victoria and Albert Museum (London, England), 472
Vintage (Kinsale, Irish Republic), 541–42

Wales, 10–11, 449–50
Wales, tour, 662–78
Walks, see Hiking
Wallace Collection (London, England), 472
Waterford (city), Irish Republic, 382–89, 704
 essay, 382–83
 hotels, 388
 local transportation, 385–86
 museums, 384–85, 386
 music, 387
 nightclubs and nightlife, 387
 pubs, 389
 restaurants, 388–89
 shopping, 386
 sights and activities, 383–85
 sins, 387
 special events, 386
 sports, 387
 theater, 387
 tourist information, 385
Waterford (County), Irish Republic, 563
Waterside Inn (Bray-on-Thames, England), 533–34
Waterville, Irish Republic, 718–19
Waterville Golf Club (Waterville, Irish Republic), 417
Waterways and coastal cruises, 429–35
Weald, England, 577–78
Wells, England, 603
Welsh Marches, England, 449
Wentworth Golf Club (Virginia Water, England), 413–14
Westmeath (County), Irish Republic, 563
West Penwith, England, 598–99
Westport, Irish Republic, 750–51
Wexford, Irish Republic, 390–97, 696–97
 essay, 390–91
 hotels, 395–96
 local transportation, 393–94
 museums, 392, 393
 music and nightlife, 395
 pubs, 397
 restaurants, 396–97
 shopping, 394
 sights and activities, 391–93
 sins, 395
 special events, 394–95
 sports, 395
 theater, 395
 tourist information, 393
Wexford County Museum (Enniscorthy, Irish Republic), 475
Wexford Festival Opera (Wexford, Irish Republic), 496
Wheatsheaf Coffee Shoppe (Morpeth, England), 549

Whitstable, England, 556, 570–71
Wicklow (County), Irish Republic, 563
Wicklow Mountains (Cos. Wicklow and Dublin, Irish Republic), 459
Wicklow Way (from Marley Park, near Sandyford, to Luggala, near Sally Gap, Irish Republic), 464
Wight, Isle of, *see* Isle of Wight
Wigmore Hall (London, England), 481
Winchcombe, England, 611
Winchester, England, 589–90
Windermere, England, 616–17
Windrush, England, 607
Windsor Festival (Windsor Castle, England), 497
Wine bars
  Dublin, 287
  London, 361
Wolds Way (from Filey to North Ferriby, England), 463
Worthing, England, 504

York, England, 398–409
  antiques and auctions, 504
  essay, 398–99
  hotels, 406–7
  local transportation, 403
  museums, 400, 401–2, 403
  music, 405
  nightclubs and nightlife, 406
  pubs, 409
  restaurants, 407–8
  shopping, 404
  sights and activities, 400–402
  sins, 406
  special events, 404–5
  sports, 405
  theater, 405
  tourist information, 402–403
York Festival (York, England), 492
Yorkshire Dales, England, 449
Youghal, Irish Republic, 702–3
Young Vic Theatre (London, England), 481

GET YOUR TRAVEL ADVICE AND GO!

Stephen Birnbaum brings you
the very best travel advice in the world in the Get 'em and Go travel guides, each revised and updated annually.

Canada, 1983	$11.95
Caribbean, Bermuda, and the Bahamas, 1983	$11.95
Europe, 1983	$13.95
Great Britain and Ireland, 1983	$11.95
Hawaii, 1983	$11.95
Mexico, 1983	$11.95
South America, 1983	$11.95
United States, 1983	$11.95

Stephen Birnbaum brings you
the best of *Disneyland* and *Walt Disney World* in the only official guides to the most famous and most popular tourist attractions in America.

Disneyland, 1983	$4.95
Walt Disney World, 1983	$4.95

Look for all these guides in bookstores across America.
To order directly by mail or to inquire about Houghton Mifflin travel books, write to:

> Special Sales Manager
> Travel Guides Department GG
> Houghton Mifflin Company
> 2 Park Street
> Boston, MA 02108

Send your check or money order for the price listed plus $1.00 for shipping and tax (where applicable). Allow 4 weeks for delivery.